ISBN 978-1-5282-3519-8
PIBN 10917741

1 MONTH OF
FREE
READING

at
www.ForgottenBooks.com

By purchasing this book you are eligible for one month membership to ForgottenBooks.com, giving you unlimited access to our entire collection of over 1,000,000 titles via our web site and mobile apps.

To claim your free month visit:

www.forgottenbooks.com/free917741

English
Français
Deutsche
Italiano
Español
Português

www.forgottenbooks.com

Mythology Photography **Fiction**
Fishing Christianity **Art** Cooking
Essays Buddhism Freemasonry
Medicine **Biology** Music **Ancient
Egypt** Evolution Carpentry Physics
Dance Geology **Mathematics** Fitness
Shakespeare **Folklore** Yoga Marketing
Confidence Immortality Biographies
Poetry **Psychology** Witchcraft
Electronics Chemistry History **Law**
Accounting **Philosophy** Anthropology
Alchemy Drama Quantum Mechanics
Atheism Sexual Health **Ancient History**
Entrepreneurship Languages Sport
Paleontology Needlework Islam
Metaphysics Investment Archaeology
Parenting Statistics Criminology
Motivational

V. 2

INDEX

TO

VOLUME II.

1921.

Issued under the Authority of the
EMPIRE PARLIAMENTARY ASSOCIATION
(United Kingdom Branch),
Westminster Hall, Houses of Parliament,
LONDON, S.W.1.

=	Answer(s).	Newfld.	= Newfoundland.
=	Africa.	N.L. & C.	= National Liberal and Conservative.
=	Amendment.		
=	Australia.	N.S.W.	= New South Wales.
=	Australian Commonwealth.	N.Z.	= New Zealand.
		Q.	= Question(s).
=	British Columbia.	Q. & A.	= Question(s) and Answer(s).
=	Board of Trade.		
=	Canada.	q.v.	= quod vide.
=	Coalition-Liberal.	Ref.	= Reform.
=	Constitutional Democrat.	Ry. or Rys.	= Railway or Railways.
		S. Africa	= South Africa.
=	Conference.	S.A.P.	= South African Party.
=	Country Party.	Soc.	= Socialist.
=	Coalition-Unionist.	sqq.	= sequitur (and following pages).
=	Farmers' Union.		
=	Government.	supra	= above.
=	Independent.		
=	Independent Liberal.	S.W. Africa	= South-West Africa.
=	Independent Unionist.	Tas.	= Tasmania.
=	below.	T.U.	= Trade Union.
=	Labour.	T.U.s	= Trade Unions.
=	Liberal.	U.	= Unionist.
=	League of Nations.	U.K.	= United Kingdom.
=	Nationalist.	U.S.A.	= United States of America.
=	National.	Vic.	= Victoria.
=	National Progressive.	W. Aust.	= Western Australia.

INDEX.

A 2

Malan, Rt. Hon. F. S., on *(contd.)*
Regulation of Wages Bill : Introducing Bill, 448
South-West Africa Mandate (A.), 914, 916
German Language in S.W. African Schools (A.), 915, 916
Scope of Mandate, 914
Unemployment Expenditure : Labour Party's Misunderstanding of Vote in Loan Estimates : Application of Vote : Cost of Building : Housing Scheme in operation : Irrigation Scheme : Two Kinds of Unemployment : " Poor Whites " : Cost of White Agricultural Labour : Govt. Policy, 937-8
Malan, M. L. (Nat., S. Africa), on Land Settlement Amendment Bill : Preference to Returned Soldiers, 217-18
Malcolm, A. S. (Ref., N.Z.), on Conf. of Prime Ministers of Empire and Continuous Representation in London : an Imperial Constitution : Imperial Federation : Powers of Taxation : Dominion Representation : Relations with U.S.A., 640-4
Defence and the Education Dept. : N.Z. and the Navy : Imperial Unity : " Standing Out " of a War, 173-4
a Discussion on Imperial Affairs (Q.), 404
Maloney, Dr. W. (Lab., Aust. Com.), on Conf. of Prime Ministers of Empire : Anglo-Japanese Treaty, 617
New Hebrides : Settlers' Preference for British Flag, etc., 877-8
Malta, and Proportional Representation, 520
Mandated or Mandatory Territories
Consultation of Inhabitants of, 493, 495, 496, 913
Included under Overseas Trade Amendment Bill, 497
Q. & A. on, in House of Commons, 498
Mandates of L. of N., *vide under that head, and under countries concerned*
Not given by L. of N., but by Allied and Associated Powers, 911
Mandatory Power, Peoples choosing their own, 913
Manion, R. J. (N.L. & C., Can.), on Address : Work of the Govt. summarised, 322
Manitoba Experiment in Proportional Representation, 34, 853
Manufactures (Aust. Com.)
Extension Urged, 885-6
Potentialities of, 883
Value of, 135
Relative to that of Primary Industries, 884

Maori Views on
Diplomacy, 182-3
Immigration Restriction Bill (N.Z.), 182-3
Marais, Senator Hon. C. G. (S. Africa), on
Marriage Law Amendment Bill : Moving that the Petitioning Clergy be heard by the Senate, 942 ; Further Motion by, 943
Native Affairs Bill and the Nationalist Party, 214
Marine Engineers, Strike of (Aust. Com.), 145
Maritime Strike (Aust. Com.), 138
Markets for
Germany, 797
South Africa, 929
Marks, W. M. (Nat., Aust. Com.), on Cost of Contribution to British Fleet on Population Basis, 611
Marlborough, Duke of, on Agriculture Bill (U.K.), 48
Marriage, Divorce, etc., Legislation on, in
Newfoundland, 946
New Zealand, 429, 430, 434, 752
South Africa, 451, 938
South Australia, 154, 396
United Kingdom, 69, 939
Marriage Amendment Act (N.Z.)
Passed, 430
Provisions of, as
Introduced, 429 & *n.*
Passed, 429-30 & *n.*
Debates on Bill, in
House of Representatives, 432
Legislative Council, 430
Marriage Law Amendment Act (S. Africa)
Passed, 942, 943
Provisions of, 451, 938
Debates on Bill, in
House of Assembly, 939
Senate, 942
Marriage Register (N.Z.)
Divorces to be entered on, Act, *re*, 429
Married Ex-Soldiers (Can.)
Allowances to, for Children, Increased, 94
Totally or Partially Disabled : Pension Increased, 94
Married Women
Naturalisation of (Can.)
Q. & A. on, in House of Commons (Can.), 778
and Infant Children, Status of, under Nationality Act (Aust. Com.), 369-70
Marriott, J. A. R. (C.-U., U.K.), on National Expenditure, Seconding Resolution to Limit, 49
Rhodesia's Constitutional Status, 746
Martial Law in Ireland, 38-9, 244, 246
Marwick, J. S. (S.A.P., S. Africa), Motion by, on Asiatic Problem for Segregation of Asiatics, 689

VACHER & SONS, LTD., Westminster House, S.W.1.—95373.

JOURNAL OF THE
PARLIAMENTS
OF THE EMPIRE

Vol. II.—No. 1.   January, 1921.

Issued under the Authority of the
EMPIRE PARLIAMENTARY ASSOCIATION
(United Kingdom Branch),
WESTMINSTER HALL, HOUSES OF PARLIAMENT,
LONDON, S.W.1.

Price to Non-Members 10s. Net.

CONTENTS.

AUSTRALIA.

Commonwealth Parliament.

State Parliaments.

New South Wales.

Victoria.

Queensland.

South Australia.

Western Australia.

NEW ZEALAND.

INTRODUCTION.

The present quarterly issue of the JOURNAL OF THE PARLIAMENTS OF THE EMPIRE constitutes the first number of the second volume. It may be thought that the commencement of the second year in the existence of the JOURNAL affords a convenient opportunity to review the position to which it has attained, and to record something concerning the reception it has secured from the members of the Empire Parliamentary Association throughout the Parliaments of the British Commonwealth. A reference, however, to the Introductions appearing in the JOURNALS of last year, where the individual and collective appreciation of members of the Dominion Parliaments was recorded, renders it unnecessary to produce further testimony to prove that the JOURNAL has, at any rate, accomplished what it set out to do, viz., to provide a satisfactory summary of the proceedings of general interest occurring in the Parliaments of the Empire, in order that the members of those Parliaments may be kept constantly informed of each other's point of view and legislative proposals.

Many of the varied subjects dealt with throughout the past year have formed common problems for the legislators of the Empire, and the fact that information concerning the methods of treatment of them in the different Parliaments has been made readily available in the pages of the JOURNAL has undoubtedly proved of practical utility. In more than one case the framework of a Bill introduced into one Parliament has been based upon information given in the JOURNAL as to the terms of a Bill dealing with the same subject in another Parliament; while there is not the least doubt, from the evidence that has been put before the Editor, that statesmen and legislators generally are finding it of increasing importance, as a preparation for both official and informal Conferences, to understand the attitude adopted towards outstanding public questions by the leading men of diverse political opinions in the Parliaments of the Empire.

The present number of the JOURNAL records the discussion and treatment of many subjects of great importance as between the nations of the British Commonwealth. The relations of the Empire to the outside world are dealt with in the course of several debates of considerable interest and significance occurring in the Parliaments of the United Kingdom, the Australian Commonwealth and New Zealand. In those Parliaments pronouncements and discussions upon such matters as the League of Nations, the next Imperial Conference, the constitutional position of the Dominions, defence policy (both naval and military), immigration of coloured races (including references to Indian fellow-subjects), the treatment of mandated territories, indentured labour, etc., have taken place, and require the earnest consideration of all responsible students of inter-Imperial and international politics.

Other subjects which may be said to come within the wider category, and also to have arisen directly or indirectly from the war, are those relating to the treatment of enemy property (in the United Kingdom and South African Parliaments), the granting of emergency powers to the Government (in the United Kingdom and New Zealand), the land settlement of soldiers (in Canada and South Africa), shipbuilding (in Australia and Newfoundland), naturalisation (in Canada), and other matters.

In the sphere of Parliamentary activity which may be described as, in a sense, local, but which at the same time conveys a meaning and a message to all the nations within the Empire, fall the legislation and discussions in the United Kingdom Parliament concerning Ireland, national expenditure, unemployment, etc.; in the Canadian and Australian Commonwealth Parliaments on industrial disputes; and in the South Australian Parliament on venereal diseases. The last-named Bill goes further, it is believed, in the direction of compulsion than any previous proposals for legislation in this connection.

Special interest attaches to much of the domestic legislation passed in the United Kingdom Parliament during the latter part of the last Session, notably that concerning the employment of women and children (arising from the conventions and recommendations of the International Labour Organisation), agriculture, the safeguarding of the dye-making industry, etc.

In South Africa the local legislation relating to native affairs, to currency and banking, to profiteering and to housing are worthy of particular attention ; while in New Zealand the proposal to create an elective executive, and the attempt in Western Australia to abolish the Upper House are both of constitutional significance.

So far as can be seen at present, the only country of the British Commonwealth which will have to choose a new Parliament before the next issue of the JOURNAL is the Union of South Africa. The election on 8th February, which follows upon the new combination that has occurred between the South African and Unionist parties as a result of General Smuts' recent appeal for the formation of a moderate party, is being watched with much interest by members of other Parliaments.

In response to many requests, a fairly exhaustive Index to the last volume of the JOURNAL is being despatched to members with the present number. It is believed that this Index will greatly facilitate a ready reference to subjects that have been discussed and legislated upon, and to the speakers who have taken part ; and it is hoped that as a result the value of the JOURNAL to legislators and students of affairs will be materially enhanced.

THE EDITOR.

EMPIRE PARLIAMENTARY ASSOCIATION
(*United Kingdom Branch*),
WESTMINSTER HALL,
HOUSES OF PARLIAMENT,
LONDON, S.W.1.

25*th January*, 1921.

UNITED KINGDOM.

The business of the Session was resumed on 19th October, 1920, at the conclusion of the Autumn Recess. Both Houses sat regularly until 23rd December, on which date the King's Speech was read and Parliament was Prorogued until 15th February, 1921. In the last issue of the JOURNAL *the proceedings of Parliament were summarised up to the adjournment on 16th August. Business transacted between the date of reassembly in October and the end of the Session is dealt with in the following pages.*

LEAGUE OF NATIONS.

(Discussion on Work: List of States.)

In the House of Commons on 22nd December, 1920, during the debate on the Third Reading of the Consolidated Fund (Appropriation) (No. 2) Bill, a statement on the League of Nations was made by the Lord President of the Council, who had returned a short time previously from Geneva after attending as a British delegate the First Assembly of the League.

DEBATE IN HOUSE OF COMMONS.

The Lord President of the Council (the Right Hon. A. J. Balfour) said the termination of the Assembly of the League appeared to supply a fitting occasion on which to survey the work of the first eleven months, or thereabouts, of the League's existence. The Council met, he thought, eleven times in the course of those eleven months. Though he hoped its meetings would not be so frequent in the course of the next twelve months, it was deliberately contemplated that it should meet regularly every two months, and more often if emergencies required. At the beginning of its proceedings this year, the Assembly represented 42 separate nations. It now represented 48 separate nations and would doubtless represent more in the future. The organisation work had been heavy this year, and while the rules of procedure laid down would, no doubt, require modification at times, on the whole he thought their labours in that department had really proved creditable, very largely owing to the admirable Secretariat by which they were served.

The partition of expenditure between the different members of the League was admittedly and notoriously unfair.

The chief victims happened to be the members of the British Empire. He believed that on the principle of the Postal Union it would be found that the British Empire paid about 40 per cent. of the total expenditure incurred by the League. " I need hardly say," remarked Mr. Balfour, " that the statesmen of our Dominions did not sit down silently under this pecuniary difficulty, and a good deal of time was very properly occupied in discussing it."

International Court of Justice.

With regard to the establishment of a permanent Court of International Justice, the Assembly had passed the scheme and it now remained for acceptance by the nations. There was only one point which raised a good deal of debate. It was whether the appeal to the Court should be made compulsory on both parties, or, to put the matter in another way, whether it should be in the power of any given nation to compel another nation to come before the Court over any dispute or difficulty which might have arisen between them. The Council of the League turned it from an obligatory into a voluntary system, and the Assembly, by a large majority, confirmed that decision.

The plan actually adopted was to pass the scheme in a voluntary form, and then to have an additional protocol or diplomatic instrument which any nation might sign, declaring its adhesion to the obligatory form. " It has been signed already, I need hardly say," Mr. Balfour proceeded, " in the first, but not the second, form by this country and by, I believe, all the members of the British Dominions, and probably by a large number of other nations. I doubt not it will be universally signed, and as soon as more than half the nations belonging to the League have signed the document the Court will come into legal international existence."

Amendments to Covenant.

The Scandinavian Governments had prepared before the Assembly a very carefully considered and thought-out body of amendments to the Covenant, but the Assembly were of opinion that to begin to amend the Pact before the League had been in existence for a year would be to show impatience. It was decided that any amendment to the Pact should first go through the mill of careful consideration by a body appointed by the Council, then by the Council, and that a report should be submitted to the next Assembly under conditions which would enable them to judge what ought or ought not to be done in the way of modifying the instrument on which their very existence was founded. That, he thought, was a satisfactory solution.

The Assembly had deferred for a year the setting up of a permanent scheme under which non-permanent members were to be elected from time to time.

Economic Work.

Dealing with the economic work of the League, Mr. Balfour said it had been decided to hold an international conference upon transit at Barcelona next year (1921) and possibly it would carry out a very important work. The Council had adopted the Ter Meulen scheme* which was laid before the international conference held at Brussels a few months ago with the object of doing something to mitigate the present formidable difficulties which stood in the way of the international exchange of goods owing to the deficiency of credit. One of the great troubles under which the economic world was now groaning was that those who produced could not sell and those who wanted to do so could not buy.

"Of course," said Mr. Balfour, " I shall neither attempt to describe in minute detail nor to defend the proposal put forward, which is to make it possible for any country which requires imports for the essential needs of life . . . to see whether in some shape or another, either in the shape of what in this country we would call Crown lands —national lands — or in the shape of a particular source of revenue, or in any other shape, it has assets on which borrowing may legitimately take place. If it has these public assets on which borrowing may legitimately take place, the League of Nations proposes to find the machinery to value these assets, and it would be possible for the borrowing country to issue bonds upon these assets, and issue these bonds in payment of goods imported. Everything, of course, turns upon whether the exporting country will take these bonds in payment for the goods. That is obviously the first crux of this tremendous problem, but if the matter is put, as it were, under the League of Nations, so that there could be no question of Stock Exchange difficulties, and no interference with national pride such as would take place if the nation had to go, say, to a Council of Foreign Bondholders, or some other organisation of that kind . . . it is, I think, extremely probable that this scheme will prove useful."

---

* A movement has been started to secure the co-operation of the British Government, the bankers and the insurance companies in establishing a system of credit insurance for export trade in connection with the Ter Meulen scheme.

He was authorised by the President of the Board of Trade to say that the Government were seriously considering whether, so far as this country was concerned, the scheme of these bonds might not be supplemented by some form of insurance which would make their currency and their utility far more certain.

Political Work: Disarmament.

Turning to the political work of the League, Mr. Balfour said that all the preliminary arrangements were now being carried out that the free town of Dantzig should come under the protection of the League and carry out the management of its own affairs with a High Commissioner appointed by the League, whose business it would be, among other things, to do all he could to improve and perfect the relations between Dantzig and its Polish neighbours. " It is with a feeling of disappointment," the right hon. gentleman continued, " that I speak on the next subject . . . the subject of disarmament. I believe, indeed I am sure, that what has been done by the League of Nations is all that could be done. I admit what has been done is very little. All you can say is that we have moved, and the movement we have made is in the right direction. . . . I hope that the next Assembly will see the modest step which has been taken carried still further, and that the progress, the very small progress, which the world is making in this all-important subject will be of increasing rapidity and ever-growing success." Traffic in arms, Mr. Balfour remarked, was also an unsatisfactory matter, because although a Convention was signed by all the important Powers in connection with it, the Convention had not been ratified.

Mandates: Other Efforts.

Not much had yet been decided on the question of mandates. As to the method of control and criticism, the Council had devised a scheme which on the whole they believed to be fair both to the mandatory Power and to the population of the mandated territories. All the mandates had been put in, but the only ones examined and approved were the " sea mandates " dealing with South-West Africa, New Guinea, and the territories mandated to New Zealand and Japan.

With regard to two great philanthropic efforts in which the League had engaged, so far success in the campaign against typhus was small, but he hoped it would increase. In the case of the repatriation of prisoners of war, under the admirable and energetic efforts of Dr. Nansen a great deal had been done. Those efforts had more than half solved the problem, and the only reason it was not fully solved was that adequate money had not so far been provided.

The right hon. gentleman concluded by remarking that he was more than ever convinced that the experiment they had begun was one they could never afford to drop. The League of Nations might be, and would be, modified, but it seemed to him absolutely incredible that they could ever consent to go back to the international disorganisation which preceded it.

Labour and the League.

The Right Hon. J. R. Clynes (Vice-Chairman of the Parliamentary Labour Party) expressed the view that at future Assemblies of the League the British delegation should include representatives not actually within the personnel of the Government. With regard to the Labour Bureau of the League, certain matters were settled at Washington nearly twelve months ago of great importance from the economic and industrial standpoint. Was it not a fact that if legislative action were not taken before 26th January the British Government would have failed to comply with the decisions as to the conditions of employment for expectant mothers ? He felt certain that the trading, the financial, and the banking communities, and, indeed, all who were interested in the progress and improvement of industrial life, could find no better guarantee for improvement in trade and economic conditions than could be given by an effective, working League of Nations.

He shared keenly the disappointment expressed by Mr. Balfour as to what was done at the Assembly on the great question of disarmament. " All the countries which count in this matter of armament," Mr. Clynes proceeded, " must agree on some common plan, if all countries are to be liberated from the pressure and the waste that we have suffered in the past on account of armaments. Therefore, we should do our best to go abreast of other countries, and so far as we can to give a lead to other countries, and, while in no way placing ourselves in a condition of danger, to create that spirit of peace which will bring all the leading countries of the world that really count in this matter to one common policy, so that disarmament may take place on an extensive scale, if not completely, at one time. To this end I should like to see a more enthusiastic advocacy on our part of the impossibility of private or financial interests in any way inspiring or dominating supplies of armaments in any one country."

In this country, as in others, Mr. Clynes added, organised Labour could have done more to create a public opinion in

favour of the League. There were those in the Labour world
who said that capitalist Governments could not be trusted to
keep out of war. If that were true, there was all the greater
need for making their peace machinery more perfect, so as to
keep capitalist Governments under such conditions as would
make peace more probable than if there were no peace
machinery at all. He believed also that there were those who
thought that if the Governments of the world were Labour
Governments there would be peace perpetually. He could not
share that optimism, for, whatever else they might change,
they could not change human nature.

The Labour Bureau.

The **Right Hon. G. N. Barnes** (Labour, *Glasgow*, *Gorbals*),
who was one of the delegates of the United Kingdom to the
Assembly, said he thought he might claim to have been a non-
Government delegate. They might with profit, he thought,
include one woman in future delegations as an adviser or in
some other capacity.

The delegates of the British Government at Washington
did not vote for the particular Convention to which Mr. Clynes
had referred, but in order to carry out their obligation under the
Pact the Government should submit the Convention to the
House of Commons. The Government were not compelled to
do this by 26th January. They might plead exceptional
circumstances and comply with the obligation if they submitted it within six months of that date. There was also the
Convention about the eight hours' day. That had not been
carried out. One of the reasons was because it conflicted with
an arrangement made by the Ministry of Transport on the one
side and the railwaymen's union on the other. He thought
it would have been a generous thing to do if the railwaymen
had brought themselves within the terms of the Washington
Convention.

The Labour Bureau was intended to be the ears and eyes
of labour throughout the world, to ascertain where conditions
might be improved, and submit proposals. He believed they
were carrying out that part of their work with efficiency and
commending themselves usefully to organised labour throughout the world.

Disarmament.

The **President of the Board of Education** (the **Right Hon.
Herbert Fisher**) said he was chairman of the sub-committee
at Geneva which was appointed to deal with the question of
disarmament. It had been asked whether any steps had

already been taken with the view of approaching the members of the League in the matter. " We ascertained," said Mr. Fisher, " that the military commission had already prepared a *questionnaire* which is to be submitted to the Council, and if approved by the Council will be circulated among the members of the League. I have had an opportunity of seeing that *questionnaire*, which is a searching inquiry into the nature of armaments in the different countries, but until replies to that *questionnaire* have been received, obviously it is impossible to take any definite steps."

The majority of the committee were of opinion that the most hopeful way of tackling the problem was by a simultaneous and proportionate reduction of armaments, although they were perfectly well aware of the difficulties in the way. But they came to the conclusion that, short of that, it might be possible to obtain a universal arrest of armaments, and accordingly a resolution was submitted to the Assembly inviting the Council of the League to submit to the different Governments, who were members of the League, a plan to the following effect. The members of the League were to be asked whether they could enter into an undertaking not to increase their military and naval expenditure for a period of two years over and above the level of the military and naval expenditure in the next Budget, subject to two reservations. First of all it was subject to the possibility of the nation being called upon to undertake some military enterprise at the invitation of the Council of the League, and, secondly, subject to exceptional circumstances, notified as such to the Council of the League.

The resolution was not passed without some opposition, but he thought he was right in saying that thirty-four States voted for it, without, of course, committing their respective Governments. They voted for it as a plan which seemed to be practicable and eminently suited for submission by the Council to the various members of the League, and he hoped he was not too sanguine in expressing the hope that sooner or later this plan would be so submitted.

The discussion on the subject came to an end with the speech of Mr. Fisher.

List of States.

A statement regarding the League was made in the House of Commons at question time on 8th November, when **Sir Harry Brittain** (Coalition Unionist, *Acton*) asked the Prime Minister whether he was able to inform the House as to the names of the Sovereign States which had joined the League of Nations, together with the respective amounts so far subscribed by each for the purpose of supporting the necessary machinery ?

The Prime Minister (the Right Hon. D. Lloyd George) said: "During 1919-1920 His Majesty's Government have paid the sum of £23,000, and during the current financial year (1920-1921) £21,948 12s. These two sums together constitute the proportional share of His Majesty's Government under the present distribution among members of the League of the total budget of the League up to 31st December, 1920.

"I regret that I am not in a position to state the amounts actually subscribed by other members of the League. . . . The following is a list of the States* which have joined the League of Nations :—

Argentine Republic.	Liberia.
Belgium.	Netherlands.
Bolivia.	Norway.
Brazil.	Panama.
British Empire.	Paraguay.
Canada.	Persia.
Australia.	Peru.
South Africa.	Poland.
New Zealand.	Portugal.
India.	Roumania.
Chile.	Salvador.
Colombia.	Serb-Croat-Slovene
Czecho-Slovakia.	State.
Denmark.	Siam.
France.	Spain.
Greece.	Sweden.
Guatemala.	Switzerland.
Italy.	Uruguay.
Japan.	Venezuela."

* In the course of his statement to the House of Commons on 22nd December, Mr. Balfour indicated the changes made in the above list as the result of the meeting of the Assembly. He explained that Greece was not re-elected on the Council of the League, and China was selected for the vacant place. The following six States had been admitted to the League : Austria, Bulgaria, Costa Rica, Finland, Albania and Luxemburg.

ENEMY PROPERTY.

(Statement of Government Policy.)

An important statement was made in the House of Commons by the Chancellor of the Exchequer on 28th October regarding the property of German nationals.

The Right Hon. F. D. Acland (Independent Liberal, Cornwall, Camborne) asked a question in these terms :—

"Whether the Chancellor of the Exchequer could make any statement in regard to the announcement by the British Government of their intention not to exercise their rights under Paragraph 18 of Annex II. to Part VIII. of the Treaty of Versailles to seize the property of German nationals in this country in the case of voluntary default by Germany in respect of her reparation obligations."

The Chancellor of the Exchequer (the Right Hon. Austen Chamberlain) replied as follows : —

" I am glad to have an opportunity of making a statement on this matter, which has given rise to a good deal of misconception. The paragraph in question reads as follows : —

' The measures which the Allied and Associated Powers shall have the right to take, in case of voluntary default by Germany, and which Germany agrees not to regard as acts of war, may include economic and financial prohibitions and reprisals and in general such other measures as the respective Governments may determine to be necessary in the circumstances.'

Rights not Renounced.

" His Majesty's Government have not renounced their right to take measures such as are contemplated in this paragraph. They have merely declared that among the measures which they might take in given circumstances there will not be included a seizure of the property of German nationals in this country, whether such property is in the United Kingdom or under United Kingdom control, and whether it is in the form of bank balances or of goods in British bottoms or of goods sent to this country for sale.

" This decision was not taken in consequence of any representations from Germany, nor was it dictated by regard for German interests. The matter has been under consideration for a long time and it was hoped that it might be decided in connection with the general discussion of reparation questions at the Spa Conference or at the Conference proposed to be held at Geneva. In view, however, of the postponement of the latter, His Majesty's Government felt it to be impossible to continue to maintain a threat which injuriously affected British interests without offering any real security for the execution of the Treaty, since, so long as private German property in this country, and, in particular, private bank balances belonging to Germans were exposed to seizure, it was fairly certain that, if the moment ever arrived when we desired to put Paragraph 18 into operation, there would be no appreciable property to seize. The paragraph thus operated merely

B

to keep business away from London and to make Germans keep their balances in neutral currencies, a course which was inconvenient to all parties and involved clear loss to this country without any countervailing advantage.

" I may add, by way of further commentary, that there has actually been a campaign in certain of the German newspapers in favour of the handing over of these particular German assets by the German Government to the Reparation Commission in order to punish the individual German owners for sending money abroad.

Freedom of Action.

" With regard to the criticism that this action was taken by His Majesty's Government on their own responsibility, without obtaining the concurrence of the Allied Governments, I would say that the words of the paragraph clearly leave it ' to the respective Governments ' to determine what action may be necessary under the paragraph. In the opinion of His Majesty's Government it would have been both unnecessary and undesirable to seek to share the responsibility of the decision they have taken with the other Allies, thus both limiting their own freedom of action under the Treaty and giving the appearance of desiring to dictate to other Governments as to their action under the paragraph. As a matter of courtesy the decision reached* was immediately communicated to the other Powers through the Ambassadors' Council, and also to the Reparation Commission through the British Delegate."

Further questions and answers on the subject included the following:—

Colonel J. W. Greig (Coalition Liberal, *Renfrew, W.*): " Does the relinquishment of a right of retention or reprisal against German property in British hands or under their control apply only to German property which has come here since the peace was signed, or to other German property already in our hands before that date ? "

The Chancellor of the Exchequer : " It refers only to the property which has come here since."

---

* The Foreign Office issued in January the text of the Agreement arrived at between the British and German Governments. It provides for the immediate restoration to British nationals of property and interests held by them in Germany which have been subject to exceptional war measures, but have not been completely liquidated. As regards German property in the United Kingdom restoration is limited to household furniture and effects, personal belongings, and implements of trade up to a total value of £500, and this concession will only apply to applicants whose income is certified not to exceed £400 a year at the current rate of exchange.

IMPERIAL CONFERENCE.
(Meeting of Prime Ministers, 1921.)

In the House of Commons on 11th November an announcement was made by the Prime Minister on the subject of the next Imperial Conference.*

Commander Oliver Locker-Lampson (Coalition Unionist, *Huntingdon*) asked whether it was intended to summon an Imperial Conference next year and, if so, upon what date.

The Prime Minister (the Right Hon. D. Lloyd George) replied : —

" I have been anxious for some time past to renew as soon as possible that personal consultation between Prime Ministers which produced such good results in the last two years of the War and at Paris. I recently made inquiries of my colleagues in the Dominions as to the date which would be most generally suitable for them, and I am glad to say that a meeting with the Prime Ministers of the Empire has been arranged for the middle of June, 1921."

Mr. Percy A. Hurd (Coalition Unionist, *Frome*) asked whether it had been considered desirable to hold the Conference at Ottawa, and the Prime Minister answered, " That was discussed."

In reply to a further question on 17th November,

The Leader of the House (the Right Hon. A. Bonar Law) said : " I should like to explain that the meeting of Prime Ministers summoned for June, 1921, will be a meeting on the lines of the Imperial War Cabinet meetings which took place in 1917 and 1918, to deal with the many urgent problems of common interest which call for the co-ordination of policy and action by the different Governments of the Empire. It

---

* An official statement was subsequently issued explaining the nature of the forthcoming Conference. It is to be a business meeting, on the lines of the Imperial War Cabinet meetings which took place in 1917 and 1918, to deal with the many urgent problems of common Imperial interest which call for the co-ordination of policy and action by the different Governments of the Empire. The success of those meetings led to the conclusion that they should, as far as possible, take place annually, and they were, in fact, continued at Paris in 1919 under the title of Meetings of the British Empire Delegation, and only discontinued in 1920 in view of the urgency of the problems of domestic reconstruction in every part of the Empire. It is not proposed to hold in 1921 the Special Constitutional Conference contemplated by the Imperial War Conference resolution of 1917.

will not be the special Constitutional Conference contemplated by Resolution IX. of the Imperial War Conference, 1917. The agenda will, of course, be a matter for subsequent settlement with the Dominion Ministers. There is general agreement that Imperial defence matters will require joint examination in the near future, but I am not yet in a position to say precisely what arrangements will be made for their discussion."

Major the Hon. H. O'Neill (Unionist, *Antrim, Mid.*) asked the following supplementary question :

" Are we to understand from the right hon. gentleman that the very important question of the readjustment of the constitutional relations between different parts of the Empire will be debarred from being discussed at the forthcoming Conference ? "

The Leader of the House gave the following further answer : —

"No, Sir. We have been in negotiation with the Dominions on this matter. There has been a good deal of unrest in regard to it and there is a general feeling that it would not be right to suppress it."

BRITISH EMPIRE EXHIBITION (GUARANTEE) ACT.

An Act to enable the Board of Trade to guarantee part of the expenses of a British Empire Exhibition, to be held in London in 1923 " or such earlier date as may be possible," was given the Royal Assent on 23rd December.

The Act empowers the Board of Trade on such terms and conditions as they think fit and as the Treasury may approve, to guarantee, up to £100,000, any loss which may result from the holding of the Exhibition. It is made a condition of the guarantee that the Exhibition shall be conducted by an executive committee and a general manager approved by the Board.

DEBATE IN HOUSE OF COMMONS.

The Bill came on for Second Reading in the House of Commons on 1st November.

The Secretary to the Overseas Trade Department (the Right Hon. F. G. Kellaway) quoted from a White Paper issued on the subject as follows : —

" The objects of the Exhibition are to foster Inter-Imperial interests from both a commercial and a political standpoint, and to demonstrate the natural resources of the territories of the Empire, and the inventive and manufacturing energy of its peoples.   The Exhibition will be privately organised, but is receiving official recognition and support.   His Majesty the King has given it his patronage, and H.R.H. the Prince of Wales has consented to act as President of the General Committee.''

The Government's guarantee, he explained, was to be given, subject to private guarantees amounting to £500,000 being forthcoming.   The idea of the Exhibition, which originated, he thought, with Lord Strathcona, was supported by the Dominions Royal Commission appointed in 1912.   The Commission stated in their report that they found a general feeling not only in the United Kingdom, but also in the Dominions, that Inter-Imperial Exhibitions were likely to have an increasing tendency to promote Imperial trade, and that such exhibitions should afford a valuable opportunity to British manufacturers for developing their trade in the growing markets of the Dominions.   At a Conference held in 1919, at which were present representatives of the United Kingdom and of all the Great Dominions, it was decided that the proposal should be pushed ahead, not only with the objects which were originally behind the idea, but in order to provide a memorial of the great part played by the Empire during the War.   There was a great opportunity behind the idea of demonstrating, not only to the world, but to every part of the Empire, the almost unlimited resources which Providence had placed within the ambit of the Empire.

Empire Trade Possibilities.

" The possibilities of Imperial trade within the Empire have not only not been sufficiently carried through," said Mr. Kellaway, " but they have not been sufficiently realised. It was a regrettable feature in the tendency of British trade during the years before the War that the percentage of the trade done with the Overseas Empire showed a diminution. . . .   I am glad to say that since the signing of the Armistice there has been a steady improvement in this important respect."

" In 1913," Mr. Kellaway continued, " our exports to the Empire Overseas amounted to £208,900,000, or 32·9 per cent. of the total bulk of our exports.   In 1919 our exports were £215,300,000, and there is no comparison possible between those two figures, because of the change in the value of money, but the percentage, which is the important point, had fallen from 32·9 in 1913 to 22·4 in 1919.   The figures for the first six months of this year are much more satisfactory.   During those six months the exports to the Empire Overseas totalled £236,700,000 or 30·6 per cent. of the total bulk of our exports."

The Right Hon. Sir F. Banbury (Coalition Unionist, *City of London*) : " Including India ? "

The Secretary to the Overseas Trade Department : " Yes, all oversea parts of the Empire. . . . There is no question that there are great possibilities of doing much more in increasing the percentage of the trade which this country does with our Empire overseas. We are dealing with a population of the Empire, roughly, of 450,000,000—I think 441,000,000 is the closest figure yet given. . . . I believe an exhibition of this kind will enable much more to be done in increasing the trade between the Dominions and ourselves, and I believe it does that without raising any acute fiscal controversy or any political question likely to arouse controversy."

Sir F. Banbury said he did not think that was a proper time to spend £100,000 on any object, however good it might be.

Sir John Rees (Coalition Unionist, *Nottingham, E.*) asked whether or not India would receive space equivalent to the predominant part she played in the foreign trade of the Empire ? If that question was answered in the affirmative, would the Government of India pay for stalling her goods and for sending her exhibits here ? It was of the utmost importance that the cotton of India and of Nyassaland—Empire grown—should be provided for.

Labour's Approval.

The Right Hon. J. R. Clynes (Vice-Chairman of the Parliamentary Labour Party) observed that, looking at the matter from the standpoint of internal Empire trade, he thought everything could be said to commend a Bill of that kind. He took the view that there was a certain form of expenditure which could be shown to be the truest economy, and at times they could make, assist, and expand trade by a certain degree of expenditure upon trade, or upon those contingencies which tended to make trade. This was a proposal which offered to Parliament a little opportunity of doing great good to Empire trade. " While I cannot claim to speak for every hon. member of the Labour Party," Mr. Clynes added, " I think I am safe in saying that this step is one which will assist in diminishing unemployment, and in improving trade, and therefore it should have the support of every Labour member in this House."

Mr. J. M. Hogge (Independent Liberal, *Edinburgh, E.*) was not impressed with the arguments about the utility of these exhibitions. The truth was they did not want an exhibition in this country to encourage trade in the Empire. What they wanted was a new Government that would cease to interfere with trade, and would allow traders and business men to get on with their own business and develop the resources inside the Empire without any of the grandmotherly assistance given by the members of the present Government.

Mr. J. D. Kiley (Independent Liberal, *Whitechapel***)** asked why should the British Government alone undertake this guarantee? "If any of the Dominions themselves had put up some of their money," he said, "and had then come and invited our Government to join with them, the Minister in charge would have had some good ground for coming before us. Are the Dominions putting up any money whatsoever? As I understand, they are not putting up a single penny, and yet we on their behalf are prepared to put up our money in order to push the trade of the Dominions."

The Second Reading of the Bill was carried on a division by 205 votes against 30. The Bill subsequently passed unamended through its remaining stages in the House of Commons.

DEBATE IN HOUSE OF LORDS.

On 18th December the Bill was briefly discussed in the House of Lords on Second Reading.

The Secretary of State for the Colonies (Viscount Milner) said these large International Exhibitions were sometimes nothing more than shows and opportunities of amusement. But every care was being taken that in this instance the Exhibition should be thoroughly well arranged and calculated to give really valuable information to those who were interested in the economic development of the Empire. It was a condition of the guarantee that the executive committee and the general manager of the Exhibition should be appointed with the approval of the Board of Trade.

The Marquis of Crewe was convinced that the project would be received with general sympathy, if only because the great Dominions, speaking generally, were taking a most keen interest in the plan. He could not help feeling that the more liberty that was allowed to the promoters to run the machine in their own way and with the experience of past Exhibitions the more the project was likely to succeed.

The Earl of Meath believed he was correct in saying that was the first time the British Government had ever guaranteed money for such a purpose. That showed an enormous advance in the attitude of the Government towards Imperial questions.

The Second Reading was agreed to and the Bill was then passed through its other stages without further discussion.

GOVERNMENT OF IRELAND ACT.

In the list of measures which received the Royal Assent on the closing day of the Session was the Government of Ireland Act. The King's Speech contained the following reference to this important piece of legislation : —

I have given My assent to a Bill for the better government of Ireland. This Act, by setting up two Parliaments and a Council of Ireland, gives self-government in Irish affairs to the whole of Ireland, and provides the means whereby the people of Ireland can of their own accord achieve unity. I sincerely hope that this Act, the fruit of more than thirty years of ceaseless controversy, will finally bring about unity and friendship between all the peoples of My Kingdom.

Appended is a summary of the principal provisions of the Act : —

TWO PARLIAMENTS AND COUNCIL OF IRELAND.

The Act provides for the establishment of two Parliaments, one for Southern Ireland and one for the six North-eastern counties of Ulster, viz., Antrim, Armagh, Down, Fermanagh, Londonderry and Tyrone. The area of the Northern Parliament includes the parliamentary boroughs of Belfast and Londonderry. Each Parliament is to consist of a Senate and a House of Commons.

With a view to the eventual establishment of a Parliament for the whole of Ireland, and to bringing about harmonious action between the Parliaments and Governments of Southern Ireland and Northern Ireland, and to the promotion of mutual intercourse and uniformity in relation to matters affecting the whole of Ireland, a Council of Ireland is to be constituted.

The Council is to consist of a President, nominated by the Lord-Lieutenant, and forty other persons, viz., seven members of each Senate and thirteen members of each House of Commons. The election of members of the Council is to be the first business of the Senates and Houses of Commons.

Power is given to the two Parliaments by identical Acts agreed to by an absolute majority of members of each House of Commons to establish, in lieu of the Council, a Parliament for the whole of Ireland to consist of two Houses. The date at which that Parliament is established is subsequently referred to in the Act as the date of Irish union.

LEGISLATIVE POWERS.

The two Parliaments first established are to have power respectively to make laws for the peace, order, and good government of Southern Ireland and Northern Ireland. They are not, however, to have power to make laws in respect of the following matters, which are reserved to the Imperial Parliament :—

The Crown, or the property of the Crown, or the Lord Lieutenant except as respects the exercise of his executive power in relation to Irish services.

Making of peace or war, or matters arising from a state of war.

The Navy, the Army, the Air Force, the Territorial Force, or the defence of the Realm, including questions of pensions and allowances.

Treaties or relations with foreign States or with other parts of the King's Dominions, or procedure connected with the extradition of criminals.

Dignities or titles of honour, treason, naturalisation, aliens and domicile.

Trade outside the area of each Parliament, bounties on the export of goods, quarantine, and navigation (including merchant shipping) except as respect regulation of harbours and local health regulations.

Submarine cables, wireless telegraphy, aerial navigation, and lighthouses.

Coinage, trade marks, copyright, and patent rights.

The making by either of the Irish Parliaments of laws interfering with religious equality, or taking property without compensation is prohibited.

EXECUTIVE AUTHORITY.

The executive power will continue vested in His Majesty and as respects Irish services will be exercised by the Lord Lieutenant on the King's behalf. The Ministers of Northern and Southern Ireland respectively will constitute Executive Committees of the Irish Privy Council to advise the Lord Lieutenant in the exercise of his executive power in relation to Irish services. " Irish services " are defined as all public services in connection with the administration of civil government, except reserved services. These latter include, in addition to those mentioned above, the following services to be reserved for the periods mentioned :—

Control of Royal Irish Constabulary and Dublin Metropolitan Police and appointment of magistrates for three years, or until the date of Irish union.

Post Office, including designs for stamps, registration of deeds and Public Record Office of Ireland until the date of Irish union, or the passage of identical Acts by the two Parliaments making provision for the transfer of these services.

Land Purchase Acts until otherwise provided by the Imperial Parliament.

The power of making laws with respect to railways, fisheries, and the contagious diseases of animals (not being powers relating to reserved matters) are to be entrusted to the Council of Ireland and not to the two Parliaments. The Council is also given powers with respect to Private Bill legislation and may consider questions bearing on the welfare of either part of Ireland on which it may, by resolution, make suggestions to the Parliament concerned. It will also particularly be the duty of the Council to consider what Irish services ought in the common interest to be administered by a body having jurisdiction over the whole of Ireland.

The Act prescribes the number of members of each House of Commons, the method of their election, the constitution of the Senates and other details. After the appointed day Ireland is to return forty-six members to serve in the Parliament of the United Kingdom.

FINANCIAL PROVISIONS.

The two Parliaments are empowered to make laws with respect to taxation other than Customs Duties, Excise Duties, Excess Profits Duty, Corporation Profits Tax, or other tax on profits, and Income Tax.

Ireland's contribution to Imperial expenditure is for the first two years to be at the rate of £18,000,000 per annum. Subsequently the proportion is to be such as the Joint Exchequer Board determine to be just, having regard to the relative taxable capacities of Ireland and the United Kingdom. The proportion is to be subject to revision at the end of every fifth financial year.

Land purchase annuities are to be collected by the two Governments in their respective areas and will be retained by them.

Provision is made to ensure that after the date of Irish union consideration is given to the question of the transfer of Customs and Excise to the Parliament and Government of Ireland.

In place of the Supreme Court of Judicature in Ireland the Act provides for the establishment of Supreme Courts in both Southern and Northern Ireland, with a court having appellate jurisdiction throughout the whole of Ireland to be called the High Court of Appeal for Ireland.

In the event of either House of Commons not being properly constituted power is given for the dissolution of the Parliament in question by Order in Council and for the exercise of the powers of Government by the Lord Lieutenant with the assistance of a committee of Privy Councillors. The Act would, in such case, be operated by a legislative assembly consisting of the committee and other persons appointed by the King for the purpose.

The Act is to come into operation on " the appointed day," namely, the first Tuesday in the eighth month after the month in which it was passed, or such other day not more than seven months earlier or later as may be fixed by Order in Council.

The Government of Ireland Act 1914 is repealed as from the passing of the present Act.

DEBATE IN HOUSE OF COMMONS.

The Second Reading and part of the Committee stage of the Bill in the House of Commons were taken before Parliament adjourned in August for the Autumn Recess. Proceedings on the Bill were resumed on 22nd October when the House of Commons went into Committee and considered a further financial resolution relating to the measure.

The Right Hon. Sir Laming Worthington-Evans (Minister without Portfolio) gave an outline of the Government's amended proposals regarding the finance of the Bill. He pointed out that for two years Ireland was to make a contribution of £18,000,000 towards Imperial services, viz., £10,080,000 from the Southern Parliament and £7,920,000 from the Northern Parliament. He had put down an amendment empowering the Joint Exchequer Board at any time after the end of the second financial year to reduce the contribution of £18,000,000, having regard to the relative taxable capacity of Ireland and of the United Kingdom, if they came to the conclusion that a less sum should be justly contributed by the two Governments. The Joint Exchequer Board might also vary the proportions of the contribution as between the Southern and Northern Parliaments. The contribution would be subject to periodical revision.

He claimed that the Imperial contribution proposed by the Government was not only just, but extremely moderate. If the Government had desired to exact their pound of flesh from Ireland, the Imperial contribution would be fixed not at £18,000,000, but at £22,250,000, which was the contribution Ireland was making in the current year. Ireland would therefore, according to the Estimates, be left with a surplus revenue of £4,250,000 a year. In addition the Government had decided to make a free gift of the existing land annuities amounting at present to £3,250,000, which would be available as additional revenue for Ireland. An amendment had been put down by the Government with regard to the grant to each Parliament to provide for the necessary buildings and equipment. It omitted the limit of £1,000,000 and threw upon the Imperial Exchequer the duty of paying such sums as the Joint Exchequer Board might certify to be necessary for the purpose.

Generous Proposals.

The Government's proposals were infinitely more generous to Ireland and gave far greater powers to the Irish Parliaments than had been proposed in any Home Rule measure hitherto introduced. They were sufficient to enable the Parliaments to enter upon their duties without fear that their efforts would be stultified by want of money.

The Right Hon. Sir Donald Maclean (Chairman of the Independent Liberal Party in Parliament) said the Government expressly contemplated that the Southern Parliament would not be set up, and, therefore, he suggested that, as business men, they should confine their attention to the Northern Parliament.

The Right Hon. Sir Edward Carson (Leader of the Ulster Unionist Party) remarked that, as he understood the Government's amendments, if the Southern Parliament did not function there would be something else in its place to which the taxation of the Bill would be relevant. He was very anxious if the Bill became law that the finance should be a success, and he could not but believe that the British Government wished that both Parliaments, if they functioned, should run smoothly as regarded finance.

Lieut.-Colonel the Hon. Walter Guinness (Coalition Unionist, *Bury St. Edmunds*) observed that the finance of the Bill could not be a success unless it had popular support in Ireland. The Bill satisfied only one section of opinion in six out of 32 Irish counties. He agreed that the Government could not afford to satisfy the murder gang, but they could and must provide for a saner element amongst Sinn Fein.

Major J. W. Hills (Coalition Unionist, *Durham*) contended that it would be necessary to give Ireland the control of Customs and Excise. They could not expect the two Irish Governments to do any useful work unless they had the authority and responsibility that fiscal autonomy would give them.

The Financial Resolution was agreed to without a division.

On 28th October the House resumed consideration of the Bill in Committee and this stage of the measure was completed on the following day. The Report Stage was begun on 8th November and concluded on 10th November.

Third Reading.

On 11th November the Bill came up for Third Reading, and the debate was opened by,

The Right Hon. W. Adamson (Leader of the Parliamentary Labour Party), who, in moving the rejection of the measure, said that in following that course the Labour Party were acting in a perfectly consistent manner. Instead of providing a satisfactory solution of the problem, the Government policy, if allowed to develop upon the present disastrous lines, would inevitably have the gravest consequences to the Empire. Already their methods of government in Ireland had done almost irreparable damage to their prestige and reputation for good government among the other nations of the world. Their stupid, senseless, mailed-fist policy in Ireland was simply taking away from them much of the credit they earned in the War as the champion of small peoples. No one regretted the murders and reprisals that were taking place in Ireland more than the Labour Party. It was his personal opinion that if the 1914 Act had been put into operation the whole Irish question would have been settled and done with. But the legitimate rights of the Irish people had been withheld from them, and now, when they put forward a claim which possibly a considerable section of the people of this country considered to be an illegitimate claim, how could they be blamed ?

"The great bulk of the Irish people in the South and West," Mr. Adamson said, "are undoubtedly demanding complete independence and the recognition of an Irish Republic, but I do not believe that in their heart of hearts they really want a Republic. They are simply putting forward their maximum demand. The Labour Party do not believe in an Irish Republic. They do not think that it would be good for the people of this country or for Ireland. At the same time the Labour Party believe that the Irish people should be given the right to determine for themselves, and if you give them that right you give them perfect freedom of choice. . . . Let the army of occupation be withdrawn and let arrangements be made at once for the calling together of a Constituent Assembly elected on the basis of proportional representation by a free, equal and secret vote. That, in our opinion, would create such a response from Irishmen from all parts of the world as has never been given to any former proposal put forward by the respective Governments of Great Britain." The Constituent Assembly should draw up a Constitution for Ireland, on the understanding that that Constitution would be accepted subject to two conditions. The first was that it afforded protection to the minority, and the second that it would prevent Ireland from becoming a military or naval menace.

He appealed to the Government to withdraw the Bill and to get one put on the Statute Book at the earliest possible moment that would settle this question on a basis more in accordance with the feeling of the people of Ireland.

A World Question.

Lieutenant-Colonel John Ward (Liberal, *Stoke-on-Trent*) said it was a moral certainty that if they were to wait until they got a measure through that House that was unanimously approved of by the whole of Ireland, they would never deal with the subject at all. It would be most regrettable if, on principle, any Labour man walked into the Lobby against a measure that was going to give additional help to the Irish people in managing their own affairs. This had become a world question, and it was necessary that they should do something at once to show that they were prepared to give the Irish people an opportunity of governing themselves.

The Right Hon. H. H. Asquith (Leader of the Independent Liberal Party) asked what did the Bill amount to in the form in which they were now asked to give it their final assent? It amounted to the grant to one part of Ireland, the north-east corner of Ireland—what was sometimes very inaccurately

described as Ulster—of a Parliament which confessedly the
majority of that area did not want. They were content to
accept it, not with enthusiasm, not even with conviction,
because in their opinion it interposed an effectual, and, so
far as they could foresee, a permanent barrier to the attainment of Irish national union. On the other hand it offered to
what was called the South of Ireland—again the term was a
misnomer, for what was called the South of Ireland really
meant, in point of area and of population, by far the greater
part of Ireland—a Parliament not only which they did not
want, but which, judging by all the evidence, they would not
work. All the probabilities pointed to the so-called Southern
Parliament of Ireland being from the first still-born and a
dead letter.

Crown Colony Government.

That probability had appeared to the framers of the
Bill as so imminent that on the Report Stage they introduced a
clause expressly to provide that·in the event of the South of
Ireland repudiating this so-called boon the legislation and
administration of the larger part of the island should be
committed to a non-elected and irresponsible body of Crown
nominees. If the Bill passed into law it would provide
not even an instalment of hope or promise, let alone of
practical result, for the solution of that problem. After
speaking of the deterioration in the condition of Ireland
in regard to the maintenance of law and order, Mr. Asquith
said that in some respects, at any rate to the superficial
observer, there had never been a blacker or more un-
promising moment than the present. But he did not take
that view.

If they could only impress upon the Irish people that they
were ready and willing to meet them in a frank and generous
spirit, not to secure the triumph either of the minority or of the
majority in that country, but—consistently with the provision of every safeguard, both for strategic and Imperial
interests, and for the protection of minorities, be it in the
North or in the South—to give to them the great boon of absolute
self-government in regard to their own internal affairs and get
the Irish people to come together on that basis to deal with
the British people, the latter on that basis were perfectly
prepared to come together and deal with them. But it
must be a joint effort.

"If we can only do that," Mr. Asquith added, "I have
believed and still believe that we can within a measurable
distance of time banish these old controversies . . . and

bring at last to fruition the long-delayed and often-frustrated hopes of the best friends of both Ireland and England in a union of peace."

Always at Cross Purposes.

The Prime Minister (the Right Hon. D. Lloyd George) said the Government were only too anxious to respond to Mr. Asquith's appeal in the spirit in which it was made. There was nothing with which Great Britain would be better pleased than a frank reconciliation with Ireland. "The British people are not a vindictive people," the right hon. gentleman proceeded. "To them it would be a source of joy and pleasure to extend the right hand of fellowship to Ireland and let the past be forgiven and forgotten, so that the two nations should proceed together side by side to solve the great problems of the Empire and the problems of humanity." It was, he continued, one of the curses of the relations of the two countries that they had always been at cross purposes. Nothing baffled one more in dealing with Ireland than the atmosphere of suspicion in which the whole problem was considered and discussed. There was suspicion in Ireland, towards Ireland, and from Ireland.

The trouble had been not so much in discussing particular details, as in scattering the cloud of suspicion that obscured the intentions and the good will of one nation towards the other. Until that suspicion was removed they would get no measure that would be accepted by the Irish people. Mr. Asquith had put forward proposals of a very extreme character. He had been driven to propose something which gave Ireland the power to set up an Army and a Navy. He even proposed that Ireland should have foreign relations.

Mr. Asquith: "My proposal is to give Ireland no power which is not given to one of the Dominions."

The Prime Minister: "I quite agree. Undoubtedly Australia not only has the power to have an army, but has an army. Canada not only has the power to have an army, but has an army, and Australia has a navy as well. What I want to point out is that if you try to satisfy Ireland in her present rather aggressive and, if I may say so, unreasoning frame of mind you are driven to proposals that Irishmen in their better temper would never dream of putting forward."

Ireland's Whole Interest.

The Leader of the Labour Party, the Premier went on to say, had also been driven by that very desire to put forward proposals quite unacceptable to the vast majority of the

workers of England. Mr. Adamson had talked about giving
Irishmen the right to self-determination and gave the illustration of Czecho-Slovakia. He set before them the spectacle
of the *débris* of the Austrian Empire after a shattering war
as something that Great Britain ought to apply in principle
when it came to deal with Home Rule for Ireland. That was
inconceivable. The whole interest of Ireland was in the closest
association with the United Kingdom. If in the Assembly
of which Mr. Adamson had spoken the Sinn Feiners said what
they wanted was an independent Irish Republic, would the
right hon. gentleman give it to them ?   Ireland in a moment
of temper would give an answer which would be disastrous
to her own future and would not represent in the least
her real mind.   Therefore, let them not talk about self-
determination.

Did anyone deny that what the Government proposed
meant conferring upon Ireland a measure of self-government
of the most generous character ?

Mr. J. Devlin* (Nationalist, *Belfast, Falls*) : " Yes."

The Prime Minister, continuing, said that his hon. friend
was bound to deny it. What was wanted was an atmosphere
in Ireland where they could get calm consideration of what
the Imperial Parliament suggested, and what further suggestions Ireland had to make.   On behalf of the Government he
had invited spokesmen who claimed that they had authority
to speak on behalf of the Irish people to come forward and
discuss the Government's proposals, and to put forward any
alternative proposals of their own, subject to certain well-
defined conditions.

No Independence.

" The independence of Ireland as a Sovereign State,"
said Mr. Lloyd George, " we would not recognise, not merely
because it would be injurious to the United Kingdom, but
because it would be injurious to Ireland. . ' . .   We could
not consent to anything which would weaken the strategic
security of the United Kingdom by depriving us of complete
control over the harbours of Ireland for strategic purposes.
I am glad that Mr. Asquith accepts that position."

Mr. Asquith : " I have said so several times."

The Prime Minister : " Yes, but let me point out to my
right hon. friend that when he talked about Dominion Home
Rule he did not quite mean it."

---

* Early in August Mr. Devlin was suspended from the service of the
House for disregarding the authority of the Chair. On 22nd October his
suspension was terminated by a resolution of the House.

Mr. Asquith : " I would give to Ireland the same power —neither greater nor less—as is given to the self-governing Dominions."

The Prime Minister : " It shows the danger of using these phrases. Australia has complete strategic control over her own harbours, and so has Canada. Can anyone contend that Canada, and Australia and South Africa have not the most complete strategic control over their own harbours ? "

Mr. Adamson : " And they have not been a menace to this country."

The Prime Minister : " I agree, and that is the difficulty. If my right hon. friend will take the trouble to read the documents which the persistence of an hon. member has induced the Government to publish, I am not so sure that he will be quite so pleased when he sees them. He will also see what a menace the creeks of Ireland could be to the security of the Empire, how they plotted to use them, how they did use them, and how they would have used them much more fatally to the detriment of this country if we had not had a complete grip on them. That grip we mean to retain. . . . It is not well that a small nation like Ireland should be tempted, lured by the enemies of Britain, into a course that would be disastrous to herself."

No Separate Army and Navy.

The Government, said the Premier, could not consent to anything which would enable Ireland to organise an army and a navy of her own. If powers were given to Ireland to raise a conscript army it would be a menace to Britain, and he warned Labour members, who had been taking a leading part in opposing conscription, that if they were to have an army of that kind in Ireland, which under full powers of Dominion Home Rule would be given to it, conscription in Great Britain would be inevitable. As for a navy, there were smaller countries than Ireland that had navies and it did not need an expensive navy to be formidable to this country. Submarine bases, submarines, and small craft would be dangerous. It was tempting Ireland. With regard to Ulster, the Government were in honour bound not to consent to any scheme of self-government for Ireland which would involve the coercion of Ulster into acceptance.

Fiscal autonomy in principle the Government had conceded to a much larger extent than in the Act of 1914. There were provisions in the Bill that would enable the Council of Ireland, when there was Irish union, even to have powers to take into consideration the transferring of Customs and Excise to the Irish Parliament. Autonomy was something which the Government had never ruled out of discussion, but it could only be discussed with people who accepted the conditions that he had laid down on behalf of the Government as to the relations between Ireland and Great Britain.

Position of Ulster.

Sir Edward Carson remarked that as Ulster was chided with not being enthusiastic about the Bill he wished to say that he saw no reasons for being enthusiastic towards any change that would bring about a diminution of the position of Ulster people as citizens of the United Kingdom. The Ulster people, having accepted the view of the Government that it was essential they should be put under a Parliament of their own, which they did not ask for, had set themselves to get ready for that Parliament, and had resolved to work it in the best interests of their own country and of the Empire.

" I desire to say frankly to the House," Sir Edward proceeded, " that I do see a great change in that direction in Ulster . . . and I am now even better fitted than before to give the pledge that Ulster will do its best to perform the obligations put upon it under this Bill." The right hon. gentleman went on to say that the Bill set up a procedure for a union of the whole of Ireland, which would be a real and not a sham unity. In his belief no other scheme was so statesmanlike, or so near to self-determination, which was so loosely defined, had ever yet been brought before that Parliament. He hoped with all his heart that in the long run the Bill would lead to unity and peace in Ireland, but it must be given a fair trial. If hon. gentlemen opposite proceeded to try to thwart its working, or to encourage others for political or other purposes in Ireland to try to do so, they might readily succeed in that purpose, but they would be doing the greatest disservice to Ireland and to Great Britain that could be conceived.

They were told that the South and West would not function in the Parliament set up there. If Ulster did what he hoped and believed she would do in setting up an example and precedent of good, fair, honest government, of government not for sections or factions, but for all, her example might be followed by the rest of Ireland, and in that way there might be brought about a peace which was not at the moment anticipated.

Nationalist View.

Mr. Devlin said no one in the House was so anxious as he was to see an ending to the long and bitter quarrel between the two nations. Even in the midst of the horrors which he thought British rule had brought on Ireland he never could work himself up to a hatred of the British people, and if he were convinced that the Bill would terminate the unhappy quarrel of centuries he would hesitate before he voted against it. But he frankly confessed that he did not think any proposal submitted by any Government could be so foreign in its ultimate end to that purpose as this proposal. He was firmly convinced that if a great scheme of Dominion Home Rule were introduced for Ireland, with what all sane men could regard as adequate safeguards for North-East Ulster, it would undoubtedly satisfy the overwhelming sentiment of the people of Ireland. The Act of 1914 had been assailed from many quarters, but his own belief was that if the Government had taken the financial clauses of the Act and made them satisfactory it would have been a solution of the Irish problem. It was now understood that the genuine reason why the present proposal had been brought forward was simply to clear away from the Statute Book the Act of 1914—a betrayal as gross as the Act of Union.

On a division the amendment for the rejection of the Bill was negatived by 183 votes against 52 and the Third Reading was then agreed to.

DEBATE IN HOUSE OF LORDS.

The Bill came up for Second Reading in the House of Lords on 23rd November and the debate was continued on the two following days.

The Lord Chancellor (Lord Birkenhead), after explaining in detail the provisions of the measure, said that as they were repeatedly told that nobody wanted the Bill it was right that he should make plain to their Lordships that the arrangements for establishing and working their Parliament, and all the ancillary institutions which were involved in the establishment of that Parliament, had reached a high degree of progress in Ulster at the present moment. When their Lordships came to pass criticism upon the Bill let them at least not ignore that for the first time it enabled them to show to the whole world by irrefutable testimony that the Irish question was an Irish question alone, and it was in the power of Irishmen to reach a complete solution to-morrow. " Here, within the pages of this Bill," said the Lord Chancellor, " we make it plain to the whole world that we have set up an authority, which consists of Irishmen and Irishmen alone, which, if they can bridge over—and, with discussion, I hope they will

c 2

succeed in bridging over—their controversies may procure for them a degree of self-government which has exceeded what has been put forward by any great Irish leader or Nationalist until the claim for a separate Republic was made."

It was obvious, the noble Lord continued, that he would be asked two questions. He would be asked what was to happen supposing that the Sinn Fein representatives in Ireland declined to take any part in the election of the Southern Parliament, or, if they took part in it, refused to present themselves and take the Oath. Supposing that happened, they would be governed, until they saw that they had a better alternative, as a Crown Colony. He would also be asked what was to happen supposing the Sinn Feiners, or the majority in Ireland, fraudulently affected to become members of the Southern Parliament; supposing, in other words, that they were elected and having taken the Oath proceeded to declare a Republic, or to violate the Oath. He did not believe that, with all their mental and moral idiosyncrasies, the Sinn Fein Party would, in fact, adopt that course, but if they did the existence of that Irish Parliament would be brought to an end by any means that might be appropriate and necessary. It might involve, conceivably, the conquest of the South of Ireland.

He was of opinion that this was incomparably the most promising measure which had ever been introduced upon the subject of Home Rule.

Motion for Rejection.

The **Earl of Dunraven** moved the following amendment to the motion for the Second Reading :—

"That this House declines to proceed with a Bill which meets with no support from the great majority of the Irish people and affords no prospect of any permanent settlement."

The noble Earl said he thought it was very important, in order to satisfy Irish sentiment, that Ireland should be restored to her former status of a kingdom. He was sure that they could never have a permanent settlement and permanent peace in Ireland until they had moderate opinion —and that was really the great bulk of public opinion—behind the law and in favour of maintenance of the law. He was equally certain that they would never satisfy that moderate public opinion and get it openly to support the law until it was satisfied on the financial point. It never would be satisfied until they gave to Ireland full fiscal and financial control over her own affairs. The Bill did not give that or anything like it, and it was on that ground he asked their

Lordships not to proceed with it, because it was fatally and vitally faulty in the one point on which they could not amend it in that House.

Identifying himself with moderate opinion, he thought they had a right to expect far larger, more just, and more generous provisions than were contained in the financial clauses of the Bill.

Lord Oranmore and Browne believed that if the Bill was ever to have a chance of being successfully put into force three things were necessary. In the first place the financial provisions must be largely and generously revised. In the second place, ample safeguards must be supplied for the Unionists of the South and West, as to representation in both the Lower and Upper House, whether those safeguards complied with the ethics of democracy or not. In the third place provision must be made, if Ulster could not be included in the Irish Parliament at present, for a plebiscite or referendum from time to time, whether by counties or otherwise, to see whether she, or any part of Ulster, was prepared to change her mind and was ready to try and solve with Southern Unionists the problem of whether Ireland was able to govern herself.

Responsible Government.

Viscount Haldane said there was one feature in the Bill for which he valued it much. It offered to Ireland responsible government. Students of the British Empire knew that responsible government was something which had been given very tardily. If responsibility was placed where power was in Ireland he had the same belief about Ireland that he had practical verification of in the case of Canada. " The circumstances, of course, vary in some ways," said Lord Haldane, " but unless you have the courage to take your life in your hand and go to the fullest extent with this, then do not swither between the two things : either say that you are out-and-out coercionists, or say you will take the full step. That has been the case throughout the experience of the British Empire. We have found as we have gathered courage that disturbances have become lessened and have finally disappeared in so far as we have made it the interest of the people themselves to put an end to them."

Viscount Grey of Fallodon said the Bill seemed to him to stereotype partition, and on finance he went further, perhaps, than many noble Lords were prepared to go who thought the provisions of the Bill on finance were inadequate. To that day even moderate Irishmen believed that the reason why financial control was not given in the Bill was that people in England were still anxious that Ireland should not have her fair opportunities and fair scope.   The best way to get rid of that suspicion would be to treat Ireland as a self-governing Dominion and say frankly that they would take nothing from Ireland except what Ireland was prepared voluntarily to contribute.   If, instead of saying that if peace were offered they would give fiscal freedom to Ireland, the Government would give that fiscal freedom in the hope that it would produce peace, something might be made of the Bill.

It was true, he said, that Ireland was a domestic question, but it transcended in importance all other domestic questions as regarded their international relations.   The Irish race was a unit : only a small proportion of it was in Ireland, and as long as Ireland was irreconcilable, the influence in the most important parts of the world would be sinister, malignant and detrimental in foreign countries and in the self-governing Dominions.

It was quite true that the self-governing Dominions, as they read of those intolerable murders in Ireland, were entirely in sympathy with anything the Government might do to punish criminals.   But this question of murder was transitory.   The abiding case of the Irish question was not in those things which were horrible symptoms of it.   It lay much deeper and there had been growing in the self-governing Dominions a feeling of surprise, and they asked, " Why cannot you do for Ireland something of the same sort of thing as is done for ourselves ? " On the settlement of the Irish question depended, he thought, not merely a great deal in foreign relations, but something in their relations with the self-governing Dominions.   Urging the Government to improve the Bill, he quoted the example of South Africa and asked whether in all their history this country had ever lost by giving too much.   He counselled Ministers to " take courage from the history of the Empire."

The Earl of Donoughmore said that under the Bill the Government were offering to the Parliament in Dublin less financial authority than was now enjoyed by the Channel Islands or the Isle of Man.   He wondered any British Government could think that such a position could be accepted by any body of sensible men for five minutes.

Lord Killanin described the measure as a pure partition Bill, and said the policy of partition was hateful to every Irishman.

The Earl of Midleton moved the adjournment of the debate for a fortnight in order to permit of negotiations taking place with reference to the financial proposals in the Bill, the question of a Second Chamber, and other matters.

Control of Finances.

The Marquis of Crewe agreed with a remark that had fallen from another noble Lord, that the Bill had been framed simply from the point of view and in the interests of the six counties of Ulster. He thought that the design and composition of the Exchequer Board was a fatal blot on the Bill and it was one of the matters which the Government ought to be asked to reconsider. He would certainly give Ireland control over all her finances, yet at the same time it would seem to him reasonable—and he believed it would be regarded as reasonable in Ireland—that a lump sum, or the equivalent of a lump sum, should be paid in reduction of the National Debt as a final clearing up of the financial position between the two countries. They had been told that, failing this Bill, Southern Ireland would be subjected to Crown Colony government. As an old Colonial Secretary he protested most strongly against any statement of the kind.

The government—a government without any representation or consent—which was going to be imposed upon Ireland bore no sort of resemblance to Crown Colony government. Crown Colony government in all important cases was representative government. What Crown Colony government did closely resemble was the position of Irish members at Westminster since the Union. Ireland had not had responsible government but representative government, just as in Crown Colony government there was a body of representative members always liable to be outvoted by the official majority, but able to state their views. What really was proposed was the sort of government which might be imposed upon some pagan Protectorate—upon people who were in themselves assumed to be completely unfit for any form of representative government.

Reply for the Government.

The Secretary of State for Foreign Affairs (Earl Curzon of Kedleston) said the march of events had brought a great number of them—he believed they were the majority of that House—to the conviction that some form of Home Rule must be conceded to Ireland. When the Government were told that nobody wanted this Bill, after all the men in that House who spoke for 1,250,000 of the population of Northern Ireland had told them that they did want it; and when they were told by their critics in foreign countries that they ought to defer to the principle of self-determination, at least that was the principle on which they had acted so far as Ulster was concerned. He believed that when the Bill was passed the

Ulstermen would take it and would set up their Parliament in Belfast, and that without vindictiveness, without partiality, and without provocation they would show how Irishmen could govern themselves and could govern other Irishmen who did not agree with them

Instead of thinking that they were building up a wall with big bricks that was to sever the two sections of the Irish people from each other, he believed they were building a flimsy wall that would be kicked over by the common sense and moderation of that people before many years had gone by. Turning to the question of finance, the noble Earl observed that whatever be the case for or against fiscal autonomy in relation to a united Ireland and a single Parliament, how could they possibly give fiscal autonomy to two Irelands and two Parliaments ? The proposition was altogether unthinkable. " I say this," continued the noble Earl, " that if any real proposal for fiscal autonomy for a united Ireland and a single Parliament were put forward by a body competent to speak for the majority in Ireland and offering prospects of settlement, we will go a long way to meet it.

" If Ireland came with one accord and with one voice and said, ' Give us our Customs, give us our Excise, give us our Income Tax,' do you think there is any British Government that would steel itself to immediate refusal ? No. Under such conditions an Irish body, or an Irish Parliament, speaking with the authority that I described, would have the game in its own hands and would almost be able to exact such reasonable terms from any British Government as it might desire to exact."

De Valera's " No."

The noble Earl reminded the House that the Prime Minister had deliberately said he was open to receive any responsible suggestion coming from representative quarters in Ireland, either on the finance of the Bill or on anything else. But while that was his attitude and while no reply was made to him, from across the Atlantic there was thunder—the implacable " No " of De Valera. It was always that sinister figure in the background that was confounding their best efforts. Having urged the House not to accept Lord Midleton's motion to adjourn the debate, the noble Earl asked their Lordships not to cast this Bill away, but to take it, use it as a basis, use it as a platform from which to move out and do something better. " If you refuse it," he said, " once again you plunge Ireland into the old unending and cruel strife."

Their Lordships divided first on Lord Midleton's amendment to adjourn the debate for a fortnight, which was negatived by 177 votes against 91. Another division followed on Lord Dunraven's amendment to the Second Reading motion, which was negatived by 164 votes against 74. Thereafter, the Bill was read a second time.

During the subsequent stages of its progress through the Upper House the Government suffered a number of defeats and the Bill was amended in various important particulars.

COMMONS AND AMENDMENTS.

The Lords' amendments to the Bill were considered at length by the House of Commons and discussed in detail. In the course of the discussion on 16th December, some references were made to the application of the system of Proportional Representation to the new Parliaments in Ireland and the experiences of the Dominions were cited.

Proportional Representation: Dominion Experience.

The Right Hon. Sir Edward Carson (Leader of the Ulster Unionist Party) said: " I was very much struck in looking through an excellent new Journal,* referred to at a meeting over which you, Sir, presided this morning, of representatives of Parliaments of the Empire,† on reading a statement by the Prime Minister of New Zealand on this system of Proportional Representation. He said that in New Zealand, and I think he also mentioned Australia, where it has been tried, it has been proved to be the most absolute failure, and has brought about the most unexpected results by the way in which these quotas and other matters are worked in these elections, and by the scientific manœuvring that goes on as regards the bringing in of people who really would never have a chance otherwise of election. I do not know where a great success in this system has ever been achieved.

Mr. Aneurin Williams (Liberal, *Durham,* *Consett):* " Belgium ! "

---

* Reference is made to this JOURNAL, Vol. I., No. 4, at page 715.

† This refers to the Annual Meeting of the United Kingdom Branch of the Empire Parliamentary Association over which the Speaker (the Right. Hon. J. W. Lowther) had presided that morning in the Rooms of the Association, Westminster Hall.

Sir Edward Carson : " We have many Parliaments in the Empire, subordinate Parliaments, and I do not believe in any of them it has been a success."

Mr. Aneurin Williams : " Oh, yes, in many cases it has." (Hon. Members : " Where ? ") : " In Manitoba, in Australia, in Tasmania, in New Zealand, in South Africa."

Sir Edward Carson : " I have referred to the opinion of the Prime Minister of New Zealand who is nearer to the working of this thing, and I hope many Members of the House will read what he said upon this system."

Agreed Changes in Bill.

Amongst the changes in the text which eventually, after considerable discussion, were the subject of agreement between the two Houses, was the insertion of the provision that there should be a Senate for each of the two Parliaments. The constitution of the Council of Ireland was altered as compared with the proposal in the Bill when read a third time in the House of Commons, and it was also decided that if the first attempt to elect a Parliament in either part of Ireland failed another Parliament might be summoned at any time within three years from 1st June, 1921, unless a resolution declaring that it was inexpedient that this should be done was passed by both Houses of the United Kingdom Parliament. There was a good deal of controversy over the last-named alteration in the Bill and the form of words adopted represented the final result of the negotiations between the two Houses. Other changes effected are embodied in the summary of the text of the Act, which was under discussion until almost the eve of the Prorogation.

IRISH LAND BILL.

The Right Hon. Sir Laming Worthington-Evans (Minister without Portfolio) introduced in the House of Commons on 11th November a Bill " to amend the law relating to the occupation and ownership of land in Ireland." In order to redeem a promise made when the Government of Ireland Bill was first presented, the Government, it has been announced, will reintroduce these proposals for the completion of land purchase in Ireland next Session and ask Parliament to pass them into law. In the Session just ended the measure was not taken beyond the stage of formal First Reading.

The Bill is to come into force on an appointed day which is to be not more than three nor less than two and a half years after the date of its passing. On that day all tenanted land throughout Ireland will, be vested in either the Land Commission or the Congested Districts Board with the following exceptions :—

(1) Land purchased under previous Acts or which is subject to actual agreement to purchase.

(2) All untenanted land intended to be let for a residence, or which is a demesne, home farm, park, garden, or pleasure ground occupied in connection therewith.

(3) All holdings which have a potential or actual building value.

(4) Any holding not exceeding £200 in rateable value which the owner cultivates and on which he resides ; and

(5) All land held by the State, by local authorities, and by public utility companies.

The terms of purchase provide that the annual instalment payable by the tenant is to be at the rate of 5¼ per cent. instead of 3¼ per cent. as at present. The Bill enacts that the landlord shall be paid in bonds bearing interest at the rate of 5 per cent.—the remaining ¼ per cent. charged to the tenant representing sinking fund—and the Treasury is authorised to create a new capital stock of that denomination. The bonds are to be redeemable by means of periodical drawings.

Provision is made for compensating vendors who have sold under the Act of 1909 in respect of the old three per cent. stock, if any portion of it is required to be realised.

The value of the land to be brought under compulsory purchase under the measure is estimated at £70,000,000.

IRISH PEACE PROPOSALS.

(Prime Minister's Announcement: Martial Law, &c.)

During the closing weeks of the year rumours were freely circulated regarding approaches to the Government from Ireland for a settlement of the Irish question. In these circumstances an announcement of Government policy—a double policy—by the Prime Minister on 10th December created considerable interest. The Premier's statement was made in reply to a question from Mr. Asquith and was not the subject of debate.

STATEMENT IN HOUSE OF COMMONS.

The Prime Minister (the Right Hon. D. Lloyd George) said that during the last few weeks the Government had been in touch with intermediaries who had been anxious to bring about a better understanding. There had been no negotiations, but certain people who offered their services had seen both sides and had thus enabled the Government to arrive at certain conclusions about the position in Ireland. The Government were convinced that the majority of the people of Ireland of all sections were anxious for peace and for a fair settlement. The Government on their side were no less anxious for peace and a fair and lasting settlement, and in that respect he felt confident they represented the views of the whole of the people of Great Britain. On the other hand, the Government were also very regretfully convinced that the section which controlled the organisation of murder and outrage in Ireland was not yet ready for a peace that would accept the only basis on which peace could be concluded—an acceptance which would be consistent with the unbroken unity of the United Kingdom.

"Their communications," said the Premier, "are all conceived in the spirit of proposals from an independent belligerent Power offering peace to another independent belligerent with whom they are at war, and to whom they are in a position to dictate. In these circumstances the Government determined on the double policy which I propose now to declare. On the one hand they feel they have no option but to continue, and indeed to intensify, their campaign against that small but highly organised and desperate minority who are using murder and outrage in order to obtain the impossible and bring peace neither to Ireland nor to Great Britain; but, on the other hand, to open and encourage every channel whereby the forces in Ireland which are really anxious for an honourable settlement can find expression and so lead to negotiations which may produce a real and lasting peace.

"This is the general policy of the Government, and I want the House to understand that this is a considered policy that aims on the one hand at the repression of crime and on the other at preparing the way towards a better understanding between the two peoples."

Offer to Sinn Fein M.P.'s.

Continuing, the right hon. gentleman referred to a resolution passed by the Galway County Council, a body which had proclaimed its adhesion to the Republican Party and he rather thought to the Dail Eireann. That resolution revealed the first area of dry land which had shown itself after the deluge of unconstitutionalism in that part of the country. A telegram had also been sent to him by Father O'Flanagan, but although he called himself, in the absence of Mr. De Valera, acting president of Sinn Fein, his action had been repudiated by the heads of the organisation which, in the judgment of the Government, was responsible for murder in Ireland. The resolution of the Galway County Council condemned the murders and condemned reprisals. The Council said they believed the present unfortunate state of affairs was detrimental to the interests of both countries in such a crisis of the world's affairs. They, therefore, as adherents of Dail Eireann, requested that body to appoint three delegates, and they suggested that for that purpose the British Government should withdraw the bar on the meeting of Dail Eireann.

"At the present moment," Mr. Lloyd George proceeded, "that body is not permitted to meet, and of course we cannot recognise it, for to recognise it as a separate body is to recognise that the part of the country which it represents constitutes a separate republic apart from the United Kingdom. . . . But when you come to the members individually they are the people who have been elected under the constitution of this country to this House. . . . They are not permitted to meet at the present moment, and the question is whether it is desirable that they should be permitted to do so in order to consider the new situation which has arisen in Ireland. There are very practical difficulties in the way. Some of these members have, in our judgment, been guilty of crimes which would make them liable to prosecution and punishment, whether in Ireland or Great Britain, or in any other civilised country in the world.

"We cannot possibly grant to those who have been guilty of crimes of violence . . . of very brutal murder, a safe conduct which we would not grant to any British member of the House of Commons in similar circumstances. . . . We must, therefore, make an exception in the case of those men."

Reply to County Council.

The full text of the reply which it was proposed to send to the Galway County Council was communicated to the House by the Premier. The following is an extract : —

"The first necessary preliminary to the re-establishment of normal conditions is that murder and crimes of violence shall cease. It is to that end that the efforts of the Irish Executive have been constantly directed, and until it has been attained no progress can be made towards a political settlement. The Government are prepared to facilitate the meeting together for this purpose of persons duly elected to represent constituencies in Ireland or any part of Ireland. There are, however, certain individuals who are gravely implicated in the commission of crime so serious that the Government cannot consent to abandon their elementary duty of bringing such persons to trial. To all members except these individuals a safe conduct would be granted by the Government. It should be clearly understood that His Majesty's Government must insist that effective measures be taken to ensure the cessation of murder and other crimes of violence and the surrender of all arms unlawfully held."

The reply to be sent to Father O'Flanagan, which was similar in character, was also read by the Premier. The right hon. gentleman, answering a question from the Opposition side, said the Government were prepared to furnish a list of those Sinn Fein members of Parliament to whom they would give a safe conduct. Due protection would be afforded to those who had a safe conduct by the police and by the whole forces of the Crown, who would be available against any possible attack upon them.

Martial Law.

The Government were determined to do all in their power to break up the terrorists, because he did not think it would be possible for Ireland to recover that independence which was essential to her if she was to make peace, until those men had been brought to justice, or at any rate to surrender. The Government had, therefore, been driven to the conclusion, especially in the last two very terrible years, that they must take stronger action in certain disturbed areas in Ireland.

" What is the position, more particularly in the south-west of Ireland ? " asked Mr. Lloyd George. " You have got there organised insurgent forces. Until recently they dwelt, I will not say in complete immunity, but in something approaching it, in their own towns and villages. The very strong action which has been taken has forced them to take to the hills, and there they are organising bands. They attack the police. They ambush the police. They intimidate men of their own race who are tired of this terrorism. It is necessary that they should be captured and broken up. . . . In this area an attack was made upon the police by men who were dressed in British uniforms and trench helmets. That has added to the difficulty. . . . We have decided to proclaim in that quarter of Ireland martial law and to mete out exactly the same treatment to these people as would be done if they were open rebels.

" There is no doubt at all that if these men were open rebels, with some distinctive mark showing that they were rebels armed openly for the purpose of shooting down soldiers, the soldiers would not only have the right but it would be their duty to shoot back. Treachery should not be a protection.

We are only meting out the ordinary rules of civilised warfare."

Surrender of Arms.

"What is proposed to be done is this. First of all there will be a proclamation of martial law, and then under that a proclamation will be issued. The effect will be to demand the surrender of all arms and uniforms by a certain date within that area. The surrender can be made either to an officer of the Crown, or to the police, or to a military officer, or to the parish priest provided the parish priest surrenders them afterwards to the proper officer in the area. . . . After a certain date unauthorised persons found in possession of arms in the specified areas to which martial law is applied will be treated as rebels, and will be liable on conviction by a military court to the penalty of death. The same penalty will be applied to the unauthorised wearing of the uniforms of any of His Majesty's forces, and to the aiding and abetting and harbouring of rebels. . . . Ample notice will be given to enable all persons in those areas who have been so misguided as to array themselves against order and law, and the authority of the Crown in those areas, to surrender their arms under the conditions specified. Trial will be by a military court.

"I deeply regret that it should be necessary to do this, or to declare martial law. I would infinitely have preferred that the control of the administration of the whole of Ireland should be in the hands of the civil authorities, but the recent outrages which have taken place have made it necessary that we should take these steps in this part of Ireland." The right hon. gentleman added that the Government were eager for peace. They proposed to encourage every authority, every organisation, every individual who was prepared to assist in the negotiations for peace in Ireland. They were, however, convinced that peace was impossible so long as these forces were perpetrating outrage and intimidating the population, because the people themselves were afraid to talk peace.

In reply to questions the Prime Minister said it was essential that action should be taken immediately. The question of an amnesty would be a matter for discussion when peace was made. It was the intention of the Government to go on with the Government of Ireland Bill.

REPRISALS IN IRELAND.

(Vote of Censure Moved.)

A Vote of Censure on the Government in respect of Ireland was moved on behalf of the Labour Party on 20th October and was supported by the Independent Liberal Party. The resolution, which was proposed by the Right Hon. Arthur Henderson (Labour, *Widnes*), was in these terms : —

" That this House regrets the present state of lawlessness in Ireland and the lack of discipline in the armed forces of the Crown, resulting in the death or injury of innocent citizens and the destruction of property ; and is of opinion that an independent investigation should at once be instituted into the causes, nature, and extent of reprisals on the part of those whose duty is the maintenance of law and order."

The Chief Secretary for Ireland (Lieut.-Colonel the Right Hon. Sir Hamar Greenwood), in reply, declared that there was in Ireland a deliberate, organised, highly-paid conspiracy to smash the British Empire. He did not want reprisals even on notorious Sinn Feiners. He wanted them to be arrested and, if guilty of crime, to be tried. The best and the surest way to stop reprisals was to stop the murder of policemen, soldiers, and loyal citizens.

On a division following a full debate the motion was negatived by 346 votes against 70.

AGRICULTURE ACT.*

The Agriculture Act—one of the principal Government measures of the year—reached the Statute Book on the last day of the Session. It was the subject of very full discussions in both Chambers, and the longest sitting of the present Parliament—twenty-two and a half hours—was mainly due to the fact that the House of Commons devoted 13 hours of that time to the consideration of amendments made by the House of Lords.

MINIMUM PRICES, &c.

The Act continues in force the temporary provisions of the Corn Production Act, 1917, but provides that the operation of that Act may be terminated by an Order in Council made on an Address presented to the Crown by both Houses of Parliaments. Such an Order will not

---

* For summary of Bill as introduced and preliminary discussions, see JOURNAL, Vol. I., No. 3, page 449.

take effect, however, until the expiration of the fourth year subsequent to the year in which it is made.

Minimum prices are to be based on the following minimum prices for 1919, the standard year :—

Wheat	..	..	..	68s. per quarter of 504 pounds.
Oats	..	..	..	46s. per quarter of 336 pounds.

The Act provides for the appointment of three Commissioners whose duty it will be in 1921 and each subsequent year to fix minimum prices for that year. These prices are to rise or fall in comparison with those of the standard year in the same proportion as the ascertained rise or fall in the cost of production. The cost of production is to be ascertained by the Commissioners each year as soon as possible after the completion of the harvest.

ENFORCEMENT OF PROPER CULTIVATION.

Power is conferred on the Minister of Agriculture to enforce proper cultivation :—

(A) If arable or grass land, not being a park, garden, or pleasure ground, or land adjoining a mansion or garden attached to it, or woodland, is not being cultivated according to the rules of good husbandry.

(B) If the production of food on such land can, in the national interest and without injuriously affecting the persons interested in the land or altering the general character of the holding, be maintained or increased by an improvement in the existing method of cultivation.

(C) If the occupier or the owner of the land has unreasonably neglected to execute the necessary works of maintenance.

It is laid down in the Act that an order with respect to cultivation shall not interfere with the discretion of the occupier as to the crops to be grown. A right of appeal to an arbitrator is provided to determine whether the order is properly made.

If a landlord is required to execute repairs and fails to comply, the tenant may be authorised by the Minister to execute the works and recover the cost from the landlord.

Unreasonable failure to comply with a notice requiring the execution of any work is made an offence punishable by fine. The Minister of Agriculture is empowered to execute the work and to recover the cost from the person in default.

MISMANAGEMENT OF ESTATES, &C.

If, after consultation with the Agricultural Committee, the Minister is of opinion that the owner of an estate grossly mismanages it so as to prejudice materially the production of food, or the welfare of those engaged in its cultivation, he may, after a public inquiry, appoint a receiver and manager. The owner may appeal to the High Court against such an order.

" Necessary works of maintenance " are defined as follows :—

(A) Maintenance and clearing of drains, embankments, and ditches.

(B) Maintenance and proper repair of fences, stone walls, gates, and hedges.

(C) Execution of repairs to buildings.

D

The Minister may serve a notice upon the occupier of land requiring him to cut down or destroy injurious weeds. The expression "occupier" includes in this case an authority responsible for maintaining a public road.

Part II. of the Act provides for the amendment of the Agricultural Holdings Acts.

A landlord who gives notice to a tenant to quit, unless the notice is given for any one of the reasons specified in the Act, is liable to pay compensation for the disturbance of the tenant. The compensation is to be a sum representing the loss or expense directly attributable to the quitting of the holding unavoidably incurred by the tenant. It is to be computed at an amount equal to one year's rent, but if proved to be in excess of that amount the whole loss is to be recoverable up to a maximum equal to two years' rent.

If the landlord refuses a demand by a tenant for arbitration as to the rent of a holding and as a consequence the tenant terminates the tenancy by notice, the tenant is entitled to compensation. On the other hand, compensation is not payable if a landlord gives a tenant notice to quit because of the failure of the latter to agree to a demand by the landlord for arbitration as to the rent of a holding.

The Act makes provision under certain conditions for the payment of compensation for disturbance in respect of allotment gardens and of cottages held by agricultural labourers under a farmer. The law as to compensation for improvements made by the tenant is amended and provision is made for compensation in the case of a tenant who has continuously adopted a higher standard of farming than is required by his contract of tenancy.

On the other hand, the Act provides that corresponding compensation shall be payable to the landlord in the case of the deterioration of a holding by a tenant.

As regards market garden improvements, the Act contains provisions enabling an arbitrator or the Agricultural Committee to apply to a holding, or any part of a holding, the conditions known as "the Evesham Custom" under which the tenant who determines his tenancy is only entitled to compensation for market garden improvements if he can find another tenant willing to take his place and to undertake his liability for compensation.

DEBATE IN HOUSE OF COMMONS.

After undergoing examination by a Standing Committee, the Bill came back to the House of Commons, and the Report stage was begun on 2nd November. This stage of the measure occupied the time of the House at eight further sittings, and it was not until 25th November that the motion for Third Reading was taken.

Lieut.-Colonel G. L. Courthope (Coalition Unionist, Rye), proposed, as an amendment to the Third Reading motion, the rejection of the Bill. Everybody agreed, he said, that the desire to increase production and to re-establish, if possible, a rural population, was a laudable one, but the Bill would be an obstacle rather than an assistance to the furtherance of those aims. The Bill proposed to maintain in peace time the War policy of interference. It was true that the forms of interference might not be exercised very frequently. But, so far as he was aware, the sword of Damocles never fell, and yet it was quite sufficient to destroy the appetite of the unfortunate man who sat beneath it.

If the Bill were passed in anything like its present form it would be a sword of Damocles—a fear of interference coming Heaven knows when or where—hanging over the whole agricultural community. It would tend to poison the relationship between a landlord and his tenants, and possibly to some extent also between employer and employed, although the latter was a small point compared with the former. He believed, therefore, that in that respect, the Bill would do more harm than good. Although the minimum prices were ample to provide a handsome profit to the wheat grower on the good wheat land, they were not enough to induce the occupier of second-rate wheat land to devote that land to wheat.

The Right Hon. Sir F. Banbury (Coalition Unionist, *City of London*), in seconding the amendment, said that unless people were certain when they entered into arrangements that these would be sacred, there would be no likelihood of the future of farming being as successful even as it was in the bad times beginning somewhere about the 'eighties.

A Transitional Stage.

The Right Hon. George Lambert (Liberal, *Devon, South Molton*) observed that it was absolutely impossible to forecast the future of agriculture, which was in a transitional stage, and he did not hail with delight the Government's attempt to lay down a permanent policy for the future.

The Right Hon. F. D. Acland (Independent Liberal, *Cornwall, Camborne*) thought that, taken altogether, the Bill provided something like a fairly stable basis for the future progress of the agricultural industry. Certainly, if they looked within the industry there would be much more peace there than if the Corn Production Act had just been allowed to expire. In that case they would have had no Wages Board, and the farmer would have been at the mercy of a return to the prices of the 'nineties. He would have had no extra compensation for disturbance, there would have been no provision to induce landlords to keep their estates up to the highest mark of which they were capable, and there would have been no increased security for the tenant of the tied cottage. He believed that the Bill gave a greater feeling of all-round security and on it wonderful things might be built.

Mr. George Edwards (Labour, *South Norfolk***)** was perfectly convinced that the Bill would increase food production and lead to the better cultivation of the land. Although it had been said that the Bill did not give any security to the farmer, if they were going to give the farmer security of capital then it was to all intents and purposes security of tenure. When a landlord knew that if he turned a tenant out of his farm he was liable to pay compensation he would think twice before he took such a course. The agricultural labourer was never going back to his position in pre-war days. The Bill would do something to increase his comfort and lift him higher in the social scale. If they wanted to abolish unrest and keep the agricultural labourers contented they must pass the Bill.

Importance of Agriculture.

The Parliamentary Secretary to the Ministry of Agriculture (the Right Hon. Sir A. Griffith-Boscawen) remarked that an Agriculture Bill which did not deal with the problem of the agricultural labourer and try to better his condition would not be worth having. The Wages Board, which was made permanent, was not popular with farmers, but had done most excellent work. It had improved the wages of the labourers and had kept peace on the farm as peace had not been preserved in any other industry. There had often in the past been far too much difference of opinion between landlord and tenant. He looked forward to the time—and he hoped that Bill might help to accomplish it—when everybody in agriculture would recognise that their interests were identical and that they were engaged in one of the greatest of the national industries.

Replying to critics of the Bill, the right hon. gentleman asked what could the alternative policy be? They were agreed that increased production could only be obtained by means of the maintenance of more land under the plough. That must be done by making the conditions of the farmer such that he would risk his capital on arable land without running grave danger of losing it. If they guaranteed prices it followed that there must be a certain amount of control. If the State was willing to undertake a big financial burden it had a right to see that the land was properly cultivated— to see that there were no bad and indifferent farmers. The land of this country was too small in extent and too valuable to allow it to be badly farmed. They all agreed also that a bad landlord had no place in the country to-day any more than an indifferent farmer. If compensation for disturbance were not enacted in that Bill or in some other measure in the immediate future they would have an agitation either for complete fixity of tenure, with a Land Court, or else for nationalisation.

He maintained that the Bill dealt fairly with all classes who were interested in the soil. It was the only measure which could be carried at the present moment to deal with the agricultural situation.

On a division the amendment was negatived by 161 votes against 12 and the Bill was then read a third time.

DEBATE IN HOUSE OF LORDS.

On 30th November the Second Reading debate on the Bill was commenced in the House of Lords.

The Minister of Agriculture (Lord Lee of Fareham) said it was his sincere conviction that the safety of the realm might be largely bound up in the passing of that Bill, which was not designed primarily as a measure of agricultural reform, but as an essential provision of national defence shown to be necessary as a result of the lessons of the late War. The national returns showed that since 1918 there had been a reduction of over 450,000 acres of arable land and since 1870 a reduction of over 3,000,000 acres. Farmers would never grow cereals simply for the sake of the guarantees, but the Government had confidence that the insurance against loss which these guarantees would afford would encourage the growing of cereals whenever market conditions appeared reasonably favourable.

With regard to the powers taken under the Bill to enforce proper cultivation, there was no question of applying war methods to peace farming. He could only assume that what critics and opponents genuinely feared was a possible resumption of some kind of grass ploughing campaign such as was carried out on a wholesale scale in 1917 and 1918 at the greatest crisis of the War. There was no possibility of such a thing unless the very life of the nation were again at stake. An important amendment was inserted in the Bill in the House of Commons under which no order could in any circumstances be made which would interfere with the discretion of the farmer with regard to the crops that would be grown on a particular piece of land.

He could conceive that self-interest might possibly dictate the conversion of the whole of England into a grazing ranch; but the national need would be entirely ignored. And the occupation of land involved national obligations as well as individual self-interest.

A Social Aspect.

" It is true," said Lord Lee, " that the Bill is not designed in any sense as a measure of social reform, but incidentally, if passed, it may prevent a great injury to our social fabric. Everyone admits, I suppose, that the maintenance, and indeed the increase, of our rural population is of vital importance from both a political and hygienic standpoint. But the substitution on a large scale of grass land for arable is a direct negative to that policy ; it is not only opposed to the national interest, but, if persisted in, must have one result— the result of creating a new army of landless men who are skilled land workers and who, having lost their employment, will embark upon what, I venture to say, would prove an irresistible agitation for the breaking up of farms and for the nationalisation of the land. There have been rumbles of it already. I am quite convinced that that tendency would not be in the interests either of farmers or of landlords, whilst at the same time it is a contingency which cannot lightly be dismissed."

In that part of the Bill which dealt with the amendment of the Agricultural Holdings Acts, the purpose the Government had in view, the noble lord observed, was to make it easy to get rid of a bad tenant while making it difficult, or at any rate expensive, to get rid of a good one. He did not believe that the good landlords—and they were in a great majority— had anything to fear from that portion of the Bill. As a matter of fact, as between the good landlord and the good tenant these compensation clauses would hardly ever come into effect, whilst on the other hand they did constitute a much needed and effective protection to the good tenant against the rare case of the harsh, oppressive, and capricious landlord. " This Bill," added Lord Lee, " cannot be fairly described as a farmer's charter ; still less as a landlord's scourge. It is, if anything, a consumer's insurance."

Rejection Moved.

At the close of Lord Lee's speech the debate was adjourned for a week. When the proceedings on the Bill were resumed on 7th December,

The Marquis of Lincolnshire moved the rejection of the Bill, which, he contended, was bad for agriculture, was dangerous to the public—inasmuch as it must impose fresh millions of taxation on an already exhausted nation—and was repugnant to Liberal and Free Trade principles.

The Earl of Selborne believed that the Bill was based on considerations of national welfare and national safety. What would happen if the Bill were rejected and they relapsed into the policy of *laissez faire* which existed before the War? The process of the conversion of arable land to grass would go on at an ever-increasing rate, and if war took place twenty-five years hence this country would not find itself with the same proportion of grass and arable land as it had in 1914, but something very much less.

The Marquis of Crewe said the Bill finally pronounced the doom of independent systems of British farming. The industry of agriculture was to be made the subject of public inspection in a way which no other industry in this country had been or apparently would be. Anything like a large system of wheat storage had been in the main, as he understood, rejected by the experts, but—if the Government really believed that a sudden outbreak of war had to be guarded against—it would be worth their while to consider whether they ought not to combine the provisions of the Bill with other provisions which would ensure the existence of a six months' supply (or whatever it might be) of wheat in the country at a given moment.

Need for Agricultural Population.

The Secretary of State for the Colonies (Viscount Milner) said they were not considering an ordinary economic question which could be measured in hundreds of thousands or millions of pounds. It was the existence of this country as a great country which was at the back of the effort to promote the highest agricultural development of which they were capable. " I believe we are very near getting to a point where our agricultural industry will be entirely secondary and our agricultural population reduced to most dangerously low proportions," said Lord Milner. " I need not dwell upon the social consequences of that, the effect upon the physique or upon the character of the people. There is nothing in the world so steady as a strong agricultural population. I look with real alarm at the possibility of the agricultural people in this country, the people living on the land and by the land, being reduced to a perfectly inconsiderable and negligible minority."

He commended to their Lordships the all-important question of protecting the trade balance of this country by producing at home everything they could produce and not adding to the enormous weight of what they in any case must buy.

The Duke of Marlborough supported the Bill on the ground of the importance of food production as a weapon in national defence.

Viscount Chaplin said that if they could depend on prices continuing he would not have a moment's hesitation in moving the rejection of what he regarded as one of the worst Bills he had ever seen introduced into Parliament.

After further debate, their Lordships divided and the amendment to reject the Bill was negatived by 123 votes against 85. Thereafter the Second Reading was agreed to.

During the subsequent proceedings on the Bill in the Upper House the provisions of the measure were made the subject of numerous amendments, and these entailed considerable discussion in both Chambers. Finally, shortly before midnight on the date of the Prorogation, the two Houses were at last in agreement respecting the changes effected in the measure. The extent to which the Act differs from the Bill as originally introduced will be seen on reference to Vol. I., No. 3, of the JOURNAL (page 449), where a full summary is given of the text of the measure as first presented.

NATIONAL EXPENDITURE.

The sitting of the House of Commons on 9th December was set apart for a debate on National Expenditure. In the course of the proceedings the Chancellor of the Exchequer made a full statement explaining the steps taken by the Cabinet to curtail expenditure and the general financial policy of the Government.

DEBATE IN HOUSE OF COMMONS.

The Right Hon. George Lambert (Liberal, *Devon, South Molton*) opened the debate by moving a resolution in these terms : —

" That this House resolves that it will not sanction Expenditure for 1921-22 in excess of £808,000,000, the amount estimated as being necessary for a normal year by the Chancellor of the Exchequer on the 23rd October, 1919."

He urged that in order to avoid disaster it was necessary that there should be a sharp reversal in their financial policy.

The war habit of freely spending—he might say recklessly and extravagantly spending—must be ruthlessly broken. Expenditure must come off in chunks of tens of millions.

Mr. J. A. R. Marriott (Coalition Unionist, *Oxford*) seconded the motion. The situation at which they had arrived, he said, was so incomparably grave that they must all be prepared to postpone the achievement of the objects for which they cared most. He believed in the Education Act of 1918 and hoped to see it carried out in its fullest implications. But in view of the gravity of the financial situation the more elaborate provisions of that Act ought to be postponed for a period of years until they had reached financial equilibrium. Much as he believed in the social value of education, he did not think that at the present time the country could afford to spend £73,000,000 a year upon it.

Chancellor's Statement.

The Chancellor of the Exchequer (the Right Hon. Austen Chamberlain) drew attention to the progress of reduction in expenditure. In 1918-19 their gross expenditure was over £3,140,000,000. In 1919-20 it was reduced to £2,106,000,000, but they were borrowing to make both ends meet. This year, apart from the provision for the redemption of debt, it was reduced to £1,282,000,000. There had been, it must be admitted, a great change since the Budget was framed. To the over-hopefulness, over-confidence, over-lending, over-borrowing, over-trading, and over-speculation of the earlier months of the year there had succeeded a reaction which, he thought, had now tended to go too far in the opposite direction. Trade was stagnant. Orders were hard to obtain. Instead of fresh orders being placed, old orders were being cancelled. A feeling of anxiety and unrest was a natural consequence, and must affect the Budget estimate of revenue and, in its ultimate consequences, the Budget estimate of expenses.

The Budget estimate of expenditure was £1,418,300,000, of which £234,000,000 was not expenditure in the ordinary sense, but repayment of debt. The actual estimate of expenditure in the ordinary sense was £1,184,300,000, which included a sum of £20,000,000 for supplementary estimates to be presented in the course of the year. Mr. Chamberlain proceeded to explain that an additional £58,000,000 would be required for supplementary estimates, distributed as follows:—

Army	£40,000,000
Navy and Air Force	£8,000,000
Civil Service	£10,000,000

Savings made or in sight, however, practically afforded a set-off to the additional expenditure. The Budget total, therefore, was practically unaffected up to that date, but there must be some additional charge as the result of steps the Government might be called upon to take to deal with unemployment. There might also be additional charges as a result of the coal strike and the loss of railway revenue it involved.

Redemption of Debt.

On the revenue side the Budget estimate was also £1,418,000,000, and he was advised that at present there was no reason to anticipate that it would not be collected. He thought the year would end with between £200,000,000 and £230,000,000 or £234,000,000 for the redemption of debt. In the current year they would repay something over £90,000,000 of foreign debt, including obligations in the United States, Canada, Japan, Holland, the Argentine, and in Uruguay.

The right hon. gentleman went on to speak of the policy of the Government in regard to debt redemption and deflation. " I have," he said, " sternly set my face against further inflation starting a new cycle of increased costs and increased wages, but I have felt all the time that any sudden deflation on a great scale would produce a crisis as surely as, and more quickly than, a continuous steady inflation. My policy, therefore, in that respect is to avoid renewed inflation and, if it be in any way possible, gradually, very gradually, to deflate as opportunity offers, and as the conditions of the time permit with safety ; and as regards debt reduction, my policy has been that when we could redeem debt, we should redeem all the debt that we could, just because I saw that the good times would not always last and that we must try and lighten the load before the bad times came upon us."

Turning to the liquidation of Departments and of War services, Mr. Chamberlain stated that thirteen Departments had already been closed altogether. Of 90 trading accounts arising out of the Vote of Credit, 56 had been closed and 14 were being closed as rapidly as they could be. All War subsidies would have stopped by the end of the financial year—the bread subsidy, the coal mines subsidy, the railway subsidy, and the subsidy for the postal service.

Principles of Next Budget.

The Cabinet were acting upon the following principles in preparing the Budget for the financial year 1921-22 : —

General.—To the extent to which reforms—in themselves desirable in order to improve conditions in the United Kingdom—involved further burdens upon the Exchequer or the rates the time was not opportune for initiating them or putting them into operation. Instructions had been given to all spending Departments that except with fresh Cabinet authority schemes involving expenditure not yet in operation were to remain in abeyance.

Winding-up of Departments.—Ministry of Munitions and Ministry of Shipping would be wound up this financial year. Ministry of Food as a separate Government Department would cease to exist at the close of the year, and such powers as might still be found necessary would be transferred to another Department.

Military Expenditure.—The Cabinet were convinced of the necessity of curtailing military expenditure to the utmost extent compatible with the fulfilment of Imperial obligations and national safety. The principal field for economy was in the Near and Middle East, and the position in those regions was being fully explored with a view to further drastic reductions of expenditure the moment the situation permitted. In Mesopotamia, Sir Percy Cox, the High Commissioner, was actively engaged in the creation of an Arab State and the Provisional Government was pressing forward the creation of an Arab army which would provide a substitute for the British forces.

Naval Expenditure.—While determined to maintain the Navy at a standard of strength which should adequately secure the safety of the Empire and its maritime communications, the Cabinet, before sanctioning a programme of new construction, were bound to satisfy themselves that the lessons of the War had been definitely ascertained, more particularly as regarded the place and usefulness of the capital ship in future naval operations. They had, therefore, decided that the Committee of Imperial Defence should institute at once an exhaustive investigation into the whole question of naval strength, as affected by the latest development of naval warfare.

Air Expenditure.—The utmost economy would be enforced in the administration of the air programme, and the position and function of the Air Force would be examined in relation to the Army and the Navy.

State and Unemployed.

The Right Hon. J. R. Clynes (Vice-Chairman of the Parliamentary Labour Party) said he was unable to congratulate the Chancellor of the Exchequer on the case he had presented in opposition to the motion, but, at the same time, the Labour Party could not vote for the motion. It was not business at such a time to bind the Government to a particular figure and thereby prevent certain expenditure which it might be wise to incur. He was glad the Chancellor had announced that, whatever the Government proposed to save upon, it was not intended to try to economise in regard to insurance for unemployment. He regarded it as a State duty so to organise a State service of work as to turn unemployed men from being what they were, a sea of waste, into the producers of a bountiful supply of wealth, of which this country was still really in need.

" If private employers of labour cannot find these men work," said Mr. Clynes, " they have an excellent and unquestionable right to turn to the State and insist that the State shall do more than merely hand out a small dole to them barely to keep them alive. This policy of doles is itself the worst evidence of the policy of waste of which to a great extent the Government has been guilty." Mr. Clynes proceeded to say that the most cheerful of Ministers must have his moments of gloom when he turned to the immediate commercial, industrial, and economic outlook. The situation was unusually grave, and yet enormous profits were being made in some businesses. The workman was expected to submit to what was termed his " minimum wage." Would it not be equally fair to require capital to submit to maximum profits ?

An Amendment.

Sir Godfrey Collins (Coalition Unionist, *Greenock*) moved the following amendment to the motion : —

" That this House realising that the reduction of national expenditure will tend to a diminution of the necessarily high cost of living and in order to secure a sound financial position with reduced taxation in the future, urges His Majesty's Government in preparing the Estimates for the coming year to reduce to the utmost extent possible the expenditure in all public services."

The Right Hon. Sir Donald Maclean (Chairman of the Independent Liberal Party in Parliament) declared that the death-bed repentance they had that day was called for at least two years ago. The financial situation in this country demanded that the financial position should control policy. " I think," Sir Donald remarked, " we should shut down all fresh legislation next year, and let this House fling itself upon the financial situation as revealed by the Budget and the Estimates. Let us double the number of days ; instead of 20 days, let us have 40 days for the Estimates next year. I am not arguing that that should be a permanent alteration in the rules of procedure, but we are face to face with a wholly exceptional position. If this House really means business, that is a feasible, practical suggestion, and it is only in and through this House that the financial situation can be really, fundamentally stabilised again."

The Prime Minister (the Right Hon. D. Lloyd George) observed that it was a reflection upon Parliament to imagine there was any section of it that was not anxious to economise in public expenditure. The present difficulty was not one that was confined to this country, but was experienced by every great country that had been engaged in the War. " We are the only country that is paying its way," said the Premier. "We are doing more than that. We are not only paying our way, but are reducing our debt. We are naturally anxious, and worried, and apprehensive, but there is not a country in Europe that is not full of admiration for the way in which we are facing our difficulties." The right hon. gentleman added that with bad trade in front of them —it was general throughout the world —and with additional expenditure on the Exchequer due to unemployment, that was not the time for developing even the most beneficent schemes, whether for education or health. Until the country had bridged over the present period of exceptional difficulty they would have to do much more marking time than any of them would really like to do.

On a division the amendment, moved by Sir Godfrey Collins, was carried by 321 votes against 66. It was then put as the substantive motion and adopted by 307 votes against 30.

EMERGENCY POWERS ACT.

When Parliament reassembled at the close of the Autumn Recess the country was in the midst of a national strike of coal miners, and four days after the business of the Session had been resumed the Home Secretary introduced an Emergency Powers Bill. This was rapidly passed through both Houses and was given the Royal Assent on 29th October.

The Act provides that if at any time it appears to His Majesty that any action has been taken, or is immediately threatened, by any persons or body of persons of such a nature and on so extensive a scale as to be calculated, by interfering with the supply and distribution of food, water, fuel, or light, or with the means of locomotion, to deprive the community, or any substantial portion of it, of the essentials of life, a proclamation may be issued declaring that a state of emergency exists.

No such proclamation is to be in force for more than one month, without prejudice to the issue of another proclamation at or before the end of the period.

The occasion of making a proclamation of emergency is to be communicated to Parliament forthwith, and if Parliament is not sitting at the time a proclamation is to be issued for it to meet within five days.

So long as a proclamation of emergency is in force regulations may be made for securing the essentials of life to the community. Those regulations may confer on the Government such powers and duties as may be necessary for the preservation of the peace, for securing and regulating the supply and distribution of food, water, fuel, light, and other necessities, for maintaining the means of transit or locomotion, and for any other purposes essential to the public safety and the life of the community.

No Military or Industrial Conscription.

There are two provisos to this Section, viz. :—

That nothing in the Act is to be construed to authorise the making of any regulation imposing any form of compulsory military service or industrial conscription.

That no regulation shall make it an offence for any person or persons to take part in a strike, or peacefully to persuade any other person or persons to take part in a strike.

Regulations are to be laid before Parliament, and are not to continue in force after seven days from that time except upon a resolution passed by both Houses.

Persons guilty of offences against the regulations may be tried by courts of summary jurisdiction. The maximum penalty provided for is imprisonment for three months, or a fine of £100, or both, together with the forfeiture of any goods or money in respect of which an offence has been committed.

The Act does not apply to Ireland.

DEBATE IN HOUSE OF COMMONS.

On 25th October the Bill was debated in the House of Commons on the order for the Second Reading.

The Leader of the House (the Right Hon. A. Bonar Law) denied that the Bill was an attack on trade unions. The powers asked for were possessed by the Government of every great country. Moreover, in the past, Parliament itself had recognised a marked distinction between an ordinary industrial dispute and action which interfered with the life of the community.

In the Act of 1875 it was made not only illegal, but a criminal offence, for anyone engaged in supplying the essentials of life to strike without giving sufficient notice. Such an emergency would be a critical thing in the life of this country, and nobody in the House doubted that it might arise. The Bill had been drafted for some months and, apart from the coal strike, the Government had decided that it must be carried during the current Session, because no Government could be left without such powers when the Defence of the Realm Regulations had lapsed.

It was not provocative to let those in the country who were concerned know precisely what the action of the Government must be if an emergency arose.

The Right Hon. W. Adamson (Chairman of the Parliamentary Labour Party) moved the rejection of the Bill. He thought it a matter for profound regret that the Government had introduced the measure at that particular moment. For a week 1,200,000 mine workers had been on strike and a considerable number of other workers were involved, but little or no disturbance had taken place. He warned the Government that action of that kind was calculated to arouse the suspicions of the working classes. Mr. Bonar Law had said that it was not intended to use this legislation in ordinary disputes as to wages and working conditions, but only in the event of a dispute that would involve the national life. It would, however, be impossible for the present or any other Government to discriminate in that way.

Panic Legislation.

Panic legislation was always dangerous and the Government would be well advised to withdraw the Bill. He assured the Government that if they intended to pass legislation of that kind in a permanent form the Labour Party would fight it every inch of the way.

The Right Hon. H. H. Asquith (Leader of the Independent Liberal Party) agreed that the community ought to be protected through its constitutional agency—the authority of the Government—against privation and avoidable suffering and loss. But while he believed all parties in the House would be glad to consider carefully devised legislation for that purpose, to attempt legislation of that kind in the atmosphere which at the moment surrounded them was calculated to prejudice the object they had in view. So far as the present emergency was concerned the Government were amply equipped for dealing with it. So far as the future was concerned, it was desirable that the powers of the Executive should be defined clearly by legislative action—whatever those powers might be—but further discussion should be suspended until a more convenient season.

The Right Hon. J. R. Clynes (Vice-Chairman of the Parliamentary Labour Party) said he could not think that a Govern-

ment—with all the limitations which they believed the existing Government had—could seriously think of framing
legislation designed to undermine the power and authority
of the trade union movement. " If that authority and that
power are undermined," Mr. Clynes remarked, " it will be due,
not to the action of the Government. It will be due to the
outside follies of the trade union movement itself." The
Labour Party granted that during strikes food must be produced, imported, distributed, and supplied to the various
shops. But no one of those steps need rest upon a Bill
of that kind. " In the main what does the Bill do," asked
the right hon. gentleman. " It threatens bodies of men with
the penalties of the law. The Home Secretary has had long
enough experience in every branch of the law . . . to know
that if you make threats when you are dealing with enormous
numbers of men . . . your threats are so many empty words.
. . . Your large bodies of men will not be deterred from any
tendency to misdeeds by the term of three months' imprisonment, or by fines of £200."

Labour's Risk.

The Right Hon. Lord Robert Cecil (Independent Unionist,
Hitchin) thought that some measure of the kind was necessary.
He was not sure Labour members always realised that a
general strike was really different in kind from the old
industrial disputes. It was a matter for them very carefully
to consider whether the general strike was a weapon
that really could be used in a constitutional country, and
whether they were not running very grave risks of losing
support and popularity in the country, and ultimately
the chance of seriously affecting the legislation in the
way they desired by adopting tactics and methods of that
kind.
The Right Hon. Sir Donald Maclean (Chairman of the
Independent Liberal Party in Parliament) remarked that if the
measure received its Second Reading there would on the
morrow be created an atmosphere outside that House which
would be distinctly harmful to the progress of friendly negotiations in the coal strike.
The Right Hon. J. H. Thomas (Labour, *Derby*) did not
believe that the majority not only of members of the House
of Commons, but of the trade unionists of the country, would
for a moment desire to lay it down that in an industrial
dispute the duty of the Government was not clearly to feed
the community as a whole. He did not believe, however,
there was any advantage to the Government in pressing

forward this measure at the moment, and he urged the Prime Minister to withdraw the Second Reading motion.

Premier and the Bill.

The Prime Minister (the Right Hon. D. Lloyd George) said that even a trade union Government would find it just as necessary to be equipped with this Bill as a Government which was commonly called a Capitalist Government. The Bill was not an attack upon trade unionism, but was rendered necessary by the contingencies with which the Government had been confronted not merely this year, but last year. Mr. Thomas said the Government had these powers under the Defence of the Realm Act, but that was not the advice they got from the Departments. They were powers which were vital to the carrying on of the essential services of the nation in the event of there being a strike.

"This," continued the Prime Minister, " is only a Bill to equip us with the necessary powers for the fair distribution of the necessaries of life. What is there unkindly about it ? It is said to be provocative. Is it provocative to ask the House to give us powers to enable us to see that the working classes are not without food when other neighbourhoods have plenty, and not without coal when others have it in abundance ? Is it provocative to ask the House to give us the necessary powers to see that the lighting stations are running and that the trams are running as far as possible ? How can that be regarded as provocative ? Frankly, I can see no signs of irritation and exasperation being caused by this Bill."

Proceeding the right hon. gentleman said the railwaymen and the miners were the two most formidable parties in the Triple Alliance. They had heard for months and months about an alliance between the various trades that had in their hands the whole carriage of commodities inside the country and to the country. Just think of the position they would be in with a complete paralysis of transport and no powers ! No Government could accept the responsibility for those contingencies which were discussed and decided upon and were common talk in the trade union world without making preparations for them.

On a division the amendment to reject the Bill was negatived by 257 votes against 55, and the Second Reading was then agreed to. The measure was subjected to detailed consideration in Committee and, after amendment in various respects, was read a third time.

E

DEBATE IN HOUSE OF LORDS.

On 28th October the Bill was passed through all its stages in the House of Lords at one sitting.

The Secretary of State for the Colonies (Viscount Milner), in moving the Second Reading, pointed out that during the discussions in the Commons the necessity for the powers conferred by the Bill, and of their being kept permanently in reserve in case of emergency, was admitted on all sides. He claimed that the exceptional powers the Bill conferred were so hedged round with safeguards of every kind that it would be practically impossible for any Government to abuse those powers. This was not an offensive, but a defensive, measure. " If it is admitted that there are dangers arising from industrial strife on its vast modern scale which must be guarded against," the noble Viscount added, " then I say that I do not think it is possible to guard against them in any manner less subversive of the liberties of the subject, or more calculated to maintain the power and authority of Parliament to protect the subject."

The Marquis of Crewe explained that he did not in any way propose to oppose the Second Reading. Industrial disputes in these days might affect the whole life of the nation and it might be that those who engaged in such strife had in their minds not merely the improvement of certain material conditions in their industry—a rise in wages, or a shortening of hours—but social and economic changes which might affect the whole structure of society. Practically all the safeguards in the Bill, however, were introduced by way of amendments made in the other House and its terrors had been greatly reduced in its passage through that House.

Lord Buckmaster did not think there was to be found in the Bill itself any definite protection against an unreasonable or excessive use of its powers. If an emergency was declared to exist the whole of the Bill became operative at once, and the declaration of the emergency must, as it seemed to him, rest in the uncontrolled opinion of the Government, whatever it might be, that was for the moment in power. That was a very grave matter, because some Governments were more nervous than others, and no one could say what the character of the Governments of this country might be in the next twenty years. The temptation that was placed in the hands of any Government when once Parliament enabled them to effec their will by a stroke of the pen and the assent of their own majority in the House of Commons was a very strong one which needed to be carefully and jealously watched.

The Bill having been read a second time, some amendments were made in Committee, and, thereafter, the Third Reading was agreed to.

UNEMPLOYMENT: GOVERNMENT PLANS.

On various occasions after the reassembly of Parliament in October the subject of unemployment was raised in the House of Commons, and Ministerial statements were made from time to time outlining the measures proposed by the Government to deal with the problem. On 21st December the whole question was fully discussed on the Second Reading of the Consolidated Fund (Appropriation) (No. 2) Bill and the debate was notable for a series of suggestive speeches from members representing both Capital and Labour.

DEBATE IN HOUSE OF COMMONS.

The Minister of Labour (the Right Hon. T. J. Macnamara), in opening the discussion, said that for between three and four months the cloud of industrial depression had cast its shadow over them—a shadow which had grown deeper as the weeks had gone on. The prime necessity was to set the wheels of trade going round again, and the Government appreciated the urgency of that side of their task. Side by side with it was the immediate necessity to do all that was humanly possible to mitigate hardship and relieve distress. The right hon. gentleman gave the House the following figures as the numbers of registered unemployed on 10th December :—

Ex-Service men	265,000
Civilian men	148,000
Women	131,000

Beyond these, he said, there was a margin, perhaps a wide margin, of persons unemployed but not registered. A Cabinet Committee was appointed in August to devise plans with a view to meeting the depression which might arise during the winter, and the measures which were to be taken had already been announced. Proceeding to re-state them, the Minister of Labour referred first to negotiations proceeding with the building trades to secure that large bodies of ex-Service men should be taken into those trades in order especially that housing arrears might be made up as rapidly as possibly.

Offer to Building Trades.

Proposals submitted by the Government to the National Federation of Building Trade Operatives on 18th December

E 2

were read to the House in full by Dr. Macnamara. Following is a summary of them : —

(A) Absorption into the building industry of a large body of ex-Service men as adult apprentices or trainees to be commenced forthwith.

(B) Numbers to be absorbed should be on the basis of one in five, calculated on the number of skilled men in the whole industry, but the proportion would vary in different trades. Total number admitted to be not less than 50,000.

(c) Government to make a training grant of £5 per head for each man admitted to the trade unions concerned and trained in any of the trades in the building industry.

(D) Subject to the trade unions accepting this augmentation of labour the Government accept the principle of a guaranteed rate of pay on housing operations for time lost owing to wet or inclement weather, viz., 50 per cent. for time lost up to 22 hours per week; 75 per cent. for time lost in excess of 22 hours.

The right hon. gentleman stated that a special conference* of the building trade unions was to be summoned to consider these proposals.

Road and Municipal Schemes.

Proceeding, the Minister of Labour explained the steps that were being taken to provide work in connection with the construction of new arterial roads and the repair and reconditioning of main roads. In addition local authorities were putting in hand relief work and the Government had decided to appoint a Committee under the chairmanship of Lord St. Davids, at whose disposition they would ask Parliament to place a sum of £3,000,000 for the purpose of assisting those authorities in carrying out approved schemes. It was proposed to amend the Unemployment Insurance Act by asking Parliament to pass a Bill† immediately temporarily

---

* The Conference was held in London on 30th December, and the result was that a reply was sent to the Minister of Labour expressing regret that there was no guarantee against the consequences of unemployment. The letter also stated that only those sections which might be diluted would be entitled to any wet-time allowance, and the decision of the Conference was to consult the members of the unions on the Government's offer.

† A one-clause Bill was introduced and passed through all its stages in both Houses amending the Act in the manner described. It received the Royal Assent on 23rd December.

suspending the provision in the Act that there should be four weeks' employment and contributions as a condition precedent to the receipt of benefit.

The Right Hon. J. R. Clynes (Vice-Chairman of the Parliamentary Labour Party) said the Minister of Labour was a very optimistic man if he believed that the four lines of action he had outlined would within the next four months absorb any number of the million or so people who were out of work. The personnel of the unemployed was very different now from a few years ago. " We cannot," Mr. Clynes observed, "say to men who have saved their country and offered their lives to that end that they have not now a claim far above any claim which they ever had upon the Government and the country in relation to the unemployment problems of previous years."

Duty of the State.

The test of a Government in relation to unemployment in the future, the right hon. gentleman proceeded, would be in regard to how far the State could secure the masses of the people in employment and in a state of contentment. Also, the permanent policy of the Government must be not to wait to yield to pressure, but themselves to initiate and look ahead, and so to arrange the affairs of the State in regard to industry as to be able always to absorb into useful service that margin of workers who were certain always to be thrown out of employment when serious periods of depression were reached. To work on voluntary lines and to have a policy that would make such provision would tend to win public trust and confidence for Parliament and Governments. To get their mills and factories restored to the full level of employment, trade and commerce with all the other parts of the world must be set going again.

The Right Hon. Lord Hugh Cecil (Coalition Unionist, Oxford University) did not believe any action the State could undertake would ever be a true, far-reaching solution of the unemployment problem. " What I want to see," said the noble lord, " is a patriots' league of abundance of which employers and employed should all be members and in which the rule should be that no member of the league should ever take part in any industrial action which tended to restrict production. . . . The wealth of the world is something which could be indefinitely extended if only you could get the enterprise, industry, and talent of the human race to co-operate in the interests of abundance."

New Line Suggested.

Sir Allan Smith (Coalition Unionist, *Croydon*) said the discussion that day had ignored the cause of unemployment, viz., that the cost of production of the commodities of this country exceeded the selling price of the article. The first obligation of the Government, in a great measure, was to leave the employers and the trade unions alone.

The trade unions and the employers, knowing their own minds in each industry, were far better able to look after their domestic affairs than anyone outside. The first duty of the employers and trade unions was to sit down and settle all disputes, so that they would come back to the position which they had in certain industries prior to the War when they had agreements regulating these matters. The employers must come together and see to what extènt, at least in the larger branches of industry, each branch was capable of carrying its own load of unemployment, because that would be the first thing to settle industrial unrest. It would be the first thing to give the workman freedom to open out to the fullest extent on his job, because he knew that it would not put him in an evil position and bring about his early discharge.

" At the moment it is alleged," said the hon. member, " and is no doubt psychologically true, that if there is not work for a man to do, the employer or his representative discharges him, knowing full well that the care of that man, after he is discharged, is a matter not for the employer but for the State, and the employer has done his part by paying his contributions under the Unemployment Act. If the employers and workers were to care for unemployment personally, that objectionable feature of the State burden and the State exercise of a right would be removed. It would be a mutual burden to be looked after by the people who look after these men while in employment, and perform the counterpart of looking after them when out of employment. Not only so, but if such an arrangement were made, the duty of the employers in conjunction with the trade unions would be to look after employment, and unemployment might well be left to look after itself."

The hon. Member added that the Government ought seriously to consider the statement he made that they would never be able to bring this country back to its pre-War position as a manufacturing country until they took off the stranglehold of the Excess Profits Duty.

World Impoverished by War.

The Prime Minister (the Right Hon. D. Lloyd George) observed that unemployment was suffering which seemed to him inseparable from the trading activities of the world. The question had been treated rather as if it were something attributable to causes which were confined to Great Britain. That was not the case. With the exception of France, every country in the world was suffering from unemployment, and with that exception, too, unemployment was better in this country, even in percentages, than in any other country in the world. The present period of unemployment was undoubtedly due to the fact that the War had impoverished the world. Their customers were insolvent, and Europe could not buy. She was bankrupt. She could hardly feed herself. Until Europe started again, until Europe was able to buy, the prospects would remain very serious. Europe would recover more quickly if she could have peace, and she was getting peace gradually.

Some very able business men were of opinion that it was possible to start some sort of credit insurance system that would enable this country to do business with Central Europe and give Central Europe time to pay. If that were feasible it would be more helpful than any scheme for road-making, because it would start business again.

Problem of Emigration.

"I do not like to say it," remarked the Premier, "but I think we shall have to face the problem of emigration. It is an unpleasant suggestion, but I mean emigration within the Empire. There was one thing that the War proved, and that was that the men who leave us are not lost to us. The most remarkable fact was that they were there when we wanted them. They were the first men to come to our assistance, first from Canada, first from Australia, and so on. I met two as fine Australian soldiers during the War as one could wish to meet, and they were Welshmen who came to see me at Downing Street. I found that they had come from my own village. That applies to everybody. Almost without exception these young fellows who went out to our Dominions during the last few years enlisted, and were the first to enlist, when the War came.

"Therefore, when we talk about emigration we are really not sending these virile young men away and losing their strength; quite the reverse. They went there, and they brought a partner back to fight with them. They are a strength to the Empire, whether they are in Canada, Scotland, England, Wales, Ireland, Australia, or New Zealand. There is a greater sense of comradeship, a greater feeling that we are one people, one country. Spread them over the Empire and you strengthen not merely the Empire, but the old country as well.   I should like to see a considered scheme, considered in conjunction with the Dominions, for finding employment for men for whom I am afraid it would be difficult for us to find permanent employment in this country for some time to come, certainly until the world is restored to something like normal conditions.   That is one of the problems which I hope to see discussed when we have this meeting of Imperial Premiers in the month of June in this country.   These are the lines on which I would like to see the problem considered."

Referring to the speech of Sir Allan Smith, the right hon. gentleman observed that if an industry said, " leave us alone ; we will solve our own problem of unemployment," it would probably be found that when a certain point was reached the State had to help over the same stile.

After further speeches the House proceeded to the discussion of other subjects.

EMPLOYMENT OF WOMEN, YOUNG PERSONS, AND CHILDREN ACT.

On the day of the Prorogation of Parliament the Royal Assent was given to the Employment of Women, Young Persons, and Children Act.   The Government introduced the Bill, which has now become law, early in the Session in order to give effect to certain Conventions of the International Labour Organisation of the League of Nations which met at Washington in 1919 and at Geneva in 1920.   During the examination of the Bill by a Standing Committee a provision for the establishment of the two-shift system was struck out, and thereafter a Departmental Committee, of which Mr. T. W. Inskip, M.P., was chairman, was appointed to inquire into that system.   This Committee recommended the adoption of the system for a period of five years, and when the Bill again came before the House of Commons a provision to that effect was inserted.

The Act provides that no child under the age of 14 years shall be employed in any industrial undertaking or in any ship other than vessels upon which only members of the same family are employed, or school or training ships.

Every shipmaster is required to keep a register of all persons under the age of sixteen years employed on board his vessel or a list of them in the articles of agreement, and of the dates of their births.

Industrial undertakings include mines, quarries and other works for the extraction of minerals from the earth.

EMPLOYMENT IN SHIFTS.

The Home Secretary may, on the joint application of the employer and a majority of the workpeople in a factory or workshop, make orders authorising the employment of women and young persons of the age of 16 and upwards at any time between the hours of 6 a.m. and 10 p.m. on any weekday except Saturday, and between the hours of 6 a.m. and 2 p.m. on Saturday, in shifts averaging not more than eight hours per day.

It is provided that if a joint representation is made to the Home Secretary by organisations representing a majority of the employers and workers in an industry to the effect that orders ought not to be made in respect of factories and workshops in that industry the power to make orders shall cease to be exerciseable as regards that industry unless the representation is withdrawn, and, if required, any order previously made in respect of a factory or workshop in that industry shall, on the expiration of a period not exceeding four months, cease to have effect.

An order may permit the employment in a factory or workshop in shifts of young persons under the age of 16 years who are already in employment at the date of the commencement of the Act.

The provision with respect to the employment of women and young persons in shifts is to remain in force for a period of five years.

The expression " child " means a person under the age of fourteen years ; " young person " means a person who has ceased to be a child and who is under the age of eighteen ; and "woman" means a woman of the age of eighteen or upwards.

DEBATE IN HOUSE OF COMMONS.

When the Bill was discussed on the Report Stage in the House of Commons on 26th, 29th and 30th November, the new clause making provision for the employment of women and young persons in shifts was considered at great length.

The Home Secretary (the Right Hon. E. Shortt) pointed out that Home Office inspectors quite voluntarily in their reports put it forward as their view that women employed on the two-shift system during the War were very anxious for that system to continue. The proposal was that certain provisions that were adopted during the War should be continued for a limited period of time in order that they might be thoroughly investigated and that the permanent provision eventually decided upon should be based on the widest experience. The factory system was to be overhauled with a view to further amendments of the law.

The Right Hon. J. R. Clynes (Vice-Chairman of the Parliamentary Labour Party) strongly objected to legislation of that kind. He did not think it a good thing for the trades and industries of the country to repose in the Home Office power, on application, to vary or extend the working hours in different occupations. If there were a real demand from certain industries—the glass, the chemical, or the tinplate— let it be shown that there was some measure of agreement among employers and employed for the two-shift system, and let there be legislation in statutory terms instead of handing over the matter to a State Department.

The Right Hon. G. H. Roberts (Labour, *Norwich***)** thought they would view with great apprehension anything calculated to extend the possibilities of young persons and women being employed in the very early hours of the morning or late at night. These continuous shifts must undoubtedly have a prejudicial effect upon health.

The Second Reading of the new clause was carried by 148 votes to 66 and, after amendment in various particulars, was added to the Bill. The measure was read a third time on 30th November and sent to the House of Lords, where it was passed in time to allow it to become law as stated.

WOMEN AND YOUNG PERSONS (EMPLOYMENT IN LEAD PROCESSES) ACT.

An Act to make provision for the better protection of women and young persons against lead poisoning was given the Royal Assent on 23rd December. It was introduced and passed to carry out a recommendation of the general conference at Washington in 1919 of the International Labour Organisation of the League of Nations.

The Act prohibits the employment of women or young persons in any of the following operations :—

Work at a furnace where the reduction or treatment of zinc or lead ores is carried on.

Manipulation, treatment, or reduction of ashes containing lead, the desilverising of lead, or the melting of scrap lead or zinc.

Manufacture of solder or alloys containing more than ten per cent. of lead.

The manufacture of any oxide, carbonate, sulphate, chromate, acetate, nitrate, or silicate of lead.

Mixing or pasting in connection with the manufacture or repair of electric accumulators.

The cleaning of workrooms where any of the above processes are carried on.

It is made unlawful to employ women or young persons in any process involving the use of lead compounds unless regulations prescribed by the Act are complied with. These provide, *inter alia,* for the drawing away from persons employed of dust or fume from a lead compound by an efficient exhaust draught, periodical medical inspection of workers, prohibition of bringing food or drink into workrooms, and provision of sufficient and suitable cloakroom, washing, and mess-room accommodation, and of special protective clothing.

Samples of any substance suspected to contain a lead compound may, if it is for use in a process in which women and young persons are employed, be taken by a factory inspector.

DEBATE IN HOUSE. OF COMMONS.

The Bill had a friendly reception in both Houses. On 1st November, the date of Second Reading in the House of Commons,

The Home Secretary (the Right Hon. E. Shortt) explained that what the Washington Conference recommended was the minimum standard to which every country ought at least to attain. That did not in the least prevent any country from either continuing to be better than the recommendations or, if not better now, becoming better. So far as this country was concerned, legislation would make very little difference, because where they differed from the recommendations they were better, and would remain better.

Major J. W. Hills (Coalition Unionist, *Durham*) observed that all the regulations prescribed in the Bill had been in force for many years in British pottery works, and their effect in diminishing the evil of lead poisoning had been great. That had been the case especially as it affected women.

The Second Reading was agreed to without a division, and the further proceedings on the Bill were uneventful.

DYESTUFFS (IMPORT REGULATION) ACT.

Only three weeks before the close of the Session the President of the Board of Trade presented the Dyestuffs (Import Regulation) Bill, and the measure became law on the date of the Prorogation.

With a view to the safeguarding of the dye-making industry, the Act prohibits the importation into the United Kingdom of all synthetic organic dyestuffs, colours, and colouring matters, and all organic intermediate products used in their manufacture.

The Board of Trade are given power by licence to authorise, either generally or in any particular case, the importation of any of the goods, or any class or description of the goods, whose importation is so prohibited.

For the purpose of advising them with respect to the granting of licences the Board are required by the Act to constitute a committee consisting of five persons concerned in the trades in which goods of this class are used, three persons concerned in the manufacture of such goods, and three other persons not concerned in either capacity, of whom one is to be chairman of the committee.

If on an application for a licence the committee are satisfied that the goods in question are wholly produced or manufactured in some part of the King's Dominions a licence shall be granted.

A committee consisting of persons concerned in the trades of dye-maker or dye-user and others is to be constituted by the Board of Trade

for the purpose of advising them with respect to the efficient and economical development of the dye-making industry.

The Act is to continue in operation for ten years from 15th January,
1921.

DEBATE IN HOUSE OF COMMONS.

On 7th December the Bill was debated in the House of
Commons on the motion for Second Reading.

**The President of the Board of Trade (the Right Hon. Sir
Robert Horne)** said that a great industry had been built up in
Germany by the extraction of dyes from coal-tar, and many
natural dyes were now entirely out of the market because of
the competition of synthetic dyes which had been produced by
that system. England had the credit of the original inventor
of the system, but unfortunately they had before the War
completely lost the industry to Germany. When the War
broke out the textile industry in this country was threatened
with disaster owing to the fact that it was cut off from practically its only supplies of dyes. The Government made
arrangements with the dye-users of the country to set up a firm,
British Dyes, Ltd., into which the Government put £1,700,000,
the whole capital of the Company being something over
£4,000,000.

" The foundation upon which the setting up of the British
Dyes Corporation was based," Sir Robert Horne said, " was
getting rid of our dependence on outside sources of supply,
but besides the great necessity of dyes for our own industries
during the War we discovered something else. We discovered
that the country which has the largest dye-making industry
has got within its borders a very powerful agent in the waging
of war." The right hon. gentleman explained that the German
dye industry produced a very great amount of the materials
necessary for the manufacture of explosives, and Britain was
very severely handicapped because it had no such industry on
which it could call for that kind of production. He said that
to-day the Germans were sending dyes to this country at prices
with which the British Dyestuffs Corporation at the moment
could not compete. If that was allowed to go on they might
very soon clear out the dye-making industry from this country.
He denied that it was " Protection in its worst form," as had
been said, to deal with an industry, which everyone agreed
must be defended, by a system which imposed no duty and
which allowed the importation, with no cost, of all the country
required.

Major H. Barnes (Independent Liberal, *Newcastle-on-Tyne,
E.*) moved an amendment for the rejection of the Bill on the

ground that, under the pretext of providing for national defence, it reintroduced the vicious protectionist system of prohibition and licences, which would inflict grave injury upon the textile industries of the country.

The Right Hon. H. H. Asquith (Leader of the Independent Liberal Party) doubted very much whether the seriousness of the competition to which the British industry was exposed was due so much to the greater cheapness of the competing article as to its superior quality and attractiveness.

On a division the amendment was negatived by 277 votes against 72 and the Bill was read a second time. There was a good deal of further discussion on the measure during its subsequent stages, and the final form in which it took its place on the Statute Book was the result of amendments made in both Houses.

ADMINISTRATION OF JUSTICE ACT.

An Act to amend the law with respect to the administration of justice, the constitution of the Supreme Court, and other matters was given the Royal Assent on the date of the Prorogation. Introduced by the Lord Chancellor (Lord Birkenhead) after the reassembly of Parliament in the Autumn, the measure had a smooth passage through both Houses.

Section I. of the Act gives power to try matrimonial causes " of any prescribed class " at Assizes and for that purpose confers on any Commissioner of Assize all powers and duties vested in the Probate, Divorce and Admiralty Division of the High Court under the enactments relating to divorce and matrimonial causes.

The class of cases which may be so tried is to be prescribed by the Lord Chancellor, with the concurrence of the Lord Chief Justice of England and the President of the Probate, Divorce and Admiralty Division.

TRIALS WITHOUT JURY: OTHER PROVISIONS.

Under Section II., relating to any action or other matter requiring to be tried in the High Court, the court or a judge shall, on the application of either of the parties, order the trial to be without a jury if satisfied that this is the more convenient course.

The consent of both parties to such an order is required where the action is one in which fraud is alleged, or in which damages are claimed in respect of libel, slander, malicious prosecution, false imprisonment, seduction, or breach of promise of marriage.

Similar provision is made in Section III. with respect to the trial of any action in County Courts and other inferior courts of civil jurisdiction. Actions which, if tried in the High Court, would require a jury are excepted from this provision. All actions arising under the Increase of Rent and Mortgage Interest (Restrictions) Act, 1920, are to be tried without a jury.

Section IV. prescribes that if a defendant has admitted the charge made against him before the examining justices, the Grand Jury at Quarter Sessions or Assizes, on the production of a certificate to that effect, shall return a true bill as respects that charge without hearing witnesses.

Other Sections provide for an extension of the Admiralty jurisdiction of the High Court, the precedence of the President of the Probate, Divorce and Admiralty Division of the High Court next after the Master of the Rolls, and the empowerment of ex-judges of the Supreme Court on request of the Lord Chancellor to sit as judges.

RECIPROCAL ENFORCEMENT OF JUDGMENTS.

Section IX. deals with reciprocal enforcement of judgments in the United Kingdom and in other parts of His Majesty's Dominions.

It provides that where a judgment has been obtained in a superior court in any part of His Majesty's Dominions outside the United Kingdom to which Part II. of the Act extends, the judgment creditor may apply to the High Court in England or Ireland, or to the Court of Session in Scotland within twelve months, or such longer period as the court may allow, to have the judgment registered in that court.

Certain exceptions (as for instance where the original court acted without jurisdiction, the judgment was obtained by fraud, or the judgment was in respect of a cause of action which for reasons of public policy could not have been entertained by the registering court) are laid down in the Act.

In Section X. it is provided that where a judgment has been obtained in the United Kingdom the court shall, on proof that the judgment debtor is resident in some part of His Majesty's Dominions outside the United Kingdom, issue to the judgment creditor a certified copy of the judgment.

Part II. of the Act may, by Order in Council, be applied to any territory under His Majesty's protection, or in respect of which a mandate is being exercised.

In Part III. of the Act which relates to miscellaneous matters, it is laid down (Section XV.) that questions relating to foreign law arising in an action which is being tried by a judge with a jury in any court in England or Wales shall be decided by the judge alone.

DEBATE IN HOUSE OF COMMONS.

On 20th December the Bill was passed through all its stages in the House of Commons, having come down from the Upper House a few days previously.

The Attorney-General (the Right Hon. Sir Gordon Hewart) said the provision with respect to the trial of divorce cases at Assizes did not, of course, enable any person who was not at present entitled to a divorce to obtain one, but made it simpler, quicker, and cheaper for a person to obtain the divorce to which he was entitled.

Major-General the Hon. Sir Newton Moore (Coalition Unionist, *Islington, N.*) asked, in respect of the enforcement in the United Kingdom of judgments obtained in superior courts in other British Dominions, whether any arrangement had been made, so far, in regard to reciprocity between the Dominions referred to.

The Attorney-General explained that the whole question had been carefully and repeatedly considered at Colonial conferences and otherwise, and he thought he could safely say that there would be reciprocity in the matter.

Sir Newton Moore : " I presume that certain enactments will have to be brought forward before this clause can become operative between the Dominions?"

The Attorney-General : " Not before this clause can become operative, but no doubt before it can have complete effect."

The Bill passed through the Lower House without amendment.

MINISTRY OF HEALTH BILL.

The Ministry of Health (Miscellaneous Powers) Bill was introduced just before Parliament adjourned in August, and discussion upon it was accordingly reserved until the Autumn. The proposals of the Bill will be found summarised in the JOURNAL, Vol. I., No. 4, page 641. They related to matters connected with housing, public health, and the machinery of local government administration. The Bill was severely attacked in the House of Commons from the point of view of its possible effect in adding to the burdens of the Exchequer and the local rates. The Government agreed to drop a number of its clauses, and six were, in fact, omitted during the examination of the measure by a Standing Committee.

DEBATE IN HOUSE OF LORDS.

The Bill came up for Second Reading in the House of Lords on 14th December, when, in explaining the objects of the measure,

Viscount Sandhurst said that no charge at all was made on the Exchequer and clause after clause was drawn with the intention of saving or lightening the burden of the rates.

Lord Strachie moved the rejection of the Bill on the ground that it had not received adequate consideration.

Viscount Galway said that various provisions in the Bill must mean an increase of bureaucratic staffs. They were getting tired of bureaucratic staffs, and he was a little surprised that the Government did not see the handwriting on the wall.

The Marquis of Salisbury observed that some of the provisions of the Bill were good and he would be rather sorry if an adverse fate befell them. He suggested that the Government should drop all the contentious clauses and only pass those on which there was general agreement.

The Secretary of State for Foreign Affairs (Earl Curzon of Kedleston) said he would be reluctant to accept that proposal for the reason that there might be certain differences of opinion as to what were the controversial points of the Bill. He would also hesitate as a general proposition to accept the position that it was part of the function of a Government responsible for introducing a Bill that had controversial elements, when the measure came to their Lordships, to ask the House at the first sitting at which it was taken to carry into law only those portions of the Bill about which there was no dispute and indefinitely to postpone the rest. That would be a dangerous precedent to set up.

The Marquis of Salisbury : " In the week before Christmas ? "

The Secretary of State for Foreign Affairs suggested that the Bill should be read a second time that night and that the Committee stage should be taken after Christmas.

On a division the motion that the Bill be then read a second time was defeated by 57 votes against 41, and the Bill was accordingly rejected.

GOLD AND SILVER (EXPORT CONTROL, ETC.) ACT.

The Royal Assent was given to this Act on 23rd December. Its object is to control the exportation of gold and silver coin and bullion, and to prohibit the melting or improper use of gold and silver coin.

The Act extends the Customs and Inland Revenue Act, 1879 (which enables the exportation of certain articles to be prohibited) so as to include gold or silver coin and gold or silver bullion.

A Customs penalty of £100 is prescribed in the case of failure to comply with any condition attached to a licence for export.

The expression " gold or silver bullion " includes gold and silver partly manufactured, and any mixture or alloy containing gold or silver.

It is made unlawful by the Act, except under a licence granted by the Treasury, to melt down, break up, or use otherwise than as currency, gold or silver coin for the time being current in the United Kingdom or in a British Possession or foreign country.

The penalty laid down is a fine of £100 or imprisonment for two years, or both.

During the debate on the Second Reading of the Bill in the House of Commons on 29th November,

The Financial Secretary to the Treasury (the Right Hon. Stanley Baldwin) said the Government were anxious, and the Bankers as trustees of the gold supply of the country were anxious, too, to see this legislation made part of the permanent financial equipment of the country.

After the Second Reading the Bill went to a Standing Committee and subsequently was read a third time.

During the passage of the Bill through the House of Lords it was explained that the Bill continued certain War powers which could not be dispensed with. The measure had an uneventful passage through the Upper House and became law as stated.

CRIMINAL LAW AMENDMENT.

Reference was made in the last number of the JOURNAL by way of a footnote to the fact that a Joint Select Committee of Lords and Commons had been appointed to consider the Government's Criminal Law Amendment Bill, the similar measure introduced by the Bishop of London, and the Sexual Offences Bill. The Committee, which reported in December, evolved a single measure on the basis of the Government Bill embodying such alterations in the law as seemed, in their opinion, to be desirable and necessary. It is expected that this measure will be introduced next Session and its provisions will then be summarised in the JOURNAL.

CANADA.

The following summary deals with some further Acts and discussions of the Fourth Session of the Thirteenth Parliament (which opened on 26th February and was adjourned on 1st July, 1920) and is in continuation of the summaries published in Vol. I., Nos. 2, 3 and 4 of the JOURNAL.

NATURALISATION ACTS, 1914 AND 1920.

(Treatment of Enemy Aliens: Uniformity of Legislation, &c.).

This Act, which was assented to on 1st July, 1920, repeals the Naturalisation Act of 1919 and revives that of 1914 with certain amendments.

The Act provides that where the Governor-in-Council, upon the report of the Secretary of State of Canada, is satisfied that a certificate of naturalisation granted by the Secretary of State under this Act or any Naturalisation Act heretofore in force in Canada has been obtained by false representation or fraud, or by concealment of material circumstances, or that the person to whom the certificate was granted has shown himself by act or speech to be disaffected or disloyal to His Majesty, the Governor-in-Council shall by Order revoke the certificate. He shall also revoke a certificate of naturalisation in any case in which he is satisfied that the person to whom the certificate was granted either

(A) has, during any war in which His Majesty is engaged unlawfully traded or communicated with the enemy or with the subjects of any enemy State, or been engaged in or associated with any business which is to his knowledge carried on in such manner as to assist the enemy in such war ; or

(B) has, within five years of the date of the grant of the certificate, been sentenced by any Court in His Majesty's dominions to imprisonment for a term of not less than twelve months, or to a term of penal servitude, or to a fine of not less than five hundred dollars ; or,

(c) was not of good character at the date of the grant of the certificate ; or

(D) has since the date of the grant of the certificate been for a period of not less than seven years ordinarily resident out of His Majesty's dominions otherwise than as a representative of a British subject, firm or company carrying on business, or an institution established in His Majesty's dominions, or in the service of the Crown, and has not maintained substantial connection with His Majesty's dominions ; or

(E) remains, according to the law of a State at war with His Majesty, a subject of that State ;

and that (in any case) the continuance of the certificate is not conducive to the public good.

Before making a report on the case the Secretary of State may refer it to an inquiry held by a Commission constituted for the purpose by the Governor-in-Council upon the recommendation of the Secretary of State or by the Superior Court of the province in which the case arises ; and the Secretary of State shall by notice given to or sent to the last known address of the holder of the certificate give him an opportunity of claiming that the case be referred for such inquiry.

The Act further provides that where a person to whom a certificate of naturalisation has been granted in some part of His Majesty's dominions is resident in Canada, the certificate may be revoked in accordance with the above by the Governor-in-Council, with the concurrence of the Government of that part of His Majesty's dominions in which the certificate was granted.

Where a certificate of naturalisation is revoked, the Governor-in-Council may, upon the recommendation of the Secretary of State, direct that the wife and minor children (or any of them) of the person whose certificate is revoked shall cease to be British subjects, and any such person shall thereupon become an alien, but otherwise their nationality shall not be affected by the revocation, and they shall remain British subjects, provided that the wife within six months after the date of the order of revocation may make a declaration of alienage, and thereupon she and any minor children of her husband and herself shall cease to be British subjects, and provided that the Governor-in-Council shall not make any such order in the case of a wife who was at birth a British subject, unless he is satisfied that if she had held a certificate of naturalisation in her own right the certificate could properly have been revoked under this Act.

Where a certificate of naturalisation is revoked the former holder thereof shall be regarded as an alien and as a subject of the State to which he belonged at the time the certificate was granted, and shall thereafter for the purpose of this Act, and of the Immigration Act, be deemed never to have been naturalised.

The Naturalisation Act of 1914 is amended so as to provide that where an alien is a subject of a State at war with His Majesty it shall be lawful for a wife, if she was at birth a British subject, to make a declaration that she desires to resume British nationality, and thereupon the Secretary of State, if he is satisfied that it is desirable that she be permitted to do so, may grant her a certificate of naturalisation.

It is also provided that where a certificate of naturalisation has been granted in Canada since 4th August, 1914, to a person who, at or at any time before, the grant of the certificate, was the subject of a country which at the date of the grant was at war with His Majesty, the Governor-in-Council may, on the recommendation of the Secretary of State, refer for inquiry (as above) the question whether it is desirable that the certificate should be revoked, and if such question is answered in the affirmative, he may revoke the certificate, but this provision shall not apply to a person who at birth was a British subject.

No certificate of naturalisation shall, before the expiration of a period of ten years after the termination of the war, be granted in Canada to any subject of a country which at the time of the passing of this Act (1914) or at any time since 4th August, 1914, was at war with His Majesty ; but this provision shall not apply to a person who,

(A) having served in His Majesty's forces or in the forces of His Majesty's Allies or of any country acting in naval or military

F 2

co-operation with His Majesty was not discharged from such service
by reason of his enemy nationality, sympathy or associations ; or
    (B) is a member of a race or community known to be opposed
to the enemy governments ; or
    (C) was at birth a British subject ; or
    (D) was domiciled and continuously resided in Canada for a
period of at least ten years immediately preceding 7th July, 1919,
and who establishes to the satisfaction of the Secretary of State
that he has always during his residence conducted himself as a good
and loyal citizen and that his allegiance to His Majesty will not be
affected by sympathy or association with the enemy State of which
he was formerly a subject.

DEBATE IN HOUSE OF COMMONS.

In moving for leave to introduce the Bill on 17th June,
The Minister of Justice (the Right Hon. C. J. Doherty) recalled that in connection with the Franchise Act considerable
discussion arose with regard to the effect of certain provisions
of the Naturalisation Act of 1919—provisions which excluded
the naturalising of persons of former enemy alien nationality
for a period of ten years following the war.

Concurrent British Legislation.

The discussion proceeded upon the understanding that the
British legislation of 1918 had so operated as to make it necessary, if they were to preserve a uniformity between their
legislation and the British naturalisation legislation, that they
should adopt this provision making it impossible to naturalise
for the period of ten years the class of aliens which he had
mentioned. In connection with that discussion he had
ventured to express a very strong hope that it would be found
possible to come to such an understanding as would cause
to disappear the supposed necessity of their adopting that
absolutely prohibitive legislation for the purpose of maintaining uniformity in the naturalisation legislation. He was
glad to say that he had not been over-sanguine ; that it
was possible for them to so modify the provisions referred
to as to remove the impossibility during the period of time
in question of naturalising the class mentioned, without
causing their legislation not to be uniform with that of the
United Kingdom upon the subject of Imperial naturalisation. One of the purposes of this Bill was not to abolish
entirely the provision, but to make it possible to grant
certificates of naturalisation to persons of proved loyalty who
before the passage of the Act had resided in Canada for a period
of ten years. The misunderstanding with regard to the effect
of the British naturalisation disappeared upon careful examination of the legislation. The British Parliament, in

naking the particular enactment to which he had referred,
was careful, inasmuch as there was no consultation with the
Dominions on the subject, to make it, not as an enactment to
form part of the Imperial Naturalisation Act of 1914, but as
a substantial enactment in the United Kingdom.   That had
eft them their liberty in the matter.   It was a misapprehension
o suppose that this was a matter of legislation imposed upon
hem by the Act of the British Parliament.   The Act of 1914
tself was an Act passed in virtue of an agreement and was
actually passed by the Canadian Parliament before it was
passed by the British Parliament.

For the purpose of clearness it had been thought desirable
that they should remodel the form of the Act as it was passed
ast year.   It seemed to them desirable that they should keep
clear by themselves the provisions of the Act of 1914 and any
amendment that might be made to it—that was the Act the
uniformity of which they must maintain—and deal separately
as the British Parliament did, with other provisions not
forming part of it.   For that purpose this present Bill repealed
the Act of 1919, revived the Act of 1914, inserting in it those
amendments which properly formed part of it and were
necessary for maintaining uniformity between their Act of
1914 and the British Act of 1914, and thus enacting such
provisions as formed no part of it as substantial provisions
standing by themselves, and among which was the provision
which would make it possible, not to do away with the ten-
year requirements generally, but in meritorious cases, for
persons of former enemy alien nationality who had resided
ten years in the country, to be naturalised before the expiry
of the ten-year period from the expiry of the Act in 1919.

Naturalisation of Women.

Mr. W. D. Euler (Liberal, *Waterloo, N. Riding, Ont.*) :
" I should like to know whether in the new Bill which the
Minister is introducing he includes a provision for the personal
naturalisation of women as well as men.   I think that would
be desirable."

The Minister of Justice : " That is a matter which was
dealt with in the original Act of 1914, the Act that was then
decided upon.   If we should depart from the agreement then
reached, which was embodied in both the British and our
legislation upon that subject, we should then be making in
the provisions of the original Act a distinction which would
differentiate our legislation, and just as the British Government and Parliament did not think it proper to modify that
without consultation with the other Dominions, if we modify
it we would be departing from uniformity.   Therefore, there

is not contained in the present Bill a provision for a separate
and distinct naturalisation on the part of married women,
of whom I understand the hon. member is speaking."

Speaking during the Committee stage on 21st June,

The Minister of Justice said that there was the advantage
that the two Acts of 1914—their Act, which was, by the way, the
first, and the British Act of 1914—continued to be concurrent
legislation. In the British system they had retained their
Act of 1914 and amended it, and it seemed desirable that they
should maintain in force their Act of 1914 and proceed by
amending it. They would then always have clearly in the
amending sections of this Bill, and any amendments made in
the future, clauses relating to legislation concurrent with that
of the Mother Country and the other Dominions. They had
deemed it desirable to revive the Act of 1914, making any
amendments now necessary apply directly to it instead of
retaining the Act of 1919, which itself would require amendment. It was a matter of their proceeding by consent and
concurrently. It placed the British Parliament and themselves, in dealing with this kind of legislation, in this position,
that they had to conform to those things which had been
previously discussed before either of them legislated.

Mr. S. W. Jacobs (**Liberal,** *George Etienne Cartier, Que*):
" I should like to ascertain from the Minister if the British
Government has concurred in the change which is now pro-
posed by this legislation."

The Minister of Justice : " Yes, the British Government
has most fully concurred." The Minister went on to say that
the British Parliament was scrupulously careful not to enact
anything that would be necessary to the general Imperial
naturalisation without previous consultation with the
Dominions.

Mr. Euler pointed out that while the Act permitted
naturalisation of those who had previously lived in Canada
for ten years, it did not make provision for those who might
attain the full ten-year residence in Canada after 1909. As
the law stood now, the effect of it would be that any person
of former alien enemy nationality who was resident in Canada
on 7th July, 1909, could now be naturalised, but a man who
came to Canada in the fall of 1909, or in 1910, 1911, 1912,
1913, could not obtain naturalisation until 1929.

The Minister of Justice thought the Committee would be
unanimous on this point, that the provision that suspended
for a time the naturalisation of people who had just come into
the country since the war was a proper precaution under the
circumstances. They were extending the benefit of citizenship to a certain class of people for whom exemption from the
provisions of the law, as applicable to those who were coming

in, was granted ; and he did not think it unfair to say that they should extend this benefit only to those whom they had had for ten years under their eye before the termination of the war.

Mr. Joseph Archambault (Liberal, *Chambly and Verchères, Que.*) inquired whether the clause allowing a member of a race known to be opposed to the enemy governments would apply to a citizen of Alsace-Lorraine whose sympathy was with France and opposed to the enemy government but who was a subject of Germany.

The Minister of Justice replied that during the war, once any French authority was prepared to vouch for the feelings of a citizen of Alsace-Lorraine, they never treated him as an alien enemy.

Mr. W. H. White (Liberal, *Victoria, Alta.*) drew attention to the fact that there was a very large class of settlers in Western Canada who came in 1909 and 1910, and took up land with the full understanding that they could become citizens and receive their naturalisation papers and patents after the expiration of a certain time. It appeared very unfair to deny them the rights of citizenship under the circumstances.

Mr. H. A. Mackie (Unionist, *Edmonton, E. Riding, Alta.*) said that these people were probably the ones who came from Galicia. They were under Austria at one time. Western Galicia was now classed as Polish territory, and all who came from that portion of Galicia under Polish dominion were able to get their naturalisation papers without further difficulty. The only question that remained was as to those who came from Eastern Galicia, and they were counted as alien enemies as they came from German Galicia.

After further discussion the Bill was read a third time and passed on 21st June.

DEBATE IN THE SENATE.

The Leader of the Senate and Minister of Civil Re-establishment (Senator the Hon. **Sir James Lougheed**), in moving the Second Reading of the Bill on 25th June, said that in 1914 the Parliament of Canada passed a Naturalisation Act as the result of an agreement between the Imperial authorities and the Government of Canada. It was the outcome of an agreement among the different parts of the Empire with a view to making naturalisation uniform and common throughout the whole Empire. In 1919 after the Armistice was arrived at, and after public opinion had been excited over what should constitute the naturalisation of alien enemies, they repealed the Act of 1914 and passed a new Act. Probably the most prominent feature of the later measure was a prohibition as to the naturalisation of certain enemy aliens until they had put in a residence of ten years in the Dominion. It was afterwards discovered that there had been a misunderstanding between their Government and the Imperial authorities. The opinion was that Great Britain had acted similarly. It had been found that that was not the case, and, owing to certain amendments which were made at the time, it had been thought desirable to return to the Act of 1914.

Senator the Hon. H. Bostock (Leader of the Opposition) understood that the object of this legislation was to enable the Government to deal with a question that arose under the Franchise Act in another place. When this Bill became law the Government would be able to give naturalisation to aliens who lived in this country prior to the coming into effect of the Act of 1914, but who had not taken out naturalisation papers. He thought he was right in stating that there was another improvement in this Naturalisation Act, inasmuch as certain powers which before were left entirely in the hands of the Secretary of State would now be exercised by the Governor-in-Council on the advice of the Secretary of State. That brought the matter to the attention of the whole Government and in a way was, he thought, an additional advantage to the whole country.

After further discussion the Bill was passed, with a few minor amendments, on 28th June.

OPIUM AND NARCOTIC DRUG AMENDMENT ACT.

(International Convention: League of Nations, &c.)

This Act is intended to bring into force, so far as Canada is concerned, the International Opium Convention signed at The Hague in 1912. The original Bill (*vide* JOURNAL OF THE PARLIAMENTS OF THE EMPIRE, Vol. I., No. 2, page 335) was considerably amended during the last Session of Parliament and the following summary gives the main points of the Act.

The Act amends the Opium and Drug Act of 1911 by inserting the word " Narcotic " before the word " Drug," which means and includes any substance (whether alone or in conjunction with any other substance) mentioned in the Schedule to the Act or which may be added to such Schedule under the authority of the Act. It is provided that any person who deals in any drug, who gives, sells or furnishes any drug to any person other than a duly authorised and practising physician, veterinary surgeon or dentist, or to a *bona fide* wholesale druggist, or to a druggist carrying on a business in a *bona fide* drug store, and any druggist who gives, sells or furnishes any drug except upon a written order or prescription signed by a duly authorised and practising physician, veterinary surgeon or dentist, or who, without the authority of the prescribing physician, veterinary surgeon or dentist, uses any prescription to sell any drug on more than one occasion, shall be guilty of a criminal offence, and shall be liable upon summary conviction to a fine not exceeding one thousand dollars and costs and not less than five hundred dollars and costs, or to imprisonment for a term not exceeding one year, or to both fine and imprisonment.

With the approval of the Governor-in-Council, the Minister presiding over the Department of Health shall have power to issue licences for the import, export, sale, manufacture and distribution of any drug, to name the ports and places in Canada where any drug may be exported or imported, to prescribe the manner in which any raw opium, prepared opium or any drug is packed and marked for export, to prescribe the record that shall be kept by any licensee in connection with the export, import, receipt, sale, disposal and distribution of any drugs mentioned in such licence, and to make other necessary regulations.

It is further provided that every physician, veterinary surgeon, dentist and druggist, pharmacist or chemist shall make to the Minister, when required, a declaration in the prescribed form, stating that he is engaged in the sale or distribution of opium, morphine, cocaine and their respective salts or derivatives, or otherwise, as the case may be.

The provisions of the Act regarding penalties for improper export and import, manufacture, etc., do not apply to preparations and remedies or to preparation for external use which do not contain more than a specified amount of drugs.   No person, however, shall sell for administration or administer to a child under two years of age, any remedy or preparation containing opium, morphine, heroin or codeine, the sale of which is permitted by this subsection.

DEBATE IN HOUSE OF COMMONS.

The President of the Council (Hon. N. W. Rowell), in moving the Second Reading of the Bill on 26th April, said the Bill was necessary to carry out the obligations they had assumed under the International Opium Convention, and in the interest of public health and the welfare of the people. The first legislation that they had in Canada in connection with the importation of opium was the Act of 1908 introduced by the hon. member for Maisonneuve (Mr. Lemieux), then Minister of Labour.   That legislation grew out of an investigation carried on by the present Leader of the Opposition (Mr. Mackenzie King), when Deputy Minister of Labour, into certain anti-Asiatic riots in the City of Vancouver, which disclosed the extent to which the manufacture and sale of opium were being carried on in the Dominion of Canada. One of the effects of that legislation was greatly to decrease the importation of opium into Canada. The Act of 1911 followed what was known as the Shanghai Conference, and was intended to give effect to some of the important decisions of that Conference. That legislation continued on the Statute books unaltered until last year, when a Bill was passed through the House which provided for prohibiting import except under licence. That was the condition of the legislation at the present time.

The Act of 1908 dealt only with opium. The Act of 1911 went further and dealt with derivatives of opium—morphine, heroin and codeine as well as with cocaine.

In the United States they had had what was known as the Harrison Act passed in 1914. That Act was amended in 1918 and made much more stringent. The United States Government took almost complete control of the traffic in these drugs by reason of that legislation. One of the results appeared to have been that those interested in the trade imported these drugs into Canada, and then by smuggling gained access to the American market. In fact that was complained of by a Committee appointed by the United States Government to investigate the matter.

The important changes introduced into the legislation by the new Bill might be summarised briefly. First of all, in the definition of drugs itself, it was made perfectly clear that the prohibitions of the Act applied not only to the drug itself but to any preparations of it, subject to the exceptions provided in the Bill. Secondly, under the International Opium Convention, it was required—in order to limit the extent of this traffic as much as it was possible to do so by legislation and regulation—that not only should there be a limit to the purposes for which drugs might be imported, and for which they might be exported to other countries that had adopted regulations, but also that the ports of import or export should be named so that it might be possible to check up what was coming in and going out ; and it was also required that the packages which contained these drugs should also be marked in such a way as to indicate their character. These were the requirements of the International Convention and this legislation provided for such regulations.

Mr. Rowell went on to explain the reasons for the International Convention (*vide* JOURNAL OF THE PARLIAMENT OF THE EMPIRE, Vol. I., No. 2, page 336).

Speaking in Committee on 28th April,

The President of the Council said that they were not requiring in the Bill, so far as the particular matters of licence and record were concerned, anything that was not required by the International Opium Convention. Their legislation in that respect did not go nearly so far as the American legislation which was intended to carry out the provisions of the convention ; it did not go so far as the legislation of some other countries. Quite apart from any question of public interest, they were obligated by the terms of the Convention, which was approved by the Government in 1914 and which did not go into effect until the ratification of the Treaty of Peace, to put this legislation through.

Mr. W. F. Cockshutt (Unionist, *Brantford, Ont.*) : " If it is found that this Act is unworkable, or oppressive, if it is opposed by a large number of the people who are affected by it, will it be necessary for us to go back to the League of Nations if we want to make amendments to the Act ? . . . Is legislation respecting our domestic affairs to be forced upon us by international obligation instead of by national or imperial authority ? I think that is a very important point, and I should like to know if the legislation mentioned in the Treaty of Peace is going to be obligated upon this country for all time or until we are relieved of the obligation by the League of Nations which imposed it."

The President of the Council : " This country is under obligation to carry out its contracts, the same as any other party who makes one. We have entered into a contract by joining in this Convention. If we do not desire to adhere to its terms we should have to withdraw from it in the manner provided in the contract. As long as our legislation keeps within the terms of the Convention we have absolute freedom of action."

Mr. Cockshutt : " And to amend legislation ? "

The President of the Council : " We have absolute right to amend anything we like, but we should not violate the terms of the Convention so long as we are a party to it."

The Hon. W. S. Fielding (Liberal, *Shelburne and Queen's, N.S.*) : " If we desire to be relieved of our obligation, what will be the procedure before we can get out ? "

Mr. P. McGibbon (Unionist, *Muskoka, Ont.*) : " I never understood that the League of Nations was going to interfere in our domestic affairs, and I think it is a bad principle if we have bound ourselves to something as far-reaching as that."

The President of the Council : " All we have to do is to serve notice denouncing the Convention. One year after the notice is served, the Convention terminates so far as we are concerned."

After further discussion the Bill was read a third time and passed on 3rd May.

INCOME WAR TAX AMENDMENT ACT.

This Act, which was assented to on 1st July, 1920, amends the Income.War Tax Act of 1917 in certain particulars.

The Act provides that income tax shall be assessed, levied and paid on the income during the preceding year of every person (1) residing or ordinarily resident in Canada or (2) who remains in Canada during any calendar year for a period or periods equal to one hundred and eighty-three days; or (3) who is employed in Canada; or (4) who, not being a resident of Canada, is carrying on a business in Canada; or (5) who, not being a resident of Canada, derives income for services rendered in Canada to any person resident or carrying on business in Canada but only upon that portion of the income so earned by such non-resident.

The several taxes and surtaxes prescribed by the Income War Tax Act of 1917 are increased by the addition of five per cent. on any income of five thousand dollars or more for the year 1919 or each subsequent calendar year.

Dividends or shareholders' bonuses shall be taxable income of the taxpayer in the year in which they are distributed. Income accumulating in trust for the benefit of unascertained persons, or of persons with contingent interests, shall be taxable in the hands of the trustees or other like persons acting in a fiduciary capacity, as if such were the income of an unmarried person.

The Act also provides for the payment of one quarter of the tax with the return of the income and of the balance by instalments with interest; penalties for understating the amount of income; payment of income by trustees, assignees, executors, etc., before distribution; refund of over-payments and obtaining information.

If the Minister suspects that the taxpayer is about to leave Canada, he may demand payment of taxes within ten days. Non-payment of the tax within the specified time shall render the goods of the taxpayer liable to confiscation.

DEBATE IN HOUSE OF COMMONS.

Addressing the House in Committee of Ways and Means on 4th June,

The Minister of Finance (Hon. Sir Henry Drayton) said that the richer man must relatively pay much more than the man with the small income. The tax as it now stood commenced with the lowest rate of four per cent. of normal tax on the small income; that was four per cent. on all incomes exceeding $1,000 in the case of unmarried persons and $2,000 in the case of married persons, and it ran from there to $6,000. After you reached an income of $6,000, the tax on everything over that was eight per cent., no matter how large the income was. The first surtax started with a tax of one per cent. on the amount by which an income exceeded $5,000, and did not exceed $6,000; then the tax was two per cent. on the amount by which an income exceeded $6,000 and did not exceed $8,000, and so on.

In moving the Second Reading of the Bill on 8th June, the Minister stated that it carried into effect the taxation changes as to incomes proposed in the Budget speech (*vide* JOURNAL OF THE PARLIAMENTS OF THE EMPIRE, Vol. I., No. 3, page 500).

Explaining in Committee the section dealing with dividends and shareholders' bonuses, the Minister said that where companies did not pay dividends but issued stock, which was really a bonus, to their shareholders, the stock dividend was treated the same as money.

Mr. J. A. Currie (Unionist, *Simcoe, N. Riding, Ont.*) said that the United States Government undertook to tax stock dividends. The question was argued before the Supreme Court and the Court held that this was surplus of the company, and that although stock was issued against it, it was not taxable. He did not think it was good policy to say that stock dividends were taxable.

The Minister of Finance, referring to the section dealing with persons liable to income tax, said that the object of subsection 5* was to cover the case of such men as mining engineers who, having their address outside of Canada, spent five or six months of their time in the country and derived a very substantial income from work they did there. It was thought that they should pay a tax on that income. They had an arrangement at present under which people who came from the United States into Canada and engaged in work from which they derived an income might have credited to them by the United States authorities in respect of income tax any amount which they paid to them on that account.

Mr. J. A. Robb (Liberal, *Chateauguay-Huntingdon, Que.*) asked whether, if persons residing in the British Isles and having investments in Canada paid income tax to the Canadian Government, they were exempt from taxation in the British Isles.

The Minister of Finance : " That is a question that has given a great deal of trouble and to which we have given much consideration. The whole matter is now being considered by a Royal Commission in the Old Country, and we hope to make some satisfactory progress in the matter. At present no such relief is given as my hon. friend suggests."

Speaking in Committee on 9th June,

Mr. Joseph Archambault (Liberal, *Chambly and Verchères, Que.*) suggested that the exemption in respect of each child should be increased from $200 to $500. Everyone knew that one of the causes of race suicide and voluntary sterility was the high cost of the upkeep of children.

---

* See No. (5) in the summary of the Act.

The Minister of Finance pointed out that the exemption for children applied in Great Britain, where the exemption for the first child was, if he remembered rightly, $200 with a smaller exemption for each subsequent child.

The Hon. Rodolphe Lemieux (Liberal, *Maisonneuve, Que.*) was surprised that the Government should refuse to encourage large families.

Mr. Michael Clark (Independent, *Red Deer, Alta.*) could not honestly give his assent to the proposition that a man ought to be helped in his parental duties by being exempted from his State duties.

Mr. P. F. Casgrain (Liberal, *Charlevoix–Montmorency, Que.*) drew attention to the taxing of earned and unearned incomes. At present under their law there was no difference in taxation depending on where the income came from. In England he was told a distinction was drawn between incomes derived from real estate and securities and those which were earned.

The Minister of Finance stated that a distinction was drawn in some countries. It was not drawn in the United States, nor in Australia, nor in New Zealand as he recollected. It was drawn in part in Great Britain, but the difference was not very great. For some reason, probably having regard to the cost, the value of money and the demand made by investors for money, the Parliament of the Mother Country made that difference only on incomes up to £2,000. Having regard to the fact that after all they in Canada required outside capital probably as much as any other country did, because they required to develop all their resources and their position was different from that of Great Britain where the resources were well developed and the necessity for new capital was not as great as it was in Canada, he came to the conclusion that it was better to follow the example given by other countries which were seeking development, such as Australia, New Zealand and the United States.

Speaking on an amendment proposed by **Mr. Hume Cronyn (Unionist,** *London, Ont.*), to the effect that amounts paid to charities up to ten per cent. of the taxpayer's net income should be exempt from taxation, **Mr. Michael Clark** said that he would be sorry to describe as charity anything that was carefully protected from being taxed by the State.

The Hon. W. S. Fielding (Liberal, *Shelburne and Queen's, N.S.*) said that a great deal of charitable work was done by individual effort on the part of the people ; and unless they could encourage this individual effort, the charitable institutions of the country might suffer.

Mr. Hume Cronyn's amendment was negatived, and, after further discussion, the Bill was read a third time and passed on 26th June.

BUSINESS PROFITS WAR TAX AMENDMENT ACT.

This Act, which was assented to on 1st July, 1920, amends the Business Profits War Tax Act of 1916, by reducing the scale of the tax.

The Act provides that the profits earned during any accounting period ending in the year 1920 which do not exceed ten per cent. per annum upon the capital employed shall be exempt from the Business Profits War Tax. Upon profits exceeding ten per cent. and not exceeding fifteen per cent. on capital there shall be paid a tax equal to twenty per cent. of such profits ; on profits between fifteen and twenty per cent., a tax equal to thirty per cent. of the profits ; on profits between twenty and thirty per cent., a tax of fifty per cent. ; and on profits exceeding thirty per cent., a tax of sixty per cent.

In any business with a capital of not less than $25,000 and under $50,000, a tax shall be paid of twenty per cent. of the amount by which the profits earned during any accounting period ending in the year 1920 in such business exceed ten per cent. per annum.

DEBATE IN HOUSE OF COMMONS.

Speaking on 4th June in Committee of Ways and Means on the resolution upon which the Act was based,

Mr. S. W. Jacobs (**Liberal,** *George Etienne Cartier, Que.*) drew attention to the fact that in many cases the amount which was charged by the Government under the excess profits tax was very much larger than the amount charged on a business with a capitalisation twice as large. He thought that was a glaring anomaly.

The Minister of Finance (**Hon. Sir Henry Drayton**) said that in all taxes of this kind the one consideration was the amount of money actually employed, and there was no doubt that where they had an active, energetic management which, by extra work and superior business acumen, turned over its capital four or five times a year as compared with another that turned its capital over only once or twice a year, the same amount of capital was utilised to a far greater extent and with greater advantage to the country.

The Minister went on to say that he did not attempt to defend the business profits tax as a matter of principle. It was an absolute necessity, and after all it afforded one rough-and-ready way, and a fairly effective way, of recovering to the nation exorbitant profits. It would be entirely improper to change the tax this year.

Mr. Ernest Lapointe (**Liberal,** *Quebec East*) stated that there were certain exemptions which would be continued under the new Bill. For instance, all companies or associations, 90 per cent. of whose capital was owned by a province or a municipality, were exempt from the provisions of this measure. He thought that in certain cases this constituted a discrimination which was unfair.

The Minister of Finance said that the only people that were benefited one way or another or that were hurt one way or another, were the shareholders who had been getting a profit, which had been defined to be an excessive profit, during the war period, and therefore had to pay something out of these excessive profits.

Mr. Lapointe claimed that when a province or municipality chose to enter the business of trading or manufacturing it should be placed in exactly the same position as other traders or manufacturers.

Speaking in Committee on 8th June,

Mr. J. A. Robb (**Liberal,** *Chateauguay–Huntingdon, Que.*) said that an income tax was absolutely sound, every person paid ; but a business profits tax did not work out to the advantage of the country. In his Budget speech the Minister of Finance clearly intimated that activity and production had been lessened during the past year. Why ? Because money that would have been used to extend business and enlarge industries was gathered in by the Government, and there was no incentive for industries to go on and extend their business. The best way to avoid the controversy as between public ownership and private ownership was to get back to the promises made by the predecessor of the Minister of Finance (Sir Thomas White) and to do away with this business profits tax, which was an injury to their industries and to Canada.

After further discussion the Bill was read a third time and passed.

DEBATE IN THE SENATE.

Speaking in Committee on 21st June,

The Leader of the Senate and Minister of Civil Re-establishment (Senator the Hon. Sir James Lougheed) said that they were exempting 10 per cent. instead of 7 per cent. In the next paragraph, 20 per cent. superseded 25 per cent. Thirty per cent. took the place of 50 per cent. The next paragraph imposed a tax of 50 per cent. in place of the 75 per cent. charged at present. In the following paragraph 60 per cent. was imposed instead of 75 per cent. In the next sub-section 20 per cent. was substituted for 25 per cent.

Senator the Hon. H. Bostock (Leader of the Opposition) thought it would have been very much more in the interest of the country to base the tax on the profits made out of a business rather than to tax the dividends, as this really did. As he understood it, the difference between the way that this tax was collected in England and the way it was fixed in Canada was that in England they took so much per cent. of the profits of a business without any reference to the amount of capital invested in it ; but the system under which they had acted was to tax the profits according to the dividends they represented on the capital. Then they had a graduated tax instead of a fixed tax. The result was that a man who had a business with a small amount of capital, but who through his energy and enterprise managed to make considerable profits, was taxed much more highly than a man who did not make such large profits on his business.

After further discussion the Bill was read a third time and passed by the Senate on 22nd June.

SPECIAL WAR REVENUE AMENDMENT ACT.

This Act, which was assented to on 1st July, 1920, amends the Special War Revenue Act of 1915 by imposing stamp taxes on bills of exchange, etc., excise taxes on certain specified articles of luxury, and a sales tax. The principle of the proposed taxes was explained and discussed in the Debate on the Budget. (*Vide* JOURNAL OF THE PARLIAMENTS OF THE EMPIRE, Vol. I., No. 3, page 498.)

The Act provides that subject to certain provisions, no person shall transfer a bill of exchange or promissory note to a bank in such manner as to constitute the bank the holder thereof, unless there is affixed thereto a stamp of the value of, if the amount of the money for which the bill or note is drawn or made (i.) does not exceed $100, two cents ; (ii.) exceeds $100, for every $100 or portion thereof, two cents. The stamp tax on bills payable on demand shall be deemed to be drawn for an amount not exceeding $100. Stamp taxes are also imposed on promissory notes given for advances, documents containing a promise to pay or pledge of securities, overdrafts, bank cheques, sale or transfer of stock, etc.

An excise tax of ten per cent. is imposed on the total purchase price of certain articles of clothing in excess of a specified price, ivory goods, cut glass, sporting goods, jewellery, etc. ; of fifteen per cent. on certain classes of furniture, etc. ; of twenty per cent. on cigar and cigarette cases, certain gold and silver articles, etc.; of fifty per cent. on articles of gold not otherwise provided for. Taxes of ten or fifteen per cent. are levied on so much of the amount paid in excess of the price specified in the Act for carpets and rugs, footwear, and certain articles of clothing. These taxes are to be paid by the purchaser to the vendor at the time

G

of sale. A tax of three per cent. is levied on chewing gum, of five per cent. on pianos, of ten per cent. on pleasure boats, cameras, confectionery, firearms, etc., subject to certain conditions as to price and quality; of fifteen per cent. on automobiles retailing for less than $3,000 each, and of twenty per cent. above that figure. Taxes are also imposed on wines and spirits.

The Act further provides that in addition to the present duty of excise and customs a tax of one per cent. shall be imposed on sales and deliveries by manufacturers and wholesalers, on jobbers and on the duty-paid value of importations, but in respect of sales by manufacturers to retailers or consumers, or on importation by retailers or consumers, the tax payable shall be two per cent. The tax shall be payable by the purchaser to the wholesaler or manufacturer at the time of such sale.

DEBATE IN HOUSE OF COMMONS.

Speaking in Committee on 9th June on the proposed resolution precedent to the amendment of the Special War Revenue Act, 1915,

The Minister of Finance (Hon. Sir Henry Drayton) said that he need add very little to what he said in his Budget speech. The Government stood absolutely on the question of principle, that revenue was required, and could be got out of expenditures of the character designated.

Mr. Michael Clark (Independent, *Red Deer, Alta.*) held that these taxes on imports were not excise taxes at all. The essential feature about an excise duty was that it could be levied only on home goods. There was no pretence that this was so in the case of these particular duties.

The Minister of Finance said that what they wanted was to get a maximum of revenue with a minimum of inconvenience from those classes of people who could best afford to pay, a tax so designed that it would not be possible for the person who should pay it to make somebody else pay it for him, and at the same time to charge profits on that tax as part of his expenses. That was the main reason why the burden of collecting the taxes had been placed upon the retailer. As regarded the great bulk of these luxury taxes, if they got saving instead of extravagance, they were not going to have a great amount of money raised. On the other hand, if the people continued to spend in the way they had been doing in the past, these luxury taxes would be very productive.

The Hon. Rodolphe Lemieux (Liberal, *Maisonneuve, Que.*) considered that these taxes on luxuries were more or less taxes on necessities.

The Minister of Finance thought that the man who bought should know he could get an essential without paying any tax at all; and that he should have the option of paying a tax for the more expensive articles if he liked, and should then pay that tax without any added profit—either to the manufacturer, to the wholesaler, or to the retailer—on that tax.

After further discussion in Committee, especially with regard to the collection and incidence of the proposed excise taxes, the Bill embodying the resolutions was introduced on 16th June, and passed on 26th June.

PENSION AMENDMENT ACT.

(Statement by Chairman of Committee on Pensions, &c.)

This Act, which was assented to on 1st July, 1920, increases the scale of pensions for ex-soldiers and their dependants and amends certain details of the Pension Act of 1919. These increases were explained by Mr. Hume Cronyn, the Chairman of the Committee on Pensions and Re-establishment, in presenting the Committee's final report to the House of Commons on 22nd June.

In addition to the increases in pensions, etc., explained in Mr. Hume Cronyn's statement (see below), the Act provides, *inter alia*, that when a pensioner has been sentenced to imprisonment for a period of six months or more, no pension shall be paid to him for the period of his imprisonment, though the Commission has discretion to pay the pension or part of it to his dependants. No pension shall be paid in respect of a child who, if a boy, is over the age of sixteen or, if a girl, over the age of seventeen, except when such child and those responsible for its maintenance are without resources and such child is unable owing to physical or mental infirmity occurring before the age of twenty-one to provide for its own maintenance, or except when such child is under the age of twenty-one and taking a course of instruction.

In cases of total disability the Act provides for the following allowances in addition to his pension in accordance with rank : Commander and Captain under three years' seniority (Naval) or Lieutenant-Colonel (Militia), not exceeding $90 per annum ; Lieutenant-Commander (Naval) or Major (Militia), not exceeding $390 per annum ; Lieutenant (Naval) or Captain (Militia), not exceeding $650 per annum.

It is further provided that when a member of the forces, previous to his enlistment or during his service. was maintaining one or both of his parents, an amount not exceeding $180 per annum may be paid to him for each of such.parents as long as he continues such maintenance.

In cases where a member of the forces has died leaving a widow or a widow and children or orphan children entitled to pension in addition to a parent or person in the place of a parent who previous to his enlistment or during his service was wholly or to a substantial extent maintained by him, the Commission may, in its discretion, award a pension to each parent or person, not exceeding $180 per annum. Pensions to parents are always subject to review, and each unmarried son is assumed to be supporting the parents with whom he resides to the extent of not less than $10 a month.

When a person of the rank of Warrant Officer or above in any of His Majesty's forces, other than those of Canada, or a member of the Allied forces who was domiciled and resident in Canada at the beginning of the war, has died as a result of the war and his widowed mother, widow or children have been awarded a smaller pension than they would have been entitled to under the Act in respect of his death, such dependants shall be entitled, during the continuance of their residence in Canada, to such additional pension as will make the total of the two pensions received by them equal to the pension that would have been awarded if the person aforesaid had died in the Military service of Canada.

The Act also provides that South African War pensions, Fenian Raid and North-West Rebellion pensions shall, during the continuance of the residence of the recipients in Canada, be brought up to the rates set forth in the present Act.

DEBATE IN HOUSE OF COMMONS.

Speaking on the motion commending the final report of the Committee on Pensions and Re-establishment to the consideration of the Government, on 22nd June,

Mr. Hume Cronyn (Unionist, *London, Ont.*) said that the report under consideration recommended certain increases in pensions. The Pension Bill of the country, if these recommendations were adopted, would be increased by nearly $8,000,000. The number of disability pensioners at the end of the fiscal year was 69,583; if they added to these the dependent pensioners, the wives and children of disability pensioners, and the children of widows, they found the total number of beneficiaries to be 177,035. The amount which would be paid to these pensioners for a period of twelve months on the present scale was estimated at over $25,000,000. If they added to this sum the increases suggested, they found their annual pension bill totalled about $33,000,000.

Pension Increases.

The history of pension legislation since the beginning of the Great War showed a steadily ascending curve in the scale of pensions adopted. The first provision was arrived at just five years ago, when $264 a year was fixed as a pension for the totally disabled of the rank and file, a similar amount being awarded to widows or dependent widowed mothers of those who were killed. In June of 1916 the total disability pension was raised to $480 and that to widows and mothers to $382. In October of 1917 the pension for a totally disabled private soldier was raised to $600 per annum, and that of the widow and mother to $480 a year. In June of last year a bonus of 20 per cent. was recommended. The result of this bonus was that a totally disabled member of the forces below the rank of lieutenant received $750 a year, while his widow or dependent parent was entitled to $576 per annum.

Recommendations.

A fourth increase was now being recommended to be given effect by way of bonus. The permanent figures which were arrived at in 1917 were taken as the standard or basic rate. The bonus being one of 50 per cent. the result was that a totally disabled member of the rank and file would receive $900 in all. The pension of the widow or widowed mother, fixed in 1917 at $480 a year, would be increased by a bonus of 50 per cent. or $240.

This increase of pensions from 20 per cent. to 50 per cent. had been recommended by the Committee to apply only to the cases of those pensioners who were resident in Canada; so far as pensioners resident outside of Canada were concerned, the recommendation was that the present bonus of 20 per cent. should be continued for another year.

The increased pension had been recommended because of the steadily advancing cost of living. In many parts of Canada there was certainly no margin left for any unforeseen emergencies, such as illness, etc.

A proportionate amount of the $900 which under the new scale would be awarded to the totally disabled members of the rank and file, would be paid to those suffering from disabilities which were less than total. The result of these various increases was to bring to a parity the pensions paid to or in respect of all ranks below that of Captain; and it was estimated that the added cost thereof to the country would amount to $3,650,000 per annum.

Dependent Parents.

Pensions to dependent parents were increased in like manner as those to widows; that was to say: the dependent father or mother of a soldier who died leaving neither widow or children, would receive by way of pension a bonus of precisely the same amount as would have been paid to his widow. Under the Pension Act the pensions of mothers were subject to a deduction if they were in receipt of an independent income from outside sources, and the Act was so construed that if any widowed mother owned her own house, or had the advantage of free lodgings, she was held to be in receipt of an independent income of from $10 to $15 a month. The Committee felt that a change in the law was called for, and accordingly recommended that the advantage of free lodgings should not be counted against the pensioner, nor, so long as she resided in Canada, should her pension be reduced because of her income from outside sources, unless that income exceeded the sum of $20 a month.

Married Men and Children.

In addition to these increases, the Committee suggested that larger pensions in certain other cases should be awarded. At the present time, if a total disability pensioner was married he was entitled to an increase in his pension of $180 a year. It was proposed that this pension should be made $300 per annum. If he had one boy of 16 or under, or a girl of 17 or under, his pension had been increased by $144 a year : it was suggested that this allowance should be increased to $180 a year. For a second child he received $10 a month ; it was now suggested that this should be increased to $12 a month : and for each subsequent child below the above ages, instead of receiving an additional $8 a month he would be allowed $10 a month. These increases would be allowed in proportion to those whose disabilities were less than 100 per cent. The widow of a deceased soldier had had her pension increased for her first child, if under the ages above-mentioned, by $180 a year. No change was suggested in this allowance, but the allowances on behalf of subsequent children were increased to those proposed for similar children of totally disabled pensioners.

Comparison with other Countries.

Amounts payable annually to those of the rank and file, permanently totally disabled under the new scale suggested for Canada and under the existing rates so far as known in the countries of the Allied belligerents were : —

	Single man.	Man and wife.	Man, wife and child.	Man, wife and 2 children.	Man, wife and 3 children.	Each additional child.
	$	$	$	$	$	$
Canada	900.00	1,200.00	1,380.00	1,524.00	1,644.00	120.00
Great Britain ..	506.13	632.66	727.56	803.46	879.42	75.92
Australia ..	379.60	569.40	695.93	790.74	854.01	63.26
New Zealand ..	506.13	759.20	885.73	1,012.25	1,138.80	126.53
South Africa ..	379.60	506.13	601.12	685.36	759.20	63.26
United States ..	1,200.00	1,200.00	1,200.00	1,200.00	1,200.00	nil
France	480.00	480.00	540.00	600.00	660.00	60.00
Italy	243.33	291.99	318.75	345.51	372.27	26.76

"Helpless" Allowance.

The present maximum for helpless allowance (" helpless " connoting a condition in which the sufferer is unable to make use of some one or more of the functions daily exercised by the normal man) was $450 per annum. The report recommended that the minimum allowance should hereafter be $250 a year to be increased when the conditions warranted to a maximum of $750.

Gratuities and their Commutation.

In Canada, a man who was only disabled to an extent of less than 5 per cent. was not paid a pension but was awarded a gratuity up to $100 to compensate for the disability from which he suffered. Other countries refused to give pensions to those whose disability was less than 10 per cent., or in some cases 20 per cent. The Canadian Act, however, provided for small pensions in these cases. A private unmarried soldier whose disability was rated from 5 to 9 per cent. was awarded $30 a year. The man in the same class suffering a disability of from 10 to 14 per cent. received double that amount. There had been for some time past a strong body of opinion, both among the disabled men and elsewhere, in favour of allowing these smaller pensions to be commuted. As over 40 per cent. of the disabled men now in receipt of pensions suffered from a disability of less than 15 per cent., it would be understood the question was of interest to nearly 30,000 pensioners. The Committee recommended that the option should be given to all pensioners whose disabilities were rated below 15 per cent. either to continue to receive the pensions now awarded, or to commute the same and accept in lieu thereof a cash payment. It was obvious the man whose disability was not permanent could not receive so large a payment as he whose body had been so injured as to suffer a disability throughout his life ; in these latter cases, when it was clear the disability was permanent, the man rated between 5 and 9 per cent. would be entitled to $300, and the man between 10 and 14 per cent. to double that amount.

In the event of the disability of a pensioner who commuted his pension increasing in after years, he was protected by a provision in the Act which would allow him to again submit his case to the Pension Board.

The Act to amend the Pension Act according to the above recommendations was introduced into the House of Commons by the Prime Minister (Right. Hon. Sir Robert Borden) on 22nd June, and, after some discussion in Committee, was passed on 23rd June.

SOLDIERS' SETTLEMENT BOARD.

(Statement as to work accomplished.)

On 7th May, 1920, the Minister of the Interior made a statement in Committee of Supply on the work carried out by the Soldiers' Settlement Board.

The Minister of the Interior (Hon. Arthur Meighen*) stated that the Soldiers' Settlement Board was constituted in 1917, first of all only for the purpose of assisting in the settlement of returned soldiers on Dominion lands. Certain work was done, certain entries were made, and assistance was given by the board to settlers on soldier grants or homestead lands. A year ago last December power was taken and exercised under Order in Council, extending the work of the board to settlement on purchased lands, and enabling the board to give assistance by way of loans for improvements, stock, and equipment, a power it previously did not have. These powers so exercised as early as 1918 were confirmed by legislation a year ago; and acting upon the Orders in Council and subsequent legislation the board had performed a very large achievement entailing a considerable financial commitment.

The Soldiers' Settlement Act contemplated assistance to returned soldiers of the Canadian Expeditionary Force, of the United Kingdom, and of the United Kingdom's Allies in the Great War, within certain restrictions set out in the definition. Under that legislation some fifty thousand men had applied to the Soldiers' Settlement Board, men almost wholly of the Canadian Expeditionary Forces, and the work of the board had since consisted in the reception and disposition of those applications and of assistance to the men who were deemed to be qualified to receive that assistance under the Act.

The soldiers' settlement work divided itself into three distinct branches. There was, first, the agricultural branch; secondly, the lands and loans branch; and thirdly, what was known as the home branch. The agricultural branch had to do with the acceptance of applications from soldiers; with the deliberation as to whether or not the applicants were such as should be granted assistance; with the training of men who were found to require training; and with the determination of the extent and character of stock and equipment which the men should receive; and finally with the supervision of the farming operations of the men after they were placed on the land.

---

*Now the Right Hon. Arthur Meighen, Prime Minister of the Dominion (see JOURNAL, Vol. I., No. 3, at page 464).

Qualification and Loan Boards.

There was a qualification board at each district office of the Soldiers' Settlement Board, of which district offices there were altogether eighteen in Canada. These qualification boards received the 50,423 applications that came in up to 21st March last, and since that time had accepted a total of 36,830 men. There had also been accepted for training 1,556 men, and the rest had been either not finally disposed of or had been rejected. After the men were passed as fitted to come under the Act, their selection of land, if they desired land to be purchased, was passed upon by what were known as loan boards, who received the appraisal of the land at the hands of specially qualified appraisal officers, and upon that appraisal, or after such further inspection as was demanded, they stated whether or not, at the price the soldier was prepared to pay for the land, the board should be advised to advance assistance against that land and to what amount. These loan boards were situated in every district office of the Settlement Board in Canada.

Advances.

The board had purchased lands and had also loaned for the purpose of discharging encumbrances on lands already owned ; it had purchased stock and equipment and loaned against stock and equipment to the soldier settler and had as well loaned to the soldier settler who located upon Dominion lands or soldier grants. The operations of the board up to the 27th March, 1920, entailed a financial commitment on the Dominion of $58,741,605.

The total of settlers under the Act aggregated 19,181 at the present time. Of the 15,234 who received loans, 9,981 settled on purchased land ; 2,779 received advances on lands they already owned to remove encumbrances and for improvements or for stock ; 2,564 received advances on Dominion lands, soldier grants.

The board advanced for the purpose of the purchase of land up to 90 per cent. of the purchase price after the valuation was approved of by the board's officers, but provided that no single advance exceeded $4,500 for that purpose. Having regard to stock and equipment, the board advanced $7,500. The total advance *per capita* to all who had received the benefit of the Act averaged $3,700.

The terms of repayment as respected land and improvement advances were repayment in 25 years with interest at 5 per cent. amortised. The terms of repayment of advances for stock and equipment were, he thought, six years with free interest for two years.

Advice of Supervisors.

The Home Branch of the Department had to do particularly with the giving of assistance to the wives of settlers. It was the duty of the field supervisors of the department, who were attached to each district office, and who were skilled agriculturists, to visit all the men, particularly those who graded low, and help them by advice and suggestion, report upon their progress and upon the condition of their stock and equipment and make any other suggestions that would enable the board to be helpful to them.

Estimate for Year.

The estimate for the year to come was fixed at $50,000,000. There would undoubtedly be losses, but a survey of the operations of the year led him to the opinion that the proportion of losses would not in the aggregate be a serious one, that it would be at all events very much smaller than the great advantages which the country would undoubtedly secure, not only by the increase in the production of those first essentials, but by the addition to the stable unwavering section of their population of so large a proportion of the returned men of Canada.

Applications from Abroad.

The Act as it stood to-day admitted to its benefits returned soldiers in England of the Army of Great Britain, as well as the Army of France, of the United States and their other Allies. They had first, however, to take care, so far as they could, of the unexpected avalanche of applications from their own men. Last year they established in England a Board of two, whose duties were to select from applicants of the British Army those who had sufficient money and sufficient stamina, so far as they could be gauged, and the right kind of experience that would make them the best prospects at least of success in Canada.

INDUSTRIAL DISPUTES INVESTIGATION AMENDMENT ACT.

This Act, which was assented to on 1st July, 1920, facilitates the establishment of Boards of Conciliation for the settlement of industrial disputes.

The Act extends the interpretation of " Employer " to any number of persons, companies or corporations acting together, or who in the opinion of the Minister have interests in common (Sec. 1).

The application to refer disputes to Boards of Conciliation and the statutory declarations accompanying them, shall be signed, if made—

(A) by an employer who is an individual, by the employer himself ;

(B) by an employer which is a partnership, firm or association, by a majority of the partners or members ;

(C) by an employer which is an incorporated company or corporation, by someone of its duly authorised managers or by one or more of the principal executive officers ;

(D) by employees who are members of a trade union, by two of its officers authorised in writing by a majority of the union members affected. If such authorisation is obtained by a vote taken in whole or in part at a meeting, such meeting shall be called on not less than three days' notice and the vote shall be by ballot ;

(E) by employees some or all of whom are not members of a trade union, by two of their number authorised in writing by a majority of such employees.

When there is more than one party to the application, it shall be signed by or on behalf of each employer or trade union or of the employees of each employer interested, or by or on behalf of a majority of such (Sec. 2).

Witnesses before the Board shall be entitled to a minimum allowance of $4 per day (Sec. 4).

It is further provided that employers and employees shall give at least thirty days' notice of an intended change affecting conditions of employment with respect to wages and hours ; and in the event of such intended change resulting in a dispute, until the dispute has been finally dealt with by a Board, and a copy of its report has been delivered through the Registrar to both the parties affected, neither of those parties shall alter.

The Minister may, on or without application, order a Board or recommend an inquiry (Sec. 5).

DEBATE IN THE SENATE.

Applications for Boards.

The Minister of Labour (Senator the Hon. G. D. Robertson) moving the Second Reading of the Bill on 6th April, said that the proposed amendments did not contemplate any change in the principles laid down in the Act, but were submitted for the purpose of ensuring more prompt and efficient and economical administration of the law. The first amendment referred to boards being established where several employees in the same industry were affected. Numerous instances had arisen of workmen in the employ of perhaps half a score or more of employers having disputes with their respective employers, and desiring that the differences be referred to a board of conciliation. It was necessary to obtain the consent of each individual employer to the establishment of the board ;

otherwise a separate board would have to be established for each employer. He believed it was desirable to amend the Act so that one board might be established to deal with a dispute in which there were several employers, members of an association, so that the employers' association might be called upon to act in the same capacity as would the individual employers. Either an employer or ten or more workmen might make an application for a board. Each party selected his own representative upon the board. The two members so selected had the opportunity of agreeing upon a third. In the event of their being unable to agree, it then became the duty of the Department of Labour to appoint the third member, who should act as chairman of the board.

As the Act now stood, it was possible for a relatively small minority of members of a labour organisation to make application for and be entitled to a board. The officer of the department felt that a substantial number, probably a majority of the members of the organisation, or, if the men were unorganised, a majority of the men affected by the dispute, ought to be obtained before the board was established.

Section 34 referred to the fees of witnesses who might be called by a board to give evidence before it. At present the fees were governed by the fees paid in the province where the inquiry was held. It was proposed to make a flat rate of $2 a day (subsequently amended to $4 a day).

Strikes and Lock-outs.

The Act of 1907 provided that after a board had been established there should be no lock-out upon the part of the employers nor any strike on the part of the employees, pending the rendering of the report by the board. It was proposed to amend the Act so as to make it clear that it would be unlawful for an employer to engage in a lock-out or for an employee to participate in a strike until the board's report had been received by the department and had been communicated to both the parties represented before the board.

Section 63a of the Act at the present time permitted the establishment of a board by the department if a strike had actually occurred. The experience of the departmental officials was that some strikes might have been avoided had it been within the power of the Minister to establish a Board of Conciliation before the strike actually occurred. It was therefore proposed to amend the section by inserting after the word " occurred," the words " or seems to the Minister to be imminent," so that an inquiry might be conducted without waiting for an actual strike or lock-out to occur.

In 1919, out of ninety-five cases in which boards were established, about seventy-one strikes were averted.

Senator the Hon. L. O. David (*Que.*) asked whether the Government had considered the question of whether they could bind the parties to abide by the decisions of the board, as had been done in certain countries for some time.

The Minister of Labour said that outside the State of Kansas he did not know of any country where the findings of the Boards of Arbitration were compulsory. The system of arbitration and adjustment of disputes that had been adopted by their Canadian railroads was an ideal one. In 1918, by mutual consent, the railway employees and the railroads agreed that there should be no strikes or lock-outs during the continuation of the war. They set up a tribunal on which each side had equal representation, and they agreed that any dispute which might arise between any individual organisation and a railroad which could not be adjusted by direct negotiation should be referred to this tribunal, consisting of twelve men, and that its decisions should be accepted as final by both parties. Notwithstanding that the war had been over for about a year and a half the arrangement still continued with marked success.

The Department of Justice, he thought, was inclined to the view that the Act could not be applied to an individual industrial plant in a given city or province except with the consent of both parties to the dispute ; neither could it be forcibly applied to establish a board as between a municipality and its employees. The Trades and Labour Congress at its Convention last year, at which 900 members were present, went on record as being in favour of extending the scope of the Act. Some employees or associations of employers in communications to the department had gone on record as being in favour of widening its scope to cover all industries. He was inclined to the opinion, based upon the views of the Department of Justice, that it was not practicable except with the consent of the provinces concerned.

Senator the Hon. Frederic Nicholls (*Ont.*) had failed to learn of one single case in which the two parties had been able to agree upon a chairman. As a rule the labour representative would not agree to any chairman that might be suggested by the employer, and thus the onus of the appointment of the chairman was thrown upon the Labour Department, which usually appointed a county judge. The board of conciliation rarely awarded the entire increase demanded. In the great majority of cases it was a question of splitting the difference, which might mean a very heavy burden on the employer. He would like to suggest that instead of the Department of Labour selecting for appointment one out of a number of county court judges, there should be for one province a permanent judge who would be independent and would learn in the course of years to weigh evidence pro and con much better than it might be done by a judge appointed only occasionally.

The Minister of Labour pointed out that legislation somewhat similar to their Industrial Disputes Investigation Act was in effect in Australia for many years. Australia had not only a permanent chairman, but a permanent board, and the law finally became a dead letter because the board could not keep pace with the work that came to it to be done.

Senator the Hon. John Milne (*Ont.*) stated that the international unions of America had control in Canada as well as in the United States. He would like to ask just how the question of international unions was going to be reconciled with the proposition that the Minister of Labour now made regarding Canada. They could deal with Canada, but they must remember that they had to deal with the United States as well.

The Minister of Labour replied that every international union had its separate Canadian unit, and that the members of the international unions in Canada exercised local autonomy and independence in the handling of their own business in this country, to just as great an extent as the Parliament of Canada handled its business without interference by the British Government. The fact that the Canadian railways adopted what was known as the McAdoo Award, in the United States, was the very key which locked the door upon strikes on railroads in Canada during the war. The minority in each of the railway organisations could not decline to accept what the majority of the members agreed to as applicable to their conditions in the United States.

Speaking in Committee on 7th April,

Senator the Hon. Frederic Nicholls said that he thought it would make for industrial peace and lessen unrest if there was a general conference of the majority of the employers engaged in an industry with representatives of a majority of the unions that might be identified with that industry. It was unfair that the minority of a union should ferment trouble and create unrest to the disadvantage of a majority of the same union that might not be in sympathy or accord with their action. It was equally important that the majority of employers should also be taken into consideration, and any decision arrived at should be uniform.

The Minister of Labour said that the Act applied only to public utilities such as mines and transportation companies. It was not within the jurisdiction of the Federal Department of Labour to interfere in private industry.

After further discussion the Bill was read a third time and passed on 13th April.

DEBATE IN HOUSE OF COMMONS.

The **Minister of the Interior** (Hon. Arthur Meighen), explaining to the House in Committee on 3rd May the extended interpretation of " employer," said the amendment was designed to permit the establishment of a single board to deal with a dispute in which a number of individual employers were concerned having interests in common. Cases occurred in which demands presented on behalf of labour, and resultant disputes, affected several different companies engaged in the same industry. In such cases, as the law now stood, it had not been found possible to establish a joint board without first obtaining the consent of the several employers concerned. It had sometimes happened that such consent had been withheld, and the inability of the Department of Labour to establish a joint board had been followed by a strike. The amendment provided that in such cases the Minister might require the employers, all of whom were affected, to select an arbitrator.

With regard to Section 2 the Minister explained that the majority of the members of a trade union must authorise (the application to refer a dispute to a board)—not a majority of those who happened to be present at a meeting but a majority of all the members must act.

The **Hon. W. L. Mackenzie King** (Liberal, Leader of the Opposition) said that most industrial disputes had grown out of a group of men, not the whole body, having a grievance often affecting only a handful of men, which, if they did not have an opportunity of having investigated, would lead to a very serious situation. As he saw the amendment of the Minister, he was going to place it in the hands of one or two labour leaders, or one or two employers to decide as to whether or not there was going to be an investigation of the dispute. It practically put the control of the situation in the hands of the leaders of either party, and he did not think it was going to work advantageously.

The **Minister of the Interior** said that the difference was just this. Under the old law there might be a very small meeting, and consequently a very small minority might precipitate the whole proceedings ; but in the end the others were all affected by it. What the law now said was : Where all are affected by this, a majority must requisition for a board in the first place.

Mr. Mackenzie King thought, with reference to the establishment of a board by the Minister of Labour without application, that where no action was taken the Government of the day would be blamed for not having intervened ; and, on the

other hand, if the Government did take action, if it went into
the dispute on its own initiative, and trouble arose, the Government would be told it had no business to interfere.

The Minister of the Interior said that it seemed to him
that if the Minister had power to appoint a board after it was
too late to avoid all the consequences of a strike, he ought to
have power to appoint a board before the crisis was reached.

Speaking on 10th May,

The Hon. Rodolphe Lemieux (Liberal, *Maisonneuve, Que.)*
said that this legislation—the credit for the drafting of which
must be given to the Leader of the Opposition—enjoyed to-day
a world reputation. It had been adopted by several States
of the Union, by some of the British Dominions, and now
there was before the French Parliament legislation based on
their Industrial Disputes Act. He would ask his hon. friend
(Mr. Meighen) not to " denature " the spirit of this legislation,
not to press the amendment whereby some employees might
at any given moment by a mere whim ask for a board when
no board was really needed.

After further discussion the Bill was read a third time
and passed by the House of Commons on 11th May.

CANADIAN WHEAT BOARD ACT.

This Act, which was assented to on 1st July, provides for
the renewal of the Canadian Wheat Board and the control of
the wheat market, should such a course prove desirable.

The Act provides that the Governor in Council may appoint a
Canadian Wheat Board consisting of not more than twelve members,
one of whom shall be named as Chairman and be the chief executive
officer. The Board shall make investigations to ascertain what supplies
of wheat are available from time to time, their location and ownership,
transportation and elevator facilities, and all conditions connected with
their marketing. The Board shall have power, *inter alia*, to take delivery
of wheat in Canada at any point ; to pay in advance to producers or
other persons delivering wheat to the Board the price per bushel set out
in the schedule to be prepared by the Board ; to sell wheat so delivered
to millers in Canada at such prices as the Board sees fit, the price being
governed by the prices obtainable in the world's markets ; to sell wheat
so delivered in excess of domestic requirements to purchasers overseas ;
to fix maximum prices or margins of profit at which flour and other
products made from wheat delivered to millers may be sold, and to
fix standards of quality ; to purchase flour from millers at prices fixed
by the Board and to sell the same in Canada or other countries ; to control
the export and sale of flour out of Canada ; to buy and sell wheat and
wheat products at any point in Canada ; to control the buying and

selling of wheat in Canada ; and to order any person holding wheat to sell the same to any purchaser named by the Board on such terms as the Board may direct.

As soon as the Board has received full payment for all wheat delivered to it, and its operational expenses have been deducted, the balance shall be distributed *pro rata* among all producers and others holding participation certificates.

The Board may appoint an executive committee of three. No facilities shall be given at any grain exchange for trading in wheat futures.

The Act shall come into force upon proclamation by the Governor in Council, and shall continue in force until 15th August, 1921.

DEBATE IN HOUSE OF COMMONS.

In moving that the House should go into Committee on 24th June to consider a proposed resolution respecting the Canadian Wheat Board, **The Minister of Trade and Commerce (the Right Hon. Sir George Foster)** said that the measure was simply an enabling one, and he hoped that it would not be necessary to put it into force. The reason for the legislation arose out of the condition of the wheat markets not only in Canada but in Europe and in the United States. Last year the Canadian Wheat Board was formed because conditions then existing made it necessary that there should be an agency for the marketing of wheat and its products in Canada—an agency which should be able to take up with other agencies in Europe and in the United States the work of purchasing and selling. Last year concentrated Government buying was the rule, and as there was but one purchaser it became necessary that there should be one seller to meet that purchaser and transact the business with a fair chance of its successful despatch. France, Great Britain and Italy particularly were closely united in their purchases, so that there was not even competition between the three great Government buyers.

Last year they were faced with this, that there was in the European market no buyer who was prepared to say what he would buy, when he would buy, or what price he would give. No grain could be sold, and consequently it had to remain in the hands of the farmer or stored. Therefore the Wheat Board was appointed to become the purchaser and seller of wheat and wheat products. The Board received the grain from the farmers whenever it was deliverable, and an advance payment of what might be the ultimate price was arranged to be paid by the banks on the security of the Government, so that there was no stoppage of the flow of the wheat from the farmers' possession to the head of the lakes or the

H

seaboard. The Wheat Board thus stood to purchase and market the wheat for the whole crop season, and after expenses of administration were borne, what remained of the ultimate price received was distributed *pro rata* amongst the original producers of the grain. A very large proportion of the wheat product of last season had already been disposed of.

So far as they could tell, France and Britain and Italy had not de-controlled the wheat and flour trade. As to neutral countries, practically all of them, he believed, had Government control. Europe was the great recipient for the surplus wheat and wheat products of Canada. Australia this year would have no surplus to market. As far as European countries were concerned the general idea might be said to be that there would be a deficit of crops for the sustenance of the peoples of Europe, owing to lack of production, or to the almost absolute confusion of transport which existed. Another thing that confronted European countries was lack of credit. If they could get credits from the United States, one of the conditions would certainly be that the country to whom she extended credit should buy wheat from the United States and not from any other country. It was possible that during the coming crop season they might be faced by a condition in Europe just as urgent as was the condition last year, and if their policy was right based on such conditions last year, then to meet the same conditions this year, some such policy would be necessary to win out.

In the United States the trade had been de-controlled, but there was a power which if it became necessary could bring back control at any time.

The Hon. W. L. Mackenzie-King (Liberal, Leader of the Opposition) thought that the uncertainty as to whether or not the Government intended to exercise any power under this enabling legislation was one which might seriously affect the relations between the grain merchants and the farmers.

Mr. H. H. Stevens (Unionist, *Vancouver Centre, B.C.*) stated that the principle of the Bill was the principle of paternalism. It approached the principle of the socialisation of industrial control.

During the war which made necessary the appointment of the Grain Supervisor, and later of the Wheat Board, Great Britain bought virtually for the whole of Europe. To-day all the neutral countries and all the Allied countries were buying for themselves. In all those countries, including Great Britain, de-control had been brought to almost vanishing point. Canada was practically the only country to-day—the Russian wheat market being virtually closed—which could supply the European market with the hard wheat which they must have to mix with their soft wheat, and there was very little evidence that there would be any difficulty in the marketing of Canadian wheat through ordinary channels. The business of an industry involving $500,000,000 would be handled by three men, with the unlimited credit of Canada behind them. He did not believe in the fixation of prices. It was the very point which would shortly be coming up before the Privy Council in regard to the Board of Commerce, whether or not that board had a right to step in and fix a price.

The Minister of the Interior (Hon. Arthur Meighen) stated that if it were the case that they had flour made from Canadian wheat selling more cheaply in England than in Canada, it was because in free trade England the Government left trade to itself to the extent of fixing the price of flour and of making up the loss to the miller and to the baker. It fixed the price of both bread and flour. As regarded their wheat they consumed at home about one-quarter or about one-fifth; they sold in the European market about three-quarters or four-fifths. The very thing that they were assailed for doing in relation to wheat selling here, England was doing in relation to wheat-buying over there.

The Hon. T. A. Crerar (Independent,* Marquette, Man.) thought that it was necessary, under the conditions that existed a year ago, to create the Wheat Board, and he was bound to say that under the disorganised conditions of world trade in grain resulting of necessity from the war, the operation of the board had entirely justified its existence. He thought the Minister of the Interior furnished the only argument that constituted a real reason why the board should be continued for another year, and that was the possibility of unified buying again in Europe. Everyone who knew anything of the European situation must realise that conditions there were very unstable, and in these circumstances he thought, perhaps, there was justification for the Government assuming the power which they were asking for under this legislation. It was another thing to have that control woven into the fabric of their laws as a permanent policy of the country.

The Bill was read a second time, considered in Committee and passed on 28th June.

---

* Though hitherto described as " Independent " in this JOURNAL it should be noted that Mr. Crerar is the leader of the Farmers' Party in the House of Commons.

INDIAN AMENDMENT ACT.

(Education and Enfranchisement.)

This Act, which was assented to on 1st July, 1920, amends the Indian Act so as to provide for the enfranchisement of Indians and the attendance of Indian children at schools.

Schools.

The Act empowers the Governor in Council to establish (A) day schools in any Indian reserve for the children of such Reserve ; (B) industrial or boarding schools for the Indian children of any reserve, district, or territory designated by the Superintendent General ; or to declare any school to be an industrial or boarding school. The Superintendent General may provide for the transport to and from boarding or industrial schools and prescribe standards in all schools. The chief and council of any band that has children in a school is granted the right of inspection.

Every Indian child between the ages of seven and fifteen years who is physically able shall attend such day, industrial or boarding school as may be designated by the Superintendent General for the full periods during which such school is open each year. Provided, however, that no Protestant child shall be assigned to a Roman Catholic school and no Roman Catholic to a Protestant school. The Act provides for the appointment of an officer to enforce the attendance of Indian children at school and to investigate cases of truancy, and imposes penalties on guardians and parents failing to cause a child to attend school after notice.

The Act further provides that any Indian woman who marries any person other than an Indian, or a non-treaty Indian, shall cease to be an Indian in every respect within the meaning of the Act, except that she shall be entitled to share equally with the members of the band to which she formerly belonged, in the distribution of their annuities.

Enfranchisement.

The Superintendent General may appoint a Board to consist of two officers of the Department of Indian Affairs and a member of the Band (to be nominated by the Council of the Band) to which the Indians under investigation belong, to enquire and report as to the fitness of any Indian to be enfranchised. The attitude of any Indian towards his enfranchisement shall be a factor in determining the question of fitness. On approval of the report of the Superintendent the Governor in Council may order enfranchisement at the expiration of two years or earlier, if requested by the Indian, after which any law making distinction between the legal rights of Indians and those of His Majesty's other subjects shall cease to apply. Upon enfranchisement letters patent for his land shall be issued to the Indian who shall receive his share of the funds of the band. When a majority of the members of a band is enfranchised, the public land or other public property of the band shall be equitably allotted to its members and the residue may be sold, the proceeds being placed to the credit of the funds of the band.

DEBATE IN HOUSE OF COMMONS.

Speaking upon the Bill in Committee of the House on 23rd June,

Mr. F. B. Stacey (**Unionist,** *Fraser Valley, B.C.*) said the Bill brought to the front certain phases of the Indian question which were very vital at the present time to British Columbia. It contained two main features : the first clause dealing with compulsory education and the second clause providing for the enfranchisement of certain Indians who were now wards of the Government. He had heard it stated that Canada had no clearly defined Indian policy ; that while the Government in co-operation with the churches of the country had set out to improve the moral and social status of the Indian youth, it had not made any adequate provision for their full and subsequent citizenship. The Bill was an honest and carefully thought-out measure to promote with reasonable celerity the social and civic welfare of the descendants of the original inhabitants of the country. There were about 100,000 Indians in Canada ; approximately a quarter of these were in British Columbia. These Indians represented all grades and conditions of civilisation and progress from the aboriginal state to comparative social and financial comfort. It was estimated that probably less than half of these Indians had ever had an opportunity to secure even a rudimentary education, and of those who had had the opportunity a very considerable number had refused to attend the schools provided. While there were many natives who were financially easy, and many more who were intellectually qualified to a very high degree, not a single Indian from British Columbia had up to the present time made application for enfranchisement.

Relation of Indians to Country.

It must be said that a number of Indians from British Columbia appeared before the Committee to oppose the passage of the Bill. Their attitude was based upon the two-fold objection, first, that they formed a kind of protectorate under the British Crown and that, therefore, Parliament had no authority to pass the Bill ; second, that they claimed tribal ownership under aboriginal title and Royal Proclamation of 1763 and were entitled to an interest in all the lands of the Provinces.

First, they must bear in mind that when the discoverers claimed the territory and formally took possession, the natives were recognised not as the owners of the land but as inhabitants

of the country ; they had absolutely no conception of ownership. If they considered the relation of the Indian tribes
to the Dominion there was no fixed date which might be
regarded as the time at which the whole question was definitely
decided. Their present condition was the result of long and
gradual growth. The present relation of the Indian tribes
to this country had been the result of a century or more
of mutual understandings and arrangements through, first
the Imperial Government, then the Colonial Government,
and finally the Dominion or Provincial Government. They
each in turn dealt generously with the Indians, who were
always regarded as the country's wards.

After giving the history of the relations of the Indian
tribes to the Government, Mr. Stacey said that during the last
20 years $4,632,288.14 had been expended for Indian purposes
in British Columbia, so that as a matter of fact a policy much
more generous than that adopted by the Crown Colony had
been in operation during the days of Confederation.

Objects of Bill.

Speaking on the provisions of the Bill, Mr. Stacey said
that children were kept at home for the slightest reason or
excuse ; irregularity in attendance prevailed everywhere,
but disinterested and patriotic educators of the Indian
population of the West were practically a unit in strongly
urging the Government to adopt a compulsory educational
system, in so far as it affected the attendance of the children
of the native population.

It was not believed that any wholesale process of
enfranchisement would follow the passage of the Bill, but
it was very strongly believed that it was necessary for the
Department to exercise the power of initiative so that when
these people were in a position to assume their proper place
in the life of the country, the machinery of the Government
should enable them to do so.

Mr. Ernest Lapointe (Liberal, *Quebec East*), speaking on
the motion for the Third Reading of the Bill on 25th June,
was opposed to changing entirely and in a very arbitrary way
the whole system which had been in force in the past. As
to the enfranchisement of Indians, the system should be
improved through educational processes. The Indians should
be led to ask for their own enfranchisement, but should
not be coerced, as they would be if this Bill was passed.
He was disposed to favour the new clauses concerning
education.

Mr. W. A. Boys (Unionist, *Simcoe, S. Riding, Ont.*) said
that if an Indian should not be found fit, he was not

immediately enfranchised and he was not enfranchised against his will. He asked the House to consider the case of an Indian who was a good business man ; he could not engage in barter, sale, or exchange without writing to Ottawa and getting the assent of the Superintendent General. Was there anything to be gained by surrounding such an Indian with protection of that kind ? This was a step leading to the ultimate goal which every one of the Indians sought, namely, as fast as possible to take his place in this country with the white man and to get away from the guardian and ward feature which they all admitted was obnoxious.

After further consideration the Bill was read a third time and passed by the House of Commons on 25th June,

DEBATE IN THE SENATE.

In moving the Second Reading of the Bill in the Senate on 28th June,

The Leader of the Senate and Minister of Civil Re-establishment (Senator the Hon. Sir James Lougheed) said that hon. gentlemen would probably appreciate the necessity of the effect given to this compulsory feature. The Indian had not those characteristics which made it proper to leave to his discretion whether he should assume responsibility or not. Up to the present time, and for some time to come, he was, and would be, the ward of the nation, but that condition must terminate some time ; and when it was found that the Indian possessed the personal qualities and the qualities of experience and education necessary to the assumption of his duties as a citizen, the Government might take the steps necessary to declare him a citizen and thus separate him from the Indian privileges which to-day he was enjoying.

Senator the Hon. H. Bostock (Leader of the Opposition) said he thought that the compulsory enfranchisement of the Indians meant that eventually the reserves would be broken up and that the Government would be relieved of the necessity of looking after the reserves and the affairs of the Indians, as they did at the present time. Indians lived together in a community under the guidance and rule of chiefs, and it was their custom to meet together in council and to arrange their own affairs. They had been trained in that way and if they were compulsorily enfranchised their whole system was broken up. The fact that the Indian could not get credit was not altogether an argument in favour of the Bill. Legislation of this kind would be unacceptable to the Indians and would have the effect of stirring up serious dissatisfaction and unrest among them.

After further discussion and consideration in Committee, the Bill was reported by the Senate without amendment.

DOMINION ELECTIONS ACT.

A summary of the Dominion Elections Bill, dealing with the election of members of the House of Commons and the electoral franchise, as introduced in the House of Commons on 11th March, 1920, was given in the JOURNAL OF THE PARLIAMENTS OF THE EMPIRE, Vol. 1, No. 2, page 337.* The following are among the principal amendments to the Bill, which received the Royal assent on 1st July, 1920 :—

To Section 29 (1) (Qualification of Electors) is added Clause (D) providing that any Indian who has served in the Naval, Military or Air Forces of Canada in the late war shall be qualified to vote, unless such Indian is otherwise disqualified under this section.

Section 40 (1) (Nomination of Candidates) is amended by providing that the Governor in Council shall fix the day for the nomination of candidates *and* the day for polling, and the days so fixed shall be named in the writ of election. At any general election the same days shall be fixed for the nomination of candidates and for polling respectively, in all electoral districts.

For the purpose of a Dominion election the voters' lists shall (Sec. 32) be those prepared for the polling divisions under the laws of the province within *two* years immediately preceding the writ of election.

Under Section 19 (1) the Chief Electoral Officer is appointed by name, and shall hold office on the same tenure as a puisne Judge of the Supreme Court of Canada.

Rule 1 of Schedule A (Sec. 32) is amended by authorising the returning officer to appoint an additional registrar to each city, town or incorporated village which has a population of over four thousand for each additional four thousand persons. Registrars shall within *three* days after the closing of registration prepare a complete and final list for each polling division.

The Act also provides (Sec. 101) that whenever under the Canada Temperance Act a vote is to be taken, the procedure to be followed shall, in lieu of the procedure therein directed, be the procedure laid down in this Act with such modifications as the Chief Electoral Officer may direct as being necessary by reason of the difference in the nature of the question to be submitted, and with such omissions as he may specify on the ground that compliance with the procedure laid down is not required.

---

* Under Conduct of Elections on page 338 of Vol. I, Section 78 should read " All sums, *except* when less than $10 must be vouched for   . . ."

AUSTRALIA.

Commonwealth Parliament.

The following summary is in continuation of the proceedings of the First Session of the Eighth Parliament, commenced in Vol. I., No. 3 of the JOURNAL. *Parliament adjourned on 26th November, 1920.*

NEW GUINEA ACT.

(Government of Territory: League of Nations: " White Australia," &c.)

The object of this Act, which received assent on 30th September, 1920, is to make provision for the acceptance from the League of Nations of a mandate for the administration of the former colony of German New Guinea, and to provide for the civil government thereof.

A summary of the Bill appeared in the last number of the JOURNAL (No. 4), page 692.

An amendment in the Bill relating to forced labour will be found reported under the speech of Mr. Tudor in the following discussion (see page 117).

DEBATE IN HOUSE OF REPRESENTATIVES.

In moving the Second Reading on 14th September, 1920, **The Prime Minister (the Right Hon. W. M. Hughes)** said that it was a measure to make provision for the acceptance of the mandate for and to establish civil administration in those islands which were once comprised under the generic term of New Guinea. The territories and islands comprised in the Bill were : Kaiser Wilhelm's Land, on the mainland of the Island of New Guinea ; the Bismarck Archipelago, containing the large islands of New Britain and New Ireland, the Admiralty Islands, and the German Solomons. The Governor of German New Guinea surrendered them all to the Australian Naval and Military Forces on 17th September, 1914 ; and they had all been occupied, and were still occupied, by the Commonwealth of Australia. Prior to the German Treaty coming into operation, the occupation had been by military force against a belligerent country. But by the Treaty Germany renounced her right, title and interest in those islands, in favour of the principal Allied

and Associated Powers, which had since agreed and had
announced, in Paris, on 7th May, 1919, that a mandate in
the case of these islands should be held by Australia.

The Bill did three things—(1) provides for the acceptance
of the mandate when issued ; (2) provides for a skeleton or
provisional government ; and (3) accepts the obligations
laid down in the Covenant of the League of Nations as regards
a mandate of the Pacific Island class.

The delay in issuing the mandate had been a matter of
some embarrassment ; and it was thought desirable to establish a civil government at once, on a provisional basis, in lieu
of the military government which then exercised authority,
and which was no longer appropriate, because Australia was
no longer holding the islands by force of arms against an
enemy.

New Zealand had passed an Act for the government of
her Samoan Possessions. South Africa had acted in like
manner. New Zealand had obtained from the Imperial
Government an order, under the Foreign Jurisdiction Acts,
upon which to base her legislative power. South Africa had
legislated under her own Constitution. The present Bill was
an exercise of the powers of the Commonwealth under its
Constitution. Apart from the Treaty and the agreement to
confer a mandate, there was also Section 122 of the Constitution, which empowered the Commonwealth to make laws for
the government of any territory placed by the King under
the authority of, and accepted by, the Commonwealth.

Obligations under Mandate.

Provision was made in the Bill for the exercise of
executive and legislative power in the Territory, and the Bill
would enable all the necessary measures to be taken, and all
the necessary governmental machinery to be set up. It
must not be forgotten that, while they were legislating in
regard to those islands, they had not sovereign power over
them, as they had over Papua. Theirs was a position of
trust, and they were responsible to the League of Nations,
or the Allied and Associated Powers, who were the signatories
of the treaties, and who, either in their capacity as the Council
of the League of Nations, or as the principal chief Allied
and Associated Powers, would look to Australia to carry
out her trust faithfully, and to whom the Commonwealth
must make report from time to time as to the manner in which
it was carrying out its obligations. These obligations were
accepted in the Bill ; and the League could rely on their
being carried out, in accordance with the traditions of British
Government of native races.

The Covenant of the League of Nations provided for three classes of mandates, A, B, and C, and it would be noted that the mandate, as far as Australia was concerned, was in Class C. This class was entirely distinct. If they were to take as an analogy the tenures of land they might say that it was a leasehold tenure, which, if it did not give the right of conversion into freehold, for all practical purposes gave such rights as were given only to freeholders. The terms of reference to the C class of mandates in the Covenant, paragraph 6 of Article 22, were worthy of being quoted. They were as follow : —

There are territories, such as South-West Africa and certain of the South Pacific Islands, which owing to the sparseness of their population, or their small size, or their remoteness from the centres of civilisation, or their geographical contiguity to the territory of the Mandatary, and other circumstances, can be best administered under the laws of the Mandatary as integral portions of its territory, subject to the safeguards above-mentioned in the interests of the indigenous population.

These safeguards were set out in the Bill as follow : —

(1) The slave trade is prohibited in the Territory.

(2) No forced labour shall be permitted in the Territory, except for essential public works and services, and then only for adequate remuneration.

(3) The traffic in arms and ammunition shall be controlled in the Territory in accordance with the principles contained in the Convention signed at Brussels on 2nd July, 1890, and known as the General Act of the Brussels Conference, or any Convention amending the same.

(4) The supply of intoxicating spirits and beverages to the natives of the Territory is prohibited.

(5) The military training of the natives of the Territory, otherwise than for purpose of internal police and the local defence of the Territory, is prohibited.

(6) No military or naval base shall be established or fortifications erected in the Territory.

(7) Freedom of conscience, and, subject to the provisions of any Ordinance for the maintenance of public order and morals, the free exercise of all forms of worship, shall be allowed in the Territory.

Subject to those conditions Australia had a mandate over these islands which enabled them to make the same laws in relation thereto as they could make for the Commonwealth itself.

Mandatory.

Under Class B mandates the mandatory Power was compelled to maintain the principle of the open door, which applied to both men and goods, that was to say, it could not exclude the nationals of any of the signatories to the Covenant, nor could it impose any bar against the importation of goods. On the other hand, under Class C mandates, such as theirs was, they might impose whatever restrictions they pleased upon both men and goods. He need hardly point out how vitally the difference between Class B and Class C mandates affected Australia; and, seeing that the islands were contiguous to the mainland of Australia, and that German New Guinea marched with the dividing line of Papua for 600 or 700 miles, it must be apparent that it was vitally important that whatever conditions applied, for example, to German New Guinea, must necessarily affect Papua.

As to immigration, trade and commerce, and shipping, the Parliament of the Commonwealth would have the same unfettered discretion as it had on the mainland of Australia.

Shipping and Trade.

In regard to shipping alone, and the trade it carried, this meant that Australia would be able to secure for herself, not only the trade in regard to commodities taken to and brought from these islands, but also the control of the shipping that conveyed them. It would be realised what a tremendous handicap it would have been for Australia had they lost control of the trade and shipping of these islands.

In 1918 the exports of German New Guinea amounted to £514,000, and imports, £325,000.

Potentialities of Territory.

He did not accept the statement of the recent Royal Commission that " the extent of land available for settlement was comparatively limited " as the last word to be said on the matter. He ventured to say with all respect to the Commissioners that they had not gone very far, and consequently could not have seen very much. He considered New Guinea was, potentially, a very rich country. It had nearly a million native inhabitants. The Government were then making arrangements with a small party of scientists to go to German New Guinea, and take stock of what the country possessed. Not one acre of the land there had passed from the possession of the Crown. Of course, a large area had previously been sold to German settlers, but that land had been taken over under the provisions of the peace treaty, and was being vested in a public trustee under the Act. They hoped to provide opportunities for their enterprising young men who had come back from the War. They were very sure, for example, and did not require scientists to tell them, that New Guinea would grow copra. They knew that the bulk of the export from the country was copra. In all human probability there was oil there. It would grow sago, and such things as coffee and rice, and it would grow rubber. It was probable that its metalliferous wealth was considerable. New Guinea was quite a different country from Papua, and was, he believed, an incomparably better one. The possibilities of trade, and what that trade would mean to Australia in wealth and opportunity, could hardly be exaggerated.

The Hon. F. G. Tudor (Leader of the Opposition) said that there was nothing in the Bill to prevent the White Australia policy being absolutely abrogated in the mandated Territories. They ought to provide that the Commonwealth Acts should apply to the Territories unless specifically exempted by the Commonwealth Parliament, instead of as provided in the Bill, viz., that Commonwealth Acts should not apply to the Territories unless expressed to apply thereto or unless applied by ordinance.

Mr. Tudor quoted the report of the recent Royal Commission in connection with the mandated territories to show that the estimated revenue of £168,500 would practically balance the estimated present cost of administration.

An amendment moved by Mr. Tudor was adopted by which the reservation is deleted from the provision " No forced labour shall be permitted in the Territory except for essential public works and services, and then only for adequate remuneration," thus leaving the prohibition of forced labour absolute.

Dr. Earle Page (Farmers' Union, *Cowper, N.S.W.*) could see no objection to the form of government and procedure provided for in the Bill. There was no alternative but government from outside the Territory, and the appointment of an Administrator whose Ordinances should be subject to disallowance by the Commonwealth Parliament was a system which offered a complete safeguard to the natives.

Mr. Frank Brennan (Labour, *Batman, Vic.*) said he was against the vaunting ambition of those who were anxious to add to the already huge unused mainland of Australia other great undeveloped territories. In his view it could only be harmful and dangerous. So far from these territories forming a buffer which would add to the strength of the defences of Australia, the truth was that they were, and must be, a source of weakness.

The Treasurer (the Right Hon. Sir Joseph Cook), in reply to a reference to the question of international control of the Territories, said that such control would have meant an open floor for men and goods. Australia would not be safe if there were unrestricted opportunities to crowd the coloured races of the world into her backyard. The White Australia policy would have been menaced by the occupation of these surrounding islands by people who had no sympathy with Australian ideals and objectives.

The Bill was read a third time on 16th September.

DEBATE IN THE SENATE.

In moving the Second Reading on 17th September, 1920,
The Minister for Repatriation (Senator the Hon. E. D. Millen)
said that in accepting the mandate in the terms in which it
had been issued, the fact was brought home to them that, in
assuming the new status achieved by Australia as the result
of her warlike efforts, they were, at the same time, committing themselves to take up new burdens. These might
be found a little inconvenient in the early years of the
Australian control of the Territories, but they were inseparable
from the position. When Australia first commenced operations in the early days of the war, it was made quite clear in
that chamber that Australia was seeking, not additional acres,
but additional safety. To insure their objective they required
some guarantee against the Territories being occupied for
any purpose which at any time might become injurious to
Australian interests, and that was secured by the acceptance
of the mandate. There would be undoubted burdens to be
borne in discharging the responsibility of looking after and
controlling the islands, but with those burdens there would
also go opportunities. What they were it was perhaps
impossible, at that juncture, to speak of with any confidence,
so little was known of the Territories and their economic
possibilities. The area of the mandated Territories was
159,800 square miles, populated, it was estimated, by 947,000
natives and some 2,000 Europeans.

German Property.

In the first place, the whole of the lands in the Territories
were Crown Lands. Not a single acre had been alienated.
It was quite true that the German Government sold certain
lands to German planters ; but as the result of the war and
the subsequent Treaty of Peace, those lands were taken over
by the Commonwealth, and were given into the possession
of a trustee, the dispossessed enemy nationals having to look
to their own Government for compensation. The money
which might be received by the Australian Government under
that arrangement would be available to pay compensation to
Australians similarly dispossessed of property in Germany.
It was a clearing-house scheme, but for the purposes of the
Bill it deprived the Germans of any claim to freehold in the
mandated Territories, unless the Australian Parliament saw
fit to give it to them later on.

Provisional Nature of Measure.

The purpose of the Bill was to create a provisional government in the islands. The reason was that they were then all under military occupation, and it was thought highly desirable to terminate military and substitute civil administration at the earliest possible moment. It was not pretended that the Bill embodied a final and complete scheme of Government, but a start had to be made. It was then proposed to authorise this skeleton administration, and thenceforward to obtain Parliamentary sanction for such filling in of the obvious gaps as experience might dictate. The control of Parliament over anything and everything that would be done in the civil administration was secured by the Bill itself. There was power to issue ordinances for the control of the Territories, but all these had to be submitted to Parliament, and could be disallowed just as ordinary regulations under the main Commonwealth Acts might be.

Senator the Hon. J. Earle (*Tasmania*) hoped that the Government would set about the task of devising some practical method for the development of the mandated Territories. In this connection he had previously advocated a utilisation of all the powers which the Government possessed by reason of their ownership of a line of steamers, by means of which they would be able to maintain a better shipping service to Papua and the other territories than had hitherto been provided. There were great possibilities in these possessions, and he hoped the Government would bend their best energies to providing a better service between them and the mainland.*

Plea for Administration by Colonial Office.

Senator H. E. Pratten (*N.S.W.*) said he was not altogether convinced that the administration of the islands by Australia was ultimately going to be as successful as administration would be through the Colonial Office from London. This territorial and governmental expansion of the Commonwealth to alien races and territories, moving out into the world, was bound sooner or later to create very delicate problems. He was hopeful that, in the not distant future, some attempt would be made to link up the whole of the islands under the British flag in the Pacific into one Government. Some considered opinions favoured the seat of Government of the islands of the Pacific being placed in Fiji, and that the already British Colonial Office administered Pacific Islands, such as

---

* See summary " Pacific Mail Contract," page 120.

Fiji, Tonga, and the Gilbert and Ellice groups, should branch out, and include also the New Zealand administered Samoa, and the Australian administered New Guinea and the Solomon Islands.

The Bill was passed by the Senate on 23rd September without amendment.

PACIFIC MAIL CONTRACT.

In reply to a question by the Hon. Sir Robert Best (Nat., *Kooyong, Vic.*) on 28th July, 1920,

The Prime Minister (the Right Hon. W. M. Hughes) stated that it had been decided to enter into a new mail contract with Burns, Philp and Company for twelve months from 1st August, 1920, for the carrying out of a three-weekly service to Papua, Rabaul, and the Solomon Islands, and a two-monthly service to Lord Howe Island, Norfolk Island, and the New Hebrides, for a total subsidy of £40,000 per annum.

The Company is to be allowed freedom to increase freights and fares subject to the Controller of Shipping being satisfied as to the reasonableness of any such increases, the present rates to be increased in the first instance by 20 per cent.

The contract will provide for uniform rates of freights and fares to be charged in respect of each service, and provision will also be made with the view of preventing any discrimination or preference as to cargo space or otherwise.

LEAGUE OF NATIONS.

(Representation at Geneva Assembly: "White Australia.")

In the House of Representatives on 17th September, 1920, the Prime Minister made a statement as to the representation of the Australian Commonwealth at the Assembly of the League of Nations at Geneva commencing on 15th November, in the course of which he referred to the importance of the subjects to be considered by the League, and to the principle of a " White Australia."

The Prime Minister (the Right Hon. W. M. Hughes) stated, in connection with the first session of the Assembly of the League of Nations at Geneva on 15th November, that it had been decided that Senator the Hon. E. D. Millen (Minister for Repatriation) would attend the Conference as the representative of Australia, and take with him competent official assistance in the person of Mr. G. S. Knowles of the Attorney General's Department.

The whole world, Mr. Hughes added, was now in a state of flux, and the League of Nations, by its advice and by its power, could exercise a potent influence on their destinies. The mandates had not been officially issued, and many questions relating to the Australian quota of defence, to the means by which the world's peace should be maintained, and disease, labour troubles, and other matters dealt with the world over, were in the hands of this, the only, international body that had, as it were, the sanction of law behind it. The League, of course, had yet to prove itself competent to deal with all the great questions that were entrusted to it, but its influence already was considerable. Australia was a signatory, and, perhaps, had more to lose than any other nation from the deliberations of the Conference. Many of the things for which Australian soldiers had fought had not yet, as it were, crystallised and assumed so definite a shape as to preclude the possibility of such alterations as would be fatal to Australian interests.

He did not know any man who was more competent to represent the Commonwealth at that great world gathering than his friend and colleague, Senator Millen. The Senator would go to the Conference with a clear understanding that he represented the Commonwealth Parliament and Australia on those questions. On certain of the questions to which he had alluded in a general way there was no room for difference of opinion. They could not listen to anyone who spoke about any encroachment on the principle of a White Australia. Senator Millen, who held the Australian view, recognised that fact already. There were other matters on the agenda paper which left any amount of room for difference of opinion, and as to those, of course, Senator Millen would exercise his own discretion.

DEFENCE POLICY.

(League of Nations; "White Australia"; Defence of Pacific; Disarmament; Naval Defence; Military Training; Air Force. &c.)

In September the Prime Minister made a comprehensive statement to the House of Representatives on Defence Policy, in which he dealt with the International situation, and referred to the League of Nations, the "White Australia" policy, the Defence of the Pacific, Australia's duty regarding naval defence, the next International Defence Conference, the Citizen Forces for Military Defence, and Aviation.

The speeches of general interest have been extracted from the subsequent debates dealing with various items of Defence expenditure, *e.g.*, that of the Leader of the Opposition on Disarmament, the Treasurer on Naval Defence, and the Minister for Defence in the Senate on proposed Military measures, universal military training, munitions supply, etc.

HOUSE OF REPRESENTATIVES.

The Prime Minister (the Right Hon. W. M. Hughes), on 9th September, in making a statement in the House of Representatives in connection with the Defence Policy, said it was very clear that a cursory survey of the world as it then existed, the teachings of history, and the experience of the ages, showed very clearly that only by sufficient preparations for effective national defence could the political integrity and the freedom of nations be maintained. He need not occupy the attention of the House in submitting the view that, although Australia must be defended, she need not undertake the task herself, but might rely on the protection of the British Navy, or on the good offices of the League of Nations.

The main factors, as he saw them, in the determination of the scale of defence by sea, land, and air which it was necessary for Australia to maintain in the immediate future, broadly grouped themselves under four headings—first, the International situation ; second, the League of Nations as regards the obligations it imposed on Australia, and then as regards the protection it afforded them ; third, Australia's partnership in the British Empire ; and fourth, the special conditions of Australia, including her geographical situation and the Australian policies and ideals, especially the White Australia policy.

International Situation.

The world war was over, but it could hardly be said that world peace was yet in sight. Peace Treaties had been ratified by the Allied Powers, but not yet by the associated power of the United States of America, with Germany, Austria and Bulgaria ; and the ratification of the treaties with Hungary and Turkey might shortly be expected. But the world was not at peace. He had often said that had it not been for the world's cataclysm of the great war the present state of affairs would have been considered the most menacing that had confronted them during the last fifty years. When people spoke of peace he asked them to look at Russia, seething with internal conflict, and engaged in open war with Poland. He asked them to look at the aftermath of war—those phenomena of a world's shortage of goods, economic upheavals, disorganisation of finance and trade, and revolutionary propaganda. All these promised very little in the way of assurance of permanent peace.

And then there was a Germany which, if they were to judge by deeds, and not by words, was still unrepentant, lacking the power to strike, but having the desire as keenly accentuated as ever. The whole world was disturbed by propaganda which menaced its peace, and the political integrity of nations — propaganda which, whether spoken of as Bolshevism or Sinn Feinism, or by whatever name, nevertheless did most certainly disturb and menace the peace of the world. In any case, the world as they saw it to-day was obviously not a world in which any prudent nation could afford to allow its war insurance policy to lapse, and to trust to luck for protection against invasion.

League of Nations.

The League of Nations represented a noble ideal, and its acceptance by the greater part of the civilised world was the only hope of the world—the only hope of enduring peace—and on its ultimate success depended the future of civilisation. But the League was yet in its infancy, and it was Utopian to expect from it in its present state of development that protection which would, if there were no obligations on Australia, render unnecessary any preparations for her own defence. War could not be banished from the world by the stroke of a pen.

He thought it only proper to say that the League of Nations was the most hopeful machinery yet devised by man for the settlement of International disputes by an appeal to reason rather than to force. It was machinery which, it was hoped, in days to come would enable nations to think internationally, and to submit their quarrels to its arbitrament, in exactly the same way as individual citizens submit theirs to the decision of municipal courts. But the success of the League depended on the growth of the peace spirit. They would be living in a paradise of fools if they did not recognise that the will to war existed as keenly in the mind of man as ever it did. Until for that will to war had been substituted a desire for peace they could not expect the League of Nations of itself to be sufficient. They had lately seen how powerless it was to deal with a de facto state of war.

The position was most suggestive, particularly to Australians situated as they were. There was Poland, but a stone's throw from the greatest military forces that the League had at its disposal. It was a basic principle of the League that the territorial integrity of every member of the League must be respected, and that every violation of that integrity was an act of war, and must be regarded as an act of war by every other member of the League.   Yet they had seen Poland overrun by those latest missionaries of the gospel of peace, the Bolshevists, and left to her own resources.   If Poland were free to-day, she owed her freedom to her own valour. If that applied to Poland, within a stone's throw of the great military resources of the League of Nations, how much more did it apply to Australia, in her geographical and political isolation ?

Obligations under League.

In explaining the obligations and privileges of Australia in connection with the League of Nations, Mr. Hughes said that if the Commonwealth had desired to beat its sword into a ploughshare, they could not have signed the Covenant, which imposed upon them a solemn obligation to furnish their quota of the international army.   This quota of an army which must be sufficient to maintain the peace of the world would be determined not merely on the basis of population, but by the geographical situation of the nation member, and by the intensity of the probable danger to civilisation which might enter through its doors.

"White Australia" Policy.

There were some interests, however, that could not be submitted to the arbitrament of the League.   So much was recognised by the League itself, and expressed in the Covenant. Great Britain, for example, could not submit the freedom of the seas, as interpreted by Germany, to the arbitrament of any League.   America could not submit the Monroe doctrine, nor could Australia submit the question of a White Australia. And Australia must be prepared, just as Great Britain and America, if necessary, to fight to the death in support of that principle, which they in Australia believed to be absolutely vital to their own existence.   A White Australia was the most vital part of their policy.   The same policy was calculated to be one of the most fruitful means of provoking international complications.   However, he did not believe that there were any Australians who would not readily declare that, on this principle, there could be no concession whatever.   He had had the honour to place the position of the Commonwealth before the great Peace Conference, and whether the people of Australia agreed with him or not politically, he thought the overwhelming bulk of them would endorse his attitude on that subject.   They must always be ready to defend that principle. They could not hope to maintain it merely by pious or blatant declarations of their intentions. Behind all that there must be some force—the utmost resources of the nation.

Obligations to British Empire.

But quite apart from their obligations with regard to the White Australia policy and their other ideals, there also rested upon them the important obligations as a partner in the great British Empire. Australia must provide an adequate Defence Force which could do its part in defending that Empire. Australia's membership of the League of Nations did not at all imply any weakening of her status as a member of the British Empire. Much as might 'be said against the Empire, no single factor had been more effective in preserving the peace of the world, and advancing mankind, than it had been.

They could not leave to Great Britain and the British Navy the sole task of defending an Empire upon whose stability Australia's very existence depended. Great Britain was staggering under a load of debt, the like of which the world had never seen. The load which the people of the Mother Country were bearing was incomparably greater than that of Australia, while her resources were not to be compared with those of Australia.

Geographical Position of Australia.

Australia was a continent almost as big as Europe, but was as remote as possible from European nations. To the north-west and north of Australia there were 750,000,000 people—half the population of the entire world, and about 150 times the population of Australia—living nearer to Australia than the nearest people of European race. Irkutsk, on Lake Baikal, in the middle of Siberia, was nearer to Australia than any part of British South Africa, or any land inhabited by people of European extraction, except, of course, New Zealand.

Australia was, as it were, the advance guard of the white population of the world, ringed about by half the population of the world, and set down in an ocean which was one-third of the size of the surface of the whole globe. They had to defend a coastline of 12,000 miles. In addition, they had taken over the control of huge islands in the Pacific, involving new obligations and responsibilities. Australia had a vast overseas shipping trade worth £250,000,000 per annum, to say nothing of the coastal trade.

Importance of Pacific.

Until 1906 the centre of the Empire's naval policy was in the Mediterranean. Owing to the menace of the German navy, it shifted to the North Sea. As a result of the war, the centre of gravity had again shifted. Between 1916 and 1920 the Pacific had assumed a new importance, for which the opening of the Panama Canal was in some degree responsible, but to which the development of all the Pacific countries, such as Japan, the Western coast of America, and Australia had also contributed.

A sane policy for Australia involved taking cognisance of their geographical situation, their future greatness, their opportunities, and their dangers, all of which were obvious, their dangers no less than their opportunities, their isolation and their distance from the rest of the world no less than their great resources. It was very evident that if they were to maintain Australia as their own, and to continue to live as a free people, they must be prepared to defend themselves.

Imperial Defence Conference.

They hoped that there would come from the Imperial Defence Conference, which he believed would meet next year, a real Imperial defence policy, in which Australia would be able to co-operate and do her share. Under the scheme they anticipated that there would be expected from Australia a given quota, and that there would be allotted to them and the other Dominions a given sphere of operations. He thought he would be doing a wrong to Australia if he did not say that, although they had not done their share in the naval defence of the Empire as compared with Britain, they had, when compared with other Dominions, done more than their share. Australia had done her share in times of war, and he trusted that they would be able to do their part in times of peace. As Australia's quota and sphere of operations under a scheme of Imperial defence had not yet been determined, whatever proposals the Government might then put forward could only be regarded as tentative.

Military—Citizen Forces.

They had in the Australian Imperial Force a highly trained personnel which, in the immediate years, could, if necessity arose, be organised and placed in the field for the defence of Australia ; and the Government proposed to invite the co-operation and assistance of the members of that Force to form the basis upon which the future Armies of Australia should be trained. Each year, approximately, 16,000 young men, physically fit for military service, and within the training areas, reached the age of eighteen years. It was proposed to recommence the training of this young manhood that year, but, owing to the financial position, only to a limited degree.

The experience of the Australian Imperial Force had demonstrated that to give effective recruit training a much longer period than that laid down in the Defence Act was necessary, and that once the training had been carried out there was no necessity to spread the period of training over such a number of years as was then provided in the Act. Proposals would, therefore, be brought forward by the Government to amend the Defence Act to concentrate the periods over a lesser number of years, and to give a longer period of training in the first year.* In 1913-14 there were 54,051 persons in the Citizen Forces then liable for training. In the present year there would be 108,000. The number of Permanent Forces in 1913-14 was 2,627. This year it was 2,603. The total military expenditure for the present year was estimated at £3,250,000.

Navy: First Line of Defence.

As part of a world-flung Empire, Australia must consider the Navy her first line of defence. They had an island continent, and it would be a bad day if they had to defend Australia within Australia. Britain had relied on her Navy for nearly 1,000 years, and never since the time of William the Conqueror had any navy successfully invaded Britain. Britain had always defended herself on the seas. He said emphatically that either on the sea or in the air must Australia endeavour to fight her enemies. Sea-power had long been recognised as essential to the political integrity of sea-girt nations. Quite recently there had been tremendous conflicts between the greatest military Power and the greatest naval Power the world had ever seen. In Napoleon's day they had seen the same, and on all occasions the greatest naval Power had been victorious. That was a lesson they must not forget.

It was on the sea that Australia's destiny lay, and it was on the sea that they must uphold their freedom. The air, that new element which man had now conquered, was but the sea in another form, and it was on the sea and in the air that they would have to look to their defence. By a general consensus of opinion, naval mastery still depended upon capital ships and not on submarines and light cruisers. The battleship was still a deciding factor in naval warfare.

* See Statement by the Minister for Defence, page 132.

This, of course, created for Australia a serious situation, because the maintenance of a great battle fleet was beyond the capacity of five million people. They must remedy that by setting about immigration in earnest.* In the meantime they must cut their coat according to their cloth. He hoped he had not said anything which might lead his fellow-citizens to think that he decried submarines or light craft. They were essential, but the decisive factor in a naval engagement was the battleship ; and for Australia the first line of defence was the sea. The estimate for this year for naval purposes was £3,959,991, which sum included £710,000 for transport purposes and trading vessels under the control of the Navy.

Aviation.

It might confidently be expected that aviation and those scientific methods of warfare which developed so rapidly during the war and which, particularly during the latter portion of the conflict, were resorted to so freely, might develop still further. No doubt that development would completely revolutionise warfare ; and let it be hoped that it would make war impossible. That, he thought, was the earnest prayer of every civilised man. The possibilities of aviation were infinite.

It was proposed to place such a sum on the Estimates as would encourage commercial aviation. Such inducements would be afforded as were hoped would encourage the manufacture of engines and aeroplanes in Australia. The Government would not hesitate to give a substantial bonus for that purpose. It was believed that commercial aviation would afford that reserve of personnel and machines which, in an emergency, would be necessary to their fighting forces. It was proposed to place a sum of £500,000 on the Estimates for the purposes of military aviation, and £100,000 for civil aviation.

Reduction of Armaments: "War to End War."

Mr. F. Brennan (Labour, *Batman, Vic.*), on 22nd September, during the consideration in Committee of Supply of part of the proposed expenditure for defence purposes, the total amount of which is £7,100,000, said that the very first item " Warlike Stores, including machine guns, etc.,": was, he hoped, an offence to the standard-bearers of democracy in Australia generally, and a repudiation of the accepted terms of the Treaty of Peace which ended the disastrous war which for over five years disgraced the so-called civilised world.

---

* A Statement as to the policy in regard to immigration will be found on page 136.

One of the outstanding features of that Treaty of repudiation into which they had entered was the reduction of armaments. The vote spelt at least one thing which they could understand, and that was an increase of armament—an increase of weapons of destruction, an increase of what a Minister in another place (the Senate) described as the money spent upon " our so-called policy of insurance." It was a further instalment of money wasted upon that policy of so-called insurance, upon which so many millions of pounds had been already wasted, and an addition to the debt saddled upon the people of Australia and every other country.

Mr. M. Charlton (Labour, *Hunter, N.S.W.*) said that as one who had justified the recent war he had been under the impression whilst the struggle was in progress that it was a war to end wars. But it appeared to him that Australia, and, indeed, every other country, was now engaged in preparing for future wars. It was the duty of public men in every land to bend their best energies to the task of preventing wars, and that could not be done by making preparations for war. There ought to be as little expenditure as possible in connection with defence, and he believed that the Australian compulsory military training system* should come to an end.

The Hon. F. G. Tudor (Leader of the Opposition) said that when they were discussing the Peace Treaty they had been told that there was to be a general disarmament. Where was the evidence of it in the Estimates? Instead of disarming, they were all the time building up. Under the Peace Treaty Germany was placed in a much better position than any other country, for the Allies had said, in effect, to Germany, ' We shall disarm you. We shall free you of this load of taxation in connection with armaments, but we shall pile up the expenditure upon every other nation."

The Assistant Minister for Defence (Hon. Sir Granville Ryrie) said a great many people pinned their faith to the League of Nations as the instrument to prevent future wars. He did not share that belief, but he thought that they should give the League of Nations a trial. If a tribunal such as the League would prevent war in the future he would support it heart and soul, for it was most desirable that everything possible should be done to prevent war with all its attendant horrors. He did not believe that the League of Nations would prevent future wars, and in support of his opinion he might repeat an argument he had used on other occasions. For years they had been passing legislation in the Common-wealth and State Parliaments for the settlement of industrial

---

* See Statement by the Minister for Defence in the Senate, page 131.

disputes. They had laid it down that parties to a dispute
must come before certain tribunals. At first it was fondly
believed that, as they had set up Arbitration Courts, there
would be no further strikes ; but, so far from that being the
case, since the introduction of this class of legislation strikes
in Australia had increased by 100 per cent. A similar result,
he thought, might be anticipated with regard to international
disputes, for the settlement of which the League of Nations
had been brought into being ; so, under the League scheme,
they should be prepared for the resort to force by some of the
nations included in the League.

Mr. J. E. Fenton (Labour, *Maribyrnong, Vic.*), speaking
later in the Debate on a motion to reduce the proposed vote
by £1, quoted figures from a Budget paper laid before the
British House of Commons showing reductions in expenditure
upon the Army, Navy and Air Force. He quoted Mr. Austen
Chamberlain as saying that Great Britain was leading in disarmament amongst the nations of the world. "Yet in
Australia," Mr. Fenton declared, "the Government are
increasing the Defence Estimates in comparison with the
expenditure actually incurred last year."

The Minister for the Navy (Hon. W. H. Laird Smith),
in the course of his reply, said that if they compared the
amount *per capita* charged in Great Britain for the Navy
with that charged in Australia it would be found that under
the Commonwealth Estimates for the current year Australians
would pay 12s. 5d. per head, whereas in Great Britain the
rate would be 34s. 4d. Dealing with the British Army
Estimates the Minister said those for the current financial
year provided for a net expenditure of £125,000,000.

Mr. F. Anstey (Labour, *Bourke, Vic.*) said the Leader of the
Government and those who sat behind him frequently affirmed
that the recent war was specially conducted for the purpose
of finishing war. A heavy responsibility rested upon those
who said one thing to the people during one hour and denied
it the very next. The Peace declaration stipulated for the
sweeping away of the German Navy, but as for the militarism
which might have been stripped of its arms, the Treasurer
had said that the Germans still possessed 1,250,000 rifles
and 400,000 armed men. These would be inadequate for
defence purposes, and with them it would be impossible to
make war on the Allies. They were there merely that Germany
might defend her Imperial Junker class against the efforts of
the workers of Germany to establish a pure democracy.
None of the things for which Australians had been called upon
to shed their blood—the abolition of militarism, the hanging
of the Kaiser, the destruction of Junkerism, and the fulfilmen
of democracy—had been realised. " All that has been done,

declared Mr. Anstey, " is to introduce black troops into the conquered territory for the violation of their women and the destruction of those forces for which we were prepared to stand."

The Treasurer (the Rt. Hon. Sir Joseph Cook) : " Is the Hon. Member in favour of going to war with Holland to get the Kaiser ? "

Mr. Anstey : " My answer is ' Yes.' " He continued : " If the Allies were prepared to make war on Holland in order to take her ships during the period of the war they could do it to obtain the Kaiser."

The Treasurer, in reply, pointed out that they had not fought Holland or taken her ships.

The proposed vote for the Department of Defence (Military) was ultimately agreed to by 32 votes to 9.

Necessity for Naval Defence.

Speaking later (23rd September) on a proposed vote of £313,214 for the Department of the Navy,

The Treasurer, in reply to Opposition criticism, said that it was the duty of Australia to make as full a contribution as their finances would permit towards the development of as large a naval force as, in conjunction with the British Navy, would give Australia a reasonable chance of defending her shores from attack. He admitted that they could not defend Australia by themselves. Their Navy was not big enough for that ; but they could do their duty and make an adequate contribution to the sum of those forces which, next year, were to be considered by the Imperial Conference, and which would, in the end, he believed, give Australia a naval defence in the Pacific which would save them from any predatory designs that might be entertained.

Further debate on the military, naval and air services will be dealt with in the next issue of the JOURNAL, the necessary numbers of the Parliamentary Debates not having been received in time for treatment in the present issue.

IN THE SENATE.

The Minister for Defence (Senator the Hon. G. F. Pearce), on 17th September, during the debate on the Budget, said that the Government adhered to the principle of maintaining its Forces upon a Citizen Force basis. Permanent troops would only be maintained in sufficient strength for administration and instruction, and to provide the nucleus of certain technical services. A continuance of the universal training

scheme could not at once produce the Force required. The
annual intake of recruits was only about 18,000. Time was
therefore required for development. In the meantime, therefore, and appreciating the desire of the returned soldier for
some definite place in the military system, the Government
proposed to reopen voluntary enlistment. The Australian
Imperial Force would therefore be invited to join the new
Forces in their old units, and become the foundation upon
which the scheme would be built. Facilities would be given
these men to fill positions in the commissioned and non-
commissioned ranks. As universal trainees became available
they would be built on to the base thus laid, and fill the
vacancies which would occur by the effluxion of time.

Proposed Army.

The Army to be raised would be composed of two Light
Horse Divisions ; four complete Divisions ; and three fixed
Brigades, which, in certain circumstances, would be capable
of union within a fifth Division. It would be seen that the
effect of such a reorganisation would be to restore the organisation of the Australian Imperial Force, an organisation tested
and proved by war. These Divisions would be supplemented
by the proportion of "extra divisional units" which war
had shown to be necessary, and which, at the same time,
were within the capacity of the Commonwealth.

It was therefore proposed to adopt a divisional organisation. The divisional commander would have complete
responsibility for the preparation for war of the Forces under
his command. An area would be allotted him, and also
personnel as "fixed machinery" of the area. For the purpose
of supply of material, etc., in its broadest sense, there would
be maintained in each State a small base office and a limited
staff. This would be part of the "fixed machinery."

Universal Training.

Under the new scheme the period over which training was
extended would be reduced to four years, in the first year
of which the requirement would be ten weeks, but in the
remaining three years the demand would be sixteen days
annually. The total period of liability would be eight years—
but in the last four years of that period the obligation would
be an annual registration only. The bulk of the training
would be done by youths in their eighteenth year. It was not
intended to effect the new scale that year, but to call up for
eight days' non-continuous training the whole of the existing
Citizen Forces—approximately 50,000 to 70,000. The object
was mainly administrative and disciplinary.

Cadet Training.

Prior to the inception of the Commonwealth each State possessed voluntary Cadet organisations, which were continued by the Commonwealth up to the inauguration of the Universal Training Scheme in 1911, the adoption of which was the result of the late Lord Kitchener's report. The four years' training resolved itself into two clearly defined steps. Boys of fourteen and fifteen years would be given work mainly of a physical and recreational nature. Youths of sixteen and seventeen—that was to say, during the second period of Cadet training—would be given an advanced degree of physical and recreational training, but would also be prepared for graduation to the Citizen Forces.

Commonwealth Arsenal.

Prior to the outbreak of war the Government had approved of the principle of the establishment of an Arsenal. The long continuance of the war had seriously hampered the development of all that was proposed. An Arsenal would now be established which it was hoped would gradually be able to supply their peace requirements. It would be established more in the form of a munitions supply branch, aiming rather at insuring that Australian trade would be able to supply their war needs than that Government-owned factories should be designed on the scale necessary for the purpose.

Air Forces.

The funds required in this connection had been largely reduced by the splendid gift made by the British authorities of 128 aeroplanes with equipment of all kinds. There was, of course, a considerable number of personnel already trained, and it was hoped that the measures to be taken in regard to civil aviation would insure a reserve of airmen and machines.

A combined Naval and Military Air Corps would be organised under a Board, composed of flying, equipment and finance officers. As it was unnecessary at that juncture to create a separate Department, and would be wasteful to separate the naval and military sides of this service, the Corps would, for convenience, be placed under the Minister for Defence. A Bill would be submitted for the constitution, administration, and discipline of the Air Corps.

It was proposed that the permanent section of the Air Force should be used in assisting civil aviation to get on a proper basis. The personnel of that Force would be used very largely for surveying, map-making, and doing the necessary pioneering work in arranging air routes in Australia which would eventually be utilised for commercial purposes.

THE BUDGET.

On 16th September, 1920, the Budget Speech was delivered by the Treasurer* in the House of Representatives.

The Treasurer (the Right Hon. Sir Joseph Cook) said that the result of the year's operations was a substantial surplus of revenue over the expenditure. Nearly all departments of revenue contributed to the surplus, and some of them were beyond the most sanguine expectations. When they considered the difficulties and scarcity of overseas transport, the desiccating drought which had played such havoc over a great part of the continent, and other impeding causes, they had the most abundant reason to congratulate themselves on the result of the year's transactions.

The Treasurer submitted his Financial Statement, which showed the following position :

PAST FINANCIAL YEAR : 1919-20.

Revenue	£52,782,748
Expenditure out of Revenue	50,558,383
Surplus for the year	2,224,365
Surplus brought forward from the previous year	3,523,058
Total Accumulated Surplus	£5,747,423

ESTIMATES FOR NEW FINANCIAL YEAR : 1920-21.

Revenue (including £3,766,000 by new taxation)	£63,364,700
Expenditure	68,872,578
Deficiency	5,507,878
Available surplus brought forward	5,747,423
Leaving an Estimated Surplus	£239,545

The other principal matters of general interest dealt with by the Treasurer were as follows : —

Production : The total value of the primary and secondary production for the year 1918 was £298,669,000, made up as follows : Pastoral, £98,297,000 ; agriculture, £58,080,000 ; dairy, poultry and bee farming, £33,738,000 ; forestry and fisheries, £7,137,000 ; mining, £26,156,000 ; value added by manufacture, £75,261,000.

Trade : The value of trade for the past financial year, viz. £246,020,000 was much greater than in any previous year, the balance of exports over imports being £51,108,000. The total value in 1913-14 was £158,320,000, and in 1918-19, £201,750,000. The large increase in

* For the Treasurer's references to Immigration and Ship Construction see pages 136 and 137.

egard to exports was not altogether due to increased production, but
partly to the higher prices which were obtainable for their products.
Higher prices also increased the value of imports.

Manufactures : The effect of increased prices was indicated in the
greater value of output in the year 1918 as compared with 1914. The
figures were £226,000,000 and £166,000,000 respectively—a difference of
60,000,000—the number of factories and employees being almost
the same in each year. The figures for the present year would, no
doubt, show still larger increases owing to the further advance in prices.

War Expenditure : The total war expenditure to 30th June, 1920,
was £381,149,019, of which amount £70,716,184 had been paid out of
revenue, leaving as expenditure out of War Loan £310,432,835, which
figure includes a sum of £42,696,500 owing to the British Government for
the maintenance and transport of troops and for certain fleet services.

Public Debt : The public debt of the Commonwealth at 30th June,
1920, might be divided as follows : Dead-weight debt—that is, debt
behind which are no live or active assets—£340,913,884 ; debt incurred
for reconstructional and developmental purposes—£40,501,433.

Loans raised in Australia : The Second Peace Loan (£25,000,000),
which closed in September, was over-subscribed. This loan brings the
total amount raised in the Commonwealth for War and Repatriation
purposes up to £245,000,000.

Australian Note Issue* : On 30th August the sovereigns held in the
Treasury equalled 41·27 per cent. of the note issue of £57,000,000.
Largely, said the Treasurer, perhaps by force of habit, the doctrine
was subscribed to that the gold available as a security to the note issue
was that stored in the Treasury, whereas, in a national issue, the whole
gold resources of the country should be regarded as the security. In
this respect the Australian note issue, by comparison with other countries,
was certainly in an enviable position, viz. : Australia 77 per cent., Great
Britain 30, Canada 43, United States of America 58, France 15, Spain 63,
Italy 9, Netherlands 61, Switzerland 55, Sweden 40, Norway 33.

New Taxation : Of the estimated revenue for 1920-21 it was proposed to raise £3,766,000 by the following increases : Income tax, additional 5 per cent. ; beer duty 6d. per gallon ; spirits 3s. per gallon ;
tobacco, cigars, and cigarettes 8d. per lb. ; letter postage ½d.; telegrams,
1d. and proportionate increase on press rates ; telephones 25 per cent. ;
with exemptions for country districts.

The Treasurer, in pointing out that Australia had not been taxed
to the extent which was justifiable during the currency of the war, said
their taxation had been light as compared with New Zealand and the
United Kingdom, as would be seen from the following figures for the
year 1919-20, viz. : Australia (States and Commonwealth), £10 13s. 9d. ;
New Zealand, £14 0s. 3d. ; and the United Kingdom, £22 3s. 11d.

War Time Profits Tax : Whilst there was good reason to remove
this tax in its present form at the earliest moment, it was thought better,
on the whole, to allow the tax to lapse, as already provided, and to

---

* There is only one note issue in Australia, which is that of the
Commonwealth Government. It has now been transferred from the
Treasury to a Note Issue Department of the Commonwealth (Govern-
ment) Bank of Australia.

collect the assessment for this year. The introduction of new schemes of taxation at that time would have only increased the complexities of the subject to be investigated by the Royal Commission. The Government had, therefore, decided to collect war-time profits tax for the last time this year.

IMMIGRATION.

(Policy of the Government.)

On 16th September, 1920, in the House of Representatives, the Treasurer made a statement as to the policy of the Government in relation to Immigration in the course of his speech introducing the Budget.

The Treasurer (the Right Hon. Sir Joseph Cook) said that it was the intention of the Government to make a serious and urgent attempt to divert to Australia a portion of the stream of migration of their own people and race which had already set in and was steadily flowing towards the different Dominions. This was the most insistent of all the immediate problems of Australia. On the Estimates would be found a sum of £100,000 for this purpose, and if more could be usefully spent more would be provided. Arrangements had already been made with the States on the following lines, viz. : —

Commonwealth to have full control overseas.

Agents-General of the several States to form consultative committees in London.

Commonwealth to be responsible for, and have control of, all overseas organisations and transport arrangements for bringing immigrants to Australia.

Primary object of scheme to be the settlement of immigrants on the lands of Australia.

Preference to be given to British ex-Service men, the Commonwealth seeking the co-operation and assistance of the British Government in obtaining the right type of immigrant and ot passages for same.

Commonwealth to assume financial responsibility for organisation for immigrants from overseas and transport to Australia.

States to be responsible for immigrants upon arrival in Australia and for their settlement on suitable lands or employment on public works.

States to enter into an agreement with the Commonwealth, setting out in definite terms what they bind themselves to do in regard to providing land, and other forms of assistance, such as depots, sustenance general care of immigrants, employment on public works, particularly on unification of railway gauges, Murray waters scheme, etc., for (a) ex Service men, and (b) other classes of immigrants.

Commonwealth and States to co-operate and consult from time to time as to the number of immigrants who can be absorbed in the respective States, and the class of immigrant required.

Commonwealth undertakes to assist the States by way of loan for approved land settlement and public works.

SHIP CONSTRUCTION.

(Government Policy.)

The Treasurer on 16th September, 1920, during the course of the Budget Speech, made a statement as to the policy of the Government regarding shipbuilding.

The Treasurer (the Right Hon. Sir Joseph Cook) said that one of the objects the Government had in mind when it started its shipbuilding scheme was an endeavour to encourage the establishment of steel shipbuilding in Australia. During the period 27th August, 1919, to 31st July, 1920, six ships, representing a total dead-weight carrying capacity of 33,600 tons, had been completed, and were in commission. These vessels had been engaged in the carriage of cargoes of considerable value to the Commonwealth.

In the construction of these six vessels and others now under construction, about £1,600,000 had been spent in Australia in wages and material, and it was only fair to say that vessels of similar class and type could only have been purchased by the Government on the open market at a considerably higher rate than it cost to build them.

The material on hand, and work done on completed and uncompleted ships, represented not less than twelve complete vessels of 70,200 tons dead-weight carrying capacity. The total expenditure to that date showed that this tonnage had been constructed at a cost to the Government of about £28 10s. per ton dead-weight.

Arrangements had been made for the construction in Australia of two additional vessels to carry about 12,700 tons dead-weight and to steam 13 knots at sea, for the carriage of refrigerated and general cargoes. These vessels were representative of the highest and latest type of cargo-boat construction. In addition, there were then under construction fifteen 6,000-ton steamships, and two 2,300-ton wooden sailing ships.

SHIPPING ACTIVITIES.

(Government Line of Steamers.)

The Minister for Repatriation (Senator the Hon. E. D. Millen) on 25th August, as a result of a question by Senator the Hon. Josiah Thomas (*N.S.W.*), presented a statement in the Senate concerning the Commonwealth Government Line of Steamers, in the course of which it was stated :—

The fleet of 15 cargo steamers purchased in 1916 by the Prime Minister formed the nucleus of the Commonwealth Government Line, which now controls 39 vessels, of an aggregate gross tonnage of 161,068 tons. These comprise 23 Government-owned vessels (including five wooden steamers built in America) and 16 ex-enemy vessels.

The object in establishing the Line was to provide for the transportation of Australian produce to the markets of the world. The primary object was not profits, but rather to prevent Australia being isolated through the world's shipping disruption, brought about by the war.

After operating for two years, the Line showed a net profit of £903,499, adequate provision having been made for depreciation and renewal reserve. In the year 1918-19 the net profits amounted to £1,160,034. The estimated net profits for the year 1919-20 are £220,000, the decrease being accounted for by the extended maritime strike on the Australian coast, which resulted in practically the whole of the Commonwealth fleet being laid up in Australia for periods varying from two to four months.

Another factor which has materially contributed to the decrease is that, owing to the congestion of shipping, which prevailed in the whole of the ports in the United Kingdom, vessels have taken abnormally long periods to discharge and load.

Supplemental to the establishment of the Commonwealth Line, the Government has undertaken an extensive shipbuilding scheme.

The benefits to the Australian people of the establishment of the Line cannot be measured by the direct profits of its operations.

*   *   *

As showing the advantages which have been provided by the Line, it may be mentioned that Australian products, particularly wheat, were piling up in the stores, and were urgently required elsewhere for national purposes. The Government Line afforded material assistance in connection with freights, which were at times very much below the world's ruling rate. On general cargo the Commonwealth Line charged the same rates of freight as the ordinary lines, but have never exceeded £7 10s. per ton for wheat.

When the rate was fixed in February, 1918, at £7 10s., inquiries made by chartering agents in London indicated that the ruling rate for British vessels at that time might be calculated as being £11 10s. per ton. As a matter of fact, British vessels were quite unobtainable, even at that figure, and at this time neutrals refused £13 15s. per ton for the same work, i.e., full cargoes of wheat. Parcels of wheat were carried at and around £7 10s. per ton by other lines, but the rates quoted refer, as mentioned, to full cargoes.

In addition to carrying cargo overseas, many of the vessels controlled by the Line have been utilised to relieve the congestion on the coast of Australia, whilst others have been used for the carriage of phosphates from the islands.

*   *   *

The Commonwealth Line has had to face the strongest competition of the British Shipping Combine, which have threatened traders that, in the event of their shipping by the Commonwealth Line, space would not be available for them on any of the Conference boats. In some cases, this threat has been actually carried into effect. Furthermore, shippers by the Commonwealth Line are liable to lose any rebates accruing to them from shipments made by them on Combine steamers. Notwithstanding this opposition, the Commonwealth Line has received a fair share of support, and recent advices from the officials of the Line indicate that for some time past there has been a steady weekly increase in the amount of privately-owned cargo shipped by the Commonwealth vessels from the United Kingdom.

CUSTOMS AMENDMENT ACT.*

(To meet Depreciation of Foreign Exchange.)

The object of this Act, which was introduced in the House of Representatives on 14th October, 1920, and received Assent on 10th November, is to provide, where found to be desirable, for the computation of import duty on the bank rate of exchange. The Act is now in operation.

The Act provides that when the bank rate of exchange of any country is more than 10 per cent. below the mint par rate of exchange the Minister shall refer to the Board of Trade the question whether the bank rate of exchange (as on London) should be used as the basis of the computation of the value for duty of goods imported from that country. The Board is empowered to recommend to the Minister that the bank rate of exchange be applied provided such course is not prejudicial to the manufacture of goods in Australia or the sale in Australia of those goods ; or any preference given to goods imported from the United Kingdom. The Minister acts on the Board's recommendations.

When, in the opinion of the Board, goods of any class or description, produced or manufactured in any country in respect of which the bank rate of exchange has been adopted, are being imported and sold in Australia in substantial quantities at prices below the fair market value for home consumption at the date of shipment of similar goods in the United Kingdom or Australia, and the production or manufacture of similar goods in Australia or the United Kingdom is, or likely to be, thereby adversely affected, the Board may recommend that the value for duty of such goods be computed on the mint par rate of exchange, which recommendation shall be adopted by the Minister.

The Minister may at any time refer to the Board for consideration the question as to the continuance of the application of the bank rate of exchange to any class or description of goods.

IN HOUSE OF REPRESENTATIVES.

The **Minister for Trade and Customs (Hon. W. Massy Greene)** in moving the Second Reading (26th October), after outlining the broad principles underlying the theory of foreign exchanges and the causes that had led to the present abnormal

---

* A proclamation has been issued in the Commonwealth Government "Gazette" in pursuance of this Act applying, as from the 12th November, 1920, the bank rate of exchange for the computation of customs duty on goods imported from France, Belgium, Italy and Czecho-Slovakia.

conditions, said that the law as it then stood laid it down that the home consumption value of goods must be ascertained, and that the genuine invoice must set out the price paid in the country of manufacture. It had been held that that meant the currency of the country of manufacture. The principal Act provided that the rate of exchange between currency and currency must be a fair rate of exchange, and that if there were any doubt the Minister must declare it. They believed that the law compelled the Customs Department to collect those duties on the home consumption value converted at the mint par rate of exchange as between the currencies of the various countries. This matter had been the subject of considerable controversy, and was then being tested in the Courts.

This practice had led to some extraordinary results, and there was no doubt that duties then being collected on some goods made it absolutely impossible profitably to sell them. The manufacturers of those classes of goods for which there was a world demand had raised the home consumption value of their goods in the currency of their country to the world's parity converted at the bank rate of exchange. When such goods were sold to Australia and the duty was collected and, as in the case of France, the bills converted into francs at the mint par rate of exchange, and those goods came into competition with other goods sold at the world's parity, and in regard to which duty was collected at par, the procedure simply put them out of court. The Bill was an attempt to remedy that. It was also an attempt to prevent the exporters of France and Italy, when the world demand for their goods might be not quite what it then was, using the exchange position to dump those goods in the Australian market at prices at which neither British nor other manufacturers could compete.

He wished to show that it was possible to use an exchange position for the dumping of goods should it be thought desirable to do so. Whatever the depreciation of a currency, it must be reflected in the price of goods exported from the country where it existed; but there were other influences, potent factors in the existing exchange position, which need not necessarily be reflected in those prices, of which it would eventually be possible for such countries to take advantage, if they so desired, unless, of course, in the meantime, the exchange position drifted back to its normal pre-war state. If, as was quite possible, the tendency were for prices to fall suddenly, those countries could use their exchange position to dump their goods in Great Britain and in Australia.

The fiscal policy of Australia rested on two principles, namely, preference to British goods and protection of Australian manufactures.

The Board would have to consider the position of a country, and if they decided that the bank rate of exchange could be adopted without any general detriment they would be able to grant it by means of their certificate. Power was also given the Board to deal with any particular class of goods. As soon as they were able, after granting the original certificate, to review the whole position, and to ascertain if any classes of goods were coming in at lower rates, or that the certificate would enable them to come in at such rates, the Board might meet and determine, in regard to those classes of goods, that the mint par rate of exchange and not the bank rate, should apply.

INDUSTRIAL PEACE ACT.

This Act, which was assented to on 13th September, 1920, relates to the establishment of a Council, Tribunals and Boards for the prevention and settlement of industrial disputes extending beyond the limits of any one State.

Constitution of Commonwealth Council.

The Act provides for the establishment of a Commonwealth Council of Industrial Representatives, consisting of a Chairman and an even number (not less than six nor more than eight) of other members. The Chairman shall be chosen by agreement between the representatives of employers and employees, or failing agreement, by the Governor-General. The other members shall be representative equally of the employers and of the recognised organisations of employees. The members of the Council are to hold office during the pleasure of the Governor-General, and to receive such remuneration, etc., as he directs. The Chairman shall not vote unless the voting is equal, in which case he shall have a casting vote. Two-thirds of the members shall form a quorum.

Powers of Council.

(A) To consider any matters, conditions and tendencies in any part of the Commonwealth leading or likely to lead to industrial disputes, or in any way affecting or likely to affect industrial peace;

(B) To inquire into any industrial matter brought before it by a member, or referred to it by the Governor-General, and to declare its opinion thereon.

(C) To confer with any persons or associations as to any matters affecting the prevention or settlement of industrial disputes;

(D) To appoint Committees for the purpose of any inquiry or conference;

(E) To summon any person before the Council or a Committee thereof for the purpose of conference or of giving evidence;

(F) To make reports to the Governor-General concerning any industrial matter.

The Council is also empowered to make rules, etc., for the order and conduct of its business and proceedings.

DISTRICT COUNCILS.

The Governor-General may appoint District Councils similar in constitution, powers and functions, to the principal Council, except that they inquire into and report to the latter on matters referred to them by the principal Council or by any employers, employees, association of employers or recognised organisation of employees.

SPECIAL TRIBUNALS.

Special Tribunals may be appointed by the Governor-General consisting of an equal number of representatives of employers and employees respectively, together with a Chairman to be chosen in the same manner as in the case of the Councils.

A Special Tribunal shall have cognizance of :

(A) Any industrial dispute between an organisation of employees on the one hand, and employers or association of employers on the other hand, referred to it by the persons or organisations parties thereto ; and

(B) Any industrial dispute as to which a compulsory conference has been held and agreement not reached, and which has been referred to the tribunal;

And have power to inquire into all matters relevant to the dispute from the point of production to the final disposal of the commodity by the employers, the decision of the Tribunal on the question of relevancy to be final.

No dispute as to which the hearing has commenced in the Commonwealth Court of Conciliation and Arbitration shall be referred to a Special Tribunal.

The disclosure or publication, without the consent of the person concerned, of evidence relating to any trade secret, profits or financial position is punishable by a fine of £500 or imprisonment for three months. All such evidence shall, if so desired, be taken in private.

POWERS OF SPECIAL TRIBUNAL.

A Special Tribunal has power to hear and determine any industrial dispute of which it has cognizance, and for that purpose has all powers which by the Commonwealth Conciliation and Arbitration Act 1904-1918 are given to the Court or the President under that Act.

COMPULSORY CONFERENCE.

A Special Tribunal or the Chairman thereof, or the Minister may, for the purpose of preventing or settling industrial disputes, summon any person to attend at a conference. Where an agreement is not reached at such a conference the dispute may be referred to a Special Tribunal.

ENFORCEMENT OF AWARDS.

Any order or award made by a Special Tribunal shall be binding on the parties and may be enforced as an award of the Commonwealth Court of Conciliation and Arbitration, and is not challengeable in any Court on any account whatever. Any agreement made in writing as to an industrial dispute before a Special Tribunal or at any compulsory conference may be filed with the Industrial Registrar and thereupon be binding and enforceable as if it were an award of the Court.

LOCAL BOARDS.

In relation to any Special Tribunal, the Governor-General may appoint a Local Board or Boards to exercise jurisdiction within such limits as are prescribed or as are defined by the Special Tribunal. A Local Board shall consist of a Chairman and an even number (not less than four nor more than eight) of other members in the same manner as the Special Tribunals and Councils, tenure and remuneration to be as prescribed. Such Board shall have cognizance of any industrial dispute referred to it by the parties thereto, or by the Special Tribunal in relation to which it was appointed, and its powers are similar to those of a Special Tribunal, except that its determinations are subject to review by the Special Tribunal.

HIGH COURT.

When an alleged industrial dispute is referred to a Special Tribunal or a Local Board any party to the proceeding may apply to the High Court for a decision on the question whether the dispute or any part thereof exists, or is threatened, impending or probable, as an industrial dispute extending beyond the limits of any one State or on any question of law arising in relation to the dispute or to the proceeding or to any award or order, the decision of the High Court to be final and conclusive.

The Chairman of a Special Tribunal or Local Board may submit for the opinion of the High Court any question which, in his opinion, is one of law.

COMMONWEALTH COURT OF CONCILIATION AND ARBITRATION.

During the currency of any award or order by a Special Tribunal or a Local Board the Commonwealth Court of Conciliation and Arbitration shall have no jurisdiction to make any award or order inconsistent therewith.

PENALTIES.

Any contravention of this Act for which no other penalty is provided shall be punishable on conviction by imprisonment for a period not exceeding six months, or a fine not exceeding £100, or both.

DEBATE IN HOUSE OF REPRESENTATIVES.

The Prime Minister (the Right Hon. W. M. Hughes), on 9th July, in moving the Second Reading, said that in Australia, where Labour had, owing to organisation, political and industrial, been able to exercise considerable influence, the industrial problem had engaged the attention of the Commonwealth and State Legislatures for very many years. He had always held that production was not a matter which concerned the individual only. It was primarily a collective function. Society was vitally concerned in production, both in its capacity as a producer and a consumer, and it was not proper that individuals—whether they be employers or employees was immaterial—should carry on production without regard to the welfare of the community as a whole.

Failure of Arbitration Court.

In the early days of the Commonwealth they had been under the impression that their powers were much wider than the High Court had since decided them to be. It was now quite clear that the powers of the Commonwealth in relation to industrial matters were covered entirely by the words of paragraph xxxv. of section 51 of the Constitution, which read as follows : —

> " Conciliation and arbitration for the prevention and settlement of industrial disputes extending beyond the limits of any one State."

This power was a very restricted and unsatisfactory one. Very many attempts had been made to widen it, but unsuccessfully.* Under that power they had created an Arbitration Court. That Court had done excellent work; but the present position of the Court was one of great congestion. The methods of the Court were then, and always had been, cumbrous in the extreme. Normally the procedure was, first of all, for the organisation concerned to file a plaint. This, in some cases, meant that hundreds of employers had to be served throughout the Commonwealth. After the plaint had been filed, and the other parties notified, the case was then set down for hearing. The case might not come before the Court for many months.

There were two ways of settling industrial disputes. One was direct action—the strike ; the other, recourse to some form of peaceful adjustment by agreement between the parties, or by arbitration. No one would deny that experience had shown that for many reasons the Arbitration Court was not the ideal instrument for the settlement of disputes. If the cumbrous procedure of the Court, its ineffective and expensive methods of settling disputes be contrasted with the expeditious methods of such a body as the shipbuilding tribunal, it must be admitted that Parliament would be wrong if it did not indicate in the plainest manner possible that it was of opinion that industrial unrest was more likely to be allayed and disputes settled by such tribunals than by the Court. Not only did the Arbitration Court suffer by comparison with the tribunal by its failure to deal with cases expeditiously and economically but also for the reason that it had been unable to settle some very serious strikes which had paralysed the community. This was particularly shown in the seamen's dispute. The men made certain demands, and, as they were not conceded

* Constitution Alteration (Legislative Powers) 1919 *vide* JOURNAL Vol. I. No. 1, page 140.

they went on strike. A compulsory conference was called by the President of the Court. No agreement was arrived at. The President had laid it down that unions could not have strikes and arbitration, and that he would not deal with a dispute until the men involved had returned to work. He (Mr. Hughes) was not going to criticise that attitude ; it was very logical and proper. But it left the community in a most unfortunate position. The men would not return to work. A conference was called by the Government, and an agreement was arrived at after a stoppage covering some five months. Then, in the coal miners' case, the machinery of the Arbitration Court failed to bring about industrial peace, and another tribunal had to be provided. Another instance might be cited where the Arbitration Court had failed to settle a de 'facto strike, namely, the dispute between the marine engineers and their employers. During the War the Government was able to exercise powers given to it under the War Precautions Act to deal with many disputes and with many matters which ordinarily it could not touch. There was no other machinery by which a tribunal could be created.

Advantages of Tribunals and Councils.

He believed that tribunals of the kind proposed, flexible, convenient, expeditious, and economical, were much more likely to promote industrial peace, and prevent industrial turmoil, than was the Arbitration Court as it then existed. The appointment of the proposed councils and tribunals was a recognition of the principle of the round-table conference, which he thought would be agreed was the best known method of arriving at a settlement. In England the Whitley Councils had been most serviceable. They, however, were not as flexible as would be the machinery proposed in the measure. There was no limitation to the power of the councils so far as the settlement of disputes was concerned, except that which was imposed by the Constitution. The award or decision of a tribunal would be binding at law and have exactly the same effect as an award of the Arbitration Court. When it had given its award the tribunal might appoint a standing tribunal to interpret the award and give effect to it. He did not pretend that the scheme was a panacea for industrial unrest, but he did say that the measure was a distinct advance on existing legislation, and he believed it would prove of infinite service.

The Hon. F. G. Tudor (Leader of the Opposition) said that the proposed measure would wipe out the Arbitration Court, or, at any rate, it would make it very ineffective. One feature of the Bill that met with his approval was the fact that it did away with lawyers in connection with arbitration. He

believed that if lawyers were eliminated from the Arbitration
Court there would be greater expedition. In the Court as it
then was lawyers raised every technical point as against the
employees with a view to making that mode of seeking redress
too expensive for them. It was claimed by some that the
arbitration principle had failed, but he did not think that the
Court had failed, though it had not been as successful as they
had hoped. Personally, he would welcome anything that
would lead to more expedition, but he did not propose to
support any proposal that might lead to one-sided tribunals
which might be the case under the provisions of the Bill.*
They had had some experience in Victoria with Wages Boards
and the representation that was given on them. He desired
a definition of " recognised organisation " and suggested that
it should be the organisation recognised by the Trades Hall.

Recognition of Unions.

Mr. M. Charlton (Labour, *Hunter, N.S.W.*) said that no
matter how good the machinery might be for the settlement
of industrial disputes, the workers would not accept it unless
their unions had recognition. That fundamental principle of
their industrial legislation of the past was absent from the
present Bill.

The Hon. David Watkins (Labour, *Newcastle, N.S.W.*),
during the consideration in Committee, supported by Labour
members, unsuccessfully endeavoured to amend the Bill so
that " organisation of employees " should mean the *bona fide*
trade union organisation representing the industry as recognised by the Trades or Industrial Council in the district or
State concerned.

An amendment moved by the **Prime Minister** was adopted
defining " organisation " in reference to employees to mean
an association of not less than one hundred employees engaged
in any industrial pursuit or pursuits, etc.

Mr. S. M. Bruce (Nat., *Flinders, Vic.*), after explaining the
Whitley Committee's scheme and the manner of its operation,
said that the first principle of the Bill was that there should
be a Commonwealth Council, which, apparently, would
perform the same duties as the National Councils under the
Whitley scheme, save that in the latter scheme each National
Council was for one industry only, whereas the Commonwealth
Council would have to deal with matters relating to all
industries. The great benefit which one could imagine to be

---

* The Bill originally provided for the appointment of Chairmen of
Councils, etc., by the Governor-General. This was subsequently amended
as shown in the summary of the provisions of the Act.

the outcome of the scheme for a National Council would be that the employer and employee would meet together and come to quick decisions. He was afraid, however, that object would be defeated if men who were engaged in a mining industry were called upon as members of the Council to deal with shipping troubles or any other disputes in allied industries. If, however, the Council confined itself to wide questions of national importance it might be possible for it to do the necessary work, operating in conjunction with the district councils and the special tribunals provided for. Thus it was not likely to be overloaded, as was the case with the Arbitration Court.

The Hon. Austin Chapman (Nat., *Eden-Monaro, N.S.W.*) could not understand the opposition displayed to the Bill. The men who ought to cavil at the Bill were agitators who got their living by promoting strikes.

Mr. Frank Brennan (Labour, *Batman, Vic.*) said he would like to have supported the Bill if he could see that it would be of any use to the country. He thought the Arbitration Act could be amended in a direction which should make of it a very useful instrument. Without amendment it did all that the proposed measure could do. The Bill provided for compulsory conferences. So did the Arbitration Act. The Bill provided for local Councils and district Boards. The Act provided for Boards of Reference. The Government should give the Arbitration Act facilities to function, and not destroy it.

The motion for the Second Reading was, on 6th August, agreed to by 33 votes to 19, and the Bill was passed by the House of Representatives on 13th August, the official Labour members voting against it.

DEBATE IN THE SENATE.

Senator the Hon. E. J. Russell (Vice-President of the Executive Council), on 19th August, in moving the Second Reading, said he wished to make it perfectly clear that the measure was not intended to interfere with the Arbitration Court as it then existed. It was designed to provide supplementary legislation, and to create facilities for the holding of special courts in time of industrial crisis. It was sometimes questioned whether the system of arbitration in Australia had proved a success or otherwise. In his opinion, it had been instrumental in preventing a good deal of industrial trouble and direct action. The rise in the price of commodities had led to an enormous increase in industrial litigation, and the avenues by means of which the Court could be approached thus became congested with business. In all the circumstances, it was not to be wondered at that there were forty-two cases then pending before the Arbitration Court. When, however, normal times had become re-established, he was firmly of opinion that arbitration would again become popular. Under the Arbitration Act sufficient was not done to prevent industrial disputes arising. Instead they waited until the disputes had developed. Under the Constitution, their industrial powers of legislation were limited to disputes which extended beyond the boundaries of any one State. That Constitutional limitation not only destroyed the effectiveness of Commonwealth legislation, but compelled the workers to start a fight in one State with the deliberate intention of extending it to another State. He had to admit that, to a certain extent, the workers had lost confidence in the institutions that had been set up for arbitration. That was not due to a belief that the machinery had been wrongly used, but to the delay and the cost of that method for the settlement of disputes. Lawyers had to be engaged, and he had known men to be receiving refreshers of fifty guineas a day in connection with cases before the Arbitration Court. The workers should be able to secure justice without being asked to pay any such fees.

Profit-Sharing.

Senator J. F. Guthrie (*Victoria*) welcomed the introduction of the Bill, because he believed it was a genuine attempt on the part of the Government to settle disputes. The measure, however, went further, because it aimed at preventing disputes, and prevention was better than cure. The Arbitration Court had broken down under its own weight. In the past seven years there had been 2,313 disputes.

The only final solution of industrial unrest was the system of profit-sharing. He had had a good deal of experience in that matter, as he had been managing several concerns in different parts of Australia. Many years back in those businesses, as far as his powers had permitted, and in his own concerns and farms, he had introduced the profit-sharing system with satisfactory results to all. He maintained that the workers were entitled at least to a basic wage, and the capitalist was entitled to interest on his capital, and the manager, with the brains of the concern, was entitled to his good salary; but there was generally a surplus of wealth created, and in that surplus he maintained that the workers were entitled to a share in proportion to their length of service and so on. This would lead to increased production, which was the only way to decrease the cost of living.

Senator the Hon. J. H. Keating (*Tasmania*) said that for a long time he had believed that they had not paid sufficient attention as a Federal Parliament to the powers which they possessed under the Constitution. They had equal powers in regard to legislating for conciliation as they had for arbitration, but hitherto they had concentrated all their legislative efforts in the direction of arbitration. The present measure was an attempt to utilise their powers in regard to conciliation, and he trusted that it might result in the benefits anticipated.

Senator the Hon. A. Gardiner (Leader of the Opposition) said that if the passing of the Bill would make industrial matters work more smoothly he welcomed it. During the past ten years the Arbitration Acts had kept the peace. In considering industrial measures they ought to try to ascertain the real cause of industrial disputes and troubles. He ventured to say that they were educating the community. The world was being educated, and as the people of the world became more educated they would want more of what the world produced in the future than they had had in the past. When the Arbitration Courts had given the men more wages, immediately the producing section, the boot manufacturers and the clothing manufacturers, the merchants and the importers, knowing that the people were getting more wages, had increased their prices. That was the cause of industrial unrest. If the present measure was intended to bring about industrial peace it certainly was not introduced in a way that would suggest that. His party (Labour) had desired that a conference should be called before the Bill was proceeded with. But the Government were in such a hurry to pass it that they guillotined it through the other branch of the Legislature.* It had to be passed within a prescribed period. He objected to fixed awards, because the prices of necessary commodities were fluctuating to such an extent that what might be considered a living wage to-day might be totally inadequate a few months hence. He had much pleasure in opposing the Bill.

The Bill was passed by the Senate on 2nd September with minor amendments which were subsequently accepted by the House of Representatives.

---

* On the motion of the Prime Minister in the House of Representatives on 4th August the Bill was declared to be one of urgency, and limitation of debate was agreed to. The Opposition, however, desired more time for the purpose of consulting the Labour organisations and ascertaining their views on the measure.

UNEMPLOYMENT INSURANCE.

In reply to a question by Mr. W. H. Story (Nat., *Boothby,* *S.A.*) as to whether his attention had been called to the success achieved by the State Governments of Victoria and Queensland through the establishment of State Insurance,

The Acting Treasurer (the Right Hon. Sir Joseph Cook), on 21st July, admitted that such was the case. He added that the Government intended, as early as practicable, to institute a searching investigation into the question of the insurance of the workers against unemployment and sickness, with a view to the establishment of a system fair both to employers and employees.

INSTITUTE OF SCIENCE AND INDUSTRY ACT.

A Bill for the permanent establishment of a Commonwealth Institute of Science and Industry was before the last Parliament in 1919 (*see* JOURNAL, Vol. I., No. 1, page 153) but lapsed with the prorogation thereof. The present Act, which received Assent on 14th September, 1920, differs from the original Bill in that instead of three directors, only one is now provided for. Another alteration is that the Institute is to establish (a) a Bureau of Agriculture; (b) a Bureau of Industries; and (c) such other bureaux as the Governor-General determines.

State Parliaments.

New South Wales.

LARGE HOLDINGS SUBDIVISION BILL.

The object of this Bill, which was introduced in the Legislative Assembly on 19th October, 1920, is to provide for the subdivision of large land holdings, and for the appropriation and resumption of portions thereof for closer settlement and other purposes.

Definition of " Large Holding."

For the purposes of the Act any holding shall be regarded as a large holding the private lands on which when fully improved exceeds in value as freehold the sum of £20,000, exclusive of buildings; except holdings within the boundaries of any municipality or urban area, within the Western Division, or within an irrigation area. The Act shall not operate in certain specified districts until a date to be fixed by proclamation. Any holding mainly used for stud sheep and cattle breeding may also be excluded.

Duties of Owners of Holdings.

Within three months after the Act comes into operation the owner of any large holding is required to submit to the district surveyor a plan showing the boundaries of his holding and areas of all measured portions thereon, the character and position of all improvements, and such other information as may be prescribed. He shall also mark the suggested acreage and position of the area he desires to retain, such area to consist only of private lands, and not to exceed in value £20,000, exclusive of buildings. If the holding is a family holding, the retention area may be extended by an additional area of land valued at £3,000 for each member of the family above one. The owner shall also submit a statutory declaration showing the improved value of the private lands of his holding, the value of his interest in such lands, the value of the suggested retention area, the tenures under which all the lands of his holding are held, and particulars of all mortgages, etc.

Valuation Courts.

Valuation Districts may be established, and a Chairman appointed for each. Upon receipt of a copy of the plan of any holding from the district surveyor, the chairman of the district shall refer it to the Valuation Court, consisting of himself and two assessors appointed respectively by the Minister and the owner of the holding in question. The Court shall consider and determine the acreage and position of the retention area, and may also determine the improved value of the land in the open area of such holding, and the value of the respective estates or interests of all persons concerned. All valuations of land made in pursuance of the Act shall not exceed the value of such land as at 31st December, 1920.

Appropriation and Resumption.

At any time after the determination of the acreage and position of the retention area of any holding the Minister may by notification in the Government Gazette declare that the whole or portion of the open area of such holding has been appropriated (if Crown land) or resumed (if private land). The lands shall then be deemed to be vested in His Majesty the King for the purposes of this Act, the Closer Settlement Acts, and the Returned Soldiers' Settlement Acts for an estate in fee simple in possession, freed from all obligations. A certified copy of the notice shall be lodged with the Registrar-General and dealt with by him as if the same were a memorandum of transfer duly executed under the Real Property Act.

Compensation.

Every person claiming payment for land so vested shall within sixty days of the publication of the notification lodge with the Minister a notice setting forth the nature of his estate or interest in the land and an abstract of his title. If the Minister is satisfied that the claimant has a valid title and that the land is not subject to any mortgage or encumbrance, he shall within three months pay to the claimant the amount of the prescribed valuation, together with interest at 4½ per cent. from the date of resumption ; such payment to be effected by closer settlement debentures having a currency of not more than thirty-eight years and bearing interest at 4½ per cent. per annum.

Disposal of Land.

Any land appropriated or resumed under this Act may be disposed of under the provisions of the Closer Settlement Acts or Returned Soldiers' Settlement Acts. No land appropriated or resumed shall be disposed of at a price less than the improved value thereof as determined under this Act.

Penalty.

Any owner who fails or neglects to comply with the provisions of the Act shall be deemed to have given the Minister the right to appoint an assessor on the owner's behalf, and shall in addition be liable to a penalty not exceeding £10 for every day of such failure or neglect.

At the date of the latest Parliamentary Debates to hand, this Bill was in the Second Reading stage. Later advice by cable states that the Bill has been postponed, and will be re-introduced in July next.

Victoria.

General Election and New Government (Note).

The results of the General Elections for the Legislative Assembly held in Victoria on 21st October, show the state of parties as follows Nationalists 31, Labour 20, Farmers' Union 13, and Independent Labour 1.

The constitution of the new Government is as follows :—

Premier and Minister for Agriculture	Hon. H. S. Lawson.
Minister for Education, Forests, and Labour	Hon Sir Alexander Peacock.
Treasurer	Hon. W. M. McPherson.
Attorney-General	Hon. A. Robinson.
Minister for Public Works and Water Supply	Hon. F. G. Clarke.
Minister for Railways and Mines ..	Hon. S. Barnes.
Minister for Lands	Hon. D. S. Oman.
Chief Secretary	Major the Hon. M. Baird.
Assistant Minister for Agriculture ..	Hon. H. Angus.
Honorary Ministers	⎧ Hon. T. Livingston. ⎫ Hon. J. W. Pennington. ⎩ Hon. J. McWhae. Hon. A. Hicks.

Queensland.

General Election and New Government (Note).

The General Election for the Legislative Assembly was held in Queensland on 9th October, 1920, and the state of parties resulted as follows : Labour 38, Country Party 21, and Nationalists 13.

A Government was formed under Mr. E. G. Theodore as Premier, the personnel of the Cabinet being as follows :—

Premier, Chief Secretary and Secretary for Lands	Hon. E. G. Theodore.
Treasurer and Minister for Works and State Enterprises	Hon. J. A. Fihelly.
Attorney-General	Hon. J. Mullan.
Home Secretary	Hon. W. McCormack.
Secretary for Public Instruction ..	Hon. J. Huxham.
Secretary for Mines (with a seat in the Legislative Council)	Hon. A. J. Jones.
Secretary for Railways	Hon. J. Larcombe.
Secretary for Agriculture and Stock ..	Hon. W. N. Gillies.
Assistant Minister	Hon. J. H. Coyne.

South Australia.

VENEREAL DISEASES BILL.

This is a Bill to provide for compulsory treatment and notification of venereal diseases, and to prevent the spread of such diseases, and was introduced in the Legislative Council on 31st August, 1920.

Compulsory Treatment.

The Bill requires that every person suffering or suspecting he is suffering from venereal disease shall, within three days of becoming aware of his condition, consult a medical practitioner thereon (giving his name, occupation and address) or attend at some hospital, and place himself under treatment. Contravention of the above renders the offender liable to a penalty not exceeding £100 or to imprisonment up to three months. The treatment is to continue until he has received a certificate that he is free from venereal disease.

A medical practitioner who (unless under the Act) communicates to any person any name or address furnished to him as above shall be liable to a penalty not exceeding £100 and be deemed to be guilty of professionally infamous conduct.

If the Inspector-General of Hospitals has reasonable ground to believe that any person is suffering from venereal disease and is not under treatment, he may order the person to forthwith place himself under treatment, and if the person does not comply with the order, a special Magistrate may issue a warrant on the complaint of the Inspector-

General, ordering the offender to be apprehended and detained, for a period not exceeding four weeks, for clinical or other examination. If the examination shows that the person is suffering from venereal disease, and the Inspector-General reports to the Minister of Health that further detention is necessary, the Governor may order such person to be detained until he is cured or has ceased to be infectious. Any person thus detained may apply to a Judge or Special Magistrate, who on receiving a report from two medical practitioners (one nominated by the patient) that the person is cured or non-infectious, shall order his release.

Other provisions of the Bill relate to the periodical examination of persons, detained as above, on behalf of the Minister.

Treatment by Medical Practitioner : Compulsory Notification.

No person other than a legally qualified medical practitioner or a person acting under his direct instructions shall attend upon or prescribe for or supply any drug or medicine to any person suffering from venereal disease, except a registered pharmaceutical chemist who dispenses the prescription of such practitioner.

A medical practitioner shall (under penalty) report all cases of venereal disease treated by him to the Inspector-General of Hospitals, and shall give notice of any person who fails to attend for treatment within ten days, provided he has not received notice from another practitioner that such person has placed himself under treatment by him.

Prevention of Infection.

Any person who knowingly infects, or knowingly does any act likely to lead to the infection of, any other person with a venereal disease, or who, knowing himself to be suffering from the disease in an infectious stage, works in or about a factory, shop, hotel, etc., in any capacity requiring him to handle food for human consumption, shall be liable to imprisonment or a penalty not exceeding £100 ; and any person who knowingly employs a person so suffering in a like capacity shall be liable to a penalty not exceeding £100.

Any occupier of a house who knowingly permits any female suffering from venereal disease to occupy the house for the purpose of prostitution shall be liable to imprisonment or a penalty not exceeding £100.

Obligations of Parents and Guardians.

Any parent or guardian of a child suffering from venereal disease shall cause such child to be treated ; and if the parent or guardian knows that the child has failed to comply with any provision of the Act, he shall report the fact to the Inspector-General of Hospitals (A child is defined as "a person under the age of 16 years.")

Prevention of Marriage.

Any person who marries, knowing that he is suffering from venereal disease in an infectious stage, shall be liable to imprisonment for a period up to five years or a penalty not exceeding £500, or both ; and if any medical practitioner has reason to believe that a person suffering from the disease intends to contract marriage, he may report the fact to the other party to the proposed marriage and also to the parent or guardian, or to the Inspector-General of Hospitals.

Privacy of Proceedings.

Any matter coming before a Special Magistrate under the Act shall be heard in private.

Other Provisions.

The Bill also provides for the seizure of articles capable of being used unlawfully for the alleviation of venereal disease ; for the protection of medical practitioners giving certificates etc. ; for persons changing their addresses or medical advisers ; for the establishment of hospitals etc. for the treatment of the disease.

Latest Parliamentary Debates to hand show this Bill in the Second Reading stage. Progress will be reported in the next issue of the JOURNAL.

Western Australia.

PROPOSED ABOLITION OF SECOND CHAMBER.

In the Legislative Council, on 10th August, 1920, the Hon. A. H. Panton moved an amendment to the Address-in-Reply to the effect that the time had now arrived when the Government of the State could best be carried on by a single Chamber elected on an adult franchise.

DEBATE IN LEGISLATIVE COUNCIL.

The Hon. A. H. Panton (*West Province*), analysing the figures in connection with the Assembly(lower Chamber)elections of 1917, said he found that in the contested districts there were 137,755 names on the roll, and the votes recorded totalled 72 per cent. In the Council elections of 1918, in the contested provinces, there were 48,310 electors on the roll, and the votes recorded totalled 38 per cent., or just about half the percentage of the votes recorded for the Assembly. In referring to the last elections, Mr. Panton said that probably one of the most regrettable features was the Metropolitan-Suburban Province election. There were 13,322 names on the roll for the whole of that province, while only 2,594 electors exercised the franchise, leaving 10,728 electors holding property qualifications who were not even sufficiently interested to record their votes. It was evident that there was not much democracy in legislation which provided for 38 per cent. of voters reviewing the work of those who represent 138,000 people. Government in Australia was costing too much. It was ridiculous that for five million people there should be seven Parliaments, seven Governors, and 678 members of Parliament. The Legislative Council of Western Australia was costing £15,000 per annum. That expenditure was not warranted in view of the financial

straits of the country. In view of the fact that the Commonwealth Government had assumed so many of the functions of
the State Governments, whatever need there was for two
Legislative Chambers in each State prior to Federation, that
need no longer existed. The Legislative Councils existed
merely because they were traditional institutions. There was
a growing demand for their abolition in every State of the
Commonwealth. Let them (Western Australia) set an example
to the Governments in the other States, and show that they,
at any rate, were prepared to fall into line with the growing
demand of democracy as it was to-day.

The Hon. T. Moore (*Central Province*), in supporting the
amendment, said that there were many men and women in the
country of sufficient intelligence who were not entitled to vote
for the Legislative Council, simply because they had not
sufficient money to buy a home. The Legislative Council
had in the past been the means of blocking legislation which
would have been of advantage to the great masses of the people.
When dealing with different Governments, it had adopted
different attitudes. He referred to the time when a Labour
Government was in office.   As a matter of fact there never was
a Labour Government in power because the power had always
lain in the Legislative Council, which had the right to say what
legislation should go on the statute-book, and the Labour
Party had never had a majority in the Legislative Council.

The Hon. J. D. Duffell (*Metropolitan–Suburban Province*),
in opposition to the amendment, said that the bi-cameral
system was the soundest and the only system that would
guarantee to the people that sound and mature judgment
after the measures from the other Chamber had been sent for
their review and deliberation. The Legislative Council was no
respecter of Governments, as had been proved by the fact that
during the last six or seven years it had dealt more severely
with the measures sent up by the Nationalist Government
than those sent by the Labour Government. While he had
been a strong advocate of a restricted franchise for the Legislative Council, he realised that it should be elected by people
who have a stake in the country.

The Hon. Sir E. H. Wittenoom (*North Province*) also
opposed the amendment, and challenged any member to show
that the Legislative Council had ever blocked a single measure
of useful legislation. It had never shown a preference to
measures submitted by Liberal Governments. The finance
of the State would be in a better position then if the Legislative
Council had declined to agree to all the proposals brought down
during the five years of the Labour Government's administration. It had helped that Government in every direction
during its tenure of office during which 35 millions of money

from loan and revenue had been spent without leaving behind a contented person or a thriving industry. Every adult person over 21 years of age, whether educated or good or bad or industrious, had a right to vote for the Legislative Assembly, which dealt with money matters and with taxation. Surely some protection should be given to those that were thrifty. The Council was established to provide that protection, after giving the greatest freedom possible to every elector. He agreed that Australia was over-governed. The ideal of Federation was that all the best men would be gathered in the Federal Parliament, and that the rest of the legislative work should be carried on by much smaller Houses in the different States. That was the ideal, but they had realised anything but that ideal. Instead of the best men being sent to the Federal Parliament, it was very difficult for them to get there at all. The Senate (Federal Parliament) had represented one class of the community only for many years, and it had been impossible for anyone else to win a seat. The Legislative Council existed to do good. On the other hand he was in accord with those who said that one House would be quite sufficient provided it was elected on a satisfactory basis to represent all parties in the community.

The amendment was rejected on a division by 15 votes to 7.

NEW ZEALAND.

The proceedings of the First Session of the Twentieth Parlia ment, which opened on 24th June, 1920, are continued in thi issue of the JOURNAL. *The Session closed on* 11th November *but there remain some important Acts to be summarised, an these will be given in the next issue of the* JOURNAL.

TREATIES OF PEACE AMENDMENT ACT.

(Samoan Mandate: Constitutional Aspects, &c.)

The Bill for the above Act was introduced in the Hous of Representatives by the Minister of External Affairs on th 2nd September, 1920, and read a second time on 23rd Septem ber, passing the final stage on 28th September.

It was read a first time in the Legislative Council o 28th September and went through its remaining stages on 6t October, receiving the Governor-General's assent on 18t October.

The original Act, passed in 1919, was only to remain i operation for one year and had to be renewed before the 29t October, 1920.* The object of the present Act is to keep th Act of 1919 in force for another year and this is stated in single clause.

DEBATE IN HOUSE OF REPRESENTATIVES.

The Minister of External Affairs (Hon. E. P. Lee), moving the Second Reading of the Bill in the House on 23 September, said that members would remember it was antic pated that the mandate from the League of Nations would given to New Zealand for the Government of Samoa.

Under the principal Act provision was made for th acceptance by the Dominion of that mandate, and for t Government of Samoa by Order in Council because it was n known when the mandate would be issued. When th mandate was issued it would be necessary for the Governme to govern Samoa under statutory authority.

---

* See Vol. I., No. 1, of this JOURNAL, page 167.

New Zealand Position compared with Australia.

The position in Australia with regard to New Guinea was somewhat the same. Under legislation before the Commonwealth Parliament so late as August of that year it was provided that until Parliament made other provisions for the government of the territory, the Governor-General might make Ordinances having the force of law, for no fixed time. They (in New Zealand) limited the operation of that Bill to twelve months. That would leave an opportunity next Session for the whole matter to be reviewed. If the mandate were not issued in the meantime, he did not know exactly what the position would be.

The Imperial Government, under the Foreign Jurisdiction Act, gave New Zealand authority to administer the affairs of Samoa,* and at present they administered Samoa, not by reason of any mandate from the League of Nations, but purely by the authority of the principal Allied and Associated Powers.

The Constitutional Aspect.

Mr. Downie Stewart (Reform, *Dunedin West*) said he rose to ask the Minister of Justice or the Prime Minister if they would make a statement on the question of how the New Zealand Government regarded its constitutional position under the Peace Treaty. They understood from the Minister explaining the Bill that the mandate was not held from the League of Nations in the meantime, but from the Allied Powers. He raised the question last year because it seemed one of vital importance,† as a different view was taken in different parts of the Empire as to what the real position was.

If New Zealand took a mandate either from the League of Nations or from the Allied Powers, but not through the intermediary of Great Britain, it might be said they were creating for themselves a new status altogether and were claiming to be a sovereign Power. That view was held by a number of constitutional writers at home. They held that the Dominions in entering into the Peace Treaty were not only original members of the League of Nations but were individually responsible for carrying out their share of the burden of the Peace Treaty. It was pointed out by writers at home of great eminence that if it was so it might mean that New Zealand might be called upon to defend every one of the new frontiers set up in Europe. He held the view that New Zealand in signing the Peace Treaty did not intend to hold

---

* See Vol. I., No. 2, of this JOURNAL, page 365.

† See Vol. I., No. 1., of this JOURNAL, page 171.

herself out as an independent Power. It was true that the
act of signing a Peace Treaty or declaring war was usually
exercised only as a sovereign right. The Dominions had no
such intention ; they intended to act simply as component
parts of the Empire.

Parliament and Sovereign Power.

The most notable statement had been made by General
Smuts in South Africa, who claimed that the only constitutional
link in the Empire was the King of England, and he had
refused to admit that the Parliament of Great Britain was
still the sovereign Power in the Empire. They were not
following South Africa in such a view. A similar difficulty
was arising in Canada, which was tending to claim for itself
sovereign powers, and that year had appointed an Ambassador
to Washington. Such a position gave rise to grave problems,
because if Canada's Ambassador to America was to speak on
behalf of the Empire on international problems the most
serious conflicts might arise between Canada and the rest of
the Empire.

They in New Zealand believed that, while they had a very
full autonomy granted to them by Great Britain, yet the
ultimate sovereignty still rested in the Government and
Parliament of Great Britain.

In view of the grave problems that arose out of the Peace
Treaty and the responsibilities that were thrust upon the
signatories to it, it was very important that they in New
Zealand should hold to the view that in their actions in international affairs they were speaking and acting as part of the
Empire and not as a separate sovereign Power. The point
might seem academical, but those who followed what was
going on in Canada and South Africa realised what the danger
was.

The Prime Minister (the Right Hon. W. F. Massey) repeated
what he had said in the debate on the Principal Act, namely
that New Zealand was not a sovereign Power in the ordinary
sense of the term as it was generally used, but was a self-
governing nation within the British Empire.* They were
allied with the other portions of the Empire, and the King
of Great Britain and the Dominions beyond the seas was their
King. As a matter of fact the King was the stronger of the
links that bound the different parts of the Empire together.

When the Imperial War Cabinet was convened and
representatives of the British Dominions were given the right
to sit around the Council Table and take part in the govern-

---

* See Vol. I., No. 1, of this JOURNAL, page 172.

ment of the Empire they ceased to be dependencies and they became partners in the Empire. Instead of what had been done tending to disintegration there was closer union of the different countries of the Empire than ever before.

The League of Nations.

Replying to an interjection, Mr. Massey said that they had been given no reason for the long delay in sending the mandate. He was a strong supporter of the League of Nations. He believed it was a great conception and was sorry that matters had not turned out as well as many of them had expected. So far as the Dominions were concerned they had got to be prepared for anything that might come along.

The comparative failure of the League of Nations led him to say that they would not be doing their duty if they neglected their own defence either at that time or in the years to come.

Labour Views.

Mr. J. McCombs (Labour, *Lyttelton*) said that what he wanted to deal with particularly was in connection with their occupation of Samoa. The Government had not furnished them with a balance-sheet concerning the administration of the plantations, nor supplied any statement in regard to the cost of occupation, administration, or the cost of sending that special group of constables to Samoa. Parliament should be made fully acquainted with what was happening in connection with the administration of the German plantations which New Zealand had taken over. They all seemed to be delightfully vague as to the position that New Zealand occupied in relation to those plantations. It was stated that there would be a valuation made and the value set off against the portion of the war indemnity which might come to New Zealand. The value depended on whether or not the people of that country consented to the continuation of indentured labour in Samoa. New Zealand had a right to consider whether a valuation was to be made on the basis of indentured labour and was to allow out of the indemnity a valuation which might ultimately prove to be on a wrong basis altogether.

The people of New Zealand had got to be convinced that it was more to the interest of New Zealand that they should take over Samoa than that Britain should, or for that matter that America should ; because from the point of view of a naval base those of them who went to Samoa were very readily convinced that it was absolutely valueless and that the Germans made not the slightest attempt to fortify it or to make a naval base there.

Mr. H. E. Holland (Labour, *Buller*) said that the Bill was a repetition of what was in the Expiring Laws Continuance Bill, just a bold clause which repealed Section 6 of the Act* of 1919. Every member of that House knew that that Act conferred on the Government of New Zealand power to rule Samoa by Order in Council. That was a principle that he thought nearly every member of that House objected to. It did not matter to him what the Treaty of Peace or the Covenant of the League of Nations said, if the people of Samoa said something different. The people of Samoa were not involved in the war. They were the victims of a process of political and economic development over which they had no control whatever. The powers which they held over them they only held by virtue of their having wrested them from the Germans ; therefore their title so far as Samoa was concerned, whether it came from the Allied Powers or from the Council of the League of Nations, was based on the rights which the Germans held at Samoa. But however they scanned the documents that were available, they had to admit that the Samoans had not been consulted in the matter of who should exercise power over their islands.

When they raised the question of the dissatisfaction of the Samoans, they were told by the Minister of External Affairs on the one hand that there was practically no serious dissatisfaction at all. They were told by the Prime Minister, on the other hand, that there was grave dissatisfaction and that that dissatisfaction was due to the work of a certain citizen of Samoa who was a German-American.

What had the Prime Minister to say to the statements that were made to them while they were in Samoa ? The whites told in a portion of certain of their statements that " From the beginning the majority of the residents were not in favour of Samoa being placed under the control of New Zealand." He would not place complete reliance on what the white traders of Samoa said if their statements were unsupported, because they were only a minority. They had a right to be heard certainly in so far as their political and other rights were concerned ; but what did the natives say to them when their Faipules came to meet the Parliamentary party at the *Fono* at Mulinu'u, the seat of Samoan Government in Upolu ? They said, " Should the dissatisfaction of the Samoan become greater with the administration, it will then be possible

---

* The clause mentioned by Mr. Holland was deleted from the Bill referred to, the Prime Minister saying it would be dealt with as separate Bill. This is the Bill now reported (see page 158).

for the Samoans to appeal that Samoa shall be ruled from England by the Colonial Office."

That was an indication that in the Samoan mind there was dissatisfaction with New Zealand rule and the Minister knew that one of the gravest reasons for their dissatisfaction was the administration in connection with the influenza epidemic—Colonel Logan's refusal to allow assistance to be brought from Tutuila when people were dying in thousands.

Government Reply to Labour.

The Minister of External Affairs, in his reply, said the debate had drifted back to the old theme of indentured labour in Samoa. The hon. member for Buller (Mr. Holland) and his fellow-members had gone to Samoa with the desire, no doubt, of finding things wrong there, but when they got there they were grievously disappointed. Indentured labour had existed in Samoa for many years, and if the conditions had been so bad there they should have long ago heard a great deal about it from those honourable members. As a matter of fact, the conditions of the Chinese labour were good, and, with no desire, such as the Germans had, of making money out of Samoa, he was endeavouring to make the conditions much better than they had been before. The hon. member for Buller would recognise that they had to take over Samoa as they found it.

Mr. Lee proceeded : " There are large estates which have been run by Chinese labour and not by the Samoans ; and however anxious we may be gradually to instil into the minds of the Samoans that it is in their interest to develop these islands and their products, we cannot do it in five minutes." Continuing, Mr. Lee said that in the meantime they must carry on with the Chinese labour, otherwise the plantations would go to ruin. They were not carrying on Samoa as a trading proposition. They were using the revenues and the proceeds of the estates for the development of the islands ; and it was useless to come there and say there was discontent raging throughout Samoa. What were they discontented with ? If there were grievances they should hear what they were, and they had not heard one.

The funds from the plantations were being spent on the island ; a policy had been laid down of laying out roads, establishing hospitals and schools, and maintaining them, Honourable gentlemen might call the system of employing the Chinese " indenturing," but he was going to call it a " contract," because it was an agreement made between the Chinese, after landing in Samoa, and the authorities. He asked the member for Buller would he allow the Chinese to come in as free labourers if they desired to come in ?

Mr. Holland : " Certainly not the Chinese."

The Minister of External Affairs : " Then if you will not allow them to come in as free labourers or under contract, I say it would be a catastrophe to Samoa."

Imperial and Australian Governments and " Indenture."

It had been said that there had been trouble with the Imperial Government about indenturing Chinese. There was no trouble at all, except that China wanted the men to be returned after the expiration of their service.

He saw that in Australia that day they had the provision that no forced labour, as they called it, should be permitted except for essential public works and services.* In reply to an interjection, Mr. Lee said he was referring to the islands Australia controlled—New Guinea.

The House divided and the Second Reading was carried by 34 votes against 12.

DEBATE IN LEGISLATIVE COUNCIL.

Government by Authority of the King.

The Attorney-General (Hon. Sir Francis Bell), speaking on the Second Reading on the 30th September, explained the Bill and said that they would see by the Treaty of Peace, the surrender by Germany of her overseas possessions was not due to any League of Nations but to the victorious Powers and a number of nations in the League of Nations were not concerned in that. The Allied and victorious Powers assigned Samoa to His Majesty in right of his Dominion of New Zealand. No doubt when the mandate of the League of Nations was issued it would contain provisions relating to the Government of Samoa which they would have to comply with ; but in the meantime they governed Samoa as they would govern it then, after the mandate, by delegation from His Majesty the King and Emperor, and not by the delegation and authority of anyone else in the world.

If the Treaties of Peace Act was not to be made perpetual its extension was necessary. They were not in a position to provide by legislation for the matters that might arise in respect of Samoa ; and if Parliament was to pass laws itself in lieu of Orders in Council, it might be that a mandate might issue from the League of Nations which would be found inconsistent with those laws, and he supposed it would be the

---

* See pages 113, 115 and 117.

duty to call Parliament together to make the laws consistent with the mandate, whereas at present they could make the legislation, by a mere stroke of the pen, coincide with the provisions of the mandate.

SAMOAN MANDATE.

(Samoan Representation in New Zealand Parliament.)

On the occasion of the visit to Samoa of the New Zealand Parliamentary party under the leadership of Sir James Allen (then Minister of External Affairs) in February-March, 1920, the Faipules (members of the Samoan Native Parliament) had presented to Sir James Allen a number of resolutions, one of which was a request that two Samoans should be appointed to attend the meetings of the New Zealand Parliament.

Question by a Native Member.

The Hon. A. T. Ngata (**Liberal,** *Eastern Maori Electorate*) asked the Government on the 11th August (1) whether any decision had been arrived at in regard to the resolution above referred to ? (2) Whether the appointment of Samoans to the Legislative Council would not meet the case ?

Constitutional Position a Bar.

The Minister of External Affairs (**Hon. E. P. Lee**) replied : " The Government have come to a decision on the request for Samoan representation in the New Zealand Parliament, and have sent a communication to the Faipules of Samoa regretting that under existing conditions there was no power to give effect to their wishes. The present constitutional position is that Western Samoa is not an integral part of the territory of New Zealand, and until the people of Samoa, in exercise of the rights conferred by the Treaty of Peace, decide that their country shall be incorporated into the Dominion, no native or British resident of Samoa is eligible for election to the House of Representatives or for appointment to the Legislative Council."

INDENTURED LABOUR IN SAMOA.

(Colonial Office and New Zealand Government.)

The Minister of External Affairs (Hon. E. P. Lee), replying in the House of Representatives on 11th August to a question by Mr. J. McCombs (Labour, *Lyttelton*), who called attention to a statement made in the House of Commons by Colonel Amery, Under-Secretary of State for the Colonies, that he would consult the New Zealand Government regarding laying on the table of the House the correspondence between Britain and New Zealand on the indenturing of Chinese coolies for Samoa, and asked whether the Minister would lay the correspondence on the table of that (the New Zealand) House, said that such a communication had been received and that the Government had replied that they had no objection, and that as soon as advice was received that the correspondence referred to had been laid on the table of the House of Commons a copy would be furnished for the information of honourable members.

The following note is printed in the New Zealand Hansard after Mr. McCombs's question* : —

" The Hon. Sir James Allen made reference to the correspondence when speaking to the citizens at Apia on the recent visit of the Parliamentary party, and gave the purport of some of the correspondence ; and, as the Under-Secretary for the Colonies implies that there is no objection on his part, there does not seem to be any sound reason why the New Zealand Government should withhold the information."

LEAGUE OF NATIONS.

(Representation at Geneva Assembly.)

The Prime Minister (the Right Hon. W. F. Massey), speaking in the House of Representatives on 13th September, 1920 said he wished to refer to the following cablegram which had appeared in the Wellington papers with reference to the Assembly of the League of Nations at Geneva in November next : —" The Secretariat of the League of Nations has no

* Mr. H. E. Holland (Labour, *Buller*) made reference to the attitude of the Imperial Government on the question of indentured labour in speech delivered by him in the House of Representatives on 30th July 1920. (See Vol. I., No. 4, of this JOURNAL, page 725.)

received communications from Australia or New Zealand regarding their representation or subjects for discussion." He then read cablegrams between the New Zealand Government and the Secretary of State for the Colonies regarding the appointment of a representative. He said he thought it was only right to let Parliament know that the Government had requested the High Commissioner, Sir James Allen, to represent New Zealand at the meeting of the League at Geneva on the date mentioned.

NAVAL DEFENCE.

(Defence of Pacific: Foreign Policy, &c.)

The debate on the Naval Estimates took place in the House of Representatives on the 6th August, 1920, when matters of naval policy, the defence of the Pacific, and some aspects of foreign affairs were discussed.

DEBATE IN HOUSE OF REPRESENTATIVES.

Parliament and the Navy: Opposition Criticism.

Mr. T. M. Wilford (Leader of the Opposition) moved in Committee of Supply that the vote of £260,075 be reduced as an indication that the proposal to expend that amount on the upkeep of the " Chatham " was disapproved of. He said the gift of the " Chatham " by the Home Government and its acceptance by the Prime Minister without any reference to Parliament was unwarranted, unnecessary, and useless. They had been promised a day for the discussion of Lord Jellicoe's report, but that had not been given. He moved the reduction of that vote as an indication that both the procedure in obtaining the ship and the refusal to discuss the Naval policy was unwarranted, unconstitutional, and contrary to all precedent and practice in democratic government.

At a later stage Mr. Wilford said that he would rather see the contribution to the British Navy increased, and let the British Navy, while carrying out its functions of policing the world with regard to the maritime position, supply them with the kind of vessel, from time to time, that it thought would be useful to them.

The Prime Minister (the Right Hon. W. F. Massey) replied that the matter had been put in a manner that was bound to raise a bitter party question in connection with the upkeep of the " Chatham." After the assurance of an opportunity to discuss Lord Jellicoe's report, there had not been a half-hour to spare. The House would be given an opportunity of discussing that report, and he thought the discussion should take place when Lord Jellicoe was there in the capacity of Governor-General. Lord Jellicoe had recommended that New Zealand should provide during the next few years three light cruisers as well as submarines and destroyers; but that during the reconstruction period they should not be called upon for more expenditure than could be helped.

Lord Jellicoe had informed him that the vessel coming out would fit in exactly with his proposals. He reminded honourable members of the valuable work done by British light cruisers, and how badly they were wanted out there when the raider "Wolfe" laid mines around the coast. All the Dominions were doing something in the way of defence, and they would be doing less than their duty if they did not do what little was proposed in those estimates. The arrangements about the "Chatham" had arisen out of the discussion he had had with the First Lord of the Admiralty. It was arranged that the annual contribution from New Zealand to the Navy should in future be applied to the upkeep of the "Chatham." It was impossible to consult Parliament because it was not sitting and the thing had to be settled pretty soon because the warships were being disposed of.

The Defence of the Pacific.

Speaking at a later stage in the debate, Mr. Massey said that it would be the duty of those who succeeded that Government to see that New Zealand was protected to the extent her population would allow. The "Chatham" would not be the only ship in the Pacific; there would be the Australian Navy, there would be two British ships in New Zealand waters, there would be several destroyers, and there would be seven submarines. Still more important, there would be battle cruisers. He was not giving away any secrets in saying that but when people said that they were relying on one vessel in their own waters, he must state that that was not the case. He believed that the great majority of New Zealand citizens were strongly of opinion that Naval defence should not be neglected.

Mr. G. Mitchell (**Independent,** *Wellington South*) said he was glad to hear that the "Chatham" was only part of the general scheme for the defence of the Pacific. The "Chatham" was certainly going to cost a little more than they had been paying for Naval defence; but it was a question whether they had ever paid their share. If they were to have the privileges njoyed, they must be prepared to undertake their share of he responsibilities of the Empire.

The Minister of Education (Hon. C. J. Parr) said it seemed lear folly to neglect making suitable provision for the defence f the Dominions. The best they could do would be to follow he advice of the greatest sailor in the world, and contribute heir little mite to a mighty whole.

Mr. C. E. Statham (Independent, *Dunedin Central*) said New Zealand must be guided in Naval matters by the advice f the British Admiralty. That Dominion had got off lightly n its Naval expenditure, for New Zealand had reaped the ullest benefit from the work of the British Navy. As New Zealand grew, she would be faced with the necessity for maintaining a Navy of her own; but he trusted that when that ay came, that Dominion's Navy would, through the centuries o come, fly the British Flag.

Labour and the "Storm Centre."

Mr. H. E. Holland (Labour, *Buller*) said the principle of the Government acting without consulting the House was one to e condemned. Over 25 per cent. of the national income as to be used for the purpose of paying interest and providing nking funds; and if on the top of that huge burden they ere going to pile up other millions to build up a militarism i connection with that country, where was it going to end? The House had yet to learn what the Government would propose for the whole of the Naval and Military expenditure d that Dominion, and far-seeing men who knew the history d militarism would oppose militarism getting a grip on that country. But even if what the militarists said were true it vould still be a debateable matter as to which was the best form of defence. The whole suggestion was that Japan was their possible enemy, and yet Japan was the ally of Britain in the late War. He did not believe the Imperialists when they said that there was danger from Japan. The storm centre would never change to the Pacific unless the people who controlled the world's commerce desired it to change there.

New Zealand Personnel.

The Prime Minister said he felt strongly in the matter of keeping down unnecessary expenditure on militarism. He was out to enable New Zealand to do its fair share in the defence of the Empire. Lord Jellicoe had recommended that New Zealand should find five per cent. of the expenditure. With their enormous export trade, that was not too much to

M

ask—in fact, that was not being asked. All that was being asked was that New Zealand would accept the ship offered by the British Admiralty and then find the necessary expenditure to keep it running. It was part of the arrangement with the Admiralty that their own men were to be placed on the ship. There were no better sailors in the world than the young men of New Zealand, whether Europeans or Polynesians. There had been no secrecy about the matter at all. He had mentioned the matter half a dozen times to the House last Session, and there had not been a single discordant note.

Mr. Downie Stewart (Reform, *Dunedin West*) said the great value of the proposal of the Government was that it incorporated the principle of personal service on the part of New Zealand. Many supported the principle of the cash payment to Britain for the support of the Navy. The whole opinion of the British Admiralty, as he had understood it, had been gradually moving in the direction of trying to work out schemes of defence to allow of local personal service by the peoples of the Dominions. So long as they were saying " There is our payment on the counter and you have to defend us " they might as well hire foreign mercenaries to defend them. If they could, on such very favourable terms receive that ship, and gradually substitute a New Zealand personnel, they should be on the best footing for trying-out the new principle. It was essential that the whole policy of Empire defence should be harmonised at the Imperial Conferences. He took it that the proposal of the Government was a tentative measure, and that the whole position would be reviewed at the Imperial Conference of next year.

Labour Demands voice in Foreign Policy.

Mr. P. Fraser (Labour, *Wellington Central*) said the predominant note of the discussion was one which was fraught with danger to the country, and that was the propensity to constantly accept whatever policy the Imperial authorities agreed to adopt without question—without claiming a right in the direction of shaping that policy. If there was one lesson that ought to be apparent, following the past five or six years, it was that surely the time had come when the people of the world should have some say in the direction of the foreign policy on which their lives and their future depended.

The amendment was negatived and the vote of £260,45 agreed to.

DEFENCE POLICY.

(Annual Defence Report: Duty to Support Navy, &c.)

The Defence Report of the Officer Commanding the New Zealand Military Forces was laid on the Table of the House on 19th August, 1920.

The report is concerned largely with the demobilisation of the New Zealand Expeditionary Force and administration in connection therewith. In it the following lessons of the War as applied to the Dominion are emphasised :—

1. An efficient Army can quickly be organised provided every man has had a limited amount of training, and there is available an ample supply of modern equipment and highly-trained officers and non-commissioned officers.

2. The large percentage of man-power found by medical examination to be physically unfit for service points to the necessity of a thorough course of physical training for all youths.

Dealing with the question of reorganisation, the Report states that experience in carrying out the existing system of training has shown :—

1. The attempt to carry out training in sparsely-populated districts has been expensive, unproductive of efficiency, and very burdensome on the trainee and his employer.

2. The limitation of training to a Territorial Force having a maximum establishment of 30,000 has resulted in over 50 per cent. of those who are liable under the Act receiving no training, which has caused great dissatisfaction, while the physically unfit who would benefit most by the course of physical training have been exempted.

The Government is urged when considering the immediate need for economy not to overlook the vital necessity for efficiency, and to decide the future Defence policy as soon as possible in order that the Defence Department can proceed with the necessary reorganisation.

DEBATE IN HOUSE OF REPRESENTATIVES.

Mr. T. M. Wilford (Liberal, *Hutt)* opened the debate on the Defence Report on 19th August and said they were again under the difficulty that members of the House had to discuss a report they had not seen. He proposed to say something in reference to the Defence Forces, and to base his remarks on the Defence Report of 1919. On page 1 of that report, which was dated 15th August, 1919, it was stated that :—

> the experience gained amply proves that a more concentrated period of training at the ages of eighteen to twenty, inclusive, instead of extending over the ages of eighteen to twenty-five as at present, is very desirable.

M 2

The report of 1919 further said that

a condensing of seven years' present training obligations into three years would, I feel sure, prove much more economical and convenient to industrial and pastoral affairs.

He considered the period of three years was too long, and was unnecessary. He would like to know whether the Government thought three years necessary still, fo he did not.

The Minister of Defence (Hon. Sir R. Heaton Rhodes): "That is, in regard to territorials?"

Mr. Wilford: "Yes."

Continuing, Mr. Wilford asked the Government to seriously consider whether it would not be possible to further curtail the period as a result of the lessons of the War, as they had seen how quickly men could learn the necessary discipline and overtake the required training.

It would be well for the Government, in dealing with the defence of that country, to give the House a concrete proposal setting out in detail exactly what it would cos for defence on land, on sea, and in the air, and prepare a sceme for the absolute co-ordination of the three branches. H was certain there was a changed mentality in the people of that country; and, while they did not object to the encouragment of the cadet system, he thought it would be found that there was strong opinion that the training for Territorials should be reduced, and that the expenditure for highly-paid officers and staff should be curtailed as much as possible.

A Plea for Economy.

Hon. J. A. Hanan (Liberal, Invercargill) said there was demand throughout the Dominion that, where consistent with efficiency, economy should be the order of the day. The Department was attention more directed than to De They asked the Minister to give full information on expenditure had been cut down, and generally that the minimum expenditure essential to maintain an organised prepared to meet emergencies.

Physical Culture and Military Training.

When war broke out, they had to provide medical examinations, physical culture and dental They might have been spared that Bill for making fit the men who went into camp if they had re treatment when they were children. All that the need of beginning training with the child moting health and physical strength.

Referring to the Senior Cadets, Mr. Hanan said that some people urged strongly that they should go back to the Junior Cadet system under which they had boys doing drill and many exercises which they did again when they entered the Senior Cadets. Consequently the latter system was not attractive to them. The little boys should take part in games, have plenty of light, fresh air, and light exercises.

In reply to the Prime Minister's question : " Would you leave the military training out ? " Mr. Hanan said : " Yes, certainly, for the junior boys." He hoped that the policy of the Government, so far as the children were concerned, would be more in the direction of physical culture and training for manhood and citizenship.

It seemed that the Government could not make up its mind in regard to a land defence policy. By hesitating, it was undoubtedly deserving of adverse criticism.

Defence under the Education Department.

Mr. A.S. Malcolm (Reform, *Clutha***)** said he had reached the position where he thought they could afford to suspend the territorial system, at least for the present, and substitute a system o training in their primary and secondary schools and in the universities. At a later stage, Mr. Malcolm stated, tha the Defence League insisted that its scheme was a branch of their educational institutions, and he asked, therfore, why it should not be under the Education Department

The Navy New Zealand's Duty.

The value of the Navy to New Zealand was frequently forgotten, and yet their whole security depended upon the Navy. If the British Navy lost command of the sea for a few months only, the position of New Zealand would be a very unhappy one. New Zealand might be stuffed full of troops, yet they would still be subject to raids from any Power which had command of the sea.

They were not doing their share towards the upkeep of the Navy ; Britain was contributing four or five times as much per head of population as was New Zealand, if he remembered rightly.

Imperial Unity : " Standing Out " of a War.

There was another aspect of the defence question. They talked about giving their youths military training, yet when all was said and done they almost entirely overlooked —in that House especially—the essence of defence, which was the unity of the British Empire. It was a comparatively small advantage to the Imperial Government to know they had, say, a hundred thousand trained men, if the Imperial Government was not absolutely assured that in the event of war all the forces of the Empire would be at the disposal of the Empire.

The Dominions had been encouraged more and more of recent years to consider themselves as quasi-independent— entitled to stand out of any war if they cared to do so. Of course none of them could imagine any Dominion standing out of a war ; but it might easily happen that there should be a war in which the interests of Britain only were concerned— in which, at any rate, the interests of the Dominions were very small indeed—and it might be a matter of doubt then to the Imperial Government whether the Dominions would be prepared to sacrifice men and money in a war of that character. The least element of doubt in such a question would of necessity weaken the position of the Imperial Government. The most essential factor in Imperial defence was Imperial unity, towards which that House, at any rate, had done nothing, simply because it had never had a chance of even discussing the matter, though he had asked for it year after year.

He believed that his scheme had the support of the great majority of the people of that country. They did not lack patriotism, but they were weary of the present system ; they believed it had not given the results it had promised. He would like to see the matter very seriously discussed and considered.

Mr. G. Mitchell* (Independent, *Wellington South*) said he regretted that it was necessary for that country and for the whole of the Empire to continue to be prepared to defend themselves. They would all be very glad if they could do away with all military training and the expense of it, but that was not practicable. In reply to the hon. member for Clutha who was advocating a system whereby they were to hand over their Defence Department to the Education Department and to train boys up to fourteen years of age, he did not think military training could be given to them at all.

Military training should take place between the time of leaving school and twenty years of age. If they had their youths trained in the fundamental principles of movement mobilisation and shooting, it would not be necessary to give them any further training until they were mobilised to go

---

* Mr. Mitchell was on active service with the New Zealand Expeditionary Force, and held the rank of Lieut.-Colonel.

to war. It would be impossible to get any standard of military training in any of their schools, with the exception of the universities. He agreed with the Acting-Leader of the Opposition, Mr. Wilford, that their training could be cut down and that they could have just as much efficiency with far less expenditure than they had had in the past. They had been inclined always to think that unless they imported somebody to " run their show " they did not have efficiency. Their officers had proved to be the equal of any officers in the field, and he did not think it was right that they should have had an Imperial officer there throughout the war who was taken at his own valuation, plus probably 100 per cent., and they had made him practically a dictator.

The question was, were they going to adopt the policy of their Labour friends, who had cut the defence of the country out of their platform and wished to see none at all ; were they going to adopt the policy of the member for Clutha, and have a school policy only; or were they going to adopt the policy of the Defence League,* whose proposals were largely those of General Russell, who was considered one of the finest divisional commanders in the British Army ?

The Minister of Defence (Hon. Sir R. Heaton Rhodes) said he thought they had the feeling of the country shown pretty clearly during the last general election—and the feeling was echoed in that House—that they must curtail their defence scheme and cut down the Estimates where possible. At the same time there was a strong feeling among thinking people that although they might have a small body of trained men, those men should be efficient. The General Officer Commanding was working out the details of a scheme, and when it was completed he would place it before the Cabinet and after approval it would go on to the Committee of Defence. There would be no camps that year, but it was not proposed to abolish camps altogether. There would be the Cadet Force, and after that there would be a period in camp. After the Cadets had completed their period he thought that if they could put them into one camp and then pass them on to the Reserve they should be meeting the wishes of the country.

The war had shown them that the men could be trained in a short period ; and the men after three or four months' training could take their places with almost any troops in the world. But they could not train their officers and non-

---

* It would appear that Mr. Mitchell embodied in his speech the proposals of the Defence League.

commissioned officers in a short period, and they must have an efficient staff to train them.*

He thought they should get more good out of aviation by using it for civil purposes, and an Air Board had been set up to consider all questions of aviation and advise the Minister.

A Committee of Defence had been set up and as Minister of Defence he became *ex-officio* a member of that Committee.

He did not think the plan as outlined by the hon. member for Clutha would be adopted. He thought their Education Department was sufficiently loaded with the burden of education without taking on the additional burden of military training.

The motion was agreed to.

DEFENCE ESTIMATES.

(Further Debate on Policy, &c.)

The Minister of Defence brought down the Estimates of the Defence Department amounting to £550,593 in Committee of Supply on the 27th August. These gave rise to a further debate on Defence Policy. (See also pages 171 *et seq.*)

The Minister of Defence (Hon. Sir R. Heaton Rhodes) said the Estimates were for the current year, and most of the expenditure had already been incurred.

Ministers were fully aware of the demand of the country for a reduction in the expenditure on defence, and they were prepared to cut it down as far as they possibly could.

Mr. H. E. Holland (Labour, *Buller*) protested against the extraordinary amount of money involved in connection with the military system of that country in a time of peace. There was no information as to what the policy was to be. He moved the reduction of the item, " Headquarters, £8,979," by £1 —as expressing disapproval of the huge military expenditure provided for in the Estimates.

Speaking at a later stage, Mr. Holland said that no sane person would object to physical training, but people did object to the military idea being introduced into the schools. The

---

* Speaking in Committee of Supply later, and replying to a suggestion that the training of the Forces should cease at 21, the Minister of Defence said that it was not intended to go beyond 21 or 22. The present training was for seven years and it was proposed to cut that down to three years. The Cadets would be trained up to 18 and then they would spend a period in camp before being drafted to their units. Although it was proposed to suspend the camps for two or three years, it was the intention to train officers and N.C.O.'s.

platitude that in time of peace they must be prepared for war had been heard in the House that evening. It was a motto given effect to in Germany prior to the war. There was a tendency in that country and in Australia to regard Japan as an enemy, and to predict that the next war would be in the Pacific. Within the next twelve months, he predicted, there would be a fury of propaganda by the Capitalist Press in that direction.

Mr. D. G. Sullivan (Labour, *Avon*) said that he had never held that it was unnecessary to make provision for the defence of the country, but in view of the present economic position it was somewhat extraordinary that the House should now be asked to allocate this large sum. The increase in expenditure of £50,000 coming at the conclusion of the Great War which was to have ended all war was an indication that the Government was largely influenced by militarist opinion and had no faith in the League of Nations. It was thus setting a bad example to the sister Dominions and encouraging other countries to increase rather than decrease their armaments.

Mr. E. J. Howard (Labour, *Christchurch South*) said it seemed to him that the Dominion had not yet learned the lesson that it ought to have learned as a result of the medical examination to which men were put when they were called up for service. It was not possible to make boys physically fit by treating them in the way they had been treated in the cadet system. Boys that were underfed could not be made physically fit by placing a musket in their hands and marching them up and down barrack squares.

Labour and Training for the Sea.

As New Zealand was an island country its first line of defence must be on the sea, and if the Government would adopt a policy of owning its own trading ships the boys would be receiving a training that would be of service to the State from an industrial point of view and would be trained to the sea if trouble came. Again if the Government would assist in the development of the fishing industry by the introduction of trawlers they would develop a class of young man who would be useful in industry and, like the men of the North Sea, of the utmost value should trouble arise. These young men could also be trained for industrial aviation and so would form the nucleus of a corps for defence in time of need.

Mr. E. Newman (Reform, *Manawatu*) said there should be no Party issue on such an important question. It was very important that the Dominion should face the expense of defence even at the present juncture for the reason that, notwithstanding the Navy, land defence was still imperative.

The country was suffering from war-weariness, which was accentuated by the extreme scarcity of labour ; but he believed in universal military training and, while the Government might find it necessary to abandon the yearly camps just at present, he hoped that they would not abandon the principle of every fit man being trained to help to defend his country and Empire in time of need. He was against the development of militarism, but the defence vote should not be unduly reduced.

Mr. Downie Stewart (Reform, *Dunedin West*) said he hoped the member for Buller would withdraw his amendment and allow the vote to pass without a division. Even the members of the Labour Party, although they had criticised the Estimates, had expressed the opinion that some system of defence was necessary for the Dominion. The real criticism had been on the ground of expense, and all the speakers had expressed the desire of the public that the defence system should be cut down to the minimum consistent with efficiency. But the system must be a democratic system, and that involved universal training ; thence the difficulty in cutting down expense. He hoped the Government, while paying attention to public feeling, would not allow efficiency to be sacrificed for the sake of apparent economy.

Mr. Holland's motion was defeated by 43 votes against 9.

IMMIGRATION RESTRICTION ACT.

(Relations with Foreigners: Treatment of Chinese, Indians, &c.)

The Bill was read a first time in the House of Rrepresentatives on 11th August, 1920, and a report and summary of the measure appears in Vol. I., No. 4, page 729, of this JOURNAL ; it was read a second time on the 14th September and a third time on the 16th September. It passed its third reading in the Legislative Council on the 29th September after some slight technical amendments had been made by the Statutes Revision Committee, and received the Governor General's assent on 9th November.

DEBATE IN HOUSE OF REPRESENTATIVES.

The debate on the Second Reading of the above Bill took place on 14th September, 1920.

A "White" New Zealand.

The Prime Minister (the Right Hon. W. F. Massey), in moving the Second Reading of the Bill, quoted figures showing the increase of immigration, and drew attention to the large number of Asiatics. He said: "The Bill is the result of a deep-seated sentiment on the part of a huge majority of the people of this country that this Dominion shall be what is often called a 'White' New Zealand, and that the people who come here should, as far as it is possible for us to provide for it, be of the same way of thinking from the British Empire point of view—I might have said the Imperial point of view, but I say from the British Empire point of view—and that they shall be people who will be loyal to the Empire, loyal to the Crown, and loyal to this country when they become its citizens."

Continuing, Mr. Massey said that no injustice was intended to the people of any other country who came to New Zealand, and the Government had a perfect right to safeguard its immigration policy. They wanted to keep the race of the Dominion as pure as possible.

The "Royal Assent" Question.

In replying to an interjection as to whether the Royal assent to such a Bill was required, the Prime Minister quoted a resolution of the Imperial War Conference of 1918, referring back to the Conference of 1917, which said that each of the several communities of the British Commonwealth should enjoy complete control of the composition of its own population by means of restriction on immigration. He thought that gave the Government a right to pass that or any similar Bill while it was understood that they were extending the same rights to other countries of the British Empire. Replying to a further interjection, Mr. Massey said that it was just possible that the Bill would have to be reserved for the Royal assent if it affected countries with which Britain had a treaty. The poll-tax on Chinese was not to be interfered with, and he thought no increase in that tax was necessary. He anticipated a considerable decrease in Chinese immigration.

Mr. Downie Stewart (Reform, *Dunedin West*), in endorsing the Prime Minister's statement as to maintaining a " White " New Zealand, said that they had grave reason to fear that that policy was being menaced by the large influx of Asiatics. As to whether the Bill would require the Royal assent or not, he gathered from the quotation of the Prime Minister that the resolutions of the Imperial Conference merely dealt with the movements of the population within the Empire.

Under the Bill the Government took power to control the movements of foreigners coming to New Zealand from Europe and Asia, and he thought that some necessity might arise for obtaining the Imperial consent, as there were a number of such countries with which Britain was engaged by treaty. The policy of the British Government was well expressed by Mr. Joseph Chamberlain at the first Colonial Conference in 1897, when he said that his Government sympathised with the white inhabitants of those Colonies which were in close proximity to Asia in their determination not to suffer an Asiatic influx.

Relations with Foreigners.

He questioned whether they were using a form of words in the Bill which would avoid hurting the feelings of foreigners. Certain nations might be exempted from the clause requiring a permit, and he had no doubt that the Government would exclude by Order in Council all nations except the Chinese. It was not a very statesmanlike way. It was a very poor compliment to a citizen of America or of France to be told that he was dependent on the good-will of the Ministry of the day for his admission to New Zealand. One must consider what the real difficulty would be if an influx of Asiatics were rushed into the Dominion. In speaking on the introduction of Chinese into South Africa, Sir Edward Grey had said that if they allowed the Chinese in they would develop the country very rapidly, but that was not the point at issue. The question was what sort of civilisation were they building up; if it were composed of elements which were bound to conflict with their customs, their habits and their politics, then they were building on an unstable foundation. That applied very clearly and emphatically to New Zealand. He was doubtful about the retention of the poll-tax. There had been three restrictions on the introduction of Chinese into the Dominion —the poll-tax, the education test and the registration of finger-prints. The first never served its purpose ; the only other part of the Empire that submitted the Chinese to a poll-tax was Canada, and when war broke out negotiations were proceeding for the repeal of the Act and the substitution of a limitation of the numbers to be absorbed annually. He tried to look at the question from the point of view of New Zealand, but he also tried to keep in view that China was a country of four hundred million people on the borders of the Pacific with whom they could not afford to quarrel. The only reason for China submitting to their legislation was that they had no effective army and navy. They in New Zealand dared not impose it on Japan. He had pointed out to the Chinese Consul-General that New Zealand was resolved to exclude, or strictly limit, the immigration from China. The Consul said that his Government did not resent it, and that they were prepared to make an agreement with New Zealand similar to the one with Canada. What he wanted to put to the House was whether it was not a fair thing to adopt some such proposal. There was a treaty made in 1894 between Britain and China, and he submitted that the legislation was in conflict with the treaty obligations of Britain.

He did not think the oath of allegiance would be effective : if a man was coming there with traitorous intent they would not limit him by a formal lip assent to any oath of allegiance.

The "International" View-Point.

Mr. H. Holland (Labour, *Buller*) said he wished to make clear the international view-point which did not place a bar upon the individual because of the colour of his skin, or the country in which he was born. When considering the possible influx into that country of a people whose standards of living were necessarily lower than their own, and who did not know the conditions to which they were coming, then it became necessary the legislation should be framed, not only to protect the standards of life of the people of New Zealand, but also to protect the coloured immigrants who might be brought there. The Labour Party proposed that the poll-tax should be abolished. They thought that a bona fide education tax should be imposed, and that there should be a definite limitation of the number of Asiatics entering New Zealand in any given year. Referring to sub-clause (2) clause 5* he doubted the power of that Parliament to pass such a measure. It meant that Parliament was being asked to regard the fact that a man was British born as nothing at all. It was being asked to tear away from such person his natural-born rights of citizenship, and that was something that could not be defended. That clause was one which the House ought not to agree to.

· He questioned the meaning of clause 6.† He could read

---

* " A person shall not be deemed to be of British birth and parentage by reason that he or his parents or either of them is a naturalised British subject, or by reason that he is an aboriginal native, or the descendant of an aboriginal native of any dominion other than the Dominion of New Zealand or of any colony or other possession or of any protectorate of His Majesty."

† " 6. (1) The Governor-General may, by Order in Council, from time to time declare that the provisions of this part of this Act shall not apply to nations or peoples specified in such Order in Council. . . .

" (3) A person shall not be deemed to be actually of such specified nation or people by reason that he or his parents or either of them is a subject by naturalisation of any specified nation or people, or that he is an original native of any colony or possession of such specified nation or people."

one meaning into it—if a day came when it was held necessary to import cheap labour into New Zealand, the Cabinet might set aside the provisions of the Act and import such labour in defiance of the wishes of the people. There was too much government by Order in Council in New Zealand. Sub-clause 3 provided that if the Government thought it necessary to exempt a certain nation they could do so; but that individual members of that nation who were objectionable to the Government might be denied the benefit of such exemption. For instance, if a man was an Indian, the Government was given power to say to him that although they were exempting the Indian people from the provisions of the Bill, yet they would not exempt certain Indians from it. It gave the Government an opportunity to apply a class principle—it might happen that certain of the men who were figuring very prominently in the national life of India would be shut out of New Zealand by reason of the existence of that clause.

He did not take any serious exception to the oath. He agreed with the suggestion that the oath was not going to keep any one out. The only people that it would keep out would be members of the Society of Friends, whom many thought were a desirable class of immigrants.

Maori View of Diplomacy.

The Hon. A. T. Ngata (Liberal, *Eastern Maori District)* said that he had no doubt that the Bill was one of the measures which should be reserved for the Royal assent. It seemed to him that no party in that House was opposed to the restric-tion of the immigration of Asiatics. As a representative of the aboriginal race of New Zealand he sympathised with the first immigrants—the British—in the attitude they had taken up in regard to the influx of Asiatics. His reason was that the best civilisation that had so far appeared on the face of the globe was that which was represented by the British race. It might not have been the best in every respect, but in regard to morality and sense of justice it was the best that had appeared so far. For that reason everything should be done to fill up the waste places of New Zealand and Australia with descendants of the race that represented that aspect of civilisation. Referring to the suggestion of diplomacy, he thought it was a very nice suggestion, but in his opinion the time had come for the British Dominions to lay their cards on the table; they had been far too diplomatic in the past. It would be the height of diplomacy if the British Dominions were to make it known, through the Imperial Government, to the Republic of China that the people of this country did not desire any Chinese to come into it. Why should they not make that desire known by a statute ? That would express the view of the representatives of the people and would be the authoritative voice of the people of that country.

IN LEGISLATIVE COUNCIL.

Relations with India.

The Attorney-General (Hon. Sir Francis Bell), speaking in the Legislative Council on 29th September on the Third Reading, said that when the Bill had been before the Statutes Revision Committee the question had been discussed as to their duty towards their fellow subjects in India. The members of the Committee had desired that he should take the opportunity of placing on record that what had influenced them in coming to the conclusion was in no sense unfair or unjust to them. It was admitted that the Bill affected them as it did all other nations. The people of India were put on exactly the same footing as people of every other race or colour and every other foreign nation. Sir Francis Bell then quoted at length from the report of the proceedings of the Imperial War Conference of 1918, and summarised the position by saying : " India was the first time represented at the Imperial Conference in 1917, and her representatives put before the Conference certain alternative suggestions, the suggestion of reciprocity being subsequently adopted by the Conference of 1918. Then, as a result of that, the representatives of India themselves moved at the War Conference the resolutions which I have read, and nothing in this Bill departs from the letter or the spirit of those resolutions. We have endeavoured to keep strictly within the limits of the resolutions which the Indian delegates moved at the Conference. The right of visit, which they desired, has been conceded. The right of settlement they have admitted to be a matter for determination by each Government, and they have declared that they have no cause for complaint on that point."

Sir Francis Bell then moved the Third Reading of the Bill.

ELECTIVE EXECUTIVE BILL.

In the earlier part of the Session a motion by Mr. C. E. Statham (Independent, *Dunedin Central*) to the effect that the Cabinet should, if not elected by the House, at least be elected by the dominant party, was accepted by the Prime Minister as a no-confidence motion, and was defeated. A report of the debate on the question appears on pages 712, &c., of Volume I., No. 4, of this JOURNAL.

A Bill dealing with the subject was introduced by Mr. Statham in the House of Representatives and read a first time on the 13th August.

The object of the Bill is to provide for an elected Executive Council, which is, in turn, to appoint the Prime Minister; and further, to prevent a dissolution taking place without the consent of the House.

Clause 2 of the Bill provides that there shall be an Executive Council of twelve members, eleven of whom shall hold ministerial office and one to be without portfolio.

The method of election is set forth in Clause 3 of the Bill, which provides that upon the first assembling of Parliament after each general election, and as soon as the Speaker has been elected, the members shall proceed to elect ten Ministers from their number, and one Minister and one Executive Councillor, without portfolio, from the members of the Legislative Council (Clause 3, Sub-clause (1)).

Nominations of each candidate signed by six members of the House and by the candidate himself, shall be handed in to the Speaker not later than 6 p.m. of the day after the Speaker's own election (Clause 3, Sub-clause (2)).

If more than the required number of nominations be received, then an election is to take place immediately, under the supervision of the Speaker. Under certain circumstances, the Speaker is given a casting vote in case of an equality of voting (Clause 3, Sub-clauses (3) and (4)).

When the Governor-General shall have approved of the Ministers and Executive Councillor so elected, they shall appoint one of their number to be Prime Minister and shall also allocate the various ministerial portfolios (Clause 4).

The term of office of the Executive is to be for the duration of Parliament and thereafter until successors are elected, unless any of them shall die, resign, or become disqualified. If any such vacancy occurs during Session, the same is to be filled by election (Clause 8); but if during recess, then provision is made for a temporary appointment by Order in Council until Parliament re-assembles, when a fresh election to fill the vacancy is to take place in the ordinary way (Clauses 7, 8, and 9).

Nothing in the Bill is to affect the existing legislation relating to the appointment of members of the Executive as representatives of the native race (Clause 10). The right is given to every Minister to speak in both Houses of Parliament on any Bill or resolution affecting his Department or introduced by him, but not to vote except in the House in which he holds his seat (Clause 11).

Finally, neither the Executive nor any Minister shall recommend the Governor-General to dissolve the House of Representatives without the consent of the House (Clause 12).

LEGISLATIVE COUNCIL AMENDMENT ACT.

This Act passed through all stages and received the Governor-General's assent on 28th October, 1920.

The main purpose of the Act is to postpone the operation of the Act of 1914, which made the Legislative Council an elective chamber in place of a nominative one. Provision is made in Clause 3 that a date for the commencement of the Act of 1914 shall be appointed by proclamation.

There is also a technical amendment which deals with the rules for fixing boundaries of electoral divisions and the number of members to be elected by each division.

WAR REGULATIONS CONTINUANCE ACT.

("Seditious" Strikes, &c.)

The above Bill, embodying the views of the Government as to what regulations in force during the war should be continued, and what should be repealed as being no longer necessary for the public welfare, was introduced by the Prime Minister in the House of Representatives. The Bill also contains certain new proposals relating to the control of wharves in case of industrial strife. It passed its Third Reading on 31st August, 1920. It was amended in some technical details in the Legislative Council and passed its Third Reading in that Chamber on 17th September, and received the Governor-General's Assent on 6th October. There was a lengthy debate on the Second Reading in the House of Representatives, the main point at issue being the criticism by Labour members of the powers proposed to be vested in the Ministry by means of Orders in Council in regard to controlling wharves and industries.

The Act provides for the continuance of certain provisions of the War Regulations Act, 1914, and its amendments, and for the repeal of others no longer necessary.

Regulation 13 in the Second Schedule of the Act provides that the control of any wharf may be taken by the Government and no person allowed to enter such wharf except by permission.

Regulation 14 provides that any industry may be declared one which is essential for the public welfare. It describes a "seditious strike" as one which is intended to interfere with the carrying on of any industry declared by Order in Council to be an industry for the public welfare—a "seditious lock-out" is similarly described.

N

DEBATE IN HOUSE OF REPRESENTATIVES.

The Prime Minister (the Right Hon. W. F. Massey), when moving the Second Reading of the Bill on 28th July, and in reply to a suggestion by the Hon. A. T. Ngata (Liberal, *Eastern Maori Electorate*) that it should be sent to the Statutes Revision Committee, said he was quite willing that this should be done. It was an important Bill—a Bill that ought to be looked into very closely by members. He would be satisfied if members agreed to the Second Reading after he had finished.

Mr. H. Holland (Labour, *Buller*) : " It will not be agreed to without debate."

Labour Opposition to Power by Order in Council.

It was agreed, on the motion of Mr. Massey, that the Bill be read a second time, *pro 'forma*, and be referred to the Statutes Revision Committee. The debate on the Bill was taken on the 24th August, when,

Mr. H. Holland said that if it was necessary to continue any of the provisions of the war-time legislation it should have been done in a form which did not bear the title of a War Regulation Act. During the war-period the privilege of trial by jury had been taken away from any man who came before the courts charged with sedition. The whole of the law of sedition had been written anew, and to the law of seditious intent had been added the law of seditious tendency. That law was to remain, and it would be possible to drag men before the Courts charged in peace time with offences that were alleged to be extraordinarily provided for in war time.

Mr. E. J. Howard (Labour, *Christchurch South*) protested against the Bill being placed on the statute book. They were supposed to be living in a state of peace with the world, and yet the Bill proposed to bestow upon the Ministry most extra-ordinary powers. If there were provisions in the Bill which the Government thought should be enacted, then those pro-visions ought to be brought down in honest legislation in a separate Bill which the House could discuss in a proper way.

A " Reform " View.

Mr. R. A. Wright (Reform, *Wellington Suburbs*) did not think that the speeches made by the Labour members should be allowed to pass without reply. It was true that injury could be done by giving any Government too much power ; but in the regulations before them there was much that could not be set down in printed words. It was impossible to put everything in a clause in a Bill, and it had been found by experience that it was necessary to give the Governor in Council power to deal with difficult issues that might arise. He admitted the regulations relating to wharf control were drastic, but there was good reason for them. What had happened on the water-front there in Wellington? Apparently there was organised systematic pillage. During war, things worked much more smoothly than they did now, and the cost of living was cheaper then and they were not deprived of much in New Zealand. Since the War the position had changed, and instead of having peace they had trouble from one end of the country to the other. Something must be done, as it was impossible for them to continue in the state they were then in.

A "Time-Limit" Suggestion.

Mr. T. K. Sidey (Liberal, *Dunedin South*), speaking on the Third Reading on 31st August, said he thought it unreasonable that a number of those restrictive regulations should be perpetuated for all time. Most members of the House in acquiescing and offering no opposition to the measure did so because they felt that they had not yet got back to normal times and that the Government might have justification for continuing a number of the regulatons at that time. He suggested that when the Bill got to another place the Prime Minister might place some restriction on the time within which, if they had not been revoked, the regulations would go out. There was a clause under which all regulations not expressly continued were revoked. He asked whether the regulations restricting the importation of goods from late enemy countries were revoked. He believed that public sentiment in that country was against the admission of goods from an enemy country; but he doubted whether they had done the best thing in the interests of the consumers. Information he had received pointed to the fact that British and American merchants had been able to step in and buy up German goods at a very low rate, and send them out at a very high price to other countries.

The Prime Minister's Reply.

The Prime Minister (the Right Hon. W. F. Massey), in moving the Third Reading of the Bill, stated that the reason for Clause 13 was industrial trouble. He had seen the wharves in that country in the possession of strikers in 1913. Men in charge of Government stock on Somes's Island had to obtain a permit before goods could be carried to the island. It was worse than the tyranny of the Czar. What happened in 1913 might happen again, and he wanted the Government to have

N 2

power to prevent it.   No section of the people—employers or workers—should be allowed to tyrannise and cause hardship and inconvenience and perhaps some serious loss to other sections without the Government having the right to step in and prevent such a thing taking place.   The Labour members would have the country believe that the Government were a set of tyrants attempting to take away the parliamentary liberties of democracy.   The real enemies of the workers were the people who were then doing their best to stir up unrest. He believed the workers were beginning to find them out. Although the Labour members had denounced the regulations, they could not give one instance of injustice.

German Goods.

He did not agree with the statement that German goods were coming into the country.   People importing goods into that country had to declare the country of origin.   He had not forgotten what had taken place during the War, and he was not anxious to commence business with Germany.   It was almost impossible for goods to filter through from America as had been suggested.   If by chance they did they had to pay a preferential duty.   If it was proved that German goods were brought through America, and sold in New Zealand as American goods, a very heavy penalty attached.

DEBATE IN LEGISLATIVE COUNCIL.

The Attorney-General (Hon. Sir Francis Bell), in moving the Second Reading on 24th September, said that Honourable members were aware that the war regulations had been in force for a very considerable time.   Some were made under the original Act of 1914 almost immediately after the passing of that Act ; they would expire according to the terms of this Act, at the expiration of twelve months from the termination of the war with Germany.   A number of the regulations had become obsolete and ought to be revoked—they should have been revoked before—but in the discussion between the late Solicitor-General and the Government it appeared that among the regulations of certain dates there were included regulations which it was considered wise to continue.   Therefore it was not possible to revoke the regulations by reference to the date of the order in council or to the Gazette in which they appeared. After consideration it was thought just that there should be set out at length in the schedule of the Bill the regulations which the Government desired to preserve, all others being revoked.   Power was given to the Governor-General to amend those regulations to give effect to them as they stood, but not further or otherwise—the power of the Governor-General to make regulations of that restrictive nature had ceased, but the power to make more effective those regulations which were before the Council in the Schedule was preserved.

The regulations empowering the Government to take possession of wharves necessary in time of war were no less necessary in time of peace. That power the Government had never exercised ; but having had it, and knowing as they did the advantage which the possession of that power had given to the country and the advantage it had been to the peace of the country, they could not advise Parliament to dispense with it in time of peace.

He admitted the regulations relating to seditious strikes were more questionable. The matter had been thoroughly argued out in another place, and practical unanimity had been arrived at there in the conclusion that it was not safe at that time to put an end to that restraint, which, again, had been but little exercised ; but possession of the power had been of almost incalculable advantage. He moved the Second Reading of the Bill.

MASTER AND APPRENTICE BILL.

(Apprenticing Immigrant Boys on Farms.)

This Bill, which embodied the proposals of the Government in regard to the apprenticing of boys immigrating from Great Britain to New Zealand to engage in farm work, was read a first time in the House of Representatives on 11th August, 1920, and, after having been amended in Committee, passed its Third Reading on 28th September. It passed its Second Reading in the Legislative Council on 29th September, was read a third time on the 14th October, and became law on the 28th October.

An explanatory memorandum is attached to the Bill which sets forth that the first part relates to farm apprentices whose passages from England to New Zealand are assisted by the Government. The Master and Apprentice Act 1908 requires that the Indenture of Apprenticeship should be executed by the parent or guardian of the boy and by the employer. Compliance with this provision would be impossible in cases where arrangement is made for immigration of boys to be subsequently employed. The boys being under age, their own contract would not bind them, and the proposal of the Bill is that the Government shall undertake the control and care of such boys and therefore enter into arrangement with the boys' parents or guardians in the United Kingdom for the employment of the boys in New Zealand, and for the provision of proper food, clothing and comfort. It is pointed out that unless the boy is bound to remain in his employment and be subject to such control as is provided in the Master and Apprentice Act it would be impossible for the Government to perform its engagements. Further, it is stated that it would be necessary that the boys should be under some control from the time of their departure until their engagement in New Zealand. To attain these objects provision is made for an Indenture signed by the High Commissioner and the boy to become binding in England.

Special provision is made in Sub-clause (6) of Clause 2 enabling the Minister to alter the Indenture, signed in England, in a manner advantageous to the boy, but not otherwise. Sub-clause (10) of the same Clause provides that the apprenticeship shall extend to the age of 20 years. This is necessary because it is not intended to engage boys of an age less than sixteen and it is desired to engage them up to an age of somewhat over eighteen years, but under nineteen. Sub-clause (4) of Clause 2 provides that after the first year the apprentice shall receive full wages according to his age and capacity; such wages to be not less than the wages ruling in the district for lads of like age and capacity.

The second part relates to farm apprenticeship of boys already resident in New Zealand. The benefits of Part 1 are extended to such apprentices also.

AMENDMENT.

In Committee on 20th September, 1920, Sub-clause (4) of Clause 2 was amended to the effect that the amount to be paid to the apprentice during the first year should be stated in the Indenture. ·

DEBATE IN HOUSE OF REPRESENTATIVES.

The Minister of Immigration (Hon. W. Nosworthy) having explained the proposals of the Bill, moved the Second Reading on the 8th September, 1920.

Mr. G. Witty (Liberal, *Riccarton*), said that a boy coming out to go on a farm had no choice as to where he would go—whether it would be a sheep station, a cattle station, or a milk-run, and his employer might not know his business. He did not like the Bill. A boy fifteen years of age had to sign his own apprenticeship in another country—not New Zealand.

Labour Objections.

Mr. F. N. Bartram (Labour, *Grey Lynn*) suggested that the Bill should be entitled " A Bill for the Procuration of Cheap Labour for the Farming Community of this Country." The Bill was a first instalment of a system of indentured labour. The indiscriminate importation of youths for industrial purposes was fraught with great danger under any circumstances. There was no limit as to the number of such immigrants, there was no indication as to their hours of work or the conditions under which they were to work. He objected to the principle of the Government's proposal to take boys in the Old Country out of parental care. There was no justification for a wild scheme—for collecting boys from all over Great Britain and bringing them out to that country. He opposed the Bill because it was a deliberate attack on Trade Unionism; it was an attempt to take away the power of regulating all hours, wages and conditions of labour then exercised under the Industrial Conciliation and Arbitration Act.

Mr. R. McCallum (Liberal, *Wairau*) submitted that the Indenture would have to be re-executed in that country before it could have any binding effect upon the immigrating boy. Such an Indenture could have no binding effect in Great Britain.

Mr. G. Mitchell (Independent, *Wellington South*) said that many boys whom he had seen in the Old Country would be good citizens in New Zealand, and their conditions would be infinitely better if they were brought there. It was as necessary to protect the boys as it was to protect the farmers against the boys who might clear out. It was not fair that the boys should receive the usual wage only after twelve months' service. Were they to receive nothing for that period ?· If so the boys were to be subjected to a severe trial. Boys should not be taken away from Great Britain without the consent of their parents who, under the Bill, need not be parties to the Indenture. He hoped that would be amended in Committee.

ACTS PASSED.

The following Acts, which were dealt with in Vol. I., No. 4, of this JOURNAL, are amongst those which were passed into law on the dates set opposite to them, namely :—

Revocation of Naturalisation
Amendment Act ... ... 9th August, 1920.

Registration of Aliens Amendment Act ... ... 9th August, 1920.

Arms Act ... ... 6th October, 1920.

Civil List Act ... ... 28th October, 1920.

SOUTH AFRICA.

The following summary of the proceedings of the First Session of the Third Parliament of the Union of South Africa, which opened on 19th March and ended on 17th August, 1920, is in continuation of the summaries appearing in the July and October issues of the JOURNAL *(Vol. I., Nos. 3 & 4).*

ENEMY PROPERTY.

(Statement of Government Policy.)

On 16th August, 1920, in the House of Assembly, the Prime Minister made a statement setting forth the policy of the Government in regard to Enemy Property in the hands of the Custodian of Enemy Property.*

The Prime Minister (Lieut.-General the Right Hon. J. C. Smuts) said that during the last Session the Minister of Justice said it was the policy of the Government to restore in full the properties of Germans, either domiciled or resident in South Africa. That had been done. The Custodian of Enemy Property had held property and assets to the value of about thirteen millions, and he had paid out to those German subjects resident or domiciled in South Africa property to the amount of about three millions. He promised that the Government would announce its policy in regard to the balance of the assets held by the Custodian which belonged to Germans not domiciled or resident in South Africa.

Terms of the Peace Treaty.

After giving the fullest consideration the Government had come to the following conclusion : The Peace Treaty made certain provisions and they wished to keep as far as possible within the terms of that Treaty. The Government was going to make certain deductions from those repayments authorised by the Peace Treaty. The deductions authorised by the Treaty were debts due to their nationals ; statements of those debts had been sent in, and a large number had been proved to the satisfaction of the Custodian and paid out. The total amount of these debts so far as they could see was about half a million.

---

* See this JOURNAL, Vol. I., No. 4, pp. 753-6.

The property and investments held by their nationals in Germany at the outbreak of war which had been sequestrated or confiscated by the German Government, had to be repaid by the latter in terms of the Treaty. If not, they were entitled to bring them into account in making any repayment, and as these had not been paid back, the Government proposed to retain an amount of about half a million to cover them. Then there was the question of the deduction of claims of various sorts. They had found no authority in the Peace Treaty anywhere which would justify them in deducting from those assets held by the Custodian any claims for damages against the German Government. They consisted of claims the result of goods supplied by their nationals to the German Government in the Protectorate previous to the War, which the German Government had not paid for; claims for goods which at the outbreak of the War were in transit on the high seas in enemy ships; and claims for loss of life and personal effects due to enemy action during the war, such as the case of the "Galway Castle."

They were not authorised to deduct these claims under the Peace Treaty, and they could not, therefore, make any deduction from enemy properties they were holding in order to satisfy them. The Government had taken the view that it would be quite unfair to their own nationals to pay back German property and German subjects in any shape or form, and at the same time to limit the claims of South African nationals to the Reparations Commission. They should deal quite fairly with these claims, and avoid such apparent discriminations in favour of the Germans.

"Galway Castle" Claims.

In regard to the "Galway Castle" claims, General Smuts continued, the Custodian thought the total would not exceed £00,000. The Government was of opinion that all these claims should be paid on a fair basis; such a basis had been laid down by the British Government, and, he thought, had been agreed to by other Governments as well. The South African Government proposed to adopt that basis and to pay out these claims without any delay for consideration by the Reparations Commission.

In the first instance, they would be paid by the Custodian out of moneys in his possession, and he might continue to finance the matter until there were payments made into the Reparation Fund accruing to South Africa; but in the first place the Treasury would not have to bear any part of the finance. They would see that of the ten million pounds that were left, after paying out debts and properties to Germans

resident or domiciled in that country, they proposed to make
a reduction of one million—half a million in respect of property
and investments in Germany, and the other half due to their
nationals. That left nine millions. To this amount the
Government proposed to add interest at the rate of 4 per cent.
for the period during which these properties had been vested
in the Custodian, so far as they had been bearing interest
or producing dividends, for there were some, of course, which
had produced practically nothing, and in these cases the
Government did not propose to add interest. This would
add another million to the nine millions to which he had
referred, so that at the present date there was a sum of about
ten millions to be dealt with.

An Opening for Generous Treatment.

The contemplation of the Peace Treaty, General Smuts
went on to say, was that this money was to be paid over to
the Reparation Fund, but it left an opening for more generous
treatment, largely owing to the activity which General Botha
and himself had been able to bear at the Peace Conference.
They wished to avail themselves of this opening, and the
Government did not propose to pay this ten millions into the
Reparation Fund, for to do so would be equal to confiscation.
It was true that the German Government had undertaken
under the Peace Treaty to compensate all their nationals
for what losses they had suffered in this way, but even so it
would be a most difficult thing to do.

No, the South African Government was not going to
confiscate private property of people who in peace time
invested their capital in South Africa, counting on the good
faith of the people of that country and its Government. It
would be for the future welfare of South Africa to deal with the
matter in a generous manner. To repay the amounts, as was
possible, to the parties interested would lead to very great
difficulty. The Reparation Fund had such a tight grip on
the whole banking system of Europe that no one could have
any certainty, even if the Government attempted to repay
to the people directly interested, that they would have the
benefit thereof.

As a result of many inquiries they had come to the conclusion that the proper way to deal with this money was to
take it as a loan to South Africa for 30 years, at 4 per cent,
which would be paid to the German nationals. Certificates
would be issued to the people entitled to them, and in order
to prevent such certificates again escaping those people, he
intended to make them non-transferable for at least 3
years. He believed that this policy met with the accept-

of the more important parties with whom it had been possible to consult, and he also believed that it was the wish of those persons who were interested. At any rate, they agreed that it was a generous policy. It was undoubtedly the most generous action taken in any country with regard to enemy property. He (General Smuts) thought South Africa could well afford it, and that it would in the end redound to the credit of that country.

The German Indemnity.

Proceeding, General Smuts said they had property, assets and certificates to the amount of ten million to deal with. Deductions of about one million had been made, but they were provisional, and as soon as money was forthcoming from the Reparation Fund this additional million would be paid to the parties directly interested, so that in the end they would get their properties restored completely and fully from South Africa. South Africa was also entitled to what was to be paid by the Germans as indemnity. He did not expect that Germany would be able to pay the extravagant amounts which had been anticipated at one time. But it would certainly be able to pay substantial sums, and South Africa would be entitled to her share. Then they would be able to restore the deductions being made as a temporary measure from these properties and assets, and their owners would get them in full. So far as he had been able to consult people, he was sure it would be looked upon as the right course to be taken by the Government.

Property in South-West Africa.

Under the Peace Treaty, General Smuts continued, the Government also got the right to deal in the same confiscatory manner with all property in South-West Africa, but there, too, they had thought that although they possessed that abstract power, it would be wrong to make use of it. They intended to leave private property severely alone. The only properties which they were not quite certain about were certain concessions in regard to which they wanted to know whether the titles were sound. If they were, the Government would recognise them. Subject to that provision they intended to recognise private property of all sorts.

With regard to the dividends of the mining companies paid to the Government during the war, and up to the time of the purchase of the diamond properties by South African people, it was proposed to deal with the amount paid to the Government before the purchase of the properties, some six or seven hundred thousand pounds, in the same way they had dealt with enemy property in the possession of the Custodian. That was to say, certificates would be given to the people entitled to same. He thought, General Smuts said in conclusion, members would agree with him that in taking this course, which was entirely exceptional, the Government had adopted the correct line, and, above all, had acted in the best and highest interests of South Africa.

In reply to Colonel F. H. P. Creswell (Leader of the Labour Party),

The Prime Minister stated that the liquidation of properties would continue as heretofore, and every precaution would be taken to see that the best value was obtained.

CURRENCY AND BANKING ACT.*

This is an Act to conserve the specie supplies of the Union by the issue of gold certificates, to provide for the establishment of a Central Reserve Bank, and to regulate the issue of bank notes and the keeping of reserves so as to secure greater stability in the monetary system of the Union. It was introduced in the House of Assembly on 5th July, 1920.

GOLD CERTIFICATES.

The first part of the Act authorises the Treasury to receive deposits of gold coin or bullion to the value of not less than ten shillings, and to issue certificates therefor of such denominational values and in such form as the Minister of Finance may direct.

Gold certificates may not be issued for a sum in excess of :—

(A) The face value of the gold coin presented, provided such coin is not less than the least current weight prescribed by law for such coin ; and

(B) £3 17s. 10½d. per ounce standard for the gold bullion or light coin presented, subject to such charges as may be prescribed by regulation to cover the cost of refining and minting.

Subject to the provisions of any proclamation, gold certificates shall be redeemed in gold specie on demand at the Treasury or at other appointed places. They shall be legal tender for payment of any amount up to their face value ; and for every purpose for which gold or gold specie is required to be kept by the Act, they shall be regarded as gold or gold specie.

When the market price of gold in the Union exceeds £3 17s. 10½d. per standard ounce, the Governor-General may suspend the redemption of the gold certificates while such excess continues. During the suspension the Treasury may require the Banks in the Union to deposit at the Treasury

* See this JOURNAL, Vol. I., No. 4, p. 761.

the whole or any portion of their gold coin and receive gold certificates in exchange.

CENTRAL RESERVE BANK.

The second part of the Act provides for the establishment at Pretoria of a corporate body to be called " The South African Reserve Bank " (Sec. 9) with a capital of £1,000,000 of which not more than half shall be subscribed at par by the Union Banks in proportion to their paid-up capital and reserve funds. The amount remaining shall be offered to the public at par, and if it is not fully subscribed the Treasury shall take it up.

The Bank shall be managed by a Board of 11 Directors of whom three shall be nominated by the Stockholding Banks, three (representative of commerce, agriculture and another industry) shall be elected by other stockholders and five (including the Governor and Deputy-Governor) shall be appointed by the Governor-General. All directors shall be British subjects and shall reside in the Union.

After making provision for debts, depreciation in assets, etc., and after payment out of the net profits of a cumulative dividend at the rate of 6 per cent. on the paid-up capital, the surplus shall be allocated to reserve fund until that fund is equal to 25 per cent. of the paid-up capital of the Bank. Thereafter, until the reserve fund is equal to the paid-up capital of the Bank, one half of the surplus shall go to the reserve fund, and the other half equally to the Government and to the stockholders.

When the reserve fund is equal to the paid-up capital, the net profits, after payment of a dividend of 10 per cent. to the stockholders, shall be paid to the Government; but so long as gold certificates issued under the first part of the Act are unconvertible, the profits after paying a dividend of 6 per cent. shall be used for strengthening the gold reserve of the Bank.

The Bank may establish branches in any part of the Union, and with the consent of the Treasury, may establish branches outside the Union, and subject to certain restrictions may carry on the business of bankers as set out in the Act.

As to the restrictions, the Bank may not engage in trade or have a direct interest in any commercial, industrial or other undertaking, save as is elsewhere specified ; it may not advance money on mortgage of fixed property or become the owner of fixed property, except as may be necessary for its business premises ; it may not make unsecured loans or advances, draw or accept bills payable otherwise than on demand ; it may not accept money on deposit for a fixed term or allow interest on credit balances on current account.

The Bank shall have the sole right to issue bank notes in the Union for a period of twenty-five years from the commencement of the Act, but until it is in a position to issue its notes, the existing Banks may continue to issue their notes on condition that they hold gold specie to an amount equal to not less than 40 per cent. of such notes in circulation.

The notes of the Bank shall be receivable in payment of taxes, duties, debts, etc., payable to the Government or any provincial administration.

The notes issued by the Bank shall be secured to an amount of not less than 40 per cent. in gold or gold specie, and as to the remainder in commercial paper or trade bills, and by a first charge on all the assets of the Bank. (Sec. 17.) Subject to the consent of the Treasury, these reserve requirements may be suspended for 30 days, renewable for periods not exceeding 15 days upon certain conditions.

In addition to the gold reserves required by Sec. 17 (see above) to be held against its notes issued, the Bank shall hold in gold or specie a reserve of at least 40 per cent. of its deposits and bills payable, but the silver specie to be counted as part of this reserve must not exceed 20 per cent. of the total.

Each bank in the Union is required to maintain reserve balances with the Central Bank.

DEBATE IN HOUSE OF ASSEMBLY.

In the House of Assembly on 5th July, the Minister of Finance moved for leave to introduce the Bill.

Mr. J. W. Jagger (Unionist, *Cape Town, Central, Cape*) said the effect of the measure would be to maintain the costs of living much more than all the puny efforts of the Profiteering Bill to reduce them. The report of the Select Committee was by no means a unanimous one, and the report of Col. Creswell, which was defeated, showed a far better grip of the question.

The Bill also dealt with banking, and proposed the introduction of a system which had not been an entire success in the country of its origin—the United States.

The Bill proposed to introduce an unconvertible paper currency at a time when every other country was trying to rid itself of the evil of paper money. The measure also proposed to revolutionise the banking system of the Union. It took the United States some years to revise its currency system, and it sent a commission to Europe to study the question. He suggested that the measure be read a first time, but should not be pushed through that Session, so that Parliament and the country might have an opportunity of considering the matter.

The excessive issue of paper money by the banks should be dealt with without delay. But, Mr. Jagger contended, that could be done by administrative action on the part of the Government without any Bill at all. The Government should give notice to the Banks that within twelve months at the latest the embargo on the export of gold coin would be taken off.

The Right Hon. J. X. Merriman (South African Party, *Stellenbosch, Cape*) supported this view, and said the Bill had caused the gravest alarm and confusion in their financial institutions. The whole question of currency was in the melting-pot in every country in the world, and delay was the one thing that would be safe for them.

Col. F. H. P. Creswell (Leader of the Labour Party) said as long as they went on with the policy of drift they were keeping every man whose income was measured by his daily, weekly or monthly earnings in a state of doubt as to the real amount which he earned. One thing that had become even clearer as a result of the investigation of the Committee was the tremendous influence that private profit-earning institutions had over the trade of the people. In conclusion, he spoke in favour of a State Bank.

The Hon. Sir Edgar Walton (Unionist, *Port Elizabeth Central, Cape*) said they were importing sovereigns at something like 30s. each and giving them to the people at 20s. He pointed out that if the loss were thrown upon the Banks they had to pass it on, so that it was the community which was paying. He did not agree with the entire proposals of the Committee ; what was advocated was really the beginning of a State Bank.

The Minister of Finance (Hon. H. Burton): " It is nothing of the sort."

Sir Edgar Walton replied that it was the first step, and once they had taken it they had to get on with the rest.

The Minister of Finance deprecated Mr. Jagger's view on the matter. The state of affairs was a very serious one indeed. This Bill proposed to do something, and the Government intended to proceed with it.

The Bill was read a first time.

Second Reading.

In the House of Assembly on the 14th July, the Minister of Finance moved the Second Reading.

The Minister of Finance (Hon. H. Burton) said the issues involved were far too serious for the party element to be introduced. One of their great difficulties with the multiplication of experts who had appeared before the Select Committee on the Embargo on the Export of Specie was the extraordinary divergence of views. They had eventually come to the conclusion that the only sound thing to do was to approach the matter from the common-sense and practical point of view.

The Embargo Justified.

The evidence was to the effect that the embargo was justifiable. Similar action was taken by every civilised country in the world, and even to-day the only great country which had removed the embargo was the U.S.A. As to the effect of the embargo on the cost of living, if it were removed now, what would be the effect? Theoretically, prices would be increased by the embargo by a percentage equal to the gold premium, about 15 per cent., and the removal would theoretically reduce the price to the same extent on commodities, both imported and produced locally. Since February, the premium had fallen something like 31 per cent. and such evidence as they had before them with regard to the effect of the fall on the cost of prices was entirely ineffective, and there appeared to be no corresponding fall. The removal of the embargo would have a dislocating effect on the trade and finance of the country generally, and home products would suffer.

They must have a proportionate reduction in services and wages, and the experience of the world was that wage reduction was a long and laborious process which would have to apply to all industries.

Maintaining Exchange at Parity in Gold.

It was very doubtful indeed whether even if they automatically raised the South African exchange to parity in gold it would be maintained there. That was a most important point, because unless it could be maintained their whole argument fell to the ground. All the witnesses with, he thought, one exception, agreed that the movement of exchange was subject to the law of supply and demand. It would depend on the maintenance of an excess of their exports over their imports, visible and invisible, in order to maintain it.

So far as the balance of their current trade was concerned, they had during recent times been on the right side. But during those years that were past they had been unable to make the usual heavy importations of a large class of material which might very easily change that situation.   .

Disappearance of Gold.

The next question dealt with was the disappearance of gold specie from South Africa. The banks had given the clearest possible evidence on that point, and their evidence was borne out by the Treasury figures, which showed that from April, 1919 to March, 1920, £2,495,000 had gone from the banks' coffers and was no longer a medium of their commerce. If the embargo were removed now, six months or a year hence, the gold would go out of the country in a wave. The Committee could not face the responsibility of recommending the House to remove the embargo.

After referring to the experiences of the United States which he described as a creditor country to-day in a stronger position than any country of the world (their exports exceeding their imports by about $4,000,000,000) and the way in which $400,000,000 worth of gold went out of that country during the nine months after the embargo was removed in June, 19

Mr. Burton said the present reserves held by the South African banks were inadequate to the business of the country, and if the embargo were lifted then or in a year's time, and the gold premium continued, it would be impossible for the banks to continue their banking operations. There would have to be, if they removed the embargo, an immediate reduction of prices for all their industrial productions to the extent of the exchange, with most prejudicial results to South African industries at large. The value of property would also sink, not to speak of the results in the shape of unemployment.

In reference to the efflux of capital from the country, that outflow was already taking place, and they could imagine what would happen when they removed the embargo. The high rate of exchange in India had led " to remittances to England on an enormous scale." Canada was experiencing the same trouble, so much so that she had to prohibit the import of her own securities into her country in order to prevent the outflow of capital. Millions of capital had been leaving South Africa during the last few months.

They were all agreed in regard to the acceptance of the gold basis as being the soundest and the best, and that it was desirable to restore their currency to the true gold basis at the earliest possible moment. The difference of opinion was as to the manner and the time. The truth was that they could not fix any definite time for the removal of the embargo.

Modification of Banking Laws.

Mr. Burton next dealt with the modification of the currency and banking laws, and said they had three schemes submitted to them.

Mr. Strakosch's scheme had been approved by the committee which sat at Pretoria (representing the banks, the Associated Chambers of Commerce, the Chamber of Mines, etc.), with the exception of the banks. On the suggestion of Col. Creswell the whole matter was submitted to a Select Committee,[*] which came to the conclusion that this was the soundest scheme to adopt. Briefly, it proposed to send all the gold to the Treasury to be preserved, and to issue against it gold certificates representing its value, and to make these certificates inconvertible until they got back to a gold basis— until the premium disappeared—and meanwhile the notes were left convertible. They would be convertible into gold certificates. That was the scheme for preserving their specie reserves against leaving the country.

---

* See this JOURNAL, Vol. I., No. 4, p. 761.

A Central Reserve Bank.

The really important part of the Bill, Mr. Burton continued, was that which provided for a Central Reserve Bank. The gold certificate scheme was merely a temporary measure. It was inaccurate to say that they were going to flood the country with a lot more paper. Every one of those certificates would be represented by actual gold, and they would use paper instead of the latter merely in order that the gold should not leave the country. It was the view of the Government and the Committee that no arrangement should be made for the conservation of their specie reserves unless it was joined to a scheme for placing their banking system on a more satisfactory footing. Provision was made in the Bill that the Central Reserve Bank, with the consent of the Treasury, might allow gold to be exported under certain circumstances, e.g., some very important trade matters. That all referred to the period during which they were getting back to the gold basis.

Precautions for National Crisis.

It was desirable, Mr. Burton continued, that they should be able to centralise their reserves in the country so that in times of national crisis they could be brought to bear on the spot. The existing system was defective in that respect. They had a few large banks with a great many branches, but they acted separately and had no common policy, and there was an absence of legislative restriction in regard to their note issues.

After giving further particulars of the working of the Central Reserve Bank, Mr. Burton said that it was a scheme for the permanent alteration of their present system, and was a great step in the evolution of banking in South Africa. The Bill was framed mainly on the American lines, and the American system did not differ essentially from the Central Banks in other countries.

Sound Financial Position.

These were critical days in which they were living, and they were glad and proud to think that South Africa's financial position was a perfectly sound one. It was possible indeed that prices might fall, and any sudden drop was bound to have a very serious effect on the finances of the country. The present system was not to meet any crisis, and the banks would be forced to call up advances which would accentuate the position still more. He submitted that this was the psychological moment to face their difficulties boldly and courageously.

The debate was adjourned until the following day.

Labour Amendment: Rejection Moved.

The debate on the motion for the Second Reading was commenced on 15th July, 1920, when an amendment was proposed by **Mr. M. Kentridge (Labour,** *Fordsburg, Trans.*) on behalf of the Labour Party as follows :—

That in the opinion of this House :—

1. The embargo upon the exportation of gold coin from the Union be removed at a date not later than 30th June, 1921 ;

2. The Government be requested to consider the advisability of introducing without delay legislation making provision for :

(A) Such portion of the present note issue as is authorised by the present law to be based on securities deposited with the Treasury being taxed at the rate of 5 per cent. per annum on their present face value ;

(B) All other notes at present in issue being fully covered by gold ; and

(C) The establishment of a State Bank having the sole right of issuing notes and organised for the purpose of carrying on the ordinary banking business of the Union.

Mr. T. E. Drew (Labour, *Denver, Trans.*) formally seconded the amendment.

Mr. J. W. Jagger (Unionist, *Cape Town, Central, Cape*) said that while other countries were trying to do their best to get back to a gold basis, they, in that country, on the recommendation of this committee, were going to cut themselves away from it and take up a form of currency which was recognised the world over to be a great evil. Besides that, they were going to make a complete revolution in the methods of banking without any inquiry by any men who really knew much about the subject. Was it to be wondered at that a committee of this kind should have fallen entirely, with two exceptions, into the hands of an expert, who had been born and bred in a country which, prior to 1900, never knew what a old currency was ?

The committee in their report started out by laying down a very sound principle, that their currency should be based on a true gold foundation, but instead of making any progress towards that point and taking off the embargo, or fixing a definite time for its duration, the Government brought forward a Bill which made no effort at all, certainly not in the first chapter, and very little in the second, to get to a true gold foundation. It seemed to him that the reverse was going to follow and that they would have increased inflation.

It was beyond question that their currency had depreciated. That was amply proved by the fact that gold bullion was at a premium even there in South Africa. The currency had depreciated because the South African banks had issued too

o 2

many notes, the quantity having increased by over 400 per
cent. since the outbreak of the war. How could the issue
of gold certificates, which would also be paper money, bring
about a deflation of the currency ?

People were asked to increase production, but what was
the use of that when, at the same time, the banks were allowed
to issue millions of pounds' worth of paper money, the result of
which was enormously to increase prices? The most effective
way to cheapen the cost of living was to reduce the quantity
of paper money in circulation, and bring currency up to a gold
standard.

Notice should be given to the banks that the embargo
would be removed on 30th June next, then they would have to
import gold from Great Britain where they had big balances.

Capital leaving the Country.

A reason why the Minister did not see his way to raising
the embargo was because he said capital would leave the
country. He (Mr. Jagger) should say that capital in South
Africa at the present time was cheaper than in any other place
in the world, and yet he had sent money overseas himself,
for when they could only get 4 per cent. there for six months'
deposit, and 6½ per cent. on the other side, it was no use keeping
money in that country.

The cheapness of money in South Africa was encouraging
over-speculation and over-importation of goods. South Africa
was importing more goods than she could pay for, and in his
opinion they were heading straight for a crisis exactly similar
to that which they had in 1904, brought about by the cheapness
of money and the big issue of paper money by the banks.

Central Reserve Bank.

Regarding a Central Reserve Bank, Mr. Jagger said the
big expansion of notes and the reduction of the reserves which
the bank held against notes and deposits were really the cause
of Chapter 2, as far as he understood the Bill. That was
state of affairs brought about entirely by the existence of the
embargo. In reply to questions by Mr. Burton and another
Member, Mr. Jagger said he would not have put on the embargo even during the war. All these points were dealt with
very effectively in the report of the Bullion Committee of 1910
which stood to-day as the classic in regard to currency in Great
Britain.

This Bill was taken from the United States, where conditions were very different. In the United States they had at
least 40,000 banks. They had only practically three big banks

in South Africa with branches all over the country. Two of these banks had capital and reserves of over four million pounds. Even the third had over one million pounds. It was clear that in the U.S.A. the establishment of the Federal Reserve Bank had not led to a reduction of currency, but to a very considerable increase. Now that House and that country (South Africa) were asked to adopt that system, and he had not the least doubt that the same result would ultimately take place as took place in the U.S.A. They would go still higher with their inflation than at the present time.

Mr. Jagger concluded by moving the rejection of the Bill.

Mr. W. Rockey (Unionist, *Langlaagte, Trans.***)** in seconding said that a principle was being introduced in the Bill which was going to change the entire financial practice of the country.

General the Hon. J. B. M. Hertzog (Leader of the Nationalist Party) said there was no doubt that they were on the wrong course with the embargo, and the sooner they returned to the gold standard the better. A false state of prosperity was being created and the longer they went on the greater would be the reaction.

After discussing evidence given before the Select Committee, General Hertzog said he wanted to see the embargo raised as soon as possible, though without undue dislocation being caused. It was ridiculous to speak of gradually lifting the embargo. It was the only thing between them and a gold basis. He agreed that a certain amount of protection should be given to the banks to prevent a rush.

He also agreed with Mr. Jagger that the gold certificates, instead of bringing them near to the gold standard, would tend to bring them further away. The only way to check inflation was to provide for free convertibility of the notes.

One of his principal objections, General Hertzog continued, to the gold certificates was that they would close the ordinary channels for the export of gold in payment of goods purchased by them. General Hertzog totally disagreed that the parity of their gold and their paper could not be maintained. If their paper was properly covered, if it was freely convertible, the note and the sovereign must be absolutely on a parity.

Largest Producer of Gold.

Continuing, he said that South Africa was in an excellent position to secure gold at the world's price, seeing that she was the world's largest producer of gold, and he argued that clause should be inserted in the Bill that no gold should be exported until South Africa's requirements had been fulfilled; that it should be done in order to prevent the mines entering into a contract for the sale of all their gold; and he held

that in order to deal with the position the Union's Mint should
be established as soon as possible. He did not think the
British or any other Government could reasonably object to
such a procedure.

England and Gold Parity.

It would take England 20 or 25 years, General Hertzog
continued, before they could get back to gold parity ; but
must South Africa continue on that basis all those years ? He
could understand England maintaining the present position
and holding on to her gold because she felt that at any time
she might again be thrown into war. But South Africa was in
a very different position to England, which was not in a
position to supplement its gold when necessary.

Dealing with the gold certificates, he said he had no
objection to them if the embargo were lifted.

Central Bank.

Was the Central Bank to be a State Bank, General Hertzog
continued, or a concentrated bank of banks, or a bank which
was to be neither State nor commercial bank ? For years
he had realised the necessity of there being a Central Bank,
and had there been one four years ago the Government would
never have imposed the embargo, and the Bank would never
have consented to South Africa being denuded of gold. He
was in favour of the Bank becoming an institution in which
the State had the preponderating influence. It should be a
sort of monopoly for the public, an institution in which the
public was interested.

Other members having spoken, Sir Edgar Walton moved
the adjournment till the next day.

On the resumption of the debate on 16th July,

The Hon. Sir Edgar Walton (Unionist, *Port Elizabeth
Central*) said he was entirely in favour of the first chapter of the
Bill, because he was convinced that it was essential in the
interests of the people. It was impossible to adopt any other
policy than that of the embargo, and in imposing it South
Africa was following the example of every other civilised
country. South Africa was better off than any other country
in regard to the cost of living. If the embargo were lifted
exporters from South Africa would lose from 20 to 25 per cent

A Revolutionary Measure.

The second chapter of the Bill was intended to meet
situation which had not yet risen. So far as that was con
cerned it seemed to him one of the most revolutionary measure

which had ever been put before that House. They were asked to introduce an institution to do something which could be better done by the existing machinery through the Treasury under the authority of Parliament. After dealing with certain other points Sir Edgar Walton said he thought the House should hold the second portion of the Bill over for further consideration. The proposals in the first part must be carried out, as they had to protect their currency.

The Right Hon. J. X. Merriman (South African Party, *Stellenbosch, Cape*) opposed the Bill. It would, he said, revolutionise their currency system. The model of the Central Bank, he said, was America, which was finding that this system worked so badly that she had been obliged to alter it already.

Mr. R. W. Close (Unionist, *Rondebosch, Cape*) claimed that the Bill afforded the only solution at the present time. The difficulty was to realise that a theory of one generation might have to be modified in an extraordinary way in a later generation.

In regard to inconvertible certificates, the bank-note system was backed by Government securities, which were good enough for him, and he thought they were good enough for other people.

They recognised that the gold basis was the right one, but if they could not adopt heroic measures without incurring great dangers, they must endeavour to achieve the desired effect in some other way, and they sought to do it by stopping the leakage of gold through inconvertible certificates.

Necessity for Bank.

With regard to the Central Bank, he regarded this part of the Bill as the keystone. Mr. Close went on to say that according to one authority the federal system was the one which saved the financial position of America during the war, and he had heard of no movement to repeal the Act. The Banks of England, France, the Netherlands and Japan were Central Banks for the purpose of making the credit system of the countries elastic. The principle had been proved a success. The necessity for such a Bank was proved by three points—the large issue of notes without control, the depletion of the reserves, and the facilities given for speculation.

Stopping Further Inflation.

The first thing they had to do was to stop further inflation, and the Bill made provision for that. After a certain period if the Federal Bank was ready to issue its notes it would notify the Treasury, who would notify all the banks and cease issuing notes. Then would follow the period when notes would have to be returned to the Central Bank, subject to a tax on notes outstanding, and at the end of two years the banks would have to pay over to the Central Bank £ for £ on every note outstanding, and in place of the present issue they would have the security of 40 per cent. in gold and 60 per cent. in good bills. That feature worked well in America. The proposal was that the deposits of the bank should be backed by 30 per cent. in gold for time demands and 3 per cent. for time deposits. At present the reserves of the banks were used for their own purposes, but under the new system the reserves would be held by the Central Reserve Fund to be used in time of panic. The case was one for urgent treatment and should not be put off.

Sir Abe Bailey (Independent, *Krugersdorp, Trans.*) said that they must protect their industries and see that they were not destroyed. With all the great advantages that the Union was enjoying, there was not a sufficient currency in the country for trading purposes. Through that insufficiency the farmers and wool merchants had suffered great losses.

He challenged Mr. Jagger to name any articles among the necessaries of life in South Africa which had gone up in price owing to the embargo. The cost of living in America had gone up since the embargo was raised. Sweden had more gold than any country, and yet the cost of living had gone up there to a greater extent than any other part of the world. After every great war prices had risen.

Col. F. H. P. Creswell (Leader of the Labour Party) said the depreciation of the value of a man's earnings was a very serious thing. It did not affect so much the dwellers in the realms of high finance, but it did affect every man who worked for a wage or a salary. The Minister said they got it back through war bonuses, but what about the people who were not strong enough, through their organisations, to demand that their wages should again be brought back to something nearer their previous purchasing value? There had been no talk of raising their wages, nor indeed anyone's wages, until they had become strong enough to demand it.

The adjournment of the Debate was moved by Col. Creswell, who when resuming, on 19th July, pointed out that gold was the measure for regulation. Their monetary system was regulated by the freedom with which a comparatively small amount of gold could be allowed to rise or fall. He desired that they should get back as quickly as possible to the only sound basis. The Minister had laid too much stress on the fact that wages would come down. He believed they would not, but that profits would.

It was said that the consequence of raising the embargo would be to send capital out of the country, but capital in the fixed form of buildings, machinery, and all the gear of activity was not going to take to itself wings and fly away. Nor did he think (taking capital in the shape of mobile credit) that the removal of the embargo would result in any material deflation of locally-owned capital from things in that country, where it was under the owner's eye and control, into a gamble with the length of time it would take British currency and British securities to get back to a gold parity.

As to the other objection that certain of their industries had benefited by the depreciation of their currency, anything of that kind acting on the economic system was very much like alcohol acting on the human system. It produced a certain amount of activity for a time, but they had to keep applying the dose and increasing it.

Col. Creswell further said that an unsound monetary system was growing up round the vested interests, and they had had to take early steps in the matter and clearly fix a time limit beyond which the present state of affairs should not continue. Had they possessed their own Mint in South Africa before the war, the embargo would probably never have been necessary. He believed that instead of the threatened disaster if it was made clear that the embargo would be raised, say on 30th June, the banks and other financial institutions would find ways and means to get over the difficulties which they now said stood in the way.

A State Bank.

He agreed that there should be a Central Bank, but it should be one belonging to the people themselves, not to be manipulated by one portion of the community alone. It was said a State Bank would be too prone to political influences. He would like to see a great deal less financial interest in the country's politics than he feared in connection with a State Bank. He concluded by saying that he was bound to oppose both parts of the Bill tooth and nail.

After further lengthy discussion the Debate was again adjourned, and continued on 20th July, when the Minister of Finance replied.

Mr. Jagger's amendment that the Bill be read a second time six months hence was negatived.

The official Labour Amendment was negatived by 77 to 8 votes, and the Second Reading was agreed to.

On 2nd August the Bill was read a third time and sent to the Senate.

DEBATE IN THE SENATE.

In the Senate on 5th August, 1920, **The Minister of Finance (the Hon. H. Burton)** moved the Second Reading of the Bill.

Senator the Hon. C. P. Robinson said the Central Bank might be a very good State Bank, and he thought it desirable that it should be a Government monopoly ; but he urged that there should be a provision in the Bill that after a period the Government should have a right to destroy that monopoly.

Senator the Hon. P. Whiteside commented on the curious resemblance between the Central Reserve Bank and the Federal Reserve Banks of America, and he also spoke of the " strike engineered by the Money Trust in the U.S.A. against the interests of the people " as a result of Mr. Roosevelt's anti-trust legislation. The Fighting President had had to climb down, and when he (Senator Whiteside) thought of Mr. Burton versus the Money Trust of South Africa he had very little hopes indeed for that Bill. He thought that currency should, like other public utilities, be in the hands of the State ; and, in conclusion, moved that the Bill be read that day six months.

Other Stages.

Various amendments having been negatived or withdrawn, and other amendments accepted, the Third Reading was agreed to on 10th August.

NATIVE AFFAIRS ACT.

This Act has for its object the constitution of a Commission and local native councils, and provides for convening native conferences, with a view to facilitating the administration of native affairs.

The Bill and the debate on the Second Reading were summarised in the July issue of the JOURNAL (Vol. 1, No. 3, pp. 554-568).

NATIVE AFFAIRS COMMISSION.

The Act provides for the establishment of a Native Affairs Commission, to consist of the Minister of Native Affairs (as Chairman) or other person designated by him to be deputy-chairman in his absence of not less than three nor more than five other members, the duties of which shall include the consideration of any matter relating to the general administration of native affairs, or to legislation affecting the native population (other than matters of departmental administration) and the submission to the Minister of its recommendations on any such matter. It shall also make recommendations with regard to any matter of administrative routine submitted to it by direction of the Minister. In the event of the Minister not accepting the recommendation, the Commission may require it to be submitted to the Governor-General, and if he does not accept it, the Commission may require that all papers be laid before both Houses of Parliament.

Regulations as to the procedure of meetings of the Commission, qualification of members, etc., are to be made by the Governor-General.

NATIVE COUNCILS.

The Act further enables the Governor-General (on the recommendation of the Commission) to establish local councils (consisting of not more than nine natives with an officer in the public service as chairman and general advisor) for the whole or any portion of any of the native areas. (Section 5).

Any local council may, within the area for which it is established, provide for the construction and maintenance of roads, drains, etc., and for the prevention of erosion ; for an improved water supply, the suppression of diseases of stock, the destruction of noxious weeds, a suitable system of sanitation, the establishment of hospitals, improvement in methods of agriculture, afforestation, educational facilities, etc.

A local council may acquire and hold land or interest in land for carrying out any of the purposes mentioned above. It shall be the duty of each local council to advise the Commission in regard to any matters affecting the general interests of the natives it represents and also to advise the Minister or Commission upon request.

Each local council may levy a rate not exceeding one pound in any year upon each adult male native ordinarily resident in its area.

REGULATIONS.

The Governor-General may make regulations providing for the consultation of the inhabitants of areas for which a council is to be established and for the selection or election of members of the councils ; for periods of office and remuneration of such members, for the procedure of councils, etc.

EXISTING SYSTEMS : GENERAL COUNCIL.

If the application of the Act in any area for which a council is appointed is found to conflict with any system of local government established there by law, the Governor-General may, by proclamation in the *Gazette*, declare the extent to which any such system shall apply in that area and make such provisions as he deems expedient for reconciling the conflict.

Whenever it appears that any of the powers conferred upon local councils can in any two or more areas for which local councils have been established be more advantageously exercised by a body with jurisdiction over all those areas, the Governor-General may, upon recommendation of the Commission, establish a General Council to consist of such number of representatives from each of the local councils as the Governor-General may determine. The General Council shall have such of the powers of local councils as the Governor-General may allocate to it.

NATIVE CONFERENCES.

The Governor-General may (Section 16), upon the recommendation of the Commission, convene conferences of chiefs, members of native councils

or local councils and prominent natives, and of native delegates invited
from any association or union purporting to represent any native political
or economic interest, with a view to ascertaining the sentiments of the
native population of the Union in regard to any measure which may
affect them. Such conferences shall be assisted in their deliberations by
persons to be designated by the Minister of Native Affairs, who is empowered to authorise expenditure for the purpose.

DEBATE IN HOUSE OF ASSEMBLY.

In the House of Assembly on 8th July, 1920,

Mr. R. Feetham (Unionist, *Parktown, Trans.***)** said he thought
that members of the Commission should be given fixed tenure
of office, and that that should not be interfered with unless for
very good reasons. The whole idea of the Bill was that they
should have continuity in native policy.

Native Councils.

The Rev. L. P. Vorster (Nationalist, *Albert–Aliwal, Cape***)**
moved an amendment altering the wording in Clause 5
relating to the establishment of native councils, so as
to provide that " All the members of each such Council shall
be natives, not being Civil servants, and to be elected by ballot
of the ratepayers."

**General the Hon. J. B. M. Hertzog (Leader of the Nationalist
Party)** said the Bill was a necessary measure, although it did
not go far enough. The question was now whether they would
help the native to develop in his own sphere. He was in
favour of segregation, because he thought it would help the
native to advance. The European in South Africa was
animated by the desire to do absolute justice to the native.
He was opposed to giving the native the vote—it was a matter
of self-preservation for the white man—but just for that
reason he realised the necessity of the native having the right
to vote in his own affairs in his own area.

Mr. Vorster said it should be laid down that the native
areas to which the Councils would apply were to be laid down
by Parliament in future.

The Natives: Future Policy.

**The Prime Minister (Lieut.-General the Right Hon. J. C.
Smuts)** expressed his appreciation of the fact that the native
question was being discussed outside the party arenas. It
was in that spirit that the Bill had been dealt with from the
start. He reiterated what he had said during the Second
Reading debate, that it was the first instalment of the whole
policy in regard to the natives. He had realised that it was

much better to appoint a permanent Commission to deal with all native matters, one of which would be the continuation of the policy of segregation.

Turning to Mr. Vorster, the Prime Minister pointed out that the desire of the natives had been met in so far that the Europeans on the Councils would be there in an advisory capacity only. In regard to election, it would be quite impossible to lay down hard and fast rules, and where possible the Councils would be elected and in other parts they would be nominated. It would be clearly impossible to lay it down that in parts where the natives were still raw and barbarous the members of the Council should be elected.

He went on to point out that the Councils were only to be appointed for areas already set aside as native areas, or for areas to be so set aside in future. Natives living in towns, or near towns, in large numbers, did not come under the Bill, and the question of urban natives would still have to be gone into. The amendment proposed by Mr. Vorster that Councils could only be appointed for areas in future to be set aside would have the effect that nothing would be done.

There was no doubt, the Prime Minister added, that there was a movement among the natives to which the European population should not shut its eyes. Fortunately, since the introduction of the Bill before the House, a much better spirit had been manifesting itself.

Mr. Vorster's amendment was negatived.

Amendments for the extension of the powers of native Councils, so as to include afforestation and the prevention of soil erosion, the former proposed by Mr. Nathan and the second by Mr. Frost, were agreed to.

The Bill was reported with certain amendments.

On 12th July, in reply to a question by Mr. Merriman, as to the position regarding the areas in which Councils were now functioning with the greatest success, such as the Glen Grey, the Transkeian General Council and Pondoland,

The Prime Minister said there was not the least intention of doing away with Native Councils which were at present working satisfactorily in the native areas. The Glen Grey Act and its extension were not repealed by that Bill. What they proposed was to extend that beneficent system, and they had formulated a new policy in the larger terms of the present Bill.

The Position of the White Man.

On 18th July during the Third Reading,

Mr. A. S. Van Hees (**Nationalist**, *Christiana, Trans.*) moved that the Bill be read a third time that day six months, arguing

that no Native Affairs Bill should be passed which did not
lay down the principle of the maintenance of the position of the
white man.

The principle of segregation, he said, was not carried
into effect under the Bill; he objected to any educational
policy for the natives the effect of which would be that large
numbers of natives would be added to the voters' rolls in the
long run, so that they would out-vote the Europeans; and
he also objected to the provisions (Clause 16) which gave
the natives the right to express their views on all legislation
affecting them. He feared that the day might come when
they would exercise these rights to stop South Africa securing
its absolute independence.

The Prime Minister said Mr. Van Hees did not seem to
realise the importance of the matter or the responsibility of the
white race on the question. He felt sure that his views were
not shared by the old Dutch population or by the Nationalist
Party, whose leader had clearly expressed himself.

The amendment was negatived by 97 votes to 16, the
minority consisting solely of Nationalists.

DEBATE IN THE SENATE.

In the Senate on 16th July, **Senator the Hon. Sir Walter
Stanford** said he agreed with General Smuts that the future
of European civilisation in that country depended very largely
on their treatment of the Bantu population. There was an
urgent need for the appointment of the Native Affairs Commission, whose work was going to be very responsible and
very difficult. They had to acknowledge that the natives
were advancing, even in the tribes themselves, although they
were becoming more detribalised. There was a greater desire
on their part to have control of their own Councils. Let
the native rule himself, he added, but under the direction of
the European.

Senator the Hon. C. G. Marais concurred that the native
question should be considered as a non-party matter, but
why had the Nationalist Party and the natives not been consulted ?

The debate was resumed on 20th July, when

Senator the Hon. H. G. Stuart said if there was one thing
they were thankful for under Union it was the power to
bring in a Bill like that which was approved of by all parts
of the Union. They wanted to deal with the native in a spirit
of friendship. South Africa was not a white man's country
but one of white and of black men, and the latter must also be

part of their Commonwealth, and be treated with justice. The first condition for the welfare of the natives was that they should be in possession not only of land, but good land.

Senator the Hon. Sir Frederick Moor counselled their going slowly before they attempted to uproot those customs, traditions and laws which the native had kept from time immemorial to the present day, and which might be better suited to his peculiar environment and psychology than the later patchwork system of the European. He denied that the way to govern the people was to turn them off the land and make them pariahs; the essential part of native custom was the communal tenure of land, and a man had a real affection for his home.

Native Education.

Senator the Hon. Dr. Roberts, in the course of his first speech as a member of the Upper House, dealing with conditions on the Rand, said there were 300,000 natives, aged from 18 to 25, put into compounds there, and asked what effect that would have on the future of the native race? Speaking of his 40 years' experience of native education, he could not say it was a success or a failure; but as to native industrial education it had been a perfect failure. He advocated simple industries being started in native villages and locations.

The Prime Minister (Lieut.-General the Right Hon. J. C. Smuts) agreed with what had been said by Dr. Roberts in regard to industrial education. They should make the best use of the resources at their command because they were getting to the end of their human resources in South Africa. They must look upon the native as an asset and a co-worker in the great development that was ahead of them, and not as one who had to be exploited. He agreed that the native question was largely personal, and one of personal leadership. The Bill was a small beginning; but, he thought, a step in the right direction.

The Second Reading was agreed to.

NATIVE AFFAIRS.

(Vote on Expenditure.)

In Committee of Supply on the Estimates (Vote No. 24, Native Affairs, £444,059) on 13th July,

Mr. J. H. S. Gow (Labour, Commissioner Street, Trans.) desired to know if the Prime Minister would inform the House

whether there was any possibility of the Government introducing a Bill to deal with native affairs in urban areas.

Medical Service and Housing.

The Rev. J. Mullineux (Labour, *Roodepoort, Trans.*) drew
attention to the need of establishing a chair of medicine in
connection with the Native College and the training of a
larger number of native nurses for service amongst their own
people. He also pleaded for the better housing of natives in
the locations and submitted that more liberal grants should
be given for the extension of educational facilities amongst
the natives.

Mr. W. B. Madeley (Labour, *Benoni, Trans.*) suggested
to the Minister the desirability of appointing a commission
to inquire into the whole question of the relations between
whites and natives, especially in industrial areas. The
position at present was that the white man was becoming
more and more inclined to look upon the native as a beast
of burden, and it was a foolish thing to allow those who
employed these people to be the sole deciding authorities under
which the natives existed.

Natives in Urban Districts.

The Prime Minister (Lieut.-General the Right Hon. J.
Smuts), replying to various points, referred to the question
natives in the urban districts. Though local or native council
had been created in the native areas the Native Affairs
Commission was an adjunct of the Native Affairs Department
whose jurisdiction extended over the whole of the Union
and one of their principal objects would be to study and
inquire into the conditions of life of the natives in urban areas
In those areas they had an enormous accumulation of natives
No forethought had been directed to that problem, and the
conditions, both for blacks and whites, were very grave
indeed. What they wanted was an all-thought-out policy
and a good deal of research was necessary before they could
settle its main lines.

The vote was agreed to.

LAND SETTLEMENT ACTS FURTHER AMENDMENT ACT

(Settlement of Returned Soldiers, &c.)

This is an Act to enable larger advances than those made
under the Land Settlement Amendment Act of 1917 to be
made to lessees of holdings, for the better development

such holdings, and the acquisition of the necessary stock, implements, etc.

The Act amends the provision of the Land Settlement Amendment Act of 1917 (Section 12) which provided that the total amount of advances to a lessee shall not exceed £250 by substituting for £250 the sum of £500*.

The Act also empowers the Minister on prescribed terms of repayment to advance moneys to any group of lessees to enable them to acquire implements, machinery, stud stock and other things required by the members of such group for the better development of their holdings and for their joint and common use, no such advance to exceed £250 in respect of each lessee of the group.

The Minister may, on the recommendation of the land board whenever the cost of boring operations has been added to the purchase price of a holding, reduce the price of the holding if those operations have been unsuccessful, provided that the amount by which the purchase price may be reduced shall not exceed the expenditure incurred by the Minister in carrying out such boring operations.

DEBATE IN HOUSE OF ASSEMBLY.

On 16th July in the House of Assembly, during the debate on the Second Reading,

Mr. G. B. Van Zijl (Unionist, *Cape Town, Harbour*), on behalf of the Soldiers' Pensions Committee, complimented the Minister on the Bill, which had gone further than they asked.

The Rev. L. P. Vorster (Nationalist, *Alberta-Aliwal, Cape*) said it appeared as if the intention was to give greater privileges to returned soldiers, whereas the original Land Settlement Act made no distinction between these and ordinary civilians. He thought that there must be no differentiation between returned soldiers and others.

Mr. L. Geldenhuys (South African Party, *Johannesburg, North, Trans.*) said the Bill was intended for the benefit of the people of that country generally, and returned soldiers were among them.

The Question of Returned Soldiers.

On the resumption of the debate on 29th July,

Mr. M. L. Malan (Nationalist, *Heilbron, O.F.S.*) said the measure had been introduced on the recommendation of the Returned Soldiers Select Committee. Everywhere returned soldiers were getting preference and the young sons of South

---

* The sum of £500 was originally named in the principal Act, viz. : "The Land Settlement Act " of 1912, so by the present amending Act the original figure is restored.

P

Africa had to give way. Protest meetings were being held all over South Africa.

Mr. C. H. Muller (Nationalist, *Pretoria District, South, Trans.***)** pointed out that it was useless settling people on the land and not giving them enough money to carry on with, because to start them short of the necessary capital meant failure.

The Minister of Defence and Lands (Colonel the Hon. Hendrik Mentz) said that the Bill was applicable to all cases no matter whether people had been on active service or not. Every case was to be dealt with on its merits. The £500 advance provided for was a maximum, and would only be granted in cases where it was essential to grant such advances.

The Second Reading was agreed to on 4th August.*

HOUSING ACT.

The object of this Act is to provide public moneys for and confer further powers upon local authorities in respect of the construction of dwellings, and to make other provisions for facilitating such construction.

CONSTRUCTION OF DWELLINGS : HOUSING LOANS, &C.

The Act provides that any local authority may borrow money to enable it to construct approved dwellings and to carry out approved schemes or to lend money for either purpose.

An administrator of a province may establish a housing loans fund in respect of his province and advance moneys to any local authority to enable it to exercise certain powers specified below (Sections 5 and 6). The capital shall consist of such moneys as Parliament may appropriate for that fund. In no case shall the period of repayment of the total amount advanced, and interest thereon, exceed fifty years. The revenues and assets of the local authority shall constitute the security and the rate of interest will be prescribed by the Treasury.

A local authority may (Section 5) out of advances made to it by the administrator or otherwise borrowed under the Act, construct approved dwellings, and sell or let any dwellings constructed by it on conditions prescribed by the administrator. It may also acquire land and construct approved dwellings outside its area.

---

* The final report of the Select Committee of the House of Assembly on War Pensions and Returned Soldiers was published on 16th August 1920. Recognising the importance of the subject of land settlement in regard to returned soldiers, the Committee had dealt with this question in some detail, and recommended the adoption of the scheme submitted by the Returned Soldiers' Advisory Board at Johannesburg for settling returned soldiers, with neither capital nor practical experience in farming; and a system of grouping under superintendence with provision for employment with adequate wages on land development, etc., and settlement on small holdings, etc.

Any local authority may (Section 6) lend money (called a "housing loan ") to any company, society or person for the construction of approved dwellings or carrying out approved schemes. Provided that a local authority shall not grant a housing loan (A) to any company or society unless its articles of association or constitution forbid it to declare or otherwise divide profits for the benefit of its members at a higher rate than may be prescribed by the administrator ; or to (B) any person who does not satisfy the local authority that he is not the owner of any other dwelling suitable for his occupation, and that he intends to occupy personally the dwelling in respect of which the housing loan is applied for. Such individuals shall not sell the dwelling within a period of five years after the date of the registration of the mortgage bond in favour of the local authority unless he has first offered it for sale to the latter.

A housing loan shall be repaid as prescribed by the administrator, but the period for repayment of the total amount and interest shall not exceed (A) forty years for a company or society, (B) twenty years for any person.

Before approving of any scheme the administrator may require the local authority to make reasonable provision for dwellings for the poorest section of the population, including the coloured and native people.

The Act provides for proceedings to be taken in the event of a failure to make repayment, or to make reasonable progress with an approved dwelling, or to comply with any condition on which the advance has been made.

The Governor-General may from time to time grant to local authorities or to any company or society as referred to above any Crown land for the purpose of providing sites for an approved scheme, provided that the value of the land attached to such dwellings as form part of the scheme if and when sold shall be paid into the Treasury for credit to the Consolidated Revenue Account. The Minister may set apart any portion of such land for parks, recreation grounds and other public requirements.

COMPULSORY PURCHASE OF LAND.

A local authority may, with the approval of the Governor-General, acquire for the purposes of the Act by voluntary or compulsory purchase any land or interest in land situate within the area of jurisdiction of such authority. Before giving approval the Governor-General shall be satisfied that the local authority has no other land available and suitable, and is unable to acquire it by voluntary purchase on reasonable terms, etc.

PURCHASE OF MATERIALS : OTHER PROVISIONS.

A local authority may also, with the approval of the administrator, utilise any part of any town lands vested in it for the construction of approved dwellings, etc.

The Act further provides for advances by the Treasury to administrators to purchase stocks of building material and fittings for use in the construction of approved dwellings, etc.; and empowers the Minister to prohibit the construction of works or buildings if there is delay in the provision of dwelling accommodation owing to a deficiency of labour or materials (Section 15). A person who, without permission of the local authority or administrator, demolishes or uses otherwise than for residential purposes any building which was so used at the commencement of this Act, and which was reasonably fit for habitation, shall be liable on conviction to a fine or imprisonment.

The Minister may by notice in the *Gazette* prohibit the export from the Union of building materials except by permit.

A Central Housing Board shall be appointed by the Minister, of not more than five persons, including, as far as practicable, an architect and a municipal or sanitary engineer, to inquire into and report as to the necessity for the provision of dwellings, etc., and advise generally the Minister and administrators in carrying out the Act. Powers of entry and inspection of premises are given to members of the Board and other authorised persons.

DEBATE IN HOUSE OF ASSEMBLY.

In the House of Assembly on 17th June, 1920,
The Minister of Public Health (Hon. Sir Thomas Watt), in moving the Second Reading of the Bill, said that the first concern was to provide decent houses, so that people might get shelter and live in some degree of comfort; but it was hoped that the indirect effect of the Bill would be gradually to reduce rents and thus benefit the people.

The valuable report recently presented by a Committee of Inquiry drew attention to the shocking conditions under which the poorer classes, more especially the coloured and native population of their towns were living, and pointed out the necessity of providing 10,500 houses of from two to five rooms each, and also of housing between 11,000 and 12,000 natives and coloured people, who were living in the large centres. These figures did not include housing accommodation for public servants, nor dwellings which might be necessary owing to increasing population.

Government Assistance.

The Commission stated that the responsibility of supplementing private enterprise in the erection of houses should be borne by the Town Councils or other local authorities, but that, as the matter was of national importance, the Government should come to the assistance of local authorities with information and advice as to the best method to be adopted, and also give them financial assistance. The view, which was held by two out of the four commissioners, that if the Government made advances on reasonable terms that was all that it could be expected to do had been adopted by the Government and embodied in the Bill.

£500,000 for Housing Funds.

After stating that the matter could only be dealt with satisfactorily if Parliament voted the necessary moneys and exercised some measure of control, Sir Thomas Watt pointed out that the houses dealt with under the Bill were limited to five rooms, the object being to help especially the working classes and poorer members of the community. If a municipality preferred to borrow money in the open market, well and good; but the leading feature of the Bill was the establishment of a Housing Fund in each province, consisting of moneys voted from time to time by Parliament, and to be controlled by the Administrator; £500,000 would be put on that year's Loan Estimates for the purpose of starting these funds. The rate of interest to be charged by the Government would be regulated from time to time.

Compulsory Purchase of Land.

In outlining the main provisions of the Bill, Sir Thomas Watt drew special attention to the provision empowering local authorities to acquire land for the purpose indicated by compulsory expropriation in the event of an agreement not being come to with the owners. Houses for working people must be within a reasonable distance of their work, and as the success of housing schemes would largely depend upon getting suitable land at reasonable price, this power of compulsory expropriation was an absolute necessity. In all cases, of course, the fair value of the land must be paid, or would, failing agreement, be fixed by arbitration. Compulsory purchase was no new thing in South Africa, because throughout the Union land could be expropriated for such purposes as railways and schools, and no one would say that the provision of houses for the people was of less importance than either of these. The provision empowering the Administrator to purchase stocks of building materials for issue to local authorities also called for remark.

Section 15 of the Bill gave the Minister of the day unusual powers, because he might issue orders that no buildings other than dwellings might be erected in any town or area where there was a scarcity of labour or material, the object being to concentrate the efforts of employers and employees engaged in the building trade in providing houses. It was hoped that nothing would be done to check the industrial development that was going on, but they had expansion in other directions which might profitably be brought to a standstill in the interests of the houseless community.

Native and Coloured Problem.

The Housing Committee dealt at considerable length in their report on the necessity for properly housing the coloured and native population in the urban centres, and expressed the hope that the interest in the housing problem would not exhaust itself in efforts for the housing of white people only. Apart altogether from considerations of public health, there was a duty laid on the white population to ensure that no section of the community should be allowed to sink to such depths of discontent or depravity as to become a menace to the well-being of the community as a whole.

Private Enterprise.

After referring to the Central Housing Board, which would freely give any advice and assistance desired by municipalities, and advise the Minister, Sir Thomas Watt dealt with the criticism that the effect of the Bill would be to discourage private enterprise. He said that private enterprise in the building trade would not be concentrated on dwellings for the working classes unless there were some power of control, and the conservative tendencies of municipalities would not be stimulated to move in this matter unless financial assistance were to a reasonable extent given by the Government.

A Serious Economic Situation.

Mr. R. W. Close (Unionist, *Rondebosch, Cape*) said the Bill was an honest attempt on the part of the Government to cope with a serious economic situation. The local authorities were unable to exercise their present powers because if they did they had nowhere to place the people. The conversion of houses into warehouses and stores he considered was a serious factor in the situation.

His only regret in connection with the Bill, Mr. Close continued, was that the Minister had not taken his courage in both hands, and undertaken responsibility for passing a measure of town-planning. He hoped that on this Bill they would not have a discussion on private enterprise *versus* State enterprise, otherwise the Bill was going to be wrecked. What they wanted in the present case was that the State should supplement, not supplant, private enterprise.

As to the expropriation clause, he agreed with the Minister that this was the foundation of the success of the Bill.

Criticism of the Bill.

Mr. A. S. Van Hees (Nationalist, *Christiania, Trans.*) said they should be very careful about giving such wide powers as were contained in the expropriation clause. The Government ought seriously to consider the advisability of building houses for its own servants. He advocated the principle that large factories should be compelled to provide housing accommodation for the employees. If they extended the provisions of the Bill to natives, he did not consider they would be effective.

They were touching, by the expropriation and other powers given under the Bill, on the fringe of extreme Socialism and nationalisation, and he did not consider those powers should be given. He thought the work of building societies should be inquired into, and that the Government would be wise to proceed on the lines of those societies.

Bad Housing Conditions.

Mr. J. H. S. Gow (**Labour,** *Commissioner Street, Trans.*) said, with regard to the amount of £500,000 as the first instalment to be set aside by the Government, that for Cape Town alone they needed £1,500,000. The housing problem had been with them for many years, and was not the result of the War, as was frequently stated. Not only was there a shortage as far as the 10,000 houses mentioned was concerned, but there was a huge number of houses which needed to be pulled down as soon as possible. White people to-day in South Africa were living in houses which had the medical officer's badge on the door to say they were unfit for human habitation, and yet the people had to live in them. The position to-day was that private enterprise had failed, leaving it to the Government and local authorities to deal with the housing problem.

Mr. L. Geldenhuys (**South African Party,** *Johannesburg, North*) protested against giving rights to municipalities to raise large sums of money seeing that the members of municipalities were elected by people who had no stake in the town and often paid no rates at all.

Mr. J. H. H. de Waal (**Nationalist,** *Piquetberg, Cape*) said the house shortage was due primarily to the scarcity of material and, secondly, to the fact that the Government by its actions had discouraged private individuals from investing their money in house property.

The debate was adjourned.

On 18th June the Housing Bill was read a second time, and referred to a Select Committee.

In the course of the discussions in Committee on 30th July and 2nd August a new clause, proposed by Mr. A. P. J. Fourie, requiring that before approving of any housing loan and making any advance to a local authority the Administrator must be satisfied that the approval of the local authorities and the ratepayers had been given, was discussed at length, and negatived by 65 votes to 39.

The Bill was read a third time on 4th August.

IN THE SENATE.

The Bill was not debated at great length in the Senate. Some amendments were made during the Committee Stage, which was concluded on 12th August.

PROFITEERING ACT.

The Debate on the Second Reading of the Profiteering Bill (introduced in the House of Assembly on 26th March, 1920) was summarised in the JOURNAL, Vol. I., No. 3 (July, 1920) pp. 568-581. The Bill was referred to a Select Committee for consideration and report. The Bill in its final form was passed during the Session.

The Act applies, subject to certain exceptions enumerated below (Sub-section 4 of Section 1), to any article or class of articles which the Minister declares by notice in the *Gazette* to be a necessary commodity, or to be material, machinery, tools, etc., used in the production of such a commodity.

APPROVAL OF PARLIAMENT.

A notice issued as above shall be laid upon the Tables of both Houses of Parliament. This notice shall be effective unless both Houses of Parliament disapprove by Resolution.

Section 1, Sub-section (4) provides that the Act shall not apply to the sale of articles for export from the Union ; the sale of articles by public auction or competitive tender ; the sale by the producer of any article produced or derived from agricultural, stock rearing, horticultural or any farming operations whatever on land owned or occupied by him.

BOARD OF CONTROL.

The Governor-General shall constitute a Board of Control consisting of a chairman and not less than four other members with power to investigate prices, costs and profits at all stages, and to require any person to appear before it and to furnish information ; to restrict profit at any or all stages ; to compel any manufacturer, importer or distributor to supply any article which he may have in stock on the most favourable terms, in accordance with the custom of the trade, to any *bona fide* trader, etc., in a position to make satisfactory arrangements for payment, and willing to take the usual quantities ; to prohibit, regulate or restrict, subject to the approval of the Minister, the export of article required for the maintenance of the food supplies of the Union ; to order that articles shall pass from the producer, manufacturer, etc., to the consumer in as direct a line and with as few intermediaries as possible and to receive and investigate complaints that there is being or has been made or is sought to be made an unreasonable profit ; and on any such complaint the Board may by order, after giving the parties an opportunity of being heard, either dismiss the complaint or declare the profit which would be reasonable, and require the seller to repay to the complainant any amount paid by him in excess of a reasonable profit, subject to the complaint being received by the Board within one month of the date of sale.

PENALTIES FOR PROFITEERING.

If, as a result of investigations, it appears that the circumstances so require, the Board (not having already made an order in terms referred to above) shall institute criminal proceedings against the seller in a magistrate's court having jurisdiction, and if the court is satisfied that the profit charged or sought by the seller exceeds that permitted by an order of the Board or is an unreasonable profit, he shall be guilty of an offence and liable on conviction to a fine not exceeding five hundred pounds or to imprisonment without the option of a fine for a period not exceeding twelve months or both, and the court may also make such an order or repayment as the Board might have made, as indicated above.

If any person fails to comply with an order he shall be liable on conviction to a fine not exceeding fifty pounds or to imprisonment without the option of a fine for a period not exceeding one month, or to both.

LOCAL COMMITTEES.

The Governor-General may, when necessary, establish a local committee to which the Minister may assign any or all of the powers referred to above in respect of any notified articles or sales thereof, the effect of any order by a committee being the same as that of the Board.

The Governor-General may make regulations and give directions as to the constitution, powers and procedure of committees so established ; such regulations are to be laid upon the Tables of both Houses of Parliament, and shall be effective unless both Houses disapprove by Resolution. The regulations may provide for the inclusion of women on a committee.

The proceedings before the Board or any committee shall, where such proceedings are founded on a complaint, be held in public.

Every person subpœnaed to attend and give evidence before the Board or any committee, or to produce books or other documents shall be bound to obey under penalty of a fine.

Every person so subpœnaed shall be entitled to the privileges of a witness before a provincial division of the Supreme Court, except that he cannot refuse to answer any question or to produce books, etc., on the ground that either would tend to incriminate him under the Act.

A person giving false evidence shall be guilty of perjury.

INFORMATION.

The Board shall obtain from all available sources (Section 9) information as to the nature, extent and development of trusts, companies, firms, etc., etc., connected with mining, manufacturing, trade, commerce, etc., having for their purpose the regulation of price or output of commodities or services produced or rendered in the Union, or the delimitation of markets in respect thereof, or the regulation of transport rates and services, in so far as they tend to the creation of monopolies or to the restraint of trade.

Any person associated with the management of such a trust, company, etc., shall be guilty of an offence if it is proved that owing to the
operations of such a trust, company, etc., the price of any notified article
has been unreasonably enhanced or the output has been unduly restricted,
etc., and that such a person knew or must have known of such operations.
On conviction the offender shall be liable to a fine not exceeding five
thousand pounds or to imprisonment without the option of a fine for a
period not exceeding three years or both.

In the interpretation clause of the Act it is provided that in declaring
a profit to be " unreasonable profit " regard shall be had *inter alia* to :—

(A) the average gross profit earned by the seller or by persons
in the same class of business upon the sale of the notified or of a like
article during 1911, 1912, and 1913 ;

(B) interest on any increased capital employed since the commencement of 1915 ;

(C) any increase since the commencement of 1915 in the ordinary
and reasonable cost incurred by the seller in the carrying on of
the business at which the notified article is sold ; and

(D) any increase since the commencement of 1915 in the ordinary
and reasonable domestic expenditure of the seller, consequent on the
increased cost of living.

DEBATE IN HOUSE OF ASSEMBLY.

Certain amendments were moved, and for the most part
negatived, during the discussions on the clauses of the Bill
and the amendments of the Select Committee, on 5th July.

The Bill and the Farmers.

Mr. Richard Feetham (Unionist, *Parktown, Trans.***)** urged
that the Board should have power to deal with both producer
and distributors.   Agricultural produce was exempted from the
operations of the Bill, and he moved an amendment to bring
the exempted articles under the operation of Clause 9 (giving
power to deal with trusts, combines, etc.).

Mr. T. Boydell (Labour, *Durban, Greyville, Natal***)** observed
that the farmers would be the only section of the community which would be allowed to profiteer.

The Minister of Justice (Hon. N. J. De Wet) wondered why
some of those who talked so much about the farmers " grinding
down the poor " did not become farmers themselves, instead
of being highly-paid artisans.

Colonel F. H. P. Creswell (Leader of the Labour Party)
asked why, if this Bill were to do any good, should the prime
producer, the farmer alone of all persons engaged in the production and distribution of the necessaries of life, be exempted.
With regard to the recent increase in the price of bread, the
Government told them the high price was due to world scarcity.

and that they would have to pay the same amount for wheat grown in the country as for the imported wheat. That was a libel on the patriotism of the wheat growers of the country. As much wheat could be produced as they wanted at 25s. a bag. There was nothing wrong in giving a fair reward to the farmer, and the Government should take measures to fix the price above which wheat should not be bought or sold in South Africa.

The Hon. Sir Edgar Walton (Unionist, *Port Elizabeth, Central, Cape*) thoroughly agreed with the policy of exempting the farmers as producers from the operations of the Bill because they ought to be encouraged to increase their production as much as possible.

The Hon. Sir Thomas Smartt (Leader of the Unionist Party) said he did not believe that the farmers of the country had to any extent taken advantage of the high prices which had prevailed. These were due to the speculation which was rampant.

Mr. Feetham's amendment was defeated by 62 votes to 39.

Labour Representation.

On 6th July in the House of Assembly **Mr. F. Nettleton** (Labour, *Durban, Umbilo, Natal*) moved an amendment to the effect that half the members of the Board of Control—

"shall be selected from nominations submitted on behalf of the consumers, by the recognised labour organisations."

The day was past when committees consisted of one section only, and all sections of the community should be represented on it.

Mr. E. G. A. Saunders (South African Party, *Natal, Coast*) moved an amendment urging that representatives of traders, the mines, manufacturers and consumers respectively should be added.

Mr. W. H. Stuart (Unionist, *Tembuland, Cape*) opposed the amendments on the ground that they wanted men on the Board of Control who were fair, not men who were representative of a particular type of person, nor men who were "sympathetic" because they were under the domination of a particular trade union.

The Minister of Justice (Hon. N. J. De Wet) said they were not going to get a good Board of Control by tying it down to representatives of particular bodies or interests. They would get the best Board by leaving it entirely free to whatever Government had to appoint it to get the most suitable men they possibly could. He was glad that Mr. Stuart had not moved an amendment for the appointment of a representative of the natives. The natives formed by far the greater proportion of the consumers of South Africa, and if this principle

of selecting members by reason of their association with a
particular class or interest were followed, the natives undoubtedly would have a very strong claim to representation on the
Board.

Both amendments were lost.

Municipal Trading.

Mr. F. Nettleton moved a new Clause 10 :

" Notwithstanding anything to the contrary in any Act contained,
a municipality or any other local authority shall for the purpose of preventing profiteering or of reducing the cost of living, have the right
to trade (by purchase and sale) in any necessary commodity."

Col. F. H. P. Creswell (Leader of the Labour Party) said in
h's opinion the soundest part of the Bill would be the amendment now submitted. If, as they had been told, this legislation,
by the interference which it involved with private enterprise,
was going to make the business of the merchant, the house
builder, and so on, more difficult and less attractive, it meant
that there would be less activity in that direction by private
enterprise : if so, they were bound to supplement it by conferring upon local authorities such powers as were proposed in the
amendment.

Sir Abe Bailey (Independent, *Krugersdorp, Trans.***)** said
that it was quite impossible to govern people and trade with
them as well.

Mr. R. Feetham (Unionist, *Parktown, Trans.***)** said they
should not interfere with the functions of the Provincial
Councils. Labour members seemed to have no regard for
constitutional authority at all, if it stood in the way of what
they wanted for the moment.

After some discussion the amendment was negatived.

IN THE SENATE.

The Profiteering Bill was read a third time in the Senate
on 23rd July, 1920, without debate.

SPECULATION IN FOODSTUFFS PREVENTION ACT.

The purpose of this Act is to license dealers and brokers
in foodstuffs, and to prevent speculation in foodstuffs.

It provides that after the expiry of thirty days from the commencement of the Act no person shall carry on business as a dealer in foodstuffs without a licence under the Act.

No person so licensed shall either directly or indirectly carry on the business of a broker in foodstuffs, auctioneer or market agent, and no person licensed as a broker, and no auctioneer or market agent shall directly or indirectly carry on the business of a dealer in foodstuffs.

Every dealer or broker shall keep such books, accounts and vouchers as will reveal in full his transactions, such books and accounts to be accessible at all reasonable times for the inspection of any officer administering this Act or of anyone authorised by him in writing to make such inspection. Any dealer or broker not complying with these provisions shall be guilty of an offence.

No contract (Section 4) between dealers or between a dealer and broker for the sale or delivery of foodstuffs above the value of ten pounds sterling shall be valid unless it is in writing and specifies the price, quantity and weight of the commodity sold, the place from which it will be consigned, and the time within which delivery is to be made.

If a person has entered into a contract to sell foodstuffs and at the date specified under the contract for delivery there is a difference between the specified contract price and the current market price for the same or similar foodstuffs, such person, where the difference is a decrease of the contract price, shall not be entitled to recover the amount of such difference or any part thereof or any amount whatever by way of damages unless at the date of the contract he was in possession of the foodstuffs contracted to be sold, or as a producer or by reason of a contract for the purchase of such foodstuffs he had reasonable expectation that he would be able to effect delivery thereof at the date fixed under the contract.

Any person who, either directly or indirectly, accepts payment which under this Section (5) he is not entitled to recover, shall be guilty of an offence.

The Governor-General is empowered under the Act to make regulations as to the issue and conditions of licences, etc.

Any person who contravenes or fails to comply with any provision of regulation of this Act shall, if no penalty be specially provided, be liable to a fine not exceeding five hundred pounds or to imprisonment without the option of a fine for a period not exceeding six months.

DEBATE IN HOUSE OF ASSEMBLY.

In the House of Assembly on 29th July during the discussions in Committee,

Mr. E. Nathan (Unionist, *Von Brandis, Trans.*) said he thought there should be some limit in price or value to which such contracts should apply, and he moved to insert the words " above the value of £100 " in Clause (4) of the Bill,* so that any transaction below that amount would not be affected by the Bill.

Mr. C. B. Heatlie (South African Party, *Worcester, Cape)* pointed out how these contracts were entered into, and considered that the disclosure of the purchaser would seriously

---

* The Bill as amended in Select Committee contained no limitation regarding the value of the contract.

affect business. If they made it more difficult for the legitimate trader to carry on his business, either the producer would
be paid less or the consumer would be charged more, or both
might be affected. These restrictions would be got round as
easily as possible by the unscrupulous man. The honest trader
would not attempt to get round them.

Colonel W. R. Collins (South African Party, *Ermelo, Cape*)
contended that transactions to a value of under £25 should not
be brought under the Bill, and he moved to that effect.

The Minister of Justice (Hon. N. J. de Wet) said the law
would not interfere with bona-fide transactions but only
speculative transactions. He considered the Bill would
control speculation to some extent, and if it succeeded in
eliminating one-half of the number of middlemen it would
be an achievement.

Mr. Nathan said that he would accept Colonel Collins'
amendment, and it was agreed to omit " £100 " from and
insert " £25 " in his (Mr. Nathan's) amendment, which in
this form was adopted by 69 votes to 22.

On the resumption of the debate in the House of Assembly
on 30th July,

Mr. C. T. M. Wilcocks (Nationalist, *Winburg, O.F.S.*)
moved to delete the provision that transactions under £25
should be excluded, and the Bill be made to apply to transactions under £50.

The Minister of Justice moved to amend £25 to £10.

By 48 votes to 47 it was resolved that " £25 " be omitted,
and it was resolved by 56 votes to 44 that " £10 " be inserted.

The Bill as amended was adopted and set down for
Third Reading.

IN THE SENATE.

In moving the Second Reading in the Senate on 4th August

The Minister of Justice remarked that that was the third
and last of the Bills with which he had been entrusted to deal
with the cost of living. He did not think it would stop
speculation, but it would check it. It was an experimental
measure.

The Second Reading was agreed to.

NEWFOUNDLAND.

The Acts which are summarised below were passed during the First Session of the twenty-fourth Parliament, which terminated on 13th July, 1920. Owing to the non-receipt of the Parliamentary Debates from the Dominion, it is regretted that summaries of the discussions cannot be given in the present number.

PEACE TREATIES ACT.

This Act, which was passed on 13th July, 1920, gives effect as far as Newfoundland is concerned to the Treaties of Peace between His Majesty and the late enemy Powers.

The Act provides that :—

"Whereas on the twenty-eighth day of June, one thousand nine hundred and nineteen, a Treaty of Peace between the Allied and Associated Powers and Germany was signed on behalf of His Majesty, acting for Newfoundland, by the plenipotentiaries therein named ;

And whereas Treaties of Peace between the Allied and Associated Powers and Austria and Bulgaria respectively have since been signed on behalf of His Majesty, acting for Newfoundland, by the plenipotentiaries therein named ;

And whereas it is probable that a Treaty of Peace will shortly be concluded between the Allied and Associated Powers and Turkey, which will be signed on behalf of His Majesty, acting for Newfoundland, by the plenipotentiaries therein named ;

And whereas it is desirable that the Governor-in-Council should have power to do all such things as may be necessary and proper for giving effect to the said Treaties ;

Be it therefore enacted by the Governor, the Legislative Council, and House of Assembly, in Legislative Session convened, as follows :—

1. The Governor-in-Council may do all such things as he may consider necessary for carrying the said Treaties into effect, and for that purpose may make such appointments, establish such offices, and make such Orders-in-Council as he may consider necessary or expedient.

2. All such Orders-in-Council shall be published in the Royal Gazette, and shall have the force and effect of law as if enacted in this Act. Any such Order may provide for the imposition of penalties for the breach of any of the provisions thereof.

FORMER ENEMY ALIENS ACT.

This Act (a summary of the Bill was given in the JOURNAL OF THE PARLIAMENTS OF THE EMPIRE, Vol. I., No. 3, page 593) was passed on 13th July, 1920. It prevents the entry, except

by special permission, of former enemy aliens into Newfoundland, or their acquisition of property, or their employment on
ships registered in the Colony, for a period of three years.

SHIPBUILDING (AMENDMENT) ACT.

(Encouragement of Shipbuilding.)

An Act was passed on 13th July, 1920, to amend
Chapter 176 of the Consolidated Statutes of Newfoundland
(Third Series) entitled "Of the Encouragement of Ship-
building."

The Act provides that the bounty payable in respect of vessels
built in the Colony, as provided in Section 3 of Chapter 176 of the Consolidated Statutes of Newfoundland (Third Series), shall in no case exceed
the amount payable on one hundred and fifty tons ; but where a vessel
is built in excess of that tonnage and is otherwise entitled to bounty
there shall be payable to the owner thereof a bounty upon one hundred and
fifty tons in accordance with the said section.

It is further provided that where any vessel of a greater tonnage
than one hundred and fifty tons is built in the Colony, the keel of which
is laid after the passing of the Act, or was launched in the Colony during
the year 1919, and duty has been paid upon any of the materials used
in the construction of the vessel, the owner shall be entitled to be repaid
the amount of such duty upon proof to the satisfaction of the proper
Customs authorities that such duty has been paid.

SALARIES ACT.

(Ministers, Judges, &c.)

This Act, which was passed on 13th July, 1920, amends the
Act respecting Salaries of 1898 by substituting the following
amounts as the yearly salaries and allowances to be paid
the undermentioned officers.

The Governor of the Colony	$15,000
The Prime Minister	4,000
The Colonial Secretary	4,000
The Minister of Justice	4,000
The Minister of Finance and Customs	4,000
The Minister of Marine and Fisheries	4,000
The Minister of Agriculture and Mines	4,000
The Minister of Shipping	4,000
The Minister of Public Works	4,000
The Minister of Posts and Telegraphs	4,000
The Minister of Education	4,000

Each member of the Board of Works	.. ..	$250
The Sheriff	.. ..	2,760
The Comptroller and Auditor-General	.. ..	4,000
The Judge of the Central District Court ..	..	4,140
The Judge of the Harbour Grace District Court..		1,728

PROFITEERING ACT.

This Act, which was passed on 13th July, is for the purpose of checking profiteering.

The Act provides that whereas it appears that the prices of articles sold in the Colony are being enhanced in some cases by the charging of prices yielding an unreasonable profit to the persons engaged in the production, handling or distribution thereof, the Food Control Board shall have power :—

(A) To investigate prices, costs and profits at all stages, and for that purpose by order to require any person to appear before them, and to furnish such information and produce such documents as they may require ; and on any such investigation they may by order fix maximum prices ; and

(B) to receive and investigate complaints that a profit is being or has been, since the passing of this Act, made or sought on the sale of the article (whether wholesale or retail) which is, in view of all the circumstances, unreasonable, and on any such complaint, they may by order, after giving the parties an opportunity of being heard, either dismiss the complaint, or

(1) declare the price which would yield a reasonable profit ; and

(2) require the seller to repay to the complainant any amount paid by the complainant in excess of such price.

Upon a complaint being made by any person to the Board that profit upon an article sold is unreasonable the Board shall forthwith cause an investigation to be made, and if it appears to the Board that the circumstances so require, the Board shall take proceedings against the seller before a Court of summary jurisdiction, and if it is found that the price charged or sought was such as to yield a profit which is, in view of all the circumstances, unreasonable, the seller shall be liable on summary conviction to a fine not exceeding five hundred dollars or, in default of payment, to imprisonment for a term not exceeding three months ; provided that a rate of profit which does not exceed the fair average rate earned by persons in the same way of business as the seller upon the sale of similar articles under pre-war conditions shall not be deemed unreasonable.

After prescribing penalties for violation of an order by the Board and for giving false information, the Act goes on to provide that where a person convicted is a Company, the Chairman and every Managing Director and every Officer concerned in the management of the Company shall be guilty of the like offence, unless he proves that the act which constituted the offence took place without his knowledge, or without his consent.

Q

The Board also has power to require any person appearing before them under the Act to give evidence on oath, and to authorise any person to administer an oath for the purpose.

Nothing in the Act shall apply to the sale of any article for export from Newfoundland, or to the sale of any articles by public auction or competitive tender.

It is further provided that the Governor-in-Council may appoint and establish local or other committees which shall have the same powers as the Board in respect of any articles or classes of articles, or sales, except the power of the Board to fix prices ; and the effect of any order by any such committee shall be the same as that of any order of the Board.

Provision is also made for penalties for refusal to sell, and appeal from Courts of summary jurisdiction to the Supreme Court.

EDUCATION ACT AMENDMENT.

This Act, which was passed on 13th July, 1920, amends the Education Act by. creating a Department of Education under a Minister and an Advisory Board for the Department; and by appointing various educational officers.

The Act provides for the creation of a Department of Education to be presided over and managed by a Minister of Education, and the appointment of a Deputy Minister and departmental officers. Power is given to the Governor-in-Council to establish a Normal School for the purpose of affording professional training for student and other teachers, and to order an annual census of school children between the ages of six and fourteen. The powers of the Minister include the enforcement of the provisions of this Act and the Education Act, the holding of annual conferences of Supervising Inspectors, the suspension or cancellation on the recommendation of the Advisory Board or Committee thereof for inefficiency, etc., of the diploma or certificate of any Inspector or Teacher, the appointment on the nomination of the Advisory Board of a Board of Examiners to conduct all examinations of teachers and Supervising Inspectors, the distribution of all educational appropriations made by the Legislature among the various religious denominations upon a per capita basis, and the presentation to the Legislature of an annual Report of all schools assisted financially by the Government and full account of the moneys expended. The Superintendents are empowered to have the general supervision and direction of all schools, academies, colleges and training schools of their respective denominations receiving aid from the Government, to have the supervision of the Normal School, Domestic Science, Summer and Night Schools, and to make conjointly with the approval of the Minister certain rules and regulations for these purposes.

The Act further provides for an Advisory Board of the Department of Education consisting of twelve members, six to be appointed by the Governor-in-Council, of whom one shall belong to the Roman Catholic Church, one to the Church of England, one to the Methodist Church, one to the Presbyterian Church, one to the Salvation Army, and one to represent the Congregational Church ; these members shall be appointed by the Teachers' Association belonging to the Roman Catholic Church he Church of England, and the Methodist Church ; Superintendents of Education shall be *ex-officio* members of the Board. Members are to hold ffice for three years and be eligible for reappointment. The duties f the Board consist of determining the standard of admission of students b the Normal Training School, the conditions for the certification of eachers, the nomination of the Board of Examiners, the submission of egulations affecting school buildings and advice as to courses of tudy in public schools.

The Act also provides for the establishment in St. John's for higher ducation of a Church of England College, a Methodist College, a Presbyrian College and two Roman Catholic Colleges, one for males and one or females, with Boards of Directors belonging to the Roman Catholic hurch.

· The Governor-in-Council is empowered to appoint eleven Supervising inspectors belonging to the several religious denominations, who shall sit, supervise, examine, and report upon all schools assigned to them by the proper Superintendent of each denomination. Any religious enomination not provided for as regards superintendence or inspection may, by application to the Minister, select any Superintendent and upervising Inspector for its purpose.

After detailing the duties of the Supervising Inspectors the Act jovides for the appropriation of certain sums of money to be apporned amongst the several religious denominations accordirg to their rspective populations for general educational purposes, assisting Boards of Education to establish schools and supply teachers in sparsely populated lcalities and to establish Superior or High Schools in central localities i their districts, maintainirg and training Normal School teachers, tchnical, educational and manual training, providing educational facilities i places which have grown up since the previous census of Newfoundland, ad other purposes.

DEPARTMENTAL POSTS AND TELEGRAPHS ACT.

This Act, which was passed on 13th July, 1920, abolishes the office of Postmaster-General and provides, *inter alia*, for the creation of a Department of Posts and Telegraphs to be presided over by a Minister of Posts and Telegraphs appointed by the Governor-in-Council by Commission under the Great Seal. The Department shall have the supervision, control and direction of all matters relating to the postal and telegraph services of the Colony.

JOURNAL OF THE PARLIAMENTS OF THE EMPIRE

Vol. II.—No. 2.   April, 1921.

Issued under the Authority of the
EMPIRE PARLIAMENTARY ASSOCIATION
(United Kingdom Branch),
WESTMINSTER HALL, HOUSES OF PARLIAMENT,
LONDON, S.W.1.

Price to Non-Members 10s. Net.

CONTENTS.

AUSTRALIA.

Commonwealth Parliament.

State Parliaments.

New South Wales.

Queensland.

South Australia.

Western Australia.

NEW ZEALAND.

CONTENTS.

SOUTH AFRICA.

NEWFOUNDLAND.

INTRODUCTION.

The present quarterly issue of the JOURNAL being the latest that will be published before the meeting of the Prime Ministers of the Empire at the Conference in June next, members of Parliament throughout the British Commonwealth will, no doubt, first turn to those subjects recorded in this number which affect the coming Cabinet conferences.

It may, therefore, be convenient to point out that in the proceedings of the Parliament of the United Kingdom, which are summarised in this issue, references will be found in the course of the Debate on the Address to the coming Cabinet meetings, and to subjects which may be discussed there. Particular mention may be made of the debate arising on the amendment to the Address relating to the co-ordination of the problems of Imperial Defence as affecting the Empire as a whole. Again, the discussions in both Houses on the Mandatory System and its control by Parliament are of importance in this connection.

In the Canadian Parliament, considerable interest in the forthcoming gathering of Prime Ministers, and in Imperial affairs generally, has been manifested in the questions and discussions. In the Debate on the Address the meeting of Prime Ministers is given special attention, and both in this Debate, and in that on the Canadian Nationals Definition Bill, the position and status of Canada within the Empire and in relation to the outside world and the League of Nations have been discussed at some length.

In the Australian Commonwealth section, a step has been taken in this number of the JOURNAL which is contrary to the usual practice in dealing with the debates in the various Parliaments, none of which have hitherto been summarised from any source but the Official Parliamentary Debates. But in view of the fact that Mr. Hughes delivered an important speech in the House of Representatives on 8th April upon the work of the forthcoming Cabinet meetings in June, and that this was officially telegraphed in full to the Acting High Commissioner, it has been thought very necessary to include a summary in the present issue. Other proceedings of the Commonwealth Parliament which are summarised relate only to that part of the Session which ended in November, 1920, where the debates on Defence Policy and on the Nationality Act are of Imperial importance, while such Acts as the Immigration Amendment Act and the Aliens Registration Act also call for notice in this connection.

In New Zealand questions also have been asked as to the position of that Dominion in Imperial affairs, particularly in relation to the meeting of Prime Ministers. Some indication has been shown here, as in Canada, of the desire that any action taken by Ministers should be subject to approval by Parliament.

Among other subjects dealt with in this number which may be said to affect directly all the nations of the British Commonwealth are : in the United Kingdom, the Navy, Army, and Air Estimates, Oversea Settlement and Unemployment, and Trade within the Empire ; in Canada, Trade with Russia, the Naval Contribution, and the Cattle Embargo; in Australia, the Air Navigation Act, the War Precautions Act Repeal, and the Passports Act ; in New Zealand, the External Affairs Amendment Act, and Overseas Shipping and Freights ; and in South Africa the Financial and Economic Situation and Repatriation of Indians.

In the category of more local legislation, but which, nevertheless, has a distinct and important bearing on similar legislation already introduced, or perhaps to be introduced, into other countries of the Empire, may be mentioned such subjects as : in the United Kingdom, the Unemployment Problem and the Criminal Law Amendment Bill (indecent assaults on young persons, etc.); in Australia, the Industrial Peace Act (Amendment), Profiteering (N.S.W.), the proposed abolition of State Parliaments (N.S.W.), the Government Loans Subscription Bill (Queensland), and Venereal Diseases Act (S. Australia) ; in New Zealand, Industrial Conciliation and Arbitration, and the Divorce and Matrimonial Causes Amendment Act; in South Africa, the Regulation of Wages Bill, which provides for the establishment of Wages Boards to fix minimum rates of wages, etc., and Bills relating to marriage and divorce.

Since the publication of the last JOURNAL, the General Election in the Union of South Africa has been held, and has resulted in the combined South African and Unionist Parties (henceforth to be known as the South African Party), under General Smuts, securing a substantial majority over any other combination. A footnote giving the figures will be found in the South African section of the JOURNAL (see page 436), and this should be compared with the election results of 1920 appearing in the JOURNAL for April, 1920 (Vol., I. No. 2, page 382).

THE EDITOR.

EMPIRE PARLIAMENTARY ASSOCIATION
    (*United Kingdom Branch*),
    WESTMINSTER HALL,
        HOUSES OF PARLIAMENT,
            LONDON, S.W.1.

15th April, 1921.

UNITED KINGDOM.

The third Session of the third Parliament of King George V.
was opened by His Majesty in person with full State ceremonial
on 15th February, 1921.
The appended summary of the proceedings in the two Houses
covers the period up to 24th March, when Parliament adjourned
or the Easter recess.

THE ADDRESS—GENERAL DISCUSSION.

(Imperial Conference: India: Egypt: Middle East:
Ireland: House of Lords Reform, etc.)

The Debate on the Address in reply to His Majesty's
gracious Speech from the Throne was commenced in the
House of Commons on 15th February, 1921, and was brought
to a conclusion on 21st February.

In the course of the Speech from the Throne, His Majesty referred
to the visit of the Duke of Connaught to inaugurate the new Councils
in India, the forthcoming Imperial Cabinet meetings, the Irish situation,
unemployment, the removal of coal control, the reorganisation of the
railways of Great Britain, the sale of alcohol, Reform of the House of
Lords, etc.

The reference to the visit of the Dominion Prime Ministers was as
follows:—" I am glad to say that arrangements have been made to
renew that personal consultation between My Ministers here and their
colleagues overseas, which produced such good results during the last
two years of the War and during the Peace settlement. I hope that the
Prime Ministers of Canada, Australia, New Zealand, the Union of South
Africa, and Newfoundland, as well as representatives of India, will be
able to visit the country during the coming summer. I am confident
that the discussions to take place during their visits will be of the utmost
value in bringing about co-ordination both in the external and internal
policy of the Empire."

The Address was moved by Mr. J. C. C. Davidson
(Coalition Unionist, *Hemel Hempstead*), and seconded by
Mr. Henry Fildes (Coalition Liberal, *Stockport*). A general
debate followed.

DEBATE IN HOUSE OF COMMONS.

**The Right Hon. H. H. Asquith (Leader of the Independent
Liberal Party)** remarked that the Speech was more remarkable
for the things it omitted than for what it contained. No one

would gather from reading it that within the last week there
had been a Conference of the Allies in Paris at which vita.
decisions were taken revising and recasting in most important
particulars the Treaty of Versailles.

The Middle East.

Another notable omission was that the Speech contained
no mention of the situation in Mesopotamia, or the policy of
His Majesty's Government in relation to that territory and
the large group of acutely difficult problems which had sprung
up in what was called the Middle East.

He congratulated Mr. Churchill very heartily on under
taking the administration of the Colonial Office, and he wished
to ask one or two questions about the new Middle Eastern
Department, with the formation and conduct of which the
right hon. gentleman said he had been entrusted. What was
it? Was it to be independent of the War Office? Was it
to be an excrescence on the Colonial Office? And what, if
any, were to be its relations to the Foreign Office? Above
all, what was to be its policy, on what lines was it going to work
and in what direction was it going to move?

India, Egypt, Imperial Conference, Ireland.

Turning to other paragraphs in the Speech, Mr. Asquith
remarked that with regard to India he had only to say that,
without distinction of party, they looked with the greatest
goodwill and the most perfect and sanguine expectation upon
the great new adventure which was now on foot. As to
Egypt, the House would be glad to know whether the Report
submitted to the Government by Lord Milner and his
colleagues in the Mission,* of which he was the head, was to
be adopted, or was to form the basis of the policy which the
Government intended to pursue. With regard to bringing the
Dominion Prime Ministers into conference in London,

---

* The Mission, which arrived in Cairo in December, 1919, was
appointed " To inquire into the causes of the late disorders in Egypt,
and to report on the existing situation in the country and the form of the
Constitution which, under the Protectorate, will be best calculated to
promote its peace and prosperity, the progressive development of self-
governing institutions, and the protection of foreign interests." The
Mission recommended that, as between Egypt and Great Britain a
Treaty should be entered into under which Great Britain would recognise
the independence of Egypt as a constitutional monarchy with representative institutions, and Egypt would confer upon Great Britain such rights
as are necessary to safeguard her special interests, and to enable her to
furnish the guarantees which must be given to foreign Powers to secure
the relinquishment of their capitulatory rights.

"that," said Mr. Asquith, "is a wise development of a policy which has been the common property of all parties in the State for the past ten years, and from which nothing but the most beneficent results to the Empire can ensue."

Turning to Ireland, the right hon. gentleman mentioned various matters on which further information was desired from the Government, including the negotiations which took place in December between Archbishop Clune, Father O'Flanagan, and others on the one side, and the Prime Minister on the other.

Labour and Economy.

The **Right Hon. J. H. Thomas (Labour,** *Derby*) referred to a statement in the Speech that it was the Government's intention to reduce expenditure to the lowest level consistent with the well-being of the Empire. While the members of the Labour Party realised the seriousness of the financial position, they submitted that the most effective means whereby economy could be established was not by saving a few thousands on social reform or education, but by tackling the millions which were being wasted on armaments and on expeditions in Mesopotamia and other places. There was a statement in the Speech that unemployment was consequent upon the world-wide restriction of trade. He agreed entirely. But the problem could not be separated from the foreign policy of the Government. "We submit," Mr. Thomas said, "that the first and real step towards the cure of unemployment is to heal the wounds of the late War, and frankly to recognise that however much we may talk about punishment of our late enemies, every time we hit them we are hitting ourselves. In other words, the high cost of living and the problem of finding employment cannot be solved until trade and commerce are set going the world over."

With reference to the Irish situation, Mr. Thomas said that as a nation they were suffering in all parts of the world in consequence of what was taking place in Ireland. Bitterness and hatred were being caused between the English and Irish people which, if not checked, would be a real danger to the Empire.

Peace the Supreme Interest.

The **Prime Minister (the Right Hon. D. Lloyd George)** said he did not consider correct Mr. Asquith's description of the Paris Resolutions as a revision and recasting of the Treaty of Versailles. He had repeatedly reminded the House of the very important provisions introduced into the Treaty which enabled the Powers to consider proposals under what was known in France as the system of *forfait* — a system of annuities which would enable Germany to discharge her liabilities. In so far as they differed from proposals which had been put forward before, the one essentially new element introduced at the last Paris Conference was that there should be an annuity which would fluctuate according to the prosperity of the export trade of Germany.

With regard to the Turkish controversy, the supreme interest of the British Empire, of the Allies, and of the world was that peace should be established, whether in the Middle East or in Central Europe. At the ensuing Conference in London His Majesty's representatives would be animated by that supreme desire, subject to the paramount obligation to see that right was done to the Christian population of Turkey, who had suffered so severely from the excesses of Turkish misgovernment.

The Middle East : Egypt.

The new Middle East Department would probably be in the Colonial Office. The relations of the new Department would be just like the relations with the Colonial Office of any other part of the world. The Foreign Office might be brought in, as it had been in the past in reference to other parts of the territories which were under the control of the Colonial Office. The same thing applied to the War Office.

" With regard to Egypt," said the Premier, " we propose to lay the Milner Report on the Table of the House and the House will have an opportunity of discussing it. The Government are not prepared to say to what extent they can adopt that Report or even accept its recommendations, certainly not until they have had a conference with the Egyptian Ministers, who so far have not been consulted in the matter officially. It will be our business to find out exactly their views on the subject. If it had been possible I should have liked also to take into consultation the representatives of the Dominions before we come to any decision. It is a matter of most vital moment to the Empire, to the peace of the Middle East, and to our future relations, perhaps, with India."

Reform of Second Chamber.

Touching on the question of reform of the House of Lords, Mr. Lloyd George remarked that the subject was an easy one, and the appointment of a Committee careful to investigate the matter was an essential preliminary, was because the Government could not give a definite plan as to when the Committee would be able to conclude its labours that a very careful statement had been put in the King's Speech.* It was no use giving undertakings until they had in their minds a definite and clear plan with which they were prepared to proceed immediately.

The Right Hon. Lord Robert Cecil (Independent Unionist, *Hitchin*) asked whether the Committee was a fresh Parliamentary Committee or a Cabinet Committee.

The Prime Minister : " A Cabinet Committee with a view to framing a scheme. As far as outside Committees are concerned, the subject has been discussed by a very able Committee presided over by Lord Bryce. The Cabinet have certainly the responsibility of deciding the matter."

Ireland : The Cork Burnings.

Proceeding to refer to Ireland, the Prime Minister dealt first with the Report relating to the extensive destruction of premises in Cork by fire, and the question of its publication. It was not, he said, General Strickland's Report ; it was simply a Report from the area of which General Strickland was in military command—an ordinary Report of an ordinary inquiry, such as was always held after either burnings or murders. With conditions in Ireland as they were it was a very grave decision to decide to publish Reports of those inquiries. When they had a life-and-death struggle between those responsible for establishing order in Ireland and those who were resorting to methods that were not countenanced by any civilised people, they must consider what was best in the interests of re-establishing the authority of the law.

In this case there was not an agreed Report, but there was enough in it to justify the Government coming to the conclusion that there had been acts of indiscipline on the part of some of the auxiliaries. There were only very few, but the Government had taken severe measures with regard to the particular company involved. The vast majority of them were not implicated in the least. Seven of them, of whom all they could say was that they suspected them of being responsible for acts of indiscipline, although they could not identify them, had been dismissed.

Lieut.-Commander Kenworthy (Independent Liberal, *Hull, Central*) : " Dismissed ? "

The Prime Minister : " You cannot do anything beyond that without evidence against them." The right hon.

---

* The statement was as follows : ." My Ministers further trust that the work of the Committee now examining the question of the Reform of the Second Chamber will be finished in time to permit of proposals being submitted to Parliament during the course of the present Session."

gentleman went on to inform the House that the officer
in command had been suspended—they were not satisfied
that he had acted in a way that commended itself to the
judgment of the Executive—and the company had been
dissolved. "Once the trouble began," remarked the Premier,
"there is no doubt at all that from some of the lower quarters
of Cork the population came forth and joined in the attack
upon these houses and was guilty of looting, but we have
not been able to get any evidence even against these civilians,
and that is one of the things with which we are confronted.
We have taken action. We immediately instituted further
inquiries when our attention was called to the position, with
the result that we have taken the sternest disciplinary action
which it is within our power to take without direct evidence
that would identify any members of the force with a specific
act of indiscipline."

Truce Negotiations.

It was perfectly true, Mr. Lloyd George continued, that
there had been negotiations between Archbishop Clune and
himself. The Archbishop of Perth came to see him. He
was Chaplain to the Australian forces on the Western Front.
There was no doubt about his absolute loyalty to the British
Empire. He asked whether something could not be done to
stop the terrible condition of things in Ireland.

"I certainly had a good many discussions with him,"
said the Prime Minister, "and I believe he had discussion
with the leaders of Sinn Fein—with most of the leaders. He
was anxious to negotiate a truce with a view to giving Ireland
an opportunity of reconsidering her position. There was
good deal to be said for that, because I believe that if the
murder campaign stopped probably they would never resume
it so long as they have not arms in their hands. After consulting those who are responsible for order in Ireland and who
are personally interested in putting an end to all this murder
in Ireland, because they run very great personal risks, every one
of them, themselves, they strongly urged that we should agree
to no truce except on the express condition that arms should
be surrendered.

"We should have been glad to have had this truce. If
these arms had been surrendered, then I think we would have
had peace in Ireland. We even suggested that the arms
might be surrendered to their own priests, so that the surrender
might not be made the means of tracking down the insurgents,
but they declined to accept that condition. That showed
that they had not abandoned the idea of bringing independence
to Ireland by force of arms, and, until they do, there

peace for Ireland." In conclusion the right hon. gentleman replied to a suggestion that nothing had been achieved by the strong action taken by the military and the police. After comparing the condition of Ireland before and since these measures were put in operation he expressed confidence that if the British people would have patience, order would be restored to Ireland, and, with order, liberty.

After some further speeches the general debate was concluded.

DEBATE IN HOUSE OF LORDS.

The Debate on the Address in the House of Lords was concluded during the opening sitting of the Session on 15th February. The Address was moved by the Duke of Abercorn and seconded by Lord Gorell.

The Marquis of Crewe, touching upon various subjects mentioned in the King's Speech, said that Germany ought to pay and must pay everything that she could possibly pay, to the uttermost farthing of reparation. Upon that as a principle there might be little difference of opinion. If there was a difference it was likely to be as to what the possibilities of the situation were, and it would no doubt be argued by some that the attempt to make what was until the other day one of the great Powers of Europe something of a contributory State to other States for a period of no less than forty-two years could hardly meet with realised success.

Visit of Dominion Ministers.

They all welcomed the announcement of the forthcoming visit of the Dominion Ministers. "Their deliberations in concert with the Government must be of the first importance," said the noble Marquis, "and the establishment of closer personal relations between those gentlemen and leading men here is, of course, always all to the good. No doubt there will be difficult problems to discuss. I confess I have never been one of those who have believed in the difficulty of maintaining the closest possible relations between the overseas Dominions and this country, however puzzling it might seem to formulate the expression of those relations into anything like an Imperial Council or Cabinet. The really difficult problems of the British Empire, as I have often said here, consist not in the relations between this country and the Dominions, but between the overseas self-governing Dominions on the one hand and India and the Colonies on the other. Far more difficult problems are to be found in relation to those than any which have ever existed within our memory between the overseas self-governing Dominions and ourselves."

Ireland.

With regard to Ireland, the phrase was used in the Speech that there were misguided people who resorted to methods of criminal violence with the idea of establishing an independent Republic, but the gravity of the situation rested in the fact that the Government had against it the great bulk of the Irish nation. With the institution of Martial Law, the necessity of which a great many people not supporters of the Government were prepared to admit, came the beginning of so-called regular and official reprisals—a dangerous policy in a country where they would have to be friends of the people in the future. But in spite of that, so far as they could gather from the public press, the irregular reprisals still continued. They had not been put a stop to, and neither regular nor irregular reprisals had the effect of stopping the campaign of outrage and assassination, the repression of which could have been the only conceivable excuse, if it could be an excuse, for their existence. It seemed to him impossible to exaggerate the gravity of the situation in Ireland.

Statement by Secretary for Foreign Affairs.

The **Secretary of State for Foreign Affairs** (Earl Curzon of Kedleston) paid a tribute to the services rendered in successive Ministerial offices by Viscount Milner.*

The general condition of the Continent of Europe, the noble Earl proceeded to say, was undoubtedly easier, brighter, more full of hope than it was a year ago. The various States which were created by the War were occupied in building up, with great effort and amid many difficulties, their national existence. The main function of the Great Powers, still closely and happily working together, was undoubtedly the carrying out, with common consent if that were possible, of the terms of the Treaty of Versailles. The real bulwark of European peace, which carried with it the peace of the world, was the continued co-operation of the Great Powers, and more especially of Great Britain and France. That co-operation was warmly emphasised at the recent Conference at Paris. As to the contemplated trade agreement with Russia, everyone, he thought, without exception, believed that in economic

---

* Viscount Milner retired from the office of Secretary of State for the Colonies shortly before the opening of the Session, and was succeeded by the Right Hon. Winston Churchill.

arrangements lay the real chance for recovery of the Eastern parts of Europe and of Russia.

"My only concern in the matter," he observed, "has been throughout to see that if these trade relations are made they are made with people who act in a friendly manner towards us, and that we do not conclude trading relations, with all the advantages to them that would ensue, with a Government of persons who then use their position to indulge in hostile actions against us in distant parts of the world. . . . That, I think, is an entirely reasonable position to take up, and, given the existence of actual guarantees of such a nature as I have described, I think there ought to be no difficulty in arriving at an agreement with the Soviet authorities upon the matter."

Imperial Cabinet: Meeting of Dominion Ministers.

"A brief reference was made by more than one speaker," the noble Earl remarked, "to the impending meeting of the Ministers of the overseas Dominions. . . . This is not, and will not be, an Imperial Conference of the character with which some noble Lords opposite are familiar, over one of which, for instance, my noble friend, Lord Harcourt, presided. This is a revival of the experiment so successfully introduced and carried out in the years 1917 and 1918 of the War. It was the summoning of an Imperial Cabinet, which became while it lasted a new and powerful organ of government, all its members being invested with the full authority and rank of Cabinet Ministers, and its decisions being not merely decisions of the British Government but of the British Empire.

"Not merely, looking back to my recollections of those times, do I recall that the discussions were of great importance, and that we received counsels of great value, as we did, from the Dominion Ministers, but that their presence here and their co-operation with us was an immense addition to the material and moral strength of the Empire, and I believe it will be no exaggeration to say that the existence and action of that Imperial War Cabinet was itself a very important instrument in the winning of the War. The noble Duke said nothing more true than this, that the service which it rendered in war time it is equally capable of rendering—and it is perhaps almost as necessary that it should render—now that the War is over and we are in time of peace.

Problems to be Considered.

"There are all the problems he mentioned—the question of the naval, military, and air defence of the Empire, the question of the foreign policy of the Empire in future, and the question of the future constitutional organisation of this great fabric. All these matters have to be discussed. The main desire which actuates every one of us who is to sit on that body is that this amazing congeries of independent States, of free nationalities, which are held together by a mere silken thread of common ideas, by the sense that they have all a common mission in the world and own loyalty to a common law, a common language and a common King, shall be bound together by even closer ties. When these Dominion statesmen come here—and General Smuts will be one of them—I look forward with great interest to the steps that will be taken to determine the manner and form of union in the future, and to devise the instruments by which it may be carried out."

Irish Reprisals.

Turning to Ireland, the noble Earl said that as a whole he believed the Irish nation had no sympathy with those scoundrels who were a desperate—he wished he could say a despicable—minority. He could not say the latter, because the force still at their disposal was such as was judged to be responsible for the sacrifice of most valuable lives. Official reprisals were confined to the areas in Ireland which were under Martial Law and where, of course, they were conducted under the orders of the G.O.C. There were no other authorised reprisals. Where lack of discipline had been shown and where guilt had been proved, men had been dismissed; some had been sent to prison and in one case, he believed, the extreme penalty was inflicted.

The Address was agreed to and was ordered to be presented to His Majesty by the Lords with White Staves.

GERMAN REPARATION (RECOVERY) ACT.

In the House of Commons on 7th March, a date before the close of the London Conference of the Allies, the Prime Minister announced that Germany's counter-proposals on the subject of reparations had been rejected and it had been decided that the sanctions should be put into operation immediately. A few days later a Bill making provision for the application of part of the purchase price of imported German goods towards the discharge of the obligations of Germany under the Treaty of Versailles was introduced, and the measure received the Royal Assent on 24th March.

The Act provides that, after 31st March, 1921, on the importation into the United Kingdom of German goods, the importer shall pay to the Commissioners of Customs and Excise such proportion of the value of the goods, not exceeding 50 per cent., as the Treasury may from time to time prescribe.

The payment of any sum to the Commissioners shall, up to the amount paid, operate as a good discharge against the person to whom the purchase price of the goods is due, and the receipt of the Commissioners will be accepted as conclusive evidence of the payment.

The Commissioners are instructed to pay all moneys so received by them into an account which is to be applied towards the discharge of the obligations undertaken by Germany under Parts VIII. and IX. of the Treaty.

The German goods to which the Act applies are goods first consigned from Germany to the United Kingdom, and goods not so consigned being goods wholly or partially manufactured or produced in Germany, unless, in the case of goods partially manufactured or produced in Germany, 25 per cent. or more of the value of the goods is attributable to processes of manufacture undergone since the goods last left Germany.

Subject to compliance with conditions as to security for re-exportation of the goods, the Act does not apply to goods imported for exportation after transit through the United Kingdom, or by way of transhipment.

The value of imported goods is to be taken to be the amount which an importer would give for them if they were delivered to him at the place of importation, freight and insurance being payable by him, and the value is to be fixed by the Commissioners.

Power is given to the High Court to vary contracts entered into before 8th March, 1921, for the acceptance of bills of exchange or the making of advances in connection with the importation of goods if the Court is satisfied that under the provisions of the Act serious hardship would be caused.

On the recommendation of one or more committees consisting mainly of persons of financial, commercial, or industrial experience, the Board of Trade is authorised to grant relaxations of the provisions of the Act.

DEBATE IN HOUSE OF COMMONS.

The Second Reading debate on the Bill took place in the House of Commons on 14th March.

The Chancellor of the Exchequer (the Right Hon. Austen Chamberlain) said that Germany had failed again and again, in particular after particular, to discharge her liabilities under the Treaty of Versailles. It was not alone with regard to reparation that they had reason to complain. The war criminals were still untried ; disarmament was still incomplete. On all these points, desiring to meet any legitimate objection or any real difficulty which might be proved by the German Government, the Allies had modified their just demands under the Treaty in point of extent, or in point of time, or in both. Yet, in the London Conference, and in the proceedings in Germany before that Conference, the German

B

Government deliberately challenged the whole basis of the Treaty of Versailles. While Germany defaulted in her obligation and refused to carry out her duty the Allies must have recourse to penalties. They were employing both military and economic penalties.

"So far as we are concerned," said Mr. Chamberlain, "we prefer the economic sanctions to the marching of new armies." Turning to the provisions of the Bill, he explained that the pledge given by H.M. Government not to exercise the power they possessed under paragraph 18 of Annexe 2 of the Treaty to seize property of German nationals in this country or in British territory was unaffected. There must be some inconvenience caused by anything which interfered with the normal and free course of trade, but the Government desired to meet cases of difficulty and hardship. Assuming the co-operation of Germany, which would take the form of reimbursing the German exporter or producer in marks in respect of that portion of the purchase price which was withheld by the importing Government, what sums were they likely to receive? He would not pretend to give a precise estimate.

British Empire's Share.

The share of the British Empire of the reparation payable by Germany was 22 per cent. If Germany co-operated in working the scheme, the British Empire could, he believed collect its share of the fixed annuity due from Germany under the Paris proposals. "If Germany refuses to make good to her exporters any part of the price we deduct, the result will be," the right hon. gentleman observed, "an embargo upon German trade with the Allied countries carrying out the agreement. . . . That is a policy which no far-sighted German would undertake if it meant ruin to him. The only inducement for him to undertake that would be if he thought it would mean ruin to us. In the present state of trade there is no difficulty . . . for us to do without these German goods if the Germans refuse to accept the only conditions on which they can enter our markets."

Mr. Horatio Bottomley (Independent, *Hackney, S.*)**,** moving an amendment for the rejection of the Bill, remarked that he would not be suspected of any undue solicitude for Germany, whose name would be to him, so long as he lived an epithet of detestation. A more fantastic and useless measure, however, was never presented to Parliament. Having been deceived and hoodwinked by Germany for over two years on the subject of indemnities, the Allies had been inspired by the wonderful idea that, if the German Government would not pay, they would ask a handful of German manufacturers and merchants to collect the indemnities for them by a deduction of 50 per cent. of the money due to them for exports, without any guarantee that they would get one farthing back from the German Government. He condemned the Bill as economically unsound, politically inexpedient, and commercially impracticable.

Major Christopher Lowther (Independent, Cumberland, N.) seconded the amendment. They must, he said, insist on Germany acknowledging her debt, and let her find the means of paying.

Lieut.-Colonel the Hon. W. Guinness (Coalition Unionist, Bury St. Edmunds) said they all saw the disadvantages of the Bill, but the country would be prepared to face far greater disadvantages and inconveniences rather than allow the Germans to evade their just liabilities.

Trading with Germany.

Lieut.-Commander E. Hilton Young* (Coalition Liberal, Norwich) said the Bill was to be welcomed in its general principles if only because it proceeded upon the assumption that there was nothing inherently immoral in trading with Germany. Further, it proceeded on the assumption that the only way to exact reparation from Germany was by the consignment of goods hither from Germany. For those reasons it exhibited a return to common sense in some quarters which might be welcomed. At the same time he asked the House to consider the nature of the difficulties, the troubles, and the anxieties which the working of the Bill would put upon all those engaged in import trade.

The Bill would neither paralyse nor stop German trade. On the other hand, it was not possible to cherish the hopeful belief that it would have no effect upon German trade and pour so many millions for reparations into the coffers of this country. It would have a constant slight effect in drawing the advantages of trade between Germany and the rest of the world away from those countries that imposed the scheme, and towards those countries that did not impose it.

The Right Hon. H. H. Asquith (Leader of the Independent Liberal Party) observed that there was absolutely no division of opinion in the House, or so far as he knew in the country outside, as to the justice of the claim made against Germany for reparation for the war which she initiated. The question pressing that claim was purely one of practicability and

---

* Lieut.-Commander Hilton Young was appointed, at the beginning of April, Financial Secretary to the Treasury, in succession to the Right Hon. Stanley Baldwin, who has become President of the Board of Trade.

B 2

expediency. They might as a punitive measure adopt means which would have the effect of excluding German goods entirely from their market, but that would be a foolish thing to do from every point of view. Like most measures of a vindictive kind it would be found to inflict at least as much harm on those who imposed it as on those for whom it was intended. What they all desired was that some practical step should be taken by which the moral and, indeed, the legal Treaty obligations on Germany to make reparation for her misdoings in the past should materialise for the benefit of the Allies.

The matter was not half so simple as at first sight it appeared to be. After examining some of the practical difficulties of the case, Mr. Asquith said he entertained the greatest misgivings whether machinery of this kind, so complicated in its nature and so easily capable of reacting injuriously upon their own trade, both import and export, would be found to be worth while in the results achieved.

Attitude of United States.

Sir William Pearce (Coalition Liberal, *Limehouse*) pointed out that the attitude of the United States and other neutrals was quite as important as was that of the German Government. If the United States were taking part in the scheme then it would be possible to put serious pressure on Germany, and he had some hope that the sympathy of America might be secured. " If and when the German Government accept and are willing to work the scheme, and if we get the sympathy of America, there will be a satisfactory state of affairs," the hon. member said, " but if we get neither—and it is idle to disregard the possibility of getting neither—we shall have Germany diverting all her exports to America and we shall have America left with the prospect of an industrial and trade alliance with Germany."

The Prime Minister (the Right Hon. D. Lloyd George) explained that under the Bill the importer was the person who cleared the goods at the Customs and he must be responsible for paying. Proceeding to discuss some of the objections to the Bill raised in the debate, he dealt with the contention that Germany would send her goods to neutral countries.

" Does anyone imagine," he asked, " she is not sending as many goods to neutral countries now as neutral countries will take ? Of course she is. Her exports last year were £250,000,000, and at pre-war prices that amounts to about £100,000,000. Before the war she was exporting about £400,000,000 worth of goods ; that is four times as much as she is exporting now. Why is she not exporting more ? It is because the neutral countries will not take the stuff from her, and if those countries wanted German goods, Germans would be sending their goods there. Therefore, you may depend upon it that if Germany can cut us in neutral markets now, she will do it ; it is her interest to do it, and she is doing it as hard as she possibly can."

Country of Origin.

It had been asked, " How are you going to find out what is the country of origin? " That was done during the War, the Premier said, and did not require enormous machinery. They used the machinery they had in the neutral countries — the consular agencies. The Customs authorities reported : —

" The questions to be decided by the Consuls in the present instance are not so difficult as those arising during the War, seeing that their attention has to be directed solely to the origin of the goods. If the consular services carry out their duties in this respect as efficiently as during the War, there should be little risk of evasion."

Of course it was possible to create imaginary difficulties, but the fact of the matter was that commerce adapted itself to a proceeding of this kind, because it was in the interests of everybody to do it. He heard it said, " Who is to pay ? " Germany could do one of three things.

" Germany can refund the whole of the one-half ; she can honour the Treasury receipt that is given. Everybody agrees that if Germany does that it will work quite smoothly. I will assume Germany will not do that, and that the second course that she can adopt is that she can refuse to have anything whatever to do with this Bill, and refuse, either in whole or in part, to honour the Treasury receipt. In that case, I say at once, this Bill operates as a penalty. It will have the effect of excluding German goods, except such goods as we want. The goods we do not really need will be excluded by the action of Germany.

What Germany Would Lose.

" Just think what that means to Germany. It means that Germany will be deprived of £50,000,000 worth of trade with the United Kingdom. It means that Germany will be deprived of her trade with Canada, if Canada chooses to collect her share of the indemnity in this way — I have no right to assume that she will. Canada will decide for herself. It means that Germany will be deprived of her trade with India if India collects her share of the indemnity in this way.

" German goods are already excluded from Australia and therefore, so far as Australia is concerned, it does not count.

She will be deprived of millions' worth of trade with France. Supposing Italy does not come in, and it has been suggested that she will not come in. Supposing she does not, and supposing Belgium does not, Germany will be deprived of trade that comes to from £70,000,000 or £80,000,000 worth up to £100,000,000 worth with the Allies who put the Bill into operation. . . . One half of that is wages. Can Germany deprive her workmen of anything between £30,000,000 and £50,000,000 worth of wages sterling ? "

There was, said the Premier, a third course which the German Government could take. It could say, " We will not pay 50 per cent., but we will pay such a percentage as will leave the employers, the producers, with quite a fair margin of profit." They might say 20 per cent. or 30 per cent. That meant practically a tax, not upon British importers, not upon British merchants, but on the great rich industrial magnates of Germany, to pay the indemnity and compensation to this country. It was a perfectly fair proposition. He appealed to the House to assist the Government in passing the measure as a substitute for force, and as a feasible method of collecting the indemnity.

A division did not take place on the amendment and the Bill was read a second time. It passed through Committee on 16th March.

Labour Point of View.

On the motion for Third Reading on 18th March,

The Right Hon. J. R. Clynes (Chairman of the Parliamentary Labour Party) moved the following amendment : —

" Whilst desirous of securing just reparation from Germany, this House cannot accept legislation of a character which does not represent a common policy on the part of the Allies, which would only result in injury to British trade and an increase in the volume of unemployment and which has been introduced before sufficient effort has been made to secure a settlement by agreement, or a settlement through the aid of the League of Nations, or other impartial tribunal, to ascertain the extent of Germany's capacity to pay."

He remarked that the Labour Party had never said Germany must not be forced to pay, but their view was that this stage had not been reached. On the contrary, all the possibilities of a settlement by agreement, which the Prime Minister admitted was a preferable method, had not been exhausted. The Labour Party did not ask that a settlement should be arranged by the Government on any annual figure less than the average figure laid down in what was termed the Paris settlement. Failing a provisional agreement for such a number of years as might be agreed upon, it would pay Great Britain better to require the German Government to make a fresh offer to the Allies good enough for them to accept at least as a basis for discussion in the hope of a settlement by agreement being finally reached.

The Attorney-General (the Right Hon. Sir Gordon Hewart) said that nothing could be more wrong than to assume that the negotiations were at an end. It had been said that the proper course was that they should hand over to the Financial Secretary to the League of Nations the matter of financial reparation. " The prospect of a German offer, if an offer might be made," said Sir Gordon, " is not a security which appears very tempting to me, and the prospect of arbitration before the League of Nations, after all that has taken place, does not seem to me to suggest those qualities of reasonable promptitude which are necessary. I should have thought that the financial section of the League of Nations was already very busy. Why are we to call upon the League of Nations in relation to this Treaty to answer the invidious function of debt collectors ? "

On a division the amendment was negatived by 132 votes against 15, and the Bill was then read a third time.

DEBATE IN HOUSE OF LORDS.

The Second Reading debate on the Bill in the House of Lords took place on 21st March.

The Lord Chancellor (Lord Birkenhead) said their Lordships would make a great mistake if the monetary difficulties in Germany were exaggerated. At the present time Germany could compete in the neutral markets of the world, and even in the markets of Great Britain, in circumstances which gave her extraordinary advantages. There were signs of increasing and remarkable prosperity in many German industries and institutions. No one who had studied the prospects would dispute the conclusion that within a period of time which could not be remote there would be a great revival of German trade and prosperity.

The practical question would be asked, " To what is it estimated the receipts under the scheme will amount ? " Last year Germany's exports to the British Empire and Allied European countries, apart from reparation payments in kind, appeared to have amounted to a figure in the neighbourhood of £100,000,000. As the process of recovery of German trade was extremely likely to continue it was reasonable to suppose that the exports to these markets in the coming year would be considerably greater. On that assumption the yield of the charge ought to approach £100,000,000, and in that event the amount collected in the United Kingdom alone would probably exceed £30,000,000.

The amount collected in the United Kingdom ought to amount ultimately to nearly £100,000,000 a year, as in 1918 Germany sent goods to this country which at present figures would represent nearly £200,000,000.

New Uncertainty.

Lord Emmott remarked that the breakdown of the Conference was bad enough, but it was made much worse by the introduction of legislation upsetting contracts and bringing new uncertainty where certainty was the one indispensable condition for the restoration of trade. His Majesty's Government seemed never to realise the complexity of modern commercial conditions, or that interference with trade often meant the strangulation of trade.

Lord Weardale said that the statesmen of Europe had absolutely failed during two-and-a-half years to bring them within sight of agreement. He suggested to the Government that they should now turn to the great Republic of America, with its new President, and ask it kindly to intervene between this country and the German Government and endeavour to bring about an arrangement which both could accept.

The Lord Chancellor remarked that he could not think the suggestion made by Lord Weardale was of very great practical value. Many persons believed that the Government's scheme offered a reasonable promise of success, and in the absence of any other proposal—it was not suggested that they should march to Berlin—surely it was worth while to give it a trial.

On the following day the Bill passed through its remaining stages in the Upper House without further discussion.

IMPERIAL DEFENCE.

(Co-operation with the Dominions: Imperial Conference, etc.)

On 15th February a brief debate took place in the House of Commons on the subject of Imperial Defence. It arose upon an amendment to the Address in the following terms :—

But regrets that His Majesty's Gracious Speech contains no reference to the very urgent need for co-ordinating the problems and tasks of the Navy, Army, and Air Force for purposes of defence of the British Empire as a whole and for the establishment of machinery to give effect thereto.

Major-General Sir J. H. Davidson (Coalition Unionist, *Fareham*), in moving the amendment, said it was the opinion of many of those who supported him that this was a matter which the Government should take up with the least possible delay. They had machinery for dealing with their three great Services, but it was pre-War machinery. It was not only wholly ineffective to-day, but it was completely out of date. His reasons for bringing the matter forward now were briefly these : —

> In the first place the problems with which they were faced to-day were wider and more indefinite than they were before the War.

> In the second place, their Imperial liabilities were far greater to-day than they were before the War, and were far more dispersed than ever before.

He maintained that a great deal could be done in the way of economy if the three great fighting Departments were properly co-ordinated. Another reason for co-ordination was the development of the science of invention. With the introduction of the Air Force they had also a factor which required most careful consideration in regard to the defensive forces of the Empire. Any study of the problem to-day as regarded one Service alone was of little value. He would go further. He thought co-ordination must be extended not only to the three Services in this country, but to the three Services in the Dominions.

Interests of Dominions.

"The time is arriving, as most people will probably admit," said the hon. and gallant gentleman, " when the Dominions will want to recognise their liabilities in a voluntary manner. They are undoubtedly interested in the great problems which have to be solved. For instance, Australia is deeply interested in the question of the Pacific, which affects not only the Navy and the Air Force, but also the Army. Emigration will increase in the immediate future, and the power of Great Britain will be largely dispersed in the Dominions —hence the necessity for greater cohesion." In his opinion the present machinery was totally inadequate. The War Office and the Admiralty very largely conserved their problems in water-tight compartments. There was a co-ordinating link in the shape of the Committee of Imperial Defence, but the Committee had only sat once in the last two years and was not an effective link. It was necessary that the occasional meetings between the technical chiefs of the three Services should be converted into permanent meetings held daily, or at any rate several times a week.

" There is," said General Davidson, " another phase of co-ordination which we have had in the past which has proved not only ineffective but vicious, and that is the occasional missions of an advisory and consultative nature to the Dominions. I am not desirous of saying a word against Lord Jellicoe's mission, but for purposes of co-ordination in the future I suggest that kind of mission is totally inadequate."

Defence Ministry.

" In the opinion of those who have studied the subject," General Davidson continued, " the correct course is to have a Defence Ministry composed of representatives of the War Office, the Admiralty, and the Air Ministry to sit for the purpose of solving problems in a logical way. . . . I recognise fully the difficulty of altering our machinery, but I do suggest that what we require is a permanent joint advisory technical committee. It should be entirely advisory. Its members should be whole-time members. It would not mean the creation of a large General Staff, but it would ensure what is most essential, and that is economy and efficiency at a time when we have little or no money to spend."

" We have pressed this on the Government . . . but so far as I can gather the only step taken up to the present moment has been the formation of a sub-committee to consider the best means of co-ordination." Regarding the technical sub-committee, the hon Member declared that the late First Lord of the Admiralty, the late War Minister, the late Air Minister, and the late Prime Minister were all agreed on the necessity for such a body.

Separate Air Ministry.

His own opinion with regard to the future of the Air Ministry was that it was absolutely essential it should be separate. He believed that in all these matters of defence the moment had arrived when they should take stock and co-ordinate. Especially in view of the Conference of Dominion Prime Ministers which was to take place this year they should set their house in order and look ahead. Living from day to day and from hand to mouth was mortgaging their future as a great British Commonwealth.

Lieut.-General Sir A. Hunter-Weston (Coalition Unionist *Bute and North Ayrshire*) seconded the amendment on the ground of economy and its great ally efficiency. What, he asked, should the co-ordinating body be ? A Joint Defence Sub-Committee was a logical evolution of an institution

---

* The Committee of Imperial Defence.

which had been satisfactory in the past, but which required modification to bring it up to the requirements of the present. It was, therefore, eminently suited to the genius of their race, and it had, further, the great advantage that it had been accepted in principle by the Government and was within the sphere of immediately practical politics.

It was important that this organisation should be brought into active being at once in view of the impending visit of the Dominion Premiers. In order that they might be able to judge of its working it was necessary that some start should be made on the work of the Committee so that they would be able to say how best their representatives should act on it, for it was essential that the Dominions should have an equal share with themselves in the consideration of any problem of Imperial defence. They were sister nations who proved their right to equality of treatment by the services their sons had rendered in the Great War. One great advantage of a Joint Defence Sub-Committee was that on it the representatives of the Dominions found their appropriate and logical place. It was, moreover, eminently elastic, and therefore any modification of procedure or composition that the Dominions might desire could easily be given effect to.

Bond of Empire.

"With the exception of the national spirit arising from our descent from one stock and our united loyalty to one throne," said General Hunter-Weston, "there is nothing that ties the Dominions to ourselves so closely as the necessity for joint defence. We know how valuable the Dominion troops have been to us during the War, and the Dominions know that but for us the danger to their continued national existence would be very great. The inception of a skilfully-constituted, elastic, co-ordinating body, on which the representatives of the Dominions could take their place, is, therefore, one of the most hopeful and also one of the most immediately valuable means of binding the Empire together."

Referring to the land forces, the hon. and gallant gentleman said that some revision of the directing organisation was necessary, and he suggested that, "in the light of our experience since 1914, and the great evolution, if not revolution, of administrative methods which have been brought about by the conquest of the air, and by this War, a small Commission, after the manner of the Esher Commission of 1904, should be established to review our military machine generally, its attention being specially directed to the constitution of the Army Council and the allocation of the duties of the War Office."

" The Army Council itself cannot carry out such a review, because its members are hard worked individually, and are too immediately concerned. I am certain that a skilfully constituted Committee such as this would be able to suggest to the Government modifications in the existing machinery which would lead to greatly increased efficiency, to a reduction in the number of staff officers, and to a great economy in money."

An Urgent Question.

Major-General the Right Hon. J. E. B. Seely (Coalition Liberal, *Ilkeston*) said that whatever happened to the League of Nations—and everybody wished it success—it was quite certain that the British Empire would almost always be fighting, because they were responsible for such an enormous portion of the earth's surface peopled in a great part by those who would not come under the League of Nations for many generations. Therefore, this matter was very urgent, because if they were not actually fighting at that minute—he believed they were—they certainly would be with the turbulent tribe who would not agree with the *pax Britannica*.

The question arose how ought they to co-ordinate the Services in order to avoid the immense losses in men and money which took place in the late War, and which had taken place during the war in Mesopotamia, Persia, and elsewhere through the lack of proper co-ordination, very often by failure to use the right power, and sometimes because the simplest thing was to go on in the old way—send a brigade and if that did not do send a division, and if that did not do send an army corps. So gradually they got to such an amazing spectacle as that in Mesopotamia of 110,000 troops, mostly infantry, in a country which only contained about five times as many adult male inhabitants as the number of troops they had there. That was the kind of thing that was due to lack of co-ordination. It had been a physical impossibility for the Prime Minister to direct his mind to all the problems that had arisen and this most urgent one he had not had time to attend to. There was all the more reason for finding some means of retaining the absolute authority of the Prime Minister of the day and yet having somebody who could co-ordinate the Services.

Assuming the need to be proved, the only question that remained was how to do it. The objection to having a Minister of Defence was that the three great Services must each have a head and he must be supreme in his office. If they had a Minister of Defence with three Under-Secretaries under him he was sure that neither the Navy, nor the Army, nor the

Air Force would be well and wisely administered. That particular solution would not help them in one of the most urgent needs, namely, co-operation with the Dominions and in India, for most of them had not a Minister of Defence, and from what he could hear from the Dominions they were not likely to adopt that method.

Committee of Imperial Defence.

"I believe the proper plan," said General Seely, "is to have the Committee of Imperial Defence meeting not once in two years, but in permanent session, with a vice-president of the Prime Minister, responsible directly to the Prime Minister, and himself a member of the Cabinet, whose whole duty—and indeed it would take his whole time—should be to co-ordinate these three Services.

The Prime Minister (the Right Hon. D. Lloyd George) said he was entirely in sympathy with his hon. and gallant friends. As Minister of Munitions, as Minister of War, as Chancellor of the Exchequer, and as Prime Minister he saw war in all its different aspects, in so far as a civilian could see it, and it was driven into his mind then that they were suffering from a lack of co-ordination. The Departments went into the War not so much as though they were Departments of the Government, but rather as allies. The Navy was a very good ally of the War Office, and the War Office was a very sound ally of the Navy, and then they found a third ally in the Air Ministry. But they were allies, and it was very difficult to get them always to act together. He had found, wherever they touched a problem such as the question of more ammunition, there was a fight between the Departments. A great effort was made—he did not know if he would be boasting if he said during the last years of the War more especially—to get co-ordination between the Departments and he thought it was achieved to a very large extent.

"If ever we got into difficulties again—and I hope that this country and no other country will ever see anything like the conditions which existed in the last war—I should say," the Prime Minister remarked, "that one of the first things that this nation should secure would be some means by which the strength and resources might be co-ordinated more efficiently from the very start. So, entirely from the conviction resulting from experience, I am wholly in favour of the general proposition which has been advocated with such force by my hon. and gallant friends. I accept entirely their argument that the lack of co-ordination leads to extravagance, because you are apt to duplicate your efforts, and one Department will make provision for a contingency without making allowance for the fact that another Department is providing against the same contingency. So you are apt to insure and reinsure in the three Departments."

Practical Difficulties.

He had considered the matter very carefully and he would say quite frankly why the Government were not pressing it forward at the moment. General Seely deprecated the proposal to have a Minister of Defence, but that was the only really effective and direct method of dealing with the problem, because there at least they would have one who was not more interested in this or that, but was himself a Committee of Imperial Defence as a whole. But unless they had a very strong personality as Minister of Defence there was a real danger that a good " wangler," if he might use the word, in any particular Department would manage somehow or other to get his own Department attended to at the expense of the others.

As to the second proposal, which was the appointment of a Joint Committee, it had not been forced forward because everybody who would be concerned was so overwhelmed with other tasks that he could not give the constant attention which it would demand. The Ministers responsible to Parliament must be there when considering vital questions of policy affecting the Departments. But there was only one way to ensure co-ordination, and that was by having a strong chairman, who was neither in one Department nor another. The Ministers must be there, but there must also be another Minister there whose lead would be respected, not merely by the Services, but by the other Ministers as well. The whole idea of the War Cabinet was that it should consist of men who had no Departments of their own, but were able to exercise supervision over the Departments.

" There was General Smuts, whose services were invaluable," said the Premier. " There were also Lord Curzon and Lord Milner, and Mr. Barnes. Ministers did not feel that there was anything which derogated from their dignity in the procedure. Undoubtedly that is the way to do it—to have a joint Committee of this kind, with the Ministers representing the Departments, who know they have to defend their Estimates, and, of course, the experts, and with another Minister who will be in the Chair. I do not mind telling the House at once that I hope the Lord President of the Council will be able to take the Chair. He has had very considerable experience in this matter. The Leader of the House or

* The Right Hon. Arthur James Balfour.

really could not do it. We could not devote the necessary attention to it.

An Imperial Problem : Forthcoming Conference.

" A second point is that this is not merely a problem for England ; it is an Imperial problem. The defence of the Empire ought to be an Imperial concern. It is too much to ask these small islands, with the gigantic burdens they are bearing, and bearing very gladly, to undertake themselves the whole burden of the defence of this gigantic Empire in every sea, Atlantic and Pacific alike. I am looking forward to the meeting of the Prime Ministers of the Empire which will take place in June as an occasion for raising the whole problem of Imperial defence. There must be co-ordination not merely between the Services, but between the various parts of the Empire.

"When we were in trouble the Empire came to our help. We drew over a million men voluntarily from India and over a million men from the Dominions, and without their aid we could not have achieved those gigantic triumphs which now stand to the credit of the British name. But that was a spasmodic effort ; it was an effort which surged up out of a great instinct of the Empire. I agree with my hon. and gallant friends that the problem should be considered in its entirety. I also agree that the knowledge that the Empire stands together and is prepared to defend the liberties it won, will be in itself a guarantee against the shedding of blood again. I believe that if those who plunged the world into war had known of what the Empire was capable, the sword would never have been unsheathed.

" The forthcoming Conference is to be one of the most momentous Conferences in the history of the Empire. If there is a general sense that we must make common cause to defend the liberties of the world and the interests of the Empire, and if it is known that, in the event of some great upheaval like the late War, the Empire is ready in future to repeat the great effort of the past, that will be one of the soundest guarantees for peace, for this British League of Nations has also got a word to say in the settlement of the world's affairs. I am looking forward to the problems to be discussed there. You have got to get co-ordination between departments—efficiency and economy depend upon it—but you must also have co-ordination between the whole of the parts of the Empire, so that this wonderful Empire, with its infinite variety of races, will be able to give as full an account of itself in the future as it has done in the past."

Following the Premier's speech the amendment was withdrawn by General Davidson.

NAVY ESTIMATES.

Navy Estimates for 1921–22 amount to £91,186,869 gross, and £82,479,000 net, as compared with £105,283,281 and £90,872,300 in 1920–21. This is a reduction of over 14 millions on the gross estimate, and of over 8¼ millions on the net estimate. The First Lord of the Admiralty (Lord Lee of Fareham), in a printed explanatory statement, pointed out that non-recurrent War liabilities, or terminal charges, amount to about 8¼ millions, including about 3¼ millions for completion of the Light Cruisers, Air-Craft Carriers, Destroyers and Submarines, begun during the War.

Lord Lee's statement contained the following paragraph on Naval Policy : Estimates can only be based upon Policy, and the Naval Policy of the Government, as announced by my predecessor, in the House of Commons, on 17th March, 1920, is to maintain a " One-Power Standard "—*i.e.*, that our Navy should not be inferior in strength to that of any other Power. The duty of the Admiralty is to carry out that policy as economically as possible, giving full weight to the special geographical, international, and other considerations which have arisen since the War. This they are doing—in no mechanical spirit nor with insistence upon " numerical equality "—and, recognising to the full the necessity for reducing expenditure to the lowest limits compatible with national security, the Admiralty have effected drastic economies, and agreed to assume risks, which in ordinary circumstances, they would regard as difficult to reconcile with the full maintenance of the Government's declared policy.

Proposed Economies.

Amongst proposed economies Lord Lee mentioned the following : —

(A) Reduction of the number of capital ships in full commission, from 20 to 16 (as compared with 38 in March, 1914). This is the smallest number that will enable the essential sea-going and technical training of officers and men to be properly carried out.

(B) Placing in reserve of one of the four destroyer flotillas of the Atlantic Fleet.

(C) Reduction of the North American and South African Squadrons by one light cruiser each, and the complete (temporary) withdrawal of the South American Squadron.

(D) Reduction of the personnel of the Fleet during 1921, to 121,? officers and men (as compared with 127,500 in 1920, and 151,000 in 1914).

(E) Reduction of Civil Staffs at the Admiralty and other establishments, and other economies in the dockyards.

These changes are dictated, almost entirely, by the pressing need for economy, and make it incumbent upon the Admiralty to maintain the reduced Navy in a state of the highest possible efficiency. In pursuance of this policy, the retention in reserve of the eight Battleships (" Hercules," " Colossus," " Neptune," " St. Vincent," " Collingwood," " Temeraire," " Bellerophon " and " Superb ") which are armed with 12-inch guns, is no longer considered justifiable, and they are transferred to the Disposal List. The number of capital ships on the effective list is thus reduced to 30 (including H.M.A.S. " Australia "), of which 14 will be in reserve.

Replacement of Obsolete Ships.

Of these 30 ships, the older types are becoming obsolescent, and cannot be reckoned as efficient fighting units for more than a few years longer. The need for their gradual replacement by modern ships, embodying the lessons of the War, can therefore no longer be disregarded. In this connection, it must be remembered that no capital ship for the Royal Navy has been laid down and completed since 1916, and it is obvious that, as the Fleet is reduced in numbers, the ships of which it is composed must be of up-to-date type and of the highest efficiency. A sum of $2\frac{1}{2}$ millions has therefore been included in these Estimates as a first instalment for " replacement " ships.

It cannot be too strongly emphasised that, in making this long-delayed beginning with the replacement of obsolete ships, the Government neither commits itself to, nor contemplates, any building " Programmes " in answer to those of any other Power. Indeed, it trusts that it may be possible, as a result of frank and friendly discussion with the principal Naval Powers, to avoid anything approaching to competitive building, either now or in the future. But, meanwhile, it would be a dereliction of duty on the part of the Admiralty to allow the efficiency, training, or *morale* of the Royal Navy to deteriorate, through neglect to provide it with *matériel* which is equal to the best and in which it can feel confidence. It is also imperative to avoid an irrevocable loss of time and building facilities which might make it impossible to maintain our sea security if it should be threatened.

Co-operation with Dominions.

A supplemental memorandum attached to the explanatory statement issued by the First Lord included the following note on co-operation with the Dominions : —

The Imperial Conference which is to take place in June of this year will give a welcome opportunity for discussing fully with the

c

Dominion Representatives the problem of Naval Policy in relation to the Empire as a whole, and for the consideration of suggestions for mutual co-operation.

The lines on which it would be proposed to proceed are towards the development of Dominion Navies under the administrative and executive command of their own Officers, each separate Navy being the responsibility of its own Government, and imbued with the particular characteristics and spirit of its own people; all, however, working in close co-operation and under the guidance of a common doctrine. If war occurred in which the Empire as a whole took part, then the various component navies would work in harmony with the general strategical policy previously decided upon. To ensure such intelligent co-operation, common principles of command and Staff work are required. This can only be developed by a uniform system of Staff training. It is proposed to make gradual progress in this direction by the appointment of Dominion Officers to the Naval Staff at the Admiralty, and by arranging for a certain proportion of Dominion Officers each year to undergo the Naval Staff Course at the Staff College. Finally, it is hoped to arrive at a position where the Dominions themselves will be able to set up their own Staff Colleges, working on the same lines and under the same system as the Naval Staff College at home.

The machinery required to give effect to these tentative proposals regarding Imperial Naval Policy, and to ensure the building up of Navies with a common doctrine and working to a common plan, cannot be indicated until this matter has been considered in conjunction with the Dominion Representatives, and their views have been fully stated.

DEBATE IN HOUSE OF COMMONS.

On 17th March the estimates were presented to the House of Commons. On the motion to go into Committee of Supply on them,

The Parliamentary Secretary to the Admiralty (Colonel Sir James Craig) quoted from a speech delivered in the House by Mr. Long on 17th March, 1920, in which the then First Lord of the Admiralty said :—

" I believe it is a fact that the naval policies of all past Governments, whichever party they represented, have, at least, included this common principle, that our Navy should not be inferior in strength to the Navy of any other Power, and to this principle the present Government firmly adheres. . . . That is the foundation of the naval policy of His Majesty's Government."

That, said Sir James Craig, remained the policy to-day as it was a year ago. The present First Lord, speaking on the previous night at a dinner of the Society of Naval Architects said :—

" We see the Naval Committee of the United States of America laying down the principle that America shall maintain a navy at least equal to that of any other Power. That is a claim of equality which this country has never accepted in the past, and never would accept, save in connection with a great English-speaking nation that sprang from our loins and must ever hold a special place in our regard and confidence.

" The speech explained very fully," Sir James remarked,
" how the First Lord has done his utmost, I will not say to hold
out the olive branch to America in this matter, but at all
events to show, when we are discussing the policy of the Navy
at the present moment, that we are restraining ourselves and
are confining ourselves entirely to the question of maintaining
One-Power standard, and that standard a high and efficient
 one such as will maintain the real old traditions of [the British
Navy."

our New Capital Ships.

With reference to the replacement of obsolescent ships,
the Parliamentary Secretary said the ships the Admiralty
would build to replace the four oldest of their capital ships now
on the effective list would be an improvement on the " Hood "
class embodying the lessons of the late War. They also proposed to build a submarine and a minelayer, both of them
embodying the latest developments in these craft and including a number of experimental features. The opinion that
the necessity for the capital ship had survived the test of the
Great War was endorsed at the time by the Board of Admiralty
and remained unchanged. It was common knowledge that a
similar investigation in the United States had led to the same
conclusion.

**The Right Hon. H. H. Asquith (Leader of the Independent
Liberal Party):** " Will all the four battleships be laid down
during the next twelve months ? "

The Parliamentary Secretary to the Admiralty replied
that if the House sanctioned the Vote that day, it was proposed
to lay down the whole of the four ships this year.

**Lieut.-Colonel M. Archer-Shee (Coalition Unionist, *Fins-
bury*)** moved the following amendment :—

" That, in the opinion of this House, owing to the great increase in
naval strength of other Powers, it is necessary that immediate steps
be taken to further increase the strength of the Royal Navy in capital
ships, and their ancillary vessels, in order to ensure that that British
Navy be at least equal in strength to that of any other single Power."

**The Right Hon. Sir F. Banbury (Coalition Unionist, *City
of London*)** seconded the amendment.

America's Navy.

Mr. Asquith said he had not the faintest apprehension
of the intention or effect of what America was doing in the
way of building up a Navy, or that it was directed, or ever
would be directed, against this country. He was rather
disposed to regret the re-entry into their political vocabulary

c 2

of such an expression as the " One-Power standard." The
used to speak of the " Two-Power standard " in the old day
before the War.   That formula was always a crude, unsound
unscientific rule of thumb.

" The only true and trustworthy principle to guide ou
action," the right hon. gentleman remarked, " is that th
Royal Navy, in conjunction, I am happy to say, with those ɑ
our Dominions—a growing factor in our Imperial panoply·
should always be adequate to secure the safety of our sea-gi
Empire and our sea-borne supplies against any reasonabl
calculable risk.   That, in my opinion, is a much better formul
than these artificial rules of thumb, One-Power or Two-Power ɑ
Two-and-a-half-Power, or whatever you like to call it.   D
let us be on our guard against this curse of talk abou
competitive shipbuilding."

He heartily re-echoed the wish expressed in the memor
andum of the First Lord that they might have a frank an
friendly discussion with other Powers.

**The Right Hon. Sir Edward Carson (Leader of the Ulste
Unionists at Westminster)** thought the House ought to b
careful not to allow the cry for economy to affect its judgmer
in relation to the naval necessities of the Empire.   They wer
on the very limit of what was safe when they said that thei
policy was that the Navy should not be inferior in strengt
to that of any other Power.   He could not see how any reasor
able man who cared about the security of the country could sa
that four new ships was anything but the most unambitiou
programme and one laid down by the experts of the Admiralt
solely because of the present economic conditions.

Danger of Provoking Competition.

**The Right Hon. J. R. Clynes (Chairman of the Parliame
tary Labour Party)** remarked that if they pursued all that w
implied in the term " One-Power standard " they were certa
to provoke the very competition in naval armaments that
thought they were most anxious to avoid.   If their princip
object was defence they might seek, at all events, to arran
to fortify themselves against attack.   It was loathsome to hir
and to many others, to have to consider questions of nav
policy now from the standpoint of developing, extending, ɑ
expanding war-like instruments, without previously exhausti
every possible opportunity of settling these matters on a pea
ful basis.

" If really we were exposed to more powerful or potent
enemies than those to which we are exposed, I, and those
whom I speak," Mr. Clynes said, " would be the last to say
do anything that would in the slightest degree enfeeble

Navy or make it less efficient for the protection of our shores. . . If these questions of armaments, or other questions, annot be settled upon such a basis as I indicate, then it is the imperative duty of this nation to safeguard itself against any isk from outside attack."

Commander Viscount Curzon (Coalition Unionist, *Battersea,* .) urged the House to remember the Imperial nature of the uestion. The problem was vital to India and the Dominions s well as to Great Britain.

The amendment was negatived and the House assented b the motion to go into Committee. Thereafter, Votes for he men and pay of the Navy were agreed to.

DOMINIONS AND NAVAL DEFENCE.

(Meeting of Prime Ministers, June, 1921.)

On 16th March a question was addressed to the Government regarding the Dominions and a Far-Eastern Fleet.

Commander Carlyon Bellairs (Coalition Unionist, *Maid-one*) asked the Prime Minister whether he was aware that brd Jellicoe in his Report asked for a Far-Eastern Fleet of he latest type, consisting of 8 battleships, 8 battle cruisers, light cruisers, 40 destroyers, and 36 submarines, to be povided by 1924, together with all necessary auxiliaries; vnether any representations from India and the Dominions had ben officially sent in concerning this Report; and whether te subject would be fully discussed at the June conference?

The Prime Minister (the Right Hon. D. Lloyd George): Vith regard to the first part of the question the reply is in the airmative. With regard to the latter part, a few interim representations have been received, but the Dominions are dferring their considered views until the whole question of Enpire Naval policy and co-operation is discussed, as is intended, at the June Conference.

NAVAL DEFENCE.

(Canada's Contribution.)

In the House of Commons on 21st March,

Mr. Percy Hurd (Coalition Unionist, *Frome*) asked the Prime Minister whether his attention had been called to the feeling aroused in Canada by the reported statement at Vancouver of Captain Adams,* of His Majesty's ship "Aurora," that "England is to-day paying 17 dollars per head for the

---

* See also page 344.

great Navy that protects us, and that it is time Canada stepped
into the breach and assumed a fair share of the burden"; and
whether he could allay this feeling by indicating these were
proper subjects for discussion between His Majesty's Ministers
of this country and of Canada in Imperial Conference, and not
for speeches by naval officers ?

The Prime Minister (the Right Hon. D. Lloyd George)
"The Hon. Member is correct in his view as to the proper
method of discussion of questions of Dominion policy. The
' Aurora ' belongs to His Majesty's Canadian Navy, and the
discipline is, therefore, the concern of the Canadian naval
authorities."

Mr. Hurd : " Was it not a British officer that made the
statement ? "

The Prime Minister : " Yes, but he is under the discipline
of the Canadian authorities."

ARMY ESTIMATES.

Discussion of the Army Estimates for 1921-22 was commenced in the House of Commons on 15th March on the
motion to go into Committee of Supply. The estimates show
a net expenditure of £106,315,000, being a net reduction on the
amount voted in respect of the financial year 1920-21 of
£58,435,000. The maximum establishment provided for
341,000 officers and men, a decrease of 184,000. The total
compare as follows : —

	1920-21.	1921-22
Gross expenditure ..	£205,000,000	£118,915,000
Appropriations in aid	40,250,000	12,600,000
Net estimate ..	£164,750,000	£106,315,000

Total strength all ranks, 1920-21	525,000
Total strength all ranks, 1921-22	341,000

The original net estimate for 1920-21 amounted to
£125,000,000, but in December a supplementary sum of
£39,750,000 had to be voted, of which £16,000,000 was for
Mesopotamia.

Of the anticipated net expenditure £69,116,500 is allocated
for the Army at home, in the Colonies, Egypt, Constantinople,
and on the Rhine, for the Territorial and Reserve Forces,
and for non-effective charges ; £26,496,500 is set aside for the
forces in Mesopotamia and Palestine, and the balance of
£10,702,000 is to meet charges arising out of the War, including
outstanding payments for services already rendered, reinstate-
ment of properties occupied during the War, and of s

after use as transports, medals and records, and extra labour employed in the disposal of war stocks.

The total of 341,000 officers and men on the establishment of the Army, exclusive of those serving in India, is the maximum for which Parliamentary authority is required. This figure is expected to fall in the course of the financial year to about 235,000, including Colonial and native Indian troops serving outside India.

A Vote on Account of £45,000,000 was asked for, representing between four and five months' expenditure.

DEBATE IN HOUSE OF COMMONS.

The Secretary of State for War (the Right Hon. Sir Laming Worthington-Evans) explained that when the Secretary of State for the Colonies returned from the conferences he was holding in Egypt, and the policy with regard to Mesopotamia and Palestine had been finally settled, separate estimates would be presented by Mr. Churchill for the expenditure in the Middle East, and the expenditure in the Army Estimates would be repaid by an Appropriation-in-Aid. The present expenditure on the Army, he continued, was about two and a half times the pre-War expenditure, and that was more or less the difference in the value of money as between then and now.

"We have at this moment," the right hon. gentleman said, "a Regular Army of 17,000 officers and 206,000 other ranks, making a total of 223,000. On 31st of this month 8,000 of other ranks are due for discharge, so that we shall start the new financial year with 201,000 officers and other ranks. The estimates provide for an average throughout the year of 192,500 officers and other ranks, and for the numbers being reduced by 31st March, 1922, to 186,000. A severe comb-out is being undertaken throughout the various departments and Commands with the view of reducing the number of officers employed." A second economy, the War Minister went on to say, arose from the decision to disband four cavalry regiments, namely, the 5th Lancers, raised in 1858, the 19th Hussars, the 20th Hussars, and the 21st Lancers, all raised in 1861. There were at present 6,000 men in the Army Reserve, and he proposed to increase that number this year to 80,000.

Territorial Army and Yeomanry.

He was asking for a cash sum of £5,200,000 for the Territorial Army and the Yeomanry. That would make provision

for reaching a strength of 210,000 officers and other ranks
before the end of the year. "The Territorial Army," Sir
Laming observed, "is being organised as our second line,
intended to be modelled on the Regular Army, and equipped
and organised so as to provide 14 divisions complete, with a
cavalry division, with army and corps troops. . . . Of
236,000 of all ranks required to complete the establishment
of these 14 divisions we have already obtained over 100,000."
The War Office was asking for £500,000 for the provision
of improved forms of tanks. Their aim was to develop a light
tank to co-operate with the infantry—a fast moving, powerful
tank which would be more effective than cavalry. Experiments were being made with cooling devices to enable tanks to
be used in tropical countries and with tractors and trans-
porters capable of moving across country. The ultimate
practical use of tanks and armoured cars and their relation
to the other arms of the Service had not yet been finally
settled.

The general view was that mechanical means of fighting
must be developed to the fullest extent. The cost of maintenance in peace time was less, and the economy of man power
in actual warfare was likely to be greater.

**The Right Hon. Sir Donald Maclean (Chairman of the
Independent Liberal Party in Parliament)** said the House should
face the fact that with the Government's handling of things
there would be very little reduction in the cost of the Army
in the year which they were about to enter. As to the Middle
East, he protested against the whole policy of tacking on to the
Colonial Office a War Department. Such a scheme could not
commend itself in the interests of economy, sound policy, or
effective military administration.

After debate the motion to go into Committee on the
estimates was adopted. Votes for 341,000 men of all ranks
and for £45,000,000 on account of the expenditure for the
year were afterwards agreed to.

AIR ESTIMATES.

Air estimates for 1921-22 were presented to the House of
Commons and showed a total net expenditure of £18,411,000—
a reduction of £4,581,230. Excluding War liabilities the net
total of the estimates was £16,940,000. An explanatory statement issued by the Secretary of State for Air contained the
announcement that it had been decided, after consultation with
the Admiralty, to suspend the Royal Air Force Airship service.
The maintenance of such a service for fighting purposes

considerable expense would have involved a diminution of effort on services of which the fighting value had been more fully demonstrated. This step, it was stated, would result in considerable economies.

With a view to encouraging the development of Civil Aviation in a time of difficulty, it was proposed, with the sanction of Parliament, to devote a sum not exceeding £60,000 to the grant of subsidies to Civil Aerial Transport Companies. The total sum allocated to Civil Aviation (including meteorological services and the cost of headquarters staff) was again £1,000,000.

DEBATE IN HOUSE OF COMMONS.

The estimates were discussed in the House of Commons on 1st March. On the motion to go into Committee,

The Secretary of State for Air* (the Right Hon. Winston Churchill) said he pointed out two years ago that, quite apart from clearing away the gigantic *débris* and enormous mass of material which the War had left, it would take five years to make an efficient, self-respecting, well-disciplined, economically organised Air Force. About 18 months of those five years had gone and the progress had been much greater than he had ventured to hope. The training organisation of the Royal Air Force would, as it developed and perfected itself, become a great technical university for the nation, with the glamour and tradition of a gallant service super-added. Without a complete training organisation they could not have any efficient force of air squadrons; once they had that organisation it would carry a few more or a few less without any particular inconvenience or additional expense.

Thirty-Two Squadrons.

Twenty-one of the 28 fully formed service squadrons were overseas. The equivalent of three more squadrons were in Ireland; three were working with the Navy; and one was employed at home in giving refresher courses to pilots. Four additional squadrons, which were the residue of the five sanctioned by the House a few months ago, would begin forming on 1st April, and would bring the total up to 32.

The fighting squadrons and training establishments comprised 2,900 officers and about 25,000 men, with a certain number of civil assistants. It was proposed this year to

* At the beginning of April Mr. Churchill was succeeded in the office of Secretary of State for Air by Captain the Right Hon. F. E. Guest, late Patronage Secretary to the Treasury.

begin the formation on a very small scale of a Territorial Air Force, for which £20,000 was taken in the estimates. The idea was to have six squadrons stationed near centres where there was a large engineering population and aerodromes were available. He did not believe they could possibly have an Air Force which would discharge the essential and vital naval and military duties of the Empire for less than £15,000,000 or £16,000,000 a year, that was to say, £7,000,000 or £8,000,000 a year at the pre-War value of money.

In view of the grave financial stringency he did not feel justified in asking at present for more than £1,000,000 a year for civil aviation. Referring to the Admiralty decision to give up airships, the right hon. gentleman said that if any company would give a reasonable undertaking to operate the vessels and continue to experiment they should have all the airships as a free gift.

Major-General the Right Hon. J. E. B. Seely (Coalition Liberal, *Ilkeston*) said it was an indefensible arrangement that a man should be Secretary of State for the Colonies and Secretary of State for Air at one and the same time.

Civil Aviation.

Colonel J. R. P. Newman (Coalition Unionist, *Finchley*) moved :

" That to promote efficiency and economy, a closer co-operation between the Air Force and civilian air services and aircraft manufacturers is essential."

Sir W. Joynson-Hicks (Coalition Unionist, *Twickenham*) in seconding the amendment, pleaded for civil aviation, not merely because he thought it would be fatal to have no civil aviation lines while other countries had them, but because it would provide a reserve in personnel and on the factory side of aviation for their military aviation when they wanted to increase it.

After debate the amendment was withdrawn, and the motion to go into Committee on the estimates was carried by 177 votes against 50. In Committee the Votes for men— 30,880 of all ranks—and for pay—£4,794,000—were agreed to

ESTIMATES COMMITTEE.

(Parliamentary Control of Finance.)

During the discussion of Supplementary Estimates in the House of Commons on 25th February, hon. members devoted attention to the control of the House over expenditure and the Chancellor of the Exchequer subsequently made a statement on the subject.

The Chancellor of the Exchequer (the Right Hon. Austen Chamberlain) said it was the general feeling that the House had not sufficient control of finance and that the Government was not successful in securing the economies which were possible. He wished the Government and the House to be partners. The intervention of the House was not always in support of the Government when they were trying to save money, and it had been proved by experience that Committees set up by the House to restrict expenditure might end in additions to expenditure. He wanted to satisfy the feeling of members who held that one of their first duties at the present time was to control expenditure.

The Right Hon. Sir F. Banbury (Coalition Unionist, *City of London*) pointed out that the National Expenditure Committee had recommended that the Estimates Committee which was in existence in the years 1912-13-14 should again be set up, with the addition that it should have the right to have an officer of the House of Commons in the same position as the Comptroller and Auditor-General with power to investigate the expenditure of Departments and bring the result to the notice of the Committee.

The Chancellor of the Exchequer said that he saw no difficulty about granting such a Committee.

The Right Hon. J. Murray Macdonald (Liberal, *Stirling and Falkirk*) : " Would it not be necessary in the first instance to have clearly defined what the powers of Committee and officer should be ? It would be impossible now to consent to a proposal of that kind until we know precisely what are the powers and duties suggested."

The Chancellor of the Exchequer said it was clear that Sir F. Banbury's suggestion did not satisfy all the critics of the Government. He thought if they got some of the more experienced members of the House to suggest the form of the Committee and the scope of its reference they might get something that would greatly assist the Government.

[A small informal Committee, with the Right Hon. Austen Chamberlain as chairman and including the Chairman of Ways and Means (the Right Hon. J. H. Whitley) and other members of the House of Commons, was subsequently appointed to report to the House on the subject.]

PARLIAMENT AND THE MANDATORY SYSTEM.

(League of Nations and Mandates: Control by Parliament, etc.)

Discussions took place during March in both Houses of Parliament regarding the system of mandates under the League of Nations and the question of the effective control of the system by Parliament.

DEBATE IN HOUSE OF LORDS.

Lord Islington on 14th March asked the Government if an opportunity would be afforded Parliament of approving or otherwise the provisions of the Mandates for Mesopotamia and Palestine prior to their submission to the Council of the League of Nations at their coming session at Geneva.

Constitutional Aspect.

The constitutional aspect, Lord Islington said, was all the more important in view of the far-reaching issues, both at home and abroad, involved in those Mandates, for it was due to Parliament and the country that they should know the extent of the payments entailed by the assumption of a mandate. The essential principle was that the character of those Mandates, the mode of their application, the issues involved both within the mandated country and outside its borders, and the expenditure of the country assuming the Mandate, demanded that the power of Parliament should be unfettered and that full and explicit information should be placed before Parliament so that it might decide whether it approved or whether it desired to amend or refuse a mandate.

It was clear, Lord Islington continued, from the inaugural address of the new President of the United States that the precise methods now incorporated in the Articles of the Covenant of the League of Nations did not receive his sanction or support. That statement demanded from Parliament itself the most earnest reconsideration both of the form and substance of the present Covenant of the League of Nations. The noble Lord added that he thought the President's protest against world-super-government was one that they could take to themselves, and, he hoped, give effect to, in the cause of their own security in the days to come.

Mandates for Palestine and Mesopotamia.

What might be said of the Covenant of the League in its present form might be said with a certain force of the adoption of the Mandates. They were now in possession of Mandates for Palestine and Mesopotamia. One feature common to both appeared to be based on the hypothesis that all the great Associated Powers were contracting parties. They now knew that was not so. The United States was not counted amongst those contracting parties, and he thought a perusal of Articles 11 and 12 of the Mandates could only indicate that they offered something in the nature of preferential treatment to those incorporated in the League or such subjects as commerce, transit, industry, etc. The signatories to the Covenant were the sole countries that were to enjoy the privilege. " Here we find," said Lord Islington, " ground and material for very serious conflict in the future and if care is not taken and full investigation is not made by the Parliaments concerned, there will be conflict between the countries within the Covenant that enjoy the privileges and those countries that stand outside and who may be denied them. Parliament should first consider the issue which is thus involved."

Another feature, he continued, was the uneven distribution of burden imposed on the country which assumed the Mandate as compared with the privileges to be enjoyed by those who merely signed it.

The Mandate for Palestine must be considered in the light of their pledges to the Arab community. There was no doubt that the Mandates, as they stood, ran counter in very important features to those pledges.

In Mesopotamia, for 2½ years a system of administration had been adopted presenting a fundamental divergence from the original precepts solemnly declared to the Arab community and intensely unpopular to that community, ruinously expensive to the British taxpayer and carried through without the sanction of Parliament.

Control by Parliament.

After dealing with expenditure in Palestine and Mesopotamia, Lord Islington said his real object in putting the question was that the Government might tell the House that all future policy in regard to mandated territories and all details, political and economic, would be submitted to Parliament for full discussion and decision before they were referred to the approval of the Council of the League of Nations.

The Government Position.

The Secretary of State for Foreign Affairs (Earl Curzon of Kedleston), after pointing out that the questions raised ought really to have been addressed to the Colonial Office, said that the policy regarding the conferment and settlement of the Mandates had been agreed on throughout at each stage and it had been based purely on the terms of the Covenant of the League of Nations by which all obligations were settled. After preliminary discussion, it was settled at San Remo last April that under the Treaty of Sèvres the Mandates should be conferred. The next stage was the drawing up of the terms of the Mandates, and this was done, in the only way it could be done, by consultation between the Powers concerned. The terms of the Mandates were then sent, under the terms of the Covenant, to the Council of the League of Nations.

Meanwhile the terms of two of the Mandates were divulged in the papers owing to some indiscretion. There was no desire to keep back the terms, but obviously they could not be published except with the consent of all the parties to them. It was in contemplation to ask for that consent at the next meeting of the Conference. There was not the least use in publishing them before their discussion by the Council of the League. It was no use for him to submit Mandates which might conceivably come under question and revision in Parliament and then send them to the Council. The Council of the League would have the original draft and the draft as amended by Parliament and it would ask with which it had to deal. That would be objectionable and intensely derogatory to· the Council of the League. The procedure taken was not only correct, but inevitable. It did not in any way derogate from the final authority of Parliament, but it brought in Parliament at the right stage.

As regarded the Mandate for Mesopotamia, Lord Curzon said that from the day they went into the country the Government had had no desire whatever except to create some form of native administration. They had abolished and removed the Turk. What had they to suggest in his place ? Obviously, the Arab—the people of the country who had been misruled for centuries and to whom the Allies were giving a chance of independence. They had no other solution but self-determination—Arab government for what was a predominantly Arab country. No one was more anxious than the Colonial Secretary, who had now assumed charge of those countries, to reduce military expenditure and the strength of the garrison to a minimum. They desired to set up this Arab administration without delay.

Viscount Bryce said he did not find anything in the expression at the end of Article 22 to exclude the intervention of the Legislature in previous stages. There was nothing to prevent the mandatory Power when it proceeded to draft its own mandate from consulting Parliament about it. If Parliament suggested alterations in or was inclined to disapprove the Mandate, and it did so after it had come from the Council, the work that the Council had done was lost, the mandate was gone, and if the mandate had to be redrafted, they had to begin de novo. It would be much better therefore, if before the mandate went to the Council its terms were published and an opportunity given to Parliament to have a discussion.

Land Question and Forced Labour: Australian Example.

They wanted to know, Lord Bryce continued, particularly in the case of African territories, how land questions were going to be dealt with and in whom the ultimate title to the land was to rest. Was it in the mandatory? If so, upon what terms would the mandatory grant land? How far would anything in the nature of freehold title, which had already been granted in these African territories, be recognised? What provisions would be made for helping the natives to manage their own affairs and to cultivate in them a communal spirit? How far would forced labour be allowed, or would it be allowed at all?

This particular question, said Lord Bryce, arose the other day in Australia. The Commonwealth Government laid before its Legislature a Bill to define the powers that were to be exercised by Australia in the New Guinea Protectorate taken over from Germany, and the Legislature, seeing a provision which allowed forced labour for certain purposes, struck it out and forced labour disappeared entirely from the terms of the Mandate.*

Of course the Australian case was a little different from the African cases because the mandatory Power received authority to assimilate the legislation with that of the contiguous territory, and as Australia was already controlling Papua it was obviously desirable to have a uniform administration there and in the mandated territory. Still the Commonwealth Parliament assumed without question the right to alter the mandate and to amend the draft.

Parliamentary Control.

He suggested that when Great Britain prepared a mandate —as it had done for Mesopotamia and Palestine—for any of the African territories, or when it aided the South African Government in doing this, it should be submitted to the criticism of Parliament before the draft went to the Council. No mandate ought to be given under the authority of the League of Nations until the nations who assented to the giving of the mandate had had an opportunity of expressing their opinion upon it.

The League and Parliament.

The Secretary of State for Foreign Affairs, in dealing with Lord Bryce's observations, said that if they looked at Article 22 they would find that at every stage the really responsible body for giving mandates and for seeing that they were carried out was the League. It was true there was nothing in the Article to prevent a previous reference to

---

* See this JOURNAL, Vol. II., No. 1, pages 113–117.

Parliament, but there was nothing to provide for it. It clearly I was never contemplated. The authority who was really responsible was the League as represented by its Council, and the view they had taken was that it was their duty to go in the first place to the League as represented by its Council. He thought it would not have been compatible with the position assigned to the Council of the League if, before going to it, they had thrown these Mandates on the table of Parliament in each country, submitted them to criticism there, and then handed over to the League whatever had been the result. Would it really have been possible to have a sort of Committee discussion on these Mandates in advance, with amendments moved on this and that point, and something emerging at the end which might not be the view of the Government at all ?

Referring to the Mandate for Mesopotamia, Lord Curzon said that it had received a very favourable reception from papers of almost every section of opinion. He had hardly seen in any quarter the kind of criticism which he had anticipated and which he might have given been unreasonable in thinking that Parliament would have given.

Presently they would know what Geneva meant to do. He did not know what the League was going to do but he imagined that when the Mandate had passed the League it would come before Parliament. He did not think it would go through Committee in Parliament, and he did not think it ought. He thought Parliament would be asked to give a general expression of opinion about it. Supposing there was an overwhelming opinion against some particular clause or provision of the Mandate, he could quite conceive that would produce a great impression on the Government. But he failed to see anything which would justify them in thinking at that stage that if the Council of the League accepted it with or without amendment, it was then open to Parliament to pull it to pieces afterwards. That was the last way in which they would give encouragement and power to this great experiment which they were all trying to make a success. Lord Curzon concluded : " At the back of my mind there was, and has been, the making of the Council of the League a responsible body, and having put it in this very authoritative position I think we must trust it to be the guardian of what is right and proper quite as much as the Parliaments of the countries who are concerned. I make that general statement in reply to the speeches which have been delivered to-night premising all the while that we are moving in a sphere of uncertainty and that I cannot lay down a definite position about a situation which is now more in the hands of the Council of the League than in the hands of His Majesty's Government.

DEBATE IN HOUSE OF COMMONS.

On the motion for the adjournment for the Easter Recess on 24th March, a discussion was raised upon the League of Nations and the system of mandates, and the matter of control by Parliament in connection with these matters.

Mandates : Control by Parliament.

Major the Hon. W. Ormsby-Gore (Coalition Unionist, *Stafford*) called attention to the constitutional position of the House and the country in relation to the mandates, and to the League of Nations. It seemed to be imagined by some that the League of Nations was imposing upon the country and the House certain conditions involving expenditure which would not otherwise be undertaken without Parliament being previously consulted. He thought the misunderstanding had come about through the British Government preparing their draft mandates in secret and presenting those drafts to the Council of the League without previously publishing them, so that those who desired to make representations regarding them, in the House or outside, should have an opportunity of doing so. The conditions regarding the Mesopotamia and Palestine mandates were not drawn up by the League of Nations, but by the British Government without previously consulting the House of Commons.

Lieut.-Colonel M. Archer-Shee (Coalition Unionist, *Finsbury*) thought that before they accepted any mandates whatever they must insist absolutely, in the House, that they had an opportunity of seeing what the mandates were, and of examining them very carefully in debate in the House before they were presented to the League of Nations at all ; and secondly, that if the League of Nations Council carried out any alterations of those mandatory drafts, then those mandates should again come before the House, and the House should have again the opportunity of discussing the alterations and deciding whether, under the circumstances, they would accept the mandate as it came from the League of Nations Council, or whether they would re-submit it again with suggested alterations. Referring to Articles 22 and 26, Col. Archer-Shee suggested that an amendment should be proposed to the Covenant so that the power should be with the people who had to exercise the mandate and merely the criticising power with the League of Nations.*

---

* The 8th Paragraph of Article 22 referred to by Colonel Archer-Shee is as follows :—

"The degree of authority, control, or administration to be exercised by the Mandatory shall, if not previously agreed upon by the Members of the League, be explicitly defined in each case by the Council."

D

The **Right Hon. Lord Robert Cecil (Independent Unionist,** *Hitchin*) said that the Government had made certain proposals which they presented to the League. That was all that had been done so far. Continuing, he said there was no reason why the British Government should not at any moment vary or amend their propositions as they were before the Council. The obligation to administer or to assist in the administration of those countries might impose a considerable burden upon them. That was a matter on which Parliament certainly should be consulted. It was very important that these mandates should be examined in detail by the House before they were submitted to the Council.

Functions of League.

With regard to Armenia, Lord Robert said he was not sure that he thought the proposal that the territory of Armenia and the Erivan territory should be defined anew by the League of Nations was a very satisfactory one. He thought it very undesirable to put duties of that kind on the League of Nations, as it would imply some duty on the part of the League to protect a territory which they would have to define. Before that was done the League would have to be provided with some force, and he did not think it was the proper function of the League of Nations to set up as the military protectors of new States.

League of Nations not a super-State.

The **Under-Secretary of State for the Colonies (Lieut. Colonel L. S. Amery)** agreed that the whole of this business of the League of Nations and the mandates was clouded with misconception which appeared to recur continuously, however much one tried to get rid of it, namely, that the League of Nations, in some sort of sense, was a super-State, which could order them to do things they did not want to do, and impose upon them conditions of mandates which they did not approve. He thought it was a pity the term " League of Nations " was ever used, and that it would have been much clearer to have spoken of some permanent International Conference—something to make it clear that all that was aimed at was a better way than the old diplomacy of getting nations to preserve peace and to administer the territories entrusted to their charge in the interests of the subject peoples and of humanity.

Mesopotamia: " B " Mandates.

Referring to Mesopotamia, Colonel Amery said they wanted to set up a form of government which should, as as possible, become increasingly the government of the people of Mesopotamia themselves. The same applied when they were dealing with " B " Mandates. There was nothing in the position laid down which indicated any departure from the system of administration already in force in the British Colonies and Protectorates in Africa.

There was no question of the League of Nations imposing on them action involving great expenditure and future liability.

Control of Liquor.

With regard to Major Ormsby-Gore's question as to why it was that while in the Samoa and South-West African mandates there was prohibition of the sale of liquor, " B " Mandates dealt with control and not with complete prohibition, Colonel Amery said: " When you are dealing with the Pacific Islands and the aborigines of South-West Africa, you are dealing with a very primitive type of native. The Australian Commonwealth and the Union of South Africa have each set up a standard of absolute prohibition of the sale of liquor to their natives. When you are dealing with ' B " Mandates you have to face a somewhat different position. If my hon. friend went, for instance, to Lagos, he would probably meet at the club lawyers, doctors and other men of culture and refinement, and he might even wish to exercise his hospitable instincts towards them. . . . What we are aiming at there is effective control rather than complete prohibition."

Parliamentary Sanction.

Referring to the authority of Parliament in the matter of mandates, Col. Amery said it seemed to him that they were not dealing with the introduction of some new principle for which Parliamentary authority must be asked; they were dealing with an integral part of the Treaty of Versailles. That Treaty was accepted in the House, and not a single member criticised the provisions of the Article in question. Generally speaking, the process of the mandate had been one of evolution from Clause 22 of the Covenant by negotiation. The House had always the final say in every matter and, above all, in any matter that involved expenditure or legislation. Those matters on which they wanted to get agreement among a large number of nations took a long time, but it would take an absolutely impossible time if the detailed negotiations had to be thrashed out on the floor of Parliament, not only in the United Kingdom, but in Brazil and Albania and every other country which was a member of the League of Nations.

TRADE WITHIN THE EMPIRE.
(Effect of Foreign Competition.)

Trade within the Empire was the subject of a question and answer in the House of Commons on 22nd February.

Mr. R. Clough (Coalition Unionist, *Keighley***)** asked the Secretary to the Department of Overseas Trade whether his latest information from any of the parts of the British Empire showed that, as a result of high prices, British goods had been suffering from foreign competition on a cheaper scale owing to rates of exchange and other causes; and, if so, in what direction of manufactured exports this tendency was most pronounced ?

The Secretary to the Department of Overseas Trade (the Right Hon. F. G. Kellaway) : During 1920 the total volume of British exports to Empire markets was adversely affected by the scarcity of British export coal. During the same period, American and Japanese competition have proved formidable and trade was lost on account of lower prices, particularly as regards American railway material, motor vehicles, and tinplate, and cheap Japanese textiles and hardware. In these cases the encroachment was not assisted by the general level of the exchanges ; but any disadvantage in this respect was counter-balanced by ability to quote firm prices and definite dates of delivery. There is no evidence that British goods have been displaced during the past year to any serious extent · by competitive goods of European origin, but present indications suggest that more severe European competition must be anticipated in the near future.

I should add that the proportion of total British exports sold within the Empire has displayed a continuous and gratifying increase during the past year. In the last quarter of 1920 40·1 per cent. of our exports went to Empire markets, as compared with 37·1 per cent. for the year 1913.

OVERSEA SETTLEMENT AND UNEMPLOYMENT.
(Colonial Office Vote.)

On 2nd March the House of Commons discussed in Committee of Supply a supplementary estimate of £250,62 for the Colonial Office in respect of the year ending 31 March, 1921.

The Under-Secretary of State for the Colonies (Lieu Colonel L. S. Amery) explained that the revised estimate f the Oversea Settlement Scheme was £195,000 higher than tl original estimate of £500,000. Of that increase, £150,0 was in respect of free passages to ex-Service men and £45,0 for other free passages. Seven thousand more ex-Servi men and their dependants had gone to different parts of the Empire than the number estimated. With regard to the free passages for persons other than ex-Service men, the increase was due to the serious stage in the condition of trade and employment which arose during December. Amongst the measures of relief from unemployment decided upon by a Committee of the Cabinet was the provision of assistance either in the way of free passage or an allowance for outfit, clothing, and so on, or landing money for men and women who did not come within the scope of the ex-Service scheme, but were in need of assistance, and for one reason or another were able to show that they had employment, or the prospect of doing well, awaiting them in the Dominions.

"There can be no question of thinking that immediate unemployment on a large scale can be relieved by measures of settlement overseas," said Colonel Amery. "There is no question of dumping people on the Dominions because they are unemployed. The Dominions have their own unemployment problem—very serious in some cases. The number and the class of people whom they can take are very limited. Therefore it would be a great mistake to encourage the idea that when you have a great crisis of unemployment you can solve it off-hand by telling people to go to the Dominions. . . . This small grant is given only after careful investigation into each individual case, first of all by the Overseas Settlement Committee of the Treasury, and, secondly, by representatives of the Dominions concerned. No person can get assistance who is not previously passed by a representative of the Dominion to which he wishes to go as a desirable settler and one reasonably assured of employment on the other side."

Women Emigrants.

The grant of £5,000 a year to the Society for the Overseas Settlement of British Women was to be increased to £7,500, Colonel Amery said. From all the information which reached him the women selected and passed had done well. The Society had also done valuable work in warning those who were not suitable for settlement overseas that they should not go, and in discouraging girls who might be tempted to emigrate too readily by advertisements and various forms of propaganda.

Mr. Trevelyan Thomson (Liberal, *Middlesbro'*, **W.)** suggested that the money would have been more economically spent if it had been devoted to developing the home land and seeking to keep in this country some of the best of the manhood and womanhood of the nation.

The Hon. W. Ormsby-Gore (Coalition Unionist, *Stafford*) protested against the idea that if British citizens left this country for the great lands of Canada and Australia they were getting rid of them. "All this idea that you have got to conserve the manhood resources of this island is," he remarked, "a Prussian idea. It was the old German idea, the idea of State power in a narrow circumscribed area. In my view it is utterly wrong. If they go to Canada, to Australia, or to any part of the Empire they remain British citizens; they are one with us, one in every way and in every manner." He hoped that when these questions of oversea settlements were being dealt with more care would be taken by the Colonial Office in cases where they were encouraging the settlement of Crown Colonies to ensure that the same kind of care should be taken as was taken by the Governments of the great self-governing Dominions.

Emigration a Necessary Factor.

The Right Hon. Sir Donald Maclean (Chairman of the Independent Liberal Party in Parliament) said that emigration from this country to the Dominions and Crown Colonies had been one of the necessary factors of that commonwealth of nations called the British Empire. It was checked during the War and it was quite proper that the Colonial Office should at the very earliest moment set going again the machinery by which that beneficial function of the British Empire would recommence as soon as possible. He was glad that the difficult and delicate task of the overseas settlement of British women was not to be undertaken solely by the State. More detailed information about the scheme would be widely welcomed throughout the country.

Mr. T. Myers (Labour, *Spen Valley*) said that reconstruction work in their own country could be embarked upon and would produce better results with a greater measure of security to their unemployed men than they got with the purely speculative offers from overseas.

Mr. Percy Hurd (Coalition Unionist, *Frome*) urged that the settlement schemes should not exclude women. "There are," he said, "many excellent young women who have no hope here whatever, but the Governments overseas might develop settlement schemes for women in poultry farming, dairying, and agricultural pursuits, and, if necessary, the women could be trained on experimental farms in this country. I ask the hon. gentleman to think out this problem of the settlement of women. Women have worked on the land and in our munition factories, and very many opportunities would arise for them overseas if they were only given a chance."

Mr. J. E. Swan (Labour, *Barnard Castle*) moved to reduce the amount of the Vote by £50,000. There was work to done at home, he said, and, with co-ordination between Government Departments, there would be abundant scope for schemes whereby men could be employed.

Forty Thousand Settlers.

The Under-Secretary of State for the Colonies, replying, said the Committee would be interested to hear the actual figures of those who had gone to the different Dominions under the scheme since it was started in 1919—16,000 odd to Canada; 12,000 odd to Australia; nearly 8,000 to New Zealand; 3,000 odd to South Africa; 376 to Rhodesia; 26 to Kenya Colony (and in spite of the great economic difficulties in that Colony the majority of those settlers promised to do well in the end); and 780 to various other destinations, including Nyassaland. In all, some 40,000 had gone—men, women and dependants.

"I wish it to be made quite clear," said Colonel Amery, "that we do not encourage, and do not allow, a man or woman to emigrate under this scheme who is not first approved by the representative of the oversea Government concerned as a desirable settler and as a person for whom there is assured work waiting. Whole classes of industrial workers who fulfilled early Service conditions have been systematically rejected by Canada on those grounds, though many have gone at their own expense, and so have swelled the unemployment statistics of that country. We have taken anxious precautions to see that no one should get this gift to whom it would not be a benefit. . . . In few cases have we heard of failure, and I am glad to say that in the majority of cases of that kind I do not think the failure could be attributed so much to the conditions as to defects on the part of the settlers themselves."

He added that the Government did not want to push men to leave this country, but they went before the War, and the restless spirit of the race would move them to do so again. What they wanted was that those should go who were fit to go, and that those who were not fit should be discouraged from going.

The amendment was withdrawn and the Vote was agreed to.

UNEMPLOYMENT PROBLEM.

(Labour Amendment to the Address.)

On the second and third days of the Debate on the Address in the House of Commons—16th and 17th February

—the subject under discussion was unemployment. The Labour Party had tabled an amendment as follows : —

" And regrets that, in view of the serious distress consequent upon unemployment and the lack of preparedness on the part of the Government to deal with the situation, there is no mention of legislation recognising the right of the genuine unemployed to work or adequate maintenance."

The Right Hon. J. R. Clynes (Chairman of the Parliamentary Labour Party) moved the amendment. He contended that in face of the situation, which the Government itself admitted, the country was entitled to more than the hint in the King's Speech that there was to be some further extension of provisions to deal with unemployment by means of national insurance. "When we ask for either work or maintenance," said Mr. Clynes, "we ask for work first, and if that demand is not met we assert the right of willing workers to adequate maintenance from the State if the State takes no steps to provide them with productive and remunerative work in exchange for wages wherewith to keep themselves in conditions of comfort."

The Minister of Labour, after remarking that the charge of lack of preparedness on the part of the Government was not a fair one, informed the House that on 11th February the number of men and women registered as unemployed at the Employment Exchanges throughout the United Kingdom was 1,039,000, including 368,000 ex-Service men. In addition it was estimated that about 600,000 were working on systematic short time, and there was also a margin, possibly a large margin, of persons unemployed but not registered. There had been times before the War when the volume of unemployment was greater, but the present cost of living rendered it a much more poignant and grim problem than in pre-War days. The policy of the Cabinet had been, as far as possible, to see that the relief work was of a useful and productive character.

The right hon. gentleman enumerated the numbers employed as the result of the various measures adopted, and, summing up said that altogether work was provided for 70,000 persons.

On a division the amendment moved by Mr. Clynes was negatived by 262 votes against 84.

UNEMPLOYMENT INSURANCE ACT (1920) AMENDMENT ACT.

On 3rd March the Royal Assent was given to the Unemployment Insurance Act (1920) Amendment Act, which was treated as an emergency measure, and had a rapid passage through both Houses. The Act makes important changes in the scheme for unemployment insurance, including provision for an immediate increase in the amount of benefit and for raising, on 4th July, 1921, the weekly rates of contribution.

On and after 3rd March, 1921, the weekly rate of unemployment benefit is as follows :—

Men	20s.
Women	16s.
Boys (between the ages of 16 and 18)	10s.
Girls ,, ,, ,, ,, ...	8s.

On and after 4th July, 1921, the weekly rates of contribution will be :—

	Employer.	Employed.	State.
Men	6d.	5d.	2¾d.
Women ..	5d.	4d.	2¼d.
Boys	3d.	2½d.	1⅜d.
Girls	2½d.	2d.	1¼d.

The maximum periods of benefit that may be drawn are as follows :—

	Weeks.
Between 3rd March, 1921, and 2nd November, 1921 (first "special period")	16
Between 3rd November, 1921, and 2nd July, 1922 (second "special period")	16
Thereafter, in each insurance year	26

Preliminary Qualifications for Benefit.

(1) The principal preliminary qualification for benefit in the period up to 2nd July, 1922, will be the furnishing of proof of employment in insurable work in at least 20 weeks since 31st December, 1919, and of proof that the applicant is normally in insurable employment, is genuinely seeking whole-time employment and is unable to obtain it. In the case of ex-Service men and women and merchant seamen covered by the Out-of-Work Donations Scheme, the number of weeks in which employment since 31st December, 1919, must be proved is reduced from 20 to 10, and, subject to the recommendation of the Local Employment Committee, this requirement may, in proper cases, be waived altogether.

(2) Before allowing benefit under these provisions, the Minister of Labour will, wherever there appears to be any doubt as to the validity of the claim, refer it to the Local Employment Committee for their recommendation. The Local Employment Committee may either recommend the grant of the full amount of benefit, or of a smaller amount, or may make the grant subject to review at a later period, or, finally, may recommend entire rejection of the claim. The Minister is empowered to issue directions to the Local Employment Committees regarding the exercise of their powers in this connection.

Where the qualification in the preceding paragraphs cannot be satisfied, benefit may, nevertheless, in certain cases be payable—

(A) If contributions have been paid by an insured contributor under the Unemployment Insurance Acts, and have not been exhausted by the receipt of benefit, the contributor may draw benefit in respect of the unexhausted contributions to the extent of one week's benefit for every six unexhausted contributions.

(B) Applicants who have paid at least four contributions under the Unemployment Insurance Acts, 1920, may draw up to 8 weeks' benefit in the 12 months between 8th November, 1920, and 7th November, 1921.

DEBATE IN HOUSE OF COMMONS.

On 23rd February the Bill was discussed in the House of Commons.

The Minister of Labour (the Right Hon. T. J. Macnamara), in moving the Second Reading, said there were over 330,000 ex-Service men on out-of-work donation—usually of 20s. per week—which was running out, and, indeed, for numbers of them had already run out. The Bill renewed the donation at the same rate for those men and brought it into the Insurance Act. Many workpeople, men and women, were rapidly exhausting the benefit payable under the Insurance Act, a fact which made the problem an urgent one. As from the passing of the Bill, men and women who had been employed 20 weeks since 31st December, 1919, would be eligible for 16 weeks' benefit between the passing of the Bill and the end of next October, and another 16 weeks' benefit between the end of next October and the beginning of July, 1922. Thereafter, persons insured under the Act would be entitled to draw in each insurance year up to 26 weeks' benefit instead of the 15 weeks provided for in the main Act.

The Right Hon. G. N. Barnes (Labour, *Glasgow, Gorbals*): " If the first 16 weeks run out in October, how much more work must a man put in before becoming entitled to the second 16 weeks ? "

The Minister of Labour : " None; it runs right on. . . . The whole thing is covered by the 20 weeks' unemployment up to 31st December, 1919."

Ex-Service Men.

Ex-Service men, the Minister explained, would have to show ten weeks' employment since 31st December, 1919, but he would propose an amendment to ensure that no deserving case was ruled out because a man had not been able to put in that number of weeks up to the end of 1920. " I have particularly in mind," said the right hon. gentleman, " the case of men who joined the Colours before they really came into industry, and who had no industrial employment before they became soldiers. As regards unemployed disabled ex-Service men, their case is specially dealt with. We propose to give the Local Employment Committee—composed as to one-half of employers of labour, and as to the other half of workpeople—authority to deal with each case on its merits waiving, if needs be, the employment qualification of ten weeks, which is the general provision for fit men."

The Government found that, with the resources at their disposal and the additional income from the increased contributions proposed in the Bill, they could make the benefit 18s. a week for men, 15s. for women, 9s. for boys, and 7s. 6d. for girls. Regarding the finance of the scheme, the Minister said he sincerely trusted that there would be no undue anxiety respecting the future of the fund arising out of the present proposals. "They are based," he remarked, "upon an average of 9½ per cent. of unemployment amongst insured persons—not the whole body—throughout the whole period from now to the end of June or the beginning of July, 1922, taking out of the calculations 1,750,000 people who may go out of the general scheme and join special schemes in the meantime. I should explain that the corresponding proportion of unemployed persons in insured trades to-day is 13 per cent. . . . Heaven knows, we may hope that the level of 9½ per cent. will not be maintained throughout the whole period or which we are legislating. I cannot think it will. I believe our basis to be a prudent one, and we shall review the position before June, 1922."

Labour Disappointed.

The Right Hon. J. R. Clynes (Chairman of the Parliamentary Labour Party) expressed a sense of real disappointment at a measure of that kind being offered by the Government as any kind of remedy for unemployment problems. It was at best some little extension of that process of almsgiving which had done duty in legislation for the very far-reaching promises of those who had spoken for the Government outside the House, and he thought they were entitled to repeat their protest against the method of the Government in dealing with the question. That method was, to use the vehicle of the King's Speech, to use the principal pronouncements of the Prime Minister, to create in the minds of the unemployed the belief that, given authority, power, and backing, the Government would solve the problem, or at least try to.

"I know," the right hon. gentleman said, "that the Government have had some information, if not in full detail, at least in general terms, of a scheme under which, by a somewhat larger contribution from the employers and from the employed, and by a very much larger contribution from the State, a benefit could be given equal in the case of an unemployed man to a minimum of half his wages, supplemented in case he is a man with dependants and a family by sums which will bring his total family income at least up to a minimum of 75 per cent.

of his wages. Such a scheme is now in working order, and if private employers in some instances can do these things without hindrance to their business, without any blow to industry, surely it is not beyond the power of the State to come pretty near the example of the very best type of employer.

"It used to be a boast in this House that the State should be a model employer. If there is any reality in that term in conditions of such severe unemployment as this, the State should undertake to be as good a model in relation to the unemployed workers as the best type of employer in any part of the country."

The Right Hon. J. H. Thomas (Labour, *Derby*) remarked that Bolshevism had no hold in this country. It could only thrive on hungry and starving people. Because the Labour Party wanted to save their country from that, they intended to press upon the Government that the only thing that mattered to them was the unemployment problem.

After the Closure had been carried the Bill was read a second time without a division.

Rates of Benefit Increased.

The House considered the Bill in Committee on 24th February, when

Mr. Clynes moved to substitute for the rates of benefit proposed by the Government the following : —

	Per week.
For the head of a family	40s.
For other than the head of a family	25s.
For each person wholly dependent upon a person entitled to benefit under the principal Act or this Act ..	5s.

The future wealth resources of the country, said Mr. Clynes, depended upon the physique, state of health, and condition of efficiency of the mass of the wealth producers. If they were underfed and improperly housed, if they had not good food and clothing for the next six or twelve months during which the privation of unemployment might be endured, they would be less healthy, less efficient, and less physically fit for the work that would face them in later years. Therefore it was worth the while of the State to pay at the right time.

The Minister of Labour, in resisting the amendment, said that the proposal would bankrupt the Insurance Fund. He had no doubt Mr. Clynes would say that it should be a State charge, but the more the credit of the State was mortgaged the more was widened the gap between the nominal and real value of wages, which was bad enough already.

After lengthy discussion, during which the Minister of Labour announced that the Government were prepared to

increase the rate of benefit from 18s. as proposed in the Bill
to 20s., the amendment was withdrawn.

Amendments were thereafter agreed to raising the benefit
to the amounts set out in the summary of the Act. The
Committee stage was concluded in the course of the sitting
and the Bill was read a third time after a brief discussion.
It had a speedy passage through the House of Lords and
became law on the date mentioned.

CANADIAN CATTLE EMBARGO.*

(Royal Commission: Imperial Conference.)

In the House of Commons on 16th March questions were
addressed to the Government with respect to the embargo
on the importation of Canadian live cattle.

Mr. A. E. Waterson (Co-operative, *Kettering***)** asked the
Prime Minister whether, having regard to the growing evidence
that public opinion was in favour of the removal of the embargo
on Canadian cattle, and that the removal would increase the
supply of home-fed and freshly killed meat, lower the prices
of such meat and bring it within the reach of the consumers
of the country, and provide additional raw materials for
several industries, in addition to strengthening the relationship
between the Dominion of Canada and this country, the Government would take steps to introduce early legislation to secure
the removal of the embargo ?

The Prime Minister (the Right Hon. D. Lloyd George) : "In
view of the pledge which was given to Canada at the Imperial
Conference in 1917, the Government proposes to set up an
impartial inquiry as to whether the embargo could be removed
without inflicting serious injury on the agricultural industry
which is of vital importance to the nation. This inquiry
will take the form of a Royal Commission, the members of
which will be selected expressly so as to constitute an impartial
tribunal without the representation of sectional interests."

Mr. Waterson : "When is the Commission likely to begin
it work ?"

The Prime Minister : "It will be set up immediately,
and I certainly should like to see its Report before the
Imperial Conference."

Lieut.-Commander Kenworthy (Independent Liberal, *Hull,
Central***)** : "If this is a pledge, why set up a Commission ?
Why not carry out the pledge to Canada straight away ?"

Major the Hon. H. O'Neill (Coalition Unionist, *Antrim,
Mid.***)** : "Can the right hon. gentleman say whether this pledge
was given with Cabinet sanction, and, in any event, what
is the effect of a pledge given in this way at a conference by a

---

* See also page 347.

Minister, which pledge, to be carried out, requires subsequent legislation ? "

The Prime Minister : " I agree.   It was given definitely by the then Colonial Secretary (Mr. Walter Long) and the present Lord Ernle, who was then Minister of Agriculture. Both gave very definite pledges on behalf of the Cabinet. I agree it is a matter for the House of Commons to decide, and if the House of Commons is to consider the question I think it would be very considerably assisted by a perfectly impartial inquiry."

CRIMINAL LAW AMENDMENT BILL.

(Indecent Assaults on Young Persons: Brothel Keepers, etc.)

The House of Lords passed on 22nd March the Criminal Law Amendment Bill introduced by the Bishop of London. The measure now awaits consideration by the House of Commons.

As amended during its passage through the Upper House, the Bill provides that it shall be no defence to a charge or indictment for an indecent assault on a child or young person under the age of 16 to prove that he or she consented to the act of indecency.

Reasonable cause to believe that a girl was of or above the age of 16 years shall not be a defence to a charge under Sections 5 or 6 of the Criminal Law Amendment Act, 1885.

Any person convicted of an offence against Section 13 of the principal Act (summary proceedings against brothel keepers, etc.) shall be liable on summary conviction :—

    (A) To a fine of £100 or three months' imprisonment, with or without hard labour ;

    . (B) On second conviction, to a fine of £250 or six months' imprisonment ; and

    (C) On third or subsequent conviction, to a fine of £500 or twelve months' imprisonment ; or, in any case, to both fine and imprisonment.

Section five of the Punishment of Incest Act, 1908 (which requires that all proceedings under that Act are to be held in camera), is repealed

DEBATE IN HOUSE OF LORDS.

The Second Reading debate on the Bill took place in the House of Lords on 9th March.

The Bishop of London (Dr. A. F. Winnington Ingram said that last year three Bills dealing with the question were introduced—one by himself, another by the Government, and the third by Earl Beauchamp. All were referred to a Select Committee of Lords and Commons, which sat for ten months under the careful leadership of Lord Muir Mackenzie. That Committee had reported favourably of

four out of five points of his Bill.   He had not included a proposal to punish the communication of venereal disease, because
he did not desire to encumber the Bill with a very controversial
clause, and it would have been difficult to be quite sure they
were just in punishing the person who communicated venereal
disease.   Their Lordships would also see how easily it might
have led to that examination of women which had been opposed
by all the women's societies of England, had been shown
to be absolutely delusive, and had been laid aside.   Every
organised women's society had written or telegraphed to
support the Bill in the shape in which he had introduced it.

Again, he had left out the compulsory detention of young
girls in homes, and he regretted far more the omission of that
clause.   But nearly all the women of England were against it,
and even that experienced rescue worker, Mrs. Bramwell
Booth, said she was opposed to the use of any compulsion.
The phrase " a common prostitute," used in another Bill,
really defeated its whole object, because the girls they wanted
to get off the streets were not common prostitutes.   Further,
he had not pretended to deal with the flats.   Anyone who
was in the thick of rescue and preventive work must know
that the venue of prostitution in great cities had changed, and
that as a matter of fact far more was carried on in private flats
where the woman had a certain number of men each night.
They could not touch her at present, because the flat was not
a brothel, unless two or three women were living in it.

Age of Consent.

The protection of boys had also been left out of the Bill
on the advice of the Home Office, as it was felt that there
would be no prosecutions under the clause by which it was
sought to punish older women for misleading boys of 17.
Another alteration in the Bill was that 18 as the age of consent
had been reduced to 17.   " I know this will disappoint   . . .
a great many of my supporters all over the country," said the
Bishop.   " I do not say I have changed my mind at all, but
I would put it to those who are so disappointed that they do
not think this Bill worth supporting, that 17, with a clean cut
and with ' reasonable cause to believe ' taken out is a tremendous advance.   If we can get that at this time, someone else
can go on afterwards to propose bringing the age up to 18."
The Committee itself did not suggest raising the age from 16,
the rev. Prelate observed, and the Home Office were not
inclined to go with him further than the proposal in the Bill.

If they turned to other parts of the world they found that
in New South Wales, Queensland, South Australia, Western
Australia, and Tasmania, the age was 17, and in nineteen
States of the United States of America it was 18.   Therefore,

no one could say that they were going ahead of the opinion
of the civilised world in raising the age to 17. The medical
authorities reported that in the clinics of London—and only
about one-tenth of the cases went to these clinics—there
were during the first half of 1920, 15,797 new cases of venereal
disease and 214,659 attendances. A large percentage of the
patients were quite young—from 16 to 20 years of age. The
medical authorities said that seduction and desertion operated
powerfully as a cause of prostitution. If only they could safeguard the young womanhood and girlhood of the country,
they would be stopping venereal disease and dealing with it
far more effectively than it could be dealt with in other ways.

Other Proposals.

There were three proposals to deal with this appalling
evil in addition to his own.

The plan of the Society for the Prevention of Venereal
Disease was practically a very wholesale distribution of packets
and the allowing of chemists to sell preventatives, etc. It was
described in the late Commission by Sir Archibald Reid, who
when pressed as to whether this would not mean a wholesale
promiscuous prostitution of the race, did not seem to have
thought that it would really interfere with the family life of
England if that were the effect. But if that kind of thing
really came into England it was the beginning of the end.
Next there was the Society for the Combating of Venereal
Disease which was necessarily very slow and partial in its
working by means of treatment centres. Men would not go
near them. Then they had the arrangement familiar in
France—the establishment of licensed houses. Flexner's
" Prostitution in Europe " absolutely crushed the idea that
they could deal with this evil by means of licensed brothels,
by inspection.

The evil was increasing because they had not had the
courage to go to the real cure—to go higher up the stream and
prevent the evil at its source. The whole point was that they
were trying to protect the girls who were not able to take care
of themselves.

The Civil Lord of the Admiralty (the Earl of Onslow)
said that although the Government left the whole matter to
the unfettered judgment of the House and would exercise no
pressure through the Whips, they would view the progress of the
Bill sympathetically. Clause 1 (" Consent of young person
to be no defence ") was identical with the clause in the Bill
introduced last session by the Government. Clause 2 differed
from the original proposal in the Government Bill which contemplated maintaining the present age of 16. The matter
had been under the careful consideration of the Home

Secretary, who had authorised him to state that he would offer no objection to raising the age limit to 17. At the same time he would point out that the extension had been viewed with a certain amount of doubt as to its wisdom.

"Reasonable Cause to Believe."

Lord Phillimore said he was for sixteen years a Judge of Assize and had to deal with more than 100 of these cases. There were, most unfortunately, any number of girls who were prostitutes before the age of 17. The taking away of the defence of " having reasonable cause to believe " that the girl was over age and the raising of the age of consent would take from young people (who were really not committing any crime, because they were only dealing with the girl as she wished to be dealt with) every possible reasonable defence.

Viscount Cave, referring to the same aspect of the question, said that so long as it was open to a person charged to get off simply by proving the state of his own mind they would not give anything like protection to those whom they all desired to protect.

The Bill was read a second time without a division. On 5th March the measure was considered in Committee. The principal change in the Bill was due to the acceptance by the Bishop of London of an amendment moved by Lord Muir Mackenzie which provided for the abolition of " reasonable cause to believe " as a defence, but substituted the age of 16 years, instead of 17 years as proposed when the Bill was introduced.

The Bishop of London said it was clear from the discussion that it would be impossible to ask the House both to raise the age to 17 and at the same time to abolish "reasonable cause." He preferred to retain the provision as to "reasonable cause" and to sacrifice raising the age.

On subsequent dates the Bill passed through the remaining stages and was sent to the Commons.

TRIBUNALS OF INQUIRY (EVIDENCE) ACT.

The Royal Assent was given on 24th March to the Tribunals of Inquiry (Evidence) Act. The object of this Act is to enable Tribunals to be established (when considered necessary by Resolution of both Houses of Parliament) to inquire into definite matters of urgent public importance.

The Act provides that where it has been resolved by both Houses of Parliament that a tribunal should be established to inquire into a definite matter of urgent public importance, and a tribunal is appointed for the purpose either by His Majesty or a Secretary of State, the instrument by which the tribunal is appointed may provide that the Act shall apply.

In such case the tribunal shall have all the powers, rights and privileges vested in the High Court (or in Scotland the Court of Session)

E

or a judge thereof on the occasion of an action in respect of the following matters :—

(A) The enforcing the attendance of witnesses and examining them on oath, affirmation, or otherwise.

(B) The compelling the production of documents.

(C) Subject to rules of court, the issuing of a commission or request to examine witnesses abroad.

PUNISHMENT FOR CONTEMPT.

A Summons signed by one or more of the members of the tribunal may be substituted for and shall be equivalent to any formal process capable of being issued in any action for enforcing the attendance of witnesses and compelling the production of documents.

If a person duly summoned as a witness makes default in attending ; or, being in attendance, refuses to take an oath or to produce any document in his power or control, or to answer any question to which the tribunal may legally require an answer ; or does any other thing which would, if the tribunal had been a court of law having power to commit for contempt, have been contempt, the chairman of the tribunal may certify the offence of that person to the High Court, or in Scotland the Court of Session.

The Court may thereupon inquire into the alleged offence and, after hearing witnesses, punish the person as if he had been guilty of contempt of the Court.

A tribunal shall not refuse to allow any portion of the public to be present at its proceedings unless it is in the public interest expedient to do so.

On 7th March the Bill was, on the motion of the Attorney General, read a second time after a brief discussion. At the next sitting it passed rapidly through Committee and was read a third time.

The Bill underwent considerable modifications in the House of Lords, where it was read a second time on 15th March. On the Third Reading motion on 23rd March,

The Lord Chancellor (Lord Birkenhead) said that under the Bill as it left that House no citizen of this country was exposed to any risk whatever either in relation to his person or his liberty, or his purse, without a decision or a verdict of a Court of Law. All that had been done was to sanction the setting up of machinery by which a Tribunal, which was thought to be necessary by the two Houses of Parliament, acting concurrently, could be so set up without in every individual case having a separate Act of Parliament.

COAL MINES (DECONTROL) ACT.

The Royal Assent was given on 24th March to the Coal Mines (Decontrol) Act, which provided for total cessation of Government control of the coal industry on 31st March, 1921, instead of on 31st August, 1921, as laid down in the Coal Mines (Emergency) Act, 1920. The Act also made new arrangements with respect to the payment of profits out of the national " pool."

CANADA.

The Dominion Parliament assembled for the Fifth Session of the Thirteenth Parliament on 14th February, 1921.

THE ADDRESS.—GENERAL DISCUSSION.

(League of Nations: Dominion Status: Representation at Washington: Imperial Conference and Defence.)

The Address in Reply to the Governor-General's Speech, which alluded to Canada's relative prosperity, the remittance of certain taxes, unemployment insurance and old age pensions, the trade agreement concluded between Canada and the West Indies, the work of the First Assembly of the League of Nations, the revision of the Customs tariff and other legislation, was moved by Mr. James McIsaac and seconded by Mr. J. A. MacKelvie on 15th February, 1921.

DEBATE IN HOUSE OF COMMONS.

Mr. James McIsaac (Nat. Lib. and Con.,* *King's, P.E.I.*) tendered his cordial congratulations to the right honourable the Leader of the House (Right Hon. Arthur Meighen) on his elevation to the important and honourable position of Leader of the Government and Prime Minister of the nation, and paid his profound tribute of respect and admiration to Sir Robert Borden who led the Government of Canada through the dark and never-to-be-forgotten days of the world's tragedy, and who for their sakes, by his devotion to duty and self-sacrifice or the exaltation of his country, had become a casualty of the War.

Canada's Prosperity.

Canada, he continued, had emerged from the War in an exceedingly strong position industrially and financially. Their

---

* At a caucus of supporters of the Government held on 1st July, 1920, Sir Robert Borden announced that the new name of the Party would be the "National Liberal and Conservative Party." Instead, therefore, of being described as "Unionists," as in past numbers of this JOURNAL, Government supporters will receive the new designation, abbreviated as follows :—"Nat. Lib. and Con."

Owing to this and the reorganisation of the Cabinet, etc., it is feared that one or two errors may have occurred in the description of the party allegiance of individual members. If any mistake has crept in, it will be corrected in the next issue of the JOURNAL.

E 2

bank deposits had increased enormously, and by far the greater part of their loans was held by their own people. Their national wealth per capita, based on bank figures, was $2,500 as compared with $2,400 in the United States. Canada's foreign trade amounted to about $300 per head of population, whereas the per capita proportion of the foreign trade of the United States was only $87. The revised tariff, which would be presented during the Session as stated in the Speech, would be based on the principles of the national policy, having for its essential qualities the requirements of revenue and the principle of protection to Canadian labour and Canadian industries, including agriculture. Under this tariff, inaugurated by Sir John A. Macdonald, which had prevailed in Canada for over forty years, Canada's industries had developed and Canadian workpeople had found abundant and lucrative employment. No fewer than six hundred branch factories had been established in Canada by American manufacturers, representing a capital of approximately $400,000,000 and affording employment to about 87,000 people. Surely a tariff which produced such results as these was the best and the only tariff for Canada, and should be perpetuated.

Mr. J. A. MacKelvie (Nat. Lib. and Con., *Yale, B.C.*) said that he belonged to a class that had perhaps two fundamental principles in regard to their political creed. First, as regarded the larger realm of the British Empire, they believed most firmly in what they considered to be a sane system of Imperialism; they believed in maintaining the closest possible affiliation and association with the Mother Country while at the same time leaving Canada absolutely mistress in her own house. And as regarded their domestic policy, they conceived that, to say the least, any deviation from the principle which underlay a protective tariff was a course of folly leading straight forward to disaster.

The Administration.

The Hon. W. L. Mackenzie King (Liberal, Leader of the Opposition) asked by what authority his right-honourable friend and the members of his Ministry carried on the Government of the country. That was the question the administration must answer to the satisfaction of Parliament and of the country, before consideration could be given to any of the lesser matters mentioned in the Speech from the Throne. Could the will of the people be further ignored, and their rights in matters pertaining to legislation and administration be further usurped? The Ministry which met Parliament to-day had an entirely different character from the Ministry which they met when Parliament was last assembled. The

Ministry was a Unionist Ministry. Surely he (the Prime Minister) did not believe that anyone was deceived as to the character of the present administration through the use of the name " National Liberal and Conservative." The Government which he had formed to-day was a reactionary Tory administration. It was without authority from the people of the country to conduct its affairs. Twelve of the members of the administration which went before the country in 1917 had ceased to be members of the present administration. For the most part the resignations had been of those hon. members who entered the Ministry at the time they did because they believed it to be a Ministry formed for war purposes, and who joined the Ministry to give that Liberal complexion which a real coalition was expected to have. Unless the Prime Minister was prepared to say that he was entitled to the confidence of the people of the country at the present time as the leader of the War administration, by what authority did he presume to carry on the Government of the country ? When the Government of 1917 was formed, it was with the distinct understanding that the tariff would not be brought up in Parliament under that administration ; it should remain for the consideration of a Parliament that was truly representative of the people of Canada.

Plea for General Election.

" When it is recalled," declared Mr. Mackenzie King, "that since 1911 the people of this country have had no opportunity to pass upon distinctly Canadian issues, and that in the interval men who have fought for their country overseas have been denied all privilege of even hearing these issues discussed at a general election, and that only a fraction of the women of the country have had a voice in government, though all have since been admitted to the franchise ; that hundreds of thousands of citizens were disfranchised in 1917 ; and that practically all young men between the ages of 21 and 41 have never yet had opportunity of recording their votes with respect to matters of vital domestic concern, the injustice to the electorate of attempting further to prolong the life of this Parliament must be apparent to all."

The two Acts, he continued, under which this particular Parliament had come into being were the War-time Elections Act and the Military Voters' Act. Under the War-time Elections Act, rights were taken away from large numbers of people. Since that time they had been taxed without any representation in Parliament one way or the other, so that there had been a direct violation of the spirit of the constitution in that regard. He would spare the House a recital of that disgraceful chapter in their national history, whereby advantage was taken of the Military Voters' Act to coerce, in the matter of their political rights, thousands of the young men of the country who were serving the cause of freedom overseas, and whereby their votes, together with the votes of hundreds of men and women who had never seen Canada, were poured by emissaries of the Government into specially selected constituencies, with no object other than that of ensuring the defeat of candidates opposed to the administration. When they had passed by this Parliament a new Franchise Act which gave the right of the ballot to thousands of citizens who had not that right previously, for the Government to continue to carry on in view of the support that it was getting from a representation effected under those old methods was, he thought, a direct usurpation of popular government.

The Government's record in the by-elections was a tale of defeat. Since the Armistice was signed there had been in all sixteen by-elections. In the case of constituencies won by the Liberals in 1917, not one was lost. There had been eight by-elections in constituencies that were won by the Government in 1917; of the eight they had retained one and lost seven.

Since the Armistice, he pointed out, Canada was the only country among the nations of the British Empire and among the countries that formed the associated and allied Powers wherein the Government had denied to its people the right of a general election. In the United Kingdom a general election was held in 1918. Was the example of the British Parliament not one worthy of being emulated in Canada? In Australia a general election was held in December, 1919. General elections were held in New Zealand in December, 1919. South Africa had had not one but two elections since the signing of the Armistice. Were their people so inferior in the rights and duties of citizenship that they were not to be trusted in the same way as the citizens of South Africa? The island of Newfoundland had had its general election in November, 1919. " What we need to-day," concluded the Leader of the Opposition, " is to seek to restore to the people faith in our parliamentary institutions, through conceding their right of control over the Parliament of the country."

Amendment to the Address

He begged to move, seconded by the Member for Shelburne and Queen's (Hon. W. S. Fielding), that the following should be added to the Address : —

" We respectfully submit to your Excellency that your Excellency's present advisers do not possess the confidence of this House or of the country, and that their retention of office constitutes a usurpation of the powers of popular government."

Government's Position.

The Prime Minister (the Right Hon. Arthur Meighen) declared that the Government was in office by the same right that every Government was in office in Canada to-day or had ever been in office in that country—by the right of the confidence of a majority of the Parliament elected by a majority of the people. His hon. friend (the Leader of the Opposition) thought they had no right to be in office last Session, but on every vote the Government was sustained by a large majority, particularly on the vote in which he wished to declare that a dissolution should take place. In point of character, in point of purpose, and in point of aim, they were in full accord with the Government they succeeded, in every respect and to the last jot and tittle. In every respect they were a continuation of that Government. Because men retired from office feeling that for reasons of their own they could not longer give the kind of public service and the great labour required of public office, did that mean that the character or the composition of the Government was altered? Did that mean that the Government lacked public confidence? If the Government had no duty save what his hon. friend himself was willing to accord it, namely, the duty of dealing with the problems of war and the problems that grew out of the War, the Government's duty was not yet done. Was the Government absolved from the duty, yea, the necessity of dealing with every question that ordinarily came within the scope of the functions of a Government? In every year of their existence the necessities of the tariff situation were attended to. No general revision was brought on, but that was because the time had not come when a general revision could be made with advantage to the country. When did the doctrine first arise that after the great, say even the only, issue upon which an election was fought was decided, the Government ceased to function? One would have thought by his (Mr. Mackenzie King's) reference to Australia that the Australian position was quite analogous to theirs, and by his reference to New Zealand that the case was the same there. Was he aware that in New Zealand the Government was elected in 1914, and that although by the constitution of that Dominion they had only a three-year term for their Assembly, actually, by extending the life of Parliament, they went until December, 1919, over six years, and then appealed to the country? In the case of Australia the facts were very similar, although there was no extension there. In the case of Great Britain the Lloyd

George Government, which was the successor of the Asquith
administration, but which did not feel because Mr. Asquith
retired it must appeal to the country at once, carried on for
some years. It did appeal to the country late in the winter
of 1918, he thought, but only after it had held office for seven
or eight years, whereas its term by constitutional practice
was about five years. Here, in this country, while they were
elected on a War issue, they actually went to the country in
war-time. The term (of Parliament) was five years ; the
usual practice was four years ; the Government was entitled
to hold office during that term, provided it maintained the
confidence of the representatives of the people as reflected in
the Parliament elected. In the history of their country or
any other that he had any knowledge of, the only departure
from such a practice had been on occasions when some overwhelmingly important issue had arisen, when a departure of
policy of major consequence was proposed by the administration, and when, as a consequence, it was desirable that the
will of the people as to the departure should be known. These
occasions had arisen in Great Britain and Australia. Would
his hon. friend say they had arisen in Canada ? He would
like it if such an issue could be raised, but they did not propose
any radical departure of public policy in the first place. They
did not propose to give the people of that country anything
save what they had voted for almost times without number.
They (the Opposition) now had an opportunity to show the
people just where they stood on this issue (the tariff). Were
they ready to abide by the platform of 1919 ? If they were,
let the Session not go by until hon. gentlemen stood up squarely
to the Speech from the Throne and told the people of Canada
where they were on the tariff issue. That could be the only
issue if a dissolution of that Parliament took place.

Speaking on 16th February,
Mr. D. D. McKenzie (Liberal, *Cape Breton North and
Victoria, N.S.*) said that no Government could expect to
frame a tariff that would suit everybody ; it was an impossible
thing to do ; but there was enough strength of thought in
that Parliament and out of it to know that some happy
medium could be reached by which the people's interests, both
east and west, would receive proper consideration. The
Government had placed themselves on the side of the capitalist

League of Nations.

**The Minister of Trade and Commerce (the Right Hon. Sir
George Foster),** speaking of the League of Nations, said that
they had made an investment in the field of world peace.
In that work they were not simply related to the Allies, the

were not simply related to the Empire ; they were related to the world. Seventy-five per cent. of the whole population of the world was embraced within that pledge. The United States was without the League ; but if they counted the United States as not being within the League, they must count also, of a surety, upon the fact that the vast majority of her people, with their prayers and hopes, were running in the direction of the League of Nations as constituted.

The League's first working organ was the Council, which was constituted by one member from each of the five Great Powers ; and as the United States had not yet ratified the Covenant of the League, only four representatives were on the Council from the Great Powers. The four other members of the Council were provided for by election by the Assembly. The Council must have unanimity in order to carry through its measures, and that condition appeared at first to be almost a block in the way of practical working. It had not been found so, however. The next organ of the League of Nations was the Assembly. There was one vote for every nation. As now constituted there would be a possible three delegates for every one of the 47 nations that now made up the membership of the League. There were some things which, under the Covenant and in the treaties, were given to the Council alone, while there were other things that were delegated solely to the Assembly. Each had some absolute powers. They had co-ordinate powers when they worked in concert one with the other in order to come to the desired result. The Secretariat was really the staff of the Council and of the Assembly.

Speaking of the duties of the League, the Minister said there was social and economic propaganda. China, for instance, was plagued by the opium traffic, but they would never stop the opium trade until they had the co-operation of all nations. There was the illicit traffic in women and children ; there were the epidemic diseases which scourged primarily one country and which threatened to scourge the world out of that country. All these things were brought under co-ordinating influences in the different nations, and by means of the League of Nations they combined for supervision and for help in carrying out the world purpose. He never saw and never read of a convention, and certainly none on the scale of this one, which so soon got down to profitable and practical work as did the first Assembly of the League of Nations.

Mr. E. Proulx (Liberal, *Prescott, Ont.*) : " Under Article 10, if the Assembly comes to a certain decision have the delegates from each other country the power to commit their country by their votes ? "

The Minister of Trade and Commerce : " That is for the delegates of each country to arrange with their Government. If they have not done that before they left, then they must get into communication with their Government and do it. When they give their vote, they are supposed to be voicing their country's views, and not simply their own opinions; otherwise, we would not have a very strong Assembly."

Court of International Justice.

The one outstanding work of the Assembly had, he thought, been the constitution of a permanent court of international justice. If it was approved and ratified, a permanent court was called into existence, which sat continuously, consisting of eleven judges and four deputy judges with power to settle disputes between States members of the League, disputes between States members of the League and other States not members of the League, and disputes between States which were outside the League. Each nation that belonged to the League had four nominees. Each nation outside could also have its four nominees, so in that way they had a panel of possible judges. The Council and the Assembly together united in choosing from that panel eleven permanent and four deputy judges. That was the system, and it appeared to have given universal satisfaction, as being free from political influences.

The Hon. Charles Murphy (Liberal, *Russel, Ont.*) : " May I ask whether a dispute between South Africa and Great Britain could be referred to this court for hearing and settlement ? "

The Minister of Trade and Commerce : " My hon. friend has asked a very close question. South Africa is a member of the League, and as a member has the right to nominate her four judges. Canada has the same right. I am not going to enter upon the field of these very close relationships between the different parts of the Empire or upon the legal features of the matter."

Mr. Ernest Lapointe (Liberal, *Quebec East*) : " Is there any truth in the report that there was some friction or differences of opinion among the Canadian delegates, or between some of the Canadian delegation and the British delegates ? "

The Minister of Trade and Commerce : " I was driver of the team from Canada and I have no knowledge of any friction in the least. I can give a direct negative to that. Neither have I any knowledge of any friction between any of the members of the British Empire delegations, and I do not believe that any existed. We did not always vote the same way. We did not always talk the same way. Each State was perfectly independent in giving its views, and in that way I think maybe a better accord and better results were obtained than if there had been any thought of acting as a unit or if there had been coercion in any way. But there was none of that."

Quebec.

Speaking on 17th February,

Mr. L. J. Gauthier (Nat. Lib. and Con., *St. Hyacinthe Rouville, Que.*) advocated the doctrine that isolation for Quebec should come to an end. He had claimed all along that the natural ally of Quebec was Ontario. Since 1912, after the defeat of reciprocity in 1911, in the ranks of his own party, he had advocated that theory. He was not listened to. The Liberal Party wanted to retain an alliance with the West. He had no objection to the people of the West, but he had before him figures that showed that west of the Great Lakes 8 per cent. of the population were not British born. Was he going to preach an alliance with those who had not the same ideals as they had and who did not love their institutions ?

Mr. W. F. Cockshutt (Nat. Lib. and Con., *Brantford, Ont.*) said that in the old days the good old Conservative Party had the backing of the French-Canadians to a great extent. There were many respects in which the provinces of Quebec and Ontario were alike. Quebec was a manufacturing centre ; so was Ontario, and at such a time as this he took off his hat to Quebec as being probably the most stable labour province in Canada to-day.

Indemnities.

In so far as the much-vaunted League of Nations was concerned, he was still a doubter. For instance, what about disarmament ? He understood that the question was shelved. Again, for example, what about reparations ? What about indemnities ? It had always been in the order of things in the past that to the victors in war belonged the spoils. It might be a false doctrine, but it had always existed, and it seemed to him that in making peace, if they had won the war they had lost the peace, or some of the pieces at least. Did they say that after bringing that terrible ruin upon this world, that their delegates should come back without any proposal with regard to what they were going to make Germany pay ? He would like them to take up one or two of these knotty points, and tell them what they were going to make Germany do with regard to reparation to France, to Belgium, and to those devastated countries, and tell them whether there was any possibility of Canada receiving some slight share of the immense indemnity that should be paid by reason of her financial sacrifice.

Ties of Empire.

There were quite a few in Canada who were ready to pull down everything that had been built up with the greatest pains for a thousand years past. This was no time to cut the old flag down, to tear apart the few remaining threads that held Canada to the Motherland. They had but four of them remaining and yet right there in the city of Ottawa, in the Province of Ontario, and in the heart of the Dominion, they had had it recommended recently by one high in authority that the appeal to the Judicial Committee of the Privy Council should be done away with and that the Governor-General should no longer come from overseas but should be appointed in Canada. This was no time to tear down any of the safeguards which surrounded their constitution. The world was full of unrest ; the Mother Country was beset with troubles and cares, both from without and within. Would they in Canada, who had practically no grievance, give it out to the world that they, too, were full of unrest, and wanted to cut the painter ? Were they going to have an election, as they had had in South Africa recently, to decide whether or not they would stay with the Motherland ? They could not shut their eyes to the fact that the enemies of the Empire were abroad, they were sowing the seeds of discord wherever they could be sown, and the attempt was being made even in some parts of Canada to raise the red flag and to call not only for the dissolution of the British Empire, but for the overthrow of constituted government in that and other parts of the Empire. Bad as the rule might be said to be in some parts of the Empire, the world had yet to show any better constitution, any greater safeguards to their liberties, to the rights and to their religious freedom than had been brought to them by reason of the benign rule that had been handed out to the Dominions from over the seas in a very mild way, and they had not only all but much more liberty than was enjoyed in most of the countries of the world.

Speaking on 18th February,

The Hon. N. W. Rowell (Nat. Lib. and Con., *Durham,* *Ont.*) stated that, notwithstanding what had been so often said, the League was not a super-State. The League had no jurisdiction to undertake the government of the world or to settle all difficulties that might arise in various quarters of the world. The League was not organised for the purpose of making peace following the recent War. That was the task of the Supreme Council, and if peace had not been established up to date in many quarters of the world it was not because of any failure on the part of the League.

Work of Delegates at League of Nations.

Under the Treaty of Versailles the League was responsible for framing the Commission and organising the government of the Saar Basin. On that Commission was one of their Canadian citizens, Mr. Waugh of Winnipeg, and he was sure it would be a matter of gratification to them to hear from the officials of the League in Geneva the strongest testimony to the splendid service that Mr. Waugh was rendering as Chairman of that Commission. There were six Vice-Presidents who were Chairmen of the six Commissions of the Assembly, and there were six Vice-Presidents at large elected by the delegates present at the Assembly. He was sure that it was a matter of congratulation to the House and the country that the Chairman of the Canadian Delegation was chosen as one of the Vice-Presidents at large of the first Assembly at Geneva. All matters which came before the Assembly were referred for consideration and report to one of the six Commissions. In the general work of the Assembly the Minister of Trade and Commerce sat on Commissions Two (Technical Organisations) and Four (Secretariat and the Budget), the Minister of Justice on Commissions Three (Permanent Court of International Justice) and Six (Armaments, Mandates and the Economic Blockade), and himself on Commissions One (Constitutional Questions) and Five (Admission of New States).

Relation of Delegates to their Governments.

A matter that arose in discussing the relations of the Council to the Assembly, and which occasioned a good deal of discussion was : What was the position of a member of the Council in giving his vote in reference to the Government which appointed him ? Did he in giving his vote record his own opinion, or did he record the opinion of the State which named him ? If these delegates represented their Governments so that when they cast their vote the vote was that of their Governments and bound their Governments — only, of course, to the extent provided in the Covenant — they had a body of plenipotentiaries capable of negotiating and settling matters of very great international importance, and they gave to the decisions of the Council and of the Assembly a value and a dignity otherwise quite impossible. The Assembly came unanimously to the conclusion that on the proper interpretation of the Covenant, while a member might express such opinions as he saw fit and was responsible only to his own Government for his opinions, when the vote was cast it was the vote, not of the delegate, but of the State he represented, so all the voting in the Council and in the Assembly was by States, and these votes bound the States to the extent, but only to the extent, mentioned in the Covenant.

Mr. A. R. McMaster (Liberal, *Brome, Que.*): " That will mean, will it not, that the representatives must always be drawn from the party which is in control of the administration of the country which they represent ? "

Mr. Rowell: " I do not think so. The vote is cast by the chairman of the delegation and he should cast the vote in accordance with the views of his Government. But that does not prevent the representation of other sections of the people if the Government in question chooses to name them."

Article 10.

Continuing, Mr. Rowell said that Mr. Doherty, on behalf of the Canadian Delegation, presented a proposal to strike out Article 10. The Assembly decided to refer all these proposals to the Council with the request that the Council should appoint a Commission to consider these amendments and report to the next Assembly.

Raw Materials: Canadian Attitude.

Referring to two constitutional questions which arose from out of the work of Commission Number Two, he said that the first arose from the suggestion of Italy and Switzerland that the Assembly should take into consideration the question of monopolies of raw materials and of their equitable distribution to the several countries of the world. The representatives of the Government of Canada felt compelled to state clearly the position of Canada, that while she would administer her raw materials in the way that she considered just and fair to all interests involved, she could not permit any other Power to interfere with the manner in which she handled this matter of purely domestic concern. Canada in her resistance to this proposal was ably supported by the other Dominions and India ; the brunt of the fight against the proposal rested upon the Dominions of the British Empire and India. Great Britain as a member of the Council had already assented to an inquiry into the question of raw materials on the motion of the representative of Italy ; she was, therefore, not in a position to oppose the resolution of the Assembly as the Dominions were. The objections of Canada to the proposal were on three grounds ; they said that the question did not come within the scope of the Covenant ; that the League of Nations was not a super-State with power to take up any question it might see fit to take up ; but it was an agreement among States to co-operate for certain definite purposes in the manner provided in the Covenant and not otherwise, or for other purposes. They claimed that, if by any stretch of construction this question could be held to come within Article 23, then there was no right to deal with it unless, and until, an international convention was agreed upon by the members of the League, and then whatever action was taken must be pursuant to the terms of that convention. If that procedure was upheld, the convention when drafted would be submitted to the Canadian Government, and the Government, in accordance with the precedent established in dealing with important international agreements, would submit the convention to the House for consideration and approval. The people of Canada would have full opportunity of discussing and reaching a conclusion on this important matter before Canada was finally committed to the policy outlined ; on the other hand, if they said that the League had power to do this, they created at once on this side of the Atlantic a sentiment against any League of Nations which had authority to interfere in their domestic affairs.

Admission of New States.

He would now refer to the other Commission upon which he sat, Number Five (Admission of New States). No question excited more interest in the Assembly, and this interest related particularly to the admission of former enemy States. Austria and Bulgaria had applied for admission, Germany did not apply. After the most careful investigation the Commission reached the conclusion that both of these States satisfied the requirement (a sincere intention to perform their international obligations) and they recommended the admission of Austria and Bulgaria to the League. The other States admitted were Albania, Costa Rica, Finland and Luxembourg. The States rejected were : Armenia, Azerbaijan, Esthonia, Georgia, Latvia, Lichtenstein, Lithuania and Ukraine. Did the admission of a State amount to its recognition *de jure* by the Powers ? The question arose in the case of Albania. The argument of the members of the Committee, who contended that admission to the League amounted to recognition *de jure*, was that, if it did not amount to recognition *de jure*, they should not admit any State not already recognised *de jure*. In the case of Albania the Committee reported against the admission of that State until her status should be more clearly determined.　The rejection of Albania's application was moved by France and seconded by Great Britain.　South Africa moved that Albania should be admitted and was supported by Canada and a number of the smaller States.　The majority of the Commission was against the admission of Albania; the matter was carried into the Assembly, and South Africa, on the floor of the Assembly, moved the admission of Albania.　South Africa was supported by Canada, and in the discussion which ensued Great Britain and France withdrew the objections which they had made in the Committee and Albania was admitted to the Assembly.

One other question of principle came before this Committee; it was proposed, in this case by South Africa, but he believed, without full consideration, that hereafter no State should be admitted to the League unless that State entered into a treaty similar to the Minorities Treaty entered into by certain of the new Central European States as a condition of their recognition as sovereign States.　The objection to that proposal was twofold; first, they should not add to the conditions of the Covenant for admission to the League, a new condition; secondly, although that principle under the conditions existing in Europe was probably essential for the preservation of peace in Europe, it did not apply to the conditions existing in the New World.　It did not apply to the conditions existing in Canada, where, apart from the two great races and the two religions, the policy was not to perpetuate the various racial minorities which came to them from Europe and other parts of the world; the policy was not to have a little England, a little Ireland, a little Scotland, a little Belgium, a little Germany, and a little France, all over the country; the policy was to develop a Canadian nationality.　The resolution was therefore amended to meet all these objections, and it passed, Canada not voting on the matter.

Independent Attitude of the Dominions.

" Apparently one of the surprises of the Assembly, declared Mr. Rowell, " was the independent attitude of the representatives from the Dominions of the British Empire. The representatives from the majority of the States apparently went to Geneva believing that the views of the Dominions and their votes would necessarily follow the views and votes of Great Britain, and when they found this view did not prevail there was very great surprise.　When one of the Canadian delegates incidentally mentioned, by way of illustrating a certain point, that we in Canada did not even permit the statesmen of the Mother Country, for whom we had the greatest respect and admiration, to interfere with our domestic affairs, they thought it was proclaiming a revolution. They had an idea that the statesmen of Great Britain managed our affairs. . . . They had not realised that the self-governing Dominions have passed from the Colonial status and are now free self-governing and sovereign States under a common Sovereign on an equality with the Mother Country. . . . I am sure the experience of other delegates present at the Assembly will confirm the conclusion which I know I reached, that Canada had a larger liberty, a more real independence and a vastly greater influence as one of the States of the British Commonwealth than she could possibly have as an independent State outside the British Empire. While we claim the fullest freedom for the individual parts of the Empire, we must also keep in view the importance of maintaining the unity of the Empire as a whole. One is just as important as the other. When the forces of dis-integration are at work among the various peoples and nations of the world, there is no force existing to-day with such a stabilising influence for law and order and for peace and justice as the British Commonwealth of free nations."

Speaking on 21st February,

The Hon. Henri S. Béland (Liberal, *Beauce,* *Que.*) desired to congratulate the hon. member for Durham (Mr. Rowell) on the special position he took in Geneva on the important question of the distribution of natural resources. It was the affirmation and the confirmation of a policy which had been dear to the hearts of members of the Liberal Party.

Article 10.

Let them hope that the League of Nations would be a success. There were many difficulties in the path. There was this Article 10, which had prevented an important nation from joining; and in connection with this Article might he say the attitude of the Liberal Party in the Session before last, and during last Session, had been fully vindicated. Now that a memorandum had been published which revealed the attitude of the right hon. gentleman (Sir Robert Borden) who led the previous administration, they learned that he had advised the Peace Conference to do away with Article 10. When the Treaty was under consideration they on that side moved that Article 10 should be accepted only with a reserva-tion, but their motion was turned down by the then Govern-ment. Before the members of the Assembly in the month of December last the Minister of Justice moved an amendment to the Covenant of the League of Nations to strike out this famous Article 10.

F

He would have been glad had the Ministers who represented Canada at Geneva discussed Article 18 of the Covenant
which referred to the registration of treaties. Not a single
word, however, had been uttered in regard to that, though it
was a matter of public knowledge that two members who
were charter members, so to speak, of the League of Nations
had signed an important treaty between themselves and had
refused to register it with the Secretariat.

Expenses of the League.

Another feature to which he would like to refer was the
question of expenses. The share of Canada, it would be found,
would be very large. It was calculated upon the fact that
the nation was a member of the International Postal Union.
It was difficult to find a basis on which to establish the proper
proportion that each country should pay. But would they
think it was fair for Canada, with its population of 8,000,000,
to pay as much as, for instance, Great Britain with a population
of 45,000,000, or France with a population of 40,000,000 ?
What should be used as a basis was difficult to find. It could
not be based on area, it could not very well be based on
population ; perhaps it could be based on the annual budget
of each country.

Imperial Centralisation.

During the last Session he mentioned that there existed
a powerful and carefully prepared organisation to promote
in the nations within the British Empire a movement in favour
of centralisation. Some sorely tormented souls thought they
had discovered that the British Empire had reached the turning
point in its history ; something appeared to them to be wrong
with the Empire. What was their panacea ? To centralise
in London the political, the military and the naval power
of the British Empire. The British Empire was not suffering
from any incapacity. There existed two schools in England
in Canada and in the other British dominions : one school
worked for centralisation ; the other worked for local control
He wished to call attention to the visit of the Imperial
Press Conference delegates in July. The head of that delegation
appeared to them all to be Lord Burnham who, if not the most
eminent, was at least one of the eminent newspaper men
England. Dr. Béland then quoted a speech delivered b
Lord Burnham at Sydney on 28th July, to the effect that th
visitors had not come to lay down the law but to learn th
secret of the great success of the Dominion. " Nobody,
said Dr. Béland, " can take exception to those words

Continuing, Dr. Béland quoted a report of a speech delivered by Lord Burnham at Edmonton on 2nd September, which suggested the creation of a common council sitting in London on which the Dominions would be represented by resident Ministers for the purpose of taking their proper place in Imperial affairs ; and also a speech of Lord Cave at the Bar Association luncheon at Ottawa, in which it was suggested that the Imperial War Cabinet might (if the Imperial Conference should so determine) drop its middle name, and while remaining wholly voluntary and consultative might become in world affairs the nerve centre of the autonomous nations of an Imperial Commonwealth. Those who believed in a greater expansion and a greater development of Canadian autonomy would, Dr. Béland declared, read with some dismay what was being said by those important British Statesmen and public men. The question was not : Shall the British Empire dissolve, or shall the British Empire endure ? There was in Canada as, he thought, there was in every Dominion of the British Empire, only one opinion : that the British Empire should last, should endure, should persist, should continue for the good of the world ; because the British Empire could and did play an important part in the world's affairs. They on that side held to-day the view that was held by the Liberal Party at all times that the British Empire would endure only through the exercise of the largest possible measure of autonomy. Let them rebuff all attempts, patent or veiled, to sink Canada's individuality, Canada's self-consciousness, Canada's self-reliance, in a word, Canada's pride and autonomy, in the vortex of Imperial Federation.

There were two reasons, equally important, why they should resist any such attempts. One was with regard to the League of Nations. The concentration of the political powers of the British Empire would evoke suspicion in the minds of other nations ; would provoke a spirit of rivalry, or perhaps cause another race for supremacy in armaments. Furthermore, let them oppose the scheme, from whatever source it come, on the ground that any such attempt to centralise political power in the metropolis of the British Empire would tend to the disintegration of the Empire.

The Imperial Conference and Defence.

The Hon. Rodolphe Lemieux (Liberal, *Maisonneuve, Que.*) stated that they were informed from all quarters that an Imperial Conference was to be convened in London for the month of June, that Ministers from the various Dominions were to gather in London, and that they would be called upon to pronounce on the question of sharing the naval defence

of the Empire. That was the declaration made by the Prime
Minister of England. And they also had a declaration made,
it was said, by Lord Milner, that the question of Home Rule
for Egypt should also bring the Dominions together in order
that they might be consulted on that most important policy.
He left aside that last question because he could not believe
that they would be involved in it, as they had nothing to do
with Egypt. But the other declaration made by the Prime
Minister of England, that the burden of naval defence had
become too heavy for Great Britain, and that the Dominions
should be called upon to share in that defence, was a most
important issue. On many occasions the ex-Prime Minister
(Sir Robert Borden) had declared, in England and in Canada,
that their country should have a voice in the affairs of the
Empire—that Canada should be consulted on the policy of the
Foreign Office. It was true that, at the Imperial Conference
in 1911, Mr. Asquith, who was then Prime Minister of England
said that all this was a sham, that the Dominions could not
share in framing the foreign policy of Great Britain. If Canada
should be called upon with British statesmen to decide the
foreign policy of the Empire, they could see at once in what
old world troubles they might be embroiled.

Canada was a self-governing dominion, and Canada would
take part in the defence of the Empire or in the defence of
Great Britain whenever Great Britain was on her trial,
but Canada would do so of her own free will ; there would
never be any central authority in London to dictate a policy
to Canada in that regard. If it was true that an Imperial
Conference was to convene in the month of June to discuss
the problem of the part Canada should take in the naval
defence of the Empire, he said that the question transcended
all other issues and that the Government clearly had no
mandate to even discuss it ! The Government should
dissolve Parliament and ask the people by way of a referendum
what was their will with regard to this grave question.

Any organic change in their Constitution would be a
serious one and should be specifically authorised by the people

Canada's Status as a Nation.

Canada, they were told, was a nation. As he understood
the elements of international law there was lacking an essential
attribute : Canada had no sovereignty. If they were a
" nation within the Empire," what about the requisition of
their ships during the War ? There was an embargo on the
Canadian cattle, an embargo which rested upon what Sir
Charles Tupper stated was a lie. It was not true that the
Canadian cattle suffered from pleuro-pneumonia, but it was

true that free-trade England wished to protect the cattlemen and breeders of Scotland and the North of Ireland. They were a "nation within the Empire," but in 1911 when the *Rainbow* and *Niobe* came to Halifax the Canadian Government received word from the British Admiralty that Canadian ships flying the King's colours and the Canadian ensign might not go beyond the three-mile limit lest they should create complications with some other Power. He would like to know how the present so-called Canadian Navy was going round the world flying the British flag and the Canadian ensign at the same time. By what process did they obtain in 1921 that privilege which was denied in 1911 ? Canada was denied the right to conclude a commercial pact with Nigeria and the Gold Coast. When British preference was voted by the Canadian Parliament in 1897, there were obstacles in the way—the German and Belgian Treaties with Great Britain. The Prime Minister of Canada went to England where he pleaded the cause of Canada and the Mother Country, and the two Treaties were denounced. To-day they were attempting to trade with Nigeria and the Gold Coast and he hoped the precedent of Belgium and Germany would help the Minister of Trade and Commerce. Canada was a nation ; but would the Minister of Justice at least give them a hint as to when they would have a right to appoint consular agents in the various countries of the world ?

The Minister of Justice (the Right Hon. C. J. Doherty) : When we shall need them."

Representation at Washington.

Mr. Lemieux, continuing, said that a few months ago the Government was nearly defeated on the question of representation at Washington, escaping defeat by five of a majority. The question was whether or not Canada should be represented at Washington by an ambassador or semi-ambassador. "I make bold to say," said Mr. Lemieux, "that the ink which signed the approval of Parliament was not dry when loud protests were made by the British Ambassador at Washington and when louder protests were made by the Colonial Office and the Foreign Office in London, because a nation we may be, but still under the ægis of Downing Street. The Canadian Ambassador has not yet been appointed. Will my right hon. friend state to-night if that Ambassador will be appointed ? He will not be appointed."

The Minister of Justice : "I will state this, that it is no loud protest from anybody outside of Canada that has anything to do with the question whether he will be appointed or not. My hon. friend said that he would make bold to make the

statement. He certainly carried the boldness to the extreme
of making a statement entirely devoid of foundation."

Mr. Lemieux : " My right hon. friend evades the issue.
He will not say if the Ambassador will be named, and I make
bold to say once more that he will not be appointed."

The Minister of Justice : " I will also say, as I am accused
of evasion, that he will be named just as soon as Canada
decides who is to be named."

Mr. Lemieux : " This question was mooted, not last year,
but three years ago, and I think this is the third time we have
voted the money necessary to maintain a Canadian Ambassador
at Washington. It is very easy for my right hon. friend
in answer to a question, to say that he will be appointed
just as soon as we decide who shall be appointed ; but if you
never decide, no one will ever be appointed."

Great Britain, Mr. Lemieux continued, through the
Foreign Office in London, would never allow the Canadian
Government to appoint a dual ambassador at Washington
and why should the Foreign Office give Canada, which had
no sovereignty, the right to discuss with the United States
the interests of Great Britain at large ? If they were to
appoint a High Commissioner like the one they had in
London or Paris, the case would be quite different, and he
had already stated that they would see with pleasure the
appointment of a Canadian, who was familiar with Canadian
trade and Canadian affairs generally, to Washington, where
they had so many problems to discuss and settle. It was
about time that Canada should have a High Commissioner
in Washington, not attached to the British Embassy, but
speaking for himself and surveying always Canadian conditions there.

Speaking on 22nd February,

· **The Minister of Justice (the Right Hon. C. J. Doherty**
asked what more absolute evidence of the readiness to be
governed from Downing Street could be found than the
abject submission of the hon. gentleman and his friends to a
declaration which he attributed to one Prime Minister (Mr.
Asquith) as settling for ever the status of Canada ? In the
day what that Prime Minister said was unsound and untrue.
He slammed the door in the face of Sir Joseph Ward, who
made the suggestion—which, he was sure, found a response
in the hearts of ·the people of all the Dominions—that the
time had come when as sister nations they were entitled to
have their say as to what the Empire of which they were
an essential part should do ,in connection with her foreign
affairs as well as in connection with other affairs of general
interest. They had to admit that the then representative

of Canada stood silently by, and so far as silence could give acquiescence, he gave his acquiescence. Within one year after that incident other representatives of Canada were in England speaking the real voice of Canada. What Mr. Asquith said in 1911, he abandoned in 1912* ; the hon. gentleman (Mr. Lemieux) clung to it still. They wanted to see Canada, however perfectly she might have fitted herself for her rôle amongst her sister nations, with her fingers grasping close her mother's apron-strings and clamouring to be kept in the nursery. High ambition, lofty ideal for Canadians to hold ! " What is the position to-day ? " asked Mr. Doherty. " Every statesman of the United Kingdom recognises that this Empire is made up of different, distinct, self-governing nations and that it takes the commonwealth of them to make up the Empire ; that there belongs to no one of those nations the right of domination over the other; that there belongs not even to a majority of those nations the right to dominate over any one or more of them. . . . Why did His Majesty, when he was called upon to sign the Peace Treaty and wanted to bind his whole Empire, sign that Treaty distinctly on behalf of Canada, distinctly on behalf of Australia, distinctly on behalf of South Africa, distinctly on behalf of New Zealand ? Simply because what was needed was the Empire's signature, and you would not have the Empire's signature when you had the signature of but one of the nations that went to make up the Empire. Can there be any more outstanding act that His Majesty is ever called upon to do on behalf of this Empire than the signing of a treaty of that import ? Why, too, when the nations proceeded to form their Assembly of Nations, did they welcome Canada as one amongst them ? Why, when they convened their Assembly of the League of Nations, did they summon Canada to be present ? Why did they receive her delegates on a footing of equality with the delegates of the greatest States of this world ? Why did they, whatever may have been the value of what those delegates had to say, listen with respect to the voice of Canada ? The answer is obvious. Nothing of that kind could have happened if they had not at all events differed from my hon. friend as to Canada's status."

" Then," continued the Minister of Justice, " my hon. friend (Mr. Lemieux) and the hon. member for Beauce (Dr. Béland) raised the ghost that we thought had long since been laid, the ghost with which they seek to terrorise the people of Canada, the ghost of some central organisation that must necessarily be brought into existence and have conferred upon it a power to dominate Canada if Canada ventures to assert her national status. Outside of the imagination of

*Reference is made to Mr. Asquith's speech in Parliament on 22 July, 1912.

these hon. gentlemen, where can we find evidence of any such danger as that ? Who is preaching to-day the creation of a central organisation to dominate this Dominion ? "

Dr. Béland : " Lord Burnham and Lord Cave."

The Minister of Justice : " If Lord Burnham and Lord Cave are preaching such a doctrine, let me again point out that we on this side of the House are not like my hon. friend. We do not say : Lord Burnham and Lord Cave have said so ; therefore, Canada, bow down. . . . But those of us who have been proud to step out into the open field of Canada's nationhood trust to ourselves for our own protection from any threatened interference with our autonomy, if there be such threat."

The measure of Canada's nationhood, declared the Minister, was just the measure of the determination of her children to see that she had that nationhood ; and if they failed in that respect it would be because the only adversaries of Canada's nationhood, who were to be found in Canada, would have overturned the facts by their misinterpretation of them. Canada's nationhood had no enemies outside Canada ; it was not questioned abroad ; they had to come to Canada to find the thing put in question.

Meeting of Prime Ministers.

The hon. gentleman said that because there was going to be what he described as an Imperial Conference they must have a general election. Did Sir Wilfrid Laurier go to the country every time he was going to attend an Imperial Conference ? In the first place, what was going to take place in June was not an Imperial Conference. As a matter of fact, it would be a meeting of Prime Ministers to talk over and discuss matters. It was not, nor would an Imperial Conference be, a body whose decisions would bind any country represented at it. If the parties attending that Conference did, as between themselves, come to a mutual agreement that a certain course would be desirable, all that could follow from it would be that the representative of each country would go back home and submit his report first to the Government of his country and that Government, if it approved, would submit to the national Parliament the suggested projects that might have been considered and might have been agreed to at such Conference.

Mr. Lemieux : " I said that if the Prime Minister of Canada was going to a conference where he is to discuss — according to despatches which have been published of late — the share that Canada must take in the naval defence of the Empire, surely that was such an important question that he should get a mandate from the people."

The Minister of Justice replied that he was not prepared to say whether they would talk about Imperial defence ; but whatever might be talked about there, nothing would be done that would bind Canada; the whole thing was purely consultative.

Referring to the appointment of a Canadian representative at Washington, the Minister explained that it would be part of his duties to watch what was going on at Washington ; and just as, no doubt, the British Ambassador in fulfilling his function watched in the general interest of the Empire what was going on in the United States, so their Minister would watch those things in the general interest of Canada.

" Let not the hon. gentleman fear," declared the Minister, "that we are going to sacrifice the. interests of our nation because we are interested in' the affairs of other nations ; let him not suggest that we should fail to do our reasonable part to contribute to the preservation of the world's peace, and to make successfully workable this great instrument upon whose success so much depends for humanity in general and for ourselves in forming part of that humanity ; let him not suggest failure on our part to do our reasonable duty to keep Canada in a position in which she may not suffer the reproach that she alone among the nations did not interest herself in that which makes for the common good of the world ; let him not be afraid that because we are prepared to do our duty we are therefore going to expose the interests of this our own nation of which we are so proud."

French-Canadian View.

Mr. Arthur Trahan (**Liberal,** *Nicolet, Que.*) declared that during the debate on the Peace Treaty, in the second Session of 1919, the Government had treated the members of the House and the people shamefully. They had treated them in this cavalier fashion because, at that time, it was necessary to ratify the Treaty without reserve and above all without delay —England it appeared demanded it—however serious the consequences might be for Canada, and the Government, the slave of Downing Street, paid scant regard to its supporters, parliamentary institutions or the rights of the people in rushing through without consideration a treaty of which to-day they demanded the repeal of one of the most important clauses.

He was opposed to any centralisation of Imperial control, and he would add that any change in their constitutional relations with Great Britain should not come into force until it had been submitted to the approval of the Parliament of Canada and approved by the people by means of a referendum.

As for Imperial defence, he asked why should there be this military Imperialism at a time when one spoke everywhere of general disarmament.

Turning to the matter of divorce, Mr. Trahan said they spoke of legalising in Canada this social cancer which preyed on other countries. According to the opinions of the most distinguished jurists, the indissolubility of marriage was the rule, at least as far as concerned Quebec and Ontario. Divorce was contrary to the natural order of things. They could attribute the unrest which was prevalent in certain parts of Canada to the horrible ravages of divorce and the decrease in the birth-rate.

Speaking on 23rd February, ·

Mr. Joseph Archambault (Liberal, *Chambly and Verchères,* *Que.*) asked whether the present Government went before the people in 1917 with the statement that they had decided to change from the time immemorial the Canadian railway policy of private ownership to nationalisation ? Could the Minister of Marine and Fisheries (Mr. Ballantyne) say that he was elected on a policy of a Government-owned merchant marine ?

In the Speech from the Throne at the opening of the British Parliament His Majesty the King hoped that the Imperial Conference would be " of the utmost value in bringing about co-ordination, both in the external and in the internal policy of the Empire." In a recent speech before the English Speaking Union, Mr. Winston Churchill, the new Minister for the Colonies, referring to that conference, stated " that an effective policy regarding Ireland, Egypt and India would be discussed." The Prime Minister of England, in his opening speech in Parliament, spoke of the intended conference and about the Dominions taking a share in the defence of the Empire. Was it possible that the Prime Minister of Canada thought it so negligible a matter as not to interest the people of Canada ? It was their duty and their interest to have for Great Britain a loyal and devoted respect, but nobody could reasonably expect from them towards Great Britain and the Empire the same love born of the ties of kinship that was embedded in the hearts of their English-speaking compatriots. Although they piously preserved for old France a deep affection, although they had a great respect and loyalty and devotion for England there was another country which they loved more, nay, a hundred times more, than England or France, a country which deserved to occupy a first place in the hearts of every true Canadian. It was his own country.

Speaking on 24th February,

The Hon. T. A. Crerar (National Progressive,* *Marquette,* *Man.*), referring to unemployment insurance and old age pensions, said that while they might, some time in the future, give concern to the country, there existed no very great need at present.

Tariff Revision and Agriculture: Naval Defence.

The speech also contained the announcement that the Government was going to undertake tariff revision at the present Session. To leave the impression that a system of protection was of assistance to agriculture in the Dominion was ridiculous. What were their chief agricultural products? They were wheat, live stock, dairy products, potatoes, fruits; and in every one of these products the country produced away and beyond what they could possibly consume at home. Therefore it followed, as night followed day, that the value they got for all these commodities was fixed in the markets of the world, and not in the home market. Consequently when the Government made the pious declaration in the pronouncement that they were maintaining that policy to protect agriculture in Canada, they were simply " beating up against the wind." There was a distinct difference between a tariff based on the principle of protection and a tariff based on the principle of revenue, and when his hon. friends opposite endeavoured to link the two together they were simply endeavouring to mislead the people of the country.

What was needed in Canada was a programme of rigid economy in every department of the public service. He thought they in Canada might take a naval holiday. One of the greatest mistakes the Government had made, in his judgment, was the acceptance of several war vessels from the British Government, resulting in their having to incur the additional expenditure inevitably attendant upon it. They were rapidly developing a ministry of war in Canada.

Trade and Reciprocity: Imperial Conference.

It was a notable fact that their trade with Europe was falling off. In 1918 they exported to Great Britain $568,000,000 worth of goods. In 1920 that had fallen to $341,000,000. European countries were doing business with other countries of the world where the exchange was more on a parity with their own than was the case in Canada and the United States. What were the figures of their growing trade

*The party lead by Mr. Crerar, hitherto known as " United Farmers " now appears to be generally termed " National Progressive."

with the United States ?   In 1910 they exported $110,000,000 worth of goods to that country.   In 1920 their exports to their southern neighbour had grown to $560,000,000.   Was not that a desirable market to cultivate ?   Ten years ago they had an offer of reciprocity with the United States in natural products, and to the great misfortune of Canada that proposition was turned down at the time.

With regard to the Imperial Conference, Mr. Crerar held the view that before the country was committed to any scheme of joint Imperial defence the sanction of Parliament should be obtained, and he offered this word of advice to his right hon. friend that when he met the British Prime Minister and the other members of the conference he would jealously guard Canada's rights and interests.

Proportional Representation.

Speaking on 25th February,
Mr. Levi Thomson (Liberal, *Qu'Appelle, Sask.*) was in favour of proportional representation.   They had, he said, extremists among their labourers, although they were a very small proportion of the mass, and it seemed to him that for their own safety they should see that every opportunity was given to the labouring classes to be properly represented in the House.

Work of the Government.

Speaking on 28th February,
Mr. R. J. Manion (Nat. Lib. and Con., *Fort William and Rainy River, Ont.*) said that the Government had carried on Canada's part in the War.   After that they brought about demobilisation in a very able manner.   They adopted measures of soldiers' civil re-establishment and a soldier land settlement scheme which was looked upon by many people as a standard for adoption by many other countries.   They had brought in a life insurance scheme for soldiers and a pension scheme which involved a higher pension scale than that of any other country.   They established a Department of Health, and in the speech from the Throne that year they mentioned the establishment of a Department of Scientific Research.   They gave the franchise to women and brought in a Franchise Act which fair-minded people looked upon as a very high type of law.   They brought Canada through the War from a financial standpoint in such a capable manner that Canada, with the possible exception of the United States, was to-day in a better financial position than any other country that took part in the War.   They put on an Income Tax.   Finally, they had insisted on Canada taking its place as a nation in the galaxy of the nations of the Empire.

Policy of the Opposition.

Mr. J. H. Sinclair (**Liberal,** *Antigonish and Guysborough, N.S.*) said that the Prime Minister had divided the people into nation-builders and nation-wreckers. The wreckers were men who stood for freeing the necessaries of life and the implements of production from their present burden, who stood for a 40 per cent. preference to Great Britain, reciprocity on natural products with the United States, honest Government, a free Parliament, economy in administration, a decent franchise and recognition of the rights of labour.

Free Trade.

Speaking on 1st March,

Mr. Michael Clark (**National Progressive,** *Red Deer, Alta.*) claimed that the outlook of protection was always local, always sectional, always narrow, and never national. If they were to discharge the national debt, principal and interest, they must do it by the tremendous surplus which they were well able to produce of the great unprotected natural products of the country. He was glad that the present Minister of Finance stated that this year he expected to collect $40,000,000 by Income Tax, and if he got $80,000,000 next year he would not blame him. Great Britain accumulated so much wealth by her free trade that she had investments all over the world drawing interest, and the interest on these investments went into Britain in the shape of imports bought by individuals within the nation out of their wealth, but constituting an excess of imports in the nation's trade balance. At the present moment she was building 51 per cent. of the entire ships constructed in the world. Before the War she did the carrying trade of the world ; and she carried by her carrying trade the other half of her excess imports. Protection, standing as it did for special privilege, was typical Toryism.

The Minister of Militia (**Hon. Hugh Guthrie**) in reply, asked whether it was any wonder that one of the foremost planks in the tariff policy of the Farmers' party was the plank calling for free farm implements ? They were paying now only from 12½ to 15 per cent. in duty, but in spite of that tariff they were successfully bringing in and selling to a tremendous number of people in the West American farm machinery against the competition of Canadian manufacturers. It was said that they in Canada were to-day suffering, to some extent at least, from unemployment. Was it a patriotic thing, or a sound thing economically, to take the money of the people of Canada at this critical period, to send it across to the United States to give employment to the factories there,

when so many good Canadians during the last few months
had been looking for jobs in Canada?

The Governor-General and Canada's Status.

Mr. Thomas Vien (Liberal, *Lotbinière*, *Que.*) asked whether
it was not childish to try this make-believe on the Canadian
people—" Canada stands to-day in the world on a footing
of equality with other nations " ?   What other independent
nation, even the most humble, was presided over by a Governor-
General ?   What other nation would allow British newspapers
to discuss openly who should be the representative of His
Majesty the King in this country, all booming their respective
candidates ?   If they were a nation, let the right hon. gentleman (the Prime Minister) take a step further and introduce
legislation enabling Parliament to determine who should
preside over their destinies.

South African Elections.

Speaking on 2nd March,
Mr. Ernest Lapointe (Liberal, *Quebec East*) referred to the
elections in South Africa and said that after the Session
was over General Smuts considered that conditions were
rather precarious and tried to form an alliance with the
Nationalist Party.   A conference was held but the extremists
of the Nationalist Party could not modify their views to a
sufficient extent to allow General Smuts and themselves to
co-operate.   He had a majority in the House of Representatives of South Africa, but what did he do ?   He had no mandate
from the people of South Africa to carry on the affairs of the
country with a new party formed of a combination of the
South African Party and the Unionist Party.   General Smuts
was a Liberal ; General Smuts was a statesman ; General
Smuts was a great British constitutionalist ; and he found
that it was his duty to secure the mandate from the people
of South Africa, yet from his point of view it was a dangerous
course to pursue ; it was a very close fight, but it was always
safer to trust the people, and General Smuts to-day was
Premier of South Africa, and when he proceeded to the
Imperial Conference in June he would go there speaking
in no unmistakable way as the representative of the South
African people.

Importance of the Imperial Conference.

The Conference was to be a gathering of momentous
importance ; problems of extreme gravity, the solution of

which might involve tremendous responsibility on their part, would be brought before that Conference. He would read the very words that were used in the calling together of the Conference : —

" The Dominions are invited to attend the Imperial Conference in June on the lines of the Imperial War Cabinet meetings which took place in 1917 and 1918, to deal with the many urgent problems of common interest which call for co-ordination of policy and action by the different Governments of the Empire."

" I emphatically state," said Mr. Lapointe, " that the gentlemen who pretend to govern Canada at the present time have no right to represent our country at that Conference because they do not enjoy its confidence and are not entitled to speak the national voice. . . . We should set our own house in order before undertaking to rebuild the British Empire or attempting to modify the constitutional structure of other nations."

British Empire as a Single Unit.

Speaking on 3rd March,

The Hon. W. S. Fielding (Liberal, *Shelburne and Queen's, N.S.*) affirmed that the House was unanimous in its belief in the League of Nations. But when they came to deal with foreign affairs he was not desirous that Canada should play a part of her own, separate and apart from the British Empire ; he wanted the British Empire, when they came to deal with foreign affairs, to enter every conference as a unit, not as representing several places. Even in matters concerning Canada alone, even in Imperial matters in which Canada was particularly interested, his desire would naturally be that Canada should be, as she had been, represented by Canadians. He would have them go into the Conference, not merely as Canadians, but as representatives of the British Empire. A separate existence in the League of Nations was not making for that Imperial unity that they should desire, but was paving the way towards separation. The gravest position arising out of their action with respect to the League of Nations was that they were having the unfortunate spectacle of the representatives of Canada and the representatives of the Empire quarrelling in the eyes of the public at the Peace Conference and at the League of Nations. Careful observers in the public Press were noticing the quarrels between the representatives of the Mother Country and those of the Dominions, and every enemy of Great Britain and the Empire was getting aid and comfort from those quarrels.

No Question for Imperial Conference.

He believed that the Government did not know about any policy with which to go to the Imperial Conference. He agreed that conferences between Imperial ministers and overseas statesmen, the meeting together of these men and the exchange by them of information, all made for a good purpose. He did not hesitate to say, however, that from the point of view of Canada there was no question to-day which required to be submitted to an Imperial Conference. The truth was that there was a body of people over in England, not a very numerous one, that he might describe as the " Grand Order of Fussers." They were talking about a new Constitution to come before the Imperial Conference. They were always talking about what Canada wanted, and about what Australia wanted. Canada did not want anything.

Cattle Embargo.

They had one little question, important in its way, in regard to the cattle embargo. They thought that the British Government were wrong in their attitude, but they might as well let it go because, if they were maintaining the right to regulate their own trade and commerce, they were not going to claim the right to dictate to the British Government how to regulate British trade and commerce in their own way, even if it did not happen to please them (Canadians).

After further discussion Mr. Mackenzie King's amendment to the Address was negatived by 116 votes to 91.

CANADIAN NATIONALS DEFINITION BILL.

(Canadian Nationality and Status: League of Nations International Court: Imperial Relations: Citizenship: British Subjects: Empire Naturalisation Domicile, etc.)

This Bill is for the purpose of defining what constitutes Canadian National, and was introduced on 1st March, 1921.

As introduced in the House of Commons the Bill provided that :-

The following persons are Canadian Nationals, viz. :—

(A) British subjects domiciled in Canada ; ,

(B) British subjects who ordinarily reside in Canada although not domiciled there.

On 10th March the Bill was amended in Committee of the Whole House so as to provide as follows :—

1. The following persons are Canadian Nationals, viz. :—

(A) Any British subject who is a Canadian citizen within the meaning of the Immigration Act, chapter twenty-seven of the Statutes of 1919, as heretofore amended ;

(B) The wife of any such citizen ;

(C) Any person born out of Canada, whose father was a Canadian National at the time of that person's birth, or with regard to a person born before the passing of this Act whose father at the time of such person's birth possessed all the qualifications of a Canadian National as defined in this Act.

2. (A) Any person who by reason of his having been born in Canada is a Canadian National, but who at his birth or during his minority became under the law of the United Kingdom or of any self-governing Dominion of the British Empire, a National of that Kingdom or Dominion, and is still such a National, and

(B) Any person who though born out of Canada is a Canadian National, may, if of full age and not under disability, make a declaration renouncing his Canadian nationality, and on making such declaration shall cease to be a Canadian National.

DEBATE IN HOUSE OF COMMONS.

Necessity for Definition.

The Minister of Justice (the Right Hon. C. J. Doherty), in moving leave to introduce the Bill on 1st March, explained that its purpose was to define what constituted a Canadian national. The necessity for such a definition resulted, in a large measure at all events, from the fact that under different measures adopted in connection with the carrying out of the operation of the League of Nations, there were provisions made defining certain rights and privileges which might be enjoyed by the nationals of the different members of the League. Under these circumstances it was necessary, he thought, that they should make a definition by statute so that the world might know who was, and was recognised as, a Canadian national. The Bill contained one section which defined as being Canadian nationals British subjects domiciled or ordinarily resident in Canada.

Rights Conferred.

Moving the Second Reading of the Bill on 8th March, The Minister of Justice said that it was his intention, when they got into Committee, to propose amendments to the definition of a Canadian national as set forth in the Bill. What needed to be clearly understood at the outset was that

G

the Bill did not contemplate in any way to affect the status of any Canadian as a British subject. Notwithstanding its enactment they would all remain, of course, British subjects; and under the definition as proposed nobody would be a Canadian national who was not a British subject. But the purpose of the Bill was to define a particular class of British subject who, in addition to having all the rights and all the obligations of British subjects, had particular rights because of the fact they were Canadians. He thought they had always understood that without a specific statutory definition there had for a long time been such a person as a Canadian. But they had reached a stage now where there were certain specific rights created in favour of Canadians, or, to use the expression in the Bill, of Canadian nationals, as such, and should the legislation which the House last year asked to have passed by the British Parliament, clearing up any doubt as to the extra-territorial effect of their legislation, be enacted, (*vide* JOURNAL OF THE PARLIAMENTS OF THE EMPIRE, Vol. I., No. 4, page 646), as he had every reason to believe it would be, it would then be important to have a clear-cut definition of who were the people who might be affected by that legislation.

International Court and the League of Nations.

He might give an outstanding instance of where they had rights created in favour of Canadian nationals in the provisions of the convention establishing the permanent Court of International Justice. Under those provisions—which he had no doubt would meet with the approval of the House when the convention was brought down—the judges of that court were to be elected by the representatives of the different members of the League. To secure election, it was essential that a candidate should have a majority of the votes both of the Council and of the Assembly. Each country, member of the League, had a right—a right not to be exercised directly by its Government—to nominate candidates. Each country was entitled to nominate four candidates; not more than two, however, of those candidates could be nationals of the nominating country. So there they had a case where they needed to distinguish between a national and a non-national of the nominating country.

Mr. J. Bureau (Liberal, *Three Rivers and St. Maurice* *Que.*): " Will the Minister allow me a question ? He stated that a distinction has to be made between a Canadian national and a Canadian citizen. Is it on account of the League of Nations that the word ' national ' is used?"

The Minister of Justice : " We have already a definition of a Canadian citizen in the Immigration Act, but that definition is expressly limited to the Act itself, and we have no definition of a Canadian citizen which can be of general application."

There was a reason, continued Mr. Doherty, for using the word " national " rather than the word " citizen." It was to be found in this, that in the particular convention to which he referred and in the general proceedings of the League the word " national " was used in designating a person, whether subject or citizen, who formed part of the people of a particular member of the League. He was not certain that " national " was perhaps the most desirable word for England, but the word used in the French version of these proceedings by which the word " national " in their Bill should be translated was the word "ressortissant." It was obviously important that they should be able to establish just who was a Canadian national, so that it might not be suggested that if another British subject was elected and one of their men was elected, that would be a case of the election of two men who were nationals of the same member of the League. He might say that the convention as originally drafted might have been open to that suggestion, but at the instance of the representatives of Canada, among others, the wording was modified so as to make it quite clear that this question of one giving way to the other would not arise when there were elected not merely two nationals of the British Empire, but two nationals of the same member of the League. That was another instance in which they had the creation of a right in favour of the Canadian national. The recognition that each member of the League had nationals of its own being once made so clear, it seemed to him only a natural thing, even if there was no other reason for it, that Canada should take the responsibility of defining who its nationals were, and that was what the Bill proposed to do. There was no question of modifying in any way the position and status of them all as British subjects. The purpose of the Bill was only to define a certain class of British subjects—a class who had the peculiar quality of being that kind of British subjects who were nationals of Canada.

Relation to the Immigration Act.

They would see that the provisions defining " Canadian national " made such a Canadian national every British subject who came within the definition of a Canadian citizen under the Immigration Act. In addition, a provision was made with regard to certain classes of persons which followed the principles upon which the question of the quality of British subject was determined by the British Nationality Act, which they also had enacted. The definition of " Canadian citizen " in the Immigration Act limited the quality, so far as that quality resulted from birth, to the person born in Canada.

In addition to the person born in Canada, the Bill proposed to enact that the son of a Canadian national, born while his father was a Canadian national, even though he was born outside of Canada, should be a Canadian national. There was also a provision that the wife of a Canadian national should be a Canadian national. With regard to persons such as the child in question, whose quality of Canadian national resulted from the fact of his paternity, though he was born elsewhere, there was a provision analogous to that which was found in the British Nationality Act, conferring upon such a child, if he should be entitled to nationality in any other British Dominion, the privilege of renouncing his Canadian nationality. There was no need of providing for what would happen if he was entitled to become the subject of some other country, because that was already covered in the British Nationality and Naturalisation Act. Of course, if a man ceased to be a British subject he necessarily ceased to be a Canadian national.

Mr. W. D. Euler (Liberal, *Waterloo, N. Riding, Ont.*): " In the case of men who were naturalised while they were minors, because of the fact that their fathers were naturalised, but who, under the present Franchise Act, have no vote unless they obtain a voting certificate, are they considered Canadian nationals under this Bill even if they have not that certificate ?"

The Minister of Justice : "Anybody who is a British subject and who was born in this country, or who has domicile in this country as described in the Immigration Act, is a Canadian national. This proposed legislation, of course, has nothing to do with the franchise. . . . The Bill does not deal with any particular rights that are to belong to Canadian nationals ; it is concerned simply with the making of a definition."

The Hon. W. S. Fielding (Liberal, *Shelburne and Queen's, N.S.*), regretted that this was another step in the wrong direction. The word " national," as a noun, would be properly and fairly interpreted in the language of international affairs as a citizen of a sovereign State. Hitherto, they had all been glad to be British nationals. Canada was not a sovereign State ; he did not want it to become a sovereign State, and he claimed the expression " Canadian national " was rather difficult to be understood.

Separate Status.

Speaking in Committee of the whole House on 10th March,

Mr. Lucien Cannon (Liberal, *Dorchester, Que.*) said he understood that this Bill was a very important one in the it gave to Canadian citizens what might be called a separate status from that of a British subject. Had the Government in any way, shape or form conferred with the British authorities, formally or informally, with regard to this measure ?

The Minister of Justice : " No. The hon. gentleman is under a misapprehension if he thinks that this Bill modifies to the extent of one iota the status of any of us as British subjects. It did not seem to the Government necessary to ask the permission of the British Government—which, I am sure, would not have the slightest objection—how we ought to define a Canadian, still leaving that Canadian as a British subject just where he was before."

Mr. W. F. Maclean (Nat. Lib. and Con., *York, S. Riding, Ont.*) : " Our statutes, our documents and our official returns seem to go out of the way to avoid defining a Canadian. I had thought that this was the beginning of legislation in that direction."

The Minister of Justice : " I hope it is."

Mr. Maclean : " I hope that the Minister of Justice and the Government generally will do what they can to see that a Canadian is at least recognised on his own statute-book ; for he has not been so recognised in the past. When I say that I speak for the people of all the provinces. A recognition in our statutes, public documents, etc., of what a Canadian is would be a further step towards the unification of the people of this country."

Mr. Ernest Lapointe (Liberal, *Quebec, East*): " It is because I think it is a step in that direction that I heartily support the Bill."

Mr. H. B. Morphy (Nat. Lib. and Con., *Perth, N. Riding, Ont.*) : " The provision that any person born out of Canada whose father is a Canadian national at the time of that person's birth will apply to the future ; it does not cover the past."

Mr. Fielding : " Let me state a case. Twenty years ago a British subject residing in Ontario moved his family across to the United States, and a year later a son was born to them. That son to-day is nineteen years of age. Does he become a Canadian national under this Bill ? "

The Minister of Justice : " Yes."

Mr. Fielding : " The clause reads :

'Any person born out of Canada whose father was a Canadian National at the time of that person's birth.'

That person was born 19 years ago. The hon. member for North Perth says—and I agree with him there—that there was no such thing as a Canadian national, and, therefore, that does not bring the son nineteen years of age to-day, and residing in Buffalo, within this Bill."

Amendment.

The Minister of Justice : " I am disposed to think that the definition as it is in the Bill is not wide enough to cover a person born before the passing of this measure, but I think we can find a form of words that will produce that result by letting the present clause stand as it is, but by adding to it in this way : —

(c) Any person born out of Canada whose father was a Canadian National at the time of that person's birth, or with regard to a person born before the passing of this Act whose father at the time of such person's birth possessed all the qualifications of a Canadian National as defined in this Act."

Position of Wives : Comparison with Immigration Act.

Mr. W. D. Euler (Liberal, *Waterloo, N. Riding, Ont.*) pointed out what seemed to him to be a lack of consistency between Subsection (A) of Section 1 on the one hand and Subsections (B) and (C). In looking up the Immigration Act, Chapter 27, Section 2, he found the last paragraph of Subsection (F) read : —

Provided that for the purpose of this Act a woman who has not been landed in Canada shall not be held to have acquired Canadian citizenship by virtue of her husband being a Canadian citizen ; neither shall a child, who has not been landed in Canada, be held to have acquired Canadian citizenship through its father or mother being a Canadian citizen.

There was an inconsistency there. If they interpreted according to Subsection (c) and the Immigration Act, certain women and certain men would not be included, and yet Subsection (B) made no exception whatever ; it said simply " the wife of any such citizen."

The Minister of Justice explained that the first subsection in the Bill made everybody who was a Canadian citizen a Canadian national, and the two other subsections dealt with people who were not necessarily Canadian citizens. With regard to the wife, it seemed to them proper that the wife of a Canadian national should be a Canadian national. If in the Immigration Act the wife of a Canadian citizen as such, without any other condition, had become a Canadian citizen, they need not have said anything about her in this Act but they were doing so because they did not see the necessity of maintaining with regard to a Canadian national the same distinction which from the immigration point of view it was thought desirable to make in the case of a person who never was in Canada. They thought they might safely follow what was a general rule in all legislation he had seen with regard to nationality, namely, that the wife of the man had the nationality he had.

Mr. Euler : " I quite understand that it is possible for a person to be a Canadian national, and yet not be a Canadian citizen, but it seemed to me there was some conflict in the various subsections."

The Minister of Justice : " There is an intentional difference." Their reference to the Immigration Act did not make anybody a Canadian citizen who under the Immigration Act was not a Canadian citizen. The Immigration Act stood as the law, absolutely untouched.

Domicile.

Referring to the question of domicile, Mr. Doherty thought it was a wise provision in the statute (the Immigration Act) not to require, in order to enable a man to say that he had Canadian domicile that allowed him to come back into this country, that he should be able to establish positively, according to the ordinary law, that his domicile of origin had actually ceased to be his domicile, and that his actual and real domicile was in Canada. At all events, the definition was there.

Mr. Thomas Vien (Liberal, *Lotbinière, Que.*): " You are in effect reproducing it in this Bill."

The Minister of Justice : " Yes. The view as expressed in this Bill is that if it is a good enough domicile to entitle a man to come into this country, and to go back and forth freely under the Immigration Act, it is good enough to entitle him, on the one hand, to be treated as a Canadian national and, on the other hand, to subject him to the obligations of a Canadian national. It must be borne in mind that while it looms large in our eyes as a very great privilege to be a Canadian national, that privilege carries with it certain duties, and we are interested not only in seeing that those entitled to this privilege may be able to demonstrate it, but that it is made clear just who are subject to our legislation as applicable exclusively to Canadian nationals ; and that will come to have a greater importance when, as I anticipate, we have passed the amendment removing doubts as to the extra-territoriality of our legislation."

Mr. Vien thought they should not allow a person residing in Canada to claim to be a Canadian national if he had a domicile elsewhere. If he had been a member of the House at that time (1910) he would have objected to a definition which would allow a person to become a Canadian citizen without at first giving up the domicile that he had in any other country, were it France, Belgium, England or elsewhere. It was impossible to obtain national unity in that country, it was impossible to create that Canadianism which the right

hon. gentleman claimed to have fostered for the last few
years, without exacting from every person who wished to
become a Canadian citizen the abandonment of any domicile
he might have in any other country.

The Minister of Justice asked whether the hon. gentleman
knew that in order to become a British subject and to be
naturalised under the laws of Canada there was absolutely
no requirement to abandon domicile. All that was required
to become a British subject was that they should reside
in Canada for five years. There was no requirement of any
kind of domicile. They had gone further in their definition
of Canadian citizenship than was necessary to be naturalised
as a British subject. The hon. gentleman would create for
their Canadian nationalism, and the acquisition of it, conditions that no other country had dreamed of requiring.
The cases involved would be very few and far between where
the man who had complied with the requirements of their
Immigration Act had not really got his domicile in Canada.

Mr. Vien : " There is no similarity between the case of a
British subject and the case of a Canadian national. A
British subject may be such whether he lived in Australia, in
India, or in South Africa."

The Minister of Justice : " Or whether he lived in
France."

Mr. Vien : " It does not matter at all."

The Minister of Justice : " Exactly, why should it matter
here ? "

Mr. Vien : " That is why I say there is no similarity
between the principle of becoming a British subject and what
we propose to do by this law ; that is to say, to create Canadian
nationals. I would not like to say that all British subjects
will become Canadian nationals, because the Minister must
bear in mind that although it gives some advantage for those
persons who are about to be defined by the Act to be able to
claim they are Canadian nationals, it also implies
responsibility. Therefore, I would not like the Act to define
as Canadian nationals persons who do not intend to make
Canada their principal place of permanent abode."

British Subjects.

Mr. F. S. Cahill (Liberal, *Pontiac, Que.*) : " Is a British
subject under all conditions permitted to come into Canada
under the Immigration Act ; and, if so, what is a British subject
under the Act ? "

The Minister of Justice : " There are classes of British
subjects who may be excluded from Canada. That is precisely
the advantage of being a Canadian citizen. All British subject

are not entitled *de pleno* simply because they are British subjects to come into Canada ; they are likely to be excluded if they come under any of the excluding sections of the Canadian Act. When the hon. gentleman asks me what is a British subject, I would inform him that he would find enumerated in the British National Act the kinds of people who are British subjects. For instance, everybody born within the realm is a British subject ; everybody born outside the realm but of a father who is a British subject is a British subject ; and everybody naturalised under the laws of the United Kingdom or under the laws of Canada becomes by such naturalisation a British subject. A British subject is a man who owes allegiance to, and who is entitled to protection as a subject of.the British Crown. Our Canadian national will be that kind of British subject who is in special manner subject to and owes obedience to Canadian laws as administered through Parliament and the Government and ultimately His Majesty, he being King of these Dominions just as he is King of Great Britain and the entire Empire."

League of Nations and Empire Representation.

Mr. Cannon : " At the opening of the discussion the right hon. gentleman explained that this Bill is a consequence of our being a separate and distinct member of the League of Nations. The British Empire is also a member of the League of Nations ; will the British Empire have British Empire nationals, while at the same time, Australia, Canada, India, and South Africa have nationals of their own ? If so, what will be the legal difference between a British Empire national and a Canadian national ? "

The Minister of Justice : " The description of the British Empire as a distinct member of the League has always been interpreted as meaning the United Kingdom with the Crown Colonies and Dependencies."

Mr. Cannon : " Excluding the Dominions ? "

The Minister of Justice : " Yes. I may say that there has been serious criticism of the adoption of that form. It was urged at the time that the United Kingdom with the Crown Colonies and Dependencies should have been one member, and we should have been the others, all together going to make up the British Empire. We were not able to put it that way, in words."

Mr. Vien : " Why ? "

The Minister of Justice : " No reason was given that I could possibly grasp. . . . The British Empire is spoken of as one member of the League, but in the practical operation it is the United Kingdom that is that particular member, and we of the Dominions had our membership and our representation and our say on a footing of equality with the gentlemen who represented the United Kingdom. I think that when the proper opportunity comes we should urge that that misnomer be corrected, and when we do so we shall probably be able to make the reasonableness of our contention apparent."

Mr. Vien: "Is it the purpose of the Bill to establish clearly who is a Canadian national as distinguished from nationals of France or of other countries?"

The Minister of Justice: "Of course, we can only make laws that are laws in Canada. When the country defines what its nationals or its subjects or its citizens are, it does not make a law that binds an outside country. But it puts before the world its contention; in the first place, it makes them such in its own country, where its law has force, and then it puts before the world who it is that it claims as its subjects. . . . It is one of the things that is inseparable from nationality that, as each country makes its own laws, you always have the possibility of dual nationalities; I do not think you can get rid of them until you have some system of treaties or conventions."

Canadian Nationality.

Mr. D. D. McKenzie (Liberal, *Cape Breton North and Victoria, N.S.*) declared that it was fortunate for the Minister of Justice that he was a member of a Tory Government when introducing and advocating and carrying through Parliament legislation of this kind. He could recall very well conditions in that House when if a Minister of Justice in a Liberal administration would introduce anything that would look like severing from the Mother Country and cutting away the sacred ties between themselves and the Motherland woe betide them because they would hear from the stalwart gentlemen from Ontario whom he saw looking at him from the other side.

The Minister of Justice: "This does not."

Mr. McKenzie: "But it seems to be all right for the Minister of Justice to be a Nationalist. A Nationalist in this country has a significant meaning, and our Tory friends do not like to be told that they are in league with the Nationalists, that they are in league with a Nationalist who used to make openings in the British flag."

The Minister of Justice: "There are Nationalists and Nationalists."

Mr. McKenzie: "Now it is all right to put us all in the same class and say that we are all Nationalists. The Bourassa sect and everybody that followed him are all right now. . ·

I do not think the good loyal people of Ontario will like the idea that we have forsaken Canadian citizenship with all that that term meant, and that we are now Nationalists, if we take our definition of a Nationalist from what Mr. Bourassa and those behind him were preaching.   In 1867 only four provinces of Canada entered Confederation ; they each had their status before Confederation ; but when they became Canada they got that status from an Imperial Act of Parliament, and in that Imperial Act they are called the ' Dominion of Canada.'   By what right does this Parliament change the name from the ' Dominion of Canada ' to the ' Nation of Canada ' ?   We have no right, instead of calling ourselves the Dominion of Canada,' to call ourselves the ' Nation of Canada.'   That means a change in the British North America Act, and after this Act passes, wherever the name of Dominion of Canada,' occurs in the British North America Act, we shall have to substitute for it the ' Nation of Canada ' or the ' Kingdom of Canada.'   There is no ' Nation of Canada,' and no person can say for one moment that there is. Before you have a Nationalist you must have a nation. As far as I am concerned, to be a Canadian citizen and a British subject is good enough for me, and I do not find it necessary, even with all its beauty and wealth of language and fine definition, to go to France for any definition of what I am.   I am a Canadian."

The Minister of Justice :   " We are trying to give you a home-made definition."

Mr. McKenzie :   " I am a Canadian and a British subject and particularly proud of being a subject of the British Empire and under the folds of the British flag.   For that reason I submit to the Minister that I do not think we have any right to use the word ' national,' nor have we any business to declare ourselves a nation except by some convention with the Mother country.   If it is agreed to by convention that all the Dominions shall be called nations, and so forth, I shall have no fault to find ; but it is going too far for this Parliament to declare that we are no longer a Dominion of Canada, but a nation with all its responsibilities that that word implies. We must be either one thing or the other.   If we are a nation " — —

Some Hon. Members :   " Hear, hear."

Mr. McKenzie :   " We have a right to declare war.   Will my hon. friends who are saying, ' hear, hear,' say that we have a right to declare war, or to pass in this House legislation that would be a cause of war between Great Britain and any other country ?   They will have to say that we could not. But if people are satisfied with the empty shell and are content to think they are a nation when they are not, I suppose we

should not deprive them of the privilege of playing with the
idea; but there is no such thing. It is always unwise to
live under false pretences, and I see no advantage whatever
in trying prematurely to get away from our present status
to be a nation when we are really not. I think the whole
of this legislation is a useless bungle of words."

Replying to a question by Mr. Fielding on Section 2 of
the Bill, as to where declaration of alienage should be made,

The Minister of Justice said it might be desirable to specify
the place. If he fell into an error in that regard it was simply
in following the identical analogous provision contained in the
British Nationality Act and also the Canadian Act. No
particular formality was required for the declaration of
alienage as between the nationals of different parts of the
Empire. The principle laid down in the British Act with
regard to a British subject who, under the circumstances
mentioned there, renounced his British citizenship, was
followed.

Empire Naturalisation.

Mr. Cannon said that last year, in the course of the dis
cussion of the Electoral Act, it was declared by the Govern
ment that certain arrangements had been come to between
the Imperial authorities and the Overseas Dominions as t
having a uniform law of naturalisation. (*Vide* JOURNAL
OF THE PARLIAMENTS OF THE EMPIRE, Vol. I, No. 2, page 84
and Vol. II, No. 1, page 74.) The Prime Minister (Sir Robe
Borden) said, if he remembered rightly, that no amendmen
could be introduced unless the Imperial authorities wer
consulted. Did this new legislation interfere in any way wit
the arrangements made at that time and still existing betwee
the Imperial authorities and the Canadian Government?

The Minister of Justice explained that this legislation di
not touch the question of naturalisation at all. There was n
more arrangement that they must do as the Imperial Parli
ment wanted on the subject than there was that the Imperi
Parliament must do what they wanted. The arrangeme
that was come to was that because there was something th
this Parliament could give which no one else could give, a
because there was something else that the British Parliame
could give which neither they nor any one else could giv
they should make this agreement, that so long as their la
were identical, their naturalisation, which of their own for
did not apply in the United Kingdom, would by reason of t
arrangement be effective there, and *vice versa*. So long as th
laws were identical they would recognise the home naturali
tion laws as effective in Canada. To that extent there wa

understanding. The agreement was on a footing of perfect equality.

Mr. Cannon : " Is it possible for a man to be a Canadian national in Canada, that is, a Canadian citizen, and not be a British subject in any other part of the British Empire ? "

The Minister of Justice : " A man to be a Canadian national must be a British subject."

Mr. Cannon : " In Canada ? "

The Minister of Justice : " Yes."

Mr. Cannon : " Can he be a Canadian national and a British subject in Canada and not be a British subject in another part of the British Empire ? "

The Minister of Justice : " If he has the good fortune to be naturalised under Canadian law he is a naturalised British subject in Canada and will be a naturalised British subject in the United Kingdom. He may not be in Australia or in New Zealand, because they have not as yet passed the necessary legislation, and that is unfortunate. But I see no inconsistency in a man's being a Canadian national though he is not a British subject in Australia."

Mr. C. G. Power (Liberal, Quebec South) : " There is, I presume, a United Kingdom national ? "

The Minister of Justice : " I know of no Act defining one. There are lots of things that are law though they are not in Acts, and if there be no Act or law now there may be one in the future. But I think there would be a little difficulty in ascertaining who were " ressortissants " in the United Kingdom."

Mr. Power : " Am I to understand that Canada is the first of the self-governing Colonies to have nationals of its own ? "

The Minister of Justice : " I think they all have, but we are the first, so far as I know, to make the definition."

Replying to a question by Mr. Vien with regard to the agreement as to the identity of the British and Canadian laws of naturalisation, Mr. Doherty said that the agreement, so far as they could talk about an agreement, was reached at the Imperial Conference at which Sir Wilfrid Laurier represented Canada in 1911. Carrying that out the British authorities drafted an Act which they claimed carried out the understanding. That Act was circulated throughout the Dominions and they were all asked if it was acceptable to them. All of them except Canada said that it was acceptable. That was an Act which purported to make the United Kingdom Naturalisation Act effective in Canada, so that by virtue of their legislation people would find themselves entitled to have their naturalisation recognised in Canada. " We took the position," said Mr. Doherty, " that we would not submit to that ; that whoever was to be recognised in Canada as properly naturalised must be so under the enactment of the Canadian Parliament. It took us two years and a trip to England to get that acknowledged."

Mr. Vien : " I understood the right hon. gentleman to say that when the Government undertake to define our naturalisation they confer with the British Government so as to obtain some similarity between their laws and ours. Is that conference taking place also with the other self-governing Dominions so as to try and obtain that similarity with their laws ? "

The Minister of Justice : " The practice has been to transfer suggestions to the other Dominions. For instance, if the British Government made suggestions to us they would make them to the other self-governing Dominions too, and if we transmitted suggestions to the British Government, that Government would submit them to the Parliaments of the other self-governing Dominions. Why the other self-governing Dominions have not acted I have no reason of knowing."

Mr. Vien : " Was the proposed Bill discussed at the League of Nations ? "

The Minister of Justice : " No."

Mr. Vien : " Was it suggested at the Peace Conference ? "

The Minister of Justice : " Yes."

Mr. Vien : " And was it discussed as between Canada and the United Kingdom ? "

The Minister of Justice : " No."

Mr. Vien : " Is it purely on the initiative of Canada ? "

The Minister of Justice : " Yes."

Mr. Vien : " And without any understanding that any other part of the British Empire will take the same action ? "

The Minister of Justice : " Exactly ; we have no understanding as to whether any other part of the British Empire will think proper to define its nationals or not, and with all respect I think it is none of our business."

Representation on the League.

Mr. Cannon : " I understand that after this Bill is passed Canada will, at future meetings of the League, always be represented by a Canadian national."

The Minister of Justice : " I should think so."

Mr. Cannon : " Or might Canada be in the same position as South Africa was at the last meeting of the League, when she was represented by Lord Robert Cecil ? In view of the passage of this Bill, will it no longer be possible for the Government to delegate their powers, for instance, to someone else his standing ? "

The Minister of Justice : " I should think that any Canadian Government would always be able to find Canadian nationals competent to represent Canada in the Assembly of the League of Nations. I do not want to enter upon any discussion of what General Smuts thought it proper to do in regard to South Africa ; that is a matter for South Africans to settle. All hon. gentlemen will agree that on some odd occasion it might happen, when there was nothing important to be done and ornamental representation only was required, you might ask somebody on the spot to be good enough to act as Canada's representative."

The British Flag.

Mr. McKenzie : " I understand that the British flag is the only flag recognised on Canadian ships by foreign nations. Will the adoption of this measure bring about any change in that respect ? "

The Minister of Justice : " It will not affect our ships in the slightest."

The Minister of Marine and Fisheries (Hon. C. C. Ballantyne) : " The hon. member knows well that on the Canadian merchant ships we fly the red ensign the same as the British ships, except that we have the Canadian coat-of-arms on it."

Mr. Vien : " Is it recognised abroad ? "

The Minister of Marine : " Yes."

Mr. Vien : " Internationally ? "

The Minister of Marine : " I believe so."

Mr. Vien : " I understand that a few years ago our Canadian flag—a British flag with the Canadian coat-of-arms — was hauled down in the harbour of New York or Boston because it was not internationally recognised. Has this status been changed ? "

Alienage.

Mr. A. B. Copp (Liberal, *Westmoreland, N.B.*) : " After this Bill passes will it be possible for a person to be a Canadian national and also a national of some other overseas Dominion of the United Kingdom ? "

The Minister of Justice : " So long as a person who is a Canadian national did not, even though he became a national of some other Dominion, make the declaration contemplated in the Bill, he would continue to be a Canadian national. . . . I might be desirable at some time that some convention in that regard should be arrived at between the Dominions and the Mother Country."

Mr. Copp : " But if he is a national of Canada and also of another dominion or the United Kingdom and does not choose to make any declaration, which must he take ? "

The Minister of Justice : " This Bill does not undertake to say what his relationship is to any other country. According to the law of this country, if he was born, say, in Canada, and makes no declaration, he will continue to be a Canadian national."

Mr. Copp : " He can exercise all the privileges of being a Canadian national, irrespective of whether he is also a national of another country ? "

The Minister of Justice : " Yes, just as a man born in Canada, though his father, being a Frenchman, was a French citizen, may enjoy all the privileges of a British subject either in this country or in the United Kingdom."

Mr. McKenzie : " I do not think we have any right to declare here how any man can throw off the responsibility of having become a British subject."

The Minister of Justice : " The question is not one of throwing off British citizenship ; it is purely limited to his Canadian nationality, and that is what he is throwing off. The British Nationality Act, which we have enacted also, provides how a man can throw off his quality of British subject. This Act does not touch that in the slightest. A man would lose his Canadian nationality when he threw off his quality of British subject, but his merely throwing off his quality of Canadian national does not affect his quality of British subject at all."

Mr. Cannon : " Will this Bill, from an international view point, receive any application so far as Canada is concerned, outside of our territory ? "

The Minister of Justice : " No law has any application outside of the territory of the country that made it, but I think I am safe in saying that it is the universal international custom to accept a country's own definition of who its citizens and subjects are unless some other country disputes it."

The amendments to Section 1 and Section 2 were agreed to.

LEAGUE OF NATIONS.

(Article 10.)

In reply to a question by Mr. J. E. Prevost (Liberal Terrebonne, Que.), on 4th March,

The Minister of Justice (the Right Hon. C. J. Doherty) said that he had submitted to the meeting of the League of Nations held at Geneva in December, 1920, a motion asking for the elimination of Article 10 from the Covenant signed at Versailles.

that he was expressing the opinion of the Canadian Government; and that the motion was referred to a special Commission of the Council of the League for consideration and report at the next meeting of the Assembly of the League of Nations.

CONFERENCE OF PRIME MINISTERS OF THE EMPIRE.

(Approval of Parliament.)

In reply to a question by Mr. Joseph Archambault (Liberal, *Chambly and Verchères, Que.*) on 4th March,

The Prime Minister (the Right Hon. Arthur Meighen) stated that no date had yet been fixed for the next Imperial Conference and there was no intention that it should be held this year. It was anticipated, however, that a meeting of the Prime Ministers of the different parts of the Empire would be held in June next. The agenda for the meeting of Prime Ministers had not yet been settled, but it was expected that among the subjects for discussion would be the question of the renewal of the Treaty of Alliance with Japan of the 8th July, 1911, and the question of naval policy based upon the principle of co-operation ; while there would doubtless be a review and consultation upon the general course of the foreign policy of the Empire.

Should there be an indication of a general desire on the part of the House of Commons for a discussion, the Government would be prepared to arrange facilities and would welcome expressions of opinion from all quarters ; but in view of the fact that the meeting was of the nature of a conference, the Government could not depart from the invariable practice by making commitments in advance of the meeting. Necessarily any proposal resulting from the Conference and affecting Canada must be subject to the approval of the Canadian Parliament.

The Hon. Charles Murphy (Liberal, *Russel, Ont.*), on 18th March, asked whether the Prime Minister had observed a dispatch stating that the Prime Minister of Australia intended to acquaint the Australian Parliament with the subjects to be taken up at the approaching Conference in London, and to give that Parliament an opportunity of discussing them. Was it his right hon. friend's intention to give Parliament the same statement and a like opportunity ?

The Prime Minister : " I had not observed any statement by the Australian Prime Minister to the effect described by the hon. gentleman, but I had myself moved in the matter,

H

and a little earlier than he. I have already given this House, in outline, the subjects which will probably be discussed. The exact agenda has not yet reached us, but the three important topics that had been suggested were stated in an answer made about three weeks ago to the hon. member for Chambly and Verchères (Mr. Archambault), and the answer to his question went on to state that should it appear the desire of a substantial number of members that special opportunity be afforded in this House for discussion, it would be provided. . . . Should further information reach us making certain that other important topics would be considered, I will feel it my duty to state those topics or their substance to the House."

NAVAL CONTRIBUTION.

The Hon. Charles Murphy (Liberal, *Russel, Ont.*), on 15th March, brought to the notice of the Prime Minister a report which appeared in the press of a speech delivered on 14th March before the Canadian Club at Vancouver by Captain Adams* of the H.M.C.S. " Aurora," in which, when referring to the ships of the Canadian squadron, he was alleged to have said : —

" Although these small ships were very good in their way, what the Dominion required was a striking force in time of war " ;

and later, that : —

" England to-day is paying $17 a head of population for the maintenance of the great navy which protects us. It is time that Canada stepped in the breach and assumed her fair share of this burden."

Mr. Murphy asked the Prime Minister if Captain Adams, when speaking as he was alleged to have spoken, did so with the knowledge or authority of the Government, and if not would the Government bring to the attention of Captain Adams the fact that the question of Canada's naval requirements was one to be determined by the representatives of the Canadian people, and not by one of their employees, even though he were the captain of a ship.

The Prime Minister (the Right Hon. Arthur Meighen): " I do not know whether I should assume that Captain Adams is aware that the laws of Canada are made by the representatives of the Canadian people, but if I have any reason to believe that he does not know that, we will take occasion to inform him."

---

*For another question regarding this speech, see proceedings, Parliament of United Kingdom, page 267.

FRENCH COMMERCIAL TREATY.

(Question of Parliamentary Approval.)

Mr. Joseph Archambault (Liberal, *Chambly and Verchères, Que.*) on 22nd March drew the attention of the Government to an item which appeared in the Montreal papers regarding the commercial treaty with France. The item stated that the commercial treaty with France, signed on behalf of Canada by the Minister of Trade and Commerce in the month of January last, would become effective on 27th March. He had on the Order Paper a motion for the production of that treaty. When the motion came up on 4th March, the Prime Minister asked that it should stand, and on 7th March the same answer was given. Was it true that the treaty was signed on behalf of Canada in the month of January, and that it would become effective on the 27th instant? Why was the Government keeping the people at large, the manufacturers who wished to do business with France, and members of Parliament unaware of the contents of that treaty until it became effective?

The Minister of Trade and Commerce (the Right Hon. Sir George Foster) replied that the Government had not been keeping the contents of the proposed agreement secret to the detriment of manufacturers or any other business men of the country; rather the opposite was the point held in view. It was true that an agreement was come to, and that it was signed by himself when he was on the other side in the month of January, and it was signed by the then Minister of Commerce, Mr. Isaac. But it was also true that a little after that a change of Government occurred in France, and consequently the signature by the preceding Minister of Commerce was not effective. The measure had itself to be examined and agreed to by the succeeding Ministry, so that there was no treaty that was effective, either *in esse* or in the future, until it became established that the succeeding Government was of the same mind as the preceding and would carry out the effect of the agreement. That was not ascertained until last week.

Let him say a word as to why the treaty could not just at that moment be laid before the House. He had signed for Canada the proposed agreement. Both copies of it were to be sent to the French Government through the British Embassy; and when the French Government were in a position to sign— and that would not be until the succeeding Government had approved the agreement—the two copies of the agreement were to be signed in Paris and one copy sent to the Canadian Government. So that really they had not the authoritative treaty or agreement until they received that signed copy

H 2

which belonged to them and which was now on the way from France.

Mr. Archambault : " Is it true that the treaty will become effective on the 27th of this month, that is, at the end of this week ? "

The Minister of Trade and Commerce : " That is the contents of the telegram that I have received from Mr. Roy."

The Hon. W. S. Fielding (Liberal, *Shelburne and Queen's, N.S.*): " Can it become effective in Canada until it has been approved by this House ? "

The Minister of Trade and Commerce : " Yes."

Mr. Archambault : " A commercial treaty ? "

The Minister of Trade and Commerce : " Yes."

Mr. J. A. Currie (Nat. Lib. and Con., *Simcoe, N. Riding, Ont.*): " When did this House authorise the making of the treaty with France ? Are members of this House not to be consulted at all in these matters ? I have a distinct recollection of one Government in Canada being defeated on that very question."

Dr. Henri S. Béland (Liberal, *Beauce, Que.*): " May I ask the Minister of Trade and Commerce if there is any special reason why communication with the French Government should be made through the British Embassy, instead of through the Canadian High Commissioner in Paris ? "

The Minister of Trade and Commerce : " It has always been the custom that these trade agreements that are made are made through the privity and through the medium of an official of the British Government. I sent the copies which I myself signed through the British Foreign Office. They reached the French Government through that medium, and I expect they will be returned through the same medium."

Mr. Jacques Bureau (Liberal, *Three Rivers and St. Maurice, Que.*): " That was prior to our becoming a nation."

The Minister of Trade and Commerce : " Oh, no. It said that Canada became a nation a long time ago, during Sir Wilfrid Laurier's time."

TRADE WITH RUSSIA.

The Hon. Charles Murphy (Liberal, *Russell, Ont.*) on 17th March asked whether, in view of the announcement that a trade agreement had been entered into between the Government of Great Britain and the Soviet Government of Russia, the Canadian Government had taken, or was about to take, any steps to promote trade between Canada and Russia.

The Minister of Trade and Commerce (the Right Hon. Sir George Foster) : " No particular steps have been taken of late. The situation as regards Russia and Canada is simply this—that any Russian subject has a perfect right to come to Canada to make purchases and provide for payment to the Canadians from whom he makes purchases ; and Canadians have a perfect right to trade with Russian subjects. Notwithstanding the trade commissions that were sent to Russia, conditions in that country, entirely apart from the general world conditions, are unfavourable to Canadian trade. But since the Armistice there has been no embargo on trade relations between the two countries."

Mr. J. H. Sinclair (Liberal, *Antigonish and Guysborough, N.S.*) : " Do the terms of the treaty which has been completed between Great Britain and Russia apply to Canada ? "

The Minister of Trade and Commerce : " The treaty between Great Britain and the Soviet authorities has been concluded entirely irrespective of the self-governing dominions."

Mr. Murphy : " May I ask the right hon. gentleman if the conditions in Russia to which he referred militate against Canada to any greater degree than they do against Great Britain ? "

The Minister of Trade and Commerce.: " The conditions in Russia are equally unfavourable to both countries. They arise from the confused state of affairs in Russia itself and from the almost complete breakdown of transport facilities there ; those are the special conditions. Then of course there is the general trade condition of the world in the matter of exchange and credits.

CATTLE EMBARGO.*

On 9th March the House of Commons discussed a Resolution moved by Mr. William Smith, which stated that it would not be in the interests of Canada to remove the embargo on cattle going into the United Kingdom.

DEBATE IN HOUSE OF COMMONS.

Mr. William Smith (Nat. Lib. and Con., *Ontario, S. Riding*) in moving the following Resolution : —

" That, in the opinion of this House, it would not be in the interests of Canada should the Government of Great Britain remove the embargo upon cattle going into the United Kingdom."

---

* See also page 291.

said that this embargo question was one that had engaged
the attention of succeeding administrations in Canada during
the last thirty years. When the embargo was placed upon
their Canadian cattle it was felt that a stigma had been laid
upon them, because it had been generally admitted that their
herds were free from all contagious diseases. The embargo
that was imposed by Great Britain included cattle from all
other countries as well as Canada, and it was now held that
it was put on for the purpose of satisfying particularly the
Irish people. In the year 1920 Ireland sent 924,000 cattle
to England, at a value of £30,000,000, so they could imagine
what that trade meant to Ireland. Efforts were made from
time to time by different Canadian Governments to have the
embargo removed, but all their efforts failed. During the
last few weeks representations had been made to the British
Government by private individuals, who were taking the
matter in their own hands and dictating, as it were, to the
British Government what they should do in a matter of purely
domestic concern. He felt that if they succeeded they would
make one of the greatest possible mistakes so far as Canada
was concerned. If the embargo were removed they would
do in the future what they did in the past, that was, they
would send not only their finished cattle across, but also
unfinished or store cattle. His contention was this : they
should feed and slaughter their own cattle. If they shipped
across the water a 1,000-pound animal, they were sending
across 460 pounds of waste matter which could be manufactured
just as well in Canada as in the Old Country. Even labour
had been petitioning for the removal of the embargo. If
anyone could tell him how labour would be benefited in the
slightest degree by the removal of the embargo, they would
tell him something he did not know. Then they might have
difficulty with their American friends. If the embargo were
removed against Canadian cattle and not against American
cattle, there would undoubtedly be a certain amount of
irritation, and probably many of their cattle would come
through Canada to be shipped across the sea. That would
cause trouble, because American cattle were not altogether free
from disease.

    Mr. H. A. Mackie (Nat. Lib. and Con., *Edmonton,*
Riding, Alta.) stated that this matter had been the subject
of discussion for the last two or three weeks in the Provincial
Legislature of Alberta because a candidate was defeated
on this question in an election recently held in England, and
it was a sore point with every cattleman in Western Canada.
He did not know by what method of reasoning his hon. friend
arrived at the conclusion that it was necessary for England to
put a stigma on Canadian cattle in order to develop the industry.

of Canada. There was one thing that the Canadian people in Western Canada would not stand, and that was an indirect method of adopting protection in England, without a tariff, by placing a mark of inferiority on their cattle which they did not deserve.

Mr. Michael Clark (National Progressive, *Red Deer, Alta.*) had no sympathy whatsoever with the attempts to get Canadian cattle into Britain by means of the crowbar. He reminded the House that they would not for one moment stand for British statesmen interfering to-day with any tariff they liked to put on goods. If they wanted to get their cattle into Britain they must reduce their tariff against British goods and bring the ships to their shores. If they had had a Government of initiative and courage at the end of the War they would have seen the state of affairs coming to which he referred. They would have seen the wheat produced in other countries beating their Western wheat, they would have seen the cattle from Australia and from the Argentine beating their cattle — because there was a large amount of cattle being taken from both of those countries to Britain, three and four times the distance that Canada was from the Old Country—and they would have reduced the tariff and kept up some portion at least of what he ventured to describe as the " ferry-boat service " that was established during the War.

Mr. D. Sutherland (Nat. Lib. and Con., *Oxford, S. Riding, Ont.*) stated that there was no contention on the part of the British authorities to-day that this embargo was being maintained against their cattle by reason of disease ; they freely admitted that it was a system of protection in favour of those engaged in the cattle industry in the Old Country. Those who were engaged in the livestock industry in Great Britain, and who were bringing tremendous revenues to their country by reason of their sales of livestock, did not feel that their interests ought to be jeopardised by permitting importations of livestock from outlying parts of the world. If animals were shipped to Great Britain in a finished condition, as they ought to be, the farmers of Canada would benefit much more than they would by shipping out the unfinished animals.

The Hon. Rodolphe Lemieux (Liberal, *Maisonneuve, Que.*) thought that they should not let Canadian cattle lie under the stigma with which it was now being branded throughout the world. Great Britain was free to mind her own business and Canada was free to mind hers. They knew that the tie between Great Britain and Canada was very slender. Indeed, the only ties which bound them to the Mother Country were, first, the Crown ; second, the Governor-General ; and third, the appeals to the Privy Council, and then there was that right of veto which the home Government had never exercised.

He did not wish to interfere with the policies of British
statesmen when those policies concerned only the United
Kingdom ; but whenever in Great Britain a policy was
pursued which directly affected the interests or rights of
Canada, he as a Canadian, as a free man, and as a Britisher,
had a right to remonstrate politely, but firmly, with the Mother
Country ; and in the present instance he claimed it was not
meddling with British politics to protest that in this question
of the embargo, to say the least, a very grievous mistake,
nay more, a very serious wrong had been committed. They,
the members of the Canadian Parliament, speaking for the
whole people of Canada, had the right to remonstrate with
the Board of Agriculture in Great Britain and say : You have
adopted a measure prohibiting Canadian cattle from being
landed on the docks at Liverpool, Glasgow, or any other port
in the United Kingdom on the pretext these cattle are tainted
with disease. Now it had been proven beyond the shadow
of a doubt that the disease did not exist in that case, and
they protested against the libel upon their Canadian cattle.
If the British Government wished to adopt a protective
policy, which the embargo was in effect, he did not object to
that, but in that case let them say openly that it was a measure
of protection for the cattle breeders in Scotland and in the
North of Ireland.

    The Hon. W. S. Fielding (Liberal, *Shelburne and Queen's,*
N.S.) said that having stated their views fully and accurately
he did not see what there was to be gained by their continuing
to nag at the British Government. Some British politicians
occasionally argued in favour of the abolition of the embargo
but the Department of Agriculture of the British Government—
strongly supported by the landed interests of England—had
been determined to keep it up, and they would continue to
do so. Lord Crewe, who, he thought, was Leader of the Liberal
Opposition in the House of Lords, had written a strong letter
regarding the action of Lord Lee, President of the Board of
Agriculture, who preceded the member who was defeated the
other day, and he said that the agriculturalists of England
were standing behind Lord Lee in this matter, and would insist
on this regulation being kept up.

    Mr. W. F. Cockshutt (Nat. Lib. and Con., *Brantford, Ont.*)
stated that prior to the placing of the embargo an immense
export trade in live cattle had been carried on from Ontario
to the United Kingdom, and the cattle were bringing at the
time a very high price. Immediately after the embargo
was imposed, the number of cattle exported diminished very
rapidly, and the price decreased just as rapidly as the number
of cattle exported diminished, thus showing conclusively
to his mind, that they lost a very valuable market by an a

which he always considered to be a great injustice to the Dominion. Taking it for granted that the best policy was to send the finished cattle from Canada, cattle were just as much subject to sea-sickness as human beings. In justice to British people, they should not be fed on the flesh of cattle that had been killed in a seasick condition. Yet the regulations said that those animals must be slaughtered within ten days after arrival. The proposition on the face of it was not a good one.

Mr. J. W. Kennedy (National Progressive, *Glengarry and Stormont, Ont.*) said that there had been no outbreak of foot-and-mouth disease in Canada since 1884. Under present conditions, where they had large areas of pasture, and a scarcity of labour, the Canadian farmer could produce and rear far more cattle than he could finish, and it would be of great advantage to him as well as to the British farmer to have the embargo removed, and produce and rear a large number of store cattle, to be shipped over to Great Britain and be finished there.

The Minister of Agriculture (Hon. S. F. Tolmie) stated that ever since the embargo was imposed their Governments had been making efforts to secure its removal, and in 1917 the then Prime Minister (Sir Robert Borden) received a distinct promise from the Minister of Agriculture of Great Britain that the embargo would be removed. Shortly after that two delegates were sent from Canada to Great Britain to instruct the people regarding the health of Canadian cattle and also to represent the unfairness of imposing this embargo on the ground of disease in their cattle. They did this work entirely with the approval of the Minister of Agriculture of Great Britain and clearly through official channels.

At the present time they could not possibly consume the number of beef cattle produced in Canada at home. The result was they had to look for an export market. They had been shipping these cattle to the United States, but there were rumours of tariff changes over there that would prevent their cattle from going into that market if those changes were approved.

The shipping of chilled beef in competition with the Argentine and Australia would not at the present time, he was afraid, be a very profitable work to undertake. Of the million cattle passing through their inspection abattoirs less than ten per cent. were fitted for export to the British Islands in competition with those two countries, on account of their small size, their poor quality, and their lack of finish. Over there they liked very much fatter beef than they used on this side, so that when these cattle had been fed on the ranges of

Alberta, they could then be shipped profitably to Great Britain and sold to the feeders there to finish.

He thought there would be no difficulty whatever in guarding British herds against contamination by animals from the United States. It would be no trouble to permanently mark American cattle on entry so as to prevent any of them being shipped to England by taking advantage of any arrangement that might be made between Canada and Great Britain for the shipment of Canadian cattle over there.

The Prime Minister (the Right Hon. Arthur Meighen) said that the Government that was in office from 1896 to 1911 took, as far as he was aware, precisely the same position as regarded this embargo as the Government that was in power to-day. The record, for example, of the 1917 Conference on this subject was a record of about as definite and insistent a protest as any Government was capable of making. It was on the ground of the implication embodied in the British policy that their protest had all along been lodged. It was on that ground that strong and determined action was taken at the Conference, and by reason of that ground the British Minister of Agriculture at that time was good enough to say at some date Mr. Meighen was sorry the Minister did not specify—he believed that, in rather indefinite language, he fixed it as the termination of the War—the Government would see that the embargo was removed. The case of Canada to-day rested most strongly upon that promise, and, basing their claim on that promise and on the wrong done to Canada by the implication, the Government of to-day was losing no effort to have the embargo removed.

After further discussion **Mr. Michael Steele (Nat. Lib. and Con.,** *Perth, S. Riding, Ont.*) moved on 10th March an amendment to the effect that : —

"All the words after the word ' that ' in the original motion be struck out and the following substituted therefor :—

" ' This House approves and supports the policy of the Government and of previous Governments of Canada in protesting against the implication of disease in Canadian cattle by reason of the maintenance of the embargo thereon by the British Government.' "

The Prime Minister, speaking on the amendment, said he did not think this subject should be seized upon to endeavour to create in Canada a feeling against Great Britain. It seemed to him that the passing of that amendment was consonant with the historic policy of Canada, with the dignity of Canada and also with the continuous practice of that country to respect the rights of the British Parliament within their own domain

Therefore, he hoped the House would accept, as it stood, the amendment, and, if possible, that there would be no division of opinion upon it.

After further discussion the motion as amended was agreed to.

Mr. S. W. Jacobs (Liberal, *George Etienne Cartier, Que.*) on 18th March, said that he saw by the Press that a commission was to investigate shortly the matter of the embargo. He asked whether the Government had any official knowledge of that, and, if so, did it intend to be represented before or on that commission.

The Prime Minister : " The Government has received a communication from the High Commissioner to the effect that such a commission was promised by the British Prime Minister. The terms of the commission have not yet reached the Government. It will depend upon the terms of the commission what action we should take, but I would think, undoubtedly, the Government would see to it that the facts in support of Canada's contention will be fully and carefully laid before that commission."

AUSTRALIA.

Commonwealth Parliament.

The following summary is in continuation of the proceedings of the First Session of the Eighth Parliament, which commenced on 26th February, 1920, adjourned on 26th November, and reassembled on 6th April, 1921.

The Parliamentary Debates for that portion of the Session commencing in April had not reached England at the time of going to press and will be dealt with in the next issue of the JOURNAL. As, however, the full report of a speech of the Prime Minister delivered on 8th April was officially telegraphed to this country, it has been possible to include a summary of this in the present issue.

For the summaries of proceedings in the earlier part of the Session see Vol. I., Nos. 3 and 4, and Vol. II., No. 1.

CONFERENCE OF PRIME MINISTERS OF THE EMPIRE.

(Constitutional Position: Empire Naval Defence: Anglo-Japanese Alliance: League of Nations, etc.)

The Prime Minister on 8th April, 1921, addressed the House of Representatives regarding the questions to be discussed at the Conference of Prime Ministers of the Empire in June.

IN HOUSE OF REPRESENTATIVES.

Constitutional Changes.

The Prime Minister (the Right Hon. W. M. Hughes) referring to constitutional matters said : " Recently the question of constitutional changes in the relations between the Dominions and Great Britain has been discussed in the Press and on the platform, and I have been criticised for not disclosing my views in regard thereto. There seems to be an impression amongst certain gentlemen . . . that the forthcoming Conference is called to consider and to effect some great constitutional changes. These critics protested against the Australian representative being armed with plenary powers without giving Parliament an opportunity of approving or disagreeing with my views."

The Conference, Mr. Hughes continued, " is not called even to consider constitutional changes." These were to be dealt with at a subsequent conference which might be held next year at earliest, but probably at a later date.

It was painfully evident from articles in the Press, etc., that to a certain type of mind the constitution of the British Empire was far from what it should be. One object of these enthusiastic but inexperienced persons was to redraft the Empire Constitution. When challenged they repudiated the desire to establish some kind of Imperial Parliament. They wanted to gild the pill. Falling short of a grandiose Imperial scheme, they hinted at a central council endowed with powers over various parts of the Empire. They failed to realise that a thousand formulas or Imperial Councils would not keep the Empire together if either Great Britain or the various Dominions desired to drift apart.

The British Empire was not built according to plan. Philosophers and constitutionalists, happily for mankind, had no hand in its structure or development. It was not the result of a deliberate purpose. It had grown up, as it were, haphazard, and there never was a time when its structure was crystallised. It was now, as it always had been, in a state of flux.

That the Dominions should enjoy what to all practical purposes amounted to independence and self-government, and yet, while boasting of their independence, passionately insist that they were parts of an Empire one and indivisible, appeared to the foreigner both illogical and inconsistent. "I think," added Mr. Hughes, " nothing is more certain than that the surest way of destroying this mighty Empire, one of the chief bulwarks of civilisation, is to tamper with its constitution. Complete autonomy of the parts is the foundation upon which its unity rests. Neither Great Britain nor the Dominions are prepared to yield one jot or tittle with regard to their perfect freedom to govern themselves in their own way, and this assurance of perfect freedom of each of several parts ensures a spiritual unity which binds us together."

Work of the June Conference.

The June Conference had been called to deal with Empire Defence, particularly Naval Defence, with the question of the renewal of the Japanese Treaty, and questions of foreign policy, wireless, etc. The Japanese question involved foreign policy in general, and the renewal of the Japanese Treaty in particular. That being so, the question of constitutional changes did not arise, and no good purpose could be served by mere academic discussions.

League of Nations.

How stood the nations of the world to-day? Were they beating their swords into ploughshares? Not for one day since the Great War ceased had there been peace on earth. Wars of nations, of classes, internecine wars, incessant industrial turmoil, and talk of great navies and of other wars, —this had been the grim aftermath of the War to end war. It was true the League of Nations met but a few months back and considered many things. It dealt with some, avoided dealing with many more, but did not even attempt to deal with war, the great question which it was created to settle. The Council of the League, for all practical purposes another name for the representatives of the great Allied Powers, had been in frequent session, but, like the Assembly, had by inaction confessed itself for the time being powerless to bring peace to a world drenched with blood. Who in the face of all that was happening to-day could say it had fulfilled the expectations of its creator? It might be that in fulness of time the League might prove a sure and certain shield behind which the world might rest secure against the awful scourge of war, but that day was not yet. Until then they must say with Marcus Aurelius, "Wouldst thou confer upon any country the clouds of war, induce its Government to disarm."

Dominions and Foreign Policy: Need for Consultation.

War was still one of the great facts that men and nations had to face. That was a fact of such supreme moment to Australia that even if they would they dare not ignore it. Before the War it could hardly be said that Australia realised how greatly the safety of the Commonwealth depended upon the policy and acts of other nations. Owing to his remoteness from the great centres of population, and the vastness of his heritage, the Australian had become self-centred, insular in outlook, concentrating upon domestic policy which he thought essential to his welfare, without giving thought how it might affect or be regarded by other nations. Certainly no Australian dreamed that the assassination of an Austrian Grand Duke at Sarajevo would lead to a war in which Australia would spend nearly 400 millions and lose 60,000 men.

Until quite recently the Empire's foreign policy had been shaped entirely by Great Britain, and the Dominions had no voice or control over it. No doubt any other course was practically impossible; Britain had been and still was the predominating partner: she was the mother to whom all her children looked. These, although sturdy youngsters, had not reached maturity. Since any foreign policy for the Empire must depend upon naval power, and the British

Navy was owned and maintained by Great Britain, any claim by the Dominions to a voice in foreign policy was hardly justified. Time and circumstances had changed this position, and five years of war had done more than a generation of peace to develop the national spirit of the Dominions. The manner in which the Dominions had equipped and maintained armies larger than Britain herself had ever before put into the field, put the seal upon that new status which not only Britain but the world had now acknowledged.

The statesmen of Britain were the first to recognise that the Dominions should be consulted on such acts of foreign policy as might in future involve them in war. For another reason too, besides that of the increasing population, wealth and importance of the Dominions, the relations between them and Great Britain regarding foreign policy had been materially changed. It was out of foreign policy that wars were hatched. Before the War the great burden of Empire Naval Defence rested on the shoulders of Britain, but the debt and sacrifices resulting from the War made this no longer possible. The Dominions had claimed the status of nations, had earned their right to be so considered by their war efforts. They had lost tens of thousands of men, incurred debts amounting to hundreds of millions of pounds, but neither in men nor money were their losses as heavy as Britain's.

Scheme of Imperial Naval Defence.

The British Navy was not needed for the defence of Britain alone, but of the whole Empire, including the Dominions. Britain had told them plainly that she could not any longer bear the expense of maintaining this great navy, and that the Dominions must share the burden. No request could be more reasonable, and, Mr. Hughes declared, "for us there is no alternative but participation in a scheme of Imperial Naval Defence in which we play our allotted part and contribute our due quota." Continuing, he said, any scheme of Imperial Naval Defence must necessarily provide for the defence of the Pacific Ocean, where the future of Australia would have to be decided. Naval Defence was for them a Pacific question; and their foreign policy must concern itself closely with the aims and aspirations of the peoples and countries surrounding that mighty ocean. It behoved them to know and be known to their neighbours.

In considering the question of Naval Defence they must remember how far the Empire itself was dependent upon sea power. From the constitutional point of view, the nexus which held the Empire together was the Crown. It was a fundamental truth that the Empire would be impossible

under, say, a Republican Government. As the Dominions
had developed, their legislators had claimed wider and wider
powers, which Britain with her traditional policy had always
granted. To-day, while the Dominions were accorded a
place in the family of nations, and took seats in the Assembly
of the League of Nations on a footing of equality with all
other countries, constitutionally they were one by virtue of
having one King. The Prince of Wales spoke of the Empire
as a Commonwealth of Nations. " Whether we call it a
Commonwealth or an Empire," said Mr. Hughes, " is not
material. Words are nothing ; it is things that matter.
The fact is that the constitutional nexus of the Empire is the
monarchy. We in the Australian Commonwealth now call
ourselves a nation. So we are. But in the same breath we
declare ourselves part of the British Empire. . . . Whatever material prosperity or national greatness we have, have
come because of our partnership in the British Empire, which
in its turn depends for its very existence upon the British
Navy. When we speak about the British Empire, let there
be no delusion as to that on which its existence and greatness
depend. It depends upon naval power.

    " Australia's existence depends upon adequate naval
defence. ·. . . The Conference is therefore important
because we as Dominions may there express our opinion as to
what it means to us. The question then of a satisfactory
scheme of Imperial Naval Defence is one literally of life and
death to Australia."

Anglo-Japanese Treaty.

    The bearing of the Japanese Treaty upon the Naval
Defence of the Empire was obvious. As they had seen, there
had lately been much talk of strained relations between the
United States and Japan. Now in that lay the germs of great
trouble and possibilities of infinite disaster to this world
What was the hope of the world ? As he saw it, it was a
alliance and an understanding between the two great branches
of the English-speaking peoples. That was their dilemma
Their safety lay in a renewal of the Anglo-Japanese Treaty
Yet that Treaty was anathema to the Americans. America
had said that she must have the greatest navy in the world
that she must have a navy sufficiently strong to defend
herself. To defend herself against whom ? She had left the
world in no doubt, or in very little, as to whom.

    Mr. Hughes continued : " We not only have no quarrel
with America, we have no quarrel with Japan. We have our
ideals : Japan has hers. There is room in the world for both
of us. We want to live in terms of amity with all nations of the

earth. . . . Our ideal at the Conference is, as I see it, a renewal of the Anglo-Japanese Treaty in some such form, and modified if that should be deemed proper, as will be acceptable to Britain, to America, to Japan, and to ourselves. It may be said that this is impossible. It may be so ; I do not think it is impossible." As to the alleged difficulties between Japan and America, Mr. Hughes said the Japanese wanted to hold land in America, and the right to enter the United States. The Australian attitude was very much like that of the people of the Western States of America towards Japan. " It is utterly wrong," declared Mr. Hughes, "'for the Japanese people to think that, because we have passed certain laws, we regard them as our inferiors. We do not. We admire their bravery and their patriotism ; we stand amongst those who are loudest in admiration of their magnificent achievements, for no other nation has advanced so far in so short a time. But . . . we have our ideals, they have theirs." He wanted the Japanese people to understand clearly that the Australian people were anxious to remain in peace and friendship with them. Referring to Japanese laws in relation to foreigners, Mr. Hughes said that no foreigner might hold land in Japan. So far as unskilled labourers were concerned, these might not reside outside the foreign settlements except with the permission of the Prefectual Government. For all practical purposes, the foreign labourer was excluded, and under the provision just alluded to Chinese had been deported from Japan. Naturalisation was extremely difficult, if not impossible, in Japan, other than by marriage with a Japanese person. Australian treatment of Japanese would compare quite favourably, he thought, with Japanese treatment of foreigners in general.

Mr. Hughes added that whatever might be the opinion of the country on the Anglo-Japanese Treaty in its present form, he thought the interests of Australia lay in a renewal of the Treaty in some modified form. He saw no reason why the Treaty should not be renewed in a form which should be satisfactory not only to the Empire and to Japan, but to America as well.

Naval Rivalry: League of Nations or British Empire?

Australians could not shut their eyes to the fact that there was now great danger of such naval rivalry in the Pacific as would not only be a heavy drain on the nations directly affected, but which would have its reflex influences upon the whole world. An uninterrupted era of peace was impossible to contemplate while the world was resounding with the cling of naval construction.

He had always taken the attitude that while very little
could be expected from the League of Nations, yet because
peace was so desirable, and war so awful, all civilised nations
ought to do all things possible to prevent war. But he had
never been under any illusions as to the power of the League
to do this. In future the spirit of the world might be changed,
or, when the League should have perfected its machinery and
methods, great things might be expected from it.

The most powerful agency for the world's peace to-day
was the British Empire. The hope of the future peace of
the world seemed to lie in some understanding between
America, England and France. The League of Nations was
an unwieldy, clumsy contrivance. There was only one way
to prevent war, and that was for the world to turn its back
upon it ; and since the progress of the world was uneven,
some nations surging ahead of others, if war was to be prevented, there must exist amongst those who were opposed to
war the power to prevent it.

At the conclusion of Mr. Hughes' speech a debate took
place which will be summarised in the next issue of the
JOURNAL.

DEFENCE POLICY.

The following summary, which has been taken from the
debate on the Estimates 1920-21, should be read in conjunction with and continuation of that appearing in the last
issue of the JOURNAL (Vol. II., No. 1, page 121) under the
heading of " Defence Policy."

DEBATE IN HOUSE OF REPRESENTATIVES.

Military.

The Assistant Minister for Defence (Hon. Sir Granville
Ryrie), on 16th November, 1920, in asking the Committee
to pass a vote of £1,550,000 in respect of the Department of
Defence (Military) said that the amount was not excessive, and
invited careful consideration to one or two factors, particularly
the depreciation in the purchasing power of the sovereign
He thought it had been shown by the Government statistician
that the purchasing power of money had decreased to such
an extent that it now required. 35s. 10d. to purchase what
could have been obtained in 1914 for 22s. odd. In other
words, if the Government were asking for £4,200,000 this year
it would only be equivalent to the amount granted in 191
They were, however, only asking for £3,200,000, and more
than half of that amount had already been agreed to, leaving
a balance of £1,550,000. They had to consider that during

the period of the War a large amount of defence expenditure came out of loan money, and, therefore, did not affect revenue. In perusing the military expenditure during pre-War years and comparing it with the vote now proposed, honourable members might say that the Government were asking more than had been previously granted ; but such was not the case, as no money was being taken from loan.

This year they were only providing for eight days' camp training for one quota of their trainees, and a similar period of training for the militia. They had been forced to do that in an endeavour to keep the military expenditure down to an absolute minimum. He felt sure that Mr. Ryan, who was then leading the Opposition, would assist the Government.

The Hon. T. J. Ryan (**Labour,** *West Sydney, N.S.W.*) : I am prepared to assist if you can justify the expenditure."

The **Assistant Minister for Defence** : " There is an item of £36,135 for the expenses of officers, warrant and non-commissioned officers, sent abroad for instruction which honourable members may feel inclined to discuss."

The Hon. James Page (**Labour,** *Maranoa, Q.*) : " I do not think many will object to that."

The **Assistant Minister for Defence** said he was glad to have that assurance. He could not imagine objection being taken to that item of expenditure, because they must surely advance in matters of military and naval defence, and if they took into consideration the depreciated value of money the sum sought for this year was less than was granted in pre-War days. Had they gone on with their cadet training this year on the lines adopted prior to the War the amount required would have been far in excess of £1,550,000.

The perturbed state of international affairs was a good reason why they must at all hazards maintain the efficiency of the Military Forces of the Commonwealth. They were a mere handful of people, and might not be able to provide an adequate force to fully protect themselves ; but they must do something to maintain a certain state of military efficiency, otherwise the time might come when they would find themselves completely at the mercy of some foreign Power. He asked honourable members, irrespective of party, whether they as business men would hold a valuable property without protecting themselves by adequately insuring it ? Why did a business man insure his warehouse ? Was it because he believed that it was likely to be destroyed ? He did not think so.

The Hon. James Page : " But you can pay too high a rate for your insurance."

I 2

The Assistant Minister for Defence : " The premium we propose paying is one that Parliament must decide. But at the same time we must consider the consequences of uninsurance, and realise what the position would be if disaster overtook us."

The Hon. James Page said that he had been hopeful that, the War being over, they would have had a big drop in their Defence Estimates, and that the finances of the nation would thus be afforded an opportunity to recover from the severe strain put upon them during the five years of war. But they were doomed to disappointment. He did not propose to move that the Estimates be reduced even by one penny because he believed in the Government's defence policy ; but there was certainly an opportunity, particularly in reserves of munitions, to make reductions. If there was to be no war, why provide for big supplies of munitions ?

The Assistant Minister for Defence : " We do not know that there is going to be no war. The world is still in a very disturbed state."

Mr. W. J. McWilliams (Farmers' Union, *Franklyn, Tas.* said that one always found himself at a great disadvantage in discussing defence expenditure, because he was confronted with Scylla upon the one hand and Charybdis upon the other. Whilst they were animated by a desire to effect savings whereve that course was possible they knew that a terrible responsi bility would rest upon them if they carried their ideas of economy so far as to destroy the efficiency of their fightin force.

Labour and Compulsory Training.

Mr. D. C. McGrath (Labour, *Ballarat, Vic.*) said the polic of the Government was not the Labour policy, which wa to amend the Defence Act so as to secure the deletion of a sections relating to compulsory training and military servic He felt sure that the time was not far distant when the majorit of the people of Australia would be siding with the Labou party in their hostility to any form of compulsory militar service. Those who had no military training whatev before the War were splendid soldiers within a month or tw of their taking up military duties, and their men general showed that they would compare favourably with the be fighting troops of the world. There was, however, a litt military clique who insisted upon telling the people that was necessary to have military camps at which boys migh be drilled in military evolutions such as " left wheel " an " right wheel." In modern warfare, however, that sort of thin did not count. It was absurd that their boys, at the mo critical period of their lives, should be asked to waste whole months every year in a military camp. Their principal need was to develop submarines and air services. They did not want any more vessels of the type of the " Australia " or the " Sydney," nor did they require any standing Army. They did not want to be at the mercy of any country when war broke out ; but he did not think that there was any fear of war for the next twenty years.

The Hon. T. J. Ryan said he had no desire to repeat the arguments, which had been so well put, that the Defence Estimates had not been reduced to the extent that they should have been—in other words, to something approaching their pre-War expenditure.

Mr. J. E. Fenton (Labour, *Maribyrnong*, *Vic*.) said that the countries with small and unwarlike populations had not suffered in the War; it was the other countries which, as generally happened with those who were always looking for fight, got more than they wanted. An attempt was being made to rush through the Defence Estimates by manu-facturing scares about the evil intentions of this country and that. Such attempts had been practised by the military caste in all countries from time immemorial. A Parliament such as the Commonwealth, however, was not so faint-hearted as to be frightened into approval of expenditure by such threats. They were supposed to have just finished a war that was undertaken to end war. Australia was far removed from the warlike countries of the world, though, he admitted, not far from the coloured races ; yet they were spending money on warlike preparations which would be better spent in the development of their resources. Australia, in pro-portion to population, was making more extensive military preparations than any other country. They had their military junkers, and a disaster like that which overwhelmed Germany would befall Australia if, like Germany, they paid heed to their junkers.

British Empire and Navy.

Mr. A. Wienholt (Nat., *Moreton*, *Q*.) said there were two arguments against spending money on the defence of Australia. The first was furnished by the League of Nations— though, frankly, he did not believe in the League. The only league he believed in consisted of Great Britain herself, the Dominions, and, above all, the British Navy.

The second argument, and this was perhaps the best of all—was that Australia was particularly well situated, in that she then had, and would have for the next twenty years, a large number of veteran soldiers. That, in itself, was a great

safeguard, but, of course, it would eventually die away.
He wished they were able to reduce the Defence Estimates,
but in the present position of the world he was not willing
to take the responsibility of voting for a reduction.

He could assure the hon. member (Mr. Fenton) that
there was no danger of the bulk of their soldiers ever becoming
"junkers." He was a great believer in the citizen soldier,
and the more they studied military history the more they
realised how extraordinarily well he acquitted himself in warfare. He was pleased to know that the Government were able
to be a little more generous towards the rifle clubs.

Navy and Aviation.

On the proposed vote for the Navy Department, £2,279,288,
also taken on 16th November,

Mr. W. G. Mahony (**Labour,** *Dalley, N.S.W.*) said that
the future welfare of Australia depended on an adequate
naval defence policy. Australia was an island continent
removed many thousands of miles from other centres of civilisation, and their strongest protection must be found on the
water. In the light of the lessons of the War they had to
consider what were the best and most economic methods of
defence to be adopted ; and one of the greatest was that it
was almost impossible for a purely naval attack to be successful
against decently equipped land forces. This was clearly
demonstrated in attacks made by the Allied Fleets on various
enemy ports. This non-success was due, first, to mine fields
and then to land fortifications ; and a striking illustration
was afforded at the Dardanelles. The Minister should furnish
assurances that the whole of these matters had been taken
into consideration.

The Minister for the Navy (**Hon. W. H. Laird Smith**)
" We have the plans all ready, and we have also the mines in
Australian waters."

Mr. Mahony : " That will be pleasing news to the public.
We do not wish to see those awful words ' Too late ' written
over the door of Australia."

Dr. Earle Page (**Farmers' Union,** *Cowper, N.S.W.*) said
he did not ask for a detailed statement of policy with respect
to the Navy Estimates, but would like to be assured that the
proposals were adequate for their safety, in the opinion
not merely of the Australian Government, but of the British
expert advisers who had investigated the provisions for the
defence of Australia. It was bad economy to try to cut
down one's insurances ; and the Defence Estimates, military
and naval, were Australia's insurance. The provisions so

out in the Estimates were considerably below the suggestions furnished by Viscount Jellicoe.

With respect to civil aviation, an amount of £100,000 had been set aside for its encouragement. He held that they should do still more.

The Minister for the Navy (Hon. W. H. Laird Smith) said that the Government were of opinion that it would not be advisable at that time and under the circumstances to launch out upon any considerable expenditure, seeing that the Imperial Conference would take place next year, at which the whole question of the defence of the Empire would be discussed.

In reference to aviation, he would point out that that matter did not come under the control of his department. But a Board was then being formed, and the whole question of aviation was being thoroughly inquired into. Meetings had been held between representatives of the Army and the Navy, and he felt sure the day was not far distant when they would have a very fine aviation corps upon the coast of Australia. The Government would afford every encouragement to private persons to enter upon aviation, knowing that during a period of war their services could be requisitioned by the Commonwealth.

Mr. W. J. McWilliams (Farmers' Union, *Franklyn, Tas.*) said the Minister had intimated that it was intended to regard the present Navy merely as something which should be continued until the Imperial Conference had been held, at which these matters would be dealt with. That was a proper course to follow, because, with a coastline such as Australia had, it was absolutely impossible for Australia, with its five million inhabitants, and in the shattered condition of its finances, to attempt to provide an adequate Navy for their defence. With all due respect to what the Minister had stated, he thought that their Navy as a fighting force was a negligible quantity. The people of Australia should not be permitted to think that they had an adequate Navy in the ordinary sense of the term. But if they maintained it until the Imperial Conference had been held, and if, in the meantime, they concentrated their energies upon what must be their chief defence in the future, namely, aeroplanes and submarines, they would be acting wisely.

One Hon. Member (Mr. A. Wienholt), in dealing with the League of Nations, had said that the league upon which he had built his faith was that between Great Britain and the rest of her Dominions. He (Mr. McWilliams) thought that that was the league to which the people of the Empire must look for their protection. In his judgment, it was a league that was big enough and strong enough for the defence of Australia as it was for the rest of the Empire.

Canada and British Naval Gift.

The Treasurer (the Right Hon. Sir Joseph Cook), in reply to a reference to the warships and submarines presented to Australia by the British Government, said that the only reason why Canada had not taken the ships was that she had not wished to inaugurate a new naval policy until the whole question had been discussed at the Conference to be called early next year. Canada had therefore merely post-poned the acceptance of the gift and the institution of a Navy of her own on the lines laid down by Lord Jellicoe until the whole matter could be discussed at the Imperial Conference.

As to the quality of the ships which had been given to Australia so generously by the British Government, and which amounted in value to £3,500,000, they were the very latest of their type, and amongst the last to be constructed in the light of the experience of the War. The submarines were the latest thing in that class of warfare.

The Hon. T. J. Ryan (Labour, *West Sydney, N.S.W.*) " Would not the reasons that induced Canada to refuse affect Australia in the same way ? "

The Treasurer : " Certainly not. We had a naval policy already in being. We had warships in being, of a type that these are really replacing. They have now been put in reserve.'

Mr. R. J. Burchell (Nat., *Fremantle, W.A.*) : " Some are at the bottom of the sea."

The Treasurer : " Yes, two of them are there as casualties of war." The very reason why they had accepted the new boats from the British Government was because they felt that they would be doing an excellent thing for Australia in accepting vessels which had just been built according to the very latest type of Admiralty construction, to take the place of their own, which were already getting a little old. They were not obsolete or useless, by any means. They were still good fighting material, but they were not the latest expression of naval efficiency.

Expenditure on Obsolete Craft.

Mr. L. L. Cunningham (Labour, *Gwydir, N.S.W.*) said it was all very well for the Treasurer to say that the sub-marines in Australia represented the very last word in efficiency. They were nothing of the kind. The " Dreadnought " type of submarine now being constructed in Great Britain—and the same policy must be carried out in every other naval nation—carried 10 in. and 12 in. guns ; so the submarine then in Australian waters would not last 24 hours.

The Minister for Home and Territories (Hon. A. Poynton) : " If your argument means anything, it means that our Naval Estimates are not high enough."

Mr. Cunningham : " No. It means that expenditure is being incurred on obsolete vessels." The same remark might be applied to their destroyers. It was certain that, if ever the war-cloud burst over that continent again, these vessels would be out of date, and consequently expenditure on them to-day was absolutely wasted.

Continuing, Mr. Cunningham said that it would be far better to suspend expenditure until they got the very latest advice from the British naval experts as to the more modern type of ship. It would be far better to have one ship of the very latest type—as they had found when war was declared— than to have five or six obsolete vessels. For all practical purposes they might as well have nothing. He believed that they were absolutely wasting money over these naval vessels. He would remind those hon. members who had been referring continually to the protection afforded them by the British Navy that even if they had the latest units of the British Navy, vessels like the " Renown," for instance, in Australian waters, there would be no dockyard accommodation for them.

The Minister for Home and Territories : " Another argument in favour of more expenditure."

Mr. Cunningham : " Not at all. It is an argument for an efficient naval policy." Supposing, for instance, that war broke out between Great Britain and Japan. What would be the use of the obsolete scrap-iron in the way of fighting ships that were now in Australian waters? He did not desire to increase the amount on the Estimates, but to change the avenues in which the money was being expended. Provision had been made for the expenditure of £930,000 on obsolete vessels ; and if that amount were split up between submarines, aeroplanes, and wireless, some good might be achieved.

Comparatively speaking, aeroplanes did not cost very much, and quite a number could be erected for the cost of one battleship, or even the maintenance of an obsolete vessel. During the War Zeppelins proved a veritable godsend to the Germans for scouting purposes, and Australia must look to aerial vessels to do scouting in the future.

The proposed vote was agreed to.

TREATIES OF PEACE (AUSTRIA AND BULGARIA).

An Act was assented to on 10th November empowering the Commonwealth Government to do all such things as are necessary and expedient for giving effect to the Treaties with Austria and Bulgaria.

AIR NAVIGATION ACT.

An Act was assented to on 2nd December, 1920, to commence in relation to the several States on such dates as will be respectively fixed by Proclamation.

The object of the Act is to enable the Governor-General to make regulations for the purpose of carrying out and giving effect to the Convention for the Regulation of Aerial Navigation signed in Paris on 13th October, 1919, and for the purpose of providing for the control of Air Navigation in the Commonwealth and Territories.

NATIONALITY ACT.

This Act, which was assented to on 2nd December, 1920, is based upon the British Nationality and Status of Aliens Act 1914-1918. The Act repeals the Commonwealth Naturalisation Act 1903-1917, and relates to naturalisation, national status of married women and infant children, loss of British nationality, etc. Part II. (Naturalisation) of the British Act has been adopted, and is reproduced in a schedule to the Commonwealth Act.

The main provisions of the Act are as follow : —

Natural-born British Subjects.

The definition thereof is copied from the British Act.

Naturalisation.

This part of the Act is based upon and closely follows the British Act. It provides (Section 7) that the Governor-General, in his absolute discretion, may grant a certificate of naturalisation to an alien who makes application and satisfies the Governor-General

(A) That he has either resided in the Commonwealth for not less than one year immediately preceding the application, with previous residence, either in the Commonwealth or in some other part of His Majesty's Dominions during four years within the last eight years before the application ; or been in the service of the Crown for not less than five years within the last eight years ; and

(B) that he is of good character and has an adequate knowledge of the English language ; and

(c) that he intends, if his application is granted, either to reside in His Majesty's Dominions, or to enter or continue in the service of the Crown.

In the case of a woman who was a British subject previously to her marriage to an alien, and whose husband has died, or whose marriage has been dissolved, the requirements as to residence shall not apply, and the Governor-General may (Section 7 (5)) in any other special case if he thinks fit, grant a certificate of naturalisation, although the required residence has not been within the last eight years before the application.

The period spent in the service of the Crown may, if the Governor-General thinks fit, be treated as equivalent to a period of residence in the Commonwealth.

Any person to whom a certificate of naturalisation has been issued under the repealed Act or under any State Act, or who has been naturalised by virtue of a certificate issued to his father or mother, may be granted naturalisation. (Section 8 (1).)

The grant of naturalisation in pursuance of the foregoing provisions is in the absolute discretion of the Governor-General, who may, with or without assigning any reason, give or withhold the certificate as he thinks most conducive to the public good, and no appeal shall lie from his decision. (Section 8 (2).)

Where an alien becomes naturalised, the Governor-General may on application of that alien include in the certificate the name of any minor child born before the date of the certificate ; but any such child may, within one year after attaining majority, by declaration of alienage, cease to be a British subject. (Section 10.)

A certificate of naturalisation granted under the British Act shall be recognised in the Commonwealth ; and also certificates issued by the Governments of certain Dominions provided they adopt Part II. of the British Act, viz., Canada, South Africa, New Zealand, and Newfoundland.

Revocation.

The summary of the Canadian Naturalisation Act in regard to revocation of naturalisation as appearing in JOURNAL, Vol. II., No. 1, page 74, may be read *mutatis mutandis* into the present summary, with the exception of all that part relating to the ten-year period in the case of former enemy subjects.*

Status of Married Women and Infant Children.

The wife of a British subject shall be deemed to be a British subject, and the wife of an alien shall be deemed to be an alien, provided that where a man ceases during the continuance of his marriage to be a British subject the wife may, by declaration, remain a British subject.

In the case of an enemy subject, the wife, if at birth a British subject, may make a declaration that she desires to resume British nationality, and if the Governor-General is satisfied that it is desirable that she be permitted to do so, he may grant her a certificate of naturalisation. (Section 18.)

A wife does not by reason only of the death of her husband or dissolution of the marriage cease to be an alien or British subject, as the case may be.

Where a person ceases to be a British subject, whether by declaration of alienage or otherwise, every minor child shall cease to be a British

* It will be noticed in the case of the Australian Act that the Governor-General may, in his absolute discretion, grant or withhold naturalisation with or without assigning any reason. Attention might also be invited to the summary of the Commonwealth Immigration Amendment Act, 1920 (JOURNAL, Vol. I., No. 1, page 137, and the present number, page 372), which provides for the exclusion of former enemy subjects for five years.

subject, unless such child does not become by the law of any other country naturalised in that country ; provided that where a widow who is a British subject marries an alien, any child of hers by her former husband shall not, by reason only of her marriage, cease to be a British subject, whether he is residing outside His Majesty's dominions or not.

Any child who has ceased to be a British subject may, within one year after attaining majority, resume British nationality by making a declaration to that effect. (Section 20.)

Loss of British Nationality.

Provision is made for the loss of British nationality by foreign naturalisation, and declaration of alienage.

Miscellaneous.

The remaining sections of the Act deal with procedure and evidence, penalties, power to make regulations, etc.

The Minister for Home and Territories (Hon. A. Poynton), in moving the Second Reading on 26th October, 1920, said that he believed that the provisions of the Bill were the most liberal ever introduced into the Commonwealth Parliament. Prior to 1903 naturalisation laws were framed by the State Parliaments, and, therefore, operated only within a State. Under these circumstances a Swede, a German, or an Italian naturalised in one State immediately became denaturalised the moment he crossed the border of the State in which he had taken out naturalisation papers. In 1903 the Commonwealth Parliament passed an Act which covered the whole Commonwealth ; but even under that if an alien were to go to New Zealand or Canada, or any other part of the British Empire, he would be treated as an alien. A number of Imperial Conferences were held in which such anomalies were discussed, and after careful consideration it was decided that a broader principle should be adopted within the Empire, and that naturalisation in any part of the Empire should be provided for, assuming, of course, that Great Britain and the Dominions adopted a similar law. While there was a unanimous decision in regard to having more comprehensive provisions for naturalisation within the Empire, there was a great difference of opinion as to who should give effect to them. At one stage it was suggested that Great Britain should legislate for the whole Empire, but as that raised the question of sovereign rights it was thought that the British Parliament should deal only with Great Britain, and that the other parts of the Empire should pass their own legislation. In 1914 the Imperial Parliament passed an Act somewhat similar to the present Commonwealth measure, and it was then necessary for the Dominions to enact a similar law. Owing to the War intervening, action in the Commonwealth was delayed, but he did not know whether they had lost anything because, as the result

experience, it had been shown that there were many defects
in the Imperial Act passed in 1914. In 1917 an amending
measure became law, and the Bill then before the House
was based on that Statute. The measure was entitled a
Nationality Bill, because it dealt with nationality in general,
and it was Empire-wide in its scope. Under the present law
in Australia an alien had to be resident in the Commonwealth
for two years before he was entitled to become naturalised.
Under the new measure, it would mean five years, but the
previous residence need not all have been spent in Australia.
Residence in the Empire was sufficient, provided that the last
twelve months of such residence shall have been in the country
granting the certificate.

The Hon. **Sir Robert Best (Nationalist,** *Kooyong, Vic.*) :
What would be the position with a foreigner—say a
German ? "

The **Minister of Home and Territories :** " There is a special
law relating to Germans. I am now naturalising Germans
who have been here for a number of years, and the limitation
has been twenty years' residence."

Sir Robert Best : " Does he have to reside here ? "

The **Minister :** " For at least twelve months."

Mr. E. Riley (Labour, *South Sydney, N.S.W.*) : " Can
a deported German come back in twelve months if he has
resided here four years ? "

The **Minister :** " No."

Mr. Riley : " How long will be required ? "

The **Minister :** " It all depends." Naturalisation under
the Bill did not give the right of free access to any Dominion
of the Empire, neither would its provisions place a man in a
better position than if he were a natural-born British subject.
I did not follow that, because the measure became law, Chinese,
Indians, or any of those prohibited under the Commonwealth
Immigration Act could come to Australia. That law remained
as it then was ; but they were broadening the scope of their
naturalisation laws to cover those whom they considered were
fit people to become citizens of the Empire. Under the
Commonwealth laws, for example, there was no power to
naturalise Syrians from Mount Lebanon. If the new measure
became law it would give the Minister the power to naturalise
them.

The Hon. **R. W. Foster (Nationalist,** *Wakefield, S.A.*) :
" I understand that the Government has the right to exclude
anyone from admission to the Commonwealth."

The **Minister :** " It is an inherent right of the Government
of Australia to refuse permission to 'anyone to land in the
country."

The Hon. F. G. Tudor (Leader of the Opposition) said that the Minister had informed the House that the measure was far more liberal than that then on the Statute Book. If he (Mr. Tudor) were asked to choose between the two, he would prefer the existing Act. The new Bill was certainly not more liberal than the existing Act, since it took away the papers of many persons then naturalised. During the recent War men were interned who had received their naturalisation papers more than twenty years before, and had not a stain on their character. The new Bill practically made permanent that practice.

IMMIGRATION AMENDMENT ACT.

(Exclusion of former Enemy Subjects : Trading with Germany, etc.)

This Act, which was assented to on 2nd December, 1920, provides for the exclusion of late enemy subjects and others, and the deportation of certain classes of persons. The same Bill was introduced in the last Parliament (see summary in JOURNAL, Vol. I., No. 1, page 137) and was passed by the House of Representatives, but lapsed with prorogation.

During the passage of the Bill through the Senate the term " anarchist " was deleted, without, however, materially modifying the provision as to the exclusion of persons opposed to organised government, etc.

IN THE SENATE.

The Vice-President of the Executive Council (Senator the Hon. E. J. Russell), in moving the Second Reading, said that it was very largely a machinery measure, and, with the exception of one clause (that relating to deportation) no new principles had been embodied in it. No deportation could take place without the accused person being first tried by a Board of Inquiry, one of whose members must be a judicial officer. These principles were not entirely new to Australia, and owing to the War they had been adopted, though in much more drastic form, in the United States of America, Canada and New Zealand had also legislated upon similar lines, while South Africa contemplated doing so. In Great Britain the Secretary of State had been vested with power to prevent any alien or person who was deemed to be undesirable from landing there without first obtaining a permit.

During consideration in Committee, on a motion by Senator W. Senior, the term "anarchist" was deleted.

Senator W. Senior (*S.A.*) said the inclusion of such a term as "anarchist" was too comprehensive. There were men, he added, like Prince Kropotkin and Leo Tolstoi, who, in their belief, were anarchists, but who differed very widely from the persons described in the latter part of the paragraph (see summary Vol. I, No. 1, pp. 137–138) with which he was in full concurrence.

DEBATE IN HOUSE OF REPRESENTATIVES.

The Hon. T. J. Ryan (**Labour,** *West Sydney, N.S.W.*) said that in his opinion the Bill was evidence that the policy of the Government was to restrict liberty as far as possible. He did not think the Minister had shown that the existing law was not sufficient to keep their population of the character that they desired it to be. The measure seemed the result of a panic that had overtaken the Government, judging by the manner in which some of its clauses were framed. The Bill provided that persons from the countries with which they had recently been at war should be prohibited immigrants for a period of five years, and for such further period as might be proclaimed by the Governor-General. That was too drastic a provision. He understood that in the United Kingdom the period fixed was only three years. Why should Australia be more restrictive than Great Britain in this connection? The views of the Government were too drastic, and, he thought, did not meet the approval of the majority of Australians. In his opinion the Prime Minister was the chief offender. He seemed to have a rooted hatred of their former enemies, which was reflected in this legislation. The Government's views regarding trade with those countries* were not in accordance with those of the majority of their population and were not sensible views. Australian commodities would pass to those countries, just as the products of those countries would reach Australia, whether Australia traded directly with them or not. This policy was victimising their own people by enabling persons in what had been neutral countries, and in other countries as well, to set up as middlemen, and make profits at the expense of Australia. Why should they prohibit immigration from Central European countries for a period of five years if Great Britain considered a period of three years was enough?

* The importation of goods containing more than 5 per cent. of enemy labour and/or material is prohibited. The embargo as to exportation has been removed by Proclamation dated 2nd December, 1920.

The Hon. J. Page (**Labour,** *Maranoa,* *Q.*), during consideration in Committee, pointed out that under the provisions
in question the Australian-born son or daughter of any person
of the nationalities mentioned, who had been out of the
country, could be debarred from returning to Australia. That
would be a monstrous thing to do.

The Minister for Home and Territories (Hon. A. Poynton)
declared that the clause would not prevent their return to
Australia. A person born in Australia was an Australian
subject, and the clause did not deal with such subjects. He
also had power to deal with all real cases of hardship.

Mr. A. Wienholt (Nationalist, *Moreton,* *Q.*) said that
" charity begins at home," and the immigrants he personally
wished to see come to Australia were ex-service men of their
own British nationality. They should certainly be given
first choice ; but when they were told that the British
Parliament had passed a similar measure in which the period
was fixed at three years he would remind the Minister that
when introducing another Bill (Nationality) a little while
back he (the Minister) had impressed on the House how
valuable uniformity in legislation was. What Great Britain
did should be a good guide to Australia.

Mr. F. Brennan (Labour, *Batman, Vic.*) said it was pretty
clearly recognised that the crying need of Australia was
rapidly increasing population, and, indeed, upon that question
rested their whole national well-being, as well as the White
Australia policy, which was so very dear to the hearts of the
people of Australia. He felt it to be a public duty on his part
to declare that it was worse than folly to be pursuing the
policy of creating and maintaining so long after the War
spirit of hatred among the nations. The truth was, of course,
that in all this international hate-mongering, which had been
evident throughout the world, Australia had always led the way.
The British Government had at least shown that it possessed
a much juster conception of what was desirable among
the nations.

Mr. P. J. Moloney (Labour, *Hume, N.S.W.*) said that
both Great Britain and France had entered into trade with
Germany. Australia stood alone in the Empire in its insistence
upon keeping the sore open ; worse than that, they were
rubbing salt into the wound. They were the only people who
were promulgating the gospel of hatred. A returned soldier
in that House had told the Minister that if the Government
fell in line with the British Act, their decision would not be
cavilled at by returned soldiers.

A motion by the Hon. T. J. Ryan for the reduction of the
period of the exclusion of former enemy subjects from five
to three years, so as to bring the Commonwealth provision

in this respect into conformity with the British law on the subject, was negatived by 32 votes to 13.

(For debate in the House of Representatives on other phases of the Act see JOURNAL, Vol. I., No. 1, page 137.)

ALIENS REGISTRATION ACT.

A similar Bill was before the last Parliament (see summary in JOURNAL, Vol. I., No. 2, page 352), but lapsed with the prorogation.

The Act as passed differs from the original Bill by the deletion of the provision (as in the English Act) requiring residential establishments to keep a record of all aliens living therein. The Act was assented to on 2nd December.

DEBATE IN HOUSE OF REPRESENTATIVES.

The Minister for Home and Territories (Hon. A. Poynton) on 4th November, in moving the Second Reading, said that according to a statement made by the Minister for Defence (Senator the Hon. G. F. Pearce) when in charge of the measure in the Senate, one of the greatest difficulties experienced by Great Britain in dealing with the foreign element in time of war was the absence of any scheme for the registration of aliens. In America they had a scheme in operation whereby the authorities could ascertain the locality in which an alien was residing, and this assisted them materially on the outbreak of war. In Great Britain the Government were at a great disadvantage, as they had no records, and the consequence was that a long time elapsed before a complete list could be compiled. Their experience in Australia had been very similar to that of Great Britain ; and, in the absence of registration, great difficulty had been experienced in ascertaining the exact locality of the aliens in their midst. The Bill provided that every alien who arrived in the Commonwealth shall immediately register ; and in this connection he might mention that they did not propose to go so far as the English law. In Great Britain the alien had not only to register, but the keepers of boarding houses, hotels, and all residential establishments had to keep a record of the aliens residing therein, and had also to report to the authorities their arrival and departure. The Commonwealth measure provided, however, that all aliens arriving in the Commonwealth shall register, and that the masters of vessels shall provide the authorities with particulars concerning aliens travelling on vessels. It was also mandatory on the part

K

of an alien to advise the Department of any change of abode. The present Bill also provided that the master or member of a crew of a vessel, who is an alien, and who enters the Commonwealth, unless he is exempt, shall register. The responsibility is thrown on the captain of a ship, unless it is a public vessel, of granting every facility for the Officers of the Customs or Immigration Departments to ascertain who is travelling on the vessel, and their nationality. The Bill did not apply to tourists, and the conditions then obtaining would remain in force.

The Hon. Sir Robert Best (Nationalist, *Kooyong, Vic.*): " How do you intend to distinguish a tourist ? "

The Minister for Home and Territories : " The tourist has to make the necessary application to travel in the Commonwealth for a certain period."

Sir Robert Best : " For how long ? "

The Minister for Home and Territories : " The time varies but it is usually from six to twelve months. Instances have arisen where an extension of time has been sought and granted. Any extension of time is determined by the Minister; and since I have been in charge of the Department there have not been many cases of this character."

WAR PRECAUTIONS ACT REPEAL.

This Act was assented to on 2nd December. It repeal the War Precautions Act 1914-1918 and makes provision fo the continuance of certain of the War Precautions Regulation

Coal.

The War Precautions (Coal) Regulations are continued in force un 31st December, 1921.

Wharves.

The War Precautions (Wharf) Regulations are deemed to remain force in relation to claims arising out of anything done under these Regu tions ; and as regards the functions exerciseable thereunder.

Primary Products.

The Prime Minister is empowered to enter, in conjunction with th State Governments, into agreements with Banking Corporations Australia for providing for the financial requirements of the States enable them to operate any scheme for the transportation and market of Australian Primary Products ; and to give guarantees that the St Governments will repay the advances made by the Bank under agreements.

ugar.

The provisions of the Commercial Activities Act 1919* relating to sugar are to continue in force until 30th September, 1923.

Companies, Firms and Businesses.

The War Precautions (Companies, Firms and Businesses) Regulations are to continue in force until 31st December, 1921.

No company in which more than one-third of the shares are held by aliens may, without the consent in writing of the Treasurer, acquire any mine, or interest in a mine, or carry on any mining or metallurgical business.

No alien may, without consent, acquire any share in any company incorporated in the Commonwealth.

Agents of Oversea Companies and Firms.

Such agents are required within three months after the commencement of this section, and thereafter within one month after the expiration of each financial year, to furnish in the prescribed form to the Collector of Customs particulars as to the name of a company, amount of capital, names and addresses of its branches (if any), and such other particulars as are required, and in the case of a firm—the name and address, name, nationality, and address of each member, amount of capital, etc.

Entry to Commonwealth.

Any British subject entering the Commonwealth may be required to subscribe an oath or affirmation of allegiance to the King, and to loyally uphold the constitution of the Commonwealth.

Unlawful Assemblies.

It is unlawful for any number of persons exceeding twenty to meet or be assembled surrounding Parliament House to make known any grievances, to discuss public affairs or matters of public interest, etc.

Amendment of Crimes Act, 1914-1915.

This Act is amended by the addition of a new section in relation to inciting or urging to the commission of an offence, and seditious words, intention or enterprise.

Loans.

Notwithstanding the provisions of any law or the regulations of any banking company, any such company may make advances to any officer or employee for the purpose of investment in any loan raised by the Commonwealth Government. Power is also taken in respect of the investment of trust funds in any such loan. This section is to continue in operation for a period of two years.

Miscellaneous.

The Act contains provisions relating to the unlawful defacement or destruction of British gold coin. It also provides for the making of regulations relating to the sale of liquor to members of the Naval or Military Forces; publication of books, etc., purporting to be records of the services of any Naval or Military Expeditionary Force raised in the Commonwealth; use of the word "Anzac"; and publication of newspapers or periodicals in foreign language.

---

* See JOURNAL, Vol. I., No. 1, page 149.

PASSPORTS ACT.

This Act, which was assented to on 2nd December, is in continuation of the main regulations under the War Precautions Act in relation to passports.

The main provisions of the Act are :—

No person who appears to an officer to be more than sixteen years of age will be permitted to embark at any place in the Commonwealth for a journey to any place abroad unless he is in possession of a duly viséed passport or other document authorising his departure.

Before an alien seaman signed on outside the Commonwealth is discharged he is obliged to lodge his passport and also any certificate of nationality or identity. The master of a vessel who discharges such a seaman without lodgment of his passport is liable to a penalty of £50, or imprisonment for three months.

Exemptions.

Any member of the Naval or Military Forces of any part of the British Dominions leaving the Commonwealth on duty.

Any member of the crew of an oversea vessel leaving any port in the Commonwealth who was a member of the crew on the last arrival of the vessel in that port ; or who signs on in Australia and is by occupation a seafaring man.

Any aboriginal native of Asia, or of any island in the East Indies, or in the Indian or Pacific Oceans, leaving the Commonwealth.

Certain exemptions are specified in the case of travel to New Zealand, Papua, and Norfolk Island.

BASIC WAGE.

(Discussion on Report of Royal Commission.)

On 23rd November the Prime Minister presented the Report of the Royal Commission which was appointed 6th December, 1919, to inquire into the cost of living in relation to the minimum or basic wage. The Commission found that the actual cost of living according to reasonable standards of comfort, including all matters comprised in the ordinary expenditure of the household for a man with a wife and three children, varied in the several State capitals from £5 6s. 2d. to £5 17s. a week.

The Prime Minister (the Right Hon. W. M. Hughes), in recapitulating the circumstances in which the Commission was appointed, said that the Leader of the Opposition (Hon. F. G. Tudor) had introduced a deputation composed of members of unions* that usually sought redress for their grievances

* Commonwealth public servants.

the Arbitration Court. The deputation had asked for the appointment of a Royal Commission to inquire into the question of the basic wage. The Commission was duly appointed. The policy of the Government was shaped generally upon the expectancy of a grant of those extended powers which a majority of the Commonwealth Parliament had on several occasions stated to be necessary. The Government had asked the people, *inter alia*, to give it those extended powers in relation to industrial matters, but this had not been done.* The present position was that the Commonwealth was unable to make industrial laws, or to give effect directly to the recommendations of that or any other Commission of the same kind, except in respect of its own public servants.

The basic wage was not a wage determined merely by the value of the work done. It rested upon a principle established long ago in the Commonwealth, and, he thought, very properly, that a wage must be paid which would enable the citizen receiving it to live according to a standard of comfort fitting and proper in a progressive community. The Commission, therefore, had not concerned itself with the question whether as a fact such wage could be paid. It had only sought to ascertain the money wage which would enable that to be done.

The basic wage proper might be said to rest on a decision given by Mr. Justice Higgins in the Sunshine Harvester Company case in 1907, in connection with which his Honour found that £2 2s. per week was a fair and reasonable wage for a man, his wife and three children. Since then the purchasing power of the sovereign had depreciated very materially. The Commission had analysed the reasons and facts that had induced his Honour to fix that rate.

Expressed in round figures, the average for the Commonwealth in the case of a man with a wife and three children as found by the Commission was about £5 16s. The report went on to state the cost of living in 1914 as from £3 4s. 11d. to £3 18s. 11d. according to the particular State.

According to the Commonwealth Statistician in 1907, the year in which 42s. a week was regarded by Mr. Justice Higgins as a fair and reasonable wage in the State of Victoria, the wage for the Commonwealth as a whole was 43s. 1d., being the average for the six States based on the Melbourne rate of 42s. So, from those figures, it would appear that 84s. 8d. now represented the equivalent of 43s. 1d. in 1907. Admittedly, therefore, the depreciation of the sovereign had

---

* See summary "Constitution Alteration (Legislative Powers)," JOURNAL, Vol. I., No. 1, page 140.

been very considerable, and had rendered it necessary to re-
adjust the money wage to meet the increased cost of living.
The Industrial Courts and wages tribunals had from time to
time made an effort to do this. At present no uniform standard
had been adopted, except by the Commonwealth Court of
Arbitration. According to the latest decisions of the tribunals,
the present basic wage for New South Wales, Queensland and
Victoria was £4, whilst the recent determination of the New
South Wales Board of Trade fixed a basic wage of £5 4s. for
the metropolitan district only. From these figures it would
seem that the average basic wage throughout Australia
was somewhere in the neighbourhood of £4 a week.

Turning to the finding of the Basic Wage Commission,
Mr. Hughes said it had to be noted that the increase proposed,
roughly about 35 per cent., was greatly in excess of any
increase ever awarded by any Court. They had to consider
its effect upon industries and upon the country. Its effect,
if it were applied, as suggested by some, to all workers, married
or single, would mean an economic revolution.

Roughly speaking, 600,000 male persons in Australia
had no dependent children. These were figures for 1911.

The Chairman of the Commission (A. B. Piddington, K.C.)
had assumed, for 1920, 1,000,000 employees and 900,000
children. But industries were now charged with the support
of 3,000,000 children, of whom 2,100,000 were non-existent.
If the basic wage of £5 16s. were applied to employees with or
without dependent children—as it had been applied since
1907—the increased burden, according to Mr. Piddington,
would be £93,000,000 per annum, and the Commonwealth
Statistician, £101,000,000. Now, the total wealth produced
in Australia in 1918 was £298,000,000. Prices had increased
since then ; but allowing for that, the burden imposed on
industry by this basic wage would be nearly 31 per cent.
Mr. Piddington had assumed that the labour costs, as expressed
in the terms of value of all goods and commodities, amounted
to 50 per cent., so the increased burden on industry, following
the payment of this basic wage to all male workers, would
in the neighbourhood of 62 per cent. What this meant might
be set out in Mr. Piddington's own words : —

If it could be supposed that the whole of the additional £93,000,0
labour costs could be passed on to the community, the increase in pri
would altogether outstrip the purchasing power of employees having
basic wage of £5 16s.

But, of the £298,000,000 produced in Australia in 1918, £113,000,0
or about 38 per cent., was exported. Whether the increased wage o
of 62 per cent. could be added to the prices asked for the 38 per ce
of our products would depend upon world prices, that is upon our
competition with all countries in the markets of the world.

I have not had time to go into details with regard to our individual export industries, but it seems certain that, as far as manufacturing industries for export are concerned, they would be ruined. With regard to primary industries, the percentage of labour costs in them is below the percentage of labour costs—carried to the last analysis—in the industries of the Commonwealth as a whole ; and, moreover, wool and—at present—wheat, enjoy a favourable position in outside markets compared with other countries. Still, the increase in the price even of the products of our primary industries would, before long, be a formidable drawback to their development, and possibly to their continuance. . . .

Another result of adding to the cost of production of goods for domestic consumption—which was 62 per cent. of the total production of 1918—the additional wages cost would be to so raise prices for such goods that all secondary industries would be liable to be ruined by importations unless the Tariff was very substantially increased.

Mr. Hughes, continuing, said that taking the statistics for 1915, if all the incomes over £156 per annum had been divided among those who had less than that amount, such persons would have received as their share only 10s. 5d. per week more. If the whole of the net profits of Australian manufacturing industries had been distributed amongst the employees, they would, during the period from 1913 to 1918, have received only from 7s. 4d. to 11s. a week more than their actual wages. So that to increase the basic wage by more than from 7s. 4d. to 11s.—the difference in the purchasing power of the sovereign during that period explaining why the amounts varied—would be impossible. The amount of wealth produced was an impassable barrier to any higher wage than could be paid by distributing the whole of the profits.

If the basic wage of £5 16s. were applied to all male workers the increase in labour costs would so increase prices that in three months the basic wage would have to be increased to £7 3s. to purchase the same amount of commodities, and, in twelve months, to £8 12s. 4d. That kind of thing would go on for ever.

True Incidence of Basic Rate.

Mr. Piddington had stated that the average basic wage in Australia was £4 per week. To secure the actual cost of living according to its true incidence, accepting the finding of the Commission of £5 16s., Mr. Piddington was of opinion that every employee should receive enough to keep a man and wife, viz., £4 per week, plus 12s. a week in respect of each dependent child. This could be done, according to Mr. Piddington, if the employer paid £4 to each employee and then paid into a pool 10s. 9d. in respect of each employee. This would raise £27,900,000 a year for the endowment of

900,000 children under the age of fourteen years. The Commonwealth could then pay to the mothers of families 12s. a week
for each child.   The total obligation of the employer would be
£4 10s. 9d., wage and tax, per week.   This, Mr. Piddington
had said, would involve an increased burden on industry
of, roughly speaking, £28,080,000, as against £93,000,000
if the basic wage were paid to all.   It would insure to a man
with a wife and three children £5 16s. ; to every man £4;
and to every man who had children 12s. a week per child.
This would adjust the basic wage to the principle upon which
it rested, namely, that the wage was not a return for the value
of labour, but a return to the citizen by virtue of his citizenship,
and was determined by the needs of the citizen so far as he
was or was not the father of a family.

Mr. Hughes, continuing, said the system was entirely
novel, and was far reaching.   How far it went none of them,
perhaps, was able to say.   He neither accepted it nor rejected
it as a principle.   On the face of it there was much to recommend it.   It appeared to be at once equitable and salutary,
and seemed to place the basic wage on sound foundations.
It seemed to create such conditions as would encourage men
to get married and to have large families.   That was the
crying need of Australia.   They wanted more people.   Their
country, with its 5,000,000 people, was confronting a situation
which might well appal a less courageous community.   He
must have time to consider the principle.   He rejected
absolutely and without reservation, because of its impossibility,
any proposal to pay £5 16s. a week to all persons in Australia
whether they had children or not.   It would bring ruin to the
country—ruin to the very men whom it was intended to
benefit.

With regard to Commonwealth Government employees,
Mr. Hughes said that there was a solemn obligation on the
Government to see that their public servants were paid an
adequate basic wage.   He was not prepared to apply the basic
wage recommended by the Commission to every person in the
public service.   As to applying the system of differentiating
between married men with dependent children and others
in the public service, opportunity must be given the Government to consider the question carefully, because where they
led the community would have to follow.   The Government
recognised that the wages of the public servants must be
increased, and, although it was not prepared to say offhand
what was a fair basic wage, it would give immediate consideration to the question.   Meanwhile, in his opinion, the
matter should be adjusted on a basis that would enable the
public servant to purchase as much with his present wage
as he could purchase in 1907, leaving him to obtain further

edress in the way of increase of salary from the Public Service
\rbitrator.

A motion by the Hon. F. G. Tudor (Leader of the Opposi-
ion) that the Government should give effect immediately
o the finding of the Commission was defeated by 36 votes
o 18, only the Labour members voting in favour of the
notion.

Members agreed on 26th November by 26 votes to 14 to a
notion by the Treasurer (the Right Hon. Sir Joseph Cook) that
he House approve the statement of the Prime Minister regard-
ig the basic wage to be paid to employees in the Commonwealth
ublic Service ; and requesting that the Government forthwith
rrange for such amount to be paid as would be equitable
nd just alike to the employees and the general public, and
'ithin the practical capabilities of the Commonwealth to
efray—payment of such basic wage to be made from 1st
lovember, 1920.*

INDUSTRIAL PEACE ACT (AMENDMENT).

A summary of the Industrial Peace Act appeared in the
JOURNAL, Vol. II., No. 1, page 141.
That Act (Section 14) is amended by the Industrial Peace
At (No. 2) as follows : —

At meetings of a Special Tribunal the opinion of the majority shall
prevail ; and where members of the Tribunal present are equally divided
in opinion, the opinion of the Chairman shall prevail.
Two-thirds of the members of a Special Tribunal shall form a
qorum.

INVALID AND OLD-AGE PENSIONS.

An Act was assented to on 2nd December to amend the
At 1908-1919 by increasing the limit of pension and income
together in the case of blind pensioners.†

---

* The decision of the Government in regard to its employees as
put into operation from 1st November, 1920, fixes the basic wage of a
married man at £4 a week with allowance of 5s. a week in respect of each
dependent child under 14 years of age. Single men and others also receive
certain allowances. In the case of salaries over £300 a year such allowances diminish on a sliding scale until they disappear at salary of £500
a year. (Differentiation is also made in favour of married men, but not
in respect of dependent children, in the application of the Cost of Living
Bonus, as distinct from the Basic Wage allowances.)
† For the limit in other cases see summary, Vol. I., No. 2, page 355.

The Amending Act provides that —

In the case of a permanently blind person who is qualified under the Act to receive a pension, the amount of pension may be at such a rate (not exceeding £39 per annum) as will make the income of the pensioner and of the pensioner's wife (or husband), together with the pension, equal to an amount not exceeding £221 per annum, or such other amount as is declared by any Act, or by any authority constituted under an Act, to be a basic wage for the portion of the Commonwealth in which the pensioner resides.

The income of the husband or wife of a permanently blind person, where the husband and wife are living apart pursuant to any decree, judgment, order or deed of separation, or where there are special reasons which, in the opinion of the Commissioner of Pensions, are adequate, shall not be taken into account in assessing the rate of pension payable to the blind person.

COMMONWEALTH BANK AMENDMENT (NOTE ISSUE) ACT.

This Act was assented to on 30th November. It provides for the transfer of the Australian note issue from the Commonwealth Treasury to the Commonwealth Bank of Australia.

The main provisions of the Act are as follow :—

No State notes are to be issued or circulated. Such notes are not legal tender.

A Note Issue Department is to be established in the Commonwealth Bank, distinct from the other departments and managed by a Board of Directors composed of the Governor of the Bank and three other Directors appointed by the Governor-General.

Upon a date to be fixed by proclamation all the assets and liabilities of the Treasurer under the Australian Notes Act 1910-1914 are to be transferred to the Note Issue Department of the Bank.

The Board is empowered to print and issue, re-issue and cancel Australian Notes in denominations of 5s., 10s., £1, £5, £10, or any multiple of ten pounds. These notes will bear the promise of the Treasurer to redeem them in gold coin on demand at the Head Office of the Bank.

A Reserve of gold coin and bullion is to be held by the Board not less than one-fourth of the amount of notes issued.*

In case of emergency the Governor-General may by proclamation authorise transfer from the Board to the Treasury of the control of and responsibility for the whole or part of the note issue.

---

* See summary of the Budget, under "Australian Note Issue," Vol. II., No. 1, page 135.

State Parliaments.

New South Wales.

PROFITEERING PREVENTION ACT.

This Act was assented to 31st December. It is designed to prevent undue profit-making; to make provision for the control and acquisition of necessary commodities and the control of necessary services; to obtain information as to the operations of trusts and other associations; to prevent unfair methods of trade competition; to promote co-operative enterprise, etc.

Undue Profit-making.

Provision is made under the Act for the constitution of a "Profiteering Prevention Court" presided over by a Judge of the Supreme Court, etc., with auxiliary judges; and the appointment of a barrister or public accountant as Commissioner of the Court for the conduct of inquiries and report and recommendation to the President. The President or Commissioner may have associated with him as assessors persons possessing special expert business knowledge appointed by the Minister on the recommendation of the President.

Trusts.

Power is taken for the investigation of the operations of trusts, etc., in order to ascertain whether they tend to the creation of monopolies or restraint of trade, etc. The President will from time to time forward a report to the Governor embodying any information acquired and any recommendations based thereon (*cf.* British Profiteering Act 1919).

Cornering.

The cornering of any necessary commodity and stores is an offence, and such commodity is liable to forfeiture. (*cf.* Necessary Commodities Control Act 1919 of Victoria.)

Unfair Methods.

Power is taken to call on any person to show cause why he should not be ordered to cease from using any unfair method of competition or discrimination in trade. If upon hearing the President is satisfied that the method is unfair, he will make a report and cause to be served on the person concerned an order requiring him to cease such unfair method within a specified time. Failure to obey the order will entail a penalty not exceeding £200 and a further penalty not exceeding £50 for every day after the first during which such failure continues, or imprisonment not exceeding six months. In the case of a corporation the maximum penalty is £500, and £100 for each additional day of non-compliance with the order. Appeal may within fourteen days be made to the Supreme Court.

Co-operative Enterprise.

With a view to the reduction of the average cost of living the Board of Trade is empowered to report to the Governor and propound schemes

for the promotion and control of co-operative enterprise for the wholesale
and retail supply of necessary commodities or the supply of necessary
services, and for the constitution of co-operative societies, banks, credit
unions, etc.

Prices.

The President is empowered to investigate complaints and fix reasonable prices and charges in respect of necessary commodities and services
(*cf.* British Profiteering Act 1919) ; and to approve schemes limiting
profits (*cf.* British Profiteering (Amendment) Bill 1920).

By notice in the *Gazette* and in prescribed newspapers the President
may from time to time after inquiry fix maximum prices, rates of
profit, etc. ; and also prohibit the increase in price of necessary commodities (*cf.* Victorian Necessary Commodities Control Act 1919) ; likewise in respect of necessary services.

Acquisition of Commodities.

The Governor may, upon the recommendation of the President,
by Proclamation in the *Gazette* or by notice to individuals, direct persons,
whether owners or otherwise, to retain and hold any specified necessary
commodity, or quantity thereof, for and on behalf of His Majesty;
possession to be given to the Minister, etc.   The owner will be entitled to
be paid by the Minister at a price fixed under the Act, or otherwise, as
mutually agreed upon, or in default of agreement, as determined by the
President.   The Minister may dispose of any such commodity as he thinks
fit.

Maximum penalty : £500 or imprisonment for six months, or both;
and in the case of a corporation, £1,000.

Supplies for Home Consumption.

Where the Governor has reason to believe that any necessary commodity is being sent out of New South Wales in such quantities that a
sufficient supply will not or may not be available for home consumption
at the fixed price, etc., he may make such regulations and orders and give
such directions as may be necessary to render available a sufficient
supply at such price.

Contravention of proclamation entails maximum penalty of £400
or imprisonment for twelve months ; and, if a corporation, £1,000.

Returns.

The Governor is empowered to require any person to furnish particulars as to any necessary commodity or service suspected to be in the
possession or under the control of such person.

Penalties.

Except where otherwise provided, for a first offence—penalty not
exceeding £100 or imprisonment not exceeding three months ; or in
the case of a corporation—maximum £200 ; provided that the President
etc., may, if satisfied that such offence was due to inadvertence, impose
a nominal penalty only.   Second or subsequent offence—maximum
£200 or imprisonment not exceeding six months, or both, and if a corporation—maximum £500.   Third or subsequent offence against provisions as to cornering, fixed prices, speculating, etc., not less than £5
nor more than £500, or imprisonment not exceeding twelve months, or
both.

Other sections of the Act deal with power to recommend taxation of excess profits in lieu of fixing prices, particular offences, penalties and forfeitures, attendance of witnesses and production of documents, etc., powers of search, inspectors etc.

PROPOSED ABOLITION OF STATE PARLIAMENTS.

A Resolution in favour of the abolition of State Parliaments and the substitution of a National Parliament with full sovereign rights was moved in the Legislative Assembly of New South Wales on 2nd September, 1920, by Mr. Bagnall.

IN THE LEGISLATIVE ASSEMBLY.

Mr. W. R. C. Bagnall (Liberal, *St. George*), moved : —

> · That in the opinion of this House, the time has arrived in the interests of effective government and economy, for the abolition of the State Parliaments and the substitution therefor of a National Parliament, with full sovereign rights, to govern the Australian nation.

He felt, he said, that he ought to add to the motion the words : " In the interests of national security," so that that would be understood to be the principal reason why he asked the House to discuss the question. He appreciated the fact that in Australia there were many schools of thought in the matter of the amendment of the Federal constitution. He was not one of those who held the view that the States as entities were ineffective as mediums for the effective government of the people. He realised that Australia owed what she was to-day to the magnificent work performed by the various States. It was solely because he felt that to-day they were faced with entirely new conditions, affecting the national welfare and security of Australia, that he asked the House to bring this question before the people for public discussion, and to join him in a propaganda movement to bring about the drastic change of the medium by which the people of Australia were governed. The Federal Parliament was to-day an anæmic structure, possessed of a few powers, which were limited, though important as affecting the well-being of Australia. Defence was a truly far-reaching national function ; but when they took away from the Federal Parliament the function of defence, they left it with functions of a more or less administrative character. Because of that fact, the people of Australia had their minds more concentrated

upon the State Parliaments ; and until they had one Parliament to concentrate upon, they would never be brought to
an appreciation of their national position.

If one took stock of the international position and the
relations of Australia to the rest of the world, he must
appreciate the extremely insecure position Australia was in
so far as her national security was concerned. It was because
there was a prospect of a serious change in the policy of
Great Britain that they were seriously menaced. To-day
they owed their safety to the strength of the British Navy ; and
as any change in the policy of Great Britain would involve
a change in the strength and effectiveness of the British
Navy, he wanted the people of Australia to appreciate what
this would mean to them. A school of political thought
in England, which was gathering strength rapidly, was
antagonistic to the idea of spending the large sum of money
required to maintain the British Navy in its present position
of pre-eminence. There was a growing feeling among the
more radical and industrial sections that all they had need
to provide for was the defence of the coast-line of the United
Kingdom, and that the safety of the other portions of the
Empire was not their concern. They said that Australia,
New Zealand and other outlying parts should look after
themselves. Unfortunately, the Government of Great Britain
was rapidly falling into the hands of the aggressive industrial
section. That was a factor which they must consider as
concerned in their national well-being.

In Australia they had a population of 5,000,000, inhabiting
a great island continent of 3,000,000 square miles. They
were some 14,000 miles from the heart of the Empire. Around
their coast-line were hundreds of islands capable of being
rapidly turned into naval bases. When they remembered
that within a short distance of Australia were some 600 odd
millions of coloured aliens, led by the Power which, so far as its
navy was concerned, now ranked second in the world, it was
no use Australia allowing the matter to go by default. So
long as the Lloyd George Government and the great political
parties of England stood for the Empire and for the pre-
eminence of the British Navy, Australians were safe and
secure. But if the forces that were to-day undermining
the strength of the British Government succeeded, the security
of Australia was menaced. These forces were growing stronger
week by week. They knew neither the outlook nor the ideal
of Empire. These large industrial organisations were composed largely of theorists, who had become infatuated with
the idea that it was possible to live in the world without
taking any active steps for the defence of their country.

Whilst the Australian people had their minds concentrated

pon State Parliaments and boundaries, it was a matter of ractical impossibility to expect a national outlook. There vas only one way of securing the attention of the people nd focussing their minds on important national problems, nd that was through the medium of one National Parliament, ossessed of full sovereign rights, containing some 200 or 300 members fully representative of the people of Australia, and which would fulfil all the functions of government now carried n by the State Parliaments. There was only one policy or such a Parliament, and that was the policy of bringing more people to Australia. When the people had achieved the necessary steps to bring about their well-being, it would be time for them to create a position similar to that which cisted in Canada, where the Central Parliament had the sovereign power, and a number of provinces carried on the ork of domestic administration.

The motion had not been discussed further when the House rose for the Christmas recess.

Queensland.

GOVERNMENT LOANS SUBSCRIPTION BILL.

The Bill, which was initiated in Committee on 18th November, provides for compulsory subscription to Government loans in the event of the amount raised voluntarily being less than the amount sought. It had not proceeded beyond the Second Reading stage when Parliament adjourned for the Christmas recess.

The following are the principal provisions of the Bill :—

Application.

The measure shall apply to every loan or part thereof raised or sought to be raised after the passing of the Act under the authority of any State Government Loan Act, but not to loans raised outside the Commonwealth of Australia and the Dominion of New Zealand.

Incidence.

If the amount subscribed voluntarily to any loan is less than the amount asked for the Treasurer may direct the Commissioner of Taxes to require further subscriptions to the loan. If the Commissioner has reason to believe that any person whose yearly average taxable income exceeds £1,000 has not subscribed in due proportion to his means, he may, subject to the direction of the Treasurer, by notice in writing, require such person to subscribe to the loan within such time and to such amount as is specified in the notice, stating a time within which any objections may be lodged with the Commissioner. The amount which any person may be so required to subscribe shall be calculated on the basis fixed by the Governor in Council as applicable to such person, and shall be subscribed by him accordingly together with any penalty in addition. The Governor in Council may, from time to time, by Order in Council published in the *Gazette*, fix the basis on which the amount required to be subscribed by any person shall be ascertained. Such basis may be either on a scale (or sliding scale) in proportion to the amount of the yearly average State income-tax paid or payable during the three years ending the 30th June immediately preceding the financial year in which the loan is raised, or the yearly average taxable income, which is defined in the Bill, in respect of any loan raised during the financial year ending 30th June, 1921, as the average taxable income for the calendar years 1917 and 1918 and the financial year 1918-1919 ; and in respect of any later loans the three corresponding later periods. The Governor in Council may fix one basis in respect of any class or classes of persons and the other basis for another class.

Provision is made for the service of notices on the agents of absentees, trustees of beneficiaries, and public officers of companies.

Objection.

Objection against any requirement may be lodged in writing with the Commissioner of Taxes. In considering the objection the Commissioner may take into account the amount, if any, invested by the objector in any previous loan raised to which the present Bill has applied.

Board of Appeal.

Any objector who is dissatisfied with the decision of the Commissioner upon an objection may appeal within a prescribed number of days to a Board of Appeal consisting of three persons, *i.e.*, the Auditor-General, the Under-Secretary of the Treasury, and the Commissioner of Taxes. The Auditor-General shall be Chairman of the Board, and in his absence the Treasurer may appoint one of the members to act as Chairman. Two members shall form a quorum. When a member of the Board is temporarily unable to act, the Treasurer may appoint a person to act in the place of such member. For the purpose of appeals the Board shall have respectively all the powers of a Commission and of the Chairman thereof under the "Official Inquiries Evidence Act 1910." An appeal shall be determined by a majority of the votes of the members present, and, in the event of there being an equality of votes, the Chairman shall have a casting vote. The decision of the Board shall be final. The Commissioner of Taxes may communicate to the members of the Board any information relating to any appeal which has come into his possession by virtue of his official position as Commissioner of Taxes.

Penalty.

Any person who is required under the measure to subscribe to any loan, and whose objection is not wholly allowed by the Commissioner, or who is not wholly exempted by the Board from obligation to subscribe, shall be liable to a penalty of an amount equal to one-fourth of the amount of subscription determined under the Bill. The payment of such penalty shall not relieve him from liability to pay the amount of the subscription determined. The amount of subscription and any amount of penalty shall be invested in the loan on behalf of the person from whom it is received or recovered. If the actual amount of subscription and penalty is not £10 or a multiple thereof, it will be calculated as the next higher amount which is a multiple of £10.

DEBATE IN LEGISLATIVE ASSEMBLY.

In the Legislative Assembly, on 17th November,

The Treasurer (Hon. F. A. Fihelly), in moving that the House resolve itself into a Committee to consider the introduction of the Bill, said the measure was drafted on the lines of a similar Bill introduced by Sir Joseph Cook in the Commonwealth Parliament. He did not think there would ever be any necessity for it to come into force. The amount of the loan would probably be £2,000,000. The Bill did not deal with the loan in any shape or form, excepting to provide for such contingencies as interest, an appeal board, exemptions and the like. The legislation at present on the statute-books would leave them free to deal entirely with the amounts and so forth. No person with an income of £1,000 or under would be called upon to pay by compulsion. The rate of interest would be fixed by the Governor in Council. There would be an assessing board and an appeal board, and then they would depend upon the legislation already passed.

Mr. W. H. Vowles (Leader of Country Party and Opposition) said he took it that the Government was asking for power to raise unlimited loans. They were told the Treasurer had cribbed the Bill from a measure introduced in the Commonwealth Parliament. In the case of the Commonwealth Government it was the result of post-war necessities —circumstances for which the Government was in no way responsible. In their own case they were asked to give extraordinary powers to a Government which had got itself into a financial difficulty through its own muddling. They had been asked to lend the Government a helping hand, but the Government would have to be frank. Their legislation would have to be honourable and straightforward, and such as would not interfere with private development. They were given to understand that if certain financial institutions and private individuals subscribed a certain amount of money during that year it would not be necessary for the Government to put the Bill into effect. On the top of that they found that the amount of money to be levied was uncertain, and the Government would have the right to compel the people to find cash for whatever amount they decided upon over and above the voluntary subscriptions made by these individuals and institutions. They were not going to give a free hand to the Government to put on the statute-books a measure that was going to be lasting, and which would give to future Governments the power to borrow to an unlimited extent by compulsion.

The Hon. W. H. Barnes (Leader of National Party) said the Treasurer had told them there was a provision in the Bill not only to give power in connection with the first £2,000,000 loan, but, in addition, for future demands which the Government might find necessary to make on the people. He wished to point out that already increased income-tax had been demanded. They were already paying per head of the population more than any of the other States ; and yet under the proposed measure they could turn up the income-tax returns and make demands upon the people to pay still further. The Government's policy had always been to take money out of circulation and to spend it on certain wild-cat schemes. The effect of the proposed measure would be to restrict enterprise and to impoverish a great number of people.

Other hon. members having spoken against the motion the House divided, and the question was resolved in the affirmative.

On 19th November,

The Treasurer in moving the Second Reading said that the Bill did not deal with the amount of any loan that might be asked for—the authority for which was contained entirely in previous measures. It merely provided that in the event of loan flotations by the Government not being fully subscribed in Queensland, compulsion might be resorted to by the Government. He would give an assurance that only £2,000,000 would be asked for. This Bill was not required to bring forward a loan at all. This was merely the compulsory part of it. They were asking for authority to collect, under compulsion, subscriptions from those who could afford to pay them, if they would not subscribe voluntarily. The Commonwealth had the same legislation, but they had an exemption of only £250. In New Zealand there was no exemption at all. This Bill was drafted on the legislation of both. He did not think there was an original clause, except that which provided for an appeal board which would hear and determine appeals against assessments. If it found that a business man required all his surplus capital for reinvestment in his business, it could make an arrangement to allow him to retain his capital.

They had had in the Treasury requests for about £4,000,000 on loans for local authorities. Did any hon. member say they were wrong in asking for a local loan of £2,000,000, and that they were not justified in using compulsion to collect £2,000,000 ? People who made fortunes out of the State should pay something towards its development. Queensland and Commonwealth taxation combined was not nearly as high as New Zealand taxation. The Government would have to curtail the loan expenditure from £300,000 per month to probably £150,000.

The penalties were much less severe than those of the

Commonwealth or New Zealand. Any penalties would be devoted to fresh investments in the loan. It should be remembered in regard to Queensland in the matter of loans, that most of the big pastoral properties and enterprises were owned by absentees. Queensland had not the same resources as New South Wales and Victoria, and the absentees in those States also would have to pay.

COMMONWEALTH BANK AGREEMENT RATIFICATION AND STATE ADVANCES ACT.

This Act, which was assented to on 6th December, provides for the ratification of an agreement between the Government of Queensland and the Commonwealth Bank of Australia with respect to the transfer to the said Bank of the business and assets of the Queensland Government Savings Bank, and to make provision for the carrying on of the State Advances business by the Savings Bank, etc.

The main provisions of the agreement are :—

Transfer to the Commonwealth (Government) Bank of Australia of the business and assets of the Queensland Government Savings Bank for a period of twenty-five years, the Queensland Government to have the option of continuing the arrangement for a further period not exceeding an additional twenty years.

The Commonwealth Bank, which takes over all the assets and property of the Savings Bank and all officers exclusively employed therein, except those of the Credit Foncier Department, will keep a separate account of the amalgamated Savings Bank business in the State of Queensland, and the resultant profit or loss on such business is to be equally shared by the respective parties.

The Queensland Government takes the profits already made by the Savings Bank amounting to £314,777 5s. (which includes accumulated reserve £230,000, and credit balance of profit and loss £72,224 17s.).

The Queensland Government will have the right to draw from time to time, at current rates of interest, 70 per cent. of increases in the amount of Savings Bank depositors' balances in Queensland for Trust Fund purposes in connection with workers' dwellings and rural loans, and will hand to the Commonwealth Bank as security therefor securities of the Queensland Government payable at Brisbane with currency not exceeding twenty-five years.

The Commonwealth Bank accepts the liabilities of the Savings Bank, as at 30th June, 1919, amounting to £14,325,069 12s. 2d. The Queensland Government pays the Commonwealth Bank £137,431 2s. 6d. in cash, and issues a deposit receipt at call for £3,086,677 3s. 3d., which latter sum represents the amount of funds of the Savings Bank on deposit with the Queensland Treasury, together with funds to its credit with the Queensland National Bank, Limited, at the date above mentioned, after deducting the sum mentioned in the third paragraph above as retained by the Queensland Government. Such deposit receipt at call bears interest at the rate of 3½ per cent. per annum, and, except by mutual arrangement, the total amount of the deposit is to remain undisturbed unless there is an excess of withdrawals over deposits in any one quarter in Queensland, in which event the Commonwealth Bank will have the right to withdraw from the Queensland Treasury at call an amount equal to 70 per cent. of such decrease in depositors' balances.

The Queensland Government agrees and undertakes to enter into a separate agreement with the Commonwealth Bank to hand over the general banking business of the State in Australia, London and abroad, including the flotation of State loans and the payment of interest thereon and the repayment of principal, such agreement to take effect as from the expiry of the existing arrangements with the Queensland National Bank, Limited, and the Bank of England.

DEBATE IN LEGISLATIVE ASSEMBLY.

The Treasurer (Hon. J. A. Fihelly), in moving the Second Reading in the Legislative Assembly, on 24th November, said that from the point of view of duplication that existed at present, it must be admitted that the saving would be extensive. In Queensland one person out of every three had an account in the Government Savings Bank. Some also had duplicate accounts in the Commonwealth Bank. They had duplicate accounts because if they placed all their savings in one bank the amount would be above the maximum allowed for drawing interest. Under the Agreement the Commonwealth Bank would raise their rate of interest to the Queensland Savings Bank's standard (3½ per cent.), and both accounts would now be available for interest-bearing purposes. It might be argued that previous Governments had submitted to them a similar agreement and had concluded that it could not be to the advantage of Queensland to ratify it. Proposals had been submitted in 1912, of which the Denham Government did not approve. One of the suggestions in 1912 was that the Queensland Government securities then held by the State Savings Bank amounting to £4,968,000 should be retained by the State, and that in lieu thereof the Commonwealth Bank should receive as an asset new debentures of a face value of £5,080,000, which, in effect, meant a loss of £112,000 to the State. That objectionable feature had been entirely eliminated, and instead of their giving the Commonwealth Bank debentures of a greater value, the Bank was now accepting their debentures at their book value and not at their market value. Under this agreement, also, the current account of £3,086,000 was to be treated as a deposit with the State at 3½ per cent. That sum would remain undisturbed unless there was an excess of withdrawals over deposits, and the only to the extent of 70 per cent. The Treasurer would advise the Governor of the Commonwealth Bank in regard to the remaining 30 per cent. of the deposits. They would have the use of 70 per cent. of the deposits without any necessity to keep a reserve fund.

To those who suggested that they were selling their birth-right, he would emphasise that they were making a good business bargain ; and it was going to simplify matters for all State Governments now and in the future. Banking should be essentially a function of the central governing body— that was the Commonwealth Government.

The Hon. W. H. Barnes (Leader of National Party) said that the Premier (Hon. E. G. Theodore) had made a statement that 70 per cent. was to be appropriated to the Government, and that the other 30 per cent. would probably go in another direction. In other words, that whilst the Government were not now able to help, in the main, to finance local authorities, in the future there would be no difficulty whatever for local authorities to get it from the Commonwealth Savings Bank. He wanted to know who had moved in connection with the Bill. Was it the Governor of the Commonwealth Bank or the Treasurer ?

The Premier : It originated at the Treasurers' conference, and was brought forward by Mr. Watt, the Federal Treasurer.

Hon. W. H. Barnes : What had been the attitude of the other States to the proposals of the Commonwealth Bank ? The little State of Tasmania had certainly gone into line ; but at conferences he had known these proposals had been turned down by the State Treasurers because they felt they were losing a grip upon one of the most important assets of the State. The position was that they were going to hand over a business of £15,000,000 to the Commonwealth which was running a business of £3,000,000 in connection with Savings Bank deposits. It was only a step towards unification. To use the Treasurer's own words, it would be parting with the birth-right of Queensland. It was the bank of the people of Queensland, and it was absolutely unfair that this legislation should be passed.

Mr. W. H. Vowles (Leader of Country Party and Opposition) said that his main objection was that they had not been requested to consider the terms of the agreement before it was signed. They could have been consulted in the House as to whether they considered it desirable to amalgamate. Personally he was opposed to it. It was too much like a start in the direction of unification.

South Australia.

VENEREAL DISEASES ACT.

This Act, which was assented to on 1st December, 1920, provides for compulsory treatment and notification of venereal diseases and prevention of the spread of such diseases. A summary of the Bill appeared in Vol. II., No. 1, page 153, and substantially it was passed as originally introduced. The principal amendments made during the passage of the Bill are indicated in the following summary which should be read in conjunction with the summary of the Bill.

The following are the principal amendments :—

Section 13 (Warning other party to proposed marriage) is amended by providing that instead of it being lawful for a medical practitioner to warn the other party to a proposed marriage ; the medical practitioner shall (under penalty), where he has reason to believe that a person suffering from venereal disease consulting him or attended or treated by him intends to contract marriage, inform the Inspector-General of Hospitals thereof, who shall inform any person whom he believes on reasonable grounds to be the other party that the person suffering from such disease is so suffering, and give like information to any parent or guardian of such party.'

Section 18 (Prevention of infection), which renders liable to maximum imprisonment of one year, or penalty not exceeding £100, any person who knowing himself to be suffering from any venereal disease in an infectious stage, works in or about any factory, shop, hotel, restaurant, house, or other place in any capacity requiring him to handle food intended for human consumption—is extended to include ships and boats, and also any person working in or about any hairdressing saloon.

Section 29. A new section is inserted providing that where the person to be compulsorily examined is a female, the medical practitioner or if more than one, one of them shall, if so desired by the person to be examined, be a female medical practitioner if available and willing to act within twenty miles of the place of examination.

DEBATE IN LEGISLATIVE COUNCIL.

In moving the Second Reading in the Legislative Council on 7th September, **the Minister of Agriculture (Hon. T. Pascoe)** said that South Australia was the last of the States to introduce legislation of this character. It gave one an idea of the magnitude of these diseases that in the Adelaide Hospital for three years, without compulsory notification, Dr. Rischbieth (surgeon in charge of the clinic for venereal disease) should have had 15,000 consultations on the subject. The passing of legislation to deal with venereal disease had been stimulated by the experience gained during the War of the effects of the ravages of the disease. In fact, it was a letter from the Prime Minister of the Commonwealth, dated 25th September, 1915, which first brought the necessity for anti-venereal legislation prominently before the South Australian Government. In that letter the Prime Minister pointed out that the alarming increase in the number of cases of venereal disease among troops in training was likely seriously to affect the efficiency and general health of the army, and that he would be glad if the Government would consider the desirableness of taking steps to provide for the compulsory notification of venereal disease. In reply to that letter the South Australian Government stated that it did not propose to introduce legislation on the matter at that time, but intended to establish night clinics, by which means it was hoped that the danger might be combated. In pursuance of that policy Dr. H. Rischbieth was appointed honorary surgeon of the department for venereal diseases at the Adelaide Hospital. After having been in charge of that department for about two and a half years, Dr. Rischbieth wrote urging the Government to pass anti-venereal legislation providing for compulsory notification. In the meantime the Commonwealth Government had been so impressed with the urgency of combating the disease that it appointed a committee, which, on 24th May, 1916, presented a report on venereal disease. The Bill was based on the recommendations of the Commonwealth Committee and also on the best medical advice available. In addition the Government had secured reports from the medical authorities administering the Acts in other States. The Bill had also been submitted to leading members of the medical profession in Adelaide and to Dr. J. H. Cumpston, the Federal Director of Quarantine, a high authority on the treatment and control of venereal disease, who reported that the Bill contained many admirable features, and that he admired some improvements on the existing legislation of the other States, particularly Clause 13 (empowering medical practitioner to inform party to intended marriage that other party is suffering from venereal disease); Clause 14 (liability of person marrying while knowingly suffering from venereal disease); and Clause 18 (liability of person knowingly suffering from venereal disease handling food in factories, shops, etc.). At a meeting of the local branch of the British Medical Association especially called to consider the draft of the Bill, a resolution was passed to the effect that the meeting approved of the general principle of the Bill provided that no certificate of inspection with or freedom from venereal disease be given without confirmation by a bacteriological or serological examination. It had, however, been deemed unnecessary to make any such provision in the Bill itself. If desired that matter might be dealt with by regulations under the Act or met by instructions to medical practitioners.

The Hon. J. Jelly (Opposition) said he supported the Government in its endeavour to eradicate venereal disease. Apparently in Victoria there was the same hesitation on the part of females to present themselves for treatment as prevailed in South Australia. That showed clearly the necessity for drastic legislation to make the reporting of venereal disease compulsory. Clause 4 of the Bill confined the treatment of the disease to medical practitioners only. Any effort to get rid of the quacks that prey on the public was deserving of whole-hearted support. Clause 18 was a necessary provision, but he saw a loophole. There was no reference to a ship or boat included in the definitions of places in which it would be illegal for infected persons to work or handle food.* The Minister had pointed out how prevalent venereal disease was in the seaports, and it seemed to him that the disease would be found in numerous cases on board shipping vessels. He was glad to notice that the Minister might arrange for free treatment. It occurred to him that all the legislation making notification compulsory would be so much waste paper unless they were prepared to supply, in necessitous cases at all events, free medical attention.

DEBATE IN HOUSE OF ASSEMBLY.

In the House of Assembly on 21st September,

Mr. J. Gunn (Socialist, *Adelaide*), in supporting the Second Reading, said that if the Act became operative, and some person was penalised under Clause 14 (liability of person marrying while suffering from venereal disease) the Government should consider what was to become of the marriage. He did not think that the offence under the clause would be sufficient grounds for annulling a marriage under their present matrimonial laws. The Bill was very necessary. One felt that they did not heed the cry of the medical profession early enough in this connection.

Mr. Peter Reidy (Nationalist, *Victoria*) said that they were going to penalise a man or woman for certain offences and things which happened after marriage. Should they not insert a provision in the Bill that before they marry they should be in possession of a certificate showing they had clean bill of health? If a person suffering from venereal

---

* This clause was subsequently amended to include provision in this respect.

disease married, the life of the other party to the contract would be ruined, and it was too late to start inflicting penalties after that had happened. Clause 14 as it stood seemed to be doing the right thing at the wrong time. He hoped some of the restrictions would be made more drastic.

In Committee, Mr. Reidy moved that the following new clause be inserted : —

1. Notwithstanding anything in any Act, it shall not be lawful for any licensed officiating person to celebrate any marriage unless each of the persons intending to contract the marriage has presented to him prior to the celebration of the intended marriage the certificate of a legally qualified medical practitioner that such person is free from venereal disease.

2. Any officiating minister of religion who is guilty of any contravention of this section shall be liable to a penalty not exceeding fifty pounds.

His principal reason for moving to insert that clause was his belief in the broad principle that prevention was better than cure. The regulations could set out the manner in which examination was to be made—by blood test or some other way.

The Commissioner for Public Works (Hon. W. Hague) opposed the new clause because it was too drastic, and would be very objectionable in many ways.

Mr. S. O'Flaherty (Socialist, *Murray*) opposed the clause because of its far-reaching effects. If it were inserted in a health Bill applying to other diseases as well as this one, then he would not hesitate to support it. Clause 14 would cover the difficulty mentioned by Mr. Reidy.

Mr. W. J. Denny (Socialist, *Adelaide*) supported the principle of the clause. He granted that the clause did not express what a large number of members would desire ; for instance, it did not say, even if the certificate was not produced, that the marriage should not be solemnised or that it should be invalid. It simply made a penalty for any officiating person. In many country places it would be impossible for a person to see a medical man, and in some cases it was urgent that marriages should be solemnised.

Mr. H. S. Hudd (Liberal, *Alexandra*) said that until medical evidence was forthcoming that such a clause was necessary, he could not support so drastic an alteration.

Mr. Gunn : " It is the law of three States in America."

Mr. Hudd : " We have two provisions already dealing with persons contemplating marriage, and we should give the Bill a trial first.''

The proposed new clause was negatived.

Western Australia.

THE STATE AND FEDERATION.

A Resolution was proposed in the Legislative Assembly on 13th October, 1920, suggesting that steps should be taken to place the financial position of the State of Western Australia, as a result of federation, before the Commonwealth Ministry.

DEBATE IN LEGISLATIVE ASSEMBLY.

Mr. E. H. Angelo (National, *Gascoyne***)** moved : —

> " That this House is of opinion that the State has suffered great financial loss through the federation of Australia, and that the time has now arrived when steps should be taken to place the position clearly and strongly before the Ministry of the Commonwealth with the view of obtaining some measure of relief."

During the nineteen years, he said, that Western Australia had been a party to the Federal compact, their monetary loss had amounted to more than 9½ millions. At the present time Western Australia had a deficit of over four millions. Had the State been able to collect all the excise and customs duties, and to impose all the direct taxation which the Federal Government had collected in Western Australia during that period, at the same time carrying on all the different departments which the Federal Government had been administering in the State, together with their proportion of War expenditure which had been paid out of revenue, they would now have been five millions to the good. This was not his opinion only. It was shared by all their ex-Treasurers, who had expressed similar opinions from time to time. He had pointed out in a recent speech a great many of the disadvantages from which Western Australia had suffered. Their factories had disappeared, and they had been asked to contribute huge sums in loans, which though raised in the State, had not entailed the expenditure of a penny there. All the manufacturing and purchasing Government stores and materials had been done in the Eastern States. Up to the present the Northern Territory had cost Australia six million pounds and Western Australia's share of it had been £400,000. They were the only State that had a northern territory of its own to develop. They had heard that the Commonwealth Government intended to proceed with the building of the Federal capital. That would cost 70 millions, and their share would be five millions. Surely they could do more good if that five millions of money were retained and utilised for the benefit of the State. He was not in favour of secession, but he wished to see a better financial arrangement made than that which they had at present. It might be urged that a convention of the different States was to take place shortly, but he would like members to understand that Western Australia would have a smaller representation than the other States, who would swamp the few members they could send from Western Australia. He suggested that Parliament should send a delegation to Melbourne—consisting of two members from the Government side, two from the Opposition, and two representing the Country Party—to put their case clearly to the Federal Government.

The Premier (Hon. J. Mitchell) said he did not suppose any member would object to the motion. He did not know that it would carry very much weight. They had suffered great financial loss through federation, but he did not think they could repair their loss by passing a motion of that kind. They paid their share of the cost of the Federal Government on a *per capita* basis, then the Federal Government returned to the States an even amount of 25s. per head of population. That was unfair to Western Australia because their contribution as consumers was very much greater than that of any other State. The Government had gone to considerable trouble to compile the facts of their case, and these facts had been submitted to the Federal Government. He did not know what more they could do.

Mr. J. T. Lutey (Labour, *Brownhill-Ivanhoe*) said that Western Australia had elected certain gentlemen to represent it in the Federal House. It would be an insult to them to pass such a motion as this. If it was suggested in the motion that representation should be made to their Federal representatives, he would support it.

Mr. R. T. Robinson, K.C. (National Liberal, *Canning*), said it was never anticipated when they joined the Commonwealth that all the avenues of direct taxation would be exploited by the Commonwealth. It had been publicly stated by the Hon. Alfred Deakin and other leaders of the first Federal convention that only as a last resort would the Commonwealth interfere with direct taxation. Long before the War, in 1909, the Federal authorities started out on direct taxation and they had gone on ever since. It was the root of all their troubles in the State. How many members knew that year after year the surplus revenue over and above expenditure had been put into the coffers of the Federal Treasury, thereby robbing the States, and that the Federal authorities had passed a Bill authorising them to do this and to break the compact that they themselves had made. A report had been made by Mr. Owen, their Commissioner of Taxation, and subsequently Under-Treasurer, who was an authority on the subject. The figures and data of that report were unchallenge-able.* The Prime Minister (the Right Hon. W. M. Hughes) came to the State and talked affably to them, but as soon as he went to Melbourne they were as far forgotten as the people in the New Hebrides. He agreed with the motion.

Mr. James Gardiner (National, *Irwin*) said that during the Federal Convention discussions it was specifically stated that the Savings Bank business would be retained by the States. However, the Commonwealth had come over with their Savings Bank, and after five years of competition the State Savings Bank deposits, less withdrawals and including interest, amounted to about £357,000, but in the case of the Commonwealth Savings Bank the excess of deposits totalled approximately £1,300,000, which was money the State could have borrowed at 4 per cent., instead of being compelled to pay £6 2s. 6d. or £6 10s. per cent.

The Hon. W. C. Angwin (Labour, *North-East Fremantle*) said they had been told about the losses, let them see what Western Australia had gained by federation. When the War broke out they were experiencing a drought, and it was necessary to finance the farmers in the interest of the State as a whole. From that time down to twelve months ago every shilling of loan money necessary for the development of the State had been provided by the Commonwealth. He agreed that a mistake had been made in regard to the money taken by the Commonwealth Surplus Revenue Fund.† The Commonwealth had no right to do that without having first consulted the States. They should get it out of their heads that they could secede from federation. They must make the best of a bad bargain. He hoped that Ministers would set about obtaining all the information necessary to supply to those who were elected to the convention, so that they might place their views before that body when it met.

The motion was still under discussion when the Session closed.

---

* Mr. Owen's report on the " Financial Relations between the State of Western Australia and the Commonwealth," showed the estimated total monetary loss of Western Australia from federation as at 30th June, 1919, to be £8,055,000.

† For particulars as to the financial arrangement between the Commonwealth and the States see " Official Year Book of the Commonwealth of Australia "—No. 6, 1913, Section XIX—Commonwealth Finance, page 778 *et seq.*

NEW ZEALAND.

The following summary deals with some further Acts and proceedings of the First Session of the Twentieth Parliament, which closed on 11th November, 1920, and is in continuation of the summaries published in Vol. I., No. 4, and Vol. II., No. 1, of this JOURNAL.

Parliament again met on 10th March, 1921, when a short session was held for the purpose of discussing the attendance of the Prime Minister at the Imperial Conference to be held in June next, and to vote supplies. Parliament was prorogued on 24th March. A summary of the proceedings will be published in the next issue of this JOURNAL.

CONFERENCE OF PRIME MINISTERS OF THE EMPIRE.

(Question of Parliamentary Sanction, etc.)

Power to Commit Country.

On 11th November, 1920,

Mr. W. E. Parry (Labour, *Auckland Central*) asked the Prime Minister, without notice, if in view of the House not being given an opportunity of discussing New Zealand's representation at the Imperial Conference next year, the Prime Minister would give the House an idea as to whether the Dominion's representative would be given power to commit New Zealand in any undertaking before reporting to Parliament.

The Prime Minister (the Right Hon. W. F. Massey) said that so far as concerned New Zealand's representation at the Imperial Conference, or Imperial Cabinet—he was not certain which it would be—the Dominion would be represented there by at least one Minister.* Possibly there might be two, and in addition to the gentlemen he had in mind there was also the High Commissioner, who was an ex-Minister and a man who knew the position of New Zealand in relation to Imperial affairs as well as any man in the country.

Mr. Parry : " Will they be able to commit New Zealand ? "

The Prime Minister said that when the representative or representatives came back they would report—to Cabinet first and to Parliament afterwards—as to what had been done, and it would then be for Parliament to say whether it agreed

---

* Official advice has since been received that Mr. Massey will be present at the Conference of Prime Ministers.

with the actions of its representatives at the Cabinet meetings or the Conference.

Discussion on Imperial Affairs.

On the same date,

Mr. A. S. Malcolm (Reform, *Clutha***)** asked the Prime Minister whether he would see that the House should have an opportunity early in the next Session of expressing an opinion on Imperial affairs. He had raised the question Session after Session, but although more or less favourable replies had always been given, the opportunity for discussion had not been afforded. He said that in no carping spirit, but Imperial affairs and relations were becoming of such importance to the country that he thought Parliament should have an opportunity of hearing not only what the representatives of the country had to report about the Imperial Conference, but the opinions of the members themselves on Imperial affairs.

The Prime Minister replied that on the different occasions when the ex-Minister of Finance, Sir Joseph Ward, and he had returned from Imperial Conferences, they had reported to the House at some length, and a full opportunity had been given on those occasions to members to express their opinions. Mr. Massey added that, supposing he were to make a suggestion that the House of Representatives should at that period of the Session, after all the other business was done, go into a discussion of Imperial affairs, that would not give satisfaction.

Mr. W. E. Parry (Labour, *Auckland Central***) :** " Would it not be better to have the discussion before the delegates leave ? "

The Prime Minister said that the representatives of New Zealand would not be delegates in the ordinary sense of the term. He would endeavour to comply with the request of the hon. member for Clutha, and would take an opportunity of devoting a day, or two days if necessary, early in the next Session to the discussion of Imperial affairs.

EXTERNAL AFFAIRS AMENDMENT ACT.

Under the provisions of the External Affairs Act, 1919,* the administration of the Cook Islands was brought under the External Affairs Department.

The object of the above Act is to restore the administration to the Cook Islands Department. It received the Governor-General's Assent on 13th October, 1920.

---

* See this JOURNAL, Vol. I., No. 1, page 176.

The measure was debated at considerable length on its Second Reading in the House of Representatives on the 5th October, 1920. In the course of the discussion references were made (*inter alia*) to the status and scope of the duties appertaining to the office of the Minister of External Affairs.

DEBATE IN HOUSE OF REPRESENTATIVES.

The Minister of External Affairs (Hon. E. P. Lee) said that it was found expedient to go back to the old system and leave the administration of the Cook Islands in the hands of the Minister representing the Native race. The administration of the Cook Islands and that of the Samoan Islands were two quite distinct matters. The Cook Islands Department had controlled those islands for a number of years, and was in direct touch with the affairs of the islands and the requirements of the inhabitants. The Cook Islands required the close attention of those experienced in their administration.

Status of Minister of External Affairs.

Mr. T. M. Wilford (Leader of the Opposition) said that, in his opinion, the whole of the islands in the Pacific which were under the jurisdiction of New Zealand should logically be under the Minister of External Affairs. At the same time, he quite thought that the Minister who represented the Maori race in the Executive Council should exercise that same representation for the Natives of the Cook Islands that he did for the Natives of New Zealand. He protested emphatically against the Minister of External Affairs losing his grip as Minister of those islands. What did the authority of the Minister of External Affairs cover at that time ? Was he going to divide his governance in connection with administration or trade with the Minister in Charge of the Cook Islands ? How did he stand in regard to Samoa ? Had he, as Minister of External Affairs, charge over Samoa, or was he still involved with the Defence Department ? Now that they had a high-sounding title like Minister of External Affairs, let them have an understanding what it meant. Did it mean that he was to direct the foreign policy of the country in relations with America and other countries, and to be the diplomatist for the Government in dealing with the Japanese ? Mr. Wilford concluded by saying that the matter with which he was most concerned was that the Minister of External Affairs was losing control of the Cook Group. He wanted to know why that was being done.

Mr. W. Downie Stewart (Reform, *Dunedin West*) said that there was something in what had been said by the Leader

of the Opposition. He thought the Minister might have
given them some better explanation as to why the change
was being made, and told them generally more about his
Department. He had always considered the title of " External
Affairs " an entire misnomer if the operations of the Department were to be confined to Samoa. It seemed to him that
a better name would have been " Department of Pacific
Affairs," because any outsider looking at their legislation
would suppose that the Minister of External Affairs would
deal with all external questions affecting New Zealand, arising
in Europe or America, or anywhere else, including matters
affecting the islands. There were several questions which
arose in connection with Samoa and the Cook Group, which
ought to be dealt with in common, and it would probably
lead to duplication and expense if the separation took place.

Dr. A. K. Newman (Liberal, *Wellington East*) said that
New Zealand had a large number of islands to control. They
had acquired Samoa, Cook Group, Kermadecs, Macquarie,
Chatham, the Auckland Islands, and so on. He had been in
great hopes that the Government would have dictated some
policy concerning the governance of all those valuable islands.
Many of the islands were almost unknown to them. The
Kermadecs were worth something, whilst Cook Islands and
Samoa were worth a great deal. The Samoan trade went
entirely away from them. The one important thing was that
they should have those islands (Samoa and Cook Islands)
under the control of one Minister, and the same with the line
of steamers, in order to carry out a policy of development.

The Prime Minister (the Right Hon. W. F. Massey) said that
members had asked why the Minister of External Affairs
should not control the Cook Islands ? Hon. members ought to
know that legally the Cook Islands were part of New Zealand.
The portfolio of the Department of External Affairs was not
set up for the purpose of controlling New Zealand, or part of
New Zealand, but countries outside New Zealand, and mostly,
as suggested by the hon. member for Dunedin West, Pacific
Countries.

Speaking on the question of trade in the islands, Mr.
Massey said that aspect had not been forgotten, but they
could not do everything at once. He looked forward to New
Zealand taking its proper place in relation to the islands of the
Pacific. He quite admitted that trade had gone from that
that ought to have come to New Zealand, though he did not
think it could be said that they were losing trade. They did
not properly realise what was going on around them. He
would remind members of the great possibilities in connection
with the opening of the Panama Canal. There was a great
deal to be done in Fiji itself, right on the line of trade between

New Zealand and Panama. Then there were the New Hebrides, a magnificent group of islands capable of producing anything that could be grown in tropical countries, and there was there a population of 60,000 natives.

He did not think they had ever sent a vessel to the New Hebrides, and it would be for the Minister of External Affairs to take up the question of the New Hebrides with the Imperial Government, and assist in bringing about a better arrangement so far as those islands were concerned than existed at that time. He had no ambition to control the New Hebrides, but it was the duty of the British Governments in the Pacific to insist upon some better arrangement for the government of those islands.

Dr. the Hon. M. Pomare (Member of the Executive representing the Native Race) said he thought a mistake had been made in bringing the Cook Islands under the External Affairs Department last year, because the two groups of islands were nearly a thousand miles apart, and matters which concerned Samoa had no correlation with matters affecting Rarotonga whatsoever. Consequently, a scheme of steamship service for Samoa could not be made to fit in with Rarotonga (Cook Islands).

Dr. Pomare then quoted figures to show that trade in the Cook Islands had not gone back, but had, he claimed, shewn a marked increase in imports, exports, and revenue year by year. The member for Hurunui (Mr. G. W. Forbes) had asked a question in regard to the request made by some of the traders in the islands for representation on the Native Council. Provision was being made for that in the form of a Bill, but any proposal would have to be sent down for the corroboration of the Rarotongans before it was submitted to Parliament, which would take time.

Mr. H. E. Holland (Labour, *Buller*) said that what they really wanted was a Bill covering the whole of the government of the Cook Islands, and such a Bill ought to be far more extensive in the powers it conferred than the present Bill; the kind of Bill they wanted was one that would go somewhere in the direction of providing for the self-government of the Cook Islands.

The Minister of External Affairs : "There is a very extensive Act on the statute-book for that purpose."

Mr. Holland : "But, still, it is an Act that does not go nearly far enough."

After commenting upon other matters raised in the debate, Mr. Holland said the Prime Minister had stressed— and rightly stressed—the fact that the Cook Islands were an integral part of New Zealand ; that being so, the people of the Cook Islands should have the same rights of representation

M

there (in New Zealand) as the Native race in New Zealand had. The Minister informed them that there was a Cook Islands Bill coming down, but why not, in that case, let the matter before them stand until the Bill came down ? A comprehensive measure, embodying the promises made to the people during the recent visit of the parliamentary party, would be far more satisfactory both to the Natives and the Whites there.

The Minister of External Affairs, in his reply, said that when Sir James Allen* visited the islands he gave the people there to understand that any legislation proposed to be introduced to Parliament in the future would be submitted to them. An amendment of the Cook Islands Act had now, in accordance with that undertaking, to be submitted to the people of the islands, and it was questionable whether it would be back in time to be put through that Session. That was one reason why the provisions of the present Bill, as brought down, were not embodied in the legislation referred to. The Government had come to the conclusion, after considering the matter from all viewpoints, and with a knowledge of what the Minister of External Affairs had to do in connection with the administration of Samoa, that the administrations of the two groups of islands were not linked together in any way, and that the affairs of the Cook Islands could be better carried out by Dr. Pomare, whose administration, it had been admitted that afternoon, had been successful.

The House divided, and the Second Reading was carried by 35 votes against 18, the Liberal and Labour members voting together in opposition.

IN THE LEGISLATIVE COUNCIL.

The Bill passed through all stages in the Legislative Council without debate on the 7th October.

COMMISSIONER TO THE UNITED STATES.

On 5th November, 1920,

Mr. T. M. Wilford (Leader of the Opposition) asked the Prime Minister whether the Government had considered the advisability of appointing a Commissioner to the United States. He pointed out that it was a matter of rema

---

* Sir James Allen (then Minister of Defence) was in charge of the Parliamentary Party which visited Samoa and the Cook Islands February-March, 1919 (see this JOURNAL, Vol. I., No. 4, at page 7 and following pages.

mong bankers and commercial men, at a conference held in
California, which he (Mr. Wilford) had attended in 1912, that
New Zealand was not officially represented in the United
States.

An Hon. Member: "Australia has such a representative."

The Prime Minister replied that the matter had not been
lost sight of, but no definite decision had yet been arrived at.
There was the possibility of important political changes in the
United States, and, as they had waited so long, the Government
thought it would be well to wait till such changes were completed. Personally, he was in favour of keeping the American
market open to New Zealand and that they should take care
to keep the Dominion represented in American markets.

Mr. Wilford pointed out that America also looked to the
New Zealand market. It was expedient to arrange some sort
of exchange and appreciate the differences in value when
trading, and for that reason a representative on the spot was
required.

OVERSEAS SHIPPING AND FREIGHTS.

(Discussion on Report: Recommendation of a Dominion Line: United States Shipping Legislation, etc.)

On 27th October, 1920, in the House of Representatives,
Mr. G. Hunter (Reform, *Waipawa*) brought up the report of
the Agricultural and Pastoral Industries, Stock, and Commerce
Committee, as the result of its enquiry into the questions of
increases in ocean freights, and of shipping tonnage available
for Dominion trade. In the course of the report a recommendation is made that a shipping line, independent of any
combination, should be established, to be assisted by the
Government; and it is further recommended that, to meet
the action of combinations of shipping companies, legislation
should be introduced, based on the United States Shipping
Act of 1916.

The following is a summary of the findings of the Committee:—

The refrigerated tonnage engaged in the services of the companies
in the New Zealand trade is sufficient for normal requirements at the
present time.

While giving full consideration to the various causes which have
operated in materially increasing the cost of running vessels as compared with pre-war times, the Committee is of the opinion that the rates
now quoted for privately-owned produce are unwarrantably high.

M 2

The evidence obtained as to combinations among shipping companies gives cause for grave concern, especially when the dependence of the Dominion upon refrigerated tonnage is realised and consideration given to the relatively small total amount of refrigerated tonnage existing in the world as compared with ordinary cargo-vessels. Thus the existence of these combinations of shipping companies owning refrigerated tonnage constitutes a position which has in it possibilities of creating trading conditions calculated to operate to the disadvantage of the community generally.

Notwithstanding the fact that sufficient refrigerated tonnage for present-day normal requirements is owned by the companies now in the New Zealand trade, the Committee is of opinion that, consequent upon the possibilities latent in the combinations existing, it is desirable, in the best interests of the Dominion, that a shipping line be established which will be entirely independent of any combination, and that the Government should assist in the establishment of such a line by guarantee, financial assistance, or otherwise.

Among the most important features of the evidence obtained was the information given to the Committee regarding the methods adopted by shipping companies or combines in preventing opposing independent lines securing outward cargo from Great Britain, among which methods the granting of freight rebates constituted an important feature. In order to combat this the Committee recommends that legislation based on that contained in the United States Shipping Act, 1916, be introduced.

The report concluded with a synopsis of Sections 14 and 15 of the Shipping Act (U.S.A.), 1916.

DEBATE IN HOUSE OF REPRESENTATIVES.

Mr. Oswald Hawken (Reform, *Egmont*), in moving that the report should lie on the table, said that he doubted whether the conditions in any other industry were so grave as in that particular industry. The official figures for the extra charge on exports alone amounted to over five millions sterling per year, which was a huge percentage of the actual value of the exports. British shipping, unfortunately, had suffered greatly in the War ; but it seemed to him that they were paying far more than they should to make up for that loss. There was another feature of the shipping charges which they should take note of : there was no doubt that shipping had to pay, and would have to pay, very heavy charges in taxation in the Old Country ; and, though they had no information as to how those charges were made up, it was quite sensible to suppose that they were paying to a very large extent the taxation which the United Kingdom imposed upon its shipping. In that way taxation might be imposed or passed on to them which they had no right to pay ; and the only way they could minimise such charges would be by obtaining shipping of their own, and thereby bring the rates down to a reasonable figure.

The Prime Minister (the Right Hon. W. F. Massey): " Shipping pays a fair share of taxation here."

Mr. Hawken : " A very small proportion as compared with he taxation there."

The Prime Minister : " That is so. What I mean is that he shipping of this country is taxed in this country."

Mr. Hawken said that he knew that; but they wanted nore shipping. Continuing, he said that it was quite apparent o the Committee—and he thought admitted by the shipping ompanies themselves—that they had an agreement as to the harges they made for their services. There was no shipping ine they could bring in as a competitor to reduce the rates. Ie thought it would be a wise step to bring in the American aw as to making the ships common carriers. He was not in favour of a Government-owned line, but he did think that l line of ships owned partly by the Government and partly y the freight-owners would be a proper combination ; he had o objection to the importers being included.

Mr. Edward Newman (Reform, *Manawatu*), speaking in favour of the findings of the Committee, said it was understood hat after the War a Committee was to be appointed—he lelieved it was appointed—by the Imperial Government— nd he thought on the suggestion of the Prime Minister of New Zealand—to regulate freights throughout the Empire ; but he ad not heard whether the Committee had taken any action, nd it would be interesting to know what proposals it had to nake.

Australian Shipping.

Hon. gentlemen would have observed what had taken place in the (Australian) Commonwealth in connection with hipping. There had been a strenuous fight going on between ested interests in shipping and the Government ships. Al- hough space was badly wanted, one heard of ships travelling mpty because the people were penalised in some way by a ystem of rebates—a most pernicious system by which people vere compelled to send their cargo for other countries by one ine or the other. He hoped the Government would realise he importance of the question and give a lead to the people.

Mr. W. D. Lysnar (Reform, *Gisborne*) after pointing out hat a Parliamentary Committee, which had considered the neat-shipping question in 1917, had recommended practically vhat the present report did, but that no legislation had yet een passed, said that the necessity of declaring the ships ommon carriers should be very apparent. He was absolutely dverse to the Government having a shipping line of their wn. They should not shoulder more than the responsibility f guaranteeing half the cost of a boat on behalf of different groups of producers, who were quite able to finance their own boats, but would not take the necessary steps. They could not separate the shipping combine from the Meat Trust. They were so intermixed that they could not separate them ; and because one operated in favour of the other was another reason why something should be done.

The Prime Minister in congratulating the Committee on the good work they had done, said that a comparison of the rates of freight charged between that country and England, and those charged between the other Dominions of the Empire and Europe or London, would be a most interesting comparison, and might be a guide as to what should be done. He had no doubt that the high taxation in Great Britain had very considerably affected the rates of freight charged to the oversea Dominions ; but there were other reasons for the tremendous increase, and they should have the fullest information. If those rates of freight continued, with the prices ruling in England and which were likely to be lower, then it was going to crush the meat industry of the country.

After referring to the setting up of the Imperial Shipping Committee, and stating its functions, Mr. Massey said he should be seriously disappointed if it did not do good work ; there was nothing of more importance to the Dominions than the matter of reasonable freights and fares between those countries and the heart of the Empire. He had expressed the opinion in England that the rates of freight must be kept down, not only for the benefit of the Dominions, but to ensure that British trade would be kept to British ships. As far as a Government shipping line was concerned, he agreed with the opinions expressed, and he felt very doubtful as to the Government of that or any other country being able to make a success of a shipping line in competition with other lines run by experts and owned by men with huge capital behind them. When the Session came to a finish he looked forward to taking up the shipping question and endeavouring to place it in a better position.

Hon. J. A. Hanan (Liberal, *Invercargill*) said they had heard from a number of hon. gentlemen representing farming districts how strongly they favoured the principle of State ownership, or State interference with private enterprise. It was suggested that the State should assist the farmers to purchase and own ships. He was one of those who believed that the ultimate result would be that they would have Empire owned ships, just as they had Empire-owned cables and an Empire-owned Navy. He hoped that the Prime Minister would advocate at the next Imperial Conference an Imperial owned shipping service. It was for the Governments of the Empire to smash the shipping combines, otherwise the workers of the world would take the question up and endeavour to destroy the monopoly.

Mr. H. E. Holland (Labour, *Buller*) objected to the general note that had been struck by a certain section of the House with respect to shipping. They admitted the exploitation that was going on, but they were not prepared to say that the people of New Zealand should own the shipping.

The debate was then adjourned.

CUSTOMS TARIFF REVISION.

On 1st November, 1920,

Mr. R. McCallum (Liberal, *Wairau*) asked the Minister of Customs if he would, before preparing his Bill for revising the tariff, to be brought before Parliament next Session, allow an advisory committee from the British Agents' Association to place its views before the Government : such committee to undertake (1) that its suggestions would have the effect of substantially protecting the consumer from exploitation, and (2) that the effect of such suggestions would not be in the direction of reducing the amount of customs revenue required by the Minister of Finance.

The Minister of Customs and Labour (Hon. Sir W. H. Herries) replied that he would be very glad to put the views of the hon. member before the Cabinet, which would, directly after the Session, go into the whole question as to what was to be done with regard to the revision of the tariff.

INDUSTRIAL CONCILIATION AND ARBITRATION BILL.

(Question of One Big Union.)

The above was a private member's Bill introduced by Mr. M. J. Savage, Labour member for Auckland, West, the main object of the measure being to enable any Union to be registered for the whole of the Dominion in respect of any trade, with branches of such union in the several " Industrial Districts " prescribed by the Industrial Conciliation and Arbitration Act, instead of independent unions in each of such districts, as provided by the Act.

The Bill passed its Second Reading in the House of Representatives and was then referred to the Labour Bills Committee, which struck out the main proposal. The Bill was eventually referred back to the Committee, but did not reach a further stage, and was included among the list of Bills dropped at the close of the Session.

The Bill proposed (*inter alia*) to amend Section 7* of the Industrial Conciliation and Arbitration Act, 1908, by adding to it the following sub-clause : —

" (3) Notwithstanding anything contained in sub-section two of this section, it shall be competent for any union, trade or calling to register a union which shall cover the whole of New Zealand in so far as that industry, calling, or trade is concerned, and each union of the said industry, calling, or trade in the various industrial districts shall be branches of the aforesaid union."

DEBATE IN HOUSE OF REPRESENTATIVES.

The One Big Union.

On 15th July, 1920,

Mr. M. J. Savage (**Labour,** *Auckland West*), in moving th Second Reading, said, in regard to Clause 2 of the Bill, tha as the law stood that day provision was simply made for th formation of unions in the various districts, but the ide underlying the Bill was to keep pace with industrial develop ment, and to provide for the formation of Dominion Union

He moved that the Bill be read a second time, and referred to the Labour Bills Committee.

The Minister of Labour (**Hon. Sir William Herries**) sa that he was glad the hon. gentleman intended to have th Bill referred to the Labour Bills Committee, as otherwi he should have had to oppose it. The Government wou oppose in every way anything in the nature of the formati of what was known as " one big union " or combination

---

* Section 7 reads as follows :—

" 7. (1) Every society registered as an industrial union sh as from the date of registration, but solely for the purposes of t Act, become a body corporate by the registered name, have perpet succession and a common seal, until the registration is cancel as hereinafter provided.

" (2) There shall be inserted in the registered name of ev industrial union the word ' employers ' or ' workers ' according such union is a union of employers or workers, and also (except the case of an incorporated company) the name of the industry connection with which it is formed, and the locality in which majority of its members reside or exercise their calling as th : ' The (Christchurch Grocers') Industrial Union of Employer ; ' The (Wellington Tramdrivers') Industrial Union of Workers.'

unions. The Government were not going to have any outside body telling them what they were to do under threat of direct action. They were not opposed to unions combining in order to procure advantages for members of their own particular trade, but they did object to their going outside the province of their particular trade and attempting to dictate to the Government as to what was to be done in questions of general policy.

Mr. P. Fraser (**Labour,** *Wellington Central*) said there was no question of "one big union." It was simply a provision to make it easy and convenient for the scattered members of an industry to have one organisation, to get one award, and meet their common employer before the Conciliation Council and Arbitration Court. For instance, they had the Union Steamship Company operating right throughout New Zealand, and the seamen felt that they would be in a better position than they were at that time if they could go to the Court with, as it were, the one employer and the one body of employees.

Mr. D. Jones (**Reform,** *Kaiapoi*): "You can get a Dominion award now."

Mr. P. Fraser: "Yes; but that is not so easily worked, or so acceptable to the men as this method would be. It is really a machinery proposal. As far as the "one big union" is concerned, this is an age of trusts, combines, and employers' federations; and it seems to me that any attempt to keep the workers from looking after their own interests and consolidating their organisations would be like Mrs. Partington's attempt to sweep back the waves of the sea."

Mr. J. P. Luke (**Reform,** *Wellington North*) said he had had an experience of dealing with "one big union," namely, the tramway men of the Dominion, a case in which it was thought a settlement would be easy, and that the employees would have had a common object in the proposal they put before the other side. Most of the tramways were publicly owned and an honest endeavour had been made by the conference to bring about a condition of things that would apply to the different tramway authorities throughout the country. After spending days and days in trying to attain that object the whole thing broke down, and he was not at all convinced that what the hon. member was contending for that day would be so beneficial to labour and the country as he anticipated. It was found impossible to bring about a settlement, largely because of the varying conditions as to rent and cost of living in the different parts of the Dominion.

It was very specious pleading to say there was no intention to hold up any industry. Whether the union were "one big union" or not, it was a proposal that, badly used, could

strangle the industries of the Dominion, and they must be
very careful in dealing with the matter.

Mr. W. A. Veitch (Independent Labour, *Wanganui*) said
that if the watersiders, for example, or the coalminers, or
the seamen, or any other body of men employed in one great
industry, desired to form themselves into one union in order
to facilitate their work and to economise in carrying it out,
it seemed to him a sound principle that they should have
power under the law to do so. After all, the question of
" one big union " which was now in the air in certain directions
and which might involve some danger, was outside the Bill.
That " one big union " might to some extent almost entirely
usurp the functions of the general Government; and he,
for one, would never stand for that principle.

Mr. D. G. Sullivan (Labour, *Avon*) said the attitude which
the Minister of Labour was adopting was the right way to
help the consolidation of the unions into " one big union," because
if unions desired closer unity and were unable to get registration under the Conciliation and Arbitration Act, the natural
course for them to pursue was to register under some other
Act, such as the Trade Unions Act.

Mr. E. J. Howard (Labour, *Christchurch South*) replying
to the speeches of the Minister of Labour and Mr. Luke, said
that if there was one Act upon the statute book that had
driven workers in the direction their hon. friends disliked
it was the Arbitration Act. Ever since the 1908 Act the
Trades Councils of the Dominion had been registered under
the Industrial Conciliation and Arbitration Act, but it had
been suddenly discovered that there was no provision for their
registration. The consequence was that the Trades and
Labour Councils which had done good work and held the
workers together, were then declared illegal organisations
and the unions were driven to some other form of organisation.
They could not register under the Trade Unions Act, and
they had no other course open but to get together as they
were doing at that time; so that their exclusion from the
benefit of the Industrial Conciliation and Arbitration Act
was doing the very thing the Minister deplored.

Mr. Savage, in his reply, said the Arbitration Act had
got to be amended to meet altered conditions, or got out of
the way. If the law was not made to meet the requirements
of those employed in industry, the unions were simply going
to cancel their registration in order to get full unity outside
the Act.

The Bill was then read a second time.

On the 8th September
Mr. Luke brought up the report of the Labour Bills Com-

mittee recommending that the Bill be allowed to proceed as amended, namely, with the " one big union " clause struck out, and other amendments.

The debate, having been interrupted, was resumed on 21st September, when

Mr. Howard moved as an amendment that the Bill be referred back to the Committee for further consideration, saying that he did so as a protest against the report.

The Minister of Labour said that he had no objection to the Bill going back to the Committee, but he could not say when the Committee could deal with it.

Mr. Howard : " I only moved that it be referred back by way of protest."

Mr. Fraser : " We want it killed right out."

Mr. Howard's amendment was eventually agreed to, eight Labour members taking part in the debate, and five others, including the Minister of Labour.

INDUSTRIAL CONCILIATION AND ARBITRATION AMENDMENT ACT.

(Status of Guilds under the Act: Amendment of Awards, etc.)

The Bill (No. 2) for the above Act was introduced into the House of Representatives by the Minister of Labour on 2nd November, 1920, within 10 days of the close of the session. Its object, as the Minister explained, was to benefit Guilds so as to give them a status under the Arbitration Act.

The Bill was strenuously opposed by the Labour Party and was considerably amended during its passage, one of the most important clauses (clause 4)* being withdrawn, whilst another clause (clause 3, which became section 2 of the Act)

---

* Clause 4 was introduced as an amendment to Section 11 of the Industrial Conciliation and Arbitration Act, 1908 (Section 11 is quoted in Mr. Sullivan's speech *vide* page 420) by adding the following proviso :—

" Provided that if there is only one registered industrial union in the same locality or industrial district connected with the same industry or related industries to which the members of the union applying for registration might, in the opinion of the Registrar, conveniently belong, the Registrar shall not have power to refuse registration on that ground in any case where the members of the union applying for registration have at a meeting called in accordance with the rules of such applicant union resolved that they do not desire to join that existing registered union."

was materially amended.   A new clause (clause 10 of the Bill, which became section 8 of the Act) was added in Committee, dealing with the powers of the Arbitration Court to amend awards given to the Court under the War Legislation and Statute Law Amendment Act, 1918.*

The Labour Party attacked this clause vigorously, but it was carried by 36 votes against 13, the Liberals voting with the Labour members for its rejection.

The Act received the Governor-General's assent on 11th November, 1921.

Section 2 of the Act provides as follows :—

2. In any proceeding before a Council or the Court relating to any industry, any organisation of employers, or any organisation of workers consisting of not less than fifteen members, connected with that industry in the locality to which the proceeding relates shall be entitled to appear and be heard in every respect as if they were parties to such proceeding if in the opinion of the Commissioner where such proceeding is before a Council, or of the Court where such proceeding is before the Court, such organisation employers or workers, or the members thereof. may in any manner be affected by any result of such proceeding. †

Section 7 provides that the salaries of the members of the Arbitration Court (Assessors) representing the employers and the workers respectively, shall be increased from £500 per annum to £750, plus allowance. Section 8 amends Section 18 of the War Legislation and Statute Law

---

* The following is an extract from the New Zealand Official Year Book, 1919, in regard to the matter :—

During last Session an important amendment of the Industrial Conciliation and Arbitration Act was passed—and included in the War Legislation and Statute Law Amendment Act—providing that on an application being made, the Arbitration Court should have power to amend any award or industrial agreement in regard to wages or hours to meet any alteration in the conditions of employment or the cost of living that may have taken place since the award or agreement was made. This legislation came into operation on the 10th December last, and between that date and the 31st March, 1919, a large number of applications have already been made to the Court. In seventeen instances the Court has made amendments in accordance with the provision referred to. A considerable number has also been made since the 31st March.

† Clause 3, before amendment, read as follows :—

In any proceeding before a Council or the Court relating to any industry, any employer or worker, or society of employer or workers, concerned or engaged in that industry shall be entitled to appear and be heard in every respect as if he or they were party or parties to such proceeding, if in the opinion of the Commissioner, where such proceeding is before a Council, or of the Court, where such proceeding is before the Court, such employer or worker or society of employers or workers, may in any manner be affected by any result of such proceeding.

Amendment Act, 1918, by repealing subsections three and four thereof, and substituting the following subsection :—

(3) The powers conferred on the Court by this section are discretionary, and may be exercised only if the Court, after taking into consideration any alteration since the date of the award or agreement in the conditions affecting the industry or industries to which such award or agreement relates and any increase or decrease since the date of the award or agreement in the cost of living affecting the workers or any class of workers engaged in any such industry or industries, and all other relevant considerations, is satisfied :—

(A) That it is just and equitable to the employers and the workers in such industry or industries that the award should be amended ; and

(B) That the economic continuance of such industry or industries will not be duly imperilled by the effect of any such amendment upon the cost of production :

Provided, however, that any award or agreement made under this clause shall provide for a fair living wage for the workers engaged in the industry or industries concerned.

The Act contains some other minor and consequential amendments.

DEBATE IN HOUSE OF REPRESENTATIVES.

On 3rd November, 1920,

Mr. J. P. Luke (Reform, *Wellington North*) brought up the report of the Labour Bills Committee, which recommended that the Bill be allowed to proceed without amendments. He moved : " That the report do lie on the table."

Mr. D. G. Sullivan (Labour, *Avon*) said he recognised that there were possibly one or two good features in the Bill, but it also contained some features which were very objectionable to the trade-union movement of the Dominion. It affected every trade-unionist in the country, and all their employers, and it affected also the unorganised workers and the unorganised employers. The Bill came down at such a late stage of the Session that it was almost impossible that it should be given the consideration it deserved. The principal objections he had to it related to clauses 3 and 4.

A "Yellow Union."

The effect of clause 3 was to allow people not parties to the dispute, and who were not even intimately affected, but who might be able to show that they were in some way concerned, to appear before the Conciliation Council or the Arbitration Court, and with the consent of the Commissioner or Judge place their view before the tribunal. Had such a

clause been embodied in the legislation in the early days, it
would have been possible to prevent almost any trade-union
from getting any award from the Court. He thought he
could see why that clause had been inserted in the Bill. It
seemed to him to have resulted from the recent proceedings in
Christchurch, where the clerks had made an attempt, and had
succeeded, in securing an award of the Court. A number of
the clerks, dissatisfied with the bad conditions under which
many of them were working, formed a union in the face of
great hostility and presented their case to the Conciliation
Council and subsequently to the Arbitration Court. When
the case came before the Conciliation Council, a number of
the clerks, under the inspiration of the employers, formed a
guild, or what was known in Europe as a "yellow union,"
went before the Conciliation Council and attempted to get a
hearing, with the definite object of resisting the claims of the
clerks' union, and so preventing an award being made for the
union. But under the existing legislation it was not possible
to allow the guild to be heard. Exactly the same thing took
place subsequently before the Arbitration Court. He wanted
the House to realise what the position was going to be if
people who were not parties to the dispute were allowed to
appear before the Court and take part in the proceedings.
It was quite possible under the terms of the Bill to have
disgruntled members of a union taking action on account of
some trivial dispute they had had with other members of the
union. If, for that reason, they had broken away from the
union, they might seek to go before the Court as a body
opposed to the union and state a case in opposition to the
union. He trusted, therefore, that the Minister would see
his way to withdraw clause 3 from the Bill. It was a very
wide clause. Owing to the use of the word "concerned," it
would be possible for all kinds of organisations to come in
and take part in proceedings before the Council or the Court.

Mr. Sullivan then proceeded to deal with clause 4 of the
Bill, which proposed to amend section 11 of the Industrial
Conciliation and Arbitration Act, 1908. He said section 11
read : —

"In order to prevent the needless multiplication of
industrial unions connected with the same industry in
the same locality or industrial district, the following
special provisions shall apply."

The House would observe the direction and force of these
words. If the clause (clause 4) became law it would enable
the registration of any number of unions in the same industry
in the same locality.

An Hon. Member : "Only two."

Mr. Sullivan said that even supposing that it were only two, the House should realise how unfair the clause was ; it did not state merely that in the event of a number of men being unable to join an existing union, or if there were just reasons why they should not join one, they should have the right to form a new one. But it actually provided they could resolve that they did not desire to join the existing registered union ; and the Registrar in the terms of the clause was then definitely compelled to grant the registration. The whole effect of the clause was to strike a blow at the very root of trade-unionism in New Zealand by enabling the registration of black-leg unions. The Bill contained one or two good clauses, but those to which he had referred were trade-union-wrecking provisions. If the Minister insisted upon them he would do more than had ever been done in that country to wreck the Conciliation and Arbitration Act, and engender such a spirit of discontent and of dissatisfaction with the Arbitration Act that unions throughout New Zealand would withdraw from registration and take other measures. He would not accuse the Minister of having deliberately struck a blow at trade-unionism, but that was the effect of the clauses.

The Minister of Labour (Hon. Sir W. H. Herries) did not want to prolong the debate, but he thought the members of the Committee would do him the justice of endorsing the fact that he was quite prepared to drop clause 4 in Committee. Therefore all the talk on that clause was mere waste of time.

Mr. H. E. Holland (Labour, *Buller*) : " Are you prepared to drop it now, unconditionally ? "

The Minister of Labour replied in the affirmative ; when the Bill went into Committee of the House. But he wanted clause 3 for certain reasons he would be glad to explain to the hon. gentleman, as he had already done to the members of the Select Committee.

Mr. J. McCombs (Labour, *Lyttelton*) said that the Minister, in response to representations made to him, had agreed to withdraw clause 4, which provided for the registration of workers' societies and organisations other than the recognised trade-unions, which had been formed under the Industrial Conciliation and Arbitration Act, for which purpose it was necessary to amend a provision that had been in the law since its inception. The offer of the Minister of Labour to withdraw clause 4, provided that clause 3 was gone on with, was a very innocent one. Clause 3 provided that any society of workers, or anybody who thought they were interested in the proceedings of the Court, or thought they might be affected thereby, could come into the Court and be heard as parties to the dispute, even if they were not parties to it, but rank outsiders. That was simply an attempt to provide facilities for the obstruction of the Arbitration Court procedure. They were actually creating machinery for a counter organisation, the sole object of which would be not to secure the settlement of industrial disputes by means of Arbitration Court awards, but to prevent awards being made. Only a Government and a Minister that were absolutely hostile to the workers and the principle of arbitration could be guilty of fathering the Bill before the House. The Minister would willingly remove clause 4 from the Bill, because, instead of allowing a second union or guild to be recognised, the union, without registration and without responsibility, could go before the Court and be heard. The Minister's proposal to drop clause 4 did not meet the position at all. It would not be met unless he were prepared to drop clause 3.

Defects of Arbitration Courts.

Mr. T. M. Wilford (Leader of the Opposition) said that it had been admitted that the Arbitration Court had in many ways failed, and he believed that the failure was largely due to the fact that there were two permanent assessors in the Court. It was impossible for anyone to be master of all trades, and it was partly on account of the constitution of the Court that so much dissatisfaction had arisen in the labour unions of that country. He had been told that there were many questions that cropped up before the Court which were so technical in their nature that the assessors, who ought to be advisers to the judge, and skilled in all the ramifications of the various disputes, were unable to assist at all. He would wipe out the permanent assessors, and would run the Arbitration Courts on the simple procedure of the Conciliation Court, except that he would remove the Conciliation Commissioner and put the Arbitration Court in the position where the Conciliation Commissioner had been when an appeal took place from the Conciliation Commissioner's finding. He would also have on the Arbitration Court two men skilled in the industry in which the dispute arose, one on behalf of the employer and one on behalf of the employee, sitting with the Arbitration Court Judge. He would have four Conciliation Commissioners for the whole of New Zealand, each trained to become an expert in a particular industry. He was quite satisfied that the industrial trouble in the country was caused by the fact that in 80 per cent. of the cases the Arbitration Court did not understand all the details of the disputes submitted for decision.

The debate having been interrupted, was resumed on the 8th November.

Mr. M. J. Savage (Labour, *Auckland West***)** said that clause 4 meant the wrecking of unionism by the formation of a lot of sections in an industry, with endless confusion and a whole lot of different demands appearing before a Conciliation Council or Arbitration Court. The Minister had agreed to drop that; but he (Mr. Savage) would point out that the difference was very small between that and the insisting upon clause 3, which would give one man or any number of men, whether they be organised or otherwise, the right to appear before a Conciliation Council with demands that might be opposed to the organised workers in a given industry. The Minister had missed with the first barrel and was putting in the second with the same effect. Where a union came forward with definite demands deliberately decided on, and found they were in conflict with a number of people—a small section—who might or might not be there at the instigation of the employers, prepared to argue in an opposite direction, it must be quite plain that there must be endless confusion. If they observed what was going on in the older countries they would find the various Governments recognising that the present-day industrial conditions were different from what they were a year or two ago, and the Governments in question were moving accordingly. Even in the Commonwealth of Australia they were moving in the direction of having local Councils, national Councils, and in a bigger way generally. In New Zealand they were going backwards apparently, with no suggestion from the Government towards bringing about a bigger and higher conception as to the industrial position. Any Conciliation Commissioner in the Dominion, if asked for his personal opinion, would be found unfavourable to the clause. The Commissioners were nearly driven out of their minds now, and this would be about the last straw. It would be absolutely impossible in a Conciliation Council to come to any decision whatever. Instead of developing the principle of conciliation the Bill would destroy it. Whatever chance there was in front of an Arbitration Court, where there were three individuals, but really one ruling, there would be absolutely none in a Conciliation Council. The clause was going to kill the Conciliation Councils as dead as a wheelbarrow. As to clause 4, it was still in the Bill, and it remained to be seen whether it was going to be withdrawn or not. He did not know that the Minister had given a definite promise or not.

The Minister of Labour : " Yes, I have."

Mr. Savage said he would like to know, then, whether the Minister would turn clause 3 into something better than it was.

The Minister of Labour : " Yes, I will amend it."

Mr. E. J. Howard (Labour, *Christchurch South*) said that clause 3 was one of the most cowardly things ever proposed

N

against Labour. It was calculated to favour the employ
of the Dominion, but it would cost them thousands u[
thousands of pounds if the Government put it on the Stat
Book. Without doubt, Labour would accept the challen
If the Government broke their side of the agreement, tl
they should not charge trades unionism if it accepted
challenge, and broke its side, and said, " Take your Arbitrat
Act, we will organise some other way."

The Hon. J. A. Hanan (Liberal, *Invercargill*) said
main reason for criticising the clause (clause 3) was beca
if a worker, an individual, was encouraged to appear " on
own " in the Court there would arise great complaints.
hoped they would not go back on the principle of collect
bargaining and organised representation on the part of ;
workers before the Court. If the clause went through
brought down, it would incite and inflame moderate Lab[
and sane trade-unionists. They had been getting along fai
well that Session, and now the Government proposed to [
through a clause that would make for industrial unrest.

Mr. E. Kellett (Independent Labour, *Dunedin North*) s;
they had been told that evening by some of the members
the extreme section of the Labour Party what they w[
prepared to do ; and he would tell members from the moder[
side of Labour that thousands of unionists not connect
with the extreme organisation looked upon this propo[
with dismay. The members on his left would tell the Ho[
quite frankly that they did not believe in arbitratio[
that they believed in another method. What the Gove[
ment had to decide was whether they were prepared to pl[
the section that he represented in the position that the Arbi[
tion Act was of no use owing to the clause that had b[
proposed ; whether the clause was to be pressed on—a cla[
which the member for Christchurch South said they w[
prepared to fight the Government on. That was what
Government and the House had to consider.

Mr. P. Fraser (Labour, *Wellington Central*) opposed
Bill, and moved as an amendment to the motion before
House, that the report be referred back to the Labour
Committee.

Mr. H. E. Holland (Labour, *Buller*), in seconding
amendment, said it was now proposed to give a number of
who held themselves too superior to the average work[
people to come into a trade union, a measure of the [
recognition before the Court as the properly organised un[
had. The people it was proposed to do this for were [
who were mostly used in times of industrial trouble t[
to smash the unions. When the workers were on st[
1891, where did the authorities rush to for their s[

constables ? Both in Australia and in New Zealand they invaded the banks to get the bank clerks, and the shops to get the shop assistants. That was in the early "nineties." The shop assistants had awakened, however, and were now organised along with the rest of the workers. The bank clerks were also beginning to awaken, and there were to be found here and there among them fearless-minded men who were prepared to stand up for living-conditions in the work which they were doing; but the bulk of the men engaged in the banks were not prepared to recognise that they were working men, and they thought themselves superior to the other workers, and wanted guilds insteads of unions. There was already a clerks' union; let the bank clerks get into those unions; there was no reason why they should form guilds; if they enrolled in the industrial unions he would venture to say that every man on the Labour benches could safely promise them the assistance of all the industrial organisations of the country. But they found that some sinister influence was at work with the bank clerks, and here was a movement to organise them into guilds, and so to bind them to their employers and use them to undermine the industrial position of the working classes. In conclusion, he wished to say that the Government could carry the measure into law through the force of their majority, but when they had carried it into law they would not be able to carry it into effect.

The Minister of Labour said he had given away quite enough in giving up clause 4, which he had already indicated he would drop, as he was afraid it would be taken advantage of not by the guilds, but by the labour organisations. It looked like a boomerang clause to him, and wanted very careful consideration. He had told them frankly that the Bill was to benefit the guilds, and it had been done on the recommendation of Judge Stringer*, who had said he thought the guilds ought to have a standing in the Arbitration Court; they were apparently increasing, and doing good work. Some members might say, " Why do they not register under the Arbitration Act ? " But it seemed to him if they did not wish to register—if they had come to some agreement with their employers which was perfectly satisfactory to them and the employers—he did not see why Parliament should force them to come under the Arbitration Act. The Minister then read the clause as he proposed to amend it.

Mr. Holland : " That would let fifteen men form a bogus union."

---

* His Honour Judge Stringer was until recently the judge of the Arbitration Court in New Zealand.

The Minister of Labour said that was the same number that could form an ordinary union. Clause 4 had allowed a second union to be formed under the Arbitration Act. That was the difference. Clause 3 did not register them; it only gave them the status to appear in the Court to object to an award. It did not give them the power to be granted an award, and they did not ask that, because they had made their award already by agreement with their employers. All he had given them was the power to come and give evidence and point out how they would be injured if that award was given to another union that was contrary to the agreement they had made with their own employers, and therefore asked to be kept out of the other union. Was there anything fairer than that? He had struck out the provision regarding individuals; some hon. members had objected to it, and he had endeavoured to meet them. He thought the guilds ought to have some recognition. When there were, say, one hundred or two hundred men in a guild, was it right for fifteen disgruntled people to form a union and then compel the others to adopt their award? This provision was to ensure that this should not be done. That was the explanation of clause 3, and he felt bound in honour to put it through. It was not going to affect the real unions in any way, but would prevent what the guilds called " bogus unions " from blocking them. The clause was not worded in quite the way the guilds wanted it, because he had told their representatives that to word the clause as they desired might result in defeating their object. They might be turned inside out, and might find the unions taking up their position, and they would then be left out in the cold.

In reply to an interjection by Mr. P. Fraser : " Why not make provision for a guild to be registered as a union " Sir W. Herries said that they could always register as a union but did not wish to. They were a fairly strong body of men. That was the explanation of the clause, and there was no sinister motive behind it. He did not wish to destroy the Arbitration Court ; he thought, with other members, that the Act would have to be amended, and he was not sure that the constitution of the Court would not have to be altered. He was inclined to favour the idea, of which some hon. members had spoken, that the assessors in a dispute should be taken from the industry into which investigation was being made.

Mr. McCombs : " There is very little in that. Only some one who knows nothing about it would suggest that."

The Minister of Labour said that he had heard people who professed to know a great deal about the matter make the suggestion.

Mr. Kellett : " I made the suggestion, and I know a great deal more about it than the hon. member for Lyttelton."

The Minister of Labour said that in any case he was not prepared to alter the whole constitution of the Arbitration Court that Session. He thought the clause should be passed by the House.

Mr. Sullivan, in replying to the remarks of the Minister of Labour in reference to guilds, said that the idea of forming these guilds had sprung not from the minds of the clerks, but from the minds of the employers as a counterblast to the formation of the Clerks' Union. The formation of these guilds would have the effect of creating the utmost bitterness in the minds of the majority of the trade unionists, and when they found themselves in the Court, compelled to fight their own fellow-workers—employees who had been taken hold of by the employers, and were being used as tools—the trade-unionists would feel the utmost bitterness, which was bound to express itself in some way or other. If the Government persisted in regarding the warnings it had received from the Labour benches purely as party propaganda, using its majority to overwhelm them, it was running upon industrial disaster.

Mr. V. H. Potter (Reform, *Roskill*) supported clause 3 of the Bill. He thought it in the interests of the workers that guilds should be permitted to register. The Bank Officers' Guild was composed of over 70 per cent. of the workers in the banks of the Dominion. They had met the bank-managers and had come to an amicable agreement, satisfactory to both sides. What was it that the extreme Labour Party demanded ? The real reason was that the extremists wanted to have all workers under their control. He attached no importance to the prophecies of the members of the Labour Party about the catastrophies that would come upon Labour if the clause were passed. The truth of the matter was that the extreme Labour section had just about killed itself, and in industrial trouble it would be proved that the majority of the workers were opposed to the unions as they were that day.

After pointing out that one of the principles of the Bank Guild was that all promotions should be made on merit only, and not on length of service, and that the whole object of the Guild was efficiency, Mr. Potter said he hoped the Minister would put clause 3 through in defiance of insinuations and threats.

Mr. Fraser's amendment was negatived by 40 votes against 18, and the motion for the committal of the Bill was then taken, when

The Minister of Labour said that if the House would agree to the committal of the Bill he would be prepared to report progress after the short title had been passed. His

reason for this was that there would be further amendme
brought down. These were not connected with the Bill
it stood.

The Bill was committed and progress reported.

On the 9th November, in Committee,

Clause 3 (Section 2 of the Act) was amended as mentior
on page 418 *ante*, and clause 10 (Section 8 of the Act) was add

The debate on the Third Reading was then taken, wl

Mr. McCombs, speaking in reference to clause 10 of '
Bill, said that while the Government had failed to redi
the cost of living in the Dominion, it now came forwi
with a proposal to keep down the cost of living, and its o
proposal for keeping down the cost of living was to redi
wages. The Prime Minister had talked largely about
prospect of breaking the vicious circle and preventing
cost of living from soaring higher. But the Governm
Statistician did not say so; he told them that the te
increase was 72·80 per cent. since the declaration of War
years ago.

The Prime Minister (the Right Hon. W. F. Massey), in rep
ing to Mr. McCombs, said that the cost of living that day v
much lower in New Zealand than in any other part of
world. Speaking with reference to clause 10 of the Bill,
said that when the clause, which had been amended on
motion that night, was passed as a section of the Act of 19
it was then intended to give discretionary power to
Arbitration Court (to amend awards); but, unfortunate
the interpretation of the Court differed from that of the
draftsman. He asked the House to give the discret
intended to be given in 1918. Up to a certain point he
not think the increases in wages affected the cost of liv
very seriously; but he did think that if they went or
they had been doing, in a very short time they would find s
of their important industries closing down, because the
creasing cost of production made it impossible for then
compete with other countries. Something was necessar
be done, and they were doing it. When members talked al
reducing the wages, they were talking nonsense. There
no one more anxious than he was, and also his colleagues
see the worker properly paid.

The Third Reading was carried by 38 votes against

IN THE LEGISLATIVE COUNCIL.

The Bill passed through all stages on 10th Novemb

MARRIAGE AMENDMENT ACT.

Women Registrars: Divorces to be entered on Marriage Register: "*Ne temere* Decree.")

The Bill for the above Act as originally introduced into the House of Representatives by the Government on 1st June, 1920, dealt with the appointment of women as Registrars of Marriages ; it provided also for the entry on the Marriage Register of dissolutions of marriages, and for the appointment of Officers of the Salvation Army as Officiating Ministers under the Act. The Bill having been referred to the Statutes Revision Committee by the Legislative Council, as the result of certain evidence taken in relation to the attitude of the Roman Catholic Church under the " *Ne temere* Decree," the Council brought in amendments which, with slight modification, were eventually incorporated in the Act.

In the meantime, before the Bill had been finally dealt with, a second Bill was introduced into the Legislative Council by the Hon. W. C. MacGregor,* whereby it was proposed to exclude from the list of Officiating Ministers under the Marriage Act any bishop, priest, etc., of the Roman Catholic

---

* The Bill introduced by Mr. MacGregor contained the following provisions :—

2. (1) It shall not be lawful for the Registrar-General to enter in the list of Officiating Ministers the name of—

(A) Any bishop, priest, or minister of the Roman Catholic church so long as a certain decree known as the " *Ne temere* Decree," or a decree or canon of the Council of Trent referred to therein, or sections 1060, 1061 and 1062 of the " Codex Juris Canonici," or any of them, continue in force in the Dominion of New Zealand :

(B) Any bishop, priest, or minister of any church, which, by any articles of religion, confession of faith, decree, edict, encyclical, canon, bull, creed, catechism, or otherwise, denies or questions, either directly or by implication, the validity, in any sense whatsoever, of marriages solemnised in accordance with the provisions of the principal Act :

(c) Any bishop, priest, or minister who, on any ground not recognised by law, has an objection to officiating in the solemnisation of marriage between any particular persons.

(2) It shall be lawful for the Governor-General, by Order in Council, to declare any Church to be such a Church as is described in paragraph (B) of subsection one hereof.

(3) It shall be lawful for the Governor-General to make regulations requiring every person who certifies the name of any minister under the provisions of . . . the principal Act to certify whether such minister comes within the provisions of paragraph (c) of subsection one hereof.

Church so long as the " *Ne temere* Decree " continued in force.
This second Bill was, on 20th October, discharged from the
Order Paper on Mr. MacGregor's own motion after he had
explained the circumstances which led him to bring the Bill
forward.

The following are the principal provisions of the Act as passed,
Section 7 being quoted *in extenso* :—

Women may be appointed to act as Registrars of Marriages
(Section 2).

On the issue of a decree absolute under the Divorce and
Matrimonial Causes Act, 1908, for the dissolution of a marriage
a notice of such dissolution is to be entered in the Marriage Register
(Section 3).

Officers of the Salvation Army may be appointed Officiating
Ministers under the Marriage Act (Section 6).

Amendment (by the Legislative Council) :—

7. (1) Every person commits an offence against this Act
and is liable on summary conviction* to a fine of one hundred
pounds, who—

(A) Alleges, expressly or by implication, that any person
lawfully married are not truly and sufficiently married ;

(B) Alleges, expressly or by implication, that the issue
of any lawful marriage is illegitimate or born out of true wedlock.

(2) " Alleges " in this section means making any verbal
statement, or publishing or issuing any printed or written statement, or in any manner authorising the making of any verbal statement, or in any manner authorising or being party to the publication
or issue of any printed or written statement.

(3) A person shall not be deemed to make an allegation
contrary to the provisions of this section by reason only of using
in the solemnisation of a marriage a form of marriage service which
at the commencement of this Act was in use by the religious
denomination to which such person belongs, or by reason only of
the printing or issue of any book containing a copy of a form of
marriage service in use at the commencement of this Act by any
religious denomination.

DEBATE IN LEGISLATIVE COUNCIL.

On 30th July, 1920,

The Hon. Oliver Samuel, having presented the report
of the Statutes Revision Committee, and having moved that
the same be laid on the table,

---

* Section 7 of the Act as originally introduced began as follows :
" Every person commits an offence against this Act and is liable on
summary conviction to *imprisonment for one year, or* a fine of," etc but
the words in italics were disagreed to by the House of Representatives
and this amendment was eventually accepted by the Legislative Council.

The **Attorney-General (Hon. Sir Francis Bell)** moved
as an amendment that the report be referred back to the
Committee for further consideration, and said that he did
so at the request of the Statutes Revision Committee. He
explained that certain persons who desired to make representations on matters not dealt with in the Bill as introduced had asked to be heard, and in another place it had been
suggested that such an opportunity should be given them
before the Statutes Revision Committee of the Council.
The Committee had heard the evidence of one side only,
and the object in reporting back to the Committee for further
consideration was that it might become publicly known
that the Committee was prepared to hear evidence on the
point he was about to refer to, and that the Committee
intended, unless such evidence contravened that put before
the Committee, to propose certain legislation on the subject.
The Committee did not assume for a moment that the evidence
so far received correctly stated the position. That evidence
showed that one denomination in that country publicly
declared by documents officially issued that marriages contracted according to the law of the land were not valid marriages. That alone might perhaps not be considered sufficient
at that time to call for the intervention of the Legislature,
though the documents produced before them, on their face,
showed that the declaration and the publication that the
marriages were invalid, were not limited to an invalidity
arising out of a mere denominational question. But the other
question was of more importance. The denomination to
which he was referring treated a marriage celebrated according
to the law of that land, but not celebrated by the priests
of the denomination, as invalid, and declared the parties
to such marriage to be living in concubinage, and required
them, in accordance with the provisions of the religious
code, to be married again by a priest of the denomination —
required them under certain religious denunciations with which
no one proposed to interfere. But the effect was that the
remarriage, or whatever they liked to call it, was carried out
and celebrated according, as far as appearances went, to the
law of that land. The marriage register of the clergyman
of every denomination was an official document required to be
kept, and was a register to which reference might be made,
and the record of the marriage entered in the Registrar-
General's register was derived from a certified copy of the
marriage register. There was evidence before the Committee
that in cases where parties had been married for years, and a
second marriage or ceremony took place — children having
been born in the meantime — the parties to the marriage
were described as bachelor and spinster; and upon an official

record it would appear by inference that the children of that union, born in lawful wedlock, were bastards. They had had evidence before them—they had had copies of the certificates of a New Zealand marriage and of a marriage in an Australian colony, and in the second certificate those people, after years of marriage, were described as bachelor and spinster, though children had been born of the first marriage. If it were found that on the marriage register of any denomination the children of an existing marriage lawfully celebrated were bastardised, whether directly or by inference, then it lay on the Legislature to see that that state of things should not continue.

The amendment was agreed to, and the Bill referred back to the Statutes Revision Committee.

The Bill passed its Third Reading in the Legislative Council on 9th September, 1920.

DEBATE IN HOUSE OF REPRESENTATIVES.

On the 28th October,

Mr. W. Downie Stewart (Reform, *Dunedin West*), in bringing up the report of the Bills Committee recommending that the amendments made by the Legislative Council (with the exception of the words already mentioned in the footnote to page 430 *ante*) be agreed to, said that one of the clauses was merely a minor amendment, but that the other clause— which was more controversial—was Clause 6* which made it a penal offence to allege, regarding marriages of persons legally married, that they were not truly and sufficiently married. Hon. members would remember that when the Bill went from there to another place it made some amendments in their marriage law which were not of a controversial nature. But while it was before the Statutes Revision Committee of another place certain evidence had been put forward on the very thorny question of the doctrine and practice of a certain Church as to the validity of certain marriages; and in consequence Clause 6 was inserted in another place.

After referring in detail to the religious controversy that had arisen in regard to the Bill and to the circumstance which had led the Committee to allow Clause 6 to stand merely cutting out the provision for imprisonment as one of the penalties imposed by the clause, Mr. Downie Stewart quoted the opinion of the Solicitor-General on Clause 6, as follows :—

---

* Clause 6 of the Bill became Section 7 of the Act as passed.

If the new Clause becomes law in its present form, the Roman Catholic Church will still be at liberty to promulgate its doctrine that the marriage of a Catholic celebrated otherwise than before a priest of the Catholic Church is not a sacrament. But that Church will be debarred from promulgating declarations that a sacramental celebration is essential to the validity of a marriage, or that marriages entered into without such a sacramental celebration are in any respect invalid as marriages ; and will be also debarred from alleging that persons so married are living together in adultery, or that their issue is illegitimate. In my opinion, that is the effect of the new clause, and I see no reason to believe that a Court of Law would interpret it otherwise.

Mr. Downie Stewart proceeded to say that if the Act did not prove satisfactory or final, and if the controversy went on, he thought that the only ultimate solution of the difficulty would be that suggested by some of the Church authorities, and that was to adopt the Continental practice of making the civil marriage the only marriage that was officially recognised by the State, and leave the parties to go through whatever religious ceremony they liked afterwards. He did not think public opinion was ripe for such a reform there yet ; but he was sure that that would be the ultimate outcome if the problem developed.

He then moved " That the report, together with the minutes of evidence, do lie on the table, and be printed."

The interrupted debate, in which many members took part, was resumed on 4th November, during the course of which·

Mr. L. M. Isitt (Liberal, *Christchurch North*) spoke at length against the measure and moved that the report be referred back to the Committee for further consideration. This amendment was negatived, and the motion " That the report of the Committee do lie on the table " was agreed to.

The Minister of Justice (Hon. E. P. Lee) then moved to the effect that the amendments made in the Legislative Council be agreed to with the exception of the words " imprisonment for one year, or,"* which he suggested should be deleted. The effect, Mr. Lee said, would then be that every person who committed an offence against the Act would be liable, on summary conviction, to a fine of £100, and the right of the Court to inflict imprisonment in the first instance would be taken away. On non-payment of the fine, to be recovered by distress, there would be, however, power under the Justices of the Peace Act to inflict imprisonment if the fine were not paid.

Mr. Lee's motion was eventually agreed to, and the Legislative Council having accepted the amendment, the Bill passed into law, receiving the Governor-General's assent on 9th November, 1920.

---

* See note, page 430 *ante.*

DIVORCE AND MATRIMONIAL CAUSES AMENDMENT ACT.

(Decree for Restitution Restored: Decree after Three Years' Separation for Insanity, etc.)

The Bill for the above Act was introduced in the Legislative Council by the Hon. J. MacGregor, and became law on the 11th November, 1920.

The principal object of the Act is to bring the divorce law of the Dominion back to what it was before the year 1907, namely, to restore the power of the Court to treat disobedience of a decree for restitution of conjugal rights as if it were desertion and sufficient ground for dissolution of marriage. Some amendments relating to the power of the Court to grant divorce on the grounds of long sentence for crime, and also of insanity, were introduced in the House of Representatives by the Government, and were assented to by the Council.

The following are the principal provisions of the Act :—

Failure to comply with a decree for restitution of conjugal rights is made a ground for divorce (Section 3).

A divorce decree may be made where the parties have been separated for three years under a decree, order, deed, etc., or where the separation has been by mutual consent. (Section 4.)

Amendments by Government.

The law as to divorce on account of crime and insanity is amended so that a decree of dissolution may be made—

On the ground that the respondent has been convicted and sentenced to imprisonment for seven years and upwards for attempting to murder, or for wounding or doing actual bodily harm to the petitioner or any child of the petitioner or respondent (Section 5 (a));

On the ground that the respondent is of unsound mind and unlikely to recover, and has been confined in an asylum for a aggregate period of seven years during ten years immediately preceding the petition (Section 5 (b));

On the ground that the respondent is of unsound mind and unlikely to recover and has been of unsound mind continuously for seven years before the filing of the petition, and has during the final three years of that period been confined in an asylum (Section 5 (c)).

ELECTIVE EXECUTIVE BILL.

The above Bill, a résumé of which was given in Vol. II, No. 1, of this JOURNAL, pp. 183-184, was thrown out in the House of Representatives on its Second Reading by 34 votes against 18, the majority of the Labour members voting with the Government for its rejection.

BANK OF NEW ZEALAND ACT.

(Government Share in Capital.)

Under the above Act, which became law on 5th November, 1920, the share of the Government in the capital of the Bank of New Zealand, as a result of the capitalisation of a portion of the Bank's Reserve Fund, is increased to £1,125,000, equal to one third of the whole share capital of the Bank, which now stands at £3,375,000.

The Act also provides for a readjustment in regard to the distribution of profits, whereby the Government obtains a substantial benefit in comparison with its former share of profits.

SOUTH AFRICA.

The First Session of the Fourth Parliament of the Union of South Africa opened on 11th March, 1921.* The following summary deals with the Parliamentary Debates of the early part of the Session, as the records of the Debates have only been received up to 24th March. The proceedings of the Session will be continued in the next number of the JOURNAL.

---

* Parliament having been dissolved on 17th August, 1920, the General Election took place on 8th February, 1921, with the result that the state of the Parties in the House of Assembly (134 members) is as follows :—

South African Party (which has absorbed the Unionist
    Party as a result of General Smuts's appeal for a
    united Party to defeat the secessionist movement) ..   78
Nationalists   45
Labour   10
Independent   1

(For the state of Parties resulting from the General Election of 10th March, 1920, see this JOURNAL, Vol. I., No. 2, page 382.) The South African Party (including the Unionists) has gained 8,503 more votes than the two Parties gained in 1920. The Nationalists have also increased their votes by 3,292. On the other hand, Labour has to record a loss of 6,977 votes, and the Independents a loss of 4,289 votes. General Smuts has a majority of 22 over the other Parties in the House of Assembly.

The new Cabinet has been constituted as follows :—

Prime Minister and Minister of Native Affairs	General the Rt. Hon. J. C. Smuts
(*General Smuts retains the Portfolio of Native Affairs but Mr. Malan will assist him with regard to the details of administration.*)	
Minister of Mines and Industries	Hon. F. S. Malan.
Minister of Finance	Hon. H. Burton.
Minister of Justice	Hon. N. J. de Wet.
Minister of Defence	Col. the Hon. H. Mentz.
Minister of Posts, Telegraphs, and Public Works.. ..	Hon. Sir Thomas Watt.
Minister of Agriculture ..	Hon. Sir Thomas Smartt.
Minister of Railways and Harbours	Hon. J. W. Jagger.
Minister of Interior, Public Health and Education ..	Hon. Patrick Duncan.
Minister of Lands	Col. the Hon. Deneys Reitz.

At the meeting of the Senate on 11th March, Senator the Hon. C. van Heerden was elected President by a majority of eight.

The House of Assembly, when it met on 11th March, re-elected the Hon. C. J. Krige as Speaker.

GOVERNOR-GENERAL'S SPEECH.

The following is a summary of the main features of the Speech of the Governor-General (H.R.H. Prince Arthur of Connaught) in opening Parliament on 11th March, 1921 :—

League of Nations.

The Governor-General referred to the fact that during the Parliamentary recess the first meeting of the Assembly of the League of Nations took place at Geneva. "The Union of South Africa was represented at the meeting, and its delegates took an active part in the proceedings." ·

South-West Africa.

"The terms of the mandate for South-West Africa," His Excellency continued. "which was entrusted to the Union by the Great Powers, have been defined by the Council of the League of Nations, and will be submitted for your information. In that territory martial law has been withdrawn, and a civil administration has been instituted. An Advisory Council has been appointed to assist the Administrator, and numerous other beneficial measures have been carried out. Several important matters affecting the territory require the legislative sanction of the Union before they can be carried into execution, and proposals to that end will be submitted to you."

Cost of Living.

Referring to more domestic matters, the Governor-General recalled that during the Session of the last Parliament a number of emergency measures had been passed, dealing with rents, profiteering, speculation in foodstuffs, and other matters bearing on the cost of living. The operation of these measures had checked the rise in the cost of living, and, in conjunction with the altered economic conditions which had set in, had tended to lower the general price levels of commodities. Proposals in reference to the continuation or otherwise or modifications of these Acts would be submitted.

Financial and Economic Situation.

After an allusion to the proposals to be made for extending the Act dealing with the financial relations between the Union and the Provinces "for a further period subject to certain modifications," pending a definite settlement of the matter, the Speech proceeded : "The waste, destruction and industrial dislocation brought about by the Great War are now producing unprecedented conditions of economic depression throughout the world. Stagnation in trade and industry, and the resulting unemployment and social unrest are everywhere creating very grave problems for Parliaments and Governments. Universal financial stringency and exchange difficulties seriously hamper international trade. Here in South Africa the effects of these world-wide conditions have been felt very suddenly, especially in the agricultural and mining industries, which depend so largely on the overseas markets for their prosperity. It is difficult to find markets abroad for some of our agricultural, pastoral and mineral exports. Several mines are either closing or curtailing their operations. Unemployment is on the increase, and is at present under

inquiry by a Commission appointed by my predecessor.   In addition to
these economic troubles, the financial position, in spite of its general
soundness, is becoming difficult, and the ordinary sources of the public
revenues are being materially affected.

Work of the Session.

" Under these circumstances my Ministers propose to concentrate
attention for this Session as far as possible on the measures which are
necessary to cope with the financial and economic situation I have referred
to.   Proposals will be laid before you dealing with unemployment. . . .
Consideration will also be given to the safeguarding of some of our
industries against unfair competition from overseas, owing to the abnormal
conditions prevailing abroad."

CONFERENCE OF PRIME MINISTERS OF THE EMPIRE.

(Agenda for Meeting, June, 1921.)

Mr. J. H. B. Wessels (Nationalist, *Bethlehem, O.F.S.)*
asked the Prime Minister, on 17th March, whether the Government was in a position to inform the House what subjects
would be discussed at the Conference of Prime Ministers
when they met in London in June, 1921, and whether the
Government of the Union of South Africa would be represented at that Conference ?

**The Prime Minister (Lieut.-General the Right Hon. J. C.
Smuts)** replied that the agenda for the Conference had not been
finally settled, but he was informed that amongst the subjects
to be discussed would be (A) the renewal of the Anglo-Japanese
Alliance ;   (B) other questions of foreign policy which may
be raised ;   (C) composition of agenda and meeting place of
Constitutional Conference to be held next year.

It was the intention of the Government of the Union to
be represented at the Conference.

INTERNATIONAL LABOUR CONFERENCE.

Mr. C. P. Robinson (South African Party, *Durban Central,
Natal)* asked the Prime Minister, on 17th March, when and
where the next International Labour Conference established
under the Peace Treaty would be held ;   how many representatives were nominated by the Government, the employers
and the trade unionists respectively ;   whether South Africa
was represented on the governing body of the International
Labour Office, and if not, whether any steps were to be taken
to ensure that such representation shall be permitted ;   whether
the recommendations of the Labour Conference were subject
to confirmation by the League of Nations ;   and, how were the
subjects to be considered by the Labour Conference arranged.

and was it competent for the South African Government to make suggestions as to the matters it considers desirable for consideration by such Conference ?

The Prime Minister (Lieut.-General the Right Hon. J. C. Smuts) replied to the effect that the next meeting would take place at Geneva in October, and that the Government was entitled to nominate two delegates as Government representatives and two as representing the organisations of employers and workers respectively. In addition, two advisers may be appointed to each delegate to advise on each separate subject of the agenda. South Africa was not directly represented on the governing body. Representations were made at the Washington Conference with a view to giving a greater proportion of representatives to countries outside of Europe, and as a result the question of the constitution of the governing body had been placed on the agenda for the forthcoming Conference. The answer to the question as to whether the recommendations of the Labour Conference are subject to confirmation by the League of Nations was in the negative. The agenda was arranged by the governing body. It was competent for any State which was a member of the League to make suggestions as to subjects for consideration.

REPATRIATION OF INDIANS.

In the House of Assembly on 16th March, in Committee on the Estimates of Additional Expenditure (Vote 20, Interior, £29,762).

Mr. T. Boydell (Labour, *Durban, Greyville, Natal*), referring to the item of £9,762 for the repatriation of Indians, said he was glad to see this vote, and he would like to know how many Indians had been repatriated as recommended by the Asiatic Commission ?

The Minister of the Interior (Hon. Patrick Duncan) said the repatriation of Indians was owing to the recommendations of the Asiatic Commission that Indians who were willing to go back to India might be encouraged to do so by the Government not merely paying the cost of their passage, but the cost of their return to their homes when they got there. A step of that kind was a cheap method of solving this problem. Up to the present 1,000 Indians had been repatriated under that scheme, and he hoped more would take advantage of it in the future.

On the 17th March in Committee on the same vote (see above), Sir Abe Bailey (South African Party, *Krugersdorp, Trans.*) drew attention to the Report recently issued by the Asiatic Inquiry Commission, a document which, he said, concerned not only every white person in South Africa, but

o

also the national life of that country. He had read th
Report and Recommendations of the Commission and, as fa
as he could see, they were the weakest product of any Com
mission which had ever gone forth. There was nothing in tha
Report which did not exist to-day. It might satisfy th
Indian community or the supporters of that community, bu
it would not satisfy a large contingent in South Africa wh
meant to assert themselves and show that the Asiatics wer
not wanted there. The Commission recommended voluntar
segregation and voluntary repatriation. They had had bot
for many years past. What was the result ? In every tow
and village in the country those people had stores, and the
were eating into the vitals of South Africa. The only poin
the Commission brought forward was that some of the evidenc
had been exaggerated, but even taking the lowest computatio
it went to show that Indians were displacing white peopl
and he hoped that every inducement would be given to ther
to return to surroundings which would be more congenial t
them than South Africa.

Mr. E. G. Saunders (South African Party, *Natal Coas*
said that the " Arab " traders, who were no more " Arabs
than he was, were really the detrimental element of the Asiati
population. If the question was to be tackled, it had to b
done in a practical way, and it could not be done for a fe
thousands, as these traders would have to be bought out.

The Minister of the Interior, in reply, said that wit
regard to the Asiatic question the item in this vote was i
connection with the voluntary repatriation of Indians, und
the suggestion made by the Commission that where India
were willing to go back the Government should pay th
expenses of their return to their homes. It was not a hero
way of dealing with the difficulty, but it was a practical way
dealing with a certain number of Indians who were ther
and wanted to go back. He did not think that any ho
member would contend that this amount of £9,700 spent
sending back 1,000 Indians had been badly spent. He agre
with Mr. Saunders and other members that this was not
policy which would ever solve the question of the Asiatics
South Africa and their relations to the European populatic
but he did not think any good purpose would be served
going into a discussion upon that question on that particul
vote. He hoped there might be other occasions during th
Session when the matter could more properly be taken u
He agreed that the problem was a very important one, that
went to the roots of the well-being of the European populati
in South Africa, and that the longer it was allowed to d
without a definite policy being adopted the more serious
would become.

CANADIAN WHEAT PURCHASE.

In the House of Assembly, on 14th March,

Mr. J. du Toit (Nationalist, *Victoria West, Cape*) asked for details as to the amount of corn and flour imported by the Government last year, the total amount paid therefor, and what had been the losses (A) on the above transactions; (B) through suspension of the import duties; and (c) through free transit over the railways.

The Minister of Finance (Hon. H. Burton) stated that 30,000 tons of Canadian wheat were imported by the Government, but no corn; that £1,375,686, less £60,000 exchange on remitting money to London, equalled £1,315,686; that the loss to the Government on above transactions was approximately £500,000; the loss to the Government owing to the suspension of the import duties on corn and flour imported into the Union since 18th February, 1920, to date, was £320,000; and that the loss through free transit over the railways was nil, all corn and flour carried over the railways being paid for by the purchasers.

DEBATE IN HOUSE OF ASSEMBLY.

In the House of Assembly, on 15th March,

Mr. J. H. H. de Waal (Nationalist, *Piquetberg, Cape*) moved that the House most strongly condemned the action of the Government in regard to the purchase and sale of Canadian flour, and was of opinion that in order to encourage the local production of foodstuffs, and in view of the danger that threatened the wheat farmers by reason of the unreasonably low price at present offered by the millers for local wheat, the Government should immediately take steps to assist the wheat farmers in particular and the wheat industry in general. Mr. de Waal said the price of wheat to-day was lower than it was the year before the War. A price of 28s. 6d. or 29s. was too low to encourage farmers to go in for wheat growing, and while the cost of other products had gone up the price of wheat had dropped.

The Government Blamed.

The blame for the present abnormal condition of affairs under which the local product was cheaper than the imported lay with the Government. He blamed them for having over-imported. They had done this without consulting the farmers, who had thus suffered the greatest damage.

Mr. D. Hugo (Nationalist, *Rouxville, O.F.S.*) seconded, and other members having supported the motion,

The **Minister of Finance** said that the Government had a
great deal of sympathy with the position in which the farmers
were placed, and would do all in its power to assist them.
But at the end of 1919 the country was in serious danger of a
shortage of the bread supply, and what the Union produced
was estimated to be a third less than the ordinary amount.

After describing the efforts which the Government then
made to secure supplies of wheat from various sources, and the
purchases of flour of, first, 10,000 tons, and then 20,000
(from Canada) at about 84s. per 200 lb. and 77s. per 200 lb.
respectively, Mr. Burton said that when the Government flour
began to arrive in South Africa the country was already
overstocked, owing to the fact that in the interval there had
been importations by millers, bakers, merchants, by the
whole community, with a view, doubtless, to making excellent
profits.

Heavy Loss Inevitable.

There was bound to be a heavy loss owing to the fall in
the price of grain, and the failure of the Government in spite
of many conferences to get the millers to come to some
arrangement with them as to the disposal of the grain. The
Government had tried to realise this flour to the best advantage,
but finally they concluded an agreement with the millers by
which it had been sold to them at 45s.

Benefit to the Consumer.

But if the State as a whole were going to lose £500,000
on this deal, there could be no doubt that the consumers had
had the benefit. These consignments of Government flour had
checked the heavy rise in the price of bread. He reminded
the House that in England the people had to pay £50,000,000
per annum during the War to stabilise the price of bread.
All the advantages of the reduction in price was not due to the
Government transaction, but the point was that since December, January and February the country had benefited by the
cheapened price of bread, which was calculated by the
Statistical Office to amount to nearly £450,000.

Suspension of Wheat Duties.

In regard to the suspension of wheat duties, and the
proposal that the grain duty should be re-introduced, Mr.
Burton said that the duties had been suspended because at
that time they were not producing sufficient supplies of wheat
in the country ; but the Government would be willing to reintroduce the duties, though they did not see the feasibility of
doing so immediately. The three months' notice clause was

put in because of the number of people who had made contracts for the importation of wheat and flour, and their shipments were still coming in.

Question of Financial Assistance.

In regard to the requests which had been made to the Government to advance money, that was, he feared, an impracticable policy. Similar requests might come from other interests, and the Government could not possibly find money to finance the whole of the industries of the country.

Railway Rates.

In regard to railway rates, there were no more preferential rates, and this, he thought, was quite right. In regard to what was called point-to-point rates, which meant that wheat from the Western Provinces would be placed on an equal footing in competition with wheat from other centres, the Government were busy examining that matter now from the railway point of view, and it was felt there might be ways of dealing with it which would meet the views of the members though they could not easily take away sources of revenue from the railway.

The motion was negatived by 68 votes to 36, the minority consisting exclusively of Nationalists.

FINANCIAL POSITION.

(Finances of the Union.)

In the House of Assembly on 14th March the Minister of Finance, in moving that the House go into Committee on the Estimates of Additional Expenditure, made a statement in regard to the financial position of the Union, and the various increased demands in respect of pensions, the relief of distress, the rise in wages and salaries in the Public Services Department, etc., and the attempts at economy that had been made and were contemplated.

DEBATE IN HOUSE OF ASSEMBLY.

The Minister of Finance (Hon. H. Burton) said that unfortunately, instead of realising the hopes of those who thought that at the end of the year they would have a surplus, the anticipated deficit of £331,000 would probably be increased. The revenue had gone up from £28,381,000, the first estimate, to £29,568,000, an increase of £1,187,000, but the expenditure had increased from £28,712,000 to £30,268,000, an increase of £1,556,000. This indicated a probable deficit for the present financial year of about £700,000.

Principal Items.

Among the principal items to be dealt with were an increase in pensions of £93,195, due to payments on account of war allowances ; provision of extra money for the higher salaries which were now going to be paid under the fifth report of the Public Service Commission ; increase of £121,000. due to the higher rates of interest payable on Treasury Bills ; a heavy increase (£199,000) for Provincial Administration £82,000 for relief of distress—£47,000 on account of unemploy-ment, mainly at Johannesburg and in the diamond fields, and £34,000 additional cost of services owing to the employment of white labour in place of native labour on irrigation works and land settlement. They had not included the latter amount in the vote, Mr. Burton added, because it was a recoverable advance, and he was happy to say that it was the invariable experience of the Native Affairs Department that these advances to natives were always recovered. This did not represent the total cost for the relief of distress, because there was an amount of £28,000 expended from loan vote in connection with the employment of 500 returned soldiers.

Co-operative Stores Loan.

The House voted £10,000 a few years ago to assist the co-operative stores started by the South Africa Industrial Co-operative Federation, but since then the Federation had found themselves in difficulties, and there was no prospect of the loan being recovered. The Chamber of Mines had offered to go to the assistance of the Federation if the Govern-ment would write off the liability, and the Government, being willing that the Federation should have the fullest opportunity of making a success of the undertaking, proposed to do this.

The Public Services Commission.

The fifth report of the Public Services Commission, Mr. Burton continued, had come at a time of waning prosperity and contracting revenue, when financially the outlook was causing the Government serious anxiety. The report mentioned the need for far-reaching changes in public service organisation, and for a more efficient and a more contented service. They were over-staffed in certain departments, and it was implied that there was room for great economy.

In regard to wages and salaries the administrative and clerical service had fallen behind the rates which had been paid to other salary and wage-earning classes during the past few years, and in view of the fact that other branches of the public services had been placed on an exceptionally favourable footing, the Government felt it was impossible to avoid, in order to play fair with the Civil Service, adopting the recommendations of the fifth report in regard to the scale of salaries, as from 1st October, 1919, the date from which the other members of the service had received their increases of pay.

Prospects of Reductions.

The increase in the cost of living had probably reached its high-water mark during the last twelve months, and the indications were that it would drop. The Government had accepted almost entirely the rates of pay laid down by the Commission for all ranks up to that of senior clerk, but the proposed reduction of the scale for secretaries, undersecretaries, chief clerks, etc., necessitated a detailed examination of the merits of each case. As a temporary measure the Government proposed to retain the existing scales, and improve them proportionately to the lower scales.

With reference to the question of economy and reorganisation, the Government proposed to take steps at once to conduct a continuous inspection of offices. The feeling was that with the machinery that they had to-day they could cope with far greater development than existed in the country at the present time. Nothing increased their expenditure so much as the creation of numerous departments and sub-departments, and nobody could help more than Parliament itself by taking a commonsense, business-like view of the matter, and by setting their face against fads. Mr. Burton added that the hours of work in the public services were to be extended by, he believed, two and a half hours per week.

General the Hon. J. B. M. Hertzog (Leader of the Nationalist Party) said the machinery which had been created was of the Government's own making, and a serious mistake had been made when they decided to give the largest cost of living allowance to the highest-paid officials. He blamed the Government for not having told the country the real position of affairs.

The Right Hon. J. X. Merriman (South African Party, Stellenbosch, Cape) moved that the debate be adjourned; nobody in the House knew what the true figures were, and if things continued to drop off they might finish up by having a £7,000,000 deficit instead of £700,000.

The Prime Minister (Lieut.-General the Right Hon. J. C. Smuts) said there was no reason for a postponement of the debate. The House at a later date when on the Estimates would have an opportunity to discuss the general financial policy and administration of the Government.

Mr. Merriman asked leave to withdraw the amendment, and the Committee stage was set down for the following day.

In the discussion in Committee on 16th March (on Vote 5, Treasury, £22,050),

Sir Abe Bailey (South African Party, *Krugersdorp, Trans.*) said they were 'now asked to produce a total revenue including that of the Provinces of £34,500,000, or over £24 per head of the European population, or £13 per head including the native population. In Great Britain, with the huge War debt, an enormous navy and a large army, it worked out at £20 per head. They were now facing a period of great depression, unrest and unemployment in South Africa, and, he thought that until Germany, Austria and other countries were set going that depression would continue. South Africa, he knew, would come right, but its finances must be taken in hand. Sound finance came before any other policy, and they had two items alone which would show a reduction of revenue of over £4,000,000.

Mr. Merriman said he saw no reason why they should not be the first Legislative Assembly to treat the finances like everything else. He was sorry the two Houses could not sit together, as they did in some countries, and deal with them as a whole, as if the Parliament were business men dealing with their own affairs.

The vote was agreed to.

PUBLIC SERVICE EXPENDITURE.

(Necessity for Economy: Reduction of War Bonus, etc.

In the House of Assembly on 18th March discussion were resumed in Committee on the Estimates of Additional Expenditure (Vote 34, Adjustment of Salaries, Wages and Allowances, £400,000).

DEBATE IN HOUSE OF ASSEMBLY.

Dr. D. F. Malan (Nationalist, *Calvinia, Cape*) pointed out that in one year salaries, wages and allowances had shown an increase of £2,769,000, and with that further £400,000 it would mean an increase of something over £3,000,000. He contended that £2,352,000 of the increase would be permanent, and the only economy which could be effected was by means of retrenchment of civil servants. He asked for an assurance from the Minister of Finance that this would be carried out in a strictly fair and impartial manner.

The Right Hon. J. X. Merriman (South African Party, *Stellenbosch, Cape*) said the money of the country was being dealt with in a free and easy way in the higher branches. He reminded members that men who were paid at the outside £1,000 a year were in a moment, on the recommendations of the Commission, put at £1,300, rising by gradation to £1,500 ; these amounts carried pensions with them, and the House was riveting on the country a burden which it could not bear. A more mischievous report was never printed, he said, and he moved that the vote stand over until they had considered its true bearings and heard what the true circumstances of the country were.

The Minister of Finance (Hon. H. Burton) opposed the motion. It was essential to pass the money before the end of the month. He pointed out that the recommendations regarding the more highly paid officials were not being carried out yet. The vote only dealt with officials on the lower scale, and it would be unfair to leave out this branch of the service while other branches had received their increases. The only thing to do was to pass these salaries, and then they would have the whole of the Civil Service on the same basis, and if reduction became necessary they could deal with them all on that basis.

Mr. Merriman's motion was negatived by 82 votes to 28 and the vote was agreed to.

The Minister of Finance made a statement in the House of Assembly on 21st March in regard to the Government's proposal to effect an economy by reducing the War bonus in the Public Service.

The Minister of Finance after moving the Second Reading of the Appropriation (Part) Bill, which asked for a provision of £7,000,000, said he wished to mention another matter out of fairness to the House and the country at large, and especially to the members both of the ordinary Public Service and the Railway Public Service. The financial position at present was such as to justify the Government taking steps to curtail their expenditure as far as they possibly could. Statistics showed that the cost of living had not merely passed its highest point some time ago, but it was now falling, and they had every reason to believe that it would fall considerably during the ensuing twelve months. In view of that and the financial position, the Government had come to the conclusion that it would be justified in reducing the amount of the war allowance or bonus to both sides of the Public Service by 25 per cent. during the first quarter of the next financial year.

Mr. T. Boydell (Labour, *Durban, Greyville, Natal*) : This is the first effect of the elections.

The Minister of Finance said he trusted that the Public Service would accept the announcement and understand the situation.

The Right Hon. J. X. Merriman (South African Party, *Stellenbosch, Cape*) asked whether it was the intention of the Government to adopt a course which had been taken in England with very great effect indeed, and to the great advantage of the country, and appoint a Committee to go into the whole question of the Estimates in a rational way,* and see whether they could not bring forward some recommendation dealing largely with financial procedure.

Mr. C. T. Wilcocks (Nationalist, *Winburg, O.F.S.*) said the Nationalists had been convinced of the necessity of economy for a long time, and had always urged it without avail. All he desired to do now was to warn the Minister against going to extremes as he had done in the past. He did not wish anything unfair to be done towards the Civil Service or to the country's general services, such as education. Everything possible should be done to avoid injustice.

Mr. J. B. Wessels (Nationalist, *Frankfort, O.F.S.*) asked for the provision of a quarter of a million to be made for the Land Bank, which had insufficient funds to carry out it purpose.

Mr. Boydell asked if the Minister of Finance had n figures to prove that the cost of living had gone down to th extent of 25 per cent. ? He must know that one of the mai reasons for lower prices to-day was that there was financi stringency, and firms were realising in many cases at a los He believed that when these stocks had been off-loade prices would steady and then begin to go up again, becau the cost of production in other parts of the world had n sufficiently declined. In addition to this, the War bonus ha never equalled the increased cost of living. He wished move the adjournment of the debate.

Mr. Boydell's motion was put and defeated, and aft further discussion the debate was adjourned.

REGULATION OF WAGES BILL.
(Wages Boards and Minimum Rate of Pay.)

The Regulation of Wages Bill was introduced the Minister of Mines and Industries (Hon. F. S. Mala) for the purpose of establishir Wages Boards, with power to minimum rates of wages, wh ch may take into consideration

---

* See page 272.

the age and experience of persons to whom the payments are made, though the scale of payment shall in no case be based upon the quantity or output of work done.

Constitution of Wages Boards.

Every Wages Board is to be constituted of not less than three, having an equal number of representatives of employers and employees, with a chairman who is neither an employer nor employee in the trade or occupation concerned. Women are eligible for membership.

Duties of Wages Board: Fixing Minimum Wage.

The duties and functions of the Wages Board include consideration of any matter referred to it by the Minister with reference to industrial conditions of any trade or occupation. It may fix minimum rates of wages payable in the area for which it is appointed, and the intervals at which such wages shall be paid. In exercising those powers, it may take into consideration the age and experience of the persons employed, and may fix a scale of rates payable to them according to their age and experience, but in no case shall such scale be based upon the quantity or output of work done. It may also fix varying rates for different portions of the area or district for which it is appointed.

Power to Summon Witnesses, Examine Books, etc.

A Wages Board may take evidence for the purpose of enquiring into any matter falling within its powers and functions and the chairman may subpœna witnesses to attend and give evidence and produce documents. The Board may examine wages sheets and books of employers in relation to the rate of wages paid by them and shall report fully to the Minister on the matters which come before it in the course of its inquiry.

Minimum Wage: Employers' Penalties.

Wherever a fixed minimum rate of wages exists under the Act for any district or area in respect of any particular trade or occupation, every employer carrying on business in that area shall pay to every person employed by him at such trade or occupation remuneration at the rate of not less than the fixed minimum wage for the period worked clear of all deductions. The penalty clauses provide for a fine not exceeding £20 and a further £5 for each day on which default is continued after conviction.

Provision of Wearing Apparel, Meals, etc.

When fixing the rates of pay in any trade or occupation in which it customary, on account of its nature, for the employee to be supplied with wearing apparel or material for personal clothing, or meals or lodging, a Wages Board shall assess the value of the apparel, meals, lodging, etc., and an employer may deduct their assessed value from the pay of the employee concerned.

Notice and Variation of Minimum Wage.

Before exercising any of these powers notice of its proposals is to be given by the Board in the " Gazette " and one or more newspapers circulating in the district concerned, and if any objections are lodged with it within a period to be stated in the notice, it shall hear those who desire to support the objections. Notice shall also be given of any minimum rate of wages fixed by it.

A Wages Board may withdraw or vary any minimum rate fixed by it, and shall reconsider such rate if the Minister so directs, whether or not application has been made for the purpose by an employer or employee or association of employers or employees.

Cases of Physical Disability.

If it appears to a Wages Board that any person employed or desiring to be employed on time work in any particular trade or occupation is affected by any infirmity or physical injury which renders her or him incapable of earning the fixed minimum time-rate of wages and that the case cannot suitably be met by employing such person on piece work, the Board may grant a permit on conditions to be specified therein exempting the employment of such persons from the provisions of the Act as to a fixed minimum time-rate of wages, and so long as such permit is in force and the conditions thereof are complied with by the employer, the latter shall not be guilty of an offence under this Act in respect of the employment of such person at a rate less than the fixed minimum time-rate of wages.

Exemptions.

The Bill exempts persons employed in any Government Department or under Provincial Administration, and persons employed in domestic service, in agriculture, and apprentices.

Joint Voluntary Boards.

The Bill further provides that the Minister may appoint a joint voluntary board of employers and employees, on application of same a wages board, if he is satisfied that such joint board is sufficiently representative of the employers and employees in the particular trade or occupation concerned in the area for which it is constituted, and any board so appointed shall perform all the duties and functions of a wage board under the Act. Voluntary agreements of both parties shall also after application is made by them, and after the Minister, if he deems expedient, has published the same in the " Gazette," become binding on a employers and employees in the area to which such agreement applie

Prosecution of an Employer, etc.

On any prosecution of an employer, it shall lie upon him to prov by the production of proper business books, wages sheets, records otherwise, that he has not paid or agreed to pay wages at less than th fixed minimum rate.

Any agreement made after the prescribed date on which a matt is under the Act to be regarded as fixed for the purposes thereof sha if in contravention thereof, be void, and any such agreement ma before that prescribed date shall become void as from that date.

The Minister may appoint wages board inspectors for the purp of investigating complaints and for securing the proper observance the Act.

DIVORCE BILL.

(To Extend Grounds for Divorce.)

A Bill was introduced on 22nd March by Mr. A. Van Hees (Nationalist) to extend the grounds for divor

It was read a first time and set down for Second Reading on 7th April.

The Bill provides that in addition to other grounds at present in force, divorce may be granted if the party against whom the decree is sought (A) is suffering from leprosy, (B) has been declared by a competent court to be insane, or (C) has been declared by a competent court under the Criminal Procedure and Evidence Act, 1917, to be an habitual criminal.

MARRIAGE LAW AMENDMENT BILL.

(Marriage with Deceased Husband's Brother, etc.)

This is a Bill to legalise marriage with a deceased husband's brother, etc., and was introduced by Mr. M. Bisset, K.C. (South African Party) in the House of Assembly on 15th March, and set down for Second Reading on 31st March.

The Bill provides that it shall be lawful for any widow to marry the brother of her deceased husband or any male related to her through her deceased husband in any more remote degree of affinity than his brother, except any ancestor or descendant from such deceased husband.

Such marriages already contracted shall be deemed valid, unless dissolved by the decree of any competent court, or unless subsequent marriage to another by either party has, during the life of the other, lawfully taken place.

Marriage with the brother of a divorced husband or of a husband by whom she has been divorced is prohibited during the lifetime of the husband.

CRIMINAL PROCEDURE AND EVIDENCE ACT AMENDMENT BILL.

A Bill to amend the Criminal Procedure and Evidence Act, 1917, in order to abolish trial by jury in criminal cases and to make other provision in lieu thereof, was introduced on 15th March by Mr. E. Nathan (South African Party) and set down for Second Reading on 31st March.

It provides for the repeal of Chapters XI. and XII. of the Act of 1917 and the substitution of a new chapter relating to trial before a Superior Court. This states that in any criminal case before a Superior Court the trial of the accused shall, save as is specially provided in Act No. 49 of 1898 of Natal or any amendment thereof or any other law conferring jurisdiction on the Native High Court of Natal, be before any one or more of the judges of the Supreme Court, provided that in any case in which only one judge presides, he may, in his discretion, summon to his assistance one or two persons (A) holding the office of magistrate, assistant magistrate, native commissioner, sub-commissioner,

or special or resident justice of the peace, or (B) barristers-at-law of not
less than ten years' standing, or (C) medical practitioners of not less than
ten years' standing, or any two of such persons to sit and act with him
as assessors in an advisory capacity on questions of fact arising upon
the trial.

Several sections of Act 31 of 1917 are consequently amended or
repealed to the extent indicated in a Schedule which follows the
provisions of the Bill.

ADMISSION OF ADVOCATES BILL.

A Bill was introduced on 22nd March by General the Hon.
J. B. M. Hertzog (Leader of the Nationalist Party) to amend
the law relating to the admission of advocates.   It was read
first time, and set down for Second Reading on 31st March.

The Bill provides that any provincial or local division of the Supreme
Court of South Africa may admit to practise as an advocate any person who
is a British subject resident in any of the Provinces of the Union who has
obtained from any of the universities supported or controlled by the
Governments of Holland, Belgium, France and Germany, and such other
universities as the Governor-General in Council may from time to time
determine, a certificate or diploma of " juris utriusque doctor " or "legum
doctor," or an equivalent degree in law, entitling him as regards professional qualifications to be admitted to practise in the Superior Courts
the country in which such university is established.

LAND FOR SETTLEMENT.

Lieut.-Colonel G. M. Claassen (South African Party,
Standerton, Trans.) asked the Minister of Lands, on 17
March, whether he was prepared to make adequate provision
in the Estimates for the coming financial year for the acquisition of additional land for settlement purposes.

The Minister of Lands (Col. the Hon. Deneys Reitz)
said that as in former years the Minister would do his
best to place a reasonable amount on the Estimates for the
purchase of land for settlement purposes.

UNION OFFICES IN LONDON.

On Loan Vote B, Public Works, £148,222, considered
in Committee on the Estimates of Additional Expenditure
on 18th March,

Dr. D. F. Malan (Nationalist, Calvinia, Cape) asked for
more information with regard to the provision and equipment

f public offices at Morley's Hotel, London, £145,000. He
riticised the expenditure of such a large amount without
eference to Parliament, declaring that it would have been
ar preferable to have assisted wool farmers. If the rumour
vere true that Morley's Hotel had been leased for 99 years to
he previous owners, of which there were still ten years to run,
ae Union would only secure Morley's Hotel for that period.
o far South Africa had paid £3,000 a year in rent for the
fnion's Offices in London, and the interest on £145,000 would
reatly and unnecessarily exceed this.

Inadequate Accommodation in London.

The Minister of Finance (Hon. H. Burton) said he doubted
hether the Government of the Union had ever made a better
urchase than this. The accommodation in London had been
tterly inadequate and unworthy of the Union for years past,
oth for the important work in the High Commissioner's
ffice and for the Trade Commissioner, in Cannon Street ;
t was not worthy of a fifth-class Dominion, or he might say
f one of the smaller Crown Colonies. He did not suppose
ey would find a finer site in London than Morley's Hotel,
hich was in the most central part of the city and faced
rafalgar Square.

The Price Paid.

Mr. Burton went on to say that the price originally
asked was £150,000, but eventually they secured it for £135,000,
he price including furniture, the greater part of which they
ould be able to sell. They had also secured 14 rooms in an
adjoining building at a rental of £450 a year. The annual
charges they would have to pay would be £11,300, and against
hat they got a rental, from sub-letting the present offices,
£6,247. The place (Morley's Hotel) belonged to the Crown,
nd he had no doubt whatever that in view of their previous
xperience they would be able to make a quite satisfactory
rrangement with the Imperial Government.

Mr. C. T. M. Wilcocks (Nationalist, *Winburg, O.F.S.)*
moved the deletion of the item relating to Morley's Hotel.

The amendment was negatived by 58 votes to 26, and
the vote was agreed to.

NEWFOUNDLAND.

Parliament met for the Second Session of the twenty-fourt
Parliament on 30th March, 1921, and the proceedings will b
summarised in the next issue of the JOURNAL.

VACHER & SONS, LTD., Westminster House, London, S.W.1.—88651.

JOURNAL OF THE
PARLIAMENTS
OF THE EMPIRE

Vol. II.—No. 3.   July, 1921.

Issued under the Authority of the
EMPIRE PARLIAMENTARY ASSOCIATION
(United Kingdom Branch),
WESTMINSTER HALL, HOUSES OF PARLIAMENT,
LONDON, S.W.1.

Price to Non-Members 10s. Net.

CONTENTS.

CANADA.

AUSTRALIA.

Commonwealth Parliament.

NEW ZEALAND.

CONTENTS.

SOUTH AFRICA.

NEWFOUNDLAND.

INTRODUCTION.

Though the last quarterly issue of the JOURNAL contained some interesting references in the various Parliaments to the Conference of Prime Ministers which is now taking place in London, the present number is remarkable for containing important discussions in the Parliaments of the United Kingdom and the four great Dominions directly upon the work and scope of the Conference. The summaries of these discussions, dealing as they do with varied points of view on many questions of vital interest to the British Commonwealth of Nations, should certainly prove of value to the Members of the different Parliaments of the Empire but probably most of all to the participants in the actual Conference now proceeding in Downing Street. For it is possible to find, within the cover of the present volume, an accurate presentation of the attitude adopted by leaders of diverse political thought in each Parliament upon the issues which are of the highest consequence to the nations of the Commonwealth in relation to the world politics of to-day.

Probably never before in the history of the Empire has so much Parliamentary consideration been devoted to the big questions at issue, and the reader of the following summaries can scarcely fail to be struck with the earnestness and high level of thought which characterise the debates in all the five Parliaments. Foreign policy and the wider aspects of defence, including such matters as the Anglo-Japanese Alliance, relations with the United States and the Pacific problem generally, have been discussed as seriously in all Parliaments as the constitutional position of the Dominions and the status they now occupy both in regard to the Empire and to the outside world.

Apart from the specific discussions upon the Conference, more than one Parliament has had under consideration questions affecting the League of Nations, mandates and defence by sea, land and air.

In Canada, significant discussions occurred on naval policy and on the appointment of a Minister at Washington; while in the Australian Commonwealth and South Africa military defence and training gave rise to interesting debates.

Of more local subjects, which nevertheless possess a direct interest for other Parliaments, the United Kingdom has matters recorded concerning the safeguarding of industries, proportional representation, and education of ex-service-men; while in a similar category may be placed the discussions in the South African and Canadian Parliaments upon the problem of Asiatic immigration.

A matter which was undoubtedly of peculiar interest to the representative Assemblies within the British Empire, possessing, as they do, a common Parliamentary tradition, was the retirement of Mr. Lowther from the Speaker's Chair of the House of Commons at Westminster. The Parliaments that may be said to have been directly concerned in this event are shown in the following pages to have been those of the United Kingdom and Canada, for while in the former Parliament the proceedings taking place upon the retirement afforded the opportunity of eloquent tributes being paid to the great work of Mr. Lowther in the Chair and to the valuable assistance he had rendered to the United Kingdom Branch of the Empire Parliamentary Association as Joint President since its inception, the fact of the retirement afforded Mr. Lowther the opportunity of proceeding to the Canadian Parliament in order to present the Speaker's Chair to the House of Commons at Ottawa, which he had been asked to do by the members of the Association in both Houses who had subscribed to the gift.

The proceedings attending the presentation of the Chair in the House of Commons at Ottawa, when the exact replica of the Speaker's Chair in the House of Commons at Westminster was handed over by Mr. Lowther to Mr. Speaker Rhodes, to stand for all time as a mark of cordial goodwill and close friendship between the Members of both Parliaments, were unique and memorable in Parliamentary records and are given in full in the following pages. Never before had the Members of all parties in both Houses of Parliament assembled together for such an occasion, and never before perhaps had the leaders of all parties in the State extended with such warmth and cordiality their greetings and appreciation to their colleagues in the "Mother of Parliaments" at Westminster.

THE EDITOR.

EMPIRE PARLIAMENTARY ASSOCIATION
(*United Kingdom Branch*),
WESTMINSTER HALL,
HOUSES OF PARLIAMENT,
LONDON, S.W.1.

1st *July*, 1921.

UNITED KINGDOM.

The business of the Session up till the Easter Recess was dealt with in the last number of the JOURNAL. *The sittings of the two Houses were resumed on 4th April, 1921, and the proceedings between that date and 20th June are summarised in the following pages.*

CONFERENCE OF PRIME MINISTERS OF THE EMPIRE.

(Defence : The Pacific: Common Foreign Policy: Anglo-Japanese Alliance : India: Subjects for Discussion : Dominions and Colonial Office, etc.)

Subjects expected to be included in the agenda for the Conference of the Prime Ministers of the Empire were discussed in the House of Commons on 17th June. The Government had been asked by a number of unofficial Members to afford facilities for debate and this sitting was specially reserved for the purpose. Amongst the visitors who listened to a portion of the debate were the Prime Minister of Canada (Mr. Meighen), the Minister of Agriculture for South Africa (Sir Thomas Smartt), the Minister of Defence for South Africa (Colonel Mentz), Mr. S. J. Crowe, M.P. (Canada), and Mr. Stacey, M.P. (Canada).

DEBATE IN HOUSE OF COMMONS.

The discussion took place on a motion by the Government for the adjournment of the House.

Major-General Sir John Davidson (Coalition Unionist, *Fareham*) said that having been closely associated with the Dominion forces during the War he had felt for some time that their strength was so enormous and so increasing that the British Empire, if working as a whole, could act for the good of the world in a military sense. There was no intention or wish on the part of the people of this country to disturb in any fundamental manner the constitutional relationship between one part of the Empire and another. The whole work of the Empire must be based in the future on the two principles of freedom and co-operation. He thought the Dominions were all agreed—in fact, only a small section of the community throughout the whole Empire were not agreed—on the advantages of maintaining the ties with the Mother Country, and particularly the tie of the Crown.

B

As to co-operation, there were a great many difficulties involved in regard to both measure and agreement. As Mr. Hughes very rightly said a few days ago, Empires and nations did not stand still. Mr. Hughes pointed out that they had to decide whether they were going to move forward on a principle of whole-hearted and unselfish co-operation, or whether they were going to decline to take advantage of the possibilities which were before them and take the other course of moving backward towards disintegration and decay. There was another tendency of movement to be considered. Old countries which were over-populated and highly industrialised were apt to recede, just in exactly the same way as new and undeveloped dominions tended to go forward very rapidly. As the focus of power and wealth moved within any group of nations from one centre to another, or from the centre to the extremities, so the incidence of responsibilities and burdens must equally and proportionately shift.

Dominions and Peace Treaties.

He did not believe that, in considering this incidence of responsibilities and burdens, there was any mechanical formula which they could follow. The only formula was mutual and voluntary agreement between the parties concerned. There had been a very evident sign in the Peace Treaties that the Dominions were prepared to accept responsibilities and take a position and status in the world generally and interest themselves in the world's affairs.

" We have seen the part they have taken in connection with the Peace Treaties and they are signatories to the League of Nations," Sir John remarked. " That is a great step forward in which Canada and South Africa are in the van, closely followed by Australia and New Zealand, with India behind, but following very rapidly also. It is all very well to say that the Dominions should accept this responsibility seeing that they have reached a state of autonomous power and be satisfied with it. There are certain anomalies involved between that condition and the condition of co-operation which we want to achieve. For instance, there is the anomaly between complete autonomy and collective action. These two things do not normally go well together. There is also the difficulty of each of the Dominions, possibly, offering separate advice to the Crown. I do not believe that these difficulties are very great or insuperable, but I think that possibly it may be desirable to effect some minor change in our constitutional practice."

His chief object was to investigate the question of Imperial defence, and, where there were autonomous Powers working together, how that co-operation which was so necessary could best be achieved between them. Certain specific problems were in front of them, and if one unfolded a map of the world and attempted to study these problems one saw that, if he put his finger on any country in any part of the globe, the British Empire was interested in one way or another up to the hilt.

Principle of Co-operation.

These problems did not affect the different parts of the Empire in the same degree, and that was where the difficulty of co-operation would come in. Was each portion of the Empire to deal with its own particular problem and to ignore the rest ? Would South Africa stand aloof saying it was no concern of hers ? Would the Dominions stand aloof, saying that Eastern Europe, the Middle East and Asia were no concern of theirs ? In what way were these burdens going to be distributed among the various parts of the British Empire ? Would they recognise that the security of one part of the Empire was the security of the whole ? Would they go in for the principle " Each for all and all for each," or some other principle ? That was the true principle of co-operation, but it needed close study and definition.

He did not wish to probe at all into the Pacific question and the question of a " White Australia." " There are," said the hon. and gallant Member, " other sides to the question, and it is extremely complicated. I know well the arguments of those who see in the Pacific problem extreme danger — the overcrowded East, the colour bar, Japan's position in China, the encroachment southward of Japan amongst the islands of the Caroline and Marshall groups, the possibility of Japan seizing the Philippine Islands, and the awakening of China. All these questions have been raised and pointed to as an extreme danger in the Far East.

" On the other hand, there are those who do not think so seriously of the situation. They point out that the distances are almost too great for war to take place, and the motives are really small. The colour question is an economic question, and if it is looked upon from the economic point of view it is easily solved. The national sentiments of those countries is generally opposed to war, and competition in armaments has only just begun.

Competition in Armaments.

" In considering these matters, however, there is one which stands out above all the rest as a matter of fundamental importance. Competition in armaments is beginning

B 2

or has begun, and if it is allowed to reach a certain point, and to pass that point, there is no stopping it, and war is the inevitable result. It is essential that that competition should be stopped at the very earliest possible moment.

" I do not mean that we should give up all idea of defending in an adequate manner the Pacific. That has to be undertaken, and possibly it will be necessary to provide naval bases and defences at places in the East. I do say, however, that it is essential that the whole situation in the Far East should be adequately reviewed by a Conference comprising not only America and ourselves but Japan as well. I believe, myself, that the sound principle is to extend the Japanese Treaty until the result of that Conference is known. I will go one step further, and point out to Australia the extreme desirability, both from the point of view of defence and from the economic point of view, of encouraging emigration to her countries and the population of her Northern belt at the earliest possible moment, and of giving every facility 'that can be given to enable that to be done. That applies also to our own Government.

" In these days everyone will agree that economic development is of far greater importance in the world than anything else. To my mind, if the whole Empire collaborates and speaks together on these important questions, it will be able to achieve a very great deal, not only for itself but for the benefit of the world at large.

The Colour Question.

" To Great Britain, Eastern Europe and Asia are of very pressing importance. I do not know whether it is sufficiently realised that we have troops in Silesia, in Constantinople, in Palestine, in Mesopotamia, in India and in China at Hong Kong. All along a perimeter of 8,000 miles there are disturbances of one sort or another and of varying degrees of importance. This country is not really fitted to undertake a function of those dimensions.

" If we are going to let this Pacific question wander on until it gets to a point where we have to compete in armaments, we cannot manage these responsibilities all over the world ourselves. I do not want to go into the colour question but it is a subject which has to be covered. It must be borne in mind that this colour question is one that may split the Empire between the East and West. The Dominions are apt to take one point of view, and our Eastern population are apt to take another point of view, and it is in the handling of this question by Indian statesmen that this matter will be very largely solved.

"But I would press the point that if the arguments are removed from the social basis and based more on the economic question—because it is more a question of the standard of life than a colour question—I am credibly informed by those who know that it will be rightly understood in India at least, and, I believe, also in Japan."

Machinery Required.

The hon. and gallant Member went on to say that they required some machinery for co-operation. They had none at the present moment, and he would like to go back to the old name of an Imperial Council. Some standing machinery of that nature was wanted, and he believed that the only satisfactory solution was to have resident Ministers from the Dominions in this country.

Spasmodic consultations once a year for a few days were of no value, and he did not believe for a moment that the mere fact of having resident Ministers meant that the Dominions would be committed to any line to which they did not want to be committed. Such a Council could deal with foreign affairs, trade and matters of defence. Fortunately, they had some machinery for Imperial Defence in this country—the Committee of Imperial Defence. If it were reconstructed on proper lines it would give them what they wanted—a real Committee of Imperial Defence with the Dominions in it.

The Prime Minister and one or two others were members of the Committee of Imperial Defence, but the Prime Ministers of the Dominions *ipso facto* should all be members as well. Technical advice should be given by a sub-committee which was in continual session and studying these matters as they changed from day to day.

A Common Foreign Policy.

Lieut.-Colonel Sir S. Hoare (Coalition Unionist, *Chelsea*), directing attention to the question, " What are to be the relations of the six British Commonwealths to the world outside," said that obviously if the unity of the Empire was to be maintained they must have a common Imperial foreign policy and a means of expressing it. If the Empire was once agreed upon the broad outlines of its foreign policy, then the details and machinery would become much more easy of solution.

He believed when, as he hoped, the Premiers of the Dominions came to consider the present position of Europe they would find that there were two dominant facts in the situation. First, they would find that, after signing the Peace Treaty, we could not altogether go back to a policy of isolation from Europe. Secondly, they would find Europe to a great extent in a state of flux and chaos. "I believe," the hon. and gallant member remarked, "when they consider the state of affairs they will come to the conclusion that the one solid fact amidst this changing sand is the Anglo-French friendship. If that is so, they will agree that the Anglo-French friendship, whether it be in its present form or whether further defined in some Treaty, must be the basis of Imperial policy in Europe."

Proceeding, he said that just as Anglo-French friendship must be the basis of their foreign policy so, perhaps, more important still, must Anglo-American policy be the basis of their world policy. He put such value upon Anglo-American friendship that there was scarcely any sacrifice he would not make to strengthen it. On that account the Conference should consider amongst its most urgent duties the removal of any differences which might at present exist between the various branches of the Anglo-Saxon race.

Anglo-Japanese Alliance.

"It seems to me," said the hon. and gallant Member, "that no alliance should be entered into or renewed that is likely to embitter our relations with any one of the six British Commonwealths or the United States. I do not think it can be denied that the Anglo-Japanese Alliance in its present form—I emphasise that reservation, its present form—has embittered feeling in the United States, and is occasioning a good deal of anxiety in Australia and other British Dominions. I say then, let the Anglo-Japanese Alliance be considered by the Imperial Premiers from that point of view. Let it be considered, if I may make this suggestion, as publicly as possible . . . If public opinion is misinformed there will be trouble either with Japan, or with America and the British Dominions."

If the Anglo-Japanese Alliance was to be renewed it must be modified to meet the just demands of China and to meet also, as far as possible, American objection. They should use the twelve months that must elapse before the Alliance came to an end for a Conference of all the Powers who had interests in the Pacific. "By that I mean," said Sir Samuel Hoare, "not only ourselves and the representatives of the six British Commonwealths, but also the United States, Japan and China. If during the next twelve months some such Conference were brought together, it would be the best means of meeting the two or three grave problems which now face all of us."

Colonel J. C. Wedgwood (Labour, *Newcastle-under-Lyme*) : " Would you include India ? "

Sir S. Hoare : " Yes, I said six British Commonwealths, and I include India. There is the racial question and Japanese emigration, and also the question of disarmament." After remarking that there was in his suggestion at least a basis for a common Imperial policy, the hon. and gallant Member said that if the Empire Premiers wanted a particular form of Imperial organisation the House of Commons would give those views their sympathetic consideration. If they desired to remove Dominion relations from the Colonial Office to some other Department they were willingly ready to make the transference.

Rights of China.

Mr. Neil Maclean (Labour, *Govan*) said that along with other members he had been pressing for a revision of the Anglo-Japanese Treaty. That Treaty was an endeavour to safeguard what this country and Japan considered to be their rights in China. What of the rights of the Chinese in China ? Were not the Chinese people to be asked to take part in the revision of this Treaty which affected the well-being of the Chinese people themselves ? Our ally broke her sacred word and had endeavoured to make of China that which she had already made of Korea—a dependency of Japan.

" The Anglo-Japanese Treaty about to be entered into," said the hon. Member, " is not a question merely for this country and Japan, or even for the Colonies; it is a question which even more vitally affects the Chinese people, and I trust that any Treaty that is going to be entered into will be a Treaty which will square, as the Leader of the House assured me it will square, not merely in letter, but in spirit with the terms of the Covenant of the League of Nations."

Sir J. D. Rees (Coalition Unionist, *Nottingham E.*) spoke of the importance in the Conference of doing justice to the natural and proper aspirations of their Indian fellow-subjects to acquire an equal status throughout the British Empire with the European subjects thereof.

Economy of Force.

Major-General Sir C. Townshend (Independent, *Shropshire, The Wrekin*) said the great fundamental principle of economy of force should be applied not only strategically, but commercially and politically to these questions. He would like to see the Dominions no longer make a money contribution to the British Fleet, but on the principle of economy of force the Dominions should begin to be building their own fleets.

"If you carried out that principle," the hon. and gallant Member proceeded, "we should see in the near future an Australian fleet policing the Pacific and the China Sea, we should see a Canadian fleet in the North Atlantic, and going back to the days of the East India Company when they had an Indian Navy, we should see an Indian fleet policing the Indian Ocean and the Persian Gulf, and so forth, and you would have the British fleet in home waters ready to move to any theatre which was threatened in time of war. That is simple and sound strategy.

"I would apply the same principle to the land forces. On the same system I would have the land forces framed on universal training throughout our great Empire, and if I had trouble in Egypt I would not send troops from England, but would reinforce from South Africa by the Cape-to-Cairo railway. If I had trouble in India I should not mind. Supposing we had a mutiny on the same scale or larger than in 1857, I would take that emergency by the collar by troops from Australia and India.

"That great principle of economy of force applied throughout is worthy the consideration of this Conference. . . . Last night I had the privilege of dining with the Chamber of Commerce of London, and Mr. Massey, the Premier of New Zealand, was there. It did one's heart good to hear the loyal-hearted sentiments of that fine old man. . . . He said our great Dominions were heart and soul with their English comrades."

India and the Conference.

Sir T. Bennett (Coalition Unionist, *Kent, Sevenoaks)* observed that the people of India would not like a Treaty to be renewed in which Japan was depended upon for coming to the defence of India. That was one of the points in the old Treaty which needed careful revision. Dealing with the place of India in the Conference, he said it marked a long step in advance when they heard India spoken of in that House as one of six Commonwealths sitting in a position of equality in the great gathering of the Governments of the Empire.

"I do not," said the hon. Member, "like to put the matter in a contentious way, but if it were necessary it might be put to those in the Conference who are indisposed to deal liberally with India—if there are any, and I doubt it—that India is not defenceless. She has full control over her own taxation, and soon she will be tackling the question of Imperial preference. A Committee has been, or shortly will be, set up in India for settling the terms on which preference should be given to other parts of the Empire. If such a reason were needed, that is a reason for dealing generously and fairly with India. I believe that she may count with confidence on fair and liberal treatment."

Whittled Away.

Commander Carlyon Bellairs (Coalition Unionist, *Kent, Maidstone*) remarked that what struck him most in the debate was the way in which the Anglo-Japanese Treaty had been whittled away. One Member after another had got up to say that America must be satisfied. If she was satisfied China must be satisfied, because America would not be satisfied unless the integrity and sovereignty of China were adequately provided for. Therefore they were face to face with the question whether the Treaty should be renewed at all. As time went on they would have to drop more and more the European outlook in favour of the Pacific outlook. After all, two-thirds of the population of the world was round the Pacific, two-thirds of the population of the British Empire bordered on it, and the shipping of the Pacific was likely in the near future to overtake the shipping of the Atlantic. Another aspect was the view which was likely to be taken by the people of this country of an alliance with Japan so long as Japan pursued militarist ambitions.

"We cannot," said the hon. and gallant Member, " get away from the naval armaments programme of Japan, providing for 16 super-dreadnoughts in 1928 in addition to the existing dreadnoughts, with Navy Estimates of £62,000,000 this year, representing 33 per cent. of the Estimates of Japan, and with combined Army, Navy and Air Force Estimates for the year amounting to over half the expenditure of Japan. We are profoundly anxious that the liberalising elements in Japan shall thrive, but I question whether our alliance has not really helped the militarist party in Japan rather than the liberalising tendencies."

Mr. B. C. Spoor (Labour, *Bishop Auckland*) remarked that whilst Labour desired the Imperial Conference to have very practical and beneficial results, they did not for a single moment imagine that this great association of free self-governing peoples was going to be built up merely on a commercial basis.

Dominions and Nation Status.

Mr. H. B. Betterton (Coalition Unionist, *Nottingham, Rushcliffe*) was not sure that the profound importance of the

Conference was not more fully realised in some of the Dominions than it was in this country. One result of the War undoubtedly had been that they now, perhaps for the first time, completely recognised the claim of each of the Dominions to the status of a nation within that community of nations which they called the British Empire. He did not think that claim had ever been disputed, but undoubtedly it had never been recognised as it was now.

They now admitted freely the right and the claim of the heads of the Dominion Governments to membership of the Imperial Council. Secondly, and perhaps most important of all, they admitted the representation of the Dominions in signing the Peace Treaty, which each of them separately signed as a separate Dominion. In the third place the Dominions had direct representation on the Assembly of the League of Nations ; and fourthly—and this might have the most far-reaching results—they had a direct contact with the Secretariat of the League. It was obvious that in such a situation, with a group of nations comprising the British Empire all with equal rights, the maintenance of the unity of the Empire would put to the test the highest qualities of statesmanship both in this country and in the Dominions. It was obvious, too, that with this separate identity, if a wise policy were not pursued, and unless in fundamentals at any rate there was a common purpose and a common unity which inspired both the statesmen in this country and in the Dominions, disruption might ensue.

Reading the debates in the Dominion Parliaments one saw that there were two points upon which there was no difference of opinion in any quarter. The first was that the future of the Empire lay rather in co-operation than in federation ; and, secondly, there would have to be loyalty to the connection with this country. Hon. Members had asked if Canada were committed, say by South Africa or Australia, which had racial problems, to a course of policy of which Canada could not approve, how far would Canada be bound. And conversely, was this country to accept responsibility for acts of the Dominions, whether in the Dominions or elsewhere? The possibility that these dangers might arise showed beyond all doubt that there was need for the closest co-ordination, the closest co-operation and the most intimate exchange of views.

The Economic Weapon.

Referring to Ireland, the hon. Member said they had been told that at the present time a meeting between the British Government and those who had the power to direct the olicy of Sinn Fein in Ireland was impossible. Was it too much to ask whether it was not possible to invoke the services if one or other of the representatives of the Dominion Parliaments now in this country to see whether a conference might not be called? As to Imperial defence, the last War had shown he enormous efficiency of the economic weapon.

" I believe," the hon. Member said, " that in the future he very threat of a blockade will be sufficient to bring any recalcitrant nation to book, and that, obviously, is the view f those who are responsible for the Covenant of the League f Nations, because the very first weapon under that Covenant which is to be brought into operation is the economic weapon. do suggest it would be a proper matter for the consideration f the Imperial Conference that we might, after consultation with the British Dominions, see how far the common resources f the Empire might be used in case of need as an economic weapon."

Mr. T. P. O'Connor (Nationalist, *Liverpool, Scotland*) nought the Conference offered a great opportunity which ught not to be missed of bringing to an end the stupid and isastrous struggle between England and Ireland.

Ireland and the Empire.

" I do not know a single one of the Colonial Premiers," remarked Mr. O'Connor, " who has not over and over again expressed a strong belief in the principle of Home Rule for Ireland, and I do not know a single Dominion which they represent which has not in some way or other expressed the same view. Resolutions in favour of Home Rule for Ireland have been passed no less than five times by the Legislatures of Canada, and a similar resolution was passed by the first Commonwealth Parliament in Australia."

" What the Dominions cannot understand is this. You have given them Home Rule. They are absolutely masters of their own destiny. They could have stood apart and not sent the men to you in your hour of struggle so far as their constitutional rights were concerned. Yet in face of this freedom, they rushed to the defence of the Mother-land as if they had had the decision of the question in their own Parliaments and as if their shores, and not yours, were menaced by the Germans. They therefore cannot understand why you would refuse to give to Ireland that which has proved such a magnificent success in their own case."

He sincerely hoped therefore that the Imperial Conference would deal with the question of Ireland.

Sir C. Kinloch-Cooke (Coalition Unionist, *Devonport*) suggested that on the solution of the question of migration

within the Empire rested the development of the defen(
of their common inheritance. If we were to have a trul
Imperial system of migration within the Empire it must b
a system financed by the Overseas Dominions as well as b
Great Britain.

Brigadier-General G. K. Cockerill (Coalition Unionis
Reigate) said the real task in the immediate future was t
devise some simple, but elastic machinery for these objects :-

(1) To permit the general will of the component part
of the Empire to be ascertained with greater ease an
facility than it has been ascertainable in the past.

(2) When the general will has been ascertained t
give direction to the unanimous purpose of the Empir
as so determined without friction between the componen
parts; and

(3) To strengthen, develop, and harmonise the mutua
interest, and, above all, the mutual ideals of the Empir(
whilst jealously safeguarding the authority of ever
nation in the British Commonwealth.

Imperial Defence: Organisation, etc.

Lieut.-General Sir A. Hunter-Weston (Coalition Unionis(
Bute and North Ayrshire) observed that all parts of the Empir
needed the help of the others. In other words, the Imperia
Defence of the whole was a vital necessity to each par(
Members of the House who had studied the subject had in th
past put forward a form of organisation which it was believe(
would be suited for the purpose. He referred to a Joi(
Committee of the Committee of Imperial Defence, on whi(
delegates from all the great Dominions would find their rig(
place and which also delegates from the Great Services and t(
great Departments of State concerned would be able to join.

There would be certain essential conditions. First, t(
organisation should meet frequently and regularly ; secondl(
it should be a permanent organisation with a carefully select(
secretariat ; and, thirdly, it should have as a neutral chairm(
some gentleman of Ministerial and, if possible, of Cabin(
rank who would attend all its meetings.

Colonel Wedgwood : " What powers ? "

Sir A. Hunter-Weston : " All those who think with 1
have laid it down that the question of execution must
exclusively with the Home Government and the Governme(
of the Dominions. This body should be a purely advis(
body, able to give to the Governments at home and th(
of the Dominions the best technical advice, put into
most easily assimilated form, so that men who have no ti(
to go into detail would be able to get in outline form

dvantages and disadvantages of any suggested proposal. 'he body would have to prepare a scheme for utilising at nce all our available resources. That, I think, is possible ithout any form of conscription.

" It is appalling to consider that nearly three years have assed since the end of hostilities and yet nothing definite nd practical has been done to get going on these lines."

leply for the Government.

The Leader of the House (the Right Hon. Austen Chamber- lin), having referred to the high level reached by the debate nd the thoughtful consideration it revealed of the many roblems which the Empire presents, proceeded to say that, a a responsible Minister must not pre-judge in any way the ecisions of the Conference, he spoke under considerable striction.

" The British Empire," he observed, " is one of the most arvellous productions of human, political ingenuity, or, all I rather say, of political sense among human beings. is what it is, not in the main by the set purpose of statesmen even of people, but because, given the quality of the races hich make up the Empire, their historical, their geographical nd other circumstances, common interests which have eveloped have led us to this point of common organisation nd co-operation.

" One of my hon. friends spoke in relation to one of the bjects which may come before the Conference—the slow- ss of our political movement. I am astonished at the pid advance which has been made within the last 20 or 25 ears. We find some form of Imperial gathering a necessity our present existence and no longer an accident occurring rare intervals. We find the equality of all the members the Empire within that gathering fully and absolutely cognised. We find India, the last to reach us, sitting on rms of equality with the other Dominions of the British own. That is no small achievement in itself. It is all te greater achievement because this growth of unity has been t merely consistent with, but contemporaneous with a owth of nationality, of independence, and of autonomy, every portion of the British Empire.

nity in Diversity.

" The British Empire is an example, such as the world has ver seen before, of unity in diversity and close co-operation mbined with the complete independence of the autonomous rts."

Mr. J. Jones (Labour, *Silvertown*) : "Except Ireland."

The Leader of the House : " I do not wonder that the spectacle of an Empire so constituted, when it came before the world at large, as it did during the War—and perhaps from this point of view, still more strikingly during the Peace Conference, when the British Empire appended not one signature, but each part its separate signature, to the Treaties of Peace—I do not wonder that this unity in diversity surprised and even was somewhat incomprehensible to our Allies and friends among foreign nations. I think when the Dominions and ourselves appeared as separate national members at the meeting of the League of Nations, not a little astonishment was created to find that, whilst able to act so closely and effectively together in vital matters of common concern, we could permit so much diversity of view and of hope on minor matters on which opinions differ.

" Something has been said to-day about the future Imperial organisation. One of my hon. friends observed that the British Empire forms a model for the League of Nations. I think it is a league of nations. It was Major-General Sir J. Davidson, and he dwelt on the fact that initiative in progress must come from the Dominions themselves. I think that is true. If they have suggestions to make, they will find them fall on no unfriendly ears. For myself, I will say only this, that I can conceive of no suggestion for closer co-operation for giving them a more definite and more continuous share in directing the policy of the Empire, or for giving them greater power and authority in the defence of the Empire—I can conceive of no suggestion which would commend itself to them which would not be gladly accepted by His Majesty's Government and this House of Commons."

Subjects for Discussion.

" We enter this Conference with no cut-and-dried agenda. His Majesty's Government have suggested as the principal subjects which they wish to bring before the Conference :—

" The Naval, Military and Air Defences of the Empire,

" Arrangements for securing common Imperial policy in foreign affairs,

" The question of the renewal of the Anglo-Japanese Alliance, and

" The composition and agenda and meeting place of the Constitutional Conference contemplated under Resolution 9 of the Imperial War Conference of 1917.

" A good many other questions have also been suggested —the question of emigration—or migration within the Empire ather than emigration outside the Empire—the question of mperial communication in all shapes and forms, and a host f other things. I do not know how many of these it will be ossible for the Conference to consider. Some of them, erhaps, may be discussed outside the Conference, with the olonial Office or in other ways. But, after all, an agenda is ade for man, and not man for the agenda, and if the)ominions, or any of them, desire and can find time to discuss ther questions, they will find us willing to enter into the iscussion with them.

eland.

"The hope was expressed by Mr. O'Connor that the ominion representatives might raise a discussion upon Ireland. Iy principal hesitation about making a suggestion of that nd myself would be lest the invitation to the Dominions meddle in our domestic affairs should be taken by them a first step on our part towards attempting to meddle in eirs. But if they desire it, and are no better informed pout the present law which establishes the present Government in Ireland than the hon. Member, I think that such a iscussion would be very valuable. The hon. Member implored to give Home Rule to Ireland. We have given to Ireland measure of Home Rule more liberal than has ever been roposed before in any of the Bills presented to the House of ommons from the time of Mr. Gladstone onwards.

"If—which I cannot believe—the Dominion representatives think that the hon. Member gives a correct picture of the rospects of government in Ireland, and the powers of the ish people to manage their affairs, then, indeed, I think discussion would be found to be very interesting and illumiting. We all understand, however, that the hon. Member ust sing his own sweet Irish melody on every occasion tat he can ; but it does not appear to have been indeed the sbject principally in the minds of the House when they eked to have this day set apart for this discussion.

uestion of Defence.

"As regards the question of defence, which, of course, ust always take a large place in any discussion among the fferent nations of the Empire on their own concerns, very reful preparations have been made for that discussion on te present occasion, with a view to making it as useful as we n. The proposals of the Government on this subject have en under careful consideration for some time past, and fidential memoranda have been prepared by the different

fighting Services.   These have been carefully examined from
the point of view of Imperial Defence as a whole, and co
ordinated by a sub-committee of the Committee of Imperia
Defence which has sat under the chairmanship of my right hon
friend the Lord President of the Council.*

"I do not think that this is the occasion, nor am I th
man, to review all the multifarious activities of the Committee
of Imperial Defence.   Of the valuable work it has achieved
since its inception by the present Lord President of the Council
in his Administration in 1903, and the outbreak of the Grea
War, anyone who was in the least behind the scenes in tha
great struggle will have some idea, and anyone who wen
out of office at the time I did, when the Committee had only
been functioning in its new form under the impulsion of my
right hon. friend for a couple of years, and then came bac
to find into what it had developed, and what work it had done
must feel the country owes a deep debt of gratitude to the Lor
President of the Council as the father of our first effectiv
Council of State on Imperial Defence, our first effectiv
co-ordinating organisation for that purpose.

Co-ordination of Forces.

"The House knows that, owing to the overwhelming
pressure of business, it has not been possible for the Committee
of Imperial Defence to resume their full pre-War activitie
in this last year, but a provisional solution of that difficult
has been found in the establishment of a standing Defenc
Sub-Committee, over which the Lord President of the Counc
presides, and the meetings of which are regularly attende
by the Secretaries of State for War, the Air, the Colonies an
India, the First Lord of the Admiralty, the First Sea Lor
the Chief of the Imperial General Staff, and the Chief of th
Air Staff, with representatives of the Treasury or any othe
office, as circumstances require, according to the need of th
subject discussed.

"It is, of course, the desire of His Majesty's Governmer
to promote, so far as in them lies, such co-ordination of th
Military, Naval and Air Forces of the Empire as enables ther
when the assent of their respective authorities has bee
obtained, to co-operate most quickly, most effectively, ar
with the greatest prospect of success in time of war.   But it
not for His Majesty's Government to talk with that air
command which is so natural to General Townshend, and
explain how they can move the forces of Australia here, t
forces of Canada there, and the forces of South Africa

* The Right Hon. Arthur James Balfour.

another place. Those are decisions which can be taken only by the Governments of the respective Dominions themselves.

" The measure of co-ordination and the measure of co-operation to which we can attain must be decided, and will be decided, by the free choice of the various Dominions concerned. All that is necessary for me to say, on behalf of His Majesty's Government here, is that we are fully seized with the importance of this co-operation, that we shall do everything we can to facilitate it and that any assistance we can render in that matter, and which the Dominions require of us, will be joyfully and gladly given.

Foreign Policy : Anglo-Japanese Alliance.

" Similarly we shall welcome any closer association of the Dominions with us in all matters concerning the foreign policy of the Empire. . . . The objections I have heard urged this afternoon to a renewal of the Anglo-Japanese Alliance—not in its present form but in any form—have been that the conditions which gave rise to it have passed away. But the conditions of to-day are not the conditions of yesterday; and what about the conditions of to-morrow ? We have to look not only backwards but forward into the possible combinations of the future.

" It has again been urged that the Alliance has given rise to misconception and apprehension in America. I do not believe that the intention or the results of the Anglo-Japanese Alliance do give rise to any real apprehension in America or to the Government of the United States, and I am certain that there is no reason for them to feel any such apprehension. I do not say that it may not excite a certain measure of apprehension amongst people who are ill-informed as to the obligations of the two parties, or who misconceive the resolute determination of the British people to maintain friendly relations with their American kinsmen.

" It has always been a cardinal feature of British policy to remove any apprehension which stands in the path of good relations with the United States and to cultivate those good relations to the utmost of our power. I entirely agree with what was said by Sir S. Hoare that a new competition in armaments, and that competition between this country and America, would be not merely a tragedy for those two countries, but a tragedy for the civilised world.

Pacific Powers and Co-operation.

" Of course, I must be careful not in any way to prejudice the question as to the attitude of the Conference on this

c

point, but I think it right to say at once that we should b
no party to any alliance directed against America, or ii
which we could be called upon to act against America.

" I do not, therefore, say that no continuation of th
Anglo-Japanese Alliance in a modified form is not possible
I think it may be found to be possible to reconcile our desir
for a perfect understanding and the closest co-operation witl
the United States of America with the continuation of ou
close and intimate friendship with an ally who acted loyall
when the occasion of the alliance arose, and who rendere
invaluable support from which we here in Great Britain a
well as other parts of the British Empire reaped the greates
benefit during the War.

" What, after all, must be the object of any British Govern
ment—and let me say I speak not merely of the Governmen
in this country, but of any Government in any of th
Domr ions ? Surely it must be to secure such confidence
such understanding, and such co-operation among the grea
Pacific Powers as may prevent that new competition in arma
ments of which mention has been made, and may secure th
peace of that great ocean and of the lands abutting on it.

Continued Unity and Friendship.

" I have spoken of the British Empire as, in fact, ;
league of nations, more closely knit than the other and mor
famous League which has lately come to birth. What th
steps of future development will be I do not know, but tha
a league of nations such as ours, so necessary to each, pre
serving peace for so large a portion of the world, exercisin
so immense an influence for good upon civilisation, should n
in course of time by whatever means—perhaps means we d
not now foresee—continue to develop its common constitution
organs and its opportunities of co-operation in policy and
action is to me inconceivable.

" We look back with pride on the birth of these Briti
nations across the seas. We follow their fortunes wi
affection. In the great hour of need from one end of t
Empire to the other came a common voice and a comm
resolution. If peace had not cemented, blood would ha
bound us for ever. The sacrifices which each of us made, t
graves side by side in so many quarters of the world are
pledge to us for our continued unity and friendship."

Against Federation.

Colonel Wedgwood said he observed that one of
subjects to be raised was the question of the Constitution

Conference to be held hereafter. That involved presumably the discussion of federation, and he begged the Government to avoid any form of federation for the British Empire as they would the plague.

Lieut.-Commander Kenworthy (Independent Liberal, *Hull Central*) said there was a great advantage in keeping their foreign policy apart from party, but owing to the crimes and blunders during the last few years of the present Government —their predecessors also had some blame in the matter— those days had gone. Any party that hoped to come into power during this generation would be ill-advised to bind itself to carry on blindly the policy of the right hon. gentleman. He hoped that would be made clear to the Dominion Premiers.

The Hon. W. Ormsby-Gore (Coalition Unionist, *Stafford*) said the Dominions would be extremely glad that the debate had taken place if only to remove misconceptions which existed in the minds of many in the Dominions that there were people in this country who were anxious to bring the Empire into some form of federation. No word of that had been heard in the debate. The representatives of the Dominions met as the representatives of free equal nations. That was the line which they were now developing in the Empire, and no longer were people in this country desirous of imposing the super-State. They did not want a super-State in the League of Nations or the British Empire. He was glad the Colonial Secretary was not there that afternoon if only to emphasise the urgent necessity of removing the Dominion Department from the Colonial Office. He hoped that these debates would invariably be dealt with by the Leader of the House. He believed that small questions of machinery of that kind were important because they were a symbol to the Dominions of a free State.

The debate was continued until the close of the sitting, when the motion for adjournment lapsed.

IMPERIAL DEFENCE.

(Reductions in Cavalry.)

Reductions in the number of cavalry regiments and the Defence of the Empire formed the subject of questions in the House of Commons on 7th April.

Lieut.-Colonel H. Page Croft (National Party, *Bournemouth*) asked the Prime Minister whether the Imperial Defence

Committee met and gave full consideration to the reductions in the cavalry of the United Kingdom and India, involving the disbanding in all of 67 cavalry regiments, before deciding to disband the four Regular and 45 Yeomanry regiments in the United Kingdom ?

The Prime Minister (the Right Hon. D. Lloyd George): " The answer is in the negative. The responsibility for these reductions must be taken by the Government and by Parliament."

Lieut.-Colonel Page Croft : " Was the reduction of the Indian cavalry regiments settled in the first place in this country ? Is the whole defensive position of the Empire being considered in this connection ? So long as the vast majority of the British Army are in Mesopotamia, on the Rhine, and in Palestine, does the right hon. gentleman not consider that the question of disbanding four cavalry regiments in this country should be delayed until some of the troops have returned to this country ? "

The Prime Minister : " The hon. and gallant member is raising very big issues, which were discussed at considerable length here, and I do not think that by question and answer I can possibly deal with it."

Lieut.-Colonel Page Croft: " Will the right hon. gentleman consider my suggestion ? "

The Prime Minister : " We have considered this among other methods of securing economy in this country. We had to take into account, not merely the needs of the Empire but the resources of this country."

NAVAL ARMAMENTS.

In the House of Commons on 30th May the Government was questioned regarding limitation of naval armaments.

Lieut.-Commander Kenworthy (Independent Liberal, Hu *Central*) asked the Prime Minister whether his attention had been called to the unanimous passing in the United State Senate of the amendment of Senator Borah authorising and requesting the President to invite the Government of Japan and His Majesty's Government to consider the mutual limitation of naval armaments ; whether he would consider inviting Parliament to pass a resolution in similar terms and, in the meantime, if he would give directions for the cessation of expenditure on new construction for His Majesty's Navy until such time as the result of the action of the United States Senate was apparent ?

The Prime Minister (the Right Hon. D. Lloyd George):
" Yes, Sir. I have observed the proceedings in the United
States Senate. We have not yet received an invitation from
the President."

Lieut.-Commander Kenworthy: " May I have an answer
to the second part of the question, whether it is advisable to
pass a similar resolution ? " (Hon. Members: " No ! ")
" May I have an answer to the third part, as to new construction ? "

The Prime Minister: " Everything will depend, of course,
on whether this resolution is put into operation."

Lieut.-Commander Kenworthy: " In view of the strength
of our naval position cannot we afford to lead the way in
stopping construction ? "

Viscount Curzon (Coalition Unionist, *Battersea S.*): " Is
it not a fact that no part of Senator Borah's resolution refers
to ships under construction now ? "

The Prime Minister: " That is so."

PEACE TREATY.

(German Reparations, Disarmament, etc.)

On 5th May the House of Commons went into Committee
of Supply and discussed the Vote for the Foreign Office. The
debate turned on the question of German observance of the
Peace Treaty, and the subject of Reparations was, in particular,
very fully dealt with in the speeches. The discussion was
taken within a few hours of the close of the meeting of the
Supreme Council of the Allies held in London during the
opening days of May.

DEBATE IN 'HOUSE OF COMMONS.

The Prime Minister (the Right Hon. D. Lloyd George)
said that when the Conference of the Allied Powers met
Germany was in default in the execution of the Treaty on
some of the most important provisions—disarmament, trial
of criminals, reparation, and four or five other clauses. The
Allies had during the past two years shown considerable
forbearance. In every case where Germany had legitimate
difficulties to encounter, where she could show that she was
doing her best to meet the demands of the Treaty, but that

conditions over which she had no control made it difficult for
her to fulfil its requirements, the Allies had made concessions,
extended time, and generally made it easier for Germany to
meet her difficulties.   There had never been a single case
that he could recall where the Allies had been unduly harsh
in.their action.   In fact, the criticism was just the other
way.

Dealing with the main cases of undoubted default on the
part of Germany, Mr. Lloyd George said that, as regards
disarmament, the Germans made a real effort after the Allied
Conference at Spa.   But there were still far too many machine-
guns and rifles unsurrendered.   In addition to that—and
this probably was the most disquieting factor—irregular
military organisations called the Einwohnerwehr and other
names were still in existence in Germany.   In Bavaria alone
there was a force of 300,000 men, a very considerable force
in East Prussia, in Würtemberg, and, he believed, in other
parts of Germany.   Those forces, added together, no doubt
would become the nucleus of a most formidable army.   They
were armed with rifles, they had machine-guns, and it was
suspected that they had a number of cannon.

France was uneasy ; she could not let down her arms ;
and therefore it was essential that Germany should carry out
that provision of the Treaty.

War Criminals.

The position with regard to war criminals was quite
unsatisfactory.   What made it all the more unsatisfactory
was that the Allied Governments made very substantial
concessions to Germany's susceptibilities by acceding to her
proposal that the trial of the accused persons should take
place before the High Court of Leipzig, a Court of un-
blemished reputation.   The Germans, however, were not
showing the same anxiety and diligence in bringing these
people to justice as they would if they had been offended
against the German laws and they were anxious to prosecute
them.

With reference to reparations, Germany by the Treaty
was to have paid £1,000,000,000 in cash and kind by 1st May
1921.   She had paid at the outside £400,000,000.   The
£1,000,000,000 was to cover the cost of the Army of Occupation as well as reparations.   As to the total amount of the
reparations, after hearing everything the German representatives had to say, and perusing everything the German
Government had to submit, the Reparations Commission
found that, after deducting the amount already received, an

after adding the Belgian debt, there was due from Germany £6,600,000,000.

The Leader of the House (the Right Hon. Austen Chamberlain) : " Gold pounds."

The Prime Minister : " Yes, gold pounds. Of that figure, France claimed 52 per cent. and the British Empire 22 per cent." The Supreme Council, the right hon. gentleman said, had considered the award of the Reparations Commission, the scheme of payments that should be submitted to Germany, the guarantees by which those payments could be ensured, and the Sanctions by which those obligations should be enforced. The Paris scheme was a scheme of 42 annuities beginning at £100,000,000 sterling per annum, increasing at intervals of two and three years until at the end of eleven years a maximum of £300,000,000 per annum would be reached. In addition it was proposed that there should be a variable sum equal to 12 per cent. of the German exports added to the fixed annuity for each year.

London Conference Proposal.

" The proposal of the London Conference," Mr. Lloyd George explained, " is that there should be one fixed sum, and that that should be £100,000,000, but that there should be a variable sum added to that per annum which will be equal to 26 per cent. of the German exports. Whether that is higher than the Paris scheme or lower depends entirely upon German prosperity. . . . The whole point of the new scheme is that Germany's annual liability will vary according to her capacity at the time."

In order to enable Germany to meet her liabilities, it was proposed that three categories of Bonds should be issued. " Series A Bonds," the Premier continued, " are for £600,000,000 gold, to be delivered by 1st July. They will bear interest at 5 per cent. with a 1 per cent. cumulative sinking fund. Series B Bonds will be for 38 milliards of gold marks or £1,900,000,000 sterling, to be delivered by the 1st November, and the interest will be the same. Series C Bonds will be delivered for the balance, which is estimated at 82 milliards of gold marks, or £4,100,000,000 sterling, to be delivered by the 1st November this year, but with this very important reservation, that the Commission is only to attach coupons to and issue these Bonds as and when it is satisfied that the payments to be made under the agreement are sufficient to provide for the interest and sinking fund.

" The first two series will be issued this year. As for the third series the date of issue will depend upon the capacity

of Germany to pay, and the Reparations Commission wi
decide that from time to time, and issue the Bonds accordin
to the capacity of Germany to pay. . . . Twenty-five pe
cent. on the exports is to be devoted, with the fixed annu
sum, to the payment of the Bonds which will be issued.]
there is a balance over and above that for any given yea
it is to be devoted to the payment of interest upon the un
issued Bonds, which represents the uncovered capital of th
debt, together with a sum equal to 1 per cent. of her export
Beyond that the interest will be wiped out. It will no
accumulate against her, and that is a very important con
cession, and I hope it will have important effects."

Methods of Payment.

Turning to the methods of payment, the Premier said th
first payment would be within 25 days and would be £50,000,00
sterling. The next item of payment would be in kind—coal
Then there were aniline dyes, timber, and material for recon
struction in France. Those sums would aggregate to ver
considerable amounts during the period of reconstruction
which was a difficult period for Germany as well as for Franc
and would probably extend over five or ten years.

The Right Hon. Lord Robert Cecil (Independen
Unionist, *Hitchin*) : " Is this against the first instalment o
£100,000,000 ? "

The Prime Minister : " It is as you get it from year t
year. In a good year you may have material worth £50,000,00
and that would be credited to Germany for that year." Th
next source of revenue, he proceeded to say, was a levy o
25 per cent. on all German exports to whatever country the
went. The collection would be, not in marks, but in th
equivalent of gold—in bills negotiable on the English marke
Germany's export trade before the War was over £500,000,00
The value of that at present prices would be somewhere abou
£1,000,000,000. If Germany had a trade of that kind, the
25 per cent. on her exports would be £250,000,000 sterlin
Other German revenues would also be pledged as security f
the payment of the interest on the Bonds.

Having explained the decisions of the Allies with respe
to the Sanctions to be enforced in the event of Germany
failure to comply with the Allied demands, Mr. Lloyd Georg
said the acceptance must come by 12th May. For te
months they had been discussing that problem unceasing
with German experts and German statesmen. She mu
make up her mind at last.

After a debate occupying the entire sitting, the Committ
reported progress.

Allied Conditions Accepted.

On 11th May, the Prime Minister, in reply to a question in the House of Commons, announced the acceptance by Germany of the Allied conditions.

The Prime Minister (the Right Hon. D. Lloyd George) said : " On 5th May on behalf of the Supreme Council I delivered a series of demands to the Ambassador for the German Government, and at 11 o'clock this morning he came and handed me the following document :

" ' MR. PRIME MINISTER,

" ' In accordance with instructions just received, I am commanded by my Government, in accordance with the decision of the Reichstag, and with reference to the resolution of the Allied Powers of the 5th of May, 1921, in the name of the new German Government, to declare, as desired, the following : —

" ' The German Government is resolved :

" ' (1) To carry out, without reserve or condition, their obligations as defined by the Reparations Commission ;

" ' (2) To accept and to carry out, without reserve or condition, the guarantees in respect of those obligations prescribed by the Reparations Commission ;

" ' (3) To carry out, without reserve or delay, the measures of military, naval, and aerial disarmament, notified to the German Government by the Allied Powers in their Note of 29th January, 1921, those overdue being completed at once and the remainder by the prescribed dates ;

" ' (4) To carry out, without reserve or delay, the trial of the War criminals, and to execute the other un-fulfilled portions of the Treaty referred to in the first paragraph of the Note of the Allied Governments of the 5th of May.

" ' I ask the Allied Powers to take note immediately of this Declaration, etc., etc.

" ' (Signed) STHAMER.'

" I immediately wired to all the other Governments—it was handed to me as President of the Supreme Council held in London—that in my opinion this is a complete acceptance of every demand."

Mr. Bottomley (Independent, *Hackney S.*) : " In view of the acceptance, will the Reparation (Recovery) Act now be suspended ? "

The Prime Minister : " No."

Dominions and Reparations.

In the House of Commons on 4th April questions **were** addressed to the Government with respect to German reparation.

Mr. C. F. White (Liberal, *Derbyshire W.*) asked the Prime Minister whether India or any of the Dominions had introduced or passed legislation similar to the German Reparation (Recovery) Act.

The Prime Minister (the Right Hon. D. Lloyd George): "The answer is in the negative, with the exception of Newfoundland."

Dr. D. Murray asked the Prime Minister the amount which would be due to Great Britain from Germany by way of reparations in the year from 1st May, 1921, to 1st May, 1922, under the Treaty of Versailles.

The Prime Minister : "Under Article 233 of the Treaty of Versailles it is the duty of the Reparations Commission to fix the amount to be paid by Germany in 1921-22 towards the discharge of her reparation liabilities. Subject to the satisfaction of the priority accorded to Belgium, the British Empire is entitled under the Spa Agreement to 22 per cent. of the amount recovered under the head of reparation. The hon. member will, however, remember that there are prior charges on all receipts from Germany for the costs of the armies of occupation and the repayment of the advances made in respect of coal deliveries."

TREATY OF PEACE (HUNGARY) ACT.

The Treaty of Peace (Hungary) Act received the Roya Assent on 12th May.

DEBATE IN HOUSE OF COMMONS.

On 20th April the Bill to confirm the Treaty came o for Second Reading in the House of Commons.

The Under-Secretary of State for Foreign Affairs (M Cecil Harmsworth) said the Hungary Treaty followed in i main features other Treaties that had been presented Parliament. They had in the forefront of it the Covenan of the League of Nations. They had military, naval and a clauses very similar to those which were found in the oth Treaties. There was the usual chapter on reparations a the chapter on labour and so forth. But he thought it wou

)e generally recognised that the work of the Peace Conference
n Paris in regard to this Treaty was easier than in the case
)f the other Treaties that were there framed, because in point
)f fact the Kingdom of Hungary had fallen to a large extent
nto its component parts before the Peace Conference took
n hand the work of constructing a Treaty. The Slav, Czech,
;lovakian, and Roumanian populations had already separated
hemselves from Hungary. As a result of the labours of the
)onference in Paris a new Hungary was created—a compact
ntity with a population of some 6,500,000 or 7,000,000
fagyars.

When there was discussion and controversy as to the
stablishment of frontiers here and there, and the allocation
f a population, he would like to observe that the Peace
)onference used throughout its deliberations Hungarian
tatistics, the results of the census of 1910. They were the
nly figures that were available, and there was this advantage
rom the point of view of a defence of the Peace Treaty that,
t all events, those figures did not err in unfairness of any
ind to the Magyar people. Having discussed the rearrange-
ient of frontiers in detail, the hon. gentleman claimed that
rhatever might be advanced in criticism of the Treaty, the
reat Powers who framed it were under no suspicion of having
ad ulterior objects in view. They had no purpose to serve
ther than the best interests of the emancipated peoples and
f European peace.

teparations.

The reparations under the Treaty of the Trianon did
ot differ materially in character from the reparations pro-
osed to be exacted by the Treaty of Versailles. It was
urely a right principle that the aggressor States should be
equired to pay for the damage done up to the limit of their
apacity to pay. If they failed to establish that principle
ley failed to remove one of the principal incentives to war.
n the case of Hungary the amount of compensation was to be
xed by the Reparations Commission, which was to draw up
ie schedule of payments, prescribing the time and manner of
ecuring and discharging by Hungary, within 30 years, dating
om 1st May, 1921, of the debt assessed by the Commission.
here was no reason to apprehend that Hungary would
eceive in the matter of reparation anything but justice at
ie hands of the Allies. He hoped and believed that new
lungary had every prospect before her of a splendid and a
rosperous future.

Colonel J. C. Wedgwood (Labour, *Newcastle-under-Lyme*),
moving the rejection of the Bill, said he thought there was

very real sympathy in that House for Hungary. Of all the Powers warring against them they had less enmity against Hungary than anybody else. To his mind the whole value of the Treaty depended upon whether or not they saw to the protection of the minorities in Hungary. If they had there a representative of Great Britain who took the decent English point of view that anti-Semitism was bad form ; if they had a representative who would keep in touch with the Minister of Labour there, and be open to hear the complaints and views of labour, things might be different. As to the repara-tion clauses, the Bill should not be allowed to pass without a protest being registered against the suicidal policy of clamour-ing for what they could not get.

Lieut.-Commander Kenworthy (Independent Liberal, *Hull Central*), in seconding the amendment, said that if it was right to hold a plebiscite for Schleswig-Holstein, or for the deter-mination of the frontiers of Upper Silesia, it was equally right to hold one for the frontiers of Hungary.

Blots on the Treaties.

The Right Hon. H. H. Asquith (Leader of the Independent Liberal Party) remarked that on the whole they might rejoice that large populations which had suffered in the past from an artificial and in many ways unsympathetic union were now in a position to work out their own future on the lines of autonomy. To talk about getting reparation in any solid or substantial sense from communities such as Hungary, or Austria, or Bulgaria, or Turkey was paying mere lip service to a political phrase. The sooner they wiped off these purely hypothetical and imaginary claims, not only from their own national estimates of possible revenue in the future, but from the whole international slate, the sooner they would recognise the absolutely clear teachings of common sense. He thought it had been one of the greatest blots upon the whole of this series of Treaties that the Great Powers did not insist, as a condition of emancipation and of the grant of autonomous rule to these countries, that they should remain as they had been, members of one economic unit.

The Lord President of the Council (the Right Hon. A. J. Balfour) said that to put off the ratification of the Treaty and go again over all the work of the Peace Conference was the last method which any sane man would adopt if he wanted to bring to an end the state of unsettlement which unfortunately prevailed in Eastern Europe. Lieut.-Commander Kenworthy was very insistent that a great deal more could have been done to secure freedom of transit between the various States There had been called together at Barcelona through th

;fforts and organisation of the League of Nations an Inter-
ational Transit Conference at which all the nations were
epresented. The result, undoubtedly, would be a great
mprovement in international transit arrangements.

As to reparations, it might be that the amount of money
o be got out of countries like Austria and Hungary was
nsignificant. But the facts ought to be examined and the
nachinery for examining them would be set to work when
he Treaty was ratified. The policy that had been adopted
vas the only one that could be adopted, namely, that they
hould leave it to a competent body to decide what these
eople could pay. The question of the protection of minorities
vas causing great anxiety to all concerned. It was a bold
tep to provide in these Treaties that unpopular minorities
hould be under some protection, or that the States which
ad been created by the War should be put under some
rotection from a body which was brought into being by the
Var. The League of Nations had been required by the
'act to undertake that duty, and he was confident that the
eague would do its best to perform it.

The amendment was negatived without a division and
he Bill was read a second time. It was not amended
uring subsequent stages, and was read a third time on
5th April.

After the Second Reading in the House of Lords on 5th
lay, the Bill had a rapid passage through the Upper House
nd became law on the date named.

LEAGUE OF NATIONS.

(International Labour Conference—Conventions.)

The first International Labour Conference under Part XIII.
f the Peace Treaty was held in Washington in October and
ovember, 1919. It adopted six Draft Conventions and six
ecommendations as follows : —

ONVENTIONS.

(1) For the establishment of an 8-hours day.

(2) Concerning unemployment statistics and labour exchanges.

(3) Relating to the employment of women before and after child.
rth.

(4) Prohibiting the employment of women at night.

(5) Fixing a minimum age for juvenile labour.

(6) Prohibiting the night-work of young persons.

RECOMMENDATIONS.

(1) Concerning unemployment insurance, the distribution of public work, and other unemployment questions.

(2) Concerning reciprocity of treatment for workers in countries other than their own.

(3) Concerning the disinfection of wool infected with anthrax spores.

(4) Concerning the protection of women and children against lead poisoning.

(5) Concerning the establishment of Government health services.

(6) Concerning the use of white phosphorus in match manufacture.

The obligations of Government in respect of decisions of the International Labour Conference are defined by Article 405 of the Peace Treaty as follows : —

" Each of the Members (of the Organisation) undertakes that it will, within the period of one year at most from the closing of the session of the Conference, or if it is impossible owing to exceptional circumstances to do so within the period of one year, then at the earliest practicable moment and in no case later than 18 months from the closing of the session of the Conference, bring the Recommendation or Draft Convention before the authority or authorities within whose competence the matter lies, for the enactment of legislation or other action. . . ."

His Majesty's Government have already secured the passing of legislation giving effect to three of the Conventions and one of the Recommendations. The measures in question are the Employment of Women and Young Persons Act and the Employment of Women and Young Persons (Lead Processes) Act which became law last Session.

DEBATE IN HOUSE OF COMMONS.

On 27th May a debate took place in the House of Commons on the subject of the Government's obligations to submit the remaining Conventions to Parliament.

The Right Hon. George Barnes* (Labour, Glasgow, Gorbals**)** moved the following resolution : —

" That, in the opinion of this House, the Conventions adopted a the International Labour Conference under the League of Nations shoul be submitted to Parliament as the competent authority."

He said that the authority or authorities referred t meant some authority other than the Government, and, s far as the Government had not brought the Convention before Parliament, he submitted that they were in defaul This Labour chapter of the Paris Peace Treaty was haile with delight by many in that House and elsewhere as an effo

---

* The Right Hon. George Barnes was one of the delegates of t British Government at the International Conference at Washington.

whereby through co-operation and goodwill they could deal with labour problems throughout the world. " If the Government make it a dead letter, and if they show by their action, or inaction, that they are concerned only with labour problems when there is a dispute, they will," said Mr. Barnes, " play right into the hands of those who do not want co-operation or goodwill, but who do want anarchy."

There were, the right hon. gentleman proceeded to remark, two outstanding Conventions—the Eight-Hours Convention and the Maternity Convention. He did not vote for the latter and, therefore, the Government were not under moral obligation in respect to it. As it was adopted by the necessary two-thirds majority, however, the Government were under obligation to submit it to Parliament, and that they had failed to do. In regard to the Eight-Hours Convention, at the time of the Washington Conference the Government were committed to legislation on the subject. The British delegates actually voted for the Convention in strict conformity with the instructions which had been given them before they left for Washington and while they were there.

Unwise Policy.

It seemed to him that the Government were plainly under an obligation not only to submit that particular Convention to Parliament, but to carry it through. Quoting a reply given in the House of Commons by the late Minister of Health,* who stated that the Government, after full consideration, had decided not to ratify the Maternity Convention, Mr. Barnes said if that fairly represented the attitude of the Government it meant knocking the bottom out of the whole Labour Organisation of the League of Nations. It would become a mere cypher in the hands of Governments, whereas it was intended to be an agency by which employers' and workmen's organisations were to be brought in to co-operate with Governments in getting results. The success of the International Labour Organisation depended, on the whole, upon results. If there was no result the Organisation would fail and that failure would delight the hearts of the Bolshevists in this and other countries. The Government's policy was unwise and would lead to trouble.

The Minister of Labour (the Right Hon. T. J. Macnamara) moved the following amendment :—

" That in the opinion of this House it is not expedient in existing circumstances to proceed with legislation to give effect to the Washington Convention on Hours of Labour."

---

* The Right Hon. Charles Addison, now Minister without Portfolio.

He said that the Government had no desire to ignore th findings of the Washington Conference. Such an attitud would, in fact, belie the past record of this country in matter affecting the social conditions of the people. The fact wa that as regarded most of these Conventions this country ha already a first-class record —he might say a record in advanc of any other country. There was a Convention on the subjec of machinery for dealing with unemployment. They passe legislation in 1909 which covered the aim of that Convention the principal point being the establishment of a system of fre public employment agencies or exchanges. They were in ; position to ratify that Convention and would do so.

Maternity Convention.

There was a Convention dealing with the employmen of women before and after child-birth. On 22nd March th then Minister of Health stated the reasons which had led th Government to decide not to ratify it. He pointed out tha they had in this country a system which was doubly capabl of dealing with these questions and that the recommendation of the Convention cut right across that system, which was fa in advance of that of any other country. Other three Con ventions had been covered by the Women, Young Person and Children's Employment Act and would be ratified. A to the matter mainly at issue, the Convention dealing with th application of the principle of the Eight-Hours Day and th 48-hours week, the Government introduced an Hours o Employment Bill in August, 1919,* to give effect to th recommendations of the Provisional Joint Committee set u by the National Industrial Council in that year, but, so fa agreement on the question had not been reached.

Examination of the Convention also disclosed the fac that there were difficulties in applying some of the provisior to the industrial circumstances of this country. The railwa trade unions and the railway companies were agreed that th limitations proposed by the Convention were not applicab to the British railway system. Then there was the questio of the hours of work of seamen, which was left over fro Washington to be dealt with at Genoa. It was not th settled, and was still outstanding, though negotiations we proceeding. Apart from that the difficulties of the provisio of the Convention with regard to overtime were not to be d regarded. The Convention did not give any recognition overtime as a regular feature of industrial work. There w in this country a strong tendency to reduce overtime througho

---

* *Vide* JOURNAL, Vol. I., No. 1, p. 74.

all industries, but the limitation could be more easily carried out by industrial agreements applicable to the various trades and to the fluctuating circumstances of industry at different periods than by the necessarily somewhat inelastic method of departmental regulation.

The Recommendations.

" As a result of agreements between employers' associations and trade unions," the right hon. gentleman observed, " an overwhelmingly large proportion of the workpeople of this country are at present covered by agreements which establish a normal week of 48 hours or less. . . . The Government would be prepared, when the opportunities of framing industrial legislation are improved by a return to normal conditions, to co-operate with the other nations who are parties to the International Labour Organisation in preparing another Convention on the same subject." With regard to the Recommendations, the first, dealing with unemployment, had four main provisions, of which the Government were prepared to accept the latter two. They could not accept the provisions dealing with the abolition of fee-charging agencies and with the proposal that recruiting of bodies of workers from one country for employment in another should be permitted only by mutual agreement.

The next Recommendation dealt with reciprocity of treatment for foreign workers. That was a proposal for equal rights for workers of all countries in all others. It depended for its execution upon agreements between the various countries and was at present under the consideration of His Majesty's Government. The special emigration aspect of the question was being considered by the International Commission which was now presided over by the late Speaker, Mr. Lowther. In conclusion the right hon. gentleman claimed that the remaining Recommendations were covered by Acts of Parliament already passed in this country.

The Ratifying Authority.

The Attorney-General (the Right Hon. Sir Gordon Hewart) said that the authority for the ratification of Conventions in this country was the Crown.

Mr. Barnes : " The Ministers of the Crown ! "

The Attorney-General : " Where the Convention is of a certain kind—if, for example, it cannot be given effect to without the expenditure of money or the passing of a Bill—then the ratification does not take place until Parliamentary

D

sanction has first been asked and obtained. But Parliamentary sanction is not that which ratifies the Convention. What ratifies the Convention is the authority of the Crown." The Conventions, Sir Gordon added, had been submitted to that House in a White Paper (Command Paper No. 627 of 1920) and legislative proposals in relation to most of them were unnecessary.

The Right Hon. Lord Robert Cecil (Independent Unionist, *Hitchin*) thought that the Government and a great many of his hon. friends who were opposed to the new international movement were making the most profound mistake. He believed very strongly that all over Europe and in this country there were grave misgivings as to the wisdom of those who were the governing classes before 1914. Now the various Governments had come forward and in solemn Conference had proposed a new system of international equality. " Labour conferences and the League of Nations," said the noble lord, " are all part of a new system based on the theory that the rivalries of nations are less important than their friendship, and that their interests are greater than their antagonism, I believe that, inarticulately and unconsciously, vast masses of the people are waiting to see whether that is a genuine offer or whether it is merely an intention to change the conduct of international affairs, or whether it is merely a new piece of camouflage or deception, or merely a last effort in what they regard as an effete and dying system."

Viscountess Astor (Coalition Unionist, *Plymouth*) said that, no doubt, this country had gone much further than other countries with regard to maternity benefit, but they wanted it to be an example to backward countries and that was why they were sorry the Government should have turned the Convention down without even discussing it.

Great Britain and the League.

The Right Hon. Arthur Henderson (Labour, *Widnes*) declared that the consequences which might follow from the attitude of the Government—consequences of an international political, and industrial character—were very serious. There was a growing feeling that this country was not so loyally behind the League of Nations, and all that the League stood for, as it was at the time of the Peace Conference. " Can we imagine," Mr. Henderson asked, " the effect that will be created if Great Britain, after giving a lead in the formation of the charter upon which the Labour Office at Geneva is expected to work, becomes cold towards the whole idea ? The consequence of the growth of such a feeling in different countries will be nothing short of disastrous."

On a division the amendment moved by the Minister of Labour was carried by 109 votes against 69.

The House thereafter proceeded to discuss the amended motion and the debate was adjourned.

COURT OF INTERNATIONAL JUSTICE.

(Hague Court of Arbitration.)

In the House of Commons on 14th June,

The Right Hon. George Barnes (Labour, *Glasgow, Gorbals*) asked the Prime Minister whether, in view of the fact that non-ratification of the Statute of the permanent Court of International Justice by the States whose representatives signed the Protocol would render impossible the constitution of the Court by the Assembly at its meeting in September next, His Majesty's Government would use its good offices with the other States, signatories of the said Protocol, to secure early ratification ?

The Leader of the House (the Right Hon. Austen Chamberlain): "It is not necessary to take any such step as is proposed in the question. The Council of the League of Nations, on whom this duty properly devolves, have issued an urgent appeal to all members of the League to expedite their signature and ratification. I do not think that isolated action of a similar character by one of the States interested would add to the strength of that appeal, and there seems no reason to doubt that sufficient ratifications will be deposited by 1st August to enable the Court to be brought into being at the next meeting of the Assembly."

Hague Court of Arbitration.

Mr. Barnes, on the same date, also asked the Prime Minister the following question : —

Whether, in view of the request addressed by the Secretary-General of the League of Nations to members of the Court of Arbitration at The Hague, His Majesty's Government had considered the question of filling the four places in the Court at The Hague accorded to the British Empire, so that full weight might be attached to the nominations to the permanent Court made on behalf of the British Empire ?

The Leader of the House : "No, Sir ; Lord Finlay is a member of the Court, and it is not proposed at present to fill the other three places. Although the new Permanent Court of International Justice will no doubt largely take the place

D 2

of The Hague Court, the latter will continue to exist, and His Majesty's Government consider it desirable to keep places vacant in case any matter is referred to it of concern to the Dominions, who are not represented separately on The Hague Court, and who should, in that event, have a voice in the selection of additional British judges."

BRITISH POLICY IN MIDDLE EAST.

(Mandates for Mesopotamia and Palestine.)

The House of Commons went into Committee of Supply on 14th June to consider a supplementary estimate for £27,197,000 in respect of Middle Eastern services under the Colonial Office.

The Secretary of State for the Colonies (The Right Hon Winston Churchill) said that the acceptance by Great Britain of mandatory power for Palestine and Mesopotamia was a very serious responsibility. They were bound to make a sincere, honest, patient, resolute effort to redeem their obligations. As soon as he had completed in January the formation of a Middle Eastern Department he endeavoured to work out a policy of military reductions by cable, but, failing to make any progress, he went to Cairo and convened a Conference of British authorities concerned in the affairs of the Middle East. What it had been impossible to arrange by telegraph proved quite easy to settle by Conference and discussion.

It was agreed at the Cairo Conference that subject to the political arrangements, which were a counterpart of these reductions, and other methods he would mention, there should be an immediate reduction of the Mesopotamia garrison from 33-battalion to a 23-battalion scale, which would be completed by 15th July. They decided on a further prospective reduction after 1st October to a 12-battalion scale, and on the immediate disposal of stock and surplus military stores in Mesopotamia, with consequent economies in storage expense and personnel. They decided upon a reduction in the number of horses from 47,000 on 1st April to 17,000 by 1st August next.

Lastly, there was a large reduction in the number of followers and in the Indian and native labour employed by the Army. The total traceable definite saving resulting from these measures amounted to £5,500,000 and a further close scrutiny of Army Estimates had enabled them to make another saving of £1,000,000. Against those savings they had, however, to set certain other charges for the Air Force, of

Arab levies, and for subsidies and charges for refugees, railways and miscellaneous civil matters. These represented a total of nearly £2,000,000, making a net total reduction of £4,500,000. If their anticipations were not overthrown by events he proposed that the estimates for next year, 1922-23, for the normal current expenditure in both Palestine and Mesopotamia together would not exceed £9,000,000 or £10,000,000.

Mesopotamia: Arab Government.

In June of last year the High Commissioner for Mesopotamia was directed by His Majesty's Government to announce the early setting up of a distinctly Arab Government under an Arab ruler in Mesopotamia, or Iraq, as it was, perhaps, more convenient to call it, and a provisional native Government had been in existence for a good many months. " It is our intention," said Mr. Churchill, " to replace this provisional Government in the course of the summer by a Government based upon an assembly elected by the people of Iraq, to instal an Arab ruler who will be acceptable to the elected assembly, and to create an Arab army for the national defence."

The British Government had no intention, the right hon. gentleman explained, of forcing upon the people of Iraq a ruler who was not of their own choice, but as the Mandatory Power they could not remain indifferent or unconcerned in a matter so vital to them. The policy definitely chosen by the British Government was to attempt to build up around the ancient capital of Baghdad, in a form friendly to Britain and to her Allies, an Arab State which could revive and embody the old culture and glories of the Arab race, and which, at any rate, would have a full and fair opportunity of doing so if the Arab race showed itself capable of profiting by it. He had caused the Emir Feisal, one of the capable sons of King Hussein, to be informed that no obstacle would be placed in the way of his candidature, that he was at liberty to proceed forthwith to Mesopotamia, and that, if he was chosen, he would receive the countenance and support of Great Britain. If the Emir Feisal should be acceptable to the people generally and to the Assembly, a solution would have been reached which offered the best prospects for a happy and a prosperous outcome.

There had lately arisen in Iraq, and particularly in the Province of Basra, a considerable movement in the direction of continuing direct British rule, but he could hold out no hope that they would be willing to continue those direct responsibilities.

"We are leaning strongly," Mr. Churchill remarked
"to what I may call the Sherifian solution, both in Mesopotami
to which the Emir Feisal is proceeding, and in trans-Jordania
where the Emir Abdulla is now in charge. We are also givin
aid and assistance to King Hussein, the Sherif of Mecca, whos
State and whose finances have been grievously affected by th
interruption of the pilgrimage, in which our Muhammada
countrymen are so deeply interested, and which we desire to se
resumed. The repercussion of this Sherifian policy upon th
other Arab chiefs must be carefully watched."

Use of the Air Force: Imperial Communications.

The 12 battalions to be maintained in Mesopotamia, wit
their ancillary units, would, it was considered, be sufficien
to hold Baghdad and the river communications which cor
nected it with the sea. There were at present six squadron
of aeroplanes in Mesopotamia and next year there would b
two more.

"The extent to which aerial control can be used in subst
tution of military force is still disputable, but with every mont
that has passed our confidence in its great utility has bee
increased. It must not be supposed that aeroplanes have n
means of acting except by using lethal force. That, of cours
is in reserve. But we hope that, by their agency, we shall b
able to keep in amicable touch with the tribes and loc
centres, and to ward off in good time movements of unrest, t
sustain and, if necessary, relieve detached posts, to kee
political officers in close relation with their districts, and
maintain a reasonable degree of order in the country. There
also a squadron of the Air Force in Palestine, and thr
squadrons in Egypt. Arrangements are being made whic
will make it possible for aeroplanes to fly regularly to and f
across the desert between Baghdad and Cairo."

Arrangements could be made to fly a certain number
commercial aeroplanes, which could carry mails and possib
passengers, and incidentally would, if they had a peacef
solution, afford a most valuable link in the chain of Imperi
communications which might ultimately result in very gre
advantage in shortening communication with India and wi
Australia and New Zealand.

Palestine: The Zionist Movement.

Turning to Palestine, the right hon. gentleman said th
at present the problem there was more acute than in Mes
potamia, though much smaller in a military sense. The on
cause of unrest arose from the Zionist movement, and fr

British pledges in regard to it. The combatant strength of the British forces in Palestine had been reduced to 5,000, and he could not hold out any hope of diminishing it in the immediate future.

The difficulty about the promise of a national home for the Jew in Palestine was that it conflicted with the regular British policy of consulting the wishes of the people in the mandated territories and of giving them representative institutions as soon as they were fit for them, which institution in this case they would use to veto any further Jewish immigration. There had been brought into Palestine under the Zionist scheme of immigration about 7,000 Jews. That immigration and the propaganda by which it had been accompanied had greatly alarmed and excited the Arab population. The Arabs believed that in the next few years they were going to be swamped by scores of thousands of immigrants from Central Europe, who would push them off the land, eat up the scanty substance of the country, and eventually gain absolute control of its institutions and destinies. There really was nothing for the Arabs to be frightened about. All the Jewish immigration was being very carefully watched and controlled both from the point of view of numbers and character.

No Jew would be brought in beyond the number who could be provided for by the expanding wealth and development of the resources of the country. There was no doubt whatever that at the present time the country was greatly under-populated.

The Word of Britain.

After paying tribute to the enormous productive results achieved by the Jewish colonies which had been established during the last 20 or 30 years in Palestine, Mr. Churchill said he saw no reason why, with care and progress there, there should not be a steady flow of Jewish immigrants into the country and that this flow should be accompanied at every stage by a general increase in the wealth of the whole existing population, and be without injury to any of them. The British Government could not possibly agree to allow the Jewish colonies to be wrecked, or all future immigration to be stopped, without definitely accepting the position that the word of Britain no longer counted throughout the East and the Middle East.

" If representative institutions are conceded, as we hope they will be, to the Arabs in Palestine, some definite arrangements will have to be made in the instrument on which those institutions stand which will safeguard within reasonable

limits the immigration of Jews into the country, as they make
their own way and create their own means of subsistence.   Our
task, using a phrase of the late Lord Salisbury, will be to
persuade one side to concede and the other to forbear, but
keeping a reasonable margin of force available in order to
ensure the acceptance of the position by both parties."

If they wished to maintain their position and to discharge
their responsibilities in the Middle East, the right hon. gentleman said, England and France together must pursue a policy
of appeasement and friendship towards both Turks and Arabs.

Earl Winterton (Coalition Unionist, *Horsham***)** said there
were those who objected to Great Britain being in Mesopotamia on the ground of the mandate, but unless they were
prepared to attack the whole idea of the League of Nations
and to refuse to carry out the obligations under the Covenant,
they were in a dilemma.   Meanwhile this country was bound
to undertake the task which was imposed upon it.

A Gamble.

Colonel J. C. Wedgwood (Labour, *Newcastle-under-Lyme***)**
remarked that this arrangement in Mesopotamia was a gamble
just as much as the Dardanelles was a gamble and as justified
as was the Dardanelles gamble.   " I hope it will turn out
better," said the hon Member, " but if it is going to turn out
better, it depends not upon the right hon. gentleman's agent
in Mesopotamia, but upon his action in his own Cabinet in
straightening up the dispute between Greece and Turkey at
the present time."

The Hon. W. Ormsby-Gore (Coalition Unionist, *Stafford***)**
said that to allow Mesopotamia to go back to anarchy
and to the government of the Turk, who for 400 years allowed
nothing to be done for that country, to throw away 14,000,000
acres of fertile land, capable of growing crop after crop, was
a thing they ought not to do.   They should proceed with the
ideal which they had before them in the past, and which was
contained in Article 23 of the Treaty, namely, that it was a
sacred trust of civilisation which they had undertaken, and not
something which they were going to get anything out of and
run away directly it cost them something.

The Right Hon. Lord Robert Cecil (Independent Unionist
*Hitchin***)** agreed that the policy which Mr. Churchill had
announced was the policy which personally he had always
wished to see carried out in reference to the Middle East, but
complained that it was not done two and half years ago.

After further speeches the debate stood adjourned.

DEBATE IN HOUSE OF LORDS.

On 20th April a debate took place in the House of Lords on the subject of the mandate for Palestine.

Lord Lamington asked the Government whether, when referring the mandate to the League of Nations, attention would be called to the fact that in framing it the wishes of the inhabitants of Palestine had not been consulted as directed in Article 22 of the Convention, but that an inquiry was made by an American Commission, the report of which had never been published. He said that in a previous debate the Leader of the House admitted with great frankness that the people of Palestine had not been consulted as to whether they wished for this mandate, and that, whilst they had expressed a preference for British assistance or for a British mandate, no doubt they did not appreciate that there would be any Zionist movement in connection with it for the establishment of a national home for the Jews in that country.

That movement, after all, as was acknowledged by a very prominent member of the Jewish faith in this country, was really only the Jewish veneer for conquest. The League of Nations would stultify its action at the outset of its administration if it was not informed that the people who formed nine-tenths of the population of Palestine and Syria had never really had an opportunity of expressing an opinion as to what form of Government they desired.

An Autocracy.

Lord Sydenham trusted that the report of the American Commission would not only be handed over to the Council of the League of Nations before it discussed this mandate, which he regarded as dangerous, but that it would be made public. In Mesopotamia they were now trying to set up an Arab Government which some of the people of Mesopotamia did not want. But in Palestine they had set up an autocracy and had deprived the Palestinians of the representation which they possessed in the time of the Turkish rule. If the present rate of immigration continued the domination of the Zionists over the Arabs was only a question of time, and not a very long time. Yet that domination had apparently been ruled out by Mr. Churchill.

The Under-Secretary of State for Air (the **Marquis of Londonderry**), as representing the Colonial Office, said the Leader of the House had already explained the extent to which the inhabitants of Palestine and other mandated territories of the Middle East had been consulted. If Lord Lamington would consult the text of the Covenant he would see that the reference made in Article 22 to the wishes of the inhabitants was solely in connection with the selection of the mandatories, and not in the framing of the mandate. With regard to the report of the American Commission, it was not for His Majesty's Government to draw the attention of the Council of the League to a document which was the property of a foreign Government, and which that Government had not thought fit either to publish or to communicate to other Governments. In any case, the draft mandates for Palestine and Mesopotamia were communicated to the Council of the League of Nations in December last, so that the time for such action as was contemplated in Lord Lamington's question had passed.

Lord Lamington said he still hoped that His Majesty's Government might see fit to communicate to the League of Nations exactly the position of these mandates. He did not know whether it was *ultra vires* to ask the American Government to furnish a copy of a report in which Great Britain was so vitally concerned. But he thought at least the League of Nations might be told it was in existence and that it was highly desirable, in the interests of all parties, that the information it contained should be given to the League, so that the League might faithfully carry out the very high and responsible work of the mandates.

Veil of Mystery.

The Marquis of Crewe said he could not help feeling that it was not encouraging for the success of the work of the League of Nations that this Parliament, and equally the Parliaments of other Powers who were members of the League should be placed in the position of not being able to obtain information. It seemed to place the work of the League on a somewhat unsatisfactory basis, and being intensely desirous that that work should be approved and appreciated by the public in different countries, the fact that a thick veil seemed to be thrown over such proceedings as this appeared to him to be a bar to that general appreciation of the work of the League which they all wished to see developed.

Lord Islington said he felt that the course which was being taken by His Majesty's Government in connection with these mandates was one that was becoming more and more unsatisfactory and prejudicial to the future of the League of Nations. It was high time that there should be a very full and explicit report of the proceedings in Palestine, showing to Parliament and the public their cost and the directions in which that cost had been entailed. The same course should be followed with regard to the mandates in Africa. They were wreathed in complete darkness so far as Parliament and the public in this country were concerned.

The **Under-Secretary of State for Air,** replying to Lord Sydenham, who asked whether the United States Commission was appointed by the Peace Conference, said he thought he was right in saying that the Peace Conference suggested that there should be such a Commission, but that this suggestion did not actually take effect. In fact, it fell through, and the result was that the Americans remained and carried out this Commission by themselves.

Lord Lamington withdrew a motion he had made for papers and the debate concluded.

OVERSEAS TRADE (CREDITS AND INSURANCE) AMEND-MENT BILL.

(British Empire Extension.)

A Bill was introduced by the Government on 2nd June to extend the Overseas Trade (Credits and Insurance) Act, 1920.

Under the Bill the power of the Board of Trade to grant credits to persons and companies for the purpose of re-establishing trade between the United Kingdom and certain other countries is to include power to make arrangements for giving guarantees, whether directly or in-directly, in connection with export transactions.

The powers of the Board may be exercised in the case of a new guarantee at any time before 8th September, 1922, and in the case of the renewal of a guarantee previously given at any time before the 8th September, 1924. No guarantee is to remain in force after 8th September, 1925.

The Bill extends the operation of the Act so as to embrace any part of the King's Dominions, including any territory under His Majesty's protection, and "any territory in respect of which a mandate of the League of Nations is exercised by the Government of any part of His Majesty's Dominions."

DEBATE IN HOUSE OF COMMONS.

On 30th May the House of Commons went into Committee and considered the financial resolution on which the Bill is based.

The **Secretary of the Overseas Trade Department (Sir Philip Lloyd-Greame)** said the Government had decided to extend the export credits scheme to the British Empire as a whole and to operate it by way of guarantee of bills of exchange drawn against shipment. That would enable business to be done in the ordinary way with the maximum of Government assistance and the minimum of Government interference. The proposal to extend the scheme to the British Empire* had been received with general assent, but for special reasons the operation of the scheme would not for the present be extended to India and the British possessions in the Far East. There had been conditions operating there under which obligations were outstanding which had not been honoured to the full, and it was obviously extremely desirable that no facilities for credit should be extended if they could operate in any way to prevent those engaging in trade from taking up their whole obligations.

Lieut.-Commander Kenworthy (Independent Liberal, *Hull Central*): " Which are the mandatory areas referred to ? "

The Secretary of the Overseas Trade Department: " It extends to any area over which the British Government has a mandate." The hon. gentleman added that Government advances were not given where business could be done through the ordinary trade channels.

Major H. Barnes (Independent Liberal, *Newcastle E.*): " How much has been disbursed under the Act so far ? "

The Secretary of the Overseas Trade Department: " Contracts to advance about £2,500,000 have been made and actual advances up to about £750,000 have, I think, been made. This proposal does not extend the amount of money which is authorised by the previous Act, but it enables us to operate with the £26,000,000 authorised in the previous Act in what I hope will be a more expeditious and convenient manner."

Extension Unnecessary.

Mr. Samuel Samuel (Coalition Unionist, *Putney*) contended that so far as the British Empire was concerned the scheme was entirely unnecessary. Any firm or company whose credit was worth anything could get their shipments financed to any part of the British Empire. There were British banks by the dozen which were willing to buy commercial bills on Australia, India, Hong Kong, Ceylon, the Straits Settlements or South Africa, provided that the credit of the firm on this side was good. They did not even look at the acceptors of the bill.

Major Barnes said that no reason could be given for the proposed extension of the scheme. Its original object was to

---

* The foreign countries in respect of which the Government are prepared to entertain proposals to guarantee drafts drawn against shipments of goods are : Finland, Latvia, Esthonia, Lithuania, Poland, Czecho-Slovakia, Serb-Croat-Slovene State, Roumania, Georgia, Armenia, Bulgaria, Austria, and Hungary.

promote trade with countries which did not possess the conditions of security that existed under the British flag. In the case of the Dominions there was security, and no more reason existed for giving people facilities to trade with them than for giving facilities to trade within the United Kingdom.

Mr. Arthur Michael Samuel (Coalition Unionist, *Farnham***)** said that traders only turned to the Government to help them when their goods could not be sold through the ordinary channels of credit—that was to say, the banks and financial houses. At the present time there were thousands of pounds worth of goods ordered which they would like to send to Australia—and to people of honour and good credit in Australia. But the firms at home could not get the bills collected. They could not get paid because of the question of exchange. The bill position between England and Australia was in a frozen state.

Mr. A. Lyle-Samuel (Independent Liberal, *Eye***) :** " What ! A question of exchange within the British Empire ! "

Mr. A. M. Samuel said the hon. gentleman who had interrupted him showed his ignorance of the hampered way in which trade with Australia at present was carried on in this country.

Trading Overseas.

Mr. Lyle-Samuel observed that it was not a healthy sign in British business when they needed a Government department to enable their traders to trade overseas. The fact was they were capable of trading in every part of the world without the advice, the guidance, the leadership, the credit or the guarantees of any Government Department.

Mr. A. Green (Coalition Unionist, *Derby***)** remarked that in Australia and Canada there was great need for co-operation on the part of the whole of the people of the Empire in order that their relationship should be more closely cemented. " The banking interests," said Mr. Green, " are not inclined to help in all cases unless there is absolutely gilt-edged security for any money that they advance. I could give an illustration of an Australian firm with a turnover that would exceed the amount that is asked for even in this particular resolution, and with individual directors, I have no doubt, each of whom could sign a cheque for a quarter of a million. One of them happened to be stranded in this great city, and he could not get from his bankers in London an advance of £1,000 to enable him to carry on and to pay his passage and pay his way through the country and back to Australia. What he had to do was to borrow that money from a firm in Sydney that had credit, and to pay an excessive sum for it."

· **Mr. J. D. Kiley (Independent Liberal,** *Whitechapel*) said this credit could do something to enable trade to be resumed with Australia until such time as the Australian Government removed their embargo on cash remittances from the other side.

On a division the financial resolution was carried by 88 votes against 9.

Second Reading of the Bill.

The debate on the Second Reading of the Bill took place in the House of Commons on the 8th June.

The Secretary of the Overseas Trade Department said there had been many discussions with the banks on this subject, and no question had ever arisen of the Government doing business which they would do. As to the extension of the scheme to the British Empire, there had been trade difficulties within the Empire in the past, and he did not think they were entirely removed. "Business within the Empire," the hon. gentleman remarked, "is business which is not attended with anything like the commercial risk of business with disorganised countries, and it is business which, if ordinary facilities do not exist, we should be glad to do. It is good business, and that is not mere sentiment, because it is business in what is actually and potentially the greatest market we have got."

The Right Hon. Lord Robert Cecil (Independent Unionist, *Hitchin*) said he was certain that the unemployment in this country was due mainly to the complete breakdown of the European market, and until they could get Europe on its feet again they would not really deal with the industrial crisis with any permanence. "This is a very small step towards dealing with the reconstruction of Europe," said the noble lord, "but it is a step in that direction, and I hope that the Government are not going to allow the policy of the previous Act to be diverted into a policy of encouraging trade within the Empire. That is a very desirable thing, but it is not the policy of the original Act. I very gladly endorse any step taken to encourage trade within the Empire, but still the most essential thing is to try to get out of the terrible industrial chaos in Europe, and I should be very sorry to see any diversion of energy in other directions."

The Secretary of the Overseas Trade Department, replying to observations made in the debate, said he did not think it would be contended for a moment that the provisions of the mandates were contrary to the provisions of the Bill. "There is," he said, "no question of granting undue preference. All we are doing is to say that we shall not exclude the mandated territories from the facilities that we are giving to our own nationals. It is open to every other country to give to its nationals in those areas exactly the same credits and guarantees that we are prepared to give to our nationals."

The Bill was read a second time without a division and referred to a Standing Committee.

CANADIAN CATTLE.

(Royal Commission Appointed.)

On 2nd May announcement was made in the House of Commons of the appointment of a Royal Commission to deal with the embargo on the importation of live Canadian cattle.

Mr. Percy A. Hurd (Coalition Unionist, *Frome***)** and **Mr. A. E. Waterson (Co-operative,** *Kettering***)** having asked questions on the subject,

The Home Secretary (the Right Hon. Edward Shortt) replied : I am glad to say that the Commission is now complete, and the following are the members : —

Lord Finlay (Chairman).
Lord Askwith.
Sir Algernon Firth.
Sir Harry Peat, and
Sir Arthur Shipley.

The terms of reference of the Commission are as follows : —

"To inquire into the admission into the United Kingdom of livestock for purposes other than immediate slaughter at the ports, whether such action would increase and cheapen the meat supply of the country, and if so, to what extent, and whether it is advisable, having regard to the necessity of protecting livestock bred in the country from the introduction of disease, and of restoring their numbers after the losses to which they were subjected during the War."

DEBATE IN HOUSE OF LORDS.

On 10th May the question was briefly discussed in the House of Lords.

Lord Strachie moved that it was desirable that counsel should be allowed to appear before the Royal Commission. He said the question had arisen from the fact that at the Imperial Conference in 1917 it was urged very strongly upon His Majesty's Government that Canadian store stock should be admitted freely into this country and should not come under the law of slaughter. It so happened that two Cabinet Ministers—Mr. Walter Long and Lord Ernle—at that Imperial Conference gave a pledge that after the War store stock should be admitted from Canada.

It was considered by the Prime Minister that it was necessary to have a Royal Commission to inquire whether that pledge could be carried out without any injurious effect upon flocks and herds in this country. It was felt by agricultural interests that it was perfectly impossible for their case against the free importation of stock from abroad to be properly put before the Commission unless they were allowed to be represented by counsel.

The **Parliamentary Secretary of the Ministry of Agriculture (the Earl of Ancaster)** pointed out that it had almost invariably been the custom that a Royal Commission made its own rules as to procedure. All he was able to do was to lay before the Chairman of the Commission the views of those who held that counsel should appear and ask him to consider the case very carefully.

The motion was withdrawn.

CURRENCY IN EAST AFRICA.

(Value of the Rupee: A Standard Coin.)

Replying to a question in the House of Commons on 30th May, the Colonial Secretary made a statement on the subject of currency in East Africa.

Colonel J. C. Wedgwood (Labour, *Newcastle-under-Lyme)* asked whether the right hon. gentleman had any statement to make on the East African currency question.

The Secretary of State for the Colonies (the Right Hon. Winston Churchill) said : " As I informed my hon. and gallant friend on the 12th April, I have considered to the best of my ability, and with the assistance of my advisers, the currency question in Kenya, Uganda and Tanganyika, and I am now in a position to make a statement on the question as a whole.

" The present position is the result of the scheme embodied, as far as Kenya and Uganda are concerned, in the East Africa and Uganda Order in Council of the 26th April, 1920. That scheme was prepared at a time when the Indian rupee had risen in exchange value to about 2s. 9d., and it was decided to substitute for the Indian currency a local currency based on the florin at 2s. sterling, at which value the Indian rupee would be current until it could be replaced. Existing contracts expressed in rupees were to be interpreted in terms of the new florin. Various representations have been received since the beginning of the year on behalf of the different interests in East Africa, some urging that a change should be made, particularly in view of the fall in the exchange value of the Indian rupee, and others urging that no alteration should be made.

The Standard Coin.

"After taking these various expressions of opinion into consideration, I have decided to maintain the original scheme in its essential features, but with the modification that, as recommended by the Currency Committee appointed in Kenya in February, 1921, the standard coin will be, not a florin, but a shilling, in order to prevent too abrupt fluctuations in local values, and that rupee contracts, instead of being construed at the rate of one florin to one rupee, will be construed at the rate of two shillings to one rupee.

"Pending the supply of the new shilling currency, which will be expedited as much as possible, steps are being taken to redeem the Indian rupee coin now current in Kenya and Uganda with the florin and other local currency now available, during a limited period, after which the Indian coin will be demonetised. Formal notices on this point will be published locally. The extension of the new arrangements to the Tanganyika territory will be effected as soon as possible."

Colonel Wedgwood : "May I ask whether the wages paid to natives in East Africa, which used to be so many rupees a month, are now twice as many shillings per month, or are they being reduced from rupees to shillings, without any increase in the number of shillings paid ; and whether there is any actual increase in the wages paid to natives ? :"

Mr. Churchill : "I think my hon. and gallant friend has not fully comprehended the effect of the answer which I have just given. No doubt that is due to the fact that this is a very complicated matter, which he has just heard for the first time ; but I hope that he will study it with attention, and then he will see what the bearing of it is between the various complicated questions."

Wages of Natives.

Colonel Wedgwood : "May I ask whether this change in the currency does not mean a change in the purchasing power of the wages of the East African natives, and that their earnings are thereby reduced ? "

Mr. Churchill : "No, Sir, it means that the purchasing power of those wages is maintained, and maintained at the

E

difference between a 2s. florin and a 1s. 3d. rupee, which is the cause of much heart-burning on the part of the settlers."

The Hon. W. Ormsby-Gore (Coalition Unionist, *Stafford*): " In order that we may study the right hon. gentleman's reply, as he suggests, may we understand whether the shilling is going to be divided into 12 pence or 100 cents ; whether the original proposal was that the florin should be divided into 100 cents ; and what is the subsidiary coin below 1s. that it is proposed to introduce in these territories ? "

Mr. Churchill: " The intention is to make the shilling the half-florin."

Colonel Wedgwood : " The question is, what will the coin be which is smaller than the shilling ? Will it be the penny or the cent, and will it be 100 cents to the shilling or 100 cents to the florin ? "

Mr. Churchill: " I think I must ask for notice of the details of the currency question, but the decision to which I have come has been to retain the existing exchange value of the rupee at two shillings, as against saying that it should be dropped to the pre-war value, and to ease the situation of the local currency by creating a new shilling currency, and taking the shilling as a basic value."

Colonel Sir C. Yate (Coalition Unionist, *Melton*): " Does that mean that the Indian currency will be entirely eliminated in East Africa ? "

Mr. Churchill : " It is intended to assimilate the currency to the British type."

Mr. A. M. Samuel (Coalition Unionist, *Farnham*): " Is there any reason why this shilling should not be the ordinary shilling we use in this country, so that it should be current here and in Cape Town ? "

No further reply was made by the Colonial Secretary.

DOMINION INCOME-TAX.

A question on the subject of Dominion income-tax was addressed to the Government in the House of Commons on 26th May.

Sir Reginald Blair (Coalition Unionist, *Bow and Bromley*) asked the Chancellor of the Exchequer whether it was still the practice of the Inland Revenue to refund to preference shareholders in a colonial company colonial income-tax at the rate of income-tax payable in that colony when their income, which was a fixed percentage on their investment, had not borne any colonial tax ; if so, how much had it cost the Exchequer in the last financial year ?

The Financial Secretary to the Treasury (Mr. Hilton Young), who replied, said : " I would refer my hon. friend to the reply which the then Chancellor of the Exchequer gave to him on this subject on 2nd August, 1920.

" As indicated in that reply, this matter has been looked into again, and it has now been decided that, in the case of a preference shareholder in a Dominion company, if the preference shares are entitled to a preferential dividend at a fixed rate without participating rights in any balance of distributable profits and the shareholder's dividend has been paid at the full fixed rate, no relief from United Kingdom income-tax is to be allowed on such dividend in respect of Dominion income-tax paid by the company, except in so far as Dominion income-tax is deducted from the dividend.

" The particulars for which my hon. friend asks in the second part of his question are not available."

DOMINIONS AND LAND VALUES TAX.

A private Member's resolution authorising the appointment of a Select Committee to inquire into the incidence of local rating by public authorities and to make a report was debated in the House of Commons on 6th April. In the course of the proceedings,

The Minister of Health (the Right Hon. Sir Alfred Mond) observed that good administration—the application of the best intelligences in localities to their own local affairs—would do more in the long run for increased efficiency and lower rating than any juggling with local taxation. A strong Cabinet Committee appointed by the Prime Minister was going to take up the question with the purpose and intention of being in a position by next Session to introduce legislation.

Mr. P. W. Raffan (Liberal, *Leigh*) remarked that as the community grew, and energy and enterprise developed, so the community itself created community value which expressed itself in land value. If the local authority were able to appropriate for the purposes of the community the value which the community itself had created the whole problem would be solved immediately. It was no new remedy. Wherever this system had been adopted the problem had been solved. In a great many of the British Dominions there had already been this transfer. In the great city of Sydney for some years past the whole of the rates, with the exception of the water rate and the sewage rate, for special reasons, had been placed on land values, and every need of the city had

E 2

been met by a rate of 4½d. in the £ on the capital value of the land. What had been done there could be done in London, Manchester and Glasgow.

An Unmitigated Failure.

Mr. R. J. Lynn (Coalition Unionist, *Woodvale*) said the question of the taxation of land values was threshed out in 1909-10. The cost of collecting the tax had been something like £500,000 more than the entire tax itself.

Mr. Raffan : " There was no real tax on land values in 1909-10."

Mr. Lynn said the tax had proved an unmitigated failure.

Mr. Raffan : " It has not been a failure in the British Colonies, where it has really been tried."

Mr. Lynn remarked that Australia had done magnificently in the War, was a great country, and had done many things of which every Britisher ought to feel proud. But in the matter of finance, the hon. Member added, Australia had not made the most of that great country itself, simply because its finance had been run by a handful of faddists. He hoped Australia would pursue a manly policy, even in matters of finance.

On a division the resolution was negatived by 49 votes against 48.

SAFEGUARDING OF INDUSTRIES BILL.

On 9th May the House of Commons in Committee of Ways and Means began discussion of two resolutions on which the Safeguarding of Industries Bill (formally introduced on 31st May) was subsequently founded. The resolutions before final adoption were debated at length both in Committee and on Report.

In Part I. of the Bill, relating to the Safeguarding of Key Industries authority is given to charge on certain goods imported into the United Kingdom Customs duties equal to one-third of their value.

Goods chargeable with duty as set out in the Schedule of the Bill are :—

Optical glass and optical elements, whether finished or not, microscopes, field and opera classes, theodolites, sextants, spectroscopes and other optical instruments.

Beakers, flasks, burettes, measuring cylinders, thermometer tubing, and other scientific glassware and lamp-blown ware, evaporating dishes, crucibles, combustion boats, and other laboratory porcelain.

Galvanometers, pyrometers, electroscopes, barometers, analytical and other precision balances, and other scientific instruments, gauges and measuring instruments of precision of the types used in engineering machine shops and viewing rooms, whether for use in such shops or rooms or not.

Wireless valves and similar rectifiers, and vacuum tubes.

Ignition magnetos and permanent magnets.

Arc-lamp carbons.

Hosiery latch needles.

Metallic tungsten, ferro-tungsten and manufactured products of metallic tungsten, and compounds (not including ores or minerals) of thorium, cerium and the other rare earth metals.

All synthetic organic chemicals (other than synthetic organic dyestuffs, colours, and colouring matters imported for use as such, and organic intermediate products imported for their manufacture), analytical reagents, all other fine chemicals and chemicals manufactured by fermentation processes.

No duty is to be charged under this head on goods shown to the satisfaction of the Commissioners to have been consigned from and grown, produced or manufactured in the British Empire. Goods will be deemed to have been manufactured in the British Empire which would be treated as having been so manufactured for the purposes of section eight of the Finance Act, 1919, relating to Imperial preference.

PREVENTION OF DUMPING.

Part II. of the Bill is concerned with the Prevention of Dumping. It provides that if, on complaint being made to the Board of Trade, it appears that goods of any class or description (other than food or drink) manufactured outside the United Kingdom are being sold or offered for sale in the United Kingdom :—

(A) at prices below the cost of production as defined in the Bill ; or

(B) at prices which, by reason of depreciation in the value in relation to sterling of the currency of the country in which the goods are manufactured, are below the prices at which similar goods can be profitably manufactured in the United Kingdom ;

and that as a consequence employment in any industry in the United Kingdom is being or is likely to be seriously affected, the Board may refer the matter for inquiry to a committee.

If the committee (which is to consist of three persons from a permanent panel of persons appointed by the President of the Board of Trade mainly of commercial or industrial experience), report that goods manufactured in any country fulfil the above conditions, the Board may, by order, apply this part of the Bill to such goods. Where an order is made, Customs duties equal to one-third of the value will be chargeable on the goods in question manufactured in countries specified in the order.

The expression " cost of production " is defined as meaning :—

(A) the wholesale price at the works charged for goods of the class or description for consumption in the country of manufacture ; or

(B) if no such goods are sold for consumption in that country, the price which, having regard to the prices charged for goods as near as may be similar when so sold or when sold for exportation to other countries, would be so charged if the goods were sold in that country ;

after deducting in either case any excise or other internal duty leviable in that country.

An order under Part II. is, unless previously revoked by the Board, to continue in force for three years, or such less period as may be specified in it, and an order may be renewed from time to time.

In Part III. containing general provisions, the value of imported goods is defined as the price which an importer would give for the goods if they were delivered to him freight and insurance paid, in bond at the port of importation.

Part I. is to continue in force for a period of five years only.

DEBATE IN HOUSE OF COMMONS.

On 6th June the Bill came on for Second Reading in the House of Commons.

The Right Hon. Sir Donald Maclean (Chairman of the Independent Liberal Party in Parliament), in moving the rejection of the Bill, said that the only result of its operations must be to raise prices. That must inevitably be the effect of all protective measures. If they were driven by military necessities to preserve the industries scheduled in the Bill, the remedy was not by a tariff, which must raise prices, but by a subsidy, which would keep them low. The whole tendency of such a measure was against peace.

The President of the Board of Trade (the Right Hon. Stanley Baldwin) said that the old economic labels were really as extinct to-day as the old political labels. It was quite impossible, having regard to the circumstances of the times, to imagine a contest between Free Trade and Protection— or Tariff Reform—as they knew it before the War. This was no war measure ; nor was it a taking up of the cudgels against any other nations. It was rather like putting up an umbrella to shield their own people. He proposed later on to set down a proposal establishing a Committee to watch the development of the scheduled industries and prepare an annual report to Parliament of their progress. He hoped to devise a method by which they could say to those industries that if in a period, say, of two or three years, it was found no progress had been made, then the removal from the schedule of the industry concerned would be considered.

As regarded Part II. of the Bill, his view was that the mere fact of having it as a piece of permanent legislation would act as a deterrent so far as ordinary dumping was concerned. With regard to dumping connected with the depreciation in the value of the sterling currency, if it should be that the exchanges rectified themselves more quickly than anybody anticipated, so much the better. But it was taking the path of wisdom to bring these provisions before the House. Replying to a question by an hon. Member, Mr. Baldwin pointed out that as the Bill stood at present, dumping from the Colonies was treated in exactly the same way as dumping from other countries.

Labour Opposition.

The **Right Hon. J. R. Clynes (Chairman of the Parliamentary Labour Party)** submitted that this legislation was not the result of any well-matured and considered plan to deal with ever-increasing difficulties. How could it be said that if a country to any degree pursued the plan of restrictions on trade it could thereby secure continuity or guarantee of employment for its general body of manual workers? He believed now, more than any other time, was the moment for the freest possible conditions of trade that could be arranged between one country and another. "Ill-conditions of trade," the right hon. gentleman said, "no matter what their cause in any one part of the world, slowly express themselves later in other parts of the world, and instead of at the moment putting forward these proposals, certain, as I think they are, to intensify unemployment, it would be better for the Government to work on lines that would produce among the countries, particularly in the Parliaments of the countries, the spirit of absolute freedom of trade, the greater to increase the opportunities for providing work."

The debate was continued on the following day (7th June), when

The **Right Hon. F. D. Acland (Independent Liberal,** *Cornwall, Camborne*) remarked that if the Government would give half the time to the real pacification of Europe that they now gave to thwarting Europe's power to recover by Bills of this kind, they would improve employment ten-fold more in this country than ever this Bill would do. They were not suffering from a superabundance of goods coming into this country, but from an ineffective demand for goods from the countries of Europe.

The **Leader of the House (the Right Hon. Austen Chamberlain)** said it had been suggested that the Paris Resolutions were a mere *brutum fulmen*, an empty threat uttered at a time when the fortune of war was going against the Allies, and intended to inspire terror into the then successful Germany. The Resolutions were not presented under that guise at Paris. They were presented as a settled and considered policy which Mr. Asquith boasted was the policy of his Government and in particular of his President of the Board of Trade. The Government had restricted the Bill within the narrowest compass which they thought would serve the purpose they had in view. The House would not be well advised to reject the measure in order to adopt the subsidy alternative of members of the Opposition.

On a division, the amendment was negatived by 312 votes against 92, and the Bill was read a second time. At a subsequent sitting, the House, after protests from the Opposition, agreed to a time-table brought forward by the Government allotting five days for the Committee stage of the Bill, two days for the Report stage, and one day for the Third Reading.

RAILWAYS BILL.

Important proposals for the reorganisation and regulation of the railways on the cessation of State control on 15th August, 1921, were laid before the House of Commons by the Minister of Transport in a Bill presented on 11th May. The introduction of this scheme was foreshadowed in a White Paper published in June, 1920, and summarised in the JOURNAL, Vol. I., No. 4, page 636.

An explanatory memorandum issued by the Government states that the Bill sweeps up masses of legislation which have accumulated in the years since railways were first sanctioned by Parliament, and it is believed that the relation of the State, the railway companies, and the users will be much simplified.

The provisions of the measure will enable the railway companies to bring about economies long desired by the directors and management ; will assure to the users reasonable facilities at reasonable rates, and will, by the provision of adequate and effective cost and operating statistics, enable the proprietors to familiarise themselves with the management of their property ; will give users and the Government an insight into the need for the charges they are asked to pay for the services rendered, and will give shareholder, employee, and community accurate data upon which sound opinion may be formed as to the adequacy of the return on capital or remuneration of labour. The confidence which should spring from such accurate and full knowledge will go far to eliminate the suspicion which makes the investor unwilling and the workers discontented.

GROUPING PROPOSALS.

There is general agreement, the Ministry of Transport says, that the grouping of railways on the basis of co-operation is right in principle. It merely carries to its logical conclusion the practice of railways in the past, the object being operating economy and administrative efficiency. Six groups, composed as follows, are provided for in the Bill :—

1.—SOUTHERN, combining the South-Eastern and Chatham, the Brighton, and the South Western.

2.—WESTERN, consisting of the Great Western system, with the Welsh lines.

3.—NORTH WESTERN and MIDLAND, combining the London and North Western, the Midland, the Lancashire and Yorkshire, the North Staffordshire, and the Furness.

4.—NORTH EASTERN and EASTERN, comprising the North Eastern, Great Central, Great Eastern, Great Northern, and Hull and Barnsley.

5.—WEST SCOTTISH, consisting of the Caledonian, Glasgow and South Western, and Highland.

6.—EAST SCOTTISH, comprising the North British and Great North of Scotland.

Provision is, however, made for the variation of the grouping, provided that the Minister of Transport is satisfied that the variation is not incompatible with the efficient and economic working of the railway system of Great Britain, and that the variation is approved by a resolution passed by both Houses of Parliament. An Amalgamation Tribunal is to be set up, consisting of Sir Henry Babington Smith, Sir William Plender, and Mr. G. J. Talbot, K.C., who will confirm amalgamation schemes. The proposal is that the larger companies named above should combine as single undertakings, and should then absorb the small companies in their respective areas. If the principal companies are unable to agree, a scheme will be settled by the tribunal.

The Bill provides that undertakings are to be valued on the basis that their charging powers would be such as to produce the 1913 net revenue. Amalgamation is to take effect on 1st January, 1923, but there is power on the part of the tribunal to postpone this date. The schemes will safeguard the interests of existing officers and servants of the various constituent and subsidiary companies.

MANAGEMENT.

The proposal for the inclusion on the boards of management of the amalgamated companies of representatives of the workers and the leading administrative officials has been abandoned, as such representation is no longer desired by the trade unions representing the men. The charging powers of the grouped companies are to be fixed so as to yield, as far as practicable, an annual net revenue equivalent to the aggregate net revenues in the year 1913 of the constituent companies and the subsidiary companies absorbed by the amalgamated companies, with additional allowances in respect of capital not fully fructified in 1913 or capital spent since that year. Periodical reviews, at comparatively short intervals in the first instance, of the charges which the railway companies are authorised to make, are provided for in the Bill.

In lieu of the formation of a development fund the Bill proposes that in the case of it appearing from the experience of the past that, with the same charges in force, a company is likely to earn a surplus above the standard revenue, the benefit of that surplus is to be divided between the trading community and the railway company. In order that the railway companies may have every incentive to efficient and economical management, it is provided that 20 per cent. of the surplus shall go to them, whilst 80 per cent. will go to the trading community in the shape of a reduction of rates. By this means a community of interest towards economy on the part of railways and their customers is assured.

The Bill gives effect to the arrangement arrived at between the Government and the railway companies as to the compensation payable under the railway agreements. A compromise has been arrived at, under which the Government are to pay the railway companies £60,000,000 in two instalments of £30,000,000 each. The sums so paid are to be liable to income tax so far as they are at any time utilised for the purpose of payment of interest and dividends.

RATE FIXING PROPOSALS.

Provisions in the Bill as to the fixing of rates give effect, without any substantial alterations, to the proposals of the Rates Advisory Committee. The duties of the rates tribunal, the memorandum points out, will be both multitudinous and onerous, especially in the first few years. It will have to fix the original standard charges, adjust all existing exceptional rates, settle the conditions of carriage, hear applications for variation of standard charges and exceptional rates, and review periodically the standard charges and exceptional rates with a view to their adjustment. It is therefore proposed to establish a new court, called the " Railway Rates Tribunal." The court will consist of three permanent members, one being a lawyer, one a commercial expert, and one a railway expert. In cases of importance the court will be strengthened by the addition of two members appointed ad hoc—one chosen from a panel of traders, and one from a panel of railway experts.

An agreement arrived at between the companies and the railway trades unions and embodied in the Bill provides for the maintenance and extension of the existing national machinery for the regulation of wages and working conditions, and for the establishment of local machinery in the shape of Whitley Councils.

DEBATE IN HOUSE OF COMMONS.

On 26th May the Bill came on for Second Reading in the House of Commons.

The Minister of Transport (the Right Hon. Sir Eric Geddes) said the railways in this country were approaching, if they had not yet reached, 100 years of life. In that time they had changed very materially in their position financially and otherwise. Before the War the value of the shares of railways was declining and the difficulty of raising capital was increasing. The anxieties from which railways suffered were shared by every other transport undertaking, not only in this country, but practically throughout the world. Trams, canals, and docks in this country were all in that difficulty. The railways alone were guaranteed by the Government during the War, and to that extent they were in a happier position than any other transport undertakings. Now they had to consider their future.

On the whole he did not think that Government control had really put the railways into the present position of difficulty. It existed before; but the circumstances of the War had made the position more difficult. In the view of the Government there was no obligation upon the State to put the railways back into any pre-War position. The

Government, however, had come to a settlement with the Railway Companies' Association under which they were to pay the companies £60,000,000, of which at least £9,000,000 came back in the form of Income Tax. That settlement had been approved by over 75 per cent. of the capital invested in the railways, and, if it was confirmed by the House, it wiped off any obligation of any kind.

Economy from Grouping.

Coming to the details of the Bill, the Minister said the Government believed that by the proposed grouping far-reaching economies could be effected. He thought £25,000,000 a year was a very reasonable estimate of their amount. True, if there were advantages in competition they would have to be foregone ; but there was not much real competition before the War. The competition he hoped they would get would be the competition in prosperity of one district against another. " I would hope," said Sir Eric, " that the House will see that a railway company will develop and endeavour to promote the prosperity of the communities through which it runs if it knows that when it succeeds it will have the advantage of it." He wanted to give railways a reasonable amount of freedom in their management, and the community a proper amount of control.

A proposal had been put forward at the request of the representatives of labour and with the approval of the Government that workman directors should be included on the boards of the railway companies. Labour, however, after conference with the companies, had deliberately surrendered that offer, and the Government thought that they had made a mistake in doing so. If the Bill were adopted he believed that within a measurable time they could look forward to immense prosperity in the railway industry and a reduction of charges to users.

Labour and Nationalisation.

The **Right Hon. J. R. Clynes (Chairman of the Parliamentary Labour Party)** moved an amendment in these terms : —

" That this House cannot assent to the Second Reading of a Bill which not only fails to provide for the public ownership and control of the railways, but would prejudice the future acquisition of the railways by the State on a fair and economic basis, which provides for the payment to the railway companies of a sum far in excess of the amount due to them in consequence of temporary State control, and which, repealing the statutory limitation imposed upon railway rates, vests in a non-elected body the arbitrary power of fixing those rates."

He said that on 20th March, 1918, the Prime Minister informed a deputation of the Trades Union Congress that he was in general sympathy with their proposals for railway nationalisation, and during the General Election campaign of 1918 the Colonial Secretary* declared publicly that it was intended to nationalise the railways. On a large matter of that kind, involving such a great principle, they were entitled to a frank statement as to why the Government had changed their policy. " If the Government have deserted the cause, which at that time they publicly supported, some of us have not," remarked Mr. Clynes. " We still have unshaken faith in the wisdom . . . of making a great national need national property, placing it under national control, and running the railway system not for any sectional or financial advantage, but for the advantage of the whole nation."

Workmen as Directors : Claim Surrendered.

An objection which many of those on the Opposition side of the House had to the Bill was that it placed in a position of greater prejudice any future prospect of nationalisation. Surely if the Government could ever look forward to the nationalisation of a national enterprise of that kind, they ought not to take a line which clearly was going to increase and intensify the interests that were embedded in their railway system. It was a matter of the greatest regret that the workmen's representatives were obliged to forfeit their right to a share in the management in order to safeguard their wage conditions.

The Minister of Transport intervened to remark that the men deliberately surrendered what he told them the Cabinet had decided to invite that House to pass.

Mr. Clynes said his information was that it was under the pressure of the action of the representatives of the railway companies that at length the men, in their view, had to choose between safeguarding their wages by obtaining from the railway companies the concessions as to the National Wages Board and the claim they originally put forward for a share in the management.

Compulsory Arbitration.

He, himself, attached the greatest importance to partnership. There might be great differences of opinion upon questions of apportioning the gains of any industry. There ought to be no difference on the question of bringing into the closest

---

* The Right Hon. Winston Churchill.

co-operation the workmen and the employers, or the workmen and the State, where the State was the employer. Referring to the provision in the Bill that questions of wages and other matters relating to working conditions and rates of pay must be referred to and settled by the Central Wages Board or, on appeal, by the National Wages Board, Mr. Clynes said it raised one of the greatest issues which had ever been discussed in the realm of industry in this country—that of compulsory arbitration.

"My desire," said Mr. Clynes, "would be to create a temper, atmosphere, and spirit for arbitration; indeed, I think there are conditions which, if they are first fulfilled, would go far to produce in this country readiness on the part of the wage-earners always to submit their claims to the decision of a Court of Arbitration." Essential conditions were:—

(1) The fixing in the case of any body of workmen of minimum rates of wages.

(2) The fixing of a maximum of profit for capital to be exceeded only as the result of additional gain coming from the joint exertions of capital and labour.

(3) Such a state of incentive to service on the part of both capital and labour as would produce a margin above both the maximum and minimum.

(4) The constitution of Courts to decide differences in such a manner as would command the absolute confidence of the two parties.

(5) That the worker should share in the conduct and control of the industry in which he was employed.

Cheap Rates Essential.

The Right Hon. Sir Donald Maclean (Chairman of the Independent Liberal Party in Parliament) observed that the interest of the public in the working of the measure was an overwhelming one. Unless they could get reasonably cheap rates for passengers and goods, the outlook for the recovery of trade in this country was very black. He regretted a decision had been come to that no railway workers were to be on the boards of railway companies. He was convinced that the real way out of their labour troubles was not the imposition of a hard-and-fast system of what was called nationalisation, but co-operation.

The Right Hon. Sir F. Banbury (Coalition Unionist, *City of London*) said that under the Bill the management and control of the railways were for the most part either continued in the Ministry of Transport or vested in various tribunals or bodies set up by the Bill. The guarantee of the Government ceased, so that, though the management of the railways would not in the main be in the hands of the owners, they would have to bear the costs which bureaucratic control would entail.   In fact, this was a sort of bastard nationalisation Bill.·

The Second Reading debate was continued on 30th May, when, just before the close of the sitting, the House divided on the amendment moved by Mr. Clynes.   This was rejected by 259 votes against 65, and the Bill was read a second time. It was then referred to a Standing Committee.

THE BUDGET.

(Mr. Austen Chamberlain's Statement.)

On 25th April the Budget statement was made in the House of Commons by the Leader of the House, who undertook the duty on behalf of his recently-appointed successor in the office of Chancellor of the Exchequer—the Right Hon. Sir Robert Horne.

The position at the close of the financial year ended 31st March, 1921, and the estimate of the position at the end of March next year, were stated as follows : —

PAST FINANCIAL YEAR, 1920-21.

Revenue	£1,425,985,000
Expenditure	1,195,428,000
Surplus applied to Debt Reduction	£230,557,000

NEW FINANCIAL YEAR, 1921-22.

Revenue	£1,216,650,000
Expenditure	1,039,728,000
Estimated Surplus	£176,922,000

It was explained that the figures for 1921-22 represent both ordinary and special receipts and expenditure, not hitherto differentiated.   In other words, the totals above quoted include special receipts arising from the liquidation of war assets and expenditure necessary for the liquidation of war commitments. Set out separately the aggregate figures are :—

	Receipts.	Expenditure.	Surplus.
Ordinary	£1,058,150,000	£974,023,000	£84,127,000
Special	158,500,000	65,705,000	92,795,000
Totals	£1,216,650,000	£1,039,728,000	£176,922,000

It was shown that actual receipts in the year ended 31st March, 1921, at £1,425,985,000, were £7,685,000 in excess of the estimate, while expenditure, at £1,195,428,000, was less than the estimate by £75,740,000. Adding £6,087,000 chargeable to capital account, the entire State expenditure for 1920-21 amounted to £1,201,515,000. In addition to the surplus of £230,557,000, there were applied to the reduction of debt various sums out of revenue (included under the head of expenditure), totalling £21,266,000, so that the aggregate amount redeemed out of revenue last year was £251,823,000. The aggregate reduction effected was £259,500,000, and the total dead weight debt at 31st March last was £7,573,000,000.

Loans to Dominions and Allies.

At 31st March loans to Dominions and Allies had risen to £1,945,600,000, an increase in twelve months of £97,000,000. The provision in the current year's estimates under this head is limited to £5,000,000, to be devoted, if required, towards reconstruction. Below are the details : —

DOMINIONS :

Australia	£90,000,000	
New Zealand	29,600,000	
Canada	13,800,000	
South Africa	7,500,000	
Other Dominions and Colonies	3,100,000	
		£144,000,000

ALLIES :

Russia	£561,400,000	
France..	557,000,000	
Italy	476,800,000	
Belgium (A) War	94,400,000	
(B) Reconstruction	9,000,000	
Serbia	22,100,000	
Portugal, Roumania, Greece and other Allies	66,200,000	
Relief Loans	16,700,000	
		£1,803,600,000

Total		£1,947,600,000

It was announced that no fresh taxation was to be imposed. On the other hand the only remissions of which intimation was made were the dropping of the Excess Profits Duty which is expected to produce £120,000,000 in the current financial year) and a reduction in two of the duties that were increased in the Budget of 1920. These reductions are : —

SPARKLING WINES.—A specific duty of 15s. per gallon, in place of the existing duty of 7s. per gallon and ad valorem duty of 33 1-3 per cent.

CIGARS.—Abolition of surtax, and duty to be restricted to a specific amount of 15s. 7d. per lb.

The Leader of the House (the Right Hon. Austen Chamberlain), in making the financial statement, said that no credit had been taken in the present Budget for the sums which they might receive on Reparations account. He hoped that they were nearing payment of them, but he thought it was not wise to include them in the Budget until they were actually received, when they would go to the further redemption of debt. On the Budget figures the total cash provision which might be available for debt reduction would be £103,500,000. That was, of course, very substantially below the contribution of £259,500,000 made in the year which had just closed, but depression had succeeded to a boom in trade, and the very fact that they did so much last year might be reasonably pleaded as a justification for moving more slowly in their present temporary difficulty.

The total debt was £7,573,000,000, of which Treasury Bills and Ways and Means advances accounted for £1,275,000,000, and external debt, at par of exchange, £1,162,000,000. The whole surplus would be required to meet obligations in respect of the debt during the current year, and even then it would be insufficient without renewing a portion of the internal debt. The expenses and loss involved in the coal strike and the large terminal liabilities under the railway agreement made it impossible for them to do more. As to 1922-23, even after allowing for normal increase of revenue he could not safely anticipate an ordinary revenue of more than £950,000,000 next year to meet the ordinary expenditure of that year.

They had to provide next year for one considerable item not included in this year's estimates, namely, interest on their debt to the United States of America, which at par exchange amounted to over £40,000,000 a year. It was possible that they might not require to provide more than half of the whole year's interest on that debt in 1922-23, but even so the starting point on the expenditure side was too high.

Drastic Reductions.

Accordingly the way was being prepared for drastic reductions in next year's estimates as compared with those of this year. If the Chancellor of the Exchequer succeeded in that purpose the amount available for debt reduction out of ordinary revenue, even on the most sanguine hypothesis, would not reach £100,000,000 in 1922-23.

The Right Hon. H. H. Asquith (Leader of the Independent Liberal Party) said that the country was not in a position to indulge in adventures, either belligerent or philanthropic, without most carefully counting the cost, and without making perfectly certain, so far as human foresight could do so, that the adventure was one which would be remunerative in the strict sense of the term. Anxious as he was to see the crushing burdens of taxation reduced, they could not talk honestly and sanely of anything of the kind until they had reduced their expenditure to a point at which they had a substantial surplus every year. On the whole the influence of the House of Commons was exercised in favour of larger rather than reduced expenditure. This was a time when the House ought to take that matter seriously to heart.

The Ways and Means Resolutions were adopted after debates extending over two sittings. The Finance Bill was then introduced, and was read a Second Time on 25th May. Its progress through Committee had not been completed at the date up to which the summary of proceedings in this issue of the JOURNAL has been carried.

PROPORTIONAL REPRESENTATION BILL.

(Rejection on Second Reading.)

A Bill presented by private Members providing for the proportional representation of the electors of the House of Commons was debated on 8th April on Second Reading and was rejected.

The Bill provided that at a contested election for a parliamentary constituency where there are two or more members to be elected the election should be according to the principle of proportional representation, each elector having one transferable vote as defined by the Representation of the People Act, 1918. It also authorised the preparation of a scheme of redistribution.

DEBATE IN HOUSE OF COMMONS.

Sir Thomas Bramsdon (Independent Liberal, *Portsmouth*), in moving the Second Reading, said it was a non-party Bill applicable to the whole of the United Kingdom. A great deal was said about difficulties in connection with the voting, the counting, and other things under the system, but he did not believe there was any person of ordinary intelligence who would not find the voting perfectly simple. As to the counting,

F

he pointed out that in the recent Irish municipal elections
there were 120 contests and not one of the districts experienced
any difficulty with the counting of the votes. After referring
to the manner in which the system had been adopted on the
Continent of Europe, the hon. Member claimed that in English-
speaking countries similar progress had been made.

In some of the States of Australia, in New Zealand
Canada, South Africa, and the United States it was now ir
operation. The British Parliament had embodied propor
tional representation in several Acts because it was found to
be the most satisfactory method of ensuring the representatior
of minorities. The system had also been recently confirmed
in New South Wales and it was proposed to introduce it ir
Malta. Statements had been made by distinguished publi
men to the effect that the system had not been successful
but what could they expect from opponents? He would
quote the view of the Prime Minister of New South Wales, the
Hon. J. Storey, who said : —

" I was prejudiced against proportional representation, but I ar
bound to admit, looking at it impartially and in the interests of the
country as a whole, that I believe it to be the better of the two systems.

Though the scheme of proportional representation had
been discussed and criticised by the finest mathematical minds
he would make the bold statement that it was impossible t
gerrymander it.

Views of Opponents.

Major V. L. Henderson (Coalition Unionist, *Glasgow
Tradeston*) moved the rejection of the Bill. He said that
they had a big constituency with five Members and the
proceeded with their party to elect their five candidates the
were bound to be certain anomalies. Some of the men migh
be well-known men like Cabinet Ministers, say, the olde
men ; yet the younger men had to bear the same expense
knowing perfectly well that under this system they stood
much less chance of election. There was,. therefore, bound t
be a much greater chance of friction amongst Member
belonging to the same party than under the present system
What he said had actually happened in the working of propo
tional representation in Australia. It had led to person
bitterness amongst the candidates of the same party.

He acknowledged that under this system the expense
would not be great, but where they had Members running
a team they would be able to do much more with their mone
than an independent Member running by himself, and
would result in independent Members being wiped out

existence. That had actually happened in New South Wales, where all independent Members had ceased to hold their seats in the House. Under proportional representation it was possible for two minorities to come to an agreement by which each would transfer the surplus votes on the understanding that they would thereby each achieve their own object. Any system of election by which they would encourage bargaining was bound to degrade the whole political life of the country.

Under proportional representation the personal side of politics went absolutely by the board and the whole basis of the early representation in that House away back to the days of Edward I. would be destroyed.

Lieut.-Col. G. B. Hurst (Coalition Unionist, *Manchester, Moss Side*), in seconding the amendment, said there was no evidence of any public demand for proportional representation. The country had always shown an inflexible resistance to applying so-called philosophic and abstract generalisations of that sort to its political machinery.   •

Paper Constitutions.

The Right Hon. Sir Henry Craik (Coalition Unionist, *Scottish Universities*) remarked that their greatest political teacher, Edmund Burke, taught this nation to beware of abstract and paper constitutions. "What we want in our constitution," the right hon. gentleman said, "is what we have had—that great virtue of simplicity which is, as Swift says, the greatest ornament of all human things. Abstract paper constitutions, cunningly devised, dexterously contrived in order to bring about purely problematical ends, are not consistent with the genius of this nation. We have never had them, and we are not likely to have them."

The Right Hon. George Roberts (Labour, *Norwich*) said he was in favour of proportional representation, despite the many objections that could be advanced against it, because of the fact that more than ever in the future there was the imperative necessity of Parliament really representing the people, and phases of thought, in the country. Whether that Bill represented the ideal system or not, he was convinced that it took them a long step forward towards a truer system under which representation in Parliament was a truer reflex of opinion in the country, thereby improving the authority and sanction of Parliament and checkmating those elements in their midst which were concerned to undermine authority and the constitution of the country.

Mr. Aneurin Williams (Independent Liberal, *Consett*) said they were told that the system produced unsettled government

F 2

and small majorities. It did not produce small majorities in corresponding bodies any more than any other system. He believed that in the Commonwealth Parliament of Australia the Government at the present time had a majority of one. That had not been produced by proportional representation, because it had not yet been applied to that particular Parliament. The statement that in New South Wales the effect of the system was to prevent the return of any independent was incorrect, because in a House of 90 there were five independent Members.

Freedom of Electors : Case of New South Wales.

Mr. W. L. Burdett-Coutts (Coalition Unionist, *Abbey*) remarked that he looked upon the case of New South Wales as the only fair test of the application of proportional representation to a great popular assembly. The Hon. John Storey and his party were in power in New South Wales. How? He was in power on the strength of a minority of one in four of the whole electorate of New South Wales. Was that a system which they wanted introduced into this country? Moreover there were incidental peculiarities which had shown themselves clearly in New South Wales. The election in New South Wales was carried on upon lines which absolutely deprived the elector of all freedom and all voluntary momentum in the matter.

Could anything be more destructive of the freedom of the electors than the system which pervaded both parties in New South Wales, and which was rendered necessary by the complicated system of preferences—that was to say, the caucus of each party, who got the whole thing into their hands? They were the half-dozen clever men who, Mr. Massey said, could carry any election they liked under the preference system. So minute was the control of the caucus, and so necessary was its operation to the exercise of what should be the free right of the electors, that no elector who wanted his party to succeed dare go into the polling booth in New South Wales without one of the " How to vote " cards. They could not, the hon. member declared, have true, satisfactory, logical proportional representation unless they turned the whole of England into one constituency.

Divided Government Opinion.

The Minister of Pensions (the Right Hon. Ian Macpherson) in explaining the attitude of the Government, said that they were divided in regard to the Bill. They did not propose to utilise the services of the Whips, but they regarded the

measure as of such great importance, and as effecting so great
a constitutional change, that they could not pledge themselves,
after a Friday afternoon's debate, to bring in a Bill dealing
with that important subject, or to grant facilities for the
passage of the present measure.

The Right Hon. Lord Robert Cecil (Independent Unionist,
Hitchin) was confident that this change would produce,
broadly speaking, two great beneficial results. It would
produce a House of Commons less absolutely nominated by
the party organisation than some of the Houses which existed
before the War. It would give a greater flexibility, a greater
opportunity for people whose opinions did not happen to be
those exactly of any party to find a position in that House.
The majority would come in belonging to the great parties,
and the great organisations ; because without organisation it
would always be difficult to deal with a democratically constituted electorate. They would get a House of the same
type, but with a larger amount of independence. They would
also get a House which more directly represented the general
current of feeling in the country, and which would not have
what he regarded as a great danger—an overwhelming, un-
yielding, unmanageable majority. The change would conduce
not to revolution, not to violence, but to orderly progress and
stability.

Hon. John Storey's Speech.

Sir C. Kinloch-Cooke (Coalition Unionist, *Devonport*)
quoted from a speech of the Premier of New South Wales
in which, the hon. Member remarked, he stated that
proportional representation worked out perhaps in a
satisfactory way. As a case in point he (the Hon. John
Storey) gave the following instance of what happened in his
own electorate in New South Wales and what was likely to
happen elsewhere : —

" In my own electorate there were only two Nationalist candidates,
and five Labour men. We thought it was a certainty for one Nationalist
candidate and two Labour men. As a matter of fact there should have
been two, but the stronger man (Dr. Stopford) we thought was so much
a certainty that in order to weaken his chances as much as we could,
we voted for his friend, who had only been put up in order to give him
a run. Dr. Stopford had said to him, ' I will put you up and pay your
expenses.' He did so. I met the doctor on the evening of the first day,
and this is what he said :

" ' Well, Story, you and I are elected, anyway. You are thousands
above your quota, and I am within a little of it. You and I, therefore,
will be sure to be elected.'

" I said : ' Of course, but under this tricky system no one knows
what may happen ; but I suppose you will be elected.'

"Mr. Story went on : 'Believe me, this gentleman was not elected ; and yet so certain was he of election that he entertained his friends at a banquet. He came over and told Mr. Holman, who was the then Premier and likely to be defeated, that he would offer him his seat, as he was certain that he was going to get in.'

"Mr. Story wound up by saying : 'The election was on the Thursday and it took to the Saturday to finish counting the votes, and when the declaration was made Dr. Stopford was still 90 behind! His friend who had put in is now a Member of Parliament in New South Wales.' "*

That, observed Sir Clement, was what happened in New South Wales. He contended that proportional representation would produce a less stable Government, a weaker Executive, and no better administration.

On a division the amendment for the rejection of the Bill was carried by 186 votes against 87.

EMERGENCY POWERS ACT, 1920.

(Stoppage in Coal Trade: Proclamation.)

When Parliament reassembled on 4th April a Proclamation by His Majesty declaring that, in view of the immediate threat of cessation of work in the coal mines, "a state of emergency" existed was read in the House of Commons. The Proclamation was made under the Emergency Powers Act, 1920, which enacts that if it appears to His Majesty that any action has been taken or is immediately threatened by any person, or body of persons, of such a nature and on so extensive a scale as to be calculated by interfering with the supply and distribution of food, water, fuel, and light, or with the means of locomotion, to deprive the community, or any substantial portion of the community, of the essentials of life His Majesty may by Proclamation declare that a state of emergency exists.

On 5th April the House passed a resolution for a humble Address to His Majesty thanking him for his gracious Message.

Following the Proclamation a number of Regulations conferring extraordinary powers on the Government were made by Order in Council under the Emergency Powers Act, and following the adoption of the resolution above referred to, a motion was submitted to the House providing that these Regulations should continue in force for a period of one month,

---

* This is a quotation from an address given by the Premier of New South Wales before a private meeting of the Empire Parliamentary Association, held in the Rooms of the Association, Westminster Hall, on 16th March, 1921.

this being the procedure prescribed by the Act (*vide* JOURNAL, Vol. II., No. 1, p. 53).

A Calamitous Occurrence.

The Chancellor of the Exchequer (the Right Hon. Sir Robert Horne) said that unfortunately for the second time within six months the country was confronted with a stoppage in the coalfields. They had come through a winter of the most severe depression and had discerned only the first flicker of reviving trade when this calamitous occurrence took place. When that flicker might be relighted no man could say. The result of the last strike was to rob them of many markets to which their coal used to go. For the first time in the history of this country American coal came to Europe in large quantities. What had happened was not only a great injury to industry at a time when it had an intolerable burden to bear, but was a disaster to the coal trade itself.

Dealing with the merits of the dispute* in the industry, the right hon. gentleman said the present controversy was not really about the particular rates of wages which were being offered to the miners. The real controversy was whether the country was to come to the assistance of the coal trade with a subsidy which might run to tens of millions of pounds in a single year. Associated with that was the question whether the Government were going to impose by legislation upon the coal trade a pooling system by which the more lucrative collieries would make up the deficiency of those which were less successful. He could not think of anything more pernicious to industry as a whole than the grant of subsidies and there was no hope of a solution along that line. As to a system of pooling profits, he could not imagine anything which would so destroy the incentive to activity and enterprise.

National Settlements.

The Right Hon. J. R. Clynes (Chairman of the Parliamentary Labour Party) resented the implication that the miners were the cause of the loss of export coal trade, as matters not unconnected with foreign affairs had much to do with the breakdown. Despite what the Chancellor of the Exchequer had said, this was to the miner a question of wages figures. To the wage-earner, the coal-getter, the greater of the two questions was, surely, that of wages and the second was that of method. As to method, the whole mining community on the

---

* The dispute arose on the termination of Government control of the coal industry on 31st March, 1921, as provided for in the Coal Mines (Decontrol) Act, which received the Royal Assent on 24th March, 1921 (*vide* JOURNAL, Vol. II., No. 2, page 296).

men's side desired a continuance of the hard-won right of national settlements. It desired to continue that method for the purpose of securing and retaining fair wages.

Re-echoing an appeal by the Chancellor of the Exchequer that the discussion should proceed on the lines of trying to evolve ideas for bringing the parties together again, Mr. Clynes remarked that the question could be fought out, of course; but it might be better to think it out than to fight it out. "You may use Proclamations—they may be necessary—you may use all the King's horses and all the King's men and get the mines in your grip so far as the law is concerned, but," he added, "they will remain absolutely useless until you get the miners down into the pits."

Mr. Duncan Graham (Labour, *Hamilton***)** said the miners were anxious that the industry should be taken over or controlled by the Government in the interests of the nation. They were not so anxious for revolution as some people imagined.

Mr. Asquith's Suggestion.

The Right Hon. H. H. Asquith (Leader of the Independent Liberal Party) observed that the root of the difficulty between the two parties was very largely in the distinction between regulating wages in the coal industry upon a national or upon a district basis. From the moment when, under the stress of war, they established a system of control which was regarded by many miners as the first step towards a more complete system of nationalisation, there had been in the mining world a strong and growing dissatisfaction with the district system. He was not satisfied that further deliberations between the parties with the assistance of the Government might not show that the gap between these two things was not so unbridgable as at first sight it appeared. "I can conceive," said Mr. Asquith, "of your accepting the principle of what I may call a national standard, taking that as the basis of . . . the law by which the system of wages is to be achieved, and at the same time finding within its limits the means for elastic variation in regard to special local conditions."

The Prime Minister (the Right Hon. D. Lloyd George) said that there had been a general demand for decontrol in all industries and it included the mining industry. The subsidising of a great industry out of taxation was wrong in principle and completely indefensible. It was especially indefensible at the present time, having regard to the heavy taxation and the condition of the Exchequer. The loss before 31st March upon the working of control and the payment of wages and of guaranteed profits came to over £1,000,000 a week. As prices were falling that amount would increase, but even at the last rate it meant a loss of between £50,000,000 and £60,000,000 a year to the Exchequer unless that arrangement were terminated, and it might very well have run up to figures like £100,000,000. No Government could possibly be justified in placing a burden of that kind upon the overburdened taxpayers of the country in order to pay either wages or the profits of the mine-owners.

No Resumption of Control.

The Government would be very glad to take any steps to promote further discussion between the mine-owners and the miners' representatives. "But we must make it clear," the Premier said, " that we could not enter into any negotiations on any expectation that we could recommend to Parliament the maintenance of this industry out of the general taxation of the country. We could not enter into any discussion upon the assumption that it would be possible to resume control of the industry. With those two limitations there is a very wide field for discussion. The whole of the ordinary questions that arise in industrial disputes of what wages it is fair for workmen to demand, what wages it is fair for the owners to pay, what the industry is capable of, all these questions can be discussed."

Debate on the resolution was resumed on 6th April, when

Mr. J. C. Gould (Unionist, *Cardiff Central*) said the experience of control in the past had been to prove conclusively that it worked against the best interests of the country. In the shipbuilding and steel industries they were working in this country at a great disadvantage, because their basic cost—the cost of coal—was so high.

A Dictatorship.

Colonel J. C. Wedgwood (Labour, *Newcastle-under-Lyme*) moved an amendment to omit from the operation of the resolution certain of the regulations. Looking at these regulations, giving power to the Government to commandeer land, mines, railways and canals, and giving the Executive an absolute right of dictatorship, he could not help thinking that they must have been brought to the notice of the Government by M. Krassin or some of the other advocates of Bolshevism in Russia.

Mr. W. Graham (Labour, *Edinburgh Central*) said the difficulty of Labour members and others in their endeavour to build up a sound, decent industrial system in Great Britain had always been with the men who would not see reason and

were satisfied that nothing but wild methods would avail by
way of a solution. Regulations of that kind encouraged this
school and made the task of Labour members more difficult.
In any emergency in which they desired peace they should
interfere as little as possible with the rights, habits and usages
of the people.

The Home Secretary (the Right Hon. Edward Shortt) said
that no one who read the regulations fairly could possibly
say they were aimed at trades unions as such or at a strike
quâ strike. What the Government were doing was carrying
out a duty which they owed to the community without regard
to the cause of the emergency or to any party concerned in the
struggle.

After further debate the amendment was negatived by
285 votes against 69. The resolution, which was amended so
as to provide for slight modifications in two of the Regulations
and the omission of a third, was subsequently adopted by 270
votes against 60.

Calling out of Reserve: Royal Proclamation.

On 11th April the House of Commons took into consideration a Message from the King stating that the " present state
of public affairs and the threatened dislocation of the life of
the community occasioned by the existing strike in the coal-
mines, and its threatened extension to the railway and transport
services of the country . . . constituting a state of great
emergency within the meaning of the Acts of Parliament in
that behalf " His Majesty was, by Proclamation, about to
order the calling out of Navy, Army and Air Force Reserves.

**The Leader of the House (the Right Hon. Austen Chamber-
lain)** said that although the threat of an extension of the
dispute to the whole transport industry of the country was
suspended, it was not withdrawn. It was necessary, therefore,
that the Government should pursue the precautionary measures
on which they had already acted, and it was vital that the
community should show that in the last resort, if its life and
existence were attacked, it had the capacity and the will to
protect itself.

The question of the coal crisis was further debated on
various occasions during the period of the Session dealt with in
this number of the JOURNAL, and from time to time official
announcements were made regarding the conferences between
the parties concerned. Parliament on two occasions passed
resolutions continuing in force the Emergency Regulations
which, as a settlement had not then been reached, still remained
in operation on 20th June, the date up to which the present
record of the proceedings of Parliament has been carried.

ARMY (ANNUAL) ACT.

(Courts-Martial—Right of Appeal.)

The Army (Annual) Bill was discussed in the House of Commons in Committee on 11th April.

Major Christopher Lowther (Independent, *Cumberland, N.*) moved a new clause to provide that any member of His Majesty's forces sentenced to death by court-martial should have the right of appeal to the Court of Criminal Appeal, assisted by one or more military assessors, as the Lord Chancellor might direct. The proposal, he said, was the considered opinion of a minority of the Courts-Martial Committee set up in 1919 to go into the whole question of courts-martial. A man who joined the Army should not, by reason of becoming a soldier, forfeit the rights he would have had were he a civilian. In civil life a man convicted of a crime of which death was a penalty had, as a matter of course, a right of appeal to the Court of Criminal Appeal. In the case of the soldier there was, instead, elaborate legal machinery which eventually led up to the Judge-Advocate-General or his representative. A Court of Criminal Appeal, consisting of Judges of the High Court of many years' experience in the sifting of evidence, was not to be compared with any other body of junior opinion either in this country or in the Army.

Mr. A. Hopkinson (Coalition Liberal, *Mossley*) said the suggestion that in cases where the death sentence had been passed in the Army for a military offence the soldier should have the right of appeal to the Court of Criminal Appeal was a cruel one. The whole point of the death sentence on active service was to act as a preventive and warning. If it were carried out after weeks of delay, after a rehearing at Calcutta in the case of cases from the Indian frontier and at Cape Town where the cases came from the northern frontier of Rhodesia, the whole point of carrying out the death sentence was gone. Even the strictest Commander-in-Chief would examine the case from the point of view of how, by any means, he could save a man's life without injuring the discipline of the Army.

Humanitarian Aspect.

The evidence of two Commanders-in-Chief came before the Committee on Courts-Martial. In one case the Commander-in-Chief had commuted 89·5 of the death sentences that came to his notice—that was to say 89·5 of the cases which had not already had their sentences commuted by the

various Army authorities on the way from the court-martial
to the General Headquarters—and in the other case the
Commander-in-Chief commuted rather over 90 per cent. Was
it conceivable that any Court of Appeal, regarding cases entirely
from the legal aspect and from the point of view of strict
justice without any regard to humanity, would have commuted
sentences to that extent ?

General Sir Ivor Philipps (Coalition Liberal, *Southampton*)
said he had been an advocate for a military Court of Appeal,
but he had never suggested that it should be extended to
court-martial verdicts and decisions. His own experience
had convinced him that there was no fairer court in the world
than a court-martial.

Lieut.-Colonel John Ward (Coalition Liberal, *Stoke-on-Trent*) remarked that during the War, in their own Army,
from beginning to end possibly from 6,000,000 to 8,000,000
men were employed. Yet with all the extraordinary conditions
that obtained, when even the bravest might flinch and commit
an act of indiscipline from the purely legal point of view—
there must have been thousands upon thousands of such cases
—only 400 actual military executions took place. That was
a credit to the courts-martial and the military tribunals.

**The Under-Secretary of State for War (Colonel Sir R.
Sanders)** pointed out that the subject had been considered
by the Courts-Martial Committee and was rejected by them.
It had been debated two or three times in the House and
had always been rejected. The Government could not accept
the proposal. He did not think in a single case where a man
was executed during the War that on a point of law he would
have got off. If there was a complaint to be made against
courts-martial, it was not that the innocent man got convicted,
but that there was a great chance of the guilty man getting
off.

On a division the proposed clause was rejected by 161
votes against 63.

The Bill received the Royal Assent on 28th April.

RETIREMENT OF THE SPEAKER.

(Election of the Right Hon. J. H. Whitley to the Chair.)

On 25th April the Right Hon. J. W. Lowther announced
to the House of Commons his intention of retiring from the
Chair, after filling the office of Speaker for a period of sixteen
years. For a term of ten years prior to 1905, when he was
unanimously elected Speaker for the first time, an honour

ubsequently repeated on five occasions, Mr. Lowther was
Chairman of Ways and Means, so that for the long span of
twenty-six years he presided in one capacity or the other over
debates in the Lower House. In making his brief statement
he right hon. gentleman recalled that it was almost 38 years
since he was first elected a Member of the House of Commons,
and there now remained in that Chamber only four Members
who were colleagues of his when he first entered it.

The following day the Prime Minister moved a resolution
conveying the thanks of the House to the Speaker for his
distinguished services in the Chair.

The Prime Minister (the Right Hon. D. Lloyd George)
spoke of the gratitude which members felt to Mr. Lowther
for the personal kindness they had always received at his
hands and which had added to their affectionate regard for
him. He passed on to say that they had found in him always
" a true guardian of the privileges, a faithful trustee of the
traditions, which are interwoven with the liberties of this
land." Nothing had in recent times strengthened the hold
and the influence of Parliament upon all classes of the nation
more than the scrupulous fairness which Mr. Lowther had
shown in the Chair. Mr. Lloyd George proceeded to refer
to the Speaker's gift of humour which had been " the delight
and the security of the House." Because of it many a thunder-
cloud had been scattered when it was on the point of breaking
with disastrous consequences to the dignity of the House.
In connection with Mr. Lowther's services outside the strict
limits of the functions of the Chair, the Premier recalled that
the largest extension of the franchise ever ventured upon
in this country was due to his tact and to his direction and
guidance.

Empire Influence.

Mr. Stephen Walsh (Labour, *Ince*), in seconding the resolution, said that Mr. Lowther had achieved success in a superla-
tive degree, and had not been content with being the First
Commoner of this realm —although that in itself was a position
which might fill the spacious ambition of any man. " You
have," Mr. Walsh said to the Speaker, " developed the sense of
parliamentary institutions in every Parliament of this great
British Commonwealth, and the extremely effective work
that you have undertaken in connection with the Empire
Parliamentary Association is, I know, already producing
the very finest results throughout the British Commonwealth.
Every Member of the Parliaments under the Southern Cross,
or in Canada, or wherever the British Commonwealth extends,
feels that you are not merely the Speaker of the British House

of Commons, but that in a very real sense you are also a
Speaker for them.   In that sense you have been casting seed
upon the waters which will, I hope, bear fruit abundantly."

**The Right Hon. H. H. Asquith (Leader of the Independent
Liberal Party)** supported the resolution, and it was agreed to
nemine contradicente.

The Speaker, in returning thanks to the House, said that
twice since he entered that Chamber he had witnessed a
very large extension of the suffrage, and twice a redistribution
of political power.   " But," he added, " notwithstanding
that—and I think possibly even by reason of that—the House
has increased in usefulness and in authority.   No man will
claim that this House is a perfect human institution, but I
will say that, in my judgment, it is, of all the institutions
of a similar character which are known to the political observer,
the most admirably fashioned for expressing the will of a
high-spirited and a free people, and for promoting the welfare
of all classes of the community."

Thereafter, the Prime Minister moved that a humble
Address should be presented to His Majesty praying him to
confer some signal mark of his favour* upon Mr. Lowther
for his eminent services, and this also was agreed to *nemine
contradicente.*

New Speaker Elected.

On 27th April the House met to elect a new Speaker.

Colonel F. B. Mildmay (Coalition Unionist, *Devon, Totnes*)
moved : —

" That the Right Hon. John Henry Whitley do take the Chair of
this House as Speaker."

The hon. Member commented upon the courteous
ease with which Mr. Whitley as Chairman of Ways and
Means had controlled their debates · in Committee.   He
had an unrivalled knowledge of the rules and usages of the
House, and might be trusted to uphold order and to maintain
their privileges with authority and dignity.

The Right Hon. Arthur Henderson (Labour, *Widnes*)
in seconding the motion, said the efficient and dignified
discharge of the heavy and important duties of the House of
Commons was vital to the maintenance of public confidence
in their parliamentary institutions, and to the orderly and
constructive development of the nation's affairs.   Never was
that confidence more needed in their parliamentary institutions
than to-day, when so many of the masses of the people were

---

* It was subsequently announced that His Majesty had been pleased
to confer a Viscountcy upon the Right Hon. J. W. Lowther.

tempted to look to other machinery for securing greater changes upon which they had set their minds. They were convinced that the high traditions of the Chair would be maintained if entrusted to the guardianship of Mr. Whitley.

Mr. Ronald McNeill (Coalition Unionist, *Canterbury*), after endorsing all that had been said in personal recommendation of Mr. Whitley, said that the Speaker was appointed by the free choice of the Members of the House of Commons, and he submitted that it ought to preserve its right to choose uncoerced by the Cabinet to-day, as it was uncoerced by the Crown in the past. The Government had violated that ancient privilege first by the manner in which they selected the candidate for the Speakership, and secondly by the selection they had made. He complained particularly that there had been neglect to ascertain the views of members on the subject, and that the Government regarded their nomination of a candidate for the Chair as completely tantamount to his election. Moreover, by what they were doing now, the Government were conferring upon the Chairman of Committees for the time being a prescriptive right to succession to the Chair, and that meant that the great office of Speaker became the gift of the Government of the day.

Sir W. Joynson-Hicks (Coalition Unionist, *Twickenham*) and **Mr. Dennis Herbert (Coalition Unionist,** *Watford*) supported this protest.

Government's Attitude.

The Leader of the House (the Right Hon. Austen Chamberlain) said the Government would deeply regret if it were thought that the Executive had interfered with the traditional rights and privileges of the House. The Government took the usual steps to ascertain the general sense of the House, and, having invited Mr. Whitley to allow his name to be submitted, they could not allow anyone of their own number to stand against that right hon. gentleman. As to the other point, he desired formally to state that the Government recognised no such inherent right in a Chairman of Committees to succeed to the Chair as had been suggested in debate that day. "All that we claim," said Mr. Chamberlain, "is that the Chairman of Committees, if he has shown the right qualities, and has shown these qualities in a pre-eminent degree, and if he is the member who commends himself more than any other to the general sense of the House, should not be the single member on whom the choice of the House may not rest, because on the nomination of the Government of the day, or of some previous Government, he has earlier served the House in the office of Chairman of Committees."

The Right Hon. J. H. Whitley then, in accordance with ancient usage, submitted himself to the will of the House. Whatever might be given to him of health and strength in the future, he said, he placed in full measure at the service of the House. He came there twenty years ago rather reluctantly, for he had found his happiness in local work and in the rough and tumble of comradeship with the boys of a great industrial town. Those boys, indeed, were his university. From them he learnt most of what he knew, and a great piece of his heart was with them still.

" I care for the House of Commons—for its traditions and its history, for its record as the living instrument by which our fathers gained for us the liberties that we now enjoy," said Mr. Whitley. " I care for it, and believe in it as the instrument by which we, and our children, will build up a still fairer Commonwealth. Should it be the will of the House to place me in its Chair, I will do my uttermost to maintain its traditions, its privileges, and its independence."

The House, having unanimously called him to the Chair, Mr. Whitley took his seat in the Chair. Following congratulatory speeches from the Prime Minister and Mr. Asquith, the House immediately adjourned. On the following day the Speaker-Elect attended at the Bar of the House of Lords, and the King's approval of the choice of the House of Commons was signified. This ended the ceremonies connected with the election of the new Speaker.

LAW OF PROPERTY BILL.

In the JOURNAL, Vol. I, No. 2, page 305, was given a summary of the main provisions of the Law of Property Bill introduced by the Lord Chancellor (Lord Birkenhead) in the Second Session of the present Parliament. After Second Reading in the House of Lords the Bill was referred to a Joint Committee of both Houses. The Bill was reintroduced with amendments in the present Session, and, after full discussions at various stages was read a third time on 31st May. The measure is now awaiting consideration in the House of Commons.

BOARD OF EDUCATION VOTE.

(Higher Education for Ex-Service Men.)

The House of Commons went into Committee of Supply on 12th April, and considered a Vote of £28,014,665 for the Board of Education.

The President of the Board of Education (the Right Hon. Herbert Fisher) said that for the year 1920-21 it was estimated that 56 per cent. of the total educational expenditure would be borne by the Board and 44 per cent. by the local authorities. More than 25,000 students were beneficiaries under the scheme which made provision for the education of ex-service students at university and technical colleges. They were serious students, their work was well reported upon, and there had been only four failures. Fifteen thousand of them had come into the universities straight from the ranks, and the vast majority belonged to families that had never before been represented at any of the British universities. It must be one of the unforeseen circumstances of the War that the desire to secure a university education for a clever son or daughter might be spread far and wide through the artisan families in this country.

After dealing with the growth of educational expenditure in recent years, a growth not confined to this country—both in France and in England the budget of the Ministry of Education had more than trebled itself since the War owing to the rise in general prices and the demand of teachers for better salaries—the right hon. gentleman pointed out that in respect of higher education an increased sum of £1,310,000 was asked for. In the reign of Queen Victoria the cause of secondary education in this country was advocated by Matthew Arnold, who complained that there was no system of cheap, good secondary education available for children of the poorer members of the middle class or the best products of the elementary schools.

Desire for Education.

If Matthew Arnold were alive to-day he would find that in addition to the old public schools, no fewer than 1,157 secondary schools for boys and girls were now in receipt of grants from the Board of Education, that those schools were educating 334,000 children, some of them paying small fees and others coming from the public elementary schools with free places. He would find a very general desire in all parts of the country to profit by the advantages offered by these secondary schools. If he visited any of the great industrial towns in the North and interrogated local authorities, he would discover that there was not one of them which could not easily fill one, two, or three additional secondary schools.

He would, indeed, criticise the very general tendency exhibited by the parents to withdraw their children before they had derived full advantage from the general increase of education offered by these institutions. But he would find

G

that the local authorities were increasing their allowance and pressing parents to enter into engagements to keep their children at school at least till the age of 16, and that there had been an improvement in the response to this attitude. He would be struck by the fact that the highway from the elementary school to the university had been considerably broadened, and that more had been done in that respect by the deliberate action of the State in this country than in any other country in the world.

He would note that 67 per cent. of the students in the secondary schools came up from the elementary schools, and that of the 200 pupils to whom State scholarships to the universities were awarded in 1920, 152 were previously educated in public elementary schools.

Equality of Opportunity.

" We hear a great deal now about class antagonism and class consciousness," said Dr. Fisher. " There should, how-ever, be nothing sectarian in a sound system of public education. On the contrary, its purpose should be to afford easy passage from class to class, to spread elementary notions of science through the community, and to convey to the spirit of the time that knowledge which will be an influence for good on the ideas of the country. . . . My belief is that recent changes, bringing as they do the different spheres of education into closer connection with one another, linking the elementary school with the continuation school, the technical school, the secondary school and then again with the technical colleges and universities, will enable more value to be extracted from our educational system and that we have now made pro-vision for the only form of equality which should attract the allegiance of thinking men—that is equality of educational opportunity."

Sir Philip Magnus (Coalition Unionist, *London University*) observed that organisation was not the most important factor in any system of education. Much more depended upon the character, the ideas, and the ideals of their teachers.

Mr. Dan Irving (Socialist, *Burnley*) said that if there was one thing the nation could not afford to save money upon it was expenditure on education. If education was free in this country all parts of it ought to be equally free to those who were fitted to take advantage of it. What sense was there in making an elementary school free and charging fees which closed the door of the secondary school to a large number of children who were fitted from an educational point of view to take advantage of it ?

After further debate the Vote was agreed to.

CANADA.

The following summary is in continuation of the proceedings of the Fifth Session of the Thirteenth Parliament which commenced on 14th February, 1921 (vide Vol. II., No. 2, for the first part of the Session). Owing to the number of important questions discussed, it has been necessary to hold over the summary of several Bills and discussions upon them until the next issue.

CONFERENCE OF PRIME MINISTERS OF THE EMPIRE.

(Subjects for Discussion: Constitutional Position: Foreign Relations: Imperial War Cabinet: Dominion Status: Representation of Parties: Anglo-Japanese Alliance: Defence: Disarmament.)

On 25th April, the Prime Minister made a statement in the House of Commons on the subjects to be discussed at the Conference of Prime Ministers to be held in London. This was followed by a general debate on 27th April.

DEBATE IN HOUSE OF COMMONS.

The Prime Minister (the Right Hon. Arthur Meighen) stated that last October he concurred in a proposal made by the Prime Minister of the United Kingdom that there should be held not later than June next a meeting of the Prime Ministers of the Empire. Since the last meeting at the Peace Conference in Paris there had been no opportunity for personal and direct consultation between the Prime Ministers on the broad issues of policy in such external matters as might be of common concern. Views were exchanged more than a year ago concerning the holding of such a meeting during 1920 ; but it was concluded at the time that this would be impracticable ; and the same conclusion was reached when, later in the year, one of the other Dominion Prime Ministers suggested a meeting immediately following the first assembly of the League of Nations. It now appeared that the middle of June next was a feasible date for all concerned.

Subjects for Discussion.

" The proposal was made and accepted last October," continued the Prime Minister, " on the basis that the June

G 2

meeting would be of a special and preliminary character having in view the necessity of discussing : —

(1) Preparation for the special Constitutional Conference contemplated in Resolution 9 of the Imperial War Conference of 1917 to be held at a later date, this preparatory discussion to include such questions as the meeting place, date, composition and agenda.

At the same time it was considered that the June meeting would afford an opportunity for discussing certain other matters of common concern which are of an urgent or important nature, such as : —

(2) A general review of the main features of foreign relations, particularly as they affect the Dominions.

(3) The question of the renewal of the Anglo-Japanese Alliance, which is indeed only a part of the general subject of foreign relations, but which is especially urgent since under the terms of the Alliance a decision should be reached this year.

(4) Preliminary consideration for the proposed Constitutional Conference, of some working method for arriving at a common understanding as to policy in such external affairs as concern all parts of the Empire.

Since that time various other subjects have been suggested for inclusion in the agenda of the June meeting. These subjects, however, in view of their technical character and of the fact that they are not of the same urgency, would seem to belong to the agenda of the Imperial Conference proper whenever its next regular Session is held ; and since it is very desirable that the special meeting of Prime Ministers in June— which is not a meeting of the Imperial Conference—should not be of a prolonged character, it seems unlikely that any considerable attention can be given to such questions, which represent an extension of the original programme. The Canadian Government have already expressed a doubt as to the inclusion of some of these questions.

These additional questions, the first two of which were proposed by the Governments of Australia and India respectively, and the remainder by the British Government, are as follows :

(5) Inter-Imperial communication by land, sea and air.

(6) The position of British Indians in other parts of the Empire.

(7) Naval, military and air defence.

(8) The recommendations of the Overseas Settlement Conference recently held in London.

(9) The development of civil aviation.

(10) The reports of the Imperial Shipping Committee appointed as a result of resolutions 11 and 24 of the Imperial War Conference of 1918.

(11) The findings of the Technical Commission appointed to discuss the question of Imperial Wireless communications.

(12) The question of German reparations, including the division as between the various parts of the British Empire of any amounts received.

(13) Imperial Statistical Bureau.

(14) Imperial patents.

In these circumstances it will be seen that the proposed agenda cannot be regarded as a hard-and-fast arrangement. It seems more likely that no subjects will be discussed that are not included in the above list, but on the other hand it seems most unlikely that all of these questions can be taken up, or indeed, in the view of the Canadian Government, that more than the first four will be closely discussed. Circumstances may develop which will render conclusions desirable in some of the other subjects. In respect of many of them it would seem that the meeting could do no more than take cognizance of proposals to be considered later."

Mr. Ernest Lapointe (Liberal, *Quebec East*): " The Prime Minister has given four subjects which he states have been definitely settled as subjects to be submitted for the consideration of the Conference. No one of these four subjects relates to Imperial defence. On the other hand, the Prime Minister of Great Britain has stated in the British House of Commons that the whole scheme of Imperial defence will be considered at the Conference. Can my right hon. friend give us any further information as to that subject ? "

The Prime Minister : " No, there is no other information that I can give. It has been placed on the agenda of the British Government. It has been submitted by them as one of their proposals with regard to the agenda, and that, doubtless, is the basis for the statement made by the Prime Minister of Great Britain. The subjects I have mentioned will not constitute the full agenda of the Imperial Conference."

Constitutional Relations.

On a motion for Committee of Supply on 27th April,
The Right Hon. Sir Robert Borden (Nat. Lib. and Con., *King's, N.S.*) quoted the resolution of 1917, which read : —

" The Imperial War Conference are of the opinion that the readjustment of the constitutional relations of the component parts of the Empire is too important and intricate a subject to be dealt with during the war, and that it should form the subject of a special Imperial Conference to be summoned as soon as possible after the cessation of hostilities.

" They deem it their duty, however, to place on record their view that any such readjustment, while thoroughly preserving all existing powers of self-government and complete control of domestic affairs, should be based upon a full recognition of the Dominions as autonomous nations of an Imperial Commonwealth, and of India as an important portion of the same, should recognise the right of the Dominions and India to an adequate voice in foreign policy and in foreign relations, and should provide effective arrangements for continuous consultation in all important matters of common Imperial concern, and for such necessary concerted action, founded on consultation, as the several Governments may determine." ·

After outlining the evolution of constitutional government in Great Britain, he recalled that British statesmen freely predicted that the grant of responsible government to the North American colonies marked the first stage of a movement which would speedily and inevitably bring about the disintegration of the Empire. It had precisely the contrary effect, and the reason for this seemed to him very plain. If there were errors in the administration controlled by the people of a country, the remedy lay in the hands of the people themselves, but if there were errors in an administration by a government controlled by the Governor or by the Colonial Office, the criticism turned upon the Governor as an Imperial Officer, or upon the Colonial Office in its administration of the affairs of the Colony. Naturally all this tended to weaken the tie which bound the Colony to the Mother Country. "I would like to emphasise the point," said Sir Robert, "that the movement for responsible government in Canada is the basis of the present constitution of the Empire. A group of free democracies, enjoying complete powers of self-government in their domestic affairs, and acting in close association with the Mother Country, has proved during the late War that unity is strongest when it is based upon freedom and autonomy."

The Imperial Conference, he continued, received its present form in 1907. It sat under the presidency of the Prime Minister of the United Kingdom, and, in his absence, under that of the Colonial Secretary. It was initiated under the name of the Colonial Conference in 1887, for the purpose of consultation. That consultation was originally between the Colonial Secretary and the Governments of the Dominions as subordinates ; but the Conference now existed for consultation between the Government of the United Kingdom and the Governments of the Dominions on the basis of equal rights and equal status.

Foreign Relations of the Empire.

Under some vague theory of trusteeship, the Government of the United Kingdom conducted for many years the more important questions touching the foreign relations of their Empire. He should remind the House, however, that these did not include everything that might be classed within the term "foreign relations" (e.g., trade and immigration). "But," he declared, "there are the higher questions of foreign relations hitherto determined by the British Government as to which the Dominions in the future must have a recognised voice and influence. To that question the Constitutional

Conference, as provided by the resolution of 1917, must address itself. I am not so unwise as to hazard any prediction as to the method which will be adopted. I am, however, of those who believe that the voice of the Dominions will exercise an important influence upon the great questions which affect our foreign relations. Moreover, I am confident that this influence will be so exercised as to assist in the avoidance of treaties or understandings which might involve the Empire in war. Indeed, at the present day, I think Great Britain might hesitate to engage in war against a strong public opinion in either Canada or Australia. Further, the voice and influence of the Dominions should tend more and more to turn the attention of British statesmen to the enormous task which confronts the Empire in the governance and development of the vast possessions which are included within its limits. . . . I may say that personally I should regret to see the Empire engage in difficult commitments, whether in Eastern Europe or Western Asia or elsewhere. We have quite enough, and perhaps more than enough, on our hands at present. I regard the effectual exercise of voice and influence by the Dominions as highly important and even essential, for this among other reasons : If the British Empire should be involved in a serious war, each Dominion must take its responsible part in the common defence or withdraw and become an independent State. A self-respecting people could hardly enjoy the advantages of union with other parts of the Empire during peace, and take no responsibility for the common security in time of danger or trouble. If we exercise no voice or influence we are committed either to ignominious withdrawal from common responsibilities, or to take part in a war as to the cause of which we have had no voice, although our united influence might have prevented its outbreak."

Imperial War Cabinet.

The genius of the British people did not lend itself to violent or sudden changes ; rather it proceeded cautiously, step by step, and as the need arose. The Imperial War Cabinet, so called, served its purpose sufficiently well during the War. It consisted of the British War Cabinet and the Prime Ministers of the Dominions, each Prime Minister being, of course, responsible to his own Parliament. In reality, the Imperial War Cabinet was the development of the Committee of Imperial Defence in which, rather than in the Imperial Conference, questions of defence and foreign relations had been discussed between Great Britain and the Dominions for several years before the War.

Canada's Status and Responsibilities.

Much ingenuity and logic had been displayed in pointing out the anomalies of the situation, and in declaring that nothing had been accomplished in advancement of status. The best answer could be given by reference to the high position which Canada took, through its representatives at Washington, in 1919, and at Geneva during recent months. There had been much alarm that the representatives of Great Britain and the Dominions did not on these occasions always see eye to eye on minor questions. They would be in an utterly false position if they were expected to re-echo on all occasions the opinions of the representatives of the United Kingdom; their points of view were not always the same as their conditions differed. On essential questions of policy he agreed that there should be a united front—not of the United Kingdom, but of the whole Empire—established by previous conference and consultation. There were those who were apprehensive of the consequence of the exercise of wide powers not by the Mother Country, but by the Dominions, and they would do well to remember that the constitution of the British Empire was based largely upon usage and convention. It would be practically impossible in any of the five democracies of the Empire to carry on government effectually if every instrument of government continually exercised its powers to the utmost extent. " It does seem to me," continued Sir Robert, " that unless there are unexpected developments the occasion is altogether inopportune for considering the problems of Imperial defence or the responsibility to be undertaken by the various parts of the Empire in that respect. Surely we have not undergone untold sacrifices merely to learn that there is to be no respite from the intolerable burden of armaments. Much depends upon the attitude of the United States towards essential co-operation for ensuring the peace of the world. I am confident that such co-operation will not be withheld, whatever may be the final decision of that great country with respect to the Covenant of the League of Nations.

"I believe that Canada has the highest opportunity for development, influence and usefulness in every sense, as a nation within the British Empire. . . . We cannot accept the status of nationhood without accepting also its responsibilities. I earnestly hope that the burden of providing for defence will be much less in the future than in the past. But, whatever the burden may be, I believe it will be less upon this country as a nation of the Empire than if we stood separate as an independent nation.

"No important step can be taken in constitutional change without the approval of Parliament and without the fullest

iscussion in Great Britain and in the Dominions. No such
hange can be effectual unless it carries public opinion in all
arts of the Empire that may be affected. The influence of the
Iritish Empire in the centuries which are behind us has been
n influence for good—perhaps the greatest influence for good
hat the world has known. Its constitutional development has
een based on principles not unlike those which inspired the
1en who framed the Covenant of the League of Nations. If
'e can make good such methods of consultation and co-
peration as will preserve to the Mother Country and to each
Iominion its full and perfect autonomy, and enable them to
cercise a united influence for the peace of the world and for
he advancement of humanity, we shall have accomplished a
reat task.

"I believe the whole Empire owes a debt of gratitude to the
pung men who associated themselves in what is known
s the Round Table Group for their fine service in arousing
ublic interest to the importance of the question with which
'e are concerned to-day. I do not agree with the conclusions
hich they have reached because I believe that the security
nd permanence of the Empire are to be found in the association
f its democracies upon a basis of autonomy, liberty and co-
peration rather than in Parliamentary federation. The
rstem for which I stand, and upon which I base my hopes
ir the future, has been tested to the utmost during the years
f the War, and the whole world bears witness to the truth
hat it has not been found wanting. It represents the strength
f five democracies, all possessing representative institutions
nd responsible government, each enjoying full autonomy and
berty in its domestic affairs and all united in effective co-
peration for the progress, development and security of the
hole."

cope of the Conference.

The Hon. W. L. Mackenzie King (Liberal, Leader of the
pposition) thought that they would all agree that as to the
onstitutional development of the British Empire his right
bn. friend was right when he said it was founded upon the
ock of responsible self-government, and that in this all-
nportant phase of constitutional development within
he Empire Canada had certainly played the leading part.
Ie thought also they would be in accord with the opinion
xpressed by his right hon. friend when as regarded the forth-
oming Conference of Prime Ministers, he said that this was not
he opportune moment to try and arrive finally at any
sttlement of some of the very important questions which were
st forth in the agenda. His purpose really was to make sure

that the House appreciated accurately the position which the
representative of Canada would be expected to take at the
forthcoming Conference. Unfortunately, in the statements
they had had placed before them of the purposes of the Conference there was a good deal that was indefinite and not a little
that was inconsistent. They understood that the Conference
would in no way have power to decide finally any of the
questions set forth in the agenda, but rather that it was to give
the Prime Ministers of the different parts of the British Empire
an opportunity of conferring together and discussing these
matters ; when they returned to their respective countries
they might make such representations to their colleagues and
to their Parliaments as they deemed wise. They understood,
that in representing Canada at the Conference his right hon.
friend would in no way commit Parliament or the country with
respect to any of the subjects that were upon the agenda.
There appeared to be a difference of point of view as to the
purposes of the Conference as set forth by different personages
who would attend. For example, the Prime Minister of Great
Britain had given out a public statement from which it would
appear that in his view the Conference was to go very much
beyond the scope of any preliminary conference for the purpose
only of discussion. Within the last few days the Secretary of
State for the Colonies, the Right Hon. Winston Churchill, had
also expressed his view in public as to the scope and significance of the Conference. He had referred to the forthcoming
Conference as a Cabinet meeting; " Imperial Peace Cabinet "
was the designation which Mr. Churchill had given to the proposed Conference of Prime Ministers in England. If it was
to be an Imperial Peace Cabinet they should know what
authority it would have to act in the name of the different
Parliaments that would be represented by the Prime Ministers
who would attend the Conference. In order to make perfectly
clear their understanding of the matter he should like to say
that they accepted his right hon. friend's view in the language
in which he presented it to the House in his statement, namely
that the Conference was one purely for the purposes of discussion and preliminary to an Imperial Conference to be held
at some subsequent time ; also that the subjects to be discussed
would be those which he had set forth, but that no decision
in any way binding Canada would be reached. He should not
leave Canada without clearly understanding that there were at
least two or three important considerations in which Parliament
would be unanimous. One was that no change in constitutional
relations should be considered in any final, binding or other way
at this preliminary conference, also that Canada should not in
any way be committed to additional financial obligations on
the score of military, naval or air defence.

Amendment.

Mr. Mackenzie King moved, seconded by Mr. Fielding, an amendment to the effect that : —

"The House, while recognising the propriety of Canada being represented at any Imperial Conference or Conference of the Prime Ministers of the Empire that may be called, desires to record its opinion that at the coming Conference no steps should be taken in any way involving any change in the relations of Canada to other parts of the Empire ; and that, in view of the present financial position of Canada, no action should be taken implying any obligation on the part of Canada to undertake new expenditure for naval or military purposes."

Danger of Restraint on Discussion.

The Prime Minister said that the practice of having a discussion preliminary to the visit of a representative of Canada to a conference of the Prime Ministers or other representatives of the Dominions and of Great Britain had not heretofore been observed. He did not remember hearing or having read of a discussion in the House specially set, looking to anything in the way of direction or restraint upon a representative who would speak at such a conference for Canada. Such action was out of harmony with the whole principle of conference. They were taking, in his judgment, a false step if Parliament took any action designed to map out the course which the representatives of Canada should take as to specific subjects which should be under discussion and review. Suppose that was to be followed to its logical conclusion in Australia, in New Zealand, in South Africa, in Newfoundland, in India, in Great Britain, and that the delegates went to the Conference directed along certain lines, or along all lines, then why did they go to the Conference at all ? The step they were asked to take was the first step towards making the consultative and conference principle of no value at all in the promotion of the common interests of the Empire. Surely it was not the part of wisdom for the House to start upon a course which, if followed, would destroy the only line that they could take as separate Dominions in association with Great Britain to promote their common concerns, and make possible their continuance as an Empire on the basis on which they now stood.

Classes of Conference.

He would endeavour to distinguish the various conferences that had been held. The Imperial Conference was the first. In 1907 a resolution was adopted by that Conference providing that a Conference should be held regularly every four years. That was a Conference of representative Ministers of the various parts of the Empire and of Great Britain. The

President of the Conference was the Prime Minister of Great Britain, but the Conference was called at the instance of the Secretary of State for the Colonies, who, as a matter of fact, usually presided. The subject matter that had been discussed from time to time at the Imperial Conferences had had to do with the concerns of the Empire as an Empire—concerns which might possibly be referred to as domestic concerns of the British Empire. It had not to do with questions of foreign policy. During the War there developed what was known as the Imperial War Cabinet. It was a meeting of the Ministers of the British Government, such as were selected, and of the Ministers of the other Governments of the Empire. Its Chairman was the Prime Minister of Great Britain, and the subject matter that was reviewed by the War Cabinet differed essentially from the subject matter that came before the Imperial Conferences. The War Cabinet had to do with matters of high policy, with matters affecting foreign affairs and particularly with matters related to the united prosecution of the War on the part of all branches of the Empire. Provision was made whereby any of the British Dominions might have a Minister of its Government present at all sessions of the Imperial War Cabinet, between its plenary sessions, dealing with War matters. At the Peace Conference at Paris the Ministers of the various Dominions considered that it would be necessary for them to meet in order to make certain arrangements and have certain discussions which, in their judgment, would be essential before the Constitutional Conference, contemplated by the resolution of the Imperial Conference of 1917, should be held. It was only last October that, in a confidential message received from the Prime Minister of Great Britain, it was suggested that, as other Prime Ministers could conveniently be present in June, Canada should be represented by its Prime Minister at a Conference to be held in Great Britain in that month.

Subjects.

The subject referred to by the Leader of the Opposition, that was, naval, military and air defences generally, was not included in those mentioned by the Prime Minister of Great Britain in his communication of October. It was, however, included in a subsequent communication. It was simply one of those that had been put forward as proper subjects for discussion, and the position Canada took with regard to it, as with regard to all others, was stated for the first time in the announcement he gave the House on 25th April.

Hon. W. S. Fielding (Liberal, *Shelburne and Queen's, N.S.*) : " Referring to the programme contained in the several statements submitted, would it be convenient to divide the list into three parts : First, what portion was proposed by His Majesty's Government of Great Britain ? Second, what portion was suggested by other parts of the Empire ? And last, but not least, what proportion of the proposals came from the Government of Canada ? "

The Prime Minister : " All the subjects have been proposed by Great Britain except No. 5, which came from Australia, and No. 6, which was proposed by India."

Mr. Fielding : " None by Canada ? "

The Prime Minister : " No."

Constitutional Conference: Ottawa as Meeting Place.

In his judgment, he continued, the meeting of the special Constitutional Conference would be held too soon if it took place before public discussion and opinion had sufficiently advanced in the Dominions to enable their representatives to confer intelligibly with relation to what might be acceptable to the countries from which they came. As to the place of meeting it was well known that Ottawa had been proposed as the proper place, it being the capital of the senior Dominion of the Empire. There was much to be said in favour of that suggestion.

Representation of Parties.

It would be recalled that the then Prime Minister of Canada (Sir Robert Borden)—he thought in 1917—suggested that the delegations of the various Dominions, at least that of Canada, should be so chosen as to afford representation to each important political party in the country. If the composition were to be decided on that basis an important if not a novel step would have been taken, and it would be well worthy of discussion whether that should be the basis of composition at any Conference to be so held.

Principles of Foreign Policy: Anglo-Japanese Alliance.

Discussing subjects Nos. 2 and 4, the Prime Minister thought it was reasonably clear what the difference was. The first was this: Was it not possible to lay down such principles of foreign policy in matters that affected the whole Empire as would appeal to all portions of that widely-scattered Empire, appeal to peoples composed of different elements in very widely-scattered communities—appeal to them as not only right in the ethical sense but as sound principles for the whole Empire? That was subject No. 2. It would easily be apparent that that was wholly different from planning out some working arrangement so that developments from time to time might be followed by the Dominions as well as by the Mother-land, whereby the Dominions could have their voice in the application of such principles of public policy as might have previously been mutually agreed upon. That was how he would express the meaning of No. 4.

Speaking of the renewal of the Japanese Alliance, the Prime Minister said that this was a subject of great and definite moment. The Anglo-Japanese Treaty dated back, he thought, to 1902. It was renewed at least once and again renewed in 1911 for a period of ten years—the assent of Canada thereto being given to it in the Committee of Imperial Defence, by the Prime Minister of Canada at that time. " The subject of renewal or non-renewal of the treaty, or its modification, has naturally been under consideration at the hands of the British Government, and if there is one Dominion to which more than another the question of renewal is of importance, it is to the Dominion of Canada. I say that with particular reference to the relationship this Dominion bears, and must always bear, as a portion of the British Empire standing.—if I may say it—between Great Britain on the one hand and the United States on the other. I need not enlarge upon how serious, or even how momentous, is the deliberation that must take place as regards the question of the renewal of that Treaty. The importance of it arises from the interest of the United States therein, and the interest of Great Britain and of Australia and other parts of the Empire ; but the importance of it to us arises, in a very great degree, out of the very great interest of the United States in the renewal or non-renewal thereof."

The purposes of the Alliance were, he thought, four in number : First, the preservation of peace in Eastern Asia and India ; second, the mutual protection of the high contracting parties in the same sphere ; third, the maintenance of the integrity of China in such a way that equal rights as to trading should be given to all countries ; fourth, a mutual obligation on the part of each country to go to the assistance of the other in the event of war ; fifth, there was a saving clause that in the event of a Treaty of Arbitration existing between one of the high contracting parties and a third Power the obligation for assistance should not apply in case of a conflict between that high contracting party and that third Power.

Mr. Ernest Lapointe : " May I ask my right hon. friend whether it is his intention to insist that a clause be inserted in the Treaty, if renewed, of the nature of the clause which was embodied in the British-French War Treaty, that it will not be binding upon Canada without the approval of the Canadian Parliament ? ''

The Prime Minister : '' The very fact that we are called to a Conference that reviews that subject indicates that Canada has the right of assent or non-assent. As to the extent to which we are bound in case war actually takes place, that is another question. We have the power of approval or dis-approval. . . . The general power of approval or disapproval involves that if we do not approve, then so far as it is not possible to be bound as part of the Empire we are not bound.''

Mr. Lapointe : '' Why was such a clause inserted in the British-French Treaty if it was not necessary ? ''

The Prime Minister : '' I presume if there is such a clause in the British-French Treaty it might be appropriate to insert one if a similar treaty is made in this case.''

Defence and Naval Policy.

Coming to the later subjects, importance undoubtedly attached to the question of wireless communications ; to the question of reparations, to the question of an Imperial statistical bureau, to the question of naval, military and air defence — great importance indeed ; also to the question of the improvement of communications by land, sea and air.

In so far as information had come to him, unless there were developments between now and the time of meeting, there did not seem any urgency for the discussion of the subject of military, naval and air defence. He said that with all the more reason because that had been a subject, which being in a large degree domestic as regarded the Empire, had always been reviewed at Imperial Conferences and not at Imperial Cabinets or meetings of Prime Ministers. The condition of the whole question of armaments the world over was such at this time that it seemed to him little progress could be made in the way of conferring between parts of an Empire as to just what the armament programme of that Empire should be. Each country would do well to leave the door open to take such steps as might seem to grow logically out of the solution of the major question —whether they were going to have some understanding as to the reduction of armaments or whether they were not.

The Prime Minister then drew attention to the memorandum presented by Sir Robert Borden to the Prime Minister of Great Britain on 15th August, 1918 (*vide* JOURNAL, Vol. I., No. 3, page 487) and especially to Clause 5 : —

'' As naval forces come to be developed upon a considerable scale by the Dominions it may be necessary hereafter to consider the establishment for war purposes of some supreme naval authority upon which each of the Dominions would be adequately represented.''

No. 5 looked forward to what might be done, but a perusal of it would show that the time had not come, so far as Canada was concerned, when any definite step contemplated therein need be taken. On that account it would occur to him that there was no need of haste in that regard.

Proposals not Binding.

"The Leader of the Opposition," concluded the Prime Minister, "asks me to be very clear and to leave Parliament in no doubt as to whether anything can be done, as he expresses it, ' of a final, binding or other nature,' unless ratified. Nothing can be done of a final and binding nature—nothing whatever. This stands to reason, because this is a conference—this is not an executive. . . . The War Cabinet was a consultative body, this is a consultative body—a body whereby the various units that compose the Empire can meet, get each other's opinions, learn each other's conditions, then come back to the Parliaments from which they are sent and, in the light of the information there gained, in the light of the impressions there driven home upon them, in the light of knowledge as to conditions, not only in their own country, but in the world at large, make such recommendations to their home Parliaments as to them seem best suited to meet the need. . . . I can give the assurance, with all the emphasis that I can command, that no step whatever will be taken binding this country—indeed, no step can be taken, whatever might be the will of the representative of Canada, which would have force or effect before ratification by the Parliament of this Dominion."

The Hon. Rodolphe Lemieux (Liberal, *Maisonneuve, Que.*) said that the question of their relations with the Mother Country and with the other parts of the Empire was perhaps the most important question from a national standpoint, affecting as it did the powers of the Canadian Parliament, and, above all, the rights of the Canadian people. But let them be frank about these Imperial Conference and Imperial Cabinet meetings ; they were in a sense much more sentimental and academic than practical, but they would be dangerous if they did not, as they intended to do to-day, clearly define the attitude which should be taken by their representatives and map out the scope of their mandate. It was proper that such Conferences should be held from time to time in order to demonstrate to the whole world the moral power of the British Empire.

Status of Canada.

They might be asked at the outset : What is the status of Canada ? He might answer at once that their status had not been altered by recent events. It mattered not what had been the effort of Canada during the last great War, it mattered not what part Canada might have taken at previous Imperial War Cabinet meetings, there was but one country in the Empire which fully possessed her sovereignty, and that was the United Kingdom. Canada was indeed a great Dominion, vested with the fullest powers of self-government, but she was not sovereign.

" No Conference of Dominion Prime Ministers," declared Mr. Lemieux, " no Imperial statesmen can object to a direction given to the right hon. gentleman by the representatives of the Canadian people in Parliament assembled. The powers which we constitutionally possess cannot be abridged by any conference, by any Imperial Cabinet, outside of this Parliament, which is the forum and the expressive power, limited though it may be by the British North America Act." They would remember, he continued, that Sir Wilfrid Laurier said on that occasion (the Conference of 1911) that Imperial unity, in which he believed, should be based on full local autonomy. The principle of autonomy in Canada, as in Australia, South Africa, Newfoundland and New Zealand, was the keystone of the whole Imperial structure.

British Preference.

At the coming Conference he did not object to the discussion of trade matters, although Canada was acting towards the Mother Country in her own way as regards the framing of tariffs. Long ago Canada cut her moorings with the Home Government on fiscal matters. They taxed the goods of the Mother Country as they saw fit. True it was that Canada a few years ago, on the initiative of the hon. Member for Shelburne and Queen's (Mr. Fielding) chose to give the Mother Country a preference ; perhaps the preference might be extended to some of the other Dominions, but always bearing in mind that in all these matters of trade Canada was absolutely free to act as she pleased. For his part he would not object to increasing the British preference. His right hon. friend, however, must not forget that he would meet at that Conference at the head of the table the present Colonial Secretary, the Right Hon. Winston Churchill, who had established a tradition for himself on the question of the British preference.

The Prime Minister : " The gentleman who will preside at the Conference will be the Prime Minister of Great Britain, who presided at the Imperial Cabinet. In his absence the Prime Minister of the senior Dominion presided."

Mr. Lemieux said that the Colonial Secretary proclaimed that, if the Dominions were going to exact from the Mother

H

Country reciprocal preference, he, having regard to British
interests, would bang, bar, and bolt the door. So his right hon.
friend should not be afraid of getting moderate instructions
from the Canadian Parliament before he met a gentleman who
had used such—should he say—violent language in reply
to the agitation started in Canada by the Minister of Trade
and Commerce, and in England by the late Mr. Joseph
Chamberlain.

Defence the Main Issue.

" I now come " said Mr. Lemieux, " to the question of
defence. Indeed, do not all these questions revolve around
our share of Imperial defence, both on land and sea ? Why
all these shams ? Let us meet boldly the issue which presents
itself as between the Dominions and the Mother Country.
The whole object of these Conferences, of all these frantic
appeals made by certain people in the Mother-land to the
Dominions, is to draft a binding agreement on the question
of Imperial defence on land and sea. Read Mr. Curtis's
book ; read the speeches of that most eminent of Imperialists,
the late Mr. Joseph Chamberlain ; follow closely his last great
campaign after the Boer War ; scan the report of the various
Conferences at which he presided when the late Sir Wilfrid
Laurier and other Dominion statesmen were convened in
London ; and you will at once realise that the whole question
at issue was that of defence. In Mr. Chamberlain's mind
the only question was whether or not the weary Titan, Old
John Bull, should carry the load alone, or should the
Dominions share the burden of expenditure. Do you not
think that.on such an issue, which involves not only a tremendous expenditure, but indeed the very future of Canada, the
hands of the right hon. gentleman should be strengthened by
an expression of opinion of the Canadian Parliament ? There
was no necessity of any binding agreement with the Mother
Country in 1914. Canada has done her share, and if there is
a timorous minority in this country, or in Great Britain
which is anxious to embalm in black and white some agreement
by which Canada should take part in the wars of the Empire
let that minority read the history of the last six years, and it
will find in that history an adequate answer. After the War
Canada took part in the Peace Congress ; and subscribed to the
Versailles Treaty. Canada as a result is now represented, and
has a voice, in the League of Nations. What is the object of
the League of Nations ? Is it to increase armaments or to
promote war ? The very contrary. The object of the League
is to put an end to all wars and to settle, by way of arbitration
all disputes between nations. Therefore Canada should share

all efforts that are made to embark her on a new race towards armaments."

No Final Decision.

His right hon. friend seemed to believe that no final decision would be arrived at by that Conference. On the other hand, the cables from the other side reminded them that this Conference would be the most important in the history of the relations of the Mother Country with her Dominions. Mr. Lloyd George was reported on the 15th March as follows :—

The defence of the Empire was a great problem, which ought to be an Imperial concern. It was too much to ask small islands to undertake the defence of this gigantic Empire in every sea. At the forthcoming conference of the Prime Ministers of the Empire the whole problem of Imperial defence would be considered. There must be co-ordination, not between the various services only, but between the several parts of the Empire.

That was a definite programme and they had a right to caution the Prime Minister (Mr. Meighen) in the discussions that would arise. He might tell his colleagues at that Conference that he might hearken to them, that he might even offer advice. But not until that advice had been backed up by public opinion in Canada, and had been ratified by the Canadian Parliament, could it be anything but advice and tentative suggestion. Their national debt had reached such a large figure as should caution any man against any further commitments. The rate of federal taxation was also being felt. Under such circumstances was this a proper moment to commit Canada to large expenditure on armaments, navies, or armies ? When trade was buoyant, when immigration had started afresh, when land settlement was on the increase in Western Canada, then they would be in a position, first, to wipe out their liabilities, second, to resume their full national development, and if there should be a balance then they should in the future meet as they did in the past their moral obligations towards the Empire.

Ties of Empire.

" I desire to repeat," declared Mr. Lemieux, " a slogan which was mightily used in 1911 : Let well enough alone. The tie that binds us to the Mother Country is slender. It is a live wire full of electricity ; but let us not bring too much pressure to bear upon it. What are our connections with the Mother Country ? The first is a Governor-General, and there are many people in this great Province of Ontario who of late

H 2

have been clamouring for the appointment of a Canadian to that post. The second connection we have with the Mother Country is the right of appeal to the Judicial Committee of the Privy Council. And here I warn the Minister of Justice (Mr. Doherty) that there is an Attorney-General in the province of Ontario who of late has been stating that we should dispense with that appeal, and he is being supported in that attitude by a larger proportion of public opinion every year. . . . After all, the great binding force between the Mother Country and the Dominions does not depend upon parchments or written constitutions, it does not depend upon flag-waving ; the tie which binds the Dominions to the Mother Country rests in the hearts of the subjects of His Majesty ; the Crown is the great bond which unites us all. .. . We Canadians are proud of our British citizenship. For us Canadians the immortal glory of England is not in Agincourt or Waterloo ; the glory of England is not her merchandise or her commerce which is transported every day on the seven seas of the world. The great glory of the Motherland is her genius for free government. . . . No binding policy at any meeting of the Imperial Cabinet, or at any conference of the Premiers—no binding policy unless the Parliament of Canada has the last say in the matter. Centralisation forced upon the people of Canada, centralisation adopted at such a Conference without a specific mandate from the people would not make for unity but spell dislocation. It will certainly not make for the happiness and contentment of the Canadian people as a whole."

Change of Status.

The Hon. N. W. Rowell (**Nat. Lib. and Con.,** *Durham, Ont.* thought that when they compared the position in 1911—the Prime Minister invited in as a favour to sit with the Committee of Imperial Defence and to hear a review of foreign policy— with the position in 1921—the Parliament of Canada exercising its proper and legitimate functions of discussing questions of foreign policy affecting the whole Empire, they had the best possible evidence of the development of their status during the past ten years. When the Prime Minister of Canada met with the Prime Minister of Great Britain and the Prime Ministers of the other Dominions in London he did so, not as the representative of a subordinate Power in the presence of a representative of a superior Power, but on an absolute equality with the Prime Minister of Great Britain and the Prime Ministers of the other Dominions of the Empire. It would be a misfortune if any constitutional conference undertook to frame a written constitution for the British Empire.

But such a Conference was necessary to put at rest all this discussion about the status of the Dominions. Why should they be discussing in this Parliament, in the Australian Parliament, in the Parliaments of New Zealand and South Africa, the question of Canada's status or the status of the Dominions ? That Imperial Conference should not create for them any new position, but by a declaration in which all the Governments of the Empire joined, they should recognise their present constitutional position and the constitutional position of all the Dominions as being equal in status with the Mother Country as self-governing nations of the British Empire.

British Empire Co-operation.

Coupled with such a declaration of status should be an outline of plans for consultation and co-operation between the Mother Country and the Dominions in matters of common concern to the whole Empire—plans which, while fully preserving the freedom and self-government of the Dominions, would ensure the strength and security of the whole.

The question of representation was not without difficulty. He was inclined to share the view that it would be desirable in this Constitutional Conference not only that the Government should be represented, but that the Opposition of the day, the different interests represented in the House of Commons, should have representation in the Conference. That, of course, could not be done by one country unless done by all countries, but then at such a Conference they should proceed as a united people rather than divided on party lines. He thought it would be a real advantage, not only to the Mother Country, but to Canada and all the other portions of the Empire, if this Conference was held in one of the Dominions, and Canada, as the senior and largest Dominion, would have the first claim.

Limitation of Armaments.

With reference to the question of defence, Mr. Rowell said that the one aspect of the matter, which apparently, to judge from statements that had been made in Great Britain, was likely to assume the greatest importance if the subject came up for serious consideration, was that of naval defence. He wished to express his entire concurrence that the time was not opportune to deal with that important problem. The cause of apprehension in 1912 was the existence of the German navy. That navy had ceased to be. It was the bounden duty of the Government to exert its influence to the utmost, to see that every honest effort was put forward to carry out the intention

of the Treaty (Versailles), the provisions of the Covenant
(League of Nations) and the recommendation of the Financial
Conference (Brussels) to secure a world-wide agreement for
the limitation of armaments. Should it be impossible after
every honest effort had been put forth to secure such an
agreement, and it appeared that no agreement was possible
through no fault of the British Empire, or any part of the
British Empire, but because other nations would still maintain
the right to settle disputes by the sword, he did not hesitate
to say that Canada should be prepared to protect her own
coasts and her own trade, and thus undertake her legitimate
share in the defence of the Empire. But that situation could
not arise before this Conference, and therefore he believed that
Canada's position at the Conference should be that they were
not prepared to consider any further steps towards increasing
their naval or military burdens until they were satisfied that
these other steps were without avail.

Principles of Foreign Policy: Canada and the United States.

Turning to foreign policy, Mr. Rowell said that the first
question that would arise was this : Shall the foreign policy
of the Empire in the future be based on the old ideas of international relationships preceding the War, or shall it be based
on the new conception subsequent to the War ? He submitted
to the Government that the Empire policy should follow the
new, and should eschew the old. There was no hope for the
future unless the British Empire gave a hand in this matter.

There should be a distinction drawn between questions
that were of interest only to one Dominion or to the United
Kingdom alone as distinguished from questions of high policy
that were of interest to the whole Empire. Take the questions
that had arisen from time to time and were arising to-day
between Canada and the United States, questions which they
took up indirectly in some cases, more directly in others, and
which they settled themselves with the United States, questions
which he hoped in the very near future they would take up
directly all the time through a Canadian Minister at Washington.
The settled policy of the Empire to-day was that on those questions exclusively affecting Canada, their view was accepted ;
and the matter was dealt with from Ottawa, London being
informed of their conclusions. A distinction should be drawn
between questions of that class and questions of high Imperial
policy affecting the whole Empire. Might he suggest certain
lines which he thought it would be in the interests of the whole
Empire to follow ? First, that the Empire had no territorial
ambitions or aggressive intentions. Second, they should stand

for the settlement of all international disputes by peaceable means. Third, the British Empire should give its whole-hearted support to the League of Nations and the establishment of a permanent court of international justice. Fourth, the British should give leadership to the movement for the limitation of armaments, endeavouring to secure the co-operation of the United States. Fifth, they should refrain from any special or exclusive alliances with other States. Sixth, they should endeavour to promote international co-operation in matters of common concern to the nations. Seventh, the recognition of Canada's special interest in all important international questions arising between the British Empire and the United States. Their geographical position, their hope that in the lifetime of many they would be a nation not of ten or fifteen millions, but of twenty-five millions of people—all these questions rendered the international relations between the British Empire and the United States of supreme concern to Canada. Eighth, he submitted to the Prime Minister that he would not be going beyond what was both in the interests of Canada and of the whole Empire if he would urge as a further principle of policy that no question of real importance arising between the British Empire and the United States should be settled without consultation with Canada. And they could not do that until they had a Canadian Minister resident at Washington. The greatest hope for permanent cordial relations between the British Empire and the United States lay in Canada's acting as an interpreter and mediator between the United States and the Empire. Ninth, if the question was of purely Canadian concern, the present well-settled practice was to accept the Canadian view as to its settlement. This principle should be extended eventually to cover questions in which the clear and paramount interest was Canadian.

Reparation and Sanctions.

Speaking on the question of reparations and sanctions, Mr. Rowell hoped the Government would not, in the division of the amount which came to the British Empire, take more than that which the Minister of Justice would advise that Canada was entitled to receive under the terms of the conditions under which Germany laid down her arms, and if more should be allotted to them the additional amount should go to Great Britain, or the peoples that had suffered more, for the purpose of restoring the devastated areas and repaying the civilian population. However far the Government of Canada might choose to go in co-operating for the enforcement of the express terms of the Treaty to which they were parties, the Government should hesitate to take part in any programme which might involve a new war, if the Minister of Justice or the Prime Minister came to the conclusion that the imposition of these sanctions outside the Treaty did amount to that. Germany should pay every dollar she agreed to pay when she laid down her arms, but so far as Canada was concerned they should not go beyond the express terms of the Treaty i1 enforcing it.

Anglo-Japanese Treaty.

Referring to Article 4 of the Anglo-Japanese Treaty —

" should either high contracting party conclude a treaty of general arbitration with a third Power, it is agreed that nothing in this agreement shall entail upon such contracting party an obligation to go to war with the Power with which such treaty of arbitration is in force "—

Mr. Rowell stated that in 1914 a new agreement was entered into between the United Kingdom and the United States with regard to the establishment of a peace commission. He believed it was generally understood that the Treaty complied with Article 4 of the Anglo-Japanese Treaty. Therefore he did not believe that there was any justification for the allegation that if a difference unfortunately did arise between Japan and the United States, the British Empire would be involved. But the Government could not ignore the feeling that did exist in the United States in reference to that alliance. " I submit for the consideration of the Government the question whether it would not be found, after careful examination, that it is in the best interest of good relations between the British Empire and the United States on the one hand and between Japan and the United States on the other, in the interests of good relations all round, that this Treaty should not be renewed, at least in its present form. Not that we love Japan less ; we do not want any alliance that will prevent us from playing the rôle of friend to every nation in the world."

Conference Unnecessary.

Mr. Michael Clark (National Progressive, *Red Deer, Alta.)* expressed a personal doubt about the value of the Conference this year at all. Mankind was stunned into an apathetic condition, and when empires had been crumbling like this, he had the gravest doubt whether even the biggest men in the Empire could not be better employed than meeting in London and embarking immediately on a fresh scheme of empire-building. There were other reasons. There was grave reason for doubting whether the Prime Minister of Britain represented the opinion of Britain at the present moment. He had still grave doubt whether the Government of Canada represented the opinion of Canada. There was only one practical question upon which ostensibly the right hon. gentleman was going to London, and that was the Anglo-Japanese Treaty. He could not see why an exchange of two or three despatches on each side should not make it perfectly plain to the Imperial Government what the mind of the Canadian Government was on the renewal or non-renewal of the Anglo-Japanese Treaty.

Might he ask the Prime Minister if he contemplated entering into any obligations whatsoever in the month of June to increase the naval and military expenditures of Canada at this time ? He said in his speech in effect that he did not. Then if he contemplated no change in the constitutional relationships, and if he contemplated taking no step to commit them to further obligations in regard to increased expenditure on armaments, whether by land or by sea, why did he not accept the amendment ?

Gladstone said : " I am absolutely sure of this that a country is in a far better position in regard to its foreign policy when it does not know it has one." Yet they had had a whole afternoon devoted to a discussion of the question how they could multiply and complicate the obligations of Canada in the direction of empire-building. He considered that the step was unnecessary at this time, because the world had had its fill of foreign policy. They could well afford to take a rest in this matter of armaments ; they could well afford to rest for awhile from artificial empire-building. If his right hon. friend was going into a conference to commence working night and day declaring that Canada was in the forefront of leadership in a movement to bring about disarmament, then he should say, " By all means, go to the Conference." But there were doubts in their minds ; there were fears that there might be commitments made along certain lines.

The Minister of Trade and Commerce (the Right Hon. Sir George Foster) said he had followed very closely the discussions which had taken place in the other Overseas Dominions, and he could not find that either there, or at home, there had been any attempt on the part of the legislatures to bind the hands of their representatives by the passage of a resolution ; in all cases they would be there with the confidence of their Parliaments behind them. He did not think that was going to contribute to the reputation and dignity of Canada, and he was quite certain that it put their representatives in an invidious position compared with the representatives of all the other parts of the Empire who would attend the Conference.

Value of Consultation.

The whole purpose of this Conference was not to come to conclusions in the concrete. If there was anything which distinguished the work of the world to-day it was the willingness of its representative men to sit round a common table and to exchange views with reference to the great interests which were confided to their charge. They had had a good deal of foreign policies and they had had a lot of world-work to do. But foreign countries still existed, international interests still existed ; inter-Imperial interests still existed, and to his mind there were many things which required at that very day conference and understanding not only between the public men of various countries, but between the public men who had to do with the Empire itself.

It was all very well on a call of a month or two next year, when the Imperial Conference met, to go to London to settle the big questions which they all admitted were to be settled in some way there ; but it was a mighty sight more important to get the benefits of personal conference first and then have the advantage of a year to think over and to pursue those personal conferences before they came up against the actual concrete solution of those big questions which would be before them within the next two years.

Never in the history of that evolution (of the constitutional liberties of the Empire) had there been on the part of English statesmen a desire to take any action as affecting Canada or the other Overseas Dominions which was not fair and square and honest and for the benefit of the Empire as a whole. As a matter of fact, nothing could be done to bind Parliament until the measures were brought back and laid before Parliament. The Prime Minister had frankly laid down his policy and his proposed line of conduct ; they should trust him and they should put no shackles about him.

Mr. Ernest Lapointe believed that they had a right to express their opinion before the discussion took place at the Conference. They had a right to tell their representatives what they wanted and what they did not want, and there was nothing in that which meant derogation from the dignity of either Parliament or the gentlemen who would represent Canada at the Conference.

Danger of Responsibility.

He quite agreed that some system must be devised for the holding of that very important Conference (the special Constitutional Conference contemplated in resolution 9 of the Imperial War Conference of 1917). It was only after the

Constitutional Conference should have taken place that the real status of Canada should be defined, and that the British Dominions should know in a clear way the true and real nature of the political union between the various parts of the Empire. Then and then only, he suggested, they would know whether it was in the interest of Canada, whether it was opportune for Canada, to take part in the shaping of the foreign affairs of the Empire, and to what extent they should do that. There was a danger in their meddling too much in foreign affairs without any reservation. As late as in 1911, at the Imperial Conference, when Australia proposed a resolution of regret that the Dominions were not consulted prior to the acceptance by the British delegates of the terms of the Declaration of London, Sir Wilfrid Laurier, speaking to the resolution, said :

"That is a thing which, in my humble judgment, ought to be left altogether to the responsibility of the Government of the United Kingdom. You ought not to give advice unless you are prepared to back the advice with all your strength."

That was the danger which faced them when they had the ambition to offer their advice regarding the foreign affairs of the British Empire. He did not think that the people of Canada were prepared to-day to say that they would put all the strength of the country or what was left of her resources, and all her manhood, behind any scheme concerning Prussia, Mesopotamia, or any other country with which the foreign affairs of the Empire might be concerned.

Speaking at Geneva last summer, his hon. friend (Mr. Rowell) said : —

"Fifty thousand Canadian soldiers under the sod in Europe is the price Canada has paid for the European statesmanship which drenched the Continent in blood."

He did not see how he could reconcile that statement with his anxiety to take part in all the conferences which might lead to a decision concerning the foreign policy of the British Empire. Canada must go slowly along that line.

Mr. Rowell " In my judgment the world's peace can only be preserved by international co-operation to preserve it by peaceful means, and that involves all nations coming in and doing their share. I think Canada should do her share with the other nations."

Mr. Lapointe : "I do not see how our giving advice to the British Foreign Office will lead to bringing that about. It is because I am afraid of taking the responsibility which our advice in every such case involves that I do not approve in the arrangement concerning the appointment of a Minister Plenipotentiary to Washington. The feature which I do not like is that our representative at Washington shall act for the

British Ambassador in his absence. If the representative of
Canada acts for the United Kingdom or for the British Empire
on such occasions, I do not see how we will escape responsibility
for his actions. He will be our nominee, appointed upon the
advice of Canadian Ministers."

Anglo-Japanese Alliance.

Speaking of the Anglo-Japanese Alliance, Mr. Lapointe
suggested the insertion of a clause in the Treaty—such a
clause was inserted in the British-French War Treaty—
stipulating that the Treaty should not be binding upon Canada
unless and until it had been approved by the Canadian Parliament. That would safeguard Canadian rights. They had
no business to tell the United Kingdom not to enter into a
War Treaty with Japan so long as the Treaty would not affect
them unless they wished it to do so. He thought their representative should insist that the Treaty, if it was renewed,
should be ratified by the Parliament of Canada. The conditions which existed in 1911 when the Anglo-Japanese Treaty
was made did not exist to-day. The only possible war would
be one with the United States, and he was not sure that Canada
should bind herself to an alliance which would compel her to
fight against that country in any struggle with Japan.

Naval Defence.

He was pleased to hear the statement that no action should
be taken with regard to naval defence. There was the all-
important argument that nothing of that kind should be done
until the Constitutional Conference had defined what was their
status in the British Empire. Then and only then would they
know exactly to what scheme of defence, naval or otherwise,
they would commit themselves, and it was only after that
Conference had taken place and its findings had been approved
by the Parliament of Canada, as well as by the other Parliaments of the Empire, that any general scheme of naval defence
should be entered upon.

Credits.

Mr. J. A. Currie (Nat. Lib. and Con., *Simcoe, N. Riding,
Ont.*) stated that there were no credits between the various
colonies and Great Britain and Canada, and something should
be done that would smooth over the question of banking and
the question of exchange as far as the British Dominions were
concerned, so that they could carry on business with a reasonable measure of success. The credit of South Africa was

first class, in fact much better than that of Canada, and they were rapidly building up their banking and financial institutions. Their Prime Minister would be at the Conference. The great Commonwealth of Australia lately debated the question whether Premier Hughes should have a free hand at the Conference, and in spite of the fact that he had only a very narrow majority, the House gave him an overwhelming vote of confidence. Canada was looked upon as the brightest gem in the crown of Empire, and the Prime Minister as her representative at the Conference should have a free hand.

Canada's Dependence.

Mr. Hermas Deslauriers (Liberal, *Sainte-Marie, Que.*) declared that if they bore in mind that they were governed under a Constitution approved by a foreign nation, that their laws were ratified by a representative of a foreign nation, that their Supreme Court of Justice was abroad, and that they had not the right to make any treaty without the signature of the representative of a foreign nation, it followed that they were not equal to the other nations of the Empire, and the people of Canada did not wish to pledge their future policy under that epithet. All the talk concerning the League of Nations and their title of sister nation was only a manœuvre on the part of the Imperialists who had dragged them into the foreign policy of England, and it was the desire of England at that moment to embroil them in her internal policy and make them espouse her quarrels in India, Egypt and even in Ireland.

Had not Lloyd George and Bonar Law declared, in the last Session of the British Parliament, that the British Isles were too small to support for long the burden of defending so vast an Empire and that they hoped in the future the Dominions would contribute their share of men and money in the future wars of the Empire ? That was the result of their great sacrifices in the last war and of their title of member of the League of Nations and sister nation. The ghost of Chamberlain should start with joy.

Japanese Immigration into Australia.

It was indisputable that the problem of yellow immigration must be settled some day or other. Since Australia possessed a vast territory, scarcely populated, it was reasonable to believe that she would offer the first mark, and under no consideration would she receive the Japanese. At that moment Australia was in difficulties with Japan with regard to Japanese immigration into Queensland. Two Australian Parliaments had adopted legislation imposing a tax of $500

on each Asiatic immigrant, and this legislation was disclaimed
by the Foreign Office through the agency of the Governor-
General of Australia, which did not prevent her being a sister
nation within the Empire on an equality with other nations.
Australia would without doubt claim at the Conference in
June the support of the Empire and her sister nations. What
attitude should they take? They should set their future
policy as an American country so as to conclude a defensive
alliance with the United States, the only nation which could
or to whose interest it was to protect them against Japan,
which could at a given moment make of Canada a second
Belgium.

Since, according to Mr. Lionel Curtis, there were only
two possible alternatives to their future policy, the Imperial
partnership which would engender sacrifices and burdens,
and independence under the sovereignty of the King of
England, they ought to choose the latter, the only one capable
of giving them timely protection.

After further discussion Mr. Mackenzie King's amendment
was negatived by 96 to 64 votes.

CONSTITUTION OF THE EMPIRE.

(Question upon Mr. Massey's Statement.)

On the Orders of the Day, 31st March,

The Hon. Charles Murphy (Liberal, *Russell, Que.*) desired
to call the Prime Minister's attention to a report published
in the London *Times* on the 17th inst. giving a summary of
a debate in the New Zealand House of Representatives on the
question of whether the Prime Minister of New Zealand should
attend the approaching Conference of Overseas Prime Ministers
in London. Mr. Massey was credited with saying :—

"He believed there would soon be an Empire Constitution and
a recognised organisation, which he thought would take the form' of
an Imperial executive, with the British Prime Minister as President.
This executive should consist of representatives of Great Britain, the
Dominions, the Dependencies and India, and it should be responsible
to the British and Dominion Parliaments. It should meet at least
biennially, and it should be responsible for foreign policy, and declaration
of war and peace."

His question was whether the Prime Minister had any knowledge of the proposed creation of such an Empire Cabinet or
Imperial Executive.

The Prime Minister (the Right Hon. Arthur Meighen) : "I
have not seen the despatch. The conception embodied in the

lespatch may be in accordance with the mind and intention
of the Prime Minister of New Zealand.   I have not subscribed
to it."

On the Orders of the Day, 6th May,

Mr. Murphy stated that the morning papers announced
that Premier Massey had arrived at Victoria on his way to the
Imperial Conference, and that he gave out an interview.
According to the despatches, Premier Massey had stated that
he was prepared to place a measure of reciprocity with Canada
on the Statute Books of New Zealand, and he also advocated
a constitution for the British Commowealth of nations and an
Imperial Executive.   The two latter he described as vital
needs of the Empire.   Might he ask if it was intended to have
a conference on this subject with Premier Massey on the part
of the Government ?

The Prime Minister : " No request has been received by
the Government for any special conference with the Prime
Minister of New Zealand on this or any other subject.   I did
observe the headline in the paper that an interview had been
given by the Prime Minister of New Zealand, but I really do
not understand that because another Prime Minister desires
to give an interview that should be the occasion of a new
expression from me.   There has been no request for an interview on this or any other subject relating to the Imperial
Conference."

MINISTER PLENIPOTENTIARY AT WASHINGTON.

Status: Relation to British Ambassador: Functions: Constitutional Aspect, etc.)

On 21st April the House in Committee of Supply discussed
the following item : —

Miscellaneous—Canadian Representation in the United States,
$60,000

(*Vide* also JOURNAL, Vol. I., No. 3, page 476, and No. 4, page 662.)

DEBATE IN HOUSE OF COMMONS.

**The Hon. W. L. Mackenzie King (Liberal, Leader of the
Opposition)** asked if any appointment at Washington had been
made up to the present time.

The Prime Minister (the Right Hon. Arthur Meighen) said
there was some urgency in regard to the matter.   The reason
that the office had not been filled up till now, was merely that

the Government had not decided on the best person to fill that very important position.

History of Responsible Government.

The Right Hon. Sir Robert Borden (Nat. Lib. and Con., *King's, N.S.*), in tracing the progress of thought in Canada with regard to responsible government and the negotiations by Canadian representatives of commercial treaties, quoted a resolution moved by Sir Alexander Galt in 1870 : —

> That it is expedient to obtain from the Imperial Government all necessary powers to enable the Government of the Dominion to enter into direct communication for such purpose with each British Possession and Foreign State.

Sir John Macdonald opposed the resolution because he thought it would tend to weaken the ties between Canada and the Mother Country. In 1878, Sir Alexander Galt was commissioned to undertake negotiations with Spain and France for better commercial relations. Lord Salisbury on that occasion was careful to say that " the negotiations must be conducted by the British Ambassador in each instance." In 1884 Sir Charles Tupper obtained fuller recognition to negotiate treaties with foreign countries.

Status of Canadian Representative.

Sir Robert Borden then read the announcement made in the House of Commons on 10th May, 1920, by the Minister of Trade and Commerce, the terms of which were agreed upon by the Governments of the United States and Canada (*vide* JOURNAL, Vol. I., No. 3, p. 476). It was perfectly apparent from the statement that the King's Minister, appointed on the recommendation of the Government of Canada, was to be in direct touch with the United States Government, that he should report directly to the Government of Canada, and that every function that was ordinarily discharged by the British Ambassador at Washington under present conditions in relation to Canadian affairs would be discharged by their Minister acting in co-operation with the British Ambassador, but possessing a perfectly independent status so far as the affairs of Canada were concerned. " This is not a step," said Sir Robert, " in the disintegration of the Empire ; it is merely carrying into effect the principle that where the interest lies there must be the responsibility and there also the action."

Mr. Thomas Vien (Liberal, *Lotbinière, Que.*): " Would the Canadian Minister be subordinate to the British Ambassador at Washington in respect of Canadian affairs ? "

Sir Robert Borden : " Not at all.   He would be the King's envoy in respect of Canadian affairs."   He thought that the establishment of the International Joint Commission was a very notable achievement of the Government of Sir Wilfrid Laurier, and described the establishment and functions of the Canadian War Mission in the United States in 1918.

He believed that the appointment of a Minister would be attended with the greatest possible benefit to Canada and would assist the supreme purpose of maintaining good relations between the British Commonwealth and the Commonwealth of the United States.

Questions Dealt With.

Among the questions dealt with in recent years between Canada and the United States there had been the following : —

The Chicago drainage canal.
Supplies of coal for Canada.
Lands of the Lake of the Woods.
The United States Merchant Marine Act.
Exportation of pulpwood from Canadian Crown lands.
Canadian and American railways.
Panamá Canal tolls.
Fishery questions on both seaboards and on the Great Lakes.

" I feel that it is highly important," declared Sir Robert, " that the appointment should be made at as early a date as possible.   Such representation will be thoroughly justified by and entirely consistent with the status of Canada under the resolution of the Imperial War Conference, but which she has acquired chiefly from the part she has taken in the war and at the Peace Conference.   General Smuts spoke of the British Empire as an inner league within the League of Nations. That very well expresses the status of the nations of the Empire at the Peace Conference and upon that status we rest our right of distinctive representation at the capital of the great neighbouring nation."

Relation to British Ambassador.

Supposing, he concluded, that a Canadian was British Ambassador at Washington, he would be responsible to the British Government and in a sense to the Governments of all the Dominions by reason of the consultation which took place in respect of the interest of the whole Empire from time to time.   The Canadian Minister, in the absence of the British Ambassador, would stand in the British Ambassador's place, and he would have precisely the same responsibilities as those which would be imposed upon the British Ambassador while acting in the same manner.

Mr. Mackenzie King : " Would he be subject to recall by the British Government in the event of his taking a step which the British Government did not approve ? "

Sir Robert Borden : " He would not be subject to recall by the British Government. If there was any difficulty of the kind, I have no doubt such questions would be settled, as all questions are, by conference between the two Governments."

Proposal not Useful.

The Hon. W. S. Fielding (Liberal, *Shelburne and Queen's, N.S.*) said that for a long time Canada had been recognised to have the right to govern her own affairs in the conduct of Canadian trade, and that right was so fully recognised to-day that he could not see what more she required in that direction. The principle had been accepted by the British Government for many years that the British Government would make no treaty having any direct reference to Canadian affairs, without putting into it a proviso that it should not apply to Canada unless the Canadian Parliament should see fit to accept it. He did not see how they could go a step further without breaking the tie. He did not want any treaty made with any foreign nation except through the instrumentality of His Majesty the King, acting, however, through the Minister responsible to the Parliament of Canada.

This proposal of an Ambassador at Washington was not a useful one. An Ambassador of Canada must go there as a subordinate to the British Ambassador. There was no help for it. They were a part of the British Empire. The word " colony " some of them did not like, but practically speaking they were a colony to-day, dependent on the Empire, and they could not be anything else so long as the Empire existed. As a mere matter of theory it was a mistake ; and when they came to the practical view, the Prime Minister of Canada could go down to Washington, fresh from a consultation with his colleagues, and deal with the question directly in a far more efficient manner than could any gentleman whom they might appoint, and who would remain at Washington constantly.

Importance of Appointment.

The Hon. N. W. Rowell (Nat. Lib. and Con., *Durham, Ont.*) rose to urge upon the Government the very great importance of making this appointment, and making it without delay,

the interests of Canada, and of the Empire. An occasional
visit by a Canadian Minister to Washington would not at all
take the place of permanent representation there by a Canadian
representative constantly protecting their interests and keeping
them fully informed of the current of sentiment there.

The United States trade with Canada a year ago was
second only to her trade with Great Britain. Before very long
the centre of the political and commercial activity of the world
would pass to a great extent from the Atlantic to the Pacific.
Canada was more vitally interested in the North Pacific
problem than was any other portion of the Empire. Canada
and the United States lay on one side and Russia, China and
Japan on the other ; and in all the problems that arose
affecting the Pacific the people on this continent would find
that they had largely common interests. It would be of
tremendous importance to them to know what were the ideals
and policies of their great neighbour to the south on questions
of international concern.

Conflict of Interests.

The Hon. Rodolph Lemieux (Liberal, *Maisonneuve, Que.*) :
" In the case of a conflict of interests and ideas between the
United States and Great Britain, the latter being an ally of
Japan, how would Canada stand in the matter ? "

Mr. Rowell replied that not only the British Government
but the Japanese Ambassador in London had made the
declaration that even under the existing Treaty the alliance had
no application to a difference, if one should arise, between
Japan and the United States—that such a contingency was
not one in which the British Empire would be involved.

On the question of Canada's status, Mr. Rowell said
that the Imperial Parliament had the residuary power of
legislation. But the use of that power was limited to constitutional convention, custom and right. The Imperial
Parliament had no right to use that power except in accordance with the well-settled principles of their Constitution.

Mr. Lemieux : " Does Pollock speak of ' The Kingdom
of Canada ? ' "

Mr. Rowell : " Yes, he does."

Mr. Lemieux : " Well, that is the Ewart doctrine."

Mr. Rowell : " I do not think it is. . . . That was
also Sir John Macdonald's view. He wanted Canada called
' The Kingdom of Canada.' "

Mr. Lemieux : " Hear, hear. I do not object to that."

Mr. Rowell continued that just as the needs of the
Dominions required that they should exercise more authority
in connection with foreign affairs than had hitherto been

I 2

exercised, then they should choose to exercise it on their own account, in co-operation always with the Mother Country. That was the spirit of the resolution of the Imperial Conference of 1917. This proposal was to put the conduct of their relations on a much more regular and permanent base. The question of their voting rights in the League of Nations was of very great moment to them. That question had been under discussion by the Senate and the Congress of the United States for months, but Canada had never been in a position to make any representation to the American Government, except through the British Ambassador.

Mr. Lemieux : " Suppose our Canadian representative is appointed, and that in dealing with those commercial questions the interests of Canada are in conflict with the interests of the Mother Country, in what position would our representative be if he shares with the British Ambassador the responsibilities of the embassy ? "

Mr. Rowell : " If any question or difference did arise, that would naturally come back to the Government of Canada and the Government of Great Britain and would be settled between them just as all questions are settled from time to time, by conference and negotiation."

Functions of Canadian Minister.

What were the functions of such a Minister ? He would take part in the negotiation of specific questions arising between the Governments of Canada and the United States. He would watch events. He would transmit to his Government from time to time reports of legislative and executive acts. He would also furnish general reports with regard to social, industrial and economic questions. One of the grave difficulties in connection with their present arrangement was lack of continuity. The establishment of personal contact was of the greatest possible advantage.

" One of the most important problems of the world to-day," declared Mr. Rowell, " having regard not only to the relations between the different Anglo-Saxon peoples, but to the peace of the world, is the maintenance of good understanding between the peoples of the British Empire and the United States. Providence has made us a liaison nation. In the course of our political development we have retained our connection with the Mother Country, and that enables us to understand their view, their attitude, their ideals and their policies on international questions as the people of the United States do not understand them. On the other hand, our close contact and constant intercourse with the American people enables us to understand them and their ideals in a way that the people of the Mother Country do not understand them. . . . If we fail to take advantage of it we shall lose one of the greatest opportunities that has ever come to us or ever will come to us to assist in maintaining a good understanding between the British Empire and the United States, not only for the benefit of Canada and the British Empire, but for the peace and progress of the world."

Responsibility to British Government.

Mr. **Ernest Lapointe** (Liberal, *Quebec East*) : " It is the Government of Canada that is going to recommend the appointment ? "

The Prime Minister: " Yes."

Mr. Lapointe : " The gentleman shall not be appointed upon the recommendation of the Imperial Government ? "

The Prime Minister: " No."

Mr. Lapointe : " It is stated that in the absence of the British Ambassador our Canadian representative will take charge of the British Embassy and will deal with British affairs. Do I understand that the British Government will trust the administration of their foreign affairs in the United States to a Canadian without having a word to say in his appointment ? "

The Prime Minister : " I think so. They have agreed to the proposal as to the appointment on terms, and one of the terms is that. I do not anticipate that there would be any difficulty myself, because the British Government would be quite certain that anyone recommended by the Government of Canada for a post of that kind would be a man of high responsibility and intimate knowledge of the affairs connected with the Embassy."

Mr. Lapointe : " Anything which is a step in the road to nationhood has my full approval. I would like to know whether the people of Canada will be responsible for the actions of their own appointee when he acts as British Ambassador, transacting purely British affairs as distinct from Canadian affairs ? "

The Prime Minister : " Inasmuch as he is named on the advice of the Canadian people he would be responsible, I think, in the same way as any other ambassador to his own country. I do not know what his responsibility to Canada would be in respect to matters purely British. It would appear to me that he would owe direct responsibility in that regard to Great Britain."

Mr Lapointe : " Why should it have been agreed that the Canadian representative will act for the British Ambassador in his absence ? "

The Prime Minister : " He is in the position second in authority there, and naturally would be first in authority in the absence of the first in authority."

Mr. Lapointe : " There are certain constitutional authorities, Mr. Curtis, for instance, who are advocates of Imperial Federation, who contend that the Dominions cannot have diplomatic representatives in foreign countries unless there is an Imperial Parliament to which those representatives are responsible, or unless there is complete independence. Can my right hon. friend give us the assurance that this appointment of a Canadian representative at Washington will not at all serve as an argument to strengthen the position of Mr. ·Curtis and those who believe as he does ? "

Grave Constitutional Departure.

Mr. W. F. Cockshutt (Nat. Lib. and Con., *Brantford, Ont.*) considered this was a very grave constitutional departure. Had Canada any constitutional right to appoint an ambassador that they did not allow South Africa, New Zealand, Australia and all the other parts of the Empire to be partakers in ? An ambassador to a foreign country could be sent only by a sovereign Power. He had not heard that they had received any particular authority from Great Britain to embark upon so important a departure as this. It was another offshoot of that evil genius, the League of Nations, and this whole thing had been largely forced upon them by that body. No man could contend that Canada was a first-class nation ; she was a first-class Power only as part of the British Empire, and it was quite good enough for them to remain in, retaining the constitutional status they had now. They had the resources but they had not the population, nor the army, nor the navy ; nor could it be contended for a moment that they were in a position to take up the full share of the white man's burden. They had no more right to appoint an ambassador to the United States than to France or Germany or Belgium or Spain or Russia or any other country in the world. It was not a matter of business ; it was a question whether or not sovereign rights were vested in Canada to make the appointment. If they had an ambassador at Washington with equal powers with the British Ambassador it was not far distant for anyone to see that these two officials would come into conflict on certain questions. If it was a matter of appointing trade agents, then let them have trade agents. If they appointed an ambassador to the United States, the question arose : Were the United States going to appoint an ambassador to Canada ? He could not possibly conceive how the Government could justify an appointment, without taking a plebiscite of

the people of Canada whether or not they were dissatisfied
with the British connection and desired to embark upon a
policy that would, with absolute certainty, lead them away
from the Motherland.

Constitutional Aspect.

   Mr. Mackenzie King said that, speaking of the legal rights
they had under the Constitution, there could be no doubt
whatever that Canada was not a nation in the sense in which
that term was used when the full rights of nationhood or the
rights of a sovereign nation were implied.   On the other hand,
if they approached the matter from the standpoint of constitutional authority, he agreed that they had the status of a nation.
It was a status they had had for a number of years, but which
had become more clearly defined in recent years.   It had been
mentioned that inasmuch as they could not amend the Constitution of Canada without the British Parliament amending
it, it was a sign of inferiority.   New Zealand and Australia
had each the right to amend their Constitutions without any
appeal to the British Government ; they were self-governing
Dominions.   He had no doubt that if they asked the British
Government to give them the same right to amend their
Constitution without referring the matter to Great Britain,
they would be given that right.   It was a matter simply of
constitutional development as to whether they took a step
which, to outward appearances, without prejudicing the unity
of the Empire as a whole, might give them still more in the
way of the status of a nation.
   He gathered from Mr. Rowell that he contended that the
King of England was also King of Canada and that a Canadian
Minister should have the same right and authority to make a
treaty in the name of the King as any Minister of the British
Government.   He agreed entirely with the point of view he
had expressed.   The British Government had, to his certain
knowledge, held that view for some time past.   As an example
Mr. Mackenzie King referred to the discussions which took
place in 1908 between himself and the then Foreign Secretary,
Sir Edward Grey, on the question of a treaty between Canada
and the Chinese Government with respect to Chinese immigration.   Sir Edward Grey took the position that a Minister of
the Crown in Canada had as much right to act in the name of
the Sovereign as any Minister of the Crown in Great Britain,
and that a Minister of the Crown in Canada might receive from
the King in England the same authority to act in the negotiating and signing of a treaty as could be given to any British
Minister.

He for one felt it was wholly in the interests of Canada to have someone represent them in an official position at Washington. There was such a thing, however, as going from one extreme to the other. He did not think Parliament should authorise any representative from Canada to assume complete control of the British Embassy at Washington. The best way to preserve friendship and unity between all parts of the British Empire was to avoid, as far as possible, any possibility of complications and misunderstandings.

Mr. T. M. Tweedie (Nat. Lib. and Con., *Calgary, W. Riding, Alta.*) thought that if they had a representative at Washington in close touch with the British Ambassador they would have the opportunity of presenting their case directly through the British Ambassador at the time the negotiations were being carried on; or of having their own representative carry on the negotiations on behalf of the Dominion. He believed that if that system had prevailed in the past Canada would have been the gainer by many hundreds of thousands of acres of territory which had been lost to them as the result of the negotiations being carried on simply by the British Ambassador without Canada having a representative at Washington. They were becoming a greater country, they were becoming more independent, but they were not separating themselves from the Motherland.

Relationship with the United States.

The Hon. T. A. Crerar (National Progressive, *Marquette, Man.*) thought that every time they had had an extension of the powers of self-government, every time they had had an addition to their autonomy as a people, the result had been a closer understanding with the Mother Country. Their close relationship with the United States, the immense volume of business they did with that country, the great extent of their boundary line contiguous to that country, the fact that they spoke the same language, the fact that they were daily mingling with each other placed their relationship with that country on a different plane from the relationship with other countries of the world. It was quite conceivable that the interests of Canada, from pressure of other business, might not receive that careful consideration from the British Ambassador at Washington which they should receive. He felt certain that this business could be much better looked after if they had their own Minister Plenipotentiary at Washington. The arrangements leading up to the appointment of a Canadian Minister Plenipotentiary were taken up with the British Government, and the present position was in entire accord with the views of the British Government and had their approval.

Change of Attitude.

Mr. D. D. McKenzie (**Liberal**, *Cape Breton N. and Victoria, N.S.*) was very proud of being a British subject and a Canadian, and he was old-fashioned enough to be prouder of being a British subject than being a Canadian. Consequently he did not feel any humiliation whatever when he required the assistance of a Britisher in the United States if he called upon the British Consul.

His right hon. friend (Sir Robert Borden) had told them that if they wanted to do anything that would attract attention in the great Empire to which they belonged the right thing to do was to send thirty-five or forty millions of money to the Old Country, where they could buy ships, and get the British Government to man them and send them up to the North Sea where they were most needed. His right hon. friend was to be congratulated upon the change of heart he had since experienced —such a change that he was now satisfied that not only could they now build ships and get the men to man them, but they were so independent of the Mother Country that they could launch out on their own account, have their own army, have their own navy, have their own system of defence, and have their own plenipotentiary at Washington.

He submitted that every interest of Canada was well looked after at Washington by the British Ambassador, and that they avoided a great deal of responsibility as a result. If they did declare war upon any country, they could not back it up, for they had not got the army or the navy requisite for the purpose. If they were going to cut loose from the wisdom and experience of British diplomacy, and their own inexperienced diplomats got into trouble, what assurance had they got that they were immediately going to have the British army and navy behind them? Being represented in the United States by the British Ambassador, they had behind them all the prestige and power of the British Empire.

Mr. Michael Clark (**National Progressive**, *Red Deer, Alta.*) said that three things were possible. They might unite with the United States. They might possibly in the long course of years become an independent country, a sovereign State. He was content for the moment that Canada should remain pretty much where she was. He thought the worst foes of the British Empire were those who imitated the little girl who had planted a flower and was always pulling it up to see how its roots were doing. The appointment of a plenipotentiary to a foreign Court was a mark of a sovereign State. If that was so, was he

not right in claiming that if they took this step they were not
following the process of evolution, but they were getting very
near to revolution ?

Sir Robert Borden declared the Minister who was to be
sent to Washington would be appointed by a sovereign power.
That sovereign power was the King, who represented the whole
Empire. The King, being the King of Canada as well as of
the United Kingdom, would see fit to appoint a Minister who,
under the instructions of the King, would be specially charged
to concern himself with and to safeguard the interests of
Canada in respect of their relations with the United States.

A High Commissioner.

The Hon. Rodolph Lemieux (Liberal, *Maisonneuve,* *Que.*)
said he would vote in favour of the item. Some years ago he
was probably one of the first to state that the time had come
for Canada to appoint, not an ambassador or semi-ambassador,
but a representative in Washington. He believed that a High
Commissioner would be more useful than an Ambassador
unless they chose to cut the painter at once and declare themselves an independent nation ; because they could not have
an Ambassador in any foreign country unless they received
that essential power of sovereignty which Canada did not
possess. Could they or could they not negotiate and sign a
treaty without the rightful interference of the Foreign Office
in London, or of the British Ambassador or Minister ? The
other day the Minister of Trade and Commerce (Sir George
Foster) laid upon the Table of the House a Treaty with France
whereon they saw the signature of the British Ambassador in
Paris. But he would support the appointment of a Canadian
representative in Washington, because they could not legislate
against geography.

Imperial Evolution.

He did not believe that any man in the House dreamed
of a permanent *status quo.* The fruit must ripen and when
the fruit had ripened it fell from the parent tree. He would
do nothing to revolutionise, but he was quite willing to
evolutionise. When the time came for Canada to take the
decisive step which should lead her to nationhood, he for one
should stand for Canada as a Kingdom.

He warned the Government that if Canada was to avoid
the other alternative, that of annexation with the United
States, they must as Canadians be very careful about the
economic situation. To-day the Americans had peacefully
invaded their prairies. They also had invaded their cities in

he Province of Ontario and in the Province of Quebec.
Therefore economically speaking American capital to a large
degree controlled the financial future of the country. English-
peaking Canada was becoming Americanised in spite of all.
f his English-speaking fellow-men were anxious to keep the
ountry British his advice to them was : Treat the French-
Canadian minority gently and generously.

Alternative of Imperial Federation.

"There is," concluded Mr. Lemieux, "the other altern-
tive, the Imperial Federation scheme, which would bring
bout, I suppose, a centralised Government. There you
would have a voice in the affairs of the Empire, but your voice
would be proportionate to your strength in the representation
f that federated Parliament of the Empire ; and it would
nean in the long run that your defence—the army and navy
f the Empire—would be controlled by a central Parliament
n London where you would have but a few votes or a few
epresentatives to give effect to your views. Then what
would happen ? A conflict would arise, because Britishers
he world over are first of all liberty-lovers, and out of such
onflict might come the break-up of the whole Imperial fabric.
My hon. friends know how the independence of the United
States was brought about : it was a case of conflict between
he Mother Country and the Thirteen Colonies. The same
hing would happen in the event of a conflict of interests in
hat central Parliament. The evolution will come slowly and
very year Canada will get a broader vision. If you are
nxious to maintain that happy state of things, let well enough
lone, have a keen respect for the autonomy of the Dominions.
Because it is one of the merits of the British system of government that the autonomy of the component parts is absolute
nd complete, and Britishers grow very sensitive when that
utonomy is in question. . . . After all, would it not be
or the pride and glory of the Mother Country to see the
Dominions which sprang from her loins increasing their
ctivities and enlarging their potentialities and having rooted
n their respective soils the standards and ideals of life that
ave made the Mother Country herself the great nation she is,
teer their own course ? "

A Company of Nations.

Mr. F. H. Keefer (Nat. Lib. and Con., *Port Arthur and
Kenora, Ont.*) declared that the King of Great Britain was
he King of their country, and he could at their request, if he

saw fit, appoint an ambassador for Canadian affairs at Washington or at any other embassy. They were bound by a
common tie, the Sovereign of all the Kingdoms, and the sooner
they let the world know, they were a company of nations bound
together by a common tie, the Throne, the better for the
English-speaking peoples. Only by following the principle
dictated by this policy should they bring about a stronger
union with that other branch of the English-speaking peoples
to the south of them and completely fulfil their destiny.

One Sovereign Nation.

The Hon. Henri S. Béland (Liberal, *Beauce, Que.*) said
that there were in the British Empire certain nations that
were on an equal footing, and they were the four Dominions,
and there was one supreme and sovereign nation, and that
was the United Kingdom. Who would contend for a moment
that they could appoint a plenipotentiary to Washington by
recommending to His Majesty the King that a man be
appointed, without the recommendation passing through the
channel of the Foreign Office or the British Government?
He strongly objected to the contention that the Dominions
and the United Kingdom were politically on an equal footing.
    He was not against appointing a representative at Wash-
ington. Canada should be represented at Washington as
Canada was represented in France. Such representation
carried with it the advantage of being on the spot, of being
in contact with the British Ambassador in Washington every
day, of being in contact with the political personages of the
great capital of the country to the south of them.

Conflict of Interests.

But coupled with those advantages, especially if they
appointed a Minister Plenipotentiary, were many dangers.
Conflicts were bound to arise between British and Canadian
interests. Who did not know that, on a certain occasion
Sir John Macdonald, who had been sitting in Washington
returned to Canada disgusted at the proceedings because the
Canadian interests had been sacrificed by the British authorities in presence of the Americans? He did not wish to bring
to the attention of the Committee the painful spectacle which
was offered in Canada at the time of the Alaskan boundary
question, when the representative of Canada was voted down
by two, the American and the British.
    He agreed with the proposition of appointing a representa-
tive at Washington; he might go so far as to agree that
discussion of purely Canadian affairs be confined as between

him and the American authorities ; but he wanted to register his opposition against the Canadian plenipotentiary acting at any time, even for one hour, as the representative of the whole British Empire. Think for a moment of the disastrous situation if their Ambassador should subordinate the British interests to the Canadian interests !

No Disintegration.

The Prime Minister said that if he thought that the step which the vote contemplated was a step towards withdrawal from the Empire, or a loosening of the bonds that bound them to the Empire, he could be relied upon to be among the first of those who would oppose it and would consistently do so at all costs. He could not follow the reasoning which led to the conclusion that they must maintain colonial status or else march towards the disintegrating of the Imperial structure. " The Imperial structure has multiplied in strength," declared the Prime Minister, " as the different Dominions of the Empire have elevated themselves step by step beyond the Colonial status. Nor do I think that this will be the end of the evolution of the Dominion into nationhood. I cannot conceive that even the relationship that this establishes would be adequately expressive of what the position of this Dominion should be in relation to the rest of the Empire when, say, we have a population here equal to the population of the United Kingdom." What they were doing now was to take a step in relation to permanent representation at Washington, parallel to that which they took in relation to the treaty-making power, having representatives of Canada really negotiate treaties and advise His Majesty in relation thereto ; and parallel to the step they had taken in respect of the International Joint Commission, when Canada virtually negotiated with the United States but when the representative was the representative of the sovereign Power, its head being the King, named on the advice of his Minister for Canada. Nor did it follow, because they took this step in relation to the United States, that it would be even natural for them to take it in relation to other countries. It might be so in the course of long years, but their position in regard to the United States differed most substantially from their position in relation to any other country in the world. " We take this step," said Mr. Meighen, " not because we are a nation and merely to express our nationhood. We take it because it will be a help to us, but it does illustrate the growing nationhood of the country ; it does illustrate the development of this country as an integral portion of the Empire ; it illustrates the evolution of this Empire as an Empire."

Extension of Representation.

Mr. Cockshutt : " Have we any constitutional right to make an appointment to the United States that is not of equal force with regard to any nation in Europe ? "

The Prime Minister : " Not at all. The United States as a foreign country is in just the same position as regards Canada as any other country ; and if the need arises to do likewise with any other country, why, then, of course, we will have the same right to do it in the same'way."

No Constitutional Change.

Mr. Fielding stated that the hon. member for Maisonneuve, speaking of the future, said that the time would come when the ripened fruit would fall off. That illustration was given fifty years ago or more by the " Little England " party. But, strange to say, with the process of time, though the fruit ripened better than ever before, it did not drop off.

Macaulay wrote some years ago : —

> " Very few propositions in politics can be so perfectly demonstrated as this—that Parliamentary government can not be carried on by two really equal and independent Parliaments in one Empire."

The position to-day was exactly what it was when Macaulay wrote. The power of the Imperial authorities—the Government and Parliament and the King—over the legislation of Canada was a very large power. There was no change in the constitution of Canada ; there was no real change in Canada's status.

Legal and Constitutional Right.

Sir Robert Borden declared that the Parliament of the United Kingdom had legal power to make a tariff for Canada It had power during the war to pass an Act for compulsory military service in Canada. It had absolutely no constitutional right to do either of these things. The legal power in the constitution of the British Empire was absolutely limited by constitutional right.

Mr. Clark asked his right hon. friend to contradict him if he was wrong when he said that no plenipotentiary or ambassador to a foreign power had ever been appointed except by a sovereign State.

Sir Robert Borden : " Canada, as one of the nations of the Empire, owes allegiance to His Majesty the King, who unquestionably is Sovereign in respect of the whole Empire and Sovereign therefore in each Dominion of the Empire. In each

Dominion he acts only upon the advice of his Ministers for that Dominion. Thus, the King is Sovereign in Canada, and Canada in respect of its allegiance to the King and in respect of its status of a nation of the British Empire, is sovereign in this essential respect, that the King, having regard to the special interest of Canada, has an absolute and perfect right to appoint a plenipotentiary to concern himself specially with the affairs of Canada in relation to any foreign country."

The item was agreed to.

COURT OF INTERNATIONAL JUSTICE.

A Bill was passed by the House of Commons on 7th May authorising the ratification and carrying into effect of the Protocol of the 16th December, 1920, accepting the Statute for the Permanent Court of International Justice of the 13th December, 1920.

Owing to the number of subjects of Imperial importance which have had to be dealt with in this number of the JOURNAL, the summary of this Bill and the discussions with reference to it will be held over to the next issue.

NAVAL POLICY.

On 27th May the House, in Committee of Supply, discussed the following vote :—

The Naval Service—to provide for the maintenance of the Royal Canadian Navy, $2,500,000.

DEBATE IN HOUSE OF COMMONS.

The Minister of Naval Service (Hon. C. C. Ballantyne) explained that he stated last year when the Naval Estimates were up that it was the intention of the Government to dispose of the *Rainbow*, the *Niobe* and the old submarines, and that they had accepted from the Mother Country one modern cruiser, two modern torpedo destroyers and two modern submarines. Those ships arrived at Halifax on 18th December last year, and at the present time they were on the Pacific coast. As to what they did with the money voted last year, they kept up the Naval College, the naval dock at Halifax and Esquimalt, and they maintained in commission, up to the time they sold them, the *Rainbow* and the *Niobe*.

They offered for sale by public tender the *Rainbow* and *Niobe*. Cash had been paid for the *Rainbow*, but only a partial payment had been paid for the *Niobe*.

After some discussion on the terms of payment,

Mr. Michael Clark (National Progressive, *Red Deer, Alta.*) trusted that they might turn their attention for a while to the vote of $2,500,000 which the Minister was asking for the Naval Service of Canada. He could not help wondering, as the old iron discussion was proceeding, how long it would be before those three vessels the Minister got last year from the British Government would be sold for old scrap iron in this way. Could he tell them how those three vessels were getting on ? Last year he (Mr. Clark) told him that he thought the Admiralty in Britain had put one over him in presenting him with those three vessels. He would like to know where this $2,500,000 was going. That was a lot of money in the present condition of the finances of the country. They had last year a national debt of $2,250,000,000, and they had just added to that $100,000,000. He would like to know how the naval dockyards were and how many naval officers they had in the Inside Service at Ottawa.

The Minister of Naval Service explained that the ships on the Pacific coast at present were the *Aurora*, two torpedo destroyers, the *Patricia* and the *Patriot*. The cruiser *Aurora* was built in 1914, was oil burning, and carried a complement of officers and men numbering 318. The two destroyers were oil burners built in 1916 and carried a personnel of about 90 each. The total number of officers and men on these three ships was something like 600. The College at Esquimalt was still carried on. Forty-five cadets entered for the last term, and the reputation that the graduates had had ever since the College was established had been a most commendable one. The course was excellent, and their young Canadian officers had done well in the British Navy, in which they had something like 38. They were going to continue the College on the same footing that had been maintained since 1911. The dockyards at Esquimalt had been closed down for nearly a year. The Halifax dockyards were being operated on very much reduced time, and their staff there was necessarily a great deal smaller than it had been. The vote they were asking for of $2,500,000 was for the operation and maintenance of the cruisers and two torpedo destroyers, two submarines, and the Colleges at Esquimalt and Halifax. The vote of $2,000,000 was no higher than the amount they spent in pre-war times.

Mr. Clark : " Would these ships be of any use if we unfortunately broke out now ? The *Niobe* and the *Rainbow* were not when the last war broke out."

The Minister of Naval Service : " The ships we have now are of the most modern type. The *Aurora* is armed with four-and six-inch guns and also torpedoes, and the destroyers are of the most modern type. We hope they will never be called upon to do anything in the way of active service, but if they are they certainly can take care of themselves."

Mr. Clark asked whether the Minister had a hope that in the near future he would be able to absorb the Canadian-trained young men in the Canadian Navy, such as it was at the present time.

The Minister of Naval Service replied that it had been the custom of the Canadian Government since the Naval Service Act was passed in 1911 to send a certain number of graduates each year to the Imperial Navy for training. They were paid by the Dominion of Canada. They had 38 there at present, and as vacancies occurred they had always this service of trained Canadian officers in the home fleet upon which to draw. Of the 34 officers now on the *Aurora* and other ships, all were Canadians with the exception of four.

Mr. Clark asked the number of naval officers employed in the office at Ottawa, how many had seen active service, and how many would be fit for active service in case of war.

The Minister of Naval Service said they had six officers at headquarters, all of whom were either Royal Canadian naval men or men from the British Navy.

Mr. I. E. Pedlow (Liberal, *Renfrew, S. Riding, Ont.*) asked the reason for the increase in the amount of the Estimate. Last year the amount was $2,000,000 ; for the current year it was $2,500,000. He should have thought, in view of the decreased cost of commodities, the Estimate would have been less for this year rather than more.

The Minister of Naval Service explained that they reduced the amount to $2,000,000 because they would not be able to get the ships from England until well on in the year. If the ships had been out there all of last year they would have wanted the $2,500,000. He therefore asked for that amount now.

Mr. Clark declared that no sentiment expressed in the House that Session had received warmer commendation from all quarters in the country than that expressed by his hon. friend from Marquette (Mr. Crerar) in his remarks in the Debate on the Address that they might very well under the present circumstances of the world take a five years' naval holiday in Canada, and a considerable portion of military holiday too (*vide* JOURNAL, Vol. II., No. 2, page 321). He knew that defence was the first duty of the State, but when the time for defending the State came Canada was not lacking, she was there as a nation, and they did wonders, and they did it all the better because they had not been spending too much money in

K

military and naval establishments before. This was a melan
choly business they had gone into—the Minister to all intent
and purposes, so far as the *Rainbow* and the *Niobe* were cor
cerned, was a dealer in scrap iron. It was said they shoul
not look a gift-horse in the mouth. He would not hav
looked at the animal at all, and he regretted that these anima
were accepted. He hoped they would take the matter int
their very serious consideration, and see if they could not kee
this business well in check. It ought to be easy, as they wer
all going to enter into the League of Nations. They had com
out of a war of unparalleled magnitude in which they suffere
terribly along with the other belligerent nations, and the
were told all along that that war was to end war, but her
they were again with a militant First Lord of the Admiralt
with fire in his eye leading them on to this business of armaments

The Minister of Naval Service said that Canada under th
Government of Sir Wilfrid Laurier decided to have a Nav
of its own. The Naval Service Act was passed in 1911
and the Government of the day decided that they would loo
after their own naval defence. He found no fault with th
policy then, and he found no fault with it now. The Nava
Service Act meant this. The Government of the day sai
to the Home Government, "Take away your ships and n
longer look after the dockyards at Halifax and Esquimal
Canada will assume that responsibility." And that respons
bility was on this Parliament to carry out the terms of th
Naval Service Act which his hon. friend (Mr. Clark) had h
full share in passing in 1911. The *Niobe* and *Rainbow* wer
brought out from England with the approval of his hon. frien
Now he would have been perfectly satisfied had they co
tinued with these two vessels.

Mr. Clark : "As training vessels."

The Minister of Naval Service stated that the vote wou
have been exactly the same as it was now. They were carryin
out the policy of the hon. Member for Red Deer and of th
Government of that day, and they were not increasing th
expenditure one iota. They had discharged 783 civilia
and naval ratings that they did not need, they had sold th
obsolete ships, and they had accepted modern ships as a fr
gift from the Mother Country. The policy followed since th
passing of the Naval Service Act must be the policy of Cana
until such time as that Act was amended or repealed. H
they not accepted these ships from the Mother Count
they would have had a disgracefully inefficient Naval Servi
a service not worth one cent to Canada, and the expenditu
would be just the same as they had now for a very efficient Nav

Under the terms of the Naval Service Act they had g
to keep the dockyards in sufficient working order to rep

any British Admiralty ships that might require repairs. They had practically closed down the dockyard at Esquimalt, but they were keeping sufficient men there to attend to any needs either of a British naval ship or one of their own ships.

Mr. Clark admitted that the Minister was pursuing a policy which was the acknowledged policy of a certain party in 1911. " There is no inconsistency whatsoever," declared Mr. Clark, " in my having supported that policy at that time as the only possible and proper naval policy for Canada, and in my saying, after the war, when another war in which we should be involved is to all human thinking considerably remote : Go easy with your naval policy. I am wholly in favour of Canada as a nation undertaking her own defence. But the Minister is inconsistent in going full steam ahead after a war just as he would have been going before the war. . . . I do not change my point of view that we might very well have waited in the present circumstances until an Imperial Conference should settle upon proper lines the question as to what each part of the Empire should do for the defence of the Empire."

Mr. A. R. McMaster (Liberal, *Brome*, *Que.*) felt it was a great mistake to take these ships from Britain. The German Navy was to-day at the bottom of the North Sea and for the time being, at least, that menace was no more. Under these circumstances would it not be the part of prudence to take a naval holiday ? The desires and hopes and prayers of all men of goodwill throughout the civilised world were centred upon the League of Nations. Was it not, then, the height of folly to go on in the same way in regard to naval matters ? Was it not unwise to contribute $200,000 to the expenses of the League and then spend ten times that amount on preparing something which, if the League was a success, would in all probability never be required ?

Mr. Ernest Lapointe (Liberal, *Quebec East*) declared that when the naval law was adopted in 1910, Sir Robert Borden and the present Prime Minister voted against that law and in favour of an amendment that no naval policy should be adopted in Canada without being first approved by the Canadian people. The issue was fought out during the campaign of 1911. Twenty-six Members were elected in the province of Quebec against the law, and after the elections they pledged themselves in Parliament that no permanent naval policy should be entered into by Canada without being first approved by the people. He asked his hon. friends when the Canadian people had since then approved the present policy. The Government had accepted those ships, as part of their permanent policy, without asking the approval, not only of the Canadian people, but of the Canadian Parliament.

K 2

The ships had been accepted, and they had to vote the money although they opposed the vote at that time. "I was opposed to that vote being accepted," declared Mr. Lapointe ; " I am still opposed to it for many reasons, one of them being that there is no settled naval policy to the present time for the British Dominions. There is going to be ar Imperial Conference next year. There is going to be a meeting of Prime Ministers this year. Conditions are such that our Prime Minister stated the other day that he would be opposed to the consideration of any naval policy at the Conference next summer. Why should we not wait until the status of the Dominions is fixed, as we are told it is going to be, at this Imperial Conference next year, before accepting, or adopting any policy as regards naval defence ? . . . We are paying an annual contribution to the League of Nations. We are members of that League. The last war was fought for the purpose of ending all wars. We should at least follow the example of those nations which are decreasing their armaments instead of increasing or entering into any new scheme."

Mr. D. D. McKenzie (Liberal, *Cape Breton North and Victoria, N.S.*) said that the Laurier policy received the full support of every man in the House. It was found that the naval policy of Laurier was not popular with some of the people in the province of Quebec, so at once there was a *volte-face* by hon. gentlemen opposite, and they at once threw to the winds the naval policy of Laurier which they had supported

He wanted to ask the Conservative party when, where and on what occasion they agreed upon a new naval policy There was not a single man of independent standing on the Government side who was in favour of this naval policy. The main body of their support, they said, they had from Ontario There was no enthusiasm in Ontario in regard to this new policy

The Government's next declaration was that they could not build ships on this side. They said it would take fifty years to build anything worth mentioning. They decided to abandon any naval policy and to take $35,000,000 and purchase some ships from the Old Country and bring them over here in the name of Canada. That was their policy It was defeated in the Senate after it had been forced through the House under closure, and they heard nothing what ever about the policy until to-night, when the Minister informed them they had a brand new Navy and naval policy and that they had wiped out the old naval policy of the Laurier administration. There was absolutely no foundation for such statement. The matter was never submitted to the people as was promised, and the Minister had no mandate to have these vessels in his possession ; nor had they the right to vote this money if they had any regard to the wishes of the people The Government did not submit the matter to the people in 1917, and the people had the right to suppose that they were not going to invest in any naval affairs or launch out on any permanent policy until the matter was pronounced upon by them. The Minister had no mandate from the people to receive this gift. The vessels were only in the way in the Old Country; they did not know where to put them and threw them off their hands on to the Minister, so that they should have the large expense in connection with them. He did not think the Minister could defend a policy of spending money just for the glory of having a Navy for which they had no use.

The various items relating to the vote were agreed to during the course of the debate.

IMPERIAL SHIPPING COMMITTEE.

Mr. J. E. Armstrong (**Nat. Lib. and Con.**, *Lambton, E. Riding, Ont.*), on 18th May, asked what action the Government had taken towards accepting the recommendation set forth in the final Report of the Royal Commission on the Natural Resources, Trade and Legislation of certain portions of His Majesty's Dominions, presented to both Houses of Parliament in March, 1917, showing that it was not desirable that the operations of the steamship companies carrying passengers between the Dominion of Canada and the United Kingdom should remain longer without some measure of Government supervision; and whether the Government intended to give effect to this legislation.

The Minister of Trade and Commerce (**the Right Hon. Sir George Foster**) gave the following reply: "The recommendations referred to have been considered by the Government and the subject matter discussed with other Overseas Premiers and the Premier of Great Britain. An Imperial Shipping Committee was appointed by the British Government in June, 1920, to inquire into and report in all matters connected with ocean freights and facilities and on all matters connected with the development and improvement of sea communications between the different parts of the Empire. On this Committee Canada and the other Overseas Dominions are represented. This Committee has been in Session and a preliminary report has been made on shipowners' liabilities under bills of lading and matters pertaining thereto. This will doubtless be followed by reports on other phases of the subject being investigated by the above-named Committee. After this investigation is finished and the reports made, what action, if any, is to be taken by the Government will have to be determined after the reception and consideration of these reports of the Committee."

IMMIGRATION.

(Statement by the Minister: Orientals.)

The Minister of Immigration (Hon. J. A. Calder), speaking in Committee of Supply on 26th April, said that the main question of policy was this : Should they at this time absolutely close the door against all immigration ?   It was asserted that every person of sound mind and body who was willing to work should be admitted to Canada, regardless of all other considera tions.   On the other hand, there were those who held that they should take into consideration economic, social and other conditions existing in Canada, and that the numbers admitted should be limited.   Then there was a middle view that they should select and allow people to come to Canada, very great care being exercised as to the classes they admitted.   It was now a little over two years since their Immigration Act was revised and consolidated.   He proposed at that time that they should clearly set out in the law the peoples of Europe and Asia that they would not admit to Canada.   That view finally did not prevail.   The House came to the conclusion that discretionary power should be placed in the hands of the Government.   They were given power to make regulations limiting the numbers that might come from certain countries and excluding those who might seek to come from other countries, or to set up instructions that might have that effect

General Policy.

As to the necessity of getting people, he did not see how there could be two opinions on that point.   The policy of total exclusion of immigrants from Canada was impracticable and it would be suicidal to the interests of Canada as a whole. So long as they had in Canada millions of acres of the finest land in the world awaiting development, and so long as there were thousands of people outside Canada capable of cultivating that land, they should not put up any unreasonable bar to prevent those people coming to their country.   The real problem was not to get people, but to shut out certain classes of people from Canada.   So long as the Federal Government and the provinces and municipalities, who had been paying money out to take care of unemployment in their cities, were still faced with the problem, did they think it would be a wise policy to allow labour, both skilled and unskilled, to flock into the country now ?   During the last three years the depart ment had encouraged mainly three classes of people to come

ʰ Canada : the farmer, the agricultural worker and the
omestic servant. Whenever a shortage of labour had existed
ʰey had not hesitated to set their agencies at work to secure
ʰhatever labour was required.

ǀumber ȯf Immigrants.

From 1907 to 1911 an average of 210,784 people entered
ǀanada for each year. The average during the last two years
ǀas 133,402. Parliament had agreed that there should be
ᵽserved for the soldiers all lands existing within fifteen miles
ʄ every railway in the West. As a consequence, during the
ǀst two or three years they had not had the privilege of
ʰviting any people to come to Canada to get free lands as they
ᵽuld in the old days. From 1897 to 1911 British immigration
ǀveraged annually 48,229 as against 68,001 during the last
ǀwo years. The average immigration from the United States
ǀuring the fifteen-year period was 43,361, whereas the average
ǀuring the last seven years was 52,794.

Most careful inquiries indicated that the Governments of
ǀrance and Belgium would not allow them to send agents there
ᵽr the purpose of drawing away their people. The suggestion
ǀas frequently made that they should endeavour to secure
ǀ large number of agriculturists from Great Britain. The
ǀgricultural population of Great Britain comprised only about
ǀfteen per cent. of the total population. Farm labour had
ǀeen unionised over there and they had been able to insist
ǀpon betteɪ hours, better living conditions and better wages.
ǀhey could not attract men from the British farms as they did.
ǀt present they had a total exclusion order against the people
ʄ Germany, Austria, Bulgaria and Turkey.

ǀestrictions.

There were in the big cities, in the small cities and in the
ǀorts of Europe, hundreds of thousands of people awaiting
ǀntry into either Canada or the United States. They had set
ǀp two restrictions in an endeavour to hold back that flood.
ǀhey had increased the money qualification ; with the excep-
ǀion of farmers, farm labourers and domestic servants, all other
ǀlasses must have $250 in cash. The other regulation was that
ǀhich required people coming from a foreign country to come
ǀn a through ticket, by continuous passage. Ordinarily they
ǀdmitted United States citizens, but in the case of undesirables
ǀho had got into the United States, and who desired to come
ǀnto Canada, they put up this bar of the through ticket.

No man could settle on the land (in Western Canada)
ǀnless he had an average capital of $7,000 or $6,000: In his
ǀudgment, the land settlement of Canada would never take
ᵽlace in a large way until the State was prepared to assist

settlers financially. He wished to refer to what had been done in the Australian colonies and New Zealand in this connection. The various States had advanced no less than £38,469,479 down to the end of 1915.

In conclusion the Minister said that there was an exclusion order at the present time against not only Chinese, but all Orientals in so far as skilled and unskilled labour was concerned. Generally speaking their policy had been to foster and encourage immigration to Canada of the classes he had mentioned. In the first place there was a limitation in so far as immigrants from enemy countries were concerned which was still in operation. In the second place, so far as the Slavonic races were concerned, while they had not stopped the entry of their nationals, they had not gone out of the way to encourage them to come to Canada during the last two or three years. As to people from the countries of Northern Europe, they encouraged all three classes from those countries. As regarded skilled and unskilled labour, on account of conditions existing in Canada they had not encouraged that movement ; as a matter of fact they had set up restrictions debarring those people entering Canada.

Mr. S. W. Jacobs (Liberal, *George Etienne Cartier, Que.* said that the artificial rules which the department made did not appeal to him, and he did not think they appealed to any person of common sense. The undesirable immigrant would find his way in by the underground route, and that was a way which was very effective. If all those people whom they brought into the country were examined at the ports of entry to find out whether they were free from anarchism and bolshevism, how was it that they had in Canada conditions such as they had within the past year or two? Surely these people never grew up in Canada. They came from the other side, the leaders actually came from the British Isles, and they were the fomenters of the discord in Canada which had been so much deplored by the Government.

Mr. Michael Clark (National Progressive, *Red Deer, Alta.* thought they would do well to see their soldiers through for a little while before they embarked, as a country, upon any larger scheme of encouraging land settlement.

Mr. W. D. Euler (Liberal, *Waterloo, N. Riding, Ont.)* was of opinion that the country to-day needed immigration in a greater degree than ever in the past ; yet the Government made the requirements more onerous. The Minister spoke concerning the probability of the admission of men from former enemy alien countries at the present time. He thought that ultimately the Minister and the country would find that their exclusion deprived Canada of productive workers capable of developing into good citizens, together with their children.

Mr. H. H. Stevens (Nat. Lib. and Con., *Vancouver Centre, B.C.*) thought that they should seek their immigration in northern Europe, not in the Balkan States, in extreme southern Europe or in Asia. He wished to address a few words to the Committee in connection with the type of immigrant with which they on the Pacific Coast were more particularly concerned. It was a question which in the last few months had been assuming very serious proportions, and it was one which he thought might well engage the attention of Parliament before the problem became even more acute than it was. He referred generally to what was known as the Oriental immigration problem. For many years they had had very severe restrictions on oriental immigration. Yet it was true that those regulations, particularly during · the last ten years, had been evaded in one manner or another and a considerable amount of Asiatic immigration had taken place. Whatever he said regarding the Chinese or Japanese was not with any racial prejudice ; his remarks were based upon exceedingly sound economic grounds. In connection with Chinese immigration they did admit students, recognising that it was a desirable thing that Chinese students should have the advantage of Western education. But they found that a very large number immediately upon obtaining access to the country were abandoning their scholastic pursuits and taking up different forms of labour. Then they admitted Chinese merchants, recognising the desirability of promoting trade, and it was found that the number of Chinese merchants entering Canada suddenly rose from three or four in a year to three or four hundred and then to over a thousand. These evasions constituted sufficient reason for the issuance, at least for the time being, of an exclusion order against Chinese immigration with the possible exception of business men, tourists and others of that character.

Agreement with Japan.

The Japanese immigration situation had been controlled very largely under regulations or agreements entered into between the Laurier Government and the Japanese Government, and brought about by a mission undertaken by the Hon. Member for Maisonneuve (Mr. Lemieux), whereby the Japanese Government voluntarily restricted their immigration. He thought they did strain the agreement somewhat, but not very seriously, though sufficiently, he believed, for the Government to give the Japanese Government a warning that they must scrupulously observe their agreement ; otherwise they would put on a complete exclusion order.

There was a recent test case in British Columbia, when a provincial law which was passed in connection with the moving about of Government coolies in British Columbia was declared *ultra vires* by the Supreme Court and the Privy Council, because it was in violation of the spirit or terms of the Anglo-Japanese Treaty, and he desired to urge upon the Minister that in the consideration of the renewal of the Treaty, Canada should reserve absolute right to control not only immigration into Canada, but the dealing with the nationals of the Japanese while they were in Canada.

Asiatic Settlers.

Within the last year there had developed in British Columbia, as in California and other Pacific Coast States, a problem which was becoming so acute that Parliament would certainly take cognizance of it before long. Three or four Japanese or Chinese would buy a piece of land and pay almost any price for it. Immediately the land adjoining depreciated in value, and they bought cheaply and thus the colony spread. They worked their coolies under conditions under which no self-respecting white man could live. Therefore it was impossible for their people to compete with them or to live alongside of communities under such conditions of life.

They held in British Columbia that it was the duty of the authorities to make it impossible for these Orientals to hold land by ownership or by lease. No Canadian was allowed to buy or own land or settle in Japan. Therefore it was not unreasonable to pass in Canada a law similar to that which obtained in regard to their own nationals in Japan. It had been contended that inasmuch as the British North America Act specifically gave to the provinces exclusive jurisdiction in matters of civil property and rights, it was within the jurisdiction of the province. But it was the opinion of the Justice Department that inasmuch as there was a Treaty between Japan and Canada, legislation as regarded Japanese nationals was within the prerogative of Parliament only. It was the duty of Parliament to legislate on the question of Japanese nationals holding or leasing land in any province or in the Dominion at large. Mr. Chamberlain gave expression to the opinion that Canada should reserve just the rights he had mentioned. Therefore they were not conflicting with any policy that had been held in the Mother-land.

Drug Traffic.

He wished to take one further general subject under review. He referred to the frightful increase of the pernicious drug habit on the Pacific Coast. This evil was not by any means restricted to British Columbia, but was gradually spreading to eastern cities, and while not wholly attributable t₁ the Asiatic, yet the basis of the traffic was Asiatic. "It i₁ the duty of this Parliament," concluded Mr. Stevens, "to deal in the most severe manner with any Oriental found indulging in or trafficking with drugs in this country. This problem is an intensely important one. Canada wants *bona-fle* settlers ; we want pioneers, but not parasites. We want men who will go and settle in the country, but we do not want a rce of persons coming into Canada who, experience shows beyond all question, are incapable of assimilation, and who will not take part in building up the country from its raw state."

Enemy Aliens.

Mr. J. T. Denis (Liberal, *Joliette, Que.*) was of opinion that te exclusion order should be rescinded now and all good cizens from Germany, and any other former enemy nation, should be admitted into Canada.

Danger of Foreign Immigration.

Speaking on 7th May,

Mr. W. A. Griesbach (Nat. Lib. and Con., *Edmonton, W. Eding, Alta.*) said that if they had one foreigner living among four men of British blood the process of assimilation would be quick and easy ; but if they had two foreigners to three men o British blood the process was slower, and the number that culd be assimilated was necessarily smaller, until the time might come when by the increase of the percentage of persons of foreign birth the process of Canadianisation might come to a standstill, and that of " foreignisation " might begin.

Mr. Griesbach then gave the following table showing the number of immigrants into Canada from 1911 to 1920 : —

Year.		British Isles.	United States.	Other Countries.	Totals.
1911..	..	123,013	121,451	66,620	311,084
1912..	..	128,121	133,710	82,406	354,237
1913..	..	150,542	139,009	112,881	402,432
1914..	..	142,622	107,530	134,726	384,878
1915..	..	43,276	59,779	41,734	144,789
1916..	..	8,664	36,937	2,936	48,537
1917..	..	8,282	61,389	5,703	75,374
1918..	..	3,178	71,314	4,582	79,074
1919..	..	9,914	40,715	7,073	57,702
1920..	..	59,603	49,656	8,077	117,336
		687,215	821,490	466,738	1,975,443

Contrasting these figures with those of the previous decade, which showed a falling off in the number of persons of British and French descent and a substantial increase in the persons

of foreign descent, Mr. Griesbach thought it reasonable
assume that the census of 1921 would disclose that there h
been a still further falling off of the British element with
very substantial increase of the foreign element.

Their problem was cautiously to admit those who were
to come. They ought to fix a definite ratio, based on statistic
and they ought not to exceed that ratio. They could n
look forward to an increased foreign immigration without gra
misgiving. The system which he laid before the Committ
was the plan of universal military service. There they had
scheme which was nation-wide, all-embracing, and backed
the supreme power of the State. The duties of citizensh
and its responsibilities would be impressed upon the foreign
and also the fact that he might some day be called upon
defend the country.

PRESENTATION OF THE SPEAKER'S CHAIR.

On 20th May a presentation to the House of Commo
of Canada of a replica of the Speaker's Chair in the Hou
Commons at Westminster was made on behalf of the Emp
Parliamentary Association, United Kingdom Branch, by t
Right Hon. James W. Lowther, late Speaker of the Bri
House of Commons and Joint President of the United Kingd
Branch of the Association.

Members of the House of Commons and of the Se
assembled in the House of Commons at 2.30 p.m., the Spe
of the House of Commons presiding. His Excellency, t
Duke of Devonshire, K.G., G.C.M.G., G.C.V.O., P.C. (Govern
General of Canada), occupied a place at the right of t
Speaker. There was present as the guest of honour t
Right Hon. James W. Lowther, LL.M., D.L., D.C.L. (Oxfo
and Leeds), LL.D. (Cambridge), M.P., accompanied
Sir Howard d'Egville, K.B.E., Secretary of the Emp
Parliamentary Association, United Kingdom Branch.

PROCEEDINGS IN HOUSE OF COMMONS.

The Speaker of the House of Commons (Hon. Edgar
Rhodes), introducing Mr. Lowther, said : " I would th
my duties were all as delightful and agreeable as the o
which devolves upon me at the moment. The conventio
have prescribed that there should be a formal introducti
of speakers on the occasion of a gathering of this charact
I am sure, however, that it is not a convention which ca

pon me to introduce the gentleman who will address you,
ecause his name is well known throughout the British
mpire. It is honoured in parliamentary circles and wherever
ritish government is known, and I need hardly say that it is
evered by the House of Commons of Canada. I present
p you the Right Honourable James W. Lowther."

The Right Hon. James W. Lowther, in making the presenta-
on, said : " Mr. Speaker, and Gentlemen of the House of
ommons of Canada : I come here to-day as the ambassador
f the Empire Parliamentary Association, United Kingdom
ranch. Every ambassador, before he is listened to, has to
resent his credentials, and I propose, if you will permit me,
erbally to follow that precedent.

" My credentials, then, are that I have been, ever since
s initiation, the President of the Empire Parliamentary
ssociation—I ought, perhaps, rather to say that I have
een a Joint President, for my colleague is the Speaker of the
Iouse of Lords for the time being, the Lord Chancellor.
he Empire Parliamentary Association is, as I think you all
now well, an association which was formed ten years ago
or the purpose of bringing into contact and communication
he Members of the different Parliaments of the United
Kingdom and of the Dominions which are all under the British
lag. That is the chief end and object, and it is carried out
n various ways. We are always delighted in London to
eceive the visits of any Members of Dominion Parliaments
vho happen to come to the Metropolis, and we believe that by
ntercommunication and by the exchange of our respective
deas, the general interests of the Empire, to which we are all
levoted, may be best furthered. I come here, then, as their
epresentative and at their request.

" But I have another qualification, I think, to which
Mr. Speaker has just referred. It is that for sixteen years
have presided over the deliberations of the House of Commons,
nd it is only a week or two ago since I stepped down from
he Chair. Now, my purpose in coming here is to carry to
vou gentlemen of the House of Commons of Canada the very
riendliest greetings and the best wishes of the Branch of the
Empire Parliamentary Association established in London.

" We heard with deep regret of the terrible calamity
which overwhelmed your Chamber in February, 1916. We
vere, I think, all the more sympathetic owing to the fact
that a similar calamity had almost one hundred years ago
overwhelmed the old Houses of Parliament at Westminster.
And when we heard that you had erected for yourselves the
magnificent building which I have had this morning an
opportunity of inspecting, a number of Members, both Peers
and Members of the House of Commons, were anxious to do

what they could to assist in completing the beautiful edific
which was being reared in Ottawa. Their first idea, I ma
tell you, was to offer you a replica of the Table in the Hous
of Commons—a table which was once described by Mr. Disrael
when he professed to be alarmed at the gesticulations of M
Gladstone, as ' this substantial piece of furniture whic
happily divides us.' On second thoughts, however, it wa
decided that a table rather connoted conference, but that
chair, a replica of the Speaker's Chair, would be more suitabl
as being more emblematic of Parliamentary institutions and mor
symbolic of the authority which rests with every Parliament.

"Now the Chair, which for the moment is veiled wit
the Union Jack, is an exact replica of the Speaker's Chai
in the House of Commons, which was erected in that buildin
in 1844. Above the Chair, in the canopy, you will observe
when the flags are removed, the Royal Coat of Arms. Thi
is carved out of a piece of oak which until recently has forme
part of the roof of Westminster Hall. The roof of West
minster Hall was erected in the time of Richard II., in the yea
1397. I think, imitating the celebrated *mot* of Napoleon
I can fairly say that from here five centuries will look dow
upon you.

"The Chair was designed by the well-known architec
Mr. Pugin, and the replica has been carried out by Sir Fran
Baines. The Chair brings to mind the names of eminen
statesmen who, from time to time, have addressed its occupan
I need only refer to the great names of Sir Robert Peel, Lor
Palmerston, Lord John Russell, Mr Disraeli, Mr. Gladstone
Mr. Asquith, Mr. Balfour, Mr. Lloyd George. The inscriptio
in front of the Chair, which you will observe when the Chai
is more open to view, recalls what I think I may call th
historical occasion. The occupants of the Chair, before
had the honour of taking it, were Mr. Shaw Lefevre, M
Denison, Mr. Peel and Mr. Gully. And, showing how lon
my parliamentary career has been, I may add that I hav
seen in the flesh everyone of those gentlemen, and I have sa
in Parliament under no less than three of them.

" But the Chair is something more than a mere gift o
friendship on the part of the Empire Parliamentary Associa
tion towards yourselves. It acknowledges, I think, in it
presentation by us and its acceptance by you, the grea
principle which has been accepted by Great Britain and b
all the Dominions within the British Empire, that governmen
of the people, by the people, and for the people is best carrie
out through parliamentary institutions. That is the best
known method by which a free people can govern themselves
and by which their aspirations or their aversions can be eithe
realised or removed.

"Les donateurs ont lieu d'espérer que ce fauteuil, pré-
enté à la Chambre des Communes de Canada, sera, dans les
ours de ce magnifique édifice, à Ottawa, un souvenir constant,
t de la bonne entente entre les membres du Parlement de la
ère patrie, et de la longue suite de traditions parlementaires,
éritées conjointement par les nations libres de l'Empire
ritannique.

"En 1818, les membres de l'Association parlementaire de
Empire du Royaume-Uni présentèrent au Sénat du Canada
ne verge noire pour remplacer celle brûlée dans l'incendie,
t espèrent que le don fait maintenant à cette Chambre,
emplaçant le fauteuil détruit dans le même incendie, soit
onsidéré comme essentiel aux procédures parlementaires et
our toujours être le symbole du bon vouloir et du grand
ésir de relations encore plus cordiales et plus intimes entre
s membres du Parlement de Westminster et de leurs collègues
u Parlement d'Ottawa.

"Finally, I would say that the Speaker's Chair is the
ymbol not only of parliamentary government as evolved
y the great constitutional elements of the commonwealth
f nations, but of authority, the authority of the individual
lected by his colleagues to preside over them, authority
o regulate debate, to maintain order and to ensure the free
xpression of all opinions. It marks, therefore, not only the
milarity and the continuity of parliamentary institutions
a the New World as in the Old, but it emphasises the principle
at without law, order and authority there can be no true
eedom. Upon the Chair itself you will find this principle
ashrined in the succinct maxim : *Libertas in Legibus.*

"It is the hope then of the donors that the parliamentary
astincts and traditions which, 'broadening down from
recedent to precedent,' have come to us in St. Stephen's,
aay flourish and abound in this country, and that when this
eneration and future generations look upon this Chair, the
ght may kindle in their hearts a spark, nay, I would rather
ay a flame, of respect and admiration and, I trust, affection
or the Old Country."

Mr. Speaker : "Your Excellency, Mr. Lowther, Gentlemen
f the House of Commons : One year ago a cablegram was
eceived by the Speaker of this House from the Secretary
f the United Kingdom Branch of the Empire Parliamentary
ssociation conveying the offer of a Speaker's Chair ' as an
biding token of goodwill between both Parliaments.'

"Acceptance would obviously involve the necessity of
oregoing a custom which has obtained in Canada almost
nce the inception of responsible government, that the retiring
peaker should take with him the Chair which he occupied
uring his term of office. But the spirit which prompted the

proposal of so fine a gift and the accompanying expression
were of such a character that no shadow of doubt as to it
acceptance could exist, and accordingly on 8th June, 1920
on the motion of the Prime Minister, seconded by the Leader
of the Opposition, it was unanimously resolved :—

> ' That the offer of a Speaker's Chair to the House of Commons
> of Canada by the Lord Chancellor and the Speaker of the House of
> Commons as Joint Presidents and by the members of the Empire
> Parliamentary Association in the House of Lords and in the House of
> Commons of the United Kingdom be most gratefully accepted, and
> that Mr. Speaker do inform the donors of the high appreciation of
> this House for the gift, and particularly. for the sympathy and good
> will which it expresses.'

" We now see the Chair in its permanent home. An object
of beauty—the finished product of expert craftsmen. It i
this, and far more than this. It comes to us surmounted b
the Royal Arms carved from the oak of old England, which ha
viewed from the roof of Westminster Hall the changing
scenes of the great Mother of Parliaments since the fourteent
century. It brings with it hallowed associations in its bein
a replica of the Chair at Westminster, a gift from our broth
parliamentarians across the sea. It will be valued becaus
it has been brought to us by one who occupied the origin
with singular acceptance and distinction during six
stirring and epoch-making years in the history of Great Brit
" As the years roll by new memories, traditions an
sentiments will mingle with those of a far-off past, challeng
and inspiring future generations to maintain those cherish
institutions which through the centuries have been insepara
associated with this ancient seat of authority.
" We gratefully accept, we thank the donors for th
treasured gift, and to you, Mr. Lowther, we are deeply grate
for the honour you have done us in making the presentat
in person."

Mr. Speaker then took the Chair.

Mr. Speaker : " To preserve the bilingual character of t
House of Commons, which was so happily recognised by yo
Mr. Lowther, I shall call upon the Deputy Speaker (Monsie
G. H. Boivin) to follow me in French."

Le Vice-President : " Qu'il plaise à Votre Excellen
monsieur l'Orateur, très honorable M. Lowther.
" C'est pour moi un grand honneur de parler aujourd'h
au nom de la députation canadienne française et au nom d
Canadiens-français de tout le pays, pour ajouter quel
mots à ceux que vient de vous adresser l'Orateur de la Cha
des communes.

"Nous trouvons au Sénat, le trône occupé par Votre Excellence, où vous représentez notre illustre Souverain, George V. Dans la Chambre des communes, le fauteuil de l'orateur est le trône du peuple, le symbole de l'autorité des citoyens. Celui qui l'occupe est le porte-parole de la députation élue aux urnes électorales, et quand il parle, il le fait avec toute l'autorité qui s'attache aux libertés conquises par des luttes plusieurs fois séculaires, depuis l'époque de la Grande Charte jusqu'à nos jours.

"Grâce au génie du peuple britannique, nos institutions parlementaires ont atteint un degré de perfection qui fait l'envie du monde entier et assure aux minorités la jouissance complète de leurs droits et de leurs prérogatives. Les généreux donateurs de ce fauteuil qui est une réplique de celui que vous avez occupé, M. Lowther, avec tant de distinction pendant seize années, ont voulu reconnaître le fait que les parlements des dominions jouissent de libertés non moins importantes que celles de l'illustre parlement du Royaume-Uni.

"De ce fauteuil de Westminster, un de vos augustes prédécesseurs, en 1867, a posé la question et a recueilli le vote qui nous a assuré l'Acte de l'Amerique britannique du Nord, sauvegarde de nos libertés, de nos droits et de nos prérogatives. C'est grâce à cet Acte que nous aurons toujours le droit, nous, de la province de Québec, d'envoyer ici soixante-cinq députés et de parler dans cette enceinte la belle langue française. C'est grâce à l'heureuse influence de cette constitution que les occupants de ce fauteuil doivent être alternativement de race anglaise et de race canadienne-française. Nous espérons que les décisions que notre représentant rendra, de ce fauteuil, seront toujours empreintes de la même connaissance de la procédure parlementaire, de la même justice, de la même impartialité et de la même courtoisie qui ont toujours caractérisé les vôtres, monsieur, pendant les seize ans que vous avez occupé le fauteuil de la mère des parlements, à Westminster.

"Laissez-moi terminer par un mot qui renferme bien plus que les quelques paroles que je viens d'adresser à cette Chambre, pour que vous le transmettiez aux généreux donateurs que vous représentez aujourd'hui. Je vous l'adresse aussi pour le long voyage que vous vous êtes imposé pour venir nous présenter ce cadeau et pour nous donner la preuve vivante que les hommes d'Etat de l'Angleterre savent parler comme nous la langue de nos ancêtres. Ce mot, monsieur, j'espère que vous y trouverez, en le traduisant, tout ce que notre cœur canadien-français y met ; c'est un des mots les plus doux et les plus expressifs de la langue française, le mot ' Merci.' "

The Prime Minister (the Right Hon. Arthur Meighen): Mr. Speaker, Your Excellency, Mr. Lowther, and Gentlemen of the Parliament of Canada :

" You, Mr. Speaker, and the Deputy Speaker as well,
have couched in very few words the sentiments that animate
us all on this occasion, sentiments that I believe are shared
not only by every member of this House but by every Canadian
worthy of the name. The presentation of this Chair is an
event of real significance. Possession of so splendid and
beautiful an ornament adds immensely to the attractions
of this chamber but what is of infinitely greater moment
it will hold before our eyes throughout the long, we hope
unending, years of parliamentary government in Canada
the symbol of the great Mother Parliament of which ours
is the offspring and the replica. It will stand as well as
evidence of that sense of fellowship felt for us in the old
land the helpful results of which we have through all our
history enjoyed.

" Every nation has made its own characteristic contribution to the world's advancement. Rome has given her
simple but sane principles of law, Greece her ideals of beauty,
Israel her ideals of religion ; Italy has brought us something,
Russia even has brought us something ; France has brought
us much. It is the peculiar glory of England that she has
given to her daughter nations the model, and to the world
the example, of popular institutions of government. Just
when the British Parliament took its birth historians hesitate
to say, neither its birth nor its growth has been marked by
any convulsion, by any easily discernible recasting or innovation. Time and events have done their work along sound
and natural lines and wisdom has always presided in the
process. This Chair will embody for us British traditions
it will remind us from day to day through the stern trials
of the future of British wisdom and British patience.

" In Canada we are not all of one race ; a large part
are of French descent. But I shall echo and anticipate the
words of those who in the ceremony of this afternoon will
especially represent French Canadians, just so far as to say
that they as well as we of Anglo-Saxon blood are attached
to the free institutions that we inherit from old England
that they believe as firmly as we in the essential rightness
and fitness of the form of government that she developed
and that now is ours.

" It is worth noting, indeed to me it is a valuable fact
that this gift from British parliamentarians to the Canadian
Parliament is carved out of English oak. The piece that
now the Royal Arms surmounting the Chair is cut from the
rafters of the great Hall of Westminster. In the blood of
every race there is something, there is some characteristic
of every leading race that accounts for its place and power
indeed for its survival. It is the sturdy oak fibre of the British

people that has carried them in triumph through the storms
and perils of a thousand years.

" We are honoured, very highly honoured, in having this
chair presented by the Right Hon. Mr. Lowther—the more
so because he has travelled from London to perform this
ceremony himself. For sixteen years, heavy, crucial, and
eventful years, Mr. Lowther has presided over the House of
Commons of Great Britain, and always with singular dignity
and capacity. The name of his family has been associated
with the public service of England ever since, or almost ever
since, there was any England to serve. Within the walls of
the British Commons for centuries back there has sat one
of his line. It is therefore a memorable event for us that he
should signalise the close of a long and distinguished service
as First Commoner in the Mother of Parliaments by coming
among us and presenting in person this visible and lasting link
between the Commons of Britain and the Commons of Canada.

" I am sure we, one and all of us, are grateful to the
United Kingdom Branch of the Empire Parliamentary Association, and particularly to the President who is here, to his
co-President, and to the Secretary Sir Howard d'Egville.
We value this Speaker's Chair as we value the sense of
fellow-citizenship in the British Empire which it is intended to
express and to ensure."

The Right Hon. Sir Robert Borden (ex-Prime Minister) :
'Mr. Speaker, Your Excellency, Mr. Lowther,—Little remains
to be said after all that has been so eloquently and appro-
priately uttered by the Speaker, the Deputy Speaker, and
the Prime Minister. May I ask to be associated with them
in profound appreciation of this gift from the Empire Parliamentary Association of the United Kingdom ; in appreciation
also of the presence of Mr. Lowther, whose name is as well
known in Canada as it is in the Mother Country, and who has
served, not only the United Kingdom but the Empire, in the
Speakership of the British House of Commons. Just one
thought, perhaps, might be added. The parliamentary institutions which we have inherited and which we hold as of right
and not of grace, were won by a common ancestry, and through
gradual evolution and development during the past five or
six centuries. I say a common ancestry advisedly, because it
was under the leadership of Norman Barons that the Saxon
people forced the Great Charter from a reluctant Norman king.

" The man who summoned the first gathering that might
be regarded as the forerunner of the Commons House of
Parliament of Great Britain, as well as that of Canada, was
a Frenchman, born in France. He well served our country
by calling together the Commons of England at Westminster
on January 20th, 1265. Thus, we can look back with

L 2

satisfaction upon the fact that Saxon and Norman, five or six
hundred years ago, stood side by side in the assertion o'
liberties that are ours to-day. With even greater satisfaction
we remember that, since the establishment of representative and
responsible government in this country, Canadians of French
descent have co-operated effectively and whole-heartedly
with those of British descent in developing our political
institutions and asserting our liberties in this Dominion,
It is perfectly true, as has been observed this afternoon, that
the present system of parliamentary government has been of
gradual evolution. One hundred years ago there was in
Great Britain representative government and responsible
government, but the House of Commons was then representative of what was called ' an educated minority.' To-day the
Parliament of the United Kingdom is representative of nearly
the whole people. In Canada the franchise began to be
extended somewhat earlier than on the other side of the
Atlantic. It now includes practically the entire community
I am sure that the influence of women in public life in both
countries will be for the best. Already in Great Britain Mr
Lowther has had the honour of having associated with him
in Parliament a lady member of the House. So we in the
near future, I imagine, may expect to see ladies sitting within
the precincts of this chamber. It is even quite possible that
some lady of distinguished parliamentary service may eventually attain the Chair, where I am sure she will preside with
great dignity and impartiality.

" Finally, Mr. Speaker, I wish to express my very great
gratification that this gift has been made. During all the
years to come it will serve as a symbol of the common purpose
of these two parliaments; and I trust that this common purpose
may ever tend toward the maintenance of liberty, autonomy
and justice towards the attainment of the highest ideals of
democracy for which it is our duty constantly to strive."

The Hon. W. L. Mackenzie King (Liberal, Leader of the
Opposition) : " Mr. Speaker, Your Excellency, Mr. Lowther,
The constituent elements of Parliament here represented are
right in regarding the present moment as one of historic
significance. There are under British parliamentary institutions two symbols of authority—the Crown, which speaks
the sovereignty of royalty ; the Speaker's Chair, which speaks
of the sovereignty of the people. That, under the ægis of
the British flag, these two sovereignties have blended into one
is a tribute not less to the character and devotion to duty of
the occupants of the British throne than to the genius of the
British peoples in the art and science of government.

" On this occasion we have these sovereignties not only
represented in the symbols I have mentioned ; we have the

)ersonified in the distinguished presence of His Excellency
he Governor-General and the presence of the eminent states-
nan who has crossed the seas to make to this Parliament and
he people of Canada the gracious gift from our brother
arliamentarians at Westminster, which by you, Mr. Speaker,
as just been accepted in terms so adequate and appropriate.

" It was said of our illustrious Queen Victoria that

> ' Statesmen at her council met
> Who knew the seasons when to take
> Occasion by the hand, and make
> The bounds of freedom wider yet.'

" We of this Parliament of Canada, reverencing British
ore, and schooled in British parliamentary traditions, recognise
n this moment such an occasion. We recognise in our
arliamentary institutions, fashioned as they are upon the
3ritish model, the greatest guarantee of freedom which a
eople can possess. We recognise that in the preservation and
xtension of the principles of government underlying our free
arliamentary institutions lies the possibility of our largest
ontribution to the freedom of mankind. Further, we recognise
hat it is around the Speaker's Chair that in the Mother of
Parliaments the battles of political freedom have been waged,
nd in appeals to the authority of the Chair, as the symbol of
people's sovereignty, that British political liberties have
een won.

" We accept, therefore, this gift with a full appreciation
f all that it signifies of what we owe of freedom to the Parlia-
nent at Westminster, and of courtesy and good-will on the
art of the members of the United Kingdom Branch of the
Empire Parliamentary Association ; and we ask you, Mr.
.owther, in conveying the thanks of this Parliament and of
he Canadian people, at the same time also to convey the
ssurance that it will be our high privilege to seek to preserve,
rith due regard to its rightful dignity and authority, and its
ncient and honourable tradition, this noble expression of the
reedom and unity of the British peoples so generously com-
nitted to our charge."

The Hon. Thomas Alexander Crerar (Leader of the National
rogressive Party) : " Mr. Speaker, Your Excellency, Mr.
.owther,—There is not much left for me to say on the present
ccasion. I am reminded, however, that it has this fortunate
spect for us. Usually the debates that take place in this
hamber are not attended with the entire unanimity that has
narked the proceedings this afternoon ; and consequently
t is a happy occasion when for the time being we can forget
ur controversies in the chamber and centre our thoughts on
united purpose. The circumstance is not an ordinary one.

We to-day, in the admirable words of Mr. Lowther, have been presented with a replica of the Speaker's Chair in the great Mother of Parliaments. That, because of the pre-eminence of British institutions and parliamentary government, is a matter of no small consequence to us. I am reminded of the fact that Canada has enjoyed now for many years the precious boon of self-government. It is a tribute to the genius of the Anglo-Saxon people that they have always endeavoured to build upon the broad foundation of freedom, and there is no finer or greater word in the whole Anglo-Saxon lexicon. We have also—and rightly and naturally so—derived our inspiration in parliamentary government from the Mother Country. We are familiar enough with history to know the struggles that have gone on in the Old Land for many centuries past, resulting in bringing the system of parliamentary government we have up to the state of perfection that we at present enjoy. It is also peculiarly fitting, Sir, that this Chair should come from the United Kingdom Branch of the Empire Parliamentary Association. That Association embraces the self-governing Dominions of the Empire, and it is a great honour to this House that we should receive from them this splendid testimony of their good-will and affection for us.

" I wish also to join my voice with those who have preceded me in saying that we are greatly honoured to-day in having with us the distinguished right hon. gentleman who for so many years presided over the deliberations of the British House of Commons. As Sir Robert Borden has stated, Mr. Lowther's name is not unknown in Canada ; in fact, it is almost as well known here as in the Mother Land ; and I am sure we all feel the deep debt of gratitude we are under to him for the trouble he has taken in coming to Canada to make this presentation in person.

" This Chair will grace this chamber long after we who are now participating in the activities of this House have passed from the stage. It will be a constant reminder to the generations who come after us of the greatness and grandeur of British parliamentary institutions, and, moreover, it will be a lasting link with the Empire to which we are proud to belong."

The Hon. Rodolphe Lemieux (Liberal, *Maisonneuve, Que.*)
" Excellence. monsieur Lowther, monsieur l'Orateur, mes chers collègues,—Je vous remercie du grand honneur que vous m' faites en m'invitant à prendre la parole à l'occasion de l'événe ment historique qui nous réunit. C'est un hommage que vous avez voulu rendre à la minorité française, et je vous en suis doublement reconnaissant.

" Au nom de mes collègues, au nom du Canada-français, je salue l'hôte distingué qui, dans la mission qu'il accomplit, renoue de très anciennes et très chères traditions entre le Parlement de la Grande-Bretagne et le Parlement du Canada. Nous avons suivi sa brillante carrière et nous savons que dans l'exercice de sa haute magistrature, il a fait respecter et aimer les institutions parlementaires. Qu'il soit le bienvenu au milieu de nous !

"Le nouveau fauteuil de l'orateur, taillé et sculpté dans la boiserie séculaire de Westminster Hall, est plus qu'un banal ornement.—C'est un emblème, c'est un symbole.

"L'éternel honneur de la mère patrie, c'est d'avoir répandu, à travers le monde, ces institutions où reposent beaucoup de sa gloire et de sa puissance.

"Trois principes sont à la base même du régime parlementaire : la *liberté*, la *justice*, l'*ordre*.

"Celui que préside aux délibérations de la représentation nationale, et qui se pénètre bien de ces principes, fondamentaux, est digne de siéger au fauteuil, qui, par une heureuse fiction, les symbolise.

"De l'aveu de tous, vous avez été, monsieur, l'un des grands '*Speakers*' dont s'honore le Parlement britannique — de ce parlement si souvent dominé par la seule dictature du génie au cours des deux derniers siècles ; de ce parlement, qui a occupé sa puissante tribune des plus grands événements de l'histoire moderne, qui, aux appels d'une éloquence généreuse et morale, a, tour à tour, proclamé l'abolition de la traite des noirs et l'émancipation des catholiques, qui a adopté l'*acte de Québec de* 1774, et concédé aux Dominions le principe du gouvernement responsable.

"Est-il besoin de rappeler que dans la longue histoire de la civilisation européenne, cheminant comme elle peut à travers les guerres, les despotismes, les révolutions, votre Parlement fut l'un des rares asiles où la parole humaine, qui a besoin de sa liberté pour avoir *toute sa puissance*, et d'un peu de sécurité pour avoir *toute sa liberté*, prit son essor ?

"Avec Chatham et Pitt, Burke et Fox, Wilberforce et O'Connell, Bright et Peel, Gladstone et Disraeli, de quels illustres ancêtres ne pouvez-vous pas vous réclamer ? Ce sont ces grands modèles qui inspirèrent Baldwin et Lafontaine, Macdonald, Cartier, McGee et celui dont la grande ombre plane encore dans cette chambre, Wilfrid Laurier.

"Me sera-t-il permis d'ajouter que, nous, Canadiens d'origine française, nous revendiquons, comme un bien de famille, l'institution du Parlement. Nos ancêtres, les barons Normands—leur signature en fait foi—arrachèrent au roi Jean Sansterre, la *Grande Charte*, et Simon de Montfort fut le premier à mettre en présence la royauté, l'aristocratie et le peuple dont l'union devait former le Parlement.

"Nous n'ignorons pas que notre langue—la plus belle qui soit tombée des lévres humaines—fut naguère la langue officielle du Parlement Anglais.

"Par un heureux retour des choses, la destinée—ou, pour mieux dire, la Providence, a voulu que les fils des vainqueurs des Plaines d'Abraham devinssent les compagnons de route des descendants des vainqueurs de Hastings, dans les immensités du Nouveau Monde.

"Notre dualité d'origine et de langue offre au monde l'un des plus intéressants spectacles. Nous avons l'illusion de croire que la diversité est l'un des éléments de la beauté et que cette dualité est le gage de l'harmonie et de l'union. Il n'y a plus ici ni vainqueurs ni vaincus. Tous, égaux devant la loi, nous voulons concourir à l'œuvre commune : le progrès et la grandeur de notre patrie, sous l'égide de la Couronne dont la devise nous est particulièrement chère, puisqu'elle exprime en un verbe dont l'accent nous est familier, l'espérance qui console et la réalité qui soutient : ' *Dieu et mon droit.*'

"Monsieur l'Orateur, profitant de vos prérogatives, vous m'avez imposé la *clôture*, une institution de date assez récente qui nous vient des Communes Anglaises. Avec votre permission, j'ajouterai quelques mots à l'adresse de Monsieur Lowther.

"Nous avons appris qu'il avait fait ses adieux à la Chambre des Communes et que bientôt il franchirait le seuil historique de la Chambre des Lords.

"Un illustre écrivain français voyageant en Angleterre, entra un jour à Westminster Hall. Il confia à un ami les impressions que voici : ' Je trouvai, dit-il, la bourgeoisie anglaise largement représentée aux Communes—mais en lisant les devises étalées sur les murs et les verrières de la Chambre des Lords, plus de doute dans mon esprit, je me retrouvais au foyer même de la vieille aristocratie normande.'

"Monsieur Lowther, vous rentrerez bientôt à Londres et nos meilleurs vœux vous accompagnent. Si nos voix françaises peuvent être entendues à travers l'océan, nous demandons à nos cousins de là-bas de vous faire bon accueil dans cette Chambre du Parlement Anglais, où, après tant de siècles, siègent encore les héritiers de l'ancienne noblesse normande."

Mr. Speaker : " I am sure I voice the unanimous desire when I express the hope that His Excellency will do us the honour of addressing us."

The Governor-General of Canada (His Excellency the Duke of Devonshire) : " Mr. Speaker, I hope I may express my grateful thanks to the House of Commons and yourself for having so made the arrangement for this historical and significant occasion as to allow me to be present. As far s I know, neither in the letter nor in the spirit have any of the ustly-guarded privileges and traditions of the House of ;ommons been in any way encroached upon, and I hope ı may take it as a happy omen for the future that the cordial elations that I have enjoyed will always exist between my ɥccessors in the distinguished office which I now have the ịonour to hold, and the members of the House of Commons.

" The ceremony we witness this afternoon will hold an ịonoured place in our parliamentary records. The present ɥd future Members of the House of Commons will, I know, lways have the same respect and veneration for this Chair ḥat their colleagues have for its prototype in the venerable ṣsembly which throughout the Empire we are proud to ạll the ' Mother of Parliaments.'

" To myself as a former Member of the House of Commons ḥe occasion is one of special interest, and that interest is ịnhanced by the fact that the presentation has been made ɟith characteristic charm and grace by an old House of ịommons friend and colleague. I am afraid that I cannot ɥnestly say that I have any reason to believe that Mr. Lowther ḍuring his long and distinguished career, first as Chairman ịf Committees and then as Speaker, had any particular reason ɔ be impressed with any utterances of mine. At any rate, ị think I can claim the satisfaction of knowing that to the ḅest of my belief I never caused him any anxiety.

" I join with you in the expression of grateful appreciation ḍ the gift and in the confidence and assurance that the spirit ɥhich prompted it is sincerely reciprocated and will still ɥrther strengthen the ties wihch bind the two Parliaments ḅgether."

Mr. Lowther : " The House will forgive me if for one ɥoment I say that in addition to the Chair and in complement ḅ it I have brought, on behalf of the Empire Parliamentary ɪssociation, this framed scroll with an inscription in front ạd a list at the back of all the Peers and the Members who ḥave subscribed toward the gift which you have so generously ạd so amiably accepted."

The proceedings were brought to a close by the singing ḍ the National Anthem by all present, and before the meeting ḍispersed, hearty cheers were given for His Excellency the ḅovernor-General and Mr. Lowther.

Expression of Thanks.

On the House meeting,

The Prime Minister begged to move, seconded by the ḷeader of the Opposition : —

" That the grateful thanks of this House be extended to the Lord Chancellor and the Speaker of the House of Commons, as

Joint Presidents, and to the members of the Empire Parliam
Association, United Kingdom Branch, for the Speaker's
presented on their behalf this day by the Right Hon. Jar
Lowther, and that Mr. Speaker do inform the donors of tl
appreciation of this House for the gift and for the expres
goodwill which accompany and will ever be associated with
of the great honour which has been shown by the welcome
the Right Hon. James W. Lowther."

The Prime Minister also moved, seconded by the I
of the Opposition, that Mr. Speaker should convey t
Lowther the thanks of the House for his visit ; an
what had been said at the formal presentation of the Spe
Chair should be printed in " Hansard " as a prefix
proceedings of the day.

These motions were agreed to.

AUSTRALIA.

Commonwealth Parliament.

The following summary is in continuation of the proceedings of the First Session of the Eighth Parliament, which was commenced in Vol. I., No. 3, of the JOURNAL.

CONFERENCE OF PRIME MINISTERS OF THE EMPIRE.

(Anglo-Japanese Treaty: League of Nations: Naval Defence: Imperial Federation: Inter-Empire Relations, etc.)

The following is a summary of the debate on the speech of the Prime Minister in the House of Representatives on 7th April (*vide* JOURNAL, Vol. II., No. 2, page 354 *et seq.*) concerning the questions to be discussed at the Conference of Prime Ministers.

DEBATE IN HOUSE OF REPRESENTATIVES.

Anglo-Japanese Treaty: Constitutional Changes.

The Hon. F. G. Tudor (Leader of the Opposition), on 13th April, said that at least 99 per cent. of the people of Australia now favour the " White Australia " policy, and desire to retain it. When they entered Federation, the percentage in favour of that policy was not so great. He, of course, was a believer in a " White Australia." He felt they should do nothing to offend the great Republic whose territory lay on the other side of the Pacific. He wished to keep friendly with the Americans. Nothing could be gained by the white races getting at loggerheads, and misunderstanding each other. But as, during the long period in which the Anglo-Japanese Treaty had had force, they had preserved the " White Australia " policy inviolate, he saw no difficulty in keeping it inviolate in the future if the Treaty were renewed, and he had no objection to any treaty that made for the peace of the world. The Prime Minister, however, had told them that the Treaty was anathema to the Americans. He (Mr. Tudor)

hoped that Mr. Hughes was hardly correct in that statement.
They might disagree with the people of the United States of
America concerning their attitude towards the League of
Nations, and might find fault with things that happened
at the Peace Conference, but he hoped that the thinking
people of the United States would not consider the Australian
support of the Treaty was influenced by any desire to prejudice
American interests.   Australia had no such desire.

The Prime Minister had told them that constitutional
changes were not to be discussed at the Conference.   The
difference between the British Parliament and the Commonwealth Parliament lay in the fact that whereas the Commonwealth's powers of legislation were bounded by a written
Constitution, Great Britain's were unlimited.   The relations
between Great Britain and the Dominions were not defined
in black and white, and his advice to those in authority,
were he permitted to give any, would be that it was wise
to let things remain as they were, without attempting to define
them, and without setting up an Imperial Council or an
Imperial Parliament, or some other body to make them more
definite.   A large number of people were content to let things
remain as they were in that matter, and would raise objections
to any hard-and-fast connection.   The people of Australia
would jealously guard their rights of self-government, and no
restrictions should be placed on them.

Mr. W. J. McWilliams (Country Party, *Franklin, Tas.*):
" Can the Conference deal with two of the chief matters on its
programme without discussing constitutional changes ? "

Mr. Tudor : " I think it can do so without laying down
hard-and-fast rules to bind Imperial relations."   He accepted
the assurance of the Prime Minister that Australia would not
be committed to any determination until it had been brought
before the Commonwealth Parliament.

The Prime Minister (the Rt. Hon. W. M. Hughes) : " The
only thing I ask this Parliament for authority to do, without
further reference to Parliament, is to renew the Anglo-Japanese
Treaty in some form acceptable to Great Britain, to Japan,
to Australia, and, if possible, to America ; provided no
renewal shall impair the principle of a ' White Australia.'
I shall not subscribe to anything that might do that, and
should bring the Treaty here were it attempted."

Mr. Tudor : " Then we shall not be committed to anything
determined by the Conference respecting foreign policy or the
Navy until Parliament has dealt with it.   As to the Anglo-
Japanese Treaty, I shall support any treaty that makes
for peace.   I shall not do anything to bring about war in this
or any other country."

League of Nations and Naval Defence.

He agreed with the Prime Minister that the League of Nations was little more than a shadow at that time, but he hoped that in the near future the League, or something in its place, would take a more substantial form, so that the various peoples might appeal to reason instead of force for the settlement of their differences, and would not continue the piling up of armaments at such huge expense.   When people felt that they were prepared for war they were less chary to fight than they would be if they were not so prepared.

Turning to the question of naval defence, he noticed that the Prime Minister had stated that last year they had spent £3,352,000 upon their Navy, although, in Mr. Hughes's opinion, it was a very insignificant force compared with that which was necessary to maintain peace even in the Pacific.   He (Mr. Tudor) agreed with that.   Mr. Hughes had stated also that Australia spent more on naval defence than all the other Dominions combined.   Naval defence in the Pacific should mean as much to the people of Western Canada as it did to Australia, but they had not prepared for it in the same way as Australia had done.   What would be Australia's contribution to the expenditure on the British Fleet on a population basis ?

Mr. W. M. Marks (**Nationalist,** *Wentworth,* *N.S.W.*): "£12,000,000 to £15,000,000."

Mr. Tudor continuing, said he unreservedly accepted the Prime Minister's assurance that they would not be committed, without the sanction of Parliament, to any huge expenditure, such as was indicated by Mr. Marks.

They had that day been informed that Australia's contribution to the expenditure of the League of Nations was £56,000 per annum.   He would rather spend £56,000 or even £560,000 per annum trying to perfect a League of Nations in order to avoid war, than he would spend thirty times that amount on naval defence in the Pacific.   He would sooner spend the larger amount to avoid war than spend it on war. If the League had already had the effect of reducing warring nations from twelve to two, the little money they had spent on it had been a good investment.   He hoped America would yet reconsider her position in regard to the League.

Imperial Federation.

Dr. Earle Page (**Leader of the Country Party**) said that the Prime Minister told them that the Conference he was about to attend would not deal with constitutional matters ; but while he was loudly proclaiming this, Mr. Massey, another Dominion Prime Minister, was before the public with a definite scheme for an alteration of the Imperial Constitution, in order to create an Imperial Council. They were dubious lest at the forthcoming Conference they might be committed by plans made for the defence of the Empire, or by conclusions arrived at upon which the people of Australia would not be able to go back. The present considered opinion of Australia was that it did not wish to be committed to any form of Imperial Federation.

The Prime Minister : " That is correct. I have always opposed it. I do not believe in it."

Dr. Earle Page, continuing, said the British Empire was a family with children of different ages. It was for the other Dominions to speak for themselves. If Canada thought it had attained the age of twenty-one years, or if South Africa thought the same, all Australia had to say was that it had not attained that stage at which it desired to leave the parental roof, and that it still wished to remain an integral part of the Empire.

Foreign Policy.

As to the foreign policy which had been outlined by the Prime Minister, he thought no one could take exception to his statement that naval defence must be the girder and guarantee of the British Empire, and without it they must perish. He was glad that the Prime Minister had given them an assurance that afternoon that whatever might be the system of naval defence proposed he would not endorse it on behalf of Australia at the Conference, but would bring it back to the Parliament and ask Members to express their approval or otherwise of the policy determined upon. The Japanese, under the Anglo-Japanese Treaty of 1911, practically agreed by Article 4 dealing with any nation that forms an arbitration treaty with Great Britain, that if war broke out between Japan and America, England would not be drawn into, it. In these circumstances, having regard to the direct declaration of Japan as set out in the Anglo-Japanese Treaty that she desires the stable government of China and is prepared to agree to the policy of the open door, there must be some way in which, by free and frank discussion of all the details of this question, they could arrive at an arrangement, such as the Prime Minister had indicated, which would satisfy Japan, America, England, Australia, and also the other Dominions of the Empire.

Inter-Empire Relations.

The Right Hon. W. A. Watt (Nationalist,* *Balaclava,* *Vic.*), during his speech, declared that he knew no one better able or more entitled to state Australian views at the Conference than the Prime Minister (Mr. Hughes).

Referring to inter-Empire relations, Mr. Watt said that during the War four important steps had been taken in the direction of increasing the importance and the responsibilities of the Dominions. All of them had probably been inevitable in the temper of the times. Some of them he thought were wise, and others dangerous; yet, notwithstanding the danger, inevitable. He did not hesitate to say, although it was a grave statement for a Member of the House to make, that merely an invisible line now stood between the oversea Dominions and complete independence. That he took to be a serious thing. Care and moderation, which happily were still distinguishing features of British statesmanship, might avert a tragic step; but the point was that the machinery had been created, and was operative, which might be used by the intemperate or the clumsy to speedily dismember the Empire.

Let them look at the four matters to which he had referred. The first was the admission of the heads of Dominion Governments to membership of the Imperial Cabinet; the second, the representation of the Dominions and their signing of the treaties concluded at the Peace Conference; the third, the direct representation of the Dominions on the Assembly of the League of Nations; and the fourth, their direct contact with the Secretariat of the League.

As to the first of these, the admission of the Dominion Prime Ministers to co-equal rank with members of the Imperial Cabinet in London, he supposed the unanimous feeling was that nothing but good could come of it, and he thought that they all devoutly hoped that it might continue. As to the second, the direct representation of the Dominions at the Peace Conference, he had always doubted its wisdom. He thought that the Empire lost in force and in political prestige by having its Delegation split up. Their Representatives should have been present, but should have been merged in the general British Delegation. All that, however, was past and gone, and, as an old sage had said, " Wise men have enough to do with things present and to come."

---

* Treasurer from 27th March, 1918, to 15th June, 1920, when he resigned office as a result of variance with his ministerial colleagues in Australia on important issues connected with his mission to England. (*Vide* JOURNAL, Vol. I., No. 3, page 519.) Mr. Watt acted as Prime Minister during Mr. Hughes's absence from Australia in connection with the Peace Conference.

Dominions and League : Need of Empire Clearing House.

It was, therefore, the third and fourth concessions to which he then wished to direct particular attention, namely their separate identity on the Assembly of the League of Nations and their direct contact with the League's Secretariat In both these lay the seed of Empire disruption. Unless something was done wisely and early to provide for the disuse of those powers or for Empire concert in a new way, trouble surely lay ahead of the British family. The expression of divergent views by British and Dominion statesmen in the Assembly of the League would inevitably weaken the prestige and influence of the Empire. Preconsultation, if it were secured and assured, would lessen the risk of that, but would not eliminate it. He knew the Prime Minister's strong desire to establish and maintain a direct channel of communication between the Dominions and the League's Secretariat, and, in his (Mr. Watt's) judgment, that was where most peril resided. The way to avoid it for the Dominions that had been given the privilege was not to use the direct wire but to talk through the central British exchange. The way to make assurance doubly sure, in their own interest especially, was to devise an Empire clearing-house, where British problems could be considered and co-ordinated before being published to the outside world. He said solemnly to those Dominions that had racial problems or racial barriers—and Australia was one of them—that that procedure was in the highest degree important, and, indeed, essential.

An Empire Partnership.

If the unity of the Empire was to be restored or preserved steps to that end must be taken at an early date. In the present condition of independence in connection with the League Secretariat all sorts of danger to them might spring up from the imprudence of other Dominions. For example, was Australia to be threatened by, or committed to, war because of some action by the Government of Canada or South Africa about which Australia had not been consulted, or of which they were entirely ignorant ? And, conversely, were the Mother land and the other Dominions to accept responsibility for the independent acts and utterances of those in Australia If not, were they to stand idly by while Australia did all its own fighting, if it came to fighting ? No ; whether they be apostles of growth or of organic union, a moment's consideration would show them that they could not run an autonomous Empire on that basis, and the sooner the people generally, as well as its leading minds, understood the delicacy of the mechanism, and the stupendous dangers with which the were playing, the better it would be for all of them.   Unfortunately, there were still some people in Australia who yearned for the glittering abstractions of independence, and at the same time hugged to their hearts the security and advantage of inter-dependence.   International recognition of the Dominions might be gratifying to their pride ; but the best salve to their pride, and the finest insurance policy they could effect, was an intimate partnership in a united British Empire.   That was not a new sentiment ; it had been uttered in another way by the Prime Minister, but it needed re-emphasis.   He was glad to hear Mr. Hughes's views about the League of Nations, because if they were to surrender the advantages of this family partnership for any allurement that rainbowed the League of Nations, they would be like Æsop's famous dog, who lost the substance in grasping at the shadow.

The Treasurer (the Right Hon. Sir Joseph Cook) : " Hear, hear ! But why should one be set against the other ? "

Mr. Watt : " Because the Prime Minister placed them in juxtaposition.   There are people who say that, while we have a League of Nations, there is no need to keep close partnership with Britain, or our alliances with other people, or to embark on a different policy.   That is the call that comes from a suicide's or fool's paradise. . . .   My faith in the League of Nations has almost faded out."

The Prime Minister : " My faith remains constant ; as it was at the beginning so it is to-day."

Mr. Watt said he was sorry that the Prime Minister had not learnt anything with the passage of time ; he (Mr. Watt) had.   His faith was altered because America had persisted in standing out of the League, and he could conceive of no potent organisation for the preservation of world peace which did not include America.   He was with the Prime Minister that the hope of the world lay in a better understanding between the great Republic of the west and the other English-speaking peoples.

Japanese Alliance and Naval Defence.

With regard to the Anglo-Japanese Alliance, Mr. Watt said that the Prime Minister's words had been welcomed by prominent Japanese thinkers.   That was a grateful sign. They were seeking to re-ally themselves with a Power which had honourably observed the compact through all the years of their peril from 1914 to 1919.   Australian policy could subsist alongside a sound alliance with Japan.

Turning to the question of naval power, Mr. Watt said that their policy was one of co-operation with Britain, particularly in southern waters.   They could never, with their population,

M

sustain a Navy which would be adequate to their huge coast-
line and their maritime interests. The Leader of the Government (Mr. Hughes) had said there was no plan of campaign
in existence. There was, as a matter of fact, a very fine plan
which had been issued to the Empire by Viscount Jellicoe.
It was the nucleus, in concept and spirit, of a partnership
in the south-eastern corner of the earth which, whatever its
magnitude, or whatever be its limitations, was the best form
of co-operation in respect of naval defence that they could have.

The Hon. Sir Robert Best (Nationalist, *Kooyong, Vic.*)
supported the views enunciated by Mr. Watt, and proceeded
to emphasise some of them, strongly urging that any alteration
in their relationship with the Mother Country must have for its
objective a more real union and a greater consolidation of the
British Empire.

Labour Views.

Mr. J. Mathews (Labour, *Melbourne Ports, Vic.*) said he
differed considerably from some of the preceding speakers
because, in his opinion, it depended not so much upon the
Empire's foreign relations as upon the settlement of its internal
troubles. If those who had control of the foreign policy of
Great Britain would only read as they passed they would
observe that not only was it undesirable and impossible for an
Empire Parliament to be brought into existence—that would
not be tolerated in any circumstances—but that the Dominions
must be held by lighter threads in future than in the past.
The Delegates should be allowed to give expression to their
opinion concerning the position in Ireland, because, whether
they liked it or not, the troubles of Ireland had been felt
upon Australia, and were reflected in Australian public life
to a remarkable degree. In other words, the sooner the
trouble in Ireland, which was causing much turmoil and
dissatisfaction, was settled the better it would be, not only for
the Commonwealth, but for the whole of the British Dominions.

Mr. M. P. Considine (Labour, *Barrier, N.S.W.*) said that
in 1924 the American Navy would be superior to the British
Navy in tonnage, armament and speed. American statesmen
declared that they were out for the greatest Navy in the world.
They wished to control the world's commerce in regard to
steel and the mercantile marine, and the natural corollary
was the biggest Navy in the world. Yet Australian statesmen
said they were going to bring about an alteration of the Anglo-
Japanese Alliance which would make oil and water mix.

The Hon. T. J. Ryan (Deputy Leader of Labour Party)
speaking on 21st April, said that the Prime Minister would
wrongly interpret the opinions of the people if he thought

they were likely to agree to any departure from the policy of having an Australian owned and controlled Navy. They did not want any departure in the nature of a contribution such as was turned down by the people of Australia, he thought, in 1910, and also by the people of Great Britain.

He did not claim that the action of Great Britain, if she should consider herself well advised in renewing the Anglo-Japanese Treaty, should be subject to the approval of the people of Australia. But he did think that, in so far as it affected Australia, or involved their people in responsibilities, t should be subject to their review.

Mr. F. Anstey (Labour, *Bourke, Vic.*) said that it was heir clear and solemn duty to Australia to at least tell the)ld Country that they were not prepared to link up with an Asiatic race in any conflict against white people. That was lear and definite.

Dr. W. Maloney (Labour, *Melbourne, Vic.*) said that after auch reading and great study of Japanese arts he had come o the conclusion that the Japanese were the greatest and most rtistic race that the world had ever seen. He felt certain hat the Prime Minister would keep imbedded in his mind hat Australians, loving the Homeland as they did, would be lad if a Treaty were arrived at with Japan with which they puld agree, and which could not, in any circumstances, be pnstrued into an agreement to take part with Japan against he United States of America.

Mr. F. Brennan (Labour, *Batman, Vic.*) hoped that by eans of a sane international policy, which he did not expect om the present Government, they would be able to sustain eir ideal of a " White Australia." He believed that, when ey had finally abandoned the baleful theory that they fed by virtue of their guns and ships ; when they were epared to extend the right hand of fellowship to the people every country in the world, whatever their colour might be, d to argue the question of immigration on sound lines of nciliation, they might hope to make Australia secure and further indulge the hope that the Commonwealth would en be effectively occupied and substantially populated by pple of the white races, people who deserved to retain it.

Mr. N. J. Makin (Labour, *Hindmarsh, S.A.*) said that ty were then so involved financially that they could not ord to incur any fresh obligations in order to provide a re adequate defence for the Commonwealth. They had Var debt of £350,000,000, and their public debt to the 30th he, 1920, totalled more than £405,000,000.

Prime Minister, concluding the debate (21st April), had repeatedly pointed out that the chief problem

M 2

before Great Britain was to draw up a Treaty that would not involve Australia or Great Britain in a struggle with the people of the United States. The hope of the world depended upon some sort of understanding between America and the Empire, and it was to find a way to realise that hope that the minds of those attending the Imperial Conference should be directed. It was unthinkable and not within the bounds of possibility that they should ever take part in a struggle against America. They could not be bound to any treaty which they themselves did not ratify, although the practical consequences of war between Britain and America, whether Japan was or was not her ally, would of course have to be faced by Australia. But even if the Anglo-Japanese Treaty be renewed, it would not bind Australia to go to war with any country in the world. The last thing that any British Government would think of would be war with the only nation which, with themselves, could hope to maintain the peace of the world. An understanding with America was essential, and they could not afford to quarrel with Japan. Australia, however, must stand by her own ideals.

Mr. Hughes promised that no defence scheme or expenditure would be incurred or pledged. Everything would be brought to the Commonwealth Parliament. He felt that he knew the opinion of Parliament, and he proposed to try to enshrine that opinion in the Treaty.

A motion by **The Hon. T. J. Ryan (Deputy Leader of the Labour Party)**, that the Australian Representative at the Conference should not be empowered to commit Australia to any agreement or understanding except on the condition that the same should be subject to the approval and ratification of the people of Australia, was defeated on a party division by 42 votes to 21.

LEAGUE OF NATIONS.

(Geneva Assembly : Pacific Islands Mandate : Financial Agreement with United Kingdom.)

On 13th April the Minister for Repatriation made a statement to the Senate concerning his mission to Europe as Australia's delegate at the Geneva Assembly of the League of Nations ; the adjustment of certain financial matters outstanding between the British and Commonwealth Governments, and other matters (*vide* JOURNAL, Vol. II., No. , page 120).

IN THE SENATE.

Financial Agreement with Great Britain.

The Minister for Repatriation (Senator the Hon. E. D. Millen) said that arising out of the War, the Commonwealth had become indebted to the British Government partly in respect of loans obtained in the early days of the War and partly in respect of amounts owing for maintenance and transport of Australian troops. Under the latter heading there were certain items, aggregating approximately £5,000,000, which still awaited adjustment. They represented claims in respect of which accounts, up to the date of the agreement, had not been finalised.

The central idea upon which the financial agreement was based was that an annuity of 6 per cent. of the total indebtedness should be paid by Australia to the Imperial Treasury. This annuity was to be devoted in the first instance to the payment of interest at the moderate rates of 3½ per cent., 4 per cent. and 5 per cent. The rate of 3½ per cent. applied to the comparatively small portion amounting to £1,263,158. The rate of 4 per cent. applied to a total of £11,500,000, and the remainder of the principal, amounting to £74,218,900, would carry interest at 5 per cent. The difference between these interest rates and 6 per cent. would be devoted towards reduction of the principal, and would repay the whole in less than thirty-seven years.

There were two items to which he wished specially to refer. There was due to the British Government the sum of £570,000 for interest which had accrued prior to July, 1917. The British Treasurer had agreed to include this in the funded debt, thus relieving Australia of the obligation of immediate payment. There was also approximately £4,000,000, being interest on the total indebtedness up to 31st March, 1921. The Commonwealth Treasurer had made provision for this on the Estimates 1920-21, but owing to the adverse state of the exchange market, it would have been difficult, and certainly very costly, even if possible, to remit this money to London at that juncture. The Imperial Treasurer had agreed to accept payment of this amount in bills at six and twelve months' date, by which time it was hoped exchange might have become easier, or, failing that, that the Commonwealth would be able to make more convenient arrangements than were possible at present. This extension had been obtained without interest.

In considering this agreement, viewed as a whole, he submitted it as first evidence that the British Government, whilst struggling with its own financial burdens, had exhibited a very generous desire to render those of Australia as little onerous as possible.

Provision was made in the last Estimates for the amount due as interest, and as the agreement required also a sinking fund, it might appear at first sight as if they would need to raise an additional amount to pay this sinking fund. But he would point out that they were already providing a sinking fund of ½ per cent. in respect of their total indebtedness in accordance with the Sinking Fund Act. That Act empowered the Treasurer to repay out of the sinking fund any moneys borrowed from the United Kingdom.

League of Nations Assembly at Geneva.

Turning to the historic gathering at Geneva, the initial meeting of the Assembly of the League of Nations, when they reviewed the tragedy of six years of war, from which the world had emerged in a pitifully shattered condition, and under the burdens of which it was doomed to struggle for many years to come, and when they learned, as they did almost daily, of increasing armaments, of those international differences, misunderstandings, and jealousies, inflammable material which a spark might ignite, they could well understand the earnestness, the pathetic hope with which all nations had watched the inaugurative meeting of the institution designed to minimise the chances of war, and to substitute friendly adjustment for the arbitrament of the sword.

Australia, like other nations, was deeply concerned in all that primarily affected the purpose of the League. But Australia, also, like other nations, had certain direct and immediate interests which she was entitled to consider, to protect and to advance. It was a source of gratification to him that his efforts for the furtherance of Australia's interest did not constitute any hostility to, or impairment of, the fundamental principles or purpose of the League.

There were two matters of outstanding concern to Australia, which, when he left for Geneva, it was thought highly probable would form the subject of discussion, viz. what was known as the Racial Equality Amendment and the Mandate for the late German possessions in the Pacific.

Racial Equality – Japan.

At the Peace Conference, the representative of the neighbour and ally, Japan, had submitted an amendment to the Covenant, which the Japanese interpreted as a recognition of the equality of all races, but which Mr. Hughes (the Prime Minister) regarded as constituting an impairment of Australia's national policy. The amendment had been carried by a substantial majority (11 to 6); but President Wilson, who was in the chair, held that as it was a matter of internal or domestic policy, the amendment could not become operative in the absence of unanimity. The Japanese delegate then intimated that Japan could not accept that decision as final, but would revive the question at a later time, when she considered it opportune to do so. This attitude was entirely frank, and to it no possible exception could be taken. In view of that declaration there had been every reason to anticipate that Japan would raise the question at Geneva, in which case he (Senator Millen) could have taken up no other stand than that adopted by the Prime Minister on the earlier occasion, and to have placed before the Assembly the reasons which made it impossible for Australia to consent willingly to any reversal of its present policy. However, the necessity did not arise. Viscount Ishii had announced in the Assembly that, while maintaining the justice and reasonableness of its cause, Japan refrained from making any concrete proposal as to the question of racial equality, but would patiently bide the time until the opportune moment should present itself. This action on the part of Japan had brought him (Senator Millen) considerable relief, as he was under the impression that if the Assembly had been called upon to record a vote, its decision would have followed that of the Peace Conference. As it was, an opportunity was afforded for further consideration of the matter, an opportunity that, it might be assumed, would not be lost sight of by those charged with the responsibility of discussing the renewal of the Anglo-Japanese Alliance.

Mandate for Pacific Islands.

After sketching the history of the Mandate (*vide* summary of debate on New Guinea Act in JOURNAL, Vol. II., No. 1, page 118, and Peace Treaty Resolution, Vol. I., No. 1, page 124) Senator Millen said that Japan had raised certain objections which had resulted in the withholding of the Mandate to Australia, as also to Japan and New Zealand. The objection was not to the issue of the Mandate or to the country nominated as Mandatory, but to the conditions to be attached to the Mandate itself. In other words, her interpretation of Article 22 was at variance with that of the majority of her associates on the Council. This difference was upon a fundamental point, and was such that if the Japanese view had been maintained it would have been impossible for Australia to accept the Mandate. Clause 5, of Article 22, dealing with Mandates of the "B" class required that the Mandatory should administer the territory "under conditions which will guarantee freedom of conscience or religion, subject only to the maintenance of public order and morals, the prohibition of abuses such as the slave trade, the arms traffic and the liquor traffic, and the prevention of the establishment of fortifications or military and naval bases and of military training of the natives for other than police purposes and the defence of territory, and will also secure equal opportunities for the trade and commerce of other members of the League."

It would be noted that that clause stipulated four conditions in the interests of the indigenous population, and, in addition, conferred a right or privilege upon all members of the League, that of equal trading opportunities. The next clause, covering " C " Mandates, read : —

"There are territories, such as South-West Africa, and certain of the South Pacific Islands, which, owing to the sparseness of their population, or their small size, or their remoteness from the centres of civilisation, or their geographical contiguity to the territory of the Mandatory, and other circumstances, can be best administered under the laws of the Mandatory as integral portions of its territory, subject to the safeguards above-mentioned in the interests of the indigenous population."

The Japanese held that the words in paragraph 6, " subject to the safeguards above-mentioned in the interests of the indigenous population," included not only the four conditions, but also the condition as to equal trading opportunities for all League members. The contrary view was that the words in paragraph 6 referred only to the four prohibitions, and could not be held to include the equal commercial opportunities secured under "B" Mandate to all League members, and further, that the words " administered under the laws of the Mandatory as integral portions of its territory," were fatal to such an interpretation. A prolonged interchange of views had taken place between the British Government and Japan, but no approach to an agreement had been made at the time of his (Senator Millen's) arrival in London, some eighteen months after the date of the letter announcing the allotment of the Mandates.

In order to make clearly understood the position which existed at Geneva, he might state that France had disclosed that she was in agreement with Japan in claiming equal trade opportunities for all members of the League, and while a Geneva a Note from the American Government to the British Government had been published in a similar strain. It would be clearly seen that the position had not been without difficulty.

He wished also to refer to an impression which had existed in certain quarters that the granting of the Mandate was the prerogative of the Assembly and not that of either the Allies or the Council. He would not attempt to go into the somewhat involved legal argument connected with the consideration of this point. Those who wished to do so were directed to a memorandum prepared by M. Hymans and adopted by the Council. The claim that authority rested with the League was based upon paragraph 8 of Article 22, which read : —

"The degree of authority, control, or administration to be exercised by the Mandatory shall, if not previously agreed upon by the members of the League, be explicitly defined in each case by the Council."

It was urged that the phrase " members of the League " could only mean the Assembly, as that was the only body in which all members of the League were represented.

Supporting the opposite view was the clause of the Peace Treaty itself in which Germany expressly surrendered to the " principal Allied and Associated Powers " all her right and interest in her overseas possessions. These Powers claimed the right of selecting the Mandatories, which right, indeed, they had already exercised. It was contended further that the clause he had just read conferred upon the Council, and not upon the Assembly, the right to determine the conditions attaching to each particular Mandate, and that the duty of the Assembly consisted in seeing that the Mandates, when issued, were properly observed by the Mandatories. This latter view was acted upon, although considerable opposition to it was manifested both in the Assembly and the Committee appointed to deal with Mandates generally. It would thus be seen that in accordance with this view the issue of the Mandate depended upon an agreement amongst the members of the Council and not upon the decisions of the Assembly. Japan's interpretation of paragraph 6 of Article 22 was the stumbling-block to such agreement.

Mr. Balfour, as Britain's principal and very distinguished delegate, had been unceasing in his efforts to arrive at an understanding with the representatives of Japan and had manifested at all times a very keen desire to further Australia's interests by securing the Mandate in the form claimed by Australia. Ultimately Japan had consented to the issue of the Mandate in the form desired by Australia, accompanying this consent with an intimation that she would, if she thought fit, ask for a revision at some later date. This declaration, Senator Millen submitted, did not in any way impair the validity of the Mandate. It would have been competent for Japan to have asked for a revision even had no declaration been made, whilst the consent of Australia would certainly be necessary before any alteration could be permitted.

Although not directly relating to the proceedings at Geneva he might say a word as to the American Note relative to Mandates which had formed the subject of recent cables

in the Press. The Note enunciated certain principles which,
if interpreted literally, applied also to those islands in respect
of which Australia had obtained its Mandate. As, however,
America appeared to be chiefly concerned regarding Yap
and Mesopotamia, he did not anticipate any results from this
expression of American views likely prejudicially to affect the
Mandate with which Australia was now vested.

League Finances.

The expenditure of the League, in his opinion, was on
an outrageously high scale, while supervision or control was
practically non-existent. The Budget for the thirteen months
ended June, 1920, was £176,807; for the following six months
£500,000 ; and for the present calendar year £1,062,500. It
was not difficult to foresee that a £2,000,000 Budget would be
asked for in the near future. Salaries and expenses were on
a lavish scale. The Secretary-General received £4,000 per
annum, plus £6,000 entertainment allowance, plus a house,
which, with exemptions from income-tax, brought the total
emoluments into the neighbourhood of £13,000. Other salaries
were quite in proportion, and the general expenditure
corresponded. The prospect of remedying this state of affairs
did not seem bright.

The Secretariat was a permanent body, while the Assembly,
to which it was theoretically responsible, met only once a year
for a month or so, and would of a certainty present each year
a changed personnel. It was, therefore, doubtful if either
effective or continuous supervision could be expected unless
some radical changes in the system were brought about.

This matter was of special importance to Australia,
because she was called upon to pay a most unfair proportion
of the League's expenditure. This arose from the fact that
the Covenant distributed the cost of the League among its
members according to the scheme of distribution employed
by the Postal Union. Under that scheme Australia was
required to pay the same amount as Great Britain and France,
and much more than many countries of bigger population and
trade. He had made a very persistent effort to secure some
immediate amelioration in this direction, and at the eleventh
hour it had been decided to authorise the preparation of a
more equitable scheme to be presented to the next Assembly.

Disappointment with League.

He had come away from the Assembly a little disappointed,
a little depressed. He hoped that the statement would not
be interpreted as indicating a want of sympathy with the

object for which the League was created. There was no justification for such an interpretation. He considered it the duty of every individual, as of every nation, to strive to make the League an effective instrument for the discharge of the high purpose for which it had been designed. He earnestly wished that he could tell Australia that he had the most complete confidence in the League and its future—that he could tell Australia that with perfect safety it could beat its swords into ploughshares and its spears into pruning-hooks. But he could not, and he conceived it to be his duty to say so plainly and definitely. "Let us," said Senator Millen, "work for the strengthening of the ideals which the League represents; meanwhile let us not be lulled into the sleep of false security, nor neglect those precautions which our circumstances require and which prudence suggests."

DEFENCE BILL.

(Military Training, etc.)

A Bill was introduced in the Senate on 7th April to amend the Defence Act 1903-1918 in connection with a new scheme of training for Senior Cadets and Citizen Forces, and also to provide for the application of the British Army Act in time of peace.

The organisation of the proposed Army under the new scheme was outlined by the Minister of Defence in the Senate on 17th September last. (*Vide* summary of Defence Policy in JOURNAL, Vol. II., No. 1, page 132.)

The main provisions of the measure relating to the new scheme of training for Cadets and Citizen Forces are as follow :—

All male inhabitants of Australia who have resided therein for six months, and are British subjects, are liable to be trained each year ending 30th June as follows :—

    (A) Junior Cadets (from 12 to 14 years of age), 90 hours ;

    (B) Senior Cadets (14 to 18 years), such drills as are prescribed, but so that the total hours of training shall not be less than 64 or more than 128 hours ;

    (C) Citizen Forces (18 to 25 years), sixteen whole-day drills or their equivalent of which not less than eight shall be whole days in ships or in camps of continuous training ;

    (D) Citizen Forces (25 to 26 years) unless otherwise directed by the Governor-General, the training is limited in each year to one muster parade or one registration.

Provided that, in the case of those allotted to the Naval Forces and Air Force and those attached to the Artillery and Engineer arms of the Military Forces and to units of the Army Service Corps, Army Medical Corps, Army Veterinary Corps and Army Ordnance Corps allotted to those arms, the training is twenty-five whole-day drills or their equivalent of which not less than seventeen are whole days in ships or in camps of continuous training.

A whole-day drill for the Citizen Forces is not less than six hours. Two half-day drills, each of not less than three hours, or four night drills each of not less than one hour and a half, are deemed to be equivalent to one whole-day drill.

In the case of Senior Cadets who reside at a distance exceeding two miles from the place of training, attendance for a less number of hours may be allowed to count for the full duration of drills, and the prescribed officers may grant leave of absence from the training required when the conditions of weather, by reason of excessive rain or heat, would render attendance a hardship, and equivalent attendance may be required in lieu thereof.

The regulations may prescribe that attendance at such drills shall be compulsory.

The Defence Act 1903-1918 already provides for payment during training. A penalty of £100 is prescribed in respect of prevention or attempted prevention by employers, or penalisation or prejudice in employment either by reduction of wages or dismissal. Parents and guardians are similarly liable.

DEBATE IN THE SENATE.

The Minister for Defence (Senator the Hon. G. F. Pearce), on 13th April, in moving the Second Reading, said that he placed the matters with which the measure dealt under the following headings : —First of all there was the interpretation of the new scheme of training for Senior Cadets and Citizen Forces, naval and military. Secondly, there was a proposal to make the Military Forces subject to the British Army Act in time of peace as well as, which was already provided, in time of war. He directed attention to the fact that the Army Act dealt practically entirely with disciplinary matters. In that respect, it was unlike the Commonwealth Defence Act, which dealt with the question of the universal training of the Citizen Forces and a variety of other subjects. There were minor amendments of the existing Act proposed in the Bill which the experience of the War had shown to be necessary. The addition of some new provisions had been rendered necessary by the adoption of a new system of training, and there were certain amendments of the existing law proposed which were consequent upon the adoption of the divisional system of organisation.

Under the Bill, it was proposed, while retaining the maximum hours of training provided for, to alter the provisions in such a way as to give latitude to meet the convenience of the Senior Cadets. As the result of experience, night drills for Senior Cadets were being practically all cut out, and half-day and day parades substituted. The curriculum of training was also being altered, and it was proposed that in the earlier years the training of the Senior Cadets should consist in the main of the encouragement of athletics, physical training, and organised games. The training was aimed rather at developing the physical and moral qualities of the Cadets, and it was only in the last year of Senior Cadet training that it became largely of a military character.

Application of Army Act.

Senator Pearce, continuing, said that at first blush he frankly confessed he had not liked the proposal of the application of the British Army Act to the Citizen Forces in time of peace. It had seemed to him that they should be able to embody, either in the Commonwealth Act, or regulations framed under it, all the provisions they wished to apply to the Australian Forces. He had considered the question from a critical point of view as to whether there would be any disadvantage to the control of their Forces or to the individuals who composed them from the proposal, and he had come to the conclusion that there would not. First of all, by the proposal, they did not give to the Imperial Legislature any control over the Australian Forces. The Commonwealth still retained control of them. The application of the Army Act would be by an Act of their own Legislature, and every amendment of the Army Act, when it had been communicated to them, would be reviewed to see whether or not it was applicable to the Australian Forces. At present the Army Act applied to their Forces only in so far as it was not inconsistent with the Commonwealth Defence Act or regulations made thereunder. It would not in any case override any of the provisions of the Commonwealth Defence Act as it then stood or as it would be amended by the passing of the Bill, nor would it override any regulation made under their legislation. As to the advantages of the proposal, Senator Pearce pointed out that under their existing law the Army Act applied to their Forces automatically in time of war. The reason for that was obvious. If the troops of the various portions of the Empire were in time of war called upon to operate together, it was clear that, so far as possible, the Act which laid down disciplinary powers in respect of the Army as a whole should be uniform.

Coming to the application of the Army Act to their Forces so far as its provisions were not inconsistent with the Commonwealth Defence Act or regulations, Senator Pearce said there was a striking illustration which would go to show that by the procedure proposed they did not give up their legislative power or any power that they then had to say what would happen to their troops even when they went to war. Under the Army Act the penalty for desertion in time of war was death. Under their Defence Act desertion to the enemy was punishable by death. But if a soldier merely deserted the Australian Army to the rear the penalty was not death, but such less penalty as might be decided by the proper authorities.

The other provisions were of a machinery character, although some of them were more or less important. Provision had been made, for instance, enabling service abroad, in certain circumstances, to be calculated for the purposes of promotion in lieu of examination. It was also provided that graduates of the Commonwealth Military College should be prevented from resigning their commissions during the first eight years of their service as officers, except in certain circumstances approved by the Minister. The Commonwealth practically gave the graduate of the Military College a university education free, and maintained him during the time he was receiving that education. It was only right, seeing that the college had been established for a specific purpose, and that such education was a gift from the nation, that the nation should expect and obtain a return from the graduate.

Senator the Hon. A. Gardiner (Labour, *N.S.W.*) questioned the success of the system of compulsory military training and suggested that the results be inquired into by the departmental experts. In his opinion it would be better to have an efficient skeleton army so that, in case of war, they would have an adequate number of officers and men well trained and capable of handling the others who would ultimately come in. The expenditure would be less, and the results more satisfactory. By endeavouring to train a large number they were failing to efficiently train even a small section of the eligible men in the Commonwealth. He realised that some training for the defence of Australia was essential. But there was another thing which was equally essential, especially in a Democracy like their own, that they did not make that training repugnant to the people.

He regretted that the Bill contained so much of the military method. It was all compulsion from beginning to end. It all went towards strengthening the power of the military authority.

Senator Elliott* (*Victoria*), speaking on 21st April, said that one of the greatest objections to the measure was the attempt to import into their Defence legislation the whole

---

* Brigadier-General H. E. Elliott, C.B., C.M.G., D.S.O., D.C.M., served with the Australian Imperial Forces in Gallipoli, Egypt, and France. He also served in the South African War, when he won the D.C.M.

of the Army Act which related to the British Standing Army and to make it applicable, without the Senate or Parliament having a chance to discuss it, to their Citizen Force, a Force which absolutely differed from the regular British Army. The British Army was recruited from men who volunteered, men who were presumed to know what were the conditions of the Service they entered, and who accepted with their eyes open the yoke of militarism; but in Australia, on the other hand, every man, irrespective of his position or class, was compelled to submit to military discipline for a certain period. The Bill provided that not only should the existing legislation of the British Parliament on the subject be adopted, but it went further by insuring that every future amendment and regulation made under the Act should be adopted by the Commonwealth. It was quite true that these regulations were to be subject to review, but who was going to keep watch? What would happen in Australia was that any regulation that did not suit Headquarters would be brought under the notice of Ministers, and steps would be taken to disallow it; while, on the other hand, if new regulations authorised by the British Parliament increased the power, already too great, which administrative Headquarters wielded in the Commonwealth, they would hear nothing about the matter until, perhaps, some scandal caused them to realise that they had been landed in a difficulty. It was wrong in principle to introduce in the Commonwealth Parliament, which had the widest of self-governing powers, legislation to allow any other Parliament to make laws for them in matters of that kind.

Senator Pratten (*N.S.W.*) said it would be extremely advantageous if the eight or nine Senators who had served Australia at the Front during the late War were to give the Senate the benefit of their experiences in relation to the measure. He agreed with Senator Elliott and Senator Foster that they should hesitate before agreeing to the continued imposition upon the people of Australia of that militarism which was typified in the War, and what went on during the War.

Senator Drake-Brockman* (*W.A.*) said that as one of those who had served in the Australian Imperial Force he had had an opportunity of appreciating the merits of the British Army Act, and so far as he knew members of the Australian Imperial Force had not suffered by reason of the Act that they were administered under it. Ex-soldiers there that afternoon had said clearly and distinctly that the form of trial used on active service for soldiers was the fairest form

---

* Brigadier-General E. A. Drake-Brockman, C.B., C.M.G., D.S.O., served with the A.I.F. in Gallipoli, Egypt, and France.

of trial that existed under any system in the world. With that he entirely agreed. He had had some little experience in the Courts of Law in at least two States of Australia, and, moreover, he had appeared in several capacities in connection with courts-martial and had presided over many of them. Therefore he had no hesitation in giving his opinion in definite terms. The Act, administered by conscientious and capable officers, was such a perfect document, and of such perfect draftsmanship, that it was just as applicable to the Citizen Forces of Australia in time of peace as it was to the Forces of Australia, or of the Empire, in time of war.

The Minister for Defence, in reply to criticism of the proposed application of the British Army Act, pointed out that if they did not train their officers under one disciplinary code in time of peace, on the outbreak of war officers had to carry out certain disciplinary measures under a system with which they were unfamiliar. That was an essential point to be considered. They were bound to apply the Army Act in time of war. Parliament had recognised that, and in the Defence Act had provided that when the Australian Forces go to war they must automatically come under the British Army Act.

Senator Foster (*Tas.*) : " Does the Minister for Defence maintain that the same disciplinary measures are required in Australia in times of peace ? "

The Minister for Defence : " No ; nor is that intended." Any punishment laid down in the British Army Act which was in excess of what was provided in the Australian Act could not be imposed. That provision would operate in time of war as well as in time of peace. He had mentioned that under the Army Act desertion was punishable by death, and that during the War, because that provision was inconsistent with the Australian Act, or was a punishment in excess of what they had provided, no Australian soldier was punished by death for desertion.

The British Army Act applied to the Regular Army and also to the British Territorial Army, which was a volunteer citizen force, and always had applied to the Volunteer Forces of Great Britain. By a clause which had been embodied in the amending Bill the Citizen Forces in their capacity as citizens would not be dealt with under the Army Act, but under the Commonwealth Defence Act. It was only when the Forces go into camp to train for war that the British Army Act would operate as far as the disciplinary code was concerned.

Dealing with a question raised by Senator Elliott, the Minister for Defence said that if Senator Elliott's intention were given effect to they would exclude from appointment to commissions, except by going through the ranks, and under going subsequent examination for promotion step by step, any Australian who had not been a member of the Citizen Forces before the outbreak of the War, although he might have served in the Australian Imperial Force during the War. It would also exclude all Australians who had served with the British Forces and obtained commissions during the War—as well as Canadians, New Zealanders, and South Africans who had rendered similar service—and who subsequent to the War took up their residence in Australia. A clause in the Bill would give the Governor-General power to grant commissions in the Citizen Forces to such men. The provision in the Bill was intended to give a wide field of choice, and, above all, to give the Commonwealth the opportunity of utilising the experience of men, no matter where they came from, and particularly of those men who had won their commissions in the field. Another clause in the Bill provided that where a Citizen Force officer had had war experience he would have preference over one who had not.

Turning to the criticism by Senator Pratten as to the imposition of militarism, the Minister declared that the Bill did not impose militarism. He sometimes rubbed his eyes when he saw the term " militarism " applied to Australia, the least military of all the nations, and one of the few that did not possess a standing army. Citizen defence was the very antithesis of militarism. The Bill was to assist in perfecting their Citizen Forces. It did not add a single permanent soldier to their Forces. It was not an Act that brought militarism, but the way it was administered. Their Permanent Forces numbered altogether about 2,000, as compared with 70,000 to 80,000 in their Citizen Forces, and were, therefore, insignificant.

The Bill was read a second time on 21st April.

In Committee—Army Act.

During consideration in Committee,

The Minister for Defence said that the Government recognised that there was room for two opinions as to the wisdom or otherwise of applying the British Army Act in time of peace. Australia was the only part of the British Empire that did not apply the Army Act to the Defence Forces in peace time. All those Dominions which applied it did so with certain qualifications, as was proposed in the measure under discussion.

Amendment.

The clause providing for the application of the Army Act in time of peace was abandoned in Committee, leaving the

N

provision for its application in time of war as it originally stood in the Defence Act, *i.e.*, so far as the Army Act is not inconsistent with the Commonwealth Defence Act. Consequential and minor amendments were made.

The Bill was read a third time in the Senate on 12th May. Progress in the House of Representatives will be reported in the next issue of the JOURNAL.

AIR DEFENCE BILL.

This Bill was introduced in the Senate on 6th April. It provides for the constitution by the Governor-General of an Air Council and a Board of Administration to be called the Air Board, and other matters relating to Air Defence. It provides also for the application of certain parts of the Commonwealth Defence Act, and the British Air Force Act, at all times, except so far as it is inconsistent with the Commonwealth Act.

DEBATE IN THE SENATE.

The Minister for Defence (Senator the Hon. G. F. Pearce) on 8th April, moving the Second Reading, said that earlier in the Session they had dealt with another phase of the subject having reference to the use of the air for commercial purposes by the passing of the Air Navigation Act (*vide* JOURNAL Vol. II., No. 2, page 368). That measure had been proclaimed and was then coming into operation. As the Air Force would be used for both the Navy and Army, the constitution of the Force must provide for both Services. In that respect the Commonwealth was following the British practice. It had been deemed inadvisable that a new Portfolio should be created for the administration of the Air Force, and it would, therefore be under the direction of the Minister for Defence.

In order that the Navy might have a voice in the control and direction of the Air Force, an Air Council had been constituted, of which the Minister for Defence was President There would be on the Council a naval member nominated by the Minister for the Navy, a military member nominated by the Minister for Defence, two technical members, and, in addition, the Controller of Civil Aviation, who would have control of the civil aviation vote, in order that civil aviation might be co-ordinated in such a way as to enable them to utilise commercial aeroplanes for naval and military purposes should war come.

For the purpose of administration they had an Air Board which would consist entirely of technical personnel. With the exception of the finance member, its members would all be flying officers.

The Air Force, on the military side, would be partly permanent, and partly composed of the Citizen Forces. There would be a permanent trained nucleus, and then a certain number of the Citizen Forces liable for training under the Defence Act would be allotted to the Air Force and do their training in that branch of the Service.

The new unit would be very technical in its character, and so they had provided for the admission of a certain number of boys into the permanent section, both naval and military. A boy so admitted would really become apprenticed to a technical trade.

Provision would be made for the attachment of naval and military officers to the Air Force for a limited period, these officers afterwards returning to their own Services. They had a Naval College and a Military College, and it was proposed that a certain number of graduates from each college should be allotted to the Air Force. It would also be necessary to have officers attached to the staff of the Chief of the General Staff in the Army, and to the First Naval Member of the Naval Board, in order to combine the operations of the Air Forces with the other branches. It was hoped by the training of these young Australians that just as they then had in the Army the possibility of filling the positions from the Inspector-General right down with Australians trained and educated in Australia, so they should be able—as they were starting on the ground-work—to train an air staff of young Australians who would be able to advise their respective chiefs in the Navy and Army as to the best means of co-operating.

The aircraft depôt, flying training school, and aeroplane squadrons would be formed, in the first place, with aircraft equipment received from the Imperial Government as a gift. The equipment for the flying-boat and seaplane squadrons would have to be imported from England, and for that purpose it was proposed to order twelve seaplanes and nine flying-boats.

The expenditure to begin with was to be £500,000.

Senator the Hon. A. Gardiner (Labour, *N.S.W.*) said that instead of spending £500,000 at the beginning on the proposed Air Service, he would rather spend the money in the manufacture of engines for aeroplanes and other military requirements. Let them begin at the right end by saying that they would have none of these elaborate preparations for the creation of another huge department to train men to do certain things. To his mind, the whole of their military training was more ostentatious than the real thing. Could it be said that the ability to "right turn" and move in column

N 2

represented the correct training of their men for war ? Was it not their ability to make boots, to turn out mechanics, and to handle the machinery for the rapid manufacture of munitions of war ? If the Minister had announced that it was the intention of the Government to establish plants within the next twelve months for the manufacture of machinery which could produce engines of various descriptions with inter-changeable parts, the Government would have been doing more for the real protection of Australia than they would be by establishing an Air Force, however it was created.

Establishment.

The Minister for Defence, speaking on 22nd April, said that the total number of machines held by the Air Board was 151. Under the Bill it was proposed to establish one flying training school, one aircraft depôt, and four squadrons, two of which would be permanent, and two citizen squadrons ; also one flying-boat squadron and a seaplane squadron with the Navy. The aeroplane squadrons would be equipped with twelve machines each, and the seaplane and flying-boat squadrons with six machines each. The reserve considered necessary was 50 per cent. of the total establishment of the unit. The personnel proposed was 160 officers and 1,500 other ranks; £500,000 had been voted for the scheme for that financial year. He thought that the establishment would cost about £600,000 in a normal financial year.

Amendment.

The provision in the Bill applying the British Air Force Act at all times so far as not inconsistent with the Australian Act and subject to such modifications and adaptations as are prescribed, was amended so as to provide for the application of the British Act only while the Australian Air Forces are on active service.

The Debate in the House of Representatives will be summarised in the next issue of the JOURNAL.

TRADE WITH GERMANY.*

In reply to a question by the Hon. Austin Chapman in the House of Representatives on 7th April, the Prime Minister (the Right Hon. W. M. Hughes) stated that there was nothing to prevent wool or any other Australian commodity being sold to Germany. The general question of resuming trade with Germany had been under consideration by the Government, and would be discussed at an early date.

* For position in regard to trade with Germany vide JOURNAL Vol. II., No. 2, footnote page 373.

NEW ZEALAND.

The following summary deals with the Special Session of Parliament, which was held (as stated in Vol. II., No. 1, at page 403, of this JOURNAL) for the purpose of considering the attendance of the Prime Minister at the Imperial Conference, held in June, and to grant supplies. Parliament met on the 10th March and was prorogued on 24th March. The Prime Minister announced that there would be a further Session later in the year after the close of the Imperial Conference.

GOVERNOR-GENERAL'S SPEECH.

(Conference of Prime Ministers.)

The Speech of the Governor-General, Lord Jellicoe, was delivered in the Legislative Council on 10th March, 1921.

Lord Jellicoe, in addressing Parliament for the first time since his assumption of office, said that, during the visits which he had paid to the principal towns and some of the country districts of the Dominion, he had been deeply impressed by the spirit of loyalty to the Crown which was so greatly in evidence, and by the cordial welcome extended to him as His Majesty's Representative.

Referring to the Imperial Conference, Lord Jellicoe said : " My Ministers believe that honourable Members of both branches of the Legislature recognise the gravity of the matters which must be considered at this Imperial Conference, and that it is essential that the Prime Ministers of the self-governing Dominions should take personal part in the discussion and determination of questions which involve the relations of the latter to each other, and also the relations of the British Commonwealth as a whole with the other nations of the world, so that there may be no question as to the continued cohesion of the Empire itself."

CONFERENCE OF PRIME MINISTERS OF THE EMPIRE.

Debate on Address: Constitutional Question: Imperial Federation: Defence and Foreign Affairs: The Pacific: Anglo-Japanese Alliance: League of Nations: Mandates: Secret Diplomacy: Reduction of Armaments, etc.)

Address in Reply.

The Address in Reply to the Governor-General's Speech was moved on the 14th March by Mr. K. S. Williams (Reform,

Bay of Plenty) and was debated on the 14th, 15th, 16th and 17th March.   In the course of the debate two amendments were moved, one by the Leader of the Opposition (Mr. T. M. Wilford) and the other by Mr. H. E. Holland (Labour, *Buller*), both of which were accepted as "no-confidence" Motions and were defeated.   Mr. Wilford's Motion took the form of a protest against the prorogation of Parliament during the Prime Minister's absence from the Dominion caused by his attending the Imperial Conference, and Mr. Holland's amendment, which is quoted *in extenso* on page 648 hereof, began with a similar protest and dealt also with the questions of reduction of armaments, secret diplomacy, the granting of self-determination to the people of Ireland, India, and Egypt, and concluded with a protest against the appointment during the Prime Minister's absence of an Acting Prime Minister not a Member of the House of Representatives.

DEBATE IN HOUSE OF REPRESENTATIVES.

The Imperial Conference.

On 14th March,

Mr. K. S. Williams (Reform, *Bay of Plenty*), in moving the Address in Reply, said that he knew that the Prime Minister would prefer to stay in New Zealand at that juncture, and had done his best to make other arrangements ; but the invitation had been made so pressing that he should attend in person, that he (Mr. Williams) did not think the Prime Minister could very well refuse it.

Supremacy on the Seas.

He hoped that the Ministers who met in Conference at Home would see that Britain was kept supreme upon the seas.   They heard rumours of what other countries were prepared to do in the way of naval construction, and they should look on money spent in that way as an insurance fund against the possibility of such a world-war descending upon them again.

Trade within the Empire.

They wanted to see better facilities for trading between the Mother Country and the Dominions, and between each of the Dominions—cheaper freight, and, if necessary, preferential tariff, so that goods manufactured in the Old Country and in the Dominions could be freighted from one part of the Empire to another, to the benefit of the people residing in them. In the past the British manufacturer had seemed to take the view that they in the Dominions should use the articles he made instead of trying to discover what they wanted and had so lost a great deal of trade, which had gone into the hands of more discerning competitors in other countries. He hoped the Prime Minister would make a note of that, and so interest the British manufacturer in trying to study what the Dominions wanted. He hoped the question of using the man-power and the capital of the Empire within the Empire would be discussed. In the past large sums of money had been spent in countries not belonging to the Empire. If they could get Empire money used within the Empire to develop it and could get their own kith and kin to come out to New Zealand to help with that development, in a very few years they should earn a place for the nation more important than that which they held at that time.

Mr. J. Craigie (Independent Liberal, *Timaru*), in seconding the Address, said he supposed it was the first time in the Parliament of New Zealand that a Member outside the Government had been asked to do so. Continuing, he said : " Our great Empire I consider a family of independent, self-governing nations, and the time has passed when Members of the House of Commons . . . can determine the fortunes of the British Empire as a whole. It is only right, therefore, that we should be represented on the great Conference that is to determine the affairs of the whole of the Empire." He considered that there should be an unwritten law that no Member should be allowed to hold office in the Imperial Cabinet until he had seen the different overseas Dominions, to get an insight into their conditions and the aspirations of their people.

. Referring to the activity of the United States in naval construction, Mr. Craigie said that they did not begrudge America her prospective great navy. He supposed they would rather see her with a great navy than any other nation in the world, outside their own. He hoped that any differences between themselves and the American Republic would be settled by peaceful arbitration.

Pacific Question.

As regarded the Anglo-Japanese Alliance, as far as he knew Japan had fulfilled her obligations to the very letter. They could not, however, disguise the fact that Japan was a country little larger in area than New Zealand, and that there were sixty millions of people penned up in that little island. A year's increase in her population was equal to the whole population of New Zealand. They must have room for expansion ;

they were a virile, clever and initiative race ; and he hoped that any expansion would be in the direction of north-eastern Asia and within their own waters. They were their (New Zealand's) neighbours in the Pacific, and so was America, and he did hope that if there was going to be rivalry it would be friendly rivalry, and that they should remain good friends with America and Japan. He was sure that the British Government of India had been beneficial, and they trusted that good relations would continue. " But the position is a delicate one," said Mr. Craigie. " They are our subjects, and we want to keep our race pure. These are matters which will come before the Conference, and no one will deny that they are delicate and embarrassing subjects to handle."

Mr. Craigie then made reference to the shipping question and the marketing of New Zealand products, saying they required a national service to take their produce Home. In his concluding remarks Mr. Craigie said that the day was past when they believed in the divine right of kings, and though they still had a monarchy they were in reality a Crown republic, and speaking of the National Anthem said : " It is not sung for the King as an individual, but for the King as the symbol of our Constitution. When ' God Save the King ' is sung it is sung as a prayer for our Empire."

Protest Against Prorogation.

Mr. T. M. Wilford (Leader of the Opposition) said that he proposed to move an amendment to the Address which was divided into two parts, the first part being : " That this House is of opinion that the Dominion should be adequately represented at the Imperial Conference." There was no possible doubt on his side of the House that the country should be represented at the Imperial Conference. It was the second part of the amendment with which he proposed to deal—" but in view of the grave issues before the country affecting every Department of State, and important questions waiting to be dealt with, it records its emphatic protest against the holding up of the country's business by the prorogation of Parliament beyond the usual time."

Mr. Wilford made reference to the national debt of the country, which he said was a matter of grave concern. When they realised that added to the public debt, which that day was £201,000,000 odd, they had also got £150,000,000 worth of mortgages running, it showed that against the private wealth of the country, which according to the Prime Minister's own statement had reached the colossal sum of £500,000,000, there was already a debt of £351,000,000. He then proceeded to criticise the financial administration of the Government generally, and gave a list of the legislation required. Continuing, he said : "Why cannot the Prime Minister go to the Imperial Conference representing this country as it should be represented, attending to Imperial problems that are of vital interest to this Dominion, but allowing the Session to go on in June so that the various questions to which I have referred may be tackled?"

Constitutional Theories Outgrown.

The Minister of Internal Affairs (Hon. W. Downie Stewart) emphasised the tremendous possibilities that devolved on the Prime Minister in going Home to the Conference. It was originally intended that the big question of the Constitutional relations of the different parts of the Empire should be dealt with at the 1922 Conference, but all indications pointed to the fact that that question could not be excluded at the coming Conference, as it was involved in the consideration of all other questions that had been set down for discussion. If this was true, then it was of outstanding importance that the Prime Minister should be present at it. Nobody could state definitely what the status of the Dominion was. One difficulty that was emerging was that during the War the Dominions had attained, it was said, an equality of status with England, and their Constitutional theories had been outgrown and were really inadequate for the present position. The problem was to reconcile the new status of the Dominions with the continued existence of the Empire and yet give full scope to the desire for autonomy which the self-governing Dominions possessed. The position was well summed up by Sir James Allen, in speaking at the Imperial Institute,* when he pointed out that the present Imperial Conference had become too ephemeral a body for the purpose of dealing with great policy questions, every one of which was constantly changing in outlook, and any one of which might give rise to a conflict of opinion between different parts of the Empire at any time. What was apparently the trend of opinion, said Mr. Downie Stewart, was that some method of continuous consultation must be evolved. The earlier enthusiasts were inclined to argue for a straight-out solution of the difficulty by the creation of an Imperial Parliament ; but more recently the tendencies seemed to indicate that some intermediate stage would have to be adopted, such as setting up an Imperial Council or Imperial Executive for the purpose of trying to

---

* The reference is apparently to an address given by Sir James Allen, High Commissioner for New Zealand, at the Royal Colonial Institute, on 2nd November, 1920, on the subject of "The Mandate for Western Samoa."

secure continuous co-operation and consultation between the different parts of the Empire. Even that was only touching the fringe of the problem, and General Smuts in South Africa had pointed out that if they did set up an Imperial Executive or Council, they were faced immediately with the question — assuming that Council arrived at a decision—Must it be a unanimous decision, or would they coerce a minority? Speaking on the point as to how far the Prime Minister should declare himself before leaving for the Conference, Mr. Downie Stewart said that his view was that, whilst they might ask the Prime Minister to declare in general outline his view of the situation, it would be unfair and unwise to ask him to give in any detail his views on questions which must arise, such as the Anglo-Japanese Alliance. Those practical problems depended for their solution on the very latest opinions derived from the most reliable sources of information, and could only be gathered by the delegates at the Conference itself. He hoped the House would agree with great unanimity to adopt the Address and that they should be able to send the Prime Minister to England with the feeling that he had practically the unanimous support of the people of the Dominion in the great task he had to undertake.

Mr. G. W. Forbes (Liberal, *Hurunui*) considered that the position of the country was such that it was absolutely necessary that Parliament should hold its Session at the proper time. At the same time he wished to see the Dominion properly represented at the Conference. He thought the Prime Minister would agree with him in saying that they ought to arrange a better method of doing business than the present, with the frequent Conferences taking away the Prime Minister from the Dominion, who was the busiest man in the country, but it was required of him under present conditions that he should be absent for many months every year or every other year. That was not a workable system of government. It was almost unthinkable that a country could be run for six months without a Prime Minister. He hoped there would be an effort to fix up more workable machinery. There was a suggestion made at one time that they should have a responsible Minister in London, and Sir James Allen had been mentioned, but that proposal was not persevered with.

The Federal View.

Mr. A. S. Malcolm (Reform, *Clutha*) said the present Session was a curious commentary on their conduct of Imperial affairs, which had apparently not been considered of sufficient importance in past years to justify the giving up of a day or two to discussion of those affairs in that House; and yet now it was apparently considered that they were of sufficient importance to justify the postponement of all legislation and the absence of the Prime Minister for four or five months. He, at any rate, was most anxious that everything possible should be done to advance Imperial interests. Apparently it had been thought inadvisable to have any other representative than the Prime Minister. Objections, for instance, had been raised to representation by the High Commissioner—objections which he thought were unsound. The High Commissioner, it was true, was the servant of the Government, but they must remember that the Imperial Conference had no Constitution, and that it was open to New Zealand to send to that Conference as its representative any person it liked.

The Prime Minister (the Right Hon. W. F. Massey): " No, it is not."

Mr. Malcolm : " It is, for this reason : that the Imperial Conference itself is an irresponsible body."

In answer to an interjection by an hon. Member, Mr. Malcolm further said that the Imperial Conference had not been set up by the Parliaments of the Empire. The Government arranged between themselves that the Prime Ministers should be asked, but there was nothing to prevent their being represented by their High Commissioner, and almost every Dominion had been represented at the initial Conference in 1887 by its Agent-General. Continuing, the hon. gentleman said that the trouble came to be that a body such as the Imperial Conference, being set up by and consisting of the Prime Ministers for the time being, it was possible for the Conference, initiated with an earnest desire to improve the constitutional relations of the Empire, to become an obstacle to that improvement. Naturally, men of strong character thought when they were in control of affairs there was no one who could do it better and few who could do it as well.

An Imperial Constitution.

To-day they were practically in the same position as they were thirty-four years ago ; but in those thirty-four years their country and the Empire might have made a very great advance towards an Imperial Constitution. The Imperial sentiment amongst the peoples of the whole of the British Empire was so strong that they had not discovered the inconveniences which were caused through their want of a federal constitution up to that time ; but as the Dominions grew, sooner or later the time was almost certain to come when some sort of binding action and some sort of constitution that would create a power, or that would be able to use executive power, must become a necessity.

The present position of affairs in the British Empire was very unsatisfactory, for the reason that the sovereignty of the Empire was going a-begging. They all knew that the practical sovereignty lay in the British Government. But the difficulty was that they had Britain, in her anxiety to do honour to New Zealand and the other Dominions, inviting them to a place at the Peace Conference and in the League of Nations as separate nations. If that was an empty compliment they were no further ahead than before ; if it meant something it meant that they were separate nations, actually independent of Great Britain. If that was so, then the sorriest thing New Zealand and the other Dominions ever did was joining the League of Nations and the Peace Conference as separate nations. It might be said, " Give the Imperial Conference time and it will become an Imperial Executive, with all the necessary authorities for the Government of the Empire." " Just fancy," said Mr. Malcolm, " an Imperial Executive consisting of men who live twenty thousand miles away from one another, and who meet one another for four, five, six, or seven weeks in the year ! An Imperial Executive ! How can such a Conference as that exercise executive powers? It cannot be done. . . . I am one of those—there are many more of the same mind—who think that the course for us to take is to follow the course pursued by the British peoples and by the American peoples throughout all history, and that is to make Parliament responsible to the people and to make the Executive responsible to Parliament."

After making reference to the history of the United States in regard to federation, Mr. Malcolm said that New Zealand, having no land neighbours, the sea had become, as it had proved in so many other ways in Britain, a uniting rather than a dividing factor, and for that very reason it would be easier to unite the units of the Empire in a federation than it was to unite the States of America. Imperial Federation would not affect their autonomy in any degree whatever.

The Prime Minister : " We would be a subsidiary Parliament."

Mr. Malcolm : " No, we would be a State Parliament."

Continuing, Mr. Malcolm said that the Premier's statement that they would be a subsidiary State was scarcely a fair way of putting it. They would be on a different plane altogether. As the Parliament of that Dominion they would not be under the authority of the Federal Parliament. They would have different functions.

The Minister of Education (Hon. C. J. Parr) : " A foreign policy of defence ? It would be taken from us."

Mr. Malcolm : . . . What control of foreign policy have we at the present time ? We have none at all."

The Prime Minister: "That is what the Executive is going to deal with next June, because that is what it is coming to."

Mr. Malcolm replied that that was not an Executive, and they must admit it. They should not lose as a Federal Parliament a tittle of the authority they at present possessed as a Parliament, but would gain a say in Imperial affairs, and in the making of war and in the declaration of peace. People took for granted that the New Zealanders who would go to the Imperial Parliament would go as New Zealanders and vote and argue as such. There was nothing more certain than that if they had half a dozen representatives from New Zealand in a Federal Parliament they would find probably three on one side and three on the other or two here, two there and two somewhere else. They would vote not as New Zealanders, but as Liberals and Conservatives.

The Prime Minister: "Exactly. Party government . . . Do you think the Empire can be run by party government?"

Mr. Malcolm: "Certainly."

The Prime Minister: "I do not."

Mr. Malcolm replied that if party government had succeeded in the British Parliament and in the Parliaments of the Dominions, most certainly it should do so in a Federal Parliament. Did they find in the Federal Parliament of the Australian Commonwealth that all the Victorians sat and voted together and that all the New South Wales representatives did the same? The locality that a man came from did not count in the Federal Parliament.

Relations with United States.

They recognised all that they owed to the Mother Country for her generosity to them. It was her Navy that had been guarding them, and towards the cost of that Navy they had been paying almost nothing. He wanted strongly to repudiate the idea that if they broke away from Great Britain they would turn to America. He ventured to say that 99 per cent. of the people of that country had no thought of turning from Great Britain in the first place, and no thought of turning to America in the second place. They desired the most friendly relations with America, but in no part of the British Empire had the indifference of the American people to the friendly advances of Britain, had the hostility of some sections of the Americans to Britain been more resented, more regretted, than in the Dominions—more in that Dominion than in Great Britain. America had always behaved as a friendly nation so far as action was concerned, but they did regret that friendly advances in so many directions were often ignored.

Power of Taxation: Representation of Dominion.

Returning to the subject of federation, Mr. Malcolm said it would, of course, be necessary to give an Imperial Federal Parliament powers of taxation. He thought that every Dominion Parliament should discuss the subject, with the hope that eventually the Dominions would be able to invite Great Britain to call a Conference to consider the question of a Government for the whole Empire.

Mr. S. G. Smith (Liberal, *Taranaki*) supported the amendment proposed by the Leader of the Opposition. The High Commissioner could represent New Zealand, but he should not be permitted to come to a definite conclusion on any question coming before the Conference without first having been advised by the country. With regard to the Anglo-Japanese question, foreign policy and other matters, no clear statement had been made by the Prime Minister. He had not, for example, made any statement with regard to a "White" New Zealand, as had been done by the leaders of the Commonwealth of Australia.

Mr. L. M. Isitt (Liberal, *Christchurch North*) said that he believed the Prime Minister was the man who ought to go. In all probability he (the Prime Minister) possessed information which it was not possible to give to the world at large—information that would affect his determination. It would have been very much wiser if Parliament had been prorogued to the usual date.

Objection to Federal Idea.

The Prime Minister, after giving an emphatic denial to a statement that had been made to the effect that he was in the habit of putting party before country, and having replied to criticisms in regard to the appointment of the Leader of the Legislative Council as Acting Prime Minister during his absence from the Dominion, and other criticisms, dealt with the speech of Mr. Malcolm, saying that he admired his speech, though he did not agree with him. He did not agree with Mr. Malcolm when he said that the Constitution of Britain was written. There was no such thing as a written Constitution for the British Empire. He hoped that they should have something in the way of a Constitution for the British Empire, at all events, before they were very much older. "What we want," said Mr. Massey, "is something that will not be elaborate, but broad and simple, and to the point, and sufficient for the purpose."

Mr. Malcolm seemed to support party Government for the Empire. He could not imagine an Imperial Parliament working satisfactorily on party lines; they would agree to certain resolutions, and the legislation would come back to the Dominion Parliaments and be dealt with on party lines. That would never do, because if they set up an Imperial Parliament, they gave it the right to tax every part of the Empire. "Does anyone imagine," said Mr. Massey, "that the Dominions, leaving New Zealand out of the question, would put up with taxation enforced by a Parliament sitting in London?"

Hon. Members: "No."

The Prime Minister: "I agree that it would never work."

There was the matter of the indemnity—the reparation fund—which had not yet been apportioned, and if there was any reparation fund it became particularly his duty to see that New Zealand got its share.

Replying to remarks made during the debate by Mr. R. McCallum (Liberal, *Wairau*), who had suggested that someone other than the Prime Minister should represent New Zealand at the Conference in London, Mr. Massey reminded the hon. Member that it was a Conference of Prime Ministers. If a Prime Minister was not able to go, it was understood he could select one of his fellow-Ministers, who would represent him and be responsible for what took place.

An Imperial Executive.

Continuing, Mr. Massey said he believed the time was coming soon when there would be a recognised organisation to deal with Imperial affairs, saying: "I believe it ought to take the form of an Imperial Executive, with the Prime Minister of the United Kingdom at the head, and the other Ministers representing the United Kingdom to be chosen by him; then at least one Minister from each of the Dominions, a representative of the Dependencies of the Empire, and perhaps two representatives of the Empire of India. That is only a suggestion. Those are the lines on which I propose to work when I get the opportunity."

He hoped that some definite arrangement would be made about a periodical meeting of the Executive, not less often than once in two years. He believed the time would come when it would meet every year, but that time was not yet. They had got the length of being partners in the Empire. There was no question about that. That did not, of course, mean that New Zealand had as much to say in the Empire's affairs as the United Kingdom, or even a large Dominion like Canada; but they were partners in the Empire on the understanding that the autonomy of any Dominion was not to be interfered with by another Dominion. It should be the business of the

Executive to do whatever might be necessary in connection with foreign affairs, such as the making of treaties or the declaration of war or the making of peace ; and the Executive should be responsible to the Parliament of the United Kingdom and to the Parliaments of the Dominions.

Defence of the Empire.

" I believe now," said Mr. Massey, " our first duty is the defence of the Empire. I am not speaking about making preparations for attacking any country. I do not believe Britain will ever attack any country, but I hope it will defend itself and will defend its Allies in the event of attack ; but it will never attack another country. That is my honest opinion."

Continuing, Mr. Massey said he would ask the representatives of the people of New Zealand to look at the defences of their ports that day. Were they adequate ? They knew very well that they were not. Something better was required. They could not go in for large expenditure until the present depression came to an end, until they had got back to normal, but they must look those things in the face. It was their first duty.

League of Nations.

Speaking on the subject of the League of Nations Mr. Massey said : " As far as the League of Nations is concerned, I would like to say that I have heard it suggested that the fact of our joining the League of Nations as an individual member of the League has weakened our connection with the Empire. I do not think so. Certainly we joined as an individual nation, one of the great family of nations of which we are all so proud ; but we joined with the object of working not only for our own interests, but also of looking after the interests of the Empire whenever the occasion may require. If I thought for one moment that our joining the League of Nations meant weakening the connection between New Zealand and the other countries of the Empire and the United Kingdom, I would say at once to the Parliament of this country that the time had come for us to withdraw from the League of Nations and do our best along with the other countries of the Empire."

Importance of Naval Defence.

He believed, he said, under present conditions, that naval supremacy was more important than military defence, because they had got in every part of the Empire thousands of men who had done their training and who would be able and, he was sure, willing to do everything for the defence of the Empire. They could depend upon them for the next ten years. He was thinking more, perhaps, of the defence that was necessary—naval defence and military defence—than anything else.

Imperial Preference and Empire Migration.

Turning to the questions of Imperial Preference and Empire Migration, Mr. Massey said :—

"There is no question that if every country of the Empire gives preference to every other country of the Empire in the way of trade and customs, that arrangement will in itself strengthen the ties that bind the Empire. We have the principle affirmed in all the Dominions of the Empire—I am not speaking of the Dependencies. It is now the law of the land. Not a great deal has been done in pushing it, but the law of the land is that of Imperial preference. I am proud of the fact, Sir, that it was arranged in the Imperial Conference when I was present. There is another matter also arranged there which is now attracting attention, and of which we have felt the effect in New Zealand : the bringing into operation of the principle that the people who desire to emigrate from the United Kingdom should be induced to stay in countries under the British flag. It is time that was done. For fifty years or more there has been a continuous stream of people going out of the United Kingdom, and a large proportion of them have found their way to countries outside the Empire. . . . I would like to see Empire migration, so that if people in one part of the Empire wanted to change their place of residence they would choose some country within the Empire, and there is plenty of opportunity. That system in actual operation has brought to this country a large number of people who, I believe, will make very desirable citizens of New Zealand—I am speaking of the Imperial ex-service men who have cast in their lot with us, and repeatedly I have heard good accounts of them. I believe that in years to come they will make good and useful citizens."

"White" New Zealand.

An Hon. Member : " We do not want the Hindus."

The Prime Minister : " When I talk of the peoples of the different countries of the Empire being on an equality and not interfering with each other, I have in mind the principle upon which we are working, and it is this : that each country within the Empire has the right to choose the people who are to be

o

the citizens of that country in years to come. That is what we are doing now."

Mr. T. M. Wilford : " That is the law."

The Prime Minister : That is the law, and it is the law not only of this country, but has been acknowledged by the Parliament of the United Kingdom and by the Sovereign himself."

Imperial Shipping.

In reply to a question by the Hon. J. A. Hanan (Liberal, *Invercargill*) : " What about an Imperial shipping service ? " the Prime Minister said that a Shipping Board had been set up to do its best for British shipping.* Up to the present not a great deal had been done, but the Board was working now, and he hoped in years to come they should have something substantial and satisfactory to show for what was intended.

In conclusion Mr. Massey said : " I do not want war, but if it ever comes I hope that we shall not be found unprepared."

The amendment was negatived by 39 votes against 25, nearly all the Liberal and Labour Members voting together in support of it, and the debate was adjourned.

The " Labour " Motion.

On the 17th March,

Mr. H. E. Holland (**Labour,** *Buller*) moved the following amendment to the Address : —

" We feel it, however, to be our duty to submit to Your Excellency—(1) That in view of the serious economic situation now developing in New Zealand, which renders it inadvisable that Parliament should go into lengthy recess, and also in view of the complete absence of any detailed reasons for holding the Imperial Conference, and failing proper provision for the democratic election of a representative by the whole of the people of New Zealand the Dominion's representative at the Imperial Conference should be the High Commissioner for New Zealand, who should be definitely instructed by the New Zealand Parliament, but with no power to commit the Dominion to any line of policy, nor to accept responsibility on behalf of the Dominion for Imperial acts, declarations of war, etc., until all such matters shall have received the sanction of both people and Parliament. (2) That the New Zealand delegate should be instructed to give loyal adherence at the Conference to the principles laid down in the Covenant of the League of Nations, of which League New Zealand is a part—Clause 8 of which reads

* *Vide* Mr. Massey's remarks on this subject in this JOURNAL Vol. II., No. 2, at page 412.

'The members of the League recognise that the maintenance of peace requires the reduction of national armaments.' The delegate should be instructed to resist every movement in the direction of increased armaments ; to oppose every suggestion making for the precipitation of war with America or any other country ; and on every occasion to urge the linking-up of the peoples of all countries in a commonwealth of industry and peace. (3) That the delegate to the Imperial Conference should declare and vote against all diplomatic secrecy, and that he should strenuously advocate that in all treaties between Great Britain and foreign Powers and all arrangements between the Dominions and Great Britain the basis shall not be for naval and military purposes, but for the purpose of social, political and economic amenities. The present Treaty between England and Japan being merely a military treaty, and both countries being members of the League of Nations, no renewal of the Treaty is required, inasmuch as Article 20 of the Covenant of the League says, ' The members of the League severally agree that this Covenant is accepted as abrogating all obligations or undertakings *inter se* which are inconsistent with the terms thereof, and solemnly undertake that they will not hereafter enter into any engagements inconsistent with the terms thereof.' (4) That the New Zealand delegate to the Imperial Conference should resolutely advocate the granting to the people of Ireland, India and Egypt that full measure of self-determination to gain which for all small nationalities the statesmen of Britain declared the recent world War was fought. (5) Finally, we feel it to be our duty to represent to Your Excellency our strong disapproval of the action of Your Excellency's Government in appointing to the position of Acting Prime Minister an honourable gentleman who is not a Member of the House of Representatives."

Representation at Imperial Conference.

Mr. Holland said that they thought the High Commissioner could better represent the Dominion because there was then nothing before them as to what was to be discussed at the Imperial Conference, and therefore whoever went should go as a watching member, with no power to commit the country to anything whatever, but only to report and get sanction or otherwise for what was done at the Conference. The people wanted to know what was being done in their name ; they should have had a specific motion before the House dealing with the invitation to the Imperial Conference. He could not find anything to uphold the Prime Minister's contention that nobody but Prime Ministers were eligible to go to the Imperial Conference. The representatives from India were not Prime Ministers.

The Prime Minister (the Right Hon. W. F. Massey): They hold a more important position than Prime Ministers. Each of those men control many times the number of people in New Zealand."

Mr. Holland, continuing, said that when Sir Joseph Ward had gone from the Dominion and presented his scheme at the

o 2

1911 Conference based on the creation of an Imperial Parliament with legislative power in Imperial affairs, with an executive of twelve, responsible not to that Imperial Parliament but to the electorates of the United Kingdom, Canada, Australia, South Africa, New Zealand, and Newfoundland, the British Prime Minister's reply had been unequivocal; he had said : —

> " Sir Joseph Ward's proposal would impair, if not altogether destroy, the authority of the Government of the United Kingdom in such grave matters as the conduct of foreign policy, the conclusion of treaties, the declaration and maintenance of peace, or the declaration of war. . . . That authority could not be shared."

An Hon. Member : " That was not the present Prime Minister."

Mr. Holland : " That is the frame of mind of the British Imperialist to-day."

The Prime Minister : " No."

Mr. Holland, after quoting extracts from published autobiographical notes of Sir Wilfrid Laurier regarding methods alleged to have been employed to influence delegates at Imperial Conferences, and also extracts from Mr. Lionel Curtis's " Problem of the Commonwealth " on the subject of the autonomy of the Dominions, proceeded to review at length what he alleged were some of the secret commitments made by various nations before, during, and after the War Having dealt with the various points raised in his amendment he concluded by saying that the Labour movement in al countries, viewing the disastrous record of the world War and the secrecy at the back of it, and at the same time recog nising that capitalism was its first cause, was determined tha there should be no mantle of darkness drawn over thei international relationships.

Extent of Self-Government.

Mr. D. G. Sullivan (Labour, *Avon***)** said that what the peopl wanted to know was the extent to which New Zealand was self-governing Dominion, able to control its own affairs on th one hand, and the extent, on the other hand, to which was controlled by the Imperial authorities. There wa nothing in the New Zealand Constitution Act defining th powers of the Imperial Government in relation to Imperi affairs as they affected New Zealand. The powers laid dow were negative—that was, they were limited to such pr posals as the Imperial Government might take exception t As he read the Act, the Imperial Government at that tim had no definite power to compel the people of that count to subscribe to any positive act. The point, therefore, th they and the people of New Zealand had to determine, in view of the developments that were taking place, had relation to the extent to which the country had to sacrifice its independence in regard to those Imperial questions. On this question might he pay a high tribute to the speech delivered by the Member for Clutha ? He disagreed with much in the latter portion of the speech, but the hon. gentleman had raised the tone of the debate quite beyond the petty considerations served up to the House by the Liberal party ; when great Imperial questions were raised through the Address in Reply, the Members of that party were apparently unable to discuss anything beyond mere domestic issues. He was interested in the suggestion of the Member for Clutha for the building up of an Imperial Executive in which there would beside the Empire's sovereignty. But what was the reason which the honourable Member put forward as the necessity for that Imperial organisation designed to strengthen the purely physical bonds which bound the Empire together ? Mr. Malcolm had said, " Some sort of Constitution and Executive is necessary in order to secure combined action in Imperial affairs " ; and, later, " A State cannot carry on a great war without a Sovereignty." The same thing was said, more or less, by the Prime Minister. If they took the speech of the honourable Member for Clutha, that of the Prime Minister, and that of the Member for Timaru, in seconding the Address, they got the fact that the only apparent aim and object in the minds of those who wanted to substitute an Imperial Executive for the strong natural ties of blood and interest which were then uniting that country to Great Britain was because those Members of the House were visualising war.

The Prime Minister : " Do you think that war is over ? "

Mr. Sullivan replied that he did not think war was over if they were to continue to be governed by people of such views or by representatives of the capitalist class. The country had to be very careful indeed as to the extent to which it was going to allow its representative " to commit the Dominion, to bind it to the Imperial chariot and follow it wherever it may be driven." If such an Imperial Executive as had been suggested were set up and allowed to operate on the present undemocratic basis—not responsible directly to the people, not elected by the people—that country and other smaller countries in the Empire might be committed to the support of declarations of war and to important Imperial acts for which it might be absolutely impossible to find moral justification. In the resolution moved by the Leader of the Labour Party there was nothing that disparaged the British Empire. The people of the country would agree with

him that they did not want to do anything that was going
to have the effect of intensifying international hostility. He
was positively alarmed at the statements of the Prime Minister
and the seconder of the Address when they pictured the dangers
of war confronting the Empire. He would conclude by saying
of the policy of the Labour Party in that country that they
did stand for closer association with the real democracy of
Great Britain, but not with exploiting financiers.

Mr. M. J. Savage (**Labour,** *Auckland West*), speaking
with reference to Mr. Malcolm's proposals, said that when
they came to look at a map of the British Empire it gave them
some idea of the difficulties with which they were confronted.
Even the Prime Minister had suggested that he would give
India representation. On what basis would India be represented ? Would it be on a population basis ? How would
the representation be nominated ? Probably by the British
Government ; certainly not on a population basis. If they
were, a country like India, with racial differences, with a
standard of living considerably below theirs, would probably
outvote them in the Councils of the Empire. He did not see
how they could stand for that, in the interests of the Indian
people as well as in their own. They could take any country
under the sun and they would have racial and economic
differences ; and in the election of anything in the nature of
an Imperial Parliament they were going to have difficulties
at that stage that seemed almost insurmountable. The
Prime Minister had stated he could not imagine an Imperial
Parliament on party lines. He (the speaker) could not
imagine a Parliament on any other lines as long as capitalism
reigned supreme ; whether it was an Imperial or a Dominion
Parliament, it was going to be on party lines as long as they
had a party conflict in industry. The Prime Minister had
stated he was in favour of an Imperial Executive. That
might mean anything. He had not told them whether its
findings were to be final, or whether the various parts of the
Empire were to be consulted before they became law. He
supposed the Prime Minister thought he was not called upon
to go into details. He (Mr. Savage) thought the situation
demanded it.

Great Britain and U.S.A.

Mr. W. E. Parry (**Labour,** *Auckland Central*) said that
the Prime Minister in his speech the previous night had endeavoured to allay any particular feeling they might have
respect to difficulties between America and Great Britain,
but he must know that there were very serious difficulties
indeed between them. If the difference of opinion in con-

nection with the exploitation of oil was not adjusted, war was practically inevitable. This was an all-important question for discussion at the forthcoming Conference.

Mr. L. M. Isitt (Liberal, *Christchurch North*) wished to enter the most earnest protest he could make against the wild and dangerous statement made by·the last speaker with reference to the possibility of a war between England and America. There was nothing better calculated to play into the hands of the belligerent spirits that existed in every nation than such unutterably unwarranted statements. There was about as much probability of war between Great Britain and America as there was of another civil war in the States themselves. He did not think they need take very much notice of the long and involved amendment, and the outburst of the extreme Labour Party, the whole thing, to his mind, being utterly insincere. The only consistent attitude for the Labour Party to take up would be to absolutely oppose any representative of the Dominion attending any such Conference, unless it were to condemn the whole thing, and voice the opinion of the extreme Labour Party.

An Imperial Parliament.

Mr. D. Jones (Reform, *Kaiapoi*) said the Labour Party had been quite consistent in moving the amendment, because to them the Empire had no meaning except as a mere shackle. He was pleased when the Prime Minister said he was opposed to an Imperial Parliament with the right of taxation. That was a right that they should never surrender as far as New Zealand was concerned. He was delighted with Mr. Malcolm's speech, though he did not agree with him. The hon. Member had said that Britain would welcome the offer of the Dominions in favour of an Imperial Parliament, with representation. Would they ? Why, in fifty years from then Britain would be the junior partner in the concern—the British population outside Britain would soon be greater than that within. Do you think," said Mr. Jones, " that Great Britain is going to surrender to us a power of representation that may put the capital city out of Britain ? No. And that idea, if nothing else, will always kill the Imperial Parliament scheme. The idea of taking the capital and putting it, say, in Auckland, or Montreal, or Delhi—these possibilities open up when you give the power of representation . . . . the idea of an Imperial Parliament is a beautiful dream ; it will never come to pass."

Naval Defence.

As far as New Zealand was concerned, the sea was their main line of defence, as it was Britain's, and soon the Dominion was going to have exports and imports worth £100,000,000 travelling to and fro on the waters. "As a business proposition, then," continued Mr. Jones, "we must increase our insurance and think more in the way of national defence than we do now. Sir, I am prepared to go back to my electors and say that in connection with our Empire we must carry a fair share of the burden, and to that end increase our subsidy as far as naval expenditure is concerned."

The House divided on the question, "That the words in the amendment moved by the honourable Member for Buller be added," and the motion was defeated by 58 votes against the eight votes of those constituting the official Labour Party.

The House adjourned at 2 a.m. on the 18th March.

DEBATE IN LEGISLATIVE COUNCIL.

On the 14th March, 1921,

The Hon. Sir William Hall-Jones, in moving the Address, said that the expression "cohesion of the British Empire" in the Governor-General's Speech seemed to him to affect the welfare of every man, woman and child in New Zealand. He believed that the words used by Mr. Lloyd George in his message of invitation to Mr. Massey to attend the Imperial Conference in June would be largely echoed by the people of New Zealand. He felt that Mr. Massey was a safe man, and did not believe he would go so far as to commit the Dominion to any course of important action without the consent and approval of Parliament.

Japanese Treaty.

With regard to foreign policy, Sir William said that he should be sorry indeed to see the self-governing Dominions claiming the right to be represented by an Ambassador in other countries. The Japanese Treaty would soon come under revision again. He looked upon Japan as a friendly nation. They had only to think of her action during the Great War where she did such excellent work—and was prepared to do more—so that when he heard or read of attacks being made and reflections cast upon her, it gave one much concern. The Japanese were an able and clever race; they had their national ambitions. They in New Zealand also had to look after the welfare of their race, and he was one who believed it would be a mistake to allow unrestricted immigration from Asiatic countries. He felt satisfied that the thinking men of Japan realised that position as much as anyone, and were the position reversed they would take much the same line as had been taken by the Dominion.

Imperial Defence.

On the question of Imperial defence, if they had .one well-considered plan which all parts of the Empire could follow—methods of training, the best class of war material, and so on—they would have the basis upon which all parts of the Empire could work. There centralisation could begin and could end. Beyond that it was certainly the duty of every part of the Empire to take sufficient steps for its own home defence. With regard to the Navy, even though they did not go in for a big or expensive Navy, they should have some useful ships which would fit in with those of Australia, and possibly Canada and South Africa, combined with Imperial ships in that part of the world or in Eastern waters, which would give reasonable protection.

German Indemnities.

Speaking on the subject of the German indemnities, Sir William said he was very pleased that the Prime Minister was of opinion that all parts of the Empire which took part in the War and incurred heavy obligations, ought to be considered in regard to any indemnity to be received.

Representation at Imperial Conference.

After dealing with the question of shipping and freights, Sir William said that it had been suggested—to his mind it was an absurd suggestion—that the High Commissioner would be a sufficient representative at the Conference; but the High Commissioner was practically a civil servant—he was not a Cabinet Minister—not even a Member of Parliament.

Let them do promptly and as worthily as they could at once—do what was required to enable the Prime Minister to go to England. It was a call of Empire, to which he believed the Parliament and the people would loyally respond, because they, like His Excellency the Governor-General, desired to see the cohesion of the British Empire maintained.

British Commonwealth: Representation in London.

The Hon. C. H. Izard, referring to the Speech, said he was pleased to find His Excellency referred to the " British Commonwealth." The expression, to his mind, was far more applicable than the " British Empire." There could be only

one person to represent the Dominion at the Conference, and
he must be the Prime Minister. It was indeed necessary that
someone should from time to time represent New Zealand
there (in England), not only for the purpose of consulting with
the members of the British Cabinet and impressing them with
the importance and requirements of their Dominion, but there
should be someone there with a sense of responsibility, able
to correct the unguarded and untrue statements which
appeared in the English Press, in signed articles, and statements made at public meetings and elsewhere by peripapetic
ex-Ministers of the Crown and others who spoke entirely
without a sense of responsibility. He trusted that one of
the first things the Prime Minister would do when he arrived
in England would be to wipe away the impression which had
been created by an ex-Minister of the Crown with regard to
the position that that country took up respecting other
races.

Migration.

They might ask their representatives to arrange with
the British Government some system by which they could
take England's surplus population that would be useful in
connection with their agricultural, manufacturing and
mercantile industries.

The Hon. Sir J. R. Sinclair regarded the suggestion that
they might be represented at the Conference by their High
Commissioner as one that they really could not consider
Questions of great importance would come up for consideration
involving responsibility that could not be taken by anyone
but a responsible Minister of the Crown.

Inter-Imperial Relations.

Not one of those questions was, in his view, as important
as that of the relations of the Dominions the one to the other
and of all to the Mother Country, in view of their having
been parties to international agreements. Had the Dominion
—he would not say acquired, because so far as he knew no
Dominion had asked for it—had they had conferred upon
them the status of independence, with all that independence
meant, or did they remain undivided parts as theretofore in
their national whole ? It had been claimed that by signing
the Peace Treaty South Africa attained the status of
Nation—that it was a sovereign State in the same sense that
the United Kingdom was, that it was directly responsible to
the League of Nations. If that were so in the case of South
Africa, it was the same with all the Dominions. Leading

Canadians had taken broadly the same view. Canada had appointed a resident Ambassador to the United States, who —in order to avoid duplication—had been incorporated in the diplomatic staff of the Mother Country.

After referring to the views of Lord Milner and of Mr. Massey regarding the status of the various parts of the Empire, Sir John Sinclair said that the views he had quoted left questions of paramount importance still to be answered. That there should be differences among leaders upon the vital question of inter-Imperial relations was disturbing. There ought to be a clear deliverance upon the question at the Conference.

Right to Withdraw from Empire Partnership.

Had the question been raised at any of the Conferences as to the removal—to use Lord Milner's words—of the last vestige of the subjection of the Dominions to the Motherland? Had any member of their Empire partnership expressed the desire to be given the moral right to withdraw? Was it open to each of the Dominions to appoint an Ambassador to other countries? The position in regard to treaties had been laid down years ago by Lord Ripon when he had said that to give Colonies the power of negotiating treaties for themselves would be to give them an international status as separate and sovereign States and would be equivalent to breaking up the Empire into a number of independent States. Did that represent the policy of to-day?

The Mandate for German Samoa had been taken by His Majesty direct from the League of Nations. They, on His Majesty's behalf, had undertaken the trust ; and it imposed upon them a duty, if he read aright, of reporting not to His Majesty's Government, but to the Council of the League. Their people had not asked for any change of status, and, with their Prime Minister, he hoped that their nation's partnership might stand as before. The Parliament of the United Kingdom had sovereign power over all. The possession of that power had given them no concern, because their nation was blessed with constitutional rulers. Was the position of a Dominion that day analogous to that of a Constitutional Sovereign, who possessed legal power, but was wholly guided by his Advisers—Advisers in the case of the Dominions being the Parliament of the Mother Country after conference with their (the Dominion) representatives? Even then, in the case of a Dominion, there would exist no restraining force if it did not " play the game," and unity in the old sense would have gone. The Dominions had been given a voice in foreign

affairs.   Before the signing of the Peace Treaty, declaration
of war by the Mother-land would have involved their Commonwealth as a whole.   Would it do so that day ?   Or might
one part be at peace, another at war ?   If it might, then they
no longer existed in an Empire partnership, and he would
ask, whence did the tribunal that had pronounced that
divorce get its jurisdiction ?

" Is it designed," said Sir John Sinclair, " that hereafter
the Dominions shall possess local autonomy, absolute, unfettered, and complete ?   Is that the meaning of Lord Milner's
words when he refers to the passing of the last vestige of
subjection on the part of the Dominions to the Mother-land ? "
Continuing, Sir John said he was one of those—and he believed
they formed a vast majority—who supported the maintenance
of a " loose tie."*

Even if there had been brought about, by whatever
means, the right in any member of their Empire partnership
to withdraw, withdrawal would none the less spell revolution.
" Have we been," he said, " without our desire and without
our knowledge, unloosed from our silken bond ?   Had those
who were responsible for the League of Nations—and it is the
child not of our nation, but of President Wilson—had they
a clear conception of its bearing upon a Commonwealth
like ours, composed of a number of separate parts bound
in one legal whole ?   The League was designed, I take it,
as a body of conciliation in time of stress.   Necessarily—
necessarily it is something more to-day.   May it become
a wedge ?   May it bring about the dismemberment, the
peaceful dismemberment, of our Empire ?   The test of any
system of arbitration must be conformity to the decisions
of its Courts.   In the case of the League of Nations non-
conformity, in the last resort, must mean industrial war or
civil war.   Is it accepted—and this to our people is a vital
question—that action which might involve our nation's
existence should be determined upon not by its own Parliaments, not by the Parliament of the Mother-land—and with
that we were well content—but by an outside body, or is it
considered that the position is sufficiently safeguarded by the
provision requiring unanimity ? "   One thing was perfectly
plain : they could not continue to exist as a Commonwealth
if all its parts were given independent status—differing
interests would grow up ; unity in the old sense would be
gone, and in the past unity had been their watchword.   Must
it not be so in the future ?   They honoured and served one
King.   They must stand or fall together.

---

* *Vide* Sir J. Sinclair's remarks on this subject, reported in the
JOURNAL, Vol. I., No. 4, at pages 718-720.

Japanese Treaty.

The Hon. W. H. Triggs, speaking of the Anglo-Japanese Treaty, said that no doubt the alliance was of considerable value to them during the War, because it had enabled them to carry out a concentration which was vitally necessary at that time. But the situation had changed, and the centre of action had shifted to the Pacific. They knew that there were possibilities—grave possibilities—of friction between the United States and Japan, and it was obvious that if they entered into any renewal of the Treaty there must be a stipulation that under no circumstances would they be dragged into war with the United States. "Why not keep ourselves free," said Mr. Triggs, "so as to be able to do our best when the time comes, in the interests of the British Empire and in the interests of civilisation at large ? "

The Irish Question.

The Hon. T. MacGibbon said the trouble in Ireland was sure to be discussed. He hoped that Mr. Massey, as their representative, would assist in solving the Irish trouble.

Irresponsible Speeches.

The Attorney-General (Hon. Sir Francis Bell) said that nothing Mr. Triggs had said with regard to Japan was spoken in a manner which could reasonably give offence, but let them put the words in his (the Attorney-General's) mouth as expressing such opinions on behalf of the Government, and it would be seen how dangerous any such expression would have been. He entirely dissented from Mr. Triggs's view, and asked hon. gentlemen who heard so much irresponsible speech and read so much irresponsible literature upon a matter which was of grave interest to them to ask themselves whether it was better to deal with a friend than to reject a friendship.

Mandates: Comparison with South Africa.

In upholding the view that the Dominions of the Crown should be represented at the Conference by their Prime Ministers, Sir Francis Bell asked what earthly use that Conference would be if it were not one of the men who were free to tell each other what the difficulties of the different parts of the Empire were, and to consider how those differences and difficulties could be reconciled ? Let them take, for instance, the differences that had arisen between South Africa and themselves as to the authority under which they exercised their respective Mandates in pursuance of the Treaty of Peace. South Africa had claimed to be a Mandatory direct of the League, and to be a sovereign Power holding authority from the League, irrespective of the Mother Country from which they (in New Zealand) derived their Constitution. "We, on the other hand," said Sir Francis, "have preferred to act under the Imperial authority, and to govern under the Imperial Foreign Jurisdiction Act. That was only an illustration of the great constitutional questions which arose and required to be discussed and considered, and in many cases to be settled by compromise. Surely the communication of the views of one Government or the other on the position of the Empire and its dangers, and the communications from the Imperial Government particularly, must be made to the men who had from their respective countries practically the mandate of authority.

Imperial Conferences.

" The Conference," said Sir Francis " is not a legislative body; it is . . . a Conference of the statesmen of the Empire, considering together the difficulties of the Empire and attempting to arrive in conference at some common course, it may be of legislation, it may be of action, it may be, in some cases, of refraining from action, in order that the Empire, in so far as it is humanly possible, may act in unison, and not as dismembered, independent parts." Speaking of the Imperial Conference of 1912, Sir Francis Bell said it was not known to that day what was said to Sir Joseph Ward (then Prime Minister) and the then Attorney-General, Sir John Findlay, because the statements were made in confidence, but they knew there was divulged to that Conference information which enabled them and the Prime Ministers of the other parts of the Empire to be seised of the condition of European affairs, and when the crisis came the different parts of the Empire were better enabled to act as parts of one Empire under the direction of the Mother Country.

They must admit that there might be times when the presence of the Prime Minister in London was infinitely more important than his presence in the Dominion.

Constitutional Questions.

There were at the present time constitutional question which had arisen within the Empire. Such questions as th basis of union, and the extent to which the various parts c the Empire could go in agreeing to define some commo principle and some elastic method which would enable those parts of the Empire which were truly autonomous to be united with the other autonomous parts under the great Mother of the nation, it was clear, could only be carefully discussed by the principal statesmen, and not by minor departmental Ministers of the Crown.

In conclusion, Sir Francis Bell said that Sir William Hall-Jones, who had held the highest position in the State,* had moved the resolution at the invitation of the Government, with an absolutely free hand to express his own views, and no trust had ever been discharged more generously ; whilst Mr. Izard, who seconded the resolution, had not been nominated to that Chamber by the Government, but by the Opposition party. Mr. Izard had consented to speak as a New Zealander without reference to party and he was grateful to him for his well-reasoned speech.

Sir William Hall-Jones, in his reply, said that he hoped that every part of the Empire would at least send their reports upon the work done under the Mandates through the Home Authorities.

The Motion before the Council was then agreed to.

---

* Sir William Hall-Jones became Premier of the Liberal Government in June, 1906, on the death of Mr. Seddon, resigning that office in favour of Sir Joseph Ward in August of the same year.

SOUTH AFRICA.

The following summary is in continuation of the proceedings of the First Session of the Fourth Parliament of the Union of South Africa which opened on 11th March, 1921. Debates in the earlier part of the Session were dealt with in Vol II., No 2, and a continuation of the summary will be published in the next number of the JOURNAL, *when several important matters, which it has been necessary to hold over, will receive attention.*

CONFERENCE OF PRIME MINISTERS OF THE EMPIRE.

(Foreign Policy: Imperial Defence: the Japanese Treaty: British Navy: Constitutional Conference; Secret Diplomacy: League of Nations, etc.)

The Prime Minister made a statement in the House of Assembly on 20th May in reference to the questions to be discussed at the Conference of the Prime Ministers of the Empire to be held in London.

DEBATE IN HOUSE OF ASSEMBLY.

On the consideration of the Prime Minister's Vote in Committee of Supply,

The Prime Minister (Lieut.-General the Right Hon. J. C. Smuts), referring to his forthcoming departure on his mission to London, stated that he proposed taking with him the Minister of Agriculture and the Minister of Defence—the former because he was anxious for his assistance in many of those questions with regard to the disposal of agricultural produce which were pressing very heavily upon them; the latter because one of the most important matters for discussion at that Conference would be the general defence position of the Empire. It was felt that the country was full of great difficulties and problems, and more than ever that was a time when the Prime Minister should be there. At the same time he felt that while a Conference like that was being held where grave questions were to be discussed which might affect South Africa, it was most important that the Prime Minister of South Africa should be present.

Limited Functions of Imperial Conference.

The so-called Imperial Cabinet, he continued, was an informal consultative body of Prime Ministers of the Empire in order to discuss large questions of policy which could only be discussed by an exchange of views such as takes place at it. He wanted to emphasise this point, because there had been a misunderstanding as to the nature of that body, not only in South Africa, but elsewhere. It could take no binding resolutions, and, whatever the discussions, they could only be of an informal character. It had no binding force, and could not be given effect to except by the Governments and Parliaments of the various parts of the Empire.

Four Subjects to be Discussed.

The subjects for discussion at this meeting were four. First, questions of foreign policy, which were not more closely specified, but which, no doubt, would cover the general aspect of the foreign policy of the Empire as a whole; secondly, the renewal of the Japanese Treaty; third, the question of Empire defence, and mostly the naval defence of the Empire; fourth, the settlement of the Agenda of the Constitutional Conference on Imperial relations, which it was proposed to hold, he believed, next year. At one stage they were told that it might be possible to add to this number. But they had not been notified of any additions.

Foreign Policy and the Need of Peace.

On these grave matters, some of the gravest now before the world, they had to speak with a certain amount of caution and restraint. The question of the foreign policy of the Empire in its larger aspect might seem to be very far away from them in South Africa, and yet there was nothing, even from their own domestic point of view in the world, more important than the foreign policy of the British Empire. It affected them vitally in their daily lives, in the marketing of their produce, and in all their industrial activities. That was why when a question of this kind was discussed by the highest body existing in the British Empire, South Africa should be represented.

Their point of view was that what they wanted, above all else in the world, was peace. The world wanted it; they wanted it in South Africa; and the British Empire wanted it perhaps more than any other combination or group of States in the world. Unless they had peace, the future outlook for all of them was very dark indeed. The voice of South Africa, so far as he was concerned at the next Conference, would be entirely in the direction of working to the utmost of their power to the securing of a real world peace. It was not only a question of external relations but of the very temper of their

P

people. It was impossible, while this condition of war was
going on all over the world, to have internal peace. People
might complain of what was happening in various parts of
the Empire, of the strikes and dislocations that were taking
place, but in his opinion it was simply a repercussion, a reaction
of the general state of the world, which continued to be a steady
state of war.

The Peace Treaty.

The Treaty of Versailles had not been followed by peace.
In regard to reparations, for once, the proper course had been
taken, and an attempt would be made to carry out the provisions of the Treaty on that point. He hoped that goodwill
and a sincere effort on the part of Germany to discharge her
obligations, followed with give-and-take on the other side,
would make that part of the Peace Treaty in future workable.
General Smuts added that when the records of the Peace
Conference were published it would appear that the two sets
of provisions in that Treaty which were most severely attacked
from the South African point of view were the settlements in
regard to Germany both in the West and in the East. It
had taken two years to justify entirely the attitude which was
taken by them at the Peace Conference, and both the Western
and the Eastern settlements of the German Peace Treaty had
been the most fruitful source of trouble. There had been
almost war over the Western settlement already. There
had been several wars over the Eastern settlement.

British Empire and European Entanglements.

The time had come when in the British Empire they should
take stock of their foreign policy, of their position about the
whole peace settlement, and the whole policy embodied in it. It
was impossible for the British Empire to continue being
entangled in these embroilments in Europe. It had not been the
traditional British policy. The wise traditional policy had been
to keep out of it, and he was sure the time had come when
they as an Empire should make the most serious effort possible
to extricate themselves from these troubles and advocate
and foster a policy of peace on the Continent of Europe.
There was, unfortunately, that great feud between the French
and the German people, which had gone on for centuries. The
time had come for the British Empire to appear on the scene
not as a party, but as a peacemaker, and see whether it was
not possible by a great effort to get Europe out of the rut into
which she had been drifting to final disaster. After all, the
British Empire had emerged from the war the most powerful

organism on earth, and it would not be a worthy part to appear to back any policy which did not bear the very highest character.

It was the proper course for the British Empire to lay down her own peaceful policy without being dragged about by any of these partisans of the Continent. If he were asked what should be the foreign policy of the Empire, he would say it should be one of trying to remove the feelings which were keeping asunder the countries of Europe, and of trying to re-establish normal conditions on the Continent. That was a policy which would be to the interest of every portion of the British Empire. Whatever power they could bring to bear from their small angle in South Africa should be brought to bear from that point and in that ratio.

The Japanese Treaty.

The Japanese Treaty did not affect them directly. It affected very largely those parts of the British Empire which bordered on the Pacific—Canada, Australia and New Zealand. To them it seemed a far-away question, and yet it was more than that, and did affect them to some extent. Mr. Hughes, the Prime Minister of Australia, in a speech which he made some months ago, said it was in the interests of Australia to renew this Treaty on certain conditions. In the first place; he wanted to safeguard her white policy. Secondly, she was very anxious that no offence should be given to America ; and subject to these conditions being fulfilled, Mr. Hughes was in favour of its renewal.

Vital Changes in the Situation since 1902.

There was no doubt that the position all over the world had changed vitally and fundamentally since 1902, when the Treaty was concluded. He supposed that if it were a question of entering into a new Treaty to-day, there would be little hesitation as to what conclusions the British Empire would come to ; but this Treaty was concluded many years ago, had been renewed several times, and either the renewal or continuation of it now must raise very great questions indeed. Since the treaty was entered into, Russia had disappeared as a trade Power, and Germany also, for the time being. The position of Japan in the East had altered completely. She had a great position now in China, Siberia, and other parts too. From a larger point of view also there was no doubt that since 1902 the friction between Japan and the Western States of America had also increased, so that from all these points of view they would see how very intricate the whole

P 2

question was. The paramount consideration that they ough
to keep before them in the future, and in the very difficul
times lying ahead, was that it was essential, as far as possible
to secure understanding and co-operation between the Britis
Empire and the United States of America. He considere
that the second essential and cardinal principle of thei
foreign policy.

Mr. F. W. Beyers (Nationalist, *Edenburg, O.F.S*): "Wha
about the fleet America is building ? "

Importance of Friendship with United States.

The Prime Minister said one thing he was certain of
that the fleet was not being built for use against the Br
Empire, or any part of that Empire. When he looked at
question as a whole, and the interests for which they stoo
the world, it seemed to him vital that every effort sh
be made to keep in touch, sympathy and contact with
great American Republic. A great and substantial po
of the British Empire adjoined the United States of Am
and was working in friendly relationship with these St
From the point of view of their interests as an Empire
European civilisation as a whole there was no doubt
should try and work with America, and remove all gr
for friction and misunderstanding with her; and that t
was subject to that consideration. He agreed that no re
should take place unless they could satisfy America b
form of the treaty that no harm to her interests could
its renewal.

Mr. C. G. Fichardt (Nationalist, *Ladybrand, O.*
" What about our old ally, France ? "

The Prime Minister : " I am speaking of the rene
the Anglo-Japanese Alliance, with which France has n
to do."

Imperial Defence.

Continuing, the Prime Minister said the third
they would deal with at the Conference was that of I
Defence, and he assumed from what he had heard an
that what was really intended was a discussion of the
question of Naval defence. That question arose in
again in regard to the Pacific at the Imperial Confere
New Zealand, and at that Conference a resolution was
he believed, calling on the Admiralty to lay down a
the naval defence of the Pacific. That plan was
been sent to the various Dominions for their consider
be elaborated upon by some other conference. The
continued, however, and nothing was done until aft

when Lord Jellicoe was sent around the Empire to consider the question of its naval defence so far as it affected the Pacific. He assumed that it was the report which he had made that was really the matter coming up for discussion.

Redistribution of Naval Units.

It was a matter of grave and urgent interest. The problem of naval defence had altered. Before the war the fighting part of the British fleet congregated in the North Sea; the need for it there existed no longer; the German fleet had disappeared, and the whole question of naval defence required readjustment and redistribution of the naval units of the Empire. The question to be considered was what part of the fleet had to remain in European waters and what part should be distributed in the Pacific, and what portions of the Dominion fleets should take part in the defence of their own countries. This grave question was one in which they in South Africa had, as it were, only a small interest. Their route, their part of the world, however important from other points of view, was not important in that direction, and, as they knew, even within the last few months the naval units which were stationed there had been decreased in number, showing the change in naval opinion in the world. The vital spots for defence were in other waters of the world.

Naval Policy of South Africa.

Replying to a question as to the strategic position, the Prime Minister said that would always remain very great, but there was no danger visible on the horizon from that point of view. The question of their naval policy was a separate one which would require a great deal of consideration from them. The whole question, as he argued it last year, and the Government still maintained the position, was that they should become directly responsible so far as their means allowed, though he admitted that their needs far transcended their financial possibilities, but they could, at any rate, move in the direction of becoming more and more able to undertake the naval defence of their country. Whether that question would be raised at the Conference he did not know; he believed something far larger and more important would be brought up. If it were, however, he and his colleagues would go thoroughly into it with the naval authorities, and they would be prepared to bring the subject before the House at another Session.

There remained another question—especially important from a South African point of view—the programme to be

put before the Constitutional Conference which it was proposed to hold next year. They had discussed, to a great
extent, their international status as a result of what happened
at Paris and after the War. There was a great deal of uncertainty and insecurity in the position as a whole. He was
certain about it, because he knew what the South Africa
Act was to-day. It was essential for them and for the other
Dominions to have a clear conception of what their status
was as members of the British Empire and their position in
the League of Nations.

South Africa's Status: Importance of Constitutional Conference.

They must settle the future relations of the Dominions,
and he thought they must discuss also this Conference system
which had been in existence now for some years as between
the various parts of the Empire and the capital, which has
held it together. He did not want to revive troubles in that
country which he hoped were passing away, and to stir up
any feeling in the House ; he would be the last man in the
world to do it. In the recent elections he took up a very
strong stand ; he saw the position of the country and fought
as hard as he could against the Republican propaganda. He
never had any intention of belittling South Africa, whose
status had always been his first consideration. He had always
tried to point out that there was no other way than Union.
That was the ideal put before South Africa : the ideal of a
country which looked after itself, which is mistress in her
own house, and independent in all essential meanings of the
word. " Yes, the open door," the Prime Minister said, in
reply to a question.

The policy was wrong which intended to cut them off
from the Empire and the League of Nations. It might have
been possible 200 years ago, but as the world was developing
and as dangers were surrounding every country in the world,
it would be impossible to cut themselves off from the Empire
and the League of Nations. While he had taken up that
attitude, and it must be one that would satisfy the needs of
the freedom-loving people of South Africa, he looked upon
the Conference of next year as one of the most important
events that was going to take place in the British Empire.
He hoped when it had met many of the disputes that had
divided them in that country would disappear. He held the
feeling that they should go to that Conference, not merely
as a Government, but that the people should have the right
to express their views.

Representation of the Dominions.

One of the things they would have to settle at the Conference meeting next month would be the representation of the Dominions at this Conference, whether it will be members of the Government, or include the various parties and not the Government only, or on what basis representation shall be. It was a matter of great importance, and he was anxious that all parties should take part in these discussions and be brought face to face with the real position, and that the resolutions which would be taken in 1922 would have behind them the weight of every considerable political factor.

The "British Commonwealth," America and League of Nations.

The Right Hon. J. X. Merriman (South African Party, *Stellenbosch, Cape*) said the speech had told them exactly what they wanted to know. The foreign policy was one of the most important questions they had to deal with. They should have no misunderstanding about the position, which was that what they called the British Empire was really the British Commonwealth. They wanted to work in harmony with the U.S.A. In dealing with that they must remember the attitude that America had taken up with regard to the League of Nations. Mr. Roosevelt had said that the League would be a fertile source of strife. Had not that been true? There had been many wars and contentions continued even now.

Importance to South Africa of Japanese Treaty.

He agreed with the Prime Minister about the Japanese. That was a very important matter, because it had to deal not only with Australia and America, but with the awakening of the whole of Asia. They have largely a control by the Anglo-Japanese Alliance, which might be one of the most important questions in the world, bearing on the future of that country more than at present. It was owing to that treaty more than anything else that Java and Sumatra had been kept in possession of a power like Holland with no army and no navy. In their own interests and those of Holland they should try and secure a renewal of the treaty.

Power of the British Navy.

In regard to Imperial Defence, the one thing that bound the British people together was the British Navy. It was policing the British Dominions. It kept the seas open for

them, and they must realise what it meant to them that
Great Britain in six weeks' time should strike and annihilate
a hostile force on the other side of the Atlantic.

Mr. N. C. Havenga (Nationalist, *Fauresmith,* **O.F.S.):**
" We have had experience of the British Navy in this country."

Mr. Merriman said they had and they ought to be very
grateful too. It would be a sorry day for them when they
did not have it. It was the British Navy that had made the
British Empire the power that it was. It was the finest
example of discipline and order and power in the world at
the present time. He hoped the Prime Minister would
shape his policy so that they took their share in that service.

Criticism of League of Nations.

In regard to the League of Nations, they were asked to
pay this year £62,000. For what? Their share of cleaning
the railway carriages in Serbia, or for taking troops to
Poland? So far as contributions were concerned, they were
placed in the category of first-class countries. Why should
they pay the same as France or Japan or China or the British
Empire? It was all done by units. They paid 25 units.
New Zealand, a fairly prosperous country with a white population of about 1½ millions, the same as they had, only paid
three units. According to the scale which had been drawn
out, they (in South Africa) ought to pay about £24,000, and
New Zealand on the same basis paid about £2,500. The
Argentine Republic, which was more populous and prosperous than that country, only paid five units. Mr. Merriman
referred to the obligation undertaken in Section 10; the
whole thing was a curious mixture of engagements of all kinds.
One section gave the League the power to interfere in their
internal affairs, and they had got to pay whatever it liked
to ask them. He hoped they would try and get out of this
League of Nations. The Prime Minister had rightly said
that it was a terrible Treaty to which they had put their
hands. One way of making it less terrible would be to get
themselves out of their entanglement with these numberless
little partners. They could not fulfil their engagements to
them and did not intend to fulfil them.

Progress was reported and leave obtained to sit again
on 23rd May.

On the resumption of the debate on 23rd May,
**General the Hon. J. B. M. Hertzog (Leader of the Nationalist
Party)** expressed his appreciation of what Mr. Merriman had
said in regard to the protection which Holland should enjoy
from England. Holland had undoubtedly done a great deal

for the civilisation of the world. He trusted that in the question he was going to refer to they would regard matters from the point of view of South Africa and as Africanders. By the continuous contact with the English in South Africa the inhabitants there better understood the English than any other section or nation in the world, with the result that the relations and bonds with other countries were often lost sight of.

Position of General Smuts at the Conference.

Continuing, General Hertzog asked the House to ask itself where the Prime Minister's policy would bring them. He had never known yet where General Smuts really stood in his politics. He certainly had spoken with caution, and only on the question of the Japanese Treaty had he expressed the views of his Cabinet so that the House could understand his meaning. He was pleased at what the Prime Minister had said about the Conference to which he was going being a mere consultative body, but how was it that General Smuts occupied the position of a Prime Minister of the Empire? Although the Conference was not that of an Empire Cabinet, the Prime Ministers were going to take part there not as Prime Ministers of South Africa, or Canada, but as Prime Ministers of the Empire, so that they were going there not to consider questions affecting their own countries, but questions affecting the Empire. General Smuts had said that no resolutions binding South Africa could be taken, but resolutions could be taken which might be binding on the Prime Minister and his colleagues, thus constituting a moral obligation and, in effect, binding South Africa.

Power of Decision held by England.

As regarded the important questions to be dealt with, General Hertzog urged the greatest caution. What power or authority did the Prime Ministers of all the Dominions have in regard to the foreign policy of the Empire? None. They could give advice, but the decision lay with the English people, and with nobody else.

Separation or Surrender of Rights.

The old conditions of the Empire had changed, he continued. Canada and Australia had said: " We are not going to assist you unless we have a say," and to that England had said: " No, we are not going to hand the decision in our foreign policy over to the Dominions." Thus the two alternatives had been created—either separation from each other or the surrender of the rights which the Dominions had.

In the Treaty of Versailles and the words of the Prime Minister there-anent he saw what the future held for the Dominions. In spite of the objections of the Dominions and the protests of the Prime Minister, that Treaty had been concluded, and to-morrow they would be told : "You helped us to conclude that Treaty : come and help us to carry it out."

England and European Politics.

General Smuts had put a terrible picture before South Africa, and had urged the necessity of their keeping outside European entanglements, but at the same time he favoured the Empire as an Empire entering these. His declaration that England had never interfered with European politics was hopelessly inaccurate. Never had a century passed that England had not interfered with European politics—in fact, England's policy since the days of Cæsar had been one of regarding itself as an integral part of the European continent. Why had America become so great ? General Hertzog added. Simply because it had always most emphatically refused to take part in European politics.

Japanese Treaty no concern of South Africa.

After appealing to the Prime Minister to take as little part in the policy of the Empire as possible, and to confine himself solely to the affairs of South Africa, General Hertzog asked what right they had to interfere in a matter like that of the Japanese Treaty ? The whole question did not concern them, and whatever advice the Prime Minister gave must eventually be to their detriment. General Smuts should say, "As Prime Minister I have nothing to do with the matter, but as a person that is my advice." Assuming that the Treaty should detrimentally affect America in ten years, America would naturally remember that South Africa had advised in the matter. If America were asked to-day whether there should or should not be a treaty, she would, of course, say "No treaty."

Objections to Defence Policy of the Empire.

In regard to defence, he protested against the Empire question being brought in again. Their defence system was daily being linked to the European military chain, the object being that in future wars South Africa and Great Britain should go hand in hand. The more they stood on their own feet the more it would keep them out of wars. In regard to the Prime Minister and his colleagues taking part in the question of naval defence, had anyone ever heard anything more ridiculous

They had not even a small barge of their own. England wanted them to take part so that they would be responsible with her for anything she did, and if eventually they had their own fleet it would have to help England. The whole object was to get them bound down.

It was a fatal step that the Prime Minister should go each year to these Conferences. He was only human and subject to influence and environment, and he might make mistakes which might have a far-reaching effect, and then on returning to South Africa he would not be able to use his influence for its benefit. If it was necessary that South Africa should be represented, then it should be by some emissary in London. Prime Ministers were wanted because they had greater influence and could bind their countries.

Constitutional Conference.

The decisions of the Constitutional Conference next year would be more far-reaching than anybody could anticipate. He regretted that the Constitutional Conference could not have been held before the one to which General Smuts was going. The resolutions of this year's Conference must unquestioningly influence those of next year. How could they lay down an Empire policy and next year deal with the constitution of the Empire? General Smuts had said that this year's Conference was to lay down the representation at next year's Conference, whether only the Government was to be represented or the whole people of South Africa. Consequently next year's Conference was to bind the people of South Africa. General Smuts had said that there had been a new form of Empire, and now next year a Conference was to be held. Was it going to bind all the members of the Empire just as the Act of Union bound all parts of South Africa? If not, why should the people be represented? He was not prepared as yet to give a reply whether his side would be represented. He would await the invitation, but neither he nor his colleagues would permit of one single right of South Africa being interfered with, and if the Conference would have the right to bind South Africa he would certainly not tolerate that.

Labour Point of View.

Mr. T. Boydell* (**Leader of the Labour Party**) said General Hertzog had not given any instance of where South

---

* Owing to the defeat of Colonel Creswell at the General Election, Mr. Boydell was elected to succeed him as Leader of the Labour Party in Parliament.

Africa would be in a better or stronger position, or would benefit by not being a member of the British Common-wealth of Nations. The day had gone by when any country could stand aside and take up a position of isolation and refuse to take any part in the politics of the world. There was no section of the community, he continued, more vitally con-cerned in foreign politics and in world politics than the working classes. When trouble came, in the bulk they had got to do the paying, and very often they had got to do the slaying. If they did not take that close interest in foreign politics that they ought to do it was not because they did not wish to do so, but because of two reasons. One was that most of them were engaged in a daily warfare in order to get their daily bread ; the second was that the peoples of the world never knew what was going on in the Foreign Office. The Parlia-ments of the world, as a rule, did not know what the Foreign Office was doing.

Labour Representation.

He was pleased that the Conference next year was to be representative of all shades of thought and opinion, and all parties that would be affected in any settlement that might be arrived at. In future the representatives of Labour should be taken more into confidence when matters like this affecting their welfare were being discussed and settled. When the principles upon which the ruling classes in the past had acted had failed to provide peace in the world, it was even more important that the principles for which Labour stood should have an opportunity of being represented and infused into the decisions which were arrived at. He hoped the Prime Minister would make it quite clear that so far as South Africa was con-cerned she was not to be committed to any definite policy until they had had an opportunity in that House of know-ing exactly what that policy was and of either ratifying or rejecting it.

Secret Diplomacy and Alliances.

Proceeding, Mr. Boydell referred to the matter of secret diplomacy and alliances. It was only now that America was building a big navy and creating a large army that England was anxious to make an alliance with her. The desire was to make an alliance with either jingoistic Japan or capitalistic America, but these alliances did not bring peace. One of the most prolific causes of war was secret diplomacy, and he wished to ask the Prime Minister whether he would work at the Conference for all treaties between nations in the future to be made public before being entered into, and sub mitted to the Parliaments of the nations affected to be either ratified or rejected. He urged him also to press for the nationalisation of munition works and the abolition of trade rivalry. There should be open markets for all nations in all countries.

Russia and Ireland.

Referring to Russia, Mr. Boydell said they wanted to know what was going to be the attitude of South Africa towards the Soviet Government ? Russia had as much right to say what form of government it wanted as any other Power. It was difficult to speak on that subject because they had not first-hand information. In regard to Ireland, he did not think it wise to meddle in other people's affairs, but the position there must be the concern of every man, woman and child, no matter what their nationality or in what part of the world they lived. He was not taking any side, but if the Prime Minister could do anything while in England to lay the foundation of what would lead up to a peaceful settlement he would deserve well not only of South Africa, but of all the civilised countries in the world.

Freedom within the British Empire.

Coming to the status of South Africa, Mr. Boydell said the Labour Party had always taken the stand that South Africa would be better off by remaining an integral part of the British Commonwealth of Nations than as one nation isolated from other nations and from Great Britain. To-day they had very nearly the maximum of freedom and political liberty in deciding their own affairs. They had a constitution which enabled them to work out their own aims and objects, which enabled South Africa to control its own destinies, and he would ask General Hertzog if he could name any case in which Great Britain had interfered with anything the South African Parliament had done. It was his opinion that if the people of South Africa had not sufficient sense to make the best use of her present Constitution, they would not have sufficient sense to make any better use of a republican constitution. Until such time as there was interference with South Africa doing what it wanted through the medium of her own constitution, he thought it was a thousand times better for her to remain as at present—an integral part of the British Empire.

Greatest Disappointment in History."

He regarded the League of Nations as the greatest disappointment in history.

Mr. J. W. Mushet (South African Party, *Liesbeck, Cape*):
" Give it a chance."

Mr. Boydell said he would like to do so if the Prime
Minister would say that it could be made a League of people's
interests. But it had already been " collared " by the world's
capitalists, for the policy of deflation which was causing
stagnation in the world to-day was decided upon by the
Finance Committee of the League in Brussels. If goodwill
and the brotherhood of man were to mean anything, then the
economic system must be altered.

The Development of Africa: Danger to White Civilisation.

Mr. G. H. Nicholls (South African Party, *Zululand, Natal*)
referred to an important omission in General Smuts's valuable
speech, and also in General Hertzog's. The question was,
what position was the South African nation, that white
Christian civilisation, going to occupy in the rapidly expanding
and developing continent of Africa ? Were they going to
allow the whole world, European and Asiatic, to come into
the heart of Africa and develop its resources to their own
enrichment, and set up forces which might strangle that
young nation of theirs while they stood by and never said
a word in their own defence ? It seemed to him that their
interests as the only civilised nation in Africa formed a fit
subject for discussion at this Imperial Conference. It was
vitally necessary that the Prime Ministers of other Dominions
should understand their position. Beyond their borders there
was a black wall. The time had arrived when they should
claim the right to be heard in counteracting any of the currents
set up by administrations on their borders that might have
an inimical effect on the native people.

East Africa: The Asiatic Menace, etc.

Mr. Nicholls went on to refer to the position in Rhodesia
and the Belgian Congo. Then there was the territory in East
Africa which had been worthless until South Africa subdued it.
The eyes of the European world were on East Africa. They
were faced with the position that all this country was open to
the Asiatic. The whole of the Western world was pouring its
wealth into Central Africa for the purpose of exploiting it.
The Asiatics were thronging it and the effect on Christianity
would be serious. It seemed appalling, he added, that the
statesmen of that country continued to focus their attention
upon high politics abroad, and ignored the terrible danger
which existed over their own borders. He advocated the

creation of a South African National branch or section of the League of Nations.

Objections to "Political Immigration" Policy.

Dr. D. F. Malan (**Nationalist,** *Calvinia, Cape*) referred to a question which he had put to General Smuts in regard to free or assisted passages given by the Imperial Government to South Africa. General Smuts had replied that all he knew about the matter was what he had read in the papers, and that South Africa had no obligation towards these immigrants. The Prime Minister should have made it his business to attend to such matters, and should have protested against such immigration taking place without consultation of the Union Government. Dr. Malan, after giving further details, declared that the whole immigration policy was part of the old Unionist policy, and carried out with definite racial objects, aiming at racial domination. Unless the Government discontinued its present policy of political immigration, South Africa would become a second Ireland.

Motion to Reduce Expenses of League of Nations.

Proceeding to deal with the League of Nations, Dr. Malan moved to reduce the vote of £62,000 for the League of Nations Secretariat to £15,000. In the first place, South Africa's share of the expenses was too large, and secondly he did so as a protest against the prostitution of the League by the Supreme Council. His conceptions of a League of Nations were that it should be a combination of nations in which not the weak but the strong nations should be bound down. He claimed that England's refusal to give up her supremacy at sea had sounded the death-knell of the League of Nations.

After a review of the historical position, Dr. Malan dealt at some length with the records of the Imperial Conferences to show that it had been decided that every year a meeting of the Imperial Cabinet was to be held to deal with questions of Imperial policy. He fully accepted the position that South Africa and the Dominions were on a footing of absolute equality with England.

Other Objections.

He quoted at length from Mr. Duncan Hall's "The British Commonwealth of Nations" to prove that General Smuts's grounds (in holding that South Africa had not the right of self-determination and could not appoint its own Governor-General) were unsound, and protested, amongst other things, that in regard to international affairs South Africa could do nothing on her own, but had to go through London, so to speak, through an international exchange.

He contended that the Conferences that had been held had not in any way tended to extend their rights and liberties, and that their object was to close up, to consolidate the Empire. There was a danger of the Prime Minister compromising and binding South Africa, and on his return he would make a party matter of what he had done, with the result that his proposals would be passed by the House. Concluding, Dr. Malan said that while accepting the basis of equality with England for South Africa, the Nationalists were not prepared to pay the price which the Prime Minister wanted them to pay.

After further discussion, progress was reported and leave obtained to sit again the next day.

On 25th May, after further discussion,

The Prime Minister, replying to criticisms that had been made, mentioned the question of the black troops on the Rhine, which had been raised by one speaker. This was a very painful question, and speaking as head of the Government he must do so with a great deal of restraint, because even now their information on the subject was very scanty. He had felt all along that a very grave mistake had been made in sending black troops to the Rhine, and he had had no hesitation in expressing his opinion about it. The Government of South Africa had gone further indeed, and in the Mandates for African Colonies there was a clause inserted at his own instance which said that the native populations of these territories should not be used for military purposes outside their own areas.

League of Nations.

In regard to the contribution to the League of Nations the same basis had been taken as in the case of the Universal Postal Bureau. It was admitted that that basis was unfair to the smaller and younger countries, and the Assembly of the League at its last meeting appointed a Committee to consider this question.

He asked the House, as a matter of very grave concern to give the institution of the League a chance. Dr. Malan had said that it had been prostituted by the Supreme Council Did he not see that that was very largely an answer to his own case against the League ? Here they had a small infant just born, unable almost to take care of itself, and next to it an association of some of the most powerful nations on earth actually in existence, fighting tooth and nail for the ground on which they are standing, some of them, no doubt, fearing that this infant would grow up. " Don't let us fight the League of Nations," the Prime Minister said, " let us fight the Supreme Council. It is not the League that is wrong ; it is the Supreme Council that may be wrong. . . . The Supreme Council may be in the melting-pot to-morrow. . . . Let us leave no stone unturned. Let us close no avenue of hope for the future of the world."

Constitutional Status.

The Debate, he continued, had shown that, in spite of the whole-hearted differences of opinion in that country, they were beginning to get to grips with the real facts that agitated them in South Africa, and to realise that difference of opinion did not necessarily imply moral obliquity. In regard to the constitution of the Dominions, and the best way of removing all obscurity from the undoubted freedom and power which belonged to their status, it had been said that this should be done by some declaration, some deed of their own ; but taking the bit between one's teeth, carrying through in a high-handed way one's own will as a nation, did not pay. There was only one proper way, that was, by coming together, talking things over, and coming to an understanding.

British Empire Defined.

Replying to General Hertzog, the Prime Minister said there was no Government of the Empire, there was no Prime Minister of the Empire, and no Minister of the Empire. The British Empire was a name for a group of free and equal States. There was no unity, no entity. This Conference was a Conference of Governments or Prime Ministers of the various States which belonged to their Commonwealth. It could take no binding action. It could consult and confer, it could exchange ideas and try to get clearness of light on a situation which to-day was as dark as any situation had been in all history, but that was all it could do. The principle involved by the League of Nations, that nations would no longer act on their own, but come together and consult, that would be the way of the British Empire League of Nations. No doubt there was a certain amount of risk of getting committed, but it all depended upon whom they sent to these conferences. He could see no alternative, no matter what Government they had, of keeping things going whether they were in the British Empire or not, except by coming together in a system of conferences and consultations such as they were proposing to hold.

Q

A Strong Stand.

A strong stand would be taken. It had been don
before. He thought that by taking a strong mandate an
expressing the principles for which they stood in a straight
forward manner, great things could be achieved, not onl
for South Africa, but for the other countries of the Empir
The voice of South Africa might yet be useful in solvin
problems which the world appeared to be finding almo;
insoluble.

Japanese Treaty and Naval Defence.

After a further allusion to the Japanese Treaty, in regai
to which there was no reason why South Africa should n
express her opinion though she was under no obligation
join the alliance, as the Treaty was between Great Brita
and Japan, the Prime Minister made a further allusion
naval defence, and appealed to the House not to dischar
"this big task in a small way." Let them take the oppo
tunity of being helpful to others. They should realise, l
added, that the British Empire had no interest in wars, b
in peace and in the peaceful development of the vario
countries comprising the Empire. If they followed the histo
of the Empire, they would find that the whole trend of develo
ment had been towards greater freedom, liberty and indepen
ence, and he could not conceive that this movement was goi
to be suddenly and artificially reversed by the Constitution
Conference. They were a group of nations working togeth
under one King, pursuing, he hoped, the same peaceful a
humanitarian end.

The Vote, as printed, was agreed to, and progress report.

LEAGUE OF NATIONS AND MILITARY ESTIMATES

In the House of Assembly, on 12th April,

Mr. J. H. B. Wessels (Nationalist, *Bethlehem,* **O.F.**)
asked whether the Government had received a letter fr
the League of Nations submitting for consideration a
approval a proposal for the acceptance by the Union Gove
ment of an undertaking not to exceed, during the two finan
years following upon the next Budget Estimates, the t
amount for military expenditure provided for in th
Estimates ; what had been the reply of the Union Gove
ment.

**The Prime Minister (Lieut.-General the Right Hon. J.
Smuts)** replied in the affirmative. The matter was still un
consideration and the House would be duly informed of
Government's decision.

UNION DEFENCE FORCES BILL.

(Registration of Citizens: Peace Training, etc.)

This Bill, which makes further provision for the Permanent Defence Force, for compulsory registration and peace training and for the training ot cadets, was introduced by the Minister of Defence, who moved the First Reading on 4th April.

PERMANENT FORCE.

The Bill provides that the Permanent Force constituted under the South Africa Defence Act, 1912, shall be reconstituted and designated the South African Permanent Force.

This Force or any portion thereof shall for all purposes be liable to be employed in like manner as, and have the same powers, duties, obligations, privileges, and indemnities as were prescribed for the Permanent Force under the South Africa Defence Act, 1912. For the purpose of section seventy-six of that Act the Union shall include the mandatory territory of South-West Africa.

PERMANENT FORCE RESERVE.

The Permanent Force may include a Headquarters Staff and instructional and administrative staffs, Field Artillery, Mounted Riflemen, Garrison Artillery, Infantry, Air Force, Engineers, Signalling and communication corps and departmental services, etc. The Bill provides for the establishment of a Permanent Force Reserve consisting of (A) members of the Permanent Force who, having completed their period of engagement in that force, are required to complete a further period of service in the South African Permanent Force Reserve ; provided that no member of the Permanent Force shall, upon the expiry of his engagement, be required to serve more than five years in the Reserve, or to serve in it after his 35th year ; (B) all other citizens, except members of the Coast Garrison Force, Active Citizen Force, or Royal Naval Volunteer Reserve, who fulfil the prescribed conditions as to age, physical fitness and military experience who are deemed suitable and engage themselves for service therein.

TRAINING REMUNERATION, ETC.

Members of the Reserve may be required to undergo short courses of training and report themselves at such times and places as may be prescribed. Any member may, under the instructions of the Minister or, in time of war, by proclamation in the *Gazette*) be called out at any time for duty with the Permanent Force and be employed under the same conditions as if he were a serving member of that force. Remuneration and conditions of service, while undertaking training or duty in that Reserve, shall be subject to the Military Discipline Code. Provision will be made for the same pension and gratuities and other consideration to his widow and dependants, or to him, as may be provided in like circumstances for members of the Permanent Force.

Registration of Citizens.

Every person (A) who, being a citizen, attains his seventeenth yea during any of the calendar years 1918, 1919, 1920 or 1921, or (B) become a citizen and reaches that age in any of the years aforesaid, is require to register during January, 1922, in the manner described und the South Africa Defence Act, 1912. If any citizen required so register is outside the Union during the whole of that month (Januar or for any other reason is not registered then, he shall, if he compli with the conditions prescribed for registration after that month, I permitted to register ; and the absence or other reason shall be a defen to any proceedings for failure to comply with the provisions of th sub-section. Any citizen failing to register shall be guilty of an offen This section shall be read as one with the provisions of Section 53 the South Africa Defence Act, 1912, and any other provisions there ancillary or incidental to that section.

Peace Training.

The course of peace training in the Active Citizen Force shall exte over a period of four years, from 1st of July in year of entry, but subj to such conditions as are prescribed. Normally the training shall completed in four years, but on grounds of educational or vocatio training or ill-health, there may be prescribed conditions under wh permission may be granted to complete the full course not later th the last day of June in the sixth year from date of entry.

The course of peace training shall include three periods of c tinuous training, of which one shall last not more than sixty days, a the other two periods taken together not more than thirty days. T longer period shall, unless otherwise prescribed on educational or ot grounds, be undergone during the first twelve months of the four-y period, and shall be reduced by one-third in the case of a citizen has completed his cadet training under the South Africa Defence A 1912, and attained a prescribed standard of efficiency in drill musketry, etc. In addition to the three periods of training, mem of the Active Citizen Force may be required to undergo as may prescribed non-continuous training during the four-year period afo said for not more than a total number of 26 days.

Uniform for Cadet Officers ; Allowances ; Etc.

Uniform clothing for cadet officers, and such scales and conditi as are prescribed and expenses thereof shall be defrayed out of mon voted by Parliament. Subject to financial provision being made Parliament, there may be granted in respect of each cadet an an allowance of an amount to be prescribed, in order to defray miscellan charges under expenses of cadet detachments.

Training of Boys while at School.

Notwithstanding anything in Section 6 of the South African Def Act, 1912, boys who are being educated at a school at which a c detachment has been established, may continue while remaining sch there to receive training as cadets until and including their twent year. Any period of such training from the 1st July in their seven year may be reckoned in addition to the provision made in Secti 6 of this Act as equivalent to peace training in the Active Citize F under such conditions as are prescribed.

DEBATE IN HOUSE OF ASSEMBLY.

In the House of Assembly on 8th April,

The Minister of Defence (Colonel the Hon. H. Mentz), in moving the Second Reading, said there was practically nothing new in that Bill ; it dealt with the same class of forces as they had in the existing law. The Defence Force of the Union consisted of the Permanent Force, the Coast Garrison, the Active Citizen Force, and the Royal Naval Volunteer Reserve. The S.A.M.R. had been used in a dual capacity as police, and in time of war they could be called up ; but it was found that they could not have good policemen and good soldiers both at the same time, and while he wanted to say everything he could in commendation of the S.A.M.R., when they had to mobilise them it was not such an easy thing making an efficient military force of them as if these same men constituted a permanent force such as was now contemplated. Most of these men were with the police to-day, and those who wanted to remain there could do so ; others could join that Permanent Force again.

Air Force.

In regard to the Air Force, although provision had been made for that in the existing law, very little was known of that force at the time the Act had been passed. Proper provision was now made for the Air Force as part of the Permanent Force. The headquarters of the squadrons would be at Pretoria and Bloemfontein.

Pension Rights for S.A.M.R., etc.

Provision was made for the pension rights for the old S.A.M.R. who had done their duty grandly on every occasion and deserved well of the country. Then there was the Permanent Force Reserve, which would be composed of men of the Permanent Force and such other citizens as were mentioned under Clause 4 (1) (h). As to the registration and training of the Active Citizen Force, the law made provision for it to-day, and notice of such training could be given ; but in view of the war and the feelings which had been aroused, they had not pressed for that registration.

Registration of Citizens from 17 to 21.

The time had now undoubtedly arrived when the Defence Force should be brought into line and the law carried out, and, therefore, provision was made (Clause 5) for the registration in January, 1922, of citizens of 17 to 21 years of age.

That, they expected, would bring in 17,000 or 18,000 men
the law provided that 50 per cent. of these might be trained
so that the maximum which they had to consider was about
8,000 or 9,000 men—not more. There was no necessity
to train even that number, but such number as the authorities
thought could be trained. The continuous training provided for was 90 days—60 days and two succeeding periods
totalling 30 days. There would be a rebate to those who
had been trained as cadets, and the longest period of training
in their case would be 40 days and two periods of 10 or 2
days. A much larger number of men would be obtained
and much less money spent if these men were trained for one
long period.

Regarding the financial side, they must not attack the
rights of men who had signed on for a fixed period. but those
who signed on " under these conditions " would get pay of
5s. per day, with an allowance which was called a " nominal
value allowance," the idea being that it was much cheaper
in practice for the State to provide uniform, rations, lodging
and medical attendance than for the individual to do so
Where a force of 2,600 men had cost £803,000, under that Bill
a force of 2,460 would cost £630,000, or an annual saving
of £173,000. They had not only to provide for the gap
occupied by the S.A.M.R., but they were on the point of
taking over the defences at Cape Town and Durban, and
for that they must have highly trained and efficient men
for that reason it was necessary to start with the training.

The debate was adjourned.

Nationalist Criticism.

On the resumption of the debate on 11th April,

Mr. J. H. H. de Waal (**Nationalist,** *Piquetburg, Cape*)
said no doubt the Defence Act required amending, and
this respect he wished to emphasise the evils of the Cadet
camps. He argued that Cadet camps should be held
every district instead of Cadets being sent far from their
homes. While the financial condition of the country was
admittedly serious, however, Colonel Mentz came forward
with proposals for the establishment of a permanent force
which would involve the country in many hundreds of thousands of pounds, and what was the object of it all, to have
such a force at a time of peace ? The speaker also criticised
the longer compulsory military training provisions, spoke
of the evils of the Cadet camps, etc., and moved that the
Bill be read six months hence.

Mr. S. A. Alberts (**Nationalist,** *Witwatersberg, Trans.*)
in seconding the amendment, said the present Act did not

In any way answer the requirements of the rural districts. The training camps lasted too long, and were held too far away from the homes of the children, which interfered with the religious character of the latter.

General J. C. G. Kemp (Nationalist, *Wolmaransstad, Trans.*) condemned the Bill, which, he said, could not have the support of the people, and in the course of his remarks referred to the attack on German West Africa as a " freebooters' attack to rob another country." The House should be very careful in dealing with a matter of this kind, because the defence of the Commonwealth affected every section of the community. Was it the Minister's intention to bind South Africa to participate in the defence of the Empire ? To that he would never give his consent. After further remarks, he moved that the order for the Second Reading be discharged, and that the subject matter of the Bill be referred to a Select Committee, with instructions to bring up an amended Bill.

General the Hon. J. B. M. Hertzog (Leader of the Nationalist Party) seconded, and said what the Government was doing was nothing but to create an out-and-out militarism, a system which not so long ago everybody had been extremely anxious to condemn. Was the Minister aware of the anxiety felt by the population in regard to their defence system ? There were portions of the Bill which he might agree with ; placed in the right hands it might be a weapon for good. Placed in the hands of a Government whose policy he and his friends were convinced was to the detriment of South Africa, it would undoubtedly prove a very evil weapon. He expressed nervousness as to what would happen at the Imperial Conference in June, and similar nervousness was displayed in other Dominions, which it was now tried to drag into the political maelstrom of Europe.

General Hertzog went on to say that he was in favour of sending the Bill to a Select Committee. The provision in the Bill aiming at the registration of young men who had reached the age in the last two or three years was one which would create the greatest dissatisfaction in South Africa. They all agreed as to the necessity of having a Defence Act, but the actions or abuse of the Government had made that Act so unpopular that it would take years to right matters.

After criticising the expenditure which would be incurred, he referred to the native Protectorates under the Union. All these had large populations. He did not say this because he was nervous of the native population's attitude ; in their Protectorates, however, they had Administrations appointed by the British Government, they had no responsibility for anything that took place there. He trusted that whatever

was done the Government would act in concert with th
Administrations in those territories, so that things might n
take place there which might seriously affect the Unio
without the latter having any say or responsibility.

He added that he hoped a truly South African flag woul
be carried in the Defence Force. They did no service t
themselves, nor to England, by bearing the Union Jack. T
him the latter was merely a piece of cloth. Once they ha
their own flag it would lead to better feelings, and remov
misunderstandings too. A Defence Act, General Hertzo
said in conclusion, must breathe the people's spirit, and mu
be a true defence measure.

The Labour View.

Mr. T. Boydell (**Leader of the Labour Party**) said th
main provision of the Bill, to set up a standing army, was
new departure. Before the War what they had was
police force to provide the nucleus of a standing arm
for an emergency, if it arose, and that method, the
submitted, was preferable to the proposals now before th
House. The police were civilians also ; they led their liv
among the people—they were not a race apart. They wei
going to set up a force of 2,600 soldiers to do soldiering
not police work. That was what they did not want to develo
Mr. Boydell went on to ask why the Bill was brought forwa
at this juncture ? It meant greater expense. The pa
he said, was ridiculously low, and he urged that the Bill
referred to a Select Committee for members to know whe
they were. There were many people who objected to pea
training as another form of conscription. He also thoug
there should be provision for the conscientious objecto
and that the standing army should not be used in any industri
dispute.

How the Forces Might be Used.

Mr. R. Feetham (**South African Party,** *Parktown, Nat*
pointed out that the Defence Force Act laid down the us
to which the Forces might be put, and they were not asked
alter that Act now. They might be used against an enem
within or without the Union, or for the prevention and su
pression of disorders within the Union. Was it reasonab
to expect that in the event of serious disorder within t
country the Union Defence Force was to be allowed mere
to look on ? Industrial trouble might arise from Europe
or native industrial disorders. Last year many people we
concerned as to the matter of the amalgamation of t

S.A.M.R., and he believed this Bill was intended to settle in a satisfactory manner the question of the officers and men who had not been absorbed into the police force. After touching upon further points in the Bill, Mr. Feetham said he deprecated the delay which would be caused by reference to a Special Committee, and supported the Second Reading.

After further discussion the debate was adjourned.

Sole Guarantee of Security.

In the course of the debate, resumed on 13th April,

Brig.-General the Hon. J. J. Byron (South African Party, *Border, Cape*) pointed out that the security of the country rested on one and only one main fact, namely, their remaining a portion of the British Commonwealth of Nations, which had command of the sea at present, and that for many years to come they could not stand alone. A consideration of that kind ought, he thought, to have prevented such expressions as they had had about the British flag. He deprecated the fact that the provision of this small Permanent Force would lead to militarism, and after reminding the House that the military life of the average man was a very short one, asked why should not the police, prison warders, messengers, etc., be recruited from the Permanent Force when they no longer made efficient soldiers ?

Interchange with Forces Overseas.

Continuing, he said the country had suffered in the past for not permitting recruiting for the Permanent Force from overseas. A further point which he thought was not taken advantage of was the interchange of members of the Permanent Force with other Forces overseas. This he looked upon as an essential part of training, and it would tend towards the solidarity of the Empire's Forces, which was so much to be desired.

Labour Support.

Mr. A. G. Barlow (Labour, *Bloemfontein North, O.F.S.*), who advocated reference to a Select Committee, said he did not fear a standing army, because he had had experience in the old days of the Republics, when the defence was left to the burghers, of an inefficient standing army. In regard to the rifle clubs, if this Bill became law and if it was not acceptable to the young men of the countryside, it would be due to the fact that the Nationalists had warned them against joining. As to camps, he had had experience of camps near

Bloemfontein, and he had never heard of all this immorality that had been spoken of. All he saw was children of Nationalists, Labourites, and S.A.P. men mixing together and having a real good time. In his opinion, all these objections which had been raised were political humbug. If those who made them were sincere in their remarks, one would expect to find their names inscribed on the scrolls of social welfare societies, but this was not so.

Air Force, Industrial Troubles, etc.

Continuing, he said he was glad that South Africa was going to have an Air Force. They knew that many of their young men had turned out to be the finest flyers in the world. If the Government supported the military side of flying, that would in time assist the commercial side. In regard to industrial troubles, they recognised it was extremely difficult to get anything into the Bill which would stop the Defence Force from being used in times of industrial riots. They wanted to put something into it which would prevent the Government, if possible, from calling out the military, as they had done in the past, to come and shoot men down in the streets. As to the flag, when the member for Smithfield appealed for their own flag, if he meant by that they wanted a Republic, cut away from the British Government altogether, and the British Commonwealth of Nations, then members of that House would fight that both in the House and outside.

The debate was adjourned.

In his reply on 15th April,

The Minister of Defence said that on the whole criticism had been directed not so much to the Bill itself as to the general defence administration ever since the Bill of 1912 was passed. He stated that the military would not be called out except in times of grave national crisis. Provision was made for the conscientious objector as the law stood to-day. Members who were after economy should vote for the Bill, because if it were rejected the cost of the present force would be greater than that proposed under the measure.

The amendment moved by Mr. J. H. H. de Waal was negatived. The amendment moved by General Kemp was lost, 27 voting for and 67 against.

The Bill was read a second time, and, on the motion of the Minister of Defence, referred to a Select Committee.

ASIATIC PROBLEM.*

(Policy of Segregation or Repatriation: Indian Position:
League of Nations: Attitude of Government:
Future Legislation.)

DEBATE IN HOUSE OF ASSEMBLY.

On 3rd May,
Mr. J. S. Marwick (South African Party, *Illovo, Natal*)
moved : —

That this House requests the Government, in drafting the
legislation recently foreshadowed by the Minister of the Interior
as a result of the report of the Asiatic Inquiry Commission, to consider the advisability of embodying therein provisions which (as
would appear to be feasible in view of Section 147 of the South
Africa Act) will allocate to the Asiatic community separate and
distinct areas, both rural and urban, in the Union, where they may
develop in accordance with their own differing needs and standards
of civilisation, due regard being had in such legislation to the interests
of the present and future European and native population of South
Africa.

The report of the Commission, he said, was an entirely
unsatisfactory document. When the Commission dealt with
the ownership of land by Asiatics they had no evidence before
them. To-day they owned land in Maritzburg and Durban
to such an extent that the position had become alarming.
In those towns the economic side of the problem was also
very much emphasised, the result being that the Europeans
were in danger of being ousted from almost every class of
employment.

Segregation.

The Commission had come to the conclusion that segregation was necessary. In effect their verdict was in favour of
those who complained of the encroachments of the Indian,
but their judgment was unsatisfactory. The evidence before
them from the farmers was that, while recognising the existing
tenure of land by the Asiatics, and that they should not be
interfered with, no further acquisition of land by purchase,
lease or other means by Asiatics should be allowed.

After giving details as to the position of the Indians in
Natal, Mr. Marwick went on to say that unless the contact
of the Asiatics either with Europeans or Natives was, to some
extent, regulated, they would have a state of affairs under

---

* *Vide* "Repatriation of Indians," JOURNAL, Vol. II., No. 2,
page 439.

which the white man would steadily retrogress, and would be overwhelmed and submerged. They needed a common objective which would take the white population of that country away from their racial difficulties and their petty squabbles of the past, and cause them to bend their energies to the building up of a great nation.

Racial Antagonism.

Mr. H. G. Mackeurtan (South African Party, *Durban, Umbilo, Natal*) supported the motion. To-day there were more Asiatics in Natal than there were Europeans ; either the two races would fuse or they would not, and if they failed to do so there was bound to be a difficult problem to face. The antagonism was almost a daily part of the life of Natal, and it was not a trade or social antagonism, but a racial antagonism which was found on both sides, and was based on the complete and transcendental difference between the two civilisations. The question was a sheer one of self-preservation. He thought it was due to the Government to find some solution.

He could not see, Mr. Mackeurtan continued, that repatriation was practical or entirely just. They could not expect to repatriate Indians who had been born in Natal and were South Africans to-day. The most they could do was to repatriate those who voluntarily wanted to go. They could only find a partial solution, and that was in a just segregation within specified areas. They should, it appeared to him, make that segregation compulsory, and have it fairly and properly done, which would allow the Indians to develop on their own peculiar lines in their own areas.

Attitude of the Government of India.

Were they to listen for all time to the Government of India ? Many Indians claimed South African nationality and why should they claim the Government of India ? The report stated that compulsory segregation would lead to passive resistance, but if he thought a thing was absolutely right and should be done in the interests of the community passive resistance would not stop him. He asked the House to adopt a middle course, which he admitted was a palliative but was better than doing nothing.

Four Aspects of the Problem.

Mr. T. Boydell (Leader of the Labour Party) said this had become something more than a racial question—it had become a trade and economic question. There were four aspects of the problem—residential, the land-owning difficulty, trading difficulties, and the difficulty of competition between the Indian worker and the white. He instanced ways in which the purchase of houses by Indian traders had made the housing problem more acute, and went on to show that there was an increasing invasion of the tailoring, cabinet-making, painting and French polishing trades by the Indians. A new phase had now developed, and that was the merchants and the traders who found themselves in competition with the Indian trader. There was also the social phase. In certain parts of Durban, Europeans and Indians were living in the same house, and their children were playing together in the streets. He did not want to see the prosperity of the Indians interfered with, but they wanted to make it possible for the European to be prosperous. They (the Labour Party) had always advocated that every possible inducement, and, if necessary, compensation should be given to those Indians in Natal and other parts of South Africa to return to India. There they had the opportunity of getting full civic and political rights and taking a share in the government of their country.

Mr. Boydell added that the Government did a great wrong not only to the Indians individually, but to South Africa, when they confiscated the gold and jewellery of those who were returning to India, and sent them out of the country without their life-long savings. He contended that the Government had aggravated the problem instead of helping to solve it.

Protection for Indian and European Workers.

He intended to propose an addition to the motion, because they wanted something which would protect the European from unfair competition, and the Indians from being unduly exploited. It was as follows :—

> And also to include in such legislation provision for maintaining European standards of civilisation by the adoption of the principle of equal pay for equal work ; and further, that the Government be requested to embark upon a more vigorous policy of encouraging and inducing the repatriation of Asiatics.

Repatriation of all Indians.

Mr. C. G. Fichardt (**Nationalist**, *Ladybrand*, *O.F.S.*) said the Indians would spread. They had enough trouble already with the segregation of their own natives in South Africa. It was a matter of self-preservation ;

and the world had taught them within the last few years
that when it came to that there was very little question of
justice. The only solution, he claimed, was repatriation
of the whole lot. He was immoral enough to say they must
look to the future of their own race first, and repatriate even
those Indians who were South African born.

Mr. Mackeurtan : " How would you repatriate them ? "

Mr. Fichardt : " By law. We made no difficulty about
deporting Europeans, and why about repatriating Indians ? "

A Mandate for the Premiers' Conference.

He would like to know, the speaker continued, whether
that question would be discussed on the other side when
the Prime Minister went to the Conference, and whether
he would take a mandate from that House. He hoped that
there would be no obligations placed on South Africa in the
interests of other countries ; he realised what had happened
in the past, a wish being later translated into a command.

Origin of Christianity in Asia: Difficulty of Segregation, etc.

The Right Hon. J. X. Merriman (South African Party,
Stellenbosch, Cape) said he did not think Mr. Fichardt saw
what a very serious question that was. They talked about
the psychology of the East and West. Did Mr. Marwick
know that their Christian religion came from Asia ? Did
he know that India was a continent, that there were ever so
many people there at different stages of civilisation, speaking
hundreds of different languages, and having different religions ?
Did he know what segregation meant ? They might get
people into a place, but how were they going to keep them
there ? Even the United States of America, with its vast
population, had not been able to segregate its natives. Here
they had a population of about 120,000 white people and they
were proposing to take upon themselves to segregate an equal
number of people somewhere else. Were the Indians, Mr.
Merriman added, such a bad part of their population ? Even
Mr. Boydell had pointed out how useful they were, and how
they were advancing in what were called the peaceful forms
of European civilisation.

Breaking Faith with India and League of Nations.

What was the League of Nations doing ? Did the hon
Member know that they were partners in that League ? They
had got an equal voice in it with various other nations, and

:hat was their status. Certain things were distinctly laid
Iown which as a member of the League they had got to obey.
They were bound by the terms of their status, and if they
)roke faith with India they broke faith with the League of
Nations. To his mind both segregation and repatriation were
mpracticable. He would counsel them to be careful. They
1ad taken their religion from Asia, and unless they were
areful they might have to take something else from Asia.

Attitude of the Government.

The Minister of the Interior (Hon. Patrick Duncan) said
his was a question in which they had to look not only within
he borders of South Africa, but beyond those borders. The.
)anacea of being a " free and independent republic " was not
;oing to help them in regard to the Asiatic question. The
;overnment had announced that, in view of the seriousness
nd the far-reaching character of the question, it was
mpossible for them to bring before Parliament that Session
egislation in connection with the report of the Asiatic
Commission.

Mr. F. W. Beyers (Nationalist, *Edenburg, O.F.S.*) : " A
policy of procrastination."

Seriousness of the Problem.

The Minister of the Interior said this was a case in which
Ie who made haste made little speed. While it would have
)een wrong if the Government had plunged into legislation
his Session, he welcomed that discussion because it had placed
pefore the House vividly the problems which were bound up
n the question and the difficult issues which they raised.
Iore and more they saw rising up against each other, so to
Speak, the European civilisation on the one hand and the
Asiatic on the other. India was to-day attaining a political
Status and power. If India were not a member of the British
Empire, she would be far more dangerous to them than she
Vas now.

Continuing, he said that the position in South Africa in
egard to the Asiatic menace was not serious outside Natal,
nd gave figures showing that the numbers in certain places
Iad not increased as had been alleged. So far as they could
find out, the numbers in the Transvaal were not seriously
ncreasing ; in fact, the figures, so far as they went, showed
I slight decrease. In Natal, however, the position was very
Serious indeed. The latest census figures showed that Asiatics'
pumbered 135,000 compared to 122,000 Europeans.

Asiatic Immigration formerly favoured.

It came strangely from Mr. Mackeurtan when he, in effect, asked why the Indian Government should be considered in this matter. Did he not remember that it was at the urgent request of the Natal Government, through the Imperial Government, that the immigration of Asiatics was allowed to go on ? Whenever the people of South Africa had made up their minds in regard to Indian immigration, their decision had never been thwarted either by the British or Indian Government.

Possible Legislation next Session.

It was his intention to go into the matter fully during the recess, and he hoped the Government would be able to introduce legislation next Session, although he would make no rash promises in this direction. Referring to the question of repatriation, he added that the instructions of the Government were that voluntary repatriation should be prosecuted as vigorously as possible.

Mr. W. B. Madeley (**Labour,** *Benoni, Natal*) : " And then you stop their goods from going out. Is that not an effectual bar ? "

The Minister of the Interior said it was not. If it were said that the Indians were not allowed to take their personal ornaments, even if they were of gold, he would agree ; but he could not agree that they should be allowed to take unlimited amounts of gold coin with them. They were allowed to take gold or gold coin to the value of £25, and the restriction was made simply to prevent indiscriminate taking of gold away from South Africa. Since the repatriation scheme started about 1,400 Indians had left the country, and he was quite certain that the scheme would be taken up by a very large number.

Decision would affect other Powers.

In conclusion, replying to Mr. Fichardt, he stated that any policy with regard to Asiatics would be decided by the Parliament, which was the arbiter. Mr. Fichardt seemed to think that it could decide that question without reference to the outside world at all ; but it brought them up against other Powers, whether they liked it or not. Could the United States of America work its will with a few Japanese in California ?

The debate was adjourned.

NEWFOUNDLAND.

The Second Session of the twenty-fourth Parliament commenced on 30th March, 1921.

GOVERNOR-GENERAL'S SPEECH.

(Debate on the Address.)

The Governor-General in his speech at the opening of Parliament stated that the policy of the regulation of the marketing of the Colony's staple product was placed in the hands of the Codfish Exportation Board. The practical application by the Board of the policy so unanimously adopted had met with difficulties inherent in all policies which sought to regulate the trade of nations. He felt quite certain that should the matter come before them as legislators they would approach its consideration with one ambition only, the welfare of Newfoundland, her commerce and her people.

Labrador Boundary.

His Excellency referred to the long-standing dispute between Newfoundland and the Province of Quebec which had, by agreement between the parties, been referred to the adjudication of His Majesty's Privy Council. The final agreement to that effect was signed in London by the Attorney-General of Canada and the Attorney-General of Newfoundland in November, and progress had already been made in the preparation of the Colony's case.

Revenue.

The revenue for the last fiscal year, His Excellency continued, showed a substantial surplus over all expenditure ; but the world depression which they must necessarily share with all other countries would cause a large shrinkage in revenue for the current fiscal year. The revenue was so largely dependent upon *ad valorem* duties on imports that while the finances of the Colony benefited by the greatly increased cost of imported goods during the War and immediately afterwards, the present readjustment of world conditions, with largely reduced cost of goods, must have a corresponding effect in reducing Customs returns.

The Estimates of expenditure and the Budget would indicate the efforts made by the Government to deal with the

R

financial problems in the readjustment of the Colony's expenditures, so that the great annual burden which the War
entailed might be met without curtailment and the necessary
public services efficiently maintained. This would necessitate
a temporary curtailment of certain large expenditures which
previous Administrations had felt justified in undertaking out
of the inflated revenues of the War period.

German Indemnity.

His Excellency said they had kept in close touch with the
Imperial Authorities in the matter of Newfoundland's claims
against the German Government, and he anticipated that
certain legislation intended to harmonise the Statute Laws o
Newfoundland with those of Great Britain in the matter o
the German Indemnity would be submitted to the House fo
consideration.

Imperial Conference.

With reference to the Conference of the Prime Ministe
in London in June, His Excellency stated that he had bee
authorised by the Prime Minister to accept the invitation c
his behalf. He appreciated the great importance of Britain
oldest Colony being represented at the Conference.

DEBATE IN HOUSE OF ASSEMBLY.

Fisheries Policy.

Mr. J. H. Scammel (Government Party, *St. Barbe*), in pr
posing on 30th March the appointment of a Select Committ
to draft an Address in Reply to the Governor-General's Spee
thought that it would be agreed that the reference of paramou
importance was to the Fishery Regulations. No policy h
excited more controversy during the past season. At the l
Session of the House two Acts of vast importance in relati
to their staple industry were passed without dissenting vo
he referred to the Codfish Standardisation Act and the
in relation to the export of salt codfish. The first of th
Acts provided the means whereby rules and regulations w
drafted, having chiefly for their object the improvemen
their cure of fish and the proper inspection of all car
destined for the foreign markets. In view of the keen a
war competition they were facing in the markets, the t
had arrived when it behoved them to take steps to imp
their cure if they were to expect anything like decent pr
from abroad. There had been a marked improvement
round and the result had reacted largely to their benefit in

narkets. The regulations framed under the Exportation Act vere primarily designed with a view to the sustaining of prices broad, and consequently ensuring to their fishermen at home he minimum price with which they could possibly decently xist.

Labrador Boundary.

Another matter of wide importance was the Labrador oundary question. They were all aware that until this matter was finalised the development of their resources in abrador must be held in abeyance. They all knew the ntold possibilities of their water power, mineral and timber ealth and the great future for employment that awaited tem in that dependency.

German Indemnity.

Reference was made to the passing of legislation in conformity with English legislation with regard to the paying out of the German indemnity of their share of the losses sustained dring the War. He felt sure that any legislation of that nture would receive the support of the whole House, as they were all anxious to be recouped as speedily as possible fr the losses they met and the expenses incurred in their share d the struggle.

Imperial Conference.

He thought that the invitation to the Prime Minister to atend the Imperial Conference in June was a sign that although they might be small and insignificant they were not overlooked by the Imperial authorities and that it was only their due right to be represented at the Imperial Conference.

Protection of Children.

The Bill dealing with delinquent and neglected children in St. John's had been drafted on the recommendation of the Social Council, an organisation that had the support of all religious denominations. It was modelled and styled after the English Acts 1906-8 and partly after the Acts of the same nature passed by the Province of Ontario. Those of them who had lived in St. John's must of necessity have recognised the pressing need of passing some sort of legislation giving properly authorised persons authority to deal with delinquent and neglected children.

Depression.

They in Newfoundland were only bearing their fair share the depression which was affecting the whole world as the aftermath of the War. They were passing through a period unprecedented in the country's history and the Government was indeed confronted with serious problems, but he felt they had reached rock bottom and that things would be brighter from now on.

Captain George Jones (Government Party, *Twillingate*), in seconding the motion, said that they were confronted with the fact that the Dominion was passing through troublesome times. In common with all the world they had to suffer from the after-effects of the War ; the period of depression they were passing through was world-wide. The returns to their people from the fisheries last season were not very satisfactory, either as regarded catch or price.

Natural Resources.

It would be a great thing for Newfoundland if the oil-wells that were to be found could be opened, so that they could produce their own supply of oil, and perhaps a great deal more for export. Recent operations had proven beyond a doubt that there were very extensive coal deposits in Newfoundland, and he could see no reason why coal-boring on a very large scale could not be carried out. With the great wealth in timber, water-power and minerals of Labrador developed as they could be, might they not hope that the time would soon come when they would not be so entirely dependent upon the fisheries for their support.

Criticism of Government Policy.

The Hon. Sir Michael Cashin (Leader of the Opposition) declared that there was not one ray of hope in the Address, not one statement telling them what had been done in the past twelve months or what would be done in the next twelve months. It struck him that it was about time for Newfoundland to wake up. What was troubling them on the other side of the House was not the Labrador Boundary ; it was whether they would not have to hand the country over to England or Canada.

After criticising the Government's policy with regard to the fisheries, the Leader of the Opposition said that the great trouble was where they were going to get the wherewithal to supply the fishermen the coming year. The Government was in the worst predicament since responsible government was granted them. When they handed over the Government about eighteen months ago there was an overflowing Exchequer of practically four millions of dollars, but when all the bills were paid by the present Government not one cent of that would be left. It was said that at the end of the fiscal year

the revenue would be $3,000,000 short. When they handed
over the administration of affairs to the present Government
the imports were $26,000,000, and they were now reduced to
seven or eight millions.

Effect of Falling Prices.

The Prime Minister (Hon. R. A. Squires) said that their
Customs revenue was dependent upon an *ad valorem* duty
on imported goods. Inflated prices of imported goods meant
inflated revenues. They were anxious that prices should
decrease and that must mean reduced Customs returns. Prices
were going down ; revenue was going down, and the problem
of readjustment had to be faced at this Session of the House.
He wished to impress upon each hon. Member the necessity
for serious consideration of the grave problems which Newfoundland must face in the after-War reconstruction period.

Mr. W. Walsh, (*Placentia and St. Mary's*) declared that the
Leader of the House told them in a serious tone how important
was the Labrador Boundary question. If the Administration
followed in the present course, which would surely lead to the
destruction of the country, the Dominion of Canada would
have no fear whether or not they would be successful in this
suit, as Labrador would in any case go to Canada in a very
short time.

Members' Salaries.

Every hon. Member who held a seat in the House had had
his salary increased from two hundred to one thousand dollars.
The Departmental heads had their salaries increased from
twenty-four to forty hundred dollars, and now they were told
there was to be a curtailment.

They were told by the mover of the Address in reply
that the catch of fish was not large enough. He could truth-
fully say that in the district of Placentia and St. Mary's there
were ten thousand quintals of fish unsaleable and unmarketable
and these people were depending on the pauper's dole ; and
then they were asked to swallow the dose of camouflage
contained in the Speech from the Throne.

THE BUDGET.

In the absence of the Minister of Finance and Customs,
owing to illness, the annual financial statement was delivered
by the Prime Minister in the House of Assembly on 25th May.

The Prime Minister (Hon. R. A. Squires) said : "During
the period of War the contesting nations paid for the War in

blood ; now that the War is over, we in common with others have to make our payments in money. Newfoundland was glad as a patriotic Colony of our great Empire to bear its responsibility to the Empire and to civilisation through its fighting forces on both sea and land and through its sacrifices at home, and now we have to face the post-War problems of reorganisation, reconstruction and deflation, and at the same time carry the large liabilities which the War has entailed. Deflation, reconstruction and reorganisation after the world turmoil of four years' War are naturally difficult and trying problems, and we have to approach them in a spirit of serious- ness and self-sacrifice. The trade depression throughout the world has seriously affected Newfoundland, and while we are fortunate in not having in our Colony a depression so serious and a trade disorganisation so extreme as in many other countries, yet we have to realise that Newfoundland is now passing through a period of trade depression, deflation and liquidation which demands the serious consideration of every patriotic Newfoundlander."

Revenue and Expenditure.

Their chief source of revenue, he continued, was Customs returns, practically the whole of which was an *ad valorem* duty on imported goods. In November last the high prices which had prevailed dropped almost suddenly, with the consequent result of a great depreciation in Customs returns.

During the previous year the leading importing merchants had brought into this country goods estimated at a value of seven million dollars over and above the natural requirements for that year. Their decision to make these large importa- tions was undoubtedly due to the fact that the termination of War did not, as was expected, cause an early depression in values, but instead prices continued to advance, and in view of the situation the importers felt that for their own protection large importations should be made. As a consequence last year's revenue was augmented by an estimated amount of two million dollars over and above the duties which would be collected on normal supplies for that year, with the result that the quantities of imports during the present fiscal year were proportionately reduced because of the large stocks on hand. This had necessarily meant a corresponding reduction in revenue. In addition, there was a shortage in revenue due to general trade depression throughout the world.

He estimated that the total revenue from all sources to the 30th day of June next would be $8,244,104. The ex- penditure during the current fiscal year amounted to a total of approximately $11,171,821.

This left a credit balance as at the 30th day of June next
of $73,469.32. That was to say, the Colony liquidated its
liabilities as on the 30th day of June next and started the next
fiscal year with a credit balance of $73,469.32 in the Surplus
Trust Account.

Salaries of Public Servants.

In the Estimates as tabled there had been no reduction
in the salaries of civil servants. It was proposed that the
salaries of civil servants as voted should remain in the Estimates as at last year, and that a special Bill should be introduced making a percentage reduction in all civil servants'
salaries, including the salary of His Excellency the Governor,
the Judges of the Supreme Court, Ministers of the Crown, and
the sessional indemnity of members of the House of Assembly
and Legislative Council. It was also proposed that a Civil
Service Commission of three should be appointed to examine
into the various public services of the Colony and report to
His Excellency the Governor in Council as to what steps
might be taken to maintain the efficiency of the service at a
substantially reduced cost.

War Expenditure.

They had to bear the interest burdens on a War expenditure of approximately $16,000,000. They had to face an
estimated annual expenditure of $1,750,000 due immediately
and directly to the participation of Newfoundland in the War.
This sum included interest on War expenditure, pensions for
soldiers and sailors, increased hospital, sanatorium and other
services to suitably provide for those who suffered during the
War.

Tariff Revision.

A commission would be appointed for the purpose of a
revision of the tariff, so that at the next Session of the Legislature such might be considered and taxation placed upon a
more equitable basis than it was at present.

The year 1919-20 was the first year since 1912-13 that
the imports had exceeded the exports; then the amount of
difference was $1,339,476, last year the excess of imports
over exports amounted to $5,667,950.

Their total funded debt as a Colony on 30th June would
be approximately $49,000,000.

Railway Problem.

The Newfoundland Railway problem had not worked out
very satisfactorily during the past year under the joint

management created by the appointment of the Railway Commission whose term of office expired on the 30th June next. The operations of the Railway would not be continued under the control of the Railway Commission after that date. If the Reid Newfoundland Company was not in a position to further finance its undertakings and carry out its contractual obligations to the Government, the Company might find it necessary to wind up its operations in Newfoundland, when the many important legal and financial matters outstanding between the Government and the Company would have to be determined by legal or other proceedings, and the railway and steamship systems operated by a receiver, so that the public transportation services of the Colony might not be interfered with, in which event entirely new arrangements must necessarily be made for the management and operation of the railway and coastal systems. In any event, a programme for railway and coastal reorganisation would be submitted to the Legislature at its next Session.

Summary of Proposals.

The resolutions which he proposed to submit to the Committee might be summarised as follows :—(1) The imposition of a special War Surtax of 25 per cent. on present total duties ; in the case of spirits, 50 per cent. (2) A reduction and adjustment of the export tax on fish. (3) An adjustment on imported sole leather. (4) The preference recently given to kerosene oil when imported in wood packages to be repealed. (5) The exemption clause in the Income War Tax Act, 1918, to be made clearer in certain particulars and clergymen exempted from income taxation (6) The irregular practice of a sturdy ten years' growth by which free entries had been permitted and drawbacks and refunds given without special statutory authority to be declared illegal. (7) Home industries to be protected by the proposed enactment of special " Dumping " legislation. (8) The bank tax, formerly collected under the Business Profits Act, to be continued.

JOURNAL OF THE
PARLIAMENTS
OF THE EMPIRE

Vol. II.—No. 4.   October, 1921.

Issued under the Authority of the
EMPIRE PARLIAMENTARY ASSOCIATION
(United Kingdom Branch),
WESTMINSTER HALL, HOUSES OF PARLIAMENT,
LONDON, S.W.1.

Price to Non-Members 10s. Net.

CONTENTS.

CONTENTS.

NEWFOUNDLAND.

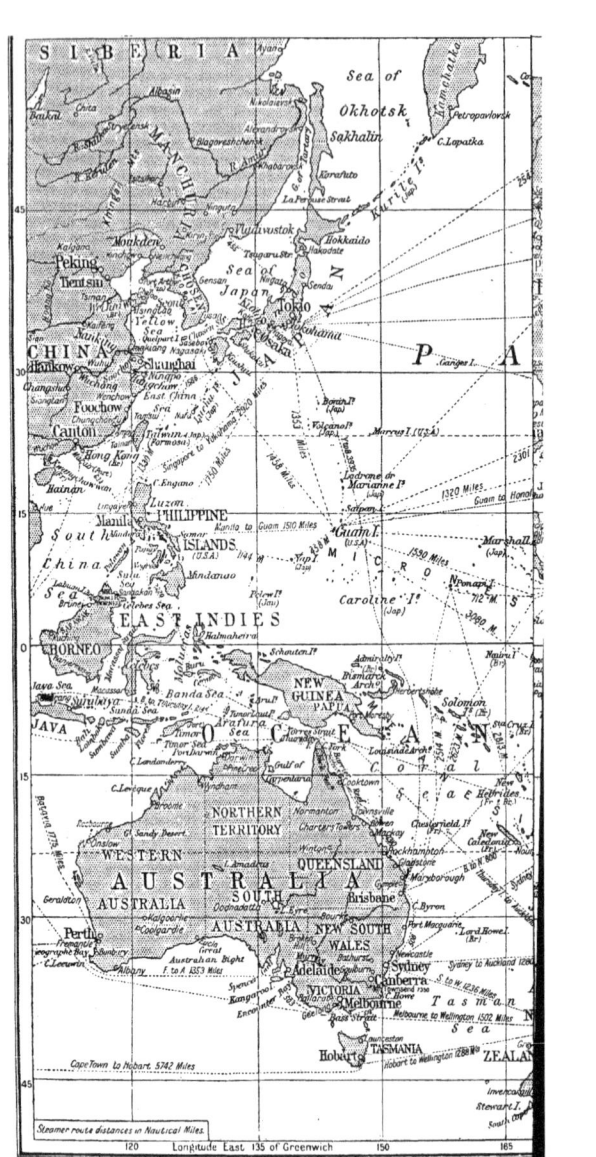

illustrating the regions which will be dealt

INTRODUCTION.

While the last issue of the JOURNAL was remarkable for containing discussions in no less than five Parliaments upon the work of the Conference of Prime Ministers of the Empire then sitting in London, the present number may be said to be equally important, both from the international and the inter-Imperial standpoints, on account of the discussions it contains upon the coming Conference at Washington. This Conference and the Pacific question generally, and also the results of the Conference of Prime Ministers, which may be said to be intimately connected with the Pacific as well as with other vital subjects, have been considered in the Parliaments of the United Kingdom and the Australian Commonwealth; while matters having a distinct bearing upon the forthcoming Conference will be found discussed in other Parliaments.

So intimate a connection has the present number with the issues of the Washington Conference, as viewed by more than one nation of the British Commonwealth, that it has been thought advisable to publish at the commencement a map of the Pacific, which has been specially prepared in order to illustrate the regions which will be dealt with at the Conference, with particular reference to the distances between the various points of strategic importance. Though it has not been customary to publish maps in the JOURNAL, it is believed that the discussions will be more readily followed by means of this map, and, therefore, that the departure will be welcomed on this occasion by Members of the Empire Parliamentary Association in the different Parliaments of the Empire.

The discussions in the Parliament of the United Kingdom which are summarised in the present issue contain a great deal of information of interest to the whole Empire; not only are international matters dealt with in the discussions on the Pacific, the Conference of the Supreme Council, the League of Nations Mandates, International Labour Conference, etc., but the statements and references to the Conference of Prime Ministers show something of the value of the gatherings where the statesmen of the Empire are able to exchange views upon questions of common concern.

In the discussion which took place in the Parliament of the Australian Commonwealth, the references to limitation of armaments, the Anglo-Japanese Treaty, and the wider question of the representation of the Dominions in Foreign

Affairs cannot fail to arrest the attention of Members in al
Parliaments; while the constitutional aspects of Empire
relationship resulting from the War have been discussed in
the Parliaments of the United Kingdom, Australia and South
Africa.

Various points of importance to the League of Nations
and to the Permanent Court of International Justice have been
considered in the Parliaments of the United Kingdom, Canada
Australia and South Africa; matters relating to Defence have
found a prominent place in general discussions, and, more
specifically, in the Union Parliament of South Africa.

The present issue of the JOURNAL may also be said to
convey information of importance in regard to proposed
measures for the development or safeguarding of the resources
and trade of the Empire. Discussions upon Trade and Tariff
occupy a considerable proportion of the debates of all
Parliaments which are summarised in the present issue
reciprocity with the United States finds a place in the
Canadian discussions and Preferential Trade in the deliberations of both Canada and Australia. It is of particular
interest to compare the provisions for the prevention
dumping outlined in the Safeguarding of Industries Act
the United Kingdom with the proposals for anti-dumping
duties brought forward in the Parliament of the Australian
Commonwealth.

Matters of more local but still of common interest to all
the nations of the British Commonwealth relate to such
questions as Finance and Unemployment (discussed in the
United Kingdom and South African Parliaments); Proportional Representation (discussed in the Canadian Parliament); Marriage Laws (United Kingdom and South African
Parliaments); Railways and Licensing (United Kingdom
Parliament); Right of Ministers to sit in either Chamber
(Canadian Parliament); Venereal Diseases Bill (Newfoundland Parliament) and other questions. With regard to the
last-named Bill, it is interesting to compare the legislation
which has been summarised in previous issues of the JOURNAL

THE EDITOR

EMPIRE PARLIAMENTARY ASSOCIATION
(*United Kingdom Branch*),
WESTMINSTER HALL,
HOUSES OF PARLIAMENT,
LONDON, S.W.1.

15th October, 1921.

UNITED KINGDOM.

In the last number of the Journal the business of the Session was dealt with up till 20th June, 1921. The proceedings of Parliament between that date and 19th August, when both Houses adjourned till 18th October, with an arrangement that they should be called upon to meet earlier should occasion require, are summarised in the present issue. Owing to pressure on space, however, it has been necessary to hold over until the next number summaries of the proceedings in respect of some half-dozen measures which were under consideration during the portion of the Session to which attention is devoted in the succeeding pages.

PACIFIC AND FAR EASTERN POLICY.

Conference at Washington: Anglo-Japanese Agreement: Imperial Conference, etc.)

In reply to a question by the Right Hon. H. H. Asquith statement was made by the Prime Minister in the House of Commons on 11th July with reference to the Pacific and the Far East.

The Prime Minister (the Right Hon. D. Lloyd George) said that when he told the House during the previous week that he hoped to be in a position to make a statement on Pacific and Far Eastern questions that day, he was awaiting replies to conversations which had taken place between the Secretary of State for Foreign Affairs and the representatives of the Governments of the United States, Japan and China the result of discussions in the Imperial Cabinet.

"I am very glad to be able to inform the House to-day that the views of the Government of the United States reached me last night, and are extremely satisfactory. The Chinese Government is also favourable. We have not yet had a formal reply from the Government of Japan, but we have good reason to hope that it will be in the same sense. Now that these views have been received, I am glad to be at liberty to inform the House of Commons fully regarding the course which our discussions in the Imperial Cabinet took. I do this with particular satisfaction, because it will show how very valuable a step forward we have been able to take by common consent in the sphere of foreign affairs.

B

Imperial Policy.

" The broad lines of Imperial policy in the Pacific and the Far East were the very first subjects to which we addressed ourselves at the meetings of the Imperial Cabinet, having a special regard to the Anglo-Japanese Agreement, the future o China, and the bearing of both those questions on the relation of the British Empire with the United States.

" We were guided in our deliberations by three main considerations. In Japan, we have an old and proved Ally. The agreement of 20 years' standing between us has been of very great benefit, not only to ourselves and her, but to the peace of the Far East. In China there is a very numerous people, with great potentialities, who esteem our friendship highly, and whose interests we, on our side, desire to assist and advance. In the United States we see to-day, as we have always seen, the people closest to our own aims and ideals with whom it is for us not merely a desire and an interest but a deeply-rooted instinct, to consult and co-operate.

" Those were the main considerations in our meeting and upon them we were unanimous. The object of our discussions was to find a method combining all these three factors in a policy which would remove the danger of heavy naval expenditure in the Pacific, with all the evils which such an expenditure entails, and would ensure the development of all legitimate national interests of the Far East.

Anglo-Japanese Agreement not Denounced.

" We had, in the first place, to ascertain our exact position with regard to the Anglo-Japanese Agreement. There had been much doubt as to whether the notification to the League of Nations made last July constituted a denunciation of the Agreement in the sense of Clause 6.

" If it did, it would have been necessary to decide upon some interim measure regarding the Agreement pending full discussions with the other Pacific Powers, and negotiations with this object in view were, in point of fact, already in progress. If, on the other hand, it did not, the Agreement would remain in force until denounced, whether by Japan or by ourselves, and would not be actually determined until months from the date when notice of denunciation was given.

" The Japanese Government took the view that no notice of denunciation had yet been given. This view was shared by the Secretary of State for Foreign Affairs ; but, as considerable doubt existed, we decided, after a preliminary discussion in the Imperial Cabinet, to refer the question to the Lord Chancellor, who considered it with the Law Officers

f the Crown, and held that no notice of denunciation had yet
een given.

he Agreement and League of Nations Covenant.

" It follows that the Anglo-Japanese Agreement remains
i force unless it is denounced, and will lapse only at the
xpiration of 12 months from the time when notice of denun-
iation is given.   It is, however, the desire of both the British
impire and Japan that the Agreement should be brought into
omplete harmony with the Covenant of the League of Nations,
ad that wherever the Covenant and the Agreement are incon-
istent the terms of the Covenant shall prevail.   Notice to
tis effect has now been given to the League.

" The broader discussion of Far Eastern and Pacific policy
t which we then turned showed general agreement on the
main lines of the course which the Imperial Cabinet desired
t pursue.   I have already explained that the first principle
o our policy was friendly co-operation with the United States.
Ie are all convinced that upon this, more than any single
fétor, depends the peace and well-being of the world.   We
alo desire, as I have stated, to maintain our close friendship
ad co-operation with Japan.

" The greatest merit of that valuable friendship is that it
hrmonises the influence and activities of the two greatest
Aiatic Powers and thus constitutes an essential safeguard to
tl well-being of the British Empire and the peace of the East.
We also aim at preserving the "open door" in China, and at
giing the Chinese people every opportunity of peaceful
progress and development.

Pesident Harding's Invitation.

" In addition to these considerations, we desire to safe-
gurd our own vital interests in the Pacific and to preclude
ar competition in naval armaments between the Pacific
Powers.   All the representatives of the Empire agreed that
ou standpoints on these questions should be communicated
wih complete frankness to the United States, Japan and China
wih the object of securing an exchange of views which might
led to more formal discussion and conference.

" The Secretary of State for Foreign Affairs accordingly
hel conversations last week with the American and Japanese
Ambassadors and the Chinese Minister, at which he communi-
cad to them the views of the Imperial Cabinet and asked in
tul for the views of their respective Governments.   He
expressed at these conversations a very strong hope that this
exhange of views might, if their Governments shared our

desire in that respect, pave the way for a Conference on the problems of the Pacific and the Far East.

" The views of the President of the United States were made public by the American Government this morning . . . Mr. Harding has taken the momentous step of inviting the Powers to a Conference on the limitation of armaments to be held in Washington in the near future, and he also suggests a preliminary meeting on Pacific and Far Eastern questions between the Powers most directly interested in the peace and welfare of that great region which is assuming the first importance in international affairs

" I need not say that we welcome with the utmost pleasure President Harding's wise and courteous initiative. In saying this I know that I speak for the Empire as a whole. The world has been looking to the United States for such a lead, I am confident that the House will esteem it as an act of far-seeing statesmanship and will whole-heartedly wish it success, I need hardly say that no effort will be lacking to make it so on the part of the British Empire, which shares to the full the liberal and progressive spirit inspiring it.

Value of the Imperial Conference.

" Let me add only one word as to the part played in the events by the gathering of the Imperial Conference in Downing Street. I venture to say that the action that we have taken could not have been taken in so prompt, effective, and unanimous a fashion but for the intimate personal consultation between the Prime Ministers of the Empire and the representatives of India which this gathering has enabled us to enjoy. We have taken counsel together without reserve. With this result before us, I need not elaborate the inestimable value of that intimate collaboration in the conduct of the Empire's affairs."

Commander Carlyon Bellairs (Coalition Unionist, Maidstone) : " In regard to the difficulty of the legal point as to whether the Alliance with Japan was denounced, and which was referred to the Lord Chancellor, may I ask whether the Law Officers of the Crown were unanimous on the point that the Alliance had not been denounced ? "

The Prime Minister : " The Lord Chancellor consulted the Law Officers before giving his opinion to the Imperial Cabinet."

Lieut.-Colonel J. Ward (Coalition Liberal, Stoke-on-Trent) : " Would the right hon. gentleman inform the House and the world in general whether, in these negotiations with reference to the future of the Pacific, China is to be treated as a Sovereign State and her representatives left to give the decision of her

Chinese Government without the interference of any other Asiatic Power ? "

The **Prime Minister** : " China will be treated as what he is, an independent Power. We made the same communication to the Chinese Government as to the other Governments."

Sir J. D. Rees (Coalition Unionist, *Nottingham, East*) : Will India be specially represented at the Conference ? "

The **Prime Minister** : " We must consider that."

CONFERENCE OF PRIME MINISTERS OF THE EMPIRE.

Statement by the Prime Minister: Constitutional
   Conference : Communications : Naval Defence :
   Anglo-Japanese Alliance: Pacific Conference, etc.)

In the House of Commons on 18th August, the adjournment of the House was moved from the Treasury Bench by Colonel Leslie Wilson (Chief Coalition Unionist Whip) to enable the Prime Minister to make a statement on the work of the Imperial Conference, and also to allow of the discussion of certain other subjects which, owing to lack of time, could not be debated on the Consolidated Fund Bill.

DEBATE IN HOUSE OF COMMONS.

Mr. J. M. Hogge (Independent Liberal, *Edinburgh, E.*) said the House welcomed the Conference of the Dominion Premiers in this country. These recurring Conferences must result in an increase of goodwill and of good relations between the different parts of the Empire, and in making more secure what he considered to be the best, the biggest, and the most real League of Nations, namely, the federation of free nations included in the British Empire.

The **Prime Minister (the Right Hon. D. Lloyd George)** agreed that in itself a Conference of this character was of value in the consolidation of the Empire. The last few years had witnessed a very remarkable development in the Constitution of the Empire and in its growth. When, in August, 1914, this country declared war there was not a single Dominion from which they could have levied any contribution either in men or in money. The Dominions were not involved in the dispute except as members of the British Empire. It concerned something that had no particular interest for them up to that moment ; but they never hesitated for one hour.

Rallied to the Flag.

Without a single exception they rallied to the Flag, an
the aid they gave to the Mother Country astonished not merel
the world, but even the great enthusiasts of Empire in th
country. "The Dominions," the Prime Minister proceedec
"sent millions of men to our aid—arid there were no fine
troops in the battlefields of Europe or of Asia than the troop
that came from the Dominions. That is an acknowledge
fact. India sent 1,250,000 troops to our aid. All these wei
sent voluntarily. We could not have compelled a sing
Canadian, Australian, New Zealander or South African 1
come to our assistance. They came of their own free will, the
came with alacrity, they came without loss of time ; and it
not too much to say that the fact that they came made tl
difference in the event. They made history, and they mae
great history.

"The whole course of human affairs has been alter
because the British Empire has been proved to be a fact an
not, what a good many people who knew nothing about
imagined, a fiction. That altered the character—the cons
tutional character—of the Empire." What happened ther
In 1917, Mr. Lloyd George continued, the Dominion Premie
and the representatives of India were invited to join the Briti
Cabinet that was directing the War. Before 1914 they to
no part in the direction of Imperial affairs. He did not kne
what measure of consultation there was on Imperial questio,
but he did not think there was much. In 1917 and 19,
however, the representatives of Canada, Australia, N
Zealand, South Africa and India sat continuously with te
War Cabinet and in the War Cabinet as members of te
War Cabinet directing the Great War.

The Leader of the House (the Right Hon. Austen Chamb-
lain) : "And Newfoundland."

The Prime Minister : "Yes, and Newfoundland ab.
I am glad to be reminded of that. It was a new depart e
and a very important departure. Then came the Peace C-
ference. The representatives of the Dominions and of In a
constituted part of the British Delegation and sat in alr st
constant session in Paris, directing the policy of the Br h
Empire. My right hon. friend the President of the Coun *
and I represented the British Empire inside the Confere e,
but there was no action taken by us that had not been s -
mitted beforehand to the British Empire Delegation, on w h,
the Dominions and India were represented.

---

* The Right Hon. A. J. Balfour. .

Determining the Constitution.

"We held constant Conferences or Cabinets in Paris, where the whole of the Empire was represented, where representatives of all parts of the Empire took part in the discussions, and where they had exactly the same voice in determining British policy as any member of the British Cabinet. That was a further development. In the War they had been in our War Councils ; in the Peace they were part of the Cabinet that decided the policy of the British Empire and determined the destinies of Europe. Events of that character imperceptibly, without writing down rules and regulations, without framing written constitutions, determine the Constitution of the Empire. It was one of those developments to which Britain is accustomed, ' broadening down from precedent to precedent.'

"The meeting we had recently was purely a continuation of what happened in Paris, and before that in the War Cabinet. The Prime Ministers of the Empire and the representatives of India came and sat at our Council Table in Downing Street, and discussed the foreign policy of the Empire.

"What it means is this : They came in 1914 to support us in a policy which they had had no voice in determining ; they merely came to the aid of the Mother Country. It is true that they approved of our action thoroughly and whole-heartedly. If they had not, probably there would not have been the same measure of support, but before that there had been no consultation. They only say now : ' We gave you 2,250,000, or nearly 2,500,000 of picked men, and we incurred enormous debts in supporting your policy. As we may be committed in the future by the Crown which holds us together, by the Crown which is ours as much as it is yours, to a given policy, before we send our sons to fight for that policy we ought to have a voice in fashioning that policy.' We say, ' That is right ; not only is it right, but we are glad to have your advice and your counsel.'

"There are distractions and there are excitements which render it very difficult to preserve an even balance of judgment when you are right in the middle of things. Here they come from the ends of the earth—people who take a more detached view, people who, perhaps, are able to judge more calmly, or, at any rate, from a different standpoint ; and we are glad to have their advice, to have their counsel, to have their wisdom put into the common stock in the work of directing the affairs of the Empire, upon whose decisions the fate of mankind depends more than upon any other nation's decisions. Therefore, we were glad to welcome them, and we were glad to have a very full and frank discussion upon the foreign policy

of the British Empire.   My noble friend the Foreign Secretary*
made an extremely luminous statement on the world position.
There was full discussion upon that, and after the discussions
we came to a common understanding as to the lines of our
policy.   We discussed questions like Silesia, Asia Minor,
Reparations, the Disarmament of Germany—— "

Lieut.-Comdr. the Hon. J. Kenworthy (Independent Liberal
Hull, Central) : " Ireland ? "

The Prime Minister : " No, we did not discuss Ireland.
We certainly should not have objected to discussing Ireland,
but we did not.   They have their difficulties in regard to
Ireland just as much as we have, and they were not particularly
anxious.   It is not a sort of question that you go into of your
own free will.   Therefore, there was no burning desire——

Mr. Percy Hurd (Coalition Unionist, *Frome*) : " Except
on the part of General Smuts."

The Prime Minister : " No, that is not quite fair.   There
was no burning anxiety on his part.   He acted a perfectly
straightforward and honourable part, and there was nothing
he did which they were not fully informed upon ; and, whatever he did, he did it with the full assent of the Sovereign and
the Ministers of this country."

Lieut.-Colonel H. Page Croft (National Party, *Bourne-*
mouth) : " Not as a representative of the Conference."

The Prime Minister : " Not as a representative of the
Conference, but purely as an individual.

" We discussed the whole of the foreign policy of the
Empire and it was an additional source of strength, in going
into the Conference last week,† to know —the Foreign Secretary
and myself —that we represented not merely the views of the
United Kingdom, but the views of the whole British Empire.
It was not merely a source of strength to us, but it made an
impression upon all those who were there—the knowledge
that we represented this very great and powerful Empire that
had contributed so substantially to victory in the late War.

Constitutional Aspect of the Empire.

" It had been decided, sometime during the War, that
we should have a discussion upon the constitutional aspect of
the Empire, and I was bound to put that down on the Agenda ;
but the general feeling was that it would be a mistake to lay
down any rules or to embark upon definitions as to what the
British Empire meant.   To do so would be to limit its utility.
To do so, I think, would be to weaken its unity.   It is that

* The Marquess Curzon of Kedleston.
† The meeting of the Supreme Council of the Allies in Paris.

ndefinable thing that makes the British Empire united, potent. You are defining life itself when you are defining the British Empire. You cannot do it, and therefore we came to the conclusion that the fact was the thing that mattered. When the War came there were 2,250,000 men—— "

Sir J. D. Rees (Coalition Unionist, *Nottingham, East*): " Including India ? "

The Prime Minister : " Yes, including India. That is much better than written rules. They were consulted in the Peace Conference ; they were now consulted, and there was an understanding that on all questions of foreign policy they should be informed and, in so far as distance would permit, that they should be consulted. That is what matters. We do not want to interfere with their internal affairs, and they do not want to interfere with ours ; but they all want to feel that they are part of this amazing organisation, which is the first thing of its kind that the world has ever seen. Therefore we decided—and the British representatives at that Conference cordially agreed—that it was better not to enter into definitions, not to lay down rules, and not to say that the British Empire henceforth shall be one, two, three, four, five. That is not what makes the Empire, and that is the conclusion we came to. I think the House of Commons will agree that it was the wise thing to do. It has grown, developed, consolidated in a way which nothing could make possible but the gigantic events which, in testing it, were bound either to break it or to solidify it. There is no doubt at all that the events of the last few years have consolidated the Empire in a way which probably generations would not have done otherwise.

No Constitutional Conference: Improvement of Communications.

" We came to the conclusion, therefore, that we would have no Constitutional Conference. The thing that matters is as frequent Conferences as time and distance will permit. After all, it is very difficult for Imperial Ministers to come here from the other end of the earth once a year when they have got very important affairs of their own to attend to and, I have no doubt, very considerable difficulties. There are party controversies, probably, even there, and there are unreasonable people who criticise Governments even in the Southern Seas. It is the sort of thing that does not change with latitude or longitude or climate. It seems to be inherent in the heart of man and to be part of his original sin.

" It is quite impossible for the Ministers to come frequently, considering the time which is expended in passing from, say, Australia and New Zealand. Canada is not so distant, and

South Africa is not so distant, but Australia and New Zealand
are a totally different proposition, and we discussed the
question of the possibilities of improving communications
There was an understanding that the Prime Ministers of the
Dominions would have the full right to communicate direct
with the Prime Minister of this country, but communication
by cable are not a means by which you can have real consultation, because a man may have a particular point of view and
may alter it after hearing what is to be said on the other side
and the difficulty is to arrange any method by which we could
meet a little more frequently. We discussed it at great
length, and there were all sorts of suggestions made as t
speedy cruisers, which I am told are not very comfortable
and even airships."

An Hon. Member : " You can telephone."

The Prime Minister : " You can telephone a message, but
not a mission, from one end of the earth to the other. There
fore it is very difficult.

" I think I should like experiments in airships to proceed
a little further before I care to go to Australia on one of these
airships. . . . We are holding up these airships for
short time until the Australian Prime Minister has an oppor
tunity of consulting his colleagues as to the extent to which
they would like to go in that matter. . . . The most effecti
way undoubtedly of securing the unity of the Empire, and
securing it by means of conference, is that through improved
communications the Prime Ministers should meet oftener
order to confer together.

Naval Defence : Dominions Contributions.

" The two questions, I think, which occupied most of o
time apart from foreign policy were the questions of the Angl
Japanese Alliance and the Pacific. Egypt was also discuss
and the naval defence of the Empire.

" They were all agreed when we came to the question
naval defence that at any rate the Empire must have a nav
force which is equal to that of any other country in the wor
. . . But when it came to a question of contribution the
was a general feeling—I think I can go to that extent—that it
was unfair to leave the whole burden of the naval defence
the Empire with the Mother Country. The extent to wh
the Dominions should contribute—the best method of c
tribution—that must be left to each Dominion, and to Ind
to consider themselves. We cannot dictate, we can
direct, and I am not sure that it will be very helpful if
even make suggestions, because they are each naturally ver
I will not say resentful, because that would not be a fair w

—but they are each very anxious to guard their own independence in these respects.

" There are some who would like to contribute in one form and some in another—some by means of naval stations, some by means of oiling stations, some by means of having a fleet of their own. Each of these questions must be considered by the Dominions with their own Parliaments, and it is not a matter where we could presume in the least to dictate or prescribe, and where it would not be wise even to suggest. The proposals must come from themselves, and they are consulting their own Parliaments upon that particular question.

The Pacific: Anglo-Japanese Alliance.

" On the question of the Pacific, there was a good deal of discussion on the Japanese Alliance. Upon that our feeling is his. The Alliance is an existing Alliance, and until twelve months' notice is given that Alliance continues. When you come to the question of whether you will give notice you must consider how that Alliance has operated. There was a real test of that Alliance in the late War, and no man who watched what happened can come to any other conclusion than that it was loyally and faithfully interpreted and carried out by our Japanese Ally. Just see what happened. There you had the Pacific raided by fast German cruisers and our ships sunk. We had to depend upon the help of New Zealand and of Australia.

" Between them they sent to our assistance from 500,000 to 600,000 first-class troops. India sent more than 1,000,000 across seas which it would have been difficult for us to guard. We had to guard the Atlantic. We had to guard the Mediterranean very largely. We had to guard the North Sea—a gigantic operation even for our immense fleet. . . . There was that immense ocean, the Pacific, the Southern Atlantic, and the Indian Ocean—the greatest seas of the world. How were we to guarantee that 500,000 troops could cross thousands of miles of seas, and 1,000,000 troops from India could cross the Indian Ocean, and that no raider would sink them ? . . . We could not have done it but for the fact that our Japanese Ally came to our aid. The Australian Prime Minister and the New Zealand Prime Minister said so. They said, ' We could never have sent our troops into that vast ocean at that time unless we had had that guarantee.'

" We could not have given the guarantee, certainly at the beginning of the War, had it not been for the Japanese Fleet giving their assistance in chasing the raiders. It was invaluable. It was one of the determining factors of the War.

They loyally, faithfully, in the letter and in the spirit, carried out their obligation.

Accord with the United States.

" Is it to be suggested that we should now turn round and say to them, ' You stood by us in trouble, but we do not need you any longer, so good-bye ' ? Would anyone behave like that in business ? The British Empire must behave like a gentleman, and when you come to deal with a country that has stood by you in trouble—stood well by you—are you to bring the Alliance to an end when trouble is over ? I say that that would not be becoming of the British Empire in dealing with a faithful Ally.

" And let me say this : I do not believe there is any country in the world, whether it likes the Japanese Alliance or does not like it, that would think any better of the British Empire if we broke off the Alliance—not one. They might appear to be glad for the moment that we had done it, but in their hearts they would despise us for doing it. That does not mean that we are to continue an Alliance of this kind against anyone else, and certainly not against the United States of America. It is a cardinal principle of British policy, and must be, that we should act in as complete accord with the United States of America as any two countries can. I do not know of any country in the world with whom it is more important that we should act in concert than with the United States of America. So much so that it is very difficult to get an English man to regard an American as a foreigner. There is a different feeling ; there is a sense of fraternity.

" It is cardinal that we should act in concert with the United States of America ; but I do not see why it is impossible to remember your obligations to Japan, preserve your friend ship for that great country, and, at the same time, preserve a spirit of fraternity with the United States of America.

Pacific Conference: Value of an Understanding.

" This is one of the questions upon which I had hoped would have been possible, and still hope it will be possible to have a discussion. If an Alliance with Japan could merge in a greater understanding with Japan and the United States of America in all the problems of the Pacific, that would be a great event; and it would be a guarantee for the peace of the world, because the problems of humanity may be to-day in the Atlantic Ocean, yesterday in the German Ocean, and they may pass to-morrow into the Pacific, and, when they do, the Powers that are most greatly concerned in Pacific matters are the United States of America, Japan and the British Empire."

The Hon. W. Ormsby-Gore (Coalition Unionist, *Stafford*): 'And China."

The Prime Minister: "Certainly, China. Those four great countries are primarily concerned in having a complete understanding with regard to the Pacific, but the surest way to make a success of any Disarmament Conference is, first of all, to come to an understanding upon the Pacific. I do not myself believe that you will attain the same measure of success in a Disarmament Conference until you have attained that complete understanding. I believe Disarmament would be much easier if you could get that clear understanding first, and I am still hopeful that that view will be taken. The British Empire as a whole were all agreed in the desire to have complete friendship with the United States of America, and to make arrangements which would remove every conceivable prospective obstacle to such friendship.

"Nothing would please the British Dominions, as well as the Mother Country, more than a settlement which would make them feel that the British Empire and the United States of America could work side by side in a common partnership for the restoration of the peace of the world—for guaranteeing the peace of the world. I do not know of any guarantee that would be equal to that of the United States of America and the British Empire in agreement upon the great principles upon which world-policy ought to be based. That is an absolute guarantee of the peace of the world, and I am still hopeful that such an understanding as would establish a scheme of that kind will ensue as a result of the coming Conference in Washington. Those are some of the great problems which we have discussed."

The right hon. gentleman went on to remark that it was difficult to say anything about Egypt at the moment, because negotiations were going on with some very distinguished representatives of that country. He was sincerely desirous of an understanding being reached which would render it possible to make Egyptian freedom and British interests coincide, and that they might work together for the benefit of that ancient and renowned country. He was very sanguine that such an arrangement could be achieved.

Distinct Advance.

The problems discussed at the Imperial Conference presented a distinct advance in the working of Empire and were full of lessons. "There," continued the Prime Minister, "you had four or five nations sitting round that table, different

races, some of them absolutely different civilisations. There
were New Zealand, Australia, Canada and South Africa.
There were Englishmen, Scotchmen, Welshmen and Frenchmen. There were Englishmen and Dutchmen from South
Africa ; men of different races, who within recent years had
been fighting each other with a fierce antagonism. I remember
the conflict on the floor of this House ; I took a little part in
it. There they were all meeting for a common purpose as free
nations.

"We never interfere with them. They never interfere
with us. They did not feel there was anything which derogated
from their national dignity to come there for common council
in this great bond of nations. On the contrary, it gave an
added dignity and an added strength.

Freedom of the Dominions.

"Take the Peace Conference. Supposing they had been
there as separate independent nations, holding no allegiance
to the British Crown. They would not have had one-fifth of
the power and dignity they had as representatives of nations
inside the British Empire.

"There was one man sitting on a Commission—the Prime
Minister of Canada—deciding questions of the Turkish Empire.
There was another sitting on a Commission deciding the fate
of Poland and the Eastern frontiers of Germany. Why were
they there ? If they had been independent nations, they
would not have sat so high in the Council Chamber. It was
the fact that they were independent nations inside the British
Empire which gave them all this power, and they knew it, and
they are proud of it. It has not derogated from the individual
freedom of any one of them—not one.

"That is full of lessons at this moment which I hope will
not be lost—of freedom inside the British nation, national
freedom, national pride, national development which has been
possible inside this great League of Nations, the first great
successful League of Nations, the first great successful League
of Free Nations the world has ever seen. India is simply a
the first step on the road to self-government. She will
develop. There is nothing that will give a greater satisfaction
than the feeling that she also has pride in the Empire. They
have fought for their national claims. They have fought for
their Indian rights in Natal and elsewhere. But they were
all proud of being in the British Empire.

"It was a great spectacle to see these men of many
nations, these men of different civilisations, of older civilisations than ours, more varied in many respects, richer than
ourselves, bringing from the store of the old and the new

he old civilisation, the old strength, the old wisdom that has
ome from the far centuries to the vigour of the New. World ;
nd all constituting the strength of this great new Empire
hich is, we believe, destined to play a worthy part in the
istory of the world."

levelopment of the. Empire.

The Right Hon. Sir Donald Maclean (Chairman of the
ndependent Liberal Party in Parliament) re-echoed the Prime
linister's remarks regarding the great services of the Dominions
nd India in the War.

There was, he proceeded, no more interesting statement
(a philosophic nature made by the Prime Minister than
hen he referred to the instinctive way in which the British
Empire had been developed. Barely a quarter of a century
ao, Professor Seeley, speaking of the growth of the British
Empire, said, " They conquered the world in a fit of absence of
mnd." That was a rhetorical way of expressing exactly
mat the Prime Minister had been so graphically telling them
tat day. There was the working through the problems of
te world of the British sub-conscious instinct for free government through free peoples in all parts of the world. He
welcomed, as he was sure the House did and the Empire would
d, the emphatic declaration of the Prime Minister that the
whole Conference came with complete unanimity to the
dfinite conclusion that any attempt to reduce the Constitution
othe great commonwealth of nations to a written basis would
b destructive of its future development on really great lines.
They ought to acknowledge the great sacrifices which the
sf-governing Dominions had made in attending these Con-
fences at the centre of the Empire.

He hoped that what the Prime Minister had said about
naval armaments was indicative of his determination that
th financial—and more than the financial—resources of the
Empire would be utilised to the smallest possible extent in
mitary and naval armaments.

Washington Conference.

No doubt in the coming Conference at Washington grave
isues might be retarded in their progress towards a better
ste of things, or very much assisted, by the spirit in which
th whole task was undertaken.

He hoped and believed—and in the situation as between
th United States and Japan it would be folly to close one's
md to the facts—that their whole effort would be based
upn an endeavour to achieve through what might happen

at Washington a settlement, at any rate, of the principle which might remove that menace to the hopes of Disarmament throughout the world. The main difficulty in the way of any Disarmament at the present time was not military in the land sense. It was the naval trouble. He was certain it was the wish of the country that the Prime Minister himself should, if possible, be present at the epoch-making Conference at Washington.

As regards Egypt, he hoped there would be no avoidable delay in dealing with that most urgent problem. He was thankful to hear that in the deliberations of the Imperial Conference it was the united intention that their self-governing Dominions and India should take their share in the shaping of the foreign policy of the future. He regarded that, even if it stood entirely by itself, as well worth the meeting of the Conference. The time had gone when the fate of millions of men and the shattering of the lives and happiness of the peoples on earth could be decided by old gentlemen discussing the affairs——

The Leader of the House : " What about my right hon friend the Prime Minister ? "

Sir Donald Maclean said he was not referring to the Prime Minister, but to the old European diplomacy of the past He hoped the foreign policy of this great Commonwealth of Nations, as they called the British Empire, would be shaped on different lines from those which existed of old in the countries and which caused wicked wars that ought to have been avoided, or fought by the men who caused them.

Influence of Dominions.

The Hon. W. Ormsby-Gore, after observing that old fashioned doctrines in the direction of a hard-and-fast Imperial Federation were not held by any considerable section of people in this country, said he rejoiced that the proposed Imperial Conference to deal with constitutional matter was not to take place, but that they were going to trust, a heretofore, to the meetings between the responsible statesmen of the various self-governing Dominions.   He believed the fact that countries so democratic as Australia and Canada were to be associated with foreign policy would be the most valuable check upon the reaction which might easily take place in this country, where foreign politics had been so essentially the affair of the Foreign Office, and so little the affair of the democratic House of Parliament. That day had ceased with the War, and the one thing that would prevent possibly an almost natural reaction in an ancient country like this was the fact that the Dominions would demand to know from the who came to the Imperial Conference all that it was right should be known and made public, and to be fully associated with their executive Governments in any action or commitments that might be undertaken.

He was glad there was to be a better system of communicating information from the Foreign Office to the Imperial Government and to the Imperial Premiers in particular. The real difficulty was to bring the self-governing Dominions into touch with the information.

" To begin with," the hon. Member said, " I would suggest that the High Commissioners of the self-governing Dominions should be kept as closely informed as possible by the Foreign Office of anything which it is reasonable and right should be communicated to them for communication to their respective Governments. I attach enormous importance to developing machinery of that kind for bringing the Empire and those distant Dominions into a position whereby they will not say, ' We cannot give you advice upon this or that matter because we have not got the information.' It is essential that just as our Prime Minister and our Foreign Secretary have information, so in the Dominions their Prime Ministers and Ministers of Defence should have the same information. Nothing should be hidden from any of the Governments responsible for advising His Majesty upon the external policy of the Empire."

India's Position in the Empire.

Referring to India, the hon. Member expressed his great satisfaction that Indian representatives were being brought into the counsels of the Imperial Conference and the meeting of Premiers. India was making rapid strides in the direction of self-government. If that goal was to be reached by India it was perfectly clear it would not be reached by India thinking only of her own internal affairs, but by being associated with all the work of the Empire. He hoped the precedent established at the recent Imperial Conference would never be gone back upon, but that it was a clear realisation by the Dominions and Great Britain of the rightful position of India inside the Empire.

Turning to other questions, Mr. Ormsby-Gore said that very North American newspaper thought that Britain and Japan by the Alliance had obtained unfair positions for themselves in Chinese markets and spheres of influence, and the like. All through the length and breadth of the North American continent there was a profound sympathy for the Chinese position. " I believe," the hon. Member remarked, " that the future of the Anglo-Japanese Alliance depends in the long

C

run upon the ability of the British Foreign Office and th
Japanese Government to go hand in hand, and really to main
tain the "open door" in China with equal opportunities for th
trade and commerce of all nations. With that object th
Japanese and ourselves should use a helping hand to assis
China back on to her feet again."

With reference to Imperial Defence, the more latitud
there was so far as the Dominions were concerned, the bette
provided there was something in the nature of an Imperi
Higher Staff College for all arms. He believed that was abse
lutely vital. Australian sailors and soldiers should hav
every encouragement to come to England and go through
course of higher training in conjunction with British officer
Indian officers, and senior officers of all arms throughout th
Empire.

Dominions and Empire Responsibilities.

He was rather surprised that one question did not com
up at the Imperial Conference, viz., the relation of the se
governing Dominions to the enormous responsibilities whi
Great Britain had to bear in the way of administration a
civil duties in the Crown Colonies and the rest of the Empi.

"Unless the Dominions come along and help us in th
matter," observed Mr. Ormsby-Gore, "unless they get som
of our experience and some of our traditions, then I can for
see considerable difficulties in the future. I am one of th
who rejoice that Samoa is to be administered by N
Zealand, and New Guinea by Australia. These two gr
Dominions will thus have direct experience in the administ
tion of less forward peoples. They will probably make m
takes, such as we made at the start, but I hope that the s
governing Dominions will come along on this question, beca
I see that the coming problems for the British Empire e
enormously complicated by the colour problem, and by e
fact that the British Empire is composed of men of every r
and every creed, living in every clime, Arctic and tropical.

As for Egypt, he hoped for a full recognition of r
national desire for independence, together with a recognit n
of British Imperial interests.

India and Japanese Treaty.

Sir J. D. Rees pointed out that in addition to provid g
1,000,000 troops during the War, India contributed in c h
out of her comparatively slender resources no less t n
£100,000,000 towards the expenses of the War. It s
believed in India that there was something in the An o
Japanese Treaty which bound Japan to come in and help G

Britain if they had internal difficulties in India. That feeling had given rise to resentment on the part of the Indian people, who were now arousing themselves, as a strong man from his sleep, and developing that race conscience and national pride which created that kind of feeling in them. The Anglo-Japanese Treaty had no such stipulation. It had no connection whatever with the internal government of India. There was, therefore, no reason whatever why anyone in India, or anyone with any interest in India, should feel the slightest jealousy or resentment towards Japan.

Referring to the Navy, the Hon. Member said it was the British Navy that made possible the co-existence of all the parts of that great Empire.

Lieut.-Comdr. Kenworthy complained that the Government were permitting trade in munitions of war to take place with the Greeks and the Turks in Asia Minor. The Covenant of the League of Nations contained specific pronouncements against the private trade in armaments and yet they were calmly encouraging that obscene traffic with these two belligerents. As regards the Anglo-Japanese Alliance, he said if it meant that their hands were tied in defending the rights of China, or what was worse, if it was to be used as an excuse for Foreign Office support for predatory concession hunters in China, it was a very serious matter if they were to allow it to be renewed without some protest. The conduct of the Japanese Government in Korea must and should be taken into full consideration when the Alliance came up for renewal in twelve months' time. He did not believe any empire or nation would benefit by being allied to an Imperialistic Power.

Austria found that, and the people of this country would find to their cost that, unless the Alliance carried with it the understanding that Imperialistic projects were not to be undertaken under its shadow, it would do them immense harm.

The speech of the hon. and gallant Member brought to a close that portion of the debate which related to the proceedings of the Imperial Conference.

CONFERENCE OF THE SUPREME COUNCIL.

(Upper Silesia: Asia Minor: Russian Famine: League of Nations: Disarmament Conference, etc.)

The motion for the Second Reading of the Consolidated Fund (Appropriation Bill) in the House of Commons on 16th August afforded an opportunity for the Prime Minister to make a statement on the decisions of the Supreme Council of the Allies at the meeting in Paris during the previous week.

DEBATE IN HOUSE OF COMMONS.

The Prime Minister (the Right Hon. D. Lloyd George) said that this was in many respects the most important meeting held since the declaration of peace. There were questions which menaced the solidarity of the Alliance, and he felt that the unity of the Allies was a guarantee for the peace of Europe. It was a matter of great gratification that at the end of the meeting a resolution was passed, not merely that the Alliance should continue, but that the spirit of the Alliance was as strong as ever.

The question which gave them the greatest anxiety was that of Silesia. Settled on its merits, geographically, economically, statistically, it never seemed to him, nor to any of his associates, to present any insuperable, or even any very great, difficulties ; but it was complicated by the introduction of other elements which converted it into rather a menacing problem. There were large sections of French public opinion who believed that the taking away of the coal mines, the zinc mines and the iron works of Germany was essential to the security of their country. That he believed to be a delusion. Then there were questions of arrangements which had been made for working the mines, and these rather complicated the problem. Silesia was not a Polish province ; out of a population of 5,100,000, some 4,000,000 was German.

The Industrial Triangle.

Reviewing the history of the question, the Prime Minister reminded the House that in the first draft of the Peace Treaty the whole of Upper Silesia was given to Poland. The Germans challenged the provisional decision of the Allies on the ground that Upper Silesia was German in population, and the Allies accepted the view of the British delegation, which met in Paris, that a case had been made for referring the matter to the decision of the population of Upper Silesia. The total votes cast were 1,190,000 —707,000 for Germany and 479,000 for Poland. There was complete agreement between the Allies that the Western part of Upper Silesia was overwhelmingly German ; also, that Pless and Rybrick, which voted Polish, should be assigned to Poland. The importance of that lay in the fact that the future development of the coal measures was in the direction of Pless and Rybrick.

The dispute centred round the very important industrial triangle wedged in between these areas. The towns were German, the villages Polish. The direction, the engineering the planning—that was German. The skilled workmen were

German; the unskilled were Polish. The miners were divided, but, taking the areas as a whole, the substantial majority was German. The British and Italian experts agreed that this area ought to be accorded to Germany upon the basis of population. On the other hand, the French experts took a different view. The French had exactly the same interest in the matter as the British and the Italians, namely, that of doing justice between the parties ; but they were undoubtedly moved by another factor—that of security, by taking the mines and the zinc and the iron away from Germany and handing them over to Poland.

"That was not a consideration which was included in the Treaty . . . and therefore we regarded it as being outside the purview of our considerations," said the Premier.

Question Referred to League of Nations.

The Polish insurrection and the subsequent refusal of the British Government to recognise what had been done as a *fait accompli* were next touched upon by Mr. Lloyd George, who declared that the only decision which would govern the fate of Upper Silesia was that of the body created by the Treaty of Peace acting upon the principles laid down by the Treaty. Coming to the meeting of the Supreme Council which had just been held in Paris, he said it was soon apparent that complete unanimity was quite impossible. There was always the complication of that element of security. Therefore France would not have agreed to any recommendation acceptable to the other Allies.

"Under those conditions," the Prime Minister proceeded, "we agreed, quite unanimously, to refer the question to the Council of the League of Nations. It may be said that it could have been done earlier. . . . I am certain that the proposal came at the only moment when it would have been acceptable, and at the only moment when it was likely to succeed. It is not for me, and not for anybody else, to dictate to the Council of the League how they are to deal with the problem, but I am assuming that they are not going to pretend to deal with it themselves, or to sit in judgment and hear remedies, and decide it for themselves. I am assuming that they will refer it either to a committee of jurists or to an arbitrator, and there is a provision for both in the Treaty. But it is very important that before anything has happened, France, Italy, Japan and ourselves are pledged to accept the decision of whatever body is nominated by the Council to deal with it. It means that the parties will undoubtedly appear before the judicial tribunal appointed by the League. It will be tried just like any other frontier question upon the document—the basic document.

There will be the evidence, there will be the documents, there will be all the considerations relevant to the trial of the case, and judgment will be given by the arbitrator or by the jurists in the ordinary way, and all parties will accept it.

"It is the most important question that has yet been referred to the League, and, undoubtedly, the reputation, the position and the influence of the League will be considerably enhanced if it successfully deals with this most complicated problem." The Prime Minister added by way of explanation that the League would deal with the whole question of Upper Silesia—and not a part of it—on the basis of the Treaty.

The "Sanctions": Germany and her Obligations.

The Premier went on to say that there was another troublesome question as to the economic and military Sanctions imposed by the Conference of London upon the Germans when they failed to carry out two or three of the most important obligations under the Treaty. No doubt the economic Sanctions on the Rhine, especially the Customs Sanction, were irksome and injurious. As Germany had accepted better arrangements with respect to reparations, and was doing her best to carry them out, the Allies, accordingly, had agreed to terminate these Customs barriers on the Rhine. With regard to the military Sanctions, the French felt that there were some of the clauses of the Treaty which had not yet been carried out, notably those with regard to Disarmament, and they proposed that the military Sanctions should be kept for some time longer. The matter was to be referred to the Military Committee sitting in Paris, and it was proposed to deal with it at the next meeting of the Supreme Council.

There was a general feeling that the time had come for a gradual reduction of the military burdens imposed upon Germany in the matter of occupation and of controls. Up to the present their cost had absorbed almost the whole amount which ought to be available for reparations, and they were a source of constant irritation. The sooner Europe settled down to normal the better. "We have decided," said Mr. Lloyd George, "gradually to reduce some of these Commissions of control to the narrowest possible limit, and with regard to the cost of the Armies of Occupation we hope to be able to perfect an arrangement which will be more satisfactory to everybody all round." He quite understood the nervousness of the French people; but the real security of France depended upon three things :—

(1) The disarmament of Germany. It was impossible to create an atmosphere of peace until France felt

free from menace, and once the German armies were dispersed it would be impossible to build up great armaments in secret.

(2) The recollection by the Germans of the ruin which the Great War had brought upon their own country.

(3) The knowledge that whoever provoked war wantonly brought the whole world upon him, and in the end the greater the initial success the greater the disaster that would fall upon the aggressor.

It was the knowledge that if there were a wanton attack the world would come to the rescue that was the real security of France.

Asia Minor : Advice to Greece.

Describing it as " another very difficult problem " for the Supreme Council, the Prime Minister dealt with the position of affairs in Asia Minor. The Greeks and Turks refused the compromise suggested by the Allies. Compulsion was ruled out as impossible. It was said that they might have referred the matter to the League of Nations. That would have been an unkindness to the League. How could they have dealt with it ? They had only the means which the Allies could have placed at their disposal, and there was no Allied Power which would have sent an army for the purpose of enforcing a decision. Therefore, the Allies had to leave both the Greeks and the Turks to fight it out.

" I am sorry to say," remarked Mr. Lloyd George, " that not only do I think that was the only course, but I am afraid it is the best course. . . . The Mustapha Kemal Turks undoubtedly had an exaggerated idea of their own prowess. They conquered Asia Minor very easily. They gained some very easy victories in Cilicia and they had . . . a contemptuous estimate of the Greeks' military capacity. Their realisation that they were wrong in both those instances will make them none the worse neighbours for Greeks, or Italians, or Frenchmen, or British. The Turk accepts a fact in the end when it is really driven into his mind. . . . There are Greek enthusiasts, on the other hand, who, I have no doubt, will realise soon that there are limits to what Greek resource and Greek valour and Greek skill can accomplish in the fastnesses of Asia Minor. War has one merit, in that it does in the end teach a respect for facts. I think both these races will be easier to deal with when their own limitations have been brought thoroughly clearly to their minds. That is what is being done."

He sincerely trusted that the Greeks would not make the mistake which Bulgaria made in 1913 when, after a series of

very brilliant victories, which dazzled her people and blinded
the vision of some of her statesmen, she insisted upon
exaggerated terms, and put forward extravagant claims which
raised for her a host of enemies, antagonised old friends, and
ended in her downfall.   As a sincere friend of Greece he trusted
that Greek statesmanship would not repeat that error.   If it
did he was certain it would end in disaster to Greece.   Moderation in victory was more important to a nation even than
victory itself.

Russian Famine: Allied Decision.

The distressing topic of the Russian famine, a most
appalling catastrophe, also engaged the attention of the
Supreme Council.   Mr. Hodgson, the British trade representative in Moscow, said that in the districts bordering the Volga
the crops had completely failed, and he calculated that
35,000,000 people would require relief.   The Supreme Council
decided to create an international Commission to study the
possibilities of rendering immediate aid to the starving population.   On that Commission the British Government had
appointed three men : —

> Sir Philip Lloyd-Greame, Secretary to the Overseas
Trade Department,
> Sir John P. Hewett, a man of great Indian experience
and
> Mr. Wardrop, who was Consul in Moscow for some
years.

There had been suggestions of relief from organisations
in America, from the Red Cross, and from private benefactors.
All were valuable, but this was such a gigantic catastrophe
that it had to be dealt with upon a much bigger scale, and it
was the feeling in Paris that there must be a great international
effort.   The problem of transport had to be dealt with.   He
thought there were a few hundred locomotives and a few
hundred wagons more or less broken down ; but the whole
economic organisation of Russia was in an appalling state.
Transport had broken down, and in the parts of Russia where
the peasants had corn they declined to part with it except in
return for such commodities as boots, clothes, agricultural
implements or something else they needed.

As to the organisation of the famine area, it was very
difficult to know how to deal with the situation.   No one
in Paris wanted to introduce the political element.   The
only desire was to find a means to save these millions of people
and to prevent the spread of the epidemic which would
inevitably follow the famine.

Lines of Relief Work.

First of all they had to induce the people in the neighbouring areas who had corn to bring it in. They could not do that unless they organised some means by which the peasants could be induced to part with the corn. It could only be done by an organised exchange of commodities. Lord Curzon, who was Viceroy of India when one of the greatest famines fell upon that country, and 60,000,000 people were affected, said that one of the most important things was to prevent great movements of the population. They had to get an organisation in Russia which would keep the people in their areas and deal with them there. They could only do that by complete co-operation with the Government machinery in the Volga area, and they must have the most complete guarantee that whatever relief was given went to the people who were suffering. They did not want to set up committees in the Volga to govern, but at any rate the people who had the experience and the only people who had the resources must, to that extent, have the control of the administration of the relief which they dispensed.

If the Soviet Government wanted to create confidence, if they wanted to get the trading community to come in to assist them at this juncture, they must say that they would recognise all the obligations which had been incurred for supplies already sent to Russia. He did not want to take advantage of this dire calamity for the purpose of obtaining acceptance of that principle, but he knew that it was the best way of dealing with the matter. " I have gone into it very carefully," said the Premier, " and I have found that this stood in the way. They themselves admit that you must get the peasants to part with their corn. They themselves admit that there is only one way of doing so, that is by giving goods. I say there is only one way of getting the goods there, and that is by restoring that confidence among the trading community that will make the trading community feel that they can send their goods there without any danger of their obligations being confiscated in the future."

Mr. Asquith's Comments.

The Right Hon. H. H. Asquith (Leader of the Independent Liberal Party) said he thought on the whole the Prime Minister's survey was the most satisfactory statement they had received on the international situation since the time of the Armistice. As regards the appalling catastrophe with which Russia was threatened, they were all glad to hear that measures of a practical kind were contemplated. The best contribution—apart, of course, from generosity in the expenditure of money and the purchase of necessaries—which the British Empire could render was to utilise to the fullest extent the unique famine experience of their great Anglo-India Administration. He was delighted to hear that Sir J. P. Hewett had been selected by the Government for that purpose. They must depend in the long run on the co-operation of the local authorities in Russia and that might be very difficult to secure.

With reference to the Sanctions imposed upon Germany, he thought the Supreme Council had, if somewhat tardily, pursued in their latest determination a very wise policy. As to Asia Minor, and the relations between Greece and Turkey, of all the loose ends and ragged edges left by the War that was perhaps the most difficult to handle and to patch up again. The Treaty of Sèvres was there, an unratified, unrecognised, and inchoate international instrument, which he thought it was safe to predict would never become, in its present form, part of the public law of Europe. It was horrible and disappointing that this ancient cockpit of secular feuds should, after three years of so-called peace, once again be the scene of an internecine conflict between warring ambitions and covetousness.

" It seems to me," Mr. Asquith observed, " a melancholy and an impotent conclusion that the Great Powers of Europe should be unable to do anything practical to stop this endless effusion of blood and temper. For the moment, I confess I have nothing more to suggest than that we should be rigidly neutral and that, so far as we can, we should restrain and contract the area of conflict within the narrowest possible geographical limits."

Upper Silesia.

The right hon. gentleman proceeded to say with reference to Upper Silesia that he could not altogether assent to the Prime Minister's view that what was now wisely being done in the invocation as arbiter of the League of Nations might not have been done sooner with better effect. The action taken was the most gratifying and hopeful indication that they had yet seen of a real, whole-hearted desire and determination on the part of the Allied Powers to give to the League of Nations the kind of authority and to enable them to discharge the sort of functions which it was the object of the Covenant to entrust to them. The great step which had been taken by the President of the United States and his country in inviting a general Conference on Disarmament for the first time, gave them a solid and assured hope that the world was going to escape from the old devastating *régime* of international animosity and competitive forces and enter upon a *régime* of international adjustment.

The Right Hon. J. H. Thomas (**Labour,** *Derby*) believed that the attitude the Prime Minister had adopted in connection with Upper Silesia was in harmony with the overwhelming feeling of the great mass of men and women in this country. They were not anti-French, but they believed that the view of a crushed and down-trodden Germany was contrary not only to the best interests of their own country, but to the best interests of the future peace of the world. The League of Nations, which up to now had been treated somewhat contemptuously, had been given a fair opportunity to perform some useful work. He associated himself with the Prime Minister's plea with regard to Russia, but was sorry the right hon. gentleman made any reference to Russia undertaking an obligation with regard to her debts. He had frequently stated that he believed one of the first things the Bolshevik Government ought to have done was to recognise Russia's obligations, but he regretted that the matter should enter in any way into the grave human appeal involved in the problem of the Russian famine. The appeal was to humanity over and above any political consideration.

As to the Sanctions, Labour Members had never hesitated to point out that economically they were unsound, and that the application of them would prove disastrous.

General Botha's Plea.

The Right Hon. G. N. Barnes (**Labour,** *Glasgow, Gorbals*) expressed his sincere gratification at the speech of the Prime Minister, especially in its reference to Silesia. "When the Prime Minister was talking this afternoon," Mr. Barnes proceeded, " the scene came back to me of a discussion by the British Empire Delegation of the conditions which had been tentatively agreed should be pressed upon the Germans. I remember especially one Sunday evening when we met in the rooms of the Lord Privy Seal, and what struck me this afternoon looking back upon that event was the part played in it by the late General Botha. We met on the 19th anniversary of the Treaty signed in South Africa following that war. Rather singularly Lord Milner happened to be sitting next to General Botha, and when this matter of Silesia was under consideration, General Botha touched Lord Milner on the shoulder and reminded him of a meeting of a similar character 19 years before on that very day.

" He reminded Lord Milner that upon that occasion he had been pleading for moderate terms to be imposed upon, as he was then, the enemy. On this occasion, on the 19th anniversary of that great event, he was in Paris pleading for like generosity to animate thòse who were meeting as victors over Germany. Therefore it was with special satisfaction that my mind travelled back to that time, because I was one of those who, with General Botha and others, induced the Prime Minister to try and induce those he was meeting daily to reconsider this question of Silesia, amongst other questions. As the right hon. gentleman rightly said, the settlement which was then reached was that the fate of Silesia was to be determined by the free vote, so far as it could be ascertained, of the people living there, modified only by geographical and economic considerations. I think it is a matter of some little pride that our Prime Minister, not only now, but last May, has stood four square to all the opposition from Frenchmen or anybody else for the strict maintenance of the agreement which was then arrived at.

Maintenance of Treaty Terms.

" I congratulate the Prime Minister, the House and the country upon having taken, through the right hon. gentleman, a part which is entirely honourable to ourselves ; and, as Mr. Thomas has just said, the Prime Minister has behind him in this action the full concurrence of the great mass of the people of this country in standing strictly for the maintenance of the terms of that Treaty."

Lieut.-Colonel the Hon. Walter Guinness (Coalition Unionist, *Bury St. Edmunds*) remarked that the country would respond very readily to the Prime Minister's eloquent appeal in the name of humanity, but since the Trade Agreement with Russia there had been little evidence that the Russian Government were in a frame of mind which would make the problem of relief an easy one. They must make certain that trains, rolling stock and material sent in response to the call of the starving millions in Russia would not afterwards be used to rivet Bolshevism even more tightly upon that unfortunate and suffering people. With reference to Asia Minor, if the Allies were united there would be very little difficulty in bringing Greece and Turkey to reason. It was now time to cease making suggestions and to begin to give orders.

Mr. Aneurin Williams (Independent Liberal, *Consett*) earnestly hoped that the war in Asia Minor would end in a Greek rather than a Turkish victory. If it was a Greek victory there would be some hope for civilisation in that part of the world in the future.

The House subsequently turned to the discussion of other subjects.

LEAGUE OF NATIONS MANDATES.

(East Africa, Mesopotamia and Palestine.)

A debate took place in the House of Lords on 23rd June respecting the Mandates for East Africa, Mesopotamia and Palestine.

DEBATE IN HOUSE OF LORDS.

Lord Parmoor, who called attention to the draft Mandate for East Africa, said that, if properly exercised, the mandate principle appeared to be one of the most beneficent results which had come from the late War. Form B mandates, which were mandates in tropical Africa, would apply to an area of 600,000 square miles and to a population of about 12,000,000. Respecting the form of the Mandate for East Africa, the noble lord referred to the Article providing : —

"For the eventual emancipation of all slaves, and for as speedy an elimination of domestic and other slavery as social conditions will allow."

The last return he had seen, issued by the Foreign Office in 1913, gave the number of slaves in German East Africa as 185,000. What was meant by "the eventual emancipation of all slaves ? " It might mean, as regards time, postponement to the Greek Kalends. Article 5 said : —

"Shall prohibit all forms of forced or compulsory labour, except for essential public works and services, and then only in return for adequate remuneration."

The line between forced or compulsory labour and slavery was a very fine one. Did the phrase "except for essential public works and services" mean works or services which could not be carried out without forced labour ? If so, were the Government prepared to give any limit within which they might hope that this form of slavery would once and for all be destroyed ? With respect to the provision that strict control should be exercised over the traffic in arms and ammunition and the sale of spirituous liquors, he thought the matter could not be dealt with effectively without absolute prohibition.

The Duke of Sutherland, in reply, said the Covenant of the League regarded the mandate as a trust for the benefit of the mandated area and not for the mandatory. This was emphasised in the use of the word tutelage. He did not think there would be any difficulty in differentiating between forced labour and the conditions of slavery. The East African

Mandate was a type of the B class. The draft mandate for the other British mandated territories which were included in the same category —namely, the portions of Togoland and the Cameroons mandated to Great Britain—followed this model, *mutatis mutandis.*

Mesopotamia and Palestine.

Lord Islington moved for a return stating the total military expenditure incurred in each of the territories administered since the acceptance of the mandate of the League of Nations by Great Britain.

As to the mandates for Mesopotamia and Palestine, they had recently, he said, a very full statement in the House of Commons by the Secretary of State for the Colonies.* Whilst the expenditure which Mr. Churchill asked the House of Commons to accept was materially reduced as compared with the previous year the sum involved was still enormous. He had to ask for £35,500,000 of British money as the irreducible minimum to meet the necessities imposed by the previous obligations which had been undertaken. That sum represented approximately 1s. in the £ in income-tax. The taxpayer might come to realise that rulers in some other countries were not unwise in insisting on the avoidance of this new form of burden with its countless obligations and overwhelming expense. The real offenders in the matter were the Executive Government, who ought to have estimated the cost, and in consultation with Parliament throughout should have framed and adopted a more prudent policy, having regard to the financial capacity of the country.

Goodwill and a clear understanding with Turkey must, in a large measure, be the basis of their continued good relations with the Moslem world throughout the East, and it was to be regretted that this was not realised two years ago. He presumed that the expense involved in the civil administration of Iraq and Kurdistan would be met by taxation within the country itself, and that there would not be an additional burden upon the taxpayers of the United Kingdom. As regards an official statement concerning the position of the mandates for Africa, they had hitherto been singularly ill-informed.

Parliament and Mandates.

A report on the subject of the administration of the mandated area was to be made annually to the Council of the League of Nations, but he hoped that a report would also be

* *Vide* JOURNAL, Vol. II., No. 3, p. 490.

sent home and subjected to the consideration of Parliament every year. The Government had been much too prone in the last two years to shield themselves and their unconstitutional conduct behind the shadowy form of the League of Nations. That was a point that could not be emphasised too much in insisting upon all these questions being brought before the Parliament representing the peoples upon whom these responsibilities were imposed. He advocated the appointment of a strong and impartial Royal Commission which should be sent out to the countries in question next winter with a specific reference to report to Parliament on the whole subject.

Viscount Bryce urged that in any steps to deal with the difficult problem of Kurdistan the scheme ought to include provision for the safety of the Nestorian and Assyrian Christians, and, if possible, their restoration to the territories from which they were expelled, and the giving to them of full protection there. Parliament ought to be kept apprised at every stage of what was being done to create a mandate and to administer it, and should have due opportunities of expressing an opinion upon it. He suggested that a Joint Committee of the two Houses should be set up to report upon the best method of administering the mandatory system compatible with the control and opinion of Parliament. They were still rather in a mist as to how the mandate system was going to work.

The first step to dispel that mist was to have a clear grasp of the relations between the three parties in the matter—His Majesty's Government, the League of Nations and Parliament. They should put upon a permanent footing the principles upon which the League of Nations was to work, bearing in mind that this country could not shuffle off its responsibilities to the League of Nations, but must be responsible in the face of the world for what it did as a mandatory Power.

Lord Sydenham said the mandates entailed responsibilities and unknown expenditure on this country. On the other hand, they might be said in a certain sense to destroy the sovereign rights of the mandatory Power and to set up what might almost amount to international control over territories in which the responsibility for maintaining order would fall wholly upon this country. Whatever Government was set up in Mesopotamia would tumble to pieces absolutely unless British forces stood behind it. Those forces must be paid for entirely by this country and no one at that stage could estimate what the cost would be. Very little expenditure need have been applied to Palestine, but for the Mandate—which must evidently have been drafted with capable Zionist assistance—and the ill-advised action of the Zionists themselves.

The **Archbishop of Canterbury** observed that there was danger in unconsciously laying down rules and setting precedents with regard to these mandated territories, which might be quoted hereafter as representing the method by which the thing had come into operation.

Civil Administration in Mesopotamia.

The **Duke of Sutherland** gave detailed replies to various specific questions addressed to the Government in the course of the debate.

He remarked that the civil administration of Mesopotamia was expected to pay its way, although the Government might have to take a Vote for the accumulated deficit up to 31st March last. The British officers employed in Mesopotamia would fall into two distinct categories. The first category was that of an advisory staff attached to the Arab Ministers, the Arab district officers and the Arab army. All the advisory staff would be servants of His Majesty's Government and not of the Mesopotamian Government. They would be seconded to Mesopotamia for a period of years and their pay would be met from Mesopotamian revenues. The second category was that of officers of technical and scientific services, such as railways, posts, telegraphs, agriculture, etc. These would be servants of the Mesopotamian Government and their number depended entirely on the wishes of that Government. With regard to Kurdistan, the policy was to reduce the number of British officers to an absolute minimum. Kurdistan was to remain for the present in direct relations with the High Commissioner, and would not be placed under the Mesopotamian Government. As to Togoland, their part consisted of a strip adjoining the Gold Coast and contained no ports, railways or industries. The administration cost very little and was carried out by increasing slightly the staff of the Gold Coast. There was no military expenditure in the Togoland mandated territory. That part of the Cameroons for which Britain was to receive a mandate would be administered by the Nigerian Government. An expansion of revenue after the development of trading facilities was looked to as the remedy for the deficit which in the current year was estimated at £78,900 ; but it was too early, especially in view of the present fall in the value of many tropical products, to forecast the future trade prospects of the province.

As to the Tanganyika territory, the finances were managed on the same lines as those of an ordinary British Protectorate which was in receipt of a grant-in-aid, and the estimated deficit for 1920-21 was £164,000. This, together with a loan of £750,000, was to be provided from the British Exchequer, precisely as in the case of the loans to Nyasaland and Somaliland. The natives of the country would be treated with justice and consideration. It was laid down in the draft mandate that their rights and interests should be respected and safeguarded.

Foreign Secretary's Statement.

The Secretary of State for Foreign Affairs (the Marquess Curzon of Kedleston) remarked that they were moving in an area of considerable obscurity, but it was an obscurity for which the Government were not responsible. Not even a trained lawyer could attach a clear meaning to many phrases of the Covenant.

" I myself am not certain," said the noble Marquess, "that it was not a mistake in policy that, when the Allied statesmen met in Paris, in their extreme anxiety to get the League of Nations put upon what one may call the International Statute Book they rushed, almost with precipitation, to discuss questions which would, as we see now, have been much better solved if they had been postponed. I cannot help thinking that if, instead of drawing up these regulations for the better government of the world in the future, they had endeavoured to end the War and to secure the peace of the world as it then was, we should have been much further advanced in conditions of peace than we now are.

" We do not want to utter reproaches to those who have passed away from the active scene of politics. But many of our difficulties in the sphere of international affairs do, in my judgment, arise from the wrong turn that was taken when the Conference first assembled in Paris."

America and the Mandates.

Turning to a question asked by Lord Islington as to whether the draft mandates had been communicated to the American Government before submission to the League of Nations, the noble Marquess explained the circumstances which rendered it impossible to do exactly what the American Government desired. The Council of the League pointed out to the American Government, however, in a letter dated March, 1921, that there would be a considerable postponement before the discussion on the mandates took place ; they cordially invited the American Government to assume connection with the League and to take part in the discussions ; and they felt confident that, by the ordinary channels of information—as was the case—the draft mandates would be in the hands of the American Government before that date.

The American Government, under President Harding, had resumed a more active interest in the affairs of the world. The more they got America to resume with them in peace that co-operation to which they owed so much in War, in the form best suited to her own feelings and desires, the better it would be for the rapid recovery of the peace of the world.

"During the past weeks," the Marquess Curzon proceeded, "the head of the President's Administration in America, quite apart from the view that he may entertain concerning the League of Nations itself . . . has expressed a strong view that, as one of the Allied and Associated Powers, America is entitled to be consulted before the mandates are finally settled. There is force and reason in that view, and I am not disposed to differ from it ; and I believe that the League of Nations are likely to reply that, holding those views themselves, they have decided again to postpone the consideration of the mandates, and that they trust that the Government who are concerned will enter into communication with the American Government in the interval. By the interval I mean before the meeting of the Assembly in September. We shall all agree that there must be a period to this uncertainty, and for my own part . . . if that suggestion comes to me from the League of Nations I shall be quite prepared to . . . enter into discussions as suggested."

There remained, said the noble Marquess, the point about publicity and about the right of Parliament to have a voice in these matters. As an act of courtesy the Government thought they would best be discharging their duty by handing over the draft mandates to the Council of the League, and he could conceive that in a short time the mandates might assume a form in which they were legitimately open for discussion by Parliament.

Lord Islington withdrew his motion and the debate closed

Attitude of the United States.

In the House of Commons on 27th June,

The Hon. W. Ormsby-Gore (Coalition Unionist, Stafford) asked the Prime Minister what had been decided by the Council of the League of Nations at their June meeting at Geneva regarding the drafts of the A and B mandates ; and whether those drafts would now be communicated officially to the American Government by the British and French Governments respectively, in accordance with the request of the American Government in their Note to the British Government, dated 20th November, 1920.

The Under-Secretary for Foreign Affairs (**Mr. Cecil Harms-worth**), who replied, said : "A letter has just been received from the President of the Council of the League, in which the suggestion is made that, in view of the intimation from the United States Government that they could not accept any decision reached on this question without their approval, the Powers concerned should make every effort to arrive at a solution of the points under discussion between them and the United States so as to enable the Council to settle the whole question of mandates before the next meeting of the Assembly. His Majesty's Government will consider the best means of giving effect to this suggestion."

INTERNATIONAL LABOUR CONFERENCE.

(Government and the Washington Conventions.)

On 27th May a debate took place in the House of Commons on the subject of the Government's obligations to submit to Parliament certain Conventions adopted at the first International Labour Conference at Washington. The debate, which was summarised in the last issue of the JOURNAL (*vide* p. 483), stood adjourned, and the question was again raised on 1st July.

DEBATE IN HOUSE OF COMMONS.

The Minister of Labour (the Right Hon. T. J. Macnamara) at the outset of the resumed debate moved :—

"That this House approves the policy of His Majesty's Government respecting the several Conventions and Recommendations of the International Labour Conference at Washington in November, 1919."

The right hon. gentleman stated the position of the Government in regard to the Conventions and Recommendations.

CONVENTIONS.

(1) For the establishment of an eight-hours day.

The Government proposed to send a letter to Geneva explaining the difficulties which here confronted them and intimating that they would be very glad to take part in a reconsideration of this Convention, probably drawn on rather more elastic lines, at a future Congress of the International Labour Organisation.

(2) Dealing with unemployment and with the establishment of a system of free public employment agencies or exchanges.

This Convention was covered by existing British legislation and the Government proposed to ratify it.

(3) Relating to the employment of women before and after child-birth.

The Government were unable to ratify this Maternity Convention, for the reason that the Washington Convention would cut right across the arrangements which had been built up in this country—arrangements in advance of those in any other country in the world—under the National Health Insurance Act and in connection with maternity and child welfare centres throughout the world.

(4) Prohibiting the employment of women during the night.

This Convention had been covered by the Women, Young Persons, and Children (Employment) Act, 1920,* and would be ratified.

(5) Fixing a minimum age for the admission of children to industrial employment.

This Convention was covered by the above-mentioned Act of 1920, and would be ratified.

(6) Prohibiting night work in the case of young persons employed in industry.

This Convention was also covered by the same Act, and would be ratified.

The net result was that His Majesty's Government were prepared to ratify four out of the six Conventions.

RECOMMENDATIONS.

(1) Concerning unemployment insurance, distribution of public work, and other unemployment questions.

The first and second Articles referring to fee-charging employment agencies and the recruitment of bodies of workers in other countries the Government had not been able to accept. They were not agreed to by the British representatives at Washington. The third and fourth Articles dealt with unemployment insurance and co-ordination of public work. These two Articles would be accepted. As regarded unemployment insurance, they had in this country a scheme more comprehensive than any other in the world.† As regarded the co-ordination of work undertaken under public authority the Article represented the existing practice in this country.

(2) Concerning reciprocity of treatment for workers in countries other than their own.

For long the British treatment of foreign workers had been fully up to the standard of this Recommendation without reciprocal agreements. But as the general question fell within the terms of reference of the International Commission on Emigration the Government thought that they should await the report of the Commission on that point.

(3) Concerning the disinfection of wool infected with anthrax spores.

This Recommendation was covered by the Anthrax Prevention Act 1919.

(4) Concerning the protection of women and children against lead poisoning.

This had been fully dealt with in the Women and Young Persons (Employment in Lead Processes) Act, 1920.

(5) Concerning the establishment of Government health services.

This Recommendation represented existing British policy.

(6) Concerning the use of white phosphorus in the manufacture of matches.

---

* *Vide* JOURNAL, Vol. II., No. 1, p. 64.
† *Vide* p. 775.

This Recommendation was anticipated in this country by the White Phosphorus Matches Prohibition Act so long ago as 1908.

The Secretary-General of the League of Nations was informed in January, 1921, of the acceptance of the last four Recommendations and he would be duly notified of the Government's acceptance of the two most important Articles of the first Recommendation. The second Recommendation, as he had said, was still under examination.

The Government's Obligations.

The Right Hon. G. N. Barnes* (**Labour,** *Glasgow, Gorbals*) said the Government had come under an obligation to bring each Convention or Recommendation before the competent Authority. So far as the Eight Hours' Convention was concerned they had not complied with the technical requirements of the documents they had signed, but, for the time being, he accepted the position that Parliament was now recognised as the competent Authority under the Treaty. There was an obligation resting upon the Government to submit the Eight Hours' Convention to that House and there was a moral obligation resting upon them to adopt it, because the British delegates voted for it at Washington according to their instructions. He admitted that the Washington Convention did not square with the agreement made with the railway workers in this country. The Convention should be ratified, and if that were impossible under present conditions, then a special Conference should be held to strike the railways out of it.

He appealed for support for the Labour Organisation and the Labour Chapter of the Peace Treaty, not as a mere declaration of rights or of hopes, but as something to which they were all committed, to enable all countries to march forward together, to lift Labour questions out of the rut of strike and lock-out into the region of moral law and social justice.

The Right Hon. J. R. Clynes (**Chairman of the Parliamentary Labour Party**) said the two things that mattered to Labour were the maternity question and the question of working hours. On these matters the Government had wholly failed in their duty, even in the first step of giving the House of Commons an opportunity of discussing and ratifying, if it thought fit to do so, the Washington decisions. As regards these international conferences and decisions the question was, "Were they to be the leaders or the laggards?" It was true that, in many respects, they occupied a front place, but they could still do much by example and by leadership.

---

* The Right Hon. George Barnes was one of the British Government representatives at the International Conference at Washington.

The Leader of the House (the Right Hon. Austen Chamberlain) submitted that the accomplishment of all their hopes and ideals was not possible as long as some of the greatest nations of the world, and especially some of the greatest industrial nations, took no part in these Conferences, were no parties to their decisions, and did not act with others in the general endeavour. " We must," said the right hon. gentleman, "have these Conventions drawn with sufficient wisdom, with sufficient moderation, with sufficient patience, and with sufficient elasticity to enable them to be readjusted to the varied conditions of the different countries, and we must seek to secure, as members of the organisation, and as parties to the legislation involved, other great industrial nations who are at present no party to the Conference."

On a division, the motion approving the policy of the Government was carried by 164 votes against 53.

COLONIAL OFFICE VOTE.

(British Policy in Middle East : Developing Empire Resources, etc.)

On 14th June (*vide* JOURNAL, Vol. II., No. 3, p. 490) the House of Commons debated at length the subject of British policy in Mesopotamia and Palestine on a supplementary estimate for £27,197,000 presented by the Colonial Office in respect of Middle Eastern Services. The debate stood adjourned and was resumed on 14th July, when the Vote for £529,104 for the Colonial Office came on for discussion in Committee of Supply.

DEBATE IN HOUSE OF COMMONS.

The Right Hon. H. H. Asquith (Leader of the Independent Liberal Party) pointed out that the Secretary of State for the Colonies in his speech on 14th June said the estimates for next year for Mesopotamia and Palestine would not exceed £9,000,000 or £10,000,000. Supposing that all the economies were realised, that sum still made a very serious demand upon the House of Commons and the taxpayers of this country.

" My considered and deliberate judgment is, as I told the House more than a year ago, that the primary duty of the Executive Government at this moment in that part of the world is to put an end to the liabilities, as," said the right hon.

gentleman, " neither on the grounds of obligation nor on grounds of interest have we any stake in Mesopotamia—and the same is true in Palestine—at all commensurate with the demands that are being made upon the sorely-tried British taxpayer. The Government tell us that they must contract expenditure on social interests of primary importance, but we are asked now to vote £27,000,000—an estimate which I agree with Mr. Churchill compares very favourably with the estimates of last year or the year before."

The Secretary of State for the Colonies (the Right Hon. Winston Churchill) : " Or of the beginning of the year."

Mr. Asquith : " I agree, it compares very favourably with the beginning of the year. He has asked for £27,000,000, and the only prospect he holds out is that of its being reduced next year to £9,000,000 or £10,000,000. But that prospect depends upon a number of the most shifting, shadowy, nebulous and unsubstantial hypotheses that have ever been presented to the House."

Sir J. D. Rees (Coalition Unionist, *Nottingham, East*) asked how could they keep Mesopotamia if they made it hateful to the electors of this country. He could not help thinking that one of the reasons which had led to undue expenditure and extravagant administration in Mesopotamia, in Palestine and elsewhere was the Covenant of the League of Nations. " I believe the League of Nations to be a most excellent thing," the hon. Member observed. " I believe now there is every prospect, owing to President Harding—not President Wilson —of our getting one that may do good. But up to now the sentimental socialism which occupies every page of the Covenant has always fostered extravagant administration."

Immigrant Jews in Palestine.

Sir W. Joynson-Hicks (Coalition Unionist, *Twickenham*), speaking of Palestine, remarked that he believed he was not far wrong in saying that very nearly half of the immigrant Jewish population was being maintained by public works, which had to be paid for out of the funds of either Great Britain or the Arabs. As regards the Mandate for Palestine, he could not help feeling that the Arabs were really entitled to ask whether Great Britain had fulfilled her obligations of honour to the Arab population.

Earl Winterton (Coalition Unionist, *Horsham*) interjected the remark that the immigrants were paid for by the general population of Palestine, and not by the Arabs alone.

Sir W. Joynson-Hicks said that 90 per cent. of the population were Arabs and Christians, and only 10 per cent. Jews. Therefore, at all events 90 per cent. of the cost of those public works must come out of Arab and Christian pockets. The Arabs had come to feel, rightly or wrongly, that the British administration of Palestine was becoming to some extent Judean, and that was what was causing the present unrest in that country.

Mr. T. Shaw (Labour, *Preston*) remarked that the Labour Party wanted Great Britain to get out of Mesopotamia at the earliest possible moment. So far as Palestine was concerned, they desired, as far as possible, and in strict accordance with the promise made, that Great Britain should leave the management of that country to the people who lived in it. The future of Mesopotamia and Palestine depended upon a lasting peace with Turkey.

The Right Hon. Sir Donald Maclean (Chairman of the Independent Liberal Party in Parliament) moved to reduce the amount of the Vote by £500.

Colonies and Protectorates: Tropical Diseases.

The Under-Secretary of State for the Colonies (Hon. Edward Wood) said he wished to confine himself to endeavouring to give some picture of the principal events of last year in the Colonies and the Protectorates of the Empire.

He pointed out that all of them practically had shared a common experience, inasmuch as to the vigorous activities that were induced by the keen demand of the world for what they had to offer during the War there had succeeded a period of economic stagnation and paralysis. The circumstances of the day had led to a great many propositions being advanced to the Colonial Office through the local Governments for particular help to meet particular sets of difficulties, and he was sorry to confess that it was necessary in these days to acknowledge that, however willing might be the spirit, the flesh, interpreted in terms of ready money, and rigidly bound by economic laws, was sadly weak. He thought that on the whole it was sounder to try, as and when one could, to spend what money one could in endeavouring to aim at the permanent development of the permanent resources, both in human life and in agriculture, with which these various places were endowed.

It was quite impossible to profess any satisfaction with the state of health in many parts of their Colonies where the mortality of their British fellow-subjects was what it was to-day. He expressed the thanks of the Government to a Committee presided over by Lord Chalmers which had recently reported after an inquiry with the object of determining how best to link more closely the problems of research in the Colonies with universities and other allied institutions in the country. More and more forces in different parts of the world were being mobilised in the pursuit of disease.

United States Co-operation.

It was with the keenest pleasure that a few weeks ago the Colonial Office was able to welcome the representatives of the International Health Board of the Rockefeller Foundation, who were good enough to come over from the United States to confer with them as to the possibility of closer co-operation in their beneficent and valuable work. He had every hope that from those consultations extremely important results would emerge.

Wherever they began to tackle the problems of research, or of its application, they were every time confronted with the question of medical personnel. In this matter the Colonial Secretary had the assistance of a strong Committee presided over by Sir Walter Egerton, and some of their recommendations had already been adopted. Remarking upon the difficulty of the problem, the hon. Member pointed out, as an illustration, that the unification of a Colonial medical service was not an easy matter. In all these matters of administration the Colonial Office was dealing with some 40 to 50 different Governments, in an infinite variety of conditions and infinitely differing in their financial resources.

He was satisfied that, as with human life, so with plants, animals, trees, and so on, they had only begun to make their own the secrets that science and scientific discovery had to unfold to them if they really applied themselves to learn them. To mention only one instance, there was the development, now approaching fruition, of the West Indian Agricultural College of Trinidad. That development had been powerfully stimulated by the recent preferential trade agreement between the West Indies and their great Dominion neighbour—Canada.

Improving Communications.

In West Africa the scientific side of agricultural departments was being strengthened with the same object. In East Africa a proposal was now being considered, which, he hoped, would shortly reach fruition, of turning the Amari Institute in Tanganyika into a central research institute for the whole of East Africa. In conjunction with other developments it was necessary to push on with the building of railways in Nyasaland, in East Africa and in West Africa, and to link up those railways with the sea through wharves, harbours and docks, and by way of the sea with the outside world.

He would postulate three conditions on the successfu
fulfilment of which he believed the future of the Britisl
Empire principally to depend : —

(1) Co-operation between themselves and the self
governing Dominions and India.

(2) The wisdom with which they in England and
that House might be able to guide those communities
not yet self-governing, along the path of constitutiona
development.

(3) The measure of harmony that they were abl
to achieve between the diversity of civilisations, races
creeds, colours, and traditions that composed thei
commonwealth.

They had heard foreigners express some astonishment a
the great variety of constitutions under which different part
of the British Empire were administered and lived. But th
result of it was that all the time there was going on al
over the Empire a process of organic growth in this matte
which took on its peculiar colour and local circumstance
according to the condition of the particular Colonies concerned

Rhodesia : Responsible Government.

Proceeding to discuss the question of responsible govern
ment in Rhodesia, the hon. Member said that whenever an
in whatever way the termination of the administration o
the British South Africa Company took place, he hoped n
party would forget the gratitude that it ought to be prepare
to offer to the Company for all they had done for the develop
ment of that country, and through that country of Africa an
the Empire. He had heard considerable doubt expresse
whether the financial position of Rhodesia was sufficientl
strong to warrant the granting of responsible governmen
to-day, but he could find no grounds for such pessimism.

"Whatever scheme is suggested," the Under-Secretar
continued, " should be amply examined from all points o
view, as it may affect, in the judgment of some, but not i
mine, the Imperial taxpayer. That point will be fully ex
plored. It is also vital and desirable that every opportunit
should be taken to ascertain the free, independent, and con
sidered judgment of the people of Rhodesia. These ar
questions which are primarily for them to settle for themselves
I should think it very unwise to force or prejudge their con
clusions in advance of their freely expressed opinions."

Earl Winterton : " Does the hon. gentleman includ
Northern Rhodesia ? "

The Under-Secretary of State for the Colonies : " I would certainly say the same of Northern Rhodesia, although I was confining my remarks to Southern Rhodesia. I should think those are wrong who say that the report of Lord Buxton's Committee in any way prejudges, or prejudices, the question of the possible entry of Rhodesia at some date, far or near, into the Union of South Africa. That question is and ought to be left entirely free for the consideration of the Rhodesian people themselves."

Kenya Colony: A Difficult Problem.

The reconciliation of the different races within the Empire, the Under-Secretary went on to observe, was at once the most far-reaching and perplexing of the problems with which they were confronted. The magnet of interest in the matter had been Kenya. There it was not a comparatively simple problem of two races, but of at least three or four. Public attention had been particularly aimed at two topics. In the first place there was the position of Indians in Kenya—a controversy in which he ventured to think the interests of the original native population had sometimes been in some danger of being ignored and overlooked.

The other matter on which public interest had fastened was the question of forced native labour. The arrival in this country of the Governor, Lieut.-General Sir E. Northey, would give the Colonial Secretary an opportunity of conferring with him on this and other matters that were exercising in one direction or another a great deal of public interest. However good the policy that they in England endeavoured to apply to these regions of the world, he suggested that ultimately, if it was to succeed, it depended on two things :

(1) On education, in the sense that the main value of education was in the formation of character in those to whom it was brought.

(2) On the actual personnel of the Colonial Service, because they were the living incarnation in which Western ideals were presented to the population with whom they were in contact.

Sir A. Steel-Maitland (Coalition Unionist, *Birmingham, Erdington*) said the problems which were being raised in Kenya were absolutely fundamental to the principles which were the only justification of British rule. Whatever remedial measures might be taken at the moment, the Colonial Secretary and the Under-Secretary should agree to have the subject considered by some really strong body, appointed to review the whole policy of British government in East Africa, the principle on which it was secured, and the principle on which it should be based.

East Africa: The Test Question.

Colonel J. C. Wedgwood (Labour, *Newcastle-under-Lyme*) contended that East Africa was the test question for the British Empire as to whether they were really the hypocrites that some people thought they were, or whether they found themselves in these African Colonies with the intention of carrying out their sentiment of being there in the interests of the aboriginal inhabitants. The Royal Commission which had been proposed would be a very admirable solution provided they could see that a Commission was imbued not with the commercial spirit, but with the altruistic spirit of Sir Arthur Steel-Maitland and the Under-Secretary.

Sir S. Hoare (Coalition Unionist, *Chelsea*) also advocated the appointment of a small Royal Commission to go into all the problems of Kenya and the East African Dependencies It seemed to him that the time had come for a comprehensive survey of the system of Crown Colony government all over the British Empire. He believed they would never get effective administration, at any rate in the smaller and poorer Dependencies, unless they had a single-graded Colonial Service It was in the poor and least progressive Colonies that they really wanted the best officials.

Mr. J. A. R. Marriott (Coalition Unionist, *Oxford*) suggested that the constitutional status given to Rhodesia should not be the restricted local responsible government proposed by the Buxton Committee, but that Southern Rhodesia should take its place in the great Union of South Africa.

The Colonial Secretary.

The Secretary of State for the Colonies, who wound up the debate, referred to the "really formidable advance in British West Africa since his first venture in official life at the Colonial Office 15 years ago. The East African group had not made the progress, and at the present moment could not show the strength, that had been achieved in West Africa There was a good deal of progress, but far less than might have been achieved if a more consistent policy of development had been pursued.

As to the racial problem in East Africa, they had the white settler, the Indian immigrant, and the large native population. The inter-play and inter-clash of these races afforded some of the most delicate and baffling problems that any man could be invited to decide upon. They were bound to regard the native populations as the greatest trust that was confided to them, because they were the most helpless of the population.

"The case of the Indian," Mr. Churchill continued, "is one of very great difficulty, first of all because of the relations between the Indian and the white, and, secondly, because of the relations between the Indian and the native, which are by no means so ideal as is sometimes suggested. In the main, we must make a continuous effort to live up to the principle that racial distinctions do not determine the status or position of any man in the British Empire who is otherwise qualified to occupy a position or exercise a function of responsibility."

The right hon. gentleman went on to say that he knew something of the white settlers in East Africa and in Rhodesia. He described the kind of things they had to struggle against and expressed the hope that when the House dealt with their problems and difficulties they would approach them in a sympathetic spirit and with a feeling that these pioneers must not be the people who were always to be sacrificed.

Royal Commission the Last Remedy.

With regard to East Africa, he had been pressed from various quarters to institute a Royal Commission on labour conditions, on the relations of the different races, and on the problems generally. It would be very easy for him to save himself all further trouble for at least a year by acceding to that request, but it was the last remedy which should be employed. He hoped to be able to take up the questions connected with East Africa in the course of the next few weeks with General Northey. Only in the event of the proposals which he would make for dealing with these matters proving unsatisfactory did he think that they ought to fall back on the desperate remedy of a Royal Commission.

He was very anxious not to say anything about the future of Rhodesia which would prejudice the discussion he must have with the representatives of the Rhodesian Council, who were about to start for England. He agreed with what had been said as to the extreme importance of not appearing to dictate to that Colony what course it should adopt, whether it should be in the direction of assuming responsible government, with all its obligations, or, on the other hand, in the direction of joining the Union Government of South Africa. He was fully alive to the importance of developing the profitable possessions of the Crown, and just for that reason he grudged very much every shilling of military expenditure in Mesopotamia and the Middle East.

With reference to Mesopotamia, the 45 battalions which were there had fallen to 22, and the authorities on the spot had now submitted a proposal to reduce the force to eight battalions in the course of next year. That was attributed to the improved condition of the country and the political situation and the great increase in the influence of the Air arm. The air route between Baghdad and Cairo was now in operation. He adhered to everything he had previously said about the importance of a satisfactory settlement with Turkey as bearing on the peace of Mesopotamia and Palestine.

The amendment of Sir Donald Maclean was negatived by 123 votes against 43, and the total Vote was then agreed to.

IMPERIAL COMMUNICATIONS.

(Conference of Prime Ministers of the Empire and Airships.)

In the House of Commons, on 4th August, the Secretary of State for the Colonies announced the decision of the Imperial Conference on airships.

Mr. A. B. Raper (Coalition Unionist, *Islington, East*) asked what was the decision of the Conference regarding airships, and what action the Air Ministry had taken, or purposed taking, regarding the airships, airship plant and equipment and both the service and civilian airship personnel?

The Secretary of State for the Colonies (the Right Hon. Winston Churchill): "The decision taken as to the disposal of the airships is best explained by quoting the following Resolution adopted on the 2nd August:—

'The Conference, having carefully considered the report of Mr. Churchill's Committee on Imperial Communications, are of opinion that the proposals contained therein should be submitted for the consideration of the Governments and Parliaments of the different parts of the Empire.

On the understanding that the cost will be in the region of £1,800 per month, they recommend that, pending such consideration, the existing material, so far as useful for the development of Imperial air communication, should be retained.'

"With regard to the disposal of the service and civilian airship personnel, the former will be absorbed within the

Royal Air Force, while the latter (all of whom are serving on temporary engagements) have already been given notice, or will receive notice."

Mr. Raper asked in the House of Commons on 20th July the estimated time by airship for the following journeys : England—Egypt, England—Karachi, England—Johannesburg, and England—Perth (Western Australia).

The Secretary of State for Air (Capt. the Right Hon. F. E. Guest) : "Assuming that the ground organsiation is complete, and a regular service established, it is estimated that the following times will be taken : —

					Days.
England —Egypt	..	..	..	..	2¼
England —Karachi	..	..	..	..	5
England —Johannesburg		..	..	..	7
England —Perth (Western Australia)					10½ "

West Indies: Proposed New Cables.

A number of questions regarding the improvement of communications with the West Indies were asked in the House of Commons on 21st June. They included the following :—

Sir Samuel Hoare (Coalition Unionist, *Chelsea*) asked the Secretary of State for the Colonies whether the proposal to lay new cables from Bermuda to Barbados, Trinidad and British Guiana would immediately be carried into effect ; and what steps were being taken to ensure the use of British wireless for British Honduras.

The Under-Secretary of State for the Colonies (Hon. E. Wood): 'As a result of inquiries regarding the cost of carrying out the proposal for a new cable from Bermuda, it has been thought desirable to suspend negotiations in the hope that the total cost of the scheme to the West Indian Colonies and to His Majesty's Government may be substantially reduced in the near future. Improvements are being effected in the wireless station in British Honduras with a view to ensuring direct communication with the naval station in Jamaica."

Lieut.-Colonel M. Archer-Shee (Unionist, *Finsbury*) : " Is the hon. gentleman aware that the State-owned cable to Australia has been an enormous financial success ; and cannot the Government come forward and help the communications of the Empire more liberally ? "

The Under-Secretary of State for the Colonies : " I can assure my hon. and gallant friend that the Government are anxious to do everything they can in the direction he suggests. The whole matter is at present under review."

NAURU AND OCEAN ISLANDS.

(Disposal of the Phosphate Deposits.)

Questions were put in the House of Commons on variou
occasions regarding the method of dealing with the outpu
of phosphates from Nauru and Ocean Islands. On 22nd
June,

The Hon. W. Ormsby-Gore (Coalition Unionist, *Stafford*
inquired, *inter alia*, whether the Phosphate Commissioner
had entered into a contract with Mr. G. V. Parker, giving th
latter a monopoly in the distribution of all phosphate
obtained from these islands on account of the British Govern
ment, and whether under the contract the whole of the amoun
received by this country must be sold in this country, o
might any of it be sold to Canada or other British Dominion
or Colonies.

The Minister of Agriculture (the Right Hon. Sir A. Griffith
Boscawen) said the Commissioners under the Nauru Islan
Agreement were Mr. A. R. Dickinson, appointed by Hi
Majesty's Government ; Mr. H. B. Pope, appointed by th
Government of the Commonwealth of Australia ; and M
A. F. Ellis, appointed by the Government of New Zealand
The first two received salaries of £2,000 a year, and the Ne
Zealand Commissioner received £1,000 a year. In accordan
with Article 2 of the Agreement, these salaries were payabl
from the proceeds of the sales of phosphates. The Phosphat
Commissioners and not the Ministry of Agriculture were th
responsible body for making sales of Nauru phosphate. Th
Ministry had no information as to the tonnage available, o
as to the methods by which the phosphate would be markete
in England by Mr. G. V. Parker.

Mr. Ormsby-Gore: "Am I to understand that in th
Island, which is the property of the British Government, th
Government have handed over all responsibility to thre
Commissioners, who can charge what they like for thes
phosphates without the Government having any say in th
matter whatever ? "

The Minister of Agriculture : "What the Governmen
have done is simply pursuant to the terms of the Act o
Parliament which was passed about a year ago."

Contracts by Commissioners.

Replying on 11th July to Mr. W. Forrest (Coalitio
Liberal, *Pontefract*),

The Minister of Agriculture said : " It is understood that the Phosphate Commissioners have entered into a contract with the South Wales Basic Slag Company, Limited, for the supply of Nauru and Ocean Islands phosphates available for shipment from Nauru and Ocean Islands to the United Kingdom between March, 1921, and the end of 1922, with a minimum of 125,000 to 215,000 tons, and that the Commissioners have also provisionally entered into a contract with the Slag Phosphate Company, Limited, for the supply of the phosphate available for shipment during the five years 1923 to 1927, with a minimum of 100,000 to 150,000 tons per annum.

" In each case the selling price to these two companies is the cost price as laid down in the Nauru Island Agreement, and the price at which these companies may dispose of the material is the cost price plus an agreed profit, which is a moderate one, so that agriculture will receive the fullest possible benefit from the arrangements made. Both of the companies mentioned are, I understand, represented by Mr. G. V. Parker."

Treatment of Phosphates.

The right hon. gentleman added that the advertisements issued by the Slag Phosphate Company, Limited, described the mixture they were placing on the market as slag phosphate, and stated that it was composed of about one-half of basic slag and the remainder of phosphates from Nauru and Ocean Islands. He therefore saw no reason to suppose that agriculturists were likely to be misled into a belief that the material offered was high-grade basic slag. An average analysis of Nauru and North African phosphates—the figures as to Nauru had been supplied by the Phosphate Commissioners—was as follows : —

	Nauru phosphate.	North African phosphate.
	Per cent.	Per cent.
Tribasic phosphate of lime	85·28	63·35
Phosphoric acid content	39·05	29
Lime	—	47·45
Carbonic acid	2·29	18·05
Oxide of iron and alumina under ..	1·0	1·5
Insoluble	—	4

The price of 3s. per unit which was being charged for the mixture of basic slag and ground phosphate was understood to be based upon cost price plus a limited profit, and compared favourably with the current prices of superphosphate and slag.

E

NATAL PROVINCIAL COUNCIL AND ASIATICS.

Action by the Natal Provincial Council in respect ⟨
Asiatics formed the subject of questions in the House ⟨
Commons on 11th August.

Sir J. D. Rees (Coalition Unionist, *Nottingham, Eas*
asked the Secretary of State for the Colonies whether a
Ordinance which had the effect of preventing Asiatics i
future from acquiring the municipal vote had passed tł
Natal Provincial Council ; if so, whether such Ordinanᴄ
had received the assent of the Governor-General ; and, if no·
whether any representation on this subject had been receive
from the Government of India ?

**The Secretary of State for the Colonies (the Right Hoɪ
Winston Churchill) :** " An Ordinance of the nature indicatec
dealing with the township franchise, was recently passe
by the Natal Provincial Council, but I am not yet in a positio
to state the decision of the Union Government with regar
to it. I do not know whether any representations have bee
made by the Government of India."

Earl Winterton (Coalition Unionist, *Horsham*) : " Wouĺ
it not be an entirely unprecedented action in the case of
self-governing Dominion for the Governor-General to refus
his assent to any Ordinance passed ? Would it not raise
question of the gravest constitutional importance to tł
whole of the self-governing Dominions ? "

The Speaker (the Right Hon. J. H. Whitley) : " If tł
matter is of such constitutional importance it seems desirabl
that a question should be put upon the Paper."

NEW ZEALAND DIVORCE LAW.

In the House of Commons, on 20th July,

Mr. A. Rendall (Liberal, *Thornbury*) asked the Attorneɣ
General whether his attention had been drawn to the neᴡ
Matrimonial Causes Act, passed recently in Nëw Zealanᴅ
granting divorce after three years of separation ; whethᴇ
under this law a British subject, after one year of residencᴇ
having obtained electoral status in New Zealand, whiᴄ
established domicile, could obtain there a dissolution of a
English marriage, founded on a judicial separation decrᴇ
given in the English High Court over three years previouslɣ
and, as if such person remarried in New Zealand and returnᴇ

to England, he would be a bigamist here, did the Government propose to introduce legislation to rectify this anomaly?

The Attorney-General (the Right Hon. Sir Gordon Hewart) : "It is true that a British subject after one year's residence in New Zealand obtains electoral status, but it does not, I think, follow that domicile is thereby established, and under the provisions of the New Zealand Divorce Acts a married person must be domiciled for two years in New Zealand before instituting proceedings there for divorce. There are good grounds for believing that the provisions of the Act of 1920 with reference to divorce founded on a decree of judicial separation are confined to decrees of judicial separation pronounced by the Supreme Court of New Zealand, and, if this view be correct, the last part of the question does not arise."

OVERSEAS TRADE (CREDITS AND INSURANCE) AMENDMENT ACT.

This Act received the Royal Assent on 28th July. Its objects were described in the JOURNAL, Vol. II., No. 3, page 197, where also will be found a summary of debates on the subject in the House of Commons. The Act extends the application of the provisions of the Statute passed in 1920 to the British Empire as a whole, including mandated territories, and enables the Government to facilitate export transactions by arranging to guarantee bills of exchange drawn against shipment.

BRITISH TRADE WITH NEW ZEALAND.

(Efforts to Supply Requirements of Importers.)

In the House of Commons on 11th August a question was put respecting British trade with New Zealand.

Sir Robert Clough (Coalition Unionist, *Keighley***)** asked the President of the Board of Trade if his attention had been called to the fact that the Prime Minister of New Zealand stated at Bradford that New Zealand importers were disappointed and annoyed when, after making inquiries, they were told that English firms could not supply their needs; whether such cases were ever brought to his notice, and, if so, what were the causes; and whether, in cases of this nature,

he would make special efforts to prevent Dominion busine
going to other countries ?

**The Secretary to the Overseas Trade Department (S
Philip Lloyd-Greame) :** " The answer to the first part of tl
question is in the affirmative. Instances of British firr
being unable to supply the requirements of importers in Ne
Zealand were brought to the notice of the Department
Overseas Trade in the earlier part of last year, when Britis
manufacturers were still unable to cope with their ordei
but I am not aware of any such cases having occurred durir
the current year.

" Every effort is made and will continue to be ma(
by His Majesty's Trade Commissioners in the Dominioi
and by the Department to secure that the requirements
importers in the Dominions be met from this countr
I may add that both the New Zealand Government ar
traders in this country have expressed their appreciatic
of the work done by His Majesty's Trade Commissioner
New Zealand."

EX-SERVICE MEN AND OVERSEAS SETTLEMENT.

(Free Passages within the Empire.)

In the House of Commons on 22nd June the questi(
of the settlement of ex-Service men overseas was raised.

Sir Clement Kinloch-Cooke (Coalition Unionist, *Devonpo*
asked the Prime Minister how many ex-Service men ai
women had been migrated with the assistance of State fun
since the Armistice; what amount had been expended (
this migration ; what amount had been expended in migrati(
out of the National Relief Fund ; and what moneys were n(
in hand ?

**The Parliamentary Secretary to the Admiralty (Mr. L.
Amery),** who replied, said : " The number of warrant boo
issued to ex-Service men and women entitling them and the
dependents to free passages within the Empire under t
Government free passage scheme from the commencement
the scheme in April, 1919, to the end of May last was 30,90
covering in all 54,040 individuals. During this period £895,0
was paid for passages. Since the 1st January last £32,7
has been spent out of public funds in providing addition
assistance, making in all the sum of £927,700. It is not
present proposed to continue this supplementary assistan
beyond the 30th June. The total sum allocated by t

National Relief Fund for purposes of overseas settlement was £375,000. Of this amount £365,000 has been actually expended or has been earmarked for expenditure. The balance from this source still available for distribution is, therefore, approximately £10,000."

Lieut.-Colonel Page Croft (National Party, *Bournemouth***) :** " Is it not very much cheaper and in the interests of economy that every facility should be given to intending emigrants to emigrate, rather than that they should receive Unemployment Benefit lasting, perhaps, for a whole year ? "

The Right Hon. G. N. Barnes (Labour, *Glasgow, Gorbals***) :** " Are steps taken to see that these men reside in the Overseas Dominions, and is track kept of them in the event of their leaving for other countries ? "

The Parliamentary Secretary to the Admiralty : " As far as possible we do try to keep in touch with them. We have a great deal of correspondence from them, and on the whole they have done very satisfactorily."

British Emigrants in 1920.

Mr. Percy Hurd (Coalition Unionist, *Frome***)** asked in the House of Commons on 20th July what was the number of emigrants from the United Kingdom in the year 1920.

The Parliamentary Secretary to the Board of Trade (Sir W. Mitchell-Thomson), in reply, presented the following table : —

Country of Future Permanent Residence.	Persons of 12 years of age and upwards.		Children under 12.	Total.
	Males.	Females.		
British North America	47,546	49,478	21,813	118,837
Australia	10,374	13,261	5,339	28,974
New Zealand ..	5,303	6,885	2,665	14,853
British South Africa ..	6,290	6,737	2,130	15,157
India (including Ceylon)	5,225	5,394	1,569	12,188
Other parts of the British Empire	5,052	2,775	758	8,585
Total British Empire	79,790	84,530	34,274	198,594
United States ..	30,227	37,664	9,260	77,151
Other Foreign Countries	4,965	3,205	1,187	9,357
Total British Emigrants, 1920 ..	114,982	125,399	44,721	285,102

IRISH PEACE NEGOTIATIONS.

(Government's Offer to Sinn Fein.)

During the greater part of that period of the Session t‖ which the present issue of the JOURNAL relates the negotiation‖ for peace in Ireland were proceeding between His Majesty'‖ Government and the representatives of Sinn Fein. Th‖ result was that with the exception of brief official statement‖ from time to time dealing with various developments in th‖ situation the subject of Ireland was not discussed in the Hous‖ of Commons. The question was, however, raised in th‖ House of Lords on two or three occasions.

DEBATE IN HOUSE OF LORDS.

The principal debate took place on 19th August, whe‖ the Secretary of State for Foreign Affairs moved a Resolutio‖ for the adjournment of the House until 18th October excep‖ that the public interest required that the House should me‖ at any earlier time.

The Secretary of State for Foreign Affairs (the Marque‖ Curzon of Kedleston) said that the moving of the Resolutio‖ sprang exclusively from the situation in Ireland. As regard‖ the terms of the offer which had been made for the settleme‖ of the Irish problem, no one could say that they were n‖ generous enough. The Government had offered all that cou‖ be given or offered without compromising the safety of t‖ realm, the sovereignty of the King, and the unity of t‖ Empire. "Many British Governments," the noble Marque‖ observed, "might have given or attempted to give less, b‖ I doubt whether, in the circumstances of the case, you wou‖ have found any Government, whatever its political complexio‖ which would have been disposed to give more."

Upon the manner in which this particular offer w‖ received, he continued, would depend, to a large extent, t‖ future history not only of Ireland, but of England. Cou‖ anyone deny that here, at last, was offered a great act ‖ renunciation—one might almost call it an act of sacrifice‖ anyhow, a very broad and liberal and notable concessi‖ for a proud country to make. None could fail to ha‖ been struck by the extraordinary—it would not be an exa‖ geration to say the unprecedented—unanimity of praise a‖ support with which the Government's proposals had be‖ received in every part of the civilised world. Looking at t‖

thing from its political aspect, it was difficult to believe that any body of responsible men would reject the particular form and quality of independence, of Dominion status, which was offered to Ireland.

Value of Dominion Status.

"Is it conceivable," the noble Marquess asked, "that the representatives of Ireland, if they have, as no doubt they have, a genuine interest in her future, will reject the status of Canada, of Australia, of New Zealand, with all that it means and involves and leads up to ?   Is it conceivable that they will reject that status in order to be like Finland or Esthonia, or Latvia or one of the smaller States that have acquired what on paper looks like real independence, but in value and status is not to be compared with the political constitution to which I have referred ?

"Neither can I believe it possible that public opinion in Ireland, any more than here, will willingly consent to a resumption of that cruel, wicked, pitiful and disastrous form of civil war upon which we have been engaged during the last year in that country.   It may be, of course, that circumstances will compel the resumption of that struggle.   It will not be we who will voluntarily take it up, and if a revival of that issue is compelled it is scarcely possible to believe that history will not visit with the severest condemnation those who are responsible for beginning again that which we have fortunately for the moment put aside.

"Will these men in Ireland of whom I speak be so ill-advised as to think that if they reject this offer they are going to get thereby complete separation, or, if they get complete separation, that they are going to do good business for Ireland ?   As regards their obtaining complete separation, this country and this Empire stand like a rock.   We all of us know that in no circumstances would either we, or a Government composed of noble lords opposite, or any Government that one can conceive in this country, take the step of granting complete independence, complete severance, from this Kingdom and this Empire to Ireland.

Results of Severance.

"Is it to be believed that any responsible man in Ireland really conceives. that, even were they to obtain complete severance from this country, they would gain thereby ? . . . Infallibly it would mean civil war in Ireland itself.   That would be the first stage ; and the second stage would be the ruin, political and economic, of Ireland herself. . • •

Were we driven to contemplate any such alternative as I have described we, that is the British Government—and I am sure we speak here for the British nation—should accept the challenge, and we should not quail before the difficult task that might lie ahead of us.''

The Marquess of Crewe said that he rejoiced at the step which His Majesty's Government had taken. If they had to be at all critical at a time when no one desired to be critical, some of them would say that the same step might have been taken earlier. Nobody could say that it would not be possible, if this country put forth its whole strength, to conquer the South and West of Ireland completely, and to exterminate, if that became necessary in the course of reconquest, all those who had been fighting on behalf of the Irish Republic. But that could only be done at an impossible cost—not merely the cost of life, but it could hardly be done without cost of honour and without outraging the consciences of the people of this country.

Referring to the analogy of South Africa, the noble Marquess said that after the South African War the prospect of a happy and united South African Dominion did not seem hopeful to many, and to some who hoped for it ultimately it appeared that the prospect must be very remote. If they had not been permitted to do what they were able to do he thought it was quite possible that they might have had an Irish situation in South Africa.

Protection of Loyalists.

The Marquess of Salisbury had on the Paper a notice to ask the Government whether, having regard to the profound dissatisfaction felt by many loyal subjects of His Majesty, both in Great Britain and Ireland, with the course of the Irish policy of the Government and to the position assumed by Mr. de Valera towards this country and to the Republican Oath of his followers, the Government proposed to proceed further with the negotiations. He said that when the terms offered to Mr. de Valera were revealed they came with something like a shock upon a large number of people in this country.

He wished to know what, in any arrangement to which the Government could come, they proposed to do in order to protect the interests of the loyalists in Ireland. Had the Government considered what could be done in giving them terms of migration from the disaffected areas ? Were the Government going to leave the ex-Service men at the mercy of their enemies ? He was glad to hear what the Marquess Curzon said about the claim of Ireland for separation, and he did not believe the Government would give way on that.

Yet what hope had they, if that be so, that they would come to terms with the followers of Mr. de Valera ? He did not ask the Government to break off the negotiations, but he earnestly hoped that they would not allow the fair name and fair fame of this country any longer to be dragged in the mire.

The Earl of Selborne remarked that it was wholly inconsistent with the safety and welfare of the Empire, or of England, that there should be a Sinn Fein Army in Ireland. He uttered his most solemn protest against that unexpected feature of the terms offered. He believed they were leading up to a tremendous disaster in the future by establishing within these two islands two different sets of Customs-houses. The Marquess of Crewe asked them to remember what had happened in South Africa and drew his moral.

Element of Future Strife.

"Let me draw another moral," said the noble Earl. "Why was it that, after self-government had been granted to the Transvaal and to the Orange Free State, the Union of South Africa was brought about within three years ? . . . It was this : The statesmen of all the four Colonies, statesmen of both races, Boer and British, saw that if they did not have a Union there would be civil war. This civil war would arise from two forces only ; it would be a war of railway rates and a war of Customs. That is exactly the element of future strife, of bitter strife, that you are introducing between Ireland of the future and Great Britain of the future."

The Earl of Donoughmore said he had no use for any loyalist whose mind was set on deserting Ireland in her hour of trial, and they did not want facilities for migration. He believed there was a majority in Ireland, a vast but inarticulate majority, who would prefer the Imperial connection.

The Lord Chancellor (Viscount Birkenhead) observed that it would be disastrous if it were not plainly realised by those to whom the offer was addressed that it contained the Government's last word in the direction of concession and compromise.

Consequences of a Breakdown.

Let no one blind himself to the conclusion that if this attempt at negotiation broke down they would find themselves committed to hostilities upon a scale never heretofore undertaken by this country against Ireland.

"Let us plainly understand," said the noble and learned Viscount, "what the nature of the sacrifices involved will be, sacrifices in respect of life, sacrifices less grave, but grave enough in our present situation, in respect of treasure. We shall find ourselves bound to take—and in the unhappy contingency indicated we shall not shrink from—whatever measures may be necessary in order to prevent the secession of a constituent part of these islands from the British Constitution. And with immense depression, if we be forced to adopt that course, we shall apply ourselves to it in the same spirit and with the same determination with which the Northern part of the United States protested and struggled against the secession of the South."

After further debate the Resolution of the Secretary of State for Foreign Affairs was agreed to.

SAFEGUARDING OF INDUSTRIES ACT.*

The Royal Assent was signified on 19th August to the Safeguarding of Industries Act. In the last number of the JOURNAL (Vol. II., No. 3, p. 506) an epitome was given of the provisions of the measure as introduced by the Government and also of the Second Reading debate in the House of Commons on 6th and 7th June.

KEY INDUSTRIES.

Part I. of the Act relates to the safeguarding of Key Industries. It provides that there shall be charged on the following goods imported into the United Kingdom Customs duties equal to one-third of their value :—

Optical glass and optical elements, whether finished or not, microscopes, field and opera glasses, theodolites, sextants, spectroscopes and other optical instruments.

Beakers, flasks, burettes, measuring cylinders, thermometers tubing, and other scientific glassware and lamp-blown ware, evaporating dishes, crucibles, combustion boats, and other laboratory porcelain.

Galvanometers, pyrometers, electroscopes, barometers, analytical and other precision balances, and other scientific instruments, gauges and measuring instruments of precision of the types used in engineering machine shops and viewing rooms, whether for use in such shops or rooms or not.

Wireless valves and similar rectifiers, and vacuum tubes.

Ignition magnetos and permanent magnets.

Arc-lamp carbons.

Hosiery latch needles.

Metallic tungsten, ferro-tungsten and manufactured products of metallic tungsten, and compounds (not including ores or minerals) of thorium, cerium and the other rare earth metals.

All synthetic organic chemicals (other than synthetic organic dyestuffs, colours, and colouring matters imported for use as such, and organic intermediate products imported for their manufacture), analytical

* cf. Customs Tariff (Industries Preservation) Bill (Australia), p. 893

re-agents, all other fine chemicals (except sulphate of ·quinine of vegetable origin) and chemicals manufactured by fermentation‚processes.

No duty is chargeable under this section on goods which are shown to the satisfaction of the Commissioners to have been consigned from and grown, produced or manufactured in the British Empire. 'Goods are deemed to have been manufactured in the British Empire which would be treated as having been so manufactured for the purposes of Section 8 of the Finance Act, 1919, which relates to Imperial Preference.

PREVENTION OF DUMPING.

Prevention of Dumping is dealt with in Part II. The Act provides that if, on complaint being made to the Board of Trade, it appears that goods of any class or description (other than articles of food or drink) manufactured outside the United Kingdom are being sold or offered for sale in the United Kingdom—

(A) at prices below the cost of production as defined in the Act ; or

(B) at prices which, by reason of depreciation in the value in relation to sterling of the currency of the country in which the goods are manufactured, not being a country within His Majesty's Dominions, are below the prices at which similar goods can be profitably manufactured in the United Kingdom ;

and that by reason thereof employment in any industry in the United Kingdom is being or is likely to be seriously affected, the Board may refer the matter for inquiry to a Committee.

No matter involving a question of depreciation of currency is to be so referred unless the Board are satisfied that the value of the currency of the country in question in relation to sterling is less by 33⅓ per cent. or upwards than the par value of exchange. The Board must direct the Committee to report on the effect which the imposition of a duty under Part II. on goods of any particular class or description would exert on employment in any other industry using the same kind of goods as material.

PERMANENT COMMITTEE PANEL.

If a Committee (which is to consist of five persons selected by the President of the Board of Trade from a permanent panel of persons mainly of commercial or industrial experience) report that goods manufactured in any country fulfil the conditions specified above the Board may, by Order, apply this part of the Act to such goods. There are two provisos :—

(1) Part II. is not to be applied to any goods unless the Committee report that production in the industry manufacturing similar goods in the United Kingdom is being carried on with reasonable efficiency and economy.

(2) No order is to be made which is at variance with any treaty, convention, or engagement in force with any foreign State.

Where an order is made under Part II. Customs duties equal to one-third of the value will be chargeable on the goods in question manufactured in any of the countries specified in the Order. The expression "cost of production" is defined as meaning the current sterling equivalent of ninety-five per cent. of—

(A) the wholesale price at the works charged for goods of the class or description for consumption in the country of manufacture, subject to the deduction of the amount of any excise or other similar internal duty leviable in that country and included in the price ; or

(B) if no such goods are sold wholesale for consumption in the country of manufacture, the price at the wórks (subject to the like deduction) which would have been reasonable if the goods had been so sold and in determining what price would have been reasonable regard shall be had to the wholesale prices charged for goods as near as may be similar.

An Order under Part II., unless previously revoked by the Board, continues in force for three years, or such less period as may be specified, and an order may be renewed from time to time. Part I. came into operation on 1st October, 1921, and is to continue in force for a period of five years.

DEBATE IN HOUSE OF COMMONS.

Five days were allotted for the Committee Stage of the Bill in the House of Commons under a time-table adopted by resolution of the House. This stage began on 29th June and was concluded on 20th July. Two days were given for the discussion of the measure on the Report Stage. On the 10th August,

Major H. Barnes (Independent Liberal, *Newcastle, East*) moved a new clause to provide that the Act should not apply to goods imported for the purpose of being used in shipbuilding or ship-repairing. He said that if the Government were determined to spare no other industry, there was at least some ground for their making a concession in this case, because even most Protectionist countries, such as Germany and America, exempted from their tariff materials required for shipbuilding.

Sir Godfrey Collins (Independent Liberal, *Greenock*), in seconding the amendment, remarked that this country had built up its shipbuilding industry on a policy of free imports.

The Hon. Alexander Shaw (Coalition Liberal, *Kilmarnock*) said the shipbuilding industry was in for a period of fierce competition. It was greatly handicapped already, but if it could get the best and cheapest materials in the world, and if in respect of those materials it could be placed on a par with its competitors, then he believed that the skill of the British builder and of British management would carry it through and would place the industry in the same position as before the War.

The President of the Board of Trade (the Right Hon. Stanley Baldwin) said that this was not a Bill to bring in a general tariff. It was a Bill to try to stop dumping when that dumping caused serious unemployment. No matter what the industry might be, it was entitled to protection if it could make out its case that employment in it was being seriously affected by dumping from either of the two sources mentioned in the Bill.

On a division the proposed new clause was negatived by 198 votes against 81.

Captain Wedgwood Benn (Independent Liberal, *Leith***)** proposed a new clause to exempt goods used for educational or scientific purposes. This was negatived by 231 votes against 80.

Position of Allied Countries.

·During the debate on 11th August the question of the application of the Act in the case of Allied countries was considered.

Mr. A. Lyle-Samuel (Independent Liberal, *Eye***)** moved to exempt the goods of any country allied or associated, with the United Kingdom during the War from the operation of the provisions with respect to dumping. The Bill, he said, put them in the miserable position of injuring their Allies at a time when France was desperately anxious about her financial position.

The President of the Board of Trade said that this was a Bill for the safeguarding of English industries. If dumping were a bad thing it made no difference, so far as this country was concerned, whether goods were dumped from countries with which previously we had been at War, or were Allies, or which were neutral. It was true that in existing conditions it was extremely improbable—it was impossible at the moment —that the dumping duty would apply to any of their late Allies, but after all, they did not want to lock the stable door after the horse had gone. They were trying to make provision for possible harm to their trade throughout the next three years. For that reason it was essential, whether the danger was imminent or not, to have all the countries included. It was not the intention to denounce the existing commercial treaties at the present time. " I am as anxious as anyone can be," said the right hon. gentleman, " for the development of trade between ourselves and Allied nations, due regard being kept all the time to the interests of our own people."

Mr. G. Terrell (Coalition Unionist, *Chippenham***)** observed that the fact that the foreign commercial treaties were not to be denounced indicated a complete change of policy on the part of the Government.

The President of the Board of Trade said that on 6th July the following announcement on the subject was made in the House :—

" It is ,not the intention of the Government to denounce any commercial treaties at the present time. If the inquiries provided for in the Bill disclose cases of dumping due to depreciation of exchange where an Order would be at variance with the terms of a commercial treaty, the desirability of denouncing such treaty will be considered."

Mr. Terrell said that was the first notice they had been given as regards France that to put the Bill into operation it would be necessary to denounce the Commercial Treaty with France. He complained of the way the Bill was being whittled down.

On a division the amendment was negatived by 169 votes against 59.

At the conclusion of the Report Stage the Speaker stated that he would endorse his certificate on the Bill to the effect that it was a Money Bill within the meaning of the Parliament Act.

Third Reading : The Paris Resolutions.

The Third Reading debate in the House of Commons took place on 12th August, when,

The Right Hon. H. H. Asquith (Leader of the Independent Liberal Party), in moving the rejection of the Bill, said it was difficult to know whether to treat it as a serious fiscal proposal or as an ephemeral political freak. One thing that was clear was the futility of attempting to father it upon the Resolutions of the Paris Conference of 1916. The Bill was directed in effect—he would not say with intention—not against their ex-enemies, but, more than against any other Power, against their Allies in France. The safeguarding of the Key Industries might really be almost laughed out of court, and dumping was practically non-existent. So far as concerned some of the industries whose products were essential in time of war, the proper way of giving State encouragement was by the open participation of the State by means of a subsidy. That was not to be lightly recommended, but it had the advantage that whatever was done was done in the light of day and they could limit the profits, as they sought to do in the case of the dye industry, so that the surplus might be applied to scientific research.

The Leader of the House (the Right Hon. Austen Chamberlain) remarked that at one time Mr. Asquith was very proud of the Paris Resolutions—so much so that he wished it publicly known that they were drafted by the British Government.

Mr. Asquith said he had never repudiated in any shape or form the Paris Resolutions, or ceased to defend them.

The Leader of the House : " No, but the right hon. gentleman's defence takes the form of saying that they mean nothing. Yet these particular Resolutions, dealing not with a temporary emergency arising during the War, but with permanent measures to be taken after the War, are the proper and true foundations of the measure he is now asking the House to reject." Mr. Chamberlain observed regarding the schedule of Key Industries, that not an industry was included which was not essential to national existence during war. As an alternative to the Bill, Mr. Asquith spoke of a system of subsidy and participation in commercial enterprise. He could not imagine a more fatal policy alike for the public exchequer and for the interests of industry.

After a debate occupying the entire sitting, the amendment was negatived by 176 votes against 54, and the Bill was read a third time.

DEBATE IN HOUSE OF LORDS.

On 15th August the Bill came up for Second Reading in the House of Lords.

Lord Emmott, in proposing its rejection, said the movement of a large and active political section was towards Protection even more extreme than that Bill, although at present they dare not ask for the taxation of food. The measure was not liked by Protectionists, because it was not what the Protectionist really wanted. It was loathed by Free Traders, and it created suspicion and dislike in the minds of a great many business men, apart from party. The Bill proposed wrong and ineffective methods for protecting Key Industries. It proposed safeguards against economic dumping which were not at present required, and were likely to do more harm than good. It set up barriers against imports from countries with depreciated exchanges which, if effectual in excluding their goods, would tend to add to the root causes of the evil it was sought to combat.

Lord Sheffield said there were two driving forces behind the Bill. First of all there was the desire of producers in a number of trades to get protection. Secondly, there was the feeling of resentment against Germany on account of the

way she dragged this country into the War and her conduct
of the War.   Both of them, he thought, were bad forces.

Lord Colwyn thought the Government had acted very
wisely in dealing with those trades which were essential for
national safety.

An Unsettling Effect.

The Marquess of Crewe remarked that there was not a
word in the Bill which carried out the principles or the aims
of the Paris Resolutions, the purpose of which was the declaration of an economic concert between those who were then
fighting together as Allies.   The real objection to the measure
was that it was bound to have a thoroughly unsettling effect
upon trade generally and an even more unsettling effect
upon industry.   The protests against the Bill represented the
fears of organised industries concerning what was going to
happen under it.

The Chancellor of the Duchy of Lancaster (Viscount Peel),
replying for the Government, said that a good deal of the
criticism in the debate had been directed not so much against
the provisions of the Bill as against an imaginary measure
of general tariff reform.   Lord Emmott had asked what
would be the effect of these proposals on German reparations
The amount of the payment under German reparations on
goods coming to this country had been reduced from 50 per
cent. to 26 per cent.   It had no effect whatever as a tariff
because for some months now the Germans had paid that
amount over to their exporters, and, therefore, it did not
affect the question of the export.

On a division the amendment for the rejection of the Bill
was negatived by 69 votes against 43, and the Second Reading
was then agreed to.

In Committee on 17th August an amendment was carried
against the Government excluding from articles on which
a duty may be levied under Part II. " articles for use in the
practice of husbandry, agriculture, or the raising of stock."
Another amendment was also made to limit the operation of
the provisions with respect to dumping to two years.   The
Bill was, thereafter, read a third time and was returned to the
Commons.   In the Lower House the amendments were
disagreed to on the ground that they infringed " the sole
and undoubted right of the Commons to impose taxation."

The Upper House, thereupon, decided not to insist upon
the amendments.

TRADE WITH GERMANY.

(Imports into the United Kingdom for first three months of 1921.)

A statement on the subject of imports into the United Kingdom consigned from Germany was printed in the Official Report of the House of Commons, in reply to a question by Sir William Barton (Independent Liberal, *Oldham*), on 21st June.

The Secretary to the Overseas Trade Department (Sir Philip Lloyd-Greame) said the returns which were being regularly obtained with regard to imports from Germany were prepared in quarterly periods. Prior to the War the corresponding figures were only prepared in respect of an annual period, and the total imports were, therefore, given in the following table : —

	Three months Jan.-March, 1921.	Year 1914
Class II.	£	£
Raw materials and Articles mainly unmanufactured.	120,000	4,076,000
Class III.		
Articles wholly or mainly manufactured :—		
A. Articles completely manufactured and ready for consumption.	3,870,000	15,882,000
B. Articles manufactured but requiring to pass through some process of adaptation or combination before entering into consumption.	2,513,000	13,383,000
C. Articles partly manufactured ..	826,000	4,472,000

In the period January–March, 1921, the six largest of the items separately returnable for statistical purposes included in the above totals were : —

	£
Finished dyestuffs obtained from coal tar, other than alizarine and synthetic indigo	472,104
Crude zinc	338,925
Toys, other than dolls and metal and wooden toys	291,205
Gloves of cotton	206,772
Wire, other than uninsulated electric and fencing wire ..	156,278
Machines and machinery not elsewhere specified	129,588

F

RAILWAYS ACT.

State control of the railways came to an end on 15th August, 1921. During the month of May the Minister of Transport (the Right Hon. Sir Eric Geddes) presented to Parliament a Bill embodying the Government's proposals for the reorganisation and regulation of the railways in Great Britain after their decontrol. A full summary of the provisions of the measure and of the Second Reading debate in the House of Commons was published in the JOURNAL, Vol. II., No. 3, p. 510.

In the course of the exhaustive discussions which subsequently took place, the Bill was amended in various particulars, but the principles on which it was based remained unaltered and the text need not, therefore, be repeated. The grouping of companies underwent some changes, and as the original proposals of the Bill in this respect were set out in the last issue of the JOURNAL, the new groupings are now given : —

1. Southern : London and South Western ; London, Brighton, and South Coast ; South Eastern ; and London, Chatham and Dover.

2. Western : The Great Western and the Welsh Companies.

3. North Western, Midland and West Scottish : London and North Western ; Midland ; Lancashire and Yorkshire ; North Staffordshire ; Furness ; Caledonian ; Glasgow and South Western ; and Highland

4. North Eastern and East Scottish : North Eastern ; Great Central ; Great Eastern ; Great Northern ; Hull and Barnsley ; North British ; and Great North of Scotland.

In the debates in both Houses the importance was emphasised of certain provisions giving effect to an agreement arrived at between the companies, the Government, and the railwaymen's unions respecting the method of dealing with wages and conditions of service in the future. These provisions are to the effect that : —

(A) All questions relating to rates of pay, hours of duty, or other conditions of service of employees are, in default of agreement between the companies and the unions, to be referred to the Central Wages Board or, on appeal, the National Wages Board.

(B) Arrangements are to be made for establishing for each railway company one or more councils consisting of officers of the company and representatives of the men employed by the company.

(C) The Central Wages Board is to be composed of eight representatives of the companies and the same number of representatives of the employees.

(D) The National Wages Board is to comprise six representatives of the companies, six representatives of the employees, and four representatives of the users of railways, with an independent chairman.

The Bill was passed through the House of Commons under a time-table and was debated in the House of Lords on Second Reading on 11th August. It received the Royal Assent on 19th August.

LICENSING ACT.

On 17th August the Royal Assent was given to the Licensing Act. This measure, introduced by the Government only about a month before the adjournment of Parliament in August, was based upon the recommendations of a Round Table Conference, consisting of Members of the House of Commons representing various interests, who at the invitation of the Government met during the summer under the chairmanship of the Attorney-General in order to determine whether agreed legislation could be presented to Parliament. During the greater part of the War period and until the date when the new Act came into operation the Liquor Trade was conducted under the regulations of the Central Control Board, which, consequent upon the passing of this legislation, has now ceased to exist.

The Act limits the number of hours during which intoxicating liquor may be sold on week days in licensed premises or clubs, for consumption on or off the premises, to eight. These hours are to begin not earlier than 11 a.m and there must be a break of at least two hours after noon. The latest hour of sale is 10 p.m.

The above provisions apply to the country generally. A special exception is made in the case of the metropolis, where the number of hours is extended to nine and the latest closing hour may be 11 p.m.

The Act also provides that the licensing justices for any licensing district outside the metropolis may, in order to meet the special requirements of the district, increase the maximum number of hours to eight and a half, and fix 10.30 p.m. as the latest closing hour. They may also allow sales to begin at 9 a.m., instead of 11 am.

The permitted hours provisionally specified in the Act, but subject to variation by the licensing justices, are :—

London .. 11.30 a.m. to 3 p.m. 5.30 p.m. to 11 p.m.
. Elsewhere .. 11.30 a.m. to 3 p.m. 5.30 p.m. to 10 p.m.

SUNDAY HOURS.

On Sundays, Christmas Day and Good Friday the number of hours restricted to five. Of these not more than two are to be between noon and 3 p.m., and not more than three between 6 p.m and 10 p.m. These hours are to be fixed by the licensing justices. The Act provides for total Sunday closing in Wales and in Monmouthshire.

In the case of licensed premises or clubs in respect of which the licensing justices are satisfied that they are structurally adapted and bona fide used for the purpose of habitually providing, for the accommodation of persons frequenting the premises, substantial refreshments to

F 2

which the sale and supply of intoxicating liquor is ancillary, liquor ma:
be sold or supplied during an extra hour after the permitted hours in th
evening.

During that additional hour liquor must be sold or supplied only fo
consumption at a meal supplied at the same time in such portion of th
premises as is usually set apart for the service of meals. Otherwis
no intoxicating drink must be consumed on the premises and the drinkin
bar is to be closed.

The Act does not prohibit or restrict—

The sale of intoxicating liquor to any person residing in an
licensed premises or club.

The supply of liquor for consumption on licensed premises t
any private friends of the licence holder *bona fide* entertained by hir
at his own expense.

The consumption of liquor with a meal in any licensed premise
or club within half an hour after the conclusion of the permitte
hours, provided the liquor was supplied during permitted hours an
served at the same time as the meal.

STATE MANAGEMENT.

Other provisions forbid the " long pull," the hawking of liquor, an
the sale of liquor on credit for consumption in licensed premises and club
The management of the areas in England and Scotland where the liqu
trade is under State management is transferred from the Central Contr
Board to the Home Secretary and the Secretary for Scotland.

These areas are four in number, viz. :—In England : the Carlis
District and the Enfield Lock District. In Scotland : the Cromar
Firth District and the Gretna District.

DEBATE IN HOUSE OF COMMONS.

In moving the Second Reading of the Bill in the House (
Commons on 22nd July,

The Attorney-General (the Right Hon. Sir Gordon Hewar
said the problem with which the Round Table Conference ha
to deal was that of adapting to a time of peace the lesso
learned during the period of the War. After explaining son
of the provisions, he mentioned that under the Bill the *bon
fide* traveller would disappear. The *bona-fide* traveller was
person who took a *bona-fide* walk in order to get a *mala-fi
drink.* The Bill represented a sincere and honest effort
express what was ascertained to be the highest comme
measure of agreement.

Mr. Horatio Bottomley (Independent, *Hackney, Sou*)
moved the rejection of the Bill, which, he declared, was bas
on an utterly wrong conception of the problem with whi
it had to deal. It represented merely a whittling down of
the cant provisions which had emanated since that unfortun
declaration of the Prime Minister in the early days of the W
that they were fighting three enemies of which the great
and most formidable was drink.

The **Right Hon. Sir Donald Maclean (Chairman of the Independent Liberal Party in Parliament)** regretted that the Bill sought to increase the facilities for obtaining alcoholic drink, although it prevented a rush back to the 1913 conditions. The Dominions had gone in the direction of the complete prohibition of alcoholic consumption. The great competitive nation of the United States had taken action which, with all its drawbacks—he agreed they must be many and serious—was to the point, though there was no use people thinking it was a complete success.

Wasteful Expenditure.

Could they in the United Kingdom afford on the economic side to spend, as they did last year, £469,700,000 on the purchase of alcoholic liquors? He admitted that the Chancellor of the Exchequer got £197,000,000 in taxation out of it; but, of course, they could not afford wasteful expenditure of that kind.

Colonel J. Gretton (Unionist, *Burton*) said that this was only a small Bill and subsequently the wider issues of the licensing question would have to be faced.

Mr. P. W. Raffan (Independent Liberal, *Leigh*) remarked that he and other members especially interested in temperance were unable to give unqualified approval to all the proposals in the measure, but they did not intend to oppose it. They looked forward, however, to the time when the House would pass legislation dealing drastically with this question, not on the lines of imposing on the people restrictions against their will, but in the direction of giving to them in their respective districts the right to deal with liquor control in the way they thought best.

The Leader of the House (the Right Hon. Austen Chamberlain) said he could not believe it was the desire of any considerable section of the community to go back to pre-War conditions in the liquor trade without any change, and he was sure it was not the desire of the trade. This was a very moderate Bill which would prevent them on the one hand from reverting to the pre-War conditions, and, on the other hand, from being swept into wild and extreme measures which would be found here, as in other countries, extremely difficult of enforcement and would not respond to the needs and conditions of the people.

Advance in Public Tone.

The Right Hon. J. R. Clynes (Chairman of the Parliamentary Labour Party) observed that there was good ground

to congratulate themselves upon the gradual advance i
public tone and social habit on the part of men and wome
in this country of all classes in regard to the use of alcoholi
drink. It was in the direction of the improvement (
individual tastes that the real solution of the problem was t
be found.

The amendment was withdrawn and the Bill was rea
a second time without a division. One of the respects i
which, during its subsequent passage through Parliamen
attempts were made to amend the Bill was by the omissio
of the provision extending Sunday closing to Monmouthshir
Amendments designed to secure this result were defeated i
both the House of Commons and the House of Lords.

CORN PRODUCTION ACTS (REPEAL) ACT.

(Abolition of Guaranteed Prices for Home-grown Cereals.)

During the Session of 1920 was passed the Agricultu
Act (*vide* JOURNAL, Vol. II., No. 1, p. 40), which continue
in force the temporary provisions of the Corn Production Act
It also provided that minimum prices for cereals shou
be based upon the minimum prices for 1919, which was to b
taken as the standard year : —

Wheat	..	..	..	68s. per quarter of 504 lbs.
Oats..	..	..	..	46s. per quarter of 336 lbs.

Power was conferred on the Minister of Agriculture
enforce proper cultivation of land and provision was also ma
to ensure the good management of estates. Part II. of th
Act amended the Agricultural Holdings Acts in the direction
granting tenants the right of compensation for disturbance.
On 27th June, 1921, the Government introduced a B
repealing the Corn Production Acts 1917 and 1920, includi
Part I. of the Agriculture Act. After full debates in bot
Houses this measure was given the Royal Assent on 19t
August.

While enacting the repeal as from 1st October, 1921, of the A
in question, provision is made in the measure for payments to farm
in respect of the current year's harvest on the basis of £3 per acre
wheat and £4 per acre for oats.

Provisions contained in the Corn Production Acts relating to t
destruction of injurious weeds growing upon any land are continued
force.

The Act specifies that the State shall provide during the pres
financial year a sum of £1,000,000 for promoting agricultural deve

ment, including the establishment of scholarships and maintenance grants for the sons and daughters of agricultural workmen and others.

The Ministry of Agriculture in England and Wales, and the Board of Agriculture in Scotland, are empowered to take steps to secure the voluntary formation and continuance of local joint conciliation committees for the purpose of dealing with wages, or hours, or conditions of employment.

These committees are to be representative of persons (whether owners or occupiers of agricultural land) employing workmen in agriculture and of such workmen.

Persons who are members of a district wages committee will, until the expiration of two years from the date of the passing of the Act, or until a joint conciliation committee is formed, whichever first happens, be a joint conciliation committee for the purpose named.

DEBATE IN HOUSE OF COMMONS.

The Second Reading of the Bill was moved in the House of Commons on 4th July, and the debate was concluded on the following day.

The Minister of Agriculture (the Right Hon. Sir Arthur Griffith-Boscawen) said that as the result of the measure agriculture would be entirely decontrolled. Guaranteed prices, control of cultivation and the Wages Board would all disappear after the coming harvest. Payment in respect of the crops of this year's harvest was to be made by a composition instead of proceeding under the methods laid down by the Act of last year. It was a serious matter for the Government to reverse a policy so recently adopted, but they had been compelled by the financial situation to take this step. Since the Act of last year was passed the fall in prices had been infinitely heavier and more sudden than anybody anticipated. The bill which would have to be presented to the House in respect of this year's guarantees was accordingly very heavy. Taking the acreage of last year the payment would amount to something like £19,000,000. Unless Parliament terminated Part I. of the Act the total cost to the State in respect of the succeeding years would be simply gigantic.

Ministers decided that there was to be no subsidising of industry, and the Government came to the conclusion that under the circumstances the present agricultural policy could not be continued. It had been claimed that the Wages Board should be retained even though the guaranteed prices and the control of cultivation disappeared, but he was convinced that the substitution of voluntary conciliation councils or committees for the board would be an advantage. The Wages Board was intended to fix minimum wages. In practice it had fixed rigid standard wages, applicable to all alike, without any regard to questions of fitness or skill. That had a fatal effect. The minimum wages were actually maximum, but in addition the question of hours was introduced, and in the agricultural industry they could not have rigid factory hours. He had warned the farmers that the worst thing they could do was to attempt big cuts in wages so as to try to get back to pre-War conditions, and he did not believe they would do it.

Greater Educational Facilities.

He hoped to see a further establishment of farm institutes in different counties, where the farmers' sons could go for a short course in the winter, and their women folk receive daily instruction in the summer. He also hoped to see certain free places allotted there for selected sons of agricultural labourers. By giving greater facilities for education and by substituting goodwill and conciliation for coercion and compulsory methods, he was not certain that, grievous as it was to have to abandon a policy deliberately adopted, in the long run the Bill would not make for what was best in agriculture.

Mr. W. R. Smith (**Labour,** *Wellingborough*), in moving the rejection of the Bill, said that if the Wages Board had adopted coercive measures it was because employers had withheld from their workpeople wages which were legally theirs. Increases of wages had been agreed to by both sides. If, when they were fixed, the orders of the Board were not carried out it was not too much to ask that those who failed to obey the law should be prosecuted. All round there were attempts on the part of farmers to reduce wages and force men back to the old conditions.

The Right Hon. Sir Donald Maclean (**Chairman of the Independent Liberal Party in Parliament**) observed that if there was one Key Industry that wanted safeguarding it was the agricultural industry. It was far more important to protect the food of the people than the manufacture of microscopes. He was very glad indeed that the finances of the country were to be relieved of this appalling charge. He could not ally himself in any full degree with the argument that the Government had no right to alter their policy in accordance with the financial position in which they found themselves. What he was anxious about on that point was that the farmers should have fair treatment. As to the Wages Board, speaking generally public opinion would view with the greatest disfavour the turning of the agricultural labourer adrift on the sea of purely economic conditions at the present moment.

The Report stage was concluded on 25th July, and during the same sitting the Bill was read a third time by 193 votes against 66.

DEBATE IN HOUSE OF LORDS.

On 2nd and 3rd August the Bill was debated on the Order for Second Reading in the House of Lords.

Lord Strachie moved an amendment declaring that the House refused to assent to a partial and lop-sided repeal of the Agriculture Act, 1920.

Viscount Milner said he deplored equally the abandonment of the guarantees and the extinction of the agricultural Committees, which had a valuable effect in raising the general standard of agriculture. It seemed to him absolutely inevitable that, as a result of what they were now doing, the amount of land which was poorly farmed, or not farmed at all, would considerably increase. He had hoped they had learnt as one of the lessons of the War that agriculture was something more than just one kind of business by which people might make a living, and that it was absolutely vital to the life of the State that the people engaged in it, whether landowners, or farmers, or labourers, must be regarded as engaged in a form of national service.

The Earl of Selborne remarked that because he foresaw the consequences he deplored the repeal of the Corn Production Acts. Within less than a generation a vast area of land in England—millions of acres—would have gone down to grass and that meant a still further decrease in the rural population. He regarded that as a great economic, social and political evil.

The Parliamentary Secretary to the Ministry of Agriculture (the Earl of Ancaster) said he believed that the policy of stopping subsidies and beginning to allow industries to stand on their own feet would be the first step towards relieving them of the heavy burden of taxation.

The amendment was negatived without a division, and the Second Reading of the Bill was agreed to. After discussions in Committee and on Report, the Bill was read a third time on 12th August.

UNEMPLOYMENT INSURANCE ACT.

(Reduction of Rates of Benefit, etc.)

On 1st July the Royal Assent was given to the Unemployment Insurance Act, which varies the rates of contribution and benefit laid down under previous Acts. This was the second measure passed during the present year relating to statutory insurance against unemployment. An Act* was

---

* *Vide* JOURNAL, Vol. II., No. 2, p. 286.

given the Royal Assent on 3rd March which raised the weekly
rates of unemployment benefit to the following figures : —

Men	..	..	..	..	..	..	..	20s.
Women	..	..	..	..	..	..	16s.
Boys (between the ages of 16 and 18)			..	..	10s.
Girls	..	..	..	..	..	..	..	8s.

The Act which became law in July substituted a revised
scale of benefits as under : —

Men	..	..	..	..	..	..	..	15s.
Women	..	..	..	..	..	..	12s.
Boys (between 16 and 18)		..	..	..	..	7s. 6d.
Girls	..	..	..	..	..	..	6s.

Weekly rates of contribution were increased under the
later Act and are now as follows : —

			Employer.	Employed.	State.
Men ..	..	..	8d.	7d.	3¾d.
Women	..	..	7d.	6d.	3¼d.
Boys ..	..	..	4d.	3½d.	1¾d.
Girls ..	..	..	3½d.	3d.	1⅝d.

DEBATE IN HOUSE OF COMMONS.

In asking, on 8th June, the leave of the House of Commons
to bring in the Bill effecting these further modifications,
The Minister of Labour (the Right Hon. T. J. Macnamara
said that throughout the present grave period of trade de
pression the Government had endeavoured to adapt the schem
of unemployment insurance to the needs of the situation
To-day the percentage of unemployment amongst insure
persons was 23 per cent. Two millions* of men and wome
were wholly unemployed. Another million were on shor
time. Under the Act the Government were now payin
benefit at the rate of £2,000,000 a week with an income fro
contributions of less than £350,000. The Insurance Fund
which in March last stood at £22,500,000, now stood a
£8,500,000. As things were going it would last them onl
for about another month. Therefore, he must make seriou
alterations in his scheme to meet a most serious situation.
The right hon. gentleman referred to the fact that th
Act of last March provided that unemployment benefit migh
be drawn for sixteen weeks between 3rd March, 1921, an
2nd November, 1921. The ever-deepening unemployment ha
compelled a large number of persons to draw the sixteen week

---

* On 24th June, 1921, there was a total of 2,177,899 men, wome
boys and girls out of work. On 16th September these figures h
decreased to 1,469,700.

benefit without intermission. Accordingly, many would have no assistance from the fund during part of July and August, September and October. If things did not improve the same experience would be encountered as regards the sixteen weeks' benefit which was to be allowed between 3rd November, 1921, and 2nd July, 1922. He would, therefore, ask for powers to give, if it proved to be necessary, an extension of six weeks' benefit to the sixteen provided by the Act of last March for each of those periods.

Longer Waiting Period.

He could sanction no further special schemes of contracting out of the Act till solvency was reached, and he was compelled to ask that the three days waiting period should be made six. Given an average of 1,250,000 insured persons unemployed over the whole year, July, 1921 to July, 1922, the maximum deficiency which these readjustments would give at any period would be about £16,000,000, which must meanwhile be advanced by the Exchequer. It would be repaid as circumstances became normal. To carry him on until July, 1922, the limit of £10,000,000 borrowing power in the Act of last March must be increased to £20,000,000, and the scheme of reduced benefits, side by side with increased contributions, must stand till the fund was again solvent.

The Right Hon. J. R. Clynes (Chairman of the Parliamentary Labour Party) said the introduction of the Bill was a most amazing step even for this Government to take. The Government had limited their action in relation to unemployment to insurance. They now had the spectacle of unemployment deepening daily in every sense of the term, and at the worst stage of the trouble, when great suffering was being endured, the Government came forward to undo a good part even of the little they had attempted in the way of providing relief or remedy by means of national insurance.

"I admit," said Mr. Clynes, "that there are individual cases of workers, and perhaps even of groups of workers, who have abused the provisions of the Act and the assistance provided under it. There is, however, no justification for withholding a reasonable degree of support from the vast majority of the workers who have no opportunity, in face of the industrial outlook, of securing employment for a considerable time to come." The right hon. gentleman pointed out that millions accumulated in the Insurance Fund during years when there was only a low percentage of unemployment, and it was a business-like proposition that they should draw upon their certain future prosperity in order to meet the difficulties of the moment. The Government should do what many of the trades unions were doing—borrow and pledge their credit for the future in order to meet the abnormal needs of the present.

He claimed that the workers in their distress, with their small allowance of £1 per week, were entitled, until the cost of living was reduced, to look to a continuance of that support unless the Government took some other steps to relieve them from the privations and hardships of unemployment. Labour, therefore, would have to offer to the measure every possible resistance.

On a division the motion for leave to bring in the Bill was carried by 221 votes against 62, and, thereafter, the measure was formally introduced.

Twelve Months' Balance-Sheet.

The Bill was debated on Second Reading in the House of Commons on 15th June.

The Minister of Labour further explained its provisions. He also placed before the House a rough forecast balance-sheet for the insurance year July, 1921—July, 1922, based on the assumption that throughout that period there would be an average of 1,250,000 insured persons unemployed. On the income side he hoped to get contributions from : —

	Millions.
Workpeople	13¾
Employers	15¼
The State	7⅓

That was a total income of just under £37,000,000. On the expenditure side he got :—

	Millions.
Benefits to be paid	46¼
Interest on debt	¾
Grants for administrative expenses	3½

That was a total expenditure of about £50,750,000, and it would leave them at the end of the year still owing about £13,750,000. The maximum debt would be £16,000,000, but towards the end of the period they would have begun, as the result of improving employment, to pay some of it off.

The Right Hon. John Hodge (Labour, *Gorton*), in moving the rejection of the Bill, said he hoped the Government might realise even yet that unless the workers of the country were kept physically fit for the turn of the tide—there was no doubt that trade would boom again—there would be a limitation of output. When bad times came why should the manual worker be the only person to be thrown, as it were, on the scrapheap, or to be obliged to rest content with a small unemployment donation ? The richest country in the world was treating shamefully the men who threw down their implements of labour and rallied round for the saving of the country.

Interference with Trade.

Mr. J. M. Hogge (Independent Liberal, *Edinburgh, East*) observed that every part of the legislation of the Government—the Safeguarding of Industries Bill, the German Reparation (Recovery) Act and so on—was preventing the clearing of the channels of work between this country and other countries. Twenty-eight millions of the people of this country lived and had their being in the country's export trade. It was true to say that because of the policy of the Government those 28,000,000 people were not so actively in touch with the markets of the world as they should be. To try to fob off a situation which had been created by the artificial methods by which the Government interfered with trade was pure nonsense.

The time had long since come when they should address themselves not only to the question of unemployment, but to the whole question of the revision of the Poor Law and the spending of money on Old Age Pensions. These should be brought under one sensibly controlled Department of State.

Mr. Austin Hopkinson (Coalition Liberal, *Mossley*) discussed a suggestion made in the debate that each industry should provide for its own unemployment problem. Under such conditions it would happen that those employers who took a purely selfish view of the matter, and tried to add to their profits in time of great prosperity by increasing the number of men they employed, would be supported in that policy by those who did the reverse. There would be no inducement to those who endeavoured, even if it meant a loss in booming trade, to provide a certainty of employment for those whom they employed, and the suggestion, therefore, was worthless.

The only outcome to real prosperity and real contentment in industry was for as many people as possible in that industry to become capitalists. He did not necessarily say they should become rich men living on income from investments, but they should carefully refrain from spending all they had earned and week by week, it might be to a very small extent, accumulate savings—in other words, accumulate capital. "Individual freedom for the wage-earner can never come," said the hon. Member, "until, apart from any collective capital which he holds in trade unions, he has also that personal and private capital which will enable him to stand as a free man face to face with his employer and as a free man face to face with his own trade union."

Government and Employers.

The Right Hon. J. R. Clynes said the Government could do much to prevent unemployment by doing a little to curb the tendency which was now shown by many employers to take advantage of the conditions of the labour market and of the comparative helplessness of workmen, because of the depletion of their trade union funds, to insist upon reductions of wages altogether in excess of anything which could be defended or justified.

The amendment for the rejection of the Bill was negatived by 214 votes against 83, and, having been read a second time, the measure was committed to a Standing Committee. The Bill came back to the House and was discussed on Report on 27th June. When the measure came on for Third Reading on the following day, the Right Hon. J. R. Clynes, for the Labour Party, again moved its rejection, but the amendment was negatived by 240 votes against 81.

In the House of Lords, on 29th June, the Bill was read both a first and second time without a division. Next day it was passed through the remaining stages and subsequently became law on the date mentioned.

THE FINANCE ACT.

(Co-operative Societies and Corporation Tax.)

The Budget, introduced on 25th April, was summarised in the last number of the JOURNAL (*vide* p. 516), and the progress of the Finance Bill was also referred to. Portions of five sittings of the House of Commons were devoted to the consideration of the Bill in Committee, and this stage was completed on 12th July.

DEBATE IN HOUSE OF COMMONS.

The Report Stage was taken on 18th and 19th July. On the latter date the Government suffered a defeat on Clause 43, which provides that interest on certain State loans is not to be treated as profits for the purposes of the Corporation Profits Tax.

Mr. J. Kidd (Coalition Unionist, *Linlithgow*) moved to add to the clause the following words : —

Where the profits are profits or surplus arising from the trading with its own members of a society registered under the Industrial and Provident Societies Acts no such Corporation Profits Tax shall be charged.

The hon. Member contended that the balance resulting from mutual trading could not possibly be a profit and should be exempt from tax. But in so far as a mutual trading society, or a co-operative society, embarked on outside profit-making trading, or seeking to exploit the public for profit, it was not entitled to exemption from the tax.

Mr. A. E. Waterson (Co-operative, *Kettering*) remarked that the Corporation Profits Tax as applied to the co-operative movement struck definitely at the principle on which the movement was based.

The Financial Secretary to the Treasury (Mr. Hilton Young) said there was no distinction between the treatment meted out by the present taxation law to co-operative societies on the one hand and life assurance societies and mutual life societies on the other.

The Right Hon. H. H. Asquith (Leader of the Independent Liberal Party) observed that Corporation Profits Tax was a special Income Tax of a peculiar kind, and every argument of policy which justified the exemption of these so-called profits of the co-operative societies from schedule D of the old Income Tax appeared to him to apply with exactly the same force to the Corporation Profits Tax.

Privileges of Corporations.

The Chancellor of the Exchequer (the Right Hon. Sir Robert Horne) said the tax in question had been applied to corporations on the main ground that they enjoyed privileges and immunities which were not given to private firms. The co-operative movement was certainly a corporation, with over £80,000,000 worth of capital in its trading and commercial organisation. Was it too much to ask it to pay £150,000 a year for the privilege of having the liberties and immunities which it derived from the Limited Liability Act ?

On a division the amendment was carried by 137 votes to 135—a defeat for the Government by a majority of two. At a later stage of the sitting a brief discussion took place on the subject of the reverse sustained by the Government.

The Right Hon. Sir Donald Maclean (Chairman of the Independent Liberal Party in Parliament) asked what steps the Government proposed to take in the matter ?

The Leader of the House (the Right Hon. Austen Chamberlain) said that having regard to the public circumstances of the day, to the many very grave issues which were under the discussion of the House, and to the small financial importance of the alteration made, the Government would accept the decision of the House. He did not see in that anything undignified on the part of the Government. It was not a process to be repeated very often by any Government, but he was certain that in the course they were taking there was nothing contemptuous of the House.

The Bill was read a third time on 29th July, subsequently passed through the House of Lords, and received the Royal Assent on 4th August.

NATIONAL EXPENDITURE.

(Appointment of an Advisory Committee of Business Men.)

Announcement was made by the Chancellor of the Exchequer in the House of Commons on 16th August of the appointment of a Committee of business men to advise the Government on the subject of the reduction of national expenditure.

The Chancellor of the Exchequer (the Right Hon. Sir Robert Horne) said the Committee would be composed as follows : The Right Hon. Sir Eric Geddes (Chairman), Lord Inchcape, Lord Faringdon, Sir Joseph Maclay and Sir Guy Granet. They would sit at the Treasury and would report to the Chancellor of the Exchequer. The terms of reference were : —

" To make recommendations to the Chancellor of the Exchequer for effecting forthwith all possible reductions in the national expenditure on Supply services, having regard especially to the present and prospective position of the revenue. In so far as questions of policy are involved in the expenditure under discussion, these will remain for the exclusive consideration of the Cabinet ; but it will be open to the Committee to review the expenditure and to indicate the economies which might be effected if particular policies were either adopted, abandoned, or modified.'

The Treasury organisation would be employed in the ordinary course for the purposes of the Committee's work and some other members of the Civil Service would be seconded for service in the Treasury under the Committee.

Mr. J. M. Hogge (Independent Liberal, *Edinburgh, East* asked whether, if the Committee did not take evidence, the same information as was supplied to them would be supplied to the Estimates Committee of the House of Commons ?

The Chancellor of the Exchequer: " The Estimates Committee of the House are appointed to investigate such Departmental estimates as they see fit to examine, and to report to the House upon the particular estimates which they do examine. The purpose of this Committee is a far wider and greater one. We want the whole expenditure of the country to be examined with regard to all the Departments, and not to have merely a fitful examination of any particular Department. We wish the matter to be taken into account as a whole, having regard to the revenue that the country may expect to have. . . . So far as the Estimates Committee are concerned, they will still have their function to perform with regard to any Departmental estimates that they see fit to examine, because, after this Committee have advised the Chancellor of the Exchequer, it will still be necessary for the Departmental estimates to be prepared, and such Departmental estimates as the Estimates Committee desire to examine will become the subject of their particular investigation."

Sir W. Pearce (Coalition Liberal, *Limehouse*) asked whether there was any obligation on the Chancellor of the Exchequer to follow the recommendations of this new Committee.

The Chancellor of the Exchequer : " Of course there can be no obligation to follow the recommendations, because that would be to put into the hands of the Committee the powers of government, and no Government could surrender those powers."

DEBATE IN HOUSE OF COMMONS.

Later in the same sitting the subject of National Expenditure and the appointment of the Committee was raised in the debate on the Second Reading of the Consolidated Fund (Appropriation) Bill.

The Right Hon. Sir Donald Maclean (Chairman of the Independent Liberal Party in Parliament) contended that it was the duty of the House of Commons to be its own business committee and to control its own finance. The scale of expenditure at the present time terrified the House and shocked the country. The real charge he had against the Government was that they were evading their responsibilities. The operation of this Committee must involve a serious derogation of the financial functions of the House.

Mr. G. Locker-Lampson (Coalition Unionist, *Wood Green*) believed that unless the Treasury could recover its control they would get into a hopeless financial morass. Let the Government ration themselves to a definite figure. Let them make up their minds as to how much expenditure this country could afford and then it would be perfectly easy to ration every department in turn.

Mr. T. W. H. Inskip (Coalition Unionist, *Bristol, Central*) urged that the question of policy dominated the question of economy.

G

Sir Godfrey Collins (Independent Liberal, *Greenock*) sai
that to call in an outside body to determine the policy of th
country was not consistent with their past history and wa
a direct slight on the House of Commons.   During the Autum
large questions of public policy, which would determine th
expenditure in 1922-23, would arise for settlement.   It was fo
the Chancellor of the Exchequer to say quite definitely, no
shielding himself behind the decision of any outside Committe
whether the country was so poor that they must curtail the
foreign policy and reduce their commitments abroad.

The Financial Position: German Reparations.

The Chancellor of the Exchequer assured the Hou
that he would not have proposed this course if he had not th
fullest conviction that it was the best method of bringing abo
the economies they all desired to see effected.   Discussing t
position of the country's finances, he said that when th
Budget was presented the Government estimated that t
surplus on ordinary and extraordinary expenditure togeth
would be £176,000,000.   It was pointed out, however, th
there was varied expenditure which would modify and redu
that surplus.   What had actually happened was thi
supplementary estimates had been presented for £91,000,00
and £7,000,000 had to be added for the cost of the Defen
Forces embodied during the coal stoppage.   That left for t
repayment of debt an available surplus of £78,000,000, inste
of £80,000,000, as estimated in the Budget.

So far as the first four and a half months of this ye
were concerned the ordinary items of revenue had shown
remarkable steadiness.   The only items upon which there h
been any serious deficiency were the Miscellaneous Receip
which were chiefly concerned with the sales of the Dispos
Board, and the Excess Profits Duty.   These two thi
together would not be sufficient to wipe out entirely the fig
of £78,000,000 which would otherwise be available for t
reduction of debt.   There would be a sum of a substan
character available from German reparations to help th
revenue in this financial year.

Mr. Horatio Bottomley (Independent, *Hackney, Sout*
" In marks or in gold ? "

The Chancellor of the Exchequer : " In gold."   The ri
hon. gentleman went on to say that he did not look at
current year's position in the gloomy way some of his h
friends were apt to do.   It was when he turned to the n
year that he found the real difficulty, for they would not
able to realise anything like the same revenue as this year,

in order to make the accounts balance they would have to reduce expenditure by at least £130,000,000. Reductions in the last three years had been : —

1919	..	..	..	..	..	£1,200,000,000
1920	..	..	..	..	..	£680,000,000
1921	..	..	..	..	..	£275,000,000

Treasury Economy Circular.

The very fact that they had been able to effect those reductions made the possible reduction next year harder to realise. In response to the Treasury Circular* one might at present estimate a reduction of at least £50,000,000. But as some of the Departments had not yet made a complete return the probability was that they would achieve a reduction of £70,000,000. That still left £60,000,000 to be deducted from the services at some point or other. He begged the House to believe that no single man could undertake all the duties that now devolved on the Chancellor of the Exchequer, and at the same time perform the great task of making the necessary investigations into the expenditure of the country.

There was no derogation from the authority of the House of Commons in setting up a Business Committee to advise him. Questions of policy, of course, must remain for the final decision of the Government. The Committee could, however, show precisely what a policy in a particular direction was costing. It would be in their power to show that particular modifications would have particular results in cost. The functions of the Estimates Committee were in no way abrogated by what the Committee who advised the Chancellor of the Exchequer were going to do. The Business Committee would advise before the estimates were prepared in the form in which they would come before the Estimates Committee. Those estimates would be subject to such scrutiny as the Estimates Committee chose to give them, and Parliament ultimately had full control over expenditure.

At the conclusion of the speech of the Chancellor of the Exchequer the subject dropped.

---

* On 13th May, 1921, a Treasury Circular was issued stating that His Majesty's Government had come to the conclusion that it was necessary to reduce ordinary Supply expenditure for 1922-23 to £90,000,000, and instructing every Department to undertake forthwith a searching examination of their current expenditure " with a view to securing the large reduction in estimates for 1922-23 which the nation imperatively demands."

MEMBERS' SALARIES IN PRINCIPAL LEGISLATURES.

A statement on the subject of the salaries paid t
Members of the principal Legislatures was made in th
House of Commons on 5th August by the Financial Secretar
to the Treasury in reply to a question addressed to him b
Mr. L. Haslam (Coalition Liberal, *Newport*).

The **Financial Secretary to the Treasury (Mr. Hilto**
Young) said that no official returns had been compiled b
His Majesty's Government on this subject since 1911, bu
the following particulars (extracted partly from th
Statesman's Year Book) might be assumed to be substantiall
correct : —

Great Britain : £400 per annum to Members of Parlie
ment.

France : 27,000 francs (£577 at current rate of exchang
per annum to Members of both Chambers. Free travellin
on all railways by means of a small payment. Pensions fe
ex-Deputies or their widows and orphans. Pensions Fun
supported by contributions from Deputies (deducted fro
their pay) as well as by gifts and legacies.

Sweden : 3,400 and 4,500 Kr. (£195 and £257 at curre
rate of exchange) for Members of both Chambers living in
outside the Capital for each ordinary Session, besides travellir
expenses. 24 or 32 Kr. a day in case of extra Session. Sala
free of Income Tax.

Italy : 15,000 lire (£180 at current rate of exchang
per annum to Members of Lower House. Members of bo
Houses travel gratis on railways.

Germany : 12,000 marks (£41 at current rate of exchang
per annum to Members of Reichstag, and allowance f
travelling expenses.

United States of America : Members of Congress. —7,5
dollars (£2,103 at current rate of exchange) per annum
Members of both Senate and House of Representatives
Delegate in Congress, with an allowance, based on distanc
for travelling expenses. *State Legislatures.*—150 to 1,5
dollars (£42 to £421 at current rate of exchange) per Sessi
for Members of both Houses, with an allowance for travellir
expenses.

STOPPAGE IN COAL TRADE : THE SETTLEMENT TERMS.

(Application of Profit-Sharing Principle.)

In the last issue of the JOURNAL (*vide* p. 524) reference was made to the prolonged stoppage in the coal trade and the measures adopted by the Government in connection therewith.

On 28th June, the Prime Minister announced that negotiations had resulted in an agreement on settlement terms, and that the demand for a national pool had been definitely abandoned.

The Prime Minister (the Right Hon. D. Lloyd George) said the main feature of the permanent settlement was that it fixed a new system for remuneration of the wage-earner—a system by which the workman shared with the employer the proceeds of the industry. He believed that no such large and scientific application of the theory of profit-sharing had ever before taken place in the history of any industry in any country. Wages would form a first charge on the industry and a standard (20 per cent. above the pre-War rate of earnings) had been set up below which they would not fall. The standard wage and the other costs of the industry being satisfied, the owner took a certain portion of the proceeds. It had been agreed that for every £100 which the workmen received in respect of his standard wage the owner should take £17. If there were further proceeds to be divided, the mine-owner and the workmen took them in the proportion of £83 to the workmen and £17 to the owner. The system was worked out according to the production of the several districts in the coalfields.

Wage Reductions.

The settlement was to last until 30th September, 1922, and three months' notice was to be given by either party if they then wished to discontinue it. The first reduction in wages was to take place in July and would not exceed 2s. per shift ; the next in August, 2s. 6d. ; and another in September, 3s. per shift. Beyond that period the permanent arrangement came into full operation and in the meantime, in order that reductions might be limited to the amounts stated, the Government would contribute up to a sum of £10,000,000 for the assistance of the industry. In many districts in which Government aid was necessary the owners as a body had agreed to forego for three months the amount of the aggregate profit which would accrue to that district under the profit-sharing scheme.

A National Board was to be set up, consisting of equal numbers of representatives of the mine-owners and miners. and also District Boards of a like character, to which all matters of controversy between the parties would be referred. Both the District Boards and the National Board would have independent chairmen, to be called in if the parties could not agree. It was hoped in that way to obtain a settlement of questions which might not otherwise be accomplished. He was very hopeful that the adoption of these principles might create new relations between Capital and Labour, not merely in the coal industry, but in all industries.

On 1st July the House of Commons agreed to vote a sum of £10,000,000 for this subvention in aid of wages.

CANADA.

The *following Summary deals with some *further Acts and discussions of the Fifth Session of the Thirteenth Parliament* (which opened on 14th February, and was prorogued on 4th June, 1921) and is in continuation of the Summaries published in Vol. II., Nos. 2 and 3 of the JOURNAL.

There remain a few important Acts passed by Parliament during this period which have not yet been dealt with. These will be summarised in the next issue of the JOURNAL.

LEAGUE OF NATIONS.

(Canada's Contribution: Mandates: Article 10.)

On 20th April the following item was discussed by the House in Committee of Supply : —

MISCELLANEOUS.—To provide for Canada's contribution towards the maintenance of the permanent Secretariat of the League of Nations, $200,000.

---

* During the month of September the Prime Minister reorganised the Cabinet and a General Election was announced for the first week of December.

The following is the personnel of the reorganised Cabinet :—

Prime Minister and Minister of External Affairs	Rt. Hon. Arthur Meighen.
Minister of Railways and Canals ..	Hon. J. A. Stewart.
Minister for Soldiers' Civil Re-establishment	Capt. the Hon. R. J. Manion.
Minister of Customs and Excise	Hon. J. B. M. Baxter.
Minister of Public Works	Hon. F. B. McCurdy.
Minister of Finance	Hon. Sir Henry Drayton.
President of the Privy Council	Dr. the Hon. L. P. Normand.
Minister of Agriculture	Dr. the Hon. S. F. Tolmie.
Minister of Labour	Sen. the Hon. G. D. Robertson.
Minister of Marine and Fisheries and Naval Service	Hon. Charles C. Ballantyne.
Minister of Trade and Commerce.. ..	Hon. H. H. Stevens.
Minister of Justice and Attorney-General	Hon. R. B. Bennett.
Postmaster-General	Hon. L. de G. Belley.
Secretary of State	Hon. Rodolphe Monty.
Minister of Health, Immigration and Colonisation	Dr. the Hon. J. W. Edwards.
Minister of Militia and Defence	Hon. Hugh Guthrie.
Solicitor-General	(Not yet appointed.)
Ministers without Portfolio	Hon. Sir Edward Kemp. Hon. E. K. Spinney. Hon. J. R. Wilson. Hon. Edmund Bristol.

DEBATE IN HOUSE OF COMMONS.

The Prime Minister (the Right Hon. Arthur Meighen) stated
that the contribution last year was $200,000 and that this yea
the same amount was asked for. The original basis of com
putation and distribution of the expenses of the League, a
agreed upon, was the Universal Postal Union's basis, whicl
placed Canada in the same rank as a first-class Power and fixed
her share on that dimension. At the last meeting of the League
a financial committee was appointed to consider the whol
subject of the budget of the League and its distribution, and
one of the Canadian representatives (Sir George Foster) was
he believed, the most active member of the committee. Th
committee made a report and it was quite confidently expected
that as a result thereof a new basis of distribution would b
arrived at.

The Minister of Trade and Commerce (the Right Hon
Sir George Foster) explained that the Universal Postal Union'
expenses were limited to 1,250,000 francs, and that sum bein
very small, it made very little comparative difference as t
whether the nations belonged to the first class or not. Th
Postal Union divided its national members into seven classes
The first-class nations paid the largest amount and the lowes
class the smallest ; and in putting in their claims to be con
sidered as first-class or any other class nations, some of th
smaller countries were ambitious and put their names in th
first rank. The members of the League of Nations, based upo
that allocation, took the same class of nationality as they di
in the Universal Postal Union. So it happened that Sout
Africa, for instance, who had a white population of about
million and a half, having been rated as a first-class nation i
the Universal Postal Union became rated as a first-class natio
in the League of Nations, and as the amount to be paid in th
gross was very much more, the allocation attributed to her wa
exactly the same as was attributed to France, to Great Britai
and to the United States of America. Canada also elected to b
called a first-class nation in the Universal Postal Union and sh
in the same way, had to contribute as a first-class natio
That was manifestly unfair, but that basis was settled in th
Treaty itself. It could only be rearranged and another bas
adopted by an amendment of the constitution. There was on
other way in which it might be done. The Swiss Confederatio
at Geneva, which was the supervising authority of the Post
Union, might take up the basis of allocation for that Unio
and might so arrange it that it would become a reasonabl
basis upon which the nations that belonged to the Leagu
might make their contributions with reasonable relation one t

another. That was being sought to be done and a committee for the purpose was appointed at the first Assembly. If that could be done and was satisfactory to the Council and to the League of Nations then the matter would be settled. If it could not be done, then it had to be rearranged by the next Assembly which would meet in September. It was agreed by resolution—approved by the Assembly—that the reasonable basis of allocation, which should be arranged by the Assembly at its next session, would be taken into account in 1921 and 1922. If Canada now paid as a first-class Power an amount equal to what Great Britain paid, she would in 1922 have the allocation placed much lower compared with what it would have been under the past allocation, and a country which had paid less than the allocation to be arranged for 1922 would pay more.

Mr. Samuel Jacobs (Liberal, *George Etienne Cartier, Que.*)**:** " Could we demand a rebate or refund when we are put in Class 2 ? "

The Minister of Trade and Commerce : " We obtain a rebate."

Technical Committees: Participation and Expenses.

The Hon. N. W. Rowell (Nat. Lib. and Con., *Durham, Ont.*) said that at Geneva the Assembly approved of the holding of a conference to consider certain international conventions relating. to international transport and communications. He understood that Canada was not represented at the Barcelona Conference held in March. If *The Times* report of the proceedings was correct, it would appear that one of the steps taken was the creation of an organisation relating to international communications and transportation in the form of a technical advisory committee and body of delegates that would meet from time to time. The question he wished to put was whether there was any discussion in the Finance Committee of the Assembly as to limiting the costs of these technical organisations to the States that actually participated in them, or whether it was assumed that all the States, members of the League, would contribute their quota?

The Minister of Trade and Commerce thought that the expenses which were authorised should be met by the League as a whole. At the same time there was a limit as to the maximum expenditure, and his impression was that as far as possible it should be kept within limits in order that the proposals and methods of work of those technical organisations might be reviewed by the Assembly before they became permanent organisations and embarked upon more or less extensive operations.

Mr. Rowell said that one could not but recognise that there might be real force in the argument that these permanent organisations were required for the needs of European countries, and it might be that they would come to the conclusion, particularly if the United States should not enter the League, that they should not join in the conventions which had been recommended. He would draw the attention of the Government to the fact that at a meeting of the Council held during the latter part of 1920, when certain special committees were appointed to investigate particular matters, the question of whether the expenses of those special committees should be charged upon the general funds of the League or against the nations that were particularly interested in the work was discussed, and it was decided in regard to the specific matters which they then had before them that the expenses should be charged against the nations that were directly concerned. He would submit to the Government that this matter should be kept in view at the next Assembly when the report was received from the Barcelona Conference, and that if it should be decided that Canada should not join in the proposed conventions, they should not be called upon to contribute to their expense.

Mr. A. R. McMaster (Liberal, *Brome, Que.*): "Was Canada represented at this Barcelona Conference?"

Mr. Rowell : "I understand that Canada had no representative there."

Mr. McMaster : "What was the purpose of the Barcelona Conference?"

Mr. Rowell replied that it was understood that there would be laid before this Conference certain draft conventions which had been worked out by a committee on communications and transit for the consideration of the members of the League. General freedom of international communication undoubtedly was a desirable thing, both on land and sea. But these conventions involved very substantial obligations upon the States that entered into them to provide freedom of transit, so far as they controlled it, to international trade and traffic; and they set up a superior authority—that was, a technical committee which was to be constituted as part of the organisation—to determine questions in dispute. From that authority there might be an appeal to the Permanent Court of International Justice. Nothing had been done there which bound Canada unless they decided to assent to it. He thought that for the sake of the future the Government of Canada should make its position quite clear that they did not think any organisation could be created under Article 23 except under a convention entered into in accordance with the provisions of that Article.

Mandates and the Liquor Traffic.

Another point to which he wished to direct attention in the hope that the Government would take it up with the Council of the League related to the question of mandates. The form of the mandates as published in *The Times* for the Central African group was not in accordance with the terms of the Covenant in one important respect. This was the provision in reference to the Central African group : —

> Other peoples, especially those of Central Africa, are at such a stage that the Mandatory must be responsible for the administration of the territory under conditions which will guarantee freedom of conscience and religion, subject only to the maintenance of public order and morals, the prohibition of abuses such as the slave trade, the arms traffic and the liquor traffic, and the prevention of the establishment of fortifications of military and naval bases, etc.

When they came to the B mandates relating to Central Africa, in respect of which there was this express provision in the Covenant, the mandates provided for the regulation rather than the prohibition of the liquor traffic. Might he draw the attention of the Government to what was stated in the British House of Commons, viz., that Germany derived a substantial part of her revenue in administering East Africa from the sale of gin to the natives, and it was asked if it was contemplated that part of the revenue of the administration should be secured in that way. He took it that the authorities were agreed that liquor traffic among the native races should be prohibited. When there was the expressed provision in the Covenant the traffic should be prohibited; there was no justification for departing from the terms of the Covenant.

Mr. W. F. Cockshutt (Nat. Lib. and Con., *Brantford, Ont.*) declared that the salaries that had been mentioned in connection with the members of the League were out of all proportion to those that should be paid to men of such high deals as were expressed with regard to the League. A list furnished to the House showed that those gentlemen got from $15,000 to $40,000 apiece per annum. Personally, he did not look upon the League of Nations as an asset to Canada. He did not think in its present chaotic shape it would stop military expenditure by a single dollar, because the League was at present no bulwark with regard to the peace of the world. He could not see that a super-force set up to rule the world would have the loyalty of all given to it in an unqualified sense, and at the same time that they should retain all the loyalty that they originally had in connection with their own country and the Empire.

Article 10.

If the despatches could be believed, the Minister of Justice was responsible for the request that Article 10 should be removed from the constitution of the League. Article 10 was a very substantial entity in the League, and he questioned very much the wisdom, both from their standpoint and that of the British Empire, of having it removed from the constitution of the League at the present time. It seemed to him strange that the Peace Treaty should be lost sight of and that they should, to all intents and purposes, lose practically the whole result of their efforts in some panacea which was intended to cure all the ills of the future.

Mr. McMaster understood that the object was not to set up a super-State to overpower all other States. To the League of Nations the nations of the world would give that consideration and concurrence which any reasonable man gave to the municipal organisation under which he lived. The great ideal which was found in the League would not sap people's individual patriotism for their respective countries, but would rather enhance it. He thought if Germany could be forced to repair the material damage done to France, and to individuals who had suffered through the War—and he understood she had offered to repair the damages in Northern France herself—he did not know whether they could expect to get very much more. If they did not allow the goods of Germany, in payment for reparation, to come into their own market, they must find some neutral market where they would compete with the goods manufactured by Great Britain and by other nations.

Mr. Ernest Lapointe (Liberal, *Quebec East*) absolutely agreed with Mr. Rowell that no part of the money contributed by Canada should go to defray the expenses of technical or other commissions in the proceedings of which they had no share and upon which they were not represented. The principle of no taxation without representation applied to the League of Nations as to any other constitutional body.

The Minister of Justice (the Right Hon. C. J. Doherty) said that he had not contended that they ought to have assumed all of the obligations that were contained in Article 10. What he did point out to the House was that Canada, while she did not approve of certain provisions of the Covenant, was placed in the position where, if she believed in the principle and wanted improvements in particular provisions, her only course was to ratify them. If she failed to do so she was on the outside, voiceless, and powerless to bring about any improvement. If she did so, then she placed herself within the League of Nations and entitled herself to representation in the forum where she could effectively appeal for amendment to the Government, for the disappearance of those clauses to which she objected, for the improvement of those clauses which she thought susceptible of improvement. The hon. gentleman (Mr. Lapointe) had asserted that they had opposed that clause in Paris. That was perfectly true. They came within an ace of succeeding in Paris. It was a fairly open secret to-day that the insertion of Article 10 was really the work of one Great Power. While the motion which he made at Geneva for the elimination of Article 10 was not passed then and there, he might say that neither was any adverse opinion expressed with regard to it upon the substance of the motion itself. It shared the fate that befell all proposed amendments ; it was determined that before proceeding to amend the Covenant there should be careful study by a commission appointed by the Council, the fruit of that study to be placed before the next meetings of the Assembly. "I must say," said the Minister, "that because of the strength of the reasons which may be invoked in support of the proposal and from the views expressed to me by representatives of different countries, I feel that we may look forward with confidence to bringing about that very great improvement in the Covenant which, in my judgment at all events, would result from the elimination of Article 10."

Mr. Jacobs : "It was suggested in the Press during the Geneva Conference last winter that the elimination of Article 10 from the Treaty was mooted in order to obtain some success in inducing the United States to enter the League. Can the hon. gentleman tell us anything about that ? "

The Minister of Justice : "That formed no part of the motive that brought about our making the proposal. The proposal was made carrying out the views which had been entertained by Canada's representatives from the time of the adoption of the Covenant. I am quite prepared to add that I have no doubt that all of the nations who formed part of the League of Nations would welcome with open arms the incoming of the United States. I think Canada would join in extending that welcome, and it would be an additional reason why we would feel that we had done good work in bringing about the elimination of that Article if it should transpire that that elimination should prove to be an important factor in determining the United States to enter the League of Nations."

Indemnities.

Mr. J. A. Currie (Nat. Lib. and Con., *Simcoe, N. Riding, Ont.*) said that if the Germans would pay in gold that portion of the indemnity which they agreed to pay in gold, the position of the Allies would be immediately relieved. The Allies owed the United States something like eleven billion dollars, on which no interest had been paid ever since the War started or they got the loan. If the Germans paid up part even of the cash indemnity, the money would be handed over to the United States, and Great Britain, France, Belgium and the other nations would be relieved of the necessity of paying cash to the United States to that amount. There was enough money standing to the credit of Germany in the United States to pay one-half of the eleven billion dollars that they owed, and there was enough gold in Germany to pay one-half. He believed Canada should put a surtax on German goods. German factories were working over-time. In Canada they had factories closed to-day that had not been closed for thirty years. If Canada and Great Britain had been relieved by the payment of indemnities in cash, the exchanges would have been straightened right away, and they and the Empire and everyone else would have been better off.

Article 10 meant not aggression but protection. It meant that every nation that signed the Covenant of the League, when its territory was threatened by any other nation, would have behind it all the other members of the League. Suppose Japan waived aside the League, went to war with the United States, and attempted to use Canada as a base. Under Article 10 all the other nations of the League would immediately come to their assistance. All the pro-Germans in the United States, and all the journals and people opposed to Great Britain, made a great cry at the last election against the signing of Article 10 by the United States. If the United States had accepted the Covenant there would have been no question about the security of the League.

Their representatives should have taken the position held by the British. He never dreamed for a moment that their delegates, after having induced the House to ratify the Treaty, virtually without any reservation, would go to the Assembly and themselves be the leaders of a movement to have Article 10 struck out. Article 10 was the backbone of the whole thing.

The question had arisen as to the advisability of nations, which were going to send delegates to the League, sending representative delegates instead of delegates appointed by the central Government. The question had been raised in all countries except, possibly, Great Britain and Canada. It was suggested that Parliament might elect its delegates and that these delegates might be representative of all Parties in the legislative body.

The item was agreed to.

PERMANENT COURT OF INTERNATIONAL JUSTICE ACT.

This Act, which was assented to on 4th June, 1921, is for the purpose of authorising the ratification and carrying into effect of the protocol of 16th December, 1920, accepting the Statute for the Permanent Court of International Justice.

The principal clauses of the Bill are given in the course of the speech of the Minister of Justice below.

DEBATE IN HOUSE OF COMMONS.

General Plan of the Court.

The Minister of Justice (the Right Hon. C. J. Doherty), introducing the Bill on 14th April, explained that it contained two clauses. The first provided for the ratification of the protocol, the other conferred power to do such things as might be necessary to carry it out. The Assembly at Geneva unanimously assented to the proposed plan for the creation of a Permanent Court of International Justice under the provisions of the Treaty and the Covenant of the League; and it was provided that the Council of the League should submit such a plan for adoption by nations who were members of the League. The view was entertained by a large portion of the representatives—the Canadian representatives shared in that view—that it was not competent for the representatives in the Assembly to assent on behalf of their respective countries to the adoption of the plan submitted. Pursuant to this view, a protocol was drawn up for signature by the different nations through their representatives, which protocol was made subject to ratification by the nations signing. Canada had signed the protocol subject to ratification. While the power of ratification was in the Crown, acting on the advice of its constitutional advisers, at the same time it was considered desirable that the executive should not take upon itself to ratify without the authorisation of Parliament.

Mr. Samuel Jacobs (Liberal, *George Etienne Cartier, Que.*) : " What would happen should the Canadian Parliament fail to ratify this protocol ? "

The Minister of Justice : " Canada would not have approved the constitution of the Court, and would, therefore, not be entitled to invoke its jurisdiction or appear before it." Continuing, the Minister said that the United States was not represented at the Assembly and was therefore not called upon to take part in this ratification. It was, however, provided under the constitution establishing the Court that

countries mentioned in the schedule to the Covenant should
have access to that Court. The Court was, therefore, open
to the United States. even though that country should not
become a member of the League. It was, perhaps, note-
worthy that a very prominent part in the preparation of the
constitution of the Court was taken by one of the most distinguished lawyers of the United States, and that even those
who did not warmly favour the League of Nations had expressed
themselves in the highest terms with regard to the establishment of this Court.

The Hon. W. S. Fielding (Liberal, *Shelburne and Queen's,
N.S.*) : " I understood my right hon. friend to say that
Canada will pay, but through the League of Nations ? "

The Minister of Justice : " Yes, but will not pay anything
more than its contribution to the League of Nations."

Precedents.

Giving a further explanation of the Bill in Committee on
28th April,

The Minister said that the project was not as new as
the League of Nations. The establishment of a Permanent
Court of International Justice, to which the nations might
have access and which would fill as between the nations the
rôle which domestic Courts filled as between the nationals of
the respective countries, had long been an object of aspiration.
The Hague Conference in 1899 and in 1907 took up this matter
of the establishment of a Court to settle international disputes.
In 1899 what was known as an Arbitral Tribunal was established. That Tribunal had not the character of a Permanent
Court as finally determined upon. It consisted simply of a
list of jurists from whom nations, when they determined to
submit differences between them to arbitration, might select
their judges. In 1907 the need for something more in the
nature of a Permanent Court again occupied the attention of
the Conference. Save upon two points, it was found possible
to reach agreement. The two points were : first, the method
of constituting and organising the Court ; and the second was
what should be the nature of the jurisdiction of the Court,
that was to say, whether that Court should have compulsory
jurisdiction. On these two points, agreement being found
impossible, the Conference did not succeed in constituting the
Tribunal.

It was provided by Article 14 of the Covenant of the
League of Nations that the Council of the League should
charge a committee to draft a plan for the constitution of a
Court to be submitted to the members of the League. The
Court was to have jurisdiction to determine such cases as might

be submitted by the nations, parties concerned therein, and, furthermore, was to have a consultative capacity upon questions that might be referred to it by the Council or by the Assembly of the League of Nations. That Committee was composed of a number of very eminent jurists.

Mr. Jacobs : " Was no Canadian present ? "

The Minister of Justice : " No Canadian was selected upon that Committee."

Equality of States and Nomination of Judges.

The Committee held their session at The Hague from 16th June to 24th July, 1920, and as a result of their labours produced the Statute establishing the Court, which, having, in passing through the Council and Assembly, been subjected to certain amendments, with which amendments it was unanimously assented to by the Assembly, was the Statute that was now before them. They solved the general lines of the settlement to meet the difference of opinion between the nations which at the previous Hague Conferences had made agreement impossible. Agreement had previously been impossible because of the great difficulty of conciliating the principle of equality of all the nations with the view very strongly entertained that the more important nations should have in the Court a guarantee of greater representation than the smaller nations. While absolute equality had not been established by the system adopted, they had got as near to absolute equality as under the circumstances it was possible to get. The question of equality became a burning question because you could not compose a Permanent Court of such a large number of members as would allow every nation to have representation upon it. The plan arrived at was this : the judges were to be elected by the Council and the Assembly of the League of Nations, a majority in each of these bodies being essential to the election of any individual, but before a person could be eligible for election it was required that he should be nominated. The power of nomination was placed in the hands of the members of the existing Arbitral Tribunal, who figured upon the list of arbitral judges established as the result of the Conference of 1899. On that list each of the nations which was party to that Convention had four judges of its nomination. The nomination had to be made by each one of these national groups, each group having the right to nominate four candidates. Of the four not more than two were to be the nationals of the country to which the nominating group belonged. There were to be in all eleven judges and four deputy judges.

H

Position of the Dominions.

Canada and the Dominions, as well as nations which had come into existence since The Hague Conventions of 1899 and 1907, not having been parties to The Hague Conferences, naturally had no members on the Arbitral Tribunal. That difficulty was overcome by a provision that those nations which had no national group on the Arbitral Court should be entitled to constitute a similar group, which had the same privileges of nominating candidates for election to the Permanent Court. No nominees could be judges on the Court if the nations naming them were not parties to the Convention. To election it was essential that the candidate should have a majority in both the Assembly and the Council. This operated to give to the nations that were members of the Council two votes ; and that was so far a concession to the most important Powers, who occupied permanently seats upon the Council. Save to that extent there was no distinction between the voting power of the different nations. The judges were appointed for a period of nine years. A judge might be re-elected.

The Hon. Rodolphe Lemieux (Liberal, *Maisonneuve and Gaspé, Que.*) : " Are they supposed to give all their time ? "

The Minister of Justice : " No, not the judges. The President of the Court is obliged to live at The Hague, which is the seat of the Court, and he gets a very much larger remuneration than the judges.

" Our position is this," continued the Minister. " We are entitled to constitute a group of four members analogous to the group on the Arbitral Tribunal. That group would be entitled to nominate four candidates for election to the Permanent Court. Of these four candidates not more than two must be Canadian nationals."

Mr. Jacobs : " May I ask if there is provision for a Canadian judge being appointed in the event of a case being tried in which Canada is interested ? "

The Minister of Justice : " If one of the two parties litigant have among the judges a national belonging to it and the other has not, then the party who has not is entitled to designate a judge for that particular case."

Mr. Lucien Cannon (Liberal, *Dorchester, Que.*) : " Would a representative of Canada be allowed to sit on the Tribunal if, for instance, the Irish question were submitted to the International Court ? "

The Minister of Justice replied that he saw no reason why a man who happened to be a Canadian should not sit. The desire was to avoid any conception that men sat in the Court representatives of their country. There was another provision that the parties electing should see to it that the great leading systems of law and the leading diverse civilisations should find representation.

Question of Compulsory Jurisdiction.

The other question, continued the Minister, whether the jurisdiction of the Court should be compulsory or subject to the consent of the parties in each particular case, was solved by the committee of jurists at The Hague in the sense of compulsory jurisdiction. The Council of the League did not accept that conclusion, and they modified the project to the extent of making the jurisdiction of the Court dependent upon the consent of the interested parties. So large a number of members of the Assembly entertained the view that the jurisdiction should be compulsory, that a special protocol was inserted to enable such nations as desired to do so to express their readiness to accept the compulsory jurisdiction of the Court as between themselves and any other nations also signing the protocol. What was contended for by those who asked for compulsory jurisdiction was that any one nation should have the right to summon another nation to appear before the Court, and that the Court should thereupon have jurisdiction whether the summoned nation consented to accept such jurisdiction or not. "In this case," declared the Minister, "the Court sits as a Court, exercising jurisdiction conferred upon it by the common consent of the nations. It does not derive its jurisdiction directly from the particular parties that are before it in the sense that its members are not selected by those particular parties. But the exercise of its jurisdiction does under the present Statute depend upon the common consent of the parties under a Treaty existing between them by which they have agreed to submit their differences to the Court, or where it is determined by some condition of the Peace Treaty itself that it is a matter for adjudication by the Permanent Court. . . . It is not intended, unless the parties should especially ask it, to introduce into its procedure the element of conciliation or compromise. The desire is to build up a jurisprudence that will result in a more complete system of international law. I think everybody was willing to join in expressing the belief that if the Court were once constituted and the nations began to submit their disputes, we might look forward in a comparatively brief period to the general acceptance by the nations of the compulsory principle. . . . The purpose of the Court is to endeavour to provide for the nations a method of administering justice and securing to each nation its respective right without the necessity for resort to force."

The Minister stated that there were no provisions dealing specifically in the Statute with the execution of the judgments. In the Covenant of the League of Nations itself with regard to certain matters powers were conferred for taking steps to enforce the decisions of the arbitration or the decisions of the Council, and it was believed that these clauses were wide enough to be made applicable, at all events in cases where there was danger of rupture of peace, to the enforcement of the judgments of the Court.

Canada had signed the general protocol. She had not committed herself in one way or the other as to making the jurisdiction compulsory. While one might believe that the compulsory principle was the sound principle, that was one thing, if everybody accepted the compulsory principle; but it was another thing, before they knew what other countries were going to accept the principle, to go and bind yourself to accept that compulsory principle.

Canada's Nationhood.

Mr. Cannon: "Am I to understand that the jurisdiction of the Tribunal is fully stated in Article 36?"

The Minister of Justice: "Article 36 provides that the jurisdiction of the Court comprises all cases which the parties refer to it, and all matters specially provided for in treaties and conventions in force."

Mr. Cannon: "Then if Article 36 gives the full jurisdiction of this new Tribunal, how can Canada, in view of her actual status as a Dominion, be interested directly or indirectly in any question to be submitted to the Tribunal, because each and every one of these questions has to be a question of an international character?"

The Minister of Justice: "To my mind, Canada may be a party to an international question. As was pointed out the other day by Sir Robert Borden, Canada and the United States have a special Tribunal established to determine international questions between them, and that is an international Tribunal."

Mr. Cannon: "The members of which are appointed by the Imperial Government."

The Minister of Justice: "Upon the recommendation of the Government of Canada. . . . Officially, it is His Majesty dealing with the United States. His Majesty is King of the entire Empire, and when the United Kingdom has a treaty to make His Majesty makes it. Similarly, when Canada has a treaty to make His Majesty makes it."

Mr. Jacobs: "Advised by his English Ministers."

The Minister of Justice: "In regard to a treaty made by Canada he is advised by his Canadian Ministers."

Mr. Jacobs: "Irrespective of the British Ministry?"

The Minister of Justice: "Quite irrespective of the British Ministry." In many of their differences upon the subject of Canada's nationhood they had differed because of this fact, that on one side they were looking at substance and on the other side they were looking at form. Those who said that His Majesty acted upon the advice of his Canadian Ministers in matters of that sort based that statement upon the fact that the advice really came from the Canadian Ministers. On the other hand, those who said that he acted through his British Ministry rested their case upon the fact that the advice was transmitted through the British Ministry. They had the forms that had survived from the old Colonial days, but they had the substance of a nation standing on a footing of equality, whose representatives tendered their advice to as King, who acted on that advice.

The Hon. N. W. Rowell (Nat. Lib. and Con., *Durham, Ont.*) declared that the progress which had been made in the settlement of international disputes by arbitration in the past twenty or thirty years was one of the most encouraging signs in the world outlook. Another encouraging feature in connection with this particular matter was that there was every ground to believe that the United States would co-operate in the work of this international Court. He was sure they all hoped the time would come when full compulsory jurisdiction might be given to the international Court.

Mr. D. D. McKenzie (Liberal, *Cape Breton N. and Victoria, N.S.*): "How can the hon. Member reconcile the submission of a sovereign State to the jurisdiction of any authority beyond its own?"

Mr. Rowell: "The State does it by its own agreement." While the commission of jurists recommended compulsory jurisdiction they pointed out that it could not go into effect unless the various States ratified a convention, and if they ratified the convention and accepted compulsory jurisdiction, then it became a treaty to which they were parties; it was no derogation from their sovereignty.

Authority of the Court.

This Court was the final tribunal for the settlement of disputes under the labour clauses of the Peace Treaty; for dealing with disputes arising under the ports, waterways and railway provisions of the Peace Treaty. It was the final authority on certain questions arising under the minority treaties, and also under the mandates. That was also true of the International Air Convention, of the Arms Traffic Convention, and of the Liquor Traffic Convention in Africa.

Then there was the very important matter, which might properly constitute one of the most important phases of the Court's jurisdiction, the provision in the Covenant which entitled the Council or the Assembly to refer any matter coming before them to the Court for an advisory opinion.

Canada and the International Aspect.

Mr. Cannon declared that the question to be decided was not whether this Tribunal should be good or bad ; it was simply whether Canada had anything to do with affairs of this kind, and he had no hesitation whatsoever in stating that he did not believe Canada was in any way interested in this matter. Canada would never be interested in any matter submitted to this Tribunal. The jurisdiction of the Court was a jurisdiction of an exclusively international character. Would Canada, as a Dominion, not as a nation—because he did not believe that Canada had achieved up to now the status of an independent or separate nation within the Empire—be interested in the Court ? They were, as a Dominion, part of the British Empire, and the British Empire as a whole, that was Great Britain and the Dominions Overseas was a single nation so far as the other nations of the world were concerned. Therefore they could not be interested in any international problem submitted to this Court, and if they were not interested, why should they elect one of the judges of the Tribunal ? He thought the people of Canada had had enough of their interference in European problems. Canada was an American country ; should Canada take part in the decisions of European problems when their all-powerful neighbour to the south refused to do so ? They had enough of their own domestic problems, and enough Imperial problems without poking their noses into matters with which they had absolutely nothing to do. Even if they should express an opinion, their opinion would not carry any weight, because the opinion which was to be expressed was the opinion of the British Government, and of no other Government. So much was that the case that treaties had been signed ever since the War which interested the whole Empire as an Empire, but the old policy of the British Empire had been continued unchanged. Their Canadian Government was not consulted, the Australian Government was not consulted, and they never would be.

Financial Aspect.

His second objection to the scheme was the financial objection. They had already for all those fancy ideas brought back from the Peace Conference by their delegates paid out hundreds of thousands of dollars, and he understood that this year their contribution to the League of Nations was $200,000.

What was the real secret of Great Britain's greatness? It was that her statesmen for many years pursued the policy of keeping their hands off the European continent. He thought that they in Canada should follow suit.

"What I object to," declared Mr. Cannon, "is the way in which Canada was treated at the Peace Conference, and I say that so long as we do not obtain from Great Britain a larger share of international freedom, so long as we remain what we are to-day, so long as we are deprived of a real and distinct nationhood, so long as we are simply a Dominion, and nothing else, within the British Empire, then let us mind our own business and confine our energies to our national problems; and Great Britain can continue in future, as she has always done in the past, to make the decisions which bind the Empire, including Canada."

Mr. Cannon asked whether the protocol had been signed already by His Majesty for the British Empire.

The Minister of Justice : " It has been signed on behalf of Great Britain by Mr. Arthur Balfour. It has been signed on behalf of Canada by the High Commissioner at Paris, under authorisation of Order in Council, and has been signed on behalf of the other Dominions by their representatives. There have been no signatures on behalf of the Empire as a whole; each one of the countries has signed through its representative, and it is now proposed that His Majesty, on behalf of each one of the Dominions, shall so sign and ratify it."

Mr. Cannon : " As far as this is concerned, we are in the same position as in the case of the Covenant of the League of Nations. Great Britain is a member and all the Dominions are separate members."

The Minister of Justice : " Yes. Although as an actual matter of fact the representatives nominally of the British Empire have acted throughout as the representatives of the United Kingdom, with the Crown Colonies and Dependencies, and the enumerated Dominions have acted through their representatives."

Mr. Cannon : " What would happen if Canada should ratify and Great Britain should not ? "

The Minister of Justice : " If Great Britain did not ratify she would not have approved the Convention. Canada would have approved the Convention and would be entitled to exercise the rights that came to her under it."

After further discussion the Bill was read a third time and passed on 7th May.

NAURU ISLAND.

(Monopoly of Raw Materials.)

The Hon. W. L. Mackenzie King (Leader of the Opposition) on 1st June asked whether it was true that the Government, through its representatives on the British Empire Delegation to the Peace Conference, agreed to the granting of a monopoly of the raw materials of Nauru Island, including the largest reserves of high-grade phosphates in the world, to the United Kingdom, Australia and New Zealand, and to the exclusion of Canada from any benefits accruing under the Mandate for the administration of Nauru Island, which Mandate the Allied and Associated Powers conferred upon the British Empire as a whole ; and, if so, why ?

The Minister of Justice (the Right Hon. C. J. Doherty) replied that he would give a definite answer later. In the meantime he might say his very strong impression was that there was no such agreement.

In reply to a further question by Mr. Mackenzie King on 4th June,

The Minister of Justice said that there was no agreement to which Canada was a party with regard to the Mandate for Nauru. The mandates were conferred by the principal Allied and Associated Powers. That for Nauru was conferred upon His Majesty, designated in the Mandate as His Britannic Majesty, who had undertaken to exercise it on behalf of the League of Nations. The Mandate so conferred, in so far as it might be considered to be conferred upon a country, was, as he understood it, conferred upon Great Britain. Canada expressed no desire to be granted a mandate for any of the countries for which mandatories were appointed.

Mr. Mackenzie King believed it was quite true that the Mandate was conferred as the Minister said. He was not so sure that it had been conferred in the name of Great Britain for the British Empire.

The Minister of Justice : " Upon His Britannic Majesty."

Mr. Mackenzie King stated that a question was asked in the British House in reference to this matter, and Mr. Asquith, speaking on 16th June, 1920, in regard to Article 10 of the agreement in reference to the Nauru Island Mandate was reported in that day's proceedings as recorded in the Hansard of the United Kingdom as having expressed himself as follows : —

We find that the Commissioners who are to carry it out, and who are to represent those three constituent but not exhaustive members of our Empire,

" shall not . . . sell or supply any phosphates to, or for shipment to, any country or place other than the United Kingdom, Australia, or New Zealand."

This is the latest form of preference ! Here is a Mandate given to the British Empire, confined as far as its practical operation is concerned to three of its constituent members, and, what is much more important, when you come to hand over the phosphates, they are to go to three selected parts of the Empire, and not to the rest.

I think South Africa and Canada are as much entitled as any other part of the Empire to have a voice in the matter.

Elsewhere in the course of the debate, Mr. Bonar Law, Leader of the House, was reported as having replied to Mr. Asquith as follows : —

The Mandate is to be given to the British Empire, which does not consist of the three parts of it concerned in this agreement ; and my right hon. friend assumed that all this had been done without any knowledge on the part of the other portions of the British Empire. He is entirely mistaken. · I was myself in Paris when the British Empire Delegation considered this subject, and it was a very difficult subject to deal with. The use of these phosphates, which had always gone to New Zealand and Australia, was vital to this country. These Dominions were vitally interested in them, and it was difficult to get any agreement which would satisfy everybody. It was, therefore, discussed in the British Empire Delegation, at which all the Dominions were present, and an agreement of this kind was come to as the best method in all the circumstances of the case.

The Right Hon. Sir Robert Borden (Nat. Lib. and Con., *King's, N.S.*) declared that the hon. gentleman was quite mistaken. The matter stood in such a position that if it ever became one of practical importance Canada could have her share of these phosphates as well as the other portions of the British Empire to which allusion had been made. Difficulty arose in the first place by reason of the action of New Zealand, but the controversy was settled by giving a mandate for the British Empire to the United Kingdom. The arrangement then made was being carried out. He had not heard of any demand from Canada for the purchase of phosphates from Nauru. If the question should become one of practical importance he had no doubt it could be regulated so as to meet any demands from Canada.

FRENCH TRADE AGREEMENT ACT.

(Treaty-making Powers: Constitutional Position.)

This Act, which received the Royal Assent on 3rd May, 1921, approves the Trade Agreement between France and Canada entered into with the object of continuing, in a modified form, trade relations between the two countries on the lines of the Conventions of 1907 and 1909, which were denounced by Canada in 1920. The Governor-in-Council is empowered to make such orders and regulations as are deemed necessary to carry out the provisions of the Agreement.

The Agreement states that, pending the conclusion of a new commercial convention, with a view to which negotiations will begin immediately, the French and Canadian Governments have agreed to the following provisions :—

> *Article* 1.—Canada shall apply to products originating in and coming from France the most favourable tariffs and taxes that are or may be granted to the products of any third Power, except those of the United Kingdom and British Possessions.
> *Article* 2.—Canada shall also accord most-favoured-nation treatment as regards exportation, transit, consumption taxes, and other internal duties.
> *Article* 3.—The French Government agrees to continue for the benefit of Canadian products imported into France, until the conclusion of the new commercial convention, the application of the *régime* laid down in the Conventions of 1907 and 1909 subject to certain modifications and additions.

This arrangement remains in force until the conclusion of a new Commercial Convention, but either of the High Contracting Parties may denounce it after four months' notice.

DEBATE IN HOUSE OF COMMONS.

Explaining the Bill to the House in Committee on 14th April,

The Minister of Trade and Commerce (the Right Hon. Sir George Foster) stated that in 1907 and 1909 there were under negotiation the Conventions, so-called, of 1907 and 1909. They had been in effect from 1910 until their cancellation, which took place in 1920. After the War had gone on a little time, France gave notice to all countries with which she had trade agreements that she would hold herself free to undertake new negotiations resulting from changes which took place on account of, and during, the War, and notice was given of the cancellation of those treaties which she accompanied with a declaration as regarded Canada that it was not because France was indisposed to retain treaty arrangements with reference to trade, but that she wanted to hold herself free— the arrangement to go on in the meantime subject to cancellation by either side on three months' notice. Therefore, the Convention was kept in force for a year and a half, or more after the notice had been made.

In the course of the tariff arrangements which were necessary in Canada, in order to get as large a revenue as possible from some articles, particularly those articles with reference to which there was a special schedule in the French Convention allowing a certain list of articles to come in at a lower rate than even the intermediate rate, it was found, as that was the minimum tariff below all other tariffs in respect of those goods, that all nations with " most-favoured-nation " treaties had a right to the same minimum as France. Therefore, not only did that class of goods which came in from France at a lower rate diminish their possible revenue, but like goods coming in, especially from Switzerland and Japan, made a larger hole in the revenue than it was thought should be allowed during the period of the War. Therefore, they gave the three months' notice to France, and in June of 1920 the Treaty was, as far as Canada was concerned, denounced, and from that time until this the importations from France had been carrying the maximum rate of duty in all cases. France, however, was not anxious that there should be a complete severance of trade interchanges between the two countries. Canada also desired, if possible, that they should be carried on in some modified form. Under the circumstances, it was absolutely impossible to undertake to make a general treaty arrangement with France, or in fact with any other European country, owing to the disorganised state of trade. After certain *pourparlers*, they agreed upon a *modus vivendi*, or trade agreement, by which, subject to four months' notice, certain interchanges of articles should take place between the two countries along a certain line of duties.

They had three schedules in the Conventions 1907 and 1909. Under schedule A France imposed only the minimum tariff upon the products of Canada named therein ; these had been chosen because they were the items for which Canada would be most likely to find a market in the French Republic. Schedule B contained a list of selected articles, the origin of which was in France, which could be imported into Canada under their intermediate tariff. Schedule C contained a list of articles not very large in number, but fairly important in the matter of export for France, and for which there were special duties other than there were in the intermediate tariff. The arrangement ultimately arrived at was that of the 152 articles in schedule A, which after the denunciation of the Treaty became subject to the French maximum tariff, all except twelve should again be allowed in under the French minimum tariff. These twelve articles were allowed into France at less than the maximum duty. The articles in schedule C, which had the lowest rate when imported into Canada, now came under their intermediate tariff. France gave them in addition the lower tariff, either the minimum or one lower than the maximum, on the articles in schedule 2 of the Bill.

The Conventions of 1907 and 1909 took in the dependencies of France. The arrangement now was made simply and solely between France and Canada as respecting either exports or imports.

The Hon. W. S. Fielding (Liberal, *Shelburne and Queen's,* *N.S.***) :** " Any concession which is granted to the French Republic under this Treaty will be given to many other nations, will it not ? "

The Minister of Trade and Commerce : " It will be given to all ' most favoured nations.' "

The Hon. Rodolphe Lemieux (Liberal, *Maisonneuve and* *Gaspé, Que.***) :** " Can my right hon. friend give a list of those nations ? "

The Minister of Trade and Commerce : " Argentina, Colombia, Denmark, Spain, Sweden, Switzerland, Venezuela and Japan. Three other countries were given special conditions —Belgium, the Netherlands and Italy."

Mr. Fielding : " All these nations get concessions under this Treaty and give nothing in return ? "

The Minister of Trade and Commerce : " France gets no concession under this Treaty that has not already been given to these countries. Consequently they do not benefit by the present arrangement made with France. If, of course, we gave to any other nation treaty or tariff benefits lower than these, the ' most favoured nations ' come in and enjoy the same."

Mr. Lemieux was gratified to know that the Canadian Government had revised their Trade Agreement with France. He would be disposed to give to France if not the British preference, the next to it. In 1920 they imported from France goods to the value of $10,609,122. Look at what they were selling to France. During the War, in 1918, Canada exported to France goods to the value of $210,526,297. In 1920, without a Treaty, without any special favour, France opened her ports to Canadian produce to the extent of $61,106,938. After the United States and Great Britain, France was the best customer they had in the world, and surely that market was worth cultivating.

Agents Required.

It was not possible to expect that trade with Canada would undergo any great expansion if only one solitary agent was maintained in France. They had just one little office, in the Commissioner-General's office, in Paris, with one agent. Paris was not all France. If they had no representatives in these cities, which were the nerve-centres of French commerce and industry, they could not develop those channels of trade which they were seeking to establish between Canada and France.

Treaty-making Powers.

As to the final signatories of the Treaty, Mr. Lemieux declared that he was a strong Canadian, and he did not object to His Majesty the King being a signatory to that Treaty, through the British Ambassador in Paris, or even through the instrumentality of the Foreign Office in London, but what he did object to was the subterfuge of the Minister of Justice (Mr. Doherty) who of late had been stating *ad nauseam* that Canada was a nation, that there was such a thing as a Canadian national, and that they enjoyed almost sovereign powers. Yet in the case of this Treaty they found that his right hon. friend (Sir George Foster), fresh from the Geneva Conference, where the sovereign rights of Canada were supposed to have been proclaimed throughout the world, went direct to the Foreign Office in London and from there by a circuitous route to the British Ambassador in Paris to get the Agreement signed. When they got down to hard-pan they found that they were still a Dominion, with no sovereignty, and that this Treaty would be non-existent but for the signatures on the parchment of Hardinge of Penshurst before that of George E. Foster.

Mr. Ernest Lapointe (Liberal, *Quebec East*) : "May I ask who appointed the gentlemen who signed the Treaty on behalf of Canada and on behalf of His Majesty ? What authority did these gentlemen have to affix their signatures to the Treaty ? "

The Minister of Trade and Commerce : " On our side I signed as representing Canada and the British Ambassador as representing the Foreign Office and on behalf of His Majesty, which was necessary in order to make the Treaty complete."

Mr. Lapointe : " The Bill says that this Agreement was entered into at Paris by representatives appointed by His Majesty. Who acted for His Majesty in the appointment of his representatives ? Was there an Order in Council appointing the two gentlemen who signed the Treaty ? "

The Minister of Trade and Commerce : " I was authorised, as far as I was concerned, by our own Government. That authority was intimated to the Foreign Office through the Colonial Secretary, and the Foreign Office sent in a despatch to the British Ambassador in Paris to sign on behalf of His Majesty's Government."

Mr. Lapointe : " I want to know if there has been any change in the method of treaty-making on the part of Canada with regard to this Treaty."

The Minister of Trade and Commerce : " There has been no change. The Treaty that was made at Washington and the Treaty that was made in 1907 were treaties which we negotiated with the privity of His Majesty's Government and were signed by the Ambassador representing Great Britain at Washington and also by the British Ambassador at Paris. The same thing was done here. There was no very great formality about it as far as I was concerned, but it was by the direction of the Foreign Office that the Treaty was signed."

Mr. Lapointe : " We have been told that we should be proud that we, a sister nation, enjoy absolute equality of status. Is it an evidence of that if our representatives have to be appointed by the Foreign Office, and if, as I know, the Treaty has been submitted to the Imperial Government before being signed and put into force ? Really, there is something wrong as to this claim of our enjoying equality of status."

Mr. Fielding : " There is nothing wrong in the making of the Treaty. The only wrong is in the humbug of professing to us that there has been any change in the status of Canada. My hon. friend (Mr. Lapointe) states that His Majesty has sanctioned these appointments. It is true that His Majesty's name is in the Bill, but in this Treaty there is no reference to His Majesty from beginning to end. My right hon. friend said there was no formality in the making of our treaties before, but he is mistaken. The Washington Agreement was not signed by the British Ambassador at Washington, but by representatives of Canada on the one side and those of the United States on the other. But it was not in the form of a treaty. If it had been a treaty, it would probably have received the signature of those designated by His Majesty strictly for that purpose."

Mr. A. R. McMaster (Liberal, *Brome, Que.***) :** " I do not see why our Minister of Trade and Commerce could not have done the whole thing himself, and I would have preferred to see him do it. I can understand that the Trade Agreement could have been made, nominally, between the King and the President of the French Republic. He would act then as King of Canada and the Minister of Trade and Commerce would act as the Minister of the King in Canada. It is quite true that the Agreement itself does not mention the name of the King, but I want to express the view, which I believe is entertained by the vast majority of the Members of this House sitting on your left, Mr. Chairman, that we accept with pleasure any change of status which brings us to a position of equality."

Mr. Lapointe : " I want to keep the name of His Majesty in any treaty concerning Canada ; but I want His Majesty to act through Canadian representatives appointed by the Canadian Government, without the intervention of the Foreign Office in London."

After further discussion, the Bill was passed by the House of Commons on 15th April.

WEST INDIES TRADE AGREEMENT ACT.

This Act, which was assented to on 3rd May, gives approval to the Agreement between the Dominion of Canada and the Governments of certain of His Majesty's Colonies in the West Indies for the extension of trade and the improvement of communications, and empowers the Governor in Council to prescribe by proclamation the day upon which the preferential treatment of the goods provided for in the agreement shall be brought into force.

Trade.

The Agreement provides for a 50 per cent. preference by Canada on all imports from the British West Indies, except tobacco and liquors. Certain articles (including sugar, cocoa beans, limes, arrowroot, grape fruit, rum and onions) imported from the Colonies into Canada are subject to special preferential treatment indicated in schedule A. Barbados, British Guiana and Trinidad give Canada a 50 per cent. preference ; British Honduras, the Leeward and Windward Islands 33½ per cent. ; Bermuda and Jamaica 25 per cent. ; and the Bahamas 10 per cent. Certain articles (including flour and liquors) are subject to special preference indicated in schedule B. The Governments of Canada or of any of the Colonies on giving six months' notice may provide that to be entitled to the above concessions the products of their respective countries shall be conveyed direct without transhipment (Articles 1-8). The agreement shall not interfere with any existing preference or the granting of any future preference by the Dominion or the Colonies to any other part of the Empire (Article 9).

Steamship Services—Eastern Group. (Barbados, Trinidad, British Guiana, Leeward and Windward Islands and Bermuda.)

The Government of Canada agrees to use its best endeavours to arrange a weekly mail, passenger and freight steamship service to come into force as soon as possible, and in any case within three years. Steamers will be from 5,000 to 6,000 tons gross, capable of maintaining an ocean speed of 12 knots, and with accommodation for 230 passengers ; cold storage shall be provided if this can be secured without unreasonable additional cost. If a subsidised service is arranged for, the Colonies shall contribute towards it proportionately up to a total amount of £27,000. In the meantime Canada undertakes to maintain a fortnightly service on the existing lines, and to supplement it with such additional passenger and freight vessels as the trade may require (Articles 10-14).

Western Group. (The Bahamas, Jamaica and British Honduras.)

The Government of Canada undertakes to provide as soon as possible, and in any case not later than 1st January, 1921, a fortnightly freight, mail and passenger service. Steamers shall not be less than 3,500 tons dead weight, with an ocean-going speed of 10 knots and accommodation for from 15 to 20 first-class passengers. If the service proves unremunerative the Colonial Governments shall contribute 25 per cent. of any loss, provided that the amounts shall not exceed in the case of the Bahamas £3,000 per annum, and in the case of British Honduras and Jamaica £5,000 per annum.

The Agreement is subject to the approval of the Canadian Parliament (Articles 15 and 16), the Colonial Legislatures, and the Secretary of State for the Colonies, and shall remain in force for ten years, after which it is terminable on twelve months' notice (Articles 17 and 18).

Cables.

The recommendation is made that the Governments should take up the question of a better cable service, the Government of Canada agreeing to institute inquiries into the possibility of arranging for such cables.

DEBATE IN HOUSE OF COMMONS.

Explaining the Bill on 19th April,

The Minister of Trade and Commerce (the Right Hon Sir George Foster) said that the relations of Canada in commercial matters with the West Indian Colonies had always been more or less close and from a time shortly after Confederation they had been improved from year to year Previous to 1897, for a considerable number of years, Canada had subsidised steamship services between her ports and the ports of the different West India Islands, and sustained the cost of those services entirely from her own Treasury. In 1897 the advantages of the British preference were given to the West India Islands without any request for a reciprocation on their part, and steamship services were continued from that date uninterruptedly at the expense of the Dominion In 1912 a conference was held in Ottawa between representatives of certain of the West India Islands and of the Canadian Government, and an arrangement was entered into That arrangement contemplated—and it was afterward approved—an Agreement to last for ten years, which would terminate in 1922. One defect of the Agreement was that it included only a portion of the West Indies. Jamaica was not a party to the arrangement, nor were the Bahamas, Bermuda and British Honduras. The Agreement was attended with an improved steamship service between Canadian ports and those islands which had availed themselves of the arrangement It was provided, however, that even those islands which were not parties to the Agreement should participate in its advantages for three years. The War intervened ; and during the course of the working out of the Agreement all the West India Islands participated in the benefits given by Canada to imports from the Colonies ; but from those Islands no parties to the Agreement they received no corresponding preference. The preference in the Agreement of 1912 amounted to 20 per cent. upon a selected list of the exports of Canada to the West India Islands, whilst Canada gave to those islands the British preference. In 1897 the total trade amounted to $2,842,968 ; in 1920 it totalled $35,124,736.

There were certain features which distinguished this Convention (of 1920) and the resultant Agreement from that of 1912. At this Convention they had representatives from all of the British West Indian Colonies, and from British Honduras on the mainland. This time they commenced by affirming the principle that all products from either of the countries should be admitted on the principles of a general preference, and that special articles might be selected for limitations or restrictions as to the amount of preference that should be granted. That resulted in practically widening the operation of preference to all the products of both countries, with the exception of tobacco and cigarettes. The West Indian Colonies divided themselves off into three groups according to the capabilities which they considered they possessed as to the amount of preference that those Colonies could give and hope to carry through their several Legislatures.

It was an Article of the Agreement that the preferences therein given did not interfere with any existing preference or with any prospective preferences that those countries might give within the British Empire.

It was felt that the increase of the preference, and the increase which had heretofore progressively taken place in Canada, called for a better steamship service between the islands and Canada. In this Agreement there was introduced for the first time an obligation on the islands to assist the service by pledging themselves to contribute certain amounts.

Bermuda was the one Colony which had found it impossible to approve of the Agreement. Bermuda did a large trade with the United States ports, particularly New York, and possibly there was some fear that if she approved of this Agreement, and thereby gave preferential treatment to Canada, the impending tariff changes in the United States might be greatly to the Island's disadvantage.

The Hon. Rodolphe Lemieux (Liberal, *Maisonneuve and Gaspé, Que.*) asked if the union of the West Indies with Canada was mooted at the Conference and if his right hon. friend was aware that resolutions in favour of such union had already been passed by some of the Legislative bodies in the West Indies ?

The Minister of Trade and Commerce said that there was complete unanimity with regard to this trade Agreement. There might not be the same unanimity with regard to political union and a discussion of the matter at that stage might not be opportune.

Speaking of the preference given to sugar, the Minister said that obviously a preference would be of little use to the British West Indies unless it came close to or a little bit in advance of the preference which was offered by the Old Country,

and in schedule A, as regarded the first item of sugar, the
extended list of preference for each degree of polarisation was
a little shade higher than the preference which had been given
by Great Britain for the same degree of polarisation on the
importation of West India sugars into the Old Country.

The Hon. W. S. Fielding (Liberal, *Shelburne and Queen's,*
N.S.) thought that the general purpose of the Agreement
would commend itself to the House and the country. There
had been for many years a large and important trade between
Canada, chiefly the Maritime Provinces, and the West Indies.
There was a natural relation between the West Indies and
themselves. They were all to the north, and the West Indies
were all to the south. They had things which the West
Indies wanted, and the West Indies had things which they
wanted.

Mr. J. H. Sinclair (Liberal, *Antigonish and Guysborough,*
N.S.) stated that the Royal Mail Packet Company was at
present running four ships on the eastern route, giving a
fortnightly service, and they were paying them a subsidy of
$340,000 a year. They were now proposing to provide a
weekly service, and he supposed that would mean that eight
vessels instead of four would be required. Did his right hon.
friend expect, when he promised a weekly service, to increase
the volume of freight correspondingly so that it would not
cost Canada an enormous amount to keep the service going?

The Minister of Trade and Commerce replied that there
was still a very large proportion of the imports into those
West Indian Islands which could be supplied by Canada and
which this added preference would help Canada to supply,
so that they might hope for a progressive increase of freights
as a result of added preferences and of increased frequency of
steamship communications.

After further discussion the Bill was read a third time
and passed.

RECIPROCITY WITH THE UNITED STATES.

On 13th April, 1921, the Hon. W. S. Fielding moved the
following amendment to a motion of the Minister of Finance
for the House to go into Committee of Supply : —

In the opinion of the House, the Government should bring in a measure
to approve, ratify and confirm the Agreement respecting reciprocal
trade between the United States and Canada, signed at Washington
on the 21st day of January, 1911, by Hon. P. C. Knox on the part of the
United States and by Hon W. S. Fielding and the late Hon. William
Paterson on the part of Canada, which Agreement remains on the Statute
Books of the United States.

DEBATE IN HOUSE OF COMMONS.

The Hon. W. S. Fielding (Liberal, *Shelburne and Queen's,* *N.S.*) said that it had always been to him a matter of profound regret that in 1911 a question of a commercial character, an economic question, was made a matter of Party controversy—that for the first time in the history of their country reciprocity became a matter of Party conflict. He wished to present the question to the House with the single desire that the House should do what he thought might be helpful in meeting a rather grave condition which had arisen to-day through the prospects of tariff legislation at Washington. The historic commercial policies of the two Parties in the United States were well known. The Republican Party was historically a protectionist Party ; the Democratic Party was historically a moderate tariff Party. The Democratic Party came into power at the elections of November, 1912, and in the Session of Congress held in the early part of 1913 the Democratic administration made changes in the tariff in the direction of either freedom of exchange or tariff reduction. Some of the very things which some of them thought were important to Canada in the reciprocity agreement came to them by the voluntary action of the Democratic Party. In the very recent national elections for the Presidency of the United States a change again occurred. The Republican Party had again come into power, and they were now face to face with a condition which should give them cause for some anxiety. At the earliest stage after the election of the Republican President, a movement was brought into the United States Congress which took form in the shape of the Fordney Bill. That Bill proposed to levy duties not on the products of Canada particularly, but on the products of the world, but which were likely to operate to the manifest disadvantage of Canada. President Wilson was no longer there to veto, the Fordney Bill was again before Congress, and they were face to face with the prospect of having these duties applied against the products of Canada.

Canada was not dependent on the United States. They had the resources, the intelligence and the patriotism to get along without the United States if it was necessary to do so. On the other hand, it was folly on their part to pretend that the United States was in any degree dependent upon Canada. The British Empire, scattered widely over the world, had all the resources of the United States, but speaking of a consolidated country the United States had within itself a greater variety of resources than any other country in the world, and

I 2

they could get along, no doubt, if they established a hostile tariff against Canada. But he did not hesitate to say that they would both get along better if they were reciprocal in their tariffs. It was a very interesting fact, and of great importance now, that the reciprocity agreement of 1911 was still on the Statute Books of the United States and was a standing offer. They were justified in assuming that it was still open to them to consider, and he thought they should do well if they proceeded along those lines. The wheat growers of the West attached great importance to their access to the American market. And in the matter of the cattle trade of the country, he thought the feeling was stronger.

There never was a time when, even apart from the question of commercial relations, it was more desirable that Canada and the United States should be on friendly terms. More than one public speaker of late had said that Canada should be the interpreter of good relations between the Mother Country and the great American Republic. What better could they do than begin by trying to establish better commercial relations ?

The Minister of Finance (Hon. Sir Henry Drayton) declared that it was true that Canada, with her eight or nine millions of people, did more business with the United States than the whole of the continent of South America, with which the United States people were at present doing so much trade. There was no issue between them as to the necessity for maintaining the very best·possible relations with their great neighbour to the south.

During the last eleven months Canada imported from the United States $792,804,843 worth of commodities. Did that not look as if they were trading very largely with the United States, or as if there was any room for complaint on the part of American shippers against the tariff system of Canada ? During the same period they exported to the United States $540,494,713 worth of goods. He wondered what his hon. friend thought of adverse balances and debts which must be paid. He wondered if he thought that there was no limit to the amount to which adverse balances could be allowed to accumulate. These adverse balances were mirrored in their currency. Last year the result was that they had a maximum of nineteen per cent. discount on their Canadian dollar, and the agitation that existed to-day in the United States had its birth in the fact that they were buying unwisely in the American market. The trouble to-day about this Fordney Bill was not that they had been buying too little but that they had been buying too much. Their adverse trade balance was much worse than it looked, because over and above the trade balance there was the full amount of the money that had to go to the United States day by day in the payment of interest and other carrying charges. The question of exchange was very largely at the bottom of the whole of this trouble.

The adoption of the reciprocity Agreement would mean that the American duties on fish, meats, bacon and hams, salted meats, lard, wheat flour, oatmeal, agricultural machinery, shingle, lumber, iron ore, cement, and bituminous coal would be raised against the Canadian exporter. The duties on all these articles to-day were lower than were called for by the reciprocity agreement. So that those exports that would be in any way helped by the reciprocity treaty amounted to only 7·2 per cent. The assistance to American goods imported into Canada would amount to 16 per cent.—more than double.

He was not going to say that they should then and there adopt retaliatory measures. But he did believe in having a tariff for Canada, and one that was in the best interests of the Canadian nation. He did not know any way by which they could compel the United States to take their goods, but they could, and he thought they ought to, reduce their purchases.

Mr. Michael Clark (National Progressive, *Red Deer, Alta.*) supported the resolution because its effect would be inevitably to increase international trade in at least one direction. They were not trading enough with the United States; they were not trading enough anywhere. An export always bought an import. The adverse balance of trade was due to definite economic causes, and the great cause of it was that they were borrowing enormously from the United States. The best way to alter the adverse balance was to stop borrowing as a nation. All these borrowings came into Canada in the shape of United States goods and constituted that adverse balance of trade which the Minister of Finance so much lamented.

He wanted to point out that with the growth of their trade with the United States last year, while their imports from the States increased, it was true also that they exported $100,000,000 more to the States than they did in the previous year, showing the truth of the fiscal theory that in the last analysis international trade was an exchange of surpluses. The adverse exchange on the dollar was due to the fact that in the States they were nearer a gold basis than Canada was; in other words, their currency was more inflated than the currency of the States. If he were asked what would be the effect upon the balance of trade of this reciprocity agreement going into operation, he should say that it would improve that balance, for the reason that they were in a very much better position to produce an excess of natural products than were the United States. To get a free market for their natural products in the United States was a certain way of enriching the agricultural population of Canada by providing them with a larger market for their products, and through the agricultural community of enriching the whole nation.

Mr. J. W. Edwards (Nat. Lib. and Con., *Frontenac, Ont.*) declared that Canada did not produce a larger excess of natural products than the United States. Comparing 1918 with 1916, Canada's exportable surplus of these articles (butter, cheese, eggs, lard and meats) increased by 72 per cent. as compared with an increase in the United States of 138 per cent.

Mr. A. R. McMaster (Liberal, *Brome, Que.*) said that the Agreement merely established a maximum rate of duties, and that under the Agreement it was left open to either party at their desire to reduce the duties below the schedules.

It was an unsound economic argument to say that if people had a surplus of similar things they could not trade in those things. He was only willing to maintain tariffs for the purpose of raising revenue. If commerce was allowed to pursue its course without restriction, exchange conditions would in process of time assert themselves. If there was a heavy discount against their money in the United States, that would tend to foster sales of Canadian goods to the United States, because their money, being worth more than Canadian money, they would be able to sell in the United States more cheaply than they otherwise could ; while if there was a heavy premium against their money in the United States, they would tend to reduce their purchases in that country. If they could get this reciprocity, limited as it was, in the markets of the United States, they would confer an inestimable benefit on the producer of foodstuffs and other natural products in Canada. They could not help the producer of natural products without helping the manufacturer, the man engaged in transportation or banking or any other department of distribution.

Mr. W. F. Cockshutt (Nat. Lib. and Con., *Brantford, Ont.*) said that the Fordney Bill was designed especially to protect the farmers of the United States from the inroads of Canadian products and products from other countries. In 1911 it was shown that the Canadian market was in every respect a better market for the Canadian farmer than the United States market, and the same could be shown to-day. The reciprocity Agreement that his hon. friend now proposed to put into force was voted down in 1911 by one of the largest majorities Canada had ever seen. The only way they could meet the Fordney Bill, if such a preposterous measure became law in the United States, was to have up their sleeves a corresponding style of argument. They had a better market than the United States. It was in Great Britain, in the Dominions overseas, in the West Indies and in other parts of the world where the British flag flew.

Mr. W. H. White (Liberal, *Victoria, Alta.*) : " Is Great Britain a better market for our cattle than the United States ? "

Mr. Cockshutt said it was prohibitory ; it said : " Your cattle are diseased, and cannot come in at any price." Let Great Britain put on £5, yes £10 per head, and they would send their cattle over there in such numbers as would pretty soon convince them that they were in the cattle business good and strong. The reason that they lost the British cattle-market was free trade with the United States. The disease was introduced into Canada from the United States, and for that reason their cattle was placarded as being infected.

Mr. Levi Thomson (**National Progressive**, *Qu'Appelle, Sask.*) said they should put no obstacle in the way of their trade with the United States in live animals. If this proposal was not accepted, and something in the nature of the Fordney Bill was put into effect, their market for live animals in the United States would practically be done away with. The acceptance of the reciprocity offer would have the effect of increasing their exports generally, at least of increasing the proportion which exports bore to imports.

Mr. R. H. Butts (**Nat. Lib. and Con.**, *Cape Breton S. and Richmond, N.S.*) declared that farmers' implements were taxed about fifty per cent. less than the products used by any other class in the Dominion. They paid the United States last year for steel and steel products alone $199,916,000. They not only took that out of the factories—they not only took it out of the labouring man, out of his family and out of his wages —but they sent the money over into a foreign country to build up another and a rival nation.

After further discussion Mr. Fielding's amendment was negatived by 100 to 79 votes.

CANADIAN TRADE.

(Preference : Reciprocity : Steamship Subsidies, etc.)

On 22nd March and 1st April, 1921, the House in Committee of Supply discussed various items for the Department of Trade and Commerce relating to the extension of Canadian trade.

DEBATE IN HOUSE OF COMMONS.

Trade Commissioners.

Speaking on 22nd March,

The Minister of Trade and Commerce (the Right Hon. Sir George Foster) said that the Director of Commercial Intelligence Service had under him the whole staff of trade commissioners. He had also the direction of the whole staff of Commercial Intelligence, which included instructions to their commissioners in different parts of the world, the reception of reports therefrom, their publication in the *Weekly Bulletin,* and all the correspondence with business men in Canada who had more or less trade in connection with the different countries in which their trade commissioners exercised their functions. They had between twenty and thirty trade commissioners. They had not yet adopted the policy of extending their trade commissionerships to the United States, but the matter was now under consideration. The knowledge that existed was so much more widely distributed with reference to the United States than to other countries that there was not the same necessity for trade commissioners.

Mr. Thomas Vien (Liberal, *Lotbinière, Que.*) declared that the purpose of appointing trade commissioners in the United States was to open up new markets in that country for Canadian industries. The American Republic had consuls in Canada, being represented in almost every town. Their own lack of organisation had, to a great degree, prevented the expansion of their export trade to the United States. When the Government brought down legislation creating the position of Canadian Ambassador at Washington, they contended that the time had come when a Canadian representative should reside in Washington and look after Canadian interests. He did not share the opinion of the Government as to the method they then suggested. He thought that their representative in Washington should by no means be linked up with the British Embassy. He should not be the Vice-Ambassador of the British Empire in Washington, he should be absolutely untrammelled and should represent Canadian interests exclusively. If Canada wished to develop her trade with the United States her duty was not to rely upon other representatives, whether they were British consuls, vice-consuls or consular agents. Canada should see to it that Canadians, who had only Canadian interests at heart, were appointed. They should not report to the British Ambassador, but directly to their Minister of Trade and Commerce for the benefit of Canadian industries.

Trade with Australia and New Zealand.

Mr. J. A. Currie (Nat. Lib. and Con., *Simcoe, N. Riding, Ont.*) said that unfortunately their trade with Australia and New Zealand, which had reached very large proportions, was now cut off, largely due to the fact that those two Dominions had no credits with Canada. He suggested that the Government should seriously take into consideration the granting of credit to Australia and New Zealand so that that trade might be continued until such time as those two countries had reached the point where normal conditions might be said to have been re-established. They had displaced Germany and England in the Australian market for most lines of manufactured goods. The depression was general so far as these two Dominions were concerned, but that condition of affairs did not extend to China, India and Japan; their credit was ample in Canada, and they could pay for anything which they bought from them. Unfortunately, Australia and New Zealand had not the funds now .to pay for goods that they would very much like to purchase from Canada.

Wheat Purchases.

Speaking on 1st April,

Mr. Currie stated that immediately on the announcement that the Canada Wheat Board would not be continued for another year, the Americans sold their entire surplus of wheat to Great Britain. It was the nations that were buying the grain. Great Britain bought grain as a nation, so did France and all the other countries, so the only rational way was to trade in grain as a nation. Through the lack of common sense of the Agrarian group the farmers of Canada lost $100,000,000. Lord Lee bought 180,000,000 bushels of wheat in the States last June. Why did he not buy in Canada? Because they had no grain board to arrange credits with him for the purchase of such a large amount of grain.

Mr. Samuel Jacobs (Liberal, *George Etienne Cartier, Que.*) pointed out that before the war they had a system in Germany and Austria under which well-known men in commercial life were appointed to act as a sort of advisory board to the Ministry.

The Minister of Trade and Commerce said he had considered the matter. In a way they were getting advice though they had no formal board. Their department was in communication with all the Boards of Trade, and with all the important centres of industrial trade activity.

Publicity.

Speaking on publicity work, the Minister said that cinematograph films illustrating manufacturing processes and activities were shown. When he was in Great Britain two years ago he had arranged a contract with one of the most prominent film exhibitors, and he was now taking a new film from them almost every month. He put them through his regular circuit, and a certain percentage of the proceeds came to Canada. These pictures had been distributed in New Zealand, Australia and South Africa.

Australia and Preference.

In answer to a question by Mr. D. C. Ross (Liberal, *Middlesex, W. Riding, Ont.*), the Minister stated that South Africa received a small preference in the Australian market on a very limited number of goods, and he thought South Africa gave three or five per cent. preference on a certain limited number of Australian goods. That was the only preference that Australia had given other than to the United Kingdom. The Government which at present existed in Australia, when it came into power, undertook a revision of the tariff. In March, 1920, it brought down a resolution which was the basis upon which was to be founded a Bill and an Act,* but the Bill itself had not yet been framed and passed by the Legislature ; only the resolution held, and the Government was acting under the resolution. By that resolution Australia gave a preference to British goods, but gave no preference to any other outside Dominion or dependency of Great Britain, but in the resolution she contemplated, after the legislation was completed, opening negotiations with Canada and New Zealand† for preference between herself and these countries. The Bill was still being discussed, and the latest advices that he had were that probably it would be the autumn of this year before it was finally passed. In the meantime the present position was that Australia made material additions to her tariff along protective lines, gave to Great Britain a fairly good preference on her products as Australia imported them, but had no other preferential arrangements either made or under negotiation.

The Hon. W. S. Fielding (Liberal, *Shelburne and Queen's, N.S.*) : "We do not give Australia a preference ? "

The Minister of Trade and Commerce : "No, we have never been successful in getting an arrangement. · · The answer I invariably get is that as soon as this Bill becomes law they will take the matter up with us."

Cattle Embargo.

Mr. F. S. Cahill (Liberal, *Pontiac, Que.*) asked whether the Government had in mind, or had attempted to negotiate

---

* See p. 879.   † See p. 879.

a treaty with England permitting live Canadian cattle to be imported into that country. They gave a preference to British goods entering Canada, and he should think that if the Government displayed sufficient activity it could, in exchange for that preference, get permission to have their live cattle landed in Britain. The cattle industry of Canada was going to be very badly crippled if their livestock was excluded from the American market by a high tariff, and shut out entirely from the British market. He would recommend that if Britain was not agreeable to admitting their live cattle, they should reduce the Customs duties on goods coming from other countries and make them equal to those prevailing on goods coming from Britain.

The Minister of Trade and Commerce thought that probably the matter would be in a better position by the Government continuing along the lines which had been followed in the past, rather than to interject into the issue a tariff question by way of reprisal.

Reciprocity.

The Hon. Rodolphe Lemieux (Liberal, *Maisonneuve and Gaspé, Que.*) recalled that in 1910 Mr. Fielding succeeded in obtaining from the Government of the United States a pact which no one could deny was the best commercial agreement ever reached by Canada with the United States. If they wished to develop trade with the United States, the larger part of that business being agricultural, what was most essential was a market for their farm products. It must be laid of his right hon. friend (Sir George Foster) that since 1911 he had been in a state of mortal sin, because he had helped by incendiary speeches to defeat the reciprocity pact that would have provided so much business for Canada.

He believed it would not be a bad thing if there were some trade agents in the principal centres of the United States. They were told by the Minister of Justice that Canada was a nation, and that so soon as it pleased the country she might appoint consular agents and even an ambassador to Washington. Why did they not appoint consular agents if they had that power?

Mail and Steamship Subsidies: Services to New-foundland, West Indies, South Africa, New Zealand and Australia.

Mr. D. D. McKenzie (Liberal, *Cape Breton N. and Victoria, N.S.*), discussing the item for mail subsidies and steamship subventions, said that Canadian trade with Newfoundland was very large, and unless they had proper means of handling it they could not hope to keep it going. It was not a local matter at all, it was the broad question of Canadian trade with a British country such as Newfoundland was, a country that was willing to trade with them. If the people of Canada found that their trade with Newfoundland was falling off, they would know that the cause to some extent was that they were not in a proper position to handle expeditiously the traffic that now existed and that had been growing very satisfactorily during the last 25 years.

The Minister of Trade and Commerce stated that their own vessels of the merchant marine were going from Halifax to St. John's, Newfoundland, which was the objective of most of the traffic. They were also putting on a service which would serve Prince Edward Island and go from there direct to St. John's. Everything that could possibly be done to keep the connection on this route, he thought, they had a right to do. .

With reference to the West Indies, the Minister said that the Royal Mail Steam Packet Company was the only regular service they had between Canada and the whole ring of West India Islands and Demerara. It was absolutely essential to have this service if they were going to promote trade between themselves and these colonies. While they had so far been carrying on this service entirely at their own expense, the West India Islands touched by that route would, under the new agreement, pay a certain proportion of the subsidy which was necessary to maintain the service.

With reference to the steamship service between Canada and South Africa, the Minister stated that last year about $10,000,000 worth of exports was carried from Canada by that route to South Africa. It was the only subsidised service they had between the two countries. During the last ten years their trade with South Africa had greatly improved. The service might be dropped, but their whole trade with South Africa might be diverted to some other country.

On the service to Australia and New Zealand the Minister said that the service carried on for a number of years from the Atlantic Ports was a freight service. For that had been substituted their own vessels, so that subsidy had been withdrawn. On the Pacific side the subsidy he was asking for was contributed by themselves and New Zealand to a passenger and freight service regularly from Vancouver and Victoria touching at Fiji and New Zealand, and going on to Australia. The year before last they gave a subsidy of $180,000, and he had reduced it to $130,000.

GOVERNMENT MERCHANT MARINE.

On 29th March, 1921, the Minister of Marine, Fisheries and Naval Service made a general statement with regard to the position of the Government Merchant Marine. The statement was subsequently discussed by the House in Committee of Supply on the following item: —

Department of Marine—Shipbuilding programme—Amount required for the construction of vessels in accordance with the Government programme, $8,330,000.

DEBATE IN HOUSE OF COMMONS.

Reasons for Government Merchant Marine.

The Minister of Marine and Fisheries (Hon. C. C. Ballantyne), in stating the reasons leading to the creation of a Government Merchant Marine, said that during the spring of 1918 the situation amounted to a race between the enemy submarines and the shipbuilding yards of the British Empire. The Government, therefore, thought it wise to enter upon shipbuilding as a war measure. Before that decision was reached the British Government was utilising their steel shipbuilding yards throughout the Dominion for the construction of steel ships for its own purposes, which ships were under British registry, the Canadian Government providing the necessary funds. The Dominion Government, therefore, came to the conclusion, and its decision received the unanimous approval of the House at that time, that it would be better for Canada in the national interests that they should build ships under Canadian registry and for the benefit of the Canadian people. The second reason for embarking upon this policy was that the Government, having a vast system of national railways, deemed it necessary to complete the chain of transportation by providing ships to carry the cargoes that would be transported over the immense railway system to their seaports for exportation. The third reason was to enable Canada to expand her export trade, and the Government had performed a very great national work in opening up new trade routes. The Government had not placed any new contracts for the construction of ships since 1919, but was simply carrying to its completion its original shipbuilding programme. The Government's reason for continuing the shipbuilding programme was the serious labour conditions which existed throughout Canada at the time of the signing of the armistice.

Post-War Shipping.

The year 1920 proved unsatisfactory to shipping interests the world over, more especially from the point of view of net earnings. The loss of tonnage that had been sustained during the War was more than overtaken, with the result that there had been throughout the year a surplus of available tonnage. The world tonnage at the commencement of the War was about 49,000,000 tons. The available tonnage at present was about 65,000,000 tons. The costs of operation that had reached abnormally high proportions during the War continued throughout the year. That, taken in conjunction with the substantial decline in freight rates, added very materially to the difficulties with which shipowners had to cope. So acute was the depression in shipping that for some considerable time there had been lying idle in different ports of the world a very large number of British ships, and at the present time there were lying idle 536 steel steamers of United States registry. Under all these unusual conditions the Canadian Government Merchant Marine might well be considered to have had a very satisfactory year.

Extent and Cost of Programme.

The entire programme when completed would comprise 63 ships, and the approximate tonnage would be 374,254 tons. For the purpose of the shipbuilding programme the sum of $20,000,000 was voted for the present fiscal year. Of the amount of $8,000,000 which would be required to complete the programme $4,665,496.01 was a re-vote. The average cost of constructing all the vessels under the programme figured out at $191.95 per deadweight ton. The average cost of the vessels constructed by the United States Shipbuilding Board was stated to be about $215 per deadweight ton. The monthly cost of a Canadian Government Merchant Marine ship of 8,100 tons was $3,705. Published figures showed the monthly wage cost of foreign ships of similar tonnage as being, for British ships, $3,924 ; American, $5,315 ; and Japanese, $2,869. The number of officers and men employed was 1,674 (868 Canadian by birth or adoption and 806 British).

Services.

The Minister then gave a list of the routes upon which these ships were plying, which included from Canada to various ports in the British Isles, the West Indies, Newfoundland, South America, Australia, New Zealand, the Mediterranean, the Straits Settlements and India. In accordance with the Trade Agreement signed with the British West Indies it was decided to equip two of the 5,100-ton vessels with passenger accommodation, in consequence of which a regular service every three weeks had been established between Canada and the Bahamas, Jamaica and British Honduras. The importance of the Merchant Marine to Canadian trade could not be too strongly emphasised. Canadian goods to the value of over $50,000,000 had been transported during the year in Canadian-built ships.

The operating account for 1920 showed net earnings of $781,460.09, and the Minister pointed out that these net earnings were before providing for interest, and equalled 2·35 per cent. interest on notes given to the Government for the full cost of the ships.

The aim of the Government throughout was to develop shipbuilding as a self-contained industry. They managed to build these ships in Canada, and the achievement was a great tribute to the Canadian workman and the Canadian shipbuilder. The design was British, but all accessories were made in Canada by Canadian manufacturers, and no serious complaints had reached the Marine Department either in regard to design, construction or equipment, down to the minutest detail.

State *versus* Private Enterprise.

Mr. D. D. McKenzie (**Liberal**, *Cape Breton N. and Victoria, N.S.*) said that the ships were probably worth less than half of what they cost, and the Minister would find that possibly he could not sell any one of his ships to-day at one-third of the price he paid for its construction. It was, therefore, a grave question for the Canadian people whether or not the expenditure of seventy-five million dollars in ships, which certainly would not pay for their operation, and which they could not get off their hands if they wanted to sell them, was a wise venture. When the necessity for building ships for war purposes had disappeared, the Minister should have finished the construction of the ships then in hand and not have ventured any further into the business of shipbuilding. They would find that in proportion to the amount of money invested they were just as badly off as they were in connection with the Government-owned railways. It was only a further evidence that Governments should, as far as possible, keep their hands off the private enterprises and allow private individuals to look after them.

Mr. Michael Clark (**National Progressive**, *Red Deer, Alta.*) said that this was a scheme which in its magnitude was now almost as serious as the railroad problem which was exercising the mind of every thoughtful Canadian. Including the contracts which were entered into with the Imperial Munitions Board, Canada had embarked upon an expenditure up to date of no less a sum than $140,000,000 in connection with this shipbuilding scheme. The value of the ships had been cut through the middle ; freights could not be had. Such schemes were as common under a protective tariff as withered leaves in autumn.

The Hon. Rodolphe Lemieux (Liberal, *Maisonneuve and Gaspé, Que.*) said he had supported this shipbuilding programme because they were officially informed that it was absolutely urgent that Canada should build ships in order to relieve the shipping situation of the Allies. They were told not so very long ago that it was impossible to build ships in Canada ; that they could hardly find riveters ; that they could not manufacture plates ; that they could not have men to man their navy. He, as a Canadian, had enough pride that, even though told by Mr. Winston Churchill that they were not able to build ships, they were, indeed, able to do it. One must not infer that he stood in favour of this huge expenditure now that the War was over. It was a well-known fact that during the last fifteen or sixteen months ships had been like a drug on the market in Great Britain, the United States and France. Government ownership was a mistake. The Minister should have stopped building immediately after the armistice. They had taught John Bull that Jack Canuck was able to take care of himself.

Mr. Edmund Bristol (Nat. Lib. and Con., *Toronto Centre, Ont.*) declared that the belief of the people in every country at that time (1918) was that the building of ships was not only a good policy from the point of view of war, but that it would prove good business. To come to the Armistice. There was some $250,000,000 invested in this industry in Canada, and practically 250,000 men dependent on it. Were the Government suddenly to cancel contracts and turn every one of these men loose, with the resultant unemployment throughout the country ? Not only did they construct better ships than those built in the United States, but they were vastly cheaper. Conditions in Canada were worse because they had to import plates from the United States for a long time, until the Government adopted a policy of establishing a plate mill in Canada, which made it possible for Canada to build every part of a ship and not be dependent on the United States. Until their railways and the railways of the United States were on a stable basis ; until there had been a world-wide readjustment of the rates of exchange ; until trade was again normal ; and until the situation in Germany and Russia and elsewhere was settled, no man could reasonably expect the business of shipping to resume its pre-War status.

Development of Canadian Trade.

The Prime Minister (the Right Hon. Arthur Meighen) said that the statement made by the Minister of Marine reflected anything but a disastrous situation. Possibly it was not as rosy as many of them expected when the programme was launched, but on the whole satisfactory ; and particularly so when compared with the experience of any other country, not excepting Great Britain herself. They supported this programme because they needed ships for the purpose of Canadian commerce. It was known that when the War was over there would be a very serious shortage of ships, and each country vied with the other in an endeavour to catch up with that shortage and to give its own people the benefit of the industry that would be entailed in the process of catching up. In that effort Canada bore a creditable part.

Speaking on 7th April,

Mr. William Duff (Liberal, *Lunenburg, N.S.*) said that the figures showed conclusively that the ships of the Merchant Marine were carrying only a small proportion of the trade of the country, and in doing so were interfering with other lines which could carry goods far better than the slow tramp steamers which the Government had built. He could give a hundred instances to show that those ships did not carry Canadian cargo, but went to all parts of the world developing trade for the benefit of foreign countries.

After discussing the financial position of the Merchant Marine, Mr. Duff declared that there was no profit on current account ; no profit on operating account ; no profit on any other account, but an absolute loss to the country in depreciation of the value of the ships and in operation of those ships of $58,669,906.22. He agreed that they should have a Canadian Merchant Marine, but a marine built with private capital. The Government were running their steamers in competition with lines to which the country was paying subsidies voted by Parliament. The only right thing for the Government to do was to dispose of those ships as early as possible either by sale or otherwise. France and England were getting clear of their publicly-owned ships by passing them over to private individuals.

Historic British Policy.

Mr. H. H. Stevens (Nat. Lib. and Con., *Vancouver Centre, B.C.*) said he would conserve these assets, realising that this particular slump which they were now passing through could not possibly continue for any lengthy period, and that the time would come when these ships would in all probability not only earn a profit on operating expenses but pay a dividend as

K

well. Great Britain's supremacy of the sea was built up on
just such a beginning as this. She made sacrifices ; she paid
amounts enormously in excess of what she really needed to have
paid the Dutch for shipping at that time. But she established
the policy of carrying her own goods in her own bottoms and
passed very rigorous laws in support of it. The United States,
with less success, had tried to do the same thing. About forty
years ago Canada occupied a very favourable position so far as
shipping was concerned ; when wooden ships were more
fashionable than steel they had a very high place in the
shipping of the world. They lost that position because of the
complete change in the type of shipping. Now they were
launching into shipping in a modern way.

Mr. J. H. Sinclair (Liberal, *Antigonish and Guysborough,*
N.S.) said that the Minister gave London, Cardiff, Havana and
Australia as new routes. Was any one of them new ? He
questioned whether he could find an important commercial
port in any part of the world where Canadian ships had not
already been. Within ten days after the Armistice the Government of Great Britain announced their policy to return all their
freight carriers to private ownership, and they had since done so.
The United States Government tried to do the same. If the
Canadian Government had followed the example of Great
Britain, they could have saved millions and millions of dollars
to the people of Canada.

If the Minister would look at the returns of the trade
between Australia and New Zealand and Canada he would find
it was very small indeed. His competitor, the New Zealand
Company, had worked up that trade and was running ships
which made 16 and 17 knots, while his could only make 11.

Speaking on 11th April,

Mr. Sinclair continued that the ships built by the Munitions
Board were just as good for the purposes of the War as the
ships built by the Government of Canada. When those ships
were finished they were turned over to the British Admiralty,
just the same as ships built by the Canadian Government
would also be turned over to the British Government for use in
the War. The Minister had put the shipping of Canada back
a decade by his so-called policy.

West Indian Trade.

The Minister of Marine and Fisheries stated that any man
who was familiar with the transportation to the West Indies
knew that the trade of those Islands was in the hands of their
American friends. The South American trade had also been
in their hands. The exports of Canada to the British West
Indian Islands—Bermuda, British Guiana and British Honduras

-in 1913 amounted to $4,967,312, but in 1920 they had increased to $15,257,014. That was what the Government ships had done in expanding trade between Canada and the British West Indies.

No one found fault with the Emergency Fleet programme which their neighbour to the south carried on. Think of the enormous shrinkage in the value both on steel and wooden ships that the Mother Country had to face. During the War Australia built just as large a mercantile fleet of steel ships as Canada did. He had read, as no doubt other hon. gentlemen had, the JOURNAL OF THE PARLIAMENTS OF THE EMPIRE, which gives a short synopsis of the Debates in the Mother of Parliaments and in all the other Parliaments of the British Empire; but he had not read a word of criticism in any of those Parliaments in respect to the great shrinkage of the value of their ships.

No country knew better how to expand her trade than the tight little island of Great Britain, and Cromwell's Navigation Act laid down the principle that imports into the United Kingdom should be in British bottoms only, and that three-fourths of the crew should be British subjects. That was the way England started to secure the supremacy of the seas. What did Germany do in 1870 ? She subsidised steel ship-building and gave preferential rates over her railways for cargoes to be carried in German bottoms. Therefore if Canada should lose a few million dollars a year he would conceive it to be a good policy for them to have built these ships and to continue to operate them. They heard a lot about Canada being a nation. Show him a nation in the world to-day that was not a maritime nation. It was high time that Canada owned her own mercantile fleet and assumed her place among the maritime nations of the world.

After further discussion a motion by the Minister of Finance (Hon. Sir Henry Drayton) to the effect that a sum not exceeding $8,330,000 should be placed at the disposal of His Majesty for a Government shipbuilding programme was passed on 13th April by 103 to 79 votes.

MILITIA ESTIMATES.

Various items of the Militia Estimates were discussed by the House in Committee of Supply on 18th and 19th April, 1921.

DEBATE IN HOUSE OF COMMONS.

Speaking on 18th April,

The Minister of Militia and Defence (Hon. Hugh Guthrie) stated that the permanent force comprised 3,865 men and

K 2

447 officers. During the War authority was granted by statute to increase the permanent force up to 10,000. It was never found necessary to do so, but it was informally agreed that it might be increased to 5,000. However, after giving the matter very full consideration, they thought it would be just as well to keep below the 4,000 mark, and recruiting for the time being had been with the idea of not exceeding that figure. Their militia regiments during the present spring were recruiting splendidly. They did not anticipate that they would train them this year at full strength, because they were not asking for a Vote sufficient for that purpose. But there was something like the old militia spirit being re-established, and he thought by the summer the figures would approximate what they were in pre-War days.

On 19th April,

Mr. M. J. Demers (Liberal, *St. John's and Iberville, Que.*) asked what the strength of the permanent force was before the War?

Training.

The Minister of Militia replied that it was 2,970 the last year before the War. With regard to the item of $1,500,000 for annual drill, the Minister said that it would enable them to train a fairly representative proportion of the various units. In cavalry there would be twenty-three regiments at 65 per cent. of strength. They would be required to train for a period of nine days. In artillery seventy-five batteries at 80 per cent. of strength would train for six days. Infantry city corps, sixty-five battalions at 65 per cent. strength, would train for nine days. Forty battalions of rural corps would train at 65 per cent. of strength, and twenty battalions would train on the same basis as the city corps, at local headquarters or local camps, for a period of nine days. Machine guns, twenty-five batteries at 65 per cent. strength, would train for nine days.

Danger of Armaments.

Mr. A. R. McMaster (Liberal, *Brome, Que.*) thought that if any one would consider the events of the last five years he would be brought to the inevitable conclusion that the policy pursued in Europe, of one country building up vast armaments against another, only resulted in the wiping out of a great proportion of the youth of all the belligerent nations in Europe. Some of them wished to raise a fresh crop of young men for the next slaughter, and if the world depended in future, as it had depended in the past, on military preparation

MILITIA ESTIMATES. **835**

or security war would come. There was no danger in the direction of their northern frontier. Their neighbours to the south were bound to them by ties of language, custom, law and relationship. Surely there was an opportunity for Canada to lead the way to reduction of armaments and military expenditure.

Mr. J. W. Edwards (Nat. Lib. and Con., *Frontenac, Ont.***)** declared that if Great Britain had been prepared as Lord Roberts would have had her prepared in 1914, and had their great neighbour to the south been in a position to take an aggressive stand at the beginning of the War, the struggle would have lasted but a short time. It was the pacifists of Europe, of Great Britain, and of other countries, who were responsible more than anybody else for the great slaughter that took place during the War.

Cadet Services.

The **Minister of Militia**, speaking on the item of $450,000 for cadet services, said that it was proposed to provide for the instruction of 85,000 cadets, their being almost that number at the present time enrolled in Canada.

The Hon. S. C. Mewburn (Nat. Lib. and Con., *Hamilton, E. Riding, Ont.***)** said his great regret was that the appropriation was not double this amount, because the inauguration of the cadet service in Canada was of the greatest benefit to the country. The high school and public school cadet corps inculcated into the youth of Canada patriotism, discipline, and the benefits of physical development.

Mr. F. N. McCrea (Liberal, *Sherbrooke, Que.***)** declared that the great percentage of the men who went over to France and did the fighting had never had military training at all until they enlisted, and they made just as good soldiers as the men who had had military training.

Mr. W. A. Griesbach (Nat. Lib. and Con., *Edmonton, W. Riding, Alta.***)** stated that in the First Division the greater proportion of the non-commissioned officers and officers were men who had seen lengthy service in the Canadian Militia, and who owed their entire adaptability to the training they had received in the Militia. To suggest now that training was of no value was not only fallacious, but also detrimental to the best interests of the country which had relied in the past, as it would probably do in the future, on trained men.

Comparison with other countries.

The **Minister of Militia** said he wanted to show that he had been reasonable. He thought that one good way was to put

Canada side by side with almost all the other civilised countries
This was the proposal :· for this year the military expenditure
proposed in these Estimates was $11,890,000, the naval
expenditure $3,726,980, and the air expenditure, including
civil aviation, $1,625,000, making a total for defence purpose
of $17,241,000, or $2.15 per head for the people of Canada
In Australia the average was $6.13 per head. In New Zealand
it was $5.82 per head. The amount in Great Britain was
$22.36 per head, and in the United States $13.13. They had
cut down the expenditure to the lowest margin of safety.

    Mr. Peter McGibbon (Nat. Lib. and Con., *Muskoka, Ont.*
asked where the British Empire would be to-day had it not
been for the trained troops of France who stood in the gap
in France and Flanders while the British Empire was getting
ready. They should get back to some sanity on this question
Canada, like every other country, must be prepared to defend
herself.

    Mr. F. S. Cahill (Liberal, *Pontiac, Que.*) asked, as regarded
expenditure in the United States, what amount was for
military purposes, as apart from naval expenditure ?

    The Minister of Militia : " These are the figures of the
last Congress : Military, $639,275,503 ; naval, $644,515,731
air, $95,000,000 ; total, $1,378,791,234. That was the ex
penditure of the National Government, but in addition to
that there was a very heavy expenditure by the States them
selves on the National Guards which were maintained in each
State.

AIR BOARD ESTIMATES.

(Progress of Civil Aviation.)

    On 23rd May the House in Committee of Supply discussed
the following items : —

    THE AIR BOARD.—Salaries, $75,000 ; Contingencies, $25,000
Civil Aviation, $700,000 ; Canadian Air Force, $825,000.

DEBATE IN HOUSE OF COMMONS.

    The Minister of Militia and Defence (Hon. Hugh Guthrie
stated that an Air Board was established by legislation in the
Spring of 1920. Last year was practically the first yea
of their operations and was largely taken up with the work
of organisation. The four items which appeared in this estimate
fairly represented the work of the Board and the expenditure

of the money. Last year they accomplished considerable work in what might be called research or exploration. The Board had established Provincial Boards throughout the Dominion, the presiding officer of these Provincial Boards being the Lieutenant-Governor of the Province. The Provincial Board met periodically and discussed the situation in regard to its own province and made recommendations to the Government. Several Provinces had agreed with the Air Board to share half the expense of all flying operations undertaken within their territory.

Survey.

The Board did a lot of valuable work last year in the Province of Quebec. It surveyed all the northern part of Quebec from Lake Saint John for a distance of 250 miles north, and he believed that the results obtained in two weeks' flying operations were far better than the work accomplished during five years of progress on the land. Air photographs had been taken of that territory showing the location of the lakes, the rivers, and the timber areas—the photographs being distinct enough to show the burnt timber and to distinguish hard from soft wood. In many cases also they showed whether the streams were navigable or not. In British Columbia they did fire ranging. In Alberta something was being done in the exploration of the northern territory. It was hoped that during the coming season the air service would be of the greatest assistance in connection with the surveys of oil lands, etc. In addition, an air line had been mapped out across the Continent, and certain landing stations had been erected, but the policy had not been to establish such stations at the expense of the Dominion ; the municipalities desiring landing stations must establish them ; the Board located them and left it to the municipalities to decide whether they wanted landing stations established at those places.

They received a very large number of aircraft from the British Government at the conclusion of the War ; he anticipated that there would have to be an appropriation for new aircraft. They were practically operating now with machines given them.

Anti-smuggling operations.

He supposed as time went on the usefulness of the airship* would be demonstrated. Only a few days ago they were

---

* Throughout the debate the word " airship " was used to imply heavier-than-air craft.

asked to act for the Government of the Dominion in connection with Customs examinations at Victoria and Vancouver.
There had been a good deal of smuggling of drugs into Vancouver and Victoria, these drugs being dropped from incoming
ships into the ocean and picked up by smaller vessels; aircraft
would be very satisfactorily used not only in the detection
of such operations, but also in their prevention. Since their
airships had taken part in the work of prevention that class of
smuggling had largely ceased.

In answer to a question by Mr. Lemieux on the commercial
value of aviation, the Minister said that there was no question
as to its being successful as a system of transportation, but it
was practically prohibitive up to the present time on account
of the cost.

Mr. A. R. McMaster (Liberal, *Brome, Que.*) declared that
the country could not afford this experimenting with civil
aviation.

The Minister of Militia thought that now that they had
started it would be unwise to stop at this time. He believed
that in civil aviation the results already obtained justified
the expenditure. Last autumn fires, which might have cost
them several millions of dollars, were located through these
civil air operations and promptly extinguished.

Service and Civil Aviation.

Mr. I. E. Pedlow (Liberal, *Renfrew, S. Riding, Ont.*) asked
what service the Canadian Air Force rendered to the country.

The Minister of Militia replied that they could not maintain a military or naval system of any kind if they had not an
air force in connection with it. The late War demonstrated
that it was absolutely impossible to operate troops without
an air service. All scouting was done by the air service now;
all artillery work was directed by the air service, as well as all
movements of troops.

Mr. Pedlow asked if it was not possible that either one
of these branches might be dispensed with entirely and the
training necessary in case of emergency made available through
one of these two services.

The Minister of Militia replied that he did not think
that would work out satisfactorily. The Civil Aviation Branch
had charge of the training of all airmen, the granting of
certificates and the prescribing of all flying conditions.
Regulations were passed prescribing the law under which all
flying was done in Canada. Just at the moment there was an
anomaly in the conditions between Canada and the United
States. Canada having become a member of the League of
Nations was bound by certain general regulations applicable

to all nations which became parties to the Covenant. In the meantime, they were providing their own regulations and had notified the United States authorities that their machines flying over Canada must comply with Canadian requirements, notwithstanding the fact that the United States had not become a member of the League of Nations.

Mr. Pedlow : " To what extent is Canada bound in this matter by her membership in the League of Nations ? "

The Minister of Militia : " Canada has given her assent as a signatory to the Covenant of the League of Nations to certain general rules applicable to all members of the League and not applicable, of course, to the United States, which has not become a member."

Mr. W. D. Euler (Liberal, *Waterloo, N. Riding, Ont.*) : :" Is there any co-operation between the two branches of the service ? "

The Minister of Militia : " They are kept separate but one Board presides over them both. Their duties are, of course, separate ; one is purely military and naval."

Mr. William Duff (Liberal, *Lunenburg, N.S.*) thought it was an absolute waste of money to have a seaplane station at Halifax.

The Minister of Militia said that the naval service nowadays must have as an adjunct a seaplane service, and the best place for that on the eastern coast they considered to be at Halifax, and on the west coast in British Columbia.. These were their two seaplane stations.

After further discussion the items were agreed to.

IMPERIAL MINERAL RESOURCES BUREAU.

The following item was discussed on 3rd June by the House in Committee of Supply : —

Miscellaneous—grant to Imperial Mineral Resources Bureau, $12,166.67.

DEBATE IN HOUSE OF COMMONS.

The Minister of Agriculture (Hon. S. F. Tolmie) said that the establishment of this Bureau was discussed at the Imperial War Conference held in London in 1917, and a committee appointed to report on it. This committee subsequently reported favourably on the project ; the organisation of the Bureau was proceeded with and was now practically completed. The expenses of the bureau during the organisation period were met by the British Government and they purposed contributing the sum of £10,000 annually to its upkeep, the Dominions being expected to contribute an equal amount. The contributions for 1920 were as follows : —

	£
Imperial Government	10,000
Government of the Dominion of Canada	2,500
Commonwealth of Australia	2,000
Government of India	2,000
Government of New Zealand	1,000
Government of Newfoundland	250

(The remainder of the contributions was divided among the Crown Colonies and Protectorates and the National Federation of Iron and Steel Manufacturers.)

The functions of the bureau were to collect, co-ordinate and disseminate information as to the resources, production, treatment, consumption and requirements of every mineral and metal ; to ascertain the scope of existing agencies with a view ultimately to avoid any unnecessary overlapping that might prevail ; to devise means whereby existing agencies could, if necessary, be assisted and improved in the accomplishment of their respective tasks ; to supplement these agencies if necessary in order to obtain any information not now collected which might be required for the purpose of the Bureau ; to advise on the development of the mineral resources of the Empire and of all particular parts thereof in order that such resources might be made available for the purposes of Imperial defence, of industry or commerce. The Bureau was controlled by a board of governors representing all portions of the British Empire. Already a considerable number of bulletins had been issued covering particularly metals or minerals, such as nickel, zinc, manganese, copper and cobalt. These dealt with occurrences throughout the world, the production and condition of the industry, also the extent to which they were dependent or independent on foreign sources of supply. The Bureau was also building up a file in which would be tabulated information regarding the mineral resources of the various portions of the British Empire, and that would be extended to cover the world. This file was of service to them since it had already been the cause of a number of inquiries from firms in Great Britain wishing to obtain minerals in Canada.

Mr. F. S. Cahill (Liberal, *Pontiac, Que.*) said that he wished to protest against the continuation of this Bureau as an outgrowth of the Imperial War Cabinet. The people of Canada had not passed on any Imperial Cabinet, and until they did they were getting ahead of themselves when they undertook to organise bureaux under the authority of an Imperial Cabinet, whether war or otherwise. During the War the Imperial Cabinet, no doubt, had some grounds for its existence and authority, but it certainly had no authority from the Canadian people to organise a bureau under an imperial understanding. This Vote should be cancelled at the earliest possible opportunity, or, at least, the name should be changed. If it were found necessary to co-operate with the other countries of the Empire, that might be advisable, but certainly they in Canada did not wish to be bound by any Imperial Cabinet at this time. The quicker the Minister and the Government cancelled these arrangements, the better it would be for the Canadian people.

The Hon. W. S. Fielding (Liberal, *Shelburne and Queen's, N.S.*) : " There is or was in London an institute known as the Imperial Institute to which Canada contributed a large sum. I do not see any reference to it in this appropriation. Is it possible that this appropriation takes the place of the appropriation for the Imperial Institute, or are they separate organisations ? "

Mr. A. R. McMaster (Liberal, *Brome, Que.*) : " They are separate."

Mr. Fielding : " We still have the Imperial Institute ? "

Mr. McMaster : " Yes."

Mr. Fielding : " And give a grant to it ? "

Mr. McMaster said that was so. This seemed to be a case of duplication. They had their Department of Mines, their Geological Survey, which had been manned in the past by men of great ability, and amongst whose personnel at the present time were found a number of men of great ability. He was afraid that this was a duplication. They had no money to spend on duplications, and on that ground it would be well to drop the Vote.

The item was agreed to.

RIGHT OF MINISTERS TO SIT IN EITHER CHAMBER.

(Senate Reform.)

On 21st March, 1921, the Hon. Rodolphe Lemieux moved the following resolution in the House of Commons :—

> " That, in the opinion of this House, it is in the interest of good government that Ministers of the Crown should be permitted to sit in either Chamber, whenever measures and policies are introduced affecting their respective departments."

DEBATE IN HOUSE OF COMMONS.

The Hon. Rodolphe Lemieux (Liberal, *Maisonneuve and Gaspé, Que.*) said that he brought the resolution forward with a view to expediting the business of the House, believing it to be worthy of adoption by Parliament. No doubt their Upper Chamber might with advantage be reformed in certain respects, but he was confident that he was right when he asserted that the mass of the people were in favour of the continuance of the bi-cameral system. He was in favour of an Upper Chamber, first, because it was instituted for the protection of minorities in their Confederation; second, because the representatives of certain of the provinces which united to form the Dominion feared that the predominance of the larger provinces in Parliament might perhaps prejudice the interests of the smaller provinces, and· they therefore insisted on the establishment of an Upper Chamber; and, third, because he had an ingrained respect for the pact of Confederation itself. Much as the Upper Chamber might be criticised, he believed that on many occasions it had given evidence of real independence of thought and action. He did not say there was no room for Senate reform. He believed there should be an age limit. He had always thought that the election of Senators might in itself be a very good reform—election by Legislatures, boards of trade, universities, and such public bodies.

Ministers in the Senate.

They could not afford to allow the Upper Chamber to be without representatives of the Government; they must face the situation that there would always be at least a leader representing the Government in that body, and there might be occasions when it would be necessary to have Cabinet Ministers in the Senate. He did think, however, that mostly all Cabinet Ministers should occupy seats in the popular Chamber and that the less there were in the Upper Chamber the better for the Government and the better for Canada. It was to be hoped that the Government, whether Liberal, Conservative or Agrarian, would always see to it that Ministers in charge of spending departments sat in the popular Chamber. In England· they had the time-honoured House of Lords; several Ministers of the Crown sat in that Chamber. There had been cases where even the Prime Minister sat in the Upper Chamber. · But in all those cases, which were probably exceptional cases, the Government was represented in the popular Chamber by most brilliant and distinguished men who really carried public opinion with them. He believed that in England the time had gone by when Prime Ministers should sit in the Upper Chamber.

But he did not see why a Minister sitting in the Upper Chamber should be debarred from appearing in the other Chamber, without having a right to vote, to explain the policies of his department and to answer questions when the Estimates of his department were scrutinised in the House. Nor did he see why the gentlemen who occupied the Government benches in the House of Commons should not be allowed to appear in the Upper Chamber to give such explanations as might be required of them. The system which he was now propounding was the system followed in France. It was simply common sense that Ministers of the Crown in Canada should have the right that when a policy was presented to the House if the Minister who had prepared and initiated that policy sat in the other Chamber he should be prepared to explain that policy to members of the House of Commons, to answer questions, to accept amendments.

At the present time, three Ministers of the Crown had seats in the Upper Chamber—the Minister of the Interior, the Minister of Labour and the Postmaster-General. The Minister of Labour was essentially a representative of the people. Last year, when the Leader of the Government (the Right Hon. Arthur Meighen) was in charge of a Bill affecting the Labour Department, he had to report progress on two or three different occasions because he was not sufficiently informed on the matter. That was a case which he thought all would admit showed the necessity, if the Minister of Labour had not a seat in the House of Commons, of an amendment to their rules so that he would be in a position when legislation affecting his department was before the House to come and explain his policies to the House. If the resolution was adopted, it would be an' object lesson that in Canada they were in accord with the principles of responsible government.

Money Votes.

The Prime Minister (the Right Hon. Arthur Meighen), referring to a debate in the Senate in 1908, said there was manifest at that time a regret that there were not more of the Ministers of the Crown in the Upper Chamber, and that more legislation did not initiate there. In so far as the spending of money was concerned that all came before the Commons, and the Commons alone. The Commons must vote each and every individual item, and, therefore, in that regard the power of consideration and criticism was vested in that assembly and its opportunity for that was ample.

It seemed to him that while they had the bi-cameral system there must be a number of Ministers in the Upper Chamber, or the Upper Chamber could not serve even that share of the public duties which it now served. He could see a very great deal of advantage indeed in having such a system as the hon. gentleman (Mr. Lemieux) urged. On the other hand, there was very much to be considered before they launched definitely on such a scheme. For example, if a Minister of the Crown in the Senate was to be allowed to come to the Commons to speak in relation to his own Estimates, but not to make a motion or to vote, he virtually could not conduct his Estimates through that House at all, because every discussion in the passage of Estimates arose on a motion that a certain Vote appearing in the Estimates be made by that House. It would seem to him that if they went a certain length they must go all the way, and they must admit that a Minister in either House could speak in the other House in relation to any subject that he desired to discuss. Was it within the power of the House of Commons by resolution to enable a Member of the Upper House to come and take his seat among them ? Must it not be done by amendment to the constitution itself ? And if that was the proper procedure, then an address from both Houses to the British Parliament would of course be the appropriate action leading to that end.

The Hon. A. K. Maclean (Nat. Lib. and Con., Halifax, N.S.) said that the practice of having as few members of the Government as possible holding seats in the Senate had always been adhered to and he thought it reflected the spirit of their Constitution. It was utterly impossible to expect one member of the Government to handle in the Senate all the Government business originating in the House of Commons. It did seem to him, therefore, quite a rational suggestion that Members of the House of Commons who were members of the Government should have the privilege of going to the Senate and there taking direction of Government legislation. It might be asked why he should not go further and say that members of the Government holding seats in the Senate should be enabled to come to this Chamber. He thought, if that were permitted, abuses might very easily creep into parliamentary practice. For instance, if a Government was very weak it might have the major portion of its membership in the Senate, contrary to the spirit of the constitution and probably against the wishes of the people. There usually were sufficient members of the Government in this Chamber to handle expeditiously the Government business, whereas that condition might not always prevail in the Senate.

Bi-Cameral System.

The Minister of Justice (the Right Hon. C. J. Doherty) thought that the proposal involved a fundamental change in their system of government and really in the British Constitution. Their parliamentary system was based upon the conception of the existence of two distinct bodies deriving their authority from two totally different sources. They had the people's Chamber, and then they had the other Chamber which did not derive its authority directly from the people, which under their system was composed of nominees of the Crown. Resulting from the different sources from which these two bodies derived their authority, there had grown up a system under which particular things belonged specially to these two bodies. The voting of money belonged to the popular Chamber. Could they conceive of this popular assembly being guided in a matter pertaining to the voting of the people's money by a gentleman who was not a representative of the people at all, whose *rôle* in the parliamentary work of the country was to act as a member of a body constituted to exercise a species of supervising and moderating influence upon the action of the popular chamber ?

Mr. W. D. Euler (Liberal, *Waterloo, N. Riding, Ont.*) said that he would attain the result that the hon. Member for Maisonneuve (Mr. Lemieux) desired not by bringing members of the Cabinet who were Senators into the House of Commons, but by ensuring that all members of the Cabinet were members of that House. To some extent, their Senate corresponded with the British House of Lords, but only two Sessions ago they decided that they were not in favour of hereditary titles. So they were not bound by the British practice in that case in any sense whatever.

The League of Nations embodied certain principles in connection with labour matters that would be of direct interest to them—unemployment insurance, old age pensions, the eight-hour day, equal pay for equal work, abolition of child labour—and if Canada was going to live up to her position in the League, they were in duty bound to deal with these subjects. But could they do so to the best advantage if the man directly in charge of labour matters in Canada had not the privilege of coming into the House of Commons ? Personally, he believed that the Senate might be abolished, but so long as they had the two Chambers he would say, let them have one or two members of the Senate in the Cabinet, but not holding portfolios.

Election of Senators.

Mr. F. B. Stacey (Nat. Lib. and Con., *Fraser Valley, B.C.*) believed that the Senate should represent the people rather than the Government of any day. The Senate should be appointed for a stated time, not, perhaps, for such a short period as four or five years, but for a longer specified time ; and they should be responsible to, and be elected by, the people. If that were done, the principle involved in the resolution would not perhaps present insuperable difficulties.

The Hon. W. L. Mackenzie King (Leader of the Opposition) asked whether it was not conceivable that some plan might be devised whereby a Minister who had a seat in the other Chamber might be permitted at least to sit beside the Minister in the House of Commons who was giving information to Parliament in regard to the subject under discussion. It was information that they had been seeking from that side of the House and which they were getting in less and less measure from hon. gentlemen opposite. It was to remedy that tendency that his hon. friend had made this suggestion which was embodied in the resolution.

Mr. Lucien Cannon (Liberal, *Dorchester, Que.*) thought that if the Senators were given the privilege of discussing openly with the Ministers elected by the people matters of legislation, the Senate would then have as much importance in the country as the House of Commons now had, and he thought that would be a great danger. A solution might lie in a middle course. They might adopt the system which was followed in England. When Ministers of the different departments were members of the House of Lords, under-secretaries represented them in the House of Commons and acted as the representatives of those departments in giving information or discussing legislation connected therewith.

Constitutional Amendments.

. The Prime Minister had asked how this change, if it were to be introduced, would be put into effect. This brought him to the subject of their powers to amend the Constitution He regretted that this question had not been more fully discussed in Parliament. He hoped before the Prime Minister left for London to meet the Prime Ministers of the other overseas Dominions opportunity would be given to the House to discuss it. Should they in future do as they had done in the past,—apply to the British Parliament—, or should they take upon themselves the power of amending their Constitution the same way that other Dominions had assumed that power?

After further discussion the motion was withdrawn.

MINISTERS AND DIRECTORSHIPS.

On 24th February, 1921, a Bill was introduced in the House of Commons by Mr. A. R. McMaster to amend the Senate and House of Commons Act so as to prohibit Ministers of the Crown from acting as directors of incorporated companies.

DEBATE IN HOUSE OF COMMONS.

Mr. A. R. McMaster (Liberal, *Brome, Que.*), explaining the Bill at its Second Reading on 4th March, said that its object was to make it incumbent upon Ministers of the Crown to resign all directorships which they held in incorporated companies when they accepted their portfolios. When Sir Robert Borden, the former Premier, accepted office in 1911 he resigned all directorships which he held, and encouraged all his colleagues to do so. The abandonment of directorships by Ministers of the Crown was in line with the best British practice. No man who was a Minister of the Crown in Canada had any time left to fulfil the duties of a director. There was always a possibility of undesirable things happening when a man was put in two conflicting positions. Where Ministers of the Crown were directors of companies there was one fiduciary interest set up in opposition to another fiduciary interest; as Ministers they were trustees for the whole people; and as directors they were trustees for the shareholders of the company. He knew that the only directorship which Sir Wilfrid Laurier ever accepted was in a mutual life insurance company. Therefore he was asking the Government to accept legislation that would merely crystallise in the form of a Statute the best prevailing practice. It might be said that they should leave this matter to the individual feeling of delicacy and propriety of the Ministers themselves. That had not been done in regard to senators and members. Under the Senate and House of Commons Act, their obligation to refrain from bringing before the House legislation in which they were interested as lawyers, for instance, was very clearly set forth, and their inability to have an interest in a contract with the Government was also very clearly set forth.

The Hon. Sir Edward Kemp (Nat. Lib. and Con., *Toronto East, Ont.*) pointed to the case of a man who publicly had his name on his letter-head or bill-head as the director of the company in which he was interested; he then became a member of a Government, and he removed his name as director; but practically his position was the same as it was before; he did not sell out, he could not dispossess himself; it was not likely that he would sacrifice his rights, and yet he might be of great service to the Government of whatever Party it might be. The men whose names appeared as directors of corporations were generally understood to be men who, in most cases, had wider experience in their country's affairs than other men, and consequently they would be more useful to Canada.

The Hon. Rodolphe Lemieux (Liberal, *Maisonneuve and Gaspé, Que.*) recalled that some years ago Parliament amended

the Judicature Act to provide that judges who had bee
appointed directors and were drawing directors' fees in join
stock companies must resign. There was a great princip
involved in this matter, and it was that the public must hav
absolute confidence in the integrity of those who administere
the law. Ministers of the Crown made the law. They decide
long beforehand what laws should be introduced, and therefor
it seemed to him that they had an equal, if not greater, respons
bility than the judges themselves. Public opinion should b
satisfied that they had no monetary interest which migh
conflict with their duty as Ministers of the Crown. Was no
the honour of being a Minister of the Crown, the honour c
being sworn in as a Privy Councillor, a reward by itself? N
man should hesitate, when accepting that honour, to pu
aside his private interests. In the Old Country of late ther
had been a hue and cry in the public Press and elsewhere agains
members of the House of Lords, Ministers of the Crown—an
that was not done very often with Ministers of the Crown—
lending their names as promoters of companies or director
of boards.

Mr. F.ʾ H. Keefer (Nat. Lib. and Con., *Port Arthur an
Kenora, Ont.*) thought the public were well protected by th
Independence of Parliament Act, Chapter 10. There it lai
down most specifically, in Section 14, that no person, directl
or indirectly, should be allowed to have any interests in an
contract or agreement, either through trustee or otherwise
if he was a Member of Parliament.

Speaking on 8th March,

Mr. H. H. Stevens (Nat. Lib. and Con., *Vancouver Centr
B.C.*) said he had not been able to find any record showing tha
Ministers of the Crown in the past had in any sense violate
the ethics or the privileges of their office in the way sough
to be remedied by the Bill. They might prevent a man wh
holds a directorship in a company from being a Minister c
the Crown or compel him to resign his directorship, but the
did not change his position as an individual, as a member c
the company, towards the Government in the slightest degree
because it stood to reason that it would certainly obtain tha
while a man might conform with the technical requirements c
the law, he would not necessarily conform with its spirit
He might resign his directorship but retain his shares, and b
in exactly the same position as he was before. It wa
desirable, he thought, that they should have in the Hous
representative citizens from every walk of life. They ofte
heard the statement made that they ought to have mor
business men holding public office, civic, Provincial an
Dominion. He did not recall any Statute of this character, o

any stated rule of this kind, set forth in any of the great authorities, Bourinot, May, or any other, as a desirable thing.

The Minister of Marine and Fisheries (Hon. C. C. Ballantyne) said that judging from the political history of Canada and other countries it was a rare thing to find a business man who had succeeded in commerce or in finance either a Member of the popular Chamber or a member of any particular Cabinet. But if the State did call that man, he must place the duties of his public office before his business interests, and henceforward devote all his attention to the administration of those public affairs to which he had been called. If one were to do what the hon. Member for Brome wished, he would have to throw all his stock holdings in various companies on the market, and take what he could get for them, and resign from all these boards. A business man would be most unwise to dispose of all his holdings and resign from all the boards on which he sat as a director in order to accept a passing honour in any particular Government that might last for only a few years. Such small legislation as this was only going to have the effect of still further discouraging business men from entering Parliament or the Government.

Mr. Lucien Cannon (Liberal, *Dorchester, Que.*) asked whether, should the tariff policy be discussed around the Council table, if the Minister of Marine was a director of several companies, and if those companies were interested in the drafting of the tariff schedules, the Minister would think of the interests of Canada first, or would he think of the interests of his business associates? A gentleman who entered the Cabinet should make his investments in such a way that neither his investments nor his business associations would interfere with his conduct of public business.

Practice in the United Kingdom.

Mr. Michael Clark (National Progressive, *Red Deer, Alta.*) preferred to see a matter of this kind settled by the good sense, discretion and high-mindedness of men in public life, rather than by the strong arm of the law. He was not aware of what the law was in the Old Country, but he knew what was the very general practice there. When Sir Henry Campbell-Bannerman made Lord Grey his Foreign Secretary, the latter did not need any law ; he was at that time chairman of the directors of the North-Eastern Railway Company, which position carried with it a salary of £5,000 a year, and he at once, of his own initiative, gave up the chairmanship. The Old Country had had for centuries large numbers of leisured people, with abundant private income, who devoted themselves

L 2

very largely to public affairs. Canada was a younge
country, and they had not that leisured class up to the presen
moment in their national history. At the same time, the soone
they followed the example of the Old Country in that respect
the better.

The Prime Minister (the Right Hon. Arthur Meighen
stated that there was no other country which he knew o
where legislation of this kind was in effect. He did no
believe it was in effect in England. The practice might be i
effect there of resigning directorships upon accession t
Cabinet position more than it was in Canada, but he though
he was safe in saying that that practice was by no mean
universal in England right up to the present time. Govern
ments now existing and Governments that had existed, bot
in federal and provincial affairs, had retained within thei
number men who still were directors of companies. Ther
might come a time when the occupation of high Governmen
office became inconsistent with the retention of directorship
or with fiduciary relations to others, but he did not think it
advent could be settled by legislation or that the severanc
could be enforced by Statute. Sir Thomas White, who occupie
the position of Minister of Finance prior to the present Ministe
(Sir Henry Drayton)—and so far as he knew that was true o
the present Minister—resigned his directorship of all the con
panies he was in. He did that because of the belief that in th
actual administration of his public office he came into too dire
contact with the interests in respect of which he was respons
ble as a director. He (Mr. Meighen) believed that in their ow
country public men of both parties on attaining office could b
depended upon, that if the relationship was so close that th
administration of their office might be open to influence, the
would drop the private interest in deference to the imperativ
demands of public welfare. He did not know where one wa
to put one's money if it was in a Canadian company—or eve
if it was in an American company—so that it would be in suc
a position as not to be affected by any act of the Governmer
of Canada or of Parliament. If they carried the attempt ma
by this legislation to the extent of the whole principle involve
they would have to go further and enact that members
Parliament should do the same, because in the end it wa
Parliament that determined the legislation and not th
Government at all.

The Hon. Thomas Crerar (Leader of the National Progressi
Party) said that before accepting office he discussed the matt
with Sir Robert Borden, who was then Prime Minister, an
as far as his own business relations were concerned it wa
clearly understood that his time was to be entirely free fro
them. He considered it was his duty to resign his directorshi

and he did so. The best approach to a solution of this question came through a high-minded sense of public duty.

After further discussion the motion for the Second Reading was negatived by 105 to 54 votes.

PROPORTIONAL REPRESENTATION.

On 4th April, 1921, the House of Commons discussed the following resolution moved by Mr. J. A. Sexsmith :—

"That in the opinion of this House in order to give each voter an equal share in the representation, some system of proportional representation should be adopted, and that a special committee of this House should be forthwith appointed, charged with an inquiry into the different systems of proportional representation, with a view to recommend one of these for adoption."

DEBATE IN HOUSE OF COMMONS.

Mr. J. A. Sexsmith (Nat. Lib. and Con., *Peterborough, E. Riding, Ont.*) stated that to-day every country in the world that had responsible government and an electoral system such as they had in Canada was seriously discussing proportional representation. He sincerely hoped that something might be done in order that they might secure in Canada a better electoral system than they had at present. The chief evil of their present system was that large and important sections of opinion were left unrepresented, and the end of all political reform should be to secure to these important sections their due and fair share of representation in the House. In the Province of Quebec, for instance, in the General Election of 1900, fifty-seven Liberals and eight Conservatives were elected. The fifty-seven Liberals secured 88,566 votes, and the eight Conservatives 103,253. The average number of votes required to elect one Conservative was 12,907, while the average number of votes to elect one Liberal was 2,344. Thus, one Liberal had the value of six Conservative votes. Under proportional representation thirty-seven Liberals would have been elected instead of fifty-seven and twenty-eight Conservatives instead of eight. Any electoral system that allowed such a condition to prevail where it was impossible to elect a Parliament that would properly reflect the opinion of all the people, which was one of the main principles of responsible government, could not possibly make for the welfare of their country, and he believed it was the duty of Parliament, which was about to make a new redistribution of seats, to see that such a condition should

no longer prevail. They found in Great Britain during the
General Election of 1874—and these were the reasons that
Mr. Balfour and many other British statesmen were looking
very seriously at the present system, which was absolutely
unfair—the Conservatives had a majority of 50 in Parliament,
although the Liberal vote polled was 1,400,000 against a total
Conservative vote of 1,200,000. In the election of 1904,
in Nova Scotia, 46,000 electors did not secure one representative,
although they had within 10,000 of half the vote.

The spirit of democracy required that an equal share of
representation should be given to each separate elector, and
not that the direction of government should be entrusted
exclusively to one class or Party. The franchise had been
extended until, at present, almost every adult in the British
Empire had the vote. Yet the people had been unable to
control government sufficiently to see that the different
elements of the nation had a fair and equal share in the councils
of the country.

Remedy for unrest.

If the Farmers' Party of to-day aimed at becoming sole
governors of the country he could not endorse such an ideal.
If, in the past, the people from the urban centres had been
governing, that was no reason or excuse for the farmers now
to say that because they had perhaps a majority of votes
they would retaliate and elect a Government to run the
country, and that the people of the cities and towns would have
to submit. If he had his way, he would dispense with all
Parties. They were living in a democratic age, but a time of
unrest. On the one hand they found unusual concentration
of wealth in the control of a few ; on the other, a growing
restlessness and frantic attempts at organisation on the part
of the wage-earning class. He believed that the remedy lay
in the adoption of a proportional representation system at
elections. He agreed with Colonel Amery when he expressed
the belief that had proportional representation been adopted
forty years ago in the British Isles a solution might have
been found of the Irish problem.

Mr. Levi Thomson (National Progressive, Qu'Appelle
Sask.) thought that extremists must be fairly numerous before
they could get representation in the House even under the
most democratic plan of proportional representation, but if
extremists in any particular line were sufficiently numerous
to obtain representation in the House under that plan, he
believed it was for the benefit of the country that they should
come there and air their views in a place where these views
could be properly met.

The Manitoba Experiment.

He believed that they should arrange that in all their cities, at least in those which were entitled to more than one representative, the constituencies should be grouped together and each elector should only have one first vote, being entitled to give second and further choices, where necessary, to other candidates. This would enable any group of people to obtain representation, provided they were sufficiently strong to be entitled to representation. In the last local election in Manitoba provision was made for the working-out of proportional representation in the City of Winnipeg. The city was granted ten representatives. The three groups which had any large representation were Labour, Liberal and Conservative. The votes cast at first choice were 42·5 per cent. Labour, 30·4 per cent. Liberal, 13·7 per cent. Conservative and 13·4 per cent. Independent. As a result of the voting, four Labour candidates, four Liberals and two Conservatives were elected. The Independents were not elected because they were a lot of dissociated groups. A fairer result could not have been obtained amongst the Parties.

If they wished to avoid the probability of minority representatives in the House, they must adopt the principle of allowing the elector more than one choice.

The Farmers generally did not want to form an exclusive political organisation, they did not want any class rule. They had had class rule in Canada since Confederation, and they wanted to do away with that. They had a platform on which they believed that members of every class could stand. They asked for proportional representation amongst other things.

Mr. G. W. Andrews (Nat. Lib. and Con., *Winnipeg Centre, Man.*) pointed out that the system was tried in Winnipeg alone, and with this extraordinary result, that in Winnipeg they had a group of three Parties only, Labour, Liberal and Conservative, whereas in the outlying parts of the province where the old system was in force, they had a group of five, Liberal, Farmer, Conservative, Labour and Independent. As a result of the election in Manitoba there was a Bill before the Manitoba House, and it had passed its Second Reading, for the purpose of carrying out the idea of the single transferable vote in every constituency in Manitoba. This did not mean group constituencies, but if there were more than three candidates the elector would be given a first, second and third preference. It was entirely possible under their present system that they might have a House, after the next election, unless there was a change, representing about one-third of the people of Canada.

Appointment of Committee.

The Minister of Immigration and Colonisation (Hon. J. A. Calder), speaking on behalf of the Government, said that one thing that bothered him was that in the case of an election method of that kind an individual, in many cases apparently, must be voting for a principle rather than for a man. Another thing that troubled him was that he saw difficulties in adopting one principle of representation for urban communities and another for rural communities. He begged to move the following amendment :—

> " A Special Committee of the House should be appointed to consider the subject of proportional representation and the subject of the single transferable vote and the desirability of the application of one or the other, or both, to elections to the House of Commons of Canada, and to report thereon to the House. . . ."

Examples abroad.

Mr. J. J. Denis (Liberal, *Joliette*, *Que.*) pointed out that at the next General Election there would be in the field the candidates of four Parties, the Unionist Party, the Liberal Party, the Agrarian Party and the Labour Party. Taking a single constituency in which four candidates were running, each representing one of those Parties, was it not true that in many cases the successful candidate would not be the man who would represent the majority of electors ? He thought it was the duty of Parliament to change the existing law in order to give effect to the will of the electorate. Proportional representation had been given effect in over ten countries, including Galicia, Denmark, Sweden, Belgium, the Netherlands, Switzerland, two or three of the Balkan States and Brazil. Wherever the system had been given a fair trial it had never been discarded.

Mr. John Harold (Nat. Lib. and Con., *Brant, Ont.*) said he would like particularly to refer to the desirability of having the transferable vote in the single-Member constituency. The adoption of proportional representation would lead to a much better condition in such constituencies from the standpoint of fairness and honesty in elections.

The Hon. T. A. Crerar (Leader of the National Progressive Party) said he was in entire accord with the principle of proportional representation. It was a significant fact that those European countries which had adopted it were, perhaps, the most orderly countries in the world, and were amongst those subject to the least political disturbance. In 1916 the British House of Commons arranged for a Speaker's conference to consider this among other matters of reform in their electoral system, and that Speaker's conference, composed of the most representative men in the British House of Commons, brought in an unanimous report in favour of the application of proportional representation in the conduct of elections in the United Kingdom.

Mr. W. F. Cockshutt (Nat. Lib. and Con., *Brantford, Ont.*) took the ground that proportional representation was entirely unsuitable to the British system of government, which was that the majority of the people should rule. Proportional representation was a help to group and class systems, both of which were most undesirable to be introduced into Canada.

Mr. A. R. McMaster (Liberal, *Brome, Que.*) said that, during the last few years, the single-seat system had tended to over-emphasise the Liberal representation of Quebec and the Conservative representation of Ontario. Anything that caused the Canadian people to divide on religious, or racial, or sectional lines was a great mistake.

A different method of Government.

Mr. Michael Steele (Nat. Lib. and Con., *Perth, S. Riding, Ont.*) believed that the fact was lost sight of that they were endeavouring to substitute not only a different method of conducting elections, but also, unconsciously, perhaps, a different method of government for what had been the practice in the British Empire for many years. Proportional representation was not perfect, as was evident from the fact that there were 257 varieties of it, and none of them was entirely satisfactory. Where Parliament and the Government must govern, it seemed to him that it was absolutely necessary that the Government should have a good strong majority so that they might not be dependent on any clique or group for their support. You could not elect a Member under the proportional representation system by a majority vote. The number of votes required to elect a Member in each of the constituencies under proportional representation was found by dividing the total number of votes passed by a number one greater than the number of representatives required ; so that any Member elected by that system must be a minority representative. Let them elect men who would support the national policy of Canada. In order to bring that about they must retain the system that they had at present. But they could not retain it if they adopted proportional representation, and if the people of each constituency divided into two, or three or four or five or six classes ; one class, perhaps, or even two classes, with their ideas on great national questions, and the balance divided up as to whether a man should be a farmer or something else, whether he should be a labouring man or something

else. The fact was that in Western Australia where they
had, he thought, the transferable vote only sixty-five per cent.
of the voters made a second choice. Disraeli said that such
schemes were "refined and fantastic schemes for the representation of the people." John Bright was opposed to the
system, and so were Gladstone and Harcourt. He was free
to admit that a system which might be very convenient for
the people of Great Britain or in the other densely populated
countries of Europe would be entirely unsuited to a sparsely
settled country like Canada.

The Hon. W. L. Mackenzie King (Leader of the Opposition)
found himself in full sympathy with the principle. What
was the system other than an endeavour to give expression to
the democratic principles of freedom and justice ? As it gave
better expression to those principles in their electoral machinery,
he, for one, strongly favoured that system.

At the end of the debate Mr. Sexsmith's motion, as
amended, and a motion by the Prime Minister (the Right
Hon. Arthur Meighen) regarding the composition of the
Committee were agreed to.

ARMISTICE DAY ACT.

An Act, introduced in the House of Commons by
Mr. H. M. Mowat (Nat. Lib. and Con., *Parkdale, Ont.*), and
assented to on 4th June, provides that throughout Canada
in each year the Monday of the week in which the eleventh day
of November occurs, being the day on which the Great War
was triumphantly concluded by an Armistice, shall be a legal
holiday and observed under the name of Armistice Day.
The holiday called Thanksgiving Day will in future be observed
on Armistice Day.

RETIREMENT OF THE GOVERNOR-GENERAL.

(Appointment of Successor.)

On 3rd June the Prime Minister seconded by the Hon. W. L.
Mackenzie King (Leader of the Opposition), moved that an
Address be presented to His Excellency the Governor-General
on his retirement from office. The Address expressed the
regret with which the country had learned of the approaching
conclusion of the Governor-General's official connection with

Canada, and referred to his unflagging zeal and devotion in the discharge of the duties devolving upon His Majesty's Representative in the Dominion during the War and the subsequent period of readjustment.

The Right Hon. Sir Robert Borden (Nat. Lib. and Con., *King's, N.S.*), speaking on the motion, said that more and more in all the Dominions the constitutional relation of the Governor-General to his Ministers had approximated to the relation of the King to the British Ministry. Especially was this true of Canada. The Duke of Devonshire was educated in public life and thus he thoroughly understood and appreciated the trend of development of constitutional relations.

The motion, in which the Senate united, was agreed to.

The Hon. Charles Murphy (Liberal, *Russell, Que.*), on 4th June, asked the Prime Minister, first, had Lord Byng been appointed Governor-General of Canada; second, if so, was the Government officially advised of the fact before the Press despatches announcing the appointment were received; third, if Lord Byng had been appointed, was the right hon. gentleman able to tell them whether his lordship had had any political or parliamentary experience apart from his military experience?

The Prime Minister (the Right Hon. Arthur Meighen) : " In answering the first question as to the appointment, I duly received information that His Majesty had been pleased to approve of the appointment of Lord Byng as Governor-General of Canada, and that the announcement would be made in the Press this morning. The answer to the second question is 'Yes.' In answer to the third question there is every reason to believe that Lord Byng has all the qualifications, including a knowledge of political matters, required for the office."

CANADIAN NATIONALS DEFINITION ACT.

This Act, a summary of which, and the discussion thereon, is given in Vol. II., No. 2, page 326, of the JOURNAL, received the Royal Assent on 3rd May, 1921.

AUSTRALIA.

Commonwealth Parliament.

The following summary is in continuation of the proceedings of the First Session of the Eighth Parliament, which commenced on 26th February, 1920, adjourned on 26th November, and reassembled on 6th April, 1921.

For summaries of proceedings in the earlier part of the Session, vide Vol. I., Nos. 3 and 4, and Vol. II., Nos. 1 and 2.

WASHINGTON CONFERENCE.

(Imperial Conference: Limitation of Armaments: Anglo-Japanese Treaty: Representation in Foreign Affairs: League of Nations, etc.)

The Hon. T. J. Ryan* (Deputy Leader of the Opposition) in the House of Representatives on 13th July, moved the adjournment of the House to call attention to a definite matter of urgent public importance, viz.—

"The attitude of Australia towards international affairs, and especially in respect to the following matters:—

"(A) The desirability of approving and supporting any move made in the direction of the preservation of the world's peace by the limitation of armaments.

"(B) The necessity of requiring, in the public interest, more exact information of the proceedings of the Imperial Conference now sitting; and

"(C) The necessity of instructing the Prime Minister of Australia that he is not to approve of any commitment with regard to foreign relations except subject to the condition that such commitment shall be ratified by the people of Australia."

DEBATE IN HOUSE OF REPRESENTATIVES.

Limitation of Armaments.

The Hon. T. J. Ryan (Deputy Leader of the Opposition) said he had taken this course as he deemed it to be a matter of very great importance that the representatives of the people of Australia in the National Parliament should give ready and willing approval and support to any movement for the permanent preservation of peace among the nations of the world. The whole of the people of the British Empire,

* The death of Mr. Ryan on 1st August has since been reported by cable.

and, he supposed, the whole of the peoples of the world, must have been gratified at the invitation extended by the President of the United States of America to a Conference at Washington, which would deal with the question of the limitation of armaments. It was necessary for them to show that although the Prime Minister happened to be in London, the Government was in Australia, and it was very desirable that their views, giving support in the direction named, should be known promptly. There had been a tendency shown lately to leave in the hands of the Prime Minister in London matters that in his opinion should be dealt with in Melbourne.

Quite apart from the distress and misery caused by war, they all desired that the tremendous burden of taxation involved in remaining prepared for war should be lifted. No one had less to gain and more to lose by war than the workers. It was hardly necessary for him to refer to the many resolutions that had been passed by the representatives of Labour, not only in Australia, but in other parts of the world, indicating their desire to have something done in the direction of not only limitation of armaments, but absolute Disarmament. It might not be possible to bring about Disarmament in the very near future, but that ought to be the ultimate object. The move taken by the President of the United States of America presented a fitting occasion for them to express their approval of such action, and to venture the hope that the result of the Conference would justify their expectations. In the course of his statement prior to leaving for England, the Prime Minister (Right Hon. W. M. Hughes) made no reference to the question of the limitation of armaments, and the fact was pointed out at the time. He (the Prime Minister) had confined himself to the narrow ground of the renewal of the Anglo-Japanese Alliance. Further, the Prime Minister had made no reference to the views or wishes of the Chinese. He was glad to note that the proposed Conference would include a representative of China, because the interests of that country were considerably involved in any Treaty which might be finally concluded between the respective Powers.

The Imperial Conference.

In the speech referred to the Prime Minister had revealed a tendency to subordinate Australia's interests, and he was showing the same in his utterances on the other side of the world. He need only call attention to the contrast between Mr. Hughes' attitude and that of the Prime Minister of Canada. He (Mr. Ryan) was expressing the views not only of the Labour Party, but of a large majority of the people of Australia, when he said that they required a great deal more information concerning the Imperial Conference than they were getting. They were receiving only reports which sounded uncommonly like the Prime Minister's own statements. It would seem that the Conference was being conducted in secret. They should be supplied, at any rate, with the respective views expressed by the representatives of the various Dominions. The reports which they had received from London would lead them to believe that the Prime Minister (Mr. Hughes) had been responsible for every successful move made at the Conference. Indeed, the right honourable gentleman almost claimed to have been responsible for the step that had been taken by the President of the United States of America. The Prime Minister was claiming credit for something which was diametrically opposed to what he had put before Parliament before he left for England. He hoped that the motion would lead to some step being taken to secure exact information of what was happening in London. And because the information they were at present receiving was inexact, and because they knew that the representative of Australia was differing from the representatives of the other great oversea interests, such as Canada and South Africa, it was all the more necessary that they should place some limitation upon his powers. Before the Prime Minister could bind Australia to any commitment regarding foreign relations, it should be determined there (in the House) that any such proposal should be subject first to ratification by the people of Australia. He was not prepared to leave this grave matter entirely in the hands of the Prime Minister, neither were the people generally.

Anglo-Japanese Treaty.

From the scanty information he had been able to obtain, it would appear that the Prime Minister of Canada favoured a referendum with regard to the Anglo-Japanese Alliance. The necessity for getting the views of the other Dominions of the Empire, particularly of Canada and of South Africa, still remained, and they should know the views of China on the matter before a conclusion was come to.

Mr. Ryan then read a cablegram which had been received from Shanghai. It was addressed to the Members of the House, and came as representing the views of eighteen different bodies. It stated that the Anglo-Japanese Alliance had been the greatest disturbing factor of peace in the Far East, and appealed to the House to direct its representative at the Conference to debar its renewal. That message, **Mr. Ryan** continued, had been sent in the hope that they **might** pay some heed to its statements. He did not wish to say a word which might be construed as hostile to the Japanese. He had no hostility to that nation. He thought that they could have friendly relations with them, and could consider their interests in the Pacific, and at the same time give due and just consideration to the representations of China on points which that country wished them to bring before their (Australia's) representative in London.

He had drawn attention to that matter entirely because he deemed it to be of paramount importance that Parliament should express its approval of and give help to any movement for the limitation of armaments. He hoped that when this limitation had been achieved a further step might be taken, and that conscription might be simultaneously abolished in all countries. As General Smuts had said, conscription was the tap-root of militarism, out of which grew war. That was a step in the right direction.

America and the League of Nations.

The Hon. W. G. Higgs (Nationalist, *Capricornia, Q.*) said that Parliament had ratified the Covenant of the League of Nations, and had thus shown its desire for the fulfilment of the objects of the League, among which was the limitation and reduction of armaments. China, which asked that the Anglo-Japanese Treaty should not be renewed, was a member of the League, all the members of which had solemnly declared that they would respect the integrity of that country and of each other. Great Britain and Japan had declared that the Treaty, although in accordance with the spirit, was not in accordance with the letter of the Covenant of the League, and had agreed to revise it, to bring it into accord with the Covenant. The Deputy-Leader of the Opposition desired that they should support the United States of America in endeavouring to bring about a reduction of armaments. He asked the House whether that country whose last President was really responsible for the League of Nations, had done right in standing out of the League, and in endeavouring to set up a new League apparently in opposition to it ? The American people did not wish to join a League that appeared coercive, and to become entangled in European complications. That had been their attitude all along, although, no doubt, owing to the War, America would find, as Australia had found, that it would be hard for any civilised country to keep out of any world-war that occurred in the future. The only way in which nations could keep out of war was by promoting and fostering the League of Nations. He believed that the final form of the Anglo-Japanese Treaty would be acceptable to the League of

Nations, and if so it must be acceptable to the United States
of America. He thought it was deplorable that America had
stood out of the League. She should have come in with the
other forty-four nations and trusted to her immense influence
to secure an amendment of the Covenant in conformity with
the desires and traditions of the American people.

Imperial Conference Reports.

The Right Hon. W. A. Watt (Nationalist, *Balaclava, Vic.*)
said he thought that the honourable gentleman (Mr. Ryan)
who had moved the motion was correct in interpreting the
unanimous view of the Australian public to be in favour of
peace, its establishment and maintenance, and a strong
yearning towards disarmament; and if they debated the
matter for weeks they would not find one dissentient from
those theories. Therefore, they need not waste time in admitting that was the expressed opinion of the representatives of
the Australian people, irrespective of parties. He would not
have risen but for the argument of the honourable Member
for West Sydney (Mr. Ryan) in regard to reports from the
Imperial Conference. The world was disturbed to its tap-roots,
and until stability returned it was a dangerous experiment
for any world-wide Empire to open its doors to other nations
so that they might hear the counsels of the overseas Dominions
and the Government of the Central Kingdom. Admitting
that it would be impolitic to admit reporters and deal with
the problems of Empire openly, the next best course would
be for the Conference to deliberate in private, and for the chairman to issue an official report at the close of each sitting or
periodically throughout the week's session. He regretted
that that course was not being followed, although the Acting
Prime Minister had suggested that an official report was issued
every day. If that was so the public were not informed of it.
In their case they heard most of what the Australian Prime
Minister had said, and practically nothing of what was said
by others. What he appealed for was a presentation of a two-
sided discussion. They should know what the views of Canada
and Australia were, and how far it was possible to reconcile
them. He had no desire but to obtain exact and safe information which the leaders of the Empire felt they ought to give.

Renewal of Anglo-Japanese Treaty.

It was true, as Mr. Ryan had said, that no man could say
whether he would be in favour of the renewal of a Treaty
the final form of which he had not seen. But in recent utterances he (Mr. Watt) had expressed the desirability of a renewal

subject to the non-forfeiture of the principles on which Australia had founded its union. He referred to the policy of a "White Australia." He had also conditioned it, as the Prime Minister had done, by a strong desire that America should be satisfied with the form of the contract. He had latterly submitted that the interests of China should be considered, and had said that he thought that Great Britain would probably be better able to influence the sympathetic consideration of Chinese interests by Japan if she were in alliance with Japan than if she had broken the Alliance. Further, he had said that he thought that Britain and part of her Dominions, including Australia and New Zealand, were much safer in a free alliance in treaty form with Japan than she would be without a treaty of that kind. The denouncement or renunciation of the Treaty after the Conference would place Japan mid-way between two alternatives,—either of remaining in a state of "splendid isolation," or seeking new alliances that might be less friendly to America and to Britain. He would sooner see the *status quo* preserved by an oriental alliance than risk a renunciation and a search for fresh partners either by Japan or Britain.

Dominions and Foreign Affairs.

As to the liberty of action that might be enjoyed by the Prime Minister to determine foreign issues for them without consent, he thought that the Prime Minister, before he left, had been quite frank on that point. He had said, for example, in regard to Defence : "I shall commit Australia to nothing without the consent of Parliament." As to the Treaty, the Prime Minister had laid down the conditions on which he would be prepared to accept a renewal, and without which he would bring it back to that House. As far as he remembered, the Prime Minister had said that he would do his best to have the Treaty in such a form that it would secure the concurrence of the authorities of the United States of America. Later on, if the cablegrams were to be trusted, he had said that it was essential that America should approve, and had gone further and suggested that America should be a party to the compact. It would be impossible, and it was unthinkable, that the Prime Minister should go away with an absolutely blank cheque on the first occasion on which the Dominions had been summoned to consider the general question of foreign policy. No man from Australia, however learned or however able, could go as an expert to a conference on general foreign policy.

The Washington Conference.

The Acting Prime Minister (the Right Hon. Sir Joseph Cook) said he agreed with all that had been said in favour of the

M

proposals for Disarmament.   Right from the beginning he had
placed his faith in the ultimate sanity of the American people,
and he had advocated with all his strength closer relationship
between the English-speaking peoples.   He believed that
offered the one hope of ultimate peace to the war-stricken world;
he saw no prospect but through some combination of that kind.
America was a nation which had emerged from the War with
her resources undiminished, and by reason of her inherent
strength, and of her position in the world, she was the one
nation able to take the leadership of this movement for Disarmament.   He was glad to see that both France and Great
Britain were giving their whole-hearted support to the leadership of the American people in this movement.   He hoped
that nothing would prevent the Conference taking place, or
prevent the happy consummation so devoutly to be wished.

Imperial Conference secrecy.

As to the secrecy of the Imperial Conference, they could
not have details of the discussions which took place within the
door of the Conference.   He took it that they had such official
reports as the rest of the Empire, including the Mother Country,
were receiving.   A *communiqué* was issued every evening
and it went over the Empire by means of the Press.   When
they sent a plenipotentiary to discuss those delicate questions
ramifying into all kinds of international by-ways and into the
sphere of diplomacy, they must be prepared to trust him.
There were some matters which might well be published to
the world.   It was for the Conference to determine what
should be given out, and it did so, and issued to the Press
every evening a statement of the day's proceedings.

Canada and the Anglo-Japanese Treaty.

Mr Watt : " Will the Acting-Prime Minister say what
objection there could be to letting us know the Canadian
view on the Anglo-Japanese Treaty ? "

The Acting-Prime Minister : " We do know it.   We have
learned what it is from the information which has been
supplied by the Conference to the Press."

Continuing, Sir Joseph Cook said that he took it that Mr
Meighen at that moment was against the renewal of the
Japanese Treaty, because from his present position he saw in
it something which was inconsistent with the relationship
which Canadian people thought they ought to shape towards
America.   He could not say at the moment what was the
attitude of the Prime Minister of South Africa on the question,
but it was well known that the New Zealand attitude agreed
with their own.   New Zealand was in favour of a renewal

but desired that care should be taken that in the renewal of the Treaty nothing should be done, if possible, to antagonisé the United States of America. That was the attitude of Australia and New Zealand, but it was not, or had not been up to the present moment, the attitude of the Canadian delegates at the Conference.

Foreign Affairs.

Mr. Ryan wanted them to instruct the Prime Minister that he was not to approve of any commitment in regard to foreign relations unless such commitment had been ratified by the people of Australia. He also wanted them to submit details of foreign relations—the details of the Anglo-Japanese Treaty, for instance—to a referendum of the people. He (Sir Joseph Cook) did not believe that that was the best way of conducting their international relationships. It would be fatal. There could be no more prolific cause of war than the universal adoption of the referendum in respect to matters of foreign policy. He ventured to say that since the Prime Minister had been in London no possible exception could be taken to any attitude that he had so far assumed. The Prime Minister had defended the interests of Australia with rare and conspicuous ability, and he marvelled at any man who could cavil at his attitude as they were hearing and reading of it every day.

Mr. Hughes' Statement.

Sir Joseph Cook then referred to the statement* made by the Prime Minister in the House prior to leaving for the Conference, in which he declared that Parliament would have the amplest opportunity of expressing its opinion on any scheme of naval defence that was decided upon before the scheme was ratified and that he was in favour of renewing the Anglo-Japanese Treaty in any form satisfactory to Britain, America and Australia, and that otherwise he should bring back the Treaty to Parliament. Nothing that the Prime Minister had done or said, Sir Joseph concluded, could give warrant for suspecting the slightest departure from the lines which he had laid down prior to leaving these shores.

Dr. Earle Page (Leader of the Country Party) said that the motion was good in that it enabled honourable Members to do two things; first, to secure by the expression of their views a much more complete record of what was transpiring at the Imperial Conference; and, secondly, to indicate a unanimous wish that Australian opinion should be represented, if possible,

---

* Vide JOURNAL, Vol. II., No. 2, p. 354.

at the Disarmament Conference, and that it was the desire
of Australia to see a reduction of armaments throughout the
world.   It had been a misfortune that the United States of
America had not become a member of. the League of Nations,
but the next best condition for the peace of the world was an
alliance of the English-speaking peoples which President
Harding had announced as one of his objectives.   He trusted
that the present movement, inaugurated by President Harding,
would be consummated at no distant date.

Ministerial Representation in London.

One other important point had been raised, namely', the
need for Australia having better representation in London,
and for a better system for dealing with their external affairs
in Australia and at Home.   Was it necessary that, whenever
a vital gathering such as had now been projected was to be
held on the other side of the world, and whenever their external
affairs were to be considered, the business of the country
should be held up just because they had not yet provided, as
other portions of the Empire had done, for a proper arrangement of their international functions ?   When the British
Minister for Foreign Affairs was away, the House of Commons
still carried on and transacted full public business.   Australia
had now come to the parting of the ways ; she had been
admitted, though not perhaps full grown, into the comity
of nations, and she discovered new national and international
obligations.   It was essential that they enter deeply into
foreign affairs.   It was inevitable that the Government of
Australia should at any time, and always, be held responsible
for its attitude towards foreign policy just as for its domestic
policy.   Their isolation was for ever gone, and it was utterly
necessary that ministerial duties should be so arranged, as to
permit a constant channel of communication between the
centre of Empire and the Commonwealth Government and
Parliament.

In his view, to submit all treaties to the direct arbitrament of the people would be impossible.   There must be
fully-credited and responsible plenipotentiaries ; and the only
way in which they could be adjudged was by making them
responsible direct to Parliament, and thus, finally, to the
people.   He maintained that the assurances which the Prime
Minister had given, that he would bring all fresh treaties back
to Parliament, were satisfactory in all respects.   He laid
down definite conditions and the Government must be looked
to to make them good.

The debate was subsequently interrupted under Standing
Order 119.   •

Message from Prime Minister: Secrecy of Conference.

In the House of Representatives on 20th July,

The Acting Prime Minister (the Right Hon. Sir Joseph Cook), having regard to the debate which had taken place in the House a few days before, submitted to hon. Members a cablegram which had been received from the Prime Minister in which he stated that Australia had been given all the information which could be given at that juncture. The representatives of the various parts of the Empire gathered round the council were charged with the grave and responsible duties of conserving the interests and of insuring the security of the Empire. They could not hope to succeed if premature disclosure were made to the whole world—and disclosure to the Parliaments would mean that—not only of the policy recommended by the Conference, but of the views of the various members and the arguments advanced for and against any suggested policy. When the Conference had finished its labours, its Recommendations—which were all subject to approval by the respective Governments, and to ratification by Parliament—would be made available to Parliament. But if the Conference were to give to the various Parliaments of the Empire wise and prudent counsel, there must be complete frankness of speech at the meetings of the Conference. It was inevitable that reference must be made to foreign countries. Every member represented a great Dominion which had special interests to protect and special problems to solve.¹ He need not point out that a great and rich country like Australia, with only 5,500,000 people, must walk warily and not shout its secrets from the house-tops.

They were members of a Conference and must be governed by the procedure which that body decided to adopt. It had been decided that information upon certain matters should come through one channel, viz., the Secretariat of the Prime Minister of Great Britain. The official *communiqué* was the only information permitted, except where the Conference otherwise decided. Wherever it had so decided he had made public the very fullest information. Further, he had kept his colleagues supplied with the fullest confidential reports.

He had stated in the most definite and unambiguous terms in Parliament that the Commonwealth would not be committed to any scheme of naval or foreign policy, or involved in any expenditure by any act of his, but that all should be subject to ratification by Parliament. For his attitude in regard to the renewal of the Anglo-Japanese Treaty and American connection therewith, he referred to his speech dealing with those matters.* He held himself bound by the declarations contained therein.

Anglo-Japanese Treaty : Approval of Parliament, etc.

In the House of Representatives on 21st July,

The Hon. T. J. Ryan (Deputy-Leader of the Opposition) said that the cablegram received from the Prime Minister was entirely out of accord with the speech made by him in the House before he left for London. He (the Prime Minister) in his cablegram said that any scheme of naval or foreign policy, or any expenditure, would be subject to the ratification of that Parliament. This was what he had said in Parliament in regard to the continuance of the Anglo-Japanese Treaty : " Long before the Australian people could approve or disapprove, the Treaty will be renewed or else allowed to lapse. If our people do not approve, that will not alter matters by onethousandth part of an inch. . . . On my return from Britain, if the Treaty as drawn up and agreed to is not satisfactory, this Parliament can say ' We will have none of it ' ; and we can renounce it." That was an entirely different statement from that in the cablegram to the effect that anything he did at the Conference would be subject to ratification by that Parliament.

The Hon. Sir Robert Best (Nationalist, *Kooyong, Vic.*): " That is as far as it may be applicable to Australia. That is the usual practice."

Mr. Ryan : " That is not the usual practice. On the contrary, the Prime Minister of Canada has insisted at the Conference that a proviso should be inserted in the Treaty making it not binding upon Canada until the Dominion Parliament approved of it. No such suggestion has been made by the Prime Minister of Australia. He says that the Treaty will be ratified or allowed to lapse long before we can say aye or nay, and if we say nay, it will not matter."

' Continuing, Mr. Ryan said they had from the Prime Minister an admission that he had made public the fullest information. He had not told them anything about the attitude of the Prime Ministers of Canada and South Africa. After the debate in the House last week, a *résumé* of the work of the Imperial Conference appeared in the Australian Press which stated that the Conference inevitably fell into three divisions. The first division included the British Ministers, who were insistent on requiring the renewal of the Treaty, and persistent in representing their inability any longer to bear the whole burden of the defence of the Empire. The

* *Vide* JOURNAL, Vol. II., No. 2, p. 358.

second division was comprised of Mr. Meighen and General Smuts. The former differed from the British Ministers regarding both the Treaty and Defence, but was predisposed to support the Treaty. In the third division were Mr. Hughes and Mr. Massey. The former approved of the Treaty provided it was rendered inoffensive to the United States, while Mr. Massey whole-heartedly supported the renewal. Mr. Meighen's objections to the Japanese Treaty were, first, that the conditions which necessitated the Treaty in 1911 did not now exist; second, that the renewal would be regarded with disfavour by the United States; and, third, that the formation of such alliances was antagonistic to the spirit of post-war times. Failing to secure denunciation, Mr. Meighen would propose the insertion of a clause exempting Canada until the Dominion Parliament approved. General Smuts concurred in the principles of Mr. Meighen's arguments, but if assured it was Imperially necessary he would support a renewal of the Treaty.

Mr. Meighen also opposed the Conference dealing with Naval Defence. He advocated that they should suspend action until the Conference decided the precise mechanism under which the Dominions could give effect to their views on foreign affairs. General Smuts arrived at a similar conclusion by a different line of reasoning, and emphatically opposed any new defence commitments as a contravention of the spirit of the League of Nations.

He (Mr. Ryan) suggested that that was an accurate summary of the attitude taken up by the various groups. He knew from his own experience of the Prime Minister (Mr. Hughes) that the statement was accurate in regard to him. It was quite clear that the Prime Ministers of Canada and South Africa were entirely in favour of the Disarmament Conference, and the attitude of General Smuts in regard to Defence commitments was diametrically opposed to the attitude of the Prime Minister of Australia. The only conclusion to which they could come after reading that summary was that the Prime Minister of Australia and his Government were really echoes of Downing Street.

The Prime Minister had said that the League of Nations was not a sufficient guarantee of the peace of the world and that they must have expenditure and still more expenditure on Defence. He (Mr. Ryan) hoped that they would have an opportunity of impressing upon the Government that they desired the views of Australia represented at any Conference dealing with the limitation of armaments. They (the Labour Party) objected to armaments, and their objective was the abolition of armaments and conscription in all countries simultaneously.

The Acting Prime Minister said that in all his diatribe the hon. Member's (Mr. Ryan's) one substantial charge was that the Prime Minister was working in harmony with Downing Street officials. What a crime to dare to agree with the Imperial authorities! He (Sir Joseph Cook) thought that the country would agree that that was what the Prime Minister went to London to do—whenever possible, consistently with the interests of Australia, to work side by side with the Imperial authorities, not seeking to create conflict between Australia and those authorities, but working with them in efficiency and unity for the good of Australia and of the Empire as a whole.

Subsequent statement by Prime Minister.

The Prime Minister (the Right Hon. W. M. Hughes), on 30th September, immediately after his return to Melbourne, delivered an important speech in the House of Representatives on the results of the Imperial Conference. During this speech, which was fully reported by cable in *The Times* of 1st October, Mr. Hughes referred to the Washington Conference.

The speech of Mr. Hughes and the subsequent discussion will be summarised as usual from the official Parliamentary debates in the next issue of the JOURNAL, as the necessary numbers had not reached this country at the time of going to Press with the present issue. In view, however, of the Conference in November and the previous discussions summarised in the present number, it has been thought useful to give a few extracts from the Press cable below.*

---

* Mr. Hughes is reported by *The Times* as having said that on the second day of the Imperial Conference he suggested that Mr. Lloyd George should invite the great nations, especially America, France and Japan, to a Conference to discuss Disarmament ; also that America and Japan should be invited to a Conference to discuss the terms of a tripartite treaty to be substituted for the Anglo-Japanese Treaty. Before the negotiations with America and Japan on the subject were concluded, Mr. Harding's invitation was received. The Imperial Conference thought that the Pacific question ought to be discussed first. Mr. Lloyd George, Lord Curzon and the Dominion Prime Ministers volunteered to attend a meeting in America for a friendly interchange of views before the main Conference. They felt that a discussion on Disarmament could have no satisfactory result unless a *modus vivendi* in the Pacific were first reached. The Powers to be invited to the preliminary discussion were America, Japan, China and the British Empire. It was pointed out to the American Government that the presence of the Australian and New Zealand Prime Ministers would be material in securing the full and cordial assent of the people of both Dominions to the decisions of the Conference. The strategic centre of the world had changed from the North Sea to the Pacific. For Australia, the Pacific problem was for all practical purposes the problem of Japan. Since America had not

WASHINGTON CONFERENCE.

(Representation of Political Parties: Naval and Military Expenditure.)

In the House of Representatives on the 15th July the following questions were put to the Acting Prime Minister regarding the Disarmament Conference at Washington.

Mr. Matthew Charlton (Labour, *Hunter, N.S.W.*) asked the Acting Prime Minister whether in regard to the Conference which President Harding proposed to convene for the discussion on Disarmament, the Government would make representations to the President, through the proper channel, so that a representative of each political Party in the Parliament of each country affected might attend in order to insure the success of the project.

The Acting Prime Minister (the Right Hon. Sir Joseph Cook) in reply said " I do not see my way to do what is suggested because I do not think it would be proper to take that course. It is for each Government that accepts President Harding's invitation to say what form of representation it will adopt. I should be very glad if something could be suggested somewhere in the world which would lead to the representation of

been favourable to a preliminary conference, it had been " regretfully dropped." The Empire delegates had no desire to injure in the slightest degree the prospects of success at Washington, so Mr. Harding's invitation had been unequivocally accepted.

" As I see it," Mr. Hughes is reported to have said, " it is impossible to discuss Disarmament without raising the principal phases of the Pacific. We are vitally interested in many of these, yet Australia will not be directly represented at a Conference at which, if Pacific problems are to be seriously considered, questions vital to its welfare will be discussed, and probably decided. It was recognition of this fact, and of the settled determination of the Australian people to stand fast to their ' White Australia ' ideals—to preserve them, if possible, by peace— that impelled me to insist so strenuously on a preliminary Pacific Conference."

On the subject of Imperial Defence, continues *The Times*, Mr. Hughes affirmed that the safety of Australia depends upon the British Navy and its capacity to strike at any threatened point. Whatever might be determined at Washington, Australia must have such naval defence as is adequate for her safety.

" Peace in the Pacific means peace for the Empire and the world." Though the Conference had decided that the Empire must have a navy at least equal to that of any other Power, that matter and the questions of air and military defence and the necessary co-operation had been deferred until after Washington.

It is reported by cable that Senator the Hon. G. F. Pearce, Minister for Defence, has been appointed to represent Australia on the British Empire Delegation to the Washington Conference.

the various political Parties for the consideration of the matter, which, in its essence, is non-Party, and of wide-world interest."

The Hon. W. G. Higgs (**Nationalist,** *Capricornia, Q.*) asked whether it was not a fact that the League of Nations had issued a book of questions, regarding naval and military expenditure of nations which were members of the League, with a view to ascertaining whether it was possible to reduce armaments consistently with the preservation of national safety, and if the Acting Prime Minister could place on the table a list of these questions ?

The Acting Prime Minister replied that his impression was that a *questionnaire* of the kind had been issued, though he was not clear about it. He suggested that the hon. Member should put his important question on the notice paper.

PACIFIC CONFERENCE.

(Proposed Meeting in London.)

In the House of Representatives on 20th July,

The Acting Prime Minister (the Right Hon. Sir Joseph Cook) in reply to the Hon. T. J. Ryan (Deputy Leader of the Opposition), who asked if he proposed to make a statement on the communication from the Prime Minister on the subject of the Washington Conference, said that the latest suggestion was for the holding of two Conferences, one to consider Pacific problems generally, and more particularly the renewal of the Anglo-Japanese Treaty, and the other to consider the question of Disarmament, which was of interest to the whole world. It was not stated where the Conferences should be held. He could not say what the opinion of Canadians might be, but it was their (Australia's) view, and, he should think, the view of Mr. Massey and General Smuts, and also that of the British Government, that the Pacific Conference should be held in London, so that the Dominion Ministers might attend. The proposal to hold this Conference had developed from the consideration of the renewal of the Treaty between Great Britain and Japan, it having been found that two other countries were vitally interested in it, and that their representatives must be consulted. One of these countries was the United States of America, whose problems in some ways resembled those of Australia, and the other country was China. He was glad that China had been invited. It would mean a great deal to the peace of the world if a working understanding could be arrived at between the Powers and China, and particularly between Japan and China.

Dominion Representation.

The Empire had been invited to send representatives. It was important that the Prime Ministers of the Dominions should be in London when the Conference was taking place, even if they had not a seat at the Conference table. Above all things, it was important that the Prime Minister of Australia should be there, because Australia had more to gain and more to lose by the decisions that might be arrived at than any other country. For Australia, the centre of all things, naval and economic, had shifted to the Pacific. There were 1,000,000,000 people whose frontiers were, roughly, on the Pacific. And the fact that needed stressing was that of those 1,000,000,000 people, one might expect to find that not all were strongly in favour of a "White Australia." Therefore whatever happened Australia must be represented at that Conference.

The Disarmament Conference would be supremely important from a world point of view, but if either one of those Conferences was to be unattended by Australia's delegate, he said at once that it should be the Disarmament Conference, because Great Britain could, if necessary, quite well represent the whole of the Empire at a gathering of that kind. If it should happen that both these Conferences took place at Washington, an entirely different situation would arise. But until it did arise, he thought they need only proceed on the assumption that the Prime Minister would return as he had promised the House he would.

IMPERIAL CONFERENCE.

(Government Immunity from Political Action.)

In the course of the debate in the House of Representatives on 21st July (*vide* also under "Washington Conference," p. 868),

Mr. W. J. McWilliams (Country Party, *Franklin, Tas.*), speaking on the vote for Supply, said that the Country Party had, rightly or wrongly, agreed to grant the Government immunity from attack for a certain period. He intended to honour that agreement in letter and in spirit. In a political experience extending over nearly a quarter of a century, this was the first time that he had granted immunity to a Government, and it would be the last. It was the promise of immunity given by the Country Party that had tied their hands last night. He did not think any honourable Member would accuse him of lack of fairness and candour, and he said,

therefore, that the amendment* amounted to the moving
of a vote of want of confidence in the Government. The
Deputy Leader of the Opposition (Mr. Ryan) would himself
admit that when a proviso was sought to be added to a Supply
motion, against the will of the Government, it must be accepted
as a challenge. If mistakes were made, they must stand
by them, but, having consented to the Prime Minister going
to England to represent Australia, it would be black-fellow's
politics to tomahawk him. He could not be accused of undue
sympathy with or liking for the right honourable gentleman
(Mr. Hughes), but, having agreed to the giving of that pledge,
he was bound to keep it.

The Hon. T. J. Ryan (Deputy Leader of the Opposition)
said that the hon. Member (Mr. McWilliams) had frankly
admitted that but for an arrangement which had been made
by his Party with the Prime Minister, prior to the departure
of the latter for London, he would have voted differently
upon the amendment which he (Mr. Ryan) had moved the day
before. That amendment, it would be recalled, had for its
object the granting of assistance by the Commonwealth
Government in respect of the continuation of the Wheat Pool
system. It was a lamentable state of affairs that, because
the Prime Minister happened to be away from Australia,
the Government of which he was the head must be considered
free to do exactly what they liked without any fear of being
turned out of office, or, indeed, of censure. He knew of no
similar circumstances in the history of Australia, or of any
part of the Empire. It was, in his opinion, quite unconstitutional, and it was certainly contrary to the desires of the
large majority of the people of Australia.

Origin of Imperial Conference.

He wished to draw public attention to the existing state
of affairs which became the more reprehensible when one
examined the nature of the Imperial Conference and the
means by which it was brought about. When hon. Members
had discussed that matter originally the undoubted impression
in their minds was that the Imperial Government had, of
their own volition, decided upon a Conference, and had
cabled urging the attendance of Dominion representatives

---

* An amendment brought in by the Labour Party, asking the
Government to take steps to insure the continuance of the Wheat Pool.
The amendment was rejected, the Country Party voting with the Government. Later an amendment brought in by the Country Party, and
supported by the Government, requesting the Government to use its
influence with the State Governments in favour of a continuance of the
Wheat Pool for another year was carried.

in London. That impression was permitted to remain until the Prime Minister was making his final remarks in reply to a certain amendment which he (Mr. Ryan) had moved. Then the House had been informed that the Prime Minister of Australia was the individual who had asked for the Conference, that the British Government had not suggested it at all, but that the Commonwealth Prime Minister had cabled London in October last urging that a Conference should be called since he considered that such a gathering was very necessary.

The Prime Minister had said, in that Chamber, that he had cabled thus : " In my opinion it is absolutely essential that the Dominion Prime Ministers should meet in London next year." Later he had informed the House that he had cabled to Mr. Lloyd George : " I most earnestly recommend that you call a meeting of the Dominion Prime Ministers next year in London—say, about June. Delay for another year most dangerous."

By his own admission, then, the Commonwealth Prime Minister was the instigator of the Conference. Hon. Members now learnt that he had used that gathering, which he himself had instigated, in order to secure immunity for his Government while he was away. And hon. Members in the Corner (the Country Party) had fallen into his trap. The business which was to have been brought before the Conference had apparently been shelved, and the Conference was now doing nothing. To make believe that something was being done, the Prime Minister of the Commonwealth had suggested that the Pacific Conference should be held in London, although public opinion was emphatically against him in that regard. Without doubt, the Prime Minister had asked that the Imperial Conference should be convened, and had then manipulated one of the Parties in that Parliament in order to secure immunity for his Government during his absence.

IMPERIAL CABINET.

In the House of Representatives on 1st June,

The Acting Prime Minister (the Right Hon. Sir Joseph Cook), in reply to a question, said he was unable to state whether the agenda of the Imperial Conference included a discussion on the subject of an Imperial Cabinet. All he could say about the Imperial War Cabinet was that it was an institution of the greatest possible usefulness during the War, all the Dominions having been taken into the confidence of the

Imperial Government. He could not conceive of anything more useful than a repetition of those Conferences, so long as care was taken that they were on the same plan, and had in view the same objective, as the War Cabinet, which he had been privileged to attend.

IMPERIAL CABINET OR CONFERENCE.

In the House of Representatives on 8th June,

Mr. J. E. West (Labour, *East Sydney, N.S.W.*) said that it was stated that the Prime Minister (the Right Hon. W. M. Hughes), in an interview in England, had referred to the Imperial Conference as a Cabinet gathering. There was a difference between a Conference and a Cabinet, and he asked the Acting Prime Minister (the Right Hon. Sir Joseph Cook) whether on behalf of the Government and the Parliament the right honourable gentleman would inform the Prime Minister that he had left Australia to attend a Conference of Prime Ministers, and that the work of that Conference must be submitted to the Parliaments of the various Dominions for endorsement ?

The Acting Prime Minister (the Right Hon. Sir Joseph Cook) : " I do not see the need for wasting money in cabling such a statement. The proposed gathering will be, as I understand it, both a Cabinet and a Conference. The Dominions have been taken into the Cabinet Councils of the Imperial Government."

Mr. James Mathews (Labour, *Melbourne Ports, Vic.*) : " What power will it have over our local Government ? "

The Acting Prime Minister : " None whatever, nor will it attempt to take any such power. So far as I know, it does not intend to do so. But the question is : ' Should we deny ourselves the privilege of being taken into consultation regarding all the tremendous issues which are arising throughout the world ? ' Are we to stand outside when they say ' Come in ? ' I hope not."

LEAGUE OF NATIONS.

(Permanent Court of International Justice.)*

In the House of Representatives on 1st June,

The Minister for Works and Railways (Hon. L. E. Groom) said that at the Assembly of the League of Nations held in Geneva last year a protocol was drawn up providing for the

---

* See also p. 797.

acceptance by the members of the League of the Statute and the jurisdiction of the Permanent Court of International Justice. That protocol had already been signed by the whole of the British Dominions which were members of the League, other than Australia, and the Government had now decided to authorise the Prime Minister to sign the protocol on behalf of Australia, and to authorise His Majesty, after the protocol had been so signed, to ratify it. The acceptance of the juris-diction of the Court did not extend to the acceptance of the compulsory jurisdiction provided for in the second paragraph of Article 36 of the Statute.

NATURALISATION OF GERMANS.

The Postmaster-General (Hon. G. H. Wise), in the House of Representatives on 16th June, stated, on behalf of the Minister for Home and Territories, that the embargo* against persons of German origin obtaining certificates of naturalisa-tion had been removed, and that they were now ön the same footing as other European aliens in the matter of obtaining certificates of naturalisation.

A

NEW HEBRIDES.

In the House of Representatives on 12th June,

The Hon. T. J. Ryan (Deputy Leader of the Opposition) brought under the notice of the Acting Prime Minister (the Right Hon. Sir Joseph Cook) some facts relating to conditions which, it was alleged, obtained in the New Hebrides. The allegations were made by the Presbyterian Church of Victoria, and were based on a letter received from one of its missionaries in the New Hebrides, extracts from which were quoted by Mr. Ryan. It was asserted by the Missionary that land was being appropriated by French settlers to the detriment of the natives, and that if the New Hebrides were not annexed by Great Britain, the French would bring in labour—it might be Tonquin, Chinese or Japanese—and in the end Australia would pay the penalty. Mr. Ryan asked that the matter be inquired into, and, if the suggested evils existed, that representations be made with a view to having them removed.

Dr. W. Maloney (Labour, *Melbourne, Vic.*) said he had visited the Islands when they (Australia) were removing the last remnant of slavery in Australia, and had found that

---

* *Vide* debate on Nationality Act, JOURNAL, Vol. II., No. 2, p. 371.

everything possible was being done to place the kanakas back
in their old homes. However, it seemed to him that the
Commonwealth Government were faced with a great difficulty.
The settlers there did not particularly want to come under
the Australian flag, but they seemed to wish to remain under
the British flag. He hoped that an amicable arrangement
might be come to between Great Britain and France in regard
to the New Hebrides. The last War had removed many
misunderstandings between the two peoples, and he trusted
that the lies which used to be in circulation about the French
would never be repeated. He thought that an exchange of
territory might be effected, France concentrating her colonising
energy upon Africa.

The Acting Prime Minister (the Right Hon. Sir Joseph
Cook) said that the New Hebrides question was a very vexed
and a very old one. The Condominium had not worked well,
yet what to put in its place was a problem. Correspondence
on the subject had been proceeding for the last ten years to his
knowledge. He thought it was rather a pity that those
important questions should be raised without some intimation
to the Government beforehand. He knew nothing whatever
about it that was fresh, and was not, therefore, in a position
to give a satisfactory answer. All he could say was that he
hoped that no friction would occur, and that they should do
their best to prevent anything of the kind. He was informed
that, just before leaving for England, the Prime Minister had
received a deputation from the Presbyterian Church regarding
the New Hebrides, and had promised to look into their complaints when in London. He took it that those who formed
the deputation were quite content to leave matters with the
Prime Minister. There the matter must rest, so far as he was
concerned, for the present.

NAURU ISLAND.

In the House of Representatives on 16th June,

The Acting Prime Minister (the Right Hon. Sir Joseph
Cook) stated that the sum of £1,483,230 had been paid by the
Commonwealth Government for the Australian interest in
the phosphate deposits in Nauru Island and Ocean Island.
During the first six months of control by the British Phosphate
Commission, 120,000 tons of phosphates had been landed in
Australia at an average price of 78s. 6d. per ton. The impor-
tations from Nauru had not yet decreased the price of
phosphates in Australia, but a reduction was expected during
the next year.

RECIPROCITY WITH NEW ZEALAND.

In the House of Representatives on 14th July,
The Minister for Trade and Customs (Hon. W. Massy Greene) stated, in reply to a question, that the consideration of the establishment of reciprocal Customs arrangements between the Commonwealth and the Dominion of New Zealand had not been lost sight of, and that a few days before a letter had been sent to the Acting-Prime Minister of New Zealand saying that the Government were prepared to enter into negotiations with the Dominion for the reciprocal treatment of goods passing between New Zealand and Australia. They should be glad to treat the Dominion most sympathetically, but until the Tariff Bill had been passed by the Senate they could not do anything further.

TARIFF.

The new Tariff, which came into operation as from 25th March, 1920, was passed by the House of Representatives on 8th July, 1921, and is now before that Chamber in connection with certain modifications recommended by the Senate.

It provides for three different rates, viz., British Preferential, Intermediate, and General. The Intermediate rate is designed for application in the case of countries with which Australia may enter into reciprocal arrangements. An outstanding feature of the new Tariff, which is strongly Protective, is the very substantial increase in the preference extended to British manufactures. The following table is a comparison with former Tariffs as regards this preference so far as concerns *ad valorem* duties : —

Preference.	1908-1911 Tariff items.	1914 Tariff items.	1920 Tariff items.
5 per cent.	237	303	24
7½ ,,	4	3	—
10 ,,	10	120	367
12½ ,,	—	—	24
15 ,,	—	—	136
20 ,,	—	—	32

In addition, considerable increase of preference is shown in many of the items subject to fixed rates.

DEBATE IN HOUSE OF REPRESENTATIVES.

In order to render the debates of 1921 intelligible to the reader, it has been thought advisable to include in the summary a portion of the debates of 1920. The 1921 discussion commences on p. 884.

The Minister for Trade and Customs (Hon. W. Massy Greene), when submitting the proposed Tariff in March, 1920,

N

said that he believed it would protect industries born during the War, would encourage others that were desirable, and would diversify and extend existing industries. The iron and steel production of Australia had increased of recent years, and particularly during the War. It was essential that they should endeavour, so far as they could, to preserve the Australian market for Australian manufactures.

British Preference.

After quoting the above table, Mr. Massy Greene said that it would be seen that the new Tariff increased the British preferential rates, not only very substantially, but also to a greater extent than ever before. There was a long list of the fixed duties showing that the preferential rate in that connection had been raised to a greater extent than previously, so that both in the case of the *ad valorem* duties and the fixed duties the preferential rate to Great Britain had been increased. What they had tried to do, particularly in regard to commodities which they were not producing, was to throw their trade as far as possible into Britain's hands.

It was the desire of the Government, and, no doubt, the desire of all hon. Members, by every means in their power, to increase the commercial ties which bound them to the Old Country ; and the Government proposed to do something of an Imperial character, which, it was hoped, would lead to closer relations between the various Dominions.

After all, this preference to Britain was the policy of Protection applied to Britain. To whatever extent they allowed British goods to enter at lower rates meant, in effect, the policy of Protection applied to British goods. He did not know anything more humorous, to his mind, than the tremendous energy with which certain advocates of Free Trade pressed for preference within the Empire and refused to recognise that, after all was said and done, it meant the policy of Protection as applied to Britain.

Whilst they were quite willing to accord this large measure of Protection to British industry, and give assistance to their kinsmen overseas, they were not asking for a *quid pro quo*. But while they were taking that attitude, he believed that that policy could not go on for ever without reciprocity. He was pleased to note that recently the British Parliament had made a start in the way of reciprocal relations with the Dominions. He hoped it was only a beginning, and that the statesmen of Britain would see their way to recognise, in some more substantial manner than they had up to that time, the value of reciprocal trade relationship which Australia was endeavouring to strengthen in the new Tariff.

Reciprocity with Dominions, etc.

In explaining the Intermediate Tariff the Minister pointed out that under the Bill reciprocal arrangements could be entered into with the other Dominions of the British Crown. In the event of the possibility of a satisfactory reciprocal agreement, there was power to extend to other Dominions on individual items the British preferential rate, or the intermediate rate, or, it might be, the general rate. They had in the past tried to arrange reciprocal Tariffs with other Dominions, but with the sole exception, he thought, of South Africa they had never been able to come to an agreement. But the embodying of this provision in a definite form placed the means at their hand to enable them to complete such an arrangement. It was holding out, as it were, an invitation to the other Dominions to come to Australia with their proposals. While Australia was doing its best to protect its traders, where it was thought they needed protection, Australia would consider these proposals, and might be able to do something to help Australian producers to get their produce more easily into other countries.

Other countries.

In regard to reciprocal arrangements with countries other than the Dominions, the Minister was empowered to extend only the intermediate Tariff—that was to say, in entering into such negotiations, he was precluded from offering to those countries what might be termed, for the purposes of the Bill, the Empire rate. The Minister was confined in his negotiations with these other countries to the intermediate Tariff.

Powers of the Ministry.

There was one very important limitation on the power of the Minister in regard to these negotiations. He was precluded from entering into negotiations which would lead to a reciprocal Tariff arrangement if he was satisfied that the economic conditions—and this applied both to the Dominions of the British Crown and to other countries—in such Dominion or other country were substantially lower than those prevailing in Australia. Importations from such Dominions or other countries would therefore fall automatically under the General Tariff and remain there until such time as their economic conditions assimilated more closely to those of Australia.

The Hon. F. G. Tudor (Leader of the Opposition)* sai
he was not keen on the innovation of the three-colum
schedule, but he was most anxious to have all their Tari
arrangements in one measure. The existing reciproca
arrangement with South Africa was probably covered by
separate measure.

The Minister for Trade and Customs : " Once this Tari
is through, all our reciprocal arrangements will be covere
by it."

Mr. Tudor : " If we have all our Tariffs in one measur
we know exactly where we are."

In 1906 the new Protection was brought forward in tha
Parliament not only in order to give Protection to the manu
facturers, but also to provide something for the worker
They had fixed certain duties on harvesters and a few othe
farming implements, but at the same time they had provide
that unless the manufacturers paid certain wages to the
employees, and sold at a certain price to the farmers, small
duties would be imposed. As soon as the manufacturers g
this additional protection they turned round and fough
not the farmer, but the worker. A case went before th
Court, which held that the new Protection was *ultra vires.*

He was anxious to see the Tariff placed upon a soun
basis, so that their artisans should be properly trained i
Australian industries. They had, by medium of the ne
Tariff, an opportunity to place Australia's industries upon
better footing than formerly.

The Minister had stated, in comparing the 1914 Tarif
which he (Mr. Tudor) had had the honour to introduce, with th
new Tariff that there were 538 items among those in regar
to which British preference figured where the duty wou
remain exactly as before. Two-thirds of Australia's impor
came from Great Britain ; and in regard to more than 500
those items there was no alteration. That fact was importan
Since the introduction of the 1914 Tariff there had been fi
years of war, and there was then greater need than ever fo
Australia to open out industrially in new directions. Th
fact that in 538 items there was no alteration proposed in th
duties on imports from Great Britain showed that the Tari
which was introduced by the Labour Government in 191
might be said to have reached high-water mark. The com
parative tables indicated that the alterations proposed. b
the new Tariff were chiefly confined to the General Tarif

---

* A Press telegram of 15th September, 1921, stated that Mr. Tud
had resigned the Leadership of the Federal Labour Party and that h
would probably be succeeded by Mr. Matthew Charlton.

While there might not be much alteration of the duties proposed in the British preference column, there were alterations proposed in the other columns of the new Tariff. He had never been anxious that they should collect a great deal of revenue through the Tariff, but that industries should be established in Australia.

It was their duty to make Australia less dependent upon other countries than she had hitherto been. During the War they had found that they were able to manufacture much that they had never attempted before, and he was convinced that the Australian workman, when supplied with the necessary machinery and tools, could hold his own with the most skilled workers of any other country.

The Hon. H. Gregory (Country Party, *Dampier, W.A.*) said he thought that when the 1914 Tariff was introduced they had reached the standard of Protection required to build up the industries of Australia. For fifteen or twenty years before they had heard it said that, in order to build up Australian industries, a higher Tariff was necessary. The Tariff had been continually increased until, with the introduction of that of 1914, he believed they had a Tariff which would enable local manufacturers to compete with the rest of the world. But the new Tariff " out-Herods Herod," largely increasing the duties on almost every article they required. There could be no argument at that time for an increased Tariff in order to build up Australian industries. Prices had increased enormously, but Australia was, and must continue, importing. This had been due to the fact not that the duties in force at the outbreak of war had been insufficient to protect Australian manufacturers, but that millions of people, and hundreds of thousands of pounds worth of machinery, had been diverted from peaceful pursuits to the manufacture of munitions of war. Machinery which had formerly been used in the manufacture of these goods had to be utilised in the production of war material. Of recent years it had been almost impossible to get goods into Australia in any shape or form. Yet, at a time like this, a new Tariff had been brought forward.

The man who produced the raw material of the country ought to be able to get the world's parity for it. The only way in which they would ever be able to progress and discharge the tremendous obligations with which they were faced was by developing the vast vacant spaces of Australia, and by encouraging people to come there. When they had a population of 15,000,000 or 20,000,000, which they would have with good government, there would be a home market for the manufacturer, who would thus be in a far better position to compete in the open markets of the world than he then was.

Primary Industries and Protection. ·

About 1913-14 the value of their primary industries was something like £170,000,000, whilst that of their manufactured products was only about £60,000,000. In 1918 the value of the primary industries was over £200,000,000, whilst that of the manufacturing industries was less than £70,000,000. They knew that one-half of the population of Australia was to be found in the State capitals. Whilst such conditions obtained, the man who went into the bush to struggle for an existence had an embargo placed on the exportation of his products.

He objected to the action of the Customs Department in imposing embargoes upon many classes of goods coming into Australia. He was not speaking of the present Minister's Administration but of a period antecedent to it.

Speaking on 6th April, 1921,

Mr. J. H. Prowse (Country Party, *Swan, W.A.*) said it would be a misnomer to call it Protection. The new Tariff was the simplest and shortest cut to the supply of money to the Exchequer. No one could soundly reason that the imposition of additional protective duties was necessary. The new Tariff would certainly have the effect of increasing the cost of living to the whole of the people of Australia, and it was unnecessary, now that the War was over, since the War itself had given the industries of Australia an immensely increased measure of protection. Other countries which before the War had extremely cheap labour, no longer had cheap labour. Wages in other countries had increased to such an extent as to afford Australia a very great deal of protection. Increased freights also constituted a big measure of protection, and the great increase in the price of coal in other lands was an immense protection to Australian manufacturers. Surely it would be admitted that in these several respects considerable and ample protection was given to their manufacturers.

It could not be gainsaid that the primary production of Australia was the greatest asset which the country possessed. It was the only source from which new money might be obtained to give stability to their national credit, and they could not afford, therefore, to disregard its importance. The effect of the new Tariff would be to inflict a further blow to the primary producer and generally to retard the progress of primary production in Australia. Under the operation of the new Tariff the price of a binder was increased by £40.

Dr. Earle Page (Leader of the Country Party) objected to the increased incidence of *ad valorem* duties. The purchasing power of money had enormously decreased. The unit figure at the present would be something over 200, where it would have been 100 about five years ago. An *ad valorem* charge, while nominally the same to-day, provided an infinitely greater degree of protection than it would have appeared to do six years ago, because, as had been the experience following upon all great wars, they were on the eve of a slump; but there would be an unprecedented slump so far as concerned the price of raw materials. The depression was bound to last for three or four years at least; and, while it continued, the people of Australia would be burdened, if the present Tariff were continued, with rates of duty which, upon the *ad valorem* scale as it then stood, would prove doubly hard.

Years ago, when the fight occurred between Free Trade and Protection in England, the struggle was not over the protection of manufactures, but was waged upon the principle of Protection or Free Trade as applied to primary products. It was strange to-day that, in an Australian Protective Tariff, there should be no mention of anything except manufactures. It was the encouragement of primary industries that was most essential of all, because, without the production of raw material, there could be no secondary industries established. Under the present conditions the various Tariffs had not succeeded in doing this. Production in Australia had actually decreased in the past ten years, as regards primary production, to the extent of some 15 per cent.

They had to-day a Protectionist House. Both the Nationalist Party and the Labour Party went to the country on a straight-out high Protective policy, and something like twelve months ago the Government brought in the new Tariff, which was undoubtedly designed not so much to provide Protection as to secure revenue.

Speaking on 8th April, 1921,

The Hon. T. J. Ryan (Deputy-Leader of the Opposition) thought that the policy of Protection was the only sound policy for a country like Australia; it was the only policy under which they could become the great self-contained nation they desired to be.

As he understood the contention of the Country Party, it was that the farmers ought to be allowed to go into the markets of the world to purchase their agricultural machinery—they desired Free Trade for such commodities. It was necessary for making Australia a self-contained country to manufacture their agricultural machinery in Australia. They must manufacture all they could manufacture, and they must have such a policy as would enable them to manufacture at a reasonable profit. Admitting the necessity for manufacturing in Australia those implements which were used in Australia, they were inevitably driven to the conclusion that there must be such a Protective Tariff as to enable that to be done against the competition of the outside world. He was prepared to go further. Having imposed a Tariff sufficient to enable the manufacture of these implements in Australia, there must be another branch of law to insure that the manufacturers did not make exorbitant or unreasonable profits ; the farmers must not be exploited by their local manufacturers.

The home market was the best market. In Australia they had room for millions of people. Their immediate duty was to populate their vast spaces. They could not do this unless they took steps to build up their great manufacturing interests. And they could do that without in any way jeopardizing the interests of their producers.

Protection and Primary Producers.

The Minister for Trade and Customs (Hon. W. Massy Greene) on 11th May, 1921, in reply to the objections raised by members of the Country Party, challenged Members to produce a solitary instance in which the adoption of Protection had proved prejudicial to the primary producers. It had been acknowledged that the protective policy of the United States of America had been the one thing which, above all others, had placed its primary producing industries where they were. Those who opposed the imposition of America's Protective Tariffs were imbued with exactly the same views as certain Members of the Australian House of Representatives, namely, that if a protective policy were adopted the result would be the ruin of the primary producing interests. When they turned to the actual results, however, they found that, in America, not only did the Tariffs not have that effect but, indeed, that the very opposite happened. The average Tariff rate in 1850, when the population of the United States was not very much greater than that of Australia to-day, was 27 per cent. In 1857 it was reduced to a little more than 18 per cent. It was raised to the average of 40 per cent. between 1862 and 1866. In 1883 the average rate amounted to 41·63 per cent., including all the free items and everything else. In 1884, after the Tariff Commission had recommended a reduction of 25 per cent., the average rate was increased to 42·60 per cent. In 1885 the duties went up to an average rate of 47·21 per cent., and after that date the average was about 47 per cent. The measure which McKinley introduced raised the average Tariff rate to 51 per cent. There were very few of the Australian duties which approximated anywhere near to that. He had not worked out the average rates under the new Australian Tariff, but it was certainly nowhere in the vicinity of 51 per cent.

The Hon. Sir Robert Best (Nationalist, *Kooyong, Vic.*) : " Hear, hear ! It is about 27 per cent."

The Minister for Trade and Customs, continuing, said he could give instance after instance of a similar kind to show that there had never been a single case in which agriculture had suffered as the result of a Protectionist Tariff. On the other hand, he could do the same to show that agriculture had suffered through a Free Trade policy, and he knew no more significant an instance than the history of agriculture in Great Britain itself.

In reply to a question by Mr. Prowse as to Argentine, where the conditions more nearly approximated those of Australia, the Minister said that he could quote some instances that would surprise Mr. Prowse. Agricultural machinery cost a great deal more there than in Australia.

New Zealand was a Free Trade country so far as agricultural implements were concerned, but he (Mr. Massy Greene) was able to show that there was not a single class of agricultural machinery that did not cost more in New Zealand than in Australia ; that was so even in respect of the reaper and binder.

The new Tariff was approved by the House of Representatives on 8th July with amendments relating only to a few of the items, and the same day a Bill to give legislative effect to the Tariff schedule was read a second and third time and reported without amendment.

In moving the Second Reading, on 8th July, 1921,

The Minister for Trade and Customs said that the Bill provided that after the Minister had negotiated with a British Dominion or a foreign country, as the case may be and before he brought his proposal to Parliament for ratification, he must obtain a report from the Tariff Board.* The only other provision of any moment was that which provided for the application of deferred duties. It would be noticed that if the Minister got from the Tariff Board a certificate that goods upon which a deferred duty was imposed were not being manufactured in Australia in sufficient or of satisfactory volume, he might defer from time to time the operation of the deferred duty.

Further progress will be reported in the next issue of the JOURNAL. The modifications which have been recommended by the Senate do not materially affect the protective nature of the Tariff, or its British Preference provisions.

---

* *Vide* Tariff Board Act, p. 888.

TARIFF BOARD ACT.

A Bill for the creation of a Tariff Board was introduced in the House of Representatives on 6th July, 1921, and finally passed by the Senate on 28th July. The Bill aims at providing legislation to protect the public from exploitation arising out of the protection given to local manufacturers by the new tariff.

The main provisions of the Bill are as follows :—

The Tariff Board shall consist of three members, one of whom shall be an administrative officer of the Department of Trade and Customs, who shall be chairman.

The Minister shall refer the following matters to the Board for inquiry and report, and shall not take any action in respect of those matters until he has received the report of the Board :—

(1) The classification of goods under all Tariff items which provide for classification under by-laws.

(2) The determination of the value of goods for duty under Section 160* of the Customs Act, 1901-1920.

(3) Any dispute arising out of the interpretation of any Customs or Excise Tariff in which an appeal is made to the Minister from the decision of the Comptroller-General of Customs.

(4) The necessity for new, increased or reduced duties, and the deferment of existing or proposed deferred duties.

(5) The necessity for granting bounties for the encouragement of any primary or secondary industry in Australia, and the effect of bounties granted.

(6) Any proposal for the application of the British Preferential Tariff or the Intermediate Tariff to any part of the British Dominions or any foreign country, together with any requests received from Australian producers or exporters in relation to the export of their goods to any such part or country.

(7) Any complaint that a manufacturer is taking undue advantage of the protection afforded him by the Tariff, and in particular in regard to his charging unnecessarily high prices for his goods, or acting in restraint of trade to the detriment of the public.

In addition, the Minister may refer to the Board for report any of the following matters :—

(1) The general effect of the working of the Customs Tariff or Excise Tariff in relation to the primary and secondary industries of the Commonwealth.

(2) The fiscal and industrial effects of the Customs Laws of the Commonwealth.

(3) The incidence between the rates of duty on raw materials and on finished or partly finished products ; and

(4) Any other matter in any way affecting the encouragement of primary or secondary industries in relation to the Tariff.

* This section places upon the Minister the duty of determining the value of goods which come into Australia, but are not sold for home consumption in the country of production.

Upon receipt of a report from the Board the Minister may, if he thinks fit, take action in respect of any of the matters dealt with by the Board in its report.

The Board shall, in the month of June each year, report to the Minister generally as to the operation of the Tariff and the development of industries, in which report shall be set out the recommendations made by the Board during the preceding year, other than any recommendations whose inclusion the Minister and the Board agree is not in the public interest.

Power is invested in the Board to summon witnesses and order the production of any document required. Penalties are provided for, *inter alia*, failure to give evidence or to produce documents, giving of false testimony, bribery of witnesses, the prevention of witnesses from attending, and for the dismissal of an employee on account of evidence given before the Board.

DEBATE IN HOUSE OF REPRESENTATIVES.

The Minister for Trade and Customs (Hon. W. Massy Greene), in moving the Second Reading, on 6th July, said that ever since Federation Australia had formed its tariffs more or less on Protectionist lines, and with the development and extension of industry there had been a tendency always to broaden the base of their policy of Protection. There had been a great need for more complete and accurate information on the many details considered when dealing with a Tariff schedule. It seemed highly desirable, therefore, that a special body should be created whose duty it would be to study from day to day not only the operation of the Tariff and its effect upon industries, but also the development of industries in Australia and the means that should be adopted to encourage further development. All the Board would be able to do was to investigate, inform and recommend. Parliament alone could fix the Tariff.

America had in 1909 created a Tariff Board of three members. They had followed that example and proposed to appoint three members under the Bill. One of the appointees would be a member of the Department of Trade and Customs, and the other two from outside. It was necessary that there should be a close liaison between the Board and the Customs Department, and it was proposed that the departmental officer should be Chairman.

The clause which dealt with the reference of certain matters to the Board was a very drastic provision. It made it mandatory on the Minister, in respect to these matters, to refer to the Board before taking action.

The Hon. H. Gregory (Country Party, *Dampier, W.A.*) : " What do you mean by taking action—say, for instance, in regard to the application of the Intermediate Tariff ? "

The Minister for Trade and Customs: "It is impossible for the Intermediate Tariff to be applied to any country until Parliament has agreed to its application. The Minister may enter into and conclude the negotiations, but before he brings to Parliament a Bill for their ratification, he must obtain the report of the Tariff Board on the subject."

Continuing, the Minister drew attention to the provision referring to the Board any complaint that a manufacturer was taking undue advantage of the protection afforded him by the tariff. If the Board found any such complaint to be justified, it might recommend that the duty be reduced or abolished, or that such other desirable action be taken. The obligation was then thrown on the Minister to bring the report before the House within seven days.

The Hon. T. J. Ryan (Deputy-Leader of the Opposition): "If there were not a Board, could not the Minister Act? Is not the interposition of the Board a fetter on the Minister?"

The Right Hon. W. A. Watt (Nationalist, *Balaclava, Vic.*): "The Bill gives the Minister a power apart from the Board which no Minister has previously had."

The Minister for Trade and Customs: "It gives new powers of investigation and report; but it does not interfere with the existing position in relation to matters which a Minister may or may not do."

Mr. Watt: "Under Clause 15 he has summary power."

The Minister for Trade and Customs: "It is not the intention of the Government to give that power to the Minister. If the Clause requires amendment, it can be amended in Committee."

The Minister referred to the Annual Report by the Board, and said that the provision withholding any recommendations was safeguarded to the extent that the Board and the Minister must agree that it was not in the public interest that they should be made known at that time.

Mr. F. Anstey (Labour, *Bourke, Vic.*) said that in his view the Bill should go in the waste-paper basket. What a farce it would be for the Board to go to the expense of drawing up a report after making exhaustive inquiries, if the Minister might say that portions of it should not be published! On a complaint that a manufacturer had taken undue advantage of the Tariff, the Board would make inquiry and report. What would be the next step? Did the Bill provide any machinery by which Parliament might act? If they were to deal with the evil at all there must be some authority with judicial power. If they did not trust the Minister, they should establish a Board and give it the judicial authority to do all the things necessary to put the law into action to prevent undue robbery of the public by the abuse of the Tariff.

Mr. Watt said that the functions of the Board were wisely drawn, and, if properly used, might be fruitful of much good. There were three features, he thought, worthy of amendment. He suggested the necessity of altering the Clause under which power was given to the Minister to "take action" upon the recommendation of the Board, so as to make it clear that that function could not be discharged by the Minister without consulting Parliament. More important changes that might be recommended by the Board should be placed in a positive legislative form. Parliament should be asked in a definite and specific way to affirm them. In minor matters, Parliament would be inclined to trust the Executive.

The Minister had acted wisely in recommending that the Chairman of the Board should be an officer of the Customs Department. As to the other two members, however, he did not think the best men could be got for fees of £5 5s. per day. Although he believed in the proposal, he was not prepared to vote for a scheme which would provide part-time men for the discharge of this important work, at least during the first three or five years. He believed it would be profitable to pay £5,000 a year each for the services of two good men.

The penalties imposed by the Bill appeared to be too Draconian in character, and he suggested that the experience in various parts of Australia was that the more severe the penalties that were inflicted the more difficult it became to secure convictions.

Mr. Gregory said that if a Board was to be appointed he wished to have a Board that could supply information to Parliament. The Tariff Board should be independent of the Minister, who should be able to refer matters to it, but the Board should report to Parliament through the Executive Council. He desired to give special protection to the consumer, and that the Board should report to Parliament in regard to the profits on trade made by manufacturers. Then the House would have an opportunity of knowing something about the enormous profits made in highly-protected industries.

The Minister for Trade and Customs: "There is not only the constitutional difficulty, but the honourable Member is proposing the creation of a price-fixing tribunal."

Mr. Gregory, continuing, said that some manufacturers refused to supply retailers unless they would sell to the public at not less than a certain price. The Board could inquire into that. Could they not say to such manufacturers that unless they supplied goods direct to the retailers and abandoned any arrangements in restraint of trade, an excise duty on their products would be imposed? It might be a straining of the Act, but it ought to be possible to bring in something of that sort. The Board should also have power to inquire into bounties or subsidies paid by foreign countries to encourage shipping, export trade, or unfair competition.

Mr. Ryan said he did not think the measure would be effective because it did not provide any effective machinery for securing proper conditions to the workers engaged in particular manufacturing industries, nor did it protect the purchaser or consumer.

The Minister for Trade and Customs: " Does the hon. Member suggest that there are no constitutional difficulties in the way of doing these things ? "

Mr Ryan: " I do. There was a decision* in the High Court of Australia where a majority of the Court held that duties of excise could not be imposed if there was some indirect purpose such as that of securing proper conditions of industry ; but I think anyone who has followed the trend of recent decisions of the High Court of Australia will come to the conclusion that, if the matter were again submitted to them, probably they would give a decision in a directly opposite direction."

Continuing, Mr. Ryan asked whether the Tariff Board was necessary, seeing that they were not giving further powers to the Minister or to the Government, and they were not proposing to impose any duty of excise to fall automatically on those who did not afford proper working conditions or who did not supply the primary producer with his machinery at fair prices.

Motion to withdraw Bill.

Mr. T. E. Fenton (Labour, *Maribyrnong, Vic.*) moved that the Bill be withdrawn for the purpose of immediately re-casting and re-introducing so as to provide for—

(A) adequate guarantees for the primary producers and consumers generally that they can obtain locally manufactured articles or goods at reasonable prices ; and

(B) the securing of proper wages and conditions for those employed in protected industries.

The motion, which was seconded by **Mr. Parker Maloney** (**Labour,** *Hume, N.S.W.*), was negatived by 27 votes to 12.

Amendments in Committee.

In Committee, on the motion of the **Minister for Trade and Customs**, the terms of reference to the Tariff Board were

---

* The " Harvester " Case, *ex parte* H. V. McKay : Commonwealth Arbitration Reports, Vol. II., p. 1.

extended to include any complaint that a manufacturer is taking undue advantage of the protection afforded him by the Tariff " in acting in a manner which results in unnecessarily high prices being charged to the consumer for his goods "; and Clause 15 was amended so as to make it clear that it is impossible for the Minister to take action (on the recommendation of the Board) which is not already provided for by Statute.

The Bill was passed by the House of Representatives on 15th July, and by the Senate on 28th July.

CUSTOMS TARIFF (INDUSTRIES PRESERVATION) BILL.*

The Minister for Trade and Customs (Hon. W. Massy Greene), in the House of Representatives on 6th July, brought in a resolution to make provision for anti-dumping duties. The resolution, if carried, will be incorporated in the Customs Tariff (Industries Preservation) Bill. At the date when the House went into recess the resolution was still under discussion, paragraph (A) only having been carried.

The resolution provides for the collection of the undermentioned duties, which shall be in addition to such duties as are payable under the Customs Tariff. The duties shall be payable in each case only on such imported goods as shall be specified in the *Gazette*, the Minister being satisfied, after inquiry and report by the Tariff Board, that the imposition of these duties is in the interest of an Australian industry. The duties, which may be cumulative, are as follows : —

(A) On specified goods, which are of a kind manufactured in Australia, sold to an importer at a price less than their fair market value at the time of shipment, a dumping duty of an amount representing the difference between the fair market value and the export price. (" fair market value " means the fair market value of the goods sold for home consumption in the country of export plus f.o.b. charges.)

(B) On specified goods produced outside Australia and sold to an importer at less than a reasonable price, a dumping below cost duty of an amount equal to the difference between a reasonable price and the export price. (" reasonable price " means the cost of production plus 20 per cent. f.o.b. charges.)

(C) On specified goods consigned to Australia for sale, which may be sold at a less than reasonable price, a dumping consignment duty of an amount equal to the difference between the wholesale selling price in Australia and a reasonable selling price. (" reasonable selling price " in this case means the fair market value plus freight, insurance, landing charges and Customs Tariff duty, plus 20 per cent. of the aggregate.)

---

* *cf.* Safeguarding of Industries Act (U.K.), p. 760.

(D) On specified goods exported to Australia which have been carried at lower than prevailing rates, at ballast rates, or freight free a dumping freight duty of 5 per cent. of the fair market value.

(The duty on any particular goods under the preceding paragraphs shall not, either severally or collectively, exceed 15 per cent. of their value for duty under the Customs Act.)

(E) A dumping exchange duty on any specified goods exported from a country the exchange value of the currency of which has depreciated, the rate of duty to be ascertained in accordance with the following schedule :—

(a) As to the franc and the lire, if the bank rate of exchange of the country of export is between 25.22 (par) and 30, no special duty shall be chargeable ; if between 30 and 35, a special *ad valorem* duty of 8½ per cent. ; between 35 and 40, 15 per cent. ; between 40 and 45, 21 per cent. ; and so on, as the exchange depreciates the rate of added duty increasing by proportionately smaller steps. Thus, with the rate of exchange at 50, the duty is 30 per cent. ; at 100, 50 per cent. ; and at 150, 61½ per cent.

(b) As to the mark, if the rate of exchange is between 25 and 30 a special *ad valorem* duty of 10 per cent. ; between 30 and 35, 18 per cent. ; between 35 and 40, 24½ per cent. ; between 40 and 45, 30 per cent. ; and so on, the duty at 50 being 37½ per cent. ; at 100, 56½ per cent. ; and at 150, 66½ per cent.

(c) As to currencies not provided for, the special duty shall be chargeable at a rate to be proclaimed.

(F) On specified goods exported from a country in which the exchange has depreciated, and sold at less than the fair market value of the same class of goods made in the United Kingdom, when sold for home consumption therein, a dumping preference duty of an amount equal to the difference between the fair market value in the United Kingdom and the export price.

(G) On specified goods wholly or partl made from material supplied from a country whose currency has depreyiated in comparison with the country in which the goods were manufactured, a dumping material duty equal to the difference between the selling price and the fair market value of the goods if made from materials of country of export.

(H) A duty to assure that, should the duty imposed by the last two preceding paragraphs be evaded by the consignment of goods to Australia, that the goods will not be sold at a less than reasonable price.

DEBATE IN HOUSE OF REPRESENTATIVES.

The Minister for Trade and Customs (Hon. W. Massy Greene), in moving the adoption of the resolution, said that the provisions they were introducing followed the Canadian model, inasmuch as they were made effective by administrative act, and by covering all three phases of dumping, namely, goods sold to Australia at a lower price than the market price in the country of production ; goods consigned to and sold in Australia at a lower price than the price in the country of production ; and goods sold in Australia at less than the cost of production.

The Canadian principle adopted.

The Australian Industries Preservation Act of 1906 contained provisions against dumping. That measure set out to do a great deal, but it relied upon a legal process. Before dumping could be proved, the Comptroller-General of Customs had to establish before a Justice of the High Court that goods were being imported at a low price with the intent to destroy or injure an Australian industry. It was almost impossible to prove intent. The result was that no action had ever been taken. The Canadian Act of 1904-7 had been a success. Its application was administrative, and the proposed Bill followed that principle, the only difference being that in every case the Minister must proceed after a report by the Tariff Board. The Bill covered the whole ground of the Canadian Act, and in addition provision would be found for subsidised and ballast freights, which were not covered by the Canadian Act, so far as he was able to learn. It would also be found that the various dumping duties were cumulative in their effect, but altogether they might not exceed 15 per cent. He had adopted that limit because it was provided in the Canadian Act, and, so far as he knew, had been effective.

The Exchange question.

The exchange provisions were perhaps the most difficult part of the Bill. He was confident that some part of the depreciated exchange must be reflected in the increased cost of production. The difficulty was to determine how much. The Canadian Act, as he understood it, provided that if, under the ruling commercial exchange rate, the mark was worth about 2 cents in Canada, while at par rate of exchange the mark was worth 24 cents, as they (Canada) might not allow for a depreciation of more than 50 per cent., it meant that the mark was worth 12 cents when it came to valuing goods for duty. That was to say, if an invoice came into Canada for 100 dollars, the value of the invoice for duty purposes would be 600 dollars instead of 100 dollars, the *ad valorem* duty being then struck on that increased value for duty. America had set out to do the same thing, but her law provided that a greater depreciation than 66⅔ per cent. was not to be allowed, and she had abandoned the method for the same reasons that they in Australia had decided not to adopt it. They felt that in many cases the Canadian method imposed absolute prohibition, and that it would be impossible, in some circumstances, to trade under it at all.

o

Canadian method criticised.

They proposed to make their method definite, and at the same time to allow for the rise and fall in the rate of exchange, fixing different rates of duty in different sets of circumstances. To his mind the Canadian method attacked the problem from the wrong angle, because everything depended upon the rate of duty that applied. Under the Canadian method you got a much higher rate of duty with a high rate of exchange. The manufacture which it might be most necessary to protect, so far as exchange advantage was concerned, might be that to which the 10 per cent. duty was applicable, whilst that least necessary to protect might be protected by a 50 per cent. rate. If the franc went to 300 to the £1, the Australian importer would have to pay less under a rate of 25 per cent. duty, plus the 75 per cent. added duty for equalisation of exchange, than the Canadian importer would have to pay under a rate of 20 per cent., after applying their (the Canadian) method of dealing with exchange.

They had not adopted the English system* because they felt it was too rigid, being probably too much in some cases and too little in others, but they had followed it in one important particular in which it differed from the Canadian Act. The Canadian provision applied to all goods coming from a country with a depreciated exchange, whereas they proposed to apply this provision to specified goods only.

The Basis of calculation.

The Minister then explained that the assumptions upon which the schedule had been based were as follows : —

(1) That the increased cost of production must be expressed in the invoice value of the goods coming from a country whose exchange is depreciated.

(2) That the increased cost will not bear a direct inverse relation to the extent of the depreciation of the currency, but will be something less.

(3) That as the depreciation progresses the increased cost will be reflected in the selling price of the goods to a greater degree, both relatively and proportionately ; and

(4) That at some point any advantage to a selling country from a further depreciation of its currency practically disappears, as it is entirely absorbed by the increased cost of production.

He had found it impossible to get any good or sufficient data upon which to base his conclusions. He had sought information from every possible source in order to find precisely the cost of manufacture of certain classes of goods as expressed

---

* *Vide* p. 760.

in terms of the currency of different countries, but the only definite information he could get was that in organised trades the cost of wages had risen in a line with the increase in the cost of living, but the wages in unorganised trades had not. He could show that the relative cost of living between England and France and between England and Germany had not risen in the same ratio as the exchange rate between those countries had fallen. Whilst the rate of exchange between Britain and France to-day was, roughly, as 1 is to 2, the increase in the cost of living was as 1 is to 1½; and whilst the exchange rate between England and Germany was as 1 is to 13, the cost of living was, approximately, as 1 is to 4½. From this they could get an approximate idea of the advantage which Germany got in selling her goods under existing exchange conditions. As currency depreciated a greater relative increase was reflected in the cost of production when selling their goods. Applying that to the schedule, it would be seen that as the exchange depreciated they increased the rate of added duty by proportionately smaller steps.

In reply to the Hon. Austin Chapman (Nationalist, *Eden-Monaro, N.S.W.*), on 19th July, who asked if they were to conclude that the Government were going to allow goods to come in from Germany, the Minister said that that matter was on " the knees of the gods." He would say nothing in regard to it other than that they had made provision for it in the schedule.

Mr. Matthew Charlton (Labour, *Hunter, N.S.W.*), said there was one objectionable feature to the resolution. The application of the anti-dumping legislation would not, after receiving assent, apply to any specific conditions. Its application depended upon what the Tariff Board might recommend, and even then the Minister might not approve of the recommendation. Unless immediate action followed upon the revelation of dumping, the importer was likely to be unfairly affected. The provisions dealing with exchange were very complex. This duty was to be levied only on specified goods. Canada found it advisable to levy an exchange duty upon all goods. There were many things which Australia could not produce, and it would be a mistake to devise a schedule embracing all their imports. He considered a better system would be for the Customs Authorities to compile a schedule of the goods which Australia produced in sufficient quantities, and to apply to such goods the anti-dumping duties. The importer would then know at once exactly what he would have to pay. It might be argued that no provision should be made for trade with Germany. If it was not being done directly, it was being done indirectly, and the sooner they realised that, the better it would be for Australia.

The Hon. H. Gregory (Country Party, *Dampier, W.A.*) said he thought the provisions in regard to the regulation of exchange should be held over for full consideration in October. The powers provided for in paragraph (c) were the most monstrous he had read. The Minister evidently intended to fix for himself what was a reasonable selling price. To the cost of the goods was to be added freight, insurance, landing and other charges, Customs Duty—which might be an *ad valorem* duty of 45 per cent., plus the customary 10 per cent.— and on the top of all these was to be an impost of 20 per cent. He had indented from the Old Country, and knew that it was possible to do it for about 5 per cent. It was all very well to say it would only apply to this or that article, and only when the Board reported, but the Board would be the creature of the Minister.

He wished to know whether the consumer was to get any consideration. The Country Party were prepared to vote for a Bill against dumping on lines similar to those followed in Canada or Japan, but it was preposterous to ask them to agree to the legislation outlined in all the parts of the motion. The Canadian Act was plain and simple, and let the public know exactly where they stood. In this Bill, however, there was clause after clause of matter most difficult to understand.

Last year a leading Sydney accountant had pointed out the effect of the Minister charging duties on the commercial rate of exchange, and that, with a general duty of 50 per cent. owing to the state of currencies in Italy, France, the United States and Japan, the impost really amounted to 160 per cent. against Italy, 100 per cent. against France, 40 per cent. against Japan, and 38 per cent. against the United States. The general preference of 10 per cent. to Great Britain was absolutely lost, it was shown, owing to the appreciated value of the dollar and the yen. The Supreme Court ruled that the Minister's method was wrong, and when the High Court* was found to be against him, the Minister prepared these proposals. Having regard to the difficulties with which the manufacturers of France had to contend, he felt that the Australian industries, as far as importations from France were concerned, were sufficiently protected. Paragraph (A) related to exports to Australia of goods of a kind manufactured or produced in Australia. He would like to add to it the words " or consigned for sale to Australia," and make it provide for all contingencies, so that if the Minister thought they were being consigned for dumping purposes he would be able to impose on them an excess duty up to 15 per cent. The Minister had promised to protect the

---

* Stewart and Sons, Ltd., *v.* Robinson (Deputy-Collector of Customs, Brisbane), 29, C.L.R., p. 55.

consumer. If the Minister would postpone the exchange part of the motion, he would be able to give further consideration to that phase of the question.

The Minister for Works and Railways (Hon. L. E. Groom) said that paragraphs (B) and (C) could not be eliminated without practically rendering paragraph (A) ineffective. If foreign manufacturers found they had large surplus stocks on hand, they could send consignments into Australia and sell the goods below the actual cost of production. The object of paragraph (C) was to prevent that. This law would only apply to those kinds of goods which were produced or manufactured in Australia, and which had been sold at less than their fair market value at time of shipment, to the detriment of an Australian industry. The Tariff Board would report on these matters. If the Minister ignored the recommendations of the Board, he would be answerable to Parliament.

The Hon. R. Foster (Country Party, *Wakefield, S.A.*): "When the goods have been brought up to a fair market value at the time of shipment, why is a penalty of 20 per cent. added ? "

The Minister for Works and Railways: "There is no penalty of 20 per cent. If the goods are imported *bona 'fide* for the purposes of trade, the importer intends to make and is entitled to make a profit. If a man is importing and selling goods without a profit, what is his object ? In assessing the price 20 per cent. will be added to allow for expenses and profit."

Mr. Edmund Jowett (Country Party, *Grampians, Vic.*) asked the Minister to consider the advisability of postponing the provisions in paragraph (A) of the schedule, which would inflict unjust disabilities on Allies which had fought with them in the War. At the end of the War, Belgium and France were in a sense finally victorious, but their virile manhood had been greatly depleted and their financial resources exhausted. He would not admit that it was any reflection on a country to have the misfortune of having its currency depreciated. At that moment the paper issues of Great Britain and Australia were depreciated. The present value of the £1 note, either British or Commonwealth, was 15s. 1d. Yet the whole trend of the debate had been that there was some reproach against those three valiant countries (France, Belgium and Italy), and that they must impose severe penalties on their industries and manufactures to neutralise the effects. The effect of a depreciated currency on a country had been greatly exaggerated. What was known as the mint par rate of exchange was to-day largely theoretical. Before the War a person in England with £100 could purchase or exchange for

2,500 francs. Owing to the fall in exchange that £100 could now buy 4,700 francs in France. But the fall had been gradual, covering a period of seven years, during which the costs in France had been rising, until now one got little more goods in France for 4,700 francs than one got for 2,500 francs before the War. The theory upon which the clause was based was fundamentally unsound. It appeared to be based on the view that they could buy for £100 of English money a larger number of francs and lire, and therefore, to the same extent, larger quantities of goods from France, Belgium and Italy. The real position was that a process of adjustment went on and gradually tended to render nugatory all those theoretical advantages of a fall in exchanges. The Ministry might do what they liked as far as imports from Germany were concerned, and he should not say them nay.

The Hon. Sir Robert Best (Nationalist, *Kooyong, Vic.*) said he wished to emphasise the point that as regards both goods and exchange they were treating France, Belgium and Italy with nothing like the degree of severity which marked the resolution passed by the British House of Commons. They (Australia) were providing a dumping duty of 15 per cent. as against the British dumping duty of 33⅓ per cent.; and for an exchange duty of 26 per cent. at the present moment against France as against 33⅓ per cent. imposed by the British Parliament. In the United States, where there were very rigid anti-trust laws, there was at the same time express provisions against their application to the export trade of America. Power was provided for the exploitation of any foreign country to permit America to dump its manufactures abroad. They (Australia) were up against that sort of thing, and they must protect themselves. They were making their dumping protection less severe than the Mother Country in regard to some goods, and precisely similar to Canada and the United States in respect of other goods. As far as concerned the exchange provisions they were not more severe than those of Canada and the United States.

Mr. James Mathews (Labour, *Melbourne Ports, Vic.*) said he hoped that these many and varied provisions would have the effect of making the Tariff truly protective, although he doubted that they would do so. He would like to have dealt as leniently as possible with their late Allies, but he recognised no nation to which he would give precedence over the Australian people. They had imposed high duties upon importations from their own kith and kin in Great Britain in order to encourage Australian manufactures. Therefore they should not fail to protect the local product against the competition of goods manufactured in France, Belgium and Italy.

Proposed Amendment.

Paragraph (A) having been agreed to, without comment, **The Hon. H. Gregory (Country Party,** *Dampier, W.A.*), in moving that paragraph (B) be amended so as to apply to paragraphs (B) and (C) the same conditions as applied in paragraph (A), said that the Minister had stated that a reasonable price represented the equivalent of the cost of production plus 20 per cent.   To ascertain it, there was added to the production value the cost of getting the goods to the coast in the country of export, and the cost of landing them in Australia. Then there was heaped up every conceivable charge that could be imposed, and upon everything else the Minister added a profit of 20 per cent.   After which, and before the goods reached the consumer, there was the ordinary duty of, perhaps, 45 per cent., plus 15 per cent.   Where did the consumer come in ?   That was one of the most wicked and preposterous proposals ever placed before Parliament.   He was satisfied with the proposal contained in paragraph (A), but they (the Country Party) desired the same conditions in respect of goods which were not produced in Australia, but the importation of which might be detrimental to an Australian industry.   He had more than once referred to the enormous duty which had had to be paid by certain people in Western Australia upon 14-gauge wire.   The primary producer was being driven off the land.   The whole of the Government's efforts in connection with the Tariff had been in the direction of increasing the cost of living and piling up the costs of production.   He could not imagine any reason why the classes of goods specified in paragraphs (B) and (C) should be subjected to an excess dumping duty beyond the impost prescribed in paragraph (A).

The proposed amendment was still under discussion when the House went into recess on 22nd July.

State Parliaments.

New South Wales.

Death of Premier : New Cabinet (Note).

The Hon. John Storey, M.L.A., the Premier, died on October 5th. The Hon. James Dooley, M.L.A., is the new Premier, and the reconstructed Ministry is as follows :—

Premier and Chief Secretary	Hon. James Dooley, M.L.A.
Minister of Agriculture	Hon. W. F. Dunn, M.L.A.
Secretary for Lands and Minister of Forests	Hon. P. F. Loughlin, M.L.A.
Secretary for Mines and Minister of Local Government	Hon. George Cann, M.L.A.
Treasurer	Hon. J. T. Lang, M.L.A.
Minister of Public Instruction	Hon. T. D. Mutch, M.L.A.
Attorney-General and Minister of Justice	Hon. E. A. McTiernan, M.L.A.
Secretary for Public Works and Minister of Railways	Hon. John Estell, M.L.A.
Minister for Labour, Industry, Health and Motherhood	Hon. J. J. G. McGirr, M.L.A.
Minister for State Industrial Undertakings and Housing	Hon. C. C. Lazzarini, M.L.A.
Assistant Minister of Justice	Hon. W. J. McKell, M.L.A.
Solicitor-General	Hon. Robert Sproule, M.L.C.
Vice-President of the Executive Council	Hon. E. J. Kavanagh, M.L.C.

Victoria.

General Election (Note).

A General Election was held in Victoria on 30th August. The result shows the state of Parties in the Legislative Assembly as follows : Nationalists, 32 ; Labour, 20 ; Farmers' Union, 12 ; and Independent Labour, 1. In the previous Parliament, the state of Parties was : Nationalists, 31 ; Labour, 20 ; Farmers' Union, 13 ; and Independent Labour, 1. The constitution of the Cabinet remains unchanged (*vide* JOURNAL, Vol. II., No. 1, p. 152).

The General Election followed the dissolution of Parliament, which was brought about by the defeat of the Government on 28th July, on a joint vote of " no-confidence " brought in by the Labour Party and Farmers' Union Party, the main subject of which was the failure of the Government to provide for the continuance of the compulsory Wheat Pool. A Referendum amongst wheat growers in Victoria, conducted by the Farmers' Union and the Agricultural Society of Victoria, held in July, had shown a large majority in favour of a compulsory Wheat Pool controlled by the wheat growers: Recent cable advices stated that the Farmers' Union Party had agreed to support the Ministry, and that they had accepted the conditions offered by the Government of a wheat guarantee of 4s. a bushel and a co-operative pool.

ELECTORAL ACT, 1920.

This Act, which was assented to on 16th June, 1921, provides that whenever a Member of the Legislative Council or of the Legislative Assembly resigns his seat in order to seek election for the Parliament of the Commonwealth of Australia, and fails to secure election to that Parliament, if he is nominated as a candidate for the vacancy occurring through his own resignation, he shall be declared elected without holding a poll : Provided always that his resignation is received within twenty-one days of the issue of the writ for the Commonwealth election with an intimation of his intention of again becoming a candidate for the vacancy caused by his own resignation should he fail to secure election to the Commonwealth Parliament.

South Australia.

Elections and New Government (Note).

A General Election of Members to the House of Assembly was held on the 9th April, with the result that the state of Parties in the House is now as follows :—Liberal Party, 25 ; Labour Party, 16 ; Farmers' and Settlers' Association, 4 ; and Ministerial Party, 1. In the last Parliament the strength of parties was :—Liberal Party, 21 ; Labour Party, 17 ; Nationalist Party, 7 ; and Farmers' and Settlers' Association, 1.

On the same day elections of Members to the Legislative Council were held in four districts. The state of Parties in the Council is now as follows :—Liberal Party, 14 ; Labour Party, 4 ; Farmers' and Settlers' Association 1 ; and Ministerial Party, 1.

The constitution of the new Cabinet remains unchanged and is as follows :—

Premier and Attorney-General	Hon. Henry N. Barwell, M.P.
Chief Secretary and Minister of Marine	Hon. J. G. Bice, M.L.C.
Treasurer and Minister of Education ..	Hon. George Ritchie, M.P.
Commissioner of Crown Lands and Immigration and Minister of Repatriation	Hon. G. R. Laffer, M.P.
Commissioner of Public Works and Minister of Railways and Industry	Hon. W. Hague, M.P.
Minister of Agriculture, Irrigation and Mines	Hon. T. Pascoe, M.L.C.

Western Australia.

General Election and New Government (Note).

A General Election took place on 12th March, 1921, resulting in the state of Parties in the Legislative Assembly as follows :—Labour, 17 ; Country Party, 16 ; Nationalist, 11 ; National Labour, 4 ; Independent Country Party, 1 ; and Independent, 1. At this Election women were eligible for candidature for the first time in Western Australia, and Mrs. A. D. Cowan, who was returned for West Perth, is the first woman to be elected to an Australian Parliament.

As in the last Government, the constitution of the new Cabinet is a coalition of the Country Party and the Nationalists, the portfolios being allotted as follows :—

Premier, Colonial Treasurer and Minister for Lands and Repatriation	The Hon. Sir James Mitchell, K.C.M.G., M.L.A.
Minister for Education, North-West, and Justice	The Hon. H. P. Colebatch, M.L.C.
Minister for Public Works, Water Supply and Trading Concerns..	The Hon. W. J. George, M.L.A.
Minister for Mines, Railways, Industries and Forests ..	The Hon. J. Scaddan, M.L.A.
Colonial Secretary and Minister for Public Health	The Hon. F. T. Broun, M.L.A.
Minister for Agriculture and the Wheat Scheme .. :. ..	The Hon. H. K. Maley, M.L.A.

NEW ZEALAND.

The Third Session of the twentieth Parliament began on the 22nd September, 1921, when the Governor-General's speech was delivered.

As no Parliamentary reports can reach this country in time for publication in this number of the JOURNAL, the usual summary will appear in the next issue.

WASHINGTON CONFERENCE.

(New Zealand Representative.)

According to a Press cable, the Prime Minister (the Right Hon. W. F. Massey) announced in the House of Representatives, on 11th October, that the New Zealand representative at the Washington Conference would be the Hon. Sir John Salmond, one of the Judges of the Supreme Court and ex-Solicitor-General of the Dominion.

SOUTH AFRICA.

The following summary deals with the proceedings of the First Session of the Fourth Parliament of the Union of South Africa which opened on 11th March, 1921, and is in continuation of the summaries commenced in Vol. II., No. 2, of the JOURNAL. *The Session closed on 4th July, 1921. A certain number of subjects have been held over for treatment in the next number of the* JOURNAL.

TREATIES OF PEACE ACT.

(Constitutional Question: South-West African Mandate, etc.)

This Bill to facilitate the carrying into effect, in so far as concerns the Union of South Africa, of certain Treaties of Peace between the King and certain other Powers, and to extend the operation of Act No. 49 of 1919 (Treaty of Peace and South-West Africa Mandate Act),* passed the Second Reading in the House of Assembly on 16th June after a brief debate, the chief discussions taking place in the Committee Stage on 17th and 20th June. The measure was passed during the Session but the Act had not been received at the time of going to press. It would appear, however, that no amendments were made during the passage of the Bill.

The Bill provided that the Governor-General might make appointments, establish offices, and do such things as appeared to him to be necessary for giving effect to any of the provisions of the Treaties of Peace between His Majesty the King and Austria, signed at Saint Germain-en-Laye, 10th September, 1919; Bulgaria, signed at Neuilly-sur-Seine, 27th November, 1919; Hungary, signed at Trianon, 4th June, 1920; and Turkey, signed at Sèvres, 10th August, 1920; and that any act of the Governor-General in that behalf should be lawful, notwithstanding any provision in any law to the contrary.

It also enacted that the provisions of Act No. 49 of 1919 should remain in operation until repealed by Parliament, anything to the contrary in Section 5 of that Act (*vide* Amendment B, Vol. I., p. 201) notwithstanding.

DEBATE IN HOUSE OF ASSEMBLY.

On 17th June, on the motion of the Minister of Finance to go into Committee on the Bill,

The Speaker (Hon. C. J. Krige), in reply to a question by General Hertzog, ruled that questions affecting the ratification

---

* *Vide* Vol. I., No. 1, of the JOURNAL, pp. 201 and 214, and Vol. I., No. 3, p. 552.

of the Peace Treaty could not be dealt with in the Treaties of Peace Bill unless its title was amended.

General the Hon. J. B. M. Hertzog (Leader of the Opposition) thereupon moved the amendment of the title to insert the words " to ratify and to facilitate the carrying into effect." Objections being raised to this being moved as an unopposed motion, General Hertzog intimated that at a later stage he would move in the direction indicated.

The House thereupon went into Committee.

Necessity of Ratification by Parliament.

On Clause 1,

General Hertzog moved that progress be reported so that the words he mentioned might be inserted in the title. He regretted that the Minister should have objected to his unopposed motion. The responsibility of any delay would rest with the Minister. He (General Hertzog) protested strongly against rights and powers being given to the Governor-General in respect of any matter the ratification of which the South African Parliament had not first been consulted on. That Parliament had never in any way been asked to ratify the Peace Treaty or otherwise. Why should it now be asked to give the Governor-General power to act in regard to giving effect to the Peace Treaty ? The question involved was an important constitutional one and had been dealt with by the Canadian Parliament. Mr. Burton had told the House that the ratification had already taken place. Who had ratified the Treaty ? The Ministers and the King could not ratify it; they could approve of it, but the ratification rested with Parliament.

Procedure in other Dominions.

In the Canadian House of Commons Sir Robert Borden, dealing with this question, had said " it was unquestionable that the Treaty should be submitted to Parliament before its ratification." Ministers in South Africa, though they had laid on the table the Peace Treaties with Austria, Hungary, Turkey and Bulgaria, had never asked Parliament to ratify them. He dealt in detail with the various treaties, pointing out that each in turn had been approved of by the Australian and New Zealand Parliaments. Ministers in South Africa, however, acted differently and treated the House with the greatest contempt. Unless Ministers followed the constitutional course the Nationalist Party would raise objections and force them to do so. For that reason he would ask the House to insert a clause first of all ratifying the Treaties referred to ; otherwise, the Minister should propose the same by resolution.

Negation of Democratic Government.

Dr. D. F. Malan (Nationalist, *Calvinia, Cape*) said the whole question of their higher status was at issue. The King could not ratify a Treaty on his own initiative. If he could, then it would make all democratic government an absolute farce. Had the King ratified the Treaties on the advice of the English Cabinet, it meant that their higher status fell away completely. Possibly the ratification had taken place on the advice of the South African Ministry, and he asked for information from **Mr.** Burton on this point.

Another question was whether the Government could act without Parliament, or whether it should have consulted Parliament. On the Versailles Treaty, Parliament had been consulted and the whole question had been discussed. Why had not that been done in this instance ?

Action of the Government explained.

The Minister of Finance (Hon. Henry Burton) pointed out that in September, 1919, the Prime Minister moved a certain resolution in reference to the Peace Treaty with Germany, to the effect that "a humble Address be presented to His Majesty praying that His Majesty may be graciously pleased to ratify and exchange ratification of the Treaty on behalf of the Union of South Africa." When that resolution was discussed hon. Members opposite said " What is the use of all this ? This all means nothing." The point was that this resolution was prior to the ratification of the Treaty with Germany.

A resolution was not submitted in that House to say they would ratify that Treaty. They did not pass an Act, which was really what General Hertzog asked should be done. There was no doubt that the introduction of such a clause as he had mentioned would be a consitutional departure of a very serious and important character in their history. The constitutional British practice had been that the King declared war and the King made peace. The British Parliament had never claimed that no Treaty of Peace may be made with a foreign Power until that Treaty was submitted to it and ratified by Act passed by Parliament.

Proceeding, Mr. Burton said that after the Treaty with Germany had been dealt with by resolution when Parliament was sitting, the other Treaties came along and Parliament was not sitting, and, perfectly constitutionally, the British Secretary of State sent a cable to the Executive of South Africa asking for its consent to the ratification of the Treaties by the King. The consent was given. General Hertzog said that because of that control by Parliament had been lost; but this was not the position, because if the Government had gone beyond its functions Parliament knew how to deal with it as it pleased. The only Treaty of which he (Mr. Burton) had no information was that with Turkey, and if there was any constitutional difficulty in regard to that he was prepared to take it out of the Bill, because he thought that would not do much harm. He emphasised that whether the Treaties were ratified or not made no difference to that Bill. The measure contained administrative powers for which the Government would have to ask whether the Treaties were ratified or not.

Sanction of Parliament insisted upon.

General Hertzog said the Minister was quite right in saying that peace was made by the King ; that was the constitutional practice of England. But it should not end there. Constitutionally, Ministers should come to Parliament and say " This is what has happened in regard to that war," and it was for Parliament to sanction what had taken place. All he asked for now was that Ministers should first of all sanction the Peace Treaties in the correct constitutional manner. He denied that Nationalists during the discussion of the Versailles Treaty had said that the ratification of the South African Parliament meant nothing as in the end the King would have to ratify the Treaty all the same.

Mr. F. J. W. van der Riet (South African Party, *Albany, Cape*) asked if there was any instance of the British Parliament ratifying Peace Treaties by resolution after the King himself had ratified ? Was it not a fact that where Parliamentary authority was required for administrative action, following ratification of Peace, confirmation must be given by the passing of an Act ?

Constitutional Doctrine of Nationalists.

Mr. W. S. Webber (South African Party, *Troyeville, Trans.*) expressed the belief that the constitutional doctrine advanced from the Nationalist benches was quite a novel one in the history of the British Constitution. The doctrine had been set up that the King having made peace through the advice of their Ministers, the latter must ask Parliament to ratify it. According to that, the peace was not peace until it was ratified by Parliament. Where were they in the interval—at war or at peace ?

'The Minister of Public Works (Hon. Sir Thomas Watt) said that the King, on the advice of the Government of South Africa, so far as that country was concerned, could make a Treaty which was binding without the authority or sanction of Parliament. The latter might or might not express disapproval of the Government.

Labour attitude.

Mr. T. Boydell (Leader of the Labour Party) said the Labour Party held that from the democratic point of view these Treaties should be ratified at some time or other by the Parliament of the country. They agreed that something should be put in the Bill, or some resolution passed by the House, in the way that was followed previously, which gave some control to Parliament, feeble though that control might be. The more they could remove these questions of war and peace from kings and governments and bring them into the hands of the people through their Parliaments, the safer would be the people in the future.

The motion to report progress was defeated by 50 votes to 39.

South-West African Mandate.

On Clause 2,

General Hertzog objected to the extension of the Mandate Act, declaring that more information should be submitted to Parliament. The Union was the guardian of the South-West, but the report of the Commission on its administration gave him the impression that the Mandate meant nothing more or less than annexation. To his mind that was a scandalous piece of international fraud. The Mandate laid it down that because the South-West lay on their borders it should, for the sake of convenience, be administered as an integral part of the Union. But that did not mean annexation, and he was not going to agree to it. The inhabitants of South-West were concerned and were entitled to demand their rights under the Peace Treaty.

Germans and Oath of Allegiance.

He went on to ask if the intention was to deport Germans in the South-West who refused to take the oath of loyalty to the King, whether it be the King of the Union or of whatever country ? If that was the intention, it would be a scandal such as would never be tolerated by America. The idea was that eventually the South-West would be an integral part of the Union and would have its representatives in Parliament. But only those people were to elect the representatives who had taken the oath of loyalty. Where did they find that in the Mandate ?

The Minister of Justice (Hon. N. J. de Wet): " No, of course not, but who should elect the representatives to Parliament but the citizens of the Union ? "

General Hertzog asked whether, under the Mandate, the Germans in German-West had the right to refuse to become citizens of the Union if they so desired.

The Minister of Justice: " Certainly, just as much as Germans in the Union have the right."

General Hertzog said "No " ; in the Union the Germans were guests, but in German-West they were the masters.

The Minister of Justice: ". Where do you find that in the Mandate or in the Peace Treaty ? "

Authority of League of Nations.

General Hertzog declared that the Union had no right in any way to use compulsion to make German-West join the Union or otherwise. Nothing could be done until that country had come of age, and to use any persuasion or compulsion would be acting as a defrauding guardian. The League of Nations was the authoritative power, the only power which could eventually give the choice to South-West as to what it wished to be done, and then the South-West was the only party to decide whether or not it desired to join the Union.

The Acting Prime Minister (Hon. F. S. Malan) said that under Clause 2 of the Mandate the Union would administer the country as an integral part of itself, etc. Clause 22 of the Peace Treaty, he reminded them, gave the Union Government the right to deport German subjects from the territory. Clause 2 referred to inhabitants, and " inhabitants " could not be regarded as the people who had been sent away or deported.

Question of citizenship.

The inhabitants of German-West were no longer German subjects under the Peace Treaty, and they were no longer citizens or subjects of any country. They could not become citizens or subjects of the Union except at their own request, and there was not the least intention of compelling them to become citizens of the Union. But there was a second class of person in South-West—the man who had gone there from the Union. What was his position ? He did not lose his citizenship of the Union. General Hertzog had spoken a good deal about the South-West population coming of age ; surely the people who had come from the Union must also be consulted as to whether the country should join the Union. At present, the German in the South-West could return to Germany and again become a German subject, or he could go on as he was and remain a citizen of no State. Clause 2 of the Mandate made it quite clear that the country or the inhabitants could never on their own account come of age.

General Hertzog had forgotten, Mr. Malan continued, that there were three kinds of mandates, and tried apparently to apply the weakest kind to the South-West. The question of annexation, or otherwise, did not crop up at all. The Germans in German South-West could exercise their own choice when they thought fit and become citizens of the Union ; they were not within Union territory and could not therefore become naturalised citizens of the Union.

Mandates not given by League of Nations.

The Minister of Justice said the report of the Commission which had been before the country for three months dealt with the legal question. It seemed to him to be quite clear that Germany surrendered her overseas possessions to the Allied and Associated Powers, and not to the League of Nations (Clause 119 in the Peace Treaty). The mandates were not given by the League of Nations to particular Powers, but by the Allied and Associated Powers. The League of Nations had in another connection taken up the position that they had nothing to do with the allocation of mandates.

Status of German subjects.

The Allied and Associated Powers had the absolute right to repatriate every German subject of European origin from those territories. He did not say whether it was an advisable or a good thing or a nice thing to do ; he was dealing with facts. The Peace Treaty had really given no rights whatever to the old German European subjects in those territories that Germany renounced. They had no status anywhere in the Treaty. It was true that there was a general provision that those people in the territories who were not able to stand by themselves formed a sacred trust to the mandatory Power. Did that refer to the Germans in South-West? If any legal man was going to argue that that referred to the Germans in South-West he simply did not agree with him. He thought the House was entitled to know what the policy of the Leader of the Opposition was in this matter. Did he agree with the Minority Report of the Commission ?

P

Indigenous Populations.

As far as the framers of the Peace Treaty saw, the Minister of Justice continued, these communities would not stand alone. It was stated in the Treaty* that there were territories such as South-West Africa, which, owing to the sparseness of their population and so on, could best be administered under the laws of the Mandatory as integral portions of its territory, subject to safeguards in the interests of the indigenous population. Were the Germans the indigenous population of German South-West ? He maintained that the Germans in those territories which were given up had no status whatever.

Administrative Powers of Union Government.

The power of administration rested with the Union Parliament, the Union Government and, if they liked, the electors of the Union standing behind the Union Parliament. If anybody wanted to take part in the administration of this mandated territory he must be a member of that supreme authority of the Union. The Mandatory Power, the Union of South Africa, had the power to apply all or any of its laws to the mandated territory. He admitted that there was not much difference between these powers and annexation so far as all practical purposes were concerned.

The future of South-West Africa, Mr. de Wet added, was indissolubly bound up with the future of the Union, and they would be committing a crime to South Africa by holding out hopes to these people that they were going to have self-determination.

Questions relating to Naturalisation, etc.

General Hertzog said he wanted the people in the South-West to realise that the Union was doing the just thing ; he wanted them to become good citizens, and he would deprecate anything that might create a division between them and the people of the Union. Referring to the question of naturalisation, he said their laws could be applied to the South-West for administrative purposes, but what the Minister of Justice stated was different—it meant that they could use their laws to turn inhabitants of other countries into subjects of their country. That right was not given. All they could do was to leave matters as they were.

Another important question was whether, under any mandate, they could ever have the right to annex the Protectorate, and a further question was how far they could go with the approval and consent of the people living in the

---

* Clause 22.

territory. The Mandate, it was true, was handed to South Africa, but it was exercised on behalf of the League of Nations. The Minister of Justice had said that there were three kinds of mandates. Quite so. The nature of the mandate depended on the degree of civilisation and development of the mandated country. First of all, there were the people falling under the Turkish Empire, who had reached such a state of development that they could select their own mandatory. That did not apply to the other mandated countries. There were the people of Central Africa, who had not reached that state of development; and then there were the countries with the sparse populations which could be best administered under the laws of the country which had been given the mandate. That applied to the South-West territory.

The Principle of Self-Government.

There was not a word to show that, as the Minister of Justice had said, they had been given the Mandate only on account of the native population. So long as they remained the Mandatory Power they had to carry out the terms and conditions of the Mandate, and report every year. He reminded the House of General Botha's words: "We do not want annexation." Similarly, President Wilson had laid it down that no country should have the right to annex another, and that every country should have the right to govern itself. That principle had been concurred in by all the belligerents. The time would come when the Union might be able to report that the mandated country could stand on its own feet, and then the League of Nations could discharge the Union from further mandatoryship.

General Hertzog argued that even if the population of the South-West consisted mainly of natives well able to govern themselves and there was only a small number of Europeans, self-government should be given to the natives. If in ten years' time there should be a fairly large number of Europeans and natives in the South-West, and the Europeans were able to govern the country, the Union Government should recommend to the League that self-government be handed to the white section, or, if the natives were fitted for self-government, to the natives.

Possibility of Incorporation in the Union.

The question which arose was whether the South-West would ever become part of the Union. It was because he was so anxious it should that he had risen to speak. If the European inhabitants desired it of their own free will, the country could become part of the Union; but that could only take place with the consent of the Council of the League of Nations, which should then make it clear to the inhabitants of the South-West that the country could either become an integral part of the Union, or continue under the Mandate until such time as they could govern themselves. But only the inhabitants of the South-West, and not the citizens of the Union living there, could vote on that point. The Mandate was given to the Union over the inhabitants of the South-West.

The Acting Prime Minister: "And future inhabitants."

General Hertzog: "No."

The Acting Prime Minister: "But the Mandate is over the country."

General Hertzog: "And its inhabitants." The question which was concerning them was one before the people were free, and he held that when it came to an issue they must take only the opinion of the people of the South-West and not of those who were subjects of other countries. In regard to the Minority Report of the South-West Commission the general principle had his hearty approval. He added, in conclusion, that he emphatically differed from the view that the Germans in the territory had no rights and had not been considered in the Peace Treaty clause.

Unalterable character of Mandate.

Mr. R. W. Close (**South African Party,** *Rondebosch, Cape*) said they were bound by the Treaty of Peace and not by President Wilson's fourteen points. The whole of the Mandate was very novel. It gave the Mandatory full powers of administration and legislation, and, save with the consent of the mandatory Power and of the Council itself, was unalterable. The future would have to look after itself. Why General Hertzog should say that the Naturalisation Law could not be applied in South-West Africa just the same as any other law it was very difficult to see. Upon the taking over of South-West Africa by the Mandatory, the Germans in that territory ceased to be German nationals, but they did not become British nationals, since the territory had not been conquered. They were not in the position of guardians who were to take matters to a stage at which these people could stand alone and go away from them if necessary.

A hopeful note.

Mr. M. Alexander (**Constitutional Democrat,** *Cape Town, Castle*) said it was clear that there could be no future for South-West Africa apart from the Union. The people of South-West Africa could be assured that, as far as the Parliament was concerned, their grievances would be dealt with and the country would be fairly treated. He saw no reason why in the future those people should not be as good and loyal South Africans as any of them.

The debate was adjourned.

German Language in Schools.

On the resumption of the debate on 20th June,

General Hertzog referred to a report which he had seen indicating that the attitude taken up by the Administration in the South-West was that, after a certain standard, German was not admitted as a medium in the Government schools. The question arose whether they, the Union authorities, had the right to take a decision like that. · They had to ask what was most in the interest of the pupils attending the schools.

A reassuring statement.

The Acting Prime Minister said that the question just raised was receiving the attention of the Administration. General Hertzog was rather exaggerating the case when he spoke of the rights of the inhabitants of the South-West. He doubted whether they could claim the German language as a right, but the matter was one which should be dealt with in a sympathetic spirit. Their Education Ordinance, laying down the two official languages, as media of instruction, was applicable to the South-West, but the Government desired to let German, along with Dutch and English, be the medium in the primary schools. After that, German would be a subject in the curriculum. The Administration had had a conference on the subject, and it was hoped to arrive at a satisfactory arrangement.

General Hertzog expressed gratification at the attitude of the Acting Prime Minister, but said he felt very strongly on the whole question, and did not wish anything to be done which might cause discontent among the Germans, or that might kindle a suppressed fire and lead to considerable difficulty in the future.

Revenue and Expenditure.

Dr. D. F. Malan (**Nationalist**, *Calvinia, Cape*) expressed the hope that the Estimates regarding revenue and expenditure in German-West would be fully discussed, as the Union Assembly was responsible in the last resort for its finances. Every year the Union would have to account to the League of Nations, and unless the House was given an opportunity of discussing the whole matter, it would be impossible to account to the League.

"A temporary trust."

Mr. F. W. Beyers (Nationalist, *Edenburg, O.F.S.*), who criticised the speech of the Minister of Justice and seriously doubted his interpretation of Clause 22* of the Peace Treaty, said it was well known that General Smuts had conceived the idea of a Mandatory Power, but it was clear that the idea never had been that the Mandatory should be eternal. It was in the very nature of a trust which was temporary.

An amendment proposed by Mr. A. S. van Hees (Nationalist) on 17th June to make the Bill operative for one year only was negatived.

The Bill passed through its remaining stages, and was ordered to be transmitted to the Senate for its concurrence.

IN THE SENATE.

In the Senate on 23rd June, in Committee on the Treaties of Peace Bill, in reply to questions, **The Acting Prime Minister (Hon. F. S. Malan)** said that the Union, under the Mandate, had the right to administer and legislate for the Protectorate. Clause 137 of the South Africa Act could, for instance, be applied there if desired. German was not to be suppressed in the schools. The time the Mandate lasted would depend on the League of Nations. The Union's naturalisation law could be applied to the Protectorate. The properties of Germans would be treated in the same way as those of Germans in the Union.

The Bill was reported without amendment, and the Third Reading set down for the following day.

DEFENCE AND NAVAL POLICY.

(Contribution to Navy, etc.)

On 6th June, the House of Assembly, in Committee of Supply on the Estimates, discussed Vote 19, Defence, £1,340,049.

DEBATE IN HOUSE OF ASSEMBLY.

The Right Hon. J. X. Merriman (South African Party, *Stellenbosch, Cape*) said if the Defence Bill† was not to be proceeded with this Session he would like to know what

---

* Relating to the different forms of Mandate.
† *Vide* Summary in the JOURNAL, Vol. II., No. 3, pp. 681-688.

necessity there was for putting down this Vote. It seemed to him that under these circumstances the amount should be very much curtailed.

Opposition to Naval Contribution.

General the Hon. J. B. M. Hertzog (Leader of the Nationalist Party) moved the deletion of the item of £85,000 contribution to the Navy. Last year, he said, the Nationalists had clearly expressed the view that they should provide for their own protection for South Africa, including naval defence. The position to-day was even more favourable than last year, and the Prime Minister himself had declared that South Africa should take her coast defences into her own hands. So long as a Vote like this remained, which resulted in nothing being done for their coast defences, they were not doing the right thing by South Africa.

It was a ridiculous argument that the £85,000 was voted because the British Navy protected them. So long as the Navy had other work it could not protect South Africa, and the War had proved that. It was absurd to say that the Navy would come there to protect them. They had contributed £85,000 towards a total of £100,000,000. The time had come for South Africa to take matters into her own hands. If it should ever be necessary to protect South Africa, then they would have no say in the matter. All that would be asked would be " In what respect shall we help? " He contended that if South Africa undertook her own coast defence her contribution to the Navy would be far greater than it was now.

Naval Contribution defended.

Mr. Merriman said that he certainly did not want them to take away this Vote. Such a course would be little short of a blunder, which was worse than a crime. The Fleet was the only mode they had of defending the shores of that country, and unless they set up something else in its place they would be defenceless. If the King went to war they were all at war. What could they depend on for that country to defend their harbours ? This subject, he added, was too large to discuss on the Estimates. When they once came to discuss their status and decide what their real position was, they would find that they were in a very different position from what was thought.

Mr. C. T. M. Wilcocks (Nationalist, *Winburg, O.F.S.*) said that during 1919-20 a great deal more money had been voted than had been required for the purposes stated, with the result that a great deal more taxation had been imposed than was necessary.

Defence Force.

The **Acting-Minister of Defence (Hon. Patrick Duncan)** intimated that the Government did not intend to go on with the Defence Force Bill during the present Session, but explained that the reason why the estimate was in the form in which it had been brought up (as if the Government were intending to proceed with the Bill) was because the permanent force which was to have been constituted under the new Act existed to a large extent already. After giving details he assured the House that there was no need to fear that large sums of money might be voted, but not spent, during the coming year.

Navy and Defence of South Africa: Aviation.

Brig.-General the Hon. J. J. Byron (South African Party, *Border, Cape*), referring to the statement by General Hertzog that the British Navy was unable to defend South Africa and had not done so during the War, said such remarks savoured rather of mediæval history than of modern times. The battle of the Falkland Islands undoubtedly saved not only South Africa, but Cape Town, and perhaps that very House, from being shelled by enemy ships. Perhaps the hon. Member also had not forgotten that he and some of his colleagues accepted the hospitality of a British warship to convey them across the ocean at a very critical time.

The hon. Member expressed his regret that aviation was included under the Defence Vote, and emphasised his opinion that a South African Air Force was not needed primarily for military purposes. If, however, the Government insisted on keeping it as a fighting force, he would urge that it be an entirely distinct branch under the administration and control of the Director.

Major G. B. van Zyl (South African Party, *Capetown, Harbour, Cape*) urged that a strong Commission should be appointed during the recess to consider what should be done in regard to the introduction of a really good, sound Defence Force Bill next Session.

After further discussion the debate was adjourned.

Acting-Minister's Reply.

In his reply on 7th June,

The **Acting-Minister of Defence** said that one of the reasons why Colonel Mentz (Minister of Defence) had gone to England was that the Prime Ministers' Conference would discuss various questions of Defence. It was probable that these questions would concern sea more than land defence, but let them not forget.that sea defence was a South African affair also, notwithstanding the fact that South Africa paid practically nothing for it.

Another reason was that the Union Government had taken over almost entirely the defence of South Africa, and intended to continue that policy gradually in regard to its coast defences as well as its inland defences. That meant that Imperial troops would be withdrawn from South Africa, which he thought all would agree was the right policy. It would also mean, however, that considerable tracts of land and buildings of great value which had belonged to the Imperial Government would be transferred to the Union Government, and such transfer would require long and careful investigation.

Referring to the difficulty felt by certain Members in understanding why the Vote could not be reduced seeing that the Defence Bill had been dropped, Mr. Duncan said it seemed to be the impression that there was no Defence Force at the present time at all, but, as he had explained, there were three batteries of artillery in existence and a considerable number of mounted men, all of whom had to be provided for in the Vote.

The appointment of a Commission was a matter which must await the Minister's return.

The discussion was again adjourned.

On 10th June,

Mr. R. B. Waterston (Labour, *Brakpan, Trans.*) moved that the Vote stand over for further consideration by the Government, and pressed for an investigation into the whole question to see whether the money which the House was being asked to spend on a Defence Force could not be spent on something useful.

The Acting-Minister of Defence assured the House that when Colonel Mentz returned he would point out to him the criticisms and requests which had been put forward, and he had not the slightest doubt that they would be given the fullest consideration. He went on to quote figures showing that a great deal of organisation work had been done in order to get the Department out of the confusion and chaos into which it had fallen.

Labour accepts Minister's statement.

Mr. T. Boydell (Leader of the Labour Party) said that in view of the statement by the Acting-Minister of Defence, the

Labour Members did not intend to support the Nationalist amendment, which seemed to be indiscriminate and haphazard and might, if carried, do injustice to many officers.

Amendments moved by Mr. Roux, General Hertzog and Mr. A. P. J. Fourie, having been negatived, and one moved by Major Van Zyl having been withdrawn, the Vote, as printed, was agreed to.

CITIZEN FORCE TRAINING.

In the House of Assembly on 10th May, in reply to a question as to the number of men who underwent training in the Citizen Force in 1913 and 1920 and how many it is proposed to train in the same force during 1921,

The Minister of Defence (Colonel the Hon. H. Mentz) replied; 23,000 men of the Coast Garrison Force and Active Citizen Force (1913), 3,669 in the Active Citizen Force underwent a modified course of peace training (1920); some 6,000 in the Coast Garrison and Citizen Force, but only under a modified course in the latter case. In the above figures no account has been taken of Defence Rifle Associations and Cadets. The figures for these were : Defence Rifle Associations, 1913, 30,000 ; 1920, 113,300 ; 1921, 116,880. Cadets, 1913, 11,300 ; 1920, 33,000 ; 1921, 35,000.

ASIATIC IMMIGRATION.

(Numbers Entering Union: Women, Minors, etc.)

In the House of Assembly on 12th April,

Mr. J. D. Heyns (Nationalist, *Middelburg, Trans.*) asked whether the Government intended to introduce legislation during the present Session prohibiting Asiatic women and minors from entering the country.

The Minister of the Interior (Hon. Patrick Duncan) said the Government did not intend to do so. In reply to further questions he informed the House that the numbers of Asiatic immigrants who were allowed into the Union during 1918, 1919 and 1921, respectively, were as follows : 1918, 10 men, 140 women and 315 children ; 1919, 216 women and 546 children ; 1920, 1 man, 337 women and 650 children. The number of Europeans and Asiatics deported for crimes (specified in Section 22 of Act 22 of 1913) in the same years were : 1918, Europeans 10, Asiatics 105; 1919, Europeans 27, Asiatics 129 ; 1920, Europeans 32, Asiatics 125. The numbers of British subjects who arrived from England during the same years and during the first three months of 1921 with passports issued by the British Government were : 1918, 463 men, 393 women and 41 children ; 1919, 1,381 men, 2,606 women and 1,173 children ; 1920, 5,693 men, 6,677 women and 1,970 children; 1921 (first three months), 1,648 men, 1,633 women and 589 children.

On 26th April, in reply to questions,

The Minister of Justice (Hon. N. J. de Wet) said there were 238 Asiatics in the prisons of the Union on 13th April.

THE BUDGET.

On 15th April, in the House of Assembly, the Minister of Finance delivered his Budget Statement.

DEBATE IN HOUSE OF ASSEMBLY.

Deficit for 1920-21.

The Minister of Finance (Hon. H. Burton) said the House would be glad to hear that the deficit anticipated for the year 1920-21 was not going to be as large as they thought it would be,* principally because they had been able to effect certain economies. Owing to this, and the better yield from Customs and Inland Revenue, their net deficit for 1920-21 would be in the neighbourhood of £250,000. He proposed to let this be carried forward and dealt with in the discussion of the following year.

Loan Account.

The expenditure on loan for 1920-21 had been £13,220,000 or £1,249,000 less than the original and additional estimates together. To meet this they had receipts from all sources to the extent of £14,343,000. If they added the costs of raising loans, £103,000, to the expenditure, the total charge against the loan account was £13,323,000, leaving a balance to be carried forward of £1,020,000. No new loans had been raised during the year, but it had been possible to meet expenditure from the issue of Treasury Bills, both locally and in England and from receipts in respect of mining leases, sale of Crown lands, etc., together with the balance brought forward.

---

* *Vide* debate on Financial Position, JOURNAL, Vol. II., No. 2, p. 444.

Rates of Interest.

The efflux of capital from the Union, as a consequence of the premium on their own currency during the earlier periods of last year, was extremely heavy.   The natural result of that was an increase in the prevailing rates of interest, which had been reflected in the Treasury Bill rate last year.   At the same time, though these rates were raised, compared with ruling rates in other countries they were on the whole favourable.   Union Treasury Bills were sold in London during the year to the extent of £3,000,000—£2,000,000 at seven, and £1,000,000 at six and three-eighths. The two millions were six months and the other million was three months.

Public Debt: Liability to the Imperial Government.

A year ago the public debt was £173,000,000 ; on 31st March, 1921, it amounted to £178,603,000.   With the exception of about £800,000 in respect of post-War expenditure, practically the whole of the expenditure of 1920-21 was of a reproductive nature, so, broadly speaking, the deadweight might be put down as £51,000,000, of which War and post-War expenditure would account for approximately £30,000,000. They had, during that year, repaid advances by the Imperial Government, and reduced their debt in that direction by £2,354,000 at a cost to the Union of £2,000,000, owing to exchange, etc., and their total liability to the Imperial Government in respect of these advances now stood at £5,032,000. The extent to which their public debt was being held more and more in that country was quite apparent : of the £1,780,000 no less than £550,000 was now located in the Union and the balance in London.

Increase in Imports.

Turning to trade, Mr. Burton said the declared value of merchandise imported was £93,405,000 in 1920, and that, as compared with £46,713,000 in 1919, showed an increase of nearly 100 per cent.   There was plenty of evidence, as he went on to show, of the extent to which people had money to spend in extravagance, and the figures were not creditable to South Africa.

Decrease in Exports.

As to exports, the declared value of South African products and manufactures was £83,532,000, as against the total export of £99,770,000 for 1919.   In coal shipped as cargo the figure in 1920 was 1,301,000 tons as against 1,992,000 tons in 1919. There were increased shipments to Egypt and the Argentine

The export of meat showed a falling off of from 44,409,000 lb. weight in 1919 to 12,662,000 lb. in 1920, and the explanation was simply that in 1919 no less than 32,000,000 lb. weight was sent to Egypt, and this year they had sent none.

After giving further details, Mr. Burton pointed out that they were in the midst of the process of deflation. "It is the adjustment of prices to a new level," he said, "throughout all classes of industry which is responsible for the uncomfortable situation in which we find ourselves to-day." Now Labour claimed that what it had gained in increased wages it was going to hold.

Gold-mining and other Industries.

Figures were quoted showing what had been done by the banks to assist the community, and the position of the gold-mining industry, owing to the depreciation of gold, etc. Mr. Burton observed "under the present condition of our industry in South Africa gold is the one article of our production here which is holding our foreign trade together." The prospects in some other industries which were still in the initial stage, *i.e.*, the coal industry and the iron and steel industry, promised well for the future.

Decrease in Revenue.

The revenue had diminished all round, and it was only the extreme and natural buoyancy apparent last year in the Customs, especially in the first nine months, that had enabled them to keep anything like their equilibrium. So far as inland revenue was concerned the striking feature was the collapse of the diamond trade. They estimated in 1921 for £1,250,000 from diamond export duty and got £812,000. Their estimate for the coming year (£300,000) would allow for a reasonable recovery, but it would be extremely rash to put the figure higher.

Income-Tax: A prosperous year.

As to income tax the Minister stated he had dealt with this from the point of view of the diamond mines, and a falling-off was expected from the gold mines. The normal tax estimated for 1921 was £1,000,000, and for 1921-22 it was estimated at £2,500,000. The year that had just ended was the most prosperous one, he supposed, in the whole history of the country, and that had been reflected in the income-tax return on the high figure for next year. Excess profits duty had been estimated at £1,300,000 for the coming year, a statement that might surprise them, because the Act makes that tax disappear; but there were still a lot of collections to be made, and the profits made during this prosperous period—fortunately for them—would have to be taxed.

Estimates: a deficit of nearly £6,000,000.

In regard to the Estimates for 1921-22, the Departments had been warned that all unessential work must be postponed and expenditure cut down; but after some curtailments by the Treasury, and after allowing for £450,000 in respect of the adjustment of pay in accordance with the report of the Public Service Commission, and another £300,000 for unemployment, the estimates of the Departments totalled the alarming figure of £32,271,000, a figure very much higher than either the expenditure or estimates for the previous year.

The deficit to be provided for was £6,846,000, to which must be added the deficit (£250,000) of 1920-21. After all possible reductions had been made, they were still left with a shortfall of nearly £6,000,000. To write that figure upon a slate and turn the writing to the wall, as some thought possible, would be a cowardly abandoning of national responsibility. They were financially sound, and must shoulder the burden.

Reduction of Cost of Living Allowance.

The first step for the Government to take was to restrict its ordinary recurrent expenditure. The sum of just over two millions was accounted for by the cost of living allowances under the provision (approximately $11\frac{1}{2}$ millions) for Union establishment. It was proposed to reduce the cost of living allowance by 25 per cent., for the first quarter of the financial year, by 50 per cent. for the next quarter, by 75 per cent. for the third, and to eliminate it altogether by the end of the year. By this they would save £1,252,000. This allowance was granted to make up for the rise in the cost of living; the cost of living was coming down, and the indications were that it would come down much more rapidly.

Members' Allowances.

It was the duty and privilege of Parliament to set an example, and therefore it was propose to treat the Members' additional allowances (of £200*) similarly: that was to say, to leave £100 of it, but to diminish the other £100 in the same way and by the same stages as the allowance of the Civil Servants.

Mr. Burton proceeded to show how they had brought down the estimates of expenditure from £32,000,000 to

* Granted last year, *vide* JOURNAL, Vol. I., No. 4, p. 762. *Vide* also p. 786 of this issue.

£29,544,000. They thus arrived at a figure of £3,979,000 to deal with, and they were entitled under the circumstances of special national emergency to help themselves from moneys ordinarily paid into Loan Account (Sale of Crown Lands, Mine Leases, etc.). This and a balance from 1919–20 not yet applied to extinction of debt, would give £1,300,000. Mr. Burton then dealt at length with taxation proposals.

On the resumption of the debate on 22nd April,

Mr. C. G. Fichardt (Nationalist, *Ladybrand, O.F.S.*) contended that the country was gradually arriving at a position somewhat resembling bankruptcy, and, comparing the taxation figures for 1921 with those of 1910, stated that in the latter year the tax per head was £11 6s. 8d., and now it had reached £22 6s. They could not go on burdening the people with taxes, and the only other way was ruthlessly to cut down expenditure. If the Government left the Empire alone and looked only after South Africa he thought that they could soon get the country out of the mess, but instead they were led into all sorts of wild orgies by " squandermaniacs."

Need for Reduction of Expenditure.

Mr. Fichardt went on to criticise various items of expenditure, such as the sum named for the brand-new Defence Force, which would probably cost more than the £800,000 which had been named; the purchase of Morley's Hotel in London; and the employment of 175 people in the High Commissioner's office. He would start the reduction of expenditure by cutting down fancy building and next their contribution to the " fantastic League of Nations."' He would also cut out the four millions for the electrification of railways, the redundant civil servants, and the grant to the Navy; reduce the Defence Force to Coast Defence, and depend on the old commando law for the rest. He moved that the Estimates be referred back to the Government, with the request that such reduction should be made as would preclude the necessity of further taxation.

The Labour View.

Mr. H. W. Sampson (Labour, *Jeppes, Trans.*) said it was a bad Budget from the Labour point of view, because it was difficult to find in it some underlying principle. Where did they find the principle of ability to pay, or that of services rendered by the State to the individual, in considering the taxation proposals ? It was the poorest, he continued, who, in the end, paid all the taxes, for they could not pass them on. The Government was not justified either in drastically cutting into the salaries of the civil servants, unless it could be shown that there had been a corresponding drop in the cost of living.

The Peace Treaty began by saying that " henceforth labour shall not be regarded as a commodity." What were they regarding labour as now ? As a commodity, pure and simple. The Minister had said that the policy of Labour Members was that what they had they would hold. This was quite true, but not in the sense the Minister meant, not in the sense of money, of wages, but in the sense that they were determined to maintain the same standard of living as they had before the War. Mr. Sampson moved that the House should not go into Committee of Supply until the Government had given a definite assurance that it would abolish the tax on wheat and flour, provide for a steeper grading of income tax, impose a tax on unimproved land values and make provision for unemployment by schemes of afforestation, etc.

Mr. L. Blackwell (South African Party, *Bezuidenhout Trans.*) said the hon. Member for Ladybrand had put forward several economies, but all these suggestions would probably not result in the saving of more than half a million of money. For the past five years the farmer had had unexampled prosperity and some of them thought it was rather undignified on the part of the farmers to take all they could in time of prosperity and then when the first wind of adversity blew to come abjectly to the Government for help. The farmers must learn that they had to stand on their own legs, like every other industry.

While other Dominions had been paying off their War debt and South Africa had not, during the War the latter had been the highest taxed British Dominion.

League of Nations.

On 25th April,

The Right Hon. J. X. Merriman (South African Party, *Stellenbosch, Cape*) commented on the extraordinary rapidity of the growth of expenditure since Union ; in 1913-14 it had been 16½ millions, roughly, whereas last year it had got to £30,100,000. Referring to the Vote of £62,000 for the League of Nations, which they were informed was only a beginning, he said he had always been opposed to the League of Nations ; he thought it a silly and wasteful expenditure, and it had taken them out of the league of their own nations—the free Commonwealths under British rule—and put them in the hands of a pack of ragamuffins. He did not like to use that word, but what did they call those interesting little republics in South or Central America which were always going to war with each other ? He thought this useless expenditure might very possibly drag them into a disastrous war. They had better be in alliance with America than even with Hayti. Referring to the Public Debt, he thought they occupied a better position in regard to that than most countries of their standing. They had borrowed, for instance, about £19,000,000 from Great Britain and had repaid £6,000,000.

General the Hon. J. B. M. Hertzog (Leader of the Opposition) said the farming community and the trader in the rural districts were faced with ruin. The Government must first place the Land Bank in a better position. He criticised the 25 per cent. reduction of the War bonus, and said the Government could get the necessary revenue by taking off the preference tariffs. What guarantee was there that these goods on which the preference was given were made in England ? They knew that quite a large proportion of goods bearing the label " Made in England " came from other countries. General Hertzog further said that as a protest against what the League of Nations was to-day the Vote should be deleted.

Mr. J. Christie (Labour, *Langlaagte, Trans.*), who also objected to the League of Nations Vote, said the departure from the gold basis was the sum and substance of all their financial troubles, and advocated the removal of the embargo.

On 27th April,

Sir Abe Bailey (South African Party, *Krugersdorp, Trans.*) reminded Members that the period of depression was owing to the world's condition. He had never heard speeches with less constructive suggestions in them than those which had been delivered by Nationalist Members. A fortnight ago the whole of the Nationalist Party had voted that millions should be spent upon a fleet to take away goods from that country ; this showed their inconsistency. He was glad to note, however, that they supported the Land Bank. The hon. Member also referred in detail to the gold mining, coal, and boot and shoe industries, and expressed himself in favour of development in the direction of roads, bridges, and afforestation, which would give employment. He hoped the Government would do everything it could to keep South Africa's credit high and develop all her resources.

The debate was continued at considerable length on 29th April, when the Minister of Defence replied to criticisms; and on 2nd, 4th and 6th of May, when the Minister of Finance replied. A vote was taken on the motion and amendments, Mr. Sampson's amendment being negatived by 92 votes to 10, and Mr. Fichardt's by 76 votes to 36. Mr. Burton's motion was agreed to.

Q

DEVELOPMENT OF INDUSTRIES.

(Board of Trade and Industries: Tariff Board, etc.)

Mr. W. R. Burch (South African Party, *Uitenhage, Cape*) moved the following resolution in the House of Assembly on 5th April, 1921 : —

> That in the opinion of this House the Government should take into consideration the advisability of introducing legislation at an early date giving effect to some of the recommendations of the Advisory Board of Industry and Science in regard to the maintenance and development of existing industries and the encouragement of new industries. This House is further of opinion that for this purpose the Government should take into consideration the creation of a permanent Tariff Board free from Customs departmental control, with statutory powers to investigate all matters relative to industries in South Africa, and to report and make recommendations thereon, the duties of the Board to include a report on the revision of the tariff on scientific and on economic lines, with a view to facilitating the progress of industries in the Union.

DEBATE IN HOUSE OF ASSEMBLY.

Mr. W. R. Burch (South African Party, *Uitenhage, Cape*) said that the only sound foundation upon which they could build their economic future was that of a permanent and creative industry. This divided itself into two branches—farming and manufacturing. Having quoted from a speech by General Smuts at Maritzburg soon after Union, in which he dwelt on the need of the extension of industries and emphasised the importance of a stable tariff, Mr. Burch went on to say that there was great cause to congratulate the Government on having, some two or three years back, appointed the Advisory Board of Industry and Science. It had worked in an extremely self-sacrificing way, and had placed much valuable information at the disposal of the Government and the House. But while it was locked up in the shape of blue books and reports it was of little practical use to the country. The people were waiting for something to be done.

South Africa's unique position.

South Africa occupied a unique strategic position in the world, while they had a unique store of raw material. These were two particularly strong points. In the third place, they had a much better supply of labour than many other countries, and industrial development would go far to solving the

·oblem of the "poor whites." Fourthly, South Africa had an
:cellent and diversified climate, and, fifthly, they had a very
·od home market. In addition to this, they had fine markets
·actically at their very door. In order to develop their
dustries the closest attention and the best brains in the
untry were required, but two artificial conditions were
·eded. One was security for capital, and the ·other was
ntinuity of ·employment with adequate remuneration.

·otection and Prosperity.

Continuing, Mr. Burch said that when he spoke of pro-
:tion he meant sane protection. He did not advocate the
position of a heavy tax to consumers, having in view the
otection of an article for which the conditions were not
·ourable. When discussing protection a very serious and
ntroversial discussion was invited, but he hoped in that
bate the primary object would be the good of the country
d the best means of securing the happiness and well-being
the people.

He saw no reason why South Africa should not have a
:ure like that of the United States, which in 1914 had
nieved a production of no less than 24,246,000,000 dollars.
·raham Lincoln said: " When we buy goods abroad we get
: goods and the foreigner gets the money; when we buy
home we get the goods and keep the money." Examples
ich Mr. Burch gave showed how, in the United States, as
: result of putting on heavy duties on certain articles, the
t of the latter had been decreased by large amounts and
: quantities produced largely increased, and these examples,
held, entirely refuted the arguments that protection
reased the cost to the consumer. As to advantage being
:en in South Africa of the increased duties to put up prices,
npetition would prevent this. If trusts or monopolies were
ated they must be dealt with by legislation.

ot and Shoe Trade.

One industry in that country was threatened with
inction—the boot and shoe industry—which employed 5,000
5,000 people last year, paid out half a million in wages, and
vided half of South Africa's requirements. The industry
ld efficiently supply the ordinary demands of the country,
already half the people had been dismissed, factories were
ing daily, and vital labour was· being lost. Australia
done what was proposed in the report, and to-day boots
e sold there cheaper than in any part of the world. Why

could they not do that ? The whole thing was the creation of
confidence in South Africa amongst people who wanted to
manufacture there.

Need of an Impartial Board.

Referring to the proposed appointment of a Tariff Board,
Mr. Burch said they had no impartial body at present capable
of advising the Government with regard to tariff or protection.
Tariffs were largely the subject of Customs control. The
Customs Department was a department for the collection of
revenue for the State ; the creation of industries' was a
separate business altogether. In addition to officials representing the Customs and industry, he thought they should
have three or five independent people on the Board to look
at the matter from the point of view of the State.

A moderate view.

Mr. C. P. Robinson (South African Party, *Durban Central,
Natal)* said the policy of the Government in regard to industries
was laid down in the King's Speech as follows : " Consideration
will also be given to the safeguarding of some of our industries
against unfair competition from overseas during the abnormal
conditions prevailing abroad." To that extent he was in
accord with the Government's policy, but not with the principle
of wholesale protection, and every time this question came
before the House the industries were in danger on the one
hand from undue pressure on the part of those who were
extreme protectionists, and on the other hand, perhaps in
greater danger, from those who adopted free trade as a principle.
The development of the country lay midway between these
two principles.

Development in recent years.

Mr. Robinson went on to speak of the extraordinary
development which had taken place during the past ten years.
In 1915-16 the value of the manufactures of the Union was
£40,500,000, and in 1917-18 nearly £61,000,000, whereas in
1911 the value was only £17,244,000. While he granted that
protection must and should take a part in the development of
their industries, he thought a great deal could be done by
a department for fostering them. Last year the House had
voted £709,533 to the Department of Agriculture, £336,455
to the Department of Mines, and £19,150 to Industries. The
Department of Industries was capable of much greater development, and he would like to see a considerable extension in that
direction.

olicy of Great Britain.

He had read, Mr. Robinson continued, the interesting
ports of the Commission appointed by the Prime Minister
1 the boot and shoe trade; also useful memorials by the
pposition, and he was unable to make up his mind as to
hich side had the most efficacious ideas. It was significant
ı see the policy of England in relation to this matter. Great
ritain had been as near a free-trade country as any other
untry in the world, but apparently now she was imposing
heavy tariff. He submitted that the Government of South
[rica should proceed on the lines of giving power to prevent
e dumping of ·boots in the country to the detriment of the
:al manufacturers. Undue dumping was what the country
eded protection against, and that was why he strongly
.vocated the establishment of a Tariff Board. He had no
sitation in seconding the proposal, but he had some doubts
to the advisability of imposing such a high tariff.

ıme objections.

The Right Hon. J. X. Merriman (South African Party,
ıllenbosch, Cape) said the consumers were going to pay for
e protection of clothes, boots, etc. The next step would
the starting of combines and the buying up of all the
tle factories, and then they would find what capitalists
re, when they had a series of industrial trusts throughout
ı country. There were constant conflicts in the United
ites trying to control the trusts, without success, but they
1 introduced a great deal of misery among the working
sses.

South Africa, Mr. Merriman continued, was not suitable
be "industrialised." They had a large native population
1 yet could not grow their own food. No country was fit
industrial development which could not grow its own food
produce so largely that it could compete, as England did,
h the whole world. They were never going to compete
h Great Britain in making manufactured articles. In
ard to the "poor whites," if there was one thing that was
ng to create more "poor whites" than another it was this
t of bastard industry that they were asked to foster.
ırds might be useful sometimes, but he did not think
y would be so in this case, and he would recommend
hon. Member for Uitenhage to get this very important
tion referred to a Select Committee, where the opportunity
ıld be afforded of examining not only the boot manu-
turers, but other manufacturers and the "poor retailers."

Question of Employment.

Mr. G. W. Hawley* (**South African Party,** *Cape Town, Gardens*) said the industries of South Africa to-day found employment for nearly 150,000 people : if these industries went out of existence, what did the last speaker propose to do with them and their dependents ?   Another important thing to consider was the coming generation of 40,000, for whom employment would have to be found.   It seemed to him that they had been dealing with the wrong end of the matter first.   Surely it was best to make certain they had got the industries before making regulations to govern them.

After referring to the difficulties created by the War, and the fact that at that time importations of butter, cheese, boots and shoes were brought down to £1,182,000, while last year they had re-ascended to £6,520,000, an increase of over 500 per cent., Mr. Hawley said this agitation for a Board was started fifteen years ago.   What they wanted was a Tariff Board which could immediately consider what could and should be done for the development of South African industries.

Major G. B. van Zyl (**South African Party,** *Cape Town, Harbour*) moved the adjournment of the debate.

The Prime Minister (Lieut.-General the Right Hon. J. C. Smuts) said the Government was anxious to make a statement of its policy on the question, and an early opportunity would be taken of doing so.

The debate was adjourned.

Statement by the Government.

In the House of Assembly on 7th April,

The Minister of Mines and Industries (Hon. F. S. Malan) said the Government had decided to appoint a Board to be known as the Customs Tariff Board, and the main reason for coming to this decision was, first, that it had been found necessary to co-ordinate the Department dealing with this question of the Tariff.   After explaining the functions of the Industry Section of the Mines Department and the Customs Department, he said it often happened that information was in the possession of one Department and not in that of the other.   It was necessary to have some machinery by which the two might be brought more closely into touch.   It had also been found necessary to give closer attention and study to the question of the tariff than could be done by the Advisory Board on Industry and Science, which met only periodically.

---

* Mr. Hawley was subsequently unseated, and at the by-election following Dr. Forsyth (Lab.) was elected with a majority of 54 over the S.A.P. candidate.

The functions and constitution of the Board were laid down as follows : —

The functions of the Board would be (A) to hear and examine complaints which might be made as to the working of the Customs or Excise tariff ; (B) to advise the Government with regard to (1) the adjustment of anomalies which may from time to time occur ; (2) the steps necessary to assist and develop the industries of the Union ; and (3) such other matters as the Government may refer to the Board for their advice and consideration.

The Board was to consist of not more than five members, of which one should be the technical and scientific adviser of the Department of Industry, the Commissioner of Customs, and the other members to be appointed by the Governor-General.

It would be laid down that in carrying out their duties and making recommendations the Board was, as far as possible, to take (A) the prices and cost of raw materials in the Union and elsewhere, and the cost of transportation from the place of production to the place of use or consumption ; (B) the cost of production of the finished article in the Union or elsewhere ; (C) the cost of transportation of the finished article from the place of production to the place of consumption, whether in the Union or elsewhere ; (D) the cost and conditions of labour in the Union and elsewhere ; (E) the prices received by the producers, manufacturers, wholesale dealers, distributors and retailers in the Union or elsewhere, the tariff and other conditions which enter into the cost of production and the cost to the consumer in the country ; (F) the effect of trusts and combines dealing with manufactured goods ; (G) everything affecting the production, manufacture, cost and price in the Union compared with other countries ; (H) the interest of the consumers in the Union.

It would be noticed that this Board would not have the power to alter the tariff ; they would have to report to the Government and, through the Government, to the House, and it would be for the House to take what steps it might consider necessary. He had confined his statement to this one part of the Tariff Commission, and did not propose at that stage to deal with the other questions raised by Mr. Burch, which, he thought, were more germane to the Budget debate.

Establishment of Board (Note).

A Board of Trade and Industries has been established, and held its first meeting on 8th July.* Its functions will be : —

(A) to hear and examine complaints to recommendations which may be made as to the working of the Customs and Excise tariffs ;

---

* It was explained by the Acting-Prime Minister in his opening address that the name originally suggested, *i.e.*, Tariff Board, had not been adopted because, whilst tariffs play an important part, they are by no means the whole of the subject, and it was felt that to call this a Tariff Board would give too narrow a conception of its functions.

(B) to advise the Government in regard to (1) the recasting of the Customs tariff and the adjustment of anomalies which may from time to time occur in these tariffs ; (2) such action as may be necessary or advisable for assisting and developing the industries of the Union ; and (3) such matters as the Government may refer to the Board for its consideration and advice.

The official notification of the constitution of the Board directs that, in considering the matters referred to it, the Board shall examine and report upon, so far as applicable, the cost of raw materials in the Union and elsewhere, and of transportation, the cost of production of the finished article, and transportation to the place of consumption ; the cost, efficiency and conditions of labour ; the price received by producers, manufacturers, wholesale dealers, distributors and retailers ; the tariff, fiscal and other conditions, which affect the cost of production and price ; the effects of trusts and combines, and the development of markets, etc.

UNEMPLOYMENT EXPENDITURE.

(Relief Work, Schemes of Development, Housing, White Labour, etc.)

The question of unemployment received considerable attention during the Session. On 20th June in the House of Assembly, Mr. Boydell (Leader of the Labour Party) moved the adjournment of the House for the purpose of discussing—

" the very unsatisfactory position which had arisen in connection with unemployment in view of the Cape Town Municipal Council's rejection of the Cape Administrator's proposals for the starting of relief works at very low wages, and to urge upon the Government the necessity of realising that the question of unemployment was primarily a national matter, and that immediate steps should be taken to push forward various development works, and also to urge that there should be no suspension of the operation of the Housing Act, in view of the fact that many persons were already committed to building under that Act, and the building of such houses would not only help to solve the housing problem, but would also provide work for many of the unemployed."

The Speaker (Hon. C. J. Krige) referred Mr. Boydell to the Loan Estimates in which there was a special Vote dealing with the unemployed of £300,000. There was also an amount of £800,000 out of Lcan Funds for Housing. Mr. Boydell was therefore reminded that there would be ample scope for debate when these Votes came up for discussion, and the Speaker reluctantly disallowed the motion.

The ruling was accepted.

On 5th July the House of Assembly discussed in Committee of Supply on the Estimates, Vote 35, Unemployment'Expenditure, £300,000.

DEBATE IN HOUSE OF ASSEMBLY.

Mr. T. Boydell (Leader of the Labour Party) wished to know what steps the Government had taken towards carrying out the recommendations in the Interim Reports of the Unemployment Commission. Apparently the £300,000 was to be used for relief work, but he and his colleagues contended that that amount could be better used to pay for a loan with which possibly some of the recommendations of the Commission could be carried out. Charity was not wanted, but work. He deprecated the idea that prosperous times were the best in which to start development, and contended that it was when private enterprise had broken down that, the State should step in and embark on schemes of development. He thought the State should exploit its own credit, and if the Banks refused to be reasonable, it should issue its own notes, but only against production. Instead of providing employment for men, however, they were retrenching hundreds. Surely the Government could keep its men going for there were any number of national works on which they could be employed.

Mr. M. Alexander (Constitutional Democrat, *Cape Town, Castle*) said that at the Elections the Government made promises of a policy of national development as a means of dealing with unemployment. He asked whether the item " Additional cost of capital services by the employment of white labour instead of native labour " meant that coloured labour was to be displaced, and if so, how were the needs of these people to be met ?

Mr. R. B. Waterston (Labour, *Brakpan, Trans.*) pointed out that while the Government had plenty of money to send the Prime Minister, the Minister of Defence, and the Minister of Agriculture, together with a large staff, to England for " a glorified picnic," and there would be money if war broke out or riots took place, they could not find it for dealing adequately with unemployment. That question could not be dealt with from the point of charity, and even £600,000 would not deal with it. " Where was the money to come from ? " it would be asked. The policy of the Labour Party could be carried out were it not for vested interests and the private banks. The unemployment problem was so bound up with the big financial houses outside that the Government would not deal with it on right lines.

"Back to the Land."

The Right Hon. J. X. Merriman (South African Party, *Stellenbosch, Cape*) reminded the House that the whole world was calling out for schemes for dealing with unemployment, yet none had been formulated, because it could not be done. Unemployment, however, could be prevented, and the surest way to do that was not to bring more factories to the country. Did not the Labour Party know that the countries where there were most factories were those where there was most unemployment ? If they wanted to kill South Africa let them industrialise it. What they should really do was to direct the people to the land, and what had the Labour Party or the Nationalists done in this direction ? They had an item of £41,000 on the Estimates, he continued, to displace native labour by white labour at three times the cost. It would do some good if they could by any means induce the wealthy landowners to take their poorer brethren by the hand, put them on the land and teach them to cultivate it and produce more. The Vote, he added, would do great harm by pauperising people.

Mr. A. S. van Hees (Nationalist, *Christiana, Trans.*) said the percentage of unemployed among the inhabitants of rural districts was larger than it was anywhere in the world. Nine per cent. of the white population were hopeless " poor whites." How was it proposed to expend the amount of money placed on the Estimates ? If on reproductive schemes, a great deal could undoubtedly be done, but to do anything permanent a great deal more should be put down. Let them spend the money on building bridges or on irrigation schemes, and excellent results would be gained. The Boer War, from which some farmers had never recovered, was, he maintained, the main cause of the present situation, and another cause was the lack of technical and trades schools. In the establishment of these schools to teach people to work he saw a great means of alleviating the position.

Mr. J. van der Merwe (South African Party, *Wakkerstroom, Trans.*) saw no reason why the Government should not go in for a loan, say of ten millions, for the purpose of irrigation and reproductive works.

Development schemes advocated.

Mr. W. J. Snow (Labour, *Salt River, Cape*) said the policy which the Labour Party wanted to see the Government adopt was that development works should be embarked upon now so that when times of prosperity returned those developments could be used. He wished the Government to make unemployment a State problem. Let the Municipalities and Provincial

Administrations do the administrative work if necessary but the Government should control the finances, so that men should not be degraded by having to work for 3s. 6d. per day, while their wives were compelled to apply for charity at the hands of the Board of Aid.

Acting Prime Minister's Statement.

The Acting Prime Minister (Hon. F. S. Malan), replying, said the speeches by Labour Members showed that there must be a great deal of misunderstanding in regard to this Vote. It was not intended for public works or railway construction, but to pay the difference between the normal wages for work done by native labour and that done by white labour. The cost of the work itself must be borne out of loans. It had been said that the Government had stopped the building of houses and development of that kind, but he held in his hand the Loan Estimates which would shortly be brought before the House, providing, in this time of stress and strain, for this very purpose of building houses a sum of £12,000,000.

Cost of Building.

Another item in the Loan Estimates was £2,000,000 odd for local work, including £800,000 for houses. All this did not seem as if they were stopping development; but let him say at once that the information he had as Minister of Industries was that a large amount of building would be going on to-day if the price of labour was at all in conformity with the reduced cost of living. The price of material had come down considerably, but organised labour to-day was at the same high mark at which it stood during the height of the War, and people were hanging back because of this.

Housing Scheme in operation.

In regard to the complaint that houses had not been provided, he had before him a return from the Railway Department which showed that last year they voted £1,000,000 as a first instalment on a Housing scheme costing £4,000,000. Since January, 1919, up to March, 1921, 720 houses had been completed for accommodating members of the railway staff, while since union 2,177 houses had been erected at a cost of £1,383,000. Referring again to the Vote of £300,000, Mr. Malan said that the item of £41,000 included in that sum formed a subsidy towards the employment of white labour on the irrigation scheme at Hartebeestpoort, while the item of £2,000 was a transfer from the ordinary Mining and Industries Vote.

Two kinds of Unemployment.

As to the two reports of the Unemployment Commission, there were two kinds of unemployment : first of all there was that arising from contraction after the War, and that existed largely in industrial centres, and was to a considerable extent of a temporary nature. He was hopeful that this period would not be very prolonged if labour and capital tackled the problem in the right spirit. The other phase of unemployment was the more permanent one of the "poor whites," who were created mainly by the flow from country to town.

Cost of White Agricultural Labour.

Whether they liked it or not, Mr. Malan continued, it was a fact that for the poor man who wanted work on the land, unless he was his own master, it was very difficult to find employment. The farmer could not afford to pay 4s. or 5s. for labour when he could get native and coloured labour for less. The two great employers of the "poor whites" were the Government and the mines. The Government employed them through the railways and the police. To find employment for these people apart from these two large employers was not an easy thing. They must create avenues for white labour in that country ; unless they did so the competition for unskilled work would be so strong, as between native and coloured on the one hand, and white on the other, that it would be impossible for the unskilled white man to maintain himself in the Union. " I think," Mr. Malan added, " we are on that road now."

The Acting Prime Minister further said that it was not the policy of the Government to increase the ranks of the unemployed. They were keeping on more men than they would if they ran purely on business lines.

After further discussion the Vote was agreed to.

MARRIAGE LAW AMENDMENT ACT.

(Marriage with Deceased Husband's Brother, etc.)

This Act legalises the marriage of a widow with her deceased husband's brother. A summary of the Bill, which was introduced in the House of Assembly on 15th March by Mr. M. Bisset, K.C., appeared in Vol. II., No. 2, of the JOURNAL, p. 451.

DEBATE IN HOUSE OF ASSEMBLY.

In moving the Second Reading in the House of Assembly on 7th April,

Mr. M. Bisset (South African Party, *South Peninsula, Cape*) said the effect of the Bill would be to carry the legislation of last year (which legalised the marriage of a man with his deceased wife's sister) to its logical conclusion, and would make the law of the Union entirely uniform throughout the four provinces. In certain provinces the marriage of a widow with her deceased husband's brother was not admissible. In the Free State, as he read it, it was, and also in the South-West Protectorate. The consolidating Bill introduced in 1910 made provision throughout the Union for marriage not only with a deceased wife's sister, but with a deceased husband's brother. On the latter provision a debate was raised, and on a division the House, by an overwhelming majority, adopted the principle of legalising marriage with a deceased husband's brother.

Progress in England and Dominions.

Before that time an enormous change had taken place in England in regard to marriage with a deceased wife's sister. On 19 occasions the House of Commons had adopted the principle by a large majority, and on 13 occasions it had been rejected by the House of Lords. In the meantime throughout most of the Dominions and the civilised world, the principle had been recognised. In 1907 marriage with a deceased wife's sister became lawful in England. Throughout the whole of that great conflict it was recognised that if it were lawful to marry a deceased wife's sister, there was no ground, in reason or logic, why the same rule should not be applied to the marriage of a widow with her deceased husband's brother.

Mr. T. Boydell (Leader of the Labour Party) : " What happened to the Bill in this House in 1910 ? "

Necessity for Piecemeal Legislation.

Mr. Bisset said the Bill in 1910 was a General Marriage Ordinance, a sort of comprehensive Act. Somebody introduced the question of mixed marriages, and that absolutely wrecked it. That was one reason why these things must be dealt with piecemeal. The movement for the principle of that Bill, he continued, had gathered a good deal of strength in England owing to the fact that a great many war widows had been taken care of by the brothers of their husbands who had been killed at the front, and between whom an attachment had been formed.

Colonel-Commandant W. R. Collins (South African Party, *Ermelo, Trans.*) supported the Second Reading.

Mr. R. W. Close (South African Party, *Rondebosch, Cape*) opposed the Bill. Mr. Bisset, he said, had appealed to the modern spirit; a thing was not right, however, merely because it was modern, and his fear was that once they started tampering with these old institutions it would become a question as to where they would stop. Such interference could only be made if the original measure was right in principle. He did not believe that the law in regard to the deceased wife's sister was right in principle.

The Government view.

The Minister of the Interior (Hon. Patrick Duncan) said from the point of view of the Government there could be no objection to the passage of this Bill. In a matter of this kind, which touched most intimately the social life of the people in regard to a restriction which hampered their freedom very materially, the onus of proving that such restrictions should be adhered to should be upon those who sought to do so. A restriction like this could be of the most galling nature, and could impose social disabilities of the most serious kind not only on men and women who wished to contract such a union, but upon their descendants.

Legislators, the Minister continued, had to consider it not only from the point of view of their own feelings, but in regard to whether such a proposal was likely to offend religious and social susceptibilities or not, and whether it was contrary to any physical laws or laws of nature. He had been unable to find, however, any solid ground for believing that the removal of such restrictions would damage any such susceptibilities or the general social welfare.

Mr. F. W. Beyers (Nationalist, *Edenburg, O.F.S.*) moved an amendment to refer the subject matter of the Bill to a Select Committee with a view to consolidating the marriage laws of the Union.

Mr. Boydell hoped the amendment would not be pressed, because he did not think that the consolidation which was proposed would have any earthly hope of passing the House. The effect would be that this Bill would be wrecked, and they would get neither consolidation nor the present measure, which was so urgently required.

Mr. M. Alexander (Constitutional Democrat, *Cape Town, Castle*) quite agreed with the idea of a consolidating Bill, but he hoped the amendment, which would have the effect of postponing this Bill until the Greek Kalends, would not be carried. The Bill was based on reason and justice.

Mr. A. A. Cilliers (Nationalist, *Harrismith, O.F.S.*) thought the various Protestant churches in the country should first be consulted in the matter.

Mr. C. E. Nixon (South African Party, *Denver, Trans.*) and **Mr. J. H. H. de Waal (Nationalist,** *Piquetburg, Cape*) supported the previous speaker.

The Minister of Mines and Industries (Hon. F. S. Malan) said, in regard to the attitude of the churches, he could not remember any resolution against marriages of the kind which the present Bill sought to legalise.

The amendment was defeated by 71 votes to 34, and the Bill passed its Second Reading.

The attitude of the Church.

In the discussion in Committee on 14th April,

Mr. R. W. Close (South African Party, *Rondebosch, Cape*) moved that the Committee report progress and ask leave to sit again on this matter. The public, he said, had not had the opportunity of considering the Bill fully, and not only the Anglican community, but another great ecclesiastical body, the Dutch Church, had also sent in either a protest or request, officially or through prominent officials, for further time in which to consider the Bill. He contended that there was no evidence of the demand for its introduction. Although no church, Mr. Close continued, had any right to dictate to Parliament as to what kind of laws Parliament should pass, as a body of organised thought of whatever denomination it had a right to express its opinion and endeavour to make it felt in regard to proposed legislation, particularly where the latter touched so nearly the principles of the Church. Another reason why he was asking for an extension of time was that he wished to prevent any law being passed which would widen the difference between the ecclesiastical and civil laws as to marriage.

Mr. M. Bisset (South African Party, *South Peninsula, Cape*) expressed surprise as to this attitude, and pointed out that this matter had been discussed in the House again and again, for it was brought up in 1872, and again in 1892, while in 1910, by an overwhelming majority, the principle embodied in the present measure was approved. It had now been reintroduced, and again approved by an overwhelming majority. Those who were strongly opposed to the measure would have ample opportunity to raise their protest. Continuing, he said he would point out that there was complete liberty of conscience in these matters, and if members of any particular Church felt that it was against their conscience to give effect to the provisions of the Bill there was no compulsion upon them to do so.

The Minister of the Interior (Hon. Patrick Duncan) pointed out that if the motion was carried it would practically mean reversing the vote the House took a week ago. There was not the slightest chance of the Church coming to any other conclusion if they had a hundred years to consider in. The Church took up the position that its law was eternal and unchangeable.

After further discussion the amendment was negatived, Mr. Close's demand for a division coming too late.

In discussion on Clause I. (*vide* JOURNAL, Vol. II., No. 2, p. 451).

Dr. D. F. Malan (Nationalist, *Calvinia, Cape*) moved after " lawful for any widow " to omit the words " to marry the husband of her deceased brother, or ".

The amendment was defeated by 62 votes to 25. The remaining clauses having been agreed to, the Bill was reported without amendment.

The Third Reading was carried on 12th May by 47 votes to 46, and the Bill ordered to be transmitted to the Senate for its concurrence.

DEBATE IN THE SENATE.

In the Senate, on 19th May,

Senator the Hon. C. G. Marais moved that, with reference to the petition of the Rev. D. S. Botha, Moderator of the Dutch Reformed Church, and the Rev. J. O. Nash, Coadjutor Bishop of Cape Town, praying to be heard at the Bar of the House in opposition to the Bill, leave be given to them to appear and be heard before the question for the Second Reading was put. The mover urged that they were now dealing with the feelings of about half of the Christian community of the Union, and it was a matter of great concern to the Church because in these matters they should do their best to prevent divisions among the people.

Senator the Hon. G. G. Munnik seconded the motion. There was, he said, a precedent of a bishop having been allowed to address the Natal House, and there was sufficient reason for following it in this case.

The Minister of Justice (Hon. N. J. de Wet) agreed that the motion was one for the Senate to deal with on its merits. There were, of course, certain precedents, but as far as that House was concerned it had to be careful. From the point of view of policy there was much to be said against the motion. Personally he had no objection to it, but he believed it would raise personal issues unless left alone or very delicately treated.

Senator the Hon. A. D. W. Wolmarans deplored that sectarian issues were being introduced into the discussion. Personally he would support the motion.

Senator the Hon. P. Whiteside thought that in view of the present theological position it was well that the reverend gentlemen should be allowed to have an opportunity of stating their views.

The motion, on being put, was defeated, on a division, by 18 votes to 16. It being moved by Senator Marais that the Bill be read " this day six months " this motion was also defeated, and after further discussion the debate on the Second Reading was adjourned.

Having passed the Second Reading on 27th May, the Bill passed through Committee, was reported without amendment, and read a third time in the Senate on 1st June.

WOMEN'S ENFRANCHISEMENT BILL.

This is a Bill to enable women to be registered as voters for the election of members of the House of Assembly and of all Provincial Councils. It was introduced by Mr. R. Feetham (South African Party, *Parktown, Trans.*) and set down for Second Reading on 14th April. The order was reached on 28th April, when the Bill was debated, discussion being resumed on 29th April and 19th May. On the latter date, Mr. Van der Merwe (South African Party, *Wakkerstroom, Trans.*) having moved the adjournment, a division was taken, which resulted in the adjournment being carried by 52 votes to 44. The Bill has not been proceeded with.

The Bill provides that, notwithstanding anything contained in the Constitution Ordinance of the Cape of Good Hope, the Charter of Natal, Transvaal Constitution Letters Patent, 1906, Orange River Colony Constitution Letters Patent, 1907, or any amendment thereof, whereby

R

persons of the male sex only are entitled to be registered as voters for the election of Members of the House of Assembly and Provincial Councils, the said Ordinance, Charter and Letters Patent and all amendments thereof shall be read and construed as if the provisions relating to the qualifications of voters included persons of the female as well as of the male sex.

Where by any law in force for the time being in any Province the possession, occupation or renting of property or premises, of a certain value, is prescribed as entitling persons to be registered as voters for the election of Members of the House of Assembly and Provincial Councils, a married woman, who is not living apart from her husband, shall be entitled to be so registered in respect of property or premises possessed, occupied or rented by her husband, provided that the value of such property or premises, as reckoned for the purposes of the husband's qualification, is at least twice the amount prescribed by such law.

Nothing in the Act is to be construed so as to deprive any man who, if the Act had not been passed, would have been entitled to be registered as a voter of the right of being so registered.

PROFITEERING AND RENTS ACT.

(Appointment of Select Committee.)

In the House of Assembly on 21st April the Minister of Justice moved, on behalf of the Minister of Finance, that a Select Committee be appointed to inquire and report whether the Rents Act, 1920 (Act No. 13 of 1920), and the Profiteering Act, 1920 (Act No. 27 of 1920), the operation of which would expire in each case on 30th June, 1921, unless otherwise determined by resolution of both Houses of Parliament, should continue in force, and if so, for how long, etc.; also to inquire as to the operation of the Speculation in Food-Stuffs Prevention Act, 1920 (Act No. 29 of 1920); and whether any of these Acts should be amended.*

After some debate an amendment to the effect that the Select Committee should also have the power of considering the repeal of the Act, moved by Mr. C. B. Heatlie (South African Party, *Worcester, Cape*), was agreed to, and the motion as amended was adopted.

On 21st June, in the House of Assembly,

The **Minister of Public Works (Hon. Sir Thomas Watt)** moved the following resolution : —

"That this House, having regard to the provisions of Section 12 of the Profiteering Act, 1920, resolves that that Act shall continue in operation until the 30th day of June, 1922."

* *Vide* Vol. I., No. 3, of this JOURNAL, p. 568 ; Vol. II., No. 1, pp. 224 and 228.

He said that the Profiteering Act, the Rents Act and Speculation in Foodstuffs Prevention Act were sent to a Select Committee of the House, which had since presented its report. The Commission, after taking fairly voluminous evidence, recommended that the Profiteering Act should be renewed for another year. There was no doubt that the effect of the Act had been to keep down profiteering and reduce the cost of living.

After some debate, the motion was agreed to and ordered to be transmitted to the Senate for its concurrence.

ACTS PASSED.

The following Acts, which have been, or will be, dealt with in the JOURNAL, are amongst those which have been passed during the Session : —

Rents Act Extension and Amendment Act, 1921.
Children's Protection Act Amendment Act.
Speculation in Foodstuffs Repealing Act.

NEWFOUNDLAND.

WAR MEASURES ACT AMENDMENT BILL.

This Bill repeals the War Measures Act of 1914 and all amendments thereof and all orders and regulations made thereunder. It further provides that all acts and things done or omitted to be done by or under the authority of or ratified by —

(A) The Governor in Council ;
(B) Any Minister or Officer of the Government of Newfoundland ;
(c) Any other Authority or person ;

which were authorised to be done or omitted by the War Measures Act or any amendments thereof are declared to be lawfully done or omitted.

VENEREAL DISEASES BILL.*

The object of this Bill is to provide for compulsory treatment and notification of venereal disease and the prevention of the spread of such diseases.

---

* *Vide* also Vol. II., No. 1, p. 153, and No. 2, p. 396.

COMPULSORY TREATMENT.

The Bill declares venereal diseases, including syphilis, gonorrhœa and chancroid, contagious, infectious, communicable and dangerous to the public health. It is provided that every person infected shall place himself under the treatment of a qualified medical practitioner, or shall apply to the Medical Health Officer, who will direct his course as to treatment. During the course of the disease he shall carry on his treatment as required by the medical practitioner, in default of which he shall be reported to the Medical Health Officer. Refusal or neglect to comply with the above provisions is subject to a penalty of not less than $25 and not more than $100. (Secs. 1 and 2.)

PREVENTION OF MARRIAGE AND SEXUAL INTERCOURSE.

Every person infected with venereal disease shall, until pronounced non-infective, abstain from marriage, sexual intercourse or any conduct likely to infect another person under penalty of a fine of not less than $100 or more than $500, or of imprisonment for a period of not less than one or more than six months. (Sec. 3.)

PROCEDURE FOR HOSPITALS, GAOLS AND PLACES OF DETENTION, ETC.

Every medical practitioner, hospital superintendent, or person in charge of gaols, reformatories, places of detention, or public and private institutions, and every person infected shall take every precaution against the spread of these diseases, as is prescribed by the Act or from time to time by the Medical Health Officer. Any person under arrest or in custody, charged with an offence against the law of Newfoundland, or who has been committed to a gaol, reformatory, or other place of detention upon conviction, if believed to be infected with or to have been exposed to infection with venereal disease, may be examined by the Medical Health Officer. If he is found to be infected, provision is made for his treatment and, if necessary, for his detention and isolation. It shall be the duty of every physician in medical charge of any gaol or place of detention, or of the inmates thereof, to report to the Medical Officer, the serial number and place of detention, before or after conviction, of any person whom he suspects or believes to be suffering from venereal disease, the report to be made within twenty-four hours after the arrival of such person at the gaol or place of detention. (Sec. 5.)

EXAMINATION AND INSPECTION.

If the Medical Health Officer is credibly informed that any person is infected with venereal disease and has infected or is liable to infect other persons, he may notify such person to consult a medical practitioner and produce a report from him within a specified time. If the report is not produced within the time stated, the Medical Health Officer may authorise any medical practitioner to examine and report on such person. If it appears that the person so notified is suffering from venereal disease the Medical Health Officer may exercise the powers vested in him by the Act in the interest of the public health and deliver to the infected person and to the medical practitioner directions as to course of conduct to be pursued, and may require him to produce from time to time evidence that such person is undergoing proper medical treatment. The Medical Health Officer, or a qualified medical practitioner appointed by him for that purpose, may enter any house, out-house or premises in the day-time for the purpose of inquiring into the state of health of any person therein, and may cause any person found infected with any venereal disease to be removed to a hospital, or may give instructions regarding measures to be adopted to prevent others being infected. (Sec. 6.) Medical practitioners who give treatment for venereal diseases must, within two days of the first visit of a patient, send to the Medical Health Officer a report stating the serial number, age, sex, marital condition of the patient, the nature and previous duration of the disease, and the probable source of infection. (Sec. 7.)

CIRCULATION OF INFORMATION : OBLIGATIONS OF PARENTS AND GUARDIANS : PREVENTION OF INFECTION.

Medical practitioners are required to supply to persons suffering from venereal disease, at the first examination, a circular of information and advice furnished by the Medical Health Officer and a copy of this Act (Sec. 8), and information is also to be distributed to hospitals. (Sec. 10.) Parents and guardians are responsible for compliance with the requirements of the Act in the case of children or minors living with them. (Sec. 11.) No person affected with venereal disease may engage in the trade of barber, waiter, butcher, confectioner, or in the handling of foodstuffs or confectionery. (Sec. 12.)

PRESCRIPTION OF DRUGS.

No druggist, pharmacist or other person not a qualified medical practitioner may prescribe or recommend any drug, medicine or other substance for the cure or alleviation of any venereal disease, or compound any drugs or medicines for that purpose from any written formula or order not written for the persons for whom the drugs or medicines are compounded and not signed by a qualified medical practitioner. (Sec. 13.)

SECRECY.

It is further provided that every person employed in the administration of the Act shall preserve secrecy, under penalty of forfeiting his office (Sec. 14) ; while every person who, publicly or privately, verbally or in writing, states or intimates that any other person has been notified or examined or otherwise dealt with under the Act, whether such statement is true or not, shall be liable to a penalty of $100 or, in default of payment, to imprisonment for three months. This shall not apply to disclosures made in good faith to the Medical Health Officer nor to any communication made to a qualified medical practitioner. (Sec. 15.)

PENALTIES.

The Bill provides that every person who violates any provision of the Act or of any regulation made thereunder, or wilfully neglects or disobeys any order or direction lawfully given by the Medical Health Officer, or hinders any officer in the performance of his duties under the Act, or without lawful authority publishes or discloses any proceedings taken under the Act or regulations, shall, where no other penalty is prescribed, be liable to a penalty of not less than $25 or more than $100, or, in default of payment, to imprisonment for a period not exceeding three months.

The Governor in Council is empowered to make regulations, which shall have the force of law, for the prevention, treatment and cure of venereal disease.

CRUELTY TO CHILDREN BILL

This Bill is for the protection of neglectd, dependent and delinquent children under the age of fourteeı

The Bill provides that any person over the age of sixten who, having the care of any child, wilfully ill-treats, neglects or abanóns such child, or causes it to be assaulted, ill-treated, neglected or abandoed in a manner likely to cause injury to health, shall be guilty of a misdemeanour and shall be liable on summary conviction to a fine not exceedig one hundred dollars, or, in default of payment, to imprisonment, wth or without hard labour, for any term not exceeding six months. A person may be convicted, notwithstanding that actual suffering or injur to health, or the likelihood of such injury, was obviated by the acton of another person ; and notwithstanding the death of the child or oung person in respect of whom the offence is committed.

The Bill prescribes regulations for the arrest of th offender and provides for the safety of children.

It is further provided that a child charged with an ffence against the laws of Newfoundland or who is brought before a Jdge under any provisions of the Bill shall not be tried or have its case disosed of in the police-court room ordinarily used, and that all persons ther than the counsel and witnesses in the case, the officers of the Courtor any Society for the Protection of Children and the immediate friendsor relatives of the child shall be excluded.

When it appears to the Judge that the public interest nd the interest of the child are best served thereby, an order may be madfor the return of the child to its parents or friends, or the Judge may pace such child under the guardianship of a Society for the Protection f Children or of a fit friend. Instead of committing a child to prison he may hand the child to the charge of a home for destitute children or Industrial School or Society for the Protection of Children, who ma permit of its adoption by a suitable person or may apprentice it to a sutable trade.

HIGH COMMISSIONER'S BILL.

This Bill is for the purpose of empowering tle Governor in Council to appoint from time to time an officerto be called the High Commissioner for Newfoundland, who will act as a representative and resident agent of the Cobny in the United Kingdom. He will be required to performsuch duties as may be assigned to him by the Governor in bouncil and carry out instructions respecting the commercil, financial and general interests of Newfoundland in the United Kingdom and elsewhere, with power to appoint such officers and others in the Office of the High Commissioner as he dee and to fix the salaries to be received by them.

LAW SOCIETY AMENDMENT BILL.

(Admission to practice in the Courts, etc.)

This Bill is for the purpose of amending the Law Society Act so hat, subject to any rules, regulations or bye-laws, made by the Benchers, the following persons and no others may be admitted to practice at the Bar in His Majesty's Courts i Newfoundland :

(1) Any person who has been admitted into and stands upon the books of he Society as a Student of the Laws for five years, has conformed hmself to its rules, and has been enrolled a Solicitor of the Supreme 'ourt.

(2) Any person who has been admitted into and stands on the books of the Soiety as a Student of Laws for three years, and who, prior to that time has had conferred upon him the degree of Bachelor, Master, or Doctoi in Arts, Law or Science (not being an honorary degree) in any of th Universities of the United Kingdom and Ireland, or of any colonial c foreign University or College having power to grant degrees, and apprved of by the Benchers.

(3) Any person who has been admitted into and stands on the books of te Society as a Student of the Laws for four years, who, prior to that dte, has actually passed the first public examination before Moderatios in the University of Oxford, or the Previous Examination in the Unversity of Cambridge or the examination in Arts for the second year in tb University of Durham, or the Matriculation examination in any of th Universities or Colleges referred to in the last subsection.

(4) Any person who has been duly called to the Bar of England, Scotland r Ireland (excluding the Bar of Courts of merely local jurisdiction).

(5) Any person who has been duly called to the Bar of any of His Majesty's Superior Courts in the colonies or provinces in which the same privilege ould be extended to Barristers from Newfoundland.

All to above must have been enrolled as Solicitors of the Supreme Court, an the term of membership of the Law Society is reducible for those whi have served in the Forces of the Crown.

The illowing persons may be admitted and enrolled as Solicitors :—

1) Any person who has been bound by contract to a practising Soliaor in Newfoundland to serve, and has served, him as his clerk for five years.

2) Any person who has served as clerk for three years and has fulfild the conditions laid down in Subsection 2 above ; provided that he Law Society may, in cases of Students who have served with he Forces of the Crown, at their discretion reduce the term to two pars.

3) Any person who has served as clerk for four years and has fulfild the conditions laid down in Subsection 3 above.

4) Any person who has been duly called to practice at the Bar of ay of His Majesty's Superior Courts in England, Scotland or Irelad ; or of the colonies or provinces in which the same privilege is exnded to Barristers from Newfoundland.

5) Any person who has been enrolled as a Solicitor of the Suprme Court of Justice in England or Ireland, or who has been a Wrer to the Signet or Solicitor in the Supreme Courts in Scotland.

(6) Any Attorney or Solicitor in any of the Superior Courts of Law or Equity in any of the colonies or provinces, where the same privileges are extended to Solicitors of the Supreme Court of New foundland.

Any of the persons referred to in Subsections 1, 2 or 3 above, who has attended a recognised Law School, with the approval of the Benchers and passed the terminal examination, may complete the time thus spent as passed in service under his articles of clerkship ; and if he has had conferred upon him the degree of Bachelor or Doctor of Laws in any of the Universities mentioned above, his period of service may be reduced by one year.

CIVIL SERVICE SALARIES.

The following resolutions have been drawn up for submission to a Committee of the whole House on the subject of Civil Service Salaries : —

1. From 1st July, 1921, there shall be deducted from the salaries of all persons in the public service of the colony, which are annually provided for by vote of the Legislature, the following amounts :—

(A) Ten per cent. of all salaries up to and including $500 ; and in addition thereto ;

(B) Fifteen per cent. of the amount by which a salary exceeds $500, up to and including $1,000.

(C) Twenty per cent. of the amount by which a salary exceeds $1,000.

2. A Bill shall be introduced to give effect to these Resolutions.

PETROLEUM EXPLORATION AGREEMENT.

A Bill has been introduced for the purpose of bringing into force an agreement between the Government and the D'Arcy Exploration Company, Limited, whereby the colony grants to the Company the exclusive right during a period of two years to prospect the unoccupied Crown lands and search for petroleum oil, bitumen, natural gas and bituminous clays and shales capable of yielding petroleum oil on distillation. The Company may select from any area such portions as it may desire for the purpose of getting petroleum, etc., therefrom, and may lease them from the Government for ninety-nine years, subject to specified conditions. If petroleum oil is discovered in commercial quantities the Company or any lessees shall proceed with all reasonable speed and continuously to develop the same. The Company is at liberty to transfer this agreement and all or any of the rights conferred by it to a syndicate or company approved by the Government.

VACHER & SONS, LTD., Westminster House, London, S.W.1.—92599